AF818953

A SELECTION OF CASES
ON
THE LAW OF TORTS

BY

JAMES BARR AMES AND JEREMIAH SMITH

NEW EDITION BY

ROSCOE POUND
CARTER PROFESSOR OF JURISPRUDENCE
IN HARVARD UNIVERSITY

CAMBRIDGE
HARVARD UNIVERSITY PRESS
1919

This edition was first published in four parts. Part I (pp. 1–167) appeared September 25, 1916; part II (pp. 168–368), December 1, 1916; part III (pp. 369–618), February 20, 1917, and part IV (pp. 619–1008), April 23, 1917.

Copyright, 1893 and 1909, by James Barr Ames.
Copyright, 1893 and 1909, by Jeremiah Smith.
Copyright, 1910, by Richard Ames.
Copyright, 1916 and 1917, by Roscoe Pound.

PREFACE

THE chief occasion for this edition is the change in the first-year curriculum in Harvard Law School, which assigned to other courses many things formerly appropriated to the course in the Law of Torts and hence treated in former editions. Thus causation is now treated in a course on the Principles of Legal Liability; certain excuses, such as consent and self-defence, are dealt with in that course, and trespass to land and conversion, which analytically might well be treated in the first chapter of this book, have been thought more appropriate to the course on the Law of Property. But the student should be warned that such matters of arrangement do not inhere in the law. They are mere matters of pedagogical expediency. He should bear in mind that the law is a unit and should be on his guard against thinking of it as made up of separate water-tight compartments. General principles which are of prime importance in connection with the subjects treated in this book are dealt with primarily in the courses on Property and on Criminal Law. Not the least important task for the student is to seek constantly for these relations between the subjects studied.

Again, the student should be warned that the arrangement proceeds upon pedagogical considerations and does not seek to set forth an analytical system. System is to be derived from study of the cases. The effort of the student to make one in connection with his summaries for review and his reading of the systematic discussions referred to in the notes will do more for him than learning in advance a system laid out by some one else. Similar reasons have led to omission of subheadings as far as consistent with convenience, leaving it to the student to systematize the main headings for himself. For other purposes an index is offered instead.

In arrangement of the cases advantage has been taken of the experience of the late Dean Thayer, who had given the matter anxious consideration for some years. Indeed the instinct of Dean Ames for teachable cases, the sagacity of Judge Smith in finding significant cases, and the judgment of Dean Thayer in matters of arrangement left little of moment for the present editor to do.

ROSCOE POUND

CAMBRIDGE, July 18, 1917

NOTE. The present volume is a reprint of the edition of 1916–17 which was not stereotyped and was soon exhausted. A few recent decisions have been added in the notes. Otherwise there is no change.

TABLE OF CONTENTS

PART I

INTERFERENCE WITH THE PERSON OR TANGIBLE PROPERTY

CHAPTER I

CHAPTER II

CHAPTER III

PART II

INTERFERENCE WITH GENERAL SUBSTANCE OR INTERESTS IN INTANGIBLE THINGS

TABLE OF CASES

CASES ON TORTS

PART I

INTERFERENCE WITH THE PERSON OR TANGIBLE PROPERTY

CHAPTER I

INTENTIONAL INTERFERENCE

Section I

Assault and Battery

I. De S. and Wife *v.* W. De S.

At the Assizes, coram Thorpe, C. J., 1348 or 1349.

Reported in Year Book, Liber Assisarum, folio 99, *placitum* 60.

I. De S. & M. uxor ejus querunt de W. De S. de eo quod idem W. anno, &c., vi et armis, &c., apud S., in ipsam M. insultum fecit, et ipsam verberavit, &c. And W. pleaded not guilty. And it was found by verdict of the inquest that the said W. came in the night to the house of the said I., and would have bought some wine, but the door of the tavern was closed; and he struck on the door with a hatchet, which he had in his hand, and the woman plaintiff put her head out at a window and ordered him to stop; and he perceived her and struck with the hatchet, but did not touch the woman. Whereupon the inquest said that it seemed to them that there was no trespass, since there was no harm done. Thorpe C. J. There is harm, and a trespass for which they shall recover damages, since he made an assault upon the woman, as it is found, although he did no other harm. Wherefore tax his damages, &c. And they taxed the damages at half a mark. Thorpe, C. J., awarded that they should recover their damages, &c., and that the other should be taken. *Et sic nota*, that for an assault one shall recover damages, &c.[1]

[1] Smith *v.* Newsam, 1 Vent. 256; Tombs *v.* Painter, 13 East, 1; Lewis *v.* Hoover, 3 Blackf. 407; Handy *v.* Johnson, 5 Md. 450; People *v.* Carlson, 160 Mich. 426; Saunders *v.* Gilbert, 156 N. C. 463; Leach *v.* Leach, 11 Tex. Civ. App. 699 *Accord.*

TUBERVILLE *v.* SAVAGE

In the King's Bench, Trinity Term, 1669.

Reported in 1 Modern Reports, 3.

Action of assault, battery, and wounding.[1] The evidence to prove a provocation was, that the plaintiff put his hand upon his sword and said, " If it were not assize-time, I would not take such language from you." The question was, if that were an assault ? The court agreed that it was not; for the declaration of the plaintiff was that he would not assault him, the judges being in town; and the intention as well as the act makes an assault.[2] Therefore, if one strike another upon the hand or arm or breast, in discourse, it is no assault, there being no intention to assault; but if one, intending to assault, strike at another and miss him, this is an assault: so if he hold up his hand against another in a threatening manner and say nothing, it is an assault. In the principal case the plaintiff had judgment.

STEPHENS *v.* MYERS

At Nisi Prius, coram Tindal, C. J., July 17, 1830.

Reported in 4 Carrington & Payne, 349.

Assault. The declaration stated that the defendant threatened and attempted to assault the plaintiff. Plea: Not guilty.

It appeared that the plaintiff was acting as chairman at a parish meeting, and sat at the head of a table, at which table the defendant also sat, there being about six or seven persons between him and the plaintiff. The defendant having, in the course of some angry discussion which took place, been very vociferous, and interrupted the proceedings of the meeting, a motion was made that he should be turned out, which was carried by a very large majority. Upon this the defendant said he would rather pull the chairman out of the chair than be turned out of the room, and immediately advanced with his fist clenched toward the chairman, but was stopped by the church-warden, who sat next but one to the chairman, at a time when he was not near enough for any blow he might have meditated to have

[1] The report of the same case in 2 Keble, 545, adds: " The defendant pleaded the plaintiff began first, and the stroke he received, whereby he lost his eye, was on his own assault, and in defense of the defendant."

[2] Blake *v.* Barnard, 9 Car. & P. 626; State *v.* Crow, 1 Ired. 375; Commonwealth *v.* Eyre, 1 S. & R. 347; Biggins *v.* Gulf R. Co., 102 Tex. 417 *Accord.* Compare Handy *v.* Johnson, 5 Md. 450.

Similarly, a mere preparation for a possible assault, but without any act indicating a present intention to do personal violence to another, is not an assault. Lawson *v.* State, 30 Ala. 14; Godwin *v.* Collins, 67 Fla. 197; Penny *v.* State, 114 Ga. 77; Gober *v.* State, 7 Ga. App. 206; Haupt *v.* Swenson, 125 Ia. 694; State *v.* Painter, 67 Mo. 84; State *v.* Milsaps, 82 N. C. 549. But compare State *v.* Hampton, 63 N. C. 13.

reached the chairman, but the witnesses said that it seemed to them that he was advancing with an intention to strike the chairman.

Spankie, Serjt., for the defendant, upon this evidence, contended that no assault had been committed, as there was no power in the defendant, from the situation of the parties, to execute his threat, — there was not a present ability, — he had not the means of executing his intention at the time he was stopped.

TINDAL, C. J., in his summing up, said: It is not every threat, when there is no actual personal violence, that constitutes an assault; there must, in all cases, be the means of carrying the threat into effect. The question I shall leave to you will be, whether the defendant was advancing at the time, in a threatening attitude, to strike the chairman, so that his blow would almost immediately have reached the chairman if he had not been stopped; then, though he was not near enough at the time to have struck him, yet, if he was advancing with that intent, I think it amounts to an assault in law. If he was so advancing that, within a second or two of time, he would have reached the plaintiff, it seems to me it is an assault in law. If you think he was not advancing to strike the plaintiff, then only can you find your verdict for the defendant; otherwise you must find it for the plaintiff, and give him such damages as you think the nature of the case requires.

Verdict for the plaintiff. Damages, 1*s*.[1]

READ *v.* COKER

IN THE COMMON PLEAS, JUNE 1, 1853.

Reported in 13 *Common Bench Reports*, 850.

ASSAULT and false imprisonment.[2] The first count charged an assault committed by the defendant on the plaintiff on the 24th of March, 1853, by thrusting him out of a certain workshop.

Plea: Not guilty "by statute," upon which issue was joined.

The cause was tried before Talfourd, J., at the first sitting in London in Easter term last. The facts which appeared in evidence were as follows: The plaintiff was a paper-stainer, carrying on business in the City Road, upon premises which he rented of one Molineux, at a rent

[1] Townsdin *v.* Nutt, 19 Kan. 282; Handy *v.* Johnson, 5 Md. 450; Fairme's Case, 5 City Hall Rec. 95; Brister *v.* State, 40 Tex. Cr. 505; Western T. Co. *v.* Bowdoin, (Tex. Civ. App.) 168 S. W. 1 *Accord.* Jones *v.* State, 89 Ark. 213 (*semble*) *Contra.*

Compare Cobbett *v.* Grey, 4 Ex. 744, *per* Pollock, C. B.; Burton *v.* State, 8 Ala. App. 295; Wells *v.* State, 108 Ark. 312; People *v.* Lilley, 43 Mich. 521; Grimes *v.* State, 99 Miss. 232; Commonwealth *v.* Roman, 52 Pa. Super. Ct. 64; Trimble *v.* State, 57 Tex. Cr. 439.

In Mortin *v.* Shoppee, 3 Car. & P. 373, defendant rode up to plaintiff's gate, plaintiff being in his garden about three yards off, and, shaking his whip, said, "Come out, and I will lick you before your own servants." Compare People *v.* Yslas, 27 Cal. 630; State *v.* Shipman, 81 N. C. 513.

[2] Only so much of the case is given as relates to the question of assault.

of 8*s.* per week. In January, 1852, the rent being sixteen weeks in arrear, the landlord employed one Holliwell to distrain for it. Holliwell accordingly seized certain presses, lathes, and other trade fixtures, and, at the plaintiff's request, advanced him £16 upon the security of the goods, for the purpose of paying off the rent. The plaintiff, being unable to redeem his goods, on the 23d of February applied to the defendant for assistance. The goods were thereupon sold to the defendant by Holliwell, on the part of Read, for £25 11*s.* 6*d.*; and it was agreed between the plaintiff and the defendant that the business should be carried on for their mutual benefit, the defendant paying the rent of the premises and other outgoings, and allowing the plaintiff a certain sum weekly.

The defendant, becoming dissatisfied with the speculation, dismissed the plaintiff on the 22d of March. On the 24th, the plaintiff came to the premises, and, refusing to leave when ordered by the defendant, the latter collected together some of his workmen, who mustered round the plaintiff, tucking up their sleeves and aprons, and threatened to break his neck if he did not go out; and, fearing that the men would strike him if he did not do so, the plaintiff went out. This was the assault complained of in the first count. Upon this evidence the learned judge left it to the jury to say whether there was an intention on the part of the defendant to assault the plaintiff, and whether the plaintiff was apprehensive of personal violence if he did not retire. The jury found for the plaintiff on this count. Damages, one farthing.

Byles, Serjt., on a former day in this term, moved for a rule *nisi* for a new trial, on the ground of misdirection, and that the verdict was not warranted by the evidence. That which was proved as to the first count clearly did not amount to an assault. [JERVIS, C. J. It was as much an assault as a sheriff's officer being in a room with a man against whom he has a writ, and saying to him, "You are my prisoner," is an arrest.] To constitute an assault, there must be something more than a threat of violence. An assault is thus defined in Buller's Nisi Prius, p. 15: "An assault is an attempt or offer, by force or violence, to do a corporal hurt to another, as by pointing a pitchfork at him, when standing within reach; presenting a gun at him [within shooting distance]; drawing a sword, and waving it in a menacing manner, &c. The Queen *v.* Ingram, 1 Salk. 384. But no words can amount to an assault, though perhaps they may in some cases serve to explain a doubtful action: 1 Hawk. P. C. 133; as if a man were to lay his hand upon his sword, and say, 'If it were not assize-time, he would not take such language,' — the words would prevent the action from being construed to be an assault, because they show he had no intent to do him any corporal hurt at that time: Tuberville *v.* Savage." So, in Selwyn's Nisi Prius (11th ed.), 26, it is said: "An assault is an attempt, with force or violence, to do a corporal injury to another, as by holding up a fist in a menacing manner; striking at another with a cane or stick, though the party striking may miss his aim; drawing a sword or bayonet; throwing a bottle or glass with intent to wound or strike; presenting a gun at a person who is within the distance to which the gun will carry; pointing a pitchfork at a person who is within reach (Genner *v.* Sparks); or by any other similar act, accompanied with such circumstances as denote at the time an intention, coupled with a present ability (see Stephens *v.* Myers), of using actual violence against the person of another." So, in 3 Bl. Comm. 120, an assault is said to be "an attempt or offer to beat another, without touching him; as if one lifts up his cane or his fist in a threatening manner at another, or strikes at him but misses him: this is an assault, *insultus,* which Finch (L. 202) describes to be 'an unlawful setting upon one's person.'" [JERVIS, C. J. If a man comes into a room, and lays his cane on the table, and says to another, "If you don't go out I will knock you on the head," would not that be an assault ?] Clearly not: it is a mere threat, unaccompanied by any gesture or action towards carrying it into effect. The direction of the learned judge as to this point was erroneous. He should have told the jury that to constitute an assault there must be an attempt, coupled with a present ability, to do personal violence to the party; instead of leaving it to them, as he did, to say what the plaintiff thought, and not what they (the jury) thought was the defendant's intention. There must be some act done denoting a present ability and an intention to assault.

A rule *nisi* having been granted,

Allen, Serjt., and *Charnock* now showed cause. The first question is, whether the evidence was sufficient, as to the first count, to justify the learned judge in putting it to the jury whether or not the defendant had been guilty of an assault. The evidence was, that the plaintiff was surrounded by the defendant and his men, who, with their sleeves and aprons tucked up, threatened to break his neck if he did not quit the workshop. [MAULE, J. If there can be such a thing as an assault without an actual beating, this is an assault.]

JERVIS, C. J. I am of opinion that this rule cannot be made absolute to its full extent; but that, so far as regards the first count of the declaration, it must be discharged. If anything short of actual striking will in law constitute an assault, the facts here clearly showed that the defendant was guilty of an assault. There was a threat of violence exhibiting an intention to assault, and a present ability to carry the threat into execution.

MAULE, J., CRESSWELL, J., and TALFOURD, J., concurring.

Rule discharged as to the first count.[1]

[1] United States *v.* Kiernan, 3 Cranch, C. C. 435; Plonty *v.* Murphy, 82 Minn. 268; People *v.* Lee, 1 Wheeler, Crim. Cas. 364; State *v.* Davis, 1 Ired. 125; Alexander *v.* Blodgett, 44 Vt. 476; Newell *v.* Whitcher, 53 Vt. 589; Bishop *v.* Ranney, 59 Vt. 316; Barnes *v.* Martin, 15 Wis. 240; Keep *v.* Quallman, 68 Wis. 451 *Accord.*

UNITED STATES v. RICHARDSON

IN THE UNITED STATES CIRCUIT COURT, DISTRICT OF COLUMBIA, NOVEMBER TERM, 1837.

Reported in 5 Cranch, Circuit Court Reports, 348.

INDICTMENT for an assault upon one Susan Shelton.

The evidence was that the defendant came into the house where Mrs. Shelton was sitting at a window. He was armed with a musket and a club; and raising the club over her head, in an attitude for striking, and within striking distance, said to her that if she said a word (or if she opened her mouth) he would strike her; and this without any provocation on her part.

Mr. Bradley and *Mr. Hoban*, for the defendant, contended that this was not, in law, an assault; that there can be no assault without a present intent to strike; and his saying, " if she opened her mouth," showed that he had not such a present intent; and they cited the old case, " if it were not the assizes, I would stab you."

But the COURT (THURSTON, J., absent) said that he had no right to restrain her from speaking; and his language showed an intent to strike upon her violation of a condition which he had no right to impose. Suppose a stranger comes to my house armed, and raises his club over my head, within striking distance, and threatens to beat me unless I will go out of and abandon my house; surely that would be an assault. So, if a highwayman puts a pistol to my breast, and threatens to shoot me unless I give him my money; this would be evidence of an assault, and would be charged as such in the indictment.

Verdict, guilty; fined ten dollars.[1]

OSBORN v. VEITCH

AT NISI PRIUS, CORAM WILLES, J., KENT SUMMER ASSIZES, 1858.

Reported in 1 Foster & Finlason, 317.

TRESPASS and assault. Pleas: Not guilty, and *son assault demesne.* Issue.

The plaintiffs were owners of a field in which the defendants were walking with loaded guns at half-cock in their hands. The plaintiffs desired them to withdraw and give their names, and on their refusal advanced towards them, apparently as if to apprehend them. The defendants half raised their guns, which they pointed towards them,

[1] United States v. Myers, 1 Cranch, C. C. 310; Keefe v. State, 19 Ark. 190; Hixson v. Slocum, 156 Ky. 487; State v. Dooley, 121 Mo. 591; State v. Herron, 12 Mont. 230; State v. Morgan, 3 Ired. 186; State v. Cherry, 11 Ired. 475; State v. Church, 63 N. C. 15; Bishop v. Ranney, 59 Vt. 316; French v. Ware, 65 Vt. 338 *Accord.*

and threatened to shoot them. The plaintiffs (one of whom was a constable) then gave them in charge to a policeman for shooting with intent, and he, with their assistance, seized and handcuffed them.

E. James submitted that there was no assault; as the guns were only at half-cock, there was no "present ability" to execute the threat. Read *v.* Coker.

Sed per WILLES, J. Pointing a loaded gun at a person is in law an assault. It is immaterial that it is at half-cock; cocking it is an instantaneous act, and there is a "present ability" of doing the act threatened, for it can be done in an instant.[1]

E. James. The assault was in self-defence; the defendants were only trespassers, and there was an attempt to apprehend them, and excess is not even assigned. Broughton *v.* Jackson, 18 Q. B. 378.

WILLES, J. It was not necessary that it should be. To shoot a man is not a lawful way of repelling an assault. No doubt the charge of shooting with intent was idle, and the assault was only a misdemeanor. The handcuffing was utterly unlawful.

Verdict for the plaintiff. Damages, one farthing.

BEACH *v.* HANCOCK

SUPERIOR COURT OF JUDICATURE, NEW HAMPSHIRE, DECEMBER TERM, 1853.

Reported in 27 New Hampshire Reports, 223.

TRESPASS, for an assault.

Upon the general issue it appeared that, the plaintiff and defendant being engaged in an angry altercation, the defendant stepped into his office, which was at hand, and brought out a gun, which he aimed at the plaintiff in an excited and threatening manner, the plaintiff being three or four rods distant. The evidence tended to show that the defendant snapped the gun twice at the plaintiff, and that the plaintiff did not know whether the gun was loaded or not, and that, in fact, the gun was not loaded.

The court ruled that the pointing of a gun, in an angry and threatening manner, at a person three or four rods distant, who was ignorant whether the gun was loaded or not, was an assault, though it should appear that the gun was not loaded, and that it made no difference whether the gun was snapped or not.

The court, among other things, instructed the jury that, in assessing the damages, it was their right and duty to consider the effect which the finding of light or trivial damages in actions for breaches

[1] State *v.* Church, 63 N. C. 15 *Accord.*

Firing a revolver in plaintiff's presence but not at him, intending to frighten him but not to do him any bodily harm, was held not to be an assault. Degenhardt *v.* Heller, 93 Wis. 662. Compare Nelson *v.* Crawford, 122 Mich. 466.

of the peace would have to encourage a disregard of the laws and disturbances of the public peace.

The defendant excepted to these rulings and instructions.

The jury having found a verdict for the plaintiff, the defendant moved for a new trial by reason of said exceptions.

Morrison and *Fitch*, for the defendant. The first question arising in this case is, Is it an assault to point an unloaded gun at a person in a threatening manner? An assault is defined to be an inchoate violence to the person of another, with the present means of carrying the intent into effect. 2 Greenl. Ev. 72. The attempt or offer with violence to do corporal hurt to another must be coupled with a present ability to constitute an assault. Roscoe's Crim. Ev. 287; 1 Russell on Crimes, 750. It is no assault to point an unloaded gun or pistol at another, &c. Blake *v.* Barnard, 9 Car. & P. 626; Regina *v.* Baker, 1 Car. & K. 254; Regina *v.* James, 1 Car. & K. 530. The court erred in instructing the jury that the pointing of a gun in an angry and threatening manner was an assault. It is well settled that the intention to do harm is the essence of an assault, and this intent is to be collected by the jury from the circumstances of the case. 2 Greenl. Ev. 73.[1]

GILCHRIST, C. J. Several cases have been cited by the counsel of the defendant to show that the ruling of the court was incorrect. Among them is the case of Regina *v.* Baker, 1 Car. & K. 254. In that case, the prisoner was indicted under the statute of 7 Will. IV. and 1 Vict. c. 85, for attempting to discharge a loaded pistol. Rolfe, B., told the jury that they must consider whether the pistol was in such a state of loading that, under ordinary circumstances, it would have gone off, and that the statute under which the prisoner was indicted would then apply. He says, also, "If presenting a pistol at a person, and pulling the trigger of it, be an assault at all, certainly, in the case where the pistol was loaded, it must be taken to be an attempt to discharge the pistol with intent to do some bodily injury."

From the manner in which this statement is made, the opinion of the court must be inferred to be, that presenting a loaded pistol is an assault. There is nothing in the case favorable to the defendant. The statute referred to relates to loaded arms.

The case of Regina *v.* James, 1 Car. & K. 530, was an indictment for attempting to discharge a loaded rifle. It was shown that the priming was so damp that it would not go off. Tindal, C. J., said: "I am of opinion that this was not a loaded arm within the statute of 1 Vict. c. 85, and that the prisoner can neither be convicted of the felony nor of the assault. It is only an assault to point a loaded pistol at any one, and this rifle is proved not to be so loaded as to be able to be discharged." The reason why the prisoner could not be convicted of the assault is given in the case of Regina *v.* St. George, 9 Car. & P.

[1] The argument for the plaintiff is omitted.

483, where it was held that on an indictment for a felony, which includes an assault, the prisoner ought not to be convicted of an assault, which is quite distinct from the felony charged, and on such an indictment the prisoner ought only to be convicted of an assault, which is involved in the felony itself. In this case, Parke, B., said: "If a person presents a pistol which has the appearance of being loaded, and puts the party into fear and alarm, that is what it is the object of the law to prevent." So if a person present a pistol purporting to be a loaded pistol at another, and so near as to have been dangerous to life if the pistol had gone off; *semble*, that this is an assault, even though the pistol were, in fact, not loaded. Ibid.

In the case of Blake *v.* Barnard, 9 Car. & P. 626, which was trespass for an assault and false imprisonment, the declaration alleged that the pistol was loaded with gunpowder, ball, and shot, and it was held that it was incumbent on the plaintiff to make that out. Lord Abinger then says, "If the pistol was not loaded, it would be no assault," and the prisoner would be entitled to an acquittal, which was undoubtedly correct, under that declaration, for the variance. Regina *v.* Oxford, 9 Car. & P. 525.

One of the most important objects to be attained by the enactment of laws and the institutions of civilized society is, each of us shall feel secure against unlawful assaults. Without such security society loses most of its value. Peace and order and domestic happiness, inexpressibly more precious than mere forms of government, cannot be enjoyed without the sense of perfect security. We have a right to live in society without being put in fear of personal harm. But it must be a reasonable fear of which we complain. And it surely is not unreasonable for a person to entertain a fear of personal injury, when a pistol is pointed at him in a threatening manner, when, for aught he knows, it may be loaded, and may occasion his immediate death. The business of the world could not be carried on with comfort, if such things could be done with impunity.

We think the defendant guilty of an assault, and we perceive no reason for taking any exception to the remarks of the court. Finding trivial damages for breaches of the peace — damages incommensurate with the injury sustained — would certainly lead the ill-disposed to consider an assault as a thing that might be committed with impunity. But at all events, it was proper for the jury to consider whether such a result would or would not be produced. Flanders *v.* Colby, 28 N. H. 34. *Judgment on the verdict.*[1]

[1] In Chapman *v.* State, 78 Ala. 463; State *v.* Yturaspe, 22 Idaho, 360; State *v.* Sears, 86 Mo. 169; State *v.* Godfrey, 17 Or. 300; McKay *v.* State, 44 Tex. 43, it was decided that a defendant who aimed an unloaded pistol at another, although perhaps liable for a civil assault, was not guilty of a criminal assault. See also 2 Green, Cr. Cas. 271 n.; Territory *v.* Gomez, 14 Ariz. 139; People *v.* Sylva, 143 Cal. 62. Such conduct was held to be a criminal assault in State *v.* Shepard, 10 Ia. 126; Commonwealth *v.* White, 110 Mass. 407; State *v.* Barry, 45 Mont. 598;

STEARNS AND WIFE *v.* SAMPSON

SUPREME JUDICIAL COURT, MAINE, 1871.

Reported in 59 Maine Reports, 568.

ON exceptions, and motion to set aside the verdict as being against law.

Trespass. The writ contained three counts: one for breaking and entering the plaintiffs' close and carrying away the household furniture; the second, for taking and carrying away the household furniture of the wife; and the third,[1] for assault on the wife.

There was evidence tending to show that after entry and notice to leave, and refusal by the wife and her mother, with an expressed determination on their part to hold possession against the defendant, the latter called in assistants and ordered them to remove the furniture, and they did remove it from some of the rooms; that upon going to one of the rooms, the door was fastened, and the assistants opened it; that the furniture, except bed, was removed from Mrs. Stearns' sleeping-room.

That the assistants remained there several days and nights.

That the defendant caused the windows to be removed; prevented food from being carried to the house; that a tenant was let into the L of the house, and had charge of the defendant's bloodhound, five months old, and permitted him to go into the house; that the furniture was removed into a house near by, and Mrs. Stearns notified of its whereabouts; that the doors fastened by Mrs. Stearns were removed; that Mrs. Stearns finally left by compulsion with an officer, and was sick several weeks.

The rulings sufficiently appear in the opinion.

The jury returned a verdict for the plaintiffs, and the defendant alleged exceptions, and also filed motions to set aside the verdict as being against law and the weight of evidence.

APPLETON, C. J. There is in the declaration a count for an assauit and battery upon the female plaintiff. In reference to this branch of the case, the following instructions were given: "Was there a trespass committed upon the female plaintiff? She is the only one who seeks for damages. Whatever may have been the injury inflicted upon the other inmates of that house, she can recover on this suit only for that which was inflicted upon her. In order to constitute an assault, it is not necessary that the person should be touched, but

Clark *v.* State, (Okl. Cr.) 106 Pac. 803; State *v.* Smith, 2 Humph. 457; Richels *v.* State, 1 Sneed, 606 (*semble*); Morison's Case, 1 Brown, Just. R. (Scotch) 394. In Commonwealth *v.* White, *supra*, Wells, J., said: "It is not the secret intent of the assaulting party, nor the undisclosed fact of his ability or inability to commit a battery, that is material, but what his conduct and the attending circumstances denote at the time to the party assaulted." Cf. Howell *v.* Winters, 58 Wash. 436.

[1] Only so much of the case is printed as relates to this count.

there should be certain indignities. In the language of one of the decisions, if the plaintiff was embarrassed and distressed by the acts of the defendant, it would amount in law to an assault." The acts and indignities which from the charge might constitute an assault were the bursting open a door, which the defendants had no right to fasten, and the inconveniences resulting from taking off the doors and taking out the windows, which made it uncomfortable for the female plaintiff to remain, where remaining, she was a trespasser. So the bringing a bloodhound by the defendant into his house, which is proved to have barked, but not to have bitten, and the making a noise therein, with other similar acts, it was contended, would amount to an assault and trespass, and of that the jury were to judge. Now, such is not the law. An assault and battery is clearly defined by R. S., c. 118, § 28, thus: "Whoever unlawfully attempts to strike, hit, touch, or do any violence to another, however small, in a wanton, wilful, angry, or insulting manner, having an intention and existing ability to do some violence to such person, shall be deemed guilty of an assault; and if such attempt is carried into effect, he shall be deemed guilty of an assault and battery." Now, the removal of a door or windows, of the owner in possession, would constitute no assault. Indeed, as has been seen, 6 Allen, 76, the owner would, in attempting it, have the right to use as much force as was necessary to overcome the resistance of the unlawfully resisting and trespassing tenant. Acts which may embarrass and distress do not necessarily amount to an assault. Indignities may not constitute an assault. Acts aggravating an assault differ materially from the assault thereby aggravated. Insulting language or conduct may aggravate an assault, but it not an assault.[1] So the acts of the defendant in taking out the windows of

[1] State *v.* Daniel, 136 N. C. 571; Degenhardt *v.* Heller, 93 Wis. 662 *Accord.* Wood *v.* Young, 20 Ky. L. Rep. 1931 *Contra.* It is not an assault to make the kissing sign to another. Fuller *v.* State, 44 Tex. Cr. 463.

Mere words, looks, or gestures, however violent or insulting, do not amount to an assault. State *v.* Borrelli, 24 Del. 349; Reimenschneider *v.* Neusis, 175 Ill. App. 172; Harvey *v.* Harvey, 124 La. 595; Bouillon *v.* La Clede Gas Light Co., 148 Mo. App. 462; State *v.* Daniel, 136 N. C. 571; Lewis *v.* Fountain, 168 N. C. 277. *A fortiori* violent language over the telephone is no assault. Kramer *v.* Ricksmeier, 159 Ia. 48.

No action lies for the shame and insult to a woman from inviting her to illicit intercourse. Davis *v.* Richardson, 76 Ark. 348; Reed *v.* Maley, 115 Ky. 816; State *v.* White, 52 Mo. App. 285. *Aliter* where accompanied by acts that put her in fear. Johnson *v.* Hohn, 168 Ia. 147; Jeppsen *v.* Jensen, 47 Utah, 536; Newell *v.* Whitcher, 53 Vt. 589. And a common carrier is liable, as a public service company, for insults to a passenger by its employees. Knoxville Co. *v.* Lane, 103 Tenn. 376.

"Injury is committed not only when a man is struck with the fist or beaten with a stick or lashed, but also when abusive language is publicly addressed to any one, or when . . . some one . . . has followed about a married woman or a young boy or girl, or when some person's modesty may be said to have been assailed." Institutes of Justinian, iv, 4, 1.

"Likewise it is an injury of this kind when one person, without actually striking another, keeps raising his hand menacingly and creates in the other the fear that he will be struck. . . . Likewise if he mocks another with indecent or indecorous gestures; or if by means of gesticulations he indicates things of such a kind that his own house, in a bleak and cold day, might distress one unlawfully occupying and illegally refusing to quit his premises, but they could in no sense be regarded as an assault upon her. One may be embarrassed and distressed by acts done " in a wanton, wilful, angry, or insulting manner," where there is no " intention nor existing ability to do some violence " to the person, and yet there be no assault. The instruction on this point is equally at variance with the common law and the statute of the State.[1]

COLE *v.* TURNER

AT NISI PRIUS, CORAM HOLT, C. J., EASTER TERM, 1704.

Reported in 6 *Modern Reports,* 149.

HOLT, C. J., upon evidence in trespass for assault and battery declared, —

First, That the least touching of another in anger[2] is a battery.

Secondly, If two or more meet in a narrow passage, and, without any violence or design of harm, the one touches the other gently, it will be no battery.[3]

Thirdly, If any of them use violence against the other, to force his way in a rude, inordinate manner, it will be a battery; or any struggle about the passage to that degree as may do hurt will be a battery.

if they were expressed in spoken words or in writing they would convey an injury." Voet, Commentary on the Pandects, xlvii, 10, § 7.

" Ignominious treatment is an injury only when it is an infringement of one of the absolute rights of personality: a right that is recognized by the law of the State as included amongst the natural rights of every freeman. Such an infringement of another's right may be regarded as offensive to good morals (*contra bonos mores*); hence the definition of *injuria* as ' an insult offered to any person against good morals ' (*contumelia contra bonos mores alicui illata*)." De Villiers, Roman and Roman-Dutch Law of Injuries, 22.

[1] Meader *v.* Stone, 7 Met. (Mass.) 147 *Accord.*

See Rex *v.* Smith, 2 Car. & P. 449; Preiser *v.* Wielandt, 48 App. Div. 569.

[2] Hostile touching or in anger. Singer Co. *v.* Methvin, 184 Ala. 554; McGlone *v.* Hanger, 56 Ind. App. 243; Booher *v.* Trainer, 172 Mo. App. 376; Hough *v.* Iderhoff, 69 Or. 568; Raefeldt *v.* Koenig, 152 Wis. 459 *Accord.*

Touching *contra bonos mores* but with no hostile intent. Richmond *v.* Fisk, 160 Mass. 34. Taking liberties with a woman. Hatchett *v.* Blacketer, 162 Ky. 266; Timmons *v.* Kenrick, 53 Ind. App. 490. Unauthorized surgical operation. Pratt *v.* Davis, 224 Ill. 300; Mohr *v.* Williams, 95 Minn. 261; Schloendorff *v.* Society, 211 N. Y. 125; Rolater *v.* Strain, 39 Okl. 572. But see Bennan *v.* Parsonnet, 83 N. J. Law, 20. *Aliter* where authorized by a minor. Bakker *v.* Welsh, 144 Mich. 632.

[3] Kerifford's Case, Clayt. 22 pl. 38 *Accord.* See, also, Steinman *v.* Baltimore Laundry Co., 109 Md. 62; Courtney *v.* Kneib, 131 Mo. App. 204.

INNES *v.* WYLIE

AT NISI PRIUS, CORAM LORD DENMAN, C. J., FEBRUARY 22, 1844.

Reported in 1 Carrington & Kirwan, 257.

ASSAULT. Plea:[1] Not guilty.

It further appeared that the plaintiff, on the 30th of November, 1843, went to a dinner of the society at Radley's Hotel, and was prevented by a policeman named Douglas from entering the room; and it was proved by the policeman that he acted by order of the defendants.

With respect to the alleged assault, the policeman said, "The plaintiff tried to push by me into the room, and I prevented him;" but some of the other witnesses stated that the plaintiff tried to enter the room, and was pushed back.

Erle addressed the jury for the defendant. There is no assault here. The policeman, who must best know what was done, says that the plaintiff tried to push into the room, and he prevented him; and preventing a person from pushing into a room is no assault, the assault, if any, being rather on the other side.

LORD DENMAN, C. J. (in summing up). You will say, whether, on the evidence, you think that the policeman committed an assault on the plaintiff, or was merely passive. If the policeman was entirely passive, like a door or a wall put to prevent the plaintiff from entering the room, and simply obstructing the entrance of the plaintiff, no assault has been committed on the plaintiff, and your verdict will be for the defendant. The question is, Did the policeman take any active measures to prevent the plaintiff from entering the room, or did he stand in the door-way passive, and not move at all?

Verdict for the plaintiff. Damages, 40*s.*

COWARD *v.* BADDELEY

IN THE EXCHEQUER, APRIL 19, 1859.

Reported in 4 Hurlstone & Norman, 478.

DECLARATION: That the defendant assaulted and beat the plaintiff, gave him in custody to a policeman, and caused him to be imprisoned in a police-station for twenty-four hours, and afterwards to be taken in custody along public streets before metropolitan police magistrates.

Pleas: First, Not guilty; third, That the plaintiff, within the Metropolitan Police District, assaulted the defendant, and therefore the defendant gave the plaintiff into custody to a police officer, who had view of the assault, in order that he might be taken before magistrates and dealt with according to law, &c.

[1] The statement of the case has been abridged.

Whereupon issue was joined.

At the trial before Bramwell, B., at the London sittings in last Hilary term, the plaintiff proved that, on the night of the 31st of October, he was passing through High Street, Islington, and stopped to look at a house which was on fire. The defendant was directing a stream of water from the hose of an engine on the fire. The plaintiff said, "Don't you see you are spreading the flames? Why don't you pump on the next house?" He went away, and then came back and repeated these words several times, but did not touch the defendant. The defendant charged the plaintiff with assaulting him, and gave him into the custody of a policeman who was standing near.

The defendant swore that, on being interrupted by the plaintiff, he told him to get out of the way and mind his own business; that the plaintiff came up to him again, seized him by the shoulder, violently turned him round, exposed him to danger, and turned the water off the fire.

The learned judge told the jury that the question was whether an assault and battery had been committed; and he asked them, first, whether the plaintiff laid hands on the defendant; and, secondly, whether he did so hostilely. The jury found that the plaintiff did lay hands on the defendant, intending to attract his attention. Whereupon the learned judge ordered the verdict to be entered for the plaintiff, reserving leave to the defendant to move to enter a verdict for him if the court should be of opinion that he had wrongly directed the jury in telling them that, to find the issue on the third plea for the defendant, they must find that the plaintiff laid his hands upon him with a hostile intention.

Shee, Serjt., in the same term, having obtained a rule *nisi* accordingly,

Beasley now showed cause. The question is, whether the intention of the plaintiff is material to be considered in order to determine whether there was an assault and battery. In Rawlings *v.* Till, 3 M. & W. 28, Parke, B., referring to Wiffin *v.* Kincard, 2 B. & P. N. R. 471, where it was held that a touch given by a constable's staff does not constitute a battery, pointed out, as the ground of that decision, that there the touch was merely to engage the plaintiff's attention. [MARTIN, B. Suppose two persons were walking near each other, and one turned round, and in so doing struck the other: surely that would not be a battery. POLLOCK, C. B. There may be a distinction for civil and criminal purposes. CHANNELL, B. It was necessary to prove an indictable assault and battery in order to sustain the plea.] The maxim, *Actus non facit reum nisi mens sit rea* applies. He referred also to Pursell *v.* Horn, 8 A. & E. 602; Archbold's Criminal Law, p. 524 (12th ed.); Scott *v.* Shepherd, 2 W. Bl. 892.

Petersdorff, Serjt., and *Francis*, in support of the rule. The learned judge's direction was defective in introducing the word "hostile."

In order to constitute an assault, it is enough if the act be done against the will of the party. There are several cases where it has been held that an assault has been committed where there was no intention to do the act complained of in a hostile way, as in the case of a prize-fight. Rex *v.* Perkins, 4 Car. & P. 537. So a surgeon assisting a female patient to remove a portion of her dress. Rex *v.* Rosinski 1 Moody C. C. 19. Here the plaintiff interfered with the defendant in the execution of his duty. In Hawkins' Pleas of the Crown, vol. i. p. 263, it is said, " Any injury whatever, be it never so small, being actually done to the person of a man in an angry, or revengeful, or rude, or insolent manner, as by spitting in his face, or any way touching him in anger, or violently jostling him out of the way, are batteries in the eye of the law." [BRAMWELL, B. I think that the jostling spoken of must mean a voluntary jostling.]

POLLOCK, C. B. I am of opinion that the rule must be discharged. The jury found that what the plaintiff did was done with the intent to attract the attention of the defendant, not with violence to justify giving the plaintiff into custody for an assault. The defendant treated it as a criminal act, and gave the plaintiff into custody. We are called on to set aside a verdict for the plaintiff, on the ground that he touched the defendant.[1] There is no foundation for the application.

MARTIN, B. I am of the same opinion. The assault and battery which the defendant was bound to establish means such an assault as would justify the putting in force the criminal law for the purpose of bringing the plaintiff to justice. It is necessary to show some act which justified the interference of the police officer. Touching a person so as merely to call his attention, whether the subject of a civil action or not, is not the ground of criminal proceeding. It is clear that it is no battery within the definition given by Hawkins.

CHANNELL, B. I am of the same opinion. Looking at the plea, it is obvious that it was not proved.

BRAMWELL, B., concurred. *Rule discharged.*

DE MARENTILLE *v.* OLIVER

SUPREME COURT, NEW JERSEY, FEBRUARY TERM, 1808.

Reported in 1 *Pennington,* 379.

THIS was action of trespass, brought by the defendant in this court, against the plaintiff *in certiorari.* The state of demand charged the defendant below, that he unlawfully, forcibly, and with great violence, with a large stick, struck the horse of the plaintiff, on the public highway, which said horse was then before a carriage, in which the plaintiff was riding, on the said public highway, to the damage of the

[1] Courtney *v.* Kneib, 131 Mo. App. 204 *Accord.* Compare Reynolds *v.* Pierson, 29 Ind. App. 273.

plaintiff fifty dollars. This cause was tried by a jury, and verdict and judgment for the plaintiff, $15 damages. It was assigned for error that the suit was brought before the justice to recover damages for an assault and battery, when, by law, such an action cannot be supported before a justice of the peace.

PENNINGTON, J.[1] To attack and strike with a club, with violence, the horse before a carriage, in which a person is riding, strikes me as an assault on the person;[2] and if so, the justice had no jurisdiction of the action.

But if this is to be considered as a trespass on the property, unconnected with an assault on the person, I think that it was incumbent on the plaintiff below to state an injury done to the horse, whereby the plaintiff suffered damage; that he was in consequence of the blow bruised or wounded, and unable to perform service; or that the plaintiff had been put to expense in curing of him, or the like. All the precedents of declarations for injuries done to domestic animals, as far as my recollection goes, are in that way; and I think, with good reason. Suppose a man, seeing a stranger's horse in the street, was to strike him with a whip, or a large stick, if you please, and no injury was to ensue, could the owner of the horse maintain an action for this act? I apprehend not. For these reasons, I incline to think, that this judgment ought to be reversed.

KIRKPATRICK, C. J. Concurred in the reversal.

Judgment reversed.

OBERLIN v. UPSON

SUPREME COURT, OHIO, JANUARY TERM, 1911.

Reported in 84 *Ohio State Reports*, 111.

DAVIS, J.[3] Under the common law of England as it has been recognized and administered in this country, a woman cannot maintain against her seducer an action for damages arising from her own seduction. This is frankly admitted by the counsel for the plaintiff in error; but they ask a reversal of the judgment below upon the ground that the plaintiff was induced to consent to the solicitations of the defendant by a betrayal of the love and confidence which had been

[1] A part of the case, relating to a point of practice, is omitted.

[2] Dodwell *v.* Burford, 1 Mod. 24; Hopper *v.* Reeve, 7 Taunt. 698; Spear *v.* Chapman, 8 Ir. L. R. 461; Reynolds *v.* Pierson, 29 Ind. App. 273; Burdick *v.* Worrall, 4 Barb. 596 (*semble*); Bull *v.* Colton, 22 Barb. 94; Clark *v.* Downing, 55 Vt. 259 *Accord.* But see Kirland *v.* State, 43 Ind. 146.

An injury to the clothes on one's back is a trespass on the person, Regina *v.* Day, 1 Cox, C. C. 207. So is the removal of an ulster from the plaintiff, Geraty *v.* Stern, 30 Hun, 426; or seizing anything in the plaintiff's hand, Scott *v.* State, 118 Ala. 115; Dyk *v.* De Young, 35 Ill. App. 138; Steinman *v.* Baltimore Laundry Co., 109 Md. 62 (*semble*); Respublica *v.* De Longchamps, 1 Dall. 111; or cutting a rope connecting the plaintiff with his slave, State *v.* Davis, 1 Hill (S. C.) 46.

[3] The statement of the pleadings and the arguments of counsel are omitted.

engendered in her by a period of courtship and by a promise of marriage made by him. Confessedly this is not an action *ex contractu* upon a promise of marriage, in which the seduction might be pleaded and proved as an aggravation of damages;[1] but it is clearly an attempt to recover *ex delicto*. There is no averment of mutual promises or of an agreement to marry; and an analysis of the amended petition discloses no more than that the defendant's promise was one of the blandishments by which he accomplished his purpose. The case, therefore, presents no exception to the common law rule; for there is no claim of fraud, violence or artifice other than mere solicitation.

The theory of the common law is that, since adultery and fornication are crimes,[2] the woman is *particeps criminis* and hence that she cannot be heard to complain of a wrong which she helped to produce. It may be conceded that some of the arguments adduced here might be fairly persuasive if addressed to the legislature. Indeed in several of the states statutes have been enacted authorizing such an action; but a careful study of the decisions in those states, limiting and construing those statutes, raises a doubt whether the legislation is a real advance upon the common law. 8 Ann. Cas. 1115, note. There is, however, no such statute in this state and the common law rule applies.

The judgment of the circuit court is *Affirmed.*[3]

SPEAR, C. J., SHAUCK, PRICE, and JOHNSON, JJ., concur.

DONAHUE, J., not participating.

[1] Berry *v.* Da Costa, L. R. 1 C. P. 331; Collins *v.* Mack, 31 Ark. 684; Hattin *v.* Chapman, 46 Conn. 607; Graves *v.* Rivers, 123 Ga. 224; Tubbs *v.* Van Kleek, 12 Ill. 446; Tyler *v.* Salley, 82 Me. 128; Sauer *v.* Schulenberg, 33 Md. 288; Sherman *v.* Rawson, 102 Mass. 395; Kelley *v.* Riley, 106 Mass. 339; Bennett *v.* Beam, 42 Mich. 346; Schmidt *v.* Durnham, 46 Minn. 227; Green *v.* Spencer, 3 Mo. 318; Musselman *v.* Barker, 26 Neb. 737; Coil *v.* Wallace, 24 N. J. Law, 291; Kniffen *v.* McConnell, 30 N. Y. 285; Spellings *v.* Parks, 104 Tenn. 351; Daggett *v.* Wallace, 75 Tex. 352; Giese *v.* Schultz, 69 Wis. 521 *Accord.*

Weaver *v.* Bachert, 2 Pa. St. 80; Wrynn *v.* Downey, 27 R. I. 454 *Contra.*

[2] But see 4 Blackstone, Commentaries, 65; 1 Bishop, New Criminal Law, § 38.

[3] Beseler *v.* Stephani, 71 Ill. 400; Woodward *v.* Anderson, 9 Bush, 624; Paul *v.* Frazier, 3 Mass. 71; Welsund *v.* Schueller, 98 Minn. 475; Robinson *v.* Musser, 78 Mo. 153; Hamilton *v.* Lomax, 26 Barb. 615; Weaver *v.* Bachert, 2 Pa. St. 80; Conn *v.* Wilson, 2 Overt. 233 *Accord.* See Desborough *v.* Homes, 1 F. & F. 6.

An action is allowed by statute in some jurisdictions. Marshall *v.* Taylor, 98 Cal. 55; Swett *v.* Gray, 141 Cal. 83; McIlvain *v.* Emery, 88 Ind. 298; Verwers *v.* Carpenter, 166 Ia. 273; Watson *v.* Watson, 49 Mich. 540; Hood *v.* Sudderth, 111 N. C. 215; Breon *v.* Henkle, 14 Or. 494. The Scotch law is to the same effect. Smith, Law of Damages in Scotland, 128. Under these statutes it has been held that there must be a real seduction: "Consent must be procured by some trick or artifice other than mere solicitation." Brown *v.* Kingsley, 38 Ia. 220. Compare Breon *v.* Henkle, 14 Or. 494.

Even without a statute a guardian is liable in damages for the seduction of his ward. Graham *v.* Wallace, 50 App. Div. 101. See also Smith *v.* Richards, 29 Conn. 232.

BELL *v.* HANSLEY

SUPREME COURT, NORTH CAROLINA, DECEMBER TERM, 1855.

Reported in 3 *Jones,* 131.

THIS was an action of trespass, assault, and battery, tried before Ellis, Judge, at the fall term, 1855, of New Hanover Superior Court.

The plaintiff proved the assault and battery; and there was evidence tending to show a mutual affray and fighting by consent.

But his Honor was of opinion, and so advised the jury, that notwithstanding the fact that the parties had mutually assented to an affray, the plaintiff was, nevertheless, entitled to recover; but that the fact relied on as a defence was proper to be considered by the jury in mitigation of damages. The defendant excepted to these instructions. *Verdict for the plaintiff. Judgment and appeal.*

NASH, C. J. This case presents the question whether, when two men fight together, thereby committing an affray, either is guilty of an assault and battery upon the other. Justice Buller, in his Nisi Prius, at page 16, says, each does commit an assault and battery upon the other, and that each can maintain an action for it. He refers to a case at Abingdon, Boulter *v.* Clark, when Serjeant Hayward appeared for the defendant, and offered to prove that the parties fought by consent and insisted that this, under the maxim *volenti non fit injuria,* applied. Parker, Chief Baron, denied it, and said, " the fighting being unlawful, the consent of the plaintiff to fight would be no bar to his action, and that he was entitled to a verdict." Mr. Stephens, in his Nisi Prius, 211, lays down the same doctrine: " If two men engage in a boxing match, an action can be sustained by either of them against the other, if an assault be made; because the act of boxing is unlawful, and the consent of the parties to fight cannot excuse the injury."

Per Curiam. Judgment affirmed.[1]

[1] Boulter *v.* Clarke, Bull. N. P. 16; Reg. *v.* Coney, 8 Q. B. D. 534, 538, 546, 549, 567; Logan *v.* Austin, 1 Stewart (Ala.) 476; Cadwell *v.* Farrell, 28 Ill. 438; Adams *v.* Waggoner, 33 Ind. 531; Lund *v.* Tyler, 115 Ia. 236; McNeil *v.* Mullin, 70 Kan. 634; Galbraith *v.* Fleming, 60 Mich. 403; Grotton *v.* Glidden, 84 Me. 589; Commonwealth *v.* Colburg, 119 Mass. 350 (*semble*); Lizana *v.* Lang. 90 Miss. 469; Jones *v.* Gale, 22 Mo. App. 637; Morris *v.* Miller, 83 Neb. 218; Stout *v.* Wren, 1 Hawks (N. C.), 420; Barholt *v.* Wright, 45 Ohio St. 177 (explaining Champer *v.* State, 14 Ohio St. 437); McCue *v.* Klein, 60 Tex. 168 (*semble*); Willey *v.* Carpenter, 64 Vt. 212; Shay *v.* Thompson, 59 Wis. 540; Miller *v.* Bayer, 94 Wis. 124 (procuring an abortion with plaintiff's consent) *Accord.*

Reg. *v.* Coney, 15 Cox, C. C. 46 (*semble*), *per* HAWKINS J.; Hegarty *v.* Shine, L. R. 4 Ir. 288, 294 (*semble*); Goldnamer *v.* O'Brien, 98 Ky. 569 (procuring an abortion with plaintiff's consent); Lykins *v.* Hamrick, 144 Ky. 80, *Contra.* If the plaintiff is injured by the defendant, both being engaged in an illegal charivari party, he cannot recover damages from the defendant. Gilmore *v.* Fuller, 198 Ill. 130.

As to injury in the course of a " friendly scuffle," see Gibeline *v.* Smith, 106 Mo. App. 545.

SECTION II

IMPRISONMENT

NOTE BY THORPE, C. J., 1348.

Reported in Year Book, Liber Assisarum, folio 104, *placitum* 85.

THERE is said to be an imprisonment in any case where one is arrested by force and against his will, although it be on the high street or elsewhere, and not in a house, &c.[1]

GENNER v. SPARKES

IN THE KING'S BENCH, TRINITY TERM, 1704.

Reported in 1 *Salkeld,* 79.

GENNER, a bailiff, having a warrant against Sparkes, went to him in his yard, and, being at some distance, told him he had a warrant, and said he arrested him. Sparkes, having a fork in his hand, keeps off the bailiff from touching him, and retreats into his house. And this was moved as a contempt. *Et per Curiam.* The bailiff cannot have an attachment, for here was no arrest nor rescous. Bare words will not make an arrest; but if the bailiff had touched him, that had been an arrest,[2] and the retreat a rescous, and the bailiff might have pursued and broke open the house, or might have had an attachment or a rescous against him; but as this case is, the bailiff has no remedy, but an action for the assault; for the holding up of the fork at him when he was within reach, is good evidence of that.[3]

[1] McNay *v.* Stratton, 9 Ill. App. 215; Price *v.* Bailey, 66 Ill. 48; Hildebrand *v.* McCrum, 101 Ind. 61; Smith *v.* State, 7 Humph. 43; Sorenson *v.* Dundas, 50 Wis. 335 *Accord.*

Compare Marshall *v.* Heller, 55 Wis. 392. For recent definitions see Westberry *v.* Clanton, 136 Ga. 795; Coolahan *v.* Marshall Field & Co., 159 Ill. App. 466; Efroymson *v.* Smith, 29 Ind. App. 451; Comer *v.* Knowles, 17 Kan. 436; New York R. Co. *v.* Waldron, 116 Md. 441; Smith *v.* Clark, 37 Utah, 116, 126.

[2] Anon. 1 Vent. 306; Anon. 7 Mod. 8; Whithead *v.* Keyes, 3 All. 495 *Accord.*

[3] If the bailiff, who has a process against one, says to him when he is on horseback or in a coach, "You are my prisoner; I have a writ against you," upon which he submits, turns back, or goes with him, though the bailiff never touched him, yet it is an arrest, because he submitted to the process; but if, instead of going with the bailiff, he had gone or fled from him, it could be no arrest, unless the bailiff laid hold of him. Horner *v.* Battyn, Bull. N. P. 62.

WOOD *v.* LANE

AT NISI PRIUS, CORAM TINDAL, C. J., DECEMBER 13, 1834.

Reported in 6 *Carrington & Payne*, 774.

TRESPASS and false imprisonment. Pleas: Not guilty; and leave and license.

It was proved by a member of the plaintiff's family that he was a flannel draper in Castle Street, Holborn, and that on the 3d of April he came home accompanied by the defendants, Cleaton and Lane; and that the plaintiff said Cleaton had arrested him at Mr. Sanders's, in Holborn; that the plaintiff's wife asked the defendant Lane, who was, in fact, clerk to Cleaton's attorney, if he had any authority, and he said he had; and being asked his name, said, " My name is Selby of Chancery Lane." Lane made several inquiries about the plaintiff's property, and said he would give him time till eight o'clock in the evening; upon which the other defendant, Cleaton, said, " How can you do that ? I will not allow you to give him any time at all." It was proved that, in fact, Mr. Selby had no bailable process against the plaintiff. A witness was also called, who proved that, in conversation with the defendant Lane on the subject, he said it was a foolish piece of business; that Mr. Cleaton had caused him to do it; that he was very sorry for it, but he thought Mr. Cleaton would indemnify him. There was some uncertainty in the evidence of the conversation whether the defendant Lane admitted or not that he had taken the plaintiff by the arm.

According to the evidence of Mr. Sanders, at whose house the transaction commenced, the plaintiff was bargaining with him for the sale of some goods, and had just made out the invoice, which was lying before him, when the defendant Cleaton came in alone, and asked the plaintiff several times to pay the amount he owed him, or some money on account. The plaintiff said he would not; upon which Cleaton went just outside the door, and returned immediately, followed by the defendant Lane, and pointing to the plaintiff, said, " This is the gentleman." The plaintiff tore up the invoice he had written, and threw it on the fire, and said, " I suppose I am to go with you." The answer given was, " Yes." The plaintiff and the two defendants went away together.

Talfourd, Serjt., for the defendant. No arrest has been proved. Sanders, who was present, says nothing of the laying hold of the plaintiff.

TINDAL, C. J. The question is, whether the plaintiff went voluntarily from Mr. Sanders's to his own house, or whether he went in consequence of the acts of the defendants. If you put your hand upon a man, or tell him he must go with you, and he goes, supposing you to have the power to enforce him, is not that an arrest? May you not arrest without touching a man?

White referred to the case of Arrowsmith *v.* Le Mesurier, 2 B. & P. N. R. 211.

TINDAL, C. J. That is a case which has often been spoken of as going to the very extreme point; but in that case the jury found that the plaintiff went voluntarily with the officer. And in this case, if you can persuade the jury that the plaintiff went voluntarily, you may succeed.

Talfourd, Serjt., then addressed the jury for the defendants. There was no real compulsion. No writ was produced. It was only an endeavor by a manœuvre to make the plaintiff do what he ought, but would not, viz., pay the money which he owed.

TINDAL, C. J., in summing up, told the jury, that, if the plaintiff was acting as an unwilling agent, at the time and against his own will when he went to his own house from that of Sanders, it was just as much an arrest as if the defendants had forced him along.

The jury found for the plaintiff. Damages, £10.[1]

PIKE *v.* HANSON

SUPERIOR COURT OF JUDICATURE, NEW HAMPSHIRE, DECEMBER TERM, 1838.

Reported in 9 *New Hampshire Reports,* 491.

TRESPASS, for an assault and false imprisonment on the 1st day of July, A.D. 1837. The action was commenced before a justice of the peace. The defendants pleaded severally the general issue. It appeared in evidence that the defendants were selectmen of the town of Madbury for the year 1836; that they assessed a list of taxes upon the inhabitants of said town, among whom was the plaintiff, and committed it to Nathan Brown, collector of said town, for collection. Brown, after having given due notice to the plaintiff, being in a room with her, called upon her to pay the tax, which she declined doing until arrested. He then told her that he arrested her, but did not lay his hand upon her; and thereupon she paid the tax.

Upon this evidence the defendants objected that the action could not be maintained, because there was no assault.

It did not appear that the defendants had been sworn, as directed by the statute of January 4, 1833. A verdict was taken for the plaintiff, subject to the opinion of the court.

[1] Chinn *v.* Morris, 2 Car. & P. 361; Pocock *v.* Moore, Ry. & M. 321; Peters *v.* Stanway, 6 Car. & P. 737; Granger *v.* Hill, 4 Bing. N.C. 212; Warner *v.* Riddiford, 4 C. B. N. S. 180 (criticizing Arrowsmith *v.* Le Mesurier, 2 B. & P. N. R. 211); Singleton *v.* Kansas City Base Ball Co., 172 Mo. App. 299 *Accord.*

To hold a man by the sleeve without professing to arrest him or leading him to believe he is not free to get away is not an imprisonment. Macintosh *v.* Cohen, 24 N. Zeal. L. R. 625.

WILCOX, J.[1] . . . But it is contended that in the present case there has been no assault committed, and no false imprisonment. Bare words will not make an arrest: there must be an actual touching of the body; or, what is tantamount, a power of taking immediate possession of the body, and the party's submission thereto. Genner *v.* Sparkes, 1 Salk. 79. Where a bailiff, having a writ against a person, met him on horseback, and said to him, "You are my prisoner," upon which he turned back and submitted, this was held to be a good arrest, though the bailiff never laid hand on him. But if, on the bailiff's saying those words, he had fled, it had been no arrest, unless the bailiff had laid hold of him. Homer *v.* Battyn, Buller's N. P. 62. The same doctrine is held in other cases. Russen *v.* Lucas & al., 1 Car. & P. 153; Chinn *v.* Morris, 2 Car. & P. 361; Pocock *v.* Moore, Ry. & M. 321; Strout *v.* Gooch, 8 Greenl. 126; Gold *v.* Bissell, 1 Wend. 210.

Where, upon a magistrate's warrant being shown to the plaintiff, the latter voluntarily and without compulsion attended the constable who had the warrant to the magistrate, it was held there was no sufficient imprisonment to support an action. Arrowsmith *v.* Le Mesurier, 2 B. & P. N. R. 211. But in this case there was no declaration of any arrest, and the warrant was in fact used only as a summons. And if the decision cannot be sustained upon this distinction, it must be regarded as of doubtful authority.

Starkie says that in ordinary practice words are sufficient to constitute an imprisonment, if they impose a restraint upon the person, and the plaintiff is accordingly restrained; for he is not obliged to incur the risk of personal violence and insult by resisting, until actual violence be used. 3 Stark. Ev. 1113. This principle is reasonable in itself, and is fully sustained by the authorities above cited. Nor does it seem necessary that there should be any very formal declaration of an arrest. If the officer goes for the purpose of executing his warrant; has the party in his presence and power; if the party so understands it, and in consequence thereof submits, and the officer, in execution of the warrant, takes the party before a magistrate, or receives money or property in discharge of his person, we think it is in law an arrest, although he did not touch any part of the body.

In the case at bar, it clearly appears that the plaintiff did not intend to pay the tax, unless compelled by an arrest of her person. The collector was so informed. He then proceeded to enforce the collection of the tax, — declared that he arrested her, — and she, under that restraint, paid the money. This is a sufficient arrest and imprisonment to sustain the action, and there must, therefore, be

Judgment on the verdict.[2]

[1] Part of the case, not relating to imprisonment, has been omitted.

[2] Johnson *v.* Tompkins, Baldw. C. C. 571, 601; Collins *v.* Fowler, 10 Ala. 858; Courtoy *v.* Dozier, 20 Ga. 369; Hawk *v.* Ridgway, 33 Ill. 473; Brushaber *v.* Stegemann, 22 Mich. 266; Josselyn *v.* McAllister, 25 Mich. 45; Moore *v.* Thompson, 92

FOTHERINGHAM v. ADAMS EXPRESS CO.

IN THE UNITED STATES CIRCUIT COURT, EASTERN DISTRICT, MISSOURI, SEPTEMBER 24, 1888.

Reported in 36 *Federal Reporter*, 252.

THAYER, J.[1] With reference to the motion for a new trial which has been filed in this case and duly considered, it will suffice to say, that I entertain no doubt that the jury were warranted in finding that plaintiff was unlawfully restrained of his liberty from about the 27th or 28th of October until the 10th of November following; that is to say, for a period of about two weeks. The testimony in the case clearly showed that during that period he was constantly guarded by detectives employed by defendant for that purpose; that he was at no time free to come and go as he pleased; that his movements were at all times subject to the control and direction of those who had him in charge; that he was urged by them on several occasions to confess his guilt, and make known his confederates; and that he was subjected to repeated examinations and cross-examinations touching the robbery, of such character as clearly to imply that he was regarded as a criminal, and that force would be used to detain him if he attempted to assert his liberty. The jury in all probability found (as they were warranted in doing) that during the time plaintiff remained in company with the detectives, he was in fact deprived of all real freedom of action, and that whatever consent he gave to such restraint was an enforced consent, and did not justify the detention without a warrant. It is manifest that the court ought not to disturb the finding on that issue.[2]

Mich. 498; Ahern v. Collins, 39 Mo. 145; Strout v. Gooch, 8 Greenl. 126; Mowry v. Chase, 100 Mass. 79; Emery v. Chesley, 18 N. H. 198; Browning v. Rittenhouse, 40 N. J. Law, 230; Hebrew v. Pulis, 73 N. J. Law, 621; Gold v. Bissell, 1 Wend. 210; Van Voorhees v. Leonard, 1 Thomp. & C. 148; Searls v. Viets, 2 Thomp. & C. 224; Limbeck v. Gerry, 15 Misc. 663; Martin v. Houck, 141 N. C. 317; Huntington v. Shultz, Harp. 452; Mead v. Young, 2 Dev. & Batt. 521; Haskins v. Young, 2 Dev. & Batt. 527; Jones v. Jones, 13 Ired. 448; McCracken v. Ansley, 4 Strob. 1; Gunderson v. Struebing, 125 Wis. 173 *Accord.*

Submission to wrongful detention by conductor of a train in consequence of his representation of authority to detain plaintiff was held an imprisonment in Whitman v. Atchison R. Co., 85 Kan. 150.

There must be reasonable ground for fear that defendant will use force. Powell v. Champion Fibre Co., 150 N. C. 12.

But compare Cottam v. Oregon City, 98 Fed. 570, deciding that a submission to arrest rather than pay an illegal license fee is not an imprisonment.

[1] A portion of the case, relating to damages, is omitted.

[2] As to "shadowing" by detectives, see Chappell v. Stewart, 82 Md. 323; People v. Weiler, 179 N. Y. 46; Schultz v. Ins. Co., 151 Wis. 537.

BIRD *v.* JONES

IN THE QUEEN'S BENCH, TRINITY VACATION, 1845.

Reported in 7 Queen's Bench Reports, 742.

THIS action was tried before Lord Denman, C. J., at the Middlesex sittings after Michaelmas term, 1843, when a verdict was found for the plaintiff.

In Hilary term, 1844, Thesiger obtained a rule *nisi* for a new trial, on the ground of misdirection.

In Trinity term, in the same year (June 5), Platt, Humfrey, and Hance showed cause, and Sir F. Thesiger, Solicitor-General, supported the rule.

The judgments sufficiently explain the nature of the case.

Cur. adv. vult.

In this vacation (9th July), there being a difference of opinion on the bench, the learned judges who heard the argument delivered judgment *seriatim.*

COLERIDGE, J. In this case, in which we have unfortunately been unable to agree in our judgment, I am now to pronounce the opinion which I have formed; and I shall be able to do so very briefly, because, having had the opportunity of reading a judgment prepared by my Brother Patteson, and entirely agreeing with it, I may content myself with referring to the statement he has made in detail of those preliminary points in which we all, I believe, agree, and which bring the case up to that point upon which its decision must certainly turn, and with regard to which our difference exists.

This point is, whether certain facts, which may be taken as clear upon the evidence, amount to an imprisonment. These facts, stated shortly, and as I understand them, are in effect as follows: —

A part of a public highway was inclosed, and appropriated for spectators of a boat-race, paying a price for their seats. The plaintiff was desirous of entering this part, and was opposed by the defendant; but, after a struggle, during which no momentary detention of his person took place, he succeeded in climbing over the inclosure. Two policemen were then stationed by the defendant to prevent, and they did prevent, him from passing onwards in the direction in which he declared his wish to go; but he was allowed to remain unmolested where he was, and was at liberty to go, and was told that he was so, in the only other direction by which he could pass. This he refused for some time, and during that time remained where he had thus placed himself.

These are the facts; and, setting aside those which do not properly bear on the question now at issue, there will remain these: that the plaintiff, being in a public highway and desirous of passing along it in a particular direction, is prevented from doing so by the orders of the defendant, and that the defendant's agents for the purpose are policemen, from whom, indeed, no unnecessary violence was to be anticipated, or such as they believed unlawful, yet who might be expected to execute such commands as they deemed lawful with all necessary force, however resisted. But although thus obstructed, the plaintiff was at liberty to move his person and go in any other direction, at his free will and pleasure; and no actual force or restraint on his person was used, unless the obstruction before mentioned amounts to so much.

I lay out of consideration the question of right or wrong between these parties. The acts will amount to imprisonment, neither more nor less, from their being wrongful or capable of justification.

And I am of opinion that there was no imprisonment. To call it so appears to me to confound partial obstruction and disturbance with total obstruction and detention. A prison may have its boundary large or narrow, visible and tangible, or, though real, still in the conception only; it may itself be movable or fixed; but a boundary it must have, and that boundary the party imprisoned must be prevented from passing; he must be prevented from leaving that place, within the ambit of which the party imprisoning would confine him, except by prison breach. Some confusion seems to me to arise from confounding imprisonment of the body with mere loss of freedom: it is one part of the definition of freedom to be able to go whithersoever one pleases; but imprisonment is something more than the mere loss of this power: it includes the notion of restraint within some limits defined by a will or power exterior to our own.

In Com. Dig. Imprisonment (G), it is said: "Every restraint of the liberty of a free man will be an imprisonment." For this the authorities cited are 2 Inst. 482; Cro. Car. 209. But when these are referred to, it will be seen that nothing was intended at all inconsistent with what I have ventured to lay down above. In both books the object was to point out that a prison was not necessarily what is commonly so called, a place locally defined and appointed for the reception of prisoners. Lord Coke is commenting on the statute of Westminster 2d,[1] *in prisona*, and says: "Every restraint of the liberty of a freeman is an imprisonment, although he be not within the walls of any common prison." The passage in Cro. Car. 209, is from a curious case of an information against Sir Miles Hobert and Mr. Stroud for escaping out of the Gate-house Prison, to which they had been committed by the king. The question was whether, under the circumstances, they had ever been there imprisoned. Owing to the sickness in London, and through the favor of the keeper, these gentlemen had not, except on one occasion, ever been within the walls of the Gate-house. The occasion is somewhat singularly expressed in the decision of the court,

[1] Stat. 13 Ed. I. c. 48.

which was "that their voluntary retirement to the close stool" in the Gate-house "made them to be prisoners." The resolution, however, in question is this: "that the prison of the King's Bench is not any local prison confined only to one place, and that every place where any person is restrained of his liberty is a prison; as if one take sanctuary and depart thence, he shall be said to break prison."

On a case of this sort, which, if there be difficulty in it, is at least purely elementary, it is not easy nor necessary to enlarge, and I am unwilling to put any extreme case hypothetically; but I wish to meet one suggestion, which has been put as avoiding one of the difficulties which cases of this sort might seem to suggest. If it be said that to hold the present case to amount to an imprisonment would turn every obstruction of the exercise of a right of way into an imprisonment, the answer is that there must be something like personal menace or force accompanying the act of obstruction, and that, with this, it will amount to imprisonment. I apprehend that is not so. If, in the course of a night, both ends of a street were walled up, and there was no egress from the house but into the street, I should have no difficulty in saying that the inhabitants were thereby imprisoned; but if only one end were walled up, and an armed force stationed outside to prevent any scaling of the wall or passage that way, I should feel equally clear that there was no imprisonment. If there were, the street would obviously be the prison, and yet, as obviously, none would be confined to it.

Knowing that my lord has entertained strongly an opinion directly contrary to this, I am under serious apprehension that I overlook some difficulty in forming my own; but, if it exists, I have not been able to discover it, and am therefore bound to state that, according to my view of the case, the rule should be absolute for a new trial.[1]

LORD DENMAN, C. J. I have not drawn up a formal judgment in this case, because I hoped to the last that the arguments which my learned brothers would produce in support of their opinion might alter mine. We have freely discussed the matter both orally and in written communications; but, after hearing what they have advanced, I am compelled to say that my first impression remains. If, as I must believe, it is a wrong one, it may be in some measure accounted for by the circumstances attending the case. A company unlawfully obstructed a public way for their own profit, extorting money from passengers, and hiring policemen to effect this purpose. The plaintiff, wishing to exercise his right of way, is stopped by force, and ordered to move in a direction which he wished not to take. He is told at the same time that a force is at hand ready to compel his submission. That proceeding appears to me equivalent to being pulled by the collar out of the one line and into the other.

[1] The concurring opinions of Williams and Patteson, JJ., are omitted.

There is some difficulty, perhaps, in defining imprisonment in the abstract without reference to its illegality; nor is it necessary for me to do so, because I consider these acts as amounting to imprisonment. That word I understand to mean any restraint of the person by force. In Buller's Nisi Prius, p. 22, it is said: "Every restraint of a man's liberty under the custody of another, either in a gaol, house, stocks, or in the street, is in law an imprisonment; and whenever it is done without a proper authority, is false imprisonment, for which the law gives an action; and this is commonly joined to assault and battery; for every imprisonment includes a battery, and every battery an assault." It appears, therefore, that the technical language has received a very large construction, and that there need not be any touching of the person: a locking up would constitute an imprisonment, without touching. From the language of Thorpe, C. J., which Mr. Selwyn cites from the Book of Assizes, it appears that, even in very early times, restraint of liberty by force was understood to be the reasonable definition of imprisonment.

I had no idea that any person in these times supposed any particular boundary to be necessary to constitute imprisonment, or that the restraint of a man's person from doing what he desires ceases to be an imprisonment because he may find some means of escape.

It is said that the party here was at liberty to go in another direction. I am not sure that in fact he was, because the same unlawful power which prevented him from taking one course might, in case of acquiescence, have refused him any other. But this liberty to do something else does not appear to me to affect the question of imprisonment. As long as I am prevented from doing what I have a right to do, of what importance is it that I am permitted to do something else? How does the imposition of an unlawful condition show that I am not restrained? If I am locked in a room, am I not imprisoned, because I might effect my escape through a window, or because I might find an exit dangerous or inconvenient to myself, as by wading through water, or by taking a route so circuitous that my necessary affairs should suffer by delay?

It appears to me that this is a total deprivation of liberty with reference to the purpose for which he lawfully wished to employ his liberty; and, being effected by force, it is not the mere obstruction of a way, but a restraint of the person. The case cited as occurring before Lord Chief Justice Tindal, as I understand it, is much in point. He held it an imprisonment where the defendant stopped the plaintiff on his road till he had read a libel to him. Yet he did not prevent his escaping in another direction.

It is said that if any damage arises from such obstruction, a special action on the case may be brought. Must I then sue out a new writ stating that the defendant employed direct force to prevent my going where my business called me, whereby I sustained loss? And if I do, is it certain that I shall not be told that I have misconceived my remedy, for all flows from the false imprisonment, and that should have been the subject of an action of trespass and assault? For the jury properly found that the whole of the defendant's conduct was continuous: it commenced in illegality; and the plaintiff did right to resist it as an outrageous violation of the liberty of the subject from the very first. *Rule absolute.*[1]

[1] Wright *v.* Wilson, 1 Ld. Raym. 739; Crossett *v.* Campbell, 122 La. 659; Balmain Ferry Co. *v.* Robertson, 4 C. L. R. (Australia) 379, aff'd [1910] A. C. 295; Queen *v.* Macquarie, 13 N. S. W. Sup. Ct. R. (Law) 264 (*semble*) *Accord.*

See Hawk *v.* Ridgway, 33 Ill. 473; Cullen *v.* Dickenson, 33 S. D. 27.

To order one to leave a boat which was moored to a wharf and, upon his refusal, to set the boat adrift is an imprisonment. Queen *v.* Macquarie, 13 N. S. W. Sup. Ct. R. (Law) 264.

Compare Herd *v.* Weardale Steel Co. [1913] 3 K. B. 771; Robinson *v.* Ferry Co. [1910] A. C. 295; Whittaker *v.* Sanford, 110 Me. 77; Talcott *v.* National Exhibition Co., 144 App. Div. 337.

CHAPTER II

NEGLIGENT INTERFERENCE

SECTION I

NEGLIGENCE AS A GROUND OF LIABILITY

WEAVER *v.* WARD

IN THE KING'S BENCH, EASTER TERM, 1616.

Reported in Hobart, 134.

WEAVER brought an action of trespass of assault and battery against Ward. The defendant pleaded that he was, amongst others, by the commandment of the lords of the council, a trained soldier in London, of the band of one Andrews, captain, and so was the plaintiff: and that they were skirmishing with their muskets charged with powder for their exercise *in re militari* against another captain and his band; and as they were so skirmishing, the defendant, *casualiter et per infortunium et contra voluntatem suam*, in discharging his piece, did hurt and wound the plaintiff; which is the same, &c., *absque hoc*, that he was guilty *aliter sive alio modo*. And, upon demurrer by the plaintiff, judgment was given for him; for, though it were agreed that if men tilt or tourney in the presence of the king, or if two masters of defence playing their prizes kill one another, that this shall be no felony, or if a lunatic kill a man, or the like; because felony must be done *animo felonico;* yet, in trespass, which tends only to give damages according to hurt or loss, it is not so; and therefore, if a lunatic hurt a man, he shall be answerable in trespass,[1] and, therefore, no man

[1] Gates *v.* Miles, 3 Conn. 64, 70; McIntyre *v.* Sholty, 121 Ill. 660; Amick *v.* O'Hara, 6 Blackf. 258, 259; Cross *v.* Kent, 32 Md. 581; Feld *v.* Borodófski, 87 Miss. 727; Bullock *v.* Babcock, 3 Wend. 391; Krom *v.* Schoonmaker, 3 Barb. 647. (imprisonment); Ward *v.* Conatser, 4 Baxt. (Tenn.) 64; Brennan *v.* Donaghey, 19 N. Zeal. Gaz. L. R. 289, affirming s. c. 2 New Zeal. Gaz. L. R. 410 *Accord.*

The rule is the same as to torts in general. Behrens *v.* McKenzie, 23 Ia. 333, 343; Chesapeake R. Co. *v.* Francisco, 149 Ky. 307; Morain *v.* Devlin, 132 Mass. 87 (nuisance); Gibson *v.* Pollock, 179 Mo. App. 188; Jewell *v.* Colby, 66 N. H. 399; Re Heller, 3 Paige, 199; Williams *v.* Hays, 143 N. Y. 442 (compare Williams *v.* Hays, 157 N. Y. 541); Williams *v.* Cameron, 26 Barb. 172; Lancaster Bank *v.* Moore, 78 Pa. St. 407, 412; Morse *v.* Crawford, 17 Vt. 499 (conversion).

A lunatic has been held liable under a statute giving an action to the widow and children of one killed by the " careless, wanton, or malicious " use of firearms. Young *v.* Young, 141 Ky. 76.

In McIntyre *v.* Sholty, *supra*, Magruder, J., said, p. 664: " It is well settled that, though a lunatic is not punishable criminally, he is liable in a civil action for any tort he may commit. However justly this doctrine may have been originally shall be excused of a trespass (for this is the nature of an excuse, and not of a justification, *prout ei bene licuit*), except it may be judged utterly without his fault; as if a man by force take my hand and strike you, or if here the defendant had said that the plaintiff ran across his piece when it was discharging, or had set forth the case with the circumstances so as it had appeared to the court that it had been inevitable, and that the defendant had committed no negligence to give occasion to the hurt.[1]

BROWN *v.* KENDALL

SUPREME JUDICIAL COURT, MASSACHUSETTS, OCTOBER TERM, 1850.

Reported in 6 *Cushing*, 292.

THIS was an action of trespass for assault and battery, originally commenced against George K. Kendall, the defendant, who died pending the suit, and his executrix was summoned in.

It appeared in evidence, on the trial, which was before Wells, C. J., in the Court of Common Pleas, that two dogs, belonging to the plain-

subject to criticism on the grounds of reason and principle, it is now too firmly supported by the weight of authority to be disturbed. It is the outcome of the principle, that, in trespass, the intent is not conclusive. Mr. Sedgwick, in his work on Damages (margin, p. 456), says that, on principle, a lunatic should not be held liable for his tortious acts. Opposed to this view, however, is a majority of the decisions and text writers."

"So long as the primitive notion prevailed that the doer of harm was absolutely responsible therefor, the insanity of the doer could afford no defence, either to a criminal prosecution or a civil action. 7 Harv. L. Rev. 446. When this notion was so far modified that misadventure or accident on the part of the doer became a defence, it would have been entirely logical for the courts to treat the acts or the omissions of lunatics as involuntary, and consequently not tortious but accidental." Burdick, Torts (2d ed.), 60. See also Ames, Law and Morals, 22 Harv. L. Rev. 97, 99–100; Hornblower, Insanity and the Law of Negligence, 5 Col. L. Rev. 278.

"827. A person who causes damage to another while in a condition of unconsciousness or in a condition of morbid disturbance of mental activity incompatible with the free determination of the will is not responsible for the damage. . . ."

"829. A person who . . . is by virtue of 827 . . . not responsible for any damage caused by him shall nevertheless where compensation cannot be obtained from a third party charged with the duty of supervision make compensation for damage in so far as according to the circumstances (e. g. according to the relative positions of the parties) equity requires compensation and he is not deprived of the means which he needs for his own maintenance suitable to his station in life and for the fulfilment of his statutory duties to furnish maintenance to others." — German Civil Code, §§ 827, 829.

[1] Underwood *v.* Hewson, 1 Stra. 596; Welch *v.* Durand, 36 Conn. 182; Atchison *v.* Dullam, 16 Ill. App. 42; Hodges *v.* Weltberger, 6 Monr. (Ky.) 337; Louisville R. Co. *v.* Sweeney, 157 Ky. 620; Chataigne *v.* Bergeron, 10 La. An. 699; Sullivan *v.* Murphy, 2 Miles (Pa.) 298; Castle *v.* Duryee, 2 Keyes, 169; Taylor *v.* Rainbow, 2 Hen. & Mun. 423 *Accord.*

See to the same effect Morgan *v.* Cox, 22 Mo. 373; Dygert *v.* Bradley, 8 Wend. 469; Jennings *v.* Fundeburg, 4 McC. 161; Tally *v.* Ayres, 3 Sneed, 677 (the injury to chattels); Wetzel *v.* Satterwhite, (Tex. Civ. App.) 125 S. W. 93 (injury to property); Wright *v.* Clark, 50 Vt. 130. Compare Osborne *v.* Van Dyke, 113 Ia. 557.

tiff and the defendant, respectively, were fighting in the presence of their masters; that the defendant took a stick about four feet long, and commenced beating the dogs in order to separate them; that the plaintiff was looking on, at the distance of about a rod, and that he advanced a step or two towards the dogs. In their struggle, the dogs approached the place where the plaintiff was standing. The defendant retreated backwards from before the dogs, striking them as he retreated; and as he approached the plaintiff, with his back towards him, in raising his stick over his shoulder, in order to strike the dogs, he accidentally hit the plaintiff in the eye, inflicting upon him a severe injury.

Whether it was necessary or proper for the defendant to interfere in the fight between the dogs; whether the interference, if called for was in a proper manner, and what degree of care was exercised by each party on the occasion; were the subject of controversy between the parties, upon all the evidence in the case, of which the foregoing is an outline.

The defendant requested the judge to instruct the jury, that "if both the plaintiff and defendant at the time of the blow were using ordinary care, or if at that time the defendant was using ordinary care and the plaintiff was not, or if at that time both plaintiff and defendant were not using ordinary care, then the plaintiff could not recover."

The defendant further requested the judge to instruct the jury, that, "under the circumstances, if the plaintiff was using ordinary care and the defendant was not, the plaintiff could not recover, and that the burden of proof on all these propositions was on the plaintiff."

The judge declined to give the instructions, as above requested, but left the case to the jury under the following instructions: "If the defendant, in beating the dogs, was doing a necessary act, or one which it was his duty under the circumstances of the case to do, and was doing it in a proper way; then he was not responsible in this action, provided he was using ordinary care at the time of the blow. If it was not a necessary act; if he was not in duty bound to attempt to part the dogs, but might with propriety interfere or not as he chose; the defendant was responsible for the consequences of the blow, unless it appeared that he was in the exercise of extraordinary care, so that the accident was inevitable, using the word inevitable not in a strict but a popular sense."

"If, however, the plaintiff, when he met with the injury, was not in the exercise of ordinary care, he cannot recover, and this rule applies, whether the interference of the defendant in the fight of the dogs was necessary or not. If the jury believe, that it was the duty of the defendant to interfere, then the burden of proving negligence on the part of the defendant, and ordinary care on the part of the plaintiff, is on the plaintiff. If the jury believe, that the act of interference in the fight was unnecessary, then the burden of proving extraordinary care on the part of the defendant, or want of ordinary care on the part of the plaintiff, is on defendant."

The jury under these instructions returned a verdict for the plaintiff; whereupon the defendant alleged exceptions.

SHAW, C. J. This is an action of trespass, *vi et armis*, brought by George Brown against George K. Kendall, for an assault and battery; and the original defendant having died pending the action, his executrix has been summoned in. The rule of the common law, by which this action would abate by the death of either party, is reversed in this Commonwealth by statute, which provides that actions of trespass for assault and battery shall survive. Rev. Sts. c. 93, § 7.

The facts set forth in the bill of exceptions preclude the supposition, that the blow, inflicted by the hand of the defendant upon the person of the plaintiff, was intentional. The whole case proceeds on the assumption, that the damage sustained by the plaintiff, from the stick held by the defendant, was inadvertent and unintentional; and the case involves the question how far, and under what qualifications, the party by whose unconscious act the damage was done is responsible for it. We use the term "unintentional" rather than involuntary, because in some of the cases, it is stated, that the act of holding and using a weapon or instrument, the movement of which is the immediate cause of hurt to another, is a voluntary act, although its particular effect in hitting and hurting another is not within the purpose or intention of the party doing the act.

It appears to us, that some of the confusion in the cases on this subject has grown out of the long-vexed question, under the rule of the common law, whether a party's remedy, where he has one, should be sought in an action of the case, or of trespass. This is very distinguishable from the question, whether in a given case, any action will lie. The result of these cases is, that if the damage complained of is the immediate effect of the act of the defendant, trespass *vi et armis* lies; if consequential only, and not immediate, case is the proper remedy. Leame *v.* Bray, 3 East, 593; Huggett *v.* Montgomery, 2 B. & P. N. R. 446, Day's Ed., and notes.

In these discussions, it is frequently stated by judges, that when one receives injury from the direct act of another, trespass will lie. But we think this is said in reference to the question, whether trespass and not case will lie, assuming that the facts are such, that some action will lie. These *dicta* are no authority, we think, for holding, that damage received by a direct act of force from another will be sufficient to maintain an action of trespass, whether the act was lawful or unlawful, and neither wilful, intentional, or careless. In the principal case cited, Leame *v.* Bray, the damage arose from the act of the defendant, in driving on the wrong side of the road, in a dark night, which was clearly negligent, if not unlawful. In the course of the argument of that case (p. 595), Lawrence, J., said: "There certainly are cases in the books, where, the injury being direct and immediate, trespass has been holden to lie, though the injury was not intentional." The term "injury" implies something more than damage; but, independently of that consideration, the proposition may be true, because though the injury was unintentional, the act may have been unlawful or negligent, and the cases cited by him are perfectly consistent with that supposition. So the same learned judge in the same case says (p. 597), "No doubt trespass lies against one who drives a carriage against another, whether done wilfully or not." But he immediately adds, "Suppose one who is driving a carriage is negligently and heedlessly looking about him, without attending to the road when persons are passing, and thereby runs over a child and kills him, is it not manslaughter? and if so, it must be trespass; for every manslaughter includes trespass;" showing what he understood by a case not wilful.

We think, as the result of all the authorities, the rule is correctly stated by Mr. Greenleaf, that the plaintiff must come prepared with evidence to show either that the *intention* was unlawful, or that the defendant was *in fault;* for if the injury was unavoidable, and the conduct of the defendant was free from blame, he will not be liable. 2 Greenl. Ev. §§ 85–92. Wakeman *v.* Robinson, 1 Bing. 213. If, in the prosecution of a lawful act, a casualty purely accidental arises, no action can be supported for an injury arising therefrom. Davis *v.* Saunders, 2 Chit. R. 639; Com. Dig. Battery, A. (Day's Ed.) and notes; Vincent *v.* Stinehour, 7 Vt. 62. In applying these rules to the present case, we can perceive no reason why the instructions asked for by the defendant ought not to have been given; to this effect, that if both plaintiff and defendant at the time of the blow were using ordinary care, or if at that time the defendant was using ordinary care, and the plaintiff was not, or if at that time, both the plaintiff and defendant were not using ordinary care, then the plaintiff could not recover.

In using this term, ordinary care, it may be proper to state, that what constitutes ordinary care will vary with the circumstances of cases. In general, it means that kind and degree of care, which prudent and cautious men would use, such as is required by the exigency of the case, and such as is necessary to guard against probable danger. A man, who should have occasion to discharge a gun, on an open and extensive marsh, or in a forest, would be required to use less circumspection and care, than if he were to do the same thing in an inhabited town, village, or city. To make an accident, or casualty, or, as the law sometimes states it, inevitable accident, it must be such an accident as the defendant could not have avoided by the use of the kind and degree of care necessary to the exigency, and in the circumstances in which he was placed.

We are not aware of any circumstances in this case, requiring a distinction between acts which it was lawful and proper to do, and acts of legal duty. There are cases, undoubtedly, in which officers are bound to act under process, for the legality of which they are not responsible, and perhaps some others in which this distinction would be important. We can have no doubt that the act of the defendant in attempting to part the fighting dogs, one of which was his own, and for the injurious acts of which he might be responsible, was a lawful and proper act, which he might do by proper and safe means. If, then, in doing this act, using due care and all proper precautions necessary to the exigency of the case, to avoid hurt to others, in raising his stick for that purpose, he accidentally hit the plaintiff in his eye, and wounded him, this was the result of pure accident, or was involuntary and unavoidable, and therefore the action would not lie. Of if the defendant was chargeable with some negligence, and if the plaintiff was also chargeable with negligence, we think the plaintiff cannot recover without showing that the damage was caused wholly by the act of the defendant, and that the plaintiff's own negligence did not contribute as an efficient cause to produce it.

The court instructed the jury, that if it was not a necessary act, and the defendant was not in duty bound to part the dogs, but might with propriety interfere or not as he chose, the defendant was responsible for the consequences of the blow, unless it appeared that he was in the exercise of extraordinary care, so that the accident was inevitable, using the word not in a strict but a popular sense. This is to be taken in connection with the charge afterwards given, that if the jury believed, that the act of interference in the fight was unnecessary (that is, as before explained, not a duty incumbent on the defendant), then the burden of proving extraordinary care on the part of the defendant, or want of ordinary care on the part of plaintiff, was on the defendant.

The court are of opinion that these directions were not conformable to law. If the act of hitting the plaintiff was unintentional, on the part of the defendant, and done in the doing of a lawful act, then the defendant was not liable, unless it was done in the want of exercise of due care, adapted to the exigency of the case, and therefore such want of due care became part of the plaintiff's case, and the burden of proof was on the plaintiff to establish it. 2 Greenl. Ev. § 85; Powers *v.* Russell, 13 Pick. 69, 76; Tourtellot *v.* Rosebrook, 11 Met. 460.

Perhaps the learned judge, by the use of the term extraordinary care, in the above charge, explained as it is by the context, may have intended nothing more than that increased degree of care and diligence, which the exigency of particular circumstances might require, and which men of ordinary care and prudence would use under like circumstances, to guard against danger. If such was the meaning of this part of the charge, then it does not differ from our views, as above explained. But we are of opinion, that the other part of the charge, that the burden of proof was on the defendant, was incorrect. Those facts which are essential to enable the plaintiff to recover, he takes the burden of proving. The evidence may be offered by the plaintiff or by the defendant; the question of due care, or want of care, may be essentially connected with the main facts, and arise from the same proof; but the effect of the rule, as to the burden of proof, is this, that when the proof is all in, and before the jury, from whatever side it comes, and whether directly proved, or inferred from circumstances, if it appears that the defendant was doing a lawful act, and unintentionally hit and hurt the plaintiff, then unless it also appears to the satisfaction of the jury, that the defendant is chargeable with some fault, negligence, carelessness, or want of prudence, the plaintiff fails to sustain the burden of proof, and is not entitled to recover.

New trial ordered [1]

STANLEY *v.* POWELL

IN THE QUEEN'S BENCH DIVISION, NOVEMBER 3, 1890.

Reported in [1891] 1 *Queen's Bench*, 86.

DENMAN, J. This case was tried before me and a special jury at the last Maidstone Summer Assizes.[2]

In the statement of claim the plaintiff alleged that the defendant had *negligently and wrongfully and unskilfully* fired his gun and wounded the plaintiff in his eye, and that the plaintiff, in consequence, had lost his sight and suffered other damage. The defendant denied the negligence alleged. After the evidence on both sides, which was conflicting, had been heard, I left the three following questions to the jury: 1. Was the plaintiff injured by a shot from defendant's gun? 2. Was the defendant guilty of negligence in firing the charge to which that shot belonged as he did? 3. Damages.

The undisputed facts were, that on Nov. 29, 1888, the defendant and several others were pheasant shooting in a party, some being inside and some outside of a wood which the beaters were beating. The right of shooting was in one Greenwood, who was of the party. The plaintiff was employed by Greenwood to carry cartridges and the game which might be shot. Several beaters were driving the game along a plantation of saplings towards an open drive. The plaintiff stood just outside a gate which led into a field outside the plantation, at the end of the drive. The defendant was walking along in that field a few yards from the hedge which bounded the plantation. As he was walking along a pheasant rose inside the plantation; the defendant fired one barrel at this bird, and, according to the evidence for the defendant, struck it with his first shot. There was a considerable conflict of evidence as to details; but the jury must, I think, be taken to

[1] Nitro-Glycerine Case, 15 Wall. 524, 538 (*semble*); Morris *v.* Platt, 32 Conn. 75, 84–90 (defendant in defending himself lawfully against A. fired a pistol at A., but accidentally hit the plaintiff); Paxton *v.* Boyer, 67 Ill. 132 (facts similar to those in Morris *v.* Platt, *supra*); Crabtree *v.* Dawson, 119 Ky. 148 *Accord.*

[2] Only the opinion of the court is given.

have adopted the version of the facts sworn to by the defendant's witnesses. They swore that the bird, when struck by the first shot, began to lower and turn back towards the beaters, whereupon the defendant fired his second barrel and killed the bird, but that a shot, glancing from the bough of an oak which was in or close to the hedge, and, striking the plaintiff, must have caused the injury complained of. The oak in question, according to the defendant's evidence, was partly between the defendant and the bird when the second barrel was fired, but it was not in a line with the plaintiff, but, on the contrary, so much out of that line, that the shot must have been diverted to a considerable extent from the direction in which the gun must have been pointed in order to hit the plaintiff. The distance between the plaintiff and the defendant, in a direct line, when the second barrel was fired, was about thirty yards. The case for the plaintiff was entirely different; but I think it must be held that the jury took the defendant's account of the matter, for they found the second question left to them in the negative. Before summing up the case to the jury, I called the attention of the parties to the doctrine which seemed to have been laid down in some old cases — that, even in the absence of negligence, an action of trespass might lie; and it was agreed that I should leave the question of negligence to the jury, but that, if necessary, the pleadings were deemed to have been amended so as to raise any case or defence open upon the facts with liberty to the court to draw inferences of fact, and that the damages should be assessed contingently. The jury assessed them at £100. I left either party to move the court for judgment; but it was afterwards agreed that the case should be argued before myself on further consideration, and that I should give judgment, notwithstanding that I had left the parties to move the court, as though I had originally reserved it for further consideration before myself.

Having heard the arguments, I am of opinion that, by no amendment that could be made consistently with the finding of the jury could I properly give judgment for the plaintiff. It was contended on his behalf that this was a case in which an action of trespass would have lain before the Judicature Acts; and this contention was mainly founded on certain *dicta* which, until considered with reference to those cases in which they are uttered, seem to support that contention; but no decision was quoted, nor do I think that any can be found which goes so far as to hold, that if A. is injured by a shot from a gun fired at a bird by B., an action of trespass will necessarily lie, even though B. is proved to have fired the gun without negligence and without intending to injure the plaintiff or to shoot in his direction.

The jury having found that there was no negligence on the part of the defendant, the most favorable way in which it is now possible to put the case for the plaintiff is to consider the action as brought for a trespass, and to consider that the defendant has put upon the record a defence denying negligence, and specifically alleging the facts, sworn to by his witnesses, which the jury must be considered to have found proved, and then to consider whether those facts, coupled with the absence of negligence established by the jury, amount to an excuse in law.

The earliest case relied upon by the plaintiff was one in the year-book 21 Hen. 7, 28 A., which is referred to by Grose, J., in the course of the argument in Leame *v.* Bray, 3 East, 593, to be mentioned presently, in these words: "There is a case put in the year-book, 21 Hen. 7, 28 A., that where one shot an arrow at a mark which glanced from it and struck another, it was holden to be trespass." Returning to the case in the year-book, it appears that the passage in question was a mere *dictum* of Rede, who (see 5 Foss' Lives of the Judges, p. 230) was at the time (1506) either a judge of the King's Bench or C. J. of the Common Pleas, which he became in October in that year, in a case of a very different kind from that in question, and it only amounts to a statement that an action of trespass may lie even where the act done by the defendant is *unintentional.* The words relied on are, "*Mes ou on tire a les buts et blesse un home, coment que est incontre sa volonte, il sera dit un trespassor incontre son entent.*" But in that very passage Rede makes observations which show that he has in his mind cases in which that which would be *prima facie* a trespass may be excused. The next case in order of date relied upon for the plaintiff was Weaver *v.* Ward, decided in 1607. There is no doubt that that case contains *dicta* which *per se* would be in favor of the plaintiff, but it also contains the following summing up of the law applicable to cases of unintentional injury by acts which are *prima facie* trespasses: "Therefore, no man shall be excused of a trespass . . . except it may be judged utterly without his fault," showing clearly that there may be such cases. That case, after all, only decided that where the plaintiff and defendant were skirmishing as soldiers of the train-band, and the one, "*casualiter, et per infortunium, et contra voluntatem suam*" (which must be translated "accidentally and involuntarily") shot the other, an action of trespass would lie, *unless* he could show that such involuntary and accidental shooting was done under such circumstances as utterly to negative negligence. Such cases may easily be supposed, in which there could be no two opinions about the matter; but other cases may, as the present case did, involve considerable conflicts of evidence and opinion which until recently a jury only could dispose of. The case of Gibbons *v.* Pepper, 4 Mod. 405, decided in 1695, merely decided that a plea merely showing that an accident caused by a runaway horse was *inevitable*, was a bad plea in an action of trespass, because, if *inevitable*, that was a defence under the general issue. It was a mere decision on the pleading, and laid down nothing as regards the point raised in the present case. The concluding words of the judgment, which show clearly the *ratio decidendi* of that case, are these: " He should have pleaded the general issue, for if the horse ran away against his will he would have been found *not guilty,* because in such a case it cannot be said with any color of reason to be a battery in the rider." The more modern cases of Wakeman *v.* Robinson and Hall *v.* Fearnley, lay down the same rule as regards the pleading point, though the former case may also be relied upon as an authority by way of *dictum* in favor of the plaintiff, and the latter may be fairly relied upon by the defendant; for Wightman, J., in his judgment explains Wakeman *v.* Robinson thus: " The act of the defendant " (viz., driving the cart at the very edge of a narrow pavement on which the plaintiff was walking, so as to knock the plaintiff down) " was *prima facie* unjustifiable, and required an excuse to be shown. When the motion in this case was first made, I had in my recollection the case of Wakeman *v.* Robinson. It was there agreed that an *involuntary* act might be a defence on the general issue. The decision indeed turned on a different point; but the general proposition is laid down. I think the *omission to plead* the defence here deprived the defendant of the benefit of it, and entitled the plaintiff to recover."

But in truth neither case decides whether, where an act such as discharging a gun is voluntary, but the result injurious without negligence, an action of trespass can nevertheless be supported as against a plea pleaded and proved, and which the jury find established, to the effect that there was no negligence on the part of the defendant.

The case of Underwood *v.* Hewson, 1 Str. 596, decided in 1724, was relied on for the plaintiff. The report is very short. " The defendant was uncocking a gun, and the plaintiff standing to see it, it went off and wounded him; and at the trial it was held that the plaintiff might maintain trespass — Strange *pro defendente.*" The marginal note in Nolan's edition of 1795, not necessarily Strange's own composition, is this: " Trespass lies for an accidental hurt; " and in that edition there is a reference to Buller's N. P., p. 16. On referring to Buller, p. 16, where he is dealing with Weaver *v.* Ward, I find he writes as follows: " So (it is no battery) if one soldier hurt another in exercise; but if he plead it he must set forth the circumstances, so as to make it appear to the court that it was inevitable, and that he committed no negligence to give occasion to the hurt, for it is not not enough to say that he did it *casualiter, et per infortunium, et contra voluntatem suam;* for no man shall be excused of a trespass, unless it be justified entirely without his default: Weaver *v.* Ward; and, therefore, it has been holden that an action lay where the plaintiff standing by to see the defendant uncock his gun was accidentally wounded: Underwood *v.* Hewson." On referring back to Weaver *v.* Ward, I can find nothing in the report to show that the court held, that in order to constitute a defence in the case of a trespass it is necessary to show that the act was *inevitable.* If *inevitable,* it would seem that there was a defence under the general issue; but a distinction is drawn between an act which is inevitable and an act which is excusable, and what Weaver *v.* Ward really lays down is that " no man shall be excused of a trespass except it may be judged utterly without his fault."

Day *v.* Edwards, D. & E. 5 T. R. 648 (1794), merely decides that where a man negligently *drives* a cart against the plaintiff's carriage, the injury being committed by the *immediate* act complained of, the remedy must be trespass, and not case.

But the case upon which most reliance was placed by the plaintiff's counsel was Leame *v.* Bray, 3 East, 593. That was an action of trespass in which the plaintiff complained that the defendant with force and arms drove and struck a chaise which he was driving on the highway against the plaintiff's curricle, which the plaintiff's servant was driving, by means whereof the servant was thrown out, and the horses ran away, and the plaintiff, who jumped out to save his life, was injured. The facts stated in the report include a statement that " the accident happened in a dark night, owing to the defendant driving his carriage on the wrong side of the road, and the parties not being able to see each other; and that if the defendant had kept his right side there was ample room for the carriages to have passed without injury." The report goes on to state: " But it did not appear that blame was imputable to the defendant in any *other* respect as to the manner of his driving. It was therefore objected for the defendant, that the injury *having happened from negligence* and not wilfully, the proper remedy was by an action on the case, and not of trespass *vi et armis;* and the plaintiff was thereupon nonsuited." On the argument of the rule to set aside the verdict the whole discussion turned upon the question whether the injury was, as put by Lawrence, J., at p. 596 of the report, immediate from the defendant's act, or consequential only from it, and in the result the nonsuit was set aside. But it clearly appears from the report that there was evidence upon which the jury might have found negligence, and indeed the defendant's counsel assumed it in the very objection which prevailed with Lord Ellenborough when he nonsuited the plaintiff. There is nothing in any of the judgments to show that if in that case a plea had been pleaded denying any negligence, and the jury had found that the defendant was not guilty of any negligence, but (for instance) that the accident happened wholly through the darkness of the night making it impossible to distinguish one side of the road from the other and without negligence on either side, the court would have held that the defendant would have been liable either in trespass or in case.

All the cases to which I have referred were before the Court of Exchequer in 1875, in the case of Holmes *v.* Mather, and Bramwell, B., in giving judgment in that case, dealt with them thus: " As to the cases cited, most of them are really decisions on the form of action, whether case or trespass. The result of them is this, and it is intelligible enough: if the act that does an injury is an act of direct force *vi et armis*, trespass is the proper remedy (if there is any remedy), where the act is wrongful either as being wilful or as being the result of negligence. Where the act is not wrongful for either of these reasons, no action is maintainable, though trespass would be the proper form of action if it were wrongful. That is the effect of the decisions."

This view of the older authorities is in accordance with a passage cited by Mr. Dickens from Bacon's Abridgment, Trespass, I., p. 706, with a marginal reference to Weaver *v.* Ward. In Bacon the word "inevitable" does not find a place. "If the circumstance which is specially pleaded in an action of trespass do not make the act complained of lawful" (by which I understand justifiable even if purposely done to the extent of purposely inflicting the injury, as, for instance, in a case of self-defence) "and only make it excusable, it is proper to plead this circumstance in excuse; and it is in this case necessary for the defendant to show not only that the act complained of was accidental" (by which I understand, "that the injury was unintentional"), "but likewise that it was not owing to neglect or want of due caution." In the present case the plaintiff sued in respect of an injury owing to the defendant's negligence, — there was no pretence for saying that it was intentional so far as any injury to the plaintiff was concerned, — and the jury negatived such negligence. It was argued that nevertheless, inasmuch as the plaintiff was injured by a shot from the defendant's gun, that was an injury owing to an act of force committed by the defendant, and therefore an action would lie. I am of opinion that this is not so, and that against any statement of claim which the plaintiff could suggest the defendant must succeed if he were to plead the facts sworn to by the witnesses for the defendant in this case, and the jury believing those facts, as they must now be taken by me to have done, found the verdict which they have found as regards negligence. In other words, I am of opinion that if the case is regarded as an action on the case for an injury by negligence the plaintiff has failed to establish that which is the very gist of such an action; if, on the other hand, it is turned into an action for trespass, and the defendant is (as he must be) supposed to have pleaded a plea denying negligence and establishing that the injury was accidental in the sense above explained, the verdict of the jury is equally fatal to the action. I am, therefore, of opinion that I am bound to give judgment for the defendant. As to costs, they must follow, unless the defendant foregoes his right.

Judgment for the defendant.[1]

[1] Alderson *v.* Waistell, 1 Car. & K. 358; The Virgo, 25 W. R. 397; Nitro-Glycerine Case, 15 Wall. 524 (*semble*); Strouse *v.* Whittlesey, 41 Conn. 559; Sutton *v.* Bonnett, 114 Ind. 243; Holland *v.* Bartch, 120 Ind. 46 (see also Bennett *v.* Ford, 47 Ind. 264); Harvey *v.* Dunlop, Hill & D. 193; Center *v.* Finney, 17 Barb. 94, Seld. Notes, 80 *Accord.*

But one who by blasting throws rocks upon the plaintiff's land is liable in trespass *quare clausum fregit*, irrespective of negligence. Central Co. *v.* Vandenheuk,

SULLIVAN v. OLD COLONY STREET RAILWAY

SUPREME JUDICIAL COURT, MASSACHUSETTS, NOVEMBER 30, 1908.

Reported in 200 Massachusetts Reports, 303.

TORT. The first count in the declaration alleged that, while the plaintiff was a passenger on an electric car of the defendant, the car was derailed at Tiverton, owing to the defendant's negligence, " whereby the plaintiff was jolted and in many ways injured externally and internally."

At the trial, plaintiff testified substantially to the same effect as the allegations in the declaration. As to the derailment, he testified that it was violent and that he was much thrown about. The evidence for the defendant tended to show that there was practically no jar when the car left the rails at Tiverton.

At the close of the evidence plaintiff requested, among others, the following ruling: —

" 1. Upon all the evidence the plaintiff is entitled to recover on the first count."

The judge refused to so rule.

The judge instructed the jury, in part, as follows: —

" The only matters, then, of damages for you to consider are these: First, what was the effect upon the plaintiff of the jolts when the car was derailed ? To what extent did they injure the plaintiff ? "

Plaintiff excepted to the charge. Verdict for defendant.[1]

SHELDON, J. No question was made at the trial but that the defendant was liable for any injury done to the plaintiff by reason of its car having left the track. But if no injury was caused by this to the plaintiff, if he suffered no damage whatever from the defendant's negligence, then he would not be entitled to recover. Although there has been negligence in the performance of a legal duty, yet it is only those who have suffered damage therefrom that may maintain an action therefor. Heaven v. Pender, 11 Q. B. D. 503, 507; Farrell v. Waterbury Horse Railroad, 60 Conn. 239, 246; Salmon v. Delaware, Lackawanna & Western Railroad, 19 Vroom, 5, 11; 2 Cooley on Torts (3d ed.), 791; Wharton on Negligence (2d ed.), sect. 3. In cases of negligence, there is no such invasion of rights as to entitle plaintiff to recover at least nominal damages, as in Hooten v. Barnard, 137 Mass. 36, and McAneany v. Jewett, 10 Allen, 151.[2] Accordingly,

147 Ala. 546; Bessemer Co. v. Doak, 152 Ala. 166; Sloss Co. v. Salser, 158 Ala. 511; Birmingham Co. v. Grover, 159 Ala. 276; Hay v. Cohoes Co., 2 N. Y. 159; Tremain v. Cohoes Co., 2 N. Y. 163; St. Peter v. Denison, 58 N. Y. 416; Sullivan v. Dunham, 161 N. Y. 290; Holland House v. Baird, 169 N. Y. 136, 140. And the same rule has been applied to trespass to the person by blasting. Sullivan v. Dunham, 161 N. Y. 290; Turner v. Degnon Co., 99 App. Div. 135.

[1] Only so much of the report is given as relates to the first count.

[2] See The Mediana, [1900] A. C. 113, 116–118; Columbus Co. v. Clowes, [1903] 1 K. B. 244.

the first and second of the plaintiff's requests for rulings could not have been given, and the rulings made were all that the plaintiff was entitled to. *Exceptions overruled.*[1]

HART v. ALLEN

SUPREME COURT, PENNSYLVANIA, OCTOBER TERM, 1833.

Reported in 2 *Watts*, 114.

ACTION on the case against owners of a vessel.[2] Plaintiff put in evidence a bill of lading of chests of tea shipped on board defendant's vessel; "to be delivered in good order, unavoidable accidents and the dangers of the river excepted. . . ." Plaintiff also proved that the teas were delivered by defendants in a damaged state, owing to their having been wet. Defendants gave evidence that the boat, when on her passage up the river, was driven by a sudden squall of wind and snow sidewise, whereby the teas were wet and damaged; that she was well fitted for the voyage; that every exertion was made to save her; and that Samuel Johnston, the captain, was a man of experience. To rebut this the plaintiff gave evidence that Samuel Johnston was not an experienced boatman or pilot.

Judgment below for plaintiff. The original defendants brought error. One of the errors assigned was as follows: —

The court below erred in charging the jury, that although the accident in this case resulted from the act of God, and could not have been prevented by any human prudence or foresight; and although it would, in this respect, come within the exception that excuses the carrier in case of loss: still, if the crew of the boat was not sufficient, or if she was not under the control of a master or pilot sufficiently skilled to perform the duties corresponding to his station, the carrier cannot avail himself of the exception, nor excuse himself from responsibility to the owner, to the extent of the injury done to the goods. And also, in substance, that if the jury think that the boat was not fit for the voyage, or the master not competent, or the crew insufficient; they ought to find a verdict for the plaintiff, whatever might be their opinion as to the real cause of the upsetting of the boat.

GIBSON, C. J. Had the judge said no more than that the carrier is bound to provide a carriage or vessel in all respects adequate to the purpose, with a conductor or crew of competent skill or ability, and that "failing in these particulars, though the loss be occasioned by

[1] Brunsden v. Humphrey, 14 Q. B. D. 141, 150 (*semble*); Vogrin v. American Steel Co., 179 Ill. App. 245; Muncie Pulp Co. v. Davis, 162 Ind. 558; Foster v. County, 63 Kan. 43; Stepp v. Chicago R. Co., 85 Mo. 229; Commercial Bank v. Ten Eyck, 48 N. Y. 305; McCaffrey v. Twenty-Third St. R. Co., 47 Hun, 404; Washington v. Baltimore R. Co., 17 W. Va. 190 *Accord.*

Compare Clifton v. Hooper, 6 Q. B. 468.

[2] Statement condensed. Only part of opinion is given.

the act of God, he shall not set up a providential calamity to protect himself against what *may* have arisen from his own folly;" there would have been no room for an exception. But the cause was eventually put to the jury on a different principle: "though the accident resulted from the act of God," it was said, "*and could not have been prevented by any human prudence or foresight,* and though it would in this respect otherwise have come within the exception that excuses the carrier in case of loss: still, if the crew of the office [?] were not sufficient, or if she were not under the control of a master or pilot sufficiently skilful to perform the duties correspondent to his station, the carrier cannot avail himself of the exception." By this the jury were instructed, in accordance, as it was supposed, with the principle of Bell *v.* Reed and Beelor, 4 Binn. 127, that want of seaworthiness has the peculiar effect of casting every loss, from whatever cause, on the carrier, as a penalty, I presume, for his original delinquency, and not for its actual or supposed instrumentality in contributing to the disaster, which is admitted to have been produced, in this instance, by causes unconnected with the master or crew, and to have been of a nature which no human force or sagacity could control.

Does such a penalty necessarily result from the nature of the contract? A carrier is answerable for the consequences of negligence, not the abstract existence of it. Where the goods have arrived safe, no action lies against him for an intervening but inconsequential act of carelessness; nor can it be set up as a defence against payment of the freight; and for this plain reason, that the risk from it was all his own. Why, then, should it, in any other case, subject him to a loss which it did not contribute to produce, or give an advantage to one who was not prejudiced by it? It would require much to reconcile to any principle of policy or justice, a measure of responsibility which would cast the burthen of the loss on a carrier whose wagon had been snatched away by a whirlwind in crossing a bridge, merely because it had not been furnished with a proper cover or tilt to protect the goods from the weather. Yet the omission to provide such a cover would be gross negligence, but, like that imputed to the carrier in the case before us, such as could have had no imaginable effect on the event. A carrier is an insurer against all losses without regard to degrees of negligence in the production of them, except such as have been caused by an act of providence, or the common enemy: and why is he so? Undoubtedly to subserve the purposes, not of justice in the particular instance, but of policy and convenience: of policy, by removing from him all temptation to confederate with robbers or thieves — and of convenience, by relieving the owner of the goods from the necessity of proving actual negligence, which, the fact being peculiarly within the knowledge of the carrier or his servants, could seldom be done. Jones on Bail. 108, 109; 2 Kent, 59, 78. Such are the rule and the reason of it, and such is the exception. But we should enlarge the rule, or to speak more properly, narrow the exception far beyond the exigencies of policy or convenience, did we hold him an insurer against even the acts of providence, as a punishment for an abstract delinquency, where there was no room for the existence of a confederacy, or the operation of actual negligence; and to carry a responsibility, founded in no principle of natural equity beyond the requirements of necessity, would be gratuitous injustice. A delinquency which might have contributed to the disaster, such, for instance, as is imputable to the owner of a ship driven on a lee shore, for a defect in the rigging or sails, would undoubtedly be attended with different consequences; for as it would be impossible to ascertain the exact effect of the delinquency on the event, the loss would have to be borne by the delinquent on a very common principle, by which any one whose carelessness has increased the danger of injury from a sudden commotion of the elements, is chargeable with all the mischief that may ensue: as in Turberville *v.* Stamp, Skin. 681, where it was adjudged, that the negligent keeping of fire in a close would subject the party to all the consequences, though proximately produced by a sudden storm; and the same principle was held by this court in The Lehigh Bridge Company *v.* The Lehigh Navigation, 4 Rawle, 9. But it would be too much to require of the carrier to make good a loss from shipwreck, for having omitted to provide the ship with proper papers, which are a constituent part of seaworthiness, and the omission of them an undoubted negligence.

. . . .

The first question, therefore, will be, whether the captain and crew of the boat had the degree of ability and skill thus indicated; and if it be found that they had not, then the second question will be, whether the want of it contributed in any degree to the actual disaster: but if either of these be found for the carrier, it will be decision [decisive ?] of the cause. It seems, therefore, that . . . the cause ought to be put, on these principles, to another jury.

Judgment reversed, and a venire de novo awarded.[1]

[1] Carlisle Banking Co. *v.* Bragg, [1911] 1 K. B. 489; Jackson *v.* Metropolitan R. Co., 2 C. P. D. 125; Steel Car Co. *v.* Chec, 184 Fed. 868; Louisville R. Co. *v.* Pearce, 142 Ala. 680; Florida R. Co. *v.* Williams, 37 Fla. 406; Perry *v.* Central R., 66 Ga. 746; Cleveland R. Co. *v.* Lindsay, 109 Ill. App. 533; City *v.* Martin, 74 Ind. 449; Hart *v.* Brick Co., 154 Ia. 741; Goins *v.* North Coal Co., 140 Ky. 323; County *v.* Collison, 122 Md. 91; Tutein *v.* Hurley, 98 Mass. 211; McNally *v.* Colwell, 91 Mich. 527; Harlan *v.* St. Louis R. Co., 65 Mo. 22; Wallace *v.* Chicago R. Co., 48 Mont. 427; Brotherton *v.* Manhattan Beach Co., 48 Neb. 563; Koch *v.* Fox, 71 App. Div. 288; Alexander *v.* City, 165 N. C. 527; St. Louis R. Co. *v.* Hess, 34 Okl. 615; Thubron *v.* Dravo Co., 238 Pa. St. 443; Anderson *v.* Southern R. Co., 70 S. C. 490; Newton *v.* Oregon R. Co., 43 Utah, 219; Sowles *v.* Moore, 65 Vt. 322; Schwartz *v.* Shull, 45 W. Va. 405; Klatt *v.* Foster, 92 Wis. 622 *Accord.*

SECTION II

INTERESTS SECURED

SPADE *v.* LYNN & BOSTON R. CO.

SUPREME JUDICIAL COURT, MASSACHUSETTS, MAY 19, 1897.

Reported in 168 *Massachusetts Reports*, 285.

TORT, for personal injuries occasioned to the plaintiff by the alleged negligence of the defendant. The declaration contained three counts.

The third count [1] alleged that while the plaintiff was a passenger in the defendant's car, and in the exercise of due care, "one of the defendant's agents or servants, in attempting to remove from the said car a certain person claimed and alleged by said defendant's agent to be noisy, turbulent, and unfit to remain as a passenger in said car, conducted himself with such carelessness, negligence, and with the use of such unnecessary force, that said agent and servant, acting thus negligently, created a disorder, disturbance, and quarrel in said car, and thereby frightened the plaintiff and subjected her to a severe nervous shock, by which nervous shock the plaintiff was physically prostrated and suffered, and has continued to suffer, great mental and physical pain and anguish, and has been put to great expense."

The defendant's answer was a general denial.

Trial in the Superior Court, before MASON, C. J.

The plaintiff testified, among other things, that the conductor in putting off an intoxicated man twitched him in such a way as to push another intoxicated man over on to the plaintiff. The evidence for the defendant tended to disprove plaintiff's claim that either of the intoxicated persons came in contact with her, or assaulted her.

The defendant requested (*inter alia*) an instruction, that there was no evidence to warrant a verdict on the third count. This request was refused.

The judge instructed the jury as follows: —

"Now there is a third count to which attention must be called. If the jury should find that there was no bodily injury to the plaintiff direct from the acts of the conductor, that is, no person was thrown against the plaintiff, if that statement is not accurate, the plaintiff still contends that if the manner of the removal was such that it occasioned fright and nervous shock that resulted in bodily injury, that she is still entitled to recover for that bodily injury. And I have to say to you as matter of law, that if the wrongful acts of the conductor, on the

[1] Only so much of the case as relates to this count is given. The arguments are omitted. The statement was compiled, by Professor Jeremiah Smith, from the bill of exceptions filed in the Social Law Library of Boston.

occasion of removing the disorderly passenger, did occasion fright and nervous shock to the plaintiff, by reason of which she sustained bodily injury, that she can recover compensation for that injury.

"It is settled law in this State that a person cannot recover for mere fright, fear or mental distress occasioned by the negligence of another, which does not result in bodily injury.

. . . .

"But when the fright or fear or nervous shock produces a bodily injury, then there may be recovery for that bodily injury, and for all the pain, mental or otherwise, which may arise out of that bodily injury. The brain and the nervous system are so closely connected with the mind, are the instruments by which the mind communicates with the body and operates upon it, that we sometimes deal with the nervous conditions as if they were mental conditions, and possibly the testimony has to some extent treated them as one. But for the purpose of the principle which I am now stating, a clear distinction exists between what is mental and what is nervous. The nervous system, the brain and the nerve fibres, are a part of the body, and injury to them is bodily injury. Now if by the wrongful acts of this defendant or its agents, there was a mental shock, fright, and it ended with that, there can be no recovery. But if that mental shock produced a bodily injury, a disturbance of the brain or nervous system which continued and caused subsequent suffering, there may be recovery for that bodily injury and all that follows from it."

To the above instructions, the defendant excepted.

Verdict for plaintiff.

ALLEN, J. This case presents a question which has not heretofore been determined in this Commonwealth, and in respect to which the decisions elsewhere have not been uniform. It is this: whether in an action to recover damages for an injury sustained through the negligence of another, there can be a recovery for a bodily injury caused by mere fright and mental disturbance. The jury were instructed that a person cannot recover for mere fright, fear or mental distress occasioned by the negligence of another, which does not result in bodily injury,[1] but that when the fright or fear or nervous shock produces a bodily injury, there may be a recovery for that bodily injury, and for all the pain, mental or otherwise, which may arise out of that bodily injury.

[1] Western Co. *v.* Wood, 57 Fed. 471; Kyle *v.* Chicago R. Co., 182 Fed. 613; McCray *v.* Sharpe, 188 Ala. 375; Bachelder *v.* Morgan, 179 Ala. 339; St. Louis Co. *v.* Taylor, 84 Ark. 42; Chicago Co. *v.* Moss, 89 Ark. 187; Green *v.* Southern R. Co., 9 Ga. App. 751; Haas *v.* Metz, 78 Ill. App. 46; Kalen *v.* Terre Haute Co., 18 Ind. App. 202; Zabron *v.* Cunard Co., 151 Ia. 345; Kentucky Traction Co. *v.* Bain, 161 Ky. 44; Wyman *v.* Leavitt, 71 Me. 227; Wilson *v.* St. Louis R. Co., 160 Mo. App. 649; Arthur *v.* Henry, 157 N. C. 438; Samarra *v.* Allegheny Co., 238 Pa. St. 469; Folk *v.* Seaboard Co., 99 S. C. 284; Chesapeake R. Co. *v.* Tinsley, 116 Va. 600; Gulf Co. *v.* Trott, 86 Tex. 412 *Accord.*

In Canning *v.* Williamstown, 1 Cush. 451, it was held, in an action against a town to recover damages for an injury sustained by the plaintiff in consequence of a defective bridge, that he could not recover if he sustained no injury to his person, but merely incurred risk and peril which caused fright and mental suffering. In Warren *v.* Boston & Maine Railroad, 163 Mass. 484, the evidence tended to show that the defendant's train struck the carriage of the plaintiff, thereby throwing him out upon the ground, and it was held to be a physical injury to the person to be thrown out of a wagon, or to be compelled to jump out, even although the harm consists mainly of nervous shock. It was not therefore a case of mere fright, and resulting nervous shock.

The case calls for a consideration of the real ground upon which the liability or non-liability of a defendant guilty of negligence in a case like the present depends. The exemption from liability for mere fright, terror, alarm, or anxiety does not rest on the assumption that these do not constitute an actual injury. They do in fact deprive one of enjoyment and of comfort, cause real suffering, and to a greater or less extent disqualify one for the time being from doing the duties of life. If these results flow from a wrongful or negligent act, a recovery therefor cannot be denied on the ground that the injury is fanciful and not real. Nor can it be maintained that these results may not be the direct and immediate consequence of the negligence. Danger excites alarm. Few people are wholly insensible to the emotions caused by imminent danger, though some are less affected than others.

It must also be admitted that a timid or sensitive person may suffer not only in mind, but also in body, from such a cause. Great emotion may and sometimes does produce physical effects. The action of the heart, the circulation of the blood, the temperature of the body, as well as the nerves and the appetite, may all be affected. A physical injury may be directly traceable to fright, and so may be caused by it. We cannot say, therefore, that such consequences may not flow proximately from unintentional negligence, and if compensation in damages may be recovered for a physical injury so caused, it is hard on principle to say why there should not also be a recovery for the mere mental suffering when not accompanied by any perceptible physical effects.

It would seem, therefore, that the real reason for refusing damages sustained from mere fright must be something different; and it probably rests on the ground that in practice it is impossible satisfactorily to administer any other rule. The law must be administered in the courts according to general rules. Courts will aim to make these rules as just as possible, bearing in mind that they are to be of general application. But as the law is a practical science, having to do with the affairs of life, any rule is unwise if in its general application it will not as a usual result serve the purposes of justice. A new rule cannot be made for each case, and there must therefore be a certain generality in rules of law, which in particular cases may fail to meet what would be desirable if the single case were alone to be considered.

Rules of law respecting the recovery of damages are framed with reference to the just rights of both parties; not merely what it might be right for an injured person to receive, to afford just compensation for his injury, but also what it is just to compel the other party to pay. One cannot always look to others to make compensation for injuries received. Many accidents occur, the consequences of which the sufferer must bear alone. And in determining the rules of law by which the right to recover compensation for unintended injury from others is to be governed, regard must chiefly be paid to such conditions as are usually found to exist. Not only the transportation of passengers and the running of trains, but the general conduct of business and of the ordinary affairs of life, must be done on the assumption that persons who are liable to be affected thereby are not peculiarly sensitive, and are of ordinary physical and mental strength. If, for example, a traveller is sick or infirm, delicate in health, specially nervous or emotional, liable to be upset by slight causes, and therefore requiring precautions which are not usual or practicable for travellers in general, notice should be given, so that, if reasonably practicable, arrangements may be made accordingly, and extra care be observed.[1] But, as a general rule, a carrier of passengers is not bound to anticipate or to guard against an injurious result which would only happen to a person of peculiar sensitiveness. This limitation of liability for injury of another description is intimated in Allsop *v.* Allsop, 5 H. & N. 534, 538, 539. One may be held bound to anticipate and guard against the probable consequences to ordinary people, but to carry the rule of damages further imposes an undue measure of responsibility upon those who are guilty only of unintentional negligence. The general rule limiting damages in such a case to the natural and probable consequences of the acts done is of wide application, and has often been expressed and applied. Lombard *v.* Lennox, 155 Mass. 70; White *v.* Dresser, 135 Mass. 150; Fillebrown *v.* Hoar, 124 Mass. 580; Derry *v.* Flitner, 118 Mass. 131; Milwaukee & St. Paul Railway *v.* Kellogg, 94 U. S. 469, 475; Wyman *v.* Leavitt, 71 Maine, 227; Ellis *v.* Cleveland, 55 Vt. 358; Phillips *v.* Dickerson, 85 Ill. 11; Hampton *v.* Jones, 58 Iowa, 317; Renner *v.* Canfield, 36 Minn. 90; Lynch *v.* Knight, 9 H. L. Cas. 577, 591, 595, 598; The Notting Hill, 9 P. D. 105; Hobbs *v.* London & Southwestern Railway, L. R. 10 Q. B. 111, 122.

The law of negligence in its special application to cases of accidents has received great development in recent years. The number of

[1] "Ordinary street cars must be run with reference to ordinary susceptibilities, and the liability of their proprietors cannot be increased simply by a passenger's notifying the conductor that he has unstable nerves." Holmes J., in Spade *v.* Lynn R. Co., 172 Mass. 488, 491. But compare Webber *v.* Old Colony R. Co., 210 Mass. 432.

actions brought is very great. This should lead courts well to consider the grounds on which claims for compensation properly rest, and the necessary limitations of the right to recover. We remain satisfied with the rule that there can be no recovery for fright, terror, alarm, anxiety, or distress of mind, if these are unaccompanied by some physical injury; and if this rule is to stand, we think it should also be held that there can be no recovery for such physical injuries as may be caused solely by such mental disturbance, where there is no injury to the person from without. The logical vindication of this rule is, that it is unreasonable to hold persons who are merely negligent bound to anticipate and guard against fright and the consequences of fright; and that this would open a wide door for unjust claims, which could not successfully be met. These views are supported by the following decisions: Victorian Railways Commissioners *v.* Coultas, 13 App. Cas. 222; Mitchell *v.* Rochester Railway, 151 N. Y. 107; Ewing *v.* Pittsburg, Cincinnati, Chicago & St. Louis Railway, 147 Penn. St. 40: Haile *v.* Texas & Pacific Railway, 60 Fed. Rep. 557.

In the following cases, a different view was taken: Bell *v.* Great Northern Railway, 26 L. R. (Ir.) 428; Purcell *v.* St. Paul City Railway, 48 Minn. 134; Fitzpatrick *v.* Great Western Railway, 12 U. C. Q. B. 645. See also Beven, Negligence, 77 *et seq.*

It is hardly necessary to add that this decision does not reach those classes of actions where an intention to cause mental distress or to hurt the feelings is shown, or is reasonably to be inferred, as for example, in cases of seduction, slander, malicious prosecution or arrest, and some others. Nor do we include cases of acts done with gross carelessness or recklessness, showing utter indifference to such consequences, when they must have been in the actor's mind. Lombard *v.* Lennox, and Fillebrown *v.* Hoar, already cited. Meagher *v.* Driscoll, 99 Mass. 281.

In the present case, no such considerations entered into the rulings or were presented by the facts. The entry therefore must be

Exceptions sustained.[1]

[1] Victorian Commissioners *v.* Coultas, 13 App. Cas. 222; Haile *v.* Tex. Co., 60 Fed. 557; St. Louis Co. *v.* Bragg, 69 Ark. 402; Braun *v.* Craven, 175 Ill. 401 (*semble*); Kansas Co. *v.* Dalton, 65 Kan. 661; Morse *v.* Chesapeake Co., 117 Ky. 11; Reed *v.* Ford, 129 Ky. 471; White *v.* Sander, 168 Mass. 296; Smith *v.* Postal Co., 174 Mass. 576; Homans *v.* Boston Co., 180 Mass. 456 (*semble*); Cameron *v.* N. E. Co., 182 Mass. 310 (*semble*); Nelson *v.* Crawford, 122 Mich. 466; Crutcher *v.* Cleveland Co., 132 Mo. App. 311; Deming *v.* Chicago Co., 80 Mo. App. 152; Rawlings *v.* Wabash Co., 97 Mo. App. 515; Ward *v.* West Co., 65 N. J. Law, 383; Porter *v.* Del. Co., 73 N. J. Law, 405 (*semble*); Mitchell *v.* Rochester Co., 151 N. Y. 107; Newton *v.* N. Y. Co., 106 App. Div. 415 (*semble*); Prince *v.* Ridge, 32 Misc. 666, 667 (*semble*); Hutchinson *v.* Stern, 115 App. Div. 791; Miller *v.* Belt Co., 78 Ohio St. 309; Ewing *v.* Pittsburgh Co., 147 Pa. St. 40; Linn *v.*Duquesne Co., 204 Pa. St. 551; Huston *v.* Freemansburg, 212 Pa. St. 548; Hess *v.* American Pipe Co., 221 Pa. St. 67; Morris *v.* Lackawana R. Co., 228 Pa. St. 198; Taylor *v.* Atlantic Co., 78 S. C. 552; Ford *v.* Schliessman, 107 Wis. 479, 483 (*semble*) *Accord.*

The damages for an admitted tort to the person may be enhanced by proof of nervous shock caused by fright induced by the defendant's misconduct. Eagan *v.*

DULIEU *v.* WHITE AND SONS

KING'S BENCH DIVISION, JUNE 5, 1901.

Reported in [1901] 2 *King's Bench*, 669.

POINT of law raised by pleadings.[1]

The statement of claim was as follows: —

"1. The plaintiff is the wife of Arthur David Dulieu, who carries on the business of a licensed victualler at the Bonner Arms, Bonner Street, Bethnal Green, in the county of London.

"2. On July 20, 1900, the plaintiff was behind the bar of her husband's said public-house, she being then pregnant, when the defendants by their servant so negligently drove a pair-horse van as to drive it into the said public-house.

Middlesex R. Co., 212 Fed. 562, 214 Fed. 747; Birmingham Co. *v.* Martini, 2 Ala. App. 653; Melone *v.* Sierra Co., 151 Cal. 113; Seger *v.* Barkhamsted, 22 Conn. 290; Masters *v.* Warren, 27 Conn. 293; Garvey *v.* Metropolitan R. Co., 155 Ill. App. 601; Pittsburgh Co. *v.* Sponier, 85 Ind. 165; McClintic *v.* Eckman, 153 Ky. 704; Newport Co. *v.* Gholson, 10 Ky. L. Rep. 938; City Co. *v.* Robinson, 12 Ky. L. Rep. 555; Green *v.* Shoemaker, 111 Md. 69; Warren *v.* Boston Co., 163 Mass. 484; Homans *v.* Boston Co., 180 Mass. 456; Cameron *v.* N. E. Co., 182 Mass. 310; Driscoll *v.* Gaffey, 207 Mass. 102; Conley *v.* United Drug Co., 218 Mass. 238; Smith *v.* St. Paul Co., 30 Minn. 169; Hollingshed *v.* Yazoo R. Co., 99 Miss. 464; Butts *v.* Nat. Bank, 99 Mo. App. 168; Breen *v.* St. Louis Co., 102 Mo. App. 479; Heiberger *v.* Missouri Tel. Co., 133 Mo. App. 452; Lowe *v.* Metropolitan R. Co., 145 Mo. App. 248; Buchanan *v.* West Co., 52 N. J. Law, 265; Consol. Co. *v.* Lambertson, 59 N. J. Law, 297; Stokes *v.* Schlacter, 66 N. J. Law, 334; Porter *v.* Del. Co., 73 N. J. Law, 405; Kennell *v.* Gershonovitz, 84 N. J. Law, 577; O'Flaherty *v.* Nassau Co., 34 App. Div. 74 (affirmed 165 N. Y. 624); Cohn *v.* Ansonia Co., 162 App. Div. 791; Pa. Co. *v.* Graham, 63 Pa. St. 290; Scott *v.* Montgomery, 95 Pa. St. 444; Ewing *v.* Pittsburgh Co., 147 Pa. St. 40 (*semble*); Linn *v.* Duquesne Co., 204 Pa. St. 551 (*semble*); Samarra *v.* Allegheny R. Co., 238 Pa. St. 469; Folk *v.* Seaboard Co., 99 S. C. 284; Godeau *v.* Blood, 52 Vt. 251; Nordgren *v.* Lawrence, 74 Wash. 305; Shutz *v.* Chicago Co., 73 Wis. 147; and even though the admitted tort is only an assault as distinguished from a battery. Kline *v.* Kline, 158 Ind. 602; Williams *v.* Underhill, 63 App. Div. 223; Leach *v.* Leach, 11 Tex. Civ. App. 699. It must be shown that there was causal connection between the fright and the shock. Hack *v.* Dady, 142 App. Div. 510.

In Homans *v.* Boston Co., *supra*, the court said, through Holmes, C. J.: "As has been explained repeatedly, it is an arbitrary exception, based upon a notion of what is practicable, that prevents a recovery for visible illness resulting from nervous shock alone. Spade *v.* Lynn Co.; Smith *v.* Postal Co., 174 Mass. 576. But when there has been a battery and the nervous shock results from the same wrongful management as the battery, it is at least equally impracticable to go further and to inquire whether the shock comes through the battery or along with it. Even were it otherwise, recognizing as we must the logic in favor of the plaintiff when a remedy is denied because the only immediate wrong was a shock to the nerves, we think that when the reality of the cause is guaranteed by proof of a substantial battery of the person there is no occasion to press further the exception to general rules." See also Spade *v.* Lynn Co., 172 Mass. 690, per Holmes, C. J.

Liability for frightening an Animal to Death. The doctrine of the principal case was carried so far in Lee *v.* Burlington, 113 Ia., 356, that no recovery was allowed for the death of a horse from fright caused by the careless conduct of the defendant. But the opposite view prevailed in Louisville R. Co. *v.* Melton, 158 Ala. 509, and Conklin *v.* Thompson, 29 Barb. 218.

[1] Portions of the statement of facts have been omitted.

"3. The defendants were also negligent in entrusting the driving of the said horses and van to their said servant, who had no knowledge or skill in driving.

"4. The plaintiff in consequence sustained a severe shock, and was and is seriously ill, and on September 29, 1900, gave premature birth to a child.

"5. In consequence of the shock sustained by the plaintiff the said child was born an idiot.

"The plaintiff claims damages in respect of the aforesaid matters."

The statement of defence, after denying the allegations contained in the statement of claim proceeded: —

"3. The defendants submit as a matter of law that the damages sought to be recovered herein are too remote, and that the statement of claim on the face thereof discloses no cause of action."

Cur. adv. vult.

KENNEDY, J. In this case the only question for the judgment of the court is in the nature of a demurrer.

. . . .

The head of damage alleged in paragraph 5 was rightly treated by the plaintiff's counsel as untenable.

The defendant's counsel summed up his contention against the legal validity of the plaintiff's claim in the statement that no action for negligence will lie where there is no immediate physical injury resulting to the plaintiff.

. . . .

This is an action on the case for negligence — that is to say, for a breach on the part of the defendant's servant of the duty to use reasonable and proper care and skill in the management of the defendant's van. In order to succeed, the plaintiff has to prove resulting damage to herself and "a natural and continuous sequence uninterruptedly connecting the breach of duty with the damage as cause and effect." Shearman and Redfield, Negligence, cited in Beven, Negligence in Law, 2d ed. p. 7. In regard to the existence of the duty here, there can, I think, be no question. The driver of a van and horses in a highway owes a duty to use reasonable and proper care and skill so as not to injure either persons lawfully using the highway, or property adjoining the highway, or persons who, like the plaintiff are lawfully occupying that property. His legal duty towards all appears to me to be practically identical in character and in degree. I understood the plaintiff's counsel to suggest that there might exist a higher degree of duty towards the plaintiff sitting in a house than would have existed had she been in the street. I am not satisfied that this is so. The wayfarer in the street, as it seems to me, has in law as much right of redress if he is injured in person or in property by the negligence of another as the man who is lawfully sitting on a side-wall or in an adjoining house. "The whole law of negligence assumes the principle of 'Volenti non fit injuria' not to be applicable," for reasons which Sir Frederick Pollock points out (The Law of Torts, by Sir F. Pollock, 6th ed. pp. 166, 167), in a passage which follows the quotation which I have just made. The legal obligations of the driver of horses are the same, I think, towards the man indoors as to the man out of doors; the only question here is whether there is an actionable breach of those obligations if the man in either case is made ill in body by such negligent driving as does not break his ribs but shocks his nerves.

Before proceeding to consider the objections to the maintenance of such a claim as that of the present plaintiff, it is, I think, desirable for clearness' sake to see exactly what are the facts which ought to be assumed for the purposes of the argument. We must assume in her favor all that can be assumed consistently with the allegations of the statement of claim. We must, therefore, take it as proved that the negligent driving of the defendants' servant reasonably and naturally caused a nervous or mental shock to the plaintiff by her reasonable apprehension of immediate bodily hurt, and that the premature childbirth, with the physical pain and suffering which accompanied it, was a natural and a direct consequence of the shock. I may just say in passing that I use the words "nervous" and "mental" as interchangeable epithets on the authority of the judgment of the Privy Council in Victorian Railways Commissioners *v.* Coultas, 13 App. Cas. 222; but I venture to think "nervous" is probably the more correct epithet where terror operates through parts of the physical organism to produce bodily illness as in the present case. The use of the epithet "mental" requires caution, in view of the undoubted rule that merely mental pain unaccompanied by any injury to the person cannot sustain an action of this kind. Beven, Negligence in Law, 2d ed. p. 77.

Now, these being the assumed facts, what are the defendants' arguments against the plaintiff's right to recover damages in this action?

First of all, it is argued, fright caused by negligence is not in itself a cause of action — ergo, none of its consequences can give a cause of action. In Mitchell *v.* Rochester Ry. Co., (1896) 151 N. Y. 107, the point is put thus: "That the result may be nervous disease, blindness, insanity, or even a miscarriage, in no way changes the principle. These results merely show the degree of fright or the extent of the damages. The right of action must still depend upon the question whether a recovery may be had for fright." With all respect to the learned judges who have so held, I feel a difficulty in following this reasoning. No doubt damage is an essential element in a right of action for negligence. I cannot successfully sue him who has failed in his duty of using reasonable skill and care towards me unless I can prove some material and measurable damage. If his negligence has caused me neither injury to property nor physical mischief, but only an unpleasant emotion of more or less transient duration, an essential constituent of a right of action for negligence is lacking. "Fear," as Sir Frederick Pollock has stated (The Law of Torts, 6th ed. p. 51), "taken alone falls short of being actual damage not because it is a remote or unlikely consequence, but because it can be proved and measured only by physical effects." It may, I conceive, be truly said that, viewed in relation to an action for negligence, direct bodily impact is, without resulting damage, as insufficient a ground of legal claim as the infliction of fright. That fright — where physical injury is directly produced by it — cannot be a ground of action merely because of the absence of any accompanying impact appears to me to be a contention both unreasonable and contrary to the weight of authority.

[The learned judge then cited cases in which an action was held to lie, where the only physical impact did not accompany but was a consequence of the fright; also a case where there was nothing in the nature of impact and yet recovery was allowed.]

If impact be not necessary, and if, as must be assumed here, the fear is proved to have naturally and directly produced physical effects, so that the ill results of the negligence which caused the fear are as measurable in damages as the same results would be if they arose from an actual impact, why should not an action for those damages lie just as well as it lies where there has been an actual impact? It is not, however, to be taken that in my view every nervous shock occasioned by negligence and producing physical injury to the sufferer gives a cause of action. There is, I am inclined to think, at least one limitation. The shock, where it operates through the mind, must be a shock which arises from a reasonable fear of immediate personal injury to oneself. A. has, I conceive, no legal duty not to shock B.'s nerves by the exhibition of negligence towards C., or towards the property of B. or C. The limitation was applied by Wright and Bruce, JJ., in the unreported case of Smith *v.* Johnson & Co., referred to by Wright, J., at the close of his judgment in Wilkinson *v.* Downton, [1897] 2 Q. B. 57, at p. 61. In Smith *v.* Johnson & Co. (unreported), a man was killed by the defendant's negligence in the sight of the plaintiff, and the plaintiff became ill, not from the shock produced by fear of harm to himself, but from the shock of seeing another person killed. The court held that this harm was too remote a consequence of the negligence.[1] I should myself, as I have already indi-

[1] See to the same effect Phillips *v.* Dickerson, 85 Ill. 11; Cleveland Co. *v.* Stewart, 24 Ind. App. 374; Gaskins *v.* Runkle, 25 Ind. App. 584; Mahoney *v.* Dankwart, 108 Ia. 321; McGee *v.* Vanover, 148 Ky. 737; Chesapeake R. Co. *v.* Robinett, 151 Ky. 778; Sperier *v.* Ott, 116 La. 1087; Renner *v.* Canfield, 36 Minn. 90; Bucknam *v.* Great Northern R. Co., 76 Minn. 373; Sanderson *v.* Great Northern R. Co., 88 Minn. 162; Hutchinson *v.* Stern, 115 App. Div. 791; Gosa *v.* Southern Ry., 67 S. C. 347; Gulf R. Co. *v.* Overton, 101 Tex. 583 (but compare Gulf R. Co. *v.* Coopwood, 16 Tex. Ct. Rep. 354); Taylor *v.* Spokane R. Co., 72 Wash. 378, rev'g 67 Wash. 96.

cated, have been inclined to go a step further, and to hold upon the facts in Smith *v.* Johnson & Co. that, as the defendant neither intended to affect the plaintiff injuriously nor did anything which could reasonably or naturally be expected to affect him injuriously, there was no evidence of any breach of legal duty towards the plaintiff or in regard to him of that absence of care according to the circumstances which Willes, J., in Vaughan *v.* Taff Vale Ry. Co., (1860) 5 H. &. N. 679, at p. 688, gave as a definition of negligence.

. . . .

In order to illustrate my meaning in the concrete, I say that I should not be prepared in the present case to hold that the plaintiff was entitled to maintain this action if the nervous shock was produced, not by the fear of bodily injury to herself, but by horror or vexation arising from the sight of mischief being threatened or done either to some other person, or to her own or her husband's property, by the intrusion of the defendants' van and horses. The cause of the nervous shock is one of the things which the jury will have to determine at the trial.

It remains to consider the second and somewhat different form in which the defendants' counsel put his objection to the right of the plaintiff to maintain this action. He contended that the damages are too remote, and relied much upon the decision of the Privy Council in Victorian Railways Commissioners *v.* Coultas, 13 App. Cas. 222.

. . . .

The principal ground of their judgment is formulated in the following sentence: "Damages arising from mere sudden terror unaccompanied by any actual physical injury, but occasioning a nervous or mental shock, cannot under such circumstances, their Lordships think, be considered a consequence which, in the ordinary course of things, would flow from the negligence of the gate-keeper."

. . . .

Why is the accompaniment of physical injury essential? For my own part, I should not like to assume it to be scientifically true that a nervous shock which causes serious bodily illness is not actually accompanied by physical injury, although it may be impossible, or at least difficult, to detect the injury at the time in the living subject. I should not be surprised if the surgeon or the physiologist told us that nervous shock is or may be in itself an injurious affection of the physical organism. Let it be assumed, however, that the physical injury follows the shock, but that the jury are satisfied upon proper and sufficient medical evidence that it follows the shock as its direct and natural effect, is there any legal reason for saying that the damage is less proximate in the legal sense than damage which arises contemporaneously? "As well might it be said" (I am quoting from the judgment of Palles, C. B., 26 L. R. Ir. at p. 439) "that a death caused by poison is not to be attributed to the person who administered it because the mortal effect is not produced contemporaneously with its administration." Remoteness as a legal ground for the exclusion of damage in an action of tort means, not severance in point of time, but the absence of direct and natural causal sequence — the inability to trace in regard to the damage the "propter hoc" in a necessary or natural descent from the wrongful act. As a matter of experience, I should say that the injury to health which forms the main ground of damages in actions of negligence, either in cases of railway accidents or in running-down cases, frequently is proved, not as a concomitant of the occurrence, but as one of the sequelæ.

. . . .

[As to Mitchell *v.* Rochester Ry. Co., 151 N. Y. 107, cited by defendant.] Shortly, the facts there were that the plaintiff, whilst waiting for a tram-car, was nearly run over by the negligent management of the defendant's servant of a car drawn by a pair of horses, and owing to terror so caused fainted, lost consciousness, and subsequently had a miscarriage and consequent illness.

. . . .

It may be admitted that the plaintiff in this American case would not have suffered exactly as she did, and probably not to the same extent as she did, if she had not been pregnant at the time; and no doubt the driver of the defendant's horses could not anticipate that she was in this condition. But what does that fact matter ? If a man is negligently run over or otherwise negligently injured in his body, it is no answer to the sufferer's claim for damages that he would have suffered less injury, or no injury at all, if he had not had an unusually thin skull or an unusually weak heart.

[After commenting on the opinion in Spade *v.* Lynn & Boston R. R., 168 Mass. 285.]

Naturally one is diffident of one's opinion when one finds that it is not in accord with those which have been expressed by such judicial authorities as those to which I have just referred. But certainly, if, as is admitted, and I think justly admitted, by the Massachusetts judgment, a claim for damages for physical injuries naturally and directly resulting from nervous shock which is due to the negligence of another in causing fear of immediate bodily hurt is in principle not too remote to be recoverable in law, I should be sorry to adopt a rule which would bar all such claims on grounds of policy alone, and in order to prevent the possible success of unrighteous or groundless actions. Such a course involves the denial of redress in meritorious cases, and it necessarily implies a certain degree of distrust, which I do not share, in the capacity of legal tribunals to get at the truth in this class of claims. My experience gives me no reason to suppose that a jury would really have more difficulty in weighing the medical evidence as to the effects of nervous shock through fright, than in weighing the like evidence as to the effects of nervous shock through a railway collision or a carriage accident, where, as often happens, no palpable injury, or very slight palpable injury, has been occasioned at the time.

I have now, I think, dealt with the authorities and the arguments upon which the defendants rely, and I have done so at greater length than I should have wished to do but for the general interest of the points involved and the difficulties which the conflict of authorities undoubtedly present. In this conflict I prefer, as I have already indicated, the two decisions of the Irish courts. They seem to me to constitute strong and clear authorities for the plaintiff's contention. It was suggested on the part of the defendants that the applicability of the judgment in Bell *v.* Great Northern Company of Ireland, 26 L. R. Ir. 428, is affected by the fact that the female in that action was a passenger on the defendant's railway, and as such had contractual rights. It appears to me that in the circumstances this fact can make no practical difference whatever. In the Irish case there was no special contract, no notice to the railway company, when they accepted her as a passenger, that she was particularly delicate, or peculiarly nervous or liable to fright. The contractual duty existed, as it often does exist, concurrently with the duty apart from contract; but the one is in such circumstances practically coextensive with the other in the rights which it gives and the corresponding liabilities which it imposes.

I hold that, if on the trial of this action the jury find the issues left to them as the jury found them in Bell *v.* Great Northern Railway Company of Ireland, 26 L. R. Ir. 428, after the direction of Andrews, J., which was approved by the Exchequer Division, the plaintiff will have made out a good cause of action.

PHILLIMORE, J.

. . . .

I think there may be cases in which A. owes a duty to B. not to inflict a mental shock on him or her, and that in such a case, if A. does inflict such a shock upon B. — as by terrifying B. — and physical damage thereby ensues, B. may have an action for the physical damage, though the medium through which it has been inflicted is the mind.

. . . .

I think there is some assistance to be got from the cases where fear of impending danger has induced a passenger to take means of escape which have in the result proved injurious to him, and where the carrier has been held liable for these injuries, as in Jones *v.* Boyce, 1 Stark. 493.

. . . .

[The learned judge thought it possible that he might have come to the same conclusion as that arrived at in Victorian Railways Commissioners *v.* Coultas, though not for the reasons which have prominence in the judgment. He also thought that he should have come to the same decision as the Massachusetts court in Spade *v.* Lynn & Boston R. R.; but that he should not have expressed it in such broad and sweeping language.]

. . . .

In the case before us the plaintiff, a pregnant woman, was in her house. It is said that she was not the tenant in possession and could not maintain trespass *quare clausum fregit* if this had been a direct act of the defendant and not of his servant (as it was). This is true: her husband was in possession. But none the less it was her home, where she had a right, and on some occasions a duty, to be; and it seems to me that if the tenant himself could maintain an action, his wife or child could do likewise. It is averred that by reason of the careless driving of the defendants' servant a pair-horse van came some way into the room, and so frightened her that serious physical consequences thereby befell her. If these averments be proved, I think that there was a breach of duty to her for which she can have damages. The difficulty in these cases is to my mind not one as to the remoteness of the damage, but as to the uncertainty of there being any duty. Once get the duty and the physical damage following on the breach of duty, and I hold that the fact of one link in the chain of causation being mental only makes no difference. The learned counsel for the plaintiff has put it that every link is physical in the narrow sense. That may be or may not be. For myself, it is unimportant.

. . . .

Judgment for plaintiff.[1]

[1] Pullman Co. *v.* Lutz, 154 Ala. 517; Spearman *v.* McCrary, 4 Ala. App. 473; Sloane *v.* So. Co., 111 Cal. 668; Watson *v.* Dilts, 116 Ia. 249; Cowan *v.* Tel. Co., 122 Ia. 379, 382 (*semble*); Purcell *v.* St. Paul Co., 48 Minn. 134, 138; Lesch *v.* Great Northern R. Co., 97 Minn. 503; Watkins *v.* Kaolin Co., 131 N. C. 536; Taber *v.* Seaboard Co., 81 S. C. 317; Simone *v.* R. I. Co., 28 R. I. 186; Mack *v.* South Co., 52 S. C. 323; Hill *v.* Kimball, 76 Tex. 210; Gulf Co. *v.* Hayter, 93 Tex. 239; Yoakum *v.* Kroeger, (Tex. Civ. App.) 27 S. W. 953; St. Louis Co. *v.* Murdock, 54 Tex. Civ. App. 249; Pankopf *v.* Hinkley, 141 Wis. 146; Fitzpatrick *v.* Gr. W. Co., 12 Up. Can. Q. B. 645; Bell *v.* Great Northern R. Co., 26 L. R. Ir. 428; Cooper *v.* Caledonia Co. (Court of Sess., June 14, 1902), 4. F. 880 *Accord.*

See Bohlen, Right to Recover for Injury Resulting from Negligence without Impact, 41 Am. L. Reg. & Rev. 141.

Mental Anguish caused by Negligence in Transmission of Telegrams. In a few states the addressee is allowed to recover damages for mental anguish resulting from the negligent failure of a telegraph company to make seasonable delivery of a message. Mentzer *v.* Western Co., 93 Ia. 752; Cowan *v.* Western Co., 122 Ia. 379; Hurlburt *v.* Western Co., 123 Ia. 295; Chapman *v.* Western Co., 90 Ky. 265; Western Co. *v.* Van Cleave, 107 Ky. 464; Western Co. *v.* Fisher, 107 Ky. 513; Graham *v.* Western Co., 109 La. 1069; Barnes *v.* Western Co., 27 Nev. 438 (*semble*); Thompson *v.* Western Co., 106 N. C. 549; Young *v.* Western Co., 107 N. C. 370; Bryan *v.* Western Co., 133 N. C. 603; Woods *v.* Western Co., 148 N. C. 1; Hellams *v.* Western Co., 70 S. C. 83 (*statutory*); Capers *v.* Western Co., 71 S. C. 29; Wadsworth *v.* Western Co., 86 Tenn. 695; Railroad *v.* Griffin, 92 Tenn. 694;

WILKINSON *v.* DOWNTON

QUEEN'S BENCH DIVISION, MAY 8, 1897.

Law Reports, [1897] 2 *Queen's Bench,* 57.

WRIGHT, J.[1] In this case the defendant, in the execution of what he seems to have regarded as a practical joke, represented to the plaintiff that he was charged by her husband with a message to her to the effect that her husband was smashed up in an accident, and was lying at The Elms at Leytonstone with both legs broken, and that she was to go at once in a cab with two pillows to fetch him home. All this was false. The effect of the statement on the plaintiff was a violent shock to her nervous sytem, producing vomiting and other more serious and permanent physical consequences at one time threatening her reason, and entailing weeks of suffering and incapacity to her as well as expense to her husband for medical attendance. These consequences were not in any way the result of previous ill-health or weakness of constitution; nor was there any evidence of predisposition to nervous shock or any other idiosyncrasy.

In addition to these matters of substance there is a small claim for 1*s.* 10½*d.* for the cost of railway fares of persons sent by the plaintiff to Leytonstone in obedience to the pretended message. As to this 1*s.* 10½*d.* expended in railway fares on the faith of the defendant's statement, I think the case is clearly within the decision in Pasley *v.* Freeman, (1789) 3 T. R. 51. The statement was a misrepresentation intended to be acted on to the damage of the plaintiff.

The real question is as to the 100*l.*, the greatest part of which is given as compensation for the female plaintiff's illness and suffering.

So Relle *v.* Western Co., 55 Tex. 308; Stuart *v.* Western Co., 66 Tex. 580; Western Co. *v.* Beringer, 84 Tex. 38.

But the weight of authority is against such recovery. Chase *v.* Western Co., 44 Fed. 554; Crawson *v.* Western Co., 47 Fed. 544; Tyler *v.* Western Co., 54 Fed. 634; Western Co. *v.* Wood, 57 Fed. 471; Gahan *v.* Western Co., 59 Fed. 433; Stansell *v.* Western Co., 107 Fed. 668; Western Co. *v.* Sklar, 126 Fed. 295; Rowan *v.* Western Co., 149 Fed. 550; Blount *v.* Western Co., 126 Ala. 105; Western Co. *v.* Krichbaum, 132 Ala. 535; Western Co. *v.* Blocker, 138 Ala. 484; Western Co. *v.* Waters, 139 Ala. 652; Peay *v.* Western Co., 64 Ark. 538 (but changed by statute, Western Co. *v.* McMullin, 98 Ark. 346); Russell *v.* Western Co., 3 Dak. 315; Internat. Co. *v.* Saunders, 32 Fla. 434; Chapman *v.* Western Co., 88 Ga. 763; Giddens *v.* Western Co., 111 Ga. 824; Western Co. *v.* Haltom, 71 Ill. App. 63; Western Co. *v.* Ferguson, 157 Ind. 64 (overruling Reese *v.* Western Co., 123 Ind. 294); West *v.* Western Co., 39 Kan. 93 (*semble*); Cole *v.* Gray, 70 Kan. 705; Francis *v.* Western Co., 58 Minn. 252; Western Co. *v.* Rogers, 68 Miss. 748; Duncan *v.* Western Co., 93 Miss. 500; Connell *v.* Western Co., 116 Mo. 34; Newman *v.* Western Co., 54 Mo. App. 434; Curtin *v.* Western Co., 13 App. Div. 253; Morton *v.* Western Co., 53 Ohio St. 431; Butner *v.* Western Co., 2 Okl. 234; Western Co. *v.* Chouteau, 28 Okl. 664; Lewis *v.* Western Co., 57 S. C. 325 (law changed by statute in 1900, Capers *v.* Western Co., 71 S. C. 29); Connelly *v.* Western Co., 100 Va. 51; Corcoran *v.* Postal Co., 80 Wash. 570; Davis *v.* Western Co., 46 W. Va. 48; Summerfield *v.* Western Co., 87 Wis. 1; Koerber *v.* Patek, 123 Wis. 453, 464 (*semble*).

[1] Only the judgment of the court is printed.

It was argued for her that she is entitled to recover this as being damage caused by fraud, and therefore within the doctrine established by Pasley *v.* Freeman, (1789) 3 T. R. 51, and Langridge *v.* Levy, (1837) 2 M. & W. 519. I am not sure that this would not be an extension of that doctrine, the real ground of which appears to be that a person who makes a false statement intended to be acted on must make good the damage naturally resulting from its being acted on. Here there is no injuria of that kind. I think, however, that the verdict may be supported upon another ground. The defendant has, as I assume for the moment, wilfully done an act calculated to cause physical harm to the plaintiff — that is to say, to infringe her legal right to personal safety, and has in fact thereby caused physical harm to her. That proposition without more appears to me to state a good cause of action, there being no justification alleged for the act. This wilful injuria is in law malicious, although no malicious purpose to cause the harm which was caused nor any motive of spite is imputed to the defendant.

It remains to consider whether the assumptions involved in the proposition are made out. One question is whether the defendant's act was so plainly calculated to produce some effect of the kind which was produced that an intention to produce it ought to be imputed to the defendant, regard being had to the fact that the effect was produced on a person proved to be in an ordinary state of health and mind. I think that it was. It is difficult to imagine that such a statement, made suddenly and with apparent seriousness, could fail to produce grave effects under the circumstances upon any but an exceptionally indifferent person, and therefore an intention to produce such an effect must be imputed, and it is no answer in law to say that more harm was done than was anticipated, for that is commonly the case with all wrongs. The other question is whether the effect was, to use the ordinary phrase, too remote to be in law regarded as a consequence for which the defendant is answerable. Apart from authority, I should give the same answer and on the same ground as the last question, and say that it was not too remote. Whether, as the majority of the House of Lords thought in Lynch *v.* Knight, (1861) 9. H. L. C. 577, at pp. 592, 596, the criterion is in asking what would be the natural effect on reasonable persons, or whether, as Lord Wensleydale thought (9 H. L. C. 587, at p. 600), the possible infirmities of human nature ought to be recognized, it seems to me that the connection between the cause and the effect is sufficiently close and complete. It is, however, necessary to consider two authorities which are supposed to have laid down that illness through mental shock is a too remote or unnatural consequence of an injuria to entitle the plaintiff to recover in a case where damage is a necessary part of the cause of action. One is the case of Victorian Railways Commissioners *v.* Coultas, 13 App. Cas. 222, where it was held in the Privy Council that illness which was the effect of shock caused by fright was too remote a consequence of a negligent act which caused the fright, there being no physical harm immediately caused. That decision was treated in the Court of Appeal in Pugh *v.* London, Brighton and South Coast Ry. Co., [1896] 2 Q. B. 248, as open to question. It is inconsistent with a decision in the Court of Appeal in Ireland: Bell *v.* Great Northern Ry. Co. of Ireland, (1890) 26 L. R. Ir. 428, where the Irish Exchequer Division refused to follow it; and it has been disapproved in the Supreme Court of New York; see Pollock on Torts, 4th ed. p. 47 (*n*). Nor is it altogether in point, for there was not in that case any element of wilful wrong; nor perhaps was the illness so direct and natural a consequence of the defendant's conduct as in this case. On these grounds it seems to me that the case of Victorian Railways Commissioners *v.* Coultas, 13 App. Cas. 222, is not an authority on which this case ought to be decided.

A more serious difficulty is the decision in Allsop *v.* Allsop, 5 H. & N. 534, which was approved by the House of Lords in Lynch *v.* Knight, 9 H. L. C. 577. In that case it was held by Pollock, C. B., Martin, Bramwell, and Wilde, BB., that illness caused by a slanderous imputation of unchastity in the case of a married woman did not constitute such special damage as would sustain an action for such a slander. That case, however, appears to have been decided on the ground that in all the innumerable actions for slander there were no precedents for alleging illness to be sufficient special damage, and that it would be of evil consequence to treat it as sufficient, because such a rule might lead to an infinity of trumpery or groundless actions. Neither of these reasons is applicable to the present case. Nor could such a rule be adopted as of general application without results which it would be difficult or impossible to defend. Suppose that a person is in a precarious and dangerous condition, and another person tells him that his physician has said that he has but a day to live. In such a case, if death ensued from the shock caused by the false statement, I cannot doubt that at this day the case might be one of criminal homicide, or that if a serious aggravation of illness ensued damages might be recovered. I think, however, that it must be admitted that the present case is without precedent. Some English decisions — such as Jones *v.* Boyce, (1816) 1 Stark. 493; Wilkins *v.* Day, (1883) 12 Q. B. D. 110; Harris *v.* Mobbs, (1878) 3 Ex. D. 268 — are cited in Beven on Negligence as inconsistent with the decision in Victorian Railways Commissioners *v.* Coultas, 13 App. Cas. 222. But I think that those cases are to be explained on a different ground, namely, that the damage which immediately resulted from the act of the passenger or of the horse was really the result not of that act, but of a fright which rendered that act involuntary, and which therefore ought to be regarded as itself the direct and immediate cause of the damage. In Smith *v.* Johnson & Co. (unreported), decided in January last,

Bruce, J., and I held that where a man was killed in the sight of the plaintiff by the defendant's negligence, and the plaintiff became ill, not from the shock from fear of harm to himself, but from the shock of seeing another person killed, this harm was too remote a consequence of the negligence. But that was a very different case from the present.

There must be judgment for the plaintiff for 100*l.* 1*s.* 10½.

Judgment for plaintiff.[1]

YATES v. SOUTH KIRKBY COLLIERIES

IN THE COURT OF APPEAL, JULY 6, 1910.

Reported in [1910] 2 *King's Bench*, 538.

APPEAL against the award of the judge of the county court of Pontefract sitting as arbitrator under the Workmen's Compensation Act, 1906.

The question raised by this appeal was whether a nervous shock received by a workman in the course of his employment was an "accident" which entitled him to compensation under the Workmen's Compensation Act, 1906. The facts as found by the county court judge were as follows: —

In October, 1909, the applicant, — a collier, forty-six years of age, who had been engaged in coal mining all his life, and for twenty-seven years had been working at the face of the coal in the pit belonging to the respondents, — while working as usual, heard a shout for help from the next working place. He ran around his loose end at once and found a fellow collier lying full length on the ground, having been knocked down by a fallen timber prop and some coal; he was bleeding all over his head and from his ears and eyes. The applicant picked him up in his arms and, with assistance, carried him away; he was not dead at the time, but died in a quarter of an hour. The effect on the applicant was such that he sustained a nervous shock, which incapacitated him from working at the coal face; he returned to his work on the Saturday, and at the order of the under-manager on the Monday following, but on neither occasion was he able to do work,

[1] Hall v. Jackson, 24 Col. App. 225; Dunn v. Western Co., 2 Ga. App. 845; Goddard v. Watters, 14 Ga. App. 722 (*semble*); Watson v. Dilts, 116 Ia. 249, 124 Ia. 249; Lonergan v. Small, 81 Kan. 48; Nelson v. Crawford, 122 Mich. 466 (*semble*); Preiser v. Wielandt, 48 App. Div. 569; Buchanan v. Stout, 123 App. Div. 648 (*semble*); Miller v. R. R. Co., 78 Ohio St. 309, 324 (*semble*); Butler v. Western Co., 62 S. C. 222 (*semble*); Western Co. v. Watson, 82 Miss. 101 (*semble*); Shellabarger v. Morris, 115 Mo. App. 566; Wilson v. St. Louis R. Co., 160 Mo. App. 649; Hill v. Kimball, 76 Tex. 210; Davidson v. Lee, (Tex. Civ. App.) 139 S. W. 904; Jeppsen v. Jensen, 47 Utah 536 *Accord.*

Threats not amounting to an Assault. Threats of bodily harm sent by letter and causing illness by reason of apprehension of bodily harm are grounds for an action. Houston v. Woolley, 37 Mo. App. 15; Grimes v. Gates, 47 Vt. 594. Compare Stevens v. Steadman, 140 Ga. 680; Degenhardt v. Heller, 93 Wis. 662.

and after describing to the under-manager and the Government inspector on the Monday the details of what happened on the Saturday he left the pit; he then consulted his doctor and has been under his care since. In November he tried again to work, and went to his old place, but though he stayed the shift he was unable to work, and his brother, who was his mate, did it for him. In January, 1910, he asked the under-manager for a by-work job, but the under-manager would not give him one, and he had not worked since.

Proceedings for compensation having been taken, the county court judge found as a fact that there was a genuine incapacity to work which was due to the nervous shock which he sustained in October, 1909, when it clearly was his duty to his employers to go to the assistance of the injured collier who shouted for help from the next working place, and that his doing so arose both "in course of" and "out of" his employment. The learned county court judge accordingly awarded the applicant compensation at 19*s.* a week to the date of the award, and 10*s.* a week till further order.

The respondents appealed.[1]

FARWELL, L. J. I am of the same opinion. It is rightly conceded that it was part of the man's duty to go to the assistance of his fellow workman. Therefore there is no question that the events arose "out of and in the course of the employment." The learned county court judge has found as a fact that there was a genuine incapacity to work, which was due to the nervous shock which the applicant sustained in October last. In my opinion nervous shock due to accident which causes personal incapacity to work is as much "personal injury by accident" as a broken leg, for the reasons already expressed by this court in the case of Eaves *v.* Blaenclydach Colliery Co., [1909] 2 K. B. 73. In truth I find it difficult, when the medical evidence is that as a fact a workman is suffering from a known complaint arising from nervous shock, to draw any distinction between that case and the case of a broken limb. I see no distinction for this purpose between the case of the guard who is not in fact physically injured by an accident to his train, but who, after assisting to carry away the wounded and dead, breaks down from nervous shock, and the case of the guard who in similar circumstances stumbles over some of the débris and breaks his leg.[2] The difficulty is to prove the facts so as to avoid the risk of malingering, but when the facts have been proved, the injury causing incapacity to work arises from the accident in the one case just as much as in the other. I am, therefore, of opinion that the judgment of the learned county court judge must be affirmed.

[1] The opinion of Cozens-Hardy, M.R., sustaining the award is omitted.

[2] "On principle, the distinction between cases of physical impact or lesion being necessary as a ground of liability for damage caused seems to have nothing in its favour — always on the footing that the causal connection between the injury and the occurrence is established. If compensation is to be recovered under the statute or at common law in respect of an occurrence which has caused dislocation of a limb, on what principle can it be denied if the same occurrence has caused unhing-

KENNEDY, L. J. I am of the same opinion. It is beyond question that the incapacity of the applicant has arisen in the course of and out of the employment; and when you have a finding of fact by the learned county court judge that there has been a nervous shock, and that that nervous shock has produced a genuine condition of neurasthenia, I think myself the recent authorities show that this judgment ought to be supported. One knows perfectly well that neurasthenia, although there may be no outward sign if you merely look at the person, is treated, and successfully treated in some cases at any rate, by a treatment of the body. Directly you have that which requires treatment of the body, it means that a portion of that body (visible or invisible does not matter) is in a state of ill-health, and, if the condition of neurasthenia produces incapacity to work which has been brought about by something in the nature of an accident which arose "out of and in the course of the employment," you have a case of "personal injury by accident" which is within the Act. *Appeal dismissed.*

SECTION III

THE STANDARD OF CARE

VAUGHAN *v.* MENLOVE

IN THE COMMON PLEAS, JANUARY 23, 1837.

Reported in 3 *Bingham's New Cases*, 468.

THE declaration alleged, in substance, that plaintiff was the owner of two cottages; that defendant owned land near to the said cottages; that defendant had a rick or stack of hay near the boundary of his land which was liable and likely to ignite, and thereby was dangerous to the plaintiff's cottages; that the defendant, well knowing the premises, wrongfully and negligently kept and continued the rick in the aforesaid dangerous condition; that the rick did ignite, and that plaintiff's cottages were burned by fire communicated from the rick or from certain buildings of defendant's which were set on fire by flames from the rick.

Defendant pleaded the general issue; and also several special pleas, denying negligence.

ing of the mind? The personal injury in the latter case may be infinitely graver than in the former, and to what avail — in the incidence of justice, or the principle of law — is it to say that there is a distinction between things physical and mental? This is the broadest difference of all, and it carries with it no principle of legal distinction. Indeed it may be suggested that the proposition that injury so produced to the mind is unaccompanied by physical affection or change might itself be met by modern physiology or pathology with instant challenge." Lord Shaw in Coyle *v.* Watson, [1915] A. C. 1, 14.

At the trial it appeared that the rick in question had been made by the defendant near the boundary of his own premises; that the hay was in such a state when put together, as to give rise to discussions on the probability of fire; that though there were conflicting opinions on the subject, yet during a period of five weeks the defendant was repeatedly warned of his peril; that his stock was insured; and that upon one occasion, being advised to take the rick down to avoid all danger, he said " he would chance it." He made an aperture or chimney through the rick; but in spite, or perhaps in consequence of this precaution, the rick at length burst into flames from the spontaneous heating of its materials; the flames communicated to the defendant's barn and stables, and thence to the plaintiff's cottages, which were entirely destroyed.

Patteson, J., before whom the cause was tried, told the jury that the question for them to consider was, whether the fire had been occasioned by gross negligence on the part of the defendant; adding, that he was bound to proceed with such reasonable caution as a prudent man would have exercised under such circumstances.

A verdict having been found for the plaintiff, a rule nisi for a new trial was obtained, on the ground that the jury should have been directed to consider, not whether the defendant had been guilty of a gross negligence with reference to the standard of ordinary prudence, a standard too uncertain to afford any criterion, but whether he had acted *bonâ fide* to the best of his judgment; if he had, he ought not to be responsible for the misfortune of not possessing the highest order of intelligence. The action under such circumstances was of the first impression.[1]

Talfourd, Serjt., and *Whately*, showed cause.

The pleas having expressly raised issues on the negligence of the defendant, the learned judge could not do otherwise than leave that question to the jury. The declaration alleges that the defendant knew of the dangerous state of the rick, and yet negligently and improperly allowed it to stand. The plea of not guilty, therefore, puts in issue the scienter, it being of the substance of the issue: Thomas *v.* Morgan, 2 Cr. M. & R. 496. And the action, though new *in specie*, is founded on a principle fully established, that a man must so use his own property as not to injure that of others. On the same circuit a defendant was sued a few years ago for burning weeds so near the extremity of his own land as to set fire to and destroy his neighbors' wood. The plaintiff recovered damages, and no motion was made to set aside the verdict. Then, there were no means of estimating the defendant's negligence, except by taking as a standard the conduct of a man of ordinary prudence: that has been the rule always laid down, and there is no other that would not be open to much greater uncertainties.

[1] Statement abridged.

R. V. Richards, in support of the rule.

First, there was no duty imposed on the defendant, as there is on carriers or other bailees, under an implied contract, to be responsible for the exercise of any given degree of prudence: the defendant had a right to place his stack as near to the extremity of his own land as he pleased, Wyatt *v.* Harrison, 3 B. & Adol. 871: under that right, and subject to no contract, he can only be called on to act *bonâ fide* to the best of his judgment; if he has done that, it is a contradiction in terms, to inquire whether or not he has been guilty of gross negligence. At all events what would have been gross negligence ought to be estimated by the faculties of the individual, and not by those of other men. The measure of prudence varies so with the varying faculties of men, that it is impossible to say what is gross negligence with reference to the standard of what is called ordinary prudence. In Crook *v.* Jadis, 5 B. & Adol. 910, Patteson, J., says, " I never could understand what is meant by parties taking a bill under circumstances which ought to have excited the suspicion of a prudent man; " and Taunton, J., " I cannot estimate the degree of care which a prudent man should take." . . .

TINDAL, C. J. I agree that this is a case *primæ impressionis;* but I feel no difficulty in applying to it the principles of law as laid down in other cases of a similar kind. Undoubtedly this is not a case of contract, such as a bailment or the like, where the bailee is responsible in consequence of the remuneration he is to receive: but there is a rule of law which says you must so enjoy your own property as not to injure that of another; and according to that rule the defendant is liable for the consequence of his own neglect: and though the defendant did not himself light the fire, yet mediately he is as much the cause of it as if he had himself put a candle to the rick; for it is well known that hay will ferment and take fire if it be not carefully stacked. It has been decided that if an occupier burns weeds so near the boundary of his own land that damage ensues to the property of his neighbor, he is liable to an action for the amount of injury done, unless the accident were occasioned by a sudden blast which he could not foresee. Turberville *v.* Stamp, 1 Salk. 13. But put the case of a chemist making experiments with ingredients, singly innocent, but when combined liable to ignite; if he leaves them together, and injury is thereby occasioned to the property of his neighbor, can any one doubt that an action on the case would lie ?

It is contended, however, that the learned judge was wrong in leaving this to the jury as a case of gross negligence, and that the question of negligence was so mixed up with reference to what would be the conduct of a man of ordinary prudence that the jury might have thought the latter the rule by which they were to decide; that such a rule would be too uncertain to act upon; and that the question ought to have been whether the defendant had acted honestly and *bonâ fide* to the best of his own judgment. That, however, would leave so vague a line as to afford no rule at all, the degree of judgment belonging to each individual being infinitely various: and though it has been urged that the care which a prudent man would take, is not an intelligible proposition as a rule of law, yet such has always been the rule adopted in cases of bailment, as laid down in Coggs *v.* Bernard, 2 Ld. Raym. 909. Though in some cases a greater degree of care is exacted than in others, yet in " the second sort of bailment, viz., *commodatum* or lending gratis, the borrower is bound to the strictest care and diligence to keep the goods so as to restore them back again to the lender; because the bailee has a benefit by the use of them, so as if the bailee be guilty of the least neglect he will be answerable; as if a man should lend another a horse to go westward, or for a month; if the bailee put this horse in his stable, and he were stolen from thence, the bailee shall not be answerable for him; but if he or his servant leave the house or stable doors open, and the thieves take the opportunity of that, and steal the horse, he will be chargeable, because the neglect gave the thieves the occasion to steal the horse." The care taken by a prudent man has always been the rule laid down; and as to the supposed difficulty of applying it, a jury has always been able to say, whether, taking that rule as their guide, there has been negligence on the occasion in question.

Instead, therefore, of saying that the liability for negligence should be coextensive with the judgment of each individual, which would be as variable as the length of the foot of each individual, we ought rather to adhere to the rule, which requires in all cases a regard to caution such as a man of ordinary prudence would observe.[1] That was in substance the criterion presented to the jury in this case, and therefore the present rule must be discharged.

[Concurring opinions were delivered by PARK, and VAUGHAN, JJ. GASELEE, J. concurred in the result.] *Rule discharged.*

[1] Metropolitan R. Co. *v.* Jackson, 3 App. Cas. 193; Hyman *v.* Nye, 6 Q. B. D. 685; Simkin *v.* London R. Co., 21 Q. B. D. 453; Smith *v.* Browne, 28 L. R. Ir. 1; Bizzell *v.* Booker, 16 Ark. 308; Western R. Co. *v.* Vaughan, 113 Ga. 354; Chicago R. Co. *v.* Scott, 42 Ill. 132; City *v.* Cook, 99 Ind. 10; Needham *v.* Louisville R. Co., 85 Ky. 423; Merrill *v.* Bassett, 97 Me. 501; Heinz *v.* Baltimore R. Co., 113 Md. 582; Chenery *v.* Fitchburg R. Co., 160 Mass. 211; Brick *v.* Bosworth, 162 Mass. 334; Keown *v.* St. Louis R. Co., 141 Mo. 86; Teepan *v.* Taylor, 141 Mo. App. 282; Brown *v.* Merrimack Bank, 67 N. H. 549; Nashville R. Co. *v.* Wade, 127 Tenn. 154; Coates *v.* Canaan, 51 Vt. 131; Fowler *v.* Baltimore R. Co., 18 W. Va. 579; Schrunk *v.* St. Joseph, 120 Wis. 223 *Accord.*

" We do not understand that an employer's liability for the negligent act of his superintendent can be measured by the latter's poise of temperament, nor that the character of a given act of the superintendent in respect of negligence can be made to depend upon his excitability or the reverse. It is the duty of a superintendent to do what an ordinarily careful and prudent man would do under the same circumstances, and the employer is liable if he fail to do this and injury results to an employé." Bessemer Land Co. *v.* Campbell, 121 Ala. 50, 60.

Also it is erroneous to charge the jury that failure to exercise the care of " an ordinary man under like circumstances " or of " a person under similar circum-

BLYTH *v.* BIRMINGHAM WATERWORKS CO.

IN THE EXCHEQUER, FEBRUARY 6, 1856.

Reported in 11 *Exchequer*, 781.

THIS was an appeal by the defendants against the decision of the judge of the County Court of Birmingham. The case was tried before a jury, and a verdict found for the plaintiff for the amount claimed by the particulars. The particulars of the claim alleged, that the plaintiff sought to recover for damage sustained by the plaintiff by reason of the negligence of the defendants in not keeping their water-pipes and the apparatus connected therewith in proper order.

The case stated that the defendants were incorporated by stat. 7 Geo. IV., c. cix., for the purpose of supplying Birmingham with water.

By the 84th section of their Act it was enacted, that the company should, upon the laying down of any main-pipe or other pipe in any street, fix, at the time of laying down such pipe, a proper and sufficient fire-plug in each such street, and should deliver the key or keys of such fire-plug to the persons having the care of the engine-house in or near to the said street, and cause another key to be hung up in the watch-house in or near to the said street. By sec. 87, pipes were to be eighteen inches beneath the surface of the soil. By the 89th section, the mains were at all times to be kept charged with water. The defendants derived no profit from the maintenance of the plugs distinct from the general profits of the whole business, but such maintenance was one of the conditions under which they were permitted to exercise the privileges given by the Act. The main-pipe opposite the house of the plaintiff was more than eighteen inches below the surface. The fire-plug was constructed according to the best known system, and the materials of it were at the time of the accident sound and in good order. The apparatus connected with the fire-plug was as follows: —

The lower part of a wooden plug was inserted in a neck, which projected above and formed part of the main. About the neck there was a bed of brickwork puddled in with clay. The plug was also enclosed in a cast iron tube, which was placed upon and fixed to the brickwork. The tube was closed at the top by a movable iron stopper having a hole in it for the insertion of the key, by which the plug was loosened when occasion required it.

The plug did not fit tight to the tube, but room was left for it to move freely. This space was necessarily left for the purpose of easily and quickly removing the wooden plug to allow the water to flow. On the removal of the wooden plug the pressure upon the main forced the water up through the neck and cap to the surface of the street.

stances " or " just such as one of you, similarly employed, would have exercised under like circumstances " amounts to negligence. Austin R. Co. *v.* Beatty, 73 Tex. 592; St. Louis R. Co. *v.* Finley, 79 Tex. 85; Louisville R. Co. *v.* Gower, 85 Tenn. 465.

On the 24th of February, a large quantity of water, escaping from the neck of the main, forced its way through the ground into the plaintiff's house. The apparatus had been laid down twenty-five years, and had worked well during that time. The defendants' engineer stated, that the water might have forced its way through the brick-work round the neck of the main, and that the accident might have been caused by the frost, inasmuch as the expansion of the water would force up the plug out of the neck, and the stopper being incrusted with ice would not suffer the plug to ascend. One of the severest frosts on record set in on the 15th of January, 1855, and continued until after the accident in question. An incrustation of ice and snow had gathered about the stopper, and in the street all round, and also for some inches between the stopper and the plug. The ice had been observed on the surface of the ground for a considerable time before the accident. A short time after the accident, the company's turncock removed the ice from the stopper, took out the plug, and replaced it.

The judge left it to the jury to consider whether the company had used proper care to prevent the accident. He thought, that, if the defendants had taken out the ice adhering to the plug, the accident would not have happened, and left it to the jury to say whether they ought to have removed the ice. The jury found a verdict for the plaintiff for the sum claimed.

Field, for the appellant. There was no negligence on the part of the defendants. The plug was pushed out by the frost, which was one of the severest ever known.

The Court then called on

Kennedy, for the respondent. The company omitted to take sufficient precautions. The fire-plug is placed in the neck of the main. In ordinary cases the plug rises and lets the water out; but here there was an incrustation round the stopper, which prevented the escape of the water. This might have been easily removed. It will be found, from the result of the cases, that the company were bound to take every possible precaution. The fact of premises being fired by sparks from an engine on a railway is evidence of negligence: Piggott *v.* Eastern Counties Railway Company, 3 C. B. 229 (E. C. L. R. vol. 54); Aldridge *v.* Great Western Railway Company, 3 M. & Gr. 515 (Id. 42), 4 Scott, N. R. 156, 1 Dowl. N. S. 247, S. C. [MARTIN, B. I held, in a case tried at Liverpool, in 1853, that, if locomotives are sent through the country emitting sparks, the persons doing so incur all the responsibilities of insurers; that they were liable for all the consequences.[1] I invited counsel to tender a bill of exceptions to that ruling. Water is a different matter.] It is the defendants' water, therefore they are bound to see that no injury is done to any one by

[1] "See Lambert *v.* Bessey, T. Raym. 422; Scott *v.* Shepherd, 3 Wils. 403. Probably an action of trespass might have been brought." [Reporter's note.]

it. An action has been held to lie for so negligently constructing a hayrick at the extremity of the owner's land, that, by reason of its spontaneous ignition, his neighbor's house was burnt down: Vaughan *v.* Menlove, 3 Bing. N. C. 468 (E. C. L. R. vol. 32). [BRAMWELL, B. In that case discussions had arisen as to the probability of fire, and the defendant was repeatedly warned of the danger, and said he would chance it.] He referred to Wells *v.* Ody, 1 M. & W. 452. [ALDERSON, B. Is it an accident which any man could have foreseen ?] A scientific man could have foreseen it. If no eye could have seen what was going on, the case might have been different; but the company's servants could have seen, and actually did see, the ice which had collected about the plug. It is of the last importance, that these plugs, which are fire-plugs, should be kept by the company in working order. The accident cannot be considered as having been caused by the act of God: Siordet *v.* Hall, 4 Bing. 607 (Id. 13).

ALDERSON, B. I am of opinion that there was no evidence to be left to the jury. The case turns upon the question, whether the facts proved show that the defendants were guilty of negligence. Negligence is the omission to do something which a reasonable man, guided upon those considerations which ordinarily regulate the conduct of human affairs, would do, or doing something which a prudent and reasonable man would not do.[1] The defendants might have been liable for negligence, if, unintentionally, they omitted to do that which a reasonable person would have done, or did that which a person taking reasonable precautions would not have done. A reasonable man would act with reference to the average circumstances of the temperature in ordinary years. The defendants had provided against such frosts as experience would have led men, acting prudently, to provide against; and they are not guilty of negligence, because their precautions proved insufficient against the effects of the extreme severity of the frost of 1855, which penetrated to a greater depth than any which ordinarily occurs south of the polar regions. Such a state of circumstances constitutes a contingency against which no reasonable man can provide. The result was an accident for which the defendants cannot be held liable.

MARTIN, B. I think that the direction was not correct, and that there was no evidence for the jury. The defendants are not responsible, unless there was negligence on their part. To hold otherwise would be to make the company responsible as insurers.

[1] Nitro-Glycerine Case, 15 Wall. 524; Thompson *v.* Chicago R. Co., 189 Fed. 723; Fort Smith Co. *v.* Slover, 58 Ark. 168; Richardson *v.* Kier, 34 Cal. 63; Nolan *v.* New York R. Co., 53 Conn. 461; Wolf Mfg. Co. *v.* Wilson, 152 Ill. 9; Cincinnati R. Co. *v.* Peters, 80 Ind. 168; Galloway *v.* Chicago R. Co., 87 Ia. 458; Schneider *v.* Little, 184 Mich. 315; Lauritsen *v.* Bridge Co., 87 Minn. 518; McGraw *v.* Chicago R. Co., 59 Neb. 397; Roberts *v.* Boston R. Co., 69 N. H. 354; Drake *v.* Mount, 33 N. J. Law, 441; Chicago R. Co. *v.* Watson, 36 Okl. 1; Ahern *v.* Oregon Co., 24 Or. 276; Houston R. Co. *v.* Alexander, 103 Tex. 594; Washington *v.* Baltimore R. Co., 17 W. Va. 190 *Accord.*

BRAMWELL, B. The Act of Parliament directed the defendants to lay down pipes, with plugs in them, as safety-valves, to prevent the bursting of the pipes. The plugs were properly made, and of proper material; but there was an accumulation of ice about this plug, which prevented it from acting properly. The defendants were not bound to keep the plugs clear. It appears to me that the plaintiff was under quite as much obligation to remove the ice and snow which had accumulated, as the defendants. However that may be, it appears to me that it would be monstrous to hold the defendants responsible because they did not foresee and prevent an accident, the cause of which was so obscure, that it was not discovered until many months after the accident had happened.

Verdict to be entered for the defendants.[1]

YERKES v. NORTHERN PACIFIC R. CO.

SUPREME COURT, WISCONSIN, NOVEMBER 29, 1901.

Reported in 112 *Wisconsin Reports,* 184.

DODGE, J. . . . Plaintiff assigns as error the definition of the due care which plaintiff was bound to exercise to avert the charge of contributory negligence, viz.: —

"The plaintiff cannot recover in this case unless you find that he was in no manner guilty of any want of ordinary care, or such care as persons of ordinary care ordinarily use, which contributed to his said injuries." [2]

That this was an incorrect and misleading definition of "ordinary care" has been declared so often by this court as to make further discussion unnecessary. The rule has been repeatedly laid down that due care is to be tested by the surrounding circumstances, and that no definition is complete or correct which does not embody that element.[3] Ordinary care is the care ordinarily exercised by the great

[1] Sharp v. Powell, L. R. 7. C. P. 253; Pearson v. Cox, 2 C. P. D. 369; Gregg v. Illinois R. Co., 147 Ill. 550, 560; Missouri R. Co. v. Columbia, 65 Kan. 390, 400; Sutphen v. Hedden, 67 N. J. Law, 324; Crutchfield v. Richmond R. Co., 76 N. C. 320; Martin v. Highland Park Co., 128 N. C. 264; Simpson v. Southern R. Co., 154 N. C. 51; McCauley v. Logan, 152 Pa. St. 202; Bradley v. Lake Shore R. Co., 238 Pa. St. 315 ("only an extreme visionary would have imagined the consequences which followed or that injury could result to person or property therefrom"); Consumers Brewing Co. v. Doyle, 102 Va. 399; Lippert v. Brewing Co., 141 Wis. 453 *Accord.*

[2] Only that part of the opinion which relates to this instruction is given.

[3] "There is no absolute or intrinsic negligence; it is always relative to some circumstances of time, place, or person." Bramwell, B., in Degg v. Midland R. Co., 1 Hurlst. & N. 773, 781. See also Bowen, L. J., in Thomas v. Quartermaine, 18 Q. B. D. 685, 694.

Bizzell v. Booker, 16 Ark. 308; Needham v. San Francisco R. Co., 37 Cal. 409; Diamond Iron Co. v. Giles, 7 Houst. 557; Atlantic R. Co. v. Moore, 8 Ga. App. 185; Chicago R. Co. v. Johnson, 103 Ill. 512; Parks v. Yost, 93 Kan. 334; Sheridan v. Baltimore R. Co., 101 Md. 50; Kelly v. Michigan R. Co., 65 Mich. 186; De Bolt mass of mankind, or its type, the ordinarily prudent person, under the same or similar circumstances, and the omission of the last qualification, " under the same or similar circumstances," or " under like circumstances," is error. Boelter *v.* Ross L. Co., 103 Wis. 324, 330; Dehsoy *v.* Milwaukee E. R. & L. Co., 110 Wis. 412; Warden *v.* Miller, *ante*, p. 67. The necessity of the omitted qualification to a correct definition of due care is especially obvious under the circumstances of this case. What would be the care of an ordinarily prudent person, standing in safety upon a stationary platform, or even standing upon the perfect and level footboard of a moving switch engine, would not be the care to be expected of one attempting to perform the services of a yard man upon a bent, declining, and defective footboard such as here presented. The attention of the jury was not called by this instruction to a very important element which they must consider in order to decide whether the plaintiff was or was not guilty of contributory negligence, and the instruction to them on the subject was therefore misleading and erroneous.

HILL *v.* GLENWOOD

SUPREME COURT, IOWA, JULY 13, 1904.

Reported in 124 *Iowa Reports,* 479.

WEAVER, J.[1] The plaintiff claims to have been injured upon one of the public walks in the city of Glenwood, and that such injury was occasioned by reason of the negligence of the city in the maintenance of the walk at the place of the accident, and without fault on his own part contributing thereto. From verdict and judgment in his favor for $665, the city appeals. In this court the appellant makes no claim that the city was not negligent, but a reversal is sought on other grounds.

. . . .

It was shown without dispute that plaintiff had been blind for many years, and this fact is the basis of the criticism upon the charge given to the jury. In the third paragraph of the charge, the court, defining negligence, said: " (3) Negligence is defined to be the want of ordinary care; that is, such care as an ordinary prudent person would exercise under like circumstances. There is no precise definition of

v. Kansas City R. Co., 123 Mo. 496; Garland *v.* Boston R. Co., 76 N. H. 556; New Jersey Exp. Co. *v.* Nichols, 33 N. J. Law, 434; McGuire *v.* Spence, 91 N. Y. 303; Connell *v.* New York R. Co., 144 App. Div. 664; Anderson *v.* Atlantic R. Co., 161 N. C. 462; Elster *v.* Springfield, 49 Ohio St. 82; Frankford Co. *v.* Philadelphia R. Co., 54 Pa. St. 345; Virginia Power Co. *v.* Smith, 117 Va. 418; Morrison *v.* Power Co., 75 W. Va. 608; Davis *v.* Chicago R. Co., 58 Wis. 646 *Accord.*

Hence it is incorrect to define ordinary care as " such care as the ordinary person uses in the transaction of the ordinary affairs of life." Hennesey *v.* Chicago R. Co., 99 Wis. 109.

[1] Only part of the opinion is given.

ordinary care, but it may be said that it is such care as an ordinarily prudent person would exercise under like circumstances, and should be proportioned to the danger and peril reasonably to be apprehended from a lack of proper prudence. This rule applies alike to both parties to this action, and may be used in determining whether either was negligent." In the eighth paragraph, referring to the plaintiff's duty to exercise care for his own safety, the following language is used: "(8) It must also appear from the evidence that the plaintiff did not in any way contribute to the happening of the accident in question by any negligence on his part; that is, by his own want of ordinary care. The plaintiff, on his part, was under obligation to use ordinary care to prevent injury when passing over any sidewalk; and if he failed so to do, and his failure in any way contributed to the happening of the accident in question, then he cannot recover herein. The evidence shows without dispute that he was blind, and this fact should be considered by you in determining what ordinary care on his part would require when he was attempting to pass over one of the sidewalks of this city." Counsel for appellant do not deny that the rules here laid down would be a correct statement of the law of negligence and contributory negligence as applied to the ordinary case of sidewalk accident, but it is urged that the conceded fact of plaintiff's blindness made it the duty of the court to say to the jury that a blind person who attempts to use the public street "must exercise a higher degree of care and caution than a person ordinarily would be expected or required to use had he full possession of his sense of sight." We cannot give this proposition our assent. It is too well established to require argument or citation of authority that the care which the city is bound to exercise in the maintenance of its streets is ordinary and reasonable care, the care which ordinarily marks the conduct of a person of average prudence and foresight. So, too, it is equally well settled that the care which a person using the street is bound to exercise on his own part to discover danger and avoid accident and injury is of precisely the same character, the ordinary and reasonable care of a person of average prudence and foresight. The streets are for the use of the general public without discrimination; for the weak, the lame, the halt and the blind, as well as for those possessing perfect health, strength, and vision. The law casts upon one no greater burden of care than upon the other. It is true, however, that in determining what is reasonable or ordinary care we must look to the circumstances and surroundings of each particular case. As said by us in Graham *v.* Oxford, 105 Iowa, 708: "There is no fixed rule for determining what is ordinary care applicable to all cases, but each case must be determined according to its own facts." In the case before us the plaintiff's blindness is simply one of the facts which the jury must give consideration, in finding whether he did or did not act with the care which a reasonably prudent man would ordinarily exercise, when burdened by such infirmity. In other words, the measures which a traveler upon the street must employ for his own protection depend upon the nature and extent of the peril to which he knows, or in the exercise of reasonable prudence ought to know, he is exposed. The greater and more imminent the risk, the more he is required to look out for and guard against injury to himself; but the care thus exercised is neither more nor less than ordinary care—the care which men of ordinary prudence and experience may reasonably be expected to exercise under like circumstances. See cases cited in 21 Am. & Eng. Enc. Law, (2d ed.) 465, note 1. In the case at bar the plaintiff was rightfully upon the street, and if he was injured by reason of the negligence of the city, and without contributory negligence on his part, he was entitled to a verdict. In determining whether he did exercise due care it was proper for the jury, as we have already indicated, to consider his blindness, and in view of that condition, and all the surrounding facts and circumstances, find whether he exercised ordinary care and prudence. If he did, he was not guilty of contributory negligence.

This view of the law seems to be fairly embodied in the instructions to which exception is taken. If the appellant believed, as it now argues, that the charge should have been more specific, and dwelt with greater emphasis upon the fact of plaintiff's blindness as an element for the consideration of the jury in finding whether he exercised reasonable care, it had the right to ask an instruction framed to meet its views in that respect. No such request was made, and the omission of the court to so amplify the charge on its own motion was not error.[1]

KEITH v. WORCESTER STREET R. Co.

SUPREME JUDICIAL COURT, MASSACHUSETTS, NOVEMBER 26, 1907.

Reported in 196 *Massachusetts Reports*, 478.

TWO ACTIONS OF TORT for personal injuries received by the plaintiff's intestate caused by her falling when stepping across street railway rails which were piled by the defendant street railway company on the highway next to the curbing, and were allowed by the street railway company and the defendant town to remain there, and which, it was alleged, constituted an obstruction of the highway.[2]

The accident happened in the daytime. The plaintiff's intestate was near-sighted, and could not recognize a friend at a distance of more than ten or twelve feet.

[1] Rosenthal v. Chicago R. Co., 255 Ill. 552; Indianapolis Traction Co. v. Crawley, 51 Ind. App. 357 (deaf man); O'Flaherty v. Union R. Co., 45 Mo. 70; Simms v. South Carolina R. Co., 27 S. C. 268. *Accord.*

[2] Statement abridged. Part of opinion omitted.

At the trial in the Superior Court, defendants requested the following instruction: —

"If the plaintiff's intestate had defective eyesight, she should take greater care in walking the street than one of good eyesight; and if she failed to use this greater degree of care, the verdict must be for the defendant."

This request was refused, subject to exception.

In the charge to the jury, the presiding judge stated: "The plaintiff contends and has got to show by a fair preponderance of the evidence that Mrs. Keith was injured, and that she was injured while she was using . . . a degree of care that a reasonably prudent and careful person, acting prudently and carefully at the time, would have exercised and should have exercised in your judgment under all the circumstances then surrounding Mrs. Keith. That means not only external circumstances, that means not only the way in which the rails were placed, the location of the car, the necessity of action on her part, but it means also with reference to her personal peculiarities as they were shown to exist upon the stand. For instance, the conduct of a perfectly sound and healthy person may be properly regarded as one thing, when the same conduct on the part of a diseased or infirm person might be regarded as something very different.

"What might be in your judgment perfectly reasonable and proper and careful on the part of a sound person might be regarded fairly by you as improper and careless on the part of an infirm person.

"So, in this case, while I cannot instruct you as a matter of law that Mrs. Keith, if you find her to be near-sighted, was bound to use a higher degree of care than a person not near-sighted, I have got to leave it to you as a matter of fact whether a near-sighted person would not, in order to be careful, have to exercise a higher degree of care than a person not near-sighted. In other words, I have got to leave it to you to determine whether or not a near-sighted person is using due care if he or she under the particular circumstances acts exactly as a person who was not near-sighted would have done. In other words, it is a matter of fact for you to determine whether Mrs. Keith was called on to do differently from a person in full possession of eyesight rather than as a matter of law for me to direct you in regard to it."

The jury found for the plaintiff in both cases.

RUGG, J. . . . The defendant asked the court to rule that if the person injured "had defective eyesight, she should take greater care in walking the street than one of good sight, and if she failed to use this greater degree of care the verdict must be for the defendant." This request properly was refused, for the reason that it directed a verdict upon a single phase of the testimony, which was not necessarily decisive. In this respect the prayer differs vitally from the one which in Winn *v.* Lowell, 1 Allen, 177, this court held should have been given.[1] We see no reason for modifying the decision in Winn *v.* Lowell, nor is it inconsistent with subsequent cases. The standard of care established by the law is what the ordinarily prudent and cautious person would do to protect himself under given conditions. There is no higher or different standard for one who is aged, feeble, blind, halt, deaf or otherwise impaired in capacity, than for one in perfect physical condition. It has frequently, in recent as well as earlier cases, been said, in referring to one under some impediment, that greater caution or increased circumspection may be required in view of these adverse conditions. See, for example, Winn *v.* Lowell, 1 Allen, 177; Hall *v.* West End Street Railway, 168 Mass. 461; Hilborn *v.* Boston & Northern Street Railway, 191 Mass. 14; Vecchioni *v.* New York Central & Hudson River Railroad, 191 Mass. 9; Hawes *v.* Boston Elevated Railway, 192 Mass. 324; Hamilton *v.* Boston & Northern Street Railway, 193 Mass. 324. These expressions mean nothing more than that a person so afflicted must put forth a greater degree of effort than one not acting under any disabilities, in order to attain that standard of care which the law has established for everybody. When looked at from one standpoint, it is incorrect to say that a blind person must exercise a higher degree of care than one whose sight is perfect, but in another aspect, a blind person may be obliged to take precautions, practice vigilance and sharpen other senses, unnecessary for one of clear vision, in order to attain that degree of care which the law requires. It may depend in some slight degree upon how the description of duty begins, where the emphasis may fall at a given moment, but when the whole proposition is stated, the rights of the parties are as fully protected in the one way as in the other. It is perhaps more logical to say that the plaintiff is bound to use ordinary care, and that in passing upon what ordinary care demands, due consideration should be given to blindness or other infirmities. This was the course pursued by the Superior Court. Neff *v.* Wellesley, 148 Mass. 487. Smith *v.* Wildes, 143 Mass. 556. But it is also correct to say that in the exercise of common prudence one of defective eyesight must usually as matter of general knowledge take more care and employ keener watchfulness in walking upon the streets and avoiding obstructions than the same person with good eyesight, in order to reach the standard established by the law for all persons alike, whether they be weak or strong, sound or deficient.

Exceptions overruled.[2]

[1] The instruction which the court held should have been given in Winn *v.* Lowell was: "If the plaintiff was a person of poor sight, common prudence required of her greater care in walking upon the streets, and avoiding obstructions, than is required of persons of good sight."

[2] Compare Fenneman *v.* Holden, 75 Md. 1; Karl *v.* Juniata, 206 Pa. St. 633; Thompson *v.* Salt Lake Co., 16 Utah 281.

MEREDITH *v.* REED

SUPREME COURT, INDIANA, MAY TERM, 1866.

Reported in 26 *Indiana Reports*, 334.

GREGORY, C. J. Meredith sued Reed before a justice for an injury done by a stallion of the latter to the mare of the former, resulting in the death of the mare. Jury trial, verdict for the defendant; motion for a new trial overruled and judgment. The evidence is in the record. The facts are substantially as follows: In May, 1865, the defendant owned a stallion, which had previously been let to mares, but owing to the sickness of the owner, was not so let during the spring of 1865. He was a gentle stallion, and had never been known by the owner to be guilty of any vicious acts. Not being in use, he had been kept up in a stable for four or five months. He was secured in the stable by a strong halter and chain fastened through an iron ring in the manger. The stable door was securely fastened on the inside by a strong iron hasp, passed over a staple, and a piece of chain passed two or three times through the staple over the hasp, and the ends firmly tied together with a strong cord. It was also fastened on the outside by a piece of timber, one end of which was planted in the ground, while the other rested against the door. The horse was thus secured on the day and night the injury occurred. The gate of the enclosure surrounding the stable was shut and fastened as usual. About 11 o'clock that night the horse was found loose on the highway, and did the injury complained of. Early the following morning the outside gate was found open; the stable door was found open, with the log prop lying some distance to one side, and the chain which had been passed through the staple was gone, and the cord with which it had been tied was found cut and the pieces lying on the floor.

There are forty-two alleged errors assigned, but many of them are not, in our opinion, so presented as to entitle them to consideration in this Court. So far as the substantial rights of the appellant are involved, all the questions properly presented resolve themselves into the inquiry as to the nature and extent of the liability of the owner of a domestic animal for injuries done by it to the personal property of another, disconnected from any trespass to real estate.

It is contended, on the one hand, that ordinary care was all the law required of the defendant in this case. On the other it is claimed that the utmost care was necessary to free him from liability. Ordinary care is all that the law required in the case in judgment. What is ordinary care in some cases would be carelessness in others. The law regards the circumstances surrounding each case, and the nature of the animal or machinery under control. Greater care is required to be taken of a stallion than of a mare; so in the management of a steam-engine, greater care is necessary than in the use of a plow. Yet it is all ordinary care; such care as a prudent, careful man would take under like circumstances. The degree of care is always in proportion to the danger to be apprehended. The case at bar was properly sent to the jury, and the verdict is fully sustained by the evidence.

The judgment is affirmed, with costs.

DENVER ELECTRIC COMPANY *v.* SIMPSON

SUPREME COURT, COLORADO, APRIL TERM, 1895.

Reported in 21 *Colorado Reports,* 371.

ACTION for damage caused to plaintiff, while passing along a public alley, by his coming in contact with one of defendants' wires heavily charged with electricity, which had become detached from its overhead fastening, and was hanging down to within about two feet of the ground. At the trial there was some evidence tending to show that the position of the wire was due to the negligence of the defendants. Verdict for plaintiff, and judgment thereon. Defendant appealed; alleging as one ground the giving of certain instructions as to the care required by defendant. Those instructions are stated in the opinion.[1]

CAMPBELL, J. . . . This court does not recognize any degrees of negligence, such as slight or gross, and logically it ought not to recognize any degrees in its antithesis, care.[2] The court instructed the jury in this case that the defendant was not an insurer of the safety of plaintiff, but that in constructing its line and maintaining the same in repair, it was held to the utmost degree of care and diligence; that in this respect it is bound to the highest degree of care, skill, and diligence in the construction and maintenance of its lines of wire and other appurtenances, and in carrying on its business, so as to make the same safe against accidents so far as such safety can, by the use of such care and diligence, be secured. If it observed such degree of care, it was not liable; if it failed therein, it was liable for injuries caused thereby.

We think the court was unfortunate in attempting to draw any distinctions in the degrees of care or negligence. It would have been safer and the better practice to instruct the jury, — which ought here-

[1] Statement abridged. Only so much of the opinion is given as relates to a single point.

[2] Compare Wilson *v.* Brett, 11 M. & W. 113; Austin *v.* Manchester R. Co., 10 C. B. 454; Grill *v.* General Collier Co., L. R. 1 C. P. 600; Steamboat New World *v.* King, 16 How. 469; Purple *v.* Union R. Co., 114 Fed. 123; Oregon Co. *v.* Roe, 176 Fed. 715; Stringer *v.* Alabama R. Co., 99 Ala. 397; Louisville R. Co. *v.* Shanks, 94 Ind. 598; Denny *v.* Chicago R. Co., 150 Ia. 460; Raymond *v.* Portland R. Co., 100 Me. 529; McPheeters *v.* Hannibal R. Co., 45 Mo. 22; Reed *v.* Telegraph Co., 135 Mo. 661; Village *v.* Holliday, 50 Neb. 229; Perkins *v.* New York R. Co., 24 N. Y. 196; McAdoo *v.* Richmond R. Co., 105 N. C. 140; Fitzgerald *v.* Grand Trunk R. Co., 4 Ont. App. 601 *Accord.*

In Wilson *v.* Brett, *supra,* Rolfe, B., said: "I could see no difference between negligence and gross negligence — . . . it was the same thing with the addition of a vituperative epithet."

after to be observed, — even in cases like the one before us, that the defendant was bound to exercise that reasonable care and caution which would be exercised by a reasonably prudent and cautious person under the same or similar circumstances. In addition to this, the jury should have been instructed that the care increases as the danger does, and that where the business in question is attended with great peril to the public, the care to be exercised by the person conducting the business is commensurate with the increased danger. But, in effect, this is what the court did. Under the facts of the case, the law required of the defendant conducting, as it did, a business so dangerous to the public, the highest degree of care which skill and foresight can attain consistent with the practical conduct of its business under the known methods and the present state of the particular art. This is the measure of the duty owed by a common carrier to a passenger for hire. Thompson's Carriers of Passengers, p. 208, and cases cited. Not for the same reason, or because the doctrine rests upon the same principle, but with even greater force should this rule apply to a person or corporation engaged in the equally, if not more, dangerous business of distributing electricity throughout a city by means of wires strung over the public alleys and streets, in so far as concerned its duty to the travelling public.

In those courts where degrees of negligence are not countenanced, nevertheless, in cases where the duty of a common carrier of passengers is laid down, the jury are told that carriers are bound to the utmost degree of care which human foresight can attain. This is upon the theory that reasonable or ordinary care in a case of that kind is the highest care which human ingenuity can practically exercise, and that, as a matter of law, courts will hold every reasonably prudent and careful man to the exercise of the utmost care and diligence in protecting the public from the dangers necessarily incident to the carrying on of a hazardous business.

Where the facts of a case naturally lead equally intelligent persons honestly to entertain different views as to the degree of care resting upon a defendant, the court ought not to lay down a rule prescribing any particular or specific degree in that case. But where all minds concur — as they must in a case like the one we are now considering — in regarding the carrying on of a business as fraught with peril to the public inherent in the nature of the business itself, the court makes no mistake in defining the duty of those conducting it as the exercise of the utmost care. It was, therefore, not prejudicial error for the court to tell the jury in this case what the law requires of the defendant, viz., the highest degree of care in conducting its business.

. . . .

Judgment affirmed.[1]

[1] Maryland R. Co. *v.* Tucker, 115 Md. 43; Cates *v.* Hall, 171 N. C. 360; Lundy *v.* Southern Tel. Co., 90 S. C. 25 *Accord.*

LAKE ERIE & WESTERN R. CO. *v.* FORD

SUPREME COURT, INDIANA, OCTOBER 23, 1906.

Reported in 167 *Indiana Reports*, 205.

GILLETT, J. Complaint by appellee to recover damages for loss of property by fire, by reason of the alleged negligence of appellant. There was a verdict and judgment in favor of appellee.[1]

. . . .

Appellant complains of appellee's instructions five and six, which were given by the court in the order indicated by their numbers. They are as follows: "(5) It is the duty of a railroad to use all reasonable precaution in running and operating its trains, and in providing its engines with proper spark-arresters, so as to prevent injury to the property of others by sparks or fire emitted or thrown therefrom. (6) If you believe from all of the evidence and circumstances in the case that at the time and prior to the destruction of the property of the plaintiff, as alleged in his complaint, there were a number of wooden buildings and structures standing on either side of the defendant's track and in close proximity thereto, including the barn or stable of said Melissa McFall in the town of Hobbs, and at such time it was, and for some time prior thereto it had been, unusually dry, thereby

See various forms of stating this general doctrine in 2 Hutchinson on Carriers, (3d. ed.) §§ 895, 896; 4 Elliott on Railroads (1st ed.) § 1585; 1 Shearman & Redfield on Negligence (6th ed.) § 51.

In Wharton on Negligence (1st ed.) §§ 636, 637, the author says that the diligence should be "that which a good carrier of the particular grade is accustomed to exert;" *i. e.*, "the diligence and skill which a good business man in his specialty is accustomed to use under similar circumstances."

For a criticism of Wharton's statement, see 1 S. & R. Negl. (6th ed.) §§ 43–50. And compare 2 Hutchinson on Carriers (3d ed.) § 897, note 13.

"It is reasonable care under the existing circumstances that one person has the right to require of another; and that degree of care becomes increased with any increase of the apparent danger involved in its absence or with the increased power of control of one of the parties whose conduct is in question. . . . A common carrier of passengers either by rail or by water has so complete a control and the consequences of negligence on his part may be so serious that he is justly held to a very high degree of care for their safety; and accordingly it has been often said, both in this and in other jurisdictions, that he is held to the exercise of the highest degree of care. But as was pointed out in Dodge *v.* Boston & Bangor Steamship Co., 148 Mass. 207, 217, 218, this phrase and similar words which have been used to convey the same idea mean simply that the carrier is bound to use the utmost care consistent with the nature of his undertaking and with a due regard for all other matters that ought to be considered in conducting the business. This conductor was not bound absolutely to exercise the highest degree of care in running his car, but only the highest degree of care which was consistent with the practical performance of all his duties in seeing that the car was run safely without unreasonable delays, and so as to provide for the safety and convenience and properly rapid transit of his passengers. What was required of him was the highest degree of care consistent with the practical management and operation of his car for the carriage of passengers, 'or in other words, the requirement [was] reasonable care according to the nature of the contract' with the passengers." Sheldon, J., in Gardner *v.* Boston R. Co., 204 Mass. 213, 216. Compare Campbell, J., in Michigan R. Co. *v.* Coleman, 28 Mich. 440, 449.

[1] Only so much of the case is given as relates to a single point.

rendering such wood buildings and structures, including the barn or stable of said Melissa McFall, and also the property of the plaintiff herein, unusually dry, inflammable, and easily set on fire by sparks and coals of fire emitted from defendant's engines in passing through said town, and that there was also at the time, and for several hours prior thereto had been, a strong wind blowing continuously across the defendant's track, in the direction of the barn or stable of said Melissa McFall, and the wooden buildings and structures near the defendant's track, including the property of the plaintiff herein, which greatly and unusually increased the danger and risk of setting fire to such buildings by sparks and coals of fire emitted or thrown from its engine in passing through said town, over ordinary times and conditions, and all of which facts and conditions the defendant knew at the time, the defendant, under such circumstances, would be required to use a greater degree of care in operating and running its engines through said town to prevent injury to such buildings or property by sparks or coals of fire emitted or thrown from its engine, than it would at ordinary times and under ordinary conditions."

Assuming, without deciding, that it was not error for the court, in its fifth instruction, to use the term "reasonable precaution," instead of the preferable one, "ordinary care,"[1] and assuming further, since the care that the company was required to exercise was, so far as the element of law was concerned, to be measured by a fixed standard, which was to be fully complied with (Wharton, Negligence [2d ed.], § 46), that it was proper to use the expression "all reasonable precaution," the question arises whether it is not likely that the jury was misled by the charge in the next instruction that in the circumstances therein hypothetically stated "a greater degree of care" was required than in ordinary conditions. The sixth instruction would have been proper, had the court charged, after stating to the jury hypothetically the conditions which existed, leaving it to them to determine whether the danger was increased, that, in the event they so found, it was their duty, in determining whether reasonable or ordinary care had been exercised, to consider the increased danger of fire, yet we cannot say that this was the fair meaning of the words in which said instruction was couched.

There has been much discussion in the books concerning the correctness of the old doctrine as to degrees of negligence. New York Central R. Co. *v.* Lockwood, (1873) 17 Wall. 357, 21 L. Ed. 627; Steamboat New World *v.* King, (1853) 16 How. 469, 14 L. Ed. 1019; Ohio, etc., R. Co. *v.* Selby, (1874) 47 Ind. 471, 17 Am. Rep. 719; Pennsylvania Co. *v.* Sinclair, (1878) 62 Ind. 301, 30 Am. Rep. 185; Wharton, Negligence (2d ed.), § 44; 6 Albany L. J. 313; 2 Ames &

[1] "Due care," "reasonable care," and "ordinary care" are synonymous terms. Neal *v.* Gillett, 23 Conn. 437; Baltimore R. Co. *v.* Faith, 175 Ill. 58; Raymond *v.* Portland R. Co., 100 Me. 529; Durant *v.* Palmer, 29 N. J. Law, 544.

Smith, Cases on Torts, 143; 21 Am. and Eng. Ency. Law (2d ed.), 459, and cases cited. While we apprehend that the adverse opinions which have been expressed concerning such doctrine were not intended to be understood as militating against the view that the legal standard of care is not the same in all relations, or to discountenance the practice of charging the jury in terms that indicate the extent of care required, as great, ordinary, or slight (1 Shearman & Redfield, Negligence [5th ed.], § 47), yet the point which we wish to enforce now is that in all cases negligence consists simply in a failure to measure up to the legal standard of care. It was said by Willes, J., in Grill *v.* General Iron Screw, etc., Co., (1866) L. R. 1 C. P. 600, 611: "Confusion has arisen from regarding negligence as a positive instead of a negative word. It is really the absence of such care as it was the duty of the defendant to use."

Here we admittedly have a case in which it was the duty of the company to exercise ordinary care, but what does an instruction mean that informs the jury that in certain circumstances a greater degree of care is required, when it has for a background an instruction, which is applicable to all circumstances, that all reasonable precaution must be used ? We think that in such a case the jury would understand that more than ordinary care was required, and it is not improbable that the effect of giving such an instruction, following an instruction like 5, would be to lead the jury to infer that the defendant's duty was raised by the circumstances recited to a pitch of intensity that could not reasonably have been attained.

It was said by this court in Meredith *v.* Reed, (1866) 26 Ind. 334, 337: "What is ordinary care in some cases, would be carelessness in others. The law regards the circumstances surrounding each case, and the nature of the animal or machinery under control. Greater care is required to be taken of a stallion than of a mare; so in the management of a steam engine, greater care is necessary than in the use of a plough. Yet it is all ordinary care." The legal standard of care required in a particular relationship is always the same, although the amount of care thus required depends upon the particular circumstances. Cleveland, etc., R. Co. *v.* Terry, (1858) 8 Ohio St. 570; Weiser *v.* Broadway, etc., St. R. Co., (1895) 6 Ohio Dec. 215. As has been observed by a modern writer: "This standard may vary in fact, but not in law." 2 Jaggard, Torts, p. 819. In an article in 3 [6] Albany, L. J. 314, it is said: "The ratio, proportion or correspondence of diligence to circumstances, of care to surroundings, is fixed and identical. And, in determining a question of diligence or negligence in either case [as between two cases previously used by way of illustration], it would be only necessary to apply the same rule to varying circumstances and persons, to demand the same ratio between varying extremes. And it is not too much to assert that all the perplexity and misunderstanding on the subject of diligence and negligence are due to the habit of confounding the specific acts and circumstances, which must always vary, with the ratio or relation between them, which remains always the same."

In 13 Am. and Eng. Ency. Law (2d ed.), 416, it is said: "The very statement of the general rule that reasonable care is required to prevent injuries to others from fire, implies that what is reasonable care must depend upon the circumstances of each particular case. It is, however, inaccurate to say, as many of the cases do, that the degree of care varies with the particular circumstances. It is only reasonable care that is required in any case; but the greater the danger, or the more likely the communication of fire and the ignition of the property of others, the more precautions and the closer vigilance reasonable care requires." As above suggested, cases can be found in which it is stated that the degree of care to be used depends upon the danger, but, as has been observed by this court, it is not every statement of the law as found in an opinion or text-book, however well and accurately put, which can properly be embodied in an instruction. Garfield *v.* State, (1881) 74 Ind. 60. The viciousness of the instruction in question lies in its tendency to lead the jury to infer that the legal standard of ordinary care was raised by the circumstances recited, thus making possible the inference that a great but undefined extent of care was required, whereas all that the law exacted was the ordinary care which the situation demanded, or such care as it is to be assumed that an ordinarily prudent man would exercise in the circumstances, were the risk his own.[1]

In this case the acts and omissions which the complaint charged as negligent were various, so that the question of what was ordinary care arose in a number of ways, and we can only conclude, in view of the misleading character of the instruction under consideration, that prejudicial error has intervened

Judgment reversed, and a new trial ordered.[2]

[1] "But it would savor too much of refinement to hold that there is any practical inaccuracy in saying that one driving a high-powered automobile must exercise a greater care toward others on a state highway than one plodding along a country road with an ox team." Rugg, C. J., in Com. *v.* Horsfall, 213 Mass. 232, 235.

[2] "The rule, that due diligence is such attention and effort applied to a given case as the ordinary prudent man would put forth under the same circumstances, seems to meet the demands of every conceivable case. . . . The ratio of diligence to circumstances being thus fixed, the two extremes may change to an infinite extent without destroying the ratio, and without giving rise to what we term negligence. The bailee who undertakes the carriage of stone for the paving of a street is held to the rule that he must use such attention and effort as the ordinary prudent man would use under like circumstances."

"The bailee, who undertakes to repair a delicate watch, is held to the rule that he must use such attention and effort as the ordinary prudent man would use under the same circumstances. The contract of the watchmaker is the same, relatively, as that of the hod-carrier. Each contracts to provide the reasonable ordinary skill and attention which a man in his position would exercise under like circumstances. The ratio, proportion, or correspondence of diligence to circumstances, of care to surroundings, is fixed and identical. And in determining a question of diligence or negligence in either case, it would be only necessary to apply the same rule to

TRACY v. WOOD

UNITED STATES CIRCUIT COURT, DISTRICT OF RHODE ISLAND, NOVEMBER TERM, 1822.

Reported in 3 Mason (U. S. Circuit Court), 132.

ASSUMPSIT for negligence in losing 764½ doubloons, intrusted to the defendant to be carried from New York to Boston, as a gratuitous bailee. The gold was put up in two distinct bags, one within the other, and at the trial, upon the general issue, it appeared that the defendant, who was a money broker, brought them on board of the steamboat bound from New York to Providence; that in the morning while the steamboat lay at New York, and a short time before sailing, one of the bags was discovered to be lost, and that the other bag was left by the defendant on a table in his valise in the cabin, for a few moments only, while he went on deck to send information of the supposed loss to the plaintiffs, there being then a large number of passengers on board, and the loss being publicly known among them. On the defendant's return the second bag was also missing and after every search no trace of the manner of the loss could be ascertained. The valise containing both bags was brought on board by the defendant on the preceding evening, and put by him in a berth in the forward cabin. He left it there all night, having gone in the evening to the theatre, and on his return having slept in the middle cabin. The defendant had his own money to a considerable amount in the same valise. There was evidence to show that he made inquiries on board, if the valise would be safe, and that he was informed, that if it contained articles of value, it had better be put into the custody of the captain's clerk in the bar, under lock and key. There were many other circumstances in the case. The argument at the trial turned wholly on the question of gross negligence, and all the facts were fully commented on by counsel. But as the case is intended only to present the discussion on the question of law, it is not thought necessary to recapitulate them.[1]

STORY, J., after summing up the facts, said, I agree to the law as laid down at the bar, that in cases of bailees without reward, they are

varying circumstances and persons, to demand the same ratio between varying extremes. And it is not too much to assert that all the perplexity and misunderstanding on the subject of diligence and negligence are due to the habit of confounding the specific acts and circumstances, which must always vary, with the ratio or relation between them, which remains always the same. It is true that there *may* be different ratios of effort and attention to the circumstances and to the results desired. A man may contract to furnish the highest skill, the most perfect means and appliances, the most assiduous attention in the accomplishment of a specific end. But, when an individual so contracts, there is the element of *special* or *positive* intention introduced, which takes the case out of the category of diligence, and renders such a contract a special and extraordinary one. The law never requires such a special, positive intention. . . ." 6 Albany Law Journ. 313, 314.

[1] Arguments omitted.

liable only for gross negligence. Such are depositaries, or persons receiving deposits without reward for their care; and mandataries, or persons receiving goods to carry from one place to another without reward. The latter is the predicament of the defendant. He undertook to carry the gold in question for the plaintiff, gratuitously, from New York to Providence, and he is not responsible unless he has been guilty of gross negligence. Nothing in this case arises out of the personal character of the defendant, as broker. He is not shown to be either more or less negligent than brokers generally are; nor if he was, is that fact brought home to the knowledge of the plaintiffs. They confided the money to him as a broker of ordinary diligence and care, having no other knowledge of him; and, therefore, no question arises as to what would have been the case, if the plaintiffs had known him to be a very careless or a very attentive man. Jones' Bail. 46. The language of the books, as to what constitutes gross negligence, or not, is sometimes loose and inaccurate from the general manner in which propositions are stated. When it is said, that gross negligence is equivalent to fraud, it is not meant that it cannot exist without fraud. There may be very gross negligence in cases where there is no pretence that the party has been guilty of fraud, though certainly such negligence is often presumptive of fraud. In determining what is gross negligence, we must take into consideration what is the nature of the thing bailed. If it be of little value, less care is required than if it be of great value. If a bag of apples were left in a street for a short time, without a person to guard it, it would certainly not be more than ordinary neglect. But if the bag were of jewels or gold, such conduct would be gross negligence. In short, care and diligence are to be proportional to the value of the goods, the temptation and facility of stealing them, and the danger of losing them. So Sir William Jones lays down the law. "Diamonds, gold, and precious trinkets," says he, "ought from their nature to be kept with peculiar care, under lock and key; it would, therefore, be gross negligence in a depositary to leave such deposit in an open antechamber; and *ordinary* neglect, at least, to let them remain on the table, where they might possibly tempt his servants." Jones' Bail. 38, 46, 62. So in Smith *v.* Horne, 2 Moore's R. 18, it was held to be gross negligence in the case of a carrier, under the usual notice of not being responsible for goods above £5 in value, to send goods in a cart with one man, when two were usually sent to see to the delivery of them. So in Booth *v.* Wilson, 1 Barn. & Ald. 59, it was held gross negligence in a gratuitous bailee to put a horse into a dangerous pasture. In Batson *v.* Donovan, 4 Barn. & Ald. 21, the general doctrine was admitted in the fullest terms. It appears to me that the true way of considering cases of this nature is, to consider whether the party has omitted that care which bailees, without hire, or mandataries of ordinary prudence usually take of property of this nature. If he has, then it constitutes a case of gross negligence. The question is not whether he has omitted that care, which very prudent persons usually take of their own property, for the omission of that would be but slight negligence; nor whether he has omitted that care which prudent persons ordinarily take of their own property, for that would be but ordinary negligence: but whether there be a want of that care, which men of common sense, however inattentive, usually take, or ought to be presumed to take of their property, for that is gross negligence. The contract of bailees without reward is not merely for good faith, but for such care as persons of common prudence in their situation usually bestow upon such property. If they omit such care, it is gross negligence.

The present is a case of a mandatary of money. Such property is by all persons, negligent as well as prudent, guarded with much greater care than common property. The defendant is a broker, accustomed to the use and transportation of money, and it must be presumed he is a person of ordinary diligence. He kept his own money in the same valise; and took no better care of it than of the plaintiff's. Still if the jury are of opinion that he omitted to take that reasonable care of the gold which bailees without reward in his situation usually take, or which he himself usually took of such property, under such circumstances, he has been guilty of gross negligence.

Verdict for the plaintiffs for $5700, *the amount of one bag of the gold; for the defendant as to the other bag.*[1]

[1] A fuller statement of the views of the learned judge may be found in the extracts, which follow, from his work on Bailments:

"Section 11. [On the subject of the various degrees of care or diligence which are recognized in the common law.] . . . There may be a high degree of diligence, a common degree of diligence, and a slight degree of diligence; . . ."

"Common or ordinary diligence is that degree of diligence which men in general exact in respect to their own concerns. . . . That may be said to be common or ordinary diligence, in the sense of the law, which men of common prudence generally exercise about their own affairs in the age and country in which they live."

"Section 16. Having thus ascertained the nature of ordinary diligence, we may now be prepared to decide upon the other two degrees. High or great diligence is of course extraordinary diligence, or that which very prudent persons take of their own concerns; and low or slight diligence is that which persons of less than common prudence, or indeed of any prudence at all, take of their own concerns. Sir William Jones considers the latter to be the exercise of such diligence as a man of common sense, however inattentive, takes of his own concerns. Perhaps this is expressing the measure a little too loosely; for a man may possess common sense, nay, uncommon sense, and yet be so grossly inattentive to his own concerns as to deserve the appellation of having no prudence at all. The measure is rather to be drawn from the diligence which men, habitually careless or of little prudence (not 'however inattentive' they may be), generally take in their own concerns."

"Section 17. Having, then, arrived at the three degrees of diligence, we are naturally led to those of negligence, which correspond thereto; for negligence may be ordinary, or less than ordinary, or more than ordinary. Ordinary negligence may be defined to be the want of ordinary diligence, and slight negligence to be the want of great diligence, and gross negligence to be the want of slight diligence. For he who is only less diligent than very careful men cannot be said to be more than slightly inattentive; he who omits ordinary care is a little more negligent than men ordinarily are; and he who omits even slight diligence fails in the lowest degree of

DOLPHIN *v.* WORCESTER STREET R. CO.

SUPREME JUDICIAL COURT, MASSACHUSETTS, OCTOBER 18, 1905.

Reported in 189 *Massachusetts Reports*, 270.

ACTION of tort under Revised Laws, chapter 111, section 267, for the death of a passenger on a street railway.[1]

prudence, and is deemed grossly negligent. . . ." Story on Bailments (8th ed.), §§ 11, 16, 17.

See also Redington *v.* Pacific Co., 107 Cal. 317, 323–324; Belt Line R. Co. *v.* Banicki, 102 Ill. App. 642; Union R. Co. *v.* Henry, 36 Kan. 565; French *v.* Buffalo R. Co., 2 Abb. Dec. 196, 200–201, 4 Keyes 108, 113–114; Cederson *v.* Navigation Co., 38 Or. 343; Lockwood *v.* Belle City R. Co., 92 Wis. 97, 111–113; Astin *v.* Chicago R. Co., 143 Wis. 477.

"The theory that there are three degrees of negligence described by the terms slight, ordinary, and gross, has been introduced into the common law from some of the commentators on the Roman law. It may be doubted if these terms can be usefully applied in practice. Their meaning is not fixed, or capable of being so. One degree, thus described, not only may be confounded with another, but it is quite impracticable exactly to distinguish them. Their signification necessarily varies according to circumstances, to whose influence the courts have been forced to yield, until there are so many real exceptions that the rules themselves can scarcely be said to have a general operation. In Storer *v.* Gowen, 18 Maine, 177, the Supreme Court of Maine says: 'How much care will, in a given case, relieve a party from the imputation of gross negligence, or what omission will amount to the charge, is necessarily a question of fact, depending on a great variety of circumstances which the law cannot exactly define.' Mr. Justice Story, Bailments, § 11, says: 'Indeed, what is common or ordinary diligence is more a matter of fact than of law.' If the law furnishes no definition of the terms gross negligence, or ordinary negligence, which can be applied in practice, but leaves it to the jury to determine, in each case, what the duty was, and what omissions amount to a breach of it, it would seem that imperfect and confessedly unsuccessful attempts to define that duty had better be abandoned.

"Recently, the judges of several courts have expressed their disapprobation of these attempts to fix the degrees of diligence by legal definitions, and have complained of the impracticability of applying them. Wilson *v.* Brett, 11 Meeson and Wels. 113; Wyld *v.* Pickford, 8 ibid. 443, 461, 462; Hinton *v.* Dibbin, 2 Q. B. 646, 651. It must be confessed that the difficulty in defining gross negligence, which is apparent in perusing such cases as Tracy et al. *v.* Wood, 3 Mason 132, and Foster *v.* The Essex Bank, 17 Mass. 479, would alone be sufficient to justify these complaints. It may be added that some of the ablest commentators on the Roman law, and on the civil code of France have wholly repudiated this theory of three degrees of diligence, as unfounded in principles of natural justice, useless in practice, and presenting inextricable embarrassments and difficulties. See Toullier's Droit Civil, 6th vol., p. 239, etc.; 11th vol., p. 203, etc.; Makeldey, Man. Du Droit Romain, 191." Curtis, J., in Steamboat *v.* King, 16 How. 469, 474 (injury to gratuitous passenger).

"Confusion has arisen from regarding negligence as a positive instead of a negative word. It is really the absence of such care as it was the duty of the defendant to use. A bailee is only bound to use the ordinary care of a man, and so the absence of it is called gross negligence. A person who undertakes to do some work for reward to an article must exercise the care of a skilled workman, and the absence of such care in him is negligence. Gross, therefore, is a word of description, and not a definition; and it would have been only introducing a source of confusion to use the expression gross negligence, instead of the equivalent, a want of due care and skill in navigating the vessel, which was again and again used by the Lord Chief Justice in his summing up." Willes, J., in Grill *v.* General Collier Co., L. R. 1 C. P. 600.

As to the standard for physicians, see McNevins *v.* Lowe, 40 Ill. 209; Small *v.* Howard, 128 Mass. 131; Luka *v.* Lowrie, 171 Mich. 122; Booth *v.* Andrus, 91 Neb. 810; McCandless *v.* McWha, 22 Pa. St. 261.

[1] Statement rewritten. Only part of case is given.

The material portions of the statute are as follows: —

"If a corporation which operates a railroad or a street railway, by reason of its negligence or by reason of the unfitness or gross negligence of its agents or servants, while engaged in its business,[1] causes the death of a passenger, or of a person who is in the exercise of due care and who is not a passenger or in the employ of such corporation, it shall be punished by a fine of not less than five hundred nor more than five thousand dollars, which shall be recovered by an indictment," and shall be paid to the executor or administrator, to the use of the widow and children or the next of kin. "Such corporation shall also be liable in damages in the sum of not less than five hundred nor more than five thousand dollars, which shall be assessed with reference to the degree of culpability of the corporation or of its servants or agents, and shall be recovered in an action of tort . . . by the executor or administrator of the deceased for the use of the persons hereinbefore specified in the case of an indictment. . . . But no executor or administrator shall, for the same cause, avail himself of more than one of the remedies given by the provisions of this section."

At the trial the plaintiff requested the following rulings: —

"6. When the duty of exercising the highest degree of care is incumbent upon the defendant, any failure upon the part of its servants to exercise that degree of care is gross negligence.

"7. The term 'gross' in the allegation gross negligence, when used with reference to the degree of care required and not fulfilled, is merely an expletive, when the degree of care required is the very highest.

"8. There are no degrees of negligence."

The plaintiff excepted to the refusal of the judge to give the rulings requested, and to such parts of the charge as were in conflict with them. The defendant had a verdict, and the case is here on these exceptions.

LORING, J. . . . The judge was right in refusing to give the sixth ruling asked for. A failure to exercise the highest degree of care is slight negligence.

3. The seventh ruling requested was wrong. The term "gross negligence" in a case where the degree of care due is the highest degree of care means that there has been a gross failure to exercise that degree of care.[2]

4. There are degrees of care in cases under R. L. c. 111, § 267, by force of that act.[3] *Exceptions overruled.*

[1] The word gross was struck out by chap. 375, Acts of 1907, § 1.

[2] Compare Martin v. Boston R. Co., 205 Mass. 16; Devine v. New York R. Co., 205 Mass. 416.

[3] For other cases of statutory degrees of negligence, see Seaboard R. Co. v. Cauthen, 115 Ga. 422; Louisville R. Co. v. Long, 94 Ky. 410; Western Tel. Co. v. Reeves, 34 Okl. 468; Davis v. Railroad Co., 63 S. C. 370. That the wanton and reckless disregard of consequences which makes a defendant liable at common law to a plaintiff not in the exercise of due care is something more than negligence gross in degree, see Birmingham R. Co. v. Pinckard, 124 Ala. 372; Denman v.

CLEVELAND ROLLING MILL CO. *v* CORRIGAN

SUPREME COURT, OHIO, FEBRUARY 26, 1889.

Reported in 46 *Ohio State Reports*, 283.

ERROR to Circuit Court of Cuyahoga County.

The plaintiff below, John Corrigan, an infant under the age of fourteen, by his guardian, sued the Rolling Mill Company for damages suffered while in the defendants' employ, and which he alleged were caused by their negligence.

The answer of the defendants alleged, among other defences, that the injury occurred solely through the plaintiff's fault.

As to this ground of defence, the Court instructed the jury in part as follows: —

It was the duty of the plaintiff to use ordinary care and prudence; just such care and prudence as a boy of his age, of ordinary care and prudence, would use under like or similar circumstances. You should take into consideration his age, the judgment and knowledge he possessed. *Verdict and judgment for plaintiff.*

The Company filed its petition in error.[1]

WILLIAMS, J. The only questions presented in this case are those arising upon the special instructions given by the Court in response to the request of the jury. These instructions, the plaintiff in error contends, are erroneous in their entirety and in detail.

1. First, it is claimed that the Court erred in the statement of the plaintiff's duty, in the opening proposition of the charge, wherein the jury were instructed that "it was the duty of the plaintiff to use ordinary care," which the Court defined to be "just such care as boys of that age, of ordinary care and prudence, would use under like circumstances," and that the jury "should take into consideration the age of the plaintiff, and the judgment and knowledge he possessed." We have found no decision of this Court upon the subject of the contributory negligence of infants, or the measure of care required of them. Elsewhere the decisions are conflicting. Each of three different rules on the subject has found judicial sanction. One rule requires of children the same standard of care, judgment, and discretion, in anticipating and avoiding injury, as adults are bound to exercise.[2] An-

Johnston, 85 Mich. 387; Banks *v.* Braman, 188 Mass. 367; Southern Mfg. Co. *v.* Bradley, 52 Tex. 587; Barlow *v.* Foster, 149 Wis. 613.

[1] Statement of facts abridged. Only so much of the case is given as relates to one point. Arguments omitted.

[2] E. g., Neal *v.* Gillett, 23 Conn. 437 (child of 13; charge that age was not to be taken into account upheld). This is universally rejected. Lynch *v.* Nurdin, 1 Q. B. 29; Washington R. Co. *v.* Gladmon, 15 Wall. 401; Government R. Co. *v.* Hanlon, 53 Ala. 70; Chicago R. Co. *v.* Murray, 71 Ill. 601; Indianapolis R. Co. *v.* Wilson, 134 Ind. 95; McMillan *v.* Burlington R. Co., 46 Ia. 231; Kansas R. Co. *v.* Whipple, 39 Kan. 531; Lynch *v.* Smith, 104 Mass. 52; Huff *v.* Ames, 16 Neb. 139; Swift *v.* Staten Island R. Co., 123 N. Y. 645; Pennsylvania R. Co. *v.* Kelly, 31 Pa. St. 372; Queen *v.* Dayton Coal Co., 95 Tenn. 458; Cook *v.* Houston Navigation Co., 76 Tex. 353; Roth *v.* Union Depot Co., 13 Wash. 525.

other wholly exempts small children from the doctrine of contributory negligence. Between these extremes a third and more reasonable rule has grown into favor, and is now supported by the great weight of authority, which is, that a child is held to no greater care than is usually possessed by children of the same age. Authors and judges, however, do not always employ the same language in giving expression to the rule. In Beach on Contributory Negligence, sec. 46, it is thus expressed: "An infant plaintiff who, on the one hand, is not so young as to escape entirely all legal accountability, and on the other hand is not so mature as to be held to the responsibility of an adult is, of course, in cases involving the question of negligence, to be held responsible for ordinary care, and ordinary care must mean, in this connection, that degree of care and prudence which may reasonably be expected of a child." The decisions enforcing this rule, that children are to be held responsible only for such degree of care and prudence as may reasonably be expected of them, taking due account of their age and the particular circumstances, are very numerous. "It is well settled," says Mr. Justice Hunt in Railroad Company *v.* Stout, 17 Wall. 657, "that the conduct of an infant of tender years is not to be judged by the same rule which governs that of an adult. . . . The care and caution required of a child is according to his maturity and capacity only, and this is to be determined in each case by the circumstances of that case." In Shearman & Redfield on Negligence, sec. 73, it is said to be "now settled by the overwhelming weight of authority that a child is held, as far as he is personally concerned, only to the exercise of such care and discretion as is reasonably to be expected from children of his own age." Another author says, "A child is only bound to exercise such a degree of care as children of his particular age may be presumed capable of exercising." Whittaker's Smith on Neg., 411.

This rule appears to rest upon sound reason as well as authority. To constitute contributory negligence in any case there must be a want of ordinary care and a proximate connection between such want of care and the injury complained of; and ordinary care is that degree of care which persons of ordinary care and prudence are accustomed to use under similar circumstances. Children constitute a class of persons of less discretion and judgment than adults, of which all reasonably informed men are aware. Hence ordinarily prudent men reasonably expect that children will exercise only the care and prudence of children, and no greater degree of care should be required of them than is usual under the circumstances among careful and prudent persons of the class to which they belong. We think it a sound rule, therefore, that in the application of the doctrine of contributory negligence to children, in actions by them or in their behalf for injuries occasioned by the negligence of others, their conduct should not be judged by the same rule which governs that of adults, and while it is their duty to exercise ordinary care to avoid the injuries of which they complain, ordinary care for them is that degree of care which children of the same age, of ordinary care and prudence, are accustomed to exercise under similar circumstances.

That portion of the charge of the Court under discussion is in substantial conformity to this conclusion. The care and prudence which a boy of the plaintiff's age of ordinary care and prudence "would use under like and similar circumstances," as expressed in the charge, is such care as "is reasonably to be expected from a boy of his age," or "which boys of his age usually exercise," as the books express it. No different effect is given to the charge of which the plaintiff in error can complain, by the direction to the jury to take into consideration the age of the boy "and the judgment and knowledge he possessed." This did not diminish the degree of care required by the previous portion of the instruction. *Judgment affirmed.*[1]

STONE v. DRY DOCK R. CO.

COURT OF APPEALS, NEW YORK, JUNE 4, 1889.

Reported in 115 *New York Reports*, 104.

APPEAL from judgment of the General Term of the Supreme Court in the first judicial department, entered upon an order made October 26, 1887, which affirmed a judgment in favor of defendant, entered upon an order nonsuiting plaintiff on trial.

This was an action to recover damages for the alleged negligence in causing the death of plaintiff's intestate, a child of seven years and three or four months old.

The facts, so far as material, are stated in the opinion.[2]

[1] Smith v. Pittsburgh R. Co., 90 Fed. 783; Warble v. Sulzberger, 185 Ala. 603; Denver Tramway Co. v. Nicholas, 35 Col. 462; Rohloff v. Fair Haven R. Co., 76 Conn. 689; Goldstein v. People's R. Co., 5 Pennewill, 306; Elwood R. Co. v. Ross, 26 Ind. App. 258; Wyman v. Berry, 106 Me. 43; Munn v. Reed, 4 All. 431; Rasmussen v. Whipple, 211 Mass. 546 (but see Angelary v. Springfield R. Co., 213 Mass. 110); Lucarelli v. Boston R. Co., 213 Mass. 454; Strudgeon v. Village, 107 Mich. 496; Consolidated Traction Co. v. Scott, 58 N. J. Law, 682; Swift v. Staten Island R. Co., 123 N. Y. 645; Laferty v. Third Ave. R. Co., 176 N. Y. 594; Lake Erie R. Co. v. Mackey, 53 Ohio St. 370; Box & Label Co. v. Caine, 11 Ohio Cir. Ct. R. N. S. 81 (Aff'd 78 Ohio St. 405); Dubiver v. City R. Co., 44 Or. 227; Rachmel v. Clark, 205 Pa. St. 314; Parker v. Washington R. Co., 207 Pa. St. 438 (but compare Mulligan v. Burrough, 243 Pa. St. 361); Texas R. Co. v. Phillips, 91 Tex. 278; Christensen v. Oregon R. Co., 29 Utah, 192; Blankenship v. Chesapeake R. Co., 94 Va. 449; Deputy v. Kimmell, 73 W. Va. 595 *Accord.*

Children are seldom made defendants in actions for negligence. Most of the discussions as to the standard of care required of children are to be found in cases where the children, or their parents or representatives, were plaintiffs seeking to recover for damage to the children alleged to be caused by defendant's negligence, and where the defendant contended that the action was barred by the contributory negligence of the child. A good discussion where defendant was an infant may be found in Briese v. Maechtle, 146 Wis. 89.

[2] Arguments and part of opinion omitted.

ANDREWS, J. The nonsuit was placed on the ground that an infant seven years of age was *sui juris*, and that the act of the child in crossing the street in front of the approaching car was negligence on her part, which contributed to her death, and barred a recovery. We think the case should have been submitted to the jury.

The negligence of the driver of the car is conceded. His conduct in driving rapidly along Canal Street at its intersection with Orchard Street, without looking ahead, but with his eyes turned to the inside of the car, was grossly negligent. Mangam *v.* Brooklyn R. R. Co., 38 N. Y. 455; Railroad Co. *v.* Gladmon, 15 Wall. 401. It cannot be asserted as a proposition of law that a child just passed seven years of age is *sui juris*, so as to be chargeable with negligence. The law does not define when a child becomes *sui juris*. Kunz *v.* City of Troy, 104 N. Y. 344. Infants under seven years of age are deemed incapable of committing crime, and by the common law such incapacity presumptively continues until the age of fourteen. An infant between those ages was regarded as within the age of possible discretion, but on a criminal charge against an infant between those years the burden was upon the prosecutor to show that the defendant had intelligence and maturity of judgment sufficient to render him capable of harboring a criminal intent. 1 Arch. 11. The Penal Code preserves the rule of the common law except that it fixes the age of twelve instead of fourteen as the time when the presumption of incapacity ceases. Penal Code, §§ 18, 19.

In administering civil remedies the law does not fix any arbitrary period when an infant is deemed capable of exercising judgment and discretion. It has been said in one case that an infant three or four years of age could not be regarded as *sui juris*, and the same was said in another case of an infant five years of age. Mangam *v.* Brooklyn R. R., *supra;* Fallon *v.* Central Park, N. & E. R. R. R. Co., 64 N. Y. 13. On the other hand, it was said in Cosgrove *v.* Ogden, 49 N. Y. 255, that a lad six years of age could not be assumed to be incapable of protecting himself from danger in streets or roads, and in another case that a boy of eleven years of age was competent to be trusted in the streets of a city. McMahon *v.* Mayor, &c., 33 N. Y. 642. From the nature of the case it is impossible to prescribe a fixed period when a child becomes *sui juris*. Some children reach the point earlier than others. It depends upon many things, such as natural capacity, physical conditions, training, habits of life, and surroundings. These and other circumstances may enter into the question. It becomes, therefore, a question of fact for the jury where the inquiry is material unless the child is of so very tender years that the Court can safely decide the fact. The trial Court misapprehended the case of Wendell *v.* New York Central Railroad Company, 91 N. Y. 420, in supposing that it decided, as a proposition of law, that a child of seven years was capable of exercising judgment so as to be chargeable with contributory negligence. It was assumed in that case, both on the trial and on appeal, that the child whose conduct was in question was capable of understanding, and did understand the peril of the situation, and the evidence placed it beyond doubt that he recklessly encountered the danger which resulted in his death. The boy was familiar with the crossing, and, eluding the flagman who tried to bar his way, attempted to run across the track in front of an approaching train in plain sight, and unfortunately slipped and fell, and was run over and killed. It appeared that he was a bright, active boy, accustomed to go to school and on errands alone, and sometimes was intrusted with the duty of driving a horse and wagon, and that on previous occasions he had been stopped by the flagman while attempting to cross the track in front of an approaching train, and had been warned of the danger. The Court held, upon this state of facts, that the boy was guilty of culpable negligence. But the case does not decide, as matter of law, that all children of the age of seven years are *sui juris*.

We are inclined to the opinion that in an action for an injury to a child of tender years, based on negligence, who may or may not have been *sui juris* when the injury happened, and the fact is material as bearing upon the question of contributory negligence, the burden is upon the plaintiff to give some evidence that the party injured was not capable, as matter of fact, of exercising judgment and discretion. This rule would seem to be consistent with the principle now well settled in this State, that in an action for a personal injury, based on negligence, freedom from contributory negligence on the part of the party injured is an element of the cause of action. In the present case the only fact before the jury bearing upon the capacity of the child whose death was in question was that she was a girl seven years and three months old. This, we think, did not alone justify an inference that the child was incapable of exercising any degree of care. But, assuming that the child was chargeable with the exercise of some degree of care, we think it should have been left to the jury to determine whether she acted with that degree of prudence which might reasonably be expected, under the circumstances, of a child of her years. This measure of care is all that the law exacts in such a case. Thurber *v.* Harlem, B. M. & F. R. R. Co., 60 N. Y. 335.[1]

Judgment reversed.

[1] Northern R. Co. *v.* Heaton, 191 Fed. 24; Little Rock Traction Co. *v.* Nelson, 66 Ark. 494 (boy ten years old); Quincy Gas Co. *v.* Bauman, 203 Ill. 295, 104 Ill. App. 600 (seven); Fishburn *v.* Burlington R. Co., 127 Ia. 483 (six); Kentucky Hotel Co. *v.* Camp, 97 Ky. 424 (seven); McMahon *v.* Northern R. Co., 39 Md. 438 (six); Purcell *v.* Boston R. Co., 211 Mass. 79; Giaccobe *v.* Boston R. Co., 215 Mass. 224 (seven); Godfrey *v.* Boston R. Co., 215 Mass. 432 (six); Weitzel *v.* Detroit R. Co., 186 Mich. 7 (nine); Ritscher *v.* Orange R. Co., 79 N. J. Law, 462 (six); Verdon *v.* Automobile Co., 80 N. J. Law, 199 (seven); Citizen's R. Co. *v.* Bell, 26 Ohio Cir. Ct. R. 691 (seven); Galveston R. Co. *v.* Moore, 59 Tex. 64 (six); Robinson *v.* Cone, 22 Vt. 213 (three); McVoy *v.* Oakes, 91 Wis. 214 (seven); Frasers *v.* Tramways Co., 20 Sc. L. R. 192 (six); Plantza *v.* Glasgow, 47 Sc. L. R. 688 (five) *Accord.*

ILLINOIS IRON AND METAL COMPANY *v.* WEBER

SUPREME COURT, ILLINOIS, APRIL 16, 1902.

Reported in 196 *Illinois Reports*, 526.

APPEAL by original defendants from the decision of the Appellate Court for the First District; 89 Ill. App. 368.

Plaintiff was a newsboy, between eleven and twelve years old, and his stand was at Dearborn and Monroe streets in the city of Chicago. He was going from his home, about four miles distant, to his place of business. By permission of the driver, he got on a wagon loaded with brick. He stood up on the rear of the wagon behind the box, and held on to the hind end-gate of the wagon. The wagon was one of a procession of loaded teams in a street-car track. The next wagon behind was owned by defendant. The end of the pole of defendant's wagon struck the plaintiff's leg, inflicting a serious wound. Plaintiff had been in the paper business since he was nine years old, and had been in the habit of riding down town on wagons.

A few jurisdictions have an absolute rule as to children under seven. Government R. Co. *v.* Hanlon, 53 Ala. 70; Chicago R. Co. *v.* Tuohy, 196 Ill. 410; Reichle *v.* Transit Co., 241 Pa. St. 1 (six); Schnurr *v.* Traction Co., 153 Pa. St. 29; Dodd *v.* Gas Co., 95 S. C. 9. Also several jurisdictions rely on presumptions as to children between seven and fourteen (or sometimes twelve). Birmingham R. Co. *v.* Jones, 146 Ala. 277; City *v.* McLain, 67 Miss. 4; Hebert *v.* Hudson Electric Co., 136 App. Div. 107; Rolin *v.* Tobacco Co., 141 N. C. 300; Dowlen *v.* Texas Power Co., (Tex. Civ. App.) 174 S. W. 674; City *v.* Shull, 97 Va. 419; Traction Co. *v.* Wilkinson, 101 Va. 394. See also (as to children over fourteen) Central R. Co. *v.* Phillips, 91 Ga. 526; Frauenthal *v.* Laclede Gas Co., 67 Mo. App. 1; Murphy *v.* Perlstein, 73 App. Div. 256; Travers *v.* Hartmann, 5 Boyce, 302.

In Berdos *v.* Tremont Mills, 209 Mass. 489, 494, Rugg, J., says: "It is common knowledge that children under the age of fourteen are lacking in prudence, foresight, and restraint, and that their curiosity and restlessness have a tendency to get them into positions of danger. There is some point in every life where these conditions are present in such degree as to deprive the child of capacity to assume risk intelligently, or to be guilty of negligence consciously. That point varies in different children for divers reasons. There is no hard and fast rule that at any particular age a minor is presumed to be able to comprehend risks or to be capable of negligence. Extreme cases can be stated which obviously fall on one side or the other of the line. In some jurisdictions it has been held that *prima facie* a child under fourteen years of age is presumed not to be capable of contributory negligence. Tucker *v.* Buffalo Cotton Mills, 76 S. C. 539, and cases cited. Tutwiler Coal, Coke & Iron Co. *v.* Enslen, 129 Ala. 336. But the sounder doctrine seems to be that age is an important though not decisive factor in determining capacity, and that the decision of that question is not helped or hampered by any legal presumption. This is the law of this Commonwealth."

Compare Jacobs *v.* Koehler Co., 208 N. Y. 416.

In Kyle *v.* Boston R. Co., 215 Mass. 260, a boy five years and eleven months old, who ran in front of an approaching car was held negligent as a matter of law. It has generally been held that children under six are not to be charged with negligence. See City *v.* Lewis, 155 Ky. 832; Johnson *v.* City, 164 Mich. 251; Love *v.* Detroit R. Co., 170 Mich. 1; Eskildsen *v.* City, 29 Wash. 583.

As to lower ages, see Morgan *v.* Bridge Co., 5 Dill. 96; Louisville R. Co. *v.* Arp, 136 Ga. 489; Indianapolis R. Co. *v.* Bordenchecker, 33 Ind. App. 138; Fink *v.* City, 115 Ia. 641; Berry *v.* St. Louis R. Co., 214 Mo. 593. Compare Gardner *v.* Grace, 1 F. & F. 359; Dorr *v.* Atlantic R. Co., 76 N. H. 160 (five and a half); Campbell *v.* Ord, 11 Sc. L. R. 54; McGregor *v.* Ross, 20 Sc. L. R. 462.

Under instructions, the substance of which is stated in the opinion, the jury found a verdict for plaintiff.[1]

CARTWRIGHT, J. . . . The first two instructions each directed the jury to find the defendant guilty, provided they should believe, from the evidence, the existence of certain facts. One of the essential facts which the law required to be found was that the plaintiff was in the exercise of ordinary care for his own safety, and each of those instructions informed the jury that the fact was proved if he was in the exercise of ordinary care for a boy of his age. They directed the jury to return a verdict for the plaintiff if they found he was in the exercise of ordinary care for a boy of his age and the defendant was negligent and the injury resulted. That was not a correct rule of law, since the question of care was not to be determined alone by the plaintiff's age, but also from his intelligence, experience, and ability to understand and comprehend dangers and care for himself. The case was one in which the defendant was entitled to correct instructions upon that question. It was a question whether plaintiff was not guilty of negligence in riding where he did, in a procession of teams, outside of the box, behind the end-gate of the wagon. The position was a dangerous one, not provided or used for passengers or intended for such use. Plaintiff had a right to ride on the wagon with the driver's consent, but it was his duty to use reasonable care for his own safety. There was a string of heavily loaded teams in the car tracks, where it was difficult, if not impossible, to turn out, and the difficulty and danger in stopping when one of a procession stops is matter of common knowledge. Cases cited as to the liability of common carriers of passengers where a car is full and a passenger rides upon the platform have no bearing on this question. Passengers are accustomed to be upon platforms and are sometimes compelled to ride there, and different rules are applied to a common carrier from those governing parties not in that relation. There was no necessity whatever for the plaintiff assuming the position that he did. These facts were not controverted or in dispute, but are gathered from his own testimony. If the damage to the plaintiff was caused by his own negligence in assuming such a position, he could not recover. In determining that question his age was to be taken into account, but it could not be said, as a matter of law, that he was too young to exercise any care for his personal safety or that he was incapable of negligence. Unquestionably, he was capable of exercising some degree of judgment and discretion and some degree of care for his own safety. He had lived in the city and had been engaged in business, and was accustomed to ride on wagons. Judge Thompson, in his Commentaries on Law of Negligence (vol. I, sect. 309), says: "Two lads of equal age and natural capacity, one of them raised in the country and the other in the city, might approach a

[1] Statement abridged. Only so much of the opinion is given as relates to a single point.

given danger, and the one would be perfectly competent to care for himself while the other would be helpless in the face of it. Therefore, the capacity, the intelligence, the knowledge, the experience, and the discretion of the child are always evidentiary circumstances, — circumstances with reference to which each party has the right to introduce evidence, which evidence is to be considered by the jury." The rule established by our own decisions is, that age is not the only element to be considered, but that intelligence, capacity, and experience are also to be taken into account. Weick *v.* Lander, 75 Ill. 93; City of Chicago *v.* Keefe, 114 Id. 222; Illinois Central Railroad Company *v.* Slater, 129 Id. 91.

. . . .

Reversed and remanded.[1]

BULLOCK *v.* BABCOCK

SUPREME COURT OF JUDICATURE, NEW YORK, OCTOBER, 1829.

Reported in 3 *Wendell,* 391.

THIS was an action of trespass, assault, and battery.

In 1816, the defendant, then being about twelve years of age, shooting an arrow from a bow, struck the plaintiff and put out one of his eyes, the plaintiff being then between nine and ten years of age. The plaintiff and defendant were schoolmates. The boys attending the school were assembled near the school-house. One of them had a bow and arrow, with which he and the defendant had been shooting at a mark. Some remark was made by the plaintiff, when the defendant said, "I will shoot you," and took the bow and arrow from another boy who then held it. The plaintiff ran into the school-house and hid behind a fire-board standing before the fire-place in the school-room. The defendant followed to the door of the school-room, and saying,

[1] Garrison *v.* St. Louis R. Co., 92 Ark. 437; De Soto Co. *v.* Hill, 179 Ala. 186 (personal standard applied to a boy brighter than his age); Jollimore *v.* Connecticut Co., 86 Conn. 314; Herrington *v.* City, 125 Ga. 58; Elk Mills *v.* Grant, 140 Ga. 727; Keller *v.* Gaskill, 9 Ind. App. 670; Cole *v.* Searfoss, 49 Ind. App. 334; Louisville R. Co. *v.* Allnutt, 150 Ky. 831; Van Natta *v.* Peoples R. Co., 133 Mo. 13; Spillane *v.* Missouri R. Co., 135 Mo. 414; Moeller *v.* United R. Co., 242 Mo. 721; David *v.* West Jersey R. Co., 84 N. J. Law, 685; Marius *v.* Motor Co., 146 App. Div. 608; Gigoux *v.* County, 73 Or. 212; Bridger *v.* Asheville R. Co., 27 S. C. 456; North Texas Construction Co. *v.* Bostick, 98 Tex. 239; Kyne *v.* Southern R. Co., 41 Utah, 368; Quinn *v.* Ross Car Co., 157 Wis. 543 *Accord.* As to experience, see Stern *v.* Bensieck, 161 Mo. 146.

Section 2901 of the Georgia Civil Code is as follows: —

"Due care in a child of tender years is such care as its capacity, mental and physical, fits it for exercising in the actual circumstances of the occasion and situation under investigation."

In Harrington *v.* Mayor, 125 Ga. 58, 60, Lumpkin, J., said: "The average child of its own age is not the standard by which to measure its legal diligence with exactness. 'Such care as the capacity of the particular child enables it to use naturally and reasonably, is what the law requires.'" Compare Bleckley, C. J., in Western & Atlantic R. Co. *v.* Young, 81 Ga. 397, 416, 417.

" See me shoot that basket," discharged the arrow. At that moment the plaintiff raised his head above the fire-board, and the arrow struck him. There was a basket standing on a desk in the direction that the arrow was aimed. When the arrow was shot, there were a number of boys in the school-room. There had been no quarrel between the boys. The plaintiff, however, on entering the school-house was frightened, and said he was afraid he would be shot. The plaintiff suffered great pain for two months, became blind of one eye, and for five years was disabled from attending school in consequence of the weakness of sight of the other eye. His mother became a widow; and when the plaintiff was able to attend school, her poverty prevented his receiving an ordinary education. This suit was commenced in 1827, within a year after the plaintiff attained his age.

The judge charged the jury that the shooting the arrow in the school-room where there were a number of boys assembled was an unlawful act; that it appeared to him to have been, at the least, grossly negligent and unjustifiable; and that, if the jury thought so, they ought to find a verdict for the plaintiff, with damages. The defendant excepted. The jury found for the plaintiff, with $180 damages, and a motion was now made to set aside the verdict.

BY THE COURT, MARCY, J. It is not, I apprehend, necessary for us to say whether the judge erred or not in his remark to the jury that, under the circumstances of the case, the act of the defendant in shooting the arrow in the school-room, where there were a number of scholars, was not lawful; for, if the act in itself was lawful, and there was not a proper care to guard against consequences injurious to others, the actor must be held responsible for such consequences.

In ordinary cases, if the injury is not the effect of an unavoidable accident, the person by whom it is inflicted is liable to respond in damages to the sufferer. Where, in shooting at butts, the archer's arrow glanced and struck another, it was holden to be a trespass. Year-Book, 21 H. VII. fol. 28. So where a number of persons were lawfully exercising themselves at arms, one, whose gun accidentally went off, was held liable in trespass for the injury occasioned by the accident. Weaver *v.* Ward. Where, in a dark night, the defendant got on the wrong side of the road, and an injury ensued to the person of the plaintiff, trespass for the damage was sustained. Leame *v.* Bray, 3 East, 593. It is decided in the case of Wakeman *v.* Robinson, if the accident happen entirely without the fault of the defendant, or any blame being imputable to him, an action will not lie. In that case, the blame imputable to the defendant was, that, his horse being young and spirited, he used him without a curb rein; that in his alarm he probably pulled the wrong rein; and that he ought to have continued on in a straight course. The blame fairly imputed to the defendant, it will be perceived, must have been slight indeed, as it certainly was in the case of the injury done by the glancing of the arrow when shooting at a mark (a lawful act), and by the accidental discharge of the musket at a training; and yet, in each of these cases, an action for the injury was maintained. Unless a rule is to be applied to this case different from that applicable to a transaction between adults, the proof was most abundant to charge the defendant with the consequences of the injury. Infants, in the same manner as adults, are liable for trespass, slander, assault, &c.[1] Bing. on Infancy, 110; 8 T. R. 335; 16 Mass. Rep. 389;

[1] The liability of an infant for his torts is universally recognized.

Trespass. Y. B. 35 Hen. VI. f. 11, pl. 18; Burnard *v.* Haggis, 14 C. B. N. S. 45; Neal *v.* Gillett, 23 Conn. 437; Wilson *v.* Garrard, 59 Ill. 51; Peterson *v.* Haffner, 59 Ind. 130; Scott *v.* Watson, 46 Me. 362; Marshall *v.* Wing, 50 Me. 62; Sikes *v.* Johnson, 16 Mass. 389; School District *v.* Bragdon, 23 N. H. 507; Campbell *v.* Stakes, 2 Wend. 137; Hartfield *v.* Roper, 21 Wend. 615, 620; Tifft *v.* Tifft, 4 Denio, 175; Conklin *v.* Thompson, 29 Barb. 218; Huchting *v.* Engel, 17 Wis. 230; Vosburg *v.* Putney, 80 Wis. 523; Vosburg *v.* Putney, 86 Wis. 278.

Conversion. Mills *v.* Graham, 1 B. & P. N. R. 140; Bristow *v.* Clark, 1 Esp. 171; Vasse *v.* Smith, 6 Cranch, 226; Oliver *v.* McClellan, 21 Ala. 675; Ashlock *v.* Vivell, 29 Ill. App. 388; Lewis *v.* Littlefield, 15 Me. 233; Caswell *v.* Parker, 96 Me. 39 (*semble*); Homer *v.* Thwing, 3 Pick. 492; Walker *v.* Davis, 1 Gray, 506; Wheeler Co. *v.* Jacobs, 2 Misc. 236; Green *v.* Sperry, 16 Vt. 390; Baxter *v.* Bush, 29 Vt. 465.

Deceit. Fitts *v.* Hall, 9 N. H. 441; Word *v.* Vance, 1 N. & McC. 197.

Defamation. Hodsman *v.* Grissell, Noy, 129; Drane *v.* Pawley, 8 Ky. Law Rep. 530; Fears *v.* Riley, 148 Mo. 49.

Negligence. Jennings *v.* Rundall, 8 T. R. 335; Dixon *v.* Bell, 1 Stark. 287; Marsh *v.* Loader, 14 C. B. N. S. 535; Latt *v.* Booth, 3 Car. & K. 292; Humphrey *v.* Douglass, 10 Vt. 71 *Accord.*

In Scott *v.* Watson, *supra*, Appleton, J., said: "Nor is his infancy any defence, for infants are liable for torts. . . . The parent is not answerable for the torts of his minor child, committed in his absence and without his authority or approval, but the minor is answerable therefor. Tifft *v.* Tifft, 4 Denio, 177. The minor is not exempt from liability, though the trespass was committed by the express command of the father. Humphrey *v.* Douglass, 10 Vt. 71.

"Nor can the defendant derive any support from the scriptural injunction to children of obedience to their parents, invoked in defence. No such construction can be given to the command, 'Children, obey your parents in the Lord, for this is right,' as to sanction or justify the trespass of the son upon the land of another, and the asportation of his crops, even though done by the express commands of his father. The defence is as unsound in its theology as it is baseless in its law." [Smith *v.* Kron, 96 N. C. 392, 397; O'Leary *v.* Brooks, 7 N. D. 554; Humphrey *v.* Douglass, 10 Vt. 71; Huchting *v.* Engel, 17 Wis. 230 *Accord.*]

May, J., dissented, saying: "I am not quite satisfied with either the law or the theology of the opinion in this case. That sins of ignorance may be winked at, is both a dictate of reason and of Scripture. It is true, as a general rule, that infants who have arrived at the age of discretion are liable for their tortious acts. But, for the protection of infants, ought not the rule to be limited to cases where the infant acts under such circumstances that *he must know or be presumed to know* that the acts which he commits are unauthorized and wrong, when it appears that in the commission of the acts he was under the control and direction of his father? Will not an opposite doctrine tend to encourage disobedience in the child, and thus be subversive of the best interests of the community? Will it not also tend to subject him to embarrassment and insolvency when he shall arrive at full age? If all the members of a family under age are to be held liable in trespass or trover for the food which they eat, when that food is in fact the property of another, but, being set before them, they partake of it, in ignorance of such fact, by the command or direction of the parent, and under the belief that it is his, will not such a doctrine be in conflict with the principle that the common law is intended as a shield and protection against the improvidence of infancy? While the decided cases upon this subject seem to be limited to cases of contract, is there not the same reason for extending it, and applying it to cases like the one before us? In all the cases which I have examined in which infants have been held liable, the proof shows acts of

2 Inst. 328. Where infants are the actors, that might probably be considered an unavoidable accident which would not be so considered where the actors are adults; but such a distinction, if it exists, does not apply to this case. The liability to answer in damages for trespass does not depend upon the mind or capacity of the actors; for idiots and lunatics, as we see by the case reported in Hobart, are responsible in the action of trespass for injuries inflicted by them. 1 Chit. Pl. 66. *Motion for a new trial denied.*[1]

SECTION IV

PROOF OF NEGLIGENCE [2]

METROPOLITAN RAILWAY COMPANY *v.* JACKSON

IN THE HOUSE OF LORDS, DECEMBER 13, 1877.

Reported in 3 Appeal Cases, 193.

THE LORD CHANCELLOR (Lord Cairns): [3] —

My Lords, in this case an action was brought by the respondent against the Metropolitan Railway Company for negligence in not carrying the respondent safely as a passenger on the railway, and for injuring his thumb by the act of one of the appellants' servants in suddenly and violently closing the door of the railway carriage.

The question is, Was there at the trial any evidence of this negligence which ought to have been left to the jury? The Court of Common Pleas, consisting of Lord Coleridge, Mr. Justice Brett, and Mr. Justice Grove, were of opinion that there was such evidence. The Court of Appeal was equally divided; the Lord Chief Justice and Lord Justice of Appeal Amphlett holding that there was evidence, the Lord Chief Baron and Lord Justice of Appeal Bramwell holding that there was not.

positive wrong committed under circumstances where the infant must have known the nature and character of his acts. If the doctrines of the opinion are to prevail in a case like this, then the common law is but the revival of the old doctrine that the parents, by eating sour grapes, have set the children's teeth on edge. The rule that a servant who acts in ignorance of the rights of his principal is to be held liable for his acts, does not fall within the principles for which I contend."

[1] Welch *v.* Durand, 36 Conn. 182; Flinn *v.* State, 24 Ind. 286; Peterson *v.* Haffner, 59 Ind. 130; Mercer *v.* Corbin, 117 Ind. 450; Commonwealth *v.* Lister, 15 Phila. 405; Vosburg *v.* Putney, 80 Wis. 523; Vosburg *v.* Putney, 86 Wis. 278 *Accord.*

[2] The topics dealt with in this section do not concern the substantive law of tort. They fall rather under the heads of procedure and evidence. But, without some knowledge of these particular subjects, it is difficult to understand the ground of decision in some of the cases on the general subject of negligence.

[3] Statement, arguments, and parts of opinions omitted.

The facts of the case are very short. The respondent in the evening of the 18th of July, 1872, took a third-class ticket from Moorgate Street to Westbourne Park, and got into a third-class compartment; the compartment was gradually filled up, and when it left King's Cross all the seats were occupied. At Gower Street Station three persons got in and were obliged to stand up. There was no evidence to show that the attention of the company's servants was drawn to the fact of an extra number being in the compartment; but there was evidence that the respondent remonstrated at their getting in with the persons so getting in, and a witness who travelled in the same compartment stated that he did not see a guard or porter at Gower Street.

At Portland Road, the next station, the three extra passengers still remained standing up in the compartment. The door of the compartment was opened and then shut; but there was no evidence to show by whom either act was done. Just as the train was starting from Portland Road there was a rush, and the door of the compartment was opened a second time by persons trying to get in. The respondent, who had up to this time kept his seat, partly rose and held up his hand to prevent any more passengers coming in. After the train had moved, a porter pushed away the people who were trying to get in, and slammed the door to, just as the train was entering the tunnel. At that very moment the respondent, by the motion of the train, fell forward and put his hand upon one of the hinges of the carriage door to save himself, and at that moment, by the door being slammed to, the respondent's thumb was caught and injured.

The case as to negligence having been left to the jury, the jury found a verdict for the respondent with £50 damages. There was not, at your lordships' bar, any serious controversy as to the principles applicable to a case of this description. The judge has a certain duty to discharge, and the jurors have another and a different duty. The judge has to say whether any facts have been established by evidence from which negligence *may be* reasonably inferred; the jurors have to say whether, from those facts, when submitted to them, negligence *ought to be* inferred. It is, in my opinion, of the greatest importance in the administration of justice that these separate functions should be maintained, and should be maintained distinct. It would be a serious inroad on the province of the jury, if, in a case where there are facts from which negligence may reasonably be inferred, the judge were to withdraw the case from the jury upon the ground that, in his opinion, negligence ought not to be inferred; and it would, on the other hand, place in the hands of the jurors a power which might be exercised in the most arbitrary manner, if they were at liberty to hold that negligence might be inferred from any state of facts whatever. To take the instance of actions against railway companies: a company might be unpopular, unpunctual, and irregular in its service; badly equipped as to its staff; unaccommodating to the public; notorious, perhaps for accidents occurring on the line; and when an action was brought for the consequences of an accident, jurors, if left to themselves, might, upon evidence of general carelessness, find a verdict against the company in a case where the company was really blameless. It may be said that this would be set right by an application to the court in banc, on the ground that the verdict was against evidence; but it is to be observed that such an application, even if successful, would only result in a new trial; and on a second trial, and even on subsequent trials, the same thing might happen again.

In the present case I am bound to say that I do not find any evidence from which, in my opinion, negligence could reasonably be inferred. The negligence must in some way connect itself, or be connected by evidence, with the accident. It must be, if I might invent an expression founded upon a phrase in the civil law, *incuria dans locum injuriae*. In the present case there was no doubt negligence in the company's servants, in allowing more passengers than the proper number to get in at the Gower Street Station; and it may also have been negligence if they saw these supernumerary passengers, or if they ought to have seen them, at Portland Road, not to have then removed them; but there is nothing, in my opinion, in this negligence which connects itself with the accident that took place. If, when the train was leaving Portland Road, the overcrowding had any effect on the movements of the respondent; if it had any effect on the particular portion of the carriage where he was sitting, if it made him less a master of his actions when he stood up or when he fell forward, this ought to have been made matter of evidence; but no evidence of the kind was given.

As regards what took place at Portland Road, I am equally unable to see any evidence of negligence connected with the accident, or indeed of any negligence whatever. The officials cannot, in my opinion, be held bound to prevent intending passengers on the platform opening a carriage door with a view of looking or getting into the carriage. They are bound to have a staff which would be able to prevent such persons getting in where the carriage was already full, and this staff they had, for the case finds that the porter pushed away the persons who were attempting to get in. So also with regard to shutting the door; these persons had opened the door, and thereupon it was not only proper but necessary that the door should be shut by the porter; and, as the train was on the point of passing into a tunnel, he could not shut it otherwise than quickly or in this sense violently. . . .

LORD BLACKBURN: —

My Lords, I also am of opinion that in this case the judgment should be reversed, and a nonsuit entered. On a trial by jury it is, I conceive, undoubted that the facts are for the jury, and the law for the judge. It is not, however, in many cases practicable completely to sever the law from the facts.

But I think it has always been considered a question of law to be determined by the judge, subject, of course, to review whether there is evidence which, if it is believed, and the counter-evidence, if any, not believed, would establish the facts in controversy. It is for the jury to say whether and how far the evidence is to be believed. And if the facts, as to which evidence is given, are such that from them a farther inference of fact may legitimately be drawn, it is for the jury to say whether that inference is to be drawn or not. But it is for the judge to determine, subject to review, as a matter of law whether from those facts that farther inference may legitimately be drawn.

My Lords, in delivering the considered judgment of the Exchequer Chamber in Ryder *v.* Wombwell, Law Rep. 4 Ex. 32, 38, Willes, J., says: " Such a question is one of mixed law and fact; in so far as it is a question of fact, it must be determined by a jury, subject no doubt to the control of the court, who may set aside the verdict, and submit the question to the decision of another jury; but there is in every case a preliminary question, which is one of law, viz., whether there is any evidence on which the jury could properly find the verdict for the party on whom the *onus* of proof lies. If there is not, the judge ought to withdraw the question from the jury, and direct a nonsuit if the *onus* is on the plaintiff, or direct a verdict for the plaintiff if the *onus* is on the defendant. It was formerly considered necessary in all cases to leave the question to the jury, if there was any evidence, even a scintilla, in support of the case; but it is now settled that the question for the judge (subject, of course, to review), is, as is stated by Maule, J., in Jewell *v.* Parr, 13 C. B. 909, 916, ' not whether there is literally no evidence, but whether there is none that ought reasonably to satisfy the jury that the fact sought to be proved is established.' "

He afterwards observes, Law Rep. 4 Ex. 42, very truly in my opinion, " There is no doubt a possibility in all cases where the judges have to determine whether there is evidence on which the jury may reasonably find a fact, that the judges may differ in opinion, and it is possible that the majority may be wrong. Indeed, whenever a decision of the court below on such a point is reversed, the majority must have been so either in the court above or the court below. This is an infirmity which must affect all tribunals."

I quite agree that this is so, and it is an evil. But I think it a far slighter evil than it would be to leave in the hands of the jury a power which might be exercised in the most arbitrary manner. . . .

[The concurring opinions of LORD O'HAGAN and LORD GORDON are omitted.]

Judgment given for the plaintiff in the court below reversed, and a nonsuit to be entered.[1]

[1] This decision and Bridges *v.* North London R. Co., L. R. 7 H. L. 213, put an end in England to a conflict of authority as to the power of the judge to withdraw the case from the jury where there was an " invitation to alight " or " slamming

KEARNEY v. LONDON, BRIGHTON & SOUTH COAST R. CO.

IN THE QUEEN'S BENCH, JUNE 15, 1870.

Reported in Law Reports, 5 Queen's Bench, 411.

DECLARATION, that the defendants were possessed of a bridge over a certain public highway, and it became their duty to maintain and keep in repair the bridge, so that it should not be injurious to any person passing under it; yet the defendants so negligently maintained the bridge, that while the plaintiff was lawfully passing under the bridge a portion of the materials of the bridge fell down and injured the plaintiff.

the door " of a compartment car. See the cases cited in 21 Halsbury, Laws of England, 445.

A like question, much discussed in the United States, is: A man, without looking or listening, attempts to cross the track of a steam railway, and is hit by a negligently managed engine. Should the judge rule that crossing without looking and listening (or crossing without stopping, looking, and listening) is, as matter of law, negligent conduct? Or should the judge tell the jury that such conduct is evidence from which negligence *may be* inferred, and that it is for them to say whether they *do* infer it? As to this, there is a conflict of authority. See discussion and collected cases in 3 Elliott on Railroads (1st ed.) § 1167; 2 Thompson, Commentaries on the Law of Negligence, Chap. 52, Article 2, §§ 1637–1661, especially §§ 1640, 1649, 1650, 1653; 33 Cyc. 1116 ff.; Beach on Contributory Negligence (3d ed.) §§ 181, 182.

Other like questions arise in case of alighting from a moving car: Puget Sound R. Co. *v.* Felt, 181 Fed. 938; Birmingham R. Co. *v.* Girod, 164 Ala. 10; St. Louis R. Co. *v.* Plott, 108 Ark. 292; Carr *v.* Eel River R. Co., 98 Cal. 366; Coursey *v.* Southern R. Co., 113 Ga. 297; Ardison *v.* Illinois R. Co., 249 Ill. 300; Louisville R. Co. *v.* Crunk, 119 Ind. 542; Walters *v.* Missouri R. Co., 82 Kan. 739; Hayden *v.* Chicago R. Co., 160 Ky. 836; Cumberland R. Co. *v.* Maugans, 61 Md. 53; Street *v.* Chicago R. Co., 124 Minn. 517; Johnson *v.* St. Joseph R. Co., 143 Mo. App. 376; Willis *v.* Metropolitan R. Co., 63 App. Div. 332; Pennsylvania R. Co. *v.* Lyons, 129 Pa. St. 113; Kearney *v.* Seaboard R. Co., 158 N. C. 521; San Antonio Traction Co. *v.* Badgett, (Tex. Civ. App.) 158 S. W. 803; Gaines *v.* Ogden R. Co., 44 Utah, 512; Breeden *v.* Seattle R. Co., 60 Wash. 522.

Boarding moving car: Central R. Co. *v.* Hingson, 186 Ala. 40; South Chicago R. Co. *v.* Dufresne, 200 Ill. 456; Chicago Traction Co. *v.* Lundahl, 215 Ill. 289; Pence *v.* Wabash R. Co., 116 Ia. 279; Jonas *v.* South Covington R. Co., 162 Ky. 171; Mabry *v.* Boston R. Co., 214 Mass. 463; Foley *v.* Detroit R. Co., 179 Mich. 586; Hull *v.* Minneapolis R. Co., 116 Minn. 349; Nolan *v.* Metropolitan R. Co., 250 Mo. 602.

Standing on platform or running board: Texas R. Co. *v.* Lacey, 185 Fed. 225; Central R. Co. *v.* Brown, 165 Ala. 493; Holloway *v.* Pasadena R. Co., 130 Cal. 177; Augusta R. Co. *v.* Snider, 118 Ga. 146; Chicago R. Co. *v.* Newell, 212 Ill. 332; Math *v.* Chicago R. Co., 243 Ill. 114; Louisville R. Co. *v.* Stillwell, 142 Ky. 330; Blair *v.* Lewiston R. Co., 110 Me. 235; Olund *v.* Worcester R. Co., 206 Mass. 544; Heshion *v.* Boston R. Co., 208 Mass. 117; Wheeler *v.* Boston R. Co., 220 Mass. 298; Lacey *v.* Minneapolis R. Co., 118 Minn. 301; Setzler *v.* Metropolitan R. Co., 227 Mo. 454; Trussell *v.* Traction Co., 79 N. J. Law, 533; Ward *v.* International R. Co., 206 N. Y. 83; Edwards *v.* New Jersey R. Co., 144 App. Div. 554; Germantown R. Co. *v.* Walling, 97 Pa. St. 55; Brice *v.* Southern R. Co., 85 S. C. 216.

Part of body protruding from car: Georgetown R. Co. *v.* Smith, 25 App. D. C. 259; Clerc *v.* Morgan's R. Co., 107 La. 370; Lange *v.* Metropolitan R. Co., 151 Mo. App. 500; Kuttner *v.* Central R. Co., 80 N. J. Law, 11; Goller *v.* Fonda R. Co., 110 App. Div. 620.

Plea: Not guilty. Issue joined.

At the trial before Hannen, J., at the sittings in Middlesex after Michaelmas Term, 1869, it appeared, according to the plaintiff's evidence, that the plaintiff, on the 20th of January, 1869, was passing along the Blue Anchor Road, Bermondsey, under the railway bridge of the defendants, when a brick fell and injured him on the shoulder. A train had passed just previously, but whether it was a train of the defendants, or of another company (whose trains also pass over the bridge), did not appear. The bridge had been built three years, and is an iron girder bridge resting on iron piers, on one side, and on a perpendicular brick wall with pilasters, on the other, and the brick fell from the top of one of the pilasters, where one of the girders rested on the pilaster.

The defendants called no witnesses,[1] but rested their defence on there being no evidence of negligence in the defendants; and also on the ground that the injury to the plaintiff's shoulder was not really caused by the falling of the brick.

As to the evidence of negligence, the learned judge told the jury that if they thought the bare circumstance of a brick falling out was not evidence of negligence, they would find for the defendants; if they thought otherwise, for the plaintiff; and the court would determine whether there was legal evidence of negligence or not, as to which he should reserve leave to the defendants to move.

The jury found a verdict for the plaintiff for 25*l*.

A rule was obtained to enter a nonsuit, on the ground that there was no evidence of negligence to leave to the jury.[2]

COCKBURN, C. J. As we have had the whole matter carefully brought before us, with the cases bearing upon the subject, I think we should gain nothing by taking further time to consider it; and, therefore, although I regret to say we are not unanimous upon the point, I think it is better to dispose of the case at once.

My own opinion is, that this is a case to which the principle *res ipsa loquitur* is applicable, though it is certainly as weak a case as can well be conceived in which that maxim could be taken to apply. But I think the maxim is applicable; and my reason for saying so is this. The company who have constructed this bridge were bound to construct it in a proper manner, and to use all reasonable care and diligence in keeping it in such a state of repair that no damage from its defective condition should occur to those who passed under it, the public having a right to pass under it. Now we have the fact that a brick falls out of this structure, and injures the plaintiff. The proximate cause appears to have been the looseness of the brick, and the vibration of a train passing over the bridge, acting upon the defective

[1] But see L. R. 6 Q. B. 760–761.

[2] Arguments omitted; also the concurring opinion of Lush, J., and the dissenting opinion of Hannen, J.

condition of the brick. It is clear, therefore, that the structure in reference to this brick was out of repair. It is clear that it was incumbent on the defendants to use reasonable care and diligence, and I think the brick being loose affords, prima facie, a presumption that they had not used reasonable care and diligence. It is true that it is possible that, from changes in the temperature, a brick might get into the condition in which this brickwork appears to have been from causes operating so speedily as to prevent the possibility of any diligence and care applied to such a purpose intervening in due time, so as to prevent an accident. But inasmuch as our experience of these things is, that bricks do not fall out when brickwork is kept in a proper state of repair, I think where an accident of this sort happens, the presumption is that it is not the frost of a single night, or of many nights, that would cause such a change in the state of this brickwork as that a brick would fall out in this way; and it must be presumed that there was not that inspection and that care on the part of the defendants which it was their duty to apply. On the other hand, I admit most readily that a very little evidence would have sufficed to rebut the presumption which arises from the manifestly defective state of this brickwork. It might have been shown that many causes, over which the defendants had no control, might cause this defect in so short a time as that it could not be reasonably expected that they should have inspected it in the interval. They might, if they were able, have shown that they had inspected the bridge continually, or that such a state of things could not be anticipated, and had never been heard of or known before. Anything which tended to rebut the presumption arising from an accident caused by the defective condition of the brickwork, which it was their duty to keep in a proper condition of repair, even if such evidence were but slight, might have sufficed; but the defendants chose to leave it on the naked state of facts proved by the plaintiff. Upon that naked state of facts it is not unimportant to see what might have been the cause of the defective condition of this brickwork. We have the fact, the datum, that the brickwork was in a defective condition, and we have it admitted that it was the defendants' duty to use reasonable care and diligence to keep it in a proper condition. Where it is the duty of persons to do their best to keep premises, or a structure, of whatever kind it may be, in a proper condition, and we find it out of condition, and an accident happens therefrom, it is incumbent upon them to show that they used that reasonable care and diligence which they were bound to use, and the absence of which it seems to me may fairly be presumed from the fact that there was the defect from which the accident has arisen. Therefore, there was some evidence to go to the jury, however slight it may have been, of this accident having arisen from the negligence of the defendants; and it was incumbent on the defendants to give evidence rebutting the inference arising from the undisputed facts; that they have not done, and I therefore think this rule must be discharged.

[LUSH, J., delivered a concurring opinion. HANNEN, J., delivered a dissenting opinion.] *Rule discharged.*[1]

[1] Affirmed in the Exchequer Chamber, L. R. 6 Q. B. 759.

Byrne *v.* Boadle, 2 H. & C. 722; Scott *v.* London Docks Co., 3 H. & C. 596; Skinner *v.* London R. Co., 5 Ex. 787; The Joseph D. Thomas, 81 Fed. 578; Hastorf *v.* Hudson River Co., 110 Fed. 669; Cincinnati R. Co. *v.* South Fork Coal Co., 139 Fed. 528; Kahn *v.* Cap Co., 139 Cal. 340; Armour *v.* Golkowska, 202 Ill. 144; Talge *v.* Hockett, 55 Ind. App. 303; Nicoll *v.* Sweet, 163 Ia. 683; Melvin *v.* Pennsylvania Steel Co., 180 Mass. 196; Hull *v.* Berkshire R. Co., 217 Mass. 361; Cleary *v.* Cavanaugh, 219 Mass. 281; Scharff *v.* Southern Construction Co., 115 Mo. App. 157; Pratt *v.* Missouri R. Co., 139 Mo. App. 502; Mullen *v.* St. John, 57 N. Y. 567; Wolf *v.* American Society, 164 N. Y. 30; Griffen *v.* Manice, 166 N. Y. 188; Kennedy *v.* McAllaster, 31 App. Div. 453; Scheider *v.* American Bridge Co., 78 App. Div. 163; Travers *v.* Murray, 87 App. Div. 552; Connor *v.* Koch, 89 App. Div. 33; Larkin *v.* Reid Co., 161 App. Div. 77; Papazian *v.* Baumgartner, 49 Misc. 244; Barnes *v.* Automobile Co., 32 Ohio Cir. Ct. R. 233; Muskogee Traction Co. *v.* McIntire, 37 Okl. 684; Edwards *v.* Manufacturers' Co., 27 R. I. 248; Patterson *v.* Brewing Co., 16 S. D. 33; Richmond R. Co. *v.* Hudgins, 100 Va. 409; Gibson *v.* Chicago R. Co., 61 Wash. 639; Carroll *v.* Chicago R. Co., 99 Wis. 399; Klitzke *v.* Webb, 120 Wis. 254; Schmidt *v.* Johnson Co., 145 Wis. 49; Snyder *v.* Wheeling Electrical Co., 43 W. Va. 661 *Accord.*

Where the declaration alleges negligence and sets forth the nature and particulars of the accident but not the particulars of the alleged negligence, plaintiff may rely upon this doctrine, if the accident is of such a kind as to indicate that it would not have happened without negligence on the part of the defendant. James *v.* Boston R. Co., 204 Mass. 158.

The doctrine applies only in the absence of explanation. Cook *v.* Newhall, 213 Mass. 392. The inference may be met by defendant's showing the real cause of the accident. Nawrocki *v.* Chicago R. Co., 156 Ill. App. 563; Parsons *v.* Hecla Iron Works, 186 Mass. 221; Cohen *v.* Farmers' Co., 70 Misc. 548; Stearns *v.* Spinning Co., 184 Pa. St. 519; Scarpelli *v.* Washington Power Co., 63 Wash. 18. By plaintiff showing by his own witnesses just how the accident happened. Buckland *v.* New York R. Co., 181 Mass. 3. Or by defendant's showing that reasonable care was employed to prevent all probable sources of accident. Thompson *v.* St. Louis R. Co., 243 Mo. 336, 355; Sweeney *v.* Edison Co., 158 App. Div. 449.

"There are many cases that hold that an unexplained accident with a machine, not liable to occur if such machine was properly constructed and in a proper state of repair, is evidence of negligence; as in Spaulding *v.* C. & N. W. R. Co., 30 Wis. 110, where it was held that the escape of fire from a passing locomotive engine, sufficient to cause damage, raised a presumption of improper construction or insufficient repair or negligent handling of such engine. To the same effect are Cummings *v.* Nat. Furnace Co., 60 Wis. 603; Kurz & Huttenlocher Ice Co. *v.* M. & N. R. Co., 84 Wis. 171; Stacy *v.* M., L. S. & W. R. Co., 85 Wis. 225; Mullen *v.* St. John, 57 N. Y. 567; Volkmar *v.* Manhattan R. Co., 134 N. Y. 418; McCarragher *v.* Rogers, 120 N. Y. 526, and many others that might be cited. Such cases lay down a very well-recognized principle in the law of negligence, but do not . . . conflict in the slightest degree with numerous authorities that go on another principle, just as well-recognized and firmly established, to the effect that undisputed proof of freedom of the machine from all discoverable defects, either in construction or repair, effectually overcomes any mere inference or presumption arising from the happening of the accident, so as to leave no question in that regard for the jury; as in Spaulding *v.* C. & N. W. R. Co., 33 Wis. 582, where this court held the inference that a locomotive engine was defective, arising merely from the escape of fire therefrom sufficient to cause damage, rebutted by conclusive proof that the engine was free from discoverable defects, so as to leave nothing on that point for the consideration of a jury." Marshall, J., Vorbrich *v.* Geuder Co., 96 Wis. 277, 284. See Green *v.* Urban Constructing Co., 106 App. Div. 460 *Accord.*

MARCEAU *v.* RUTLAND R. CO.

COURT OF APPEALS, NEW YORK, APRIL 28, 1914.

Reported in 211 *New York Reports*, 203.

WERNER, J. The question presented by this appeal is whether the case is one in which it is proper to apply the maxim *res ipsa loquitur.*[1] . . .

The phrase *res ipsa loquitur,* literally translated, means that the thing or affair speaks for itself. It is merely a short way of saying that the circumstances attendant upon an accident are themselves of such a character as to justify the conclusion that the accident was caused by negligence. The inference of negligence is deducible, not from the mere happening of the accident, but from the attendant circumstances. " It is not that, in any case, negligence can be assumed from the mere fact of an accident and an injury; but in these cases the surrounding circumstances which are necessarily brought into view by showing how the accident occurred, contain, without further proof, sufficient evidence of the defendant's duty and of his neglect to perform it. The fact of the casualty and the attendant circumstances may themselves furnish all the proof of negligence that the injured person is able to offer, or that it is necessary to offer." Shearman & Redfield on Negligence, § 59. This section was quoted with approval by Judge Cullen in writing for this court in Griffen *v.* Manice, 166 N. Y. 188, 193, and in that connection he expressed the view that " the application of the principle depends on the circumstances and character of the occurrence, and not on the relation between the parties, except indirectly so far as that relation defines the measure of duty imposed on the defendant." He quoted also from the opinion of Judge Danforth in Breen *v.* N. Y. C. & H. R. R. Co., 109 N. Y. 297, 300, in which the author said " there must be reasonable evidence of negligence, but when the thing causing the injury is shown to be under the control of a defendant, and the accident is such as, in the ordinary course of business, does not happen if reasonable care is used, it does, in the absence of explanation by the defendant, afford sufficient evidence that the accident arose from want of care on its part." In the Griffen case Judge Cullen followed this quotation from the Breen case, with the pertinent observation that he could see no reason " why the rule thus declared is not applicable to all cases or why the probative force of the evidence depends on the relation of the parties. Of course, the relation of the parties may determine the fact to be proved, whether it be want of the highest care or only want of ordinary care, and, doubtless, circumstantial evidence, like direct evidence, may be insufficient as a matter of law to establish the want of ordinary care, though sufficient to prove absence of the highest degree of

[1] The arguments of counsel and a part of the opinion are omitted.

diligence. But the question in every case is the same whether the circumstances surrounding the occurrence are such as to justify the jury in inferring the fact in issue." Thus we see that this court is definitely committed to the view that the application of the maxim *res ipsa loquitur* depends, not upon the relation of the injured person to the person or party who is charged with causing the injury, but upon the explanatory circumstances which surround the happening of the accident. The rule thus expressed has been recognized in the recent cases of Robinson *v.* Consolidated Gas Co., 194 N. Y. 37, 41, and Hardie *v.* Boland Co., 205 N. Y. 336, 341, and has been followed in many cases in the several Appellate Divisions.[1]

While it is, therefore, the settled law that the maxim is applicable to any case where the facts warrant its application, it is apparent that the employee who invokes it against his employer encounters difficulties that do not hamper the wayfarer in a public place or the passenger in a common carrier's conveyance. The man who was lawfully upon the highway need go no farther in the first instance than to prove that he was hit by a falling wall (Mullen *v.* St. John, 57 N. Y. 567) or by a flying missile (Wolf *v.* Am. Tract Soc., 164 N. Y. 30, 33; Hogan *v.* Manh. Ry. Co., 149 N. Y. 23; Volkmar *v.* Manh. Ry. Co., 134 N. Y. 418), and that the thing by which he was injured came from the premises of the defendant. The passenger who was for the time under the protection of a common carrier needs only to show that the train upon which he was riding left the track (Seyboldt *v.* N. Y., L. E. & W. R. R. Co., 95 N. Y. 562, 565) or collided with another car or train (Loudoun *v.* Eighth Ave. R. R. Co., 162 N. Y. 380) and thus caused his injuries. The reason for the rule in such cases is not far to seek. The owner of a building or structure must exercise a high degree of care to so keep it that the wayfarer on the public streets shall not be injured by falling walls or missiles. The common carrier is under the strict duty to its passenger to keep its cars and tracks in a safe condition, and in all such cases where the plaintiff "has shown a situation which could not have been produced except by the operation of abnormal causes, the onus then rests upon the defendant to prove that the injury was caused without his fault." Seyboldt *v.* N. Y., L. E. & W. R. R. Co., 95 N. Y. 565, 568. Ordinarily walls do not fall, missiles do not fly and trains are not derailed when those in control are in the exercise of the requisite care, and, therefore, the inference of negligence follows in logical sequence.

In the nature of things the injured employee who sues his employer must present a much higher degree of proof than is necessary in the case of a wayfarer or passenger. It is to be emphasized, however, that

[1] There is a conflict of authority upon the question whether the maxim *res ipsa loquitur* is applicable in an action by a servant against a master. See cases collected in an elaborate note, 6 Lawyers' Reports, Annotated, New Series, 337–363. See also 2 Labatt on Master & Servant, §§ 833, 834, 835; especially authorities cited in § 834, note 8.

the difference is one of degree and not of kind. This more onerous burden which is placed upon the employee is the natural concomitant of the relation of the parties and of their resultant obligations. The employer is bound merely to the exercise of reasonable care in providing his employee with a safe place in which to work, with proper and adequate tools, appliances and machinery, and with fellow-employees competent for the tasks to which they are assigned. If the injured employee sues at common law and seeks to invoke the maxim, he must necessarily make proof of facts and circumstances which, under the common law, exclude every inference except that of the employer's negligence. This means that the employee must himself be free from the imputation of contributory negligence; that he is not the victim of the negligence of co-employees; that the injury is not the result of some risk either inherent in the occupation or voluntarily assumed by the employee; and that the accident is one which, in the ordinary course of events, could not have happened if the employer had exercised the degree of care required of him by the common law. The same rule applies, in a modified degree, where the employee sues under the Employers' Liability Act, as the plaintiff in this case has done. In such a case the plaintiff must establish facts and circumstances which, under the statute, would entitle him to recover in the absence of a sufficient explanation by the defendant, absolving him from the imputation of negligence. The proof must not be conjectural or speculative, but must consist of evidence which, tested by the ordinary rules of experience and observation, points to the single conclusion that the employer's omission of a duty which he owes to his employee was the sole efficient cause of the accident. Ferrick *v.* Eidlitz, 195 N. Y. 248, 252.

The next question, in logical progression, is whether the plaintiff has established his case by facts and circumstances which negative the existence of any cause for the accident by which he was injured, save the negligence of the defendant. The plaintiff, as has been stated, was a locomotive fireman in the employ of the defendant. On the 25th of March, 1911, he and his engineer left Malone on engine No. 2055 for Moira to assist in bringing back a train. After arriving at Moira the engine was turned around and coupled to another engine already attached to a train, and a start was made for the return to Malone. Suddenly there occurred an explosion in the fire box of the engine which drove the doors from their fastenings, and expelled fire and boiling water into the cab, and burned and scalded the plaintiff, and blew him out of the cab to the ground with such force as to bruise him. Although this accident was of an unusual character, it will be assumed for the purposes of this discussion that it was not such an occurrence as would, in and of itself, justify the application of the maxim *res ipsa loquitur,* for the engine was then in the custody and control of the plaintiff and his engineer. The mere happening of the accident did not necessarily exclude the inference that it might have been caused by the negligence of the plaintiff, or without any negligence at all.

It was, therefore, necessary for the plaintiff to supplement the proof of the accident with evidence tending to show that it resulted from the failure of the defendant to exercise ordinary care, either in the selection of the engine or in keeping it in reasonably safe repair. In that behalf the record discloses a number of facts and circumstances that bear upon the accident very directly and cogently. It appears that the train crews employed by the defendant have nothing to do with the care and inspection of the internal and hidden parts of the engines. That work is committed to a special corps of employees whose place of duty is in the hostelry where the engines are housed, made ready for service, and turned over to the crews designated to take them out. The engineers are charged with the duty of making a report of each trip which shall specify any needed repairs that come under their observation. The engineer Francey, who was on engine 2055 at the time of the accident, testified that he had used it on various specified dates during the month preceding the day of the accident, and that he had orally reported it as leaking, although he had been turning in written reports which made no mention of the fact. While such a circumstance might ordinarily affect the credibility of a witness, all doubt upon this subject is dissipated by the testimony of the defendant's witnesses showing that the engine was inspected by the foreman of boiler makers on or about March 21st, 1911, and found to be in a leaky condition. Several of defendant's witnesses testified that the engine had been in the shop at various times during the month on account of leaking flues, and that the last repairs in this regard were made two or three days before the accident.

After the accident an examination of the engine was made which revealed the probable cause of the trouble. One of the flues, which extend longitudinally through the boiler from the rear flue sheet to another flue sheet next the smoke stack, had been pushed or blown out of its socket in the rear flue sheet so that the forward end of the flue projected several feet beyond the forward flue sheet; thus leaving an opening in the rear flue sheet through which the boiling water and steam were admitted into the fire pot where the explosion was generated. There were 342 of these flues which were each $1\frac{7}{8}$ inches in diameter and about 16 feet in length. These flues are "safe ended" into the flue sheets so that when they are in perfect condition there can be no leakage through them from the boiler. The particular flue that was blown or driven out of its place was in the bottom row of flues where there could be no inspection without taking out the "brick arch," and that could be done only when the boiler was not in steam. There can be no doubt that the explosion by which the plaintiff was injured was due immediately to the displacement of the flue; but the cause of the dislodgement of the flue is not so clear. It is a matter of common knowledge that steam, like electricity, is a capricious and fickle agency which sometimes causes unexpected and unexplainable accidents. If the plaintiff's case were wholly dependent upon evidence merely showing the happening of this explosion, it might be necessary to hold that he had not proved enough to give him the benefit of the maxim which he invokes. The ultimate question, therefore, is whether he has the support of surrounding circumstances which show that the accident was of "such a character as does not ordinarily occur where the party charged with responsibility has exercised the degree of care and caution required by law to avoid such a mishap." Henson *v.* Lehigh Valley R. R. Co., 194 N. Y. 205, 211. We think he has. The defendant's foreman testified that if a flue is loose at both ends it would be liable to move from the pressure, and that if a flue is loose at one end it is more liable to move than one that is not loose. It is undisputed that defendant's chief boiler man inspected this engine on the 21st or 22d of March and found that a number of flues, about twenty-five, were leaking. These were repaired, but the boiler still leaked on the 24th, and the explosion occurred on the 25th. Since the defendant's experts had found loose and leaking flues which they repaired, it is reasonable to infer that the displacement of another flue within two or three days was attributable to the same cause. This was not a part of the locomotive over which the plaintiff had any control, or in respect of which he had, so far as the record discloses, any duty or knowledge. The work of inspection and repair was the work of the defendant, and any failure in this regard was its failure. The almost immediate recurrence of a condition that had led to inspection and repair was circumstantial evidence which tended to show that the work had not been thoroughly done. We think, therefore, that the plaintiff was entitled to rest upon the rule of *res ipsa loquitur*, and that in the absence of a satisfactory and convincing explanation by the defendant, the plaintiff was entitled to recover.

Counsel for the defendant contends that such an explanation has been made. In that regard it appears that the locomotive was of a modern and standard type; that for several months from January, 1910, it was in the main shops of the defendant at Rutland, where it was given a thorough overhauling and sent out in perfect condition; that the complaints of leakage made in the early part of 1911 were followed by prompt inspection and complete repair. This was an explanation well calculated indeed to create a serious issue of fact, but we think it would be going too far to hold that it was conclusive as matter of law. The limitations of the rule of *res ipsa loquitur*, and the legal effect of defendant's explanation, were well stated in the charge to the jury, and we think the judgment entered on the verdict must stand.

The judgment should be affirmed, with costs.

WILLARD BARTLETT, Ch. J., COLLIN, CUDDEBACK, HOGAN, and CARDOZO, JJ., concur; HORNBLOWER, J., not sitting.

Judgment affirmed.[1]

[1] "There was much discussion by counsel of the doctrine of *res ipsa loquitur* and its relevancy to the facts of this case. The thing speaks for itself, is a principle

WING *v.* LONDON GENERAL OMNIBUS CO.

In the Court of Appeal, July 16, 1909.

Reported in [1909] 2 *King's Bench*, 652.

Fletcher Moulton, L. J., read the following judgment:[1] — This is an appeal from the judgment delivered by the judge of the county court of Middlesex held in Clerkenwell in an action in which the plaintiff sued for damages resulting from an accident which occurred while she was a passenger in a motor omnibus belonging to the defendants.

The plaintiff's claim was based on two alternative grounds: (1) that the defendants' servants, whilst in charge of the motor omnibus, were guilty of negligence causing the accident, and (2) that the motor omnibus was itself a dangerous machine, and that the defendants were liable for having placed it upon the roadway, thereby creating a nuisance, whereby the plaintiff suffered damage.

applied by the law where under the circumstances shown the accident presumably would not have occurred in the use of a machine if due care had been exercised, or, in the case of an elevator, when in its normal operation after due inspection. The doctrine does not dispense with the requirement that the party who alleges negligence must prove the fact, but relates only to the mode of proving it. The fact of the accident furnishes merely some evidence to go to the jury, which requires the defendant 'to go forward with his proof.' The rule of *res ipsa loquitur* does not relieve the plaintiff of the burden of showing negligence, nor does it raise any presumption in his favor. Whether the defendant introduces evidence or not, the plaintiff in this case will not be entitled to a verdict unless he satisfies the jury by the preponderance of the evidence that his injuries were caused by a defect in the elevator attributable to the defendant's negligence. The law attaches no special weight, as proof, to the fact of an accident, but simply holds it to be sufficient for the consideration of the jury even in the absence of any additional evidence. Womble *v.* Grocery Co., 135 N. C. 474; 2 Labatt on Master & Servant, § 834; 4 Wigmore on Evidence, § 2509. In all other respects, the parties stand before the jury just as if there was no such rule. The judge should carefully instruct the jury as to the application of the principle, so that they will not give to the fact of the accident any greater artificial weight than the law imparts to it. Wigmore, in the section just cited, says the following considerations ought to limit the doctrine of *res ipsa loquitur:* 1. The apparatus must be such that in the ordinary instance no injurious operation is to be expected unless from a careless construction, inspection, or user; 2. Both inspection and user must have been, at the time of the injury, in the control of the party charged; 3. The injurious occurrence must have happened irrespective of any voluntary action at the time by the party injured. He says further that the doctrine is to some extent founded upon the fact that the chief evidence of the true cause of the injury, whether culpable or innocent, is practically accessible to the party charged and perhaps inaccessible to the party injured. What are the general limits of the doctrine and what is the true reason for its adoption, we will not now undertake to decide. It is established in the law as a rule for our guidance and must be enforced whenever applicable, and to the extent that it is applicable, to the facts of the particular case." Walker, J., in Stewart *v.* Van Deventer Carpet Co., 138 N. C. 60, 65.

The burden of proof is not shifted; merely the burden of going forward. Sweeney *v.* Erving, 228 U. S. 233; Ferrier *v.* Chicago R. Co., 185 Ill. App. 326; Bigwood *v.* Boston R. Co., 209 Mass. 345; Alabama R. Co. *v.* Groome, 97 Miss. 201; Kay *v.* Metropolitan R. Co., 163 N. Y. 447.

[1] The arguments of counsel, concurring opinion of Vaughan-Williams, L. J., and dissenting opinion of Buckley, L. J., and part of the opinion of Moulton, L. J., dealing with another point, are omitted.

The evidence given at the trial as to the nature and circumstances of the accident was meagre in the extreme. The plaintiff deposed to nothing more than that she was a passenger in the omnibus, and that she heard breaking of glass, and knew that the omnibus had hit something, and that she heard something fall. She tried to get out, and, in so doing, hurt her foot. No other witness was called who was present at the time of the accident, but evidence was given on her behalf by a police constable, who came up afterwards, and proved that an electric standard had been broken in the accident, and that the hind step of the motor omnibus had been slightly bent. No other damage had been caused to the omnibus. He also proved that the road was in a greasy state at the time by reason of rain that had fallen during the day. He was asked by the plaintiff's counsel as to certain admissions made to him at the time by the driver and conductor of the omnibus, and proved that they stated to him that the hind part of the omnibus skidded, when going about five miles an hour, while the driver was trying to avoid two other vehicles. The defendants called no evidence except as to the quantum of damage. At the end of the plaintiff's case, counsel for the defendants submitted that there was no evidence, either of negligence or of nuisance, to go to the jury, and the learned judge gave partial effect to that contention by withdrawing from the jury the question of negligence in the driving or management of the car. The plaintiff did not take exception to this by giving a cross notice of appeal, nor was the point raised before the Divisional Court, and it is not, in my opinion, open to her counsel to raise it now. But, apart from this, I am of opinion that the learned judge was right in so doing. There was no evidence whatever that the accident was due to negligence on the part of the servants of the defendants who were in charge of the omnibus, unless the mere occurrence of the accident amounts to such evidence. In my opinion the mere occurrence of such an accident is not in itself evidence of negligence. Without attempting to lay down any exhaustive classification of the cases in which the principle of *res ipsa loquitur* applies, it may generally be said that the principle only applies when the direct cause of the accident, and so much of the surrounding circumstances as was essential to its occurrence, were within the sole control and management of the defendants, or their servants, so that it is not unfair to attribute to them a *prima facie* responsibility for what happened. An accident in the case of traffic on a highway is in marked contrast to such a condition of things. Every vehicle has to adapt its own behaviour to the behaviour of other persons using the road, and over their actions those in charge of the vehicle have no control. Hence the fact that an accident has happened either to or through a particular vehicle is by itself no evidence that the fault, if any, which led to it was committed by those in charge of that vehicle. Exceptional cases may occur in which the peculiar nature of the accident may throw light upon the question on whom the responsibility lies, but there is nothing of the kind here. The collision with the electric standard was due to the omnibus skidding, and, if we are to give any weight to the admissions made by the defendants' servants which were proved in evidence in chief as part of the plaintiff's case, that skidding was due to difficulties in avoiding other vehicles. There is certainly no evidence to negative such a probable explanation of what actually happened, and it is impossible to say that this points to negligence, or that it establishes that any negligent act of the defendants' servant was the cause of the accident. I am therefore of opinion that the learned judge acted rightly in withdrawing from the jury the issue as to the accident being due to negligence of the defendants' servants in the driving or management of the vehicle.[1]

CARMODY *v.* BOSTON GAS LIGHT CO.

SUPREME JUDICIAL COURT, MASSACHUSETTS, JANUARY 2, 1895.

Reported in 162 *Massachusetts Reports*, 539.

FOUR actions for damages occasioned to the respective plaintiffs by the escape of gas were tried together.

Plaintiffs' evidence tended to show that gas escaped into plaintiffs' apartments from defendant's pipes in the street; that plaintiffs inhaled the gas while asleep; and that the escape was due to the defective condition of the pipe.

Defendant's evidence tended to prove that the defect in the pipe and the consequent escape of gas was due to acts of third persons of which the defendant had no notice, and not to any negligence of the defendant.

The plaintiffs requested the judge to rule that there was evidence enough of want of proper care on the part of the defendant to make it responsible, on the ground that it was bound to conduct its gas in a proper manner; and that the fact that the gas escaped was *prima facie* evidence of some neglect on the part of the defendant.

The judge declined so to rule, and instructed the jury as follows:

"The mere fact that a pipe broke and the gas escaped is not of itself sufficient to establish the liability of the company. It is evidence for you to consider upon the question of neglect; but there is other evidence bearing upon this question of neglect, and so it becomes a matter for you to determine, in view of all the evidence bearing upon the question, the burden being upon the plaintiffs to satisfy you, as a result

[1] Bonham *v.* Winchester Arms Co., 179 Ill. App. 469; Prestolite Co. *v.* Skeel, 182 Ind. 593; Rice *v.* Chicago R. Co., 153 Mo. App. 35; Dalzell *v.* New York R. Co., 136 App. Div. 329 *Accord.*

The nature and circumstances of the accident itself must not only support an inference of defendant's negligence but must exclude all others. Lucid *v.* Powder Co., 199 Fed. 377.

of all the evidence, that there was in fact a neglect by the defendant, through which, and by means of which, this gas escaped."

. . . .

Upon the counsel for the plaintiffs remarking, "Your honor has not given the requests I asked for, and so I will except to that," the judge replied as follows: "Well, you asked me to say that the fact that the gas escaped is *prima facie* evidence of some neglect on the part of the defendant. I do not choose to use that expression '*prima facie* evidence,' unless the defendant consents to it. I have already told the jury that it was evidence of neglect, or of negligence, on the defendant's part, and evidence the force of which it was for them to determine in connection with any other evidence in the case bearing upon the same subject."

The jury returned a verdict for the defendant; and the plaintiffs alleged exceptions.[1]

BARKER, J. The plaintiffs asked the court to instruct the jury "that there was evidence enough of want of proper care on the part of the defendant to make it responsible, on the ground that it was bound to conduct its gas in a proper manner, and that the fact that the gas escaped was *prima facie* evidence of some neglect on the part of the defendant." This request was copied from a ruling given in Smith *v.* Boston Gas Light Co., 129 Mass. 318, where this court said of it that, as applied to the facts of that case, it could not be said to be wrong. The presiding justice in the present case declined to give the instruction, but instructed the jury in other terms, which fully and correctly dealt with the phases of the cause to which the request was addressed.

While the ruling requested is sufficiently correct if it be construed as declaring that there was enough evidence of want of proper care to be submitted to the jury, it would invade the proper province of the jury if it was understood by them to mean that there was evidence enough to require them to find the defendant negligent, and the presiding justice was not bound to give a ruling which, as applied to the case upon trial, might have been so understood. Nor was he bound to use the Latin phrase upon which the plaintiffs insisted, but might well say, in place of it, that the fact that gas escaped was evidence of neglect "and evidence the force of which it was for them to determine in connection with any other evidence in the case bearing on the same subject."

The plaintiffs' exception did not go to the charge as given, but merely to the refusal of the request. They nevertheless argue that the statement of the charge, that "the mere fact that a pipe broke and the gas escaped is not of itself sufficient to establish the liability of the company," was incorrect. But there was evidence with which

[1] Statement abridged.

the jury had to deal tending to show that the defendant had used due care to conduct its gas in a proper manner, and that the escape of gas by which the plaintiffs were injured was due to the acts of third persons of which the defendant had no notice, and not to any negligence of the defendant.

It is apparent, from the situation of the evidence and the context of the charge, that the sentence to which the plaintiffs now object could not have been understood by the jury as forbidding them to draw the inference of negligence from the facts that a pipe broke and that gas escaped; but that, as there was other evidence bearing upon the question of negligence, they must consider and weigh it all, and not come to a conclusion upon two circumstances merely.

The true construction of the ruling asked, as applied to the case at bar, would be, that, as matter of law, the breaking of a pipe and the consequent escape of gas prove negligence. The true rule is, that a jury may find negligence from those circumstances, but it is for them to say whether they will do so; and, if there are other circumstances bearing on the question, they must weigh them all.

Instructions that evidence " is sufficient to show," or " has a tendency to show," or " is enough to show," or " is *prima facie* evidence of," are not to be understood as meaning that there is a presumption of fact, but that the jury are at liberty to draw the inference from them. Commonwealth *v.* Clifford, 145 Mass. 97. Commonwealth *v.* Keenan, 148 Mass. 470. And so the instruction in a case where a number of circumstances bearing upon a question of fact are in evidence, that a part of them are not of themselves sufficient to establish the fact, coupled with explicit instructions that they are to be considered, must be understood as directing the jury to weigh together all the pertinent circumstances, and not to draw their inference from a part without considering all. *Exceptions overruled.*[1]

BENEDICK *v.* POTTS

COURT OF APPEALS, MARYLAND, JUNE 28, 1898.

Reported in 88 *Maryland Reports,* 52.

APPEAL from Circuit Court, where judgment was entered on a verdict for defendant, ordered by the court.

Defendant owned and operated, at a pleasure resort, a mimic railway, which was a wooden structure. Open cars were hoisted up an incline to the highest point of the railway, and were then run by grav-

[1] " The maxim *res ipsa loquitur* is simply a rule of evidence. The general rule is that negligence is never presumed from the mere fact of injury, yet the manner of the occurrence of the injury complained of, or the attendant circumstances, may sometimes well warrant an inference of negligence. It is sometimes said that it warrants a presumption of negligence, but the presumption referred to is not one of law, but of fact. It is, however, more correct and less con-

ity down and around a circular track to the ground. The length of the spiral track was about two thousand feet, and it made three circuits before reaching the ground. At about the middle of the last circle nearest the ground, the cars passed through a tunnel which was part of the structure. This tunnel was one hundred and fifty feet long, and completely incased that portion of the track, and hid the cars and their occupants from all observation when passing through it. The cars were provided with handles for the occupants to grasp during the rapid descent. Plaintiff was the sole occupant of the rear seat in one of the cars. The car was started and made the descent; but when it reached the ground at the end of the track the plaintiff was not in it, though as it entered the tunnel he was seen to be upon it. Search was at once made, and he was found inside the tunnel, in an unconscious condition, with a wound upon his head. After several days he was restored to consciousness. For the damages thus sustained, this suit was brought.

The car did not leave the track, no part of it was shown to be out of repair, the track was not defective, and no explanation is given in the record as to what caused the injury. The plaintiff distinctly stated that he made no effort to rise as he passed through the tunnel, and that he did not relax his grasp on the sides of the car. He was in the car when it passed into the tunnel. He was not in it when it emerged. How he got off was not shown.

Upon this state of facts the trial court instructed the jury that there was no legally sufficient evidence to show that the defendant had been guilty of negligence; and the verdict and judgment were accordingly entered for defendant. Plaintiff brought up the record by appeal.[1]

McSherry, C. J. This is an action to recover damages for a personal injury, and the single question which the record presents is whether there was legally sufficient evidence of the defendant's imputed negligence to carry the case to the jury. The facts are few and simple. [The learned judge then stated the facts.]

It is a perfectly well-settled principle that to entitle a plaintiff to recover in an action of this kind he must show not only that he has sustained an injury but that the defendant has been guilty of some negligence which produced that particular injury. The negligence alleged and the injury sued for must bear the relation of cause and effect. The concurrence of both and the *nexus* between them must exist to constitute a cause of action. As an injury may occur from

fusing to refer to it as an inference, rather than a presumption, and not an inference which the law draws from the fact, but an inference which the jury are authorized to draw, and not an inference which the jury are compelled to draw." Cobb, J., in Palmer Brick Co. *v.* Chenall, 119 Ga. 837, 842. See Sweeney *v.* Erving, 228 U. S. 233, 240; Harlow *v.* Standard Imp. Co., 145 Cal. 477; National Biscuit Co. *v.* Wilson, 169 Ind. 442; O'Neil *v.* Toomey, 218 Mass. 242; Lincoln *v.* Detroit R. Co., 179 Mich. 189; Boucher *v.* Boston R. Co., 76 N. H. 91; Ross *v.* Cotton Mills, 140 N. C. 115. But compare Thompson *v.* St. Louis R. Co., 243 Mo. 336, 353.

[1] Statement abridged.

causes other than the negligence of the party sued, it is obvious that before a liability on account of that injury can be fastened upon a particular individual, it must be shown, or there must be evidence legally tending to show, that he is responsible for it; that is, that he has been guilty of the negligence that produced or occasioned the injury. In no instance can the bare fact that an injury has happened, of itself and divorced from all the surrounding circumstances, justify the inference that the injury was caused by negligence. It is true that direct proof of negligence is not necessary. Like any other fact, negligence may be established by the proof of circumstances from which its existence may be inferred. But this inference must, after all, be a legitimate inference and not a mere speculation of conjecture. There must be a logical relation and connection between the circumstances proved and the conclusion sought to be adduced from them. This principle is never departed from, and in the very nature of things it never can be disregarded. There are instances in which the circumstances surrounding an occurrence and giving a character to it are held, if unexplained, to indicate the antecedent or coincident existence of negligence as the efficient cause of an injury complained of. These are the instances where the doctrine of *res ipsa loquitur* is applied. This phrase, which literally translated means that "the thing speaks for itself," is merely a short way of saying that the circumstances attendant upon an accident are themselves of such a character as to justify a jury in inferring negligence as the cause of that accident; and the doctrine which it embodies, though correct enough in itself, may be said to be applicable to two classes of cases only, viz., "first, when the relation of carrier and passenger exists and the accident arises from some abnormal condition in the department of actual transportation; second, where the injury arises from some condition or event that is in its very nature so obviously destructive of the safety of person or property and is so tortious in its quality as, in the first instance at least, to permit no inference save that of negligence on the part of the person in the control of the injurious agency." Thomas on Neg. 574. But it is obvious that in both instances more than the mere isolated, single, segregated fact that an injury has happened must be known. The injury, without more, does not necessarily speak or indicate the *cause* of that injury — it is colorless; but the act that produced the injury being made apparent may, in the instances indicated, furnish the ground for a presumption that negligence set that act in motion. The maxim does not go to the extent of implying that you may from the mere fact of an injury infer what physical act produced that injury; but it means that when the physical act has been shown or is apparent and is not explained by the defendant, the conclusion that negligence superinduced it may be drawn as a legitimate deduction of fact. It permits an inference that the known act which produced the injury was a negligent act, but it does not permit an inference as to what act did produce the injury. Negligence manifestly cannot be predicated of any act until you know what the act is. Until you know *what* did occasion an injury, you cannot say that the defendant was guilty of some negligence that produced that injury. There is, therefore, a difference between inferring as a conclusion of fact *what* it was that did the injury; and inferring from a known or proven act occasioning the injury that there was negligence in the act that did produce the injury. To the first category the maxim *res ipsa loquitur* has no application; it is confined, when applicable at all, solely to the second. In no case where the thing which occasioned the injury is unknown has it ever been held that the maxim applies; because when the thing which produced the injury is unknown it cannot be said to speak or to indicate the existence of causative negligence. In all the cases, whether the relation of carrier and passenger existed or not, the injury alone furnished no evidence of negligence — something more was required to be shown. For instance: In Penn. R. R. Co. *v.* MacKinney, 124 Pa. St. 462, it was said: "A passenger's leg is broken, while on his passage, in a railroad car. This mere fact is no evidence of negligence on the part of the carrier until something further be shown. If the witness who swears to the injury testifies also that it was caused by a crash in a collision with another train of cars belonging to the same carrier, the presumption of negligence immediately arises; not, however, from the fact that the leg was broken, but from the circumstances attending the fact." And so in Byrne *v.* Boadle, 2 Hurl. & Colt. 728, there was proof not only of an injury but there was evidence to show *how* the injury happened, and the presumption of negligence was applied, not because of there being an injury, but because of the way or manner in which the injury was produced. And in Howser's case, 80 Md. 146, the injury was caused by cross-ties falling from a moving train upon the plaintiff who was walking by the side of the track, and the presumption of negligence was allowed, not as an inference deducible from the injury itself, but as a conclusion resulting from the method in which and the instrumentality by which the injury had been occasioned. In the recent case of Consolidated Traction Co. *v.* Thalheimer, Court of Errors and Appeals, N. J., 2 Amer. Neg. Rep. 196,[1] it appeared that the plaintiff was a passenger of the appellant, and, having been notified by the conductor that the car was approaching the point where she desired to alight, got up from her seat and walked to the door while the car was in motion, and, while going through the doorway, she was thrown into the street by a sudden lurch and thus injured. The court said: "At all events, the fact that such a lurch or jerk occurred, as would have been unlikely to occur if proper care had been exercised, brings the case within the maxim *res ipsa loquitur*." The inference of negligence arose not from the injury to the passenger, but from the *act* that

[1] 59 N. J. Law, 474.

caused the injury. In B. & O. R. R. *v.* Worthington, 21 Md. 275, the train was derailed in consequence of an open switch, and it was held that the injury thus inflicted on the passenger was presumptive evidence of negligence — not that the mere injury raised such a presumption, but that the injury caused in the way and under the circumstances shown indicated actionable negligence unless satisfactorily explained.

Whether, therefore, there be a contractual relation between the parties or not, there must be proof of negligence or proof of some circumstances from which negligence may be inferred, before an action can be sustained. And whether you characterize that inference an ordinary presumption of fact, or say of the act that caused the injury, the thing speaks for itself, you assert merely a rebuttable conclusion deduced from known and obvious premises. It follows, of course, that when the *act* that caused the injury is wholly unknown or undisclosed, it is simply and essentially impossible to affirm that there was a negligent act; and neither the doctrine of *res ipsa loquitur* nor any other principle of presumption can be invoked to fasten a liability upon the party charged with having by negligence caused the injury for the infliction of which a suit has been brought.

Now, in the case at bar there is no evidence that the car on the track was out of repair. The car went safely to its destination, carrying the other occupants. There is no evidence that the roof of the tunnel struck the appellant, or that the fact that a small part of the central plank of the tunnel roof had been slabbed off had the most remote connection with the accident. It is a case presenting not a single circumstance showing *how* or by what agency the injury occurred, and in which, with nothing but the isolated fact of the injury having happened, being proved, it is insisted that the jury shall be allowed to speculate as to the cause that produced it, and then to *infer* from the cause thus assumed but not established, that there was actionable negligence. It is not an attempt to infer negligence from an apparent cause, but to infer the cause of the injury from the naked fact of injury, and then to superadd the further inference that this inferred cause proceeded from negligence. If in Howser's case, *supra,* there had been no other evidence than the mere *fact* of an injury, it cannot be pretended that the jury would have been allowed to speculate as to *how* the injury had occurred.

The appellant was on the car when it entered the tunnel; he was not on the car when it emerged, but was found in an unconscious state in the tunnel. There was no defect in or abnormal condition affecting the means of actual transportation. The other occupants of the car passed safely through. What caused the appellant to be out of the car is a matter of pure conjecture. No one has explained or attempted to explain how he got where he was found. Indeed, the two persons who occupied the front seat were ignorant of the appellant's absence from the car until it had reached its destination, and the appellant himself distinctly testified that he did not relax his hold to the car and did not attempt to rise, but lowered his head as he entered the tunnel. All that is certain is, that he was injured in *some* way and he asks that the jury may be allowed, in the absence of all explanatory evidence, to infer that some act of a negligent character for which the appellee is responsible, caused the injury sustained by the appellant. No case has gone to that extent and no known principle can be cited to sanction such a position. There has been no circumstance shown which furnishes the foundation for an inference of negligence; and the circumstances which have been shown obviously do not bring the case within the doctrine of *res ipsa loquitur*. There was, consequently, no error in the ruling complained of, and the judgment of the Circuit Court must be affirmed. *Judgment affirmed.*[1]

SECTION V

THE DUTY OF CARE — MISFEASANCE AND NONFEASANCE

FLINT & WALLING MANUFACTURING CO. *v* BECKETT

SUPREME COURT, INDIANA, DECEMBER 18, 1906.

Reported in 167 *Indiana Reports*, 491.

BECKETT brought this action against the Flint & Walling Manufacturing Company to recover damages for harm done to his barn and the contents thereof, owing to the fact that the company constructed a windmill thereon in such an insufficient manner that it fell upon the roof of the barn.

The complaint contained, in substance, the following statements: —

There was an air-shaft in the centre of the barn, extending from the bottom to, and projecting through, the roof. Defendant contracted with plaintiff to erect on the air-shaft a windmill consisting of a wheel, tower, etc., to be erected in a first-class manner. The defendant erected the windmill in a negligent manner; especially in the mode of fastening the tower to the air-shaft. In consequence of this defective construction, a wind of ordinary velocity caused the windmill to break and twist the air-shaft and fall about sixty feet on the roof of the barn.

Trial in the Circuit Court. Verdict for plaintiff and judgment thereon. Defendant company appealed.[2]

[1] Actiesselskabet Ingrid *v.* Central R. Co., 216 Fed. 72; Huneke *v.* West Brighton Amusement Co., 80 App. Div. 268; De Glopper *v.* Nashville R. Co., 123 Tenn. 633 *Accord.*

[2] Statement abridged. Part of opinion omitted.

GILLETT, J.

The leading contention of appellant's counsel is that the duty it owed to appellee arose out of contract, and that, as appellant was not engaged in a public employment, its obligation could only be enforced by an action on the contract for a breach thereof. The latter insistence cannot be upheld. It is, of course, true that it is not every breach of contract which can be counted on as a tort, and it may also be granted that if the making of a contract does not bring the parties into such a relation that a common-law obligation exists, no action can be maintained in tort for an omission properly to perform the undertaking. It by no means follows, however, that this common-law obligation may not have its inception in contract. If a defendant may be held liable for the neglect of a duty imposed on him, independently of any contract, by operation of law, *a fortiori* ought he to be liable where he has come under an obligation to use care as the result of an undertaking founded on a consideration.

Where the duty has its roots in contract, the undertaking to observe due care may be implied from the relationship, and should it be the fact that a breach of the agreement also constitutes such a failure to exercise care as amounts to a tort, the plaintiff may elect, as the common-law authorities have it, to sue in case or in assumpsit. It is broadly stated in 1 Comyn's Digest, Action on the Case for Negligence, A 4, p. 418, that "if a man neglect to do that, which he has undertaken to do, an action upon the case lies. . . . But, if there be not any neglect in the defendant, an action upon the case does not lie against him, though he do not perform his undertaking." Professor Pollock says: "One who enters on the doing of anything attended with risk to the persons or property of others is held answerable for the use of a certain measure of caution to guard against that risk. To name one of the commonest applications, 'those who go personally or bring property where they know that they or it may come into collision with the persons or property of others have by law a duty cast upon them to use reasonable care and skill to avoid such collision.' . . . In some cases this ground of liability may coexist with a liability on contract towards the same person, and arising (as regards the breach) out of the same facts. Where a man interferes gratuitously, he is bound to act in a reasonable and prudent manner according to the circumstances and opportunities of the case. And this duty is not affected by the fact, if so it be, that he is acting for reward, in other words, under a contract, and may be liable on the contract. The two duties are distinct, except so far as the same party cannot be compensated twice over for the same facts, once for the breach of contract and again for the wrong. Historically the liability in tort is older; and indeed it was by special development of this view that the action of assumpsit, afterwards the common mode of enforcing simple contracts, was brought into use. 'If a smith prick my horse with a nail, etc., I shall have my action upon the case against him, without any warranty by the smith to do it well. . . . For it is the duty of every artificer to exercise his art rightly and truly as he ought.' " Webb's Pollock, Torts, 533–536. This general thought also finds expression in Mr. Street's valuable work (1 Street, Foundations of Legal Liability, 92). It is there said: " The general doctrine may be laid down thus: In every situation where a man undertakes to act or to pursue a particular course he is under an implied legal obligation or duty to act with reasonable care, to the end that the person or property of others may not be injured by any force which he sets in operation or by any agent for which he is responsible. If he fails to exercise the degree of caution which the law requires in a particular situation, he is held liable for any damage that results to another just as if he had bound himself by an obligatory promise to exercise the required degree of care. In this view, statements so frequently seen in negligence cases, to the effect that men are bound to act with due and reasonable care, are really vital and significant expressions. If there had been any remedial necessity for so declaring, it could obviously have been said without violence to the principle that men who undertake to act are subject to a fictitious or implied promise to act with due care." See also Howard *v.* Shepherd, (1850) 9 C. B. (67 Eng. Com. Law) 296, 321; Coy *v.* Indianapolis Gas Co., (1897) 146 Ind. 655, 36 L. R. A. 535; Parrill *v.* Cleveland, etc., R. Co., (1900) 23 Ind. App. 638; Rich *v.* New York, etc., R. Co., (1882) 87 N. Y. 382; Dean *v.* McLean, (1875) 48 Vt. 412, 21 Am. Rep. 130; Stock *v.* City of Boston, (1889) 149 Mass. 410, 21 N. E. 871, 14 Am. St. 430; Bickford *v.* Richards, (1891) 154 Mass. 163, 27 N. E. 1014, 26 Am. St. 224; Addison, Torts (3d ed.), p. 13; 1 Thompson, Negligence (2d ed.), § 5; 1 Shearman & Redfield, Negligence (5th ed.), §§ 9, 22; Saunders, Negligence, 55, 121; 6 Cyc. Law and Proc. 688.

The position in which appellant placed this large and heavy structure, located, as it was, upon the barn, some seventy feet above the earth, was such that it was calculated to do great harm to appellee's property should it fall. We cannot doubt, in view of the terms of the contract, construed in the light of the practical construction which the parties gave to it, to say nothing of the extraneous agreement set forth in the complaint, that it was the duty of appellant to exercise ordinary care to secure the tower in such a manner that this heavy and exposed structure would not, under the action of ordinary winds, weave around and become detached from the body of the air-shaft. Insecurely fastened, as the complaint shows that this structure was, appellant was bound to apprehend that it might fall, and that, if it did, great injury would thereby be occasioned to appellee. It was also bound to apprehend, from the very care and skill which it impliedly held itself out as exercising (a circumstance calculated to throw appellee off his guard), and from the fact that an examination was difficult, that in all probability the defects would not be observed in time to avoid the injury. Indeed, as laid down in Mowbray *v.* Merryweather, [1895] 2 Q. B. 640, and Devlin *v.* Smith, (1882) 89 N. Y. 470, 42 Am. Rep. 311, appellee owed no duty, so far as appellant was concerned, to examine the tower. The contrivance was inherently dangerous, and the circumstances of placing it upon the barn, as shown, made it calculated to eventuate in harm. This being true, and as there was no intervening responsible agency between appellee and the wrong, so that the causal relation remained unbroken, we can perceive no reason for acquitting appellant of responsibility as a tort feasor. See Wharton, Negligence (2d ed.), § 438; 1 Beven, Negligence (2d ed.), 62; Roddy *v.* Missouri Pac. R. Co., (1891) 104 Mo. 234, 15 S. W. 1112, 12 L. R. A. 746, 24 Am. St. 333. It is not necessary to consider the extent to which contracts may impose obligations to exercise care for the protection of third persons, for here the relation is direct and immediate, but we quote, as showing that there is clearly a liability in tort, in such a case as this, the following general statements in 1 Shearman & Redfield, Negligence (5th ed.), § 117, with reference to the liability for selling dangerous goods: "But one who knowingly sells an article intrinsically dangerous to human life or health, such as poison, explosive oils or diseased meat, concealing from the buyer knowledge of that fact, is responsible to any person who, without fault on the part of himself or any other person, sufficient to break the chain of causation, is injured thereby. And we see no reason why the same rule should not apply to articles known to be dangerous to property."

. . . .

A number of questions are argued by appellant's counsel which are based upon the contention that the theory of the complaint was that appellant had committed a breach of contract. The latter insistence is based on the fact that the contract is set out in full in the complaint. It is often difficult to determine whether, in the statement of such a cause of action as the one under consideration, wherein the very breach of the contract also constitutes negligence, the purpose of the pleader was to rely upon a breach of contract or to charge negligence in the violation of the implied duty which was created by the undertaking of the defendant. It is true that in an action on the case for negligence, wherein the declaration or complaint is not based on mere nonfeasance it is not necessary to plead a consideration, and, therefore, where the action is based on the manner in which an undertaking was performed, or, in other words, on some misfeasance or malfeasance, the allegation of a consideration may be regarded as one of the markings of an action *ex contractu.* But we do not understand that this is a controlling consideration; on the contrary, it does not appear to admit of question that if the contract or consideration be set out as a matter of inducement only, the plaintiff's action may be regarded as one in case for a violation of the common-law duty which the circumstances had imposed upon the defendant. 1 Chitty, Pleading, *135; Dickson *v.* Clifton, 2 Wils. 319; Watson, Damages for Per. Inj., § 570; 21 Ency. Pl. and Pr., 913. We are especially impressed with the view that in code pleading, which was designed preëminently to be a system of fact pleading, a plaintiff, in suing in tort, may properly set out his contract, as constituting the underlying fact, instead of charging the defendant's undertaking in general terms, and that the plaintiff does not thereby necessarily commit himself to the theory that his action is for breach of contract. Leeds *v.* City of Richmond, (1885) 102 Ind. 372; Parrill *v.* Cleveland, etc., R. Co., *supra;* McMurtry *v.* Kentucky Cent. R. Co., (1886) 84 Ky. 462, 1 S. W. 815; Watson, Damages for Per. Inj., § 570. In the complaint before us appellee not only sets out the written contract, but he pleads a supplemental or subsidiary agreement as well, so that it can hardly be said that he relied on the written contract as the foundation of the action. He charges no breach of the contract except as it can be implied from the allegations of negligence; he alleges damages "by reason of the defendant's negligence, carelessness, imprudence, and unskilfulness in erecting, constructing, and fastening said steel tower to said air-shaft as aforesaid;" he charges, in setting forth the total amount of his damages, that they were occasioned "by reason of the defendant's negligence and failure of duty as herein alleged," and he avers that he "had no notice or knowledge of the faulty, negligent, and unskilful erection of said mill," and that he himself was without fault or negligence in the premises. In view of the general structure of the complaint, and applying to it the rule that a construction of a pleading which will give effect to all of its material allegations is to be preferred, where reasonably possible (Monnett *v.* Turpie, [1892] 133 Ind. 424), it appears to us that it must be held that the action was for the tort. But, admitting that there is room for doubt on this subject, the fact that the court below, as the record plainly shows, tried the cause on the theory that it was an action *ex delicto,* must settle the question against the contention of appellant. Lake Erie, etc., R. Co. *v.* Acres, (1886) 108 Ind. 548; Diggs *v.* Way, (1899) 22 Ind. App. 617.

. . . .

Judgment affirmed.[1]

[1] Carpenter *v.* Walker, 170 Ala. 659; Miller *v.* Fletcher, 142 Ga. 668; Zabron *v.* Cunard Co., 151 Ia. 345; Randolph *v.* Snyder, 139 Ky. 159; Springfield Egg Co. *v.* Springfield Ice Co., 259 Mo. 664; Hales *v.* Raines, 146 Mo. App. 232, 239; Robinson *v.* Threadgill, 13 Ired. Law, 39; Hobbs *v.* Smith, 27 Okl. 830 *Accord.*

KELLY *v.* METROPOLITAN R. CO.

IN THE COURT OF APPEAL, APRIL 24, 1895.

Reported in [1895] 1 *Queen's Bench,* 944.

APPEAL from an order of a judge at chambers affirming an order of a master directing that the plaintiff's bill of costs should be referred back to be drawn on the county court scale.

The action was brought to recover damages for personal injuries to the plaintiff while a passenger on the defendants' railway. The statement of claim alleged an agreement by the defendants to carry the plaintiff safely, and a breach of that agreement in negligently and improperly managing the train in which he was, so that it ran into the wall at Baker Street Station, whereby the plaintiff sustained injury. It was admitted by the defendants that the accident occurred by the negligence of the engine-driver in not turning off steam in time to prevent the train running into the dead-end at the station. A sum of 20*l.* was paid into court, and the jury returned a verdict for the plaintiff for 25*l.*

When the plaintiff's costs were taken in to be taxed, the master was of opinion that, on the authority of Taylor *v.* Manchester, Sheffield, and Lincolnshire Ry. Co., [1895] 1 Q. B. 134, the act of the engine-driver being one of omission, the action was founded on contract, and that therefore the plaintiff was only entitled to costs on the county court scale. On appeal, this decision was affirmed by Day, J.

The plaintiff appealed.

Kemp, Q. C., and *Cagney*, for the plaintiff, submitted that the action was in fact an action of tort, and was tried as such, and that the plaintiff was entitled to costs on the High Court scale.

Lawson Walton, Q. C., and *George Elliott*, for the defendants. The duty of the defendants was contractual, and they were bound to take due care not to injure the plaintiff. The act which caused the injury was an omission to turn off steam, and amounted to a nonfeasance. It was not an act of commission or misfeasance, and the defendants were not liable in tort. The distinction is dealt with in the judgment of Lindley, L. J., and A. L. Smith, L. J., in Taylor *v.* Manchester, Sheffield, and Lincolnshire Ry. Co., [1895] 1 Q. B. 134, and the present case comes within that authority.

[They also cited Foulkes *v.* Metropolitan District Ry. Co., 4 C. P. D. 267; 5 C. P. D. 157.]

A. L. SMITH, L. J., read the following judgment:[1] There appears to have been some misapprehension as to what was decided in the case of Taylor *v.* Manchester, Sheffield, and Lincolnshire Ry. Co., [1895] 1 Q. B. 134, to which I was a party.

[1] The opinion of Lord Esher, M. R., is omitted.

The plaintiff in the present case was a passenger on the defendants' railway, and whilst lawfully riding in one of their carriages was injured by its being negligently run into a dead-end by the defendants' driver.

It has been thought by the master, and also by Day, J., that, because the negligence was that the driver omitted to turn off steam, this constituted a nonfeasance or omission within what was said in the above-mentioned case, and that as the plaintiff had recovered 25*l.* and no more he was only entitled to county court costs. I am clearly of opinion that this is not what was decided, nor is any such statement to be found in that judgment.

The distinction between acts of commission or misfeasance, and acts of omission or nonfeasance, does not depend on whether a driver or signalman of a defendant company has negligently turned on steam or negligently hoisted a signal, or whether he has negligently omitted to do the one or the other. The distinction is this, if the cause of complaint be for an act of omission or nonfeasance which without proof of a contract to do what has been left undone would not give rise to any cause of action (because no duty apart from contract to do what is complained of exists), then the action is founded upon contract and not upon tort. If, on the other hand, the relation of the plaintiff and the defendants be such that a duty arises from that relationship, irrespective of contract, to take due care, and the defendants are negligent, then the action is one of tort, and as regards the County Court Acts and costs this is what was laid down in the above-mentioned case. The appeal should be allowed with costs here and below.

Rigby, L. J. I entirely agree. It appears to me that the attempt to dissect the act of the defendants' servant, and to treat the mere omission to turn off steam as a nonfeasance within the meaning of the cases referred to, altogether fails. An engine-driver is in charge of the train, and a passenger is in that train, independently of contract, with the permission of the defendants. That passenger is injured in consequence of the train being negligently brought into collision with the dead-end. The proper description of what was done is that it was a negligent act in so managing the train as to allow it to come into contact with the dead-end and so cause the accident. It is a case in which the company by their servant neglected a duty which they owed to the plaintiff — that is to say, it was a case in which an action of tort could be brought. *Appeal allowed.*[1]

[1] The settled practice allows an action against a carrier either upon contract or upon tort, as best suits the purposes of the pleader. 3 Hutchinson, Carriers (3d ed.), § 1325.

SOUTHERN RAILWAY COMPANY *v.* GRIZZLE

SUPREME COURT, GEORGIA, JANUARY 13, 1906.

Reported in 124 *Georgia Reports*, 735.

ACTION by Mrs. Grizzle against the Southern Railway Company and T. A. O'Neal.

The petition alleged, in substance, that the petitioner's husband was killed by the negligence of the railway company, and of O'Neal, who was the engineer in charge of the train, while the train was being operated over a public-road crossing. It was alleged, *inter alia*, that no bell was rung nor whistle sounded, nor the speed of the train checked, and that the requirements of the blow-post law [1] were entirely disregarded by the engineer. To this petition O'Neal demurred on several grounds. The demurrer was overruled, and O'Neal excepted.[2]

COBB, P. J. 1. An agent is not ordinarily liable to third persons for mere nonfeasance. Kimbrough *v.* Boswell, 119 Ga. 210. An agent is, however, liable to third persons for misfeasance.[3] Nonfeasance is the total omission or failure of the agent to enter upon the performance of some distinct duty or undertaking which he has agreed with his principal to do. Misfeasance means the improper doing of an act which the agent might lawfully do; or, in other words, it is the performing of his duty to his principal in such a manner as to infringe upon the rights and privileges of third persons. Where an agent fails to use reasonable care or diligence in the performance of his duty, he will be personally responsible to a third person who is injured by such misfeasance. The agent's liability in such cases is not based upon the ground of his agency, but upon the ground that he is a wrong-doer, and as such he is responsible for any injury he may cause. When once he enters upon the performance of his contract with his principal, and in doing so omits, or fails to take reasonable care in the commission of, some act which he should do in its performance, whereby some third person is injured, he is responsible therefor to the same extent as if he had committed the wrong in his own behalf. See 2 Clark &

[1] Sect. 2222. "There must be fixed on the line of said roads, and at the distance of four hundred yards from the centre of each of such road crossings, and on each side thereof, a post, and the engineer shall be required, whenever he shall arrive at either of said posts, to blow the whistle of the locomotive until it arrives at the public road, and to simultaneously check and keep checking the speed thereof, so as to stop in time should any person or thing be crossing said track on said road."

Sect. 2224. "If any engineer neglects to blow said whistle as required, and to check the speed as required, he is guilty of a misdemeanor. . . ." — Georgia Code of 1895.

[2] Only so much of the case is given as relates to a single point. Statement abridged. Part of opinion omitted.

[3] But see Mayer *v.* Thompson, 104 Ala. 611; Carter *v.* Atlantic R. Co., 84 S. C. 456; Lough *v.* Davis, 30 Wash. 204.

Skyles on Agency, 1297 *et seq.* Misfeasance may involve also to some extent the idea of not doing; as where an agent engaged in the performance of his undertaking does not do something which it is his duty to do under the circumstances, or does not take that precaution or does not exercise that care which a due regard to the rights of others requires. All this is not doing, but it is not the not doing of that which is imposed upon the agent merely by virtue of his relation, but of that which is imposed upon him by law as a responsible individual in common with all other members of society. It is the same not doing which constitutes actionable negligence in any relation. Mechem on Ag. § 572. As was said by Gray, C. J., in Obsorne *v.* Morgan, 130 Mass. 102 (39 Am. Rep. 439): "If the agent once actually undertakes and enters upon the execution of a particular work, it is his duty to use reasonable care in the manner of executing it, so as not to cause any injury to third persons which may be the natural consequence of his acts; and he cannot, by abandoning its execution midway and leaving things in a dangerous condition, exempt himself from liability to any person who suffers injury by reason of his having so left them without proper safeguards. This is not nonfeasance or doing nothing, but it is misfeasance, doing improperly." In that case the agent was held liable by the fall of a tackle-block and chains from an iron rail suspended from the ceiling of a room, which fell for the reason that the agent had suffered them to remain in such a manner and so unprotected that they fell upon and injured the plaintiff. In Bell *v.* Josselyn, 3 Gray, 309 (63 Am. Dec. 742), Metcalf, J., said: "Assuming that he was a mere agent, yet the injury for which this action was brought was not caused by his nonfeasance, but by his misfeasance. Nonfeasance is the omission of an act which a person ought to do; misfeasance is the improper doing of an act which a person might lawfully do. . . . The defendant's omission to examine the state of the pipes, . . . before causing the water to be let on, was a nonfeasance. But if he had not caused the water to be let on, that nonfeasance would not have injured the plaintiff."

In the present case the failure of the engineer to comply with the requirements of the blow-post law was not doing, but the running of the train over the crossing at a high rate of speed without giving the signals required by law was a positive act, and the violation of a duty which both the engineer and the railroad company owed to travelers upon the highway. The engineer having once undertaken in behalf of the principal to run the train, it was incumbent upon him to run it in the manner prescribed by law; and a failure to comply with the law, although it involved an act of omission, was not an act of mere nonfeasance, but was an act of misfeasance. This view is strengthened by the fact that the blow-post law renders the engineer indictable for failure to comply with its provisions. The allegations of the petition were therefore sufficient to charge O'Neal with a positive tort, for which the plaintiff would be entitled to bring her action against him.[1]

BLACK *v*. NEW YORK, NEW HAVEN, AND HARTFORD R. CO.

SUPREME JUDICIAL COURT, MASSACHUSETTS, JANUARY 2, 1907.

Reported in 193 *Massachusetts Reports*, 448.

TORT for personal injuries alleged to have been caused by the negligence of the servants of the defendant on February 7, 1903, while the plaintiff was a passenger of the defendant. Writ dated March 20, 1903.

At the trial in the Superior Court, Wait, J., at the close of the plaintiff's evidence ordered a verdict for the defendant; and the plaintiff alleged exceptions. The material evidence is described or quoted in the opinion.

KNOWLTON, C. J. This action was brought to recover for an injury alleged to have been caused by the negligence of the defendant's servants. The plaintiff was a passenger on the defendant's train, which ran from Boston through Ashmont on the evening of February 7, 1903. He testified to having become so intoxicated that he had no recollection of anything that occurred after leaving a cigar store in Boston, until he awoke in the Boston City Hospital, about four o'clock the next day. One Thompson testified " that he took the 9.23 train on the evening of February 7, 1903, at the South Station in Boston for Ashmont, and occupied a seat near the rear of the last car of the train; that there were about twenty passengers in the car, and he noticed Black sitting in the seat opposite, very erect, with his eyes closed. When the conductor came through, Mr. Black went through his pockets as if he were looking for a ticket, and not being able to find it, tendered a fifty-cent piece in payment for his fare. The conductor began to name off the stations from Field's Corner first and then Ashmont and when he said ' Ashmont,' Mr. Black nodded his head. The conductor gave him his change and his rebate check. At Ashmont, where the train stops, there is a gravelled walk, running the whole length, as a platform, then there is a flight of steps, ten or twelve, that leads up to the asphalt walk around the station, so when you go up from the steps you have to walk along this walk. The

[1] Stiewel *v*. Borman, 63 Ark. 30; Owens *v*. Nichols, 139 Ga. 475; Baird *v*. Shipman, 132 Ill. 16; Tippecanoe Loan & Trust Co. *v*. Jester, 180 Ind. 357; Ward *v*. Pullman Co., 131 Ky. 142; Consolidated Gas Co. *v*. Connor, 114 Md. 140; Ellis *v*. McNaughton, 76 Mich. 237; Orcutt *v*. Century Bldg. Co., 201 Mo. 424; Hagerty *v*. Montana Ore Co., 38 Mont. 69; Horner *v*. Lawrence, 37 N. J. Law, 46; Schlosser *v*. Great Northern R. Co., 20 N. D. 406, 411; Greenberg *v*. Whitcomb, 90 Wis. 225 *Accord*.

conductor and brakeman took Black out of the car, with one on each side. The distance from the steps of the car to the steps that lead up to the station was twenty-five feet. As they went along the platform, the conductor and trainman were on each side of him. They tried to stand him up, but his legs would sink away from him. They sort of helped him up and carried him to the bottom of the steps. When they went to the bottom of the steps, they continued, one on each side of him. Then one of the men got on one side with his arm around him and the other back of him sort of pushing him, and they took him up about the fifth or sixth step, and after they got him up there, they turned right around and left him and went down the steps. Mr. Black sort of balanced himself there just a minute and then fell completely backward. He turned a complete somersault and struck on the back of his head. The railroad men just had time to get down to the foot of the steps. There was a railing that led up those steps and the steps were about ten feet wide. Mr. Black was upon the right-hand side going up and he was left right near the railing. When he fell, he did not seize hold of anything, his arms were at his side."

On this testimony the jury might find that the plaintiff was so intoxicated as to be incapable of standing, or walking, or caring for himself in any way, and that the defendant's servants, knowing his condition, left him halfway up the steps where they knew, or ought to have known, that he was in great danger of falling and being seriously injured. They were under no obligation to remove him from the car, or to provide for his safety after he left the car. But they voluntarily undertook to help him from the car, and they were bound to use ordinary care in what they did that might affect his safety. Not only in the act of removal, but in the place where they left him, it was their duty to have reasonable regard for his safety in view of his manifest condition. The jury might have found that they were negligent in leaving him on the steps, where a fall would be likely to do him much harm. Moody *v.* Boston & Maine Railroad, 189 Mass. 277.

The defence rests principally upon the fact that the plaintiff was intoxicated, and was incapable of caring for himself after he was taken from the train, and therefore was not in the exercise of due care. If his voluntary intoxication was a direct and proximate cause of the injury, he cannot recover. The plaintiff contends that it was not a cause, but a mere condition, well known to the defendant's servants, and that their act was the direct and proximate cause of the injury, with which no other act or omission had any causal connection. The distinction here referred to is well recognized in law. . . .

We are of opinion that the jury in the present case might have found that the plaintiff was free from any negligence that was a direct and proximate cause of the injury. *Exceptions sustained.*[1]

[1] Northern R. Co. *v.* State, 29 Md. 420; Dyche *v.* Vicksburg R. Co., 79 Miss. 361; Bresnahan *v.* Lonsdale Co., (R. I. 1900) 51 Atl. 624 *Accord.*

UNION PACIFIC RAILWAY COMPANY *v.* CAPPIER

SUPREME COURT, KANSAS, APRIL 11, 1903.

Reported in 66 *Kansas Reports*, 649.

ERROR from Wyandotte District Court.

SMITH, J. This was an action brought by Adeline Cappier, the mother of Irvin Ezelle, to recover damages resulting to her by reason of the loss of her son, who was run over by a car of plaintiff in error, and died from the injuries received. The trial court, at the close of the evidence introduced to support a recovery by plaintiff below, held that no careless act of the railway company's servants in the operation of the car was shown, and refused to permit the case to be considered by the jury on the allegations and attempted proof of such negligence. The petition, however, contained an averment that the injured person had one leg and an arm cut off by the car-wheels, and that the servants of the railway company failed to call a surgeon, or to render him any assistance after the accident, but permitted him to remain by the side of the tracks and bleed to death. Under this charge of negligence a recovery was had.

While attempting to cross the railway tracks Ezelle was struck by a moving freight-car pushed by an engine. A yardmaster in charge of the switching operations was riding on the end of the car nearest to the deceased and gave warning by shouting to him. The warning was either too late or no heed was given to it. The engine was stopped. After the injured man was clear of the track, the yardmaster signalled the engineer to move ahead, fearing, as he testified, that a passenger train then about due would come upon them. The locomotive and car went forward over a bridge, where the general yardmaster was informed of the accident and an ambulance was summoned by telephone. The yardmaster then went back where the injured man was lying and found three Union Pacific switchmen binding up the wounded limbs and doing what they could to stop the flow of blood. The ambulance arrived about thirty minutes later and Ezelle was taken to a hospital, where he died a few hours afterward.

In answer to particular questions of fact, the jury found that the accident occurred at 5.35 P.M.; that immediately one of the railway employees telephoned to police headquarters for help for the injured man; that the ambulance started at 6.05 P. M. and reached the nearest hospital with Ezelle at 6.20 P.M., where he received proper medical and surgical treatment. Judgment against the railway company was based on the following question and answer: —

"Ques. Did not defendant's employees bind up Ezelle's wounds and try to stop the flow of blood as soon as they could after the accident happened? Ans. No."

See also Willes, J., in Skelton *v.* London R. Co., L. R. 2 C. P. 631, 636; Bailey *v.* Walker, 29 Mo. 407; Thorne *v.* Deas, 4 Johns. 84, 96; Hyde *v.* Moffat, 16 Vt. 271.

The lack of diligence in the respect stated was intended, no doubt, to apply to the yardmaster, engineer, and fireman in charge of the car and engine.

These facts bring us to a consideration of the legal duty of these employees toward the injured man after his condition became known. Counsel for defendant in error quotes the language found in Beach on Contributory Negligence (3d ed.), § 215, as follows: —

"Under certain circumstances, the railroad may owe a duty to a trespasser after the injury. When a trespasser has been run down, it is the plain duty of the railway company to render whatever service is possible to mitigate the severity of the injury. The train that has occasioned the harm must be stopped, and the injured person looked after; and, when it seems necessary, removed to a place of safety, and carefully nursed, until other relief can be brought to the disabled person."

The principal authority cited in support of this doctrine is Northen Central Railway Co. *v.* The State, use of Price et al, 29 Md. 420, [illegible] Am. Dec. 545. The court in that case first held that there was evidence enough to justify the jury in finding that the operatives of the train were negligent in running it too fast over a road-crossing without sounding the whistle, and that the number of brakemen was insufficient to check its speed. Such negligence was held sufficient to uphold the verdict, and would seem to be all that was necessary to be said. The court, however, proceeded to state that, from whatever cause the collision occurred, it was the duty of the servants of the company, when the man was found on the pilot of the engine in a helpless and insensible condition, to remove him, and to do it with proper regard to his safety and the laws of humanity. In that case the injured person was taken in charge by the servants of the railway company and, being apparently dead, without notice to his family, or sending for a physician to ascertain his condition, he was moved to defendant's warehouse, laid on a plank and locked up for the night. The next morning, when the warehouse was opened, it was found that during the night the man had revived from his stunned condition and moved some paces from the spot where he had been laid, and was found in a stooping posture, dead but still warm, having died from hemorrhage of the arteries of one leg, which was crushed at and above the knee. It had been proposed to place him in the defendant's station-house, which was a comfortable building, but the telegraph operator objected, and directed him to be taken into the warehouse, a place used for the deposit of old barrels and other rubbish.

The Maryland case does not support what is so broadly stated in Beach on Contributory Negligence. It is cited by Judge Cooley, in his work on Torts, in a note to a chapter devoted to the negligence of bailees (ch. xx.), indicating that the learned author understood the reasoning of the decision to apply where the duty began after the railway employees had taken charge of the injured person.

After the trespasser on the track of a railway company has been injured in collision with a train, and the servants of the company have assumed to take charge of him, the duty arises to exercise such care in his treatment as the circumstances will allow. We are unable, however, to approve the doctrine that when the acts of a trespasser himself result in his injury, where his own negligent conduct is alone the cause, those in charge of the instrument which inflicted the hurt, being innocent of wrong-doing, are nevertheless blamable in law if they neglect to administer to the sufferings of him whose wounds we might say were self-imposed. With the humane side of the question courts are not concerned. It is the omission or negligent discharge of legal duties only which come within the sphere of judicial cognizance. For withholding relief from the suffering, for failing to respond to the calls of worthy charity, or for faltering in the bestowment of brotherly love on the unfortunate, penalties are found not in the laws of men, but in that higher law, the violation of which is condemned by the voice of conscience, whose sentence of punishment for the recreant act is swift and sure. In the law of contracts it is now well understood that a promise founded on a moral obligation will not be enforced in the courts. Bishop states that some of the older authorities recognize a moral obligation as valid, and says: —

"Such a doctrine, carried to its legitimate results, would release the tribunals from the duty to administer the law of the land; and put, in the place of law, the varying ideas of morals which the changing incumbents of the bench might from time to time entertain." (Bish. Cont. § 44.)

Ezelle's injuries were inflicted, as the court below held, without the fault of the yardmaster, engineer, or fireman in charge of the car and locomotive. The railway company was no more responsible than it would have been had the deceased been run down by the cars of another railroad company on a track parallel with that of plaintiff in error. If no duty was imposed on the servants of defendant below to take charge of, and care for, the wounded man in such a case, how could a duty arise under the circumstances of the case at bar? In Barrows on Negligence, page 4, it is said: —

"The duty must be owing from the defendant to the plaintiff, otherwise there can be no negligence, so far as the plaintiff is concerned; . . . and the duty must be owing to plaintiff in an individual capacity, and not merely as one of the general public.

"This excludes from actionable negligence all failures to observe the obligations imposed by charity, gratitude, generosity, and the kindred virtues. The moral law would obligate an attempt to rescue a person in a perilous position, — as a drowning child, — but the law of the land does not require it, no matter how little personal risk it might involve, provided that the person who declines to act is not responsible for the peril." (See, also, Kenney *v.* The Hannibal & St. Joseph Railroad Company, 70 Mo. 252, 257.)

In the several cases cited in the brief of counsel for defendant in error to sustain the judgment of the trial court, it will be found that the negligence on which recoveries were based occurred after the time when the person injured was in the custody and care of those who were at fault in failing to give him proper treatment.

The judgment of the court below will be reversed, with directions to enter judgment on the findings of the jury in favor of the railway company.

All the justices concurring.[1]

HUNICKE *v.* MERAMEC QUARRY COMPANY

SUPREME COURT OF MISSOURI, DECEMBER 19, 1914.

Reported in 262 *Missouri Reports*, 560.

WOODSON, P. J. . . . I do not understand counsel for plaintiff to make the broad claim that, in the absence of the question of *emergency*, presented in this case, it would have been the duty of the defendant to have furnished medical or surgical treatment for the injured man, upon the occasion mentioned; but I do understand counsel to contend, and which I believe is the law, that when an employee is engaged in any dangerous business for the master, and while in the performance of his duties, as such, he is so badly injured that he is thereby rendered physically or mentally incapable of procuring medical assistance for himself, then that duty, as a matter of law, is devolved upon the master, and that he must perform that duty with reasonable diligence and in a reasonable manner, through the agency of such of his employees as may be present at the time.

In other words, without trying to state the law in detail governing the master's duties in all cases of this character, that duty is put in operation whenever, under the facts and circumstances of the case, the employee is thereby so injured that he or she is incapacitated from caring for himself or herself, as the case may be.

The uncontradicted evidence in this case shows that the deceased was so badly injured that he was physically incapacitated to care for himself or to engage medical or surgical treatment; also, that the character of his injuries was such as required immediate surgical attention, for it was apparent to all present that his leg was frightfully crushed, and that his life's blood was freely flowing from his body. So obvious was this that several of those present, at the time of the

[1] Allen *v.* Hixson, 111 Ga. 460; Griswold *v.* Boston R. Co., 183 Mass. 434; Stager *v.* Laundry Co., 38 Or. 480, 489; Scholl *v.* Belcher, 63 Or. 310; Ollett *v.* Pennsylvania R. Co., 201 Pa. St. 361; King *v.* Interstate R. Co., 23 R. I. 583; Riley *v.* Gulf R. Co., (Tex. Civ. App.) 16 S. W. 595 *Accord.* See also Kenney *v.* Hannibal R. Co., 70 Mo. 252.

Whitesides *v.* Southern R. Co., 128 N. C. 229 (divided court) *contra.* See also Dyche *v.* Vicksburg R. Co., 79 Miss. 361.

accident, tried by their crude methods, to stop its flow. But the highest officer of the company present, the superintendent, thought none of their remedies were worthy of trial and told them their proposed treatment would do no good. He then telephoned to Dr. Kirk, at Kimswick, the condition of the injured man, Hunicke, and requested him to come to Wicks and treat the injured man; but the doctor being previously engaged in a serious case, could not leave it. The doctor, however, telephoned the superintendent to bring the injured party to Kimswick, some two miles distant, and that he would there treat him.

The evidence shows that both Wicks and Kimswick were on the railroad and that a hand-car was present which could have been used in conveying Hunicke from the former to the latter place for treatment.

For some reason not made clear, the superintendent declined to take the injured man to Kimswick for treatment, but telephoned the facts of the injury to the manager of the company at St. Louis, some twelve or fourteen miles distant, who telephoned back to the superintendent to place the injured man on the next train and send him to St. Louis. This was done; and some three or four hours later, the train arrived in the city; and upon the arrival of the train Hunicke was speedily taken to the hospital where his limb was amputated; but in the meantime practically all of the blood of his body had flowed therefrom, and he died shortly thereafter.

In the statement of the case we have set out much of the evidence tending to show the negligence of the defendant in not procuring surgical treatment for Hunicke more promptly, and that he would not have died had he received prompt treatment. That evidence tended to show that Kimswick was only two miles distant from the place of injury and that the injured man could have been taken there on a hand-car in a very *few* minutes, probably from fifteen to twenty, at the outside. Had this been done, in all probability the flow of blood would have been stanched several hours before it was finally stopped in the city of St. Louis.

It is true that there was some evidence which tended to show that such a trip on a hand-car would have been rough and jolting, and thereby might have aggravated the flow of the blood, but conceding that to be true, it could not have caused more waste of blood than did the constant flow during the hours that passed while he was waiting for the train and being conveyed to the city of St. Louis thereon. And it seems to me that common sense would teach us that a trip on a hand-car to Kimswick would not have caused the blood to flow more freely than the trip on the train to St. Louis, six or seven times as far, would have done.

But be that as it may, when we consider those facts in connection with all the other facts and circumstances shown by the evidence, we have reached the conclusion that this, as well as the question of negligence in delaying the procurement of a surgeon, was for the jury, and that the evidence introduced was sufficient to make out a *prima facie* case for the plaintiff.

In other words, we are of the opinion that the evidence tended to show that the company was guilty of negligence in not using more diligence in procuring medical and surgical treatment for this party; also that it tended to show that said negligence was the proximate cause of his death.

. . . .

In my opinion there is no possibility of doubt but what the law is that, whenever one person employs another to perform dangerous work, and while performing that work he is so badly injured as to incapacitate him from caring for himself, then the duty of providing medical treatment for him is devolved upon the employer; and that duty in my opinion, grows out of the fact that when we get down to the real facts in all such cases, there is an unexpressed humane and natural understanding existing between them to the effect that whenever any one in such a case is so injured that he cannot care for himself, then the employer will furnish him medical or surgical treatment as the case may be.

This is common knowledge. There is not an industrial institution in this country, great or small, where that practice is not being carried on today; and that has been the custom and usage among men from the dawn of civilization down to the present day, and will continue to be practised in the future, just so long as the human heart beats in sympathy for the unfortunate, and desires to aid suffering humanity. The same principle underlies all other avocations of life. Even armies while engaged in actual warfare observe and obey this rule when possible. The soldier who refuses to render surgical or medical aid to the victim of his own sword, is eschewed by all decent men; while upon the other hand, all who administer to the wants and necessities of the sick and wounded are considered as God's noblemen and as princes among men. So universally true and deep-seated is this humane feeling among men, and so universally recognized and practised among them, that it has become a world-wide rule of moral conduct among men, brothers, friends and foes; and it says to one and all, You must exercise all reasonable efforts and means at hand to alleviate the pain and suffering and save the lives and limbs of those who have been stricken in your presence. For the violation of this rule of moral conduct there is no penalty attached save the condemnation of God and the scorn of all good men and women.

But seeing the wisdom, goodness and justice of this moral law, the law of the land laid its strong hand upon it, the same as it did upon many other good and useful customs of England, and breathed into it a living rule of legal conduct among men. It says unto all who employ labor that, because of this universally practised custom of men to furnish medical and surgical aid for those who are stricken in their presence, you must furnish the employee with such services when he is so badly injured that he is incapacitated from caring for himself.

This is but the application or extension of the common-law rule which requires the master to furnish his servant with a safe place in which to work, and safe instrumentalities with which to perform that labor.

That law grew out of the old customs and usages of the English people, of furnishing their servants with a safe place in which to work and safe instrumentalities with which to labor. So universally true was that custom that the law read into all contracts of labor an implied promise on the part of the master to furnish those safeguards to his servants. There is no statutory or written law upon the subject. It is simply what is called the unwritten or common law of England, which has been adopted by statutes in this and many other States of the Union.

So in like manner into the universal custom of employers furnishing his employees with medical aid when so badly injured that they could not care for themselves, the common law, as in the cases of the safety appliances before mentioned, breathed an implied agreement or duty on the part of the former to furnish the latter medical or surgical aid whenever he was so badly injured that he could not care for himself.

This law, like the one previously mentioned, has no statutory origin, but has ripened into a law from wise and humane usages and customs that are so old that the memory of man runneth not to the contrary, and will continue so long as the conduct of man is prompted and governed by love and humane sentiments.

As previously stated, I am firmly of the opinion that the petition stated a good cause of action against the defendant, and that the evidence was sufficient to make a case for the jury; and so believing, I think the action of the trial court in granting a new trial to the plaintiff for the first and second reasons assigned by counsel for defendant, was not erroneous, but proper.[1]

DEPUE *v.* FLATAU

SUPREME COURT, MINNESOTA, MARCH 15, 1907.

Reported in 100 *Minnesota Reports*, 299.

ACTION in the District Court for Watonwan County to recover $5000 for personal injuries. The case was tried before Lorin Cray, J., who, at the conclusion of plaintiff's testimony, dismissed the action.

[1] Ohio R. Co. *v.* Early, 141 Ind. 73; Raasch *v.* Elite Laundry Co., 98 Minn. 357 (*semble*); Salter *v.* Nebraska Telephone Co., 79 Neb. 373 (*semble*) *Accord.* See also Shaw *v.* Milwaukee R. Co., 103 Minn. 8.

It has been held also that such a duty is incidental to the relation of carrier and

From an order denying a motion for a new trial, plaintiff appealed. Reversed.

BROWN, J. The facts in this somewhat unusual case are as follows: Plaintiff was a cattle buyer, and accustomed to drive through the country in the pursuit of his business, buying cattle, hides, and furs from the farmers. On the evening of January 23, 1905, about five or 5.30 o'clock, after having been out a day or two in the country, he called at the house of defendants, about seven miles from Madelia, where he resided. His object was to inspect some cattle which Flatau, Sr., had for sale, and if arrangements could be made to purchase the same. It was dark at the time of his arrival, but he inspected the cattle in the barn, and suggested to defendant that, being unable to determine their value by reason of the darkness, he was not prepared to make an offer for the cattle, and requested the privilege of remaining over night, to the end that a bargain might be made understandingly in the morning. His request was not granted. Plaintiff then bought some furs from other members of defendants' family, and Flatau, Sr., invited him to remain for supper. Under this invitation plaintiff entered the house, paid for the furs, and was given supper with the family. After the evening meal, plaintiff and both defendants repaired to the sitting-room of the house, and plaintiff made preparation to depart for his home. His team had not been unhitched from the cutter, but was tied to a hitching post near the house. The testimony from this point leaves the facts in some doubt. Plaintiff testified that soon after reaching the sitting-room he was taken with a fainting spell and fell to the floor. He remembers very little of what occurred after that, though he does recall that, after fainting, he again requested permission to remain at defendants' over night, and that his request was refused. Defendants both deny that this request was made, and testified, when called for cross-examination on the trial, that plaintiff put on his overshoes and buffalo coat unaided, and that, while adjusting a shawl about his neck, he stumbled against a partition between the dining-room and the sitting-room, but that he did not fall to the floor. Defendant Flatau, Jr., assisted him in arranging his shawl, and the evidence tends to show that he conducted him from the house out of doors and assisted him into his cutter, adjusting the robes about him and attending to other details preparatory to starting the team on its journey. Though the evidence is somewhat in doubt as to the cause of plaintiff's condition while in defendants' home, it is clear that he was seriously ill and too weak to take care of himself. He was in this condition when Flatau, Jr., assisted him into the cutter. He was unable to hold the reins to guide his team,

passenger. Layne v. Chicago R. Co., 175 Mo. App. 35, 41. Compare Kambour v. Boston R. Co., 77 N. H. 33; Southern R. Co. v. Sewell, 18 Ga. App. 544.

It has always been regarded as incidental to the employment of seamen. The Iroquois, 194 U. S. 240; U. S. v. Knowles, 4 Sawy. 517; Scarff v. Metcalf, 107 N. Y. 211.

and young Flatau threw them over his shoulders and started the team towards home, going a short distance, as he testified, for the purpose of seeing that the horses took the right road to Madelia. Plaintiff was found early next morning by the roadside, about three quarters of a mile from defendants' home, nearly frozen to death. He had been taken with another fainting spell soon after leaving defendants' premises, and had fallen from his cutter, where he remained the entire night. He was discovered by a passing farmer, taken to his home, and revived. The result of his experience necessitated the amputation of several of his fingers, and he was otherwise physically injured and his health impaired. Plaintiff thereafter brought this action against defendants, father and son, on the theory that his injuries were occasioned solely by their negligent and wrongful conduct in refusing him accommodations for the night, and, knowing his weak physical condition, or at least having reasonable grounds for knowing it, by reason of which he was unable to care for himself, in sending him out unattended to make his way to Madelia the best he could. At the conclusion of plaintiff's case, the trial court dismissed the action, on the ground that the evidence was insufficient to justify a recovery. Plaintiff appealed from an order denying a new trial.

Two questions are presented for consideration: (1) Whether, under the facts stated, defendants owed any duty to plaintiff which they negligently violated; and (2) whether the evidence is sufficient to take the case to the jury upon the question whether defendants knew, or under the circumstances disclosed ought to have known, of his weak physical condition, and that it would endanger his life to send him home unattended.

The case is an unusual one on its facts, and " all-four " precedents are difficult to find in the books. In fact, after considerable research, we have found no case whose facts are identical with those at bar. It is insisted by defendants that they owed plaintiff no duty to entertain him during the night in question, and were not guilty of any negligent misconduct in refusing him accommodations, or in sending him home under the circumstances disclosed. Reliance is had for support of this contention upon the general rule as stated in note to Union Pacific *v.* Cappier, [66 Kan. 649, 72 Pac. 281] 69 L. R. A. 513, where it is said: " Those duties which are dictated merely by good morals or by humane considerations are not within the domain of the law. Feelings of kindliness and sympathy may move the Good Samaritan to minister to the needs of the sick and wounded at the roadside, but the law imposes no such obligation; and suffering humanity has no legal complaint against those who pass by on the other side. . . . Unless, therefore, the relation existing between the sick, helpless, or injured and those who witness their distress is such that the law imposes the duty of providing the necessary relief, there is neither obligation to minister on the one hand, nor cause for legal complaint on the other." This is no doubt a correct statement of the general rule applicable to the Good Samaritan, but it by no means controls a case like that at bar.

The facts of this case bring it within the more comprehensive principle that whenever a person is placed in such a position with regard to another that it is obvious that, if he does not use due care in his own conduct, he will cause injury to that person, the duty at once arises to exercise care commensurate with the situation in which he thus finds himself, and with which he is confronted, to avoid such danger; and a negligent failure to perform the duty renders him liable for the consequences of his neglect.

This principle applies to varied situations arising from non-contract relations. It protects the trespasser from wanton or wilful injury. Its extends to the licensee, and requires the exercise of reasonable care to avoid an unnecessary injury to him. It imposes upon the owner of premises, which he expressly or impliedly invites persons to visit, whether for the transaction of business or otherwise, the obligation to keep the same in reasonably safe condition for use, though it does not embrace those sentimental or social duties often prompting human action. 21 Am. & Eng. Enc. (2d ed.) 471; Barrows, Neg. 3. Those entering the premises of another by invitation are entitled to a higher degree of care than those who are present by mere sufferance. Barrows, Neg. 304. The rule stated is supported by a long list of authorities both in England and this country, and is expressed in the familiar maxim, "*Sic utere tuo*," etc. They will be found collected in the works above cited, and also in 1 Thompson, Neg. (2d ed.), § 694. It is thus stated in Heaven *v.* Pender, L. R. 11 Q. B. Div. 503: "The proposition which these recognized cases suggest, and which is, therefore, to be deduced from them, is that, whenever one person is by circumstances placed in such a position with regard to another that every one of ordinary sense who did think would at once recognize that if he did not use ordinary care and skill in his own conduct with regard to those circumstances he would cause danger of injury to the person or property of the other, a duty arises to use ordinary care and skill to avoid such danger." It applies with greater strictness to conduct towards persons under disability, and imposes the obligation as a matter of law, not mere sentiment, at least to refrain from any affirmative action that might result in injury to them. A valuable note to Union Pacific *v.* Cappier, 69 L. R. A. 513, discusses at length the character of the duty and obligation of those coming into relation with sick and disabled persons, and numerous analogous cases are collected and analyzed.

In the case at bar defendants were under no contract obligation to minister to plaintiff in his distress; but humanity demanded that they do so, if they understood and appreciated his condition. And, though those acts which humanity demands are not always legal obligations, the rule to which we have adverted applied to the relation existing between these parties on this occasion and protected plaintiff from acts at their hands that would expose him to personal harm. He was not a trespasser upon their premises, but, on the contrary, was there by the express invitation of Flatau, Sr. He was taken suddenly ill while their guest, and the law, as well as humanity, required that he be not exposed in his helpless condition to the merciless elements.

The case, in its substantial facts, is not unlike that of Cincinnati *v.* Marrs' Adm'x, 27 Ky. Law, 388, 85 S. W. 188, 70 L. R. A. 291. In that case it appears that one Marrs was found asleep in the yards of the railway company in an intoxicated condition. The yard employees discovered him, aroused him from his stupor, and ordered him off the tracks. They knew that he was intoxicated, and that he had left a train recently arrived at the station, and he appeared to them dazed and lost. About forty minutes later, while the yard employees were engaged in switching, they ran over him and killed him. He had again fallen asleep on one of the tracks. The court held the railway company liable; that, under the circumstances disclosed, it was the duty of the yard employees to see that Marrs was safely out of the yards, or, in default of that, to exercise ordinary care to avoid injuring him; and that it was reasonable to require them to anticipate his probable continued presence in the yards. The case at bar is much stronger, for here plaintiff was not intoxicated, nor a trespasser, but, on the contrary, was in defendants' house as their guest, and was there taken suddenly ill in their presence, and, if his physical condition was known and appreciated, they must have known that to compel him to leave their home unattended would expose him to serious danger.

We understand from the record that the learned trial court held in harmony with the view of the law here expressed, but dismissed the action for the reason, as stated in the memorandum denying a new trial, that there was no evidence that either of the defendants knew, or in the exercise of ordinary care should have known, plaintiff's physical condition, or that allowing him to proceed on his journey would expose him to danger. Of course, to make the act of defendants a violation of their duty in the premises, it should appear that they knew and appreciated his serious condition. The evidence on this feature of the case is not so clear as might be desired, but a majority of the court are of opinion that it is sufficient to charge both defendants with knowledge of plaintiff's condition — at least, that the question should have been submitted to the jury.

Defendant Flatau, Sr., testified that he was in the room at all times while plaintiff was in the house and observed his demeanor, and, though he denied that plaintiff fell to the floor in a faint or otherwise, yet the fact that plaintiff was seriously ill cannot be questioned.

Flatau, Jr., conducted him to his cutter, assisted him in, observed that he was incapable of holding the reins to guide his team, and for that reason threw them over his shoulders. If defendants knew and appreciated his condition, their act in sending him out to make his way to Madelia the best he could was wrongful and rendered them liable in damages. We do not wish to be understood as holding that defendants were under absolute duty to entertain plaintiff during the night. Whether they could conveniently do so does not appear. What they should or could have done in the premises can only be determined from a full view of the evidence disclosing their situation, and their facilities for communicating his condition to his friends, or near neighbors, if any there were. All these facts will enable the jury to determine whether, within the rules of negligence applicable to the case, defendants neglected any duty they owed plaintiff.

Order reversed.[1]

DUTCH PENAL CODE, ART. 450. One who, witnessing the danger of death with which another is suddenly threatened, neglects to give or furnish him such assistance as he can give or procure without reasonable fear of danger to himself or to others, is to be punished, if the death of the person in distress follows, by a detention of three months at most and an amende of three hundred florins at most.

GERMAN CIVIL CODE, SECTION 826. One who wilfully brings about damage to another in a manner running counter to good morals is bound to make reparation to the other for the damage.

STAMMLER, LEHRE VON DEM RICHTIGEN RECHTE, 489–490. " I am walking along the bank of a river," says Liszt in his stimulating discussion of this subject, " and I see a man fall in the water and struggle with the waves. I am able to rescue him without any peril to myself; I neglect to do so although other help is not at hand and I foresee that he must drown. In my opinion, liability under section 826 cannot be denied." [Liszt, Die Deliktsobligationen des B. G. B., 72.] Surely not.

PLANCK, BÜRGERLICHES GESETZBUCH (3d ed.), II, 995 (§ 826, note *e*). The duty to make reparation for damage under section 826 may also be grounded upon an omission. But it is presupposed that the act which was omitted must be regarded, under the circumstances of the case, as commanded by good morals and that the omission took place with the purpose of bringing about injury to the other. If one holds fast to this, the consequences which result from the foregoing principle are not as doubtful as Liszt (p. 72) seems to assume.

BENTHAM, COMPLETE WORKS (Bowring's ed.) I, 164.

There is simple corporal injury, when, without lawful cause, an individual, seeing another in danger, abstains from helping him, and the evil happens in consequence.

[1] See also Weymire *v.* Wolfe, 52 Ia. 533; Trout *v.* Watkins, 148 Mo. App. 621. Compare Texas R. Co. *v.* Geraldon, 54 Tex. Civ. App. 71.

On the whole subject, see Ames, Law and Morals, 22 Harvard Law Rev. 99, 111–113; Bohlen, The Moral Duty to Aid Others as a Basis of Tort Liability, 56 University of Pennsylvania Law Rev. 217, 316; Bruce, Humanity and the Law, 73 Central Law Journ. 335.

Explanations: — *Abstains from helping him.*

Every man is bound to assist those who have need of assistance, if he can do it without exposing himself to sensible inconvenience. This obligation is stronger in proportion as the danger is the greater for the one, and the trouble of preserving him the less for the other. Such would be the case of a man sleeping near the fire, and an individual seeing the clothes of the first catch fire, and doing nothing towards extinguishing them: the crime would be greater if he refrained from acting not simply from idleness, but from malice or some pecuniary interest.

BENTHAM, PRINCIPLES OF MORALS AND LEGISLATION, chap. xix, sec. 1, Par. xix (Clarendon Press reprint, pp. 322–323).

As to the rules of beneficence, these, as far as concerns matters of detail, must necessarily be abandoned in great measure to the jurisdiction of private ethics. . . .

The limits of the law on this head seem, however, to be capable of being extended a good deal farther than they seem ever to have been extended hitherto. In particular, in cases where the person is in danger, why should it not be made the duty of every man to save another from mischief, when it can be done without prejudicing himself, as well as to abstain from bringing it on him. This accordingly is the idea pursued in the body of the work.[1]

BENTHAM, THEORY OF LEGISLATION, transl. by Hildreth (5th ed.), pp. 65–66.

As to beneficence, some distinctions are necessary. The law may be extended to general objects, such as the care of the poor; but, for details, it is necessary to depend upon private morality. . . .

However, instead of having done too much in this respect, legislators have not done enough. They ought to erect into an offence the refusal or the omission of a service of humanity when it would be easy to render it, and when some distinct ill clearly results from the refusal; such, for example, as abandoning a wounded man in a solitary road without seeking any assistance for him; not giving information to a man who is negligently meddling with poisons; not reaching out the hand to one who has fallen into a ditch from which he cannot extricate himself; in these, and other similar cases, could any fault be found with a punishment, exposing the delinquent to a certain degree of shame, or subjecting him to a pecuniary responsibility for the evil which he might have prevented?

LIVINGSTON, DRAFT CODE OF CRIMES AND PUNISHMENTS FOR THE STATE OF LOUISIANA. Livingston, Complete Works on Criminal Jurisprudence, II, 126–127.

Article 484. Homicide by omission only, is committed by voluntarily permitting another to do an act that must, in the natural course of things, cause his death, without apprising him of his danger, if the act be involuntary, or endeavoring to prevent it if it be voluntary. He shall be presumed to have permitted it voluntarily who omits the necessary means of preventing the death, when he knows the danger, and can cause it to be avoided, without dan-

[1] A woman's head-dress catches fire: water is at hand: a man, instead of assisting to quench the fire, looks on and laughs at it. A drunken man, falling with his face downwards into a puddle, is in danger of suffocation: lifting his head a little on one side would save him: another man sees this and lets him lie. A quantity of gunpowder lies scattered about a room: a man is going into it with a lighted candle: another, knowing this, lets him go in without warning. Who is there that in any of these cases would think punishment misapplied? — Author's Note.

ger of personal injury or pecuniary loss. This rule may be illustrated by the examples put in the last preceding article: if the blind man is seen walking to the precipice by one who knows the danger, can easily apprise him of it, but does not; or if one who knows that a glass contains poison, sees him about to drink it, either by mistake or with intent to destroy himself, and makes no attempt to prevent him: in these cases the omission amounts to homicide.[1]

MACAULAY, NOTES TO DRAFT OF INDIAN PENAL CODE. Penal Code Prepared by the Indian Law Commissioners.[2] Chapter xviii [page 76]. Of Offences Affecting the Human Body. Of Offences Affecting Life.

294. Whoever does any act or omits what he is legally bound to do, with the intention of thereby causing, or with the knowledge that he is likely thereby to cause, the death of any person, and does by such act or omission cause the death of any person, is said to commit the offence of "voluntary culpable homicide."

NOTE M.[3] *On Offences Against the Body.* Notes to Draft of Penal Code, 53–56; Macaulay's Complete Works (English ed., 1875), vol. VII, pp. 493–497; Morgan and McPherson, Indian Penal Code, 225, 226, notes.

The first class of offences against the body consists of those offences which affect human life; and highest in this first class stand those offences which fall under the definition of voluntary culpable homicide.

This important part of the law appears to us to require fuller explanation than almost any other.

The first point to which we wish to call the attention of his Lordship in Council is the expression "omits what he is legally bound to do," in the definition of voluntary culpable homicide. These words, or other words tantamount in effect, frequently recur in the Code. We think this the most convenient place for explaining the reason which has led us so often to employ them. For if that reason shall appear to be sufficient in cases in which human life is concerned, it will *a fortiori* be sufficient in other cases.

Early in the progress of the Code it became necessary for us to consider the following question: When acts are made punishable on the ground that those acts produce, or are intended to produce, or are known to be likely to produce certain evil effects, to what extent ought omissions which produce, which are intended to produce, or which are known to be likely to produce the same evil effects to be made punishable?

Two things we take to be evident: first, that some of these omissions ought to be punished in exactly the same manner in which acts are punished: secondly, that all these omissions ought not to be punished. It will hardly be disputed that a jailer who voluntarily causes the death of a prisoner by omitting to supply that prisoner with food, or a nurse who voluntarily causes the death of an infant intrusted to her care by omitting to take it out of a tub of water into which it has fallen, ought to be treated as guilty of murder. On the other hand, it will hardly be maintained that a man should be punished as a murderer because he omitted to relieve a beggar, even though there might be the clearest proof that the death of the beggar was the result of the omission, and that the man who omitted to give the alms knew that the death of the beggar

[1] This proposed code was not enacted.

[2] A Penal Code prepared by the Indian Law Commissioners, and published by command of the Governor-General of India in Council; Calcutta, 1837.

[3] As to the authorship of these notes, see the preface to the English edition (1875) of Macaulay's Works. As to the code itself, see Stephen, History of the Criminal Law of England, 298–323.

was likely to be the effect of the omission. It will hardly be maintained that a surgeon ought to be treated as a murderer for refusing to go from Calcutta to Meerut to perform an operation, although it should be absolutely certain that this surgeon was the only person in India who could perform it, and that if it were not performed the person who required it would die. It is difficult to say whether a Penal Code which should put no omissions on the same footing with acts, or a Penal Code which should put all omissions on the same footing with acts would produce consequences more absurd and revolting. There is no country in which either of these principles is adopted. Indeed, it is hard to conceive how, if either were adopted, society could be held together.

It is plain, therefore, that a middle course must be taken. But it is not easy to determine what that middle course ought to be. The absurdity of the two extremes is obvious. But there are innumerable intermediate points; and wherever the line of demarcation may be drawn it will, we fear, include some cases which we might wish to exempt, and will exempt some which we might wish to include.

Mr. Livingston's Code provides that a person shall be considered as guilty of homicide who omits to save life, which he could save "without personal danger or pecuniary loss." This rule appears to us to be open to serious objection. There may be extreme inconvenience without the smallest personal danger, or the smallest risk of pecuniary loss; as in the case which we lately put of a surgeon summoned from Calcutta to Meerut to perform an operation. He may be offered such a fee that he would be a gainer by going. He may have no ground to apprehend that he should run any greater personal risk by journeying to the Upper Provinces than by continuing to reside in Bengal. But he is about to proceed to Europe immediately, or he expects some members of his family by the next ship, and wishes to be at the presidency to receive them. He, therefore, refuses to go. Surely, he ought not, for so refusing, to be treated as a murderer. It would be somewhat inconsistent to punish one man for not staying three months in India to save the life of another, and to leave wholly unpunished a man who, enjoying ample wealth, should refuse to disburse an anna to save the life of another. Again, it appears to us that it may be fit to punish a person as a murderer for causing death by omitting an act which cannot be performed without personal danger or pecuniary loss. A parent may be unable to procure food for an infant without money. Yet the parent, if he has the means, is bound to furnish the infant with food, and if by omitting to do so he voluntarily causes its death, he may with propriety be treated as a murderer. A nurse hired to attend a person suffering from an infectious disease cannot perform her duty without running some risk of infection. Yet if she deserts the sick person, and thus voluntarily causes his death, we should be disposed to treat her as a murderer.

We pronounce with confidence, therefore, that the line ought not to be drawn where Mr. Livingston has drawn it. But it is with great diffidence that we bring forward our own proposition. It is open to objections: cases may be put in which it will operate too severely, and cases in which it will operate too leniently; but we are unable to devise a better.

What we propose is this, that where acts are made punishable on the ground that they have caused, or have been intended to cause, or have been known to be likely to cause a certain evil effect, omissions which have caused, which have been intended to cause, or which have been known to be likely to cause the same effect shall be punishable in the same manner; provided that such omissions were, on other grounds, illegal. An omission is illegal (see clause 28) if it be an offence, if it be a breach of some direction of law, or if it be such a wrong as would be a good ground for a civil action.

We cannot defend this rule better than by giving a few illustrations of the way in which it will operate. A omits to give Z food, and by that omission voluntarily causes Z's death. Is this murder ? Under our rule it is murder if A was Z's jailer, directed by the law to furnish Z with food. It is murder if Z was the infant child of A, and had therefore a legal right to sustenance, which right a civil court would enforce against A. It is murder if Z was a bedridden invalid, and A a nurse hired to feed Z. It is murder if A was detaining Z in unlawful confinement, and had thus contracted (see clause 338) a legal obligation to furnish Z, during the continuance of the confinement, with necessaries. It is not murder if Z is a beggar who has no other claim on A than that of humanity.

A omits to tell Z that a river is swollen so high that Z cannot safely attempt to ford it, and by this omission voluntarily causes Z's death. This is murder if A is a peon stationed by authority to warn travellers from attempting to ford the river. It is murder if A is a guide who had contracted to conduct Z. It is not murder if A is a person on whom Z has no other claim than that of humanity.

A savage dog fastens on Z; A omits to call off the dog, knowing that if the dog be not called off it is likely that Z will be killed. Z is killed. This is murder in A, if the dog belonged to A, inasmuch as his omission to take proper order with the dog is illegal (clause 273). But if A be a mere passer-by it is not murder.

We are sensible that in some of the cases which we have put, our rule may appear too lenient. But we do not think that it can be made more severe, without disturbing the whole order of society. It is true that the man who, having abundance of wealth, suffers a fellow creature to die of hunger at his feet, is a bad man, — a worse man, probably, than many of those for whom we have provided very severe punishment. But we are unable to see where, if we make such a man legally punishable, we can draw the line. If the rich man who refuses to save a beggar's life at the cost of a little copper is a murderer, is the poor man just one degree above beggary also to be a murderer if he omits to invite the beggar to partake his hard-earned rice ? Again, if the rich man is a murderer for refusing to save the beggar's life at the cost of a little copper, is he also to be a murderer if he refuses to save the beggar's life at the cost of a thousand rupees ? Suppose A to be fully convinced that nothing can save Z's life, unless Z leave Bengal and reside a year at the Cape, is A, however wealthy he may be, to be punished as a murderer because he will not, at his own expense, send Z to the Cape ? Surely not. Yet it will be difficult to say on what principle we can punish A for not spending an anna to save Z's life, and leave him unpunished for not spending a thousand rupees to save Z's life. The distinction between a legal and an illegal omission is perfectly plain and intelligible. But the distinction between a large and a small sum of money is very far from being so; not to say that a sum which is small to one man is large to another.

The same argument holds good in the case of the ford. It is true that none but a very depraved man would suffer another to be drowned when he might prevent it by a word. But if we punish such a man, where are we to stop ? How much exertion are we to require ? Is a person to be a murderer if he does not go fifty yards through the sun of Bengal at noon in May in order to caution a traveller against a swollen river? Is he to be a murderer if he does not go a hundred yards? — if he does not go a mile? — if he does not go ten? What is the precise amount of trouble and inconvenience which he is to endure? The distinction between the guide who is bound to conduct the traveller as safely as he can, and a mere stranger, is a clear distinction. But the distinction between a stranger who will not give a halloo to save a man's life, and a stranger who will not run a mile to save a man's life, is very far from being equally clear.

It is, indeed, most highly desirable that men should not merely abstain from doing harm to their neighbours, but should render active services to their neighbours. In general, however, the penal law must content itself with keeping men from doing positive harm, and must leave to public opinion, and to the teachers of morality and religion, the office of furnishing men with motives for doing positive good. It is evident that to attempt to punish men by law for not rendering to others all the service which it is their duty to render to others would be preposterous. We must grant impunity to the vast majority of those omissions which a benevolent morality would pronounce reprehensible, and must content ourselves with punishing such omissions only when they are distinguished from the rest by some circumstance which marks them out as peculiarly fit objects of penal legislation. Now, no circumstance appears to us so well fitted to be the mark as the circumstance which we have selected. It will generally be found in the most atrocious cases of omission; it will scarcely ever be found in a venial case of omission; and it is more clear and certain than any other mark that has occurred to us. That there are objections to the line which we propose to draw, we have admitted. But there are objections to every line which can be drawn, and some line must be drawn.

SECTION VI

LIABILITY OF OCCUPIERS OF PREMISES

MAYNARD *v.* BOSTON AND MAINE RAILROAD

SUPREME JUDICIAL COURT, MASSACHUSETTS, SEPTEMBER 4, 1874.

Reported in 115 *Massachusetts Reports*, 458.

TORT for the killing of a horse on a railroad by a locomotive engine. Upon the trial, the plaintiff admitted that the horse must be considered as trespassing upon the railroad, but contended and offered evidence tending to show that by an exercise of proper care the injury to the horse might have been avoided. The defendants offered evidence to control this, and tending to show that they did all they reasonably could do to stop their train before striking the horse. There was no evidence of any wanton misconduct on their part.

The counsel for the defendants contended and asked the presiding judge to rule, that the defendants would not be liable, unless the plaintiff proved a reckless and wanton misconduct of their employees in the management of the train when the horse was killed. The presiding judge declined so to rule; but did rule that though the horse was trespassing upon the defendants' land at the time, the managers of the train could not carelessly run over him, but were bound to use reasonable care to avoid injuring him, and that if the jury found that by the exercise of reasonable care they might have avoided injuring the horse, they would be liable. The jury found for the plaintiff, and the defendants alleged exceptions.[1]

GRAY, C. J. If the horse had been rightfully upon the defendants' land, it would have been their duty to exercise reasonable care to avoid injuring the horse. But it being admitted by the plaintiff that his horse was trespassing upon the railroad, they did not owe him that duty, and were not liable to him for anything short of a reckless and wanton misconduct of those employed in the management of their train. The defendants were therefore entitled to the instruction which they requested. Tonawanda Railroad *v.* Munger, 5 Denio, 255; s. c. 4 Comst. 349; Vandegrift *v.* Rediker, 2 Zab. 185; Railroad Co. *v.* Skinner, 19 Penn. St. 298; Tower *v.* Providence & Worcester Railroad, 2 R. I. 404; Cincinnati, Hamilton & Dayton Railroad *v.* Waterson, 4 Ohio St. 424; Louisville & Frankfort Railroad *v.* Ballard, 2 Met. (Ky.) 177.

The instruction given to the jury held the defendants to the same obligation to the plaintiff as if his horse had been rightfully on their land; and made their paramount duty to the public of running the train with proper speed and safety, and their use of the land set apart and fitted for the performance of that duty, subordinate to the care of private interests in property which was upon their track without right.

Some passages in the opinion in Eames *v.* Salem & Lowell Railroad, 98 Mass. 560, 563, were relied on by the plaintiff's counsel at the argument, and apparently formed the basis of the rulings of the learned judge in the Court below. But in that case there was no evidence of any negligence or misconduct in the management of the train, and an exact definition of the defendants' liability, by reason of such negligence or misconduct, was not required. In the present case such a definition was requested by the defendants in appropriate terms, and was refused, and for that refusal their

Exceptions must be sustained.[2]

[1] Statement abridged. Arguments of counsel omitted.

[2] Grand Trunk R. Co. *v.* Barnett, [1911] A. C. 361; Louisville R. Co. *v.* Womack, 173 Fed. 752; Chesapeake R. Co. *v.* Hawkins, 174 Fed. 597; Graysonia Lumber Co. *v.* Carroll, 102 Ark. 460; Chicago Terminal Co. *v.* Kotoski, 199 Ill. 383; Neice *v.* Chicago R. Co., 254 Ill. 595; Jordan *v.* Grand Rapids R. Co., 162 Ind. 464; Burgess *v.* Atchison R. Co., 83 Kan. 497; Lando *v.* Chicago R. Co., 81 Minn. 279; Ingram-Day Lumber Co. *v.* Harvey, 98 Miss. 11; Koegel *v.* Missouri R. Co., 181 Mo. 379; Hoberg *v.* Collins, 80 N. J. Law, 425; Gulf R. Co. *v.* Dees, 44 Okl. 118; Woodward *v.* Southern R. Co., 90 S. C. 262; Norfolk R. Co. *v.* Wood, 99 Va. 156; Huff *v.* Chesapeake R. Co., 48 W. Va. 45 *Accord.*

HERRICK *v.* WIXOM

SUPREME COURT, MICHIGAN, SEPTEMBER 27, 1899.

Reported in 121 *Michigan Reports,* 384.

TRESPASS ON THE CASE for personal injuries.

Defendant was the possessor and manager of a tent show or circus. On the afternoon of an exhibition plaintiff went inside the tent and took a seat. There was a conflict of testimony as to whether plaintiff was invited into the tent by an authorized agent of defendant, or whether he entered without any invitation or other justification. A feature of the entertainment consisted in the ignition and explosion of a giant firecracker, attached to a pipe set in an upright position in one of the show rings. Plaintiff sat thirty or forty feet from the place where the cracker was exploded. At the explosion, part of the firecracker flew and struck plaintiff in the eye, whereby he lost the sight of his eye.

The judge left to the jury the question whether it was negligent in defendant to explode this firecracker in the inside of the tent and in the presence of the audience.

Then he gave, among others, the following instruction: —

"Now you must further find, in order that the plaintiff recover, that the plaintiff was in the tent, where he was injured, by the invitation of some person having authority to allow him to go in there. If he was a mere trespasser, who forced his way in, then the defendant owed him no duty that would enable him to recover under the declaration and proofs in this case." . . .

So in case of persons wrongfully upon engines, cars, or trains. Chicago R. Co. *v.* McDonough, 112 Ill. App. 315; Handley *v.* Missouri R. Co., 61 Kan. 237; Planz *v.* Boston R. Co., 157 Mass. 377; Bjornquist *v.* Boston R. Co., 185 Mass. 130; Feeback *v.* Missouri R. Co., 167 Mo. 206; Wickenburg *v.* Minneapolis R. Co., 94 Minn. 276 (boy of twelve); Johnson *v.* New York R. Co., 173 N. Y. 79; Morgan *v.* Oregon R. Co., 27 Utah, 92. But see Johnson *v.* Chicago R. Co., 123 Ia. 224; Pierce *v.* North Carolina R. Co., 124 N. C. 83. As to who is a trespasser in such a place, see Yancey *v.* Boston R. Co., 205 Mass. 162.

"A railway company may lawfully require a wilful trespasser upon one of its moving trains to immediately cease his unlawful conduct, by such means as not to indicate a willingness to deprive him of his self-control in leaving the train, the speed of the train not being so great that a personal injury to him should be expected to occur, giving due consideration to the duty of the trespasser to cease his lawlessness by all reasonable means in his power and reasonable expectation that he will use such means in attempting to do it. It is not sufficient to indicate an intentional injury that the party causing it had reasonable ground to expect that such a result was within reasonable probabilities, otherwise a violation of the duty to exercise ordinary care would, of itself, be sufficient to indicate such injury. The danger of inflicting a personal injury upon a person by the conduct of another must be such as to reasonably permit of a belief that such other either contemplated producing it, or, being conscious of the danger that it would occur, imposed such danger upon that person in utter disregard of the consequences, to warrant saying, reasonably, that the circumstances indicate willingness to perpetrate such injury." Marshall, J., in Bolin *v.* Chicago R. Co., 108 Wis. 333, 351–352. See also Hoberg *v.* Collins, 80 N. J. Law, 425, 429. But compare Palmer *v.* Gordon, 173 Mass. 410; Romana *v.* Boston R. Co., 226 Mass. 533.

Verdict of no cause of action. Judgment for defendant. Plaintiff brought error.[1]

MONTGOMERY, J. [After stating the case.] We think this instruction faulty, in so far as it was intended to preclude recovery in any event if the plaintiff was found to be a trespasser. It is true that a trespasser who suffers an injury because of a dangerous condition of premises is without remedy. But, where a trespasser is discovered upon the premises by the owner or occupant, he is not beyond the pale of the law, and any negligence resulting in injury will render the person guilty of negligence liable to respond in damages. Beach, Contrib. Neg. § 50; Whart. Neg. § 346; Marble *v.* Ross, 124 Mass. 44; Houston, etc., R. Co. *v.* Sympkins, 54 Tex. 615 (38 Am. Rep. 632); Brown *v.* Lynn, 31 Pa. St. 510 (72 Am. Dec. 768); Needham *v.* Railroad Co., 37 Cal. 409; Davies *v.* Mann, 10 Mees. & W. 546; 1 Shear. & R. Neg. § 99. In this case the negligent act of the defendant's servant was committed after the audience was made up. The presence of plaintiff was known, and the danger to him from a negligent act was also known. The question of whether a dangerous experiment should be attempted in his presence, or whether an experiment should be conducted with due care and regard to his safety, cannot be made to depend upon whether he had forced himself into the tent. Every instinct of humanity revolts at such a suggestion.

For this error the judgment will be reversed, and a new trial ordered.[2]

CINCINNATI & ZANESVILLE R. CO. *v.* SMITH

SUPREME COURT, OHIO, DECEMBER TERM, 1871.

Reported in 22 Ohio State Reports, 227.

ERROR to the Court of Common Pleas of Fayette County, reserved in the District Court.[3]

The plaintiff below, Richard Smith, sued the defendant below, the Cincinnati & Zanesville Railroad Company, to recover the value of

[1] Statement abridged. Part of opinion omitted.

[2] Rome Furnace Co. *v.* Patterson, 120 Ga. 521; Fields *v.* Louisville R. Co., 163 Ky. 673 *Accord.* See also Hector Min. Co. *v.* Robertson, 22 Col. 491; Hobbs *v.* Blanchard, 74 N. H. 116; Stuck *v.* Kanawha R. Co., 76 W. Va. 453; Peaslee, Duty to Seen Trespassers, 27 Harvard Law Rev. 403.

As to duty to observed child trespasser, see Little Rock R. Co. *v.* Barker, 39 Ark. 491, 500; Louisville R. Co. *v.* Lohges, 6 Ind. App. 288; Baltimore R. Co. *v.* Welch, 114 Md. 536. To observed helpless trespasser, see Tanner *v.* Louisville R. Co., 60 Ala. 621; Pannell *v.* Nashville R. Co., 97 Ala. 298; Martin *v.* Chicago R. Co., 194 Ill. 138; Krenzer *v.* Pittsburgh R. Co., 151 Ind. 587; Glenn *v.* Louisville R. Co., 28 Ky. Law Rep. 949. To trespasser observed in a dangerous position, see Haley *v.* Kansas City R. Co., 113 Ala. 640; Atkinson *v.* Kelley, 8 Ala. App. 571; St. Louis R. Co. *v.* Townsend, 69 Ark. 380, 383; Chicago R. Co. *v.* Kotoski, 199 Ill. 383; Richardson *v.* Missouri R. Co., 90 Kan. 292; Whitehead *v.* St. Louis R. Co., 99 Mo. 263; Mathews *v.* Chicago R. Co., 63 Mo. App. 569; Omaha R. Co. *v.* Cook, 42 Neb. 577.

[3] Statement rewritten; part of case omitted; argument omitted.

two horses alleged to have been killed through the negligence of the servants of the defendant in operating one of its trains. The inclosure of the plaintiff adjoined the railroad of the defendant; and from this inclosure, on the night on which the horses were killed, they escaped on to the railroad.

The Court, among other things, charged the jury as follows: —

The defendant's servants in this case were not bound to use extraordinary care or extraordinary means to save the plaintiff's horses. But they were bound to use what, in that peculiar business, is ordinary care and diligence; and if the loss of the horses was the result of a want of that ordinary care and diligence, the defendant is liable.

The defendant had the right to the free and unobstructed use of its railroad track. And the paramount duty of the employees is the protection of the passengers and property in the train, and the train itself.

But this being their paramount duty, they are bound to use ordinary care and diligence, so as not unnecessarily to injure the property of others.

Under the circumstances of the case, could and would reasonably prudent men, skilled in that kind of business, keeping in view as their paramount duty the protection and safety of the train, its passengers, and the property on and about it intrusted to their care, in the exercise of ordinary care have stopped the train and saved the horses? If so, and the defendant's servants did not so act, the defendant is liable in this case; otherwise the defendant is not liable.

In considering the paramount duty of the employees in the proper management of the train for the safety of passengers and property of its train, you have a right to determine whether they have other duties to perform. It is claimed the engineer had other duties than watching the track to perform, which were necessary for the safety of the passengers and property of the train, — such as gauging his steam, watching time-table, regulating his supply of water, examining his machinery, watching for the station-signal, etc. If such were the case, he had a lawful right to perform these duties, and was not bound to neglect them to save the plaintiff's horses, nor bound to watch the track while performing these duties. They were only bound, under the circumstances of the case, to use ordinary care and diligence to save the horses, — the safety of the passengers and property of the train being their paramount duty; and if the jury find from the evidence that the persons in charge of the engine were attending to the duties of the train approaching the station at the time of the accident, these duties were paramount to watching the track for trespassing animals; and if the horses were not, on that account, discovered in time to save them by using ordinary means to stop the train, the defendant is not liable.

It is claimed by the defendant's counsel that off the crossings of the railroad the servants of the railroad company have a right to presume that there are no trespassers on the roadway; that they are not bound to look out for trespassers except for the safety of passengers or property in charge. It is also claimed that inasmuch as the road at the place where the plaintiff's horses got on the track and were killed was fenced, on that account the defendant's servants in charge of the train were not bound to look out for trespassing stock. Upon this question I only can charge you this: That if the railroad was fenced at the place where the horses got on and were killed, and this was known to the defendant's employees, you have a right to look to that circumstance as reflecting upon and in determining whether the employees exercised ordinary care in the management of the train. But if they might, in the exercise of ordinary care, have discovered the animals, although they were trespassers on the roadway, other than at a crossing, in time to have prevented their destruction, it was their duty to do so; and if from such want of ordinary care they were not discovered in time to prevent their destruction, the defendant is liable for their loss to the plaintiff.[1]

WHITE, J. The whole charge is set out in the bill of exceptions. Considering its several parts in connection, and giving to the whole a fair construction, we deem it necessary only to notice two particulars in which it is objected to.

These are: 1. Whether the fact that the horses were trespassing on the track excused the servants of the defendant from the exercise of ordinary care; and, 2. Whether that fact, and the additional one that the road was fenced, excused the engineer, as respects the owner of stray animals, from looking ahead to see whether such animals were on the track or not.

In regard to the first of these particulars, it is contended on behalf of the railroad company that, as the horses were trespassing on the railroad, the company was exempt from using ordinary care to save them, and that it was only liable for what is called gross negligence.

The Court instructed the jury that the defendant had the right to the free and unobstructed use of its railroad track, and that the paramount duty of its employees was the protection of the passengers and property in the train, and the train itself. But this being their paramount duty, they were bound to use ordinary care and diligence so as not unnecessarily to injure the property of others.

We think the charge stated the law correctly. We see no good reason, in principle, why a party, so far as may be consistent with the full enjoyment of his own rights, ought not to use ordinary care so as not unnecessarily to injure the property of others.

[1] The above portions of the instructions are set out in the argument of counsel, pp. 235–237.

It is true, the rule contended for by the counsel of the plaintiff in error is sustained by a number of authorities. But the later and better considered cases are to the contrary. Illinois Central R. R. Co. *v.* Middlesworth, 46 Ill. 494; Bemis *v.* Conn., &c. R. R., 42 Vt. 375; Isbell *v.* N. Y. R. R. Co., 27 Conn. 393; Redfield's American Railway Cases, 355, 356.

The rule contended for has never been adopted in this State. It is, moreover, as respects railroad companies, inconsistent with our statute law on the subject. S. & C. 331.

The facts in the case of the C. H. & D. R. R. Co. *v.* Waterson & Kirk, 4 Ohio St. 424, cited and relied upon by the counsel of the plaintiff in error, were different from those in the case now before us, and we do not regard the rule there laid down as to the liability of the company in that case as applicable to this.

From what has been said of the charge in the first particular named, it would seem to follow that it is unobjectionable as respects the second. If it was the duty of the servants of the company, so far as was consistent with their other and paramount duties, to use ordinary care to avoid injuring animals on the track, they were, of course, bound to adopt the ordinary precautions to discover danger, as well as to avoid its consequences after it became known.

The fact that the road was fenced at the place of collision with the horses, was a circumstance to be considered in connection with the other circumstances of the case in determining whether the engineer was guilty of negligence in not looking ahead and discovering the danger in time to avoid it. The fact that the road was fenced rendered it less probable that wandering animals would be on the track; but it cannot be said that the engineer, as a matter of law, by reason of the fences, was wholly excused from keeping a lookout ahead of the train.

If the servants of the company in charge of the train, having due regard to their duties for the safety of the persons and property in their charge, could, by the exercise of ordinary care, have seen and saved the horses, we think they were bound to have done so. Bemis *v.* Conn., &c. R. R., *supra*, 381; Louis. & Nash. R. R. Co. *v.* Wainscott, 3 Bush, 149.[1] *Judgment affirmed.*

[1] Schmidt *v.* Michigan Coal Co., 159 Mich. 308; Myers *v.* Boston R. Co., 72 N. H. 175; Carney *v.* Concord St. R. Co., 72 N. H. 364; Brown *v.* Boston R. Co., 73 N. H. 568; Magar *v.* Hammond, 171 N. Y. 377; O'Leary *v.* Brooks Elevator Co., 7 N. D. 568 *Accord.* See also Houston R. Co. *v.* Garrett, (Tex. Civ. App.) 160 S. W. 111.

As to the effect of a statute prohibiting the particular trespass, see Marra *v.* New York R. Co., 139 App. Div. 707.

As to when a horse is trespassing, see Taft *v.* New York R. Co., 157 Mass. 297.

SHEEHAN *v.* ST. PAUL & DULUTH R. CO.

UNITED STATES CIRCUIT COURT OF APPEALS, SEVENTH CIRCUIT, OCTOBER 16, 1896.

Reported in 46 *U. S. Appeals*, 498.

SEAMAN, J.[1] The plaintiff at the time of his injury was neither in the relation of passenger nor of one in a public crossing or place in which the public were licensed to travel, but upon the undisputed facts was a mere intruder on the tracks of the defendant, technically a trespasser; and this record excludes any of the elements of implied license or invitation to such use which have given rise to much discussion and diversity of views in the courts. Therefore the inquiry is here squarely presented, What is the duty which a railway company owes to a trespasser on its tracks, and how and when does the duty arise? The decisions upon this subject uniformly recognize that the trespasser cannot be treated as an outlaw; and at the least that, if wantonly injured in the operation of the railroad, the company is answerable in damages. Clearly, then, an obligation is placed upon the company to exercise some degree of care when the danger becomes apparent. Is it, however, bound to foresee or assume that rational beings will thus enter as trespassers in a place of danger, and to exercise in the running of its trains the constant vigilance in view of that probability which is imposed for public crossings? There are cases which would seem to hold this strict requirement (see note, 1 Thompson on Negligence (1880), 448; East Tennessee and Georgia Railroad Co. *v.* St. John, 5 Sneed, 524); but by the great preponderance of authority, in this country and in England, the more reasonable doctrine is pronounced, in effect, as follows: That the railroad company has the right to a free track in such places; that it is not bound to any act or service in anticipation of trespassers thereon; and that the trespasser who ventures to enter upon a track for any purpose of his own assumes all risks of the conditions which may be found there, including the operation of engines and cars. Wright *v.* Boston and Maine Railroad, 129 Mass. 440; Philadelphia and Reading Railroad Company *v.* Hummell, 44 Penn. St. 375. The decision by this court, in Cleveland, Cincinnati, Chicago and St. Louis Railway Company *v.* Philips' Administrator (1), 24 U. S. Appeals, 489, adopts the view held in this line of cases, citing the authorities of which repetition here is unnecessary. The same doctrine prevails in Minnesota, where the injury in question arose. Johnson *v.* Truesdale, 46 Minnesota, 345; Studley *v.* St. Paul & Duluth R. Co., 48 Minnesota, 249. In the latter case it was held that there could be no recovery " unless the engineer saw the girl in time to avoid the accident, and then was guilty of such gross negligence in not trying to avoid it as to evince a reckless disregard of

[1] The statement and part of the opinion are omitted.

human life;" and the opinion gives this further exposition of the rule: "The defendant's engineer was under no obligation to anticipate a trespasser, or to look out for persons walking upon the track; but, upon discovering plaintiff's intestate across the cattle-guard, as he claims she was when he noticed that she was in danger, it became the engineer's duty to use proper care to avoid running her down. If he failed to exercise proper care, he would necessarily be grossly negligent and evince a reckless disregard of human life." So in Wisconsin, in Anderson *v.* Chicago, St. Paul, Minneapolis & Omaha Railway Company, 87 Wisconsin, 195, 204, it is said: "The use of a railroad is exclusively for its owners or those acting under its authority, and the company is not bound to the exercise of any active duty of care or diligence towards mere trespassers upon its track, to keep a lookout to discover or protect them from injury, except that, when discovered in a position of danger or peril, it is its duty to use all reasonable and proper effort to save and protect them from the probable consequences of their indiscretion or negligence."

The well-established and just rule which holds the railroad company to the exercise of constant and strict care against injury through its means is applicable only to the relation on which it is founded, of an existing duty or obligation. This active or positive duty arises in favor of the public at a street crossing or other place at which it is presumable that persons or teams may be met. It is not material, so far as concerns this inquiry, whether the place is one for which a lawful right of passage exists, as it is the fact of notice to the company arising out of its existence and the probability of its use which imposes the positive duty to exercise care; the requirement of an extreme degree of care being superadded because of the hazards which attend the operations of the company. The case of a trespasser on the track in a place not open to travel is clearly distinguishable in the absence of this notice to the company. There is no constructive notice upon which to base the obligation of constant lookout for his presence there, and no actual notice up to the moment the trainmen have discovered the fact of his peril. As that peril comes wholly from his unauthorized act and temerity, the risk and all positive duty of care for his safety rest with the trespasser. The obligation of the company and its operatives is not then preëxisting, but arises at the moment of discovery, and is negative in its nature, — a duty which is common to human conduct to make all reasonable effort to avert injury to others from means which can be controlled.

This is the issue presented here. It excludes all inquiry respecting the character of the roadbed, cattle-guard, locomotive, brake appliances or other means of operation, or of the speed or manner of running the train up to the moment of notice, because no breach of positive duty is involved. It is confined to the evidence relating to the discovery by the engineer and fireman of the plaintiff's peril and to the efforts then made to avert the injury; and out of that to ascertain whether, in any view which may justly be taken, it is shown that these men or the engineer in disregard of the duty which then confronted them neglected to employ with reasonable promptness the means at hand for stopping the train.[1]

BRETT, M. R., IN HEAVEN *v.* PENDER

(1883) 11 *Queen's Bench Division*, 503, 506, 507.

BRETT, M. R. . . . The action is in form and substance an action for negligence. That the stage was, through want of attention of the defendant's servants, supplied in a state unsafe for use is not denied. But want of attention amounting to a want of ordinary care is not a good cause of action, although injury ensue from such want, unless the person charged with such want of ordinary care had a duty to the person complaining to use ordinary care in respect of the matter called in question. Actionable negligence consists in the neglect of the use of ordinary care or skill towards a person to whom the defendant owes the duty of observing ordinary care and skill, by which neglect the plaintiff, without contributory negligence on his part, has suffered injury to his person or property. The question in this case is whether the defendant owed such a duty to the plaintiff.

MITCHELL, J., IN AKERS *v.* CHICAGO, &C. R. CO.

(1894) 58 *Minnesota*, 540, 544.

MITCHELL, J. Actionable negligence is the failure to discharge a legal duty to the person injured. If there is no duty, there is no negligence. Even if a defendant owes a duty to some one else, but does not owe it to the person injured, no action will lie. The duty must be due

[1] That in general there is no duty to look out for trespassers on the track or right of way, see also Cleveland R. Co. *v.* Tartt, 99 Fed. 369; Louisville R. Co. *v.* Jones, 191 Ala. 484; Goudreau *v.* Connecticut Co., 84 Conn. 406; Atlantic R. Co. *v.* McDonald, 135 Ga. 635; Curd *v.* Cincinnati R. Co., 163 Ky. 104; Baltimore R. Co. *v.* State, 114 Md. 536; Petur *v.* Erie R. Co., 151 App. Div. 578; Carter *v.* Erie R. Co., 33 Ohio Cir. Ct. Rep. 377; Laeve *v.* Missouri R. Co., (Tex. Civ. App.) 136 S. W. 1129.

Jeffries *v.* Seaboard R. Co., 129 N. C. 236 *contra*. See also Ark. Kirby's Dig. § 6607; Tenn. Shannon's Code, § 1574 (4).

As to duty of trainmen in a place where there is a known likelihood of trespassers, see Southern R. Co. *v.* Donovan, 84 Ala. 141; Bullard *v.* Southern R. Co., 116 Ga. 644; Cincinnati R. Co. *v.* Blankenship, 157 Ky. 699; Risbridger *v.* Michigan R. Co., 188 Mich. 672; Fearons *v.* Kansas City R. Co., 180 Mo. 208; Eppstein *v.* Missouri R. Co., 197 Mo. 720; Krummack *v.* Missouri R. Co., 98 Neb. 773; St. Louis R. Co. *v.* Hodge, (Okl.) 157 Pac. 60; Whelan *v.* Baltimore R. Co., 70 W. Va. 442; Whalen *v.* Chicago R. Co., 75 Wis. 654. *Contra:* Baltimore R. Co. *v.* Welch, 114 Md. 536; Boden *v.* Boston R. Co., 205 Mass. 504; Haltiwanger *v.* Columbia R. Co., 64 S. C. 7. Compare Lowery *v.* Walker, [1911] A. C. 10.

The trainmen may assume that an adult trespasser, not in obvious peril, will look out for himself. Indianapolis R. Co. *v.* McClaren, 62 Ind. 566; Campbell *v.*

to the person injured. These principles are elementary, and are equally applicable, whether the duty is imposed by positive statute or is founded on general common-law principles.[1]

LARY *v.* CLEVELAND R. CO.

SUPREME COURT, INDIANA, NOVEMBER TERM, 1881.

Reported in 78 *Indiana Reports*, 323.

LARY sued the railroad company for damage alleged to have been sustained by him, through the negligent failure of the company to repair a building standing on its grounds, and formerly used by it as a freight house. Answer, a general denial. Upon the trial, the plaintiff introduced his evidence; the defendant demurred to it, and the plaintiff joined in demurrer. The Court sustained the demurrer, and the plaintiff excepted.

The facts which the plaintiff's evidence tended to prove are substantially as follows: —

The railroad company owned half an acre of land between the railroad track and a highway. On this land was a building erected several years before for a freight house. It was no longer used as the general freight house, though still used for storing the company's wood. A part of the roof of the building was off, and had been so for some months. The plaintiff, who was twenty years of age, was in the habit of passing the building almost daily, and had noticed that part of the roof was off. In a rain storm, the plaintiff went under the platform of the old freight house, and played there with other young people. A piece of the roof was torn off by the wind. The plaintiff, being frightened at the noise, ran out, saw the piece of the roof in the air, and ran towards the highway; but before or as he reached the edge of it, this fragment of the roof fell upon him.[2]

MORRIS, C. [After stating the case.] Upon the facts thus stated, can the appellant maintain this action ?

There is no testimony tending to show that the appellant was at the freight house by the invitation of the appellee, nor that he was there for the purpose of transacting any business with the appellee. The appellant intruded upon the premises of the appellee, and is not, therefore, entitled to that protection which one, expressly or by implication, invited into the house or place of business of another, is entitled to. The appellant was a trespasser, and as such he entered upon the appellee's premises, taking the risks of all the mere omissions of the

Kansas City R. Co., 55 Kan. 536; St. Louis R. Co. *v.* Herrin, 6 Tex. Civ. App. 718. As to a child, see Pennsylvania R. Co. *v.* Morgan, 82 Pa. St. 134.

[1] "The duty must be one owed by the defendants to the plaintiffs in respect to the very matter or act charged as negligence." — PARSONS, C. J., in Pittsfield C. M. Co. *v.* Pittsfield Shoe Co., 71 N. H. 522, 531.

[2] Statement abridged.

appellee as to the condition of the grounds and buildings thus invaded without leave. We do not wish to be understood as holding or implying that if, on the part of the appellee, there had been any act done implying a willingness to inflict the injury upon the appellant, it would not be liable. But we think there is nothing in the evidence from which such an inference can be reasonably drawn. The building could be seen by all; its condition was open to the inspection of every one; it had been abandoned as a place for the transaction of public business; it was in a state of palpable and visible decay, and no one was authorized, impliedly or otherwise, to go into or under it. Under such circumstances, the law says to him who intrudes into such a place, that he must proceed at his own risk.

In the case of The Pittsburgh, &c. R. W. Co. *v.* Bingham, 29 Ohio St. 364, the question was: "Is a railroad company bound to exercise ordinary care and skill in the erection, structure, or maintenance of its station house or houses, as to persons who enter or are at the same, not on any business with the company or its agents, nor on any business connected with the operation of its road; but are there without objection by the company, and therefore by its mere sufferance or permission?" The Court answered this question in the negative.

In the case of Hounsell *v.* Smyth, 7 C. B. N. S. 731, the plaintiff fell into a quarry, left open and unguarded on the unenclosed lands of the defendant, over which the public were permitted to travel; it was held that the owner was under no legal obligation to fence or guard the excavation unless it was so near the public road as to render travel thereon dangerous. That the person so travelling over such waste lands must take the permission with its concomitant conditions, and, it may be, perils. Hardcastle *v.* The South Yorkshire R. W. Co., 4 H. & N. 67; Sweeny *v.* Old Colony, &c. R. R. Co., 10 Allen, 368; Knight *v.* Abert, 6 Barr, 472.

After reviewing the above and other cases, Judge Boynton, in the case of The Pittsburgh, &c. R. W. Co. *v.* Bingham, *supra*, says: —

"The principle underlying the cases above cited recognizes the right of the owner of real property to the exclusive use and enjoyment of the same without liability to others for injuries occasioned by its unsafe condition, where the person receiving the injury was not in or near the place of danger by lawful right; and where such owner assumed no responsibility for his safety by inviting him there, without giving him notice of the existence or imminence of the peril to be avoided."

In the case from which we have quoted, the intestate of the plaintiff was at the defendant's station house, not on any business with it, but merely to pass away his time, when, by a severe and sudden blast of wind, a portion of the roof of the station house was blown off the building and against the intestate, with such force as to kill him. The case, in its circumstances, was not unlike the one before us. Nicholson *v.* Erie R. W. Co., 41 N. Y. 525; Murray *v.* McLean, 57 Ill. 378; Durham *v.* Musselman, 2 Blackf. 96 (18 Am. Dec. 133).

In the case of Sweeny *v.* Old Colony, &c. R. R. Co., 10 Allen, 368, the Court say: —

"A licensee, who enters on premises by permission only, without any enticement, allurement, or inducement being held out to him by the owner or occupant, cannot recover damages for injuries caused by obstructions or pitfalls. He goes there at his own risk, and enjoys the license subject to its concomitant perils." Carleton *v.* Franconia Iron and Steel Co., 99 Mass. 216; Harris *v.* Stevens, 31 Vt. 79, 90; Wood *v.* Leadbitter, 13 M. & W. 838.

The evidence in this case brings it, we think, within the principles settled by the above cases.

The appellant contends that the evidence shows that the appellee was guilty of gross negligence in not repairing its freight house, and that such negligence renders it liable, though he entered upon its premises without invitation or license, as a mere intruder, and was, while such intruder, injured; and, in support of this proposition, we are referred to the following cases: Lafayette, &c. R. R. Co. *v.* Adams, 26 Ind. 76; Indianapolis, &c. R. R. Co. *v.* McClure, 26 Ind. 370; Gray *v.* Harris, 107 Mass. 492; Isabel *v.* Hannibal, &c. R. R. Co., 60 Mo. 475.

In the first of the above cases, the Court held that, where the negligence of the company was so gross as to imply a disregard of consequences or a willingness to inflict the injury, it was liable, though the party injured was not free from fault. In the second case, it was held that a railroad company, not required to fence its road, would not be liable for animals killed on its road, unless guilty of gross negligence. The phrase "gross negligence," as used in these cases, means something more than the mere omission of duty; it meant, as shown by the evidence in the cases, reckless and aggressive conduct on the part of the company's servants. "Something more than negligence, however gross, must be shown, to enable a party to recover for an injury, when he has been guilty of contributory negligence." The Pennsylvania Co. *v.* Sinclair, 62 Ind. 301. There was, in the cases referred to in 26 Ind., something more than negligence. As in the case of The Indianapolis, &c. R. W. Co. *v.* McBrown, 46 Ind. 229, where the animal was driven through a deep cut, eighty rods long, into and upon a trestle work of the company, there was aggressive malfeasance. In the Massachusetts case, the Court held that a party building a dam across a stream must provide against unusual floods. We do not think these cases applicable to the one before us.

There could be no negligence on the part of the appellee, of which the appellant can be heard to complain, unless at the time he received the injury, the appellee was under some obligation or duty to him to repair its freight house. "Actionable negligence exists only where the one whose act causes or occasions the injury owes to the injured person a duty, created either by contract or by operation of law, which he has failed to discharge." Pittsburgh, &c. R. W. Co. *v.* Bingham, *supra;* Burdeck *v.* Cheadle, 26 Ohio St. 393; Town of Salem *v.* Goller, 76 Ind. 291. We have shown that the appellee owed the appellant no such duty.

The judgment below should be affirmed.

PER CURIAM. It is ordered, upon the foregoing opinion, that the judgment below be affirmed, at the costs of the appellant.[1]

BUCH *v.* AMORY MANUFACTURING CO.

SUPREME COURT, NEW HAMPSHIRE, DECEMBER, 1897.

Reported in 69 *New Hampshire Reports,* 257.

CASE. Trial by jury and verdict for the plaintiff. March 30, 1886, the plaintiff, then eight years of age and unable to speak or understand English, was injured by the machinery in operation in the defendants' mill. The evidence tended to show that the plaintiff's brother, who was thirteen years of age, was employed as a back-boy in the mule-spinning room, and that at his request the plaintiff went into the room for the purpose of learning the work of a back-boy. The elder brother had no authority to request or permit the plaintiff to go into the mill or to instruct him, unless it could be inferred from the fact testified to by him that "he saw other boys taking their brothers to learn, as he understood from their motions." The plaintiff was in the mill for a day and a half until the accident, openly assisting more or less in the work of the back-boys. He testified that he was directed by a person not the overseer of the room, whom he saw "bossing" the other boys, to pick up some bobbins and put some waste in a box. There was evidence tending to show that Fulton, the overseer, who was in charge of and hired the back-boys and other operatives in the room, passed in the alleys near the plaintiff, and that he was well acquainted with his help. He testified that he had no knowledge of the plaintiff's presence in the room until about two

[1] Hardcastle *v.* South Yorkshire R. Co., 4 H. & N. 67; Ponting *v.* Noakes, [1894] 2 Q. B. 281; Scoggin *v.* Atlantic Cement Co., 179 Ala. 213; Gordon *v.* Roberts, 162 Cal. 506; Whitney *v.* New York R. Co., 87 Conn. 623; Garner *v.* Town, 7 Ga. App. 630; McDermott *v.* Burke, 256 Ill. 401; Northwestern El. Co. *v.* O'Malley, 107 Ill. App. 599; Knapp *v.* Doll, 180 Ind. 526; St. Joseph I. Co. *v.* Bertch, 33 Ind. App. 491; Upp *v.* Darner, 150 Ia. 403; Bransom *v.* Labrot, 81 Ky. 638; Mallock *v.* Derby, 190 Mass. 208; Flanagan *v.* Sanders, 138 Mich. 253; Dahl *v.* Valley Dredging Co., 125 Minn. 90; Schmidt *v.* Distilling Co., 90 Mo. 284; Henry *v.* Disbrow M. Co., 144 Mo. App. 350; Butler *v.* Chicago R. Co., 155 Mo. App. 287; Burrill *v.* Alexander, 75 N. H. 554; Kleinberg *v.* Schween, 134 App. Div. 493; Riggle *v.* Lens, 71 Or. 125; Clapp *v.* La Grill, 103 Tenn. 164; Stamford Oil Co. *v.* Barnes, 103 Tex. 409; Denison Light Co. *v.* Patton, 105 Tex. 621; Lunsford *v.* Colonial Coal Co., 115 Va. 346; Anderson *v.* Northern R. Co., 19 Wash. 340; West *v.* Shaw, 61 Wash. 227.

As to setting traps for trespassers, see Bird *v.* Holbrook, 4 Bing. 628; Hooker *v.* Miller, 37 Ia. 613. Compare Marble *v.* Ross, 124 Mass. 44; Loomis *v.* Terry, 17 Wend. 497; Sherfey *v.* Bartley, 4 Sneed, 58.

hours before the accident, when, aware that the boy was not an employee, he directed him to go out, and thinking he might not understand English, took him to an operative who spoke the plaintiff's language, whom he told to send the plaintiff out. The plaintiff testified that Fulton spoke to him and, as he understood, directed him to remove his vest, but that he did not understand he was ordered to leave. There was no evidence except Fulton's that the order was communicated to the plaintiff or understood by him. There was no evidence or claim that the machinery was improperly constructed or operated, or that it was out of repair. The plaintiff's hand was caught in a gearing which the back-boys were instructed to avoid, but there was no evidence that the plaintiff was given any instruction or warning whatever. There was evidence tending to prove that boys under thirteen years of age were not employed in the room, and that the place and machinery were dangerous for a child of the plaintiff's age. Subject to exception, a motion that a verdict be directed for the defendants was denied.

Carpenter, C. J. On the evidence, the jury could not properly find that the plaintiff was upon the premises of the defendants with their consent or permission. Although there was evidence tending to show that other back-boys had taken their brothers into the room for the purpose of instructing them in the business, there was no sufficient evidence that the fact that they did so was known to the defendants, and there was evidence that on the first occasion brought to their knowledge they objected. Upon this state of the evidence, a license by the defendants — whether material or immaterial — for the plaintiff's presence in the room could not legitimately be inferred. The plaintiff was a trespasser.

The defendant's machinery was in perfect order and properly managed. They were conducting their lawful business in a lawful way and in the usual and ordinary manner. During the plaintiff's presence they made no change in the operation of their works or in their method of doing business. No immediate or active intervention on their part caused the injury. It resulted from the joint operation of the plaintiff's conduct and the ordinary and usual condition of the premises. Under these circumstances, an adult in full possession of his faculties, or an infant capable of exercising the measure of care necessary to protect himself from the dangers of the situation, whether he was on the premises by permission or as a trespasser, could not recover.

The plaintiff was an infant of eight years. The particular circumstances of the accident — how or in what manner it happened that the plaintiff caught his hand in the gearing — are not disclosed by the case. It does not appear that any evidence was offered tending to show that he was incapable of knowing the danger from putting his hand in contact with the gearing, or of exercising a measure of care sufficient to avoid the danger. Such an incapacity cannot be presumed. Stone *v.* Railroad, 115 N. Y. 104, 109–111; Hayes *v.* Norcross, 162 Mass. 546, 548; Mulligan *v.* Curtis, 100 Mass. 512, 514; Cosgrove *v.* Ogden, 49 N. Y. 255, 258; Kunz *v.* Troy, 104 N. Y. 344, 351; Lovett *v.* Railroad, 9 Allen, 557, 563.

An infant is bound to use the reason he possesses and to exercise the degree of care and caution of which he is capable. If the plaintiff could by the due exercise of his intellectual and physical powers have avoided the injury, he is no more entitled to recover than an adult would be under the same circumstances. The burden was upon him, and the case might be disposed of upon the ground that he adduced no evidence tending to show that he had not sufficient reason and discretion to appreciate the particular risk of injury that he incurred and to avoid it. But it may be that evidence tending to show the plaintiff's incapacity was adduced, and that the case is silent on the subject because this particular question was not made by the defendants.

Assuming, then, that the plaintiff was incapable either of appreciating the danger or of exercising the care necessary to avoid it, is he, upon the facts stated, entitled to recover ? He was a trespasser in a place dangerous to children of his age. In the conduct of their business and management of their machinery the defendants were without fault. The only negligence charged upon or attributed to them is that, inasmuch as they could not make the plaintiff understand a command to leave the premises and ought to have known that they could not, they did not forcibly eject him.

Actionable negligence is the neglect of a legal duty. The defendants are not liable unless they owed to the plaintiff a legal duty which they neglected to perform. With purely moral obligations the law does not deal. For example, the priest and Levite who passed by on the other side were not, it is supposed, liable at law for the continued suffering of the man who fell among thieves, which they might and morally ought to have prevented or relieved. Suppose A, standing close by a railroad, sees a two-year-old babe on the track and a car approaching. He can easily rescue the child with entire safety to himself, and the instincts of humanity require him to do so. If he does not, he may, perhaps, justly be styled a ruthless savage and a moral monster; but he is not liable in damages for the child's injury, or indictable under the statute for its death. P. S., c. 278, s. 8.

"In dealing with cases which involve injuries to children, courts . . . have sometimes strangely confounded legal obligation with sentiments that are independent of law." Indianapolis *v.* Emmelman, 108 Ind. 530. "It is important to bear in mind, in actions for injuries to children, a very simple and fundamental fact, which in this class of cases is sometimes strangely lost sight of, viz., that no action arises without a breach of duty." 2 Thomp. Neg. 1183, note 3. "No action will lie against a spiteful man, who, seeing another running into danger, merely omits to warn him. To bring the case within the category of actionable negligence some wrongful act must be shown, or a breach of some positive duty; otherwise, a man who allows strangers to roam over his property would be held answerable for not protecting them against any danger they might encounter whilst using the license." Gautret *v.* Egerton, L. R. 2 C. P. 371, 375.

What duties do the owners owe to a trespasser upon their premises? They may eject him, using such force and such only as is necessary for the purpose. They are bound to abstain from any other or further intentional or negligent acts of personal violence, — bound to inflict upon him by means of their own active intervention no injury which by due care they can avoid. They are not bound to warn him against hidden or secret dangers arising from the condition of the premises (Redigan *v.* Railroad, 155 Mass. 44, 47, 48), or to protect him against any injury that may arise from his own acts or those of other persons. In short, if they do nothing, let him entirely alone, in no manner interfere with him, he can have no cause of action against them for any injury that he may receive. On the contrary, he is liable to them for any damage that he by his unlawful meddling may cause them or their property. What greater or other legal obligation was cast on these defendants by the circumstance that the plaintiff was (as is assumed) an irresponsible infant?

If landowners are not bound to warn an adult trespasser of hidden dangers, — dangers which he by ordinary care cannot discover and, therefore, cannot avoid, — on what ground can it be claimed that they must warn an infant of open and visible dangers which he is unable to appreciate? No legal distinction is perceived between the duties of the owners in one case and the other. The situation of the adult in front of secret dangers which by no degree of care he can discover, and that of the infant incapable of comprehending danger, is in a legal aspect exactly the same. There is no apparent reason for holding that any greater or other duty rests upon the owners in one case than in the other.

There is a wide difference — a broad gulf — both in reason and in law, between causing and preventing an injury; between doing by negligence or otherwise a wrong to one's neighbor, and preventing him from injuring himself; between protecting him against injury by another and guarding him from injury that may accrue to him from the condition of the premises which he has unlawfully invaded. The duty to do no wrong is a legal duty. The duty to protect against wrong is, generally speaking and excepting certain intimate relations in the nature of a trust, a moral obligation only, not recognized or enforced by law. Is a spectator liable if he sees an intelligent man or an unintelligent infant running into danger and does not warn or forcibly restrain him? What difference does it make whether the danger is on another's land, or upon his own, in case the man or infant is not there by his express or implied invitation? If A sees an eight-year-old boy beginning to climb into his garden over a wall stuck with spikes and does not warn him or drive him off, is he liable in damages if the boy meets with injury from the spikes? Degg *v.* Railway, 1 H. & N. 773, 777. I see my neighbor's two-year-old babe in dangerous proximity to the machinery of his windmill in his yard, and easily might, but do not, rescue him. I am not liable in damages to the child for his injuries, nor, if the child is killed, punishable for manslaughter by the common law or under the statute (P. S., c. 278, s. 8), because the child and I are strangers, and I am under no legal duty to protect him. Now suppose I see the same child trespassing in my own yard and meddling in like manner with the dangerous machinery of my own windmill. What additional obligation is cast upon me by reason of the child's trespass? The mere fact that the child is unable to take care of himself does not impose on me the legal duty of protecting him in the one case more than in the other. Upon what principle of law can an infant by coming unlawfully upon my premises impose upon me the legal duty of a guardian? None has been suggested, and we know of none.

An infant, no matter of how tender years, is liable in law for his trespasses. 1 Ch. Pl. 86; 2 Kent, 241; Cool. Torts, 103; Poll. Torts, 46; 2 Add. Torts, 1126, 1153; 10 Am. & Eng. Enc. Law, 668, et seq.; Humphrey *v.* Douglass, 10 Vt. 71; School District *v.* Bragdon, 23 N. H. 507; Eaton *v.* Hill, 50 N. H. 235; Bullock *v.* Babcock, 3 Wend. 391; Williams *v.* Hays, 143 N. Y. 442, 446–451; Conklin *v.* Thompson, 29 Barb. 218; Neal *v.* Gillett, 23 Conn. 437; Huchting *v.* Engel, 17 Wis. 237. If, then, the defendants' machinery was injured by the plaintiff's act in putting his hand in the gearing, he is liable to them for the damages in an action of trespass and to nominal damages for the wrongful entry. It would be no answer to such an action that the defendants might by force have prevented the trespass. It is impossible to hold that while the plaintiff is liable to the defendants in trespass, they are liable to him in case for neglecting to prevent the act which caused the injury both to him and them. Cases of enticement, allurement, or invitation of infants to their injury, or setting traps for them, and cases relating to the sufficiency of public ways, or to the exposure upon them of machinery attractive and dangerous to children have no application here.

Danger from machinery in motion in the ordinary course of business cannot be distinguished from that arising from a well, pit, open scuttle, or other stationary object. The movement of the works is a part of the regular and normal condition of the premises. Sullivan *v.* Railroad, 156 Mass. 378; Holbrook *v.* Aldrich, 168 Mass. 15; Rodgers *v.* Lees, 140 Pa. St. 475. The law no more compels the owners to shut down their gates and stop their business for the protection of a trespasser than it requires them to maintain a railing about an open scuttle or to fence in their machinery for the same purpose. Benson v. Company, 77 Md. 535; Mergenthaler v. Kirby, 79 Md. 182. There was no evidence tending to show that the defendants neglected to perform any legal duty to the plaintiff. McGuiness v. Butler, 159 Mass. 233, 236, 238; Grindley v. McKechnie, 163 Mass. 494; Holbrook v. Aldrich, 168 Mass. 15, 17, and cases cited.

Verdict set aside: judgment for the defendants.[1]

PARSONS, J., did not sit: the others concurred.

KEFFE v. MILWAUKEE AND ST. PAUL RAILWAY CO.

SUPREME COURT, MINNESOTA, JANUARY 11, 1875.

Reported in 21 *Minnesota Reports*, 207.

THE plaintiff, an infant, brought this action in the Court of Common Pleas for Ramsey County to recover damages for injuries sustained while playing upon a turn-table of defendant. The circumstances under which plaintiff was injured are thus stated in the complaint: "That in connection with said railroad" [of defendant] "defendant, before and up to the month of October, 1867, used and operated a certain turn-table, located on the lands of said defendant in said town of Northfield, which said turn-table was so constructed and arranged as to be easily turned around and made to revolve in a horizontal direction."

After minutely describing the turn-table, the complaint proceeds: "That said turn-table was situated in a public place, near to a passenger depot of the defendant, and within 120 feet from the residence and home of plaintiff. That said turn-table was unfastened and in no way protected, fenced, guarded, or enclosed, to prevent it from being turned around at the pleasure of small children, although the same could at all times be readily locked and securely fastened.

"That said turn-table . . . was in the possession and under the control of defendant, and not necessary in operating said railroad and it was the duty of said defendant to keep said turn-table fastened or in some way protected, so that children could not readily have access thereto and revolve the same. That the same was not so protected or fastened, and that said turn-table, when left unfastened, was very attractive to young children, and that while the same was being

[1] Latham v. Johnson, [1913] 1 K. B. 398; Cleveland R. Co. v. Ballentine, 84 Fed. 935; Riedel v. West Jersey Co., 177 Fed. 374; Pastorello v. Stone, 89 Conn. 286; Norman v. Bartholomew, 104 Ill. App. 667; Nelson v. Burnham Co., 114 Me. 213; Peninsular Trust Co. v. City, 131 Mich. 571; Houck v. Chicago R. Co., 116 Mo. App. 559; Hughes v. Boston R. Co., 71 N. H. 279; Leithold v. Philadelphia R. Co., 47 Pa. Super. Ct. 137; Dobbins v. Missouri R. Co., 91 Tex. 60; Bottum v. Hawks, 84 Vt. 370; Curtis v. Stone Quarries, 37 Wash. 355; Uthermohler v. Mining Co., 50 W. Va. 457; Ritz v. City, 45 W. Va. 262 *Accord.* Compare Walsh v. Pittsburg R. Co., 221 Pa. St. 463; Lyttle v. Harlem Coal Co., 167 Ky. 345.

moved by children, and at all times when left unfastened, it was dangerous to persons upon or near it.

"That defendant had notice of all the aforesaid facts before and at the time the injury herein named occurred to the plaintiff.

"That plaintiff, on September 11, 1867, was a child of tender years, without judgment or discretion, he being at that date seven years old, and that in consequence of the carelessness, negligence, and improper conduct of said defendant, in not locking, enclosing, or otherwise fastening said turn-table, and by the negligence, carelessness, and improper conduct of said defendant, its agents, and servants, in allowing said turn-table to be and remain unfastened, insecure, and improperly put in motion, it was, at the date last aforesaid, revolved by other children, over whom the parents and guardians of plaintiff had no control, and without their knowledge, and, while being so revolved, the plaintiff, being on said turn-table, had his right leg caught near the knee, between the surface of said turn-table and said abutment or wall, and between the iron rail on said turn-table and the iron rail on said abutment or wall, and said leg was thereby so bruised, broken, mangled, and fractured, as to render amputation necessary."

The complaint further alleges that the injury was caused by defendant's negligence, and without any fault or negligence on the part of the plaintiff, or his parents or guardians, etc.

The defendant having answered the complaint, and the action having been called for trial, the defendant moved for judgment on the pleadings. The motion was granted by Hall, J., and judgment entered accordingly, from which plaintiff appealed.

Bigelow, Flandrau & Clark, for respondent, relied on the opinion of Hall, J., and the cases therein cited.[1]

YOUNG, J. In the elaborate opinion of the Court below, which formed the basis of the argument for the defendant in this Court, the case is treated as if the plaintiff was a mere trespasser, whose tender years and childish instincts were no excuse for the commission of the trespass, and who had no more right than any other trespasser to require the defendant to exercise care to protect him from receiving injury while upon its turn-table. But we are of opinion that, upon the facts stated in the complaint, the plaintiff occupied a very different position from that of a mere voluntary trespasser upon the defendant's property, and it is therefore unnecessary to consider whether the proposition advanced by the defendant's counsel, viz., that a landowner owes no duty of care to trespassers, is not too broad a statement of a rule which is true in many instances.

To treat the plaintiff as a voluntary trespasser is to ignore the averments of the complaint, that the turn-table, which was situate in a public (by which we understand an open, frequented) place, was,

[1] This opinion, too long to be inserted here, will be found in 2 Cent. Law Journal, 170.

when left unfastened, very attractive, and, when put in motion by them, was dangerous to young children, by whom it could be easily put in motion, and many of whom were in the habit of going upon it to play. The turn-table, being thus attractive, presented to the natural instincts of young children a strong temptation; and such children, following, as they must be expected to follow, those natural instincts, were thus allured into a danger whose nature and extent they, being without judgment or discretion, could neither apprehend nor appreciate, and against which they could not protect themselves. The difference between the plaintiff's position and that of a voluntary trespasser, capable of using care, consists in this, that the plaintiff was induced to come upon the defendant's turn-table by the defendant's own conduct, and that, as to him, the turn-table was a hidden danger, — a trap.

While it is held that a mere licensee "must take the permission with its concomitant conditions, — it may be perils," Hounsell *v.* Smyth, 7 C. B. (N. S.) 731; Bolch *v.* Smith, 7 H. & N. 836, yet even such licensee has a right to require that the owner of the land shall not knowingly and carelessly put concealed dangers in his way. Bolch *v.* Smith, *per* Channell and Wilde, BB.; Corby *v.* Hill, 4 C. B. (N. S.) 556, *per* Willes, J.

And where one goes upon the land of another, not by mere license, but by invitation from the owner, the latter owes him a larger duty. "The general rule or principle applicable to this class of cases is that an owner or occupant is bound to keep his premises in a safe and suitable condition for those who come upon and pass over them, using due care, if he has held out any inducement, invitation, or allurement, either express or implied, by which they have been led to enter thereon." *Per* Bigelow, C. J., in Sweeny *v.* Old Colony & Newport R. Co., 10 Allen, 368, reviewing many cases. And see Indermaur *v.* Dames, L. R. 1 C. P. 274; L. R. 2 C. P. 311.

Now, what an express invitation would be to an adult, the temptation of an attractive plaything is to a child of tender years. If the defendant had left this turn-table unfastened for the purpose of attracting young children to play upon it, knowing the danger into which it was thus alluring them, it certainly would be no defence to an action by the plaintiff, who had been attracted upon the turn-table and injured, to say that the plaintiff was a trespasser, and that his childish instincts were no excuse for his trespass. In Townsend *v.* Wathen, 9 East, 277, it was held to be unlawful for a man to tempt even his neighbor's dogs into danger, by setting traps on his own land, baited with strong-scented meat, by which the dogs were allured to come upon his land and into his traps. In that case, Lord Ellenborough asks, "What is the difference between drawing the animal into the trap by his natural instinct, which he cannot resist, and putting him there by manual force?" And Grose, J., says, "A man must not set traps of this dangerous description in a situation to invite his neighbor's dogs, and, as it were, to compel them by their instinct to come into the traps."

It is true that the defendant did not leave the turn-table unfastened for the purpose of injuring young children; and if the defendant had no reason to believe that the unfastened turn-table was likely to attract and to injure young children, then the defendant would not be bound to use care to protect from injury the children that it had no good reason to suppose were in any danger. But the complaint states that the defendant knew that the turn-table, when left unfastened, was easily revolved; that, when left unfastened, it was very attractive, and when put in motion by them, dangerous, to young children; and knew also that many children were in the habit of going upon it to play. The defendant therefore knew that by leaving this turn-table unfastened and unguarded, it was not merely inviting young children to come upon the turn-table, but was holding out an allurement, which, acting upon the natural instincts by which such children are controlled, drew them by those instincts into a hidden danger; and having thus knowingly allured them into a place of danger, without their fault (for it cannot blame them for not resisting the temptation it has set before them), it was bound to use care to protect them from the danger into which they were thus led, and from which they could not be expected to protect themselves.

We agree with the defendant's counsel that a railroad company is not required to make its land a safe playground for children. It has the same right to maintain and use its turn-table that any landowner has to use his property. It is not an insurer of the lives or limbs of young children who play upon its premises. We merely decide that when it sets before young children a temptation which it has reason to believe will lead them into danger, it must use ordinary care to protect them from harm. What would be proper care in any case must, in general, be a question for the jury, upon all the circumstances of the case.

The position we have taken is fully sustained by the following cases, some of which go much farther in imposing upon the owner of dangerous articles the duty of using care to protect from injury children who may be tempted to play near or meddle with them, than it is necessary to go in this case. Lynch *v.* Nurdin, 1 Q. B. 29; Birge *v.* Gardiner, 19 Conn. 507; Whirley *v.* Whiteman, 1 Head, 610.

It is true that, in the cases cited, the principal question discussed is not whether the defendant owed the plaintiff the duty of care, but whether the defendant was absolved from liability for breach of duty by reason of the fact that the plaintiff was a trespasser, who, by his own act, contributed to the injury; and the distinction is not sharply drawn between the effect of the plaintiff's trespass, as a bar to his right to require care, and the plaintiff's contributory negligence, as a bar to his right to recover for the defendant's failure to exercise such care as it was his duty to use. But as a young child, whom the defendant knowingly tempts to come upon his land, if anything more than a technical trespasser, is led into the commission of the trespass by the defendant himself, and thus occupies a position widely different from that of an ordinary trespasser, the fact that the Courts, in the cases referred to, assumed, instead of proving, that the defendant owed to a young child, under such circumstances, a duty he would not owe to an ordinary trespasser, for whose trespass he was not in any way responsible, does not weaken the authority of those cases. And in Railroad Co. *v.* Stout, 17 Wall. 657 (a case in all respects similar to the present), the distinction insisted on by counsel is taken by Mr. Justice Hunt, and the circumstance that the plaintiff was in some sense a trespasser is held not to exempt the defendant from the duty of care. In the charge of the learned circuit judge at the trial of the last named case (reported under the title of Stout *v.* Sioux City & Pacific R. Co., 2 Dillon, 294), the elements which must concur to render the defendant liable, in a case like the present, are clearly stated.

In Hughes *v.* Macfie, 2 Hurlst. & Coltm. 744, and Mangan *v.* Atterton, L. R. 1 Exch. 239, cited by defendant's counsel, there was nothing to show that the defendants knew or had reason to apprehend that the cellar lid in the one case, or the crushing machine in the other, would be likely to attract young children into danger. It must be conceded that Hughes *v.* Macfie is not easily to be reconciled with Birge *v.* Gardiner, and that Mangan *v.* Atterton seems to conflict with Lynch *v.* Nurdin; but whether correctly decided or otherwise, they do not necessarily conflict with our decision in this case.

Much reliance is placed by defendant on Phila. & Reading R. Co. *v.* Hummell, 44 Penn. St. 375 and Gillis *v.* Penn. R. Co., 59 Penn. St. 129. In the first of these cases, the plaintiff, a young child, was injured by coming upon the track while the cars were in motion. The only negligence charged upon the defendant was the omission to give any signal at or after the starting of the train. If the plaintiff had been crossing the track, through one of the openings which the company had suffered the people in the neighborhood to make in the train while standing on the track, and the cars had then been run together upon him, without any warning, the case would more nearly resemble the present; but the facts, as they appear, show that the company used abundant care, and that it had no reason to suppose that the plaintiff was exposed to danger; and the decision is put upon the latter ground, although Strong, J., delivering the opinion of the Court, uses language which lends some support to the defendant's contention in this case. Gillis *v.* Penn. R. Co. was properly decided, on the ground that the company did nothing to invite the plaintiff upon the platform, by the fall of which he was injured, and that the platform was strong enough to bear the weight of any crowd of people which the company might reasonably expect would come upon it. Neither of these cases is an authority against, while a later case in the same court, Kay *v.* Penn. R. Co., 65 Penn. St. 269, tends strongly to support, the plaintiff's right of action in this case; and the recent case of Pittsburg, A. & M. Passenger R. Co. *v.* Caldwell, 74 Penn. St. 421, points in the same direction.

It was not urged upon the argument that the plaintiff was guilty of contributory negligence, and we have assumed that the plaintiff exercised, as he was bound to do, such reasonable care as a child of his age and understanding was capable of using, and that there was no negligence on the part of his parents or guardians, contributing to his injury. *Judgment reversed.*[1]

FROST *v.* EASTERN RAILROAD

SUPREME COURT, NEW HAMPSHIRE, DECEMBER, 1886.

Reported in 64 *New Hampshire Reports*, 220.

CASE, for personal injuries from the alleged negligence of the defendants in not properly guarding and securing a turn-table. The plaintiff, who sues by his father and next friend, was seven years old when the accident occurred, June 23, 1877, and the action was commenced June 7, 1884. Plea, the general issue and statute of limitations. A motion for a nonsuit was denied, and the defendants excepted. Verdict for the plaintiff. The facts are sufficiently stated in the opinion.

CLARK, J. The action is not barred by the statute of limitations. "Any infant, married woman, or insane person may bring any personal actions within two years after such disability is removed." G. L., c. 221, s. 7.

As a general rule, in cases where a disability exists when the right of action accrues, the statute does not run during the continuance of the disability, and it has not commenced to run against the plaintiff.

[1] Railroad Co. *v.* Stout, 17 Wall. 657; Union R. Co. *v.* McDonald, 152 U. S. 262 (slackpit); St. Louis R. Co. *v.* Underwood, (C. C. A.) 194 Fed. 363 (pile of lumber); Southern R. Co. *v.* Bunt, 131 Ala. 591; Thompson *v.* Alexander Cotton Mills Co., 190 Ala. 184 (drain containing hot water); Barrett *v.* Southern P. R. Co., 91 Cal. 296 (but see Peters *v.* Bowman, 115 Cal. 345 — pond; George *v.* Los Angeles R. Co., 126 Cal. 357 — cars standing unattended); Ferguson *v.* Columbus R. Co., 75 Ga. 637, 77 Ga. 102 (but see Savannah R. Co. *v.* Beavers, 113 Ga. 398 — excavation); City *v.* McMahon, 154 Ill. 141; Donk Bros. *v.* Leavitt, 109 Ill. App. 385; Belt R. Co. *v.* Charters, 123 Ill. App. 322 (but see American Advertising Co. *v.* Flannigan, 100 Ill. App. 452); Chicago R. Co. *v.* Fox, 38 Ind. App. 268; Lewis *v.* Cleveland R. Co., 42 Ind. App. 337; Edgington *v.* Burlington R. Co., 116 Ia. 410 (but see Anderson *v.* Ft. Dodge R. Co., 150 Ia. 465); Price *v.* Atchison Water Co., 58 Kan. 551 (reservoir); Kansas City R. Co. *v.* Matson, 68 Kan. 815 (wood pile); Osborn *v.* Atchison R. Co., 86 Kan. 440 (abandoned round house — but see Somerfield *v.* Land and Power Co., 93 Kan. 762 — unguarded canal); Bransom *v.* Labrot, 81 Ky. 638 (pile of timber); Palermo *v.* Orleans Ice Co., 130 La. 833 (gutter containing hot water); Koons *v.* St. Louis R. Co., 65 Mo. 592; Schmidt *v.*

Pierce *v.* Dustin, 24 N. H. 417; Little *v.* Downing, 37 N. H. 356. It is said that the plaintiff's next friend was under no disability, that he could have brought the action at any time within six years after the right of action accrued, and therefore the statute should apply to this case. It is an answer to this suggestion that it is the infant's action, and the failure of the next friend to bring suit within six years is no bar to the plaintiff's right of action. Wood Lim. of Act. 476.

The motion for a nonsuit raises the question whether there was evidence upon which the jury could properly find a verdict for the plaintiff. Paine *v.* Railway, 58 N. H. 611. The ground of the action is, that the defendants were guilty of negligence in maintaining a turn-table insecurely guarded, which, being wrongfully set in motion by older boys, caused an injury to the plaintiff, who was at that time seven years old, and was attracted to the turn-table by the noise of the older and larger boys turning and playing upon it. The turn-table was situated on the defendants' land, about sixty feet from the public street, in a cut with high, steep embankments on each side; and the land on each side was private property and fenced. It was fastened by a toggle, which prevented its being set in motion unless the toggle was drawn by a lever, to which was attached a switch padlock, which being locked prevented the lever from being used unless the staple was drawn. At the time of the accident the turn-table was fastened by the toggle, but it was a controverted point whether the padlock was then locked. When secured by the toggle and not locked with the padlock, the turn-table could not be set in motion by boys of the age and strength of the plaintiff.

Upon these facts we think the action cannot be maintained. The alleged negligence complained of relates to the construction and condition of the turn-table, and it is not claimed that the defendants were guilty of any active misconduct towards the plaintiff. The right of a landowner in the use of his own land is not limited or qualified like

Kansas City Distilling Co., 90 Mo. 284 (hole made by escaping steam); Berry *v.* St. Louis R. Co., 214 Mo. 593 (but see Overholt *v.* Vieths, 93 Mo. 422 — abandoned quarry; Barney *v.* Hannibal R. Co., 126 Mo. 372 — unfenced freight yard; Kelly *v.* Benas, 217 Mo. 1 — pile of lumber); Chicago R. Co. *v.* Krayenbuhl, 65 Neb. 889; Evansich *v.* Gulf R. Co., 57 Tex. 126 (but see Missouri R. Co. *v.* Edwards, 90 Tex. 65; Johnson *v.* Atlas Supply Co., (Tex. Civ. App.) 183 S. W. 31, 33); Smalley *v.* Rio Grande R. Co., 34 Utah, 423 (but see Palmer *v.* Oregon S. L. Co., 34 Utah, 466); Haynes *v.* City, 69 Wash. 419 (but see Barnhart *v.* Chicago R. Co., 89 Wash. 304); Kelley *v.* Southern R. Co., 152 Wis. 328 (but see Emond *v.* Kimberly-Clark Co., 159 Wis. 83 — pond) *Accord.*

Compare McCabe *v.* American Woolen Co., (C. C. A.) 132 Fed. 1006 (unguarded canal); Valley Planing Mill *v.* McDaniel, 119 Ark. 139; Brinkley *v.* Cooper, 70 Ark. 331; Prickett *v.* Pardridge, 189 Ill. App. 307; Stendal *v.* Boyd, 73 Minn. 53; Dahl *v.* Valley Dredging Co., 125 Minn. 90; Cooper *v.* Overton, 102 Tenn. 211.

See also Smith, Landowner's Liability to Children, 11 Harv. Law Rev. 349, 434; 7 Thompson, Negligence, § 1031; Burdick, Torts (3d. ed.), §§ 558–569.

As to the age to which the doctrine is applicable, see Belt R. Co. *v.* Charters, 123 Ill. App. 322; State Bank *v.* Mandel, 176 Ill. App. 278; Wilmes *v.* Chicago R. Co., 175 Ia. 101; Shaw *v.* Chicago R. Co., (Mo.) 184 S. W. 1151.

the enjoyment of a right or privilege in which others have an interest, as the use of a street for highway purposes under the general law, or for other purposes under special license (Moynihan *v.* Whidden, 143 Mass. 287), where care must be taken not to infringe upon the lawful rights of others. At the time of his injury the plaintiff was using the defendants' premises as a playground without right. The turn-table was required in operating the defendants' railroad. It was located on its own land so far removed from the highway as not to interfere with the convenience and safety of the public travel, and it was not a trap set for the purpose of injuring trespassers. Aldrich *v.* Wright, 53 N. H. 404. Under these circumstances, the defendants owed no duty to the plaintiff; and there can be no negligence or breach of duty where there is no act or service which the party is bound to perform or fulfil. A landowner is not required to take active measures to insure the safety of intruders, nor is he liable for an injury resulting from the lawful use of his premises to one entering upon them without right. A trespasser ordinarily assumes all risk of danger from the condition of the premises; and to recover for an injury happening to him he must show that it was wantonly inflicted, or that the owner or occupant, being present and acting, might have prevented the injury by the exercise of reasonable care after discovering the danger. Clark *v.* Manchester, 62 N. H. 577; State *v.* Railroad, 52 N. H. 528; Sweeny *v.* Railroad, 10 Allen, 368; Morrissey *v.* Railroad, 126 Mass. 377; Severy *v.* Nickerson, 120 Mass. 306; Morgan *v.* Hallowell, 57 Me. 375; Pierce *v.* Whitcomb, 48 Vt. 127; McAlpin *v.* Powell, 70 N. Y. 126; St. L., V. & T. H. R. R. Co. *v.* Bell, 81 Ill. 76; Gavin *v.* Chicago, 97 Ill. 66; Wood *v.* School District, 44 Iowa, 27; Gramlich *v.* Wurst, 86 Pa. St. 74; Cauley *v.* P. C., & St. Louis Railway Co., 95 Pa. St. 398; Gillespie *v.* McGowan, 100 Pa. St. 144; Mangan *v.* Atterton, L. R. 1 Ex. 239. The maxim that a man must use his property so as not to incommode his neighbor, only applies to neighbors who do not interfere with it or enter upon it. Knight *v.* Abert, 6 Pa. St. 472. To hold the owner liable for consequential damages happening to trespassers from the lawful and beneficial use of his own land would be an unreasonable restriction of his enjoyment of it.

We are not prepared to adopt the doctrine of Railroad Co. *v.* Stout, 17 Wall. 657, and cases following it, that the owner of machinery or other property attractive to children is liable for injuries happening to children wrongfully interfering with it on his own premises. The owner is not an insurer of the safety of infant trespassers. One having in his possession agricultural or mechanical tools is not responsible for injuries caused to trespassers by careless handling, nor is the owner of a fruit-tree bound to cut it down or enclose it, or to exercise care in securing the staple and lock with which his ladder is fastened, for the protection of trespassing boys who may be attracted by the fruit. Neither is the owner or occupant of premises upon which there is a natural or artificial pond, or a blueberry pasture, legally required to exercise care in securing his gates and bars to guard against accidents to straying and trespassing children. The owner is under no duty to a mere trespasser to keep his premises safe; and the fact that the trespasser is an infant cannot have the effect to raise a duty where none otherwise exists. "The supposed duty has regard to the public at large, and cannot well exist as to one portion of the public and not to another, under the same circumstances. In this respect children, women, and men are upon the same footing. In cases where certain duties exist, infants may require greater care than adults, or a different kind of care; but precautionary measures having for their object the protection of the public must as a rule have reference to all classes alike." Nolan *v.* N. Y. N. H. & H. Railroad Co., 53 Conn. 461.

There being no evidence to charge the defendants with negligence, the motion for a nonsuit should have been granted.

Exceptions sustained.[1]

COOKE *v.* MIDLAND GREAT WESTERN RAILWAY OF IRELAND

IN THE HOUSE OF LORDS, MARCH 1, 1909.

Reported in [1909] *Appeal Cases*, 229.

THE appellant by his father brought an action against the respondents for an injury sustained on the company's land in Meath under the circumstances stated in the headnote, the details of which are fully discussed in the judgments in this House. At the trial before Lord O'Brien, C. J., the jury found a verdict for the plaintiff for £550, and judgment was entered accordingly. The jury found that the fence was in a defective condition through the negligence of the defendants; that the plaintiff was allured through the hedge and up to the turn-table by the negligence of the defendants; and that it was by reason of the defendants' negligence and as the effective cause of it that the misfortune occurred. That judgment was affirmed by the King's Bench Division in Ireland (Palles, C. B., and Johnson, J., Kenny, J., dissenting) and was afterwards set aside by the Court of Appeal in Ireland (Sir S. Walker, L. C., FitzGibbon and Holmes, L.JJ.). Hence this appeal by the plaintiff.[2]

[1] Wilmot *v.* McPadden, 79 Conn. 367 (building in course of construction); Daniels *v.* New York R. Co., 154 Mass. 349; Ryan *v.* Towar, 128 Mich. 463 (water wheel); Peninsular Trust Co. *v.* City, 131 Mich. 571 (reservoir); Hughes *v.* Boston R. Co., 71 N. H. 279 (torpedo on right of way); Delaware R. Co. *v.* Reich, 61 N. J. Law, 635; Walsh *v.* Fitchburg R. Co., 145 N. Y. 301; Railroad Co. *v.* Harvey, 77 Ohio St. 235; Paolino *v.* McKendall, 24 R. I. 432 (unguarded fire); Uthermohlen *v.* Bogg's Run Co., 50 W. Va. 457 *Accord.*

[2] The arguments of counsel and the concurring opinions of Lords Atkinson, Collins, and Loreburn are omitted.

LORD MACNAGHTEN. My Lords, the only question before your Lordships is this: Was there evidence of negligence on the part of the company fit to be submitted to the jury? If there was, the verdict must stand, although your Lordships might have come to a different conclusion on the same materials.

I cannot help thinking that the issue has been somewhat obscured by the extravagant importance attached to the gap in the hedge, both in the arguments of counsel and in the judgments of some of the learned judges who have had the case under consideration. That there was a gap there, that it was a good broad gap some three feet wide, is, I think, proved beyond question. But of all the circumstances attending the case it seems to me that this gap taken by itself is the least important. I have some difficulty in believing that a gap in a roadside fence is a strange and unusual spectacle in any part of Ireland. But however that may be, I quite agree that the insufficiency of the fence, though the company were bound by Act of Parliament to maintain it, cannot be regarded as the effective cause of the accident.

The question for the consideration of the jury may, I think, be stated thus: Would not a private individual of common sense and ordinary intelligence, placed in the position in which the company were placed, and possessing the knowledge which must be attributed to them, have seen that there was a likelihood of some injury happening to children resorting to the place and playing with the turn-table, and would he not have thought it his plain duty either to put a stop to the practice altogether, or at least to take ordinary precautions to prevent such an accident as that which occurred?

This, I think, was substantially the question which the Lord Chief Justice presented to the jury. It seems to me to be in accordance with the view of the Court of Queen's Bench in Lynch *v.* Nurdin, 1 Q. B. 29, and the opinion expressed by Romer and Stirling, L.JJ., in McDowall *v.* Great Western Ry. Co., [1903] 2 K. B. 331.

The Lord Chancellor of Ireland puts Lynch *v.* Nurdin, 1 Q. B. 29, aside. He holds that it bears no analogy to the present case, because the thing that did the mischief there was a "cart in the public street — a nuisance." But no question of nuisance was considered in Lynch *v.* Nurdin. That point was not suggested. The ground of the decision is a very simple proposition. "If," says Lord Denman, "I am guilty of negligence in leaving anything dangerous in a place where I know it to be extremely probable that some other person will unjustifiably set it in motion to the injury of a third, and if that injury should be so brought about, I presume that the sufferer might have redress by action against both or either of the two, but unquestionably against the first." If that proposition be sound, surely the character of the place, though, of course, an element proper to be considered, is not a matter of vital importance. It cannot make very much difference whether the place is dedicated to the use of the public or left open by a careless owner to the invasion of children who make it their playground.

I think the jury were entitled and bound to take into consideration all the circumstances of the case — the mode in which the turn-table was constructed; its close proximity to the wall by which the plaintiff's leg was crushed; the way in which it was left, unfenced, unlocked, and unfastened; the history of this bit of ground and its position, shut off as it was by an embankment from the view of the company's servants at the station, and lying half derelict. After the construction of the embankment it served no purpose in connection with the company's undertaking, except that at one time a corner of it was used as a receptacle for some timber belonging to the company, and afterwards as a site for this turn-table. In other respects, and apart from these uses, it seems to have been devoted or abandoned to the sustenance of the railway inspector's goat and the diversion of the youth of Navan. It is proved that in spite of a notice board idly forbidding trespass it was a place of habitual resort for children, and that children were frequently playing with the timber, and afterwards with the turn-table. At the date of the trial, twelve months after the accident, a beaten path leading from the gap bore witness both to the numbers that flocked to the spot and to the special attraction that drew children to it. It is remarkable that not a single word of cross-examination as to either of these points was addressed to the principal witnesses for the plaintiff, Tully, the herd, and Gertrude Cooke, the plaintiff's sister; nor was any explanation or evidence offered on the part of the company. Now the company knew, or must be deemed to have known, all the circumstances of the case and what was going on. Yet no precaution was taken to prevent an accident of a sort that might well have been foreseen and very easily prevented. They did not close up the gap until after the accident. Then it was the first thing thought of. But it was too late. They did not summon any of the children who played there, or bring them before the magistrates, as a warning to trespassers and a proof that they were really in earnest in desiring to stop an objectionable practice which had gone on so long and so openly. They did not have their turn-table locked automatically in the way in which Mr. Barnes, C. E., whose evidence is uncontradicted, says it is usual to lock such machines. The table, it seems, was not even fastened. There was a bolt; but if Cooke, the father of the plaintiff, is to be believed, the bolt was rusty and unworkable. The jury were not bound to believe Fowler, a ganger in the service of the company, in preference to Cooke. Fowler, after some incautious admissions which the jury probably accepted as true, turned round and showed himself, as the Chief Justice says, to be hostile to the plaintiff. He prevaricated to such an extent that the jury were justified in disregarding everything said by him with the view of shielding his employers or saving himself from blame, whether it came out of his own head, as the nonsense he talked about rat-holes, or was suggested by counsel, as the expression of "hunting" children off the ground.

. . . .

It seems to me that the Chief Justice would have been wrong if he had withdrawn the case from the jury. I think the jury were entitled, in view of all the circumstances, on the evidence before them, uncontradicted as it was, to find that the company were guilty of negligence. I am therefore of opinion that the finding of the jury should be upheld and the judgment under appeal reversed, with pauper costs here and costs below; and I move your Lordships accordingly.

I will only add that I do not think that this verdict will be followed by the disastrous consequences to railway companies and landowners which the Lord Chancellor of Ireland seems to apprehend. Persons may not think it worth their while to take ordinary care of their own property, and may not be compellable to do so; but it does not seem unreasonable to hold that, if they allow their property to be open to all comers, infants as well as children of maturer age, and place upon it a machine attractive to children and dangerous as a plaything, they may be responsible in damages to those who resort to it with their tacit permission, and who are unable, in consequence of their tender age, to take care of themselves.[1]

[1] See Latham v. Johnson, [1913] 1 K.B. 398. In that case Hamilton, L. J., said (pp. 415–416): "Two other terms must be alluded to — a 'trap' and 'attraction' or 'allurement.' A trap is a figure of speech, not a formula. It involves the idea of concealment and surprise, of an appearance of safety under circumstances cloaking a reality of danger. Owners and occupiers alike expose licensees and visitors to traps on their premises at their peril, but a trap is a relative term. In the case of an infant, there are moral as well as physical traps. There may accordingly be a duty towards infants not merely not to dig pitfalls for them, but not to lead them into temptation. 'Allurements,' too, is a vague word. It may refer only to the circumstances under which the injured child has entered the close. Here it is hard to see how infantile temptations can give rights, however much they may excuse peccadilloes. A child will be a trespasser still, if he goes on private ground without leave or right, however natural it may have been for him to do so. On the other hand, the allurement may arise after he has entered with leave or as of right. Then the presence in a frequented place of some object of attraction, tempting him to meddle where he ought to abstain, may well constitute a trap, and in the case of a child too young to be capable of contributory negligence it may impose full liability on the owner or occupier, if he ought, as a reasonable man, to have anticipated the presence of the child and the attractiveness and peril of the object."

"Finally, what objects which attract infants to their hurt are traps even to them? Not all objects with which children hurt themselves simpliciter. A child can get into mischief and hurt itself with anything if it is young enough. In some cases the answer may rest with the jury, but it must be matter of law to say whether a given object can be a trap in the double sense of being fascinating and fatal. No strict answer has been, or perhaps ever will be, given to the question, but I am convinced that a heap of paving stone in broad daylight in a private close cannot so combine the properties of temptation and retribution as to be properly called a trap."

BOLCH *v.* SMITH

IN THE EXCHEQUER, JANUARY 30, 1862.

Reported in 7 *Hurlstone & Norman*, 736.

ACTION to recover for damage occurring as hereinafter stated. Pleas: first, not guilty; second, various special pleas. Issues thereon.[1]

At the trial, before CHANNELL, B., at the last Hampshire Summer Assizes, the following facts appeared: The plaintiff was a millwright employed in the Government dock-yard at Portsmouth. The defendant was a contractor, and had been engaged for some time in enlarging one of the docks. The men employed in the dock-yard were not allowed to leave it during the day, and water-closets had been built for their use. For the purpose of going to these water-closets, they had permission to use certain paths which crossed the dock-yard. The defendant had been permitted to erect a mortar-mill for the purpose of his work, and he built an engine-house on one side of one of these paths and the mortar-mill on the other side of the path. A revolving shaft which connected the engine with the mill was placed across the path about six inches above the level of the ground. This shaft was partly covered with a few planks not joined together, and forming an incline upwards from the ground, so that a barrow could be wheeled over it. The shaft had been on that spot covered or uncovered for five years. The plaintiff had gone along this path to one of the water-closets, and whilst returning he accidentally stumbled when near the shaft, which was in rapid motion, and on reaching out his hand to save himself his left arm was caught by the shaft, and so much lacerated that it was necessary to amputate it. There were two other paths by which the plaintiff might have reached the water-closet; but the one he used was the shortest and most convenient.

In the course of the defendant's case it appeared that the shaft had been fenced to some extent but not sufficiently.

At the close of the defendant's case, the learned judge proposed to leave it to the jury to assess the damages, supposing the plaintiff had a right of action, and then to nonsuit the plaintiff, reserving leave for him to move to set aside the nonsuit, and enter the verdict for the amount assessed by the jury. The plaintiff's counsel declined to accede to this course; whereupon the learned judge left it to the jury to say: first, whether the plaintiff was lawfully using the way in question on the day of the accident; secondly, whether the defendant was guilty of negligence in leaving the shaft in the state it was on that day. The jury answered both questions in the affirmative, and they added that they found " that the shaft was not sufficiently fenced; " and they assessed the damages at 230*l*. A verdict having been entered for the plaintiff for that amount,

[1] Statement abridged. Arguments omitted, and parts of opinions.

Coleridge, in last Michaelmas Term, obtained a rule nisi for a new trial, on the ground that the learned judge misdirected the jury in not telling them that there was no obligation on the part of the defendant to fence the shaft; and also that the verdict was against the evidence.

CHANNELL, B. I am of opinion that the rule must be absolute for a new trial. [Remainder of opinion omitted.]

MARTIN, B. I am of the same opinion. The real objection to this action is that the plaintiff has failed to establish that there was any obligation or duty on the part of the defendant to have this path in any other condition than it was at the time of the accident. That should have been established in some way. If the plaintiff could have shown any such obligation on the part of the defendant he would have made out a case, but that was a condition precedent, and the plaintiff has wholly failed to do so. The defendant had a right to erect the machinery, to erect it in the place he did, and to work it in the manner he was doing.

Then what is the true condition of the plaintiff? It is said that he had a right to go along the path across which the machinery was erected, for he was a workman employed in the dock-yard, and had liberty to use the water-closet. But that is a fallacious argument. It is true the plaintiff had permission to use the path. Permission involves leave and license, but it gives no *right.* If I avail myself of permission to cross a man's land, I do so by virtue of a license, not of a right. It is an abuse of language to call it a right: it is an excuse or license, so that the party cannot be treated as a trespasser. Inasmuch as there was another way by which the plaintiff might have gone, but voluntarily chose the one which was out of order, I think he has no right of action against the defendant, and that he ought to have been nonsuited at the trial.

WILDE, B. I am of the same opinion. It is of importance in all these cases that the facts upon which the decisions are based should be made plain. The plaintiff was one of a number of persons who obtained leave and license from the dock-yard authorities to cross the yard from one place to another. The defendant had permission from the same authorities to put up certain machinery in the yard. The plaintiff while walking along the usual track fell down, not by reason of any obstruction, but in consequence of stumbling, and in trying to save himself, his arm came in contact with a revolving shaft and was lacerated.

I will decide the case as if it were a question between the plaintiff and the owners of the yard, because if they are not responsible for putting up the shaft, a fortiori the defendant is not. Then, was there any obligation on the owners of the yard not to put up machinery that might be dangerous to persons crossing it? None of the facts tend to show that any such obligation existed. If what was put up was an obstruction to any person who used that way, the only consequence would be that he would have to go another way. That being so, it appears to me that this action cannot lie, because I agree that it is founded upon a duty, and none exists.

That disposes of the case; but I will add that I do not mean to say that if the defendant had made a hole in the yard, and had covered it in a way that was insufficient, but which appeared to be sufficient, he would not have been liable. But here there was nothing of that character. The danger was open and visible. There was nothing which could be called a " trap."

POLLOCK, C. B., concurred. *Rule absolute for a new trial.*[1]

GAUTRET v. EGERTON

IN THE COMMON PLEAS, FEBRUARY 11, 1867.

Reported in Law Reports, 2 Common Pleas, 371.

THE declaration in the first of these actions stated that the defendants were possessed of a close of land, and of a certain canal and cuttings intersecting the same, and of certain bridges across the said canal and cuttings, communicating with and leading to certain docks of the defendants, which said land and bridges had been and were from time to time used with the consent and permission of the defendants by persons proceeding towards and coming from the said docks; that the defendants, well knowing the premises, wrongfully, negligently, and improperly kept and maintained the said land, canal, cuttings, and bridges, and suffered them to continue and be in so improper a state and condition as to render them dangerous and unsafe for persons lawfully passing along and over the said land and bridges towards the said docks, and using the same as aforesaid; and that Leon Gautret, whilst he was lawfully in and passing and walking along the said close and over the said bridge, and using the same in the manner and for the purpose aforesaid, by and through the said wrongful, negligent, and improper conduct of the defendants as aforesaid, fell into one of the said cuttings of the defendants, intersecting the said close as aforesaid, and thereby lost his life within twelve calendar months next before the suit: and the plaintiff, as administratrix, for the benefit of herself, the widow of the said Leon Gautret, and A. Gautret, &c., according to the statute in such case made and provided, claimed 2,500*l.*

[1] See also Cole v. Willcutt, 214 Mass. 453; Habina v. Twin City Electric Co., 150 Mich. 41; Chesley v. Rocheford, 4 Neb. Unoff. 768, 777.

For examples of " traps," see Lowery v. Walker, [1911] A. C. 10; Rollestone v. Cassirer, 3 Ga. App. 161; Foren v. Rodick, 90 Me. 276; Hill v. President and Trustees, 61 Or. 190; Grant v. Hass, 31 Tex. Civ. App. 688; Brinilson v. Chicago R. Co., 144 Wis. 614.

The defendants demurred to the declaration, on the ground that "it does not appear that there was any legal duty or obligation on the part of the defendants to take means for preventing the said land, &c., being dangerous and unsafe." Joinder.

Crompton (*Mellish, Q. C.*, with him), in support of the demurrer. — To maintain this action, the declarations ought to show a *duty* in the defendants to keep the canal, cuttings, and bridges in a safe condition, and also that some invitation had been held out to the deceased to come there, and that the thing complained of constituted a sort of trap. Seymour *v.* Maddox, 16 Q. B. 326 (E. C. L. R. vol. 71), 19 L. J. Q. B. 525; Corby *v.* Hill, 4 C. B. N. S. 556 (E. C. L. R. vol. 93), 27 L. J. C. P. 318. The declaration is entirely wanting in all these particulars. It is not enough to show that the defendants were aware that the place in question was in an unsafe condition, and that the public were in the habit of passing along it. Hounsell *v.* Smyth, 7 C. B. N. S. 731, 29 L. J. C. P. 203.

[WILLES, J. The declaration does not even state that the deceased persons were unacquainted with the state of the place.]

Herschell, for the plaintiff Gautret. — The question raised upon this declaration is, whether there is any duty on the part of the defendants toward persons using their land as the deceased here did. That may be negligence in the case of a licensee, which would not be negligence as against a mere trespasser: and, if there can be any case in which the law would imply a duty, it is sufficiently alleged here.

[WILLES, J. It may be the duty of the defendants to abstain from doing any act which may be dangerous to persons coming upon the land by their invitation or permission, as in Indermaur *v.* Dames, Law Rep. 1 C. P. 274.[1] So, if I employ one to carry an article which is of a peculiarly dangerous nature, without cautioning him, I may be responsible for any injury he sustains through the absence of such caution. That was the case of Farrant *v.* Barnes, 11 C. B. N. S. 553, 31 L. J. C. P. 137. But, what duty does the law impose upon these defendants to keep their bridges in repair? If I dedicate a way to the public which is full of ruts and holes, the public must take it as it is. If I dig a pit in it, I may be liable for the consequences: but, if I do nothing, I am not.]

It was not necessary to specify the nature of the negligence which is charged: it was enough to allege generally a duty and a breach of it. Knowing the bridge to be unsafe, it was the duty of the defendants not to permit the public to use it. In Bolch *v.* Smith, 7 H. & N. 736, 31 L. J. Ex. 201, the defect in the fencing of the shaft was apparent: but the judgments of Channell and Wilde, BB., seem to concede that, if there had been a concealed defect, the action would have been maintainable. That shows that there is some duty in such a case as this.

[1] Affirmed in the Exchequer Chamber, L. R. 2 C. P. 311.

Potter, for the plaintiff Jones, submitted that the implied request on the part of the defendants to persons having occasion to go to the docks to pass by the way in question, raised a duty in them to keep it in a safe condition.

WILLES, J. I am of opinion that our judgment must be for the defendants in each of these cases. The argument urged on behalf of the plaintiffs, when analyzed, amounts to this, that we ought to construe the general words of the declaration as describing whatever sort of negligence the plaintiffs can prove at the trial. The authorities, however, and reason and good sense, are the other way. The plaintiff must, in his declaration, give the defendant notice of what his complaint is. He must recover *secundum allegata et probata.* What is it that a declaration of this sort should state in order to fulfil those conditions ? It ought to state the facts upon which the supposed duty is founded, and the duty to the plaintiff with the breach of which the defendant is charged. It is not enough to show that the defendant has been guilty of negligence, without showing in what respect he was negligent, and how he became bound to use care to prevent injury to others. All that these declarations allege is, that the defendants were possessed of land, and of a canal and cuttings intersecting the same, and of certain bridges across the canal and cuttings communicating with and leading to certain docks of theirs; that they allowed persons going to and from the docks, whether upon the business or for the profit of the defendants or not, to pass over the land; and that the deceased persons, in pursuance of and using that permission, fell into one of the cuttings, and so met their deaths. The consequences of these accidents are sought to be visited upon these defendants, because they have allowed persons to go over their land, not alleging it to have been upon the business or for the benefit of the defendants, or as the servants or agents of the defendants; nor alleging that the defendants have been guilty of any wrongful act, such as digging a trench on the land, or misrepresenting its condition, or anything equivalent to laying a trap for the unwary passengers; but simply because they permitted these persons to use a way with the condition of which, for anything that appears, those who suffered the injury were perfectly well acquainted. That is the whole sum and substance of these declarations. If the docks to which the way in question led were public docks, the way would be a public way, and the township or parish would be bound to repair it, and no such liability as this could be cast upon the defendants merely by reason of the soil of the way being theirs. That is so not only in reason but also upon authority. It was so held in Robbins *v.* Jones, 15 C. B. N. S. 221, 33 L. J. C. P. 1, where a way having been for a number of years dedicated to the public, we held that the owner of the adjoining house was not responsible for death resulting to a person from the giving way of the pavement, partly in consequence of its being over-weighted by a number of persons crowding upon it, and partly from its having been weakened by user. Assuming that these were private docks, the private property of the defendants, and that they permitted persons going to or coming from the docks, whether for their own benefit or that of the defendants, to use the way, the dedication of a permission to use the way must be taken to be in the character of a gift. The principle of law as to gifts is, that the giver is not responsible for damage resulting from the insecurity of the thing, unless he knew its evil character at the time, and omitted to caution the donee. There must be something like fraud on the part of the giver before he can be made answerable. It is quite consistent with the declarations in these cases that this land was in the same state at the time of the accident that it was in at the time the permission to use it was originally given. To create a cause of action, something like fraud must be shown. No action will lie against a spiteful man who, seeing another running into a position of danger, merely omits to warn him. To bring the case within the category of actionable negligence, some wrongful act must be shown, or a breach of some positive duty: otherwise, a man who allows strangers to roam over his property would be held to be answerable for not protecting them against any danger which they might encounter whilst using the license. Every man is bound not wilfully to deceive others, or do any act which may place them in danger. It may be, as in Corby *v.* Hill, 4 C. B. N. S. 556, 27 L. J. C. P. 318, that he is responsible if he puts an obstruction on the way which is likely to cause injury to those who by his permission use the way; but I cannot conceive that he could incur any responsibility merely by reason of his allowing the way to be out of repair. For these reasons, I think these declarations disclose no cause of action against the defendants, and that the latter are therefore entitled to judgment.

KEATING, J. I am of the same opinion. It is not denied that a declaration of this sort must show a duty and a breach of that duty. But it is said that these declarations are so framed that it would be necessary for the plaintiffs at the trial to prove a duty. I am, however, utterly unable to discover any duty which the defendants have contracted towards the persons whom the plaintiffs represent, or what particular breach of duty is charged. It is said that the condition of the land and bridges was such as to constitute them a kind of trap. I cannot accede to that. The persons who used the way took it with all its imperfections.

Herschell asked and obtained leave to amend within ten days, on payment of costs; otherwise judgment for the defendants.

Judgment accordingly.[1]

[1] Hounsell *v.* Smyth, 7 C. B. N. S. 731; Batchelor *v.* Fortescue, 11 Q. B. D. 474; Watson *v.* Manitou R. Co., 41 Col. 138; Bentley *v.* Loverock, 102 Ill. App. 166; Joseph *v.* Henrici Co., 137 Ill. 171; Indiana R. Co. *v.* Barnhart, 115 Ind. 399; South Bend Iron Works *v.* Larger, 11 Ind. App. 367; Dixon *v.* Swift, 98 Me. 207; Reardon *v.* Thompson, 149 Mass. 267; Blackstone *v.* Chelmsford Foundry Co.,

CAMPBELL *v.* BOYD

SUPREME COURT, NORTH CAROLINA, FEBRUARY TERM, 1883.

Reported in 88 *North Carolina Reports*, 129.

CIVIL ACTION tried at Fall Term, 1882, of Beaufort Superior Court, before Gilliam, J.

The defendant appealed.

SMITH, C. J. The defendant owns and operates a mill, that has been built and used for one hundred years, at the head of Pungo creek. A few yards below its site the creek divides, and its waters flow in two separate streams. Along its course on either side run parallel public roads each two miles distant, and from them have been constructed private ways leading up to and meeting at the mill, and affording convenient access from the roads to it. One of these ways was opened by former proprietors, and the other in the year 1867, by the defendant.

In 1875 or 1876, the defendant, with other owners of the intervening land, united in opening a connecting way, between those leading from the public roads, from near points in each, so as to form a direct passway across the two divergent streams from one road to the other,

170 Mass. 321; Vanderbeck *v.* Hendry, 34 N. J. Law, 467; Fitzpatrick *v.* Cumberland Glass Co., 61 N. J. Law, 378; Taylor *v.* Turnpike Co., 65 N. J. Law, 102; Victory *v.* Baker, 67 N. Y. 366; Larmore *v.* Crown Point Iron Co., 101 N. Y. 391; Sterger *v.* Van Sicklen, 132 N. Y. 499; Englehardt *v.* Central R. Co., 139 App. Div. 786; McCann *v.* Thilemann, 36 Misc. 145; Monroe *v.* Atlantic R. Co., 151 N. C. 374; Costello *v.* Farmers' Bank, 34 N. D. 131; Kelley *v.* City, 41 Ohio St. 263; Schiffer *v.* Sauer, 238 Pa. St. 550; Lunsford's Administrator *v.* Colonial Coal Co., 115 Va. 346 *Accord.*

But see Brinilson *v.* Chicago R. Co., 144 Wis. 614.

As to liability to children licensees, see Jansen *v.* Siddal, 41 Ill. App. 279; Cleveland R. Co. *v.* Means, (Ind. App.) 104 N. E. 785; Benson *v.* Baltimore Traction Co., 77 Md. 535; McCoy *v.* Walsh, 186 Mass. 369; Romana *v.* Boston R. Co., 218 Mass. 76; Bottum *v.* Hawks, 84 Vt. 370.

But see Knapp *v.* Doll, 180 Ind. 526 (citing cases); Wilmes *v.* Chicago R. Co., 175 Ia. 101; Lyttle *v.* Town Coal Co., 167 Ky. 345.

As to liability where there is a known, permissive, general use by the public, see Pomponio *v.* New York R. Co., 66 Conn. 528; Western R. Co. *v.* Meigs, 74 Ga. 857; Green *v.* Chicago R. Co., 110 Mich. 648; Barry *v.* New York R. Co., 92 N. Y. 289; Taylor *v.* Delaware Canal Co., 113 Pa. St. 162; Delaney *v.* Milwaukee R. Co., 33 Wis. 67. Compare Tucker *v.* Draper, 62 Neb. 66.

Liability in case of gratuitous carriage: [The judge at the trial in charging the jury] "suggested that the measure of duty towards a bare licensee is different, where the licensor accepts the duty of carrying him, from what it is where he merely permits him to pass through his premises; and I think the cases support this view. . . . I think it was competent for the jury to find, as they must be taken to have found, a failure of that ordinary care which is due from a person who undertakes the carriage of another gratuitously. The principle in all cases of this class is that the care exercised must be reasonable; and the standard of reasonableness naturally must vary according to the circumstances of the case, the trust reposed, and the skill and appliances at the disposal of the person to whom another confides a duty. There is an obvious difference between the measure of confidence reposed and responsibility accepted in the case of a person who merely receives permission to traverse the premises of another, and in the case where a person or his property is received into the custody of another for transportation: see in the case of goods, Southcote's Case, (1601) 4 Rep. 83 b. cited in Coggs *v.* Bernard, 1 Smith, without going up to the mill. Over these waters they also constructed bridges. While this direct route was opened mainly for the convenience of the defendant and his associates, whose lands were traversed, it was also used as well by the public with full knowledge of the defendant, and without objection from any one in passing between the roads.

In February, 1882, the plaintiff, with his horse, while in the use of this connecting way and passing one of the bridges, broke through, and both were precipitated into the creek, and the damage sustained for the redress of which the suit is brought.

The flooring of the bridge was sound, and there was no visible indication of weakness or decay to put a person passing over it on his guard. But the timbers underneath, and hidden by the floor, were in a rotten and unsound condition, and of this the defendant had full knowledge before the disaster.

He was at his mill and saw what occurred, and going up to the place remarked to the plaintiff that when he saw him about to enter the bridge he thought of calling him to stop, but did not do so; that the bridge was unsafe, and he regretted he did not stop the plaintiff from crossing.

These are the material facts found by the judge, under the consent of parties that he should pass upon the evidence and ascertain the facts of the case, and our only inquiry is upon the correctness of his ruling that the defendant is liable in damages to the plaintiff, and from which the defendant appeals.

The only case in our reports bearing upon the point is that of Mulholland *v.* Brownrigg, 2 Hawks, 349. There, the defendant's millpond overflowed parts of the public road, and hollow bridges had been erected, but by whom, did not appear; nor was it shown that they were built at the expense of the public. This condition of things had existed for twenty years, and the mill had been owned and operated by the defendant for the space of five years. The successive mill

L. C., 11th ed., p. 173, and the notes thereto. In the case of persons received for carriage, PARKE, B., says in Lygo *v.* Newbold, (1854) 9 Ex. 302, at p. 305: 'A person who undertakes to provide for the conveyance of another, although he does so gratuitously, is bound to exercise due and reasonable care.' In Austin *v.* Great Western Ry. Co., [1867] 2 Q. B. 442, at p. 445, BLACKBURN, J., says: 'I think that what was said in the case of Marshall *v.* York, Newcastle and Berwick Ry. Co., (1851) 11 C. B. 655, was quite correct. It was there laid down that the right which a passenger by railway has to be carried safely does not depend on his having made a contract, but that the fact of his being a passenger casts a duty on the company to carry him safely.' "

COLLINS, M. R., in Harris *v.* Perry, [1903] 2 K. B. 219, 225, 226. And see, also, Sington on Negligence, 61, 62. But compare Beard *v.* Klusmeier, 158 Ky. 153.

In the case of a gratuitous loan of a chattel, the lender owes no duty to the borrower except to give warning of any defects actually known to the lender. Gagnon *v.* Dana, 69 N. H. 264; Coughlin *v.* Gillison, [1899] 1 Q. B. 145. "A contract of gratuitous service, however, such as one of carriage, involves a duty of reasonable care, and must therefore be distinguished from a contract of gratuitous bailment or a gift, which does not." Salmond on Torts, 361.

proprietors had kept the overflowed bed of the road and the bridges in repair. The plaintiff's wagon, loaded with goods, passing a bridge, broke through, in consequence of its decayed state, and the goods were injured by the water. The action was for this injury. It was declared by the Court that as a nuisance was created by the flooding of the road, and the defendant had undertaken to remedy it in constructing the bridges, it was his duty, as that of preceding proprietors of the mill, to maintain them in a proper condition of repair, and ensure the safety of those persons who in using the road had to pass over them, and that the damage having resulted from his negligence he was liable to the plaintiff. The proposition is asserted, that inasmuch as the defendant has undertaken to remedy a nuisance of his own creating, by constructing the bridge, he undertakes also and is bound to keep it in sufficient repair, and is answerable for the consequences of his neglect to do so.

The principle of law, in more general terms and with a wider scope, is thus expressed by Hoar, J., in Combs *v.* New Bed. Con. Co., 102 Mass. 584. "There is another class of cases in which it has been held that, if a person allows a dangerous place to exist in premises occupied by him, he will be responsible for injury caused thereby, to any other person entering upon the premises by his invitation and procurement, express or implied, and not notified of the danger, if the person injured is in the use of due care."

"The principle is well settled," remarks Appleton, C. J., "that a person injured, without neglect on his part, by a defect or obstruction in a way or passage over which he has been induced to pass for a lawful purpose, by an invitation express or implied, can recover damages for the injury sustained, against the individual so inviting, and being in default for the neglect." Tobin *v.* P. S. & P. R. R., 59 Maine, 188.

Several illustrations of the principle in its different applications will be found in Wharton on Negligence, § 826, and following.

The facts of the present case bring it within the rule thus enunciated. The way was opened by the defendant and his associates; primarily, though it was for his and their accommodation, yet, permissively, to the general travelling public. It has, in fact, been thus used, and known to the defendant to be thus used, with the acquiescence of himself and the others; and under these circumstances it may fairly be assumed to be an invitation to all who have occasion thus to use it; and hence a voluntary obligation is incurred to keep the bridges in a safe condition, so that no detriment may come to travellers.

Reparation is an inseparable incident of its construction, and, as the obligation to repair rests on no other, the liability for neglect must rest on those who put the bridges there and invited the public to use them.

It is true the way might have been closed, or the public prohibited by proper notices from passing over it, and no one could complain of the exercise of the right to do so; but as long as the way is left open and the bridges remain for the public to use, it is incumbent on those who constructed and maintain them to see that they are safe for all. The law does not tolerate the presence over and along a way in common use, of structures apparently sound, but in fact ruinous, like man-traps, inviting travellers to needless disaster and injury. The duty of reparation should rest on some one, and it can rest on none others but those who built and used the bridges, and impliedly at least invite the public to use them also. For neglect of this duty they must abide the consequences.

We hold, therefore, that there is no error, and the judgment must be affirmed.

No error. *Affirmed.*[1]

GALLAGHER *v.* HUMPHREY

In the Queen's Bench, June 14, 1862.

Reported in 6 *Law Times Reports, New Series,* 684; *S. C.* 10 *Weekly Reporter,* 664.[2]

Declaration. That the defendant was possessed of a crane fixed upon the New Hibernia Wharf, in a certain passage called Montague Close, Southwark, along which passage the plaintiff and others were permitted to pass, repass, and use the same as a way to certain wharves; that the crane was used by the defendant and his servants to raise and lower goods over the passage; that the plaintiff was, with the permission of the proprietors of the passage, lawfully passing along the said passage to the said wharves; yet the defendant, by himself and his servants, so negligently, &c. managed, directed, and conducted themselves that by and through such neglect, &c., a part of said crane broke, whilst the defendant, by his servants, was using the same, and certain goods fell upon the plaintiff whilst he was passing along, &c. and broke both his legs, &c.

Pleas: 1. Not guilty. 2. That the plaintiff and others were not permitted by the proprietors of the said passage to pass, repass, and use the said passage as a way from a highway to certain wharves, as in the declaration charged. 3. That the plaintiff was not, with the permission of the proprietors of the said passage, lawfully passing along the

[1] Foster *v.* Portland Min. Co., (C. C. A.) 114 Fed. 613; Central R. Co. *v.* Robertson, 95 Ga. 430; Chicago R. Co. *v.* Reinhardt, 235 Ill. 576, 139 Ill. App. 53; Indianapolis Water Co. *v.* Harold, 170 Ind. 170; Lawson *v.* Shreveport Waterworks Co., 111 La. 73; Schaaf *v.* St. Louis Basket Co., 151 Mo. App. 35; Furey *v.* New York R. Co., 67 N. J. Law, 270; Fogarty *v.* Bogart, 59 App. Div. 114; Toledo Real Estate Co. *v.* Putney, 20 Ohio Cir. Ct. Rep. 486; Bush *v.* Johnston, 23 Pa. St. 209 *Accord.* Compare Moffatt *v.* Kenny, 174 Mass. 311.

[2] The case is reprinted from the Law Times Reports, except the opinions of Crompton, J., and Blackburn, J., which are taken from the Weekly Reporter.

said passage from the said highway to the said wharves, as in the declaration alleged.

Issue on the said pleas.

At the trial before Blackburn, J., at the Croydon Summer Assizes, 1861, it was proved that the plaintiff, the son of a laborer employed in the erection of West Kent Wharf, under a contractor for the defendant's father, had, on the day when the accident happened, taken his father's dinner, according to his usual custom, to West Kent Wharf, and on his return was obliged to pass under a crane erected on the defendant's (Hibernia) wharf, and there employed in lowering barrels of sugar. As he was passing the chain broke, and 12 cwt. of sugar fell upon him, inflicting the injuries complained of. The breakage of the chain was caused by negligence in the mode of applying the breaks, for, after the sugar had been attached the chain of the crane was allowed to run, and then the man suddenly put on the break and the jerk caused the weight to rise and fall and the chain to break. Montague Close is approached by steps from London Bridge, the gate to which was usually opened very early in the morning, and numbers of persons, to the knowledge of the defendant, used to pass along the passage, and no objection was made to persons using the way if on legitimate business. The judge left the following questions to the jury: 1st, Was the accident caused by the negligence of the defendant, or was it a pure accident over which no one could have any control? 2d, Could the boy by reasonable care have avoided the accident? 3d, Were the plaintiff and others permitted to go up Montague Close by the owners? 4th, Did the defendant on the evidence as disclosed tacitly give permission to the plaintiff to pass that way? 5th, Was the boy going to the wharf for a legitimate purpose? The jury having answered all the questions in favor of the plaintiff, a verdict was entered for him, with leave for the defendant to move to set it aside and enter a verdict on the second and third issues. The damages were assessed at £100.

A rule *nisi* having been obtained calling on the plaintiff to show cause why the verdict should not be entered for the defendant on the second and third issues, —

Shee, Serjt., (*Grady* with him,) showed cause. On the form of the rule as obtained the plaintiff is clearly entitled to succeed, as there was evidence that the defendant did by his acts tacitly give permission to the boy to pass along the close for a lawful purpose, and the jury have so found. But the plaintiff is also entitled to succeed on the broader ground. In Corby *v.* Hill, 4 C. B. N. S. 556, it was held that the defendant was liable for the negligence of his servant in placing materials in a dangerous position, and without notice, on a private road along which persons were accustomed to pass by leave of the owners; and in Southcote *v.* Stanley, 25 L. J. 339, Ex.,[1] a visitor to a person's house

[1] The reference should be 25 L. J. (N. S.) or 34 L. J.

was held entitled to recover for injuries caused by opening a glass door which was insecure, and which it was necessary for him to open. (He was then stopped by the Court.)

Petersdorff, Serjt., (*Bridge* with him,) in support of the rule. Montague Close was the defendant's private property, and no one had any right to be there without his express or implied permission. The lowering heavy goods from the warehouses by cranes is a manifestly dangerous business, and persons using the way took upon themselves whatever risks might be incidental to that business. In Hounsell *v.* Smyth, 7 C. B. N. S. 743, where the defendant was held not to be liable for leaving a quarry unfenced on waste land across which the public were allowed to pass, Williams, J., said: "No right is averred, but merely that the owners allowed persons, for diversion or business, to go across the waste without complaint; that is, that they were not so churlish as to interfere with any one who went across. But a person so using the waste has no right to complain of any excavation he may find there; he must accept the permission with its concomitant conditions, and it may be its perils." [BLACKBURN, J. Have you any authority that persons so using the way take upon themselves the negligence of the servants about the place ?] In Bolch *v.* Smith, 31 L. J. 201, Ex., where workmen employed in a dockyard were permitted to use a place as a way on which revolving machinery had been erected, it was held that the right so to use the place was only the right not to be treated as a trespasser, and that there was no obligation to fence the machinery, and no liability for insufficiently fencing it. [COCKBURN, C. J. There was the ordinary state of things in that case, and no superadded negligence.]

COCKBURN, C. J. I doubt whether on the pleadings and this rule it is competent to enter into the question of negligence, and whether the whole matter does not turn upon the question whether permission was or was not given to the plaintiff to pass along the way. But I should be sorry to decide this case upon that narrow ground. I quite agree that a person who merely gives permission to pass and repass along his close is not bound to do more than allow the enjoyment of such permissive right under the circumstances in which the way exists; that he is not bound, for instance, if the way passes along the side of a dangerous ditch or along the edge of a precipice, to fence off the ditch or precipice. The grantee must use the permission as the thing exists. It is a different question, however, where negligence on the part of the person granting the permission is superadded. It cannot be that, having granted permission to use a way subject to existing dangers, he is to be allowed to do any further act to endanger the safety of the person using the way. The plaintiff took the permission to use the way subject to a certain amount of risk and danger, but the case assumes a different aspect when the negligence of the defendant — for the negligence of his servants is his — is added to that risk and danger. The way in question was a private one leading to different wharves. On part of the way a wharf was being constructed or repaired, and the plaintiff's father was employed upon that work. It was the father's habit not to go home to his meals, and the boy used to take them to him at the wharf, and on this occasion was passing along carrying his father's dinner. The plaintiff was therefore passing along on a perfectly legitimate purpose, and the evidence is that the defendant permitted the way to be used by persons having legitimate business upon the premises. That being so, the defendant places himself by such permission under the obligation of not doing anything by himself or his servants from which injury may arise, and if by any act of negligence on the part of himself or his servants injury does arise, he is liable to an action. That is the whole question. The plaintiff is passing along the passage by permission of the defendant, and though he could only enjoy that permission under certain contingencies, yet when injury arises not from any of those contingencies, but from the superadded negligence of the defendant, the defendant is liable for that negligence as much as if it had been upon a public highway.

WIGHTMAN, J. The rule in this case was obtained on a very narrow ground. The declaration having alleged that the plaintiff and others were permitted to pass, repass, and use the way in question, and that the plaintiff was there with the permission of the proprietors of the passage lawfully passing along the passage, the defendant took issue on the fact whether such right to pass along the passage was permitted by the defendant. I think that there was evidence to show that the plaintiff had the permission of the defendant to use the way, and that he was lawfully there at the time of the accident. I entirely agree with my Lord Chief Justice that the plaintiff is also entitled to succeed on the larger ground. It appears to me that such a permission as is here alleged may be subject to the qualification that the person giving it shall not be liable for injuries to persons using the way arising from the ordinary state of things, or of the ordinary nature of the business carried on; but that is distinguishable from the case of injuries wholly arising from the negligence of that person's servants.

CROMPTON, J. I am of the same opinion. I think we should look not only to the grounds upon which this rule was granted, but to the real defence set up by my brother Petersdorff. That defence is, in effect, that the plaintiff was using the way only under the qualified permission that he should be subject to any negligence of the plaintiff or his servants. If that defence be sustainable upon the general issue, or otherwise, we should see whether it is made out, and I am of opinion that it is not made out. I quite agree with what has fallen from my Lord and my brother Wightman. There may be a public dedication of a way, or a private permission to use it subject to a qualification; for example, subject to the danger arising from a stone step or a projecting house; and in such a case the public, or the persons using the way, take the right to use it subject to such qualification; but they are not thereby to be made subject to risks from what may be called active negligence. Whenever a party has a right to pass over certain ground, if injury occurs to him while so passing from negligence, he has a right to compensation. The argument of my brother Petersdorff fails therefore upon this ground. I think, too, that it is doubtful whether even the fact that the injured person was present unlawfully would excuse negligence, though it would be an element in determining what is negligence, and what is not. In the present case, however, that question does not arise, as there is no doubt the plaintiff was there upon a legitimate errand.

BLACKBURN, J. I am of the same opinion. If the substantial defence raised existed I am not sure but what it could be raised under the present pleadings, and the leave reserved; but at any rate I think we could amend the pleadings, if necessary, to raise it. But I do not think that any such defence exists here. The plaintiff seeks to recover for the negligence of the defendant. Now, the existence of negligence depends upon the duty of the party charged with it. I concur with the judgment of the Court of Exchequer in Bolch *v.* Smith that, when permission is given to a person to pass through a yard where dangerous machinery is at work, no duty is cast upon the person giving such permission to fence the machinery against the person permitted so to pass. That decision does not touch the present case, which falls rather within the remark then made by my brother Wilde: "If persons in the condition of the defendant had left anything like a trap in route used on the premises, I am far from saying they would not be liable." This is more like the case of Corby *v.* Hill, where the matter placed upon the road is called a trap set for persons using it; and it is clear that when one gives another permission to pass over his land, it is his duty not to set a trap for him. Here the boy was passing upon a legitimate errand while the defendant's servants were employed in lowering weights. If he had sustained any injury by a weight descending, without any negligence of the defendant's servants, there is no doubt that he could not recover, but he suffered through the negligence of the persons lowering the bags, who were well aware that people were in the habit of passing below, and that danger would arise if the chain broke. I think, therefore, that it was the duty of the defendant and his servants to use ordinary care that the chain should not break. The jury have found that they neglected that duty, and I do not disagree with their finding. Our decision does not conflict with the judgment of the Court of Exchequer in Bolch *v.* Smith, or of the Common Pleas in Hounsell *v.* Smyth. *Rule discharged.*[1]

[1] Felton *v.* Aubrey, 74 Fed. 350; De Haven *v.* Hennessey, (C. C. A.) 137 Fed. 472; Standard Car Co. *v.* McGuire, 161 Fed. 527; Pomponio *v.* New York R. Co., 66 Conn. 528; Rink *v.* Lowry, 38 Ind. App. 132; Schmidt *v.* Michigan Coal Co., 159 Mich. 308; Clarkin *v.* Biwabik-Bessemer Co., 65 Minn. 483; Hyatt *v.* Murray, 101 Minn. 507; Schaaf *v.* St. Louis Basket Co., 151 Mo. App. 35; Knowles *v.*

CARSKADDON *v.* MILLS

IN THE APPELLATE COURT, INDIANA, MAY TERM, 1892.

Reported in 5 Indiana Appellate Court Reports, 22.

ACTION for damage to plaintiff's horse.[1] Trial by the court. The case made by plaintiff's evidence was in substance as follows: —

Defendant purchased a lot of land in October, 1890. Across this lot ran a road leading from one street to another, having a well-defined track made by wagons, horses, etc. The road was not a public highway, but had been used by the travelling public generally for a period of from five to fifteen years. Defendant's lot was not fenced on the front and rear, the direction in which the road ran, but was fenced on the sides. After building a house on the lot, defendant " informed " the people travelling over this roadway not to use it any longer for such purpose; but no heed was paid to this. In the latter part of December, 1890, in order the more effectually to stop the travel over the lot, the defendant stretched a strand of barbed wire across the rear end of the lot, about three feet above the ground and at right angles, or nearly so, with said road. The entire fence was upon the appellee's lot. No notice of any kind was given of this obstruction otherwise than as it advertised itself. The wire could not be seen in the dark of night and only a short distance — twenty to twenty-five feet — in daylight. There were no posts that could be seen from the road in the night when the accident hereinafter alluded to occurred. The appellant, who lived in that community, had frequently travelled over the road leading across this lot, and had no notice or knowledge of its being closed up with the wire. The last time before the accident when he passed over the lot was in September or October, 1890. At about 6 o'clock on the evening of January 1, 1891, after it had become too dark to see this wire, the appellant attempted to drive across this lot, in the road, to perform some legitimate errand on the other side. Not knowing of the presence of the wire, he drove his horse briskly ahead of him until the animal came up suddenly against the barbs, cutting a gash in its front leg four to five inches in length and two inches deep, severing the frontal muscle, from which the horse was injured, to the damage of the appellant.

Exeter Mfg. Co., 77 N. H. 268; Houston R. Co. *v.* Bulger, 35 Tex. Civ. App. 478; Houston R. Co. *v.* O'Leary, (Tex. Civ. App.) 136 S. W. 601 (explosion of car containing fireworks); St. Louis R. Co. *v.* Balthrop, (Tex. Civ. App.) 167 S. W. 246; Hoadley *v.* International Paper Co., 72 Vt. 79 *Accord.*

Illinois R. Co. *v.* Godfrey, 71 Ill. 500; Cunningham *v.* Toledo R. Co., 260 Ill. 589; Dixon *v.* Swift, 98 Me. 207; O'Brien *v.* Union R. Co., 209 Mass. 449 *Contra.* See also Fox *v.* Warner Asphalt Co., 204 N. Y. 240; Roche *v.* American Ice Co., 140 App. Div. 341; Rosenthal *v.* United Beef Co., 52 Misc. 166. Compare Knight *v.* Lanier, 69 App. Div. 454.

[1] Statement abridged.

When the appellant had closed his evidence, the learned judge observed that he had examined the law of the case, and saw no reason why a man could not fence in his own land, on his own ground, and that, [if] " a travelling man over such property taking the license into his own hand, without invitation or inducement, because others do so, suffers injury, he must put up with it."

The judge ruled that plaintiff's evidence did not make out a *prima facie* right to recover; and found for defendant; denying plaintiff's motion for a new trial. Plaintiff appealed.

REINHARD, C. J. [The learned judge said that a license may be created either by parol or by acquiescence in the use of the property for the purpose in question without objection. He *held* that plaintiff was *prima facie* a licensee, and not a trespasser.]

A mere license, however, to travel over the land of another may be revoked at any time at the pleasure of the licensor. Parish *v.* Kaspar, 109 Ind. 586; Simpson *v.* Wright, 21 Ill. App. 67; 13 Am. & Eng. Encyc. of Law, 555.

Where the license is once proved, however, or a *prima facie* case of such license has been made out, it then devolves upon the party asserting a revocation to prove it. Blunt *v.* Barrett, 54 N. Y. Sup. 548.

Consequently if the license in the present case was claimed to have been discontinued or revoked, the burden was upon appellees to show that fact.

Was such revocation established, or was there any evidence from which the court could infer the same ?

The transfer of the property, or the fencing of the same, may, under ordinary circumstances, be sufficient to amount to a revocation. Ordinarily a man has a right to use his own property as he pleases, but at the same time this gives him no right to use it to the detriment or injury of his neighbor. We think the erection of an ordinary fence around the lot, one that was not calculated to inflict injury, was proper and right, and it was the privilege of the appellees to thus close up their premises without asking of any one the permission to do so. But whenever they undertook to inclose their property under circumstances that made it dangerous to those likely to pass over it, and which the appellees must anticipate would incur injury by it, it became their duty, if such dangerous means must be employed to accomplish the purpose, to give some sort of warning.

Thus it was held in Houston, etc., R. W. Co. *v.* Boozer, 70 Tex. 530, that if the owner of the land has been accustomed to permit others to use his property to travel over to such an extent as to produce a confident belief that the use will not be objected to, he must not mislead them by failing to give a proper warning of his intention to recall the permission. See, also, Cornish *v.* Stubbs, 5 L. R. C. P. 334; Mellor *v.* Watkins, L. R. 9 Q. B. 400.

While we grant the clear right of the appellees to revoke the license, we assert as emphatically that they must do so in a manner not calculated under ordinary circumstances to inflict injury unnecessarily. Although a licensee acquires no interest, as the term is usually employed, nor property right in the real estate over which he is allowed to travel, he yet has the right not to be wilfully or even recklessly injured by the acts of the owner. It cannot be said truthfully that the owner does not owe *some* duty to a licensee.

At the time of the stretching of the wire the appellees must have known that the public would continue to travel over this lot until in some way prevented from doing so. They must have known further that a single strand of wire, without posts at the roadside, or other means calculated to attract the attention of passers-by, could not be seen in the dark, and was a dangerous obstruction, liable to injure those coming in contact with it. They must, therefore, have anticipated just such results as the one that happened to the appellant. It was their clear duty, consequently, in case they desired to make use of the dangerous wire, to shut out the public from going over their lot, to give some warning by which the presence of the wire might be detected. Had they used an ordinary fence, one constructed out of material not necessarily dangerous to life and limb even if encountered in the dark, the case might be otherwise, and notice might not have been necessary. But the stretching of the barbed wire, without notice, under the circumstances was, we think, a plain violation of duty.

The case made by the evidence is one of more than mere passive negligence. In that class of cases it is well enough settled that there is no liability to a mere licensee. Thus where the owner of premises inadvertently leaves unguarded a pit, hatchway, trap-door, cistern, or other dangerous opening, and one who is present merely by permission and not by invitation, express or implied, falls into the opening and is injured, he cannot recover, as, in such case, he enjoys the license subject to the risks. Thiele *v.* McManus, 3 Ind. App. 132. But while an owner may not be liable to one who is thus injured by mere inattention and neglect of the owner, there could be no doubt of his liability if it were shown that the obstruction was placed there purposely to keep the licensee from entering the premises, or for the very purpose of inflicting injury if an attempt be made to cross. As well might an owner give permission to his neighbor to travel over his field and then set a trap to hurt him.

Where the owner of ground digs a pit or erects other dangerous obstructions at a place where it is probable that persons or animals may go and become injured, without using proper care to guard the same, it is well settled in this state that there is a liability, and that the owner must respond in damages for any injury incurred by such negligence. Young *v.* Harvey, 16 Ind. 314; Graves *v.* Thomas, 95 Ind.

361; Mayhew *v.* Burns, 103 Ind. 328; Penso *v.* McCormick, 125 Ind. 116.

A barbed wire fence is not of itself an unlawful one, and the building of such along a public highway is not necessarily a negligent act; but yet, even in such case as that, there may be circumstances under which a person building such a fence, in a negligent manner, will be held liable for damages caused thereby. Sisk *v.* Crump, 112 Ind. 504. All these cases proceed upon the assumption that the party whose negligence caused the injury owed the other some duty which he failed to perform, for, after all, negligence is nothing more nor less than the failure to discharge some legal duty or obligation.

Even trespassers have some rights an owner is bound to respect. If a person, without permission, should attempt to cross the field of another, and tramp down his growing grain, it would not be contended, we apprehend, that this gave the owner any right to kill the trespasser, or even to seriously injure him unnecessarily. The use of spring guns, traps, and other devices to catch and injure trespassing persons or animals has been condemned both in this country and in England. Hooker *v.* Miller, 37 Iowa, 613; Deane *v.* Clayton, 7 Taunt. 489. If such means may not be employed against trespassers, we do not see upon what principle it can be held that it is proper to use them against one who has a permissive right to go upon the property where they are placed.

While in the case at bar there may be no proof of intentional injury, the facts, we think, bring the case within the principle declared in Young *v.* Harvey, *supra;* Graves *v.* Thomas, *supra;* Penso *v.* McCormick, *supra;* and Sisk *v.* Crump, *supra.*

The court should have sustained the motion for a new trial.

Judgment reversed.[1]

INDERMAUR *v.* DAMES

IN THE COMMON PLEAS, FEBRUARY 26, 1866.

Reported in Law Reports, 1 Common Pleas, 274.

THE judgment of the Court (ERLE, C. J., WILLES, KEATING, and MONTAGUE SMITH, JJ.) was delivered by [2]

WILLES, J. This was an action to recover damages for hurt sustained by the plaintiff's falling down a shaft at the defendant's place of business, through the actionable negligence, as it was alleged, of the defendant and his servants.

[1] Corby *v.* Hill, 4 C. B. N. S. 556; Rooney *v.* Woolworth, 78 Conn. 167; Graves *v.* Thomas, 95 Ind. 361; Penso *v.* McCormick, 125 Ind. 116; Morrison *v.* Carpenter, 179 Mich. 207; Wheeler *v.* St. Joseph Stock Yards Co., 66 Mo. App. 260 *Accord.* Compare Ellsworth *v.* Metheney, (C. C. A.) 104 Fed. 119; Cahill *v.* Stone, 153 Cal. 571; Martin *v.* Louisville Bridge Co., 41 Ind. App. 493; Quigley *v.* Clough, 173 Mass. 429; Phillips *v.* Library Co., 55 N. J. Law, 307; Beck *v.* Carter, 68 N. Y. 283; Hanson *v.* Spokane Valley Land Co., 58 Wash. 6.

[2] Statement and arguments omitted.

At the trial before the Lord Chief Justice at the sittings here after Michaelmas Term, the plaintiff had a verdict for 400*l.* damages, subject to leave reserved.

A rule was obtained by the defendant in last term to enter a nonsuit, or to arrest the judgment, or for a new trial because of the verdict being against the evidence.

The rule was argued during the last term, before Erle, C. J., Keating and Montague Smith, JJ., and myself, when we took time to consider. We are now of opinion that the rule ought to be discharged.

It appears that the defendant was a sugar-refiner, at whose place of business there was a shaft four feet three inches square, and twenty-nine feet three inches deep, used for moving sugar. The shaft was necessary, usual, and proper in the way of the defendant's business. Whilst it was in use, it was necessary and proper that it should be open and unfenced. When it was not in use, it was sometimes necessary, with reference to ventilation, that it should be open. It was not necessary that it should, when not in use, be unfenced; and it might then without injury to the business have been fenced by a rail. Whether it was usual to fence similar shafts when not in use did not distinctly appear; nor is it very material, because such protection was unquestionably proper, in the sense of reasonable, with reference to the safety of persons having a right to move about upon the floor where the shaft in fact was, because in its nature it formed a pitfall there. At the time of the accident it was not in use, and it was open and unfenced.

The plaintiff was a journeyman gas-fitter in the employ of a patentee who had supplied the defendant with his patent gas-regulator, to be paid for upon the terms that it effected a certain saving: and, for the purpose of ascertaining whether such a saving had been effected, the plaintiff's employer required to test the action of the regulator. He accordingly sent the plaintiff to the defendant's place of business for that purpose; and, whilst the plaintiff was engaged upon the floor where the shaft was, he (under circumstances as to which the evidence was conflicting, but) accidentally, and, as the jury found, without any fault or negligence on his part, fell down the shaft, and was seriously hurt.

It was argued, that, as the defendant had objected to the plaintiff's working at the place upon a former occasion, he (the plaintiff) could not be considered as having been in the place with the defendant's leave at the time of the accident: but the evidence did not establish a peremptory or absolute objection to the plaintiff's being employed, so as to make the sending of him upon the occasion of the accident any more against the defendant's will than the sending of any other workman: and the employment, and the implied authority resulting therefrom to test the apparatus were not of a character involving personal preference (*dilectus personæ*), so as to make it necessary that the patentee should himself attend. It was not suggested that the work was not journeyman's work.

It was also argued that the plaintiff was at best in the condition of a bare licensee or guest who, it was urged, is only entitled to use the place as he finds it, and whose complaint may be said to wear the color of ingratitude, so long as there is no design to injure him: see Hounsell *v.* Smyth, 7 C. B. N. S. 371, 29 L. J. (C. P.) 203.

We think this argument fails, because the capacity in which the plaintiff was there was that of a person on lawful business, in the course of fulfilling a contract in which both the plaintiff and the defendant had an interest, and not upon bare permission. No sound distinction was suggested between the case of the servant and the case of the employer, if the latter had thought proper to go in person; nor between the case of a person engaged in doing the work for the defendant pursuant to his employment, and that of a person testing the work which he had stipulated with the defendant to be paid for if it stood the test; whereby impliedly the workman was to be allowed an on-stand to apply that test, and a reasonable opportunity of doing so. Any duty to enable the workman to do the work in safety, seems equally to exist during the accessory employment of testing: and any duty to provide for the safety of the master workman, seems equally owing to the servant workman whom he may lawfully send in his place.

It is observable, that, in the case of Southcote *v.* Stanley, 1 H. & N. 247, 25 L. J. (Ex.) 339, upon which much reliance was properly placed for the defendant, Alderson, B., drew the distinction between a bare licensee and a person coming on business, and Bramwell, B., between active negligence in respect of unusual danger known to the host and not to the guest, and a bare defect of construction or repair, which the host was only negligent in not finding out or anticipating the consequence of.

There is considerable resemblance, though not a strict analogy, between this class of cases and those founded upon the rule as to voluntary loans and gifts, that there is no remedy against the lender or giver for damage sustained from the loan or gift, except in case of unusual danger known to and concealed by the lender or giver. Macarthy *v.* Younge, 6 H. & N. 329, 30 L. J. (Ex.) 227. The case of the carboy of vitriol [1] was one in which this Court held answerable the bailor of an unusually dangerous chattel, the quality of which he knew, but did not tell the bailee, who did not know it, and, who as a proximate consequence of his not knowing, and without any fault on his part, suffered damage.

The cases referred to as to the liability for accidents to servants and persons employed in other capacities in a business or profession which necessarily and obviously exposes them to danger, as in Seymour *v.*

[1] Farrant *v.* Barnes, 11 C. B. N. S. 553; 31 L. J. (C. P.) 137.

Maddox, 16 Q. B. 326, also have their special reasons. The servant or other person so employed is supposed to undertake not only all the ordinary risks of the employment into which he enters, but also all extraordinary risks which he knows of and thinks proper to incur, including those caused by the misconduct of his fellow-servants, not however including those which can be traced to mere breach of duty on the part of the master. In the case of a statutory duty to fence, even the knowledge and reluctant submission of the servant who has sustained an injury, are held to be only elements in determining whether there has been contributory negligence: how far this is the law between master and servant, where there is danger known to the servant, and no statute for his protection, we need not now consider, because the plaintiff in this case was not a servant of the defendant, but the servant of the patentee. The question was adverted to, but not decided, in Clarke *v.* Holmes, 7 H. & N. 937, 31 L. J. (Ex.) 356.[1]

The authorities respecting guests and other bare licensees, and those respecting servants and others who consent to incur a risk, being therefore inapplicable, we are to consider what is the law as to the duty of the occupier of a building with reference to persons resorting thereto in the course of business, upon his invitation, express or implied. The common case is that of a customer in a shop: but it is obvious that this is only one of a class; for, whether the customer is actually chaffering at the time, or actually buys or not, he is, according to an undoubted course of authority and practice, entitled to the exercise of reasonable care by the occupier to prevent damage from unusual danger, of which the occupier knows or ought to know, such as a trap-door left open, unfenced, and unlighted: Lancaster Canal Company *v.* Parnaby, 11 Ad. & E. 223, 3 P. & D. 162; *per cur.* Chapman *v.* Rothwell, E. B. & E. 168, 27 L. J. (Q. B.) 315, where Southcote *v.* Stanley, 1 H. & N. 247, 25 L. J. (Ex.) 339, was cited, and the Lord Chief Justice, then Erle, J., said: "The distinction is between the case of a visitor (as the plaintiff was in Southcote *v.* Stanley), who must take care of himself, and a customer, who, as one of the public, is invited for the purposes of business carried on by the defendant." This protection does not depend upon the fact of a contract being entered into in the way of the shopkeeper's business during the stay of the customer, but upon the fact that the customer has come into the shop in pursuance of a tacit invitation given by the shopkeeper, with a view to business which concerns himself. And, if a customer were, after buying goods, to go back to the shop in order to complain of the quality, or that the change was not right, he would be just as much there upon business which concerned the shopkeeper, and as much entitled to protection during this accessory visit, though it might not be for the shopkeeper's benefit, as during the principal visit,

[1] And see Bolch *v.* Smith, 7 H. & N. 736; 31 L. J. (Ex.) 201.

which was. And if, instead of going himself, the customer were to send his servant, the servant would be entitled to the same consideration as the master.

The class to which the customer belongs includes persons who go not as mere volunteers, or licensees, or guests, or servants, or persons whose employment is such that danger may be considered as bargained for, but who go upon business which concerns the occupier, and upon his invitation, express or implied.

And, with respect to such a visitor at least, we consider it settled law, that he, using reasonable care on his part for his own safety, is entitled to expect that the occupier shall on his part use reasonable care to prevent damage from unusual danger which he knows or ought to know; and that, where there is evidence of neglect, the question whether such reasonable care has been taken, by notice, lighting, guarding or otherwise, and whether there was contributory negligence in the sufferer, must be determined by a jury as matter of fact.

In the case of Wilkinson *v.* Fairrie, 1 H. & C. 633, 32 L. J. (Ex.) 73, relied upon for the defendant, the distinction was pointed out between ordinary accidents, such as falling down stairs, which ought to be imputed to the carelessness or misfortune of the sufferer, and accidents from unusual, covert danger, such as that of falling down into a pit.

It was ably insisted for the defendant that he could only be bound to keep his place of business in the same condition as other places of business of the like kind, according to the best known mode of construction. And this argument seems conclusive to prove that there was no absolute duty to prevent danger, but only a duty to make the place as little dangerous as such a place could reasonably be, having regard to the contrivances necessarily used in carrying on the business. But we think the argument is inapplicable to the facts of this case: first, because it was not shown, and probably could not be, that there was any usage never to fence shafts; secondly, because it was proved, that, when the shaft was not in use, a fence might be resorted to without inconvenience; and no usage could establish that what was in fact unnecessarily dangerous was in law reasonably safe, as against persons towards whom there was a duty to be careful.

Having fully considered the notes of the Lord Chief Justice, we think there was evidence for the jury that the plaintiff was in the place by the tacit invitation of the defendant, upon business in which he was concerned; that there was by reason of the shaft unusual danger known to the defendant; and that the plaintiff sustained damage by reason of that danger, and of the neglect of the defendant and his servants to use reasonably sufficient means to avert or warn him of it: and we cannot say that the proof of contributory negligence was so clear that we ought on this ground to set aside the verdict of the jury.

As for the argument that the plaintiff contributed to the accident by not following his guide, the answer may be that the guide, knowing the place, ought rather to have waited for him; and this point, as matter of fact, is set at rest by the verdict.

For these reasons, we think there was evidence of a cause of action in respect of which the jury were properly directed; and, as every reservation of leave to enter a nonsuit carries with it an implied condition that the Court may amend, if necessary, in such a manner as to raise the real question, leave ought to be given to the plaintiff, in the event of the defendant desiring to appeal or to bring a writ of error, to amend the declaration by stating the facts as proved, — in effect, that the defendant was the occupier of and carried on business at the place; that there was a shaft, very dangerous to persons in the place, which the defendant knew and the plaintiff did not know; that the plaintiff, by invitation and permission of the defendant, was near the shaft, upon business of the defendant, in the way of his own craft as a gas-fitter, for hire, &c., stating the circumstances, the negligence, and that by reason thereof the plaintiff was injured. The details of the amendment can, if necessary, be settled at chambers.

As to the motion to arrest the judgment, for the reasons already given, and upon condition that an amendment is to be made if and when required by the defendant, it will follow the fate of the motion to enter a nonsuit.

The other arguments for the defendant, to which we have not particularly adverted, were no more than objections to the verdict as being against the evidence: but it would be wrong to grant a new trial without a reasonable expectation that another jury might take a different view of the facts; and, as the Lord Chief Justice does not express any dissatisfaction with the verdict, the rule upon this, the only remaining ground, must also be discharged.

Rule discharged.[1]

Affirmed in Exchequer Chamber, L. R. 2 C. P. 311.

[1] Bennett *v.* Louisville R. Co., 102 U. S. 577; Alabama Steel Co. *v.* Clements, 146 Ala. 259; Hobart Tie Co. *v.* Keck, 89 Ark. 122; Whitney *v.* New York R. Co., 87 Conn. 623; Christopher *v.* Russell, 63 Fla. 191; Southern Express Co. *v.* Williamson, 66 Fla. 286; Horton *v.* Harvey, 119 Ga. 219; Latham *v.* Roach, 72 Ill. 179; Spry Lumber Co. *v.* Duggan, 182 Ill. 218; Calvert *v.* Springfield Electric Co., 231 Ill. 290; Laurie *v.* McCullough, 174 Ind. 477; Young *v.* People's Gas Co., 128 Ia. 290; Anderson *v.* Hair, 103 Ky. 196; Carleton *v.* Franconia Iron Co., 99 Mass. 216; McDermott *v.* Sallaway, 198 Mass. 517; Marston *v.* Reynolds, 211 Mass. 590; Jacobsen *v.* Simons, 217 Mass. 194; Samuelson *v.* Cleveland Iron Co., 49 Mich. 164; Donaldson *v.* Wilson, 60 Mich. 86; Pelton *v.* Schmidt, 104 Mich. 345; Nash *v.* Minneapolis Mill Co., 24 Minn. 501; Emery *v.* Minneapolis Exposition, 56 Minn. 460; Kean *v.* Schoening, 103 Mo. App. 77; Shaw *v.* Goldman, 116 Mo. App. 332; Montague *v.* Hanson, 38 Mont. 376; Land *v.* Fitzgerald, 68 N. J. Law, 28; Smith *v.* Jackson, 70 N. J. Law, 183; Ackert *v.* Lansing, 59 N. Y. 646; Weller *v.* Consolidated Gas Co., 198 N. Y. 98; Wilson *v.* Olano, 28 App. Div. 448; Withers *v.* Brooklyn Exchange, 106 App. Div. 255; Higgins *v.* Ruppert, 124 App. Div. 530; Massey *v.* Seller, 45 Or. 267; Newingham *v.* Blair, 232 Pa. St. 511; Freer *v.* Cameron, 4 Rich. Law, 228; League *v.* Stradley, 68 S. C. 515; Richmond R. Co. *v.*

McNEE *v.* COBURN TROLLEY TRACK COMPANY

SUPREME JUDICIAL COURT, MASSACHUSETTS, FEBRUARY 24, 1898.

Reported in 170 *Massachusetts Reports,* 283.

TORT, for personal injuries occasioned to the plaintiff by the fall of an elevator upon which he was riding while in the defendant's employ. Trial in the Superior Court, before Mason, C. J., who directed the jury to return a verdict for the defendant; and reported the case for the determination of this court. If the case should have been submitted to the jury, judgment was to be entered for the plaintiff in a sum named; otherwise, judgment on the verdict. The facts sufficiently appear in the opinion.

Moore, 94 Va. 493; Smith *v.* Parkersburg Ass'n, 48 W. Va. 232; Landry *v.* Great Northern R. Co., 152 Wis. 379 *Accord.*

As to child accompanying invitee: see Butler *v.* Chicago R. Co., 155 Mo. App. 287.

Liability to children invitees: see Miller *v.* Peck Dry Goods Co., 104 Mo. App. 609; Houck *v.* Chicago R. Co., 116 Mo. App. 559.

Liability where plaintiff departs from or goes beyond the permission or invitation: New York Oil Co. *v.* Pusey, 211 Fed. 622; Louisville R. Co. *v.* Sides, 129 Ala. 399; First Nat. Bank *v.* Chandler, 144 Ala. 286; Coberth *v.* Great Atlantic Co., 36 App. D. C. 569; Etheredge *v.* Central R. Co., 122 Ga. 853; Bennett *v.* Butterfield, 112 Mich. 96; Hutchinson *v.* Cleveland Iron Co., 141 Mich. 346; Trask *v.* Shotwell, 41 Minn. 66; Ryerson *v.* Bathgate, 67 N. J. Law, 337; Gilfillan *v.* German Hospital, 115 App. Div. 48; Castoriano *v.* Miller, 15 Misc. 254; Weaver *v.* Carnegie Steel Co., 223 Pa. St. 238; Hagan *v.* Delaware Steel Co., 240 Pa. St. 222; Pierce *v.* Whitcomb, 48 Vt. 127; Peake *v.* Buell, 90 Wis. 508; Lehmann *v.* Amsterdam Coffee Co., 146 Wis. 213.

But compare Pauckner *v.* Wakem, 231 Ill. 276.

Use for purpose not intended by owner or occupier: Thiele *v.* McManus, 3 Ind. App. 132; Smith *v.* Trimble, 111 Ky. 861; Ferguson *v.* Ferguson, (Ky.) 114 S. W. 297; Speicher *v.* New York Tel. Co., 60 N. J. Law, 242, 59 N. J. Law, 23; Clark *v.* Fehlhaber, 106 Va. 803. See also Urban *v.* Focht, 231 Pa. St. 623.

Invitee of licensee: see Brehmer *v.* Lyman, 71 Vt. 98.

In Cox *v.* Coulson, [1916] 2 K. B. 177, a spectator in a theatre was injured by the discharge of a pistol during a performance. Bankes, L. J., said: "It seems to me obvious that the duty of the invitor in a case like the present is not only confined to the state of the premises, using that expression as extending to the structure merely. The duty must to some extent extend to the performance given in the structure, because the performance may be of such a kind as to render the structure an unsafe place to be in whilst the performance is going on, or it may be of such a kind as to render the structure unsafe unless some obvious precaution is taken. As an illustration under the latter head I would instance a case where a tight-rope dancer performs on a rope stretched over the heads of the audience. In such a case the provision of a net under the rope to protect the audience in case the performer fell seems so obvious a precaution to take that in the absence of it the premises could not be said to be reasonably safe. In the present case the performance was one which included a discharge of pistols loaded with blank ammunition as one of the incidents. If the pistols had been properly loaded, it is difficult to see that the incident exposed any member of the audience in any ordinarily constructed theatre to any danger. On the other hand, if any one of the pistols was not properly loaded, what would otherwise be a safe performance became an exceedingly dangerous one, and any part of the auditorium might be rendered an extremely unsafe place to be in. Whether the circumstances were such that any negligence or want of proper care can be attributed to the appellant in relation to the loading of the pistol or in relation to the ammunition supplied for that purpose has not been investigated, and I do not think that justice can be done between the parties until this is done."

The case was submitted on briefs to all the justices.

ALLEN, J. The general condition of the elevator was such that a jury might find that the defendant would be negligent in continuing its use for carrying workmen up and down while engaged in their work, if this was done without warning them of the risk. It is true that the particular defect which caused the accident was not open to observation or easy to discover. But there was evidence tending to show that the accident was caused by the use of the elevator while it was in a condition which rendered it unsuitable for use, and that the defendant was fairly put upon inquiry as to its safety; and that the defendant's duty in this respect was different from and greater than that of the workmen themselves.

The question then remains whether the posting of the notices in the elevator [1] showed such a performance by the defendant of its duty of warning or cautioning the workmen, or such contributory negligence or assumption of the risk on the part of the plaintiff, as to entitle the defendant to have the case withdrawn from the jury. While upon the evidence reported a verdict for the defendant would be more satisfactory, we are unable to hold that the defendant was entitled to such verdict as a matter of law. As a general rule, the sufficiency of such warning or caution is a question of fact for the jury. Indermaur *v.* Dames, L. R. 1 C. P. 274; s. c. L. R. 2 C. P. 311. It is true that the plaintiff was not at liberty to shut his eyes in order to avoid reading a plain notice of warning. If it be assumed that the plaintiff must be held chargeable with a knowledge of the contents of the notice, or at least that the defendant performed its duty of cautioning the workmen by posting the notices in the elevator, we think the plaintiff still had the right to go to the jury upon the question whether the notices remained in force at the time of the accident, or had become a dead letter. There was evidence tending to show that the notices were put in the elevator a long time before the accident by a former treasurer whose connection with the company had then ceased, that they had become soiled and somewhat indistinct and torn, and that all of the defendant's workmen, including the general superintendent of the building, were in the regular habit of using the elevator to carry them up and down, and had been so for some months prior to the accident. There was room for a legitimate argument that the defendant could not have intended to keep such a rule in force forever, and to furnish an elevator for permanent use by the men at their own sole risk; and that the defendant expected the men to use it while they were engaged in its work, and that it was for the defendant's advantage that they should do so, from the saving of time thereby secured. It might be found that the plaintiff, even if he knew of the terms of the notice, might nevertheless assume that its force had ceased.

[1] These notices read as follows: "All persons riding on this elevator do so at their own risk."

If one who has posted a notice of entire prohibition permits it to be habitually disregarded, as, for instance, a notice not to ride on the platform of a street railway car, or in the baggage car of a train, a practical invitation to violate it may be inferred from habitual usage which is known to him. Long continued practice to the contrary may have the effect to supersede or show a waiver of the rule. O'Donnell *v.* Allegheny Valley Railroad, 59 Penn. St. 239; Pennsylvania Railroad *v.* Langdon, 92 Penn. St. 21; Waterbury *v.* New York Central & Hudson River Railroad, 17 Fed. Rep. 671. The notice in the present case was not one of entire prohibition, but, in the opinion of a majority of the court, the plaintiff upon the evidence had a right to go to the jury upon the question whether it still remained in force; and, according to the terms of the report, there must be

Judgment for the plaintiff.[1]

GARFIELD COAL CO. *v.* ROCKLAND LIME CO.

SUPREME JUDICIAL COURT, MASSACHUSETTS, JUNE 23, 1903.

Reported in 184 *Massachusetts Reports*, 60.

TORT, by the owner of the coal barge Western Belle, for injury to that vessel by grounding on a ledge of rock embedded in the mud at the bottom of the defendant's dock at Rockland, Maine.

In the Superior Court the case was tried by a judge without a jury.

"It appeared at the trial that defendant was part owner of a dock, and used it for the discharge of cargoes of coal consigned to it. Plaintiff had sold coal to the defendant, and sent it a barge loaded therewith." [2]

The plaintiff requested the judge to make certain rulings, including the following: —

"4. It is not necessary for the plaintiff to show that the defendant knew of the ledge; it is sufficient if its existence could have been discovered by reasonable diligence."

The judge refused to make any of the rulings, and found for the defendant. The plaintiff excepted.

LATHROP, J. . . . The general rules of law which are applicable in cases of this character are the same in England and in this country, and are the same at common law and in admiralty. They are as well stated in the case of Nickerson *v.* Tirrell, 127 Mass. 236, 239, as perhaps in any case: "The owner or occupant of a dock is liable in dam-

[1] Craney *v.* Union Stockyards Co., 240 Ill. 602; Kentucky Distilleries Co. *v.* Leonard, (Ky.) 79 S. W. 281 *Accord.* But see Burns *v.* Boston R. Co., 183 Mass. 96; Pike *v.* Boston R. Co., 192 Mass. 426.

[2] Statement rewritten. Only so much of the case is given as relates to a single point. The passage in quotation marks is taken from the report of this case in 67 Northeastern Reporter, 863.

ages to a person who, by his invitation express or implied, makes use of it, for an injury caused by any defect or unsafe condition of the dock which the occupant negligently causes or permits to exist, if such person was himself in the exercise of due care. Such occupant is not an insurer of the safety of his dock,[1] but he is required to use reasonable care to keep his dock in such a state as to be reasonably safe for use by vessels which he invites to enter it, or for which he holds it out as fit and ready. If he fails to use such due care, if there is a defect which is known to him, or which by the use of ordinary care and diligence should be known to him, he is guilty of negligence and liable to the person who, using due care, is injured thereby. Wendell *v.* Baxter, 12 Gray, 494; Carleton *v.* Franconia Iron & Steel Co., 99 Mass. 216; Thompson *v.* Northeastern Railway, 2 B. & S. 106; Mersey Docks *v.* Gibbs, L. R. 1 H. L. 93." Other cases bearing upon this point are: Smith *v.* Burnett, 173 U. S. 430; Barber *v.* Abendroth, 102 N. Y. 406; Barrett *v.* Black, 56 Maine, 498; Sawyer *v.* Oakman, 1 Lowell, 134, s. c. 7 Blatchf. 290; The John A. Berkman, 6 Fed. Rep. 535; Pennsylvania Railroad *v.* Atha, 22 Fed. Rep. 920; Smith *v.* Havemeyer, 36 Fed. Rep. 927; Manhattan Transportation Co. *v.* Mayor, 37 Fed. Rep. 160; Union Ice Co. *v.* Crowell, 55 Fed. Rep. 87. The rule is the same in England. Gibbs *v.* Liverpool Docks, 3 H. & N. 164; s. c. *nom.* Mersey Docks *v.* Gibbs, 11 H. L. Cas. 686, and L. R. 1 H. L. 93; The Moorcock, 13 P. D. 157, and 14 P. D. 64.

. . . .

It is clear that the vessel was in the defendant's dock on business, and was, therefore, there by invitation. The judge has found, and the evidence shows, that the injury was caused by a ledge of rocks embedded in the mud at the bottom of the dock. The questions of fact which he did not pass upon are whether the master was in the exercise of due care, and whether the defendant knew of the defect or could by the exercise of reasonable care and diligence have ascertained its existence.

. . . .

The fourth request should have been given. See cases cited above.

Exceptions sustained.[2]

[1] Bell *v.* Central Nat. Bank, 28 App. D. C. 580; Connolly *v.* Des Moines Inv. Co., 130 Ia. 633; Branham *v.* Buckley, 158 Ky. 848; Schnatterer *v.* Bamberger, 81 N. J. Law, 558 *Accord.*

[2] Washington Market Co. *v.* Clagett, 19 App. D. C. 12; Woods *v.* Trinity Parish, 21 D. C. 540; Nave *v.* Flack, 90 Ind. 205; Ford *v.* Crigler, (Ky.) 74 S. W. 661; Perrine *v.* Union Stockyards Co., 81 Neb. 790; Kenny *v.* Hall Realty Co., 85 Misc. 439; Glase *v.* City, 169 Pa. St. 488 *Accord.* Compare Larson *v.* Red River Transportation Co., 111 Minn. 427; Eisenberg *v.* Missouri R. Co., 33 Mo. App. 85; Henkel *v.* Murr, 31 Hun, 28; Alperin *v.* Earle, 55 Hun, 211.

INDIANAPOLIS STREET RAILWAY COMPANY *v.* DAWSON

APPELLATE COURT, INDIANA, NOVEMBER 17, 1903.

Reported in 31 *Indiana Appellate Court Reports*, 605.

FROM SUPERIOR COURT OF MARION COUNTY; Vincent G. Clifford, Special Judge.

Action by George J. Dawson against the Indianapolis Street Railway Company. From a judgment for plaintiff, defendant appeals.

ROBY, J. Action by appellee. Verdict and judgment for $500. Demurrers to first and second paragraphs of complaint overruled. Motion for a new trial overruled.

It is averred in the first paragraph of complaint, in substance, as extracted from a multitude of words, that appellant was on August 25, 1901, a corporation operating a street railway system in Indianapolis and was a common carrier for hire; that it owned a park near said city, and maintained certain attractions therein to induce persons to ride on its cars, inviting them to said park; that on the day named it gave a free band concert therein, the same having been extensively advertised prior thereto; that on said day appellee, accompanied by a lady, took passage upon one of its regular cars, and was conveyed to said park; that a large number of persons were daily transported thereto, among them a large number of lawless persons who were hostile to colored people, of whom appellee was one, their names being unknown to plaintiff, and who had long before said day entered into a conspiracy "to suppress, molest, assault, and insult colored people generally who might visit said park;" that in pursuance of such conspiracy said persons assaulted and beat appellee, and drove him from the park; that he and his companion demeaned themselves in a ladylike and gentlemanly manner, but upon arriving at the park were set upon by a large number of white boys and young men, appellee being assaulted and beaten by them; that appellant had, and had had for a long time prior to said day, full notice and knowledge of said conditions, and of the unlawful purposes aforesaid, and of acts of violence committed thereunder, but took no steps to prevent such conduct; that early in the afternoon of said day said lawless men and boys began marching and drilling openly in said park preparatory to an attack upon any colored male person who should be found there later, appellant taking no steps to prevent such conduct or to notify colored people of the danger, although it had knowledge thereof; that neither appellant nor its officers made any objection to the open and notorious gathering of white men and boys for the unlawful purpose stated; that it was negligent and indifferent in not employing and using a sufficient number of guards and policemen to maintain the peace; that two of its guards or policemen aided and abetted the wrong done appellee by standing by when he was being unmercifully beaten by said crowd of lawless white men and boys, and offering him no assistance, although they were able to do so, and could have prevented injury to him. " Wherefore, by reason of the matters therein stated, the plaintiff has been damaged," etc. The second paragraph of complaint is somewhat more extended than the first one, but for the purpose of this opinion the statement made is sufficient.

The pleading charges appellant with notice of the alleged conspiracy, with acquiescence therein, and, by its guards or policemen, with passive participation in the actual assault made upon appellee. " When one expressly or by implication invites others to come upon his premises, whether for business or any other purpose, it is his duty to be reasonably sure that he is not inviting them into danger, and to that end he must exercise ordinary care and prudence to render the place reasonably safe for the visit." Cooley, Torts (2d ed.), 718; Howe *v.* Ohmart, 7 Ind. App. 32, 38; Richmond, etc., R. Co. *v.* Moore, 94 Va. 493, 37 L. R. A. 258; North Manchester, etc., Assn. *v.* Wilcox, 4 Ind. App. 141; Penso *v.* McCormick, 125 Ind. 116, 21 Am. St. 211.

No case has been cited or found where the premises upon which the injury complained of occurred, and to which the complainant came by invitation, were made unsafe through a conspiracy of the nature set up herein. Danger usually has been attributed to some defect in the premises themselves. But as a matter of principle it is quite as reprehensible to invite one knowing an enemy is awaiting him with the intent to assault and beat him as it would be to invite him without having made the floor or the stairway secure. One attending an agricultural fair in response to a general invitation extended to the public has been awarded damages against the association where his horse was killed by target shooting upon a part of the ground allowed for such purpose. Conradt *v.* Clauve, 93 Ind. 476, 47 Am. Rep. 388.

Recoveries have also been sustained: When spectators rushed upon a race-track, causing a collision between horses being driven thereon. North Manchester, etc., Assn. *v.* Wilcox, 4 Ind. App. 141. When an opening was left in a fence surrounding a race-track through which one of the horses, running, went among the spectators. Windeler *v.* Rush County Fair Assn., 27 Ind. App. 92. Where horses were started on a race-track in opposite directions at the same time, causing collision. Fairmount, etc., Assn. *v.* Downey, 146 Ind. 503. Where a horse with a vicious habit of track bolting was permitted to run in a race, such horse bolting the track, causing injury. Lane *v.* Minnesota, etc., Soc., 62 Minn. 175, 29 L. R. A. 708. Recognizing the rule of reasonable care to make the premises safe, a recovery was denied in the absence of any evidence of the immediate cause of a horse running through the crowds. Hart *v.* Washington Park Club, 157 Ill. 9, 29 L. R. A. 492. Where a street car company maintained a park as a place of attraction for passengers over its line, the falling of a pole used by one making a balloon ascension, under a contract, injuring a bystander, recovery was allowed, the rule being announced that the company must use proper care to protect its patrons from danger while on its grounds. Richmond, etc., R. Co. *v.* Moore, 94 Va. 493, 37 L. R. A. 258. Where a street car company maintained a large stage for exhibitions, in a pleasure resort owned by it, and made a written contract with a manager, by which the latter furnished various entertainments, among which was target shooting, one injured by a split bullet was allowed to recover, it being held that he might safely rely on those who provided the exhibition and invited his attendance to take due care to make the place safe from such injury as he received, the question of due care being one for the jury. Thompson *v.* Lowell, etc., St. R. Co., 170 Mass. 577, 40 L. R. A. 345; Curtis *v.* Kiley, 153 Mass. 123.

The duty of common carriers to protect their passengers from injury on account of unlawful violence by persons not connected with their service has frequently furnished material for judicial consideration. The New Jersey Court of Errors and Appeals approved an exhaustive and carefully considered opinion delivered by the Supreme Court of that State to the effect that a passenger who, while attempting to have her baggage checked, was knocked down and injured by cabmen, in no sense servants of the carrier, scuffling on a passageway under its control, might recover against it. Exton *v.* Central R. Co., 63 N. J. L. 356, 56 L. R. A. 508. In what seems to have been a pioneer case, it was held by the Supreme Court of Pennsylvania in 1866, that it was the duty of the trainmen on a passenger-train to exert the forces at their disposal to prevent injury to passengers by others fighting in the car. Pittsburgh, etc., R. Co. *v.* Hinds, 53 Pa. St. 512. Ten years later the Supreme Court of Mississippi, after very exhaustive arguments by eminent counsel of national reputation, reached the same conclusion. New Orleans, etc., R. Co. *v.* Burke, 53 Miss. 200.

Without further elaboration it may safely be said that the unusual character of an alleged peril, from which it is averred the appellant did not use due care to protect its visitors, does not affect the right of recovery, it being otherwise justified. The demurrers were therefore correctly overruled.

Evidence was introduced of other prior assaults at said park upon colored persons, and articles previously published by daily newspapers in the city describing such occurrences were also admitted. In order to determine whether appellant used due care, it was essential to show its knowledge or means of information relative to the conditions alleged to exist, rendering it dangerous for appellee to visit the park. The evidence of similar occurrences was competent as tending to show notice of the conditions. Toledo, etc., R. Co. *v.* Milligan, 2

Ind. App. 578; City of Delphi *v.* Lowery, 74 Ind. 520, 39 Am. Rep. 98; City of Goshen *v.* England, 119 Ind. 368, 375.

The facts upon which appellant's liability depends otherwise than heretofore considered were questions for the determination of the jury. There was evidence tending to establish, and from which the jury might properly find, the existence of such facts.

Appellant and its officers appear to have displayed indifference to the conditions existing which it and they could not well help knowing. This may have been due to the idea, sometimes entertained, that as to acts of lawlessness it is a sufficient duty of citizenship to be indifferent. Such idea is entirely erroneous. *Judgment affirmed.*[1]

SWEENY *v.* OLD COLONY RAILROAD COMPANY

SUPREME JUDICIAL COURT, MASSACHUSETTS, JANUARY TERM, 1865.

Reported in 10 *Allen*, 368.

TORT to recover damages for a personal injury sustained by being run over by the defendants' cars, while the plaintiff was crossing their railroad by license, on a private way leading from South Street to Federal Street, in Boston.

At the trial in this Court, before Chapman, J., it appeared that this private way, which is called Lehigh Street, was made by the South Cove Corporation for their own benefit, and that they own the fee of it; that it is wrought as a way, and buildings are erected on each side of it, belonging to the owners of the way, and there has been much crossing there by the public for several years. The defendants, having rightfully taken the land under their charter, not subject to any right of way, made a convenient plank-crossing and kept a flagman at the end of it on South Street, partly to protect their own property, and partly to protect the public. They have never made any objection to such crossing, so far as it did not interfere with their cars and engines. There are several tracks at the crossing. The only right of the public to use the crossing is under the license implied by the facts stated above.

On the day of the accident, the defendants had a car at their depot which they had occasion to run over to their car house. It was attached to an engine and taken over the crossing, and to a proper distance beyond the switch. The coupling-pin was then taken out, the engine reversed, and it was moved towards the car house by the side track. The engine was provided with a good engineer and fireman, and the car with a brakeman; the bell was constantly rung, and the

[1] Moone *v.* Smith, 6 Ga. App. 649; Mastad *v.* Swedish Brethren, 83 Minn. 40; Rommel *v.* Schambacher, 120 Pa. St. 579 *Accord.*

But compare Woolworth *v.* Conboy, 170 Fed. 934; Lord *v.* Sherer Co., 205 Mass. 1.

defendants were not guilty of any negligence in respect to the management of the car or engine.

As the engine and car were coming from the depot, the plaintiff, with a horse and a wagon loaded with empty beer barrels, was coming down South Street from the same direction. There was evidence tending to show that, as he approached the crossing, the flagman, who was at his post, made a signal to him with his flag to stop, which he did; that, in answer to an inquiry by the plaintiff whether he could then cross, he then made another signal with his flag, indicating that it was safe to cross; that the plaintiff started and attempted to cross, looking straight forward; that he saw the car coming near him as it went towards the car house; and that he jumped forward from his wagon, and the car knocked him down and ran over him and broke both his legs. It struck the fore-wheel of his wagon and also his horse. If he had remained in his wagon, or had not jumped forwards, or had kept about the middle of the crossing, the evidence showed that he would not have been injured personally. His wagon was near the left-hand side of the plank-crossing as he went.

The defendants contended that, even if the plaintiff used ordinary care, and if the flagman carelessly and negligently gave the signal that he might cross, when in fact it was unsafe to do so on account of the approaching car, the plaintiff was not entitled to recover, because the license to people to use the crossing was not a license to use it at the risk of the defendants, but to use it as they best could when not forbidden, taking care of their own safety, and going at their own risk; and also, that if the flagman made a signal to the plaintiff that he might cross, he exceeded his authority.

But the evidence being very contradictory as to the care used by the plaintiff, and also as to the care used by the flagman, the judge ruled, for the purpose of taking a verdict upon these two facts, that the defendants had a right to use the crossing as they did on this occasion, and that they were not bound to keep a flagman there; yet, since they did habitually keep one there, they would be responsible to the plaintiff for the injury done to him by the car, provided he used due care, if he was induced to cross by the signal made to him by the flagman, and if that signal was carelessly or negligently made at a time when it was unsafe to cross on account of the movement of the car.

The jury returned a verdict for the plaintiff for $7500; and the case was reserved for the consideration of the whole Court.

J. G. Abbott and *P. H. Sears*, for the defendants. The defendants had, for all purposes incident to the complete enjoyment of their franchise, the right of exclusive possession and use of the place where the accident happened, against the owners of the fee, and still more against all other persons. Hazen *v.* Boston & Maine Railroad, 2 Gray, 574; Brainard *v.* Clapp, 10 Cush. 6; Gen. Stat. c. 63, §§ 102, 103. The defendants were not bound to keep a flagman there, or exercise the other precautions prescribed for the crossing of highways or travelled places. Gen. Stat. c. 63, §§ 64–66, 83–91; Boston & Worcester Railroad *v.* Old Colony Railroad, 12 Cush. 608. The license or permission, if any, to the plaintiff to pass over the premises did not impose any duty on the defendants, but he took the permission, with its concomitant perils, at his own risk. Howland *v.* Vincent, 10 Met. 371, 374; Scott *v.* London Docks Co., 11 Law Times (N. S.), 383; Chapman *v.* Rothwell, El. Bl. & El. 168; Southcote *v.* Stanley, 1 Hurlst. & Norm. 247; Hounsell *v.* Smyth, 7 C. B. (N. S.) 729, 735, 742; Binks *v.* South Yorkshire Railway, &c., 32 Law Journ. (N. S.) Q. B. 26; Blithe *v.* Topham, 1 Rol. Ab. 88; s. c. 1 Vin. Ab. 555, pl. 4; Cro. Jac. 158. The defendants did not hold out to the plaintiff an invitation to pass over. Hounsell *v.* Smyth and Binks *v.* South Yorkshire Railway, above cited. The allowing or making of such private crossing was not in itself such an invitation, and did not involve the duty of such precautions. The keeping of a flagman there was wholly for the purpose of preventing persons from crossing, not for the purpose of holding out invitations at any time. The signal that the plaintiff might cross was in answer to his inquiry, and was, at most, only revoking the prohibition, or granting permission; it was not holding out an invitation. The duty of the flagman was simply to warn persons against crossing; and if the flagman held out an invitation or even gave permission to the plaintiff to cross, he went beyond the scope of his employment, and the defendants are not liable on account thereof. Lygo *v.* Newbold, 9 Exch. 203; Middleton *v.* Fowle, 1 Salk. 282. Even if the defendants had carelessly held out an invitation to the plaintiff to cross, still they would not be liable; for the report shows that after such supposed invitation the plaintiff might, by the exercise of ordinary care, have avoided the injury; that the plaintiff was himself at the time in the wrong; and that his own negligence and fault contributed to the accident. Todd *v.* Old Colony & Fall River Railroad, 7 Allen, 207; s. c. 3 Allen, 18, and cases cited; Denny *v.* Williams, 5 Allen, 1, and cases cited; Spofford *v.* Harlow, 3 Allen, 177, and cases cited.

BIGELOW, C. J. This case has been presented with great care on the part of the learned counsel for the defendants, who have produced before us all the leading authorities bearing on the question of law which was reserved at the trial. We have not found it easy to decide on which side of the line which marks the limit of the defendant's liability for damages caused by the acts of their agents, the case at bar falls. But on careful consideration we have been brought to the conclusion that the rulings at the trial were right, and that we cannot set aside the verdict for the plaintiff on the ground that it was based on erroneous instructions in matter of law.

In order to maintain an action for an injury to person or property by reason of negligence or want of due care, there must be shown to exist some obligation or duty towards the plaintiff, which the defendant has left undischarged or unfulfilled. This is the basis on which the cause of action rests. There can be no fault, or negligence, or breach of duty, where there is no act, or service, or contract, which a party is bound to perform or fulfil. All the cases in the books, in which a party is sought to be charged on the ground that he has caused a way or other place to be incumbered or suffered it to be in a dangerous condition, whereby accident and injury have been occasioned to another, turn on the principle that negligence consists in doing or omitting to do an act by which a legal duty or obligation has been violated. Thus a trespasser who comes on the land of another without right cannot maintain an action, if he runs against a barrier or falls into an excavation there situated. The owner of the land is not bound to protect or provide safeguards for wrongdoers. So a licensee, who enters on premises by permission only, without an enticement, allurement, or inducement being held out to him by the owner or occupant, cannot recover damages for injuries caused by obstructions or pitfalls. He goes there at his own risk, and enjoys the license subject to its concomitant perils. No duty is imposed by law on the owner or occupant to keep his premises in a suitable condition for those who come there solely for their own convenience or pleasure, and who are not either expressly invited to enter or induced to come upon them by the purpose for which the premises are appropriated and occupied, or by some preparation or adaptation of the place for use by customers or passengers, which might naturally and reasonably lead them to suppose that they might properly and safely enter thereon.

On the other hand, there are cases where houses or lands are so situated, or their mode of occupation and use is such, that the owner or occupant is not absolved from all care for the safety of those who come on the premises, but where the law imposes on him an obligation or duty to provide for their security against accident and injury. Thus the keeper of a shop or store is bound to provide means of safe ingress and egress to and from his premises for those having occasion to enter thereon, and is liable in damages for any injury which may happen by reason of any negligence in the mode of constructing or managing the place of entrance and exit. So the keeper of an inn or other place of public resort would be liable to an action in favor of a person who suffered an injury in consequence of an obstruction or defect in the way or passage which was held out and used as the common and proper place of access to the premises. The general rule or principle applicable to this class of cases is, that an owner or occupant is bound to keep his premises in a safe and suitable condition for those who come upon and pass over them, using due care, if he has held out any invitation, allurement, or inducement, either express or implied, by which they have been led to enter thereon. A mere naked license or permission to enter or pass over an estate will not create a duty or impose an obligation on the part of the owner or person in possession to provide against the danger of accident. The gist of the liability consists in the fact that the person injured did not act merely for his own convenience and pleasure, and from motives to which no act or sign of the owner or occupant contributed, but that he entered the premises because he was led to believe that they were intended to be used by visitors or passengers, and that such use was not only acquiesced in by the owner or person in possession and control of the premises, but that it was in accordance with the intention and design with which the way or place was adapted and prepared or allowed to be so used. The true distinction is this: A mere passive acquiescence by an owner or occupier in a certain use of his land by others involves no liability; but if he directly or by implication induces persons to enter on and pass over his premises, he thereby assumes an obligation that they are in a safe condition, suitable for such use, and for a breach of this obligation he is liable in damages to a person injured thereby.

This distinction is fully recognized in the most recent and best considered cases in the English Courts, and may be deemed to be the pivot on which all cases like the one at bar are made to turn. In Corby *v.* Hill, 4 C. B. (N. S.) 556, the owner of land, having a private road for the use of persons coming to his house, gave permission to a builder engaged in erecting a house on the land to place materials on the road; the plaintiff, having occasion to use the road for the purpose of going to the owner's residence, ran against the materials and sustained damage, for which the owner was held liable. Cockburn, C. J., says: "The proprietors of the soil held out an allurement whereby the plaintiff was induced to come on the place in question; they held this road out to all persons having occasion to proceed to the house as the means of access thereto." In Chapman *v.* Rothwell, El. Bl. & El. 168, the proprietor of a brewery was held liable in damages for injury and loss of life caused by permitting a trap-door to be open without sufficient light or proper safeguards, in a passageway through which access was had from the street to his office. This decision was put on the ground that the defendant, by holding out the passageway as the proper mode of approach to his office and brewery, invited the party injured to go there, and was bound to use due care in providing for his safety. This is the point on which the decision turned, as stated by Keating, J., in Hounsell *v.* Smyth, 7 C. B. (N. S.) 738. In the last-named case the distinction is clearly drawn between the liability of a person who holds out an inducement or invitation to others to enter on his premises by preparing a way or path by means of which they can gain access to his house or store, or pass into or over the land, and in a case where nothing is shown but a bare license or permission tacitly given to go upon or through an estate, and the responsibility of finding a safe and secure passage is thrown on the passenger and not on the owner. The same distinction is stated in Barnes *v.* Ward, 9 C. B. 392; Hardcastle *v.*

South Yorkshire Railway, &c., 4 Hurlst. & Norm. 67; and Binks *v.* South Yorkshire Railway, &c., 32 Law Journ. (N. S.) Q. B. 26. In the last cited case the language of Blackburn, J., is peculiarly applicable to the case at bar. He says, "There might be a case where permission to use land as a path may amount to such an inducement as to lead the persons using it to suppose it a highway, and thus induce them to use it as such." See also, for a clear statement of the difference between cases where an invitation or allurement is held out by the defendant, and those where nothing appears but a mere license or permission to enter on premises, Bolch *v.* Smith, 7 Hurlst. & Norm. 741, and Scott *v.* London Docks Co., 11 Law Times (N. S.), 383.

The facts disclosed at the trial of the case now before us, carefully weighed and considered, bring it within that class in which parties have been held liable in damages by reason of having held out an invitation or inducement to persons to enter upon and pass over their premises. It cannot in any just view of the evidence be said that the defendants were passive only, and gave merely a tacit license or assent to the use of the place in question as a public crossing. On the contrary, the place or crossing was situated between two streets of the city (which are much frequented thoroughfares), and was used by great numbers of people who had occasion to pass from one street to the other, and it was fitted and prepared by the defendants with a convenient plank-crossing, such as is usually constructed in highways, where they are crossed by the tracks of a railroad, in order to facilitate the passage of animals and vehicles over the rails. It had been so maintained by the defendants for a number of years. These facts would seem to bring the case within the principle already stated, that the license to use the crossing had been used and enjoyed under such circumstances as to amount to an inducement, held out by the defendants to persons having occasion to pass, to believe that it was a highway, and to use it as such. But the case does not rest on these facts only. The defendants had not only constructed and fitted the crossing in the same manner as if it had been a highway, but they had employed a person to stand there with a flag, and to warn persons who were about to pass over the railroad when it was safe for them to attempt to cross with the vehicles and animals, without interference or collision with the engines and cars of the defendants. And it was also shown that when the plaintiff started to go over the tracks with his wagon, it was in obedience to a signal from this agent of the defendants that there was no obstruction or hindrance to his safe passage over the railroad. These facts well warranted the jury in finding, as they must have done in rendering a verdict for the plaintiff under the instructions of the Court, that the defendants induced the plaintiff to cross at the time when he attempted to do so, and met with the injury for which he now seeks compensation.

It was suggested that the person employed by the defendants to stand near the crossing with a flag exceeded his authority in giving a signal to the plaintiff that it was safe for him to pass over the crossing just previously to the accident, and that no such act was within the scope of his employment, which was limited to the duty of preventing persons from passing at times when it was dangerous to do so. But it seems to us that this is a refinement and distinction which the facts do not justify. It is stated in the report that the flagman was stationed at the place in question, charged among other things with the duty of protecting the public. This general statement of the object for which the agent was employed, taken in connection with the fact that he was stationed at a place constructed and used as a public way by great numbers of people, clearly included the duty of indicating to persons when it was safe for them to pass, as well as when it was prudent or necessary for them to refrain from passing.

Nor do we think it can be justly said that the flagman in fact held out no inducement to the plaintiff to pass. No express invitation need have been shown. It would have been only necessary for the plaintiff to prove that the agent did some act to indicate that there was no risk of accident in attempting to pass over the crossing. The evidence at the trial was clearly sufficient to show that the agent of the defendants induced the plaintiff to pass, and that he acted in so doing within the scope of the authority conferred on him. The question whether the plaintiff was so induced was distinctly submitted to the jury by the Court; nor do we see any reason for supposing that the instructions on this point were misunderstood or misapplied by the jury. If they lacked fulness, the defendants should have asked for more explicit instructions. Certainly the evidence as reported well warranted the finding of the jury on this point.

It was also urged that, if the defendants were held liable in this action, they would be made to suffer by reason of the fact that they had taken precautions to guard against accident at the place in question, which they were not bound to use, and that the case would present the singular aspect of holding a party liable for neglect in the performance of a duty voluntarily assumed, and which was not imposed by the rules of law. But this is by no means an anomaly. If a person undertakes to do an act or discharge a duty by which the conduct of others may properly be regulated and governed, he is bound to perform it in such manner that those who rightfully are led to a course of conduct or action on the faith that the act or duty will be duly and properly performed shall not suffer loss or injury by reason of his negligence. The liability in such cases does not depend on the motives or considerations which induced a party to take on himself a particular task or duty, but on the question whether the legal rights of others have been violated by the mode in which the charge assumed has been performed.

The Court were not requested at the trial to withdraw the case from the jury on the ground that the plaintiff had failed to show he was in the exercise of due care at the time the accident happened. Upon the evidence, as stated in the report, we cannot say, as matter of law, that the plaintiff did not establish this part of his case.

Judgment on the verdict.

After the above decision was rendered, the verdict was set aside, by CHAPMAN, J., as against the evidence.[1]

STEVENS *v.* NICHOLS

SUPREME JUDICIAL COURT, MASSACHUSETTS, FEBRUARY 23, 1892.

Reported in 155 *Massachusetts Reports*, 472.

TORT, to recover for injuries occasioned to the plaintiff by driving over a curbstone covered with snow in a private way controlled by the defendants. At the trial in the Superior Court, Mason, C. J., at the defendants' request, ruled that, upon the pleadings and the plaintiff's opening, he could not maintain the action, and ordered a verdict for the defendants; and the plaintiff alleged exceptions. The facts, so far as material to the points decided, appear in the opinion.

John L. Thorndike, for the defendants.[2]

This case bears no resemblance to Holmes *v.* Drew, 151 Mass. 578, where the defendant had constructed a brick sidewalk by the side of a public street, partly on her own land and partly in the street, without any line of separation, and so that the whole was apparently part of the street, and the defendant clearly intended that it should be used

[1] Jones *v.* New York R. Co., 211 Mass. 521; De Boer *v.* Brooklyn Wharf Co., 51 App. Div. 289 *Accord.* Compare Hillman *v.* Boston R. Co., 207 Mass. 478.

This case is often cited as though it decided that the defendant was liable to the plaintiff for harm suffered by the plaintiff on account of a defect in the premises; *e. g.*, defective planks on the crossing. For a more correct view of the real question involved see the able argument of Mr. Thorndike in Stevens *v.* Nichols, *post.*

Liability of owner or occupier of a place manifestly intended for public or general use: see Crogan *v.* Schiele, 53 Conn. 186; Howe *v.* Ohmart, 7 Ind. App. 32; Davis *v.* Central Congregational Society, 129 Mass. 367; Holmes *v.* Drew, 151 Mass. 578; Gordon *v.* Cummings, 152 Mass. 513; Kelly *v.* Southern R. Co., 28 Minn. 98; Marsh *v.* Minneapolis Brewing Co., 92 Minn. 182; Rachmel *v.* Clark, 205 Pa. St. 314.

Liability of owner or occupier who passively acquiesces in use by others: see White *v.* France, 2 C. P. D. 308; Alabama R. Co. *v.* Godfrey, 156 Ala. 202; Herzog *v.* Hemphill, 7 Cal. App. 116; Pastorello *v.* Stone, 89 Conn. 286; Etheredge *v.* Central R. Co., 122 Ga. 853; Nave *v.* Flack, 90 Ind. 205; Evansville R. Co. *v.* Griffin, 100 Ind. 221; Martin *v.* Louisville Bridge Co., 41 Ind. App. 493; Zoebisch *v.* Tarbell, 10 Allen, 385; Bowler *v.* Pacific Mills, 200 Mass. 364; Habina *v.* Twin City Electric Co., 150 Mich. 41; Moore *v.* Wabash R. Co., 84 Mo. 481, 488; Kelly *v.* Benas, 217 Mo. 1; Barry *v.* Calvary Cemetery Assn., 106 Mo. App. 358; Walsh *v.* Fitchburg R. Co., 145 N. Y. 301; Fox *v.* Warner Asphalt Co., 204 N. Y. 340; Monroe *v.* Atlantic R. Co., 151 N. C. 374; Phillips *v.* Orr, 152 N. C. 583; Railroad Co. *v.* Harvey, 77 Ohio St. 235; Breckenridge *v.* Bennett, 7 Kulp (Pa.) 95.

[2] The report in 155 Mass. 472 does not give any portion of the arguments. The following passages are extracts from the printed brief for the defendants.

as part of the street. There is no similarity between such an addition to the apparent width of a public street and the opening of a private avenue or way out of a public street. The private way could not have been, or intended to be, part of the public street, and the separation between them was plain. . . .

The absence of similarity between this case and Holmes *v.* Drew, 151 Mass. 578, has already been pointed out; but it is also submitted that that case is the first in which it has ever been held that the owner of land was under any obligation to make it safe for a person that was allowed to come upon the land for his own convenience, and for a purpose in which the owner had no interest, whether the owner gave his consent in the form of a permission or in the form of what might, in common language, be called an invitation. Such persons were called licensees, and must take the land as they found it, subject only to this, that the owner must not lead them into danger by " something like fraud." Gautret *v.* Egerton, L. R. 2 C. P. 371, 374–375; Reardon *v.* Thompson, 149 Mass. 267, 268; Pollock on Torts, 424–426. . . .

But as regards persons coming upon land at the request, actual or tacit, of the owner upon business or for a purpose in which the owner had an *interest*, it was his duty to make it reasonably safe, and he was liable for damages arising from a neglect of this duty. Indermaur *v.* Dames, L. R. 1 C. P. 274, 2 C. P. 311; Carleton *v.* Franconia Iron & Steel Co., 99 Mass. 216 (rock by wharf at which vessel unloaded); The Moorcock, 14 P. D. 64 (a similar case); Davis *v.* Central Congregational Society, 129 Mass. 367 (plaintiff attending a conference of churches at defendant's meeting-house, an object in which both parties had an interest; also, p. 371, " a dangerous place without warning "); Pollock on Torts, 415–418.

It is this *common interest*, not the form of the license or invitation, that creates the liability (Holmes *v.* North Eastern Ry. Co., L. R. 4 Ex. 254, 6 Ex. 123).

The distinction between these two classes of cases is that in one the owner of the land has an interest in the person's coming there, while in the other the authority to come upon the land is a pure *gratuity*. It is reasonable that the owner should undertake some duty in respect of the condition of the land when he brings another person there for an object in which he himself has an interest. But there is no reason why he should undertake any such duty when he makes a gift of the privilege of going upon his land. The privilege is only a gift, whether the owner gives it because it is asked for, or whether he offers it first, or asks or " invites " the other to accept it. It may in a sense be said that a person is " induced " to go upon land by a license or permisson of the owner, but the real inducement is his own convenience. When the owner asks him to walk over his land whenever it is agreeable to him, and he goes there, he does so because it is agreeable to him, and not because the owner asks him. He is in law a *licensee* going upon the land for his own convenience by the owner's permission, and not a person brought there for a purpose in which the owner has an interest.[1]

Licensees, however, have a right to expect that the owner will not create a new danger while the license continues, and he is liable for the consequences if he does create such a danger; *e. g.*, by making an excavation near a path, as in Oliver *v.* Worcester, 102 Mass. 489, 502, or by placing an obstruction in an avenue, as in Corby *v.* Hill, 4 C. B. N. S. 556, 567, or by carelessly throwing a keg into a passageway, as in Corrigan *v.* Union Sugar Refinery, 98 Mass. 577, or by negligent management of trains at a private crossing of a railway habitually used by the public with the assent of the company, as in Sweeny *v.* Old Colony Rld. Co., 10 Allen, 368; Murphy *v.* Boston & Albany Rld. Co., 133 Mass. 121; Hanks *v.* Boston & Albany Rld. Co., 147 Mass. 495; Byrne *v.* New York Central Rld. Co., 104 N. Y. 362; Swift *v.* Staten Island Rld. Co., 123 N. Y. 645; Taylor *v.* Delaware & Hudson Canal Co., 113 Pa. St. 162, 175.

The principle of these cases is stated by Willes, J., in Gautret *v.* Egerton, L. R. 2 C. P., p. 373, as follows: "If I dedicate a way to the public which is full of ruts and holes, the public must take it as it is. If I dig a pit in it, I may be liable for the consequences; but, if I do nothing, I am not."

The same principle is alluded to in June *v.* Boston & Albany Rld. Co., 153 Mass. p. 82, where the court speaks of "cases in which even unintended damage done to a licensee by actively bringing force to bear upon his person will stand differently from merely passively leaving land in a dangerous condition."

[1] Smith *v.* London Docks Co., L. R. 3 C. P. 326; Holmes *v.* Northeastern R. Co., L. R. 4 Ex. 254, L. R. 6 Ex. 123; Wright *v.* London R. Co., L. R. 10 Q. B. 298, 1 Q. B. D. 252; Berlin Mills *v.* Croteau, (C. C. A.) 88 Fed. 860; Smith *v.* Day, (C. C. A.) 100 Fed. 244; Currier *v.* Trustees, (C. C. A.) 117 Fed. 44; Rhode *v.* Duff, (C. C. A.) 208 Fed. 115; Middleton *v.* Ross, (C. C. A.) 213 Fed. 6; Alabama R. Co. *v.* Godfrey, 156 Ala. 202; Schmidt *v.* Bauer, 80 Cal. 565; Herzog *v.* Hemphill, 7 Cal. App. 116; Pauckner *v.* Wakem, 231 Ill. 276; Franey *v.* Union Stockyards Co., 235 Ill. 522, 138 Ill. App. 215; Purtell *v.* Coal Co., 256 Ill. 110; Northwestern R. Co. *v.* O'Malley, 107 Ill. App. 599; Deach *v.* Woolner, 187 Ill. App. 524; Faris *v.* Hoberg, 134 Ind. 269; Baltimore R. Co. *v.* Slaughter, 167 Ind. 330; Thiele *v.* McManus, 3 Ind. App. 132; Wilmes *v.* Chicago R. Co., 175 Ia. 101; Lackat *v.* Lutz, 94 Ky. 287; Smith *v.* Trimble, 111 Ky. 861; Kentucky Distilleries Co. *v.* Leonard, (Ky.) 79 S. W. 281; Bell *v.* Houston R. Co., 132 La. 88; Dixon *v.* Swift, 98 Me. 207; Patten *v.* Bartlett, 111 Me. 409; Elie *v.* Lewiston R. Co., 112 Me. 178; Plummer *v.* Dill, 156 Mass. 426; Gauley *v.* Hall, 168 Mass. 513; Cowen *v.* Kirby, 180 Mass. 504; Norris *v.* Nawn Contracting Co., 206 Mass. 58; Lepnick *v.* Gaddis, 72 Miss. 200; Glaser *v.* Rothschild, 221 Mo. 180; Davis *v.* Ringolsky, 143 Mo. App. 364; Bryant *v.* Missouri R. Co., 181 Mo. App. 189; True *v.* Meredith Creamery, 72 N. H. 154; Flanagan *v.* Atlantic Asphalt Co., 37 App. Div. 476; Buchtel College *v.* Martin, 25 Ohio Cir. Ct. R. 494; Smith *v.* Sunday Creek Co., 74 W. Va. 606; Ross *v.* Kanawha R. Co., 76 W. Va. 197; Hupfer *v.* National Distilling Co., 114 Wis. 279; Muench *v.* Heinemann, 119 Wis. 441 *Accord.* See also Blossom *v.* Poteet, 104 Tex. 230 (wife bringing husband's dinner to mill where he was employed); Southwestern Cement Co. *v.* Bustillos, (Tex. Civ. App.) 169 S. W. 638 (child bringing lunch to employee).

But compare Mandeville Mills *v.* Dale, 2 Ga. App. 607; Furey *v.* New York Central R. Co., 67 N. J. Law, 270; Gorr *v.* Mittlestaedt, 96 Wis. 296.

The cases above mentioned include all that are cited in Holmes *v.* Drew, 151 Mass. 580. In none of them is it held or suggested that the railway company was liable for any defect or obstruction in the crossing, or that the landowner was liable for any excavation or obstruction existing when the permission was granted.

[After citing cases where the court said that some kind of inducement or invitation was necessary to create a liability for want of care in running trains.] But it was not suggested that the inducement or invitation would create any liability for defects in the crossing itself which the company gratuitously allowed the public to use.

[Referring to cases where there is implied license to the public to use a crossing.] The probability known to the company that some one may be there in pursuance of the license is treated . . . as the ground of liability in such cases for want of care in running trains. . . . But there is nothing in any of the cases above mentioned tending to support the proposition that the knowledge of the habitual use of the crossing, pursuant to the implied permission, would create a liability for defects in the crossing itself or impose any kind of duty to make it safe or convenient.

. . . .

Holmes *v.* Drew (151 Mass. 578) does not belong to either of the two last classes of cases. The plaintiff (1) did not go there upon the defendant's land for any purpose in which the defendant was interested, and (2) the defendant did nothing to make the place less safe than it was when it was first opened to the public. The plaintiff was a volunteer, going upon the defendant's land with her full permission, but entirely for his own convenience. These distinctions do not appear to have been called to the attention of the court. The judgment, which is very short, seems to proceed upon the ground that the defendant, by paving a footway partly on her own land and allowing it to remain apparently a part of the street, showed an *intention* that it should be used by foot passengers, and that this would amount to an *implied invitation,* which imposed on her a duty to make it reasonably safe. If this is to be taken literally, a permission ceases to be a *license* if it is *intended* that it shall be used; and an invitation imposes the same duty when it is given gratuitously for the pleasure of the donee as when it is given for an object in which the giver has an interest; and the owner of land that gives permission to cross his land can escape liability only by proving that he did not *intend* the permission to be used. It is submitted that the authorities cited in that case do not support this doctrine. Two of them are cases where the invitation was to come upon the land for a purpose in which the owner had an interest, and in the three others a licensee was injured by negligence in something done after the license was given. . . .

LATHROP, J. The declaration in this case, so far as material to the questions presented at the argument, alleged that the defendants on the day of the accident were, and had been for a long time, lessees and occupants of an estate on Atlantic Avenue in Boston; that the defendants maintained a way or street down by their premises, " leading out of said Atlantic Avenue, and extending to other premises beyond; that said street was in all particulars like the public streets of the city of Boston, being paved with granite blocks, and having sidewalks, and to all appearances was a public thoroughfare; that the defendants had placed no sign or notice of any kind upon or about said street . . . which would give warning to the plaintiff or to the public that said street was private property, or dangerous, but had erected a granite curbing out into said street, extending one half the distance across the same, on a line with the rear of their estate, said granite curbing being from six to seven inches above the grade of the paving; that said obstruction was dangerous both by day and by night to all persons who entered upon or passed through said street; that on or about said day the plaintiff had business that called him to the premises that lie beyond the estate of the defendants on said street, and, supposing and assuming that said street was a highway, and being induced by the acts and omissions of these defendants to so suppose and assume, entered in and upon said street to drive through the same; that said obstruction was covered by snow at said time, and plaintiff was unable to see the same; and, while in the exercise of due care, his sleigh struck said granite curbing," and he was thrown out and injured.

The opening of the plaintiff's counsel added but little to the declaration. It stated that " the snow lay perfectly level " where the curbstone was; that the plaintiff was driving through the defendants' way " into the way lying beyond, of which it was . . . an extension," to reach the works of the company for which he was working. It also stated that, before the defendants controlled the way under the written lease, they owned the premises, erected the building, paved the way, and put in the curbstone; " that ever since this building and other buildings had been erected down there the public made use of that way, as they would use any other street in the city; that is, as much as they had any occasion to pass down there with teams or on foot."

It does not appear that the plaintiff had any right in the way, unless he had it as one of the public. There is no allegation or statement that the plaintiff had ever used the way before, or that he knew the way was paved, or noticed whether there was a sign or not. Indeed, if he was then using the way for the first time, the fair inference would be, from the statement of the condition of the snow, that the fact that the way was paved was unknown to him until after the accident, and did not operate as an inducement to enter the way. The declaration contained no allegation as to any use by the public of the way, and the statement in the opening of counsel, that the public made use of that way, was qualified by the words, " that is, as much as they had any occasion to pass down there with teams or on foot." It is difficult to see how vehicles of any description could, when the paving was sufficiently visible to act as an inducement, go over that portion of the way which the defendants controlled.

Without laying stress upon these points, we are of opinion that the declaration and the opening of the plaintiff's counsel do not show that there was any breach on the part of the defendants of any duty which they owed the plaintiff. The defendants were not obliged to put up a sign notifying travellers on the public street that the passageway was not a public way. Galligan *v.* Metacomet Manuf. Co., 143 Mass. 527; Reardon *v.* Thompson, 149 Mass. 267; Redigan *v.* Boston & Maine Railroad, *ante*, 44.[1]

Nor can the fact that the passageway was paved be considered an invitation or inducement to the public to enter upon it for their own convenience. The defendants have a right to pave it for their own use or for the use of their customers. Johnson *v.* Boston & Maine Railroad, 125 Mass. 75; Heinlein *v.* Boston & Providence Railroad, 147 Mass. 136; Reardon *v.* Thompson, 149 Mass. 267; Donnelly *v.* Boston & Maine Railroad, 151 Mass. 210; Redigan *v.* Boston & Maine Railroad, *ante*, 44.

There was in this case no allegation and no statement that the defendants had any knowledge that the public was using the passageway, or of such a condition of things that it can be said that they must have known of it. But if it be assumed that there was such use and such acquiescence that a license might be implied, the plaintiff stands in no better position. "The general rule is," as stated by Mr. Justice Holmes in Reardon *v.* Thompson, *ubi supra*, "that a licensee goes upon land at his own risk, and must take the premises as he finds them." See also Redigan *v.* Boston & Maine Railroad, *ante*, 44; Gautret *v.* Egerton, L. R. 2 C. P. 371, 374.

The licensor has, however, no right to create a new danger while the license continues. Oliver *v.* Worcester, 102 Mass. 489, 502; Corrigan *v.* Union Sugar Refinery, 98 Mass. 577; Corby *v.* Hill, 4 C. B. (N. S.) 556. So a railroad company which allows the public habitually to use a private crossing of its tracks cannot use active force against a person or vehicle crossing under a license, express or implied. Sweeny *v.* Old Colony & Newport Railroad, 10 Allen, 368; Murphy *v.* Boston & Albany Railroad, 133 Mass. 121; Hanks *v.* Boston & Albany Railroad, 147 Mass. 495. See June *v.* Boston & Albany Railroad, 153 Mass. 79, 82.

We have no occasion to consider whether the case of Holmes *v.* Drew, 151 Mass. 578, is open to the criticism that it is inconsistent with the doctrine that a person who dedicates a footway to the public use is not obliged to keep it in repair (see Fisher *v.* Prowse, 2 B. & S. 770, 780, and Robbins *v.* Jones, 15 C. B. (N. S.) 221) as we are of

[1] That is, 155 Mass.

opinion that that case has no application to the case at bar. In Holmes v. Drew, the defendant made a continuous pavement in front of his house, partly on his own land and partly on the public land; and it was held that the jury might infer from this an invitation to walk over the whole pavement. In the case at bar, the defendants merely opened a private way into a public street, and we fail to see that they thereby invited the public to use it, even though it were paved.

Exceptions overruled.[1]

TUTTLE v. GILBERT MANUFACTURING CO.

SUPREME JUDICIAL COURT, MASSACHUSETTS, OCTOBER 20, 1887.

Reported in 145 *Massachusetts Reports*, 169.

TORT, by lessee of a building against lessor. The lessee claimed, and introduced evidence to show, that, at the time of letting, the lessor agreed to repair the building and put it in safe condition; that the lessee suffered damage by reason of a defect in the building; and that the lessor failed and neglected to make repairs until after the damage to the plaintiff.

Upon the evidence, the judge ruled that plaintiff could not recover, and ordered a verdict for defendant. Plaintiff excepted.[2]

MORTON, C. J. It is the general rule that there is no warranty implied in the letting of premises that they are reasonably fit for use. The lessee takes an estate in the premises hired, and he takes the risk of the quality of the premises, in the absence of an express or implied warranty by the lessor, or of deceit. A lessee, therefore, if he is injured by reason of the unsafe condition of the premises hired, cannot maintain an action against the lessor, in the absence of warranty or of misrepresentation. In cases where lessors have been held liable for such injuries to the lessees, the liability is founded in negligence. Looney v. McLean, 129 Mass. 33. Bowe v. Hunking, 135 Mass. 380, and cases cited.

[1] McClain v. Bank, 100 Me. 437; Moffatt v. Kenny, 174 Mass. 311 *Accord.*

Hanson v. Spokane Water Co., 58 Wash. 6 *Contra.* Compare Buckingham v. Fisher, 70 Ill. 121.

Liability to one who has business with an abutting owner who has a right to use the way: see Cavanagh v. Block, 192 Mass. 63.

As to what constitutes an implied invitation, see Bryan v. Stewart, 194 Ala. 353; Baltimore R. Co. v. Slaughter, 167 Ind. 330; Pittsburgh R. Co. v. Simons, 168 Ind. 333; Stanwood v. Clancey, 106 Me. 72; Kalus v. Bass, 122 Md. 467; Walker v. Winstanley, 155 Mass. 301; Plummer v. Dill, 156 Mass. 426; Chenery v. Fitchburg R. Co., 160 Mass. 211; Tracey v. Page, 201 Mass. 62; Shaw v. Ogden, 214 Mass. 475; Romana v. Boston R. Co., 218 Mass. 76; Allen v. Yazoo R. Co., 111 Miss. 267; Black v. Central R. Co., 85 N. J. Law, 197; Heskell v. Auburn Light Co., 209 N. Y. 86.

[2] The statement has been much abridged.

The plaintiff admits the general rule, but contends that this case is taken out of it because, at the time of the letting, the defendant agreed to repair and put in a safe condition the stable floor, the unsafe condition of which caused the injury. The contract relied on is a loose one; it fixed no time within which the repairs were to be made, and it is doubtful whether the evidence proved any breach of contract on the part of the defendant. But if we assume that the contract was to make the repairs within a reasonable time, and that the jury would be justified in finding that the defendant had not performed it within a reasonable time, the question is whether, for such a breach, the plaintiff can maintain an action of tort to recover for personal injuries sustained by reason of the defective condition of the stable floor.

The cases are numerous and confusing as to the dividing line between actions of contract and of tort, and there are many cases where a man may have his election to bring either action. Where the cause of action arises merely from a breach of promise, the action is in contract.

The action of tort has for its foundation the negligence of the defendant, and this means more than a mere breach of a promise. Otherwise, the failure to meet a note, or any other promise to pay money, would sustain an action in tort for negligence, and thus the promisor be made liable for all the consequential damages arising from such failure.

As a general rule, there must be some active negligence or misfeasance to support tort. There must be some breach of duty distinct from breach of contract. In the case at bar, the utmost shown against the defendant is that there was unreasonable delay on its part in performing an executory contract. As we have seen, it is not liable by reason of the relation of lessor and lessee, but its liability, if any, must rest solely upon a breach of this contract.

We do not see how the cases would differ in principle if an action were brought against a third person who had contracted to repair the stable floor and had unreasonably delayed in performing his contract. We are not aware of any authority for maintaining such an action. If the defendant had performed the work contemplated by its contract unskilfully and negligently, it would be liable to an action of tort, because in such case there would be a misfeasance, which is a sufficient foundation for an action of tort. Such was the case of Gill *v.* Middleton, 105 Mass. 477.

The case of Ashley *v.* Root, 4 Allen, 504, does not conflict with our view, but recognizes the rule that to sustain an action of tort there must be more than a mere breach of contract.

The plaintiff now argues that he had the right to go to the jury upon the questions of warranty and deceit. It does not appear that this claim was made in the Superior Court; but it is clear that there is no sufficient evidence of any warranty that the stable was safe, or of any deceit or misrepresentation on the part of the defendant or its agent. *Exceptions overruled.*[1]

SOUTHCOTE *v.* STANLEY

IN THE EXCHEQUER, JUNE 4, 1856.

Reported in 1 *Hurlstone & Norman*, 247.

THE declaration stated that at the time of the committing of the grievances, &c., the defendant was possessed of an hotel, into which he had then permitted and invited the plaintiff to come as a visitor of the defendant, and in which the plaintiff as such visitor then lawfully was by the permission and invitation of the defendant, and in which hotel there then was a glass door of the defendant which it was then necessary for the plaintiff, as such visitor, to open for the purpose of leaving the hotel, and which the plaintiff, as such visitor, then by the permission of the defendant and with his knowledge, and without any warning from him, lawfully opened for the purpose aforesaid, as a door which was in a proper condition to be opened; nevertheless, by and through the mere carelessness, negligence, and default of the defendant in that behalf, the said door was then in an insecure and dangerous condition, and unfit to be used or opened, and by reason of the said door being in such insecure and dangerous condition and unfit, as aforesaid, and of the then carelessness, negligence, default, and improper conduct of the defendant in that behalf, a large piece of glass from the said door fell out of the same to and upon the plaintiff, and wounded him, and he sustained divers bodily injuries, and remained ill and unable to work for a long time, &c.

Demurrer and joinder therein.

Raymond, in support of the demurrer. The declaration discloses no cause of action. It is not stated that the plaintiff was in the hotel

[1] Anderson *v.* Robinson, 182 Ala. 615; Hedskin *v.* Gillespie, 33 Ind. App. 650; Shackford *v.* Coffin, 95 Me. 69; Rolfe *v.* Tufts, 216 Mass. 563; Brady *v.* Klein, 133 Mich. 422; Korach *v.* Loeffel, 168 Mo. App. 414 (but see Graff *v.* Lemp Brewing Co., 130 Mo. App. 618; Marcheck *v.* Klute, 133 Mo. App. 280); Dustin *v.* Curtis, 74 N. H. 266; Schick *v.* Fleischhauer, 26 App. Div. 210; Stelz *v.* Van Dusen, 93 App. Div. 358; Kushes *v.* Ginsberg, 99 App. Div. 417; Boden *v.* Scholtz, 101 App. Div. 1; Mitchell *v.* Stewart, 187 Pa. St. 217; Davis *v.* Smith, 26 R. I. 129 *Accord.* See also Clyne *v.* Helmes, 61 N. J. Law, 358. Compare Miles *v.* Janvrin, 196 Mass. 431, 200 Mass. 514; Flanagan *v.* Welch, 220 Mass. 186.

Sontag *v.* O'Hare, 73 Ill. App. 432; Schwandt *v.* Metzger Oil Co., 93 Ill. App. 365 (but see Cromwell *v.* Allen, 151 Ill. App. 404); Good *v.* Von Hemert, 114 Minn. 393; Glidden *v.* Goodfellow, 124 Minn. 101; Keegan *v.* Heileman Brewing Co., 129 Minn. 496; Merchants Cotton Press Co. *v.* Miller, 135 Tenn. 187; Lowe *v.* O'Brien, 77 Wash. 677 *Contra.* See Moore *v.* Steljes, 69 Fed. 518.

Liability where landlord makes repairs negligently: see Mann *v.* Fuller, 63 Kan. 664; Gill *v.* Middleton, 105 Mass. 477; Thomas *v.* Lane, 221 Mass. 447; Finer *v.* Nichols, 175 Mo. App. 525; Carlon *v.* City Sav. Bank, 85 Neb. 659; Wynne *v.* Haight, 27 App. Div. 7; Marston *v.* Frisbie, 168 App. Div. 666; Flam *v.* Greenberg, (App. Div.) 158 N. Y. Supp. 670; Wilcox *v.* Hines, 100 Tenn. 538.

as a guest, but merely as a visitor; and there is no allegation that the defendant knew of the dangerous condition of the door. To render the defendant liable, the declaration ought to have shown some contract between the plaintiff and the defendant which imposed on the latter the obligation of taking care that the door was secure; or it should have alleged some negligence on the part of the defendant in the performance of a duty which he owed to the plaintiff. [BRAMWELL, B. If a person invites another into his house, and the latter can only enter through a particular door, is it not the duty of the former to take care that the door is in a secure condition ?] He may not be aware that the door is insecure. This declaration only alleges that through the carelessness, negligence, and default of the defendant the door was in a dangerous condition; that cannot be read as involving the allegation that the defendant knew that the door was insecure. All facts necessary to raise a legal liability must be strictly averred. Metcalfe *v.* Hetherington, 11 Exch. 257. [ALDERSON, B. It is not stated that it was the duty of the defendant, as an hotel keeper, to take care that the door was secure. Suppose a person invites another to his house, and the latter runs his hand through a pane of glass, how is the former liable ?] The Court then called on

Gray, contra. The declaration shows a duty on the part of the defendant, and a breach of that duty. It is immaterial whether the injury takes place in a private house, or in a shop, or in a street; the only question is whether the person who complains was lawfully there ? The case is similar in principle to that of Randleson *v.* Murray, 8 A. & E. 109, which decided that a warehouseman who lowers goods from his warehouse is bound to use proper tackle for that purpose. [ALDERSON, B. It is the duty of every person who hangs anything over a public way to take care that it is suspended by a proper rope.] Whether it be a private house or a shop, a duty is so far imposed on the occupier to keep it reasonably secure, that if a person lawfully enters, and through the negligence of the occupier in leaving it in an insecure state receives an injury, the occupier is responsible. Here it is alleged that the defendant invited the plaintiff to come into the hotel as a visitor; that shows that he was lawfully there. [POLLOCK, C. B. The position that an action lies because the plaintiff was lawfully in the house, cannot be supported; a servant is lawfully in his master's house and yet if the balusters fell, whereby he was injured, he could not maintain an action against the master. If a lady who is invited to dinner goes in an expensive dress, and a servant spills something over her dress which spoils it, the master of the house would not be liable. Where a person enters a house by invitation the same rule prevails as in the case of a servant. A visitor would have no right of action for being put in a damp bed, or near a broken pane of glass, whereby he caught cold. ALDERSON, B. The case of a shop is different, because a shop is open to the public; and there is a distinction between persons who come on business and those who come by invitation.]

POLLOCK, C. B. We are all of opinion that the declaration cannot be supported, and that the defendant is entitled to judgment. I do not think it necessary to point out the reasons by which I have come to that conclusion; because it follows from the decision of this Court (Priestley *v.* Fowler, 3 M. & W. 1) that the mere relation of master and servant does not create any implied duty on the part of the master to take more care of the servant than he may reasonably be expected to do of himself. That decision has been followed by several cases,[1] and is now established law, though I believe the principle was not recognized until recent times. The reason for the rule is that the servant undertakes to run all the ordinary risks of service, including those arising from the negligence of his fellow-servants. The rule applies to all the members of a domestic establishment, so that the master is not in general liable to a servant for injury resulting from the negligence of a fellow-servant; neither can one servant maintain an action against another for negligence whilst engaged in their common employment. The same principle applies to the case of a visitor at a house; whilst he remains there he is in the same position as any other member of the establishment, so far as regards the negligence of the master or his servants, and he must take his chance with the rest.

ALDERSON, B. I am of the same opinion.

BRAMWELL, B. I agree with Mr. *Gray* to this extent, that where a person is in the house of another, either on business or for any other purpose, he has a right to expect that the owner of the house will take reasonable care to protect him from injury; for instance, that he will not allow a trap-door to be open through which the visitor may fall. But in this case my difficulty is to see that the declaration charges any act of commission. If a person asked another to walk in his garden, in which he had placed spring-guns or men-traps, and the latter, not being aware of it, was thereby injured, that would be an act of commission. But if a person asked a visitor to sleep at his house, and the former omitted to see that the sheets were properly aired, whereby the visitor caught cold, he could maintain no action, for there was no act of commission, but simply an act of omission. This declaration merely alleges that " by and through the mere carelessness, negligence, default, and improper conduct of the defendant," the glass fell from the door. That means a want of care, — a default in not doing something. The words are all negatives, and under these circumstances the action is not maintainable. I doubted whether the words " carelessness, negligence, and improper conduct," &c., might not mean something equivalent to actual commission, but on the best consideration which I can give the subject, it appears to me that they do not

[1] See Hutchinson *v.* The Newcastle, York, & Berwick Railway Company, 5 Exch. 343; Wiggett *v.* Fox, 11 Exch. 832. — Reporter's Note.

mean that, but merely point to a negative. If I misconstrue the declaration it is the fault of those who so framed it.

Judgment for the defendant.[1]

BEEHLER v. DANIELS

SUPREME COURT, RHODE ISLAND, MAY 1, 1894.

Reported in 18 *Rhode Island Reports*, 563.

TRESPASS ON THE CASE. Certified from the Common Pleas Division on demurrer to the declaration.

STINESS, J. The plaintiff seeks to recover for injury caused by falling into an elevator well in the defendants' building, which he entered in the discharge of his duty, as a member of the fire department of the city of Providence, in answering a call to extinguish a fire. The negligence alleged in the first count is a failure to guard and protect the well; and in the second count such a packing of merchandise as to guide and conduct one to the unguarded and unprotected well. The defendants demur to the declaration, alleging as grounds of demurrer that they owed no duty to the plaintiff; that he entered their premises in the discharge of a public duty and assumed the risks of his employment; that he was in the premises without invitation from them; and that they are not liable for consequences which they could not and were not bound to foresee.

The decisive question thus raised is, Did the defendants, under the circumstances, owe to the plaintiff a duty, for failure in which they are liable to him in damages? The question is not a new one, and we think it is safe to say that it has never been answered otherwise than in favor of the defendants. The plaintiff argues that it was his duty to enter the premises, and, consequently, since an owner may reasonably anticipate the liability of a fire, a duty arises from the owner to the fireman to keep his premises guarded and safe. An extension of this argument to its legitimate result, as a rule of law, is sufficiently startling to show its unsoundness. The liability to fire is common to all buildings and at all times. Hence every owner of every building must at all times keep every part of his property, in such condition, that a fireman, unacquainted with the place, and groping about in darkness and smoke, shall come upon no obstacle, opening, machine or anything whatever which may cause him injury. This argument was urged in Woodruff v. Bowen, 136 Ind. 431; but

[1] Whether the result in the above case is correct is a question not yet decided in most of the United States, and upon which conflicting opinions have been expressed. See Hart v. Cole, 156 Mass. 475; KNOWLTON, J., in Coupe v. Platt, 172 Mass. 458, 459; Bigelow on Torts, 7th ed., pp. 362, 363, sections 740–743, 8th ed., p. 158; Burdick on Torts, 3d ed., sect. 555; 2 Shearman & Redfield on Negligence, 4th ed., sect. 706; Barman v. Spencer, (Ind.) 49 N. E. 9, 11, 12; Beard v. Klusmeier, 158 Ky. 153; Land v. Fitzgerald, 68 N. J. Law, 28.

the court said: "We are of the opinion that the owner of a building in a populous city does not owe it as a duty at common law, independent of any statute or ordinance, to keep such building safe for firemen or other officers, who, in a contingency, may enter the same under a license conferred by law."

Undoubtedly the plaintiff in this case had the right to enter the defendants' premises, and the character of his entry was that of a licensee. Cooley on Torts, *313. But no such duty as is averred in this declaration is due from an owner to a licensee. This question is discussed in the case just cited, as also in many others. For example, in Reardon *v.* Thompson, 149 Mass. 267, Holmes, J., says: "But the general rule is that a licensee goes upon land at his own risk, and must take the premises as he finds them. An open hole, which is not concealed otherwise than by the darkness of the night, is a danger which a licensee must avoid at his peril." So in Mathews *v.* Bensel, 51 N. J. Law, 30, Beasley, C. J., says: "The substantial ground of complaint laid in the count is, that the defendants did not properly construct their planer, and, being a dangerous instrument, did not surround it with proper safeguards. But there is no legal principle that imposes such a duty as this on the owner of property with respect to a mere licensee. This is the recognized rule. In the case of Holmes *v.* Northeastern Railway Co., L. R. 4 Exch. 254, 256, Baron Channell says: 'That where a person is a mere licensee he has no cause of action on account of the dangers existing in the place he is permitted to enter.'" In Parker *v.* Portland Publishing Co., 69 Me. 173, this question is fully examined, the court holding it to be well settled, if the plaintiff was at the place where the injury was received by license merely, that the defendant would owe him no duty and that he could not recover. See also Indiana, etc., Railway Co. *v.* Barnhart, 115 Ind. 399; Gibson *v.* Leonard, 37 Ill. App. 344; Bedell *v.* Berkey, 76 Mich. 435.

There is a clear distinction between a license and an invitation to enter premises, and an equally clear distinction as to the duty of an owner in the two cases. An owner owes to a licensee no duty as to the condition of premises, unless imposed by statute, save that he should not knowingly let him run upon a hidden peril or wilfully cause him harm; while to one invited he is under obligation for reasonable security for the purposes of the invitation. The plaintiff's declaration does not set out a cause of action upon either of these grounds, and the cases cited and relied on by him fall within the two classes of cases described, and mark the line of duty very clearly. Parker *v.* Barnard, 135 Mass. 116, was the case of a police officer who had entered a building, the doors of which were found open in the night time, to inspect it according to the rules of the police department, and fell down an unguarded elevator well. A statute required such wells to be protected by railings and trap-doors. Judgment having been given for the defendant at the trial, a new trial was ordered upon the ground of a violation of statute. The court says: "The owner or occupant of land or a building is not liable, at common law, for obstructions, pitfalls, or other dangers there existing, as, in the absence of any inducement or invitation to others to enter, he may use his property as he pleases. But he holds his property 'subject to such reasonable control and regulation of the mode of keeping and use as the legislature, under the police power vested in them by the Constitution of the Commonwealth, may think necessary for the preventing of injuries to the rights of others and the security of the public health and welfare.'" Then, likening the plaintiff to a fireman, the court also says: "Even if they must encounter the danger arising from neglect of such precautions against obstructions and pitfalls as those invited or induced to enter have a right to expect, they may demand, as against the owners or occupants, that they observe the statute in the construction and management of their building." In Learoyd *v.* Godfrey, 138 Mass. 315, a police officer fell down an uncovered well in or near a passageway to a house where he was called to quell a disturbance of the peace. A verdict for the plaintiff was sustained upon the ground that the jury must have found that the officer was using the passageway by the defendant's invitation and that the evidence warranted the finding. Gordon *v.* Cummings, 152 Mass. 513, was the case of a letter carrier who fell into an elevator well, in a hallway where he was accustomed to leave letters in boxes put there for that purpose. The court held that there was an implied invitation to the carrier to enter the premises. In Engel *v.* Smith, 82 Mich. 1, the plaintiff fell through a trap-door left open in a building where he was employed. The question of duty is not discussed in the case but simply the fact of negligence. In Bennett *v.* Railroad Co., 102 U. S. 577, the plaintiff, a passenger, fell through a hatch hole in the depot floor. The court construed the declaration as setting out facts which amounted to an invitation to the plaintiff to pass over the route which he took through the shed depot where the hatch hole was.

In the present case the plaintiff sets out no violation of a statute, or facts which amount to an invitation, and, consequently, under the well-settled rule of law, the defendants were under no liability to him for the condition of their premises or the packing of their merchandise. The demurrer to the declaration must therefore be sustained.[1]

[1] Pennebaker *v.* San Joaquin Light Co., 158 Cal. 579; Lunt *v.* Post Printing Co., 48 Col. 316; Gibson *v.* Leonard, 143 Ill. 182, 37 Ill. App. 344; Thrift *v.* Vandalia R. Co., 145 Ill. App. 414; Woodruff *v.* Bowen, 136 Ind. 431; Hamilton *v.* Minneapolis Desk Co., 78 Minn. 3; New Omaha Electric Light Co. *v.* Anderson, 73 Neb. 84; Woods *v.* Miller, 30 App. Div. 232; Eckes *v.* Stetler, 98 App. Div. 76; Houston R. Co. *v.* O'Leary, (Tex. Civ. App.) 136 S. W. 601 *Accord.* But see Wilson *v.* Great Southern Tel. Co., 41 La. Ann. 1041.

Liability to police officer or other person in by permission of law: see Casey *v.* Adams, 234 Ill. 350; Eckels *v.* Maher, 137 Ill. App. 45; Blatt *v.* McBarron, 161 Mass. 21; Racine *v.* Morris, 136 App. Div. 467; Woods *v.* Lloyd, (Pa.) 16 Atl. 43;

SECTION VII

LIABILITY TO THIRD PERSONS OF MAKER OR VENDOR OF A CHATTEL

WINTERBOTTOM *v.* WRIGHT

IN THE EXCHEQUER, JUNE 6, 1842.

Reported in 10 *Meeson & Welsby,* 109.

CASE. The declaration stated, that the defendant was a contractor for the supply of mail-coaches, and had in that character contracted for hire and reward with the Postmaster-General, to provide the mail-coach for the purpose of conveying the mail-bags from Hartford, in the county of Chester, to Holyhead: That the defendant, under and by virtue of the said contract, had agreed with the said Postmaster-General that the said mail-coach should, during the said contract, be kept in a fit, proper, safe, and secure state and condition for the said purpose, and took upon himself, to wit, under and by virtue of the said contract, the sole and exclusive duty, charge, care, and burden of the repairs, state, and condition of the said mail-coach; and it had become and was the sole and exclusive duty of the defendant, to wit, under and by virtue of his said contract, to keep and maintain the said mail-coach in a fit, proper, safe, and secure state and condition for the purpose aforesaid: That Nathaniel Atkinson and other persons, having notice of the said contract, were under contract with the Postmaster-General to convey the said mail-coach from Hartford to Holyhead, and to supply horses and coachmen for that purpose, and also not, on any pretence whatever, to use or employ any other coach or carriage whatever than such as should be so provided, directed, and appointed by the Postmaster-General: That the plaintiff, being a mail-coachman, and thereby obtaining his livelihood, and whilst the said several contracts were in force, having notice thereof, and trusting to and confiding in the contract made between the defendant and the Postmaster-General, and believing that the said coach was in a fit, safe, secure, and proper state and condition for the pur-

Burroughs Adding Machine Co. *v.* Fryar, 132 Tenn. 612; Greenville *v.* Pitts, 102 Tex. 1.

But compare Kennedy *v.* Heisen, 182 Ill. App. 200; Parker *v.* Barnard, 135 Mass. 116; Learoyd *v.* Godfrey, 138 Mass. 315; Pickwick *v.* McCauliff, 193 Mass. 70.

Liability to volunteer salvor in case of fire: see Kohn *v.* Lovett, 44 Ga. 251; Gibson *v.* Leonard, 143 Ill. 182.

Liability to person who has contractual right to inspect the premises: see Dashields *v.* Moses, 35 App. D. C. 583.

pose aforesaid, and not knowing and having no means of knowing to the contrary thereof, hired himself to the said Nathaniel Atkinson and his co-contractors as mail-coachman, to drive and take the conduct of the said mail-coach, which but for the said contract of the defendant he would not have done. The declaration then averred, that the defendant so improperly and negligently conducted himself, and so utterly disregarded his aforesaid contract, and so wholly neglected and failed to perform his duty in this behalf, that heretofore, to wit, on the 8th of August, 1840, whilst the plaintiff, as such mail-coachman so hired, was driving the said mail-coach from Hartford to Holyhead, the same coach, being a mail-coach found and provided by the defendant under his said contract, and the defendant then acting under his said contract, and having the means of knowing and then well knowing all the aforesaid premises, the said mail-coach being then in a frail, weak, infirm, and dangerous state and condition, to wit, by and through certain latent defects in the state and condition thereof, and unsafe and unfit for the use and purpose aforesaid, and from no other cause, circumstance, matter, or thing whatsoever gave way and broke down, whereby the plaintiff was thrown from his seat, and, in consequence of injuries then received, had become lamed for life.

To this declaration the defendant pleaded several pleas, to two of which there were demurrers; but, as the Court gave no opinion as to their validity, it is not necessary to state them.

Peacock, who appeared in support of the demurrers, having argued against the sufficiency of the pleas, —

Byles, for the defendant, objected that the declaration was bad in substance. This is an action brought, not against Atkinson and his co-contractors, who were the employers of the plaintiff, but against the person employed by the Postmaster-General, and totally unconnected with them or with the plaintiff. Now it is a general rule, that wherever a wrong arises merely out of the breach of a contract, which is the case on the face of this declaration, whether the form in which the action is conceived be *ex contractu* or *ex delicto*, the party who made the contract alone can sue: Tollit *v.* Sherstone, 5 M. & W. 283. If the rule were otherwise, and privity of contract were not requisite, there would be no limit to such actions. If the plaintiff may, as in this case, run through the length of three contracts, he may run through any number or series of them; and the most alarming consequences would follow the adoption of such a principle. Levy *v.* Langridge, 4 M. & W. 337, will probably be referred to on the other side. But that case was expressly decided on the ground that the defendant, who sold the gun by which the plaintiff was injured, although he did not personally contract with the plaintiff, who was a minor, knew that it was bought to be used by him. Here there is no allegation that the defendant knew that the coach was to be driven by the plaintiff. There, moreover, fraud was alleged in the declaration, and found by the jury: and there, too, the cause of injury was a weapon of a dangerous nature, and the defendant was alleged to have had notice of the defect in its construction. Nothing of that sort appears upon this declaration.

Peacock, contra. This case is within the principle of the decision in Levy *v.* Langridge. Here the defendant entered into a contract with a public officer to supply an article which, if imperfectly constructed, was necessarily dangerous, and which, from its nature and the use for which it was destined, was necessarily to be driven by a coachman. That is sufficient to bring the case within the rule established by Levy *v.* Langridge. In that case the contract made by the father of the plaintiff with the defendant was made on behalf of himself and his family generally, and there was nothing to show that the defendant was aware even of the existence of the particular son who was injured. Suppose a party made a contract with government for a supply of muskets, one of which, from its misconstruction, burst and injured a soldier: there it is clear that the use of the weapon by a soldier would have been contemplated, although not by the particular individual who received the injury, and could it be said, since the decision in Levy *v.* Langridge, that he could not maintain an action against the contractor? So, if a coachmaker, employed to put on the wheels of a carriage, did it so negligently that one of them flew off, and a child of the owner were thereby injured, the damage being the natural and immediate consequence of his negligence, he would surely be responsible. So, if a party entered into a contract to repair a church, a workhouse, or other public building, and did it so insufficiently that a person attending the former, or a pauper in the latter, were injured by the falling of a stone, he could not maintain an action against any other person than the contractor; but against him he must surely have a remedy. It is like the case of a contractor who negligently leaves open a sewer, whereby a person passing along the street is injured. It is clear that no action could be maintained against the Postmaster-General: Hall *v.* Smith, 2 Bing. 156; Humphreys *v.* Mears, 1 Man. & R. 187; Priestly *v.* Fowler. But here the declaration alleges the accident to have happened through the defendant's negligence and want of care. The plaintiff had no opportunity of seeing that the carriage was sound and secure. [ALDERSON, B. The decision in Levy *v.* Langridge proceeds upon the ground of the knowledge and fraud of the defendant.] Here also there was fraud: the defendant represented the coach to be in a proper state for use, and whether he represented that which was false within his knowledge, or a fact as true which he did not know to be so, it was equally a fraud in point of law, for which he is responsible.

LORD ABINGER, C. B. I am clearly of opinion that the defendant is entitled to our judgment. We ought not to permit a doubt to rest upon this subject, for our doing so might be the means of letting in upon us an infinity of actions. This is an action of the first impression, and it has been brought in spite of the precautions which were taken, in the judgment of this Court in the case of Levy *v.* Langridge, to obviate any notion that such an action could be maintained. We ought not to attempt to extend the principle of that decision, which, although it has been cited in support of this action, wholly fails as an authority in its favor; for there the gun was bought for the use of the son, the plaintiff in that action, who could not make the bargain himself, but was really and substantially the party contracting. Here the action is brought simply because the defendant was a contractor with a third person; and it is contended that thereupon he became liable to everybody who might use the carriage. If there had been any ground for such an action, there certainly would have been some precedent of it; but with the exception of actions against inn-keepers, and some few other persons, no case of a similar nature has occurred in practice. That is a strong circumstance, and is of itself a great authority against its maintenance. It is however contended, that this contract being made on the behalf of the public by the Postmaster-General, no action could be maintained against him, and therefore the plaintiff must have a remedy against the defendant. But that is by no means a necessary consequence, — he may be remediless altogether. There is no privity of contract between these parties; and if the plaintiff can sue, every passenger, or even any person passing along the road, who was injured by the upsetting of the coach, might bring a similar action. Unless we confine the operation of such contracts as this to the parties who entered into them, the most absurd and outrageous consequences, to which I can see no limit, would ensue. Where a party becomes responsible to the public, by undertaking a public duty, he is liable, though the injury may have arisen from the negligence of his servant or agent. So, in cases of public nuisances, whether the act was done by the party as a servant, or in any other capacity, you are liable to an action at the suit of any person who suffers. Those, however, are cases where the real ground of the liability is the public duty, or the commission of the public nuisance. There is also a class of cases in which the law permits a contract to be turned into a tort; but unless there has been some public duty undertaken, or public nuisance committed, they are all cases in which an action might have been maintained upon the contract. Thus, a carrier may be sued either in assumpsit or case; but there is no instance in which a party, who was not privy to the contract entered into with him, can maintain any such action. The plaintiff in this case could not have brought an action on the contract; if he could have done so, what would have been his situation supposing the Postmaster-General had released the defendant? That would, at all events, have defeated his claim altogether. By permitting this action, we should be working this injustice, that after the defendant had done everything to the satisfaction of his employer, and after all matters between them had been adjusted, and all accounts settled on the footing of their contract, we should subject them to be ripped open by this action of tort being brought against him.

ALDERSON, B. I am of the same opinion. The contract in this case was made with the Postmaster-General alone; and the case is just the same as if he had come to the defendant and ordered a carriage, and handed it at once over to Atkinson. If we were to hold that the plaintiff could sue in such a case, there is no point at which such actions would stop. The only safe rule is to confine the right to recover to those who enter into the contract: if we go one step beyond that, there is no reason why we should not go fifty. The only real argument in favor of the action is, that this is a case of hardship; but that might have been obviated, if the plaintiff had made himself a party to the contract. Then it is urged that it falls within the principle of the case of Levy *v.* Langridge. But the principle of that case was simply this, that the father having bought the gun for the very purpose of being used by the plaintiff, the defendant made representations by which he was induced to use it. There, a distinct fraud was committed on the plaintiff; the falsehood of the representation was also alleged to have been within the knowledge of the defendant who made it, and he was properly held liable for the consequences. How are the facts of that case applicable to those of the present ? Where is the allegation of misrepresentation or fraud in this declaration ? It shows nothing of the kind. Our judgment must therefore be for the defendant.

GURNEY, B., concurred.

ROLFE, B. The breach of the defendant's duty, stated in this declaration, is his omission to keep the carriage in a safe condition; and when we examine the mode in which that duty is alleged to have arisen, we find a statement that the defendant took upon himself, to wit, under and by virtue of the said contract, the sole and exclusive duty, charge, care, and burden of the repairs, state, and condition of the said mail-coach, and, during all the time aforesaid, it had become and was the sole and exclusive duty of the defendant, to wit, under and by virtue of his said contract, to keep and maintain the said mail-coach in a fit, proper, safe, and secure state and condition. The duty, therefore, is shown to have arisen solely from the contract; and the fallacy consists in the use of that word "duty." If a duty to the Postmaster-General be meant, that is true; but if a duty to the plaintiff be intended (and in that sense the word is evidently used), there was none. This is one of those unfortunate cases in which there certainly has been *damnum*, but it is *damnum absque injuria;* it is, no doubt, a hardship upon the plaintiff to be without a remedy, but, by that consideration we ought not to be influenced. Hard cases, it has been frequently observed, are apt to introduce bad law.

Judgment for the defendant.[1]

BLOOD BALM COMPANY *v.* COOPER

SUPREME COURT, GEORGIA, OCTOBER 14, 1889.

Reported in 83 *Georgia Reports,* 857.

ACTION by Cooper against Blood Balm Company in the City Court of Atlanta. Verdict for plaintiff. Defendants brought error.[2]

BLANDFORD, J. The main question in this case arises upon the refusal of the Court below to award a nonsuit, and the solution of this question depends upon whether, where one prepares what is known as a proprietary or patent medicine, and puts it upon the market and recommends it to the world as useful for the cure of certain diseases, the bottle containing it having therewith a prescription made by the proprietor of the medicine, in which he states that it is to be taken in certain quantities, and such medicine, accompanied with this prescription, is sold by the proprietor to a druggist for the purpose of being resold to persons who might wish to use it, and the druggist sells the same to a person who uses it in the quantity thus prescribed, and it being shown that the same contains a certain article known as the iodide of potash in such quantity as proves harmful to the person thus using, the proprietor is liable. The plaintiff in error insists that there is no liability on the part of the proprietor, (1) because it was not sold by the proprietor to the person injured, but by a druggist who had purchased the same from the proprietor; and several cases are cited to sustain this position; (2) because the drug thus sold was not imminently hurtful or poisonous.

1. We are not aware of any decision of this Court upon this question, indeed there is none; and we have searched carefully not only the authorities cited by counsel in this case, but others, and we find no question like the one which arises in this record determined by any Court. In the case of Thomas *v.* Winchester, 6 N. Y. (2 Seld.) 397, 57 Am. Dec. 455, 1 Thompson, Neg. 224, referred to by counsel in this case, the question decided was, that a dealer in drugs and medicines who carelessly labels a deadly poison as a harmless medicine, and sends it so labelled into market, is liable to all persons who, without fault on their part, are injured by using it as such medicine in consequence of the false label. This comes nearer the present case

[1] The authorities on all sides of the question raised in this cause are collected and discussed in the cases that follow. See also Pollock, Torts, 6 ed., 496–497; Piggott, Torts, 231–232; 1 Jaggard, Torts, 904–909; Clerk & Lindsell, Torts, 6 ed., 511–522; Salmond, Torts, 4 ed., 415–424; Bohlen, Affirmative Obligations in the Law of Torts, 44 Am. Law Reg. 341.

[2] The statement of facts by the reporter is omitted.

than any we have been able to find, and it is relied upon by both parties as an authority; and in the notes thereto by Mr. Freeman in the American Decisions, the cases relied upon by counsel in this case are embraced and referred to, and to some extent considered. It is not denied by counsel in this case that the doctrine of the case cited (Thomas *v.* Winchester) is sound and correct law, but the present case differs from that case, and mainly in this: there the drug sold was a deadly poison, and the wrong consisted in putting a label upon the same which indicated that it was a harmless medicine; whereas in this case the medicine sold was not a deadly poison, and no label was put upon it which was calculated to deceive any one in this respect. But accompanying this medicine was a prescription of the proprietor stating the quantity to be taken, and the evidence tended to show that the quantity thus prescribed contained iodide of potash to such an extent as, when taken by the plaintiff, produced the injury and damage complained of. The liability of the plaintiff in error to the person injured arises, not by contract, but for a wrong committed by the proprietor in the prescription and direction as to the dose that should be taken.

We can see no difference whether the medicine was directly sold to the defendant in error by the proprietor, or by an intermediate party to whom the proprietors had sold it in the first instance for the purpose of being sold again. It was put upon the market by the proprietor, not alone for the use of druggists to whom they might sell it, but to be used by the public in general who might need the same for the cure of certain diseases for which the proprietor set forth in his label the same was adapted. This was the same thing as if the proprietor himself had sold this medicine to the defendant in error, with his instructions and directions as to how the same should be taken. In all the cases cited by the plaintiff in error there is no case in which the proprietor prescribed the doses and quantities to be taken of the medicine sold by him. If this medicine contained the iodide of potassium in sufficient quantity to produce the injurious consequences complained of to the defendant in error, and if the same was administered to him, either by himself or any other person, as prescribed in the label accompanying the medicine, he could, in our judgment, recover for any injury he may have sustained on account of the poisonous effect thereof. It was a wrong on the part of the proprietor to extend to the public generally an invitation to take the medicine in quantities sufficient to injure and damage persons who might take it.

A medicine which is known to the public as being dangerous and poisonous if taken in large quantities, may be sold by the proprietor to druggists and others, and if any person, without more, should purchase and take the same so as to cause injury to himself, the proprietor would not be liable. But if the contents of a medicine are concealed from the public generally, and the medicine is prepared by one who know its contents, and he sells the same, recommending it for certain diseases and prescribing the mode in which it shall be taken, and injury is thereby sustained by the person taking the same, the proprietor would be liable for the damage thus sustained. These proprietary or patent medicines are secret, or intended by the proprietors to be secret, as to their contents. They expect to derive a profit from such secrecy. They are therefore liable for all injuries sustained by any one who takes their medicine in such quantities as may be prescribed by them. There is no way for a person who uses the medicine to ascertain what its contents are, ordinarily, and in this case the contents were only ascertained after an analysis made by a chemist, — which would be very inconvenient and expensive to the public; nor would it be the duty of a person using the medicine to ascertain what poisonous drugs it may contain. He has a right to rely upon the statement and recommendation of the proprietor, printed and published to the world; and if thus relying, he takes the medicine and is injured on account of some concealed drug of which he is unaware, the proprietor is not free from fault, and is liable for the injury thereby sustained. It appears from the analysis made by the chemist in this case that this medicine contained 25 grains of the iodide of potash to two tablespoonfuls of the medicine. The testimony of the plaintiff, by witnesses learned in the profession of medicine, was that iodide of potash in this quantity would produce the effects upon a person using it shown by the condition of the defendant in error. The prescription accompanying the bottle directed the taking of one to two tablespoonfuls of the medicine, and this was done by the defendant in error, and he was thereby greatly injured and damaged.

This is not like the case of a dangerous machine or a gun sold to a person and by him given or sold to another, as in some of the cases referred to. Mr. Freeman, in his notes to the case above referred to (Thomas *v.* Winchester), alludes to all those cases; and Mr. Thompson, in his work on Negligence, refers to the same cases, and they are there fully discussed. *Judgment affirmed.*

[Remainder of opinion omitted.]

HUSET *v.* J. I. CASE THRESHING MACHINE CO.

CIRCUIT COURT OF APPEALS, EIGHTH CIRCUIT, FEBRUARY 26, 1903.

Reported in 120 *Federal Reporter*, 865.

SANBORN, Circuit Judge:[1]

Is a manufacturer or vendor of an article or machine which he knows, when he sells it, to be imminently dangerous, by reason of a concealed defect therein, to the life and limbs of any one who shall use

[1] The statement of facts is omitted.

it for the purpose for which it was made and intended, liable to a stranger to the contract of sale for an injury which he sustains from the concealed defect while he is lawfully applying the article or machine to its intended use?

The argument of this question has traversed the whole field in which the liability of contractors, manufacturers, and vendors to strangers to their contracts for negligence in the construction or sale of their articles has been contested. The decisions which have been cited are not entirely harmonious, and it is impossible to reconcile all of them with any established rule of law. And yet the underlying principle of the law of negligence, that it is the duty of every one to so act himself and to so use his property as to do no unnecessary damage to his neighbors, leads us fairly through the maze. With this fundamental principle in mind, if we contemplate the familiar rules that every one is liable for the natural and probable effects of his acts; that negligence is a breach of a duty; that an injury that is the natural and probable consequence of an act of negligence is actionable, while one that could not have been foreseen or reasonably anticipated as the probable effect of such an act is not actionable, because the act of negligence in such a case is the remote, and not the proximate, cause of the injury; and that, for the same reason, an injury is not actionable which would not have resulted from an act of negligence except from the interposition of an independent cause (Chicago, St. Paul, Minneapolis & Omaha R. Co. *v.* Elliott, 55 Fed. 949, 5 C. C. A. 347, 20 L. R. A. 582) — nearly all the decisions upon this subject range themselves along symmetrical lines, and establish rational rules of the law of negligence consistent with the basic principles upon which it rests.

Actions for negligence are for breaches of duty. Actions on contracts are for breaches of agreements. Hence the limits of liability for negligence are not the limits of liability for breaches of contracts, and actions for negligence often accrue where actions upon contracts do not arise, and vice versa. It is a rational and fair deduction from the rules to which brief reference has been made that one who makes or sells a machine, a building, a tool, or an article of merchandise designed and fitted for a specific use is liable to the person who, in the natural course of events, uses it for the purpose for which it was made or sold, for an injury which is the natural and probable consequence of sale. But when a contractor builds a house or a bridge, or a manufacturer constructs a car or a carriage, for the owner thereof under a special contract with him, an injury to any other person than the owner for whom the article is built and to whom it is delivered cannot ordinarily be foreseen or reasonably anticipated as the probable result of the negligence in its construction. So, when a manufacturer sells articles to the wholesale or retail dealers, or to those who are to use them, injury to third persons is not generally the natural or probable effect of negligence in their manufacture, because (1) such a result cannot ordinarily be reasonably anticipated, and because (2) an independent cause — the responsible human agency of the purchaser — without which the injury to the third person would not occur, intervenes, and, as Wharton says, " insulates " the negligence of the manufacturer from the injury to the third person. Wharton on Law of Negligence (2d ed.) § 134. For the reason that in the cases of the character which have been mentioned the natural and probable effect of the negligence of the contractor or manufacturer will generally be limited to the party for whom the article is constructed, or to whom it is sold, and, perhaps more than all this, for the reason that a wise and conservative public policy has impressed the courts with the view that there must be a fixed and definite limitation to the liability of manufacturers and vendors for negligence in the construction and sale of complicated machines and structures which are to be operated or used by the intelligent and the ignorant, the skilful and and the incompetent, the watchful and the careless, parties that cannot be known to the manufacturers or vendors, and who use the articles all over the country hundreds of miles distant from the place of their manufacture or original sale, a general rule has been adopted and has become established by repeated decisions of the courts of England and of this country that in these cases the liability of the contractor or manufacturer for negligence in the construction or sale of the articles which he makes or vends is limited to the persons to whom he is liable under his contracts of construction or sale. The limits of the liability for negligence and for breaches of contract in cases of this character are held to be identical. The general rule is that a contractor, manufacturer, or vendor is not liable to third parties who have no contractual relations with him for negligence in the construction, manufacture, or sale of the articles he handles. Winterbottom *v.* Wright, 10 M. & W. 109; Longmeid *v.* Holliday, 6 Exch. 764, 765; Blakemore *v.* Ry. Co., 8 El. & Bl. 1035; Collis *v.* Selden, L. R. 3 C. P. 495, 497; Bank *v.* Ward, 100 U. S. 195, 204, 25 L. Ed. 621; Bragdon *v.* Perkins-Campbell Co., 87 Fed. 109, 30 C. C. A. 567; Goodlander *v.* Standard Oil Co., 63 Fed. 400, 406, 11 C. C. A. 253, 259, 27 L. R. A. 583; Loop *v.* Litchfield, 42 N. Y. 351, 359, 1 Am. Rep. 513; Losee *v.* Clute, 51 N. Y. 494, 10 Am. Rep. 623; Curtain *v.* Somerset, 140 Pa. 70, 21 Atl. 244, 12 L. R. A. 322, 23 Am. St. Rep. 220; Heizer *v.* Kingsland & Douglass Mfg. Co., 110 Mo. 605, 615, 617, 19 S. W. 630, 15 L. R. A. 821, 33 Am. St. Rep. 481; Daugherty *v.* Herzog, 145 Ind. 255, 44 N. E. 457, 32 L. R. A. 837, 57 Am. St. Rep. 204; Burke *v.* De Castro, 11 Hun, 354; Swan *v.* Jackson, 55 Hun, 194, 7 N. Y. Supp. 821; Barrett *v.* Mfg. Co., 31 N. Y. Super. Ct. 545; Carter *v.* Harden, 78 Me. 528, 7 Atl. 392; McCaffrey *v.* Mfg. Co., (R. I.) 50 Atl. 651, 55 L. R. A. 822; Marvin Safe Co. *v.* Ward, 46 N. J. Law, 19; Burdick *v.* Cheadle, 26 Ohio St. 393, 20 Am. Rep. 767;

Davidson *v.* Nichols, 11 Allen, 514; J. I. Case Plow Works *v.* Niles & Scott Co., (Wis.) 63 N. W. 1013.

In these cases third parties, without any fault on their part, were injured by the negligence of the manufacturer, vendor, or furnisher of the following articles, while the parties thus injured were innocently using them for the purposes for which they were made or furnished, and the courts held that there could be no recovery, because the makers, vendors, or furnishers owed no duty to strangers to their contracts of construction, sale, or furnishing. A stagecoach, Winterbottom *v.* Wright, 10 M. & W. 109; a leaky lamp, Longmeid *v.* Holliday, 6 Exch. 764, 765; a defective chain furnished one to lead stone, Blakemore *v.* Ry Co., 8 El. & Bl. 1035; an improperly hung chandelier, Collis *v.* Selden, L. R. 3 C. P. 495, 497; an attorney's certificate of title, Bank *v.* Ward, 100 U. S. 195, 204, 25 L. Ed. 621; a defective valve in an oil car, Goodlander *v.* Standard Oil Co., 63 Fed. 401, 406, 11 C. C. A. 253, 259, 27 L. R. A. 583; a porch on a hotel, Curtain *v.* Somerset, 140 Pa. 70, 21 Atl. 244, 12 L. R. A. 322, 23 Am. St. Rep. 220; a defective side saddle, Bragdon *v.* Perkins-Campbell Co., 87 Fed. 109, 30 C. C. A. 567; a defective rim in a balance wheel, Loop *v.* Litchfield, 42 N. Y. 351, 359, 1 Am. Rep. 513; a defective boiler, Losee *v.* Clute, 51 N. Y. 494, 10 Am. Rep. 623; a defective cylinder in a threshing machine, Heizer *v.* Kingsland & Douglass Mfg. Co., 110 Mo. 605, 615, 617, 19 S. W. 630, 15 L. R. A. 821, 33 Am. St. Rep. 481; a defective wall which fell on a pedestrian, Daugherty *v.* Herzog, 145 Ind. 255, 44 N. E. 457, 32 L. R. A. 837, 57 Am. St. Rep. 204; a defective rope on a derrick, Burke *v.* Refining Co., 11 Hun, 354; a defective shelf for a workman to stand upon in placing ice in a box, Swan *v.* Jackson, 55 Hun, 194, 7 N. Y. Supp. 821; a defective hoisting rope of an elevator, Barrett *v.* Mfg. Co., 31 N. Y. Super. Ct. 545; a runaway horse, Carter *v.* Harden, 78 Me. 528, 7 Atl. 392; a defective hook holding a heavy weight in a drop press, McCaffrey *v.* Mfg. Co., (R. I.) 50 Atl. 651, 55 L. R. A. 822; a defective bridge, Marvin Safe Co. *v.* Ward, 46 N. J. Law, 19; shelves in a dry goods store, whose fall injured a customer, Burdick *v.* Cheadle, 26 Ohio St. 393, 20 Am. Rep. 767; a staging erected by a contractor for the use of his employees, McGuire *v.* McGee, (Pa.) 13 Atl. 551; defective wheels, J. I. Case Plow Works *v.* Niles & Scott Co., (Wis.) 63 N. W. 1013.

In the leading case of Winterbottom *v.* Wright this rule is placed upon the ground of public policy, upon the ground that there would be no end of litigation if contractors and manufacturers were to be held liable to third persons for every act of negligence in the construction of the articles or machines they make after the parties to whom they have sold them have received and accepted them. In that case the defendant had made a contract with the Postmaster-General to provide and keep in repair the stage-coach used to convey the mail from Hartford to Holyhead. The coach broke down, overturned, and injured the driver, who sued the contractor for the injury resulting from his negligence. Lord Abinger, C. B., said:

"There is no privity of contract between these parties; and, if the plaintiff can sue, every passenger, or even any person passing along the road, who was injured by the upsetting of the coach, might bring a similar action. Unless we confine the operation of such contracts as this to the parties who entered into them, the most absurd and outrageous consequences, to which I can see no limit, would ensue."

Baron Alderson said:

"I am of the same opinion. The contract in this case was made with the Postmaster-General alone; and the case is just the same as if he had come to the defendant and ordered a carriage, and handed it at once over to Atkinson. If we were to hold that the plaintiff could sue in such a case, there is no point at which such actions would stop. The only safe rule is to confine the right to recover to those who enter into the contract. If we go one step beyond that, there is no reason why we should not go fifty."

The views expressed by the judges in this case have prevailed in England and in the United States, with the exception of two decisions which are in conflict with the leading case and with all the decisions to which reference has been made. Those cases are Devlin *v.* Smith, 89 N. Y. 470, 42 Am. Rep. 311, in which Smith, a painter, employed Stevenson, a contractor, to build a scaffold 90 feet in height, for the express purpose of enabling the painter's workmen to stand upon it to paint the interior of the dome of a building, and the Court of Appeals of New York held that Stevenson was liable to a workman of Smith, the painter, who was injured by a fall, caused by the negligence of Stevenson in the construction of the scaffold upon which he was working; and Schubert *v.* J. R. Clark Co., 49 Minn. 331, 51 N. W. 1103, 15 L. R. A. 818, 32 Am. St. Rep. 559, in which a painter purchased of a manufacturer a stepladder, and one of the painter's employees, who was injured by the breaking of a step caused by the negligence of the manufacturer, was permitted to recover of the latter for the injuries he had sustained. The decision in Devlin *v.* Smith may, perhaps, be sustained on the ground that the workmen of Smith were the real parties in interest in the contract, since Stevenson was employed and expressly agreed to construct the scaffold for their use. But the case of Schubert *v.* J. R. Clark Co. is in direct conflict with the side saddle case, Bragdon *v.* Perkins-Campbell Co., 87 Fed. 109, 30 C. C. A. 567; the porch case, Curtain *v.* Somerset, 140 Pa. 70, 21 Atl. 244, 12 L. R. A. 322, 23 Am. St. Rep. 220; the defective cylinder case, Heizer *v.* Kingsland & Douglass Mfg. Co., 110 Mo. 617, 19 S. W. 630, 15 L. R. A. 821, 33 Am. St. Rep. 481; the defective hook case, McCaffrey *v.* Mfg. Co., (R. I.) 50 Atl. 651, 55 L. R. A. 822; and with the general rule upon which all these cases stand.

It is, perhaps, the more remarkable that the current of decisions throughout all the courts of England and the United States should be so uniform and conclusive in support of this rule, and that there should, in the multitude of opinions, be but one or two in conflict with it, than it is that such sporadic cases should be found. They are insufficient in themselves, or in the reasoning they contain, to overthrow or shake the established rule which prevails throughout the English-speaking nations.

But while this general rule is both established and settled, there are, as is usually the case, exceptions to it as well defined and settled as the rule itself. There are three exceptions to this rule.

The first is that an act of negligence of a manufacturer or vendor which is imminently dangerous to the life or health of mankind, and which is committed in the preparation or sale of an article intended to preserve, destroy, or affect human life, is actionable by third parties who suffer from the negligence. Dixon *v.* Bell, 5 Maule & Sel. 198; Thomas *v.* Winchester, 6 N. Y. 397, 57 Am. Dec. 455; Norton *v.* Sewall, 106 Mass. 143, 8 Am. Rep. 298; Elkins *v.* McKean, 79 Pa. 493, 502; Bishop *v.* Weber, 139 Mass. 411, 1 N. E. 154, 52 Am. Rep. 715; Peters *v.* Johnson, (W. Va.) 41 S. E. 190, 191, 57 L. R. A. 428. The leading case upon this subject is Thomas *v.* Winchester, 6 N. Y. 397, 57 Am. Dec. 455. A dealer in drugs sold to a druggist a jar of belladonna, a deadly poison, and labelled it " Extract of Dandelion." The druggist filled a prescription of extract of dandelion, prepared by a physician for his patient. The patient took the prescription thus filled, and recovered of the wholesale dealer for the injuries she sustained. In Norton *v.* Sewall, 106 Mass. 143, 8 Am. Rep. 298, a recovery was had by a third party for the sale of laudanum as rhubarb; in Bishop *v.* Weber, for the furnishing of poisonous food for wholesome food; in Peters *v.* Johnson, for the sale of saltpetre for epsom salts; and in Dixon *v.* Bell, for placing a loaded gun in the hands of a child. In all these cases of sale the natural and probable result of the act of negligence — nay, the inevitable result of it — was not an injury to the party to whom the sales were made, but to those who, after the purchasers had disposed of the articles, should consume them. Hence these cases stand upon two well-established principles of law: (1) That every one is bound to avoid acts or omissions imminently dangerous to the lives of others, and (2) that an injury which is the natural and probable result of an act of negligence is actionable. It was the natural and probable result of the negligence in these cases that the vendees would not suffer, but that those who subsequently purchased the deleterious articles would sustain the injuries resulting from the negligence of the manufacturers or dealers who furnished them.

The second exception is that an owner's act of negligence which causes injury to one who is invited by him to use his defective appliance upon the owner's premises may form the basis of an action against the owner. Coughtry *v.* Globe Woolen Co., 56 N. Y. 124, 15 Am. Rep. 387; Bright *v.* Barnett & Record Co., (Wis.) 60 N. W. 418, 420, 26 L. R. A. 524; Heaven *v.* Pender, L. R. 11 Q. B. Div. 503; Roddy *v.* Railway Co., 104 Mo. 234, 241, 15 S. W. 1112, 12 L. R. A. 746, 24 Am. St. Rep. 333. In Coughtry *v.* Globe Woolen Co., 56 N. Y. 124, 15 Am. Rep. 387, the owner of a building employed Osborn & Martin to construct a cornice, and agreed with them to furnish a scaffold upon which their men could perform the work. He furnished the scaffold and one of the employees of the contractors was injured by the negligence of the owner in constructing the scaffold. The court held that the act of the owner was an implied invitation to the employees of Osborn & Martin to use the scaffold and imposed upon him a liability for negligence in its erection. The other cases cited to this exception are of a similar character.

The third exception to the rule is that one who sells or delivers an article which he knows to be imminently dangerous to life or limb to another without notice of its qualities is liable to any person who suffers an injury therefrom which might have been reasonably anticipated, whether there were any contractual relations between the parties or not. Langridge *v.* Levy, 2 M. & W. 519, 4 M. & W. 337; Wellington *v.* Oil Co., 104 Mass. 64, 67; Lewis *v.* Terry, (Cal.) 43 Pac. 398. In Langridge *v.* Levy, 2 M. & W. 519, a dealer sold a gun to the father for the use of the son, and represented that it was a safe gun, and made by one Nock. It was not made by Nock, was a defective gun, and when the son discharged it, it exploded and injured him. The son was permitted to recover, because the defendant had knowingly sold the gun to the father for the purpose of being used by the plaintiff by loading and discharging it, and had knowingly made a false warranty that this might be safely done, and the plaintiff, on the faith of that warranty, and believing it to be true, had used the gun, and sustained the damages. The court said in conclusion:

"We therefore think that, as there is fraud, and damage, the result of that fraud, not from an act remote and consequential, but one contemplated by the defendant at the time as one of its results, the party guilty of the fraud is responsible to the party injured."

This case was affirmed in 4 M. & W. 337, on the ground that the sale of the gun to the father for the use of the son with the knowledge that it was not as represented was a fraud, which entitled the son to recover the damages he had sustained.

In Wellington *v.* Oil Co., the defendants knowingly sold to one Chase, a retail dealer, to be sold by him to his customers as oil, naphtha, a dangerous and explosive liquid. Chase sold the naphtha as oil, the plaintiff used it in a lamp for illuminating purposes, it ignited and exploded, and he recovered of the wholesale dealer. Judge Gray, later Mr. Justice Gray of the Supreme Court, said:

"It is well settled that a man who delivers an article, which he knows to be dangerous or noxious, to another person, without notice of its nature and qualities, is liable for an injury which may reasonably be contemplated as likely to result, and which does in fact result therefrom to that person or any other who is not himself in fault. Thus a person who delivers a carboy, which he knows to contain nitric acid, to a carrier, without informing him of the nature of its contents, is liable for an injury occasioned by the leaking out of the acid upon another carrier, to whom it is delivered by the first in the ordinary course of business, to be carried to its destination. Farrant *v.* Barnes, 11 C. B. (N. S.) 553. So a chemist who sells a bottle of liquid, made up of ingredients known only to himself, representing it to be fit to be used for washing the hair, and knowing that it is to be used by the purchaser's wife, is liable for an injury occasioned to her by using it for washing her hair. George *v.* Skivington, Law Rep. 5 Ex. 1."

In Lewis *v.* Terry, (Cal.) 43 Pac. 398, a dealer, knowing a folding bed to be defective and unsafe, sold it to a Mr. Apperson without informing him of the fact. His wife suffered a broken arm and other severe injuries from the negligence of the dealer in the sale of the bed, and recovered of him the damages she sustained.

The Supreme Court of Missouri, in Heizer *v.* Kingsland & Douglass Mfg. Co., in which they held that the manufacturer was not liable to a third person for negligence in the construction of the cylinder of a threshing machine, which burst and injured him, said:

"Had the defendant sold this machine to Ellis, knowing that the cylinder was defective, and for that reason dangerous, without informing him of the defect, then the defendant would be liable even to third persons not themselves in fault. Shearman & Redfield on Negligence, (4th ed.) § 117."

Turning now to the case in hand, it is no longer difficult to dispose of it. The allegations of the complaint are that the defendant prepared a covering for the cylinder of the threshing machine, which was customarily and necessarily used by those who operated it to walk upon, and which was so incapable of sustaining the least weight that it would bend and collapse whenever any one stepped upon it; that it concealed this defective and dangerous condition of the threshing rig so that it could not be readily discovered by persons engaged in operating or working upon it; that it knew that the machine was in this imminently dangerous condition when it shipped and supplied it to the employer of the plaintiff; and that the plaintiff has sustained serious injury through this defect in its construction. The case falls fairly within the third exception. It portrays a negligence imminently dangerous to the lives and limbs of those who should use the machine, a machine imminently dangerous to the lives and limbs of all who should undertake to operate it, a concealment of this dangerous condition, a knowledge of the defendant when it was shipped and supplied to the employer of the plaintiff that the rig was imminently dangerous to all who should use it for the purpose for which it was made and sold, and consequent damage to the plaintiff. It falls directly within the rule stated by Mr. Justice Gray that when one delivers an article, which he knows to be dangerous to another person, without notice of its nature and qualities, he is liable for an injury which may be reasonably contemplated as likely to result, and which does in fact result therefrom, to that person or to any other who is not himself in fault. The natural, probable, and inevitable result of the negligence portrayed by this complaint in delivering this machine when it was known to be in a condition so imminently dangerous to the lives and limbs of those who should undertake to use it for the purpose for which it was constructed was the death, or loss of one or more of the limbs, of some of the operators. It is perhaps improbable that the defendant was possessed of the knowledge of the imminently dangerous character of this threshing machine when it delivered it, and that upon the trial of the case it will be found to fall under the general rule which has been announced in an earlier part of this opinion. But upon the facts alleged in this complaint, the act of delivering it to the purchaser with a knowledge and a concealment of its dangerous condition was so flagrant a disregard of the rule that one is bound to avoid any act imminently dangerous to the lives and health of his fellows that it forms the basis of a good cause of action in favor of any one who sustained injury therefrom.

The judgment of the Circuit Court must be reversed, and the cause must be remanded to the court below for further proceedings not inconsistent with the views expressed in this opinion.

HEAVEN *v.* PENDER

IN THE COURT OF APPEAL, JULY 30, 1883.

Reported in 11 *Queen's Bench Division*, 503.

ACTION to recover damages for injuries alleged to have been sustained by the plaintiff through the negligence of the defendant. The County Court judge gave judgment for the plaintiff. The Queen's Bench Division, on appeal, ordered judgment for defendant. The plaintiff appealed to the Court of Appeal.[1]

BRETT, M. R. In this case the plaintiff was a workman in the employ of Gray, a ship-painter. Gray entered into a contract with a ship-owner whose ship was in the defendant's dock to paint the outside of his ship. The defendant, the dock-owner, supplied, under a contract with the ship-owner, an ordinary stage to be slung in the ordinary way outside the ship for the purpose of painting her. It

[1] Arguments omitted.

must have been known to the defendant's servants, if they had considered the matter at all, that the stage would be put to immediate use, that it would not be used by the ship-owner, but that it would be used by such a person as the plaintiff, a working ship-painter. The ropes by which the stage was slung, and which were supplied as a part of the instrument by the defendant, had been scorched and were unfit for use, and were supplied without a reasonably careful attention to their condition. When the plaintiff began to use the stage the ropes broke, the stage fell, and the plaintiff was injured. The Divisional Court held that the plaintiff could not recover against the defendant. The plaintiff appealed. The action is in form and substance an action for negligence. That the stage was, through want of attention of the defendant's servants, supplied in a state unsafe for use is not denied. But want of attention amounting to a want of ordinary care is not a good cause of action although injury ensue from such want, unless the person charged with such want of ordinary care had a duty to the person complaining to use ordinary care in the matter called in question. Actionable negligence consists in the neglect of the use of ordinary care or skill toward a person to whom the defendant owes the duty of observing ordinary care and skill, by which neglect the plaintiff, without contributory negligence on his part, has suffered injury to his person or property. The question in this case is whether the defendant owed such a duty to the plaintiff.

If a person contracts with another to use ordinary care or skill toward him or his property, the obligation need not be considered in the light of a duty; it is an obligation of contract. It is undoubted, however, that there may be the obligation of such a duty from one person to another although there is no contract between them with regard to such duty. Two drivers meeting have no contract with each other, but under certain circumstances they have a reciprocal duty toward each other. So two ships navigating the sea. So a railway company which has contracted with one person to carry another has no contract with the person carried, but has a duty toward that person. So the owner or occupier of a house or land who permits a person or persons to come to his house or land has no contract with such person or persons, but has a duty toward him or them. It should be observed that the existence of a contract between two persons does not prevent the existence of the suggested duty between them also being raised by law independently of the contract, by the facts with regard to which the contract is made and to which it applies an exactly similar but a contract duty. We have not in this case to consider the circumstances in which an implied contract may arise to use ordinary care and skill to avoid danger to the safety of person or property. We have not in this case to consider the question of a fraudulent misrepresentation, express or implied, which is a well-recognized head of law. The questions which we have to solve in this case are: What is the proper definition of the relation between two persons other than the relation established by contract, or fraud, which imposes on one of them a duty toward the other to observe, with regard to the person or property of such other, such ordinary care or skill as may be necessary to prevent injury to his person or property; and whether the present case falls within such definition? When two drivers or two ships are approaching each other, such a relation arises between them when they are approaching each other in such a manner that, unless they use ordinary care and skill to avoid it, there will be danger of an injurious collision between them. This relation is established in such circumstances between them, not only if it be proved that they actually know and think of this danger, but whether such proof be made or not. It is established, as it seems to me, because any one of ordinary sense who did think would at once recognize that if he did not use ordinary care and skill under such circumstances there would be such danger. And every one ought, by the universally recognized rules of right and wrong, to think so much with regard to the safety of others who may be jeopardized by his conduct; and if, being in such circumstances, he does not think, and in consequence neglects, or if he neglects to use ordinary care and skill, and injury ensue, the law, which takes cognizance of and enforces the rules of right and wrong, will force him to give an indemnity for the injury. In the case of a railway company carrying a passenger with whom it has not entered into the contract of carriage, the law implies the duty, because it must be obvious that unless ordinary care and skill be used the personal safety of the passenger must be endangered. With regard to the condition in which an owner or occupier leaves his house or property other phraseology has been used, which it is necessary to consider. If a man opens his shop or warehouse to customers it is said that he invites them to enter, and that this invitation raises the relation between them which imposes on the inviter the duty of using reasonable care so to keep his house or warehouse that it may not endanger the person or property of the person invited. This is in a sense an accurate phrase, and as applied to the circumstances a sufficiently accurate phrase. Yet it is not accurate if the word "invitation" be used in its ordinary sense. By opening a shop you do not really invite, you do not ask A. B. to come in to buy; you intimate to him that if it pleases him to come in he will find things which you are willing to sell. So in the case of shop, warehouse, road, or premises, the phrase has been used that if you permit a person to enter them you impose on yourself a duty not to lay a trap for him. This, again, is in a sense a true statement of the duty arising from the relation constituted by the permission to enter. It is not a statement of what causes the relation which raises the duty. What causes the relation is the permission to enter and the entry. But it is not a strictly accurate statement of the duty. To lay a trap means in ordinary language to do something with an intention. Yet it is clear that the duty extends to a danger the result of negligence without intention. And with regard to both these phrases, though each covers the circumstances to which it is particularly applied, yet it does not cover the other set of circumstances from which an exactly similar legal liability is inferred. It follows, as it seems to me, that there must be some larger proposition which involves and covers both sets of circumstances. The logic of inductive reasoning requires that where two major propositions lead to exactly similar minor premises there must be a more remote and larger premise which embraces both of the major propositions. That, in the present consideration, is, as it seems to me, the same proposition which will cover the similar legal liability inferred in the cases of collision and carriage. The proposition which these recognized cases suggest, and which is, therefore, to be deduced from them, is that whenever one person is by circumstances placed in such a position with regard to another that every one of ordinary sense who did think would at once recognize that if he did not use ordinary care and skill in his own conduct with regard to those circumstances he would cause danger of injury to the person or property of the other, a duty arises to use ordinary care and skill to avoid such danger. Without displacing the other propositions to which allusion has been made as applicable to the particular circumstances in respect of which they have been enunciated, this proposition includes, I think, all the recognized cases of liability. It is the only proposition which covers them all. It may, therefore, safely be affirmed to be a true proposition, unless some obvious case can be stated in which the liability must be admitted to exist, and which yet is not within this proposition. There is no such case. Let us apply this proposition to the case of one person supplying goods or machinery or instruments or utensils, or the like, for the purpose of their being used by another person, but with whom there is no contract as to the supply. The proposition will stand thus: whenever one person supplies goods, or machinery, or the like, for the purpose of their being used by another person under such circumstances that every one of ordinary sense would, if he thought, recognize at once that unless he used ordinary care and skill with regard to the condition of the thing supplied or the mode of supplying it, there will be danger of injury to the person or property of him for whose use the thing is supplied and who is to use it, a duty arises to use ordinary care and skill as to the condition or manner of supplying such thing. And for a neglect of such ordinary care or skill whereby injury happens, a legal liability arises to be enforced by an action for negligence. This includes the case of goods, etc., supplied to be used immediately by a particular person or persons, or one of a class of persons, where it would be obvious to the person supplying, if he thought that the goods would in all probability be used at once by such persons before a reasonable opportunity for discovering any defect which might exist, and where the thing supplied would be of such a nature that neglect of ordinary care or skill as to its condition or the manner of supplying it would probably cause danger to the person or property of the person for whose use it was supplied, and who was about to use it. It would exclude a case in which the goods are supplied under circumstances in which it would be a chance by whom they would be used or whether they would be used or not, or whether they would be used before there would probably be means of observing any defect, or where the goods would be of such a nature that a want of care or skill as to their condition or the manner of supplying them would not probably produce danger of injury to person or property. The cases of vendor and purchaser and lender and hirer under contract need not be considered, as the liability arises under the contract, and not merely as a duty imposed by law, though it may not be useless to observe that it seems difficult to import the implied obligation into the contract except in cases in which if there were no contract between the parties the law would, according to the rule above stated, imply the duty.

Examining the rule which has been above enunciated with the cases which have been decided with regard to goods supplied for the purpose of being used by persons with whom there is no contract, the first case to be considered is inevitably Langridge *v.* Levy, 2 M. & W. 519; 4 id. 337. It is not an easy case to act upon. It is not, it cannot be, accurately reported; the declaration is set out; the evidence is assumed to be reported; the questions left to the jury are stated. And then it is said that a motion was made to enter a nonsuit in pursuance of leave reserved on particular grounds. These grounds do not raise the question of fraud at all, but only the question of remoteness. And although the question of fraud seems in a sense to have been left to the jury, yet no question was, according to the report, left to them as to whether the plaintiff acted on the faith of the fraudulent misrepresentation, which is, nevertheless, a necessary question in a case of fraudulent misrepresentation. The report of the argument makes the object of the argument depend entirely upon an assumed motion to arrest the judgment, which raises always a discussion depending entirely on the form of the declaration, and the effect on it of a verdict, in respect of which it is assumed that all questions were left to the jury. If this was the point taken the report of the evidence and of the questions left to the jury is idle! The case was decided on the ground of a fraudulent misrepresentation as stated in the declaration. It is inferred that the defendant intended the representation to be communicated to the son. Why he should have such an intention in fact it seems difficult to understand. His immediate object must have been to induce the father to buy and pay for the gun. It must have been wholly indifferent to him whether, after the sale and payment, the gun would be used or not by the son. I cannot hesitate to say that, in my opinion, the case is a wholly unsatisfactory case to act on as an authority. But taking the case to be decided on the ground of a fraudulent misrepresentation made hypothetically to the son, and acted upon by him, such a decision upon such a ground in no way negatives the proposition that the action might have been supported on the ground of negligence without fraud. It seems to be a case which is within the proposition enunciated in this judgment, and in which the action might have been supported without proof of actual fraud. And this seems to be the meaning of Cleasby, B., in the observations he made on Langridge *v.* Levy, *supra,* in the case of George *v.* Skivington, L. R. 5 Ex. 1, 5. In that case the proposition laid down in that judgment is clearly adopted. The ground of the decision is that the article was, to the knowledge of the defendant, supplied for the use of the wife and for her immediate use. And certainly, if he or any one in his position had thought at all, it must have been obvious that a want of ordinary care or skill in preparing the prescription sold would endanger the personal safety of the wife.

In Corby *v.* Hill, 4 C. B. (N. S.) 556, it is stated by the Lord Chief Justice that an allurement was held out to the plaintiff. And Willes, J., stated that the defendant had no right to set a trap for the plaintiff. But in the form of declaration suggested by Willes, J., on p. 567, there is no mention of allurement, or invitation or trap. The facts suggested in that form are, " that the plaintiff had license to go on the road, that he was in consequence accustomed and likely to pass along it, that the defendant knew of that custom and probability, that the defendant negligently placed slates in such a manner as to be likely to prove dangerous to persons driving along the road, that the plaintiff drove along the road, being by reason of the license lawfully on the road, and that he was injured by the obstruction." It is impossible to state a case more exactly within the proposition laid down in this judgment. In Smith *v.* London & St. Katharine Docks Co., L. R. 3 C. P. 326, the phrase is again used of invitation to the plaintiff by the defendants. Again, let it be observed that there is no objection to the phrase as applied to the case. But the real value of the phrase may not improperly be said to be that invitation imports knowledge by the defendant of the probable use by the plaintiff of the article supplied, and therefore carries with it the relation between the parties which establishes the duty. In Indermaur *v.* Dames, L. R. 1 C. P. 274, L. R. 2 C. P. 311, reliance is again placed upon a supposed invitation of the plaintiff by the defendant. But, again, it is hardly possible to state facts which bring a case more completely within the definition of the present judgment. In Winterbottom *v.* Wright, 10 M. & W. 109, it was held that there was no duty cast upon the defendant with regard to the plaintiff. The case was decided on what was equivalent to a general demurrer to the declaration. And the declaration does not seem to show that the defendant, if he had thought about it, must have known, or ought to have known, that the coach would be necessarily or probably driven by the plaintiff, or by any class of which he could be said to be one, or that it would be so driven within any time which would make it probable that the defect would not be observed. The declaration relied too much on contracts entered into with other persons than the plaintiff. The facts alleged did not bring the case within the proposition herein enunciated. It was an attempt to establish a duty toward all the world. The case was decided on the ground of remoteness. And it is as to too great a remoteness that the observation of Lord Abinger is pointed, when he says that the doctrine of Langridge *v.* Levy, *supra*, is not to be extended. In Francis *v.* Cockrell, L. R. 5 Q. B. 501, the decision is put by some of the judges on an implied contract between the plaintiff and the defendant. But Cleasby, B. (p. 515), puts it upon the duty raised by the knowledge of the defendant that the stand was to be used immediately by persons of whom the plaintiff was one. In other words, he acts upon the rule above laid down. In Collis *v.* Selden, L. R. 3 C. P. 495, it was held that the declaration disclosed no duty. And obviously, the declaration was too uncertain. There is nothing to show that the defendant knew more of the probability of the plaintiff rather than any other of the public being near the chandelier. There is nothing to show that the plaintiff was more likely to be in the public-house than any other member of the public. There is nothing to show how soon after the hanging of the chandelier any one might be expected or permitted to enter the room in which it was. The facts stated do not bring it within the rule. There is an American case: Thomas *v.* Winchester, 6 N. Y. 397, 57 Am. Dec. 455, cited in Mr. Horace Smith's Treatise on the Law of Negligence, p. 88, note (t), which goes a very long way. I doubt whether it does not go too far. In Longmeid *v.* Holliday, 6 Ex. 761, a lamp was sold to the plaintiff to be used by the wife. The jury were not satisfied that the defendant knew of the defect in the lamp. If he did, there was fraud; if he did not, there seems to have been no evidence of negligence. If there was fraud, the case was more than within the rule. If there was no fraud the case was not brought by other circumstances within the rule. In Gautret *v.* Egerton, L. R. 2 C. P. 374, the declaration was held by Willes, J., to be bad on demurrer, because it did not show that the defendant had any reason to suppose that persons going to the docks would not have ample means of seeing the holes and cuttings relied on. He does not say there must be fraud in order to support the action. He says there must be something like fraud. He says: " Every man is bound not wilfully to deceive others." And then, in the alternative, he says: " or to do any act which may place them in danger." There seems to be no case in conflict with the rule above deduced from well admitted cases. I am, therefore, of opinion that it is a good, safe, and just rule.

I cannot conceive that if the facts were proved which would make out the proposition I have enunciated, the law can be that there would be no liability. Unless that be true, the proposition must be true. If it be the rule the present case is clearly within it. This case is also, I agree, within that which seems to me to be a minor proposition, namely, the proposition which has been often acted upon, that there was in a sense an invitation of the plaintiff by the defendant to use the stage. The appeal must, in my opinion, be allowed, and judgment must be entered for the plaintiff.

COTTON, L. J. BOWEN, L. J., concurs in the judgment I am about to read. [The opinion holds defendant liable, on the ground that he must be considered as having invited the workman to use the dock and all appliances provided by the dock-owner as incident to the use of the dock; and that he was under obligation to take reasonable care that at the time the appliances provided for immediate use in the dock were furnished by him they were in a fit state to be used. The opinion then proceeds as follows: —]

This decides this appeal in favor of the plaintiff, and I am unwilling to concur with the Master of the Rolls in laying down unnecessarily the larger principle which he entertains, inasmuch as there are many cases in which the principle was impliedly negatived.

Take, for instance, the case of Langridge *v.* Levy, *supra,* to which the principle, if it existed, would have applied. But the judges who decided that case based their judgment on the fraudulent representation made to the father of the plaintiff by the defendant. In other cases where the decision has been referred to, judges have treated fraud as the ground of the decision; as was done by Coleridge, J., in Blackmore *v.* Bristol & Exeter Ry. Co., 8 E. & B. 1035; and in Collis *v.* Selden, L. R. 3 C. P. 495, Willes, J., says that the judgment in Langridge *v.* Levy, *supra,* was based on the fraud of the defendant. This impliedly negatives the existence of the larger general principle which is relied on, and the decisions in Collis *v.* Selden, *supra,* and in Longmeid *v.* Holliday, *supra* (in each of which the plaintiff failed), are, in my opinion, at variance with the principle contended for. The case of George *v.* Skivington, *supra,* and especially what is said by Cleasby, B., in giving judgment in that case, seems to support the existence of the general principle. But it is not in terms laid down that any such principle exists, and the case was decided by Cleasby, B., on the ground that the negligence of the defendant which was his own personal negligence was equivalent, for the purposes of that action, to fraud, on which (as he said) the decision in Langridge *v.* Levy, *supra,* was based.[1]

In declining to concur in laying down the principle enunciated by the Master of the Rolls, I in no way intimate any doubt as to the

[1] See an elaborate criticism of George *v.* Skivington, L. R. 5 Ex. 1, in Blacker *v.* Lake, 106 Law Times Rep. (N. S.) 533, 537.

principle that any one who leaves a dangerous instrument, as a gun, in such a way as to cause danger, or who without due warning supplies to others for use an instrument or thing which to his knowledge, from its construction or otherwise, is in such a condition as to cause danger, not necessarily incident to the use of such an instrument or thing, is liable for injury caused to others by reason of his negligent act.

For the reasons stated I agree that the plaintiff is entitled to judgment, though I do not entirely concur with the reasoning of the Master of the Rolls. *Judgment reversed.*

MacPHERSON v. BUICK MOTOR COMPANY

Court of Appeals, New York, March 14, 1916.

Reported in 217 *New York Reports*, 382.

Cardozo, J. The defendant is a manufacturer of automobiles. It sold an automobile to a retail dealer. The retail dealer resold to the plaintiff. While the plaintiff was in the car it suddenly collapsed. He was thrown out and injured. One of the wheels was made of defective wood, and its spokes crumbled into fragments. The wheel was not made by the defendant; it was bought from another manufacturer. There is evidence, however, that its defects could have been discovered by reasonable inspection, and that inspection was omitted. There is no claim that the defendant knew of the defect and wilfully concealed it. The case, in other words, is not brought within the rule of Kuelling *v.* Lean Mfg. Co., 183 N. Y. 78, 75 N. E. 1098, 2 L. R. A. (n. s.) 303, 111 Am. St. Rep. 691, 5 Ann. Cas. 124. The charge is one, not of fraud, but of negligence. The question to be determined is whether the defendant owed a duty of care and vigilance to any one but the immediate purchaser.

The foundations of this branch of the law, at least in this state, were laid in Thomas *v.* Winchester, 6 N. Y. 397, 57 Am. Dec. 455. A poison was falsely labelled. The sale was made to a druggist, who in turn sold to a customer. The customer recovered damages from the seller who affixed the label. "The defendant's negligence," it was said, "put human life in imminent danger." A poison, falsely labelled, is likely to injure any one who gets it. Because the danger is to be foreseen, there is a duty to avoid the injury. Cases were cited by way of illustration in which manufacturers were not subject to any duty irrespective of contract. The distinction was said to be that their conduct, though negligent, was not likely to result in injury to any one except the purchaser. We are not required to say whether the chance of injury was always as remote as the distinction assumes. Some of the illustrations might be rejected to-day. The principle of the distinction is, for present purposes, the important thing. Thomas *v.* Winchester became quickly a landmark of the law. In the application of its principle there may, at times, have been uncertainty or even error. There has never in this state been doubt or disavowal of the principle itself. The chief cases are well known, yet to recall some of them will be helpful. Loop *v.* Litchfield, 42 N. Y. 351, 1 Am. Rep. 513, is the earliest. It was the case of a defect in a small balance wheel used on a circular saw. The manufacturer pointed out the defect to the buyer, who wished a cheap article and was ready to assume the risk. The risk can hardly have been an imminent one, for the wheel lasted five years before it broke. In the meanwhile the buyer had made a lease of the machinery. It was held that the manufacturer was not answerable to the lessee. Loop *v.* Litchfield was followed in Losee *v.* Clute, 51 N. Y. 494, 10 Am. Rep. 638, the case of the explosion of a steam boiler. That decision has been criticized (Thompson on Negligence, 233; Shearman & Redfield on Negligence, [6th ed.] § 117); but it must be confined to its special facts. It was put upon the ground that the risk of injury was too remote. The buyer in that case had not only accepted the boiler, but had tested it. The manufacturer knew that his own test was not the final one. The finality of the test has a bearing on the measure of diligence owing to persons other than the purchaser. Beven, Negligence, (3d ed.) pp. 50, 51, 54; Wharton, Negligence, (2d ed.) § 134.

These early cases suggest a narrow construction of the rule. Later cases, however, evince a more liberal spirit. First in importance is Devlin *v.* Smith, 89 N. Y. 470, 42 Am. Rep. 311. The defendant, a contractor, built a scaffold for a painter. The painter's servants were injured. The contractor was held liable. He knew that the scaffold, if improperly constructed, was a most dangerous trap. He knew that it was to be used by the workmen. He was building it for that very purpose. Building it for their use, he owed them a duty, irrespective of his contract with their master, to build it with care.

From Devlin *v.* Smith we pass over intermediate cases and turn to the latest case in this court in which Thomas *v.* Winchester was followed. That case is Statler *v.* Ray Mfg. Co., 195 N. Y. 478, 480, 88 N. E. 1063. The defendant manufactured a large coffee urn. It was installed in a restaurant. When heated, the urn exploded and injured the plaintiff. We held that the manufacturer was liable. We said that the urn " was of such a character inherently that, when applied to the purposes for which it was designed, it was liable to become a source of great danger to many people if not carefully and properly constructed."

It may be that Devlin *v.* Smith and Statler *v.* Ray Mfg. Co. have extended the rule of Thomas *v.* Winchester. If so, this court is committed to the extension. The defendant argues that things imminently dangerous to life are poisons, explosives, deadly weapons — things whose normal function it is to injure or destroy. But whatever the rule in Thomas *v.* Winchester may once have been, it has no longer that restricted meaning. A scaffold (Devlin *v.* Smith, *supra*) is not inherently a destructive instrument. It becomes destructive only if imperfectly constructed. A large coffee urn (Statler *v.* Ray Mfg. Co., *supra*) may have within itself, if negligently made, the potency of danger, yet no one thinks of it as an implement whose normal function is destruction. What is true of the coffee urn is equally true of bottles of aerated water. Torgesen *v.* Schultz, 192 N. Y. 156, 84 N. E. 956, 18 L. R. A. (N. S.) 726, 127 Am. St. Rep. 894. We have mentioned only cases in this court. But the rule has received a like extension in our courts of intermediate appeal. In Burke *v.* Ireland, 26 App. Div. 487, 50 N. Y. Supp. 369, in an opinion by Cullen, J., it was applied to a builder who constructed a defective building; in Kahner *v.* Otis Elevator Co., 96 App. Div. 169, 89 N. Y. Supp. 185, to the manufacturer of an elevator; in Davies *v.* Pelham Hod Elevating Co., 65 Hun, 573, 20 N. Y. Supp. 523, affirmed in this court without opinion, 146 N. Y. 363, 41 N. E. 88, to a contractor who furnished a defective rope with knowledge of the purpose for which the rope was to be used. We are not required at this time either to approve or to disapprove the application of the rule that was made in these cases. It is enough that they help to characterize the trend of judicial thought.

Devlin *v.* Smith was decided in 1882. A year later a very similar case came before the Court of Appeal in England (Heaven *v.* Pender, 11 Q. B. D. 503). We find in the opinion of Brett, M. R., afterwards Lord Esher, the same conception of a duty, irrespective of contract, imposed upon the manufacturer by the law itself:

"Whenever one person supplies goods or machinery, or the like, for the purpose of their being used by another person under such circumstances that every one of ordinary sense would, if he thought, recognize at once that unless he used ordinary care and skill with regard to the condition of the thing supplied, or the mode of supplying it, there will be danger of injury to the person or property of him for whose use the thing is supplied, and who is to use it, a duty arises to use ordinary care and skill as to the condition or manner of supplying such thing."

He then points out that for a neglect of such ordinary care or skill whereby injury happens, the appropriate remedy is an action for negligence. The right to enforce this liability is not to be confined to the immediate buyer. The right, he says, extends to the persons or class of persons for whose use the thing is supplied. It is enough that the goods "would in all probability be used at once . . . before a reasonable opportunity for discovering any defect which might exist," and that the thing supplied is of such a nature "that a neglect of ordinary care or skill as to its condition or the manner of supplying it would probably cause danger to the person or property of the person for whose use it was supplied, and who was about to use it."

On the other hand, he would exclude a case "in which the goods are supplied under circumstances in which it would be a chance by whom they would be used or whether they would be used or not, or whether they would be used before there would probably be means of observing any defect," or where the goods are of such a nature that "a want of care or skill as to their condition or the manner of supplying them would not probably produce danger of injury to person or property." What was said by Lord Esher in that case did not command the full assent of his associates. His opinion has been criticized "as requiring every man to take affirmative precautions to protect his neighbors as well as to refrain from injuring them." Bohlen, Affirmative Obligations in the Law of Torts, 44 Am. Law Reg. (N. S.) 341. It may not be an accurate exposition of the law of England. Perhaps it may need some qualification even in our own state. Like most attempts at comprehensive definition, it may involve errors of inclusion and of exclusion. But its tests and standards, at least in their underlying principles with whatever qualification may be called for as they are applied to varying conditions, are the tests and standards of our law.

We hold, then, that the principle of Thomas *v.* Winchester is not limited to poisons, explosives, and things of like nature, to things which in their normal operation are implements of destruction. If the nature of a thing is such that it is reasonably certain to place life and limb in peril when negligently made, it is then a thing of danger. Its nature gives warning of the consequences to be expected. If to the element of danger there is added knowledge that the thing will be used by persons other than the purchaser, and used without new tests, then, irrespective of contract, the manufacturer of this thing of danger is under a duty to make it carefully. That is as far as we are required to go for the decision of this case. There must be knowledge of a danger, not merely possible, but probable. It is possible to use almost anything in a way that will make it dangerous if defective. That is not enough to charge the manufacturer with a duty independent of his contract. Whether a given thing is dangerous may be sometimes a question for the court and sometimes a question for the jury. There must also be knowledge that in the usual course of events the danger will be shared by others than the buyer. Such knowledge may often be inferred from the nature of the transaction. But it is possible that even knowledge of the danger and of the use will not always be enough. The proximity or remoteness of the relation is a factor to be considered. We are dealing now with the liability of the manufacturer of the finished product, who puts it on the market to be used without inspection by his customers. If he is negligent, where danger is to be foreseen, a liability will follow.

We are not required at this time to say that it is legitimate to go back of the manufacturer of the finished product and hold the manufacturers of the component parts. To make their negligence a cause of imminent danger, an independent cause must often intervene; the manufacturer of the finished product must also fail in his duty of inspection. It may be that in those circumstances the negligence of the earlier members of the series is too remote to constitute, as to the ultimate user, an actionable wrong. Beven on Negligence, (3d ed.) 50, 51, 54; Wharton on Negligence, (2d ed.) § 134; Leeds *v.* N. Y. Tel. Co., 178 N. Y. 118, 70 N. E. 219; Sweet *v.* Perkins, 196 N. Y. 482, 90 N. E. 50; Hayes *v.* Hyde Park, 153 Mass. 514, 516, 27 N. E. 522, 12 L. R. A. 249. We leave that question open. We shall have to deal with it when it arises. The difficulty which it suggests is not present in this case. There is here no break in the chain of cause and effect. In such circumstances, the presence of a known danger, attendant upon a known use, makes vigilance a duty. We have put aside the notion that the duty to safeguard life and limb, when the consequences of negligence may be foreseen, grows out of contract and nothing else. We have put the source of the obligation where it ought to be. We have put its source in the law.

From this survey of the decisions, there thus emerges a definition of the duty of a manufacturer which enables us to measure this defendant's liability. Beyond all question, the nature of an automobile gives warning of probable danger if its construction is defectiye. This automobile was designed to go 50 miles an hour. Unless its wheels were sound and strong, injury was almost certain. It was as much a thing of danger as a defective engine for a railroad. The defendant knew the danger. It knew also that the car would be used by persons other than the buyer. This was apparent from its size; there were seats for three persons. It was apparent also from the fact that the buyer was a dealer in cars, who bought to resell. The maker of this car supplied it for the use of purchasers from the dealer just as plainly as the contractor in Devlin *v.* Smith supplied the scaffold for use by the servants of the owner. The dealer was indeed the one person of whom it might be said with some approach to certainty that by him the car would not be used. Yet the defendant would have us say that he was the one person whom it was under a legal duty to protect. The law does not lead us to so inconsequent a conclusion. Precedents drawn from the days of travel by stage-coach do not fit the conditions of travel to-day. The principle that the danger must be imminent does not change, but the things subject to the principle do change. They are whatever the needs of life in a developing civilization requires them to be.

In reaching this conclusion, we do not ignore the decisions to the contrary in other jurisdictions. It was held in Cadillac Co. *v.* Johnson, 221 Fed. 801, 137 C. C. A. 279, L. R. A. 1915E, 287, that an automobile is not within the rule of Thomas *v.* Winchester. There was, however, a vigorous dissent. Opposed to that decision is one of the Court of Appeals of Kentucky. Olds Motor Works *v.* Shaffer, 145 Ky. 616, 140 S. W. 1047, 37 L. R. A. (N. S.) 560, Ann. Cas. 1913B, 689. The earlier cases are summarized by Judge Sanborn in Huset *v.* J. I. Case Threshing Machine Co., 120 Fed. 865, 57 C. C. A. 237, 61 L. R. A. 303. Some of them, at first sight inconsistent with our conclusion, may be reconciled upon the ground that the negligence was too remote, and that another cause had intervened. But even when they cannot be reconciled the difference is rather in the application of the principle than in the principle itself. Judge Sanborn says, for example, that the contractor who builds a bridge, or the manufacturer who builds a car, cannot ordinarily foresee injury to other persons than the owner as the probable result. 120 Fed. 865, at page 867, 57 C. C. A. 237, at page 239, 61 L. R. A. 303. We take a different view. We think that injury to others is to be foreseen not merely as a possible, but as an almost inevitable result. See the trenchant criticism in Bohlen, *supra,* at page 351. Indeed, Judge Sanborn concedes that his view is not to be reconciled with our decision in Devlin *v.* Smith, *supra.* The doctrine of that decision has now become the settled law of this state, and we have no desire to depart from it.

In England the limits of the rule are still unsettled. Winterbottom *v.* Wright, 10 M. & W. 109, is often cited. The defendant undertook to provide a mail coach to carry the mail bags. The coach broke down from latent defects in its construction. The defendant, however, was not the manufacturer. The court held that he was not liable for injuries to a passenger. The case was decided on a demurrer to the declaration. Lord Esher points out in Heaven *v.* Pender, *supra,* at page 513, that the form of the declaration was subject to criticism. It did not fairly suggest the existence of a duty aside from the special contract which was the plaintiff's main reliance. See the criticism of Winterbottom *v.* Wright, in Bohlen, *supra,* at pages 281, 283. At all events, in Heaven *v.* Pender, *supra,* the defendant, a dock owner, who put up a staging outside a ship, was held liable to the servants of the shipowner. In Elliot *v.* Hall, 15 Q. B. D. 315, the defendant sent out a defective truck laden with goods which he had sold. The buyer's servants unloaded it, and were injured because of the defects. It was held that the defendant was under a duty "not to be guilty of negligence with regard to the state and condition of the truck." There seems to have been a return to the doctrine of Winterbottom *v.* Wright in Earl *v.* Lubbock, [1905] 1 K. B. 253. In that case, however, as in the earlier one, the defendant was not the manufacturer. He had merely made a contract to keep the van in repair. A later case (White *v.* Steadman, [1913] 3 K. B. 340, 348) emphasizes that element. A livery stable keeper who sent out a vicious horse was held liable, not merely to his customer, but also to another occupant of the carriage, and Thomas *v.* Winchester was cited and followed, White *v.* Steadman, *supra,* at pages 348, 349. It was again cited and followed in

Dominion Natural Gas Co. *v.* Collins, [1909] A. C. 640, 646. From these cases a consistent principle is with difficulty extracted. The English courts, however, agree with ours in holding that one who invites another to make use of an appliance is bound to the exercise of reasonable care. Caledonian Ry. Co. *v.* Mulholland, [1898] A. C. 216, 227; Indermaur *v.* Dames, L. R. 1 C. P. 274. That at bottom is the underlying principle of Devlin *v.* Smith. The contractor who builds the scaffold invites the owner's workmen to use it. The manufacturer who sells the automobile to the retail dealer invites the dealer's customers to use it. The invitation is addressed in the one case to determinate persons and in the other to an indeterminate class, but in each case it is equally plain, and in each its consequences must be the same.

There is nothing anomalous in a rule which imposes upon A., who has contracted with B., a duty to C. and D. and others according as he knows or does not know that the subject-matter of the contract is intended for their use. We may find an analogy in the law which measures the liability of landlords. If A. leases to B. a tumble-down house, he is not liable, in the absence of fraud, to B.'s guests who enter it and are injured. This is because B. is then under the duty to repair it, the lessor has the right to suppose that he will fulfill that duty, and, if he omits to do so, his guests must look to him. Bohlen, *supra,* at page 276. But if A. leases a building to be used by the lessee at once as a place of public entertainment, the rule is different. There injury to persons other than the lessee is to be foreseen, and foresight of the consequences involves the creation of a duty. Junkermann *v.* Tilyou R. Co., 213 N. Y. 404, 108 N. E. 190, L. R. A. 1915F, 700, and cases there cited.

In this view of the defendant's liability there is nothing inconsistent with the theory of liability on which the case was tried. It is true that the court told the jury that " an automobile is not an inherently dangerous vehicle." The meaning, however, is made plain by the context. The meaning is that danger is not to be expected when the vehicle is well constructed. The court left it to the jury to say whether the defendant ought to have foreseen that the car, if negligently constructed, would become " imminently dangerous." Subtle distinctions are drawn by the defendant between things inherently dangerous and things imminently dangerous, but the case does not turn upon these verbal niceties. If danger was to be expected as reasonably certain, there was a duty of vigilance, and this whether you call the danger inherent or imminent. In varying forms that thought was put before the jury. We do not say that the court would not have been justified in ruling as a matter of law that the car was a dangerous thing. If there was any error, it was none of which the defendant can complain.

We think the defendant was not absolved from a duty of inspection because it bought the wheels from a reputable manufacturer. It was not merely a dealer in automobiles. It was a manufacturer of automobiles. It was responsible for the finished product. It was not at liberty to put the finished product on the market without subjecting the component parts to ordinary and simple tests. Richmond & Danville R. R. Co. *v.* Elliott, 149 U. S. 266, 272, 13 Sup. Ct. 837, 37 L. Ed. 728. Under the charge of the trial judge nothing more was required of it. The obligation to inspect must vary with the nature of the thing to be inspected. The more probable the danger the greater the need of caution.

There is little analogy between this case and Carlson *v.* Phoenix Bridge Co., 132 N. Y. 273, 30 N. E. 750, where the defendant bought a tool for a servant's use. The making of tools was not the business in which the master was engaged. Reliance on the skill of the manufacturer was proper and almost inevitable. But that is not the defendant's situation. Both by its relation to the work and by the nature of its business, it is charged with a stricter duty.

Other rulings complained of have been considered, but no error has been found in them.

The judgment should be affirmed, with costs.

Willard Bartlett, C. J. (dissenting). The plaintiff was injured in consequence of the collapse of a wheel of an automobile manufactured by the defendant corporation which sold it to a firm of automobile dealers in Schenectady, who in turn sold the car to the plaintiff. The wheel was purchased by the Buick Motor Company, ready made, from the Imperial Wheel Company of Flint, Mich., a reputable manufacturer of automobile wheels which had furnished the defendant with 80,000 wheels, none of which had proved to be made of defective wood prior to the accident in the present case. The defendant relied upon the wheel manufacturer to make all necessary tests as to the strength of the material therein, and made no such test itself. The present suit is an action for negligence, brought by the subvendee of the motor car against the manufacturer as the original vendor. The evidence warranted a finding by the jury that the wheel which collapsed was defective when it left the hands of the defendant. The automobile was being prudently operated at the time of the accident, and was moving at a speed of only eight miles an hour. There was no allegation or proof of any actual knowledge of the defect on the part of the defendant, or any suggestion that any element of fraud or deceit or misrepresentation entered into the sale.

The theory upon which the case was submitted to the jury by the learned judge who presided at the trial was that, although an automobile is not an inherently dangerous vehicle, it may become such if equipped with a weak wheel; and that if the motor car in question, when it was put upon the market was in itself inherently dangerous by reason of its being equipped with a weak wheel, the defendant was chargeable with a knowledge of the defect so far as it might be discovered by a reasonable inspection and the application of reasonable tests. This liability, it was further held, was not limited to the original vendee, but extended to a subvendee like the plaintiff, who was not a party to the original contract of sale.

I think that these rulings, which have been approved by the Appellate Division, extend the liability of the vendor of a manufactured article further than any case which has yet received the sanction of this court. It has heretofore been held in this state that the liability of the vendor of a manufactured article for negligence arising out of the existence of defects therein does not extend to strangers injured in consequence of such defects, but is confined to the immediate vendee. The exceptions to this general rule which have thus far been recognized in New York are cases in which the article sold was of such a character that danger to life or limb was involved in the ordinary use thereof; in other words, where the article sold was inherently dangerous. As has already been pointed out, the learned trial judge instructed the jury that an automobile is not an inherently dangerous vehicle.

The late Chief Justice Cooley of Michigan, one of the most learned and accurate of American law writers, states the general rule thus:

"The general rule is that a contractor, manufacturer, vendor or furnisher of an article is not liable to third parties who have no contractual relations with him, for negligence in the construction, manufacture or sale of such article." 2 Cooley on Torts, (3d ed.) 1486.

The leading English authority in support of this rule, to which all the later cases on the same subject refer, is Winterbottom *v.* Wright, 10 Meeson & Welsby, 109, which was an action by the driver of a stagecoach against a contractor who had agreed with the postmaster general to provide and keep the vehicle in repair for the purpose of conveying the royal mail over a prescribed route. The coach broke down and upset, injuring the driver, who sought to recover against the contractor on account of its defective construction. The Court of Exchequer denied him any right of recovery on the ground that there was no privity of contract between the parties, the agreement having been made with the postmaster general alone.

"If the plaintiff can sue," said Lord Abinger, the Chief Baron, "every passenger or even any person passing along the road who was injured by the upsetting of the coach might bring a similar action. Unless we confine the operation of such contracts as this to the parties who enter into them the most absurd and outrageous consequences, to which I can see no limit, would ensue."

The doctrine of that decision was recognized as the law of this state by the leading New York case of Thomas *v.* Winchester, 6 N. Y. 397, 408, 57 Am. Dec. 455, which, however, involved an exception to the general rule. There the defendant, who was a dealer in medicines, sold to a druggist a quantity of belladonna, which is a deadly poison, negligently labelled as extract of dandelion. The druggist in good faith used the poison in filling a prescription calling for the harmless dandelion extract, and the plaintiff for whom the prescription was put up was poisoned by the belladonna. This court held that the original vendor was liable for the injuries suffered by the patient. Chief Judge Ruggles, who delivered the opinion of the court, distinguished between an act of negligence imminently dangerous to the lives of others and one that is not so, saying:

"If A. build a wagon and sell it to B., who sells it to C., and C. hires it to D., who in consequence of the gross negligence of A. in building the wagon is overturned and injured, D. cannot recover damages against A., the builder. A.'s obligation to build the wagon faithfully arises solely out of his contract with B. The public have nothing to do with it. . . . So, for the same reason, if a horse be defectively shod by a smith, and a person hiring the horse from the owner is thrown and injured in consequence of the smith's negligence in shoeing, the smith is not liable for the injury."

In Torgesen *v.* Schultz, 192 N. Y. 156, 159, 84 N. E. 956, 18 L. R. A. (N. S.) 726, 127 Am. St. Rep. 894, the defendant was the vendor of bottles of aerated water which were charged under high pressure and likely to explode unless used with precaution when exposed to sudden changes of temperature. The plaintiff, who was a servant of the purchaser, was injured by the explosion of one of these bottles. There was evidence tending to show that it had not been properly tested in order to insure users against such accidents. We held that the defendant corporation was liable notwithstanding the absence of any contract relation between it and the plaintiff "under the doctrine of Thomas *v.* Winchester, *supra*, and similar cases based upon the duty of the vendor of an article dangerous in its nature or likely to become so in the course of the ordinary usage to be contemplated by the vendor, either to exercise due care to warn users of the danger or to take reasonable care to prevent the article sold from proving dangerous when subjected only to customary usage."

The character of the exception to the general rule limiting liability for negligence to the original parties to the contract of sale, was still more clearly stated by Judge Hiscock, writing for the court in Statler *v.* Ray Manufacturing Co., 195 N. Y. 478, 482, 88 N. E. 1063, where he said that:

"In the case of an article of an inherently dangerous nature, a manufacturer may become liable for a negligent construction which, when added to the inherent character of the appliance, makes it imminently dangerous, and causes or contributes to a resulting injury not necessarily incident to the use of such an article if properly constructed, but naturally following from a defective construction."

In that case the injuries were inflicted by the explosion of a battery of steam-driven coffee urns, constituting an appliance liable to become dangerous in the course of ordinary usage.

The case of Devlin *v.* Smith, 89 N. Y. 470, 42 Am. Rep. 311, is cited as an authority in conflict with the view that the liability of the manufacturer and vendor extends to third parties only when the article manufactured and sold is inherently dangerous. In that case the builder of a scaffold 90 feet high, which was erected for the purpose of enabling painters to stand upon it, was held to be liable to the administratrix of a painter who fell therefrom and was killed, being at the time in the employ of the person for whom the scaffold was built. It is said that the scaffold, if properly constructed, was not inherently dangerous, and hence that this decision affirms the existence of liability in the case of an article not dangerous in itself, but made so only in consequence of negligent construction. Whatever logical force there may be in this view it seems to me clear from the language of Judge Rapallo, who wrote the opinion of the court, that the scaffold was deemed to be an inherently dangerous structure, and that the case was decided as it was because the court entertained that view. Otherwise he would hardly have said, as he did, that the circumstances seemed to bring the case fairly within the principle of Thomas *v.* Winchester.

I do not see how we can uphold the judgment in the present case without overruling what has been so often said by this court and other courts of like authority in reference to the absence of any liability for negligence on the part of the original vendor of an ordinary carriage to any one except his immediate vendee. The absence of such liability was the very point actually decided in the English case of Winterbottom *v.* Wright, *supra*, and the illustration quoted from the opinion of Chief Judge Ruggles in Thomas *v.* Winchester, *supra*, assumes that the law on the subject was so plain that the statement would be accepted almost as a matter of course. In the case at bar the defective wheel on an automobile, moving only eight miles an hour, was not any more dangerous to the occupants of the car than a similarly defective wheel would be to the occupants of a carriage drawn by a horse at the same speed, and yet, unless the courts have been all wrong on this question up to the present time, there would be no liability to strangers to the original sale in the case of the horse-drawn carriage.

The rule upon which, in my judgment, the determination of this case depends, and the recognized exceptions thereto, were discussed by Circuit Judge Sanborn, of the United States Circuit Court of Appeals in the Eighth Circuit, in Huset *v.* J. I. Case Threshing Machine Co., 120 Fed. 865, 57 C. C. A. 237, 61 L. R. A. 303, in an opinion which reviews all the leading American and English decisions on the subject up to the time when it was rendered (1903). I have already discussed the leading New York cases, but as to the rest I feel that I can add nothing to the learning of that opinion or the cogency of its reasoning. I have examined the cases to which Judge Sanborn refers, but if I were to discuss them at length, I should be forced merely to paraphrase his language, as a study of the authorities he cites has led me to the same conclusion; and the repetition of what has already been so well said would contribute nothing to the advantage of the bench, the bar, or the individual litigants whose case is before us.

A few cases decided since his opinion was written, however, may be noticed. In Earl *v.* Lubbock, [1905] L. R. 1 K. B. Div. 253, the Court of Appeal in 1904 considered and approved the propositions of law laid down by the Court of Exchequer in Winterbottom *v.* Wright, *supra,* declaring that the decision in that case, since the year 1842, had stood the test of repeated discussion. The Master of the Rolls approved the principles laid down by Lord Abinger as based upon sound reasoning; and all the members of the court agreed that his decision was a controlling authority which must be followed. That the federal courts still adhere to the general rule, as I have stated it, appears by the decision of the Circuit Court of Appeals in the Second Circuit, in March, 1915, in the case of Cadillac Motor Car Co. *v.* Johnson, 221 Fed. 801, 137 C. C. A. 279, L. R. A. 1915E, 287. That case, like this, was an action by a subvendee against a manufacturer of automobiles for negligence in failing to discover that one of its wheels was defective, the court holding that such an action could not be maintained. It is true there was a dissenting opinion in that case, but it was based chiefly upon the proposition that rules applicable to stage-coaches are archaic when applied to automobiles, and that if the law did not afford a remedy to strangers to the contract, the law should be changed. If this be true, the change should be effected by the Legislature and not by the courts. A perusal of the opinion in that case and in the Huset Case will disclose how uniformly the courts throughout this country have adhered to the rule and how consistently they have refused to broaden the scope of the exceptions. I think we should adhere to it in the case at bar, and therefore I vote for a reversal of this judgment.

HISCOCK, CHASE, and CUDDEBACK, JJ., concur with CARDOZO, J., and HOGAN, J., concurs in result. WILLARD BARTLETT, C. J., reads dissenting opinion. POUND, J., not voting.

Judgment affirmed.[1]

[1] *Liability of abstracter to third party* injured by mistake or omission in abstract of title: see Thomas *v.* Guarantee Title & Trust Co., 81 Ohio St. 432; Bremerton Development Co. *v.* Title Trust Co., 67 Wash. 268.

Liability of water company to injured citizen where it has failed to provide water for extinguishment of fires according to its contract with the municipality: see Sunderland, Liability of Water Companies for Fire Losses, 3 Mich. Law Rev. 442; Kales, Liability of Water Companies for Fire Losses — Another View, 3 Mich. Law Rev. 501; note in 19 Green Bag, 129–133.

SECTION VIII

CONTRIBUTORY CULPABLE CONDUCT OF PLAINTIFF

NEAL *v.* GILLETT

SUPREME COURT OF ERRORS, CONNECTICUT, JUNE TERM, 1855.

Reported in 23 *Connecticut Reports*, 437.

ACTION to recover for personal injury alleged to have been incurred through the negligence of the defendants. Plaintiff claimed that the defendants were guilty of gross negligence, as the cause of the injury; and that, if the jury should so find, the plaintiff was entitled to recover notwithstanding there had been on his part a want of mere ordinary care which might have essentially contributed to produce the injury complained of. The Court charged the jury in conformity to this claim of the plaintiff. Verdict for plaintiff. Motion for new trial.

SANFORD, J. [Omitting opinion on another point.] [1] The question presented upon the second point, is, whether a plaintiff is entitled to recover for an injury, produced by the combined operation of his own want of " ordinary care," and the gross negligence of the defendant. The exact boundaries between the several degrees of care and their correlative degrees of carelessness, or negligence, are not always clearly defined or easily pointed out. We think, however, that by " ordinary care," is meant " that degree of care which may reasonably be expected from a person in the party's situation " (41 E. C. L. R. 425),[2] that is, " reasonable care " (19 Conn. R. 572); and that " gross negligence " imports not a malicious intention or design to produce a particular injury, but a thoughtless disregard of consequences; the absence, rather than the actual exercise, of volition with reference to results.

What is the measure of " reasonable care " must of course depend upon the circumstances of the particular situation in which the party at the time is placed. But " reasonable care," every one, in the enjoyment of his rights, and the performance of his duties, is bound to exercise at all times and under all circumstances. When he has done that, he is answerable to no one for any consequences which ensue, for he has done all his duty; when he has done less than that he is in fault, and if an injury ensue to another in consequence of such fault,

[1] Part of case omitted; also arguments.
On the subject of this section the student may read profitably, Bohlen, Contributory Negligence, 21 Harvard Law Rev. 233; Clark, Tort Liability for Negligence in Missouri, Bull. of Univ. of Mo. Law Series, No. 12, pp. 25–43.

[2] 1 Q. B. 29, 36.

he is responsible for it; if to himself, he must bear it. If in the enjoyment of their lawful rights by two persons, at the same time and place, reasonable care is exercised by both, and an injury accrues to one of them, it must be borne by the suffering party as a providential visitation. If such care is exercised by neither party, and an injury accrues to one of them, he must bear it, for he was himself in fault. And we hold that when the gist of the action is negligence merely, — whether gross or slight, the plaintiff is not entitled to recover, when his own want of ordinary, or reasonable care, has essentially contributed to his injury; because he is himself in fault, and because of the difficulty, if not impossibility, of ascertaining in what proportions the parties respectively, by their negligence, have contributed to the production of the injury, and whether it would have been produced at all but by the combined operation of the negligence of both. When the injury is intentional, and designed, other considerations apply.

For anything this Court can see, the negligence of the defendants, however gross, might have been entirely harmless, but for the plaintiff's own wrongful contribution to the combined causes which produced his injury. And so too, for anything this Court can see, although the defendants' negligence was gross, and fully adequate to the production of the injury, yet the plaintiff's exercise of reasonable care would have saved him from its consequences.

In the recent case of Park *v.* O'Brien, 23 Conn. R. 339, this Court said, " It is necessary for the plaintiff, to prove, first, negligence on the part of the defendant, and, secondly, that the injury to the plaintiff occurred in consequence of that negligence. But in order to prove this latter point, the plaintiff must show that such injury was not caused, wholly, or in part, by his own negligence;[1] for although the defendant was guilty of negligence, if the plaintiff's negligence contributed essentially to the injury, it is obvious that it did not occur by

[1] Chicago R. Co. *v.* Levy, 160 Ill. 385; Toledo R. Co. *v.* Brannagan, 75 Ind. 490; Cincinnati R. Co. *v.* Butler, 103 Ind. 31 (but changed in case of injuries to the person, Acts of 1899, p. 58, Burns' Ann. St. § 362); Greenleaf *v.* Illinois R. Co., 29 Ia. 14 (but changed in case of actions against a common carrier, Suppl. to the Code, 1913, § 3593 *a*); Brown *v.* Illinois R. Co., 123 Ia. 239; Dickey *v.* Maine Tel. Co., 43 Me. 492; Planz *v.* Boston R. Co., 157 Mass. 377 (but changed by Acts of 1914, ch. 553); Mynning *v.* Detroit R. Co., 67 Mich. 677; Curran *v.* Warren Chemical Mfg. Co., 36 N. Y. 153; City *v.* Nix, 3 Okl. 136; Bovee *v.* Danville, 53 Vt. 183 *Accord.*

Contra, contributory negligence an affirmative defence: Inland Coasting Co. *v.* Tolson, 139 U. S. 551; Montgomery Gaslight Co. *v.* Montgomery R. Co., 86 Ala. 372; Texas R. Co. *v.* Orr, 46 Ark. 182; Atchison *v.* Wills, 21 App. D. C. 548; MacDougall *v.* Central R. Co., 63 Cal. 431; Moore *v.* Lanier, 52 Fla. 353; City *v.* Hudson, 88 Ga. 599; Hopkins *v.* Utah R. Co., 2 Idaho, 300; St. Louis R. Co. *v.* Weaver, 35 Kan. 412; Hocum *v.* Weitherick, 22 Minn. 152; Buesching *v.* St. Louis Gaslight Co., 73 Mo. 219; Nelson *v.* City, 16 Mont. 21; O'Brien *v.* Omaha Water Co., 83 Neb. 71; Valley *v.* Concord R. Co., 68 N. H. 546; New Jersey Exp. Co. *v.* Nichols, 33 N. J. Law 434; Jordan *v.* City, 112 N. C. 743; Carr *v.* Minneapolis R. Co., 16 N. D. 217; Grant *v.* Baker, 12 Or. 329; Beatty *v.* Gilmore, 16 Pa. St. 463; Carter *v.* Columbia R. Co., 19 S. C. 20; Houston R. Co. *v.* Cowser, 57 Tex. 293; Richmond Granite Co. *v.* Bailey, 92 Va. 554; Johnson *v.* Bellingham Imp. Co., 13 Wash. 455; Fowler *v.* Baltimore R. Co., 18 W. Va. 579; Hoth *v.* Peters, 55 Wis. 405.

reason of the defendant's negligence." "Hence, to say that the plaintiff must show the latter" [the want of the plaintiff's concurring negligence], "is only saying that he must show that the injury was owing to the negligence of the defendant."

The same reasonable doctrine is sanctioned by other decisions, in our own Court and elsewhere. Birge *v.* Gardiner, 19 Conn. R. 507; Beers *v.* Housatonic R. R. Co., 19 Conn. R. 566, and cases there cited.

We think, therefore, that the charge of the Court, on this point, was wrong, and that a new trial ought to be granted.

In this opinion the other judges concurred, except Ellsworth, J., who was disqualified. *New trial to be granted.*[1]

PAYNE *v.* CHICAGO & ALTON RAILROAD COMPANY

SUPREME COURT, MISSOURI, JUNE 25, 1895.

Reported in 129 *Missouri Reports*, 405.

ACTION for personal injuries alleged to be caused by the negligence of defendant. Answer: a general denial, and a plea of contributory negligence.[2]

The judge, at the request of plaintiff, gave the following instruction: —

"No. 7. One of the defences in this case interposed by the defendant is that of negligence on the part of plaintiff, Claude Payne, directly contributing to the injuries of which plaintiff complains; and the court instructs the jury that the law devolves upon the defendant the burden of proving such negligence by a preponderance of the evidence, and it is not sufficient that the jury may believe from the evidence that the plaintiff was simply guilty of negligence, but that the negligence of plaintiff, and not that of the defendant, must be the proximate or immediate cause of the injury, to excuse the defendant from liability."

In the Circuit Court plaintiff had judgment. Defendant appealed.

MACFARLANE, J. Defendant complains of instruction 7 given the jury at the request of plaintiff. The complaint is that the instruction improperly defines contributory negligence.

Contributory negligence, as the word imports, implies the concurring negligence of both plaintiff and defendant. The phrase is defined by Beach as follows: "Contributory negligence, in its legal significa-

[1] As to contributory negligence as a bar to an action for damage caused in part by defendant's failure to perform a duty imposed on him by statute, see Bishop, Commentaries on the Written Laws, §§ 117, 117 *a*, § 131, pars. 2, 3, § 134, pars. 3, 4, § 139, par. 1; Kelley *v.* Killourey, 81 Conn. 320; Catlett *v.* Young, 143 Ill. 74; Shultz *v.* Griffith, 103 Ia. 150; Hussey *v.* King, 83 Me. 568; Wadsworth *v.* Marshall, 88 Me. 263; Schutt *v.* Adair, 99 Minn. 7; Quimby *v.* Woodbury, 63 N. H. 370; Kilpatrick *v.* Grand Trunk R. Co., 72 Vt. 263.

[2] Only so much of the case is given as relates to a single point.

tion, is such an act or omission on the part of a plaintiff, amounting to a want of ordinary care, as, concurring or coöperating with the negligent act of the defendant, is a proximate cause or occasion of the injury complained of." Beach, Cont. Neg. [2 ed.] sect. 7. The definition given by Shearman & Redfield in their work on Negligence (sect. 61) is in substance and effect the same.

If the negligence of either plaintiff or defendant is the sole cause of the injury there could be no contributory negligence in the case. The question for the jury is whether the plaintiff could "by the exercise of such care and skill as he was bound to exercise, have avoided the consequence of the defendant's negligence." Lord Blackburn, L. R. 3 App. Cas. 1207. See, also, 4 Am. & Eng. Encyclopedia of Law, 18 & 19. It is clear that there could be no contributory negligence unless there was also negligence of defendant to which that of plaintiff could contribute. Unless the negligence of defendant was the proximate cause of the injury, there could be no liability. Unless the negligence of plaintiff was a proximate cause of the injury, his action, on the ground of contributory negligence, would not be defeated.

Testing the instruction by these rules, it cannot be approved. It tells the jury that "the negligence of plaintiff, and not that of defendant, must be the proximate or immediate cause of the injury to excuse the defendant from liability." They were told in effect that this result would follow though "plaintiff was simply guilty of negligence." The jury may as well have been told that to defeat a recovery on the plea of contributory negligence, it was necessary to find that the negligence of plaintiff was the sole proximate cause of the injury. The instruction ignored entirely concurring or contributory negligence of both parties, which is one essential element of contributory negligence. There are no degrees which distinguish the negligence made necessary by the law to defeat a recovery. And negligence which is proximate or a cause of the injury is sufficient. It does not matter that the concurring and coöperating negligence of defendant was negligence, *per se*, such as the violation of an ordinance, as in this case, or statute law.

The instruction is also misleading wherein it informs the jury that in order for defendant to establish its plea of contributory negligence "it is not sufficient that the jury may believe from the evidence that plaintiff was simply guilty of negligence," and as qualified or explained, by what follows, does not correctly declare the law. The negligence to defeat a recovery must be a proximate cause for the injury, but need not be the sole proximate cause.

As the evidence on the issue of contributory negligence was very clear, we think the errors in this instruction prejudicial and must cause a reversal.[1] *Judgment reversed, and cause remanded.*

[1] Remainder of opinion omitted.

Start, J., in LaFlam v. Missisquoi Pulp Company, 74 Vt. 125, 143: "The defendants, by their second request, asked for an instruction that if, by the exercise

BREESE, J., IN GALENA, &c. R. Co. *v.* JACOBS

(1858) 20 *Illinois*, 478, 496–497.

[AFTER citing decisions in other jurisdictions.] It will be seen from these cases that the question of liability does not depend absolutely on the absence of all negligence on the part of the plaintiff, but upon the relative degree of care or want of care as manifested by both parties; for all care or negligence is at best but relative, the absence of the highest possible degree of care showing the presence of some negligence, slight as it may be. The true doctrine, therefore, we think, is, that in proportion to the negligence of the defendant should be measured the degree of care required of the plaintiff; that is to say, the

of ordinary care and prudence upon the part of the plaintiff, he would not have been injured, he cannot recover. The court instructed the jury, that, if the plaintiff's want of ordinary care or his negligence contributed in any material degree to the happening of the accident, he is not entitled to recover, even though the defendants were negligent. This was in accordance with the rule as it has sometimes been stated by this court. In Magoon *v.* Boston & Maine R. R. Co., 67 Vt. 184, 31 Atl. 156, and in Hill *v.* New Haven, 37 Vt. 507, 88 Am. Dec. 613, it is said that, if the negligence or carelessness of the person injured contributes in any material degree to the production of the injury complained of, he cannot recover; but in Reynolds *v.* Boston & Maine R. R. Co., 64 Vt. 66, 24 Atl. 134, 33 Am. St. Rep. 908, the holding is that, if the negligence of the plaintiff contributes in the *least* degree to the accident, there can be no recovery. We think this is the correct rule, and that the instruction should have conformed to it. The use of the word 'material' left the jury at liberty to consider the degree of the plaintiff's negligence, which is not considered permissible in jurisdictions where the doctrine of contributory negligence prevails. To allow jurors to consider so-called degrees of negligence would, in effect, nullify this doctrine. 7 Am. & Eng. Enc. Law, (2d ed.) 379."

"Negligence contributing as an efficient cause of injury will defeat an action therefor, irrespective of the quantum of negligence of the respective parties." Jaggard, J., in O'Brien *v.* St. Paul City R. Co., 98 Minn. 205, 207–208.

"An effect often has many proximate, and many remote, causes. If the negligence of the plaintiff was one of the proximate causes of the injury, — if it directly contributed to the unfortunate result, — he cannot recover, even though the negligence of the defendant also contributed to it." Sanborn, J., in Missouri Pac. R. Co. *v.* Moseley, 57 Fed. 921, 925.

"While purporting to give a legal definition of contributory negligence, this instruction demands that such negligence shall be found the sole and direct cause of the accident — an interpretation at war with the term 'contributory' itself." Reyburn, J., in Hanheide *v.* St. Louis Transit Co., 104 Mo. App. 323, 330.

". . . if it appears that his [plaintiff's] negligence has contributed as an efficient cause to the injury of which he complains, the court will not undertake to balance the negligence of the respective parties for the purpose of determining which was most at fault. The law recognizes no gradations of fault in such case, and where both parties have been guilty of negligence, as a general rule, there can be no recovery. There is really no distinction between negligence in the plaintiff and negligence in the defendant, except that the negligence of the former is called 'contributory negligence.'" Whittle, J., in Richmond Traction Co. *v.* Martin's Adm'r, 102 Va. 209, 213.

". . . there was a lack of ordinary care on his [the deceased's] part, and where this occurs, contributing proximately to the injury, this lack will prevent a recovery, though the negligence of the other party may have much more contributed thereto." Beard, C. J., in Memphis Gas & Electric Co. *v.* Simpson, (Tenn.) 109 S. W. 1155, 1158.

American Woolen Co. *v.* Stewart, (C. C. A.) 217 Fed. 1; Birmingham R. Co. *v.* Bynum, 139 Ala. 389; St. Louis R. Co. *v.* Musgrove, 113 Ark. 599; Denver more gross the negligence manifested by the defendant, the less degree of care will be required of the plaintiff to entitle him to recover. . . . We say, then, that in this, as in all like cases, the degree of negligence must be measured and considered, and whenever it shall appear that the plaintiff's negligence is comparatively slight and that of the defendant gross, he shall not be deprived of his action.[1]

R. Co. *v.* Maydole, 33 Col. 150; Robinson *v.* Huber, (Del.) 63 Atl. 873; O'Keefe *v.* Chicago R. Co., 32 Ia. 467; Pennsylvania R. Co. *v.* Roney, 89 Ind. 453; Atchison R. Co. *v.* Henry, 57 Kan. 154; Mann *v.* City, 154 Ky. 154; Marble *v.* Ross, 124 Mass. 44; Mynning *v.* Detroit R. Co., 59 Mich. 257; Hurt *v.* St. Louis R. Co., 94 Mo. 255; Village *v.* Holliday, 50 Neb. 229; Pennsylvania R. Co. *v.* Righter, 42 N. J. Law, 180; St. Louis R. Co. *v.* Elsing, 37 Okl. 333; Weaver *v.* Pennsylvania R. Co., 212 Pa. St. 632; Weir *v.* Haverford Electric Co., 221 Pa. St. 611; McLean *v.* Atlantic R. Co., 81 S. C. 100; McDonald *v.* International R. Co., 86 Tex. 1; Hazen *v.* Rutland R. Co., 89 Vt. 94; Chesapeake R. Co. *v.* Lee, 84 Va. 642; Franklin *v.* Engel, 34 Wash. 480; Tesch *v.* Milwaukee R. Co., 108 Wis. 593 *Accord.*

[1] "The doctrine of comparative negligence no longer exists in this state." Wilkin, J., in City *v.* Holcomb, 205 Ill. 643, 646.

"The intrinsic difficulty of the subject of contributory negligence has led to three distinct lines of decisions. In England and a majority of the States of the Union, the negligence of the plaintiff which contributes to the injury is held to be an absolute bar to the action. In the States of Illinois and Georgia the doctrine of comparative negligence has been adopted, that is, if on comparing the negligence of the plaintiff with that of the defendant, the former is found to be slight and the latter gross, the plaintiff may recover. In this State we hold that although the injured party may contribute to the injury by his own carelessness or wrongful conduct, yet if the act or negligence of the party inflicting the injury was the proximate cause of the injury, the latter will be liable in damages, the negligence or wrongful conduct of the party injured being taken into consideration, by way of mitigation, in estimating the damages. In other words, if defendant was guilty of a wrong by which plaintiff is injured, and plaintiff was also in some degree negligent or contributed to the injury, it should go in mitigation of damages, but cannot justify or excuse the wrong. East Tennessee, Virginia & Georgia Railroad Company *v.* Fain, 12 Lea, 35. At the same time we hold that if a party by his own gross negligence bring an injury upon himself, or proximately contribute to such injury, he cannot recover; neither can he recover in cases of mutual negligence where both parties are equally blamable. Id. The principal difference between our rule and the English rule, as modified by the more recent decisions, is in allowing the damages to be mitigated by the conduct of the injured party. In this respect our rule meets the objection which Mr. Thompson, in his notes on contributory negligence, makes to the construction put by some of the courts on the English rule, or to the application of the rule in particular cases. 'It is,' he says, 'nothing more than a declaration that although both parties have been guilty of negligence contributing to the injury, the party who suffered the damage is to be completely exonerated, and the other party is not to be exonerated to any extent; the former is to recover of the latter without any abatement on account of his own share of the fault, all the damages which he has suffered.' 'This is,' he adds, 'manifest injustice; and yet it is practiced every day in the courts of England and in those of nearly every State in the Union.' 2 Thompson on Neg. 1155. Our rule, moreover, is merely an adaptation of the law which prevails in civil actions for assault and battery, where the conduct of the plaintiff in the way of provocation is always admissible in evidence to mitigate the damages. Jackaway *v.* Dula, 7 Yer. 82; Chambers *v.* Porter, 5 Cold. 273, 280; Suth. on Dam. 745." Cooper, J., in Louisville R. Co. *v.* Fleming, 14 Lea, (Tenn.) 128, 135. But see Southern R. Co. *v.* Pugh, 97 Tenn. 624.

UNITED STATES COMPILED STATUTES, 1913, § 8659.

IN all actions hereafter brought against any such common carrier [1] by railroad under or by virtue of any of the provisions of this Act to recover damages for personal injuries to an employee, or where such injuries have resulted in his death, the fact that the employee may have been guilty of contributory negligence shall not bar a recovery, but the damages shall be diminished by the jury in proportion to the amount of negligence attributable to such employee: Provided, That no such employee who may be injured or killed shall be held to have been guilty of contributory negligence in any case where the violation by such common carrier of any statute enacted for the safety of employees contributed to the injury or death of such employee.[2] (Act of April 22, 1908, c. 149, § 3, 35 Stat. L. 66.)

ENGLAND, WORKMEN'S COMPENSATION ACT, 1906, § 1 (c.)

IF it is proved that the injury to a workman is attributable to the serious and wilful misconduct of that workman, any compensation claimed in respect of that injury shall, unless the injury results in death or serious and permanent disablement, be disallowed.[3]

THE MAX MORRIS

SUPREME COURT OF THE UNITED STATES, NOVEMBER 17, 1890.

Reported in 137 *United States Reports*, 1.

THE case, as stated by the court, was as follows: —

This was a suit in Admiralty, brought in the District Court of the United States for the Southern District of New York, by Patrick Curry against the steamer Max Morris.[4]

The libel alleged that on the 27th of October, 1884, the libellant was lawfully on board of that vessel, being employed to load coal upon

[1] This refers to § 8657: "Every common carrier by railroad while engaging in commerce between any of the several States or Territories, or between the District of Columbia and any of the States or Territories, or between the District of Columbia or any of the States or Territories and any foreign nation or nations. . . ."

[2] See also Florida, Comp. L., 1914, § 3149; Georgia, Park's Annotated Code, 1914, §§ 2781 (2332), 2783; Iowa, Supplement to Code, 1913, § 2071; Kansas, Laws of 1911, ch. 239, § 2; Maine, Pub. L. 1910, c. 258, § 4; Mississippi, Laws of 1910, c. 135; Nebraska, Rev. St. 1915, §§ 6054, 7892; Nevada, Rev. L. § 5651 (employees in mines); Ohio, Page & Adams, Ann. Gen. Code, §§ 6245-1, 9018; South Dakota, Laws of 1907, c. 219, § 2; Texas, McEachin's Civ. St. art. 6649; Virginia, Acts of 1916, ch. 444, § 2; Wisconsin, Stat. 1915, ch. 87, § 1816 (3). Compare Arkansas, Kirby's Dig. § 6654; Illinois, R. S. c. 114, § 231; Indiana, Burns' Ann. St. § 5277 *c*; Missouri, R. S. (1909) §§ 3164, 3172.

[3] American Workmen's Compensation Acts often provide that if the employer does not elect to act under the statute, he shall be liable to an action at law by the injured employee in which contributory negligence shall be no defence. See, for example, Ohio, Page & Adams, Annotated Gen. Code, § 1465-60.

[4] Portions of opinion omitted. Argument for appellant omitted.

her by the stevedore who had the contract for loading the coal; that, on that day, the libellant, while on the vessel, fell from her bridge to the deck, through the negligence of those in charge of her, in having removed from the bridge the ladder usually leading therefrom to the deck, and in leaving open, and failing to guard, the aperture thus left in the rail on the bridge; that the libellant was not guilty of negligence; and that he was injured by the fall and incapacitated from labor. He claimed $3000 damages.

The answer alleged negligence on the part of the libellant and an absence of negligence on the part of the claimant.

The District Court, held by Judge Brown, entered a decree in favor of the libellant for $150 damages, and $32.33 as one-half of the libellant's costs, less $47.06 as one-half of the claimant's costs, making the total award to the libellant $135.27. The opinion of the District Judge is reported in 24 Fed. Rep. 860. It appeared from that that the judge charged to the libellant's own fault all his pain and suffering and all mere consequential damages, and charged the vessel with his wages, at $2 per day, for seventy-five working days, making $150.

The claimant appealed to the Circuit Court, on the ground that the libel should have been dismissed. It was stipulated between the parties that the facts as stated in the opinion of the District Judge should be taken as the facts proved in the case, and that the appeal should be heard on those facts. Judge Wallace, who heard the case on appeal in the Circuit Court, delivered an opinion, in August, 1886, which is reported in 28 Fed. Rep. 881, affirming the decree of the District Court. No decree was made on that decision, but the case came up again in the Circuit Court on the 14th of March, 1887, the Court being held by Mr. Justice Blatchford and Judge Wallace, when a certificate was signed by them stating as follows: "The libellant was a longshoreman, a resident of the city and county of New York, and was, at the time when the said accident occurred, employed as longshoreman, by the hour, by the stevedore having the contract to load coal on board the steamship Max Morris. The injuries to the libellant were occasioned by his falling through an unguarded opening in the rail on the after-end of the lower bridge. The Max Morris was a British steamship, hailing from Liverpool, England. The defendant contends, as a matter of defence to said libel, that the injuries complained of by libellant were caused by his own negligence. The libellant contends that the injuries were occasioned entirely through the fault of the vessel and her officers. The Court finds, as a matter of fact, that the injuries to the libellant were occasioned partly through his own negligence and partly through the negligence of the officers of the vessel. It now occurs, as a question of law, whether the libellant, under the above facts, is entitled to a decree for divided damages. On this question the opinions of the judges are in conflict." On motion of the claimant, the question in difference was certified to this

Court, and a decree was entered by the Circuit Court affirming the decree of the District Court and awarding to the libellant a recovery of $135.27, with interest from the date of the decree of the District Court, and $26.30 as the libellant's costs in the Circuit Court, making a total of $172. From that decree the claimant has appealed to this Court. Rev. Stat. §§ 652, 693; Dow *v.* Johnson, 100 U. S. 158.

MR. JUSTICE BLATCHFORD, after stating the case as above reported, delivered the opinion of the Court.

The question discussed in the opinions of Judge Brown and Judge Wallace, and presented to us for decision, is whether the libellant was debarred from the recovery of any sum of money, by reason of the fact that his own negligence contributed to the accident, although there was negligence also in the officers of the vessel. The question presented by the certificate is really that question, although stated in the certificate to be whether the libellant, under the facts presented, was entitled to a decree "for divided damages." It appears from the opinion of the District Judge that he imposed upon the claimant "some part of the damage" which his concurrent negligence occasioned, while it does not appear from the record that the award of the $150 was the result of an equal division of the damages suffered by the libellant, or a giving to him of exactly one-half, or of more or less than one-half, of such damages.

The particular question before us has never been authoritatively passed upon by this Court, and is, as stated by the District Judge in his opinion, whether, in a Court of admiralty, in a case like the present, where personal injuries to the libellant arose from his negligence concurring with that of the vessel, any damages can be awarded, or whether the libel must be dismissed, according to the rule in common-law cases.

The doctrine of an equal division of damages in admiralty, in the case of a collision between two vessels, where both are guilty of fault contributing to the collision, had long been the rule in England, but was first established by this Court in the case of The Schooner Catherine *v.* Dickinson, 17 How. 170, and has been applied by it to cases where, both vessels being in fault, only one of them was injured, as well as to cases where both were injured, the injured vessel, in the first case, recovering only one-half of its damages, and, in the second case, the damages suffered by the two vessels being added together and equally divided, and the vessel whose damages exceeded such one-half recovering the excess against the other vessel. In the case of The Schooner Catherine *v.* Dickinson, *supra,* both vessels being held in fault for the collision, it was said by the Court, speaking by Mr. Justice Nelson, p. 177, that the well-settled rule in the English admiralty was "to divide the loss," and that "under the circumstances usually attending these disasters" the Court thought "the rule dividing the loss the most just and equitable, and as best tending to induce care and vigilance on both sides, in the navigation."

[In Atlee *v.* Packet Co., 21 Wallace, 389, p. 395, MILLER, J., said:] "But the plaintiff has elected to bring his suit in an admiralty Court, which has jurisdiction of the case, notwithstanding the concurrent right to sue at law. In this Court the course of proceeding is in many respects different and the rules of decision are different. The mode of pleading is different, the proceeding more summary and informal, and neither party has a right to trial by jury. An important difference as regards this case is the rule for estimating the damages. In the common-law Court the defendant must pay all the damages or none. If there has been on the part of the plaintiffs such carelessness or want of skill as the common law would esteem to be contributory negligence, they can recover nothing. By the rule of the admiralty Court, where there has been such contributory negligence, or, in other words, when both have been in fault, the entire damages resulting from the collision must be equally divided between the parties. This rule of the admiralty commends itself quite as favorably in its influence in securing practical justice as the other; and the plaintiff who has the selection of the forum in which he will litigate cannot complain of the rule of that forum." This Court, therefore, treated the case as if it had been one of a collision between two vessels.

Some of the cases referred to show that this Court has extended the rule of the division of damages to claims other than those for damages to the vessels which were in fault in a collision.

. . . .

The rule of the equal apportionment of the loss where both parties were in fault would seem to have been founded upon the difficulty of determining, in such cases, the degree of negligence in the one and the other. It is said by Cleirac (*Us et Coutumes de la Mer*, p. 68) that such rule of division is a rustic sort of determination, and such as arbiters and amicable compromisers of disputes commonly follow, where they cannot discover the motives of the parties, or when they see faults on both sides.

As to the particular question now presented for decision, there has been a conflict of opinion in the lower Courts of the United States.

. . . .

All these were cases in admiralty, and were not cases of collision between two vessels. They show an amelioration of the common-law rule, and an extension of the admiralty rule in a direction which we think is manifestly just and proper. Contributory negligence, in a case like the present, should not wholly bar recovery. There would have been no injury to the libellant but for the fault of the vessel; and while, on the one hand, the Court ought not to give him full compensation for his injury, where he himself was partly in fault, it ought not, on the other hand, to be restrained from saying that the fact of his negligence should not deprive him of all recovery of damages. As stated by the District Judge in his opinion in the present case, the more equal distribution of justice, the dictates of humanity, the safety of life and limb and the public good, will be best promoted by holding vessels liable to bear some part of the actual pecuniary loss sustained by the libellant, in a case like the present, where their fault is clear, provided the libellant's fault, though evident, is neither wilful, nor gross, nor inexcusable, and where the other circumstances present a strong case for his relief. We think this rule is applicable to all like cases of marine tort founded upon negligence and prosecuted in admiralty, as in harmony with the rule for the division of damages in cases of collision. The mere fact of the negligence of the libellant as partly occasioning the injuries to him, when they also occurred partly through the negligence of the officers of the vessel, does not debar him entirely from a recovery.

The necessary conclusion is, that the question whether the libellant, upon the facts found, is entitled to a decree for divided damages, must be answered in the affirmative, in accordance with the judgment below. This being the only question certified, and the amount in dispute being insufficient to give this Court jurisdiction of the whole case, our jurisdiction is limited to reviewing this question. Chicago Union Bank *v.* Kansas City Bank, 136 U. S. 223. Whether, in a case like this, the decree should be for exactly one-half of the damages sustained, or might, in the discretion of the Court, be for a greater or less proportion of such damages, is a question not presented for our determination upon this record, and we express no opinion upon it.

Decree affirmed.[1]

SCOTT, COLLISIONS AT SEA WHERE BOTH SHIPS ARE IN FAULT, 13 Law Quarterly Review, 17.

If minor or collateral differences be disregarded, there are amongst civilized nations four different ways of dealing with collision damage where both ships are in fault.

1. To mass the total damage and divide it equally between the two ships.[2] This is the British rule, and has been the American rule. . . .

[1] PLANIOL, TRAITÉ ÉLÉMENTAIRE DE DROIT CIVIL (6 ed.) II, § 899: "It frequently happens that one who suffers damage through the fault of another is not himself exempt from all fault; he has concurred in the accident and shares responsibility therefor with the other. In this case there is what we call in practice *faute commune.* This community of fault diminishes the responsibility of the principal author of damage who now only owes a partial reparation."

GERMAN CIVIL CODE, § 254: "If any fault of the injured party has contributed in causing the injury, the obligation to compensate the injured party and the extent of the compensation to be made depends upon the circumstances, especially upon how far the injury has been caused chiefly by the one or the other party.

"This applies also even if the fault of the injured party consisted only in an omission to call the attention of the debtor to the danger of an unusually serious injury which the debtor neither knew nor ought to have known, or in an omission to avert or mitigate the injury. . . ."

[The word "debtor" is used here in the Roman sense, meaning the person bound in any sort of obligation — here the delictual obligation to make reparation for an injury due to fault.]

[2] See The Drumlanrig, [1911] A. C. 16; Steamship Devonshire *v.* Barge Leslie, [1912] A. C. 634; St. Louis Packet Co. *v.* Murray, 144 Ky. 815. But compare Murphy *v.* Diamond, 3 La. Ann. 441; New York Towboat Co. *v.* New York R. Co., 148 N. Y. 574; Union Steamship Co. *v.* Nottingham, 17 Grat. 115.

2. To leave the loss where it falls.

This is the rule in Germany, Holland, Italy, Spain, and those of the South American States which have derived their law from Spain, and was the rule in Great Britain in our Courts of Common Law previous to the Judicature Act, 1873.

3. To divide the loss proportionally to the value of the vessels in collision.

A kind of general average principle obtaining in Turkey and Egypt.

4. To divide the loss proportionally to the faults of the two vessels.

This is the rule of France, Belgium, Norway, Sweden, Denmark, Portugal, Greece, and Roumania.

See Franck, Collisions at Sea in Relation to International Maritime Law, 12 Law Quarterly Review, 260.

England, Maritime Conventions act (1911), § 1.

1. (1) Where, by the fault of two or more vessels, damage or loss is caused to one or more of those vessels, to their cargoes or freight, or to any property on board, the liability to make good the damage or loss shall be in proportion to the degree in which each vessel was in fault:

Provided that —

(a) if, having regard to all the circumstances of the case, it is not possible to establish different degrees of fault, the liability shall be apportioned equally; and

(b) nothing in this section shall operate so as to render any vessel liable for any loss or damage to which her fault has not contributed.

BUTTERFIELD v. FORRESTER

In the King's Bench, April 22, 1809.

Reported in 11 *East*, 60.

This was an action on the case for obstructing a highway, by means of which obstruction the plaintiff, who was riding along the road, was thrown down with his horse, and injured, &c. At the trial before Bayley, J., at Derby, it appeared that the defendant, for the purpose of making some repairs to his house, which was close by the roadside at one end of the town, had put up a pole across this part of the road, a free passage being left by another branch or street in the same direction. That the plaintiff left a public house not far distant from the place in question at 8 o'clock in the evening in August, when they were just beginning to light candles, but while there was light enough left to discern the obstruction at one hundred yards distance; and the witness who proved this, said that if the plaintiff had not been riding very hard he might have observed and avoided it; the plaintiff, however, who was riding violently, did not observe it, but rode against it, and fell with his horse and was much hurt in consequence of the accident; and there was no evidence of his being intoxicated at the time. On this evidence Bayley, J., directed the jury, that if a person riding with reasonable and ordinary care could have seen and avoided the obstruction; and if they were satisfied that the plaintiff was riding along the street extremely hard, and without ordinary care, they should find a verdict for the defendant, which they accordingly did.

Vaughan, Serjt., now objected to this direction, on moving for a new trial; and referred to Buller's Ni. Pri. 26,[1] where the rule is laid down, that "if a man lay logs of wood across a highway, though a person may with care ride safely by, yet if by means thereof my horse stumble and fling me, I may bring an action."

BAYLEY, J. The plaintiff was proved to be riding as fast as his horse could go, and this was through the streets of Derby. If he had used ordinary care he must have seen the obstruction; so that the accident appeared to happen entirely from his own fault.

LORD ELLENBOROUGH, C. J. A party is not to cast himself upon an obstruction which had been made by the fault of another, and avail himself of it, if he do not himself use common and ordinary caution to be in the right. In cases of persons riding upon what is considered to be the wrong side of the road, that would not authorize another purposely to ride up against them. One person being in fault will not dispense with another's using ordinary care for himself. Two things must concur to support this action: an obstruction in the road by the fault of the defendant, and no want of ordinary care to avoid it on the part of the plaintiff. *Rule refused.*

DAVIES *v.* MANN

IN THE EXCHEQUER, NOVEMBER 4, 1842.

Reported in 10 *Meeson & Welsby*, 546.

CASE for negligence. The declaration stated, that the plaintiff theretofore, and at the time of the committing of the grievance thereinafter mentioned, to wit, on, &c., was lawfully possessed of a certain donkey, which said donkey of the plaintiff was then lawfully in a certain highway, and the defendant was then possessed of a certain wagon and of certain horses drawing the same, which said wagon and horses of the defendant were then under the care, government, and direction of a certain then servant of the defendant, in and along the said highway; nevertheless the defendant, by his said servant, so carelessly, negligently, unskilfully, and improperly governed and directed his said wagon and horses, that by and through the carelessness, negligence, unskilfulness, and improper conduct of the defendant, by his said servant, the said wagon and horses of the defendant then ran and struck with great violence against the said donkey of the plaintiff, and thereby then wounded, crushed, and killed the same, &c.

The defendant pleaded not guilty.

At the trial, before Erskine, J., at the last Summer Assizes for the county of Worcester, it appeared that the plaintiff, having fettered the

[1] The book cites Carth. 194 and 451 in the margin, which references do not bear on the point here in question. — Reporter's note.

fore-feet of an ass belonging to him, turned it into a public highway, and at the time in question the ass was grazing on the off side of a road about eight yards wide, when the defendant's wagon, with a team of three horses, coming down a slight descent, at what the witness termed a smartish pace, ran against the ass, knocked it down, and the wheels passing over it, it died soon after. The ass was fettered at the time, and it was proved that the driver of the wagon was some little distance behind the horses. The learned judge told the jury, that though the act of the plaintiff, in leaving the donkey on the highway so fettered as to prevent his getting out of the way of carriages travelling along it, might be illegal, still, if the proximate cause of the injury was attributable to the want of proper conduct on the part of the driver of the wagon, the action was maintainable against the defendant; and his Lordship directed them, if they thought that the accident might have been avoided by the exercise of ordinary care on the part of the driver, to find for the plaintiff. The jury found their verdict for the plaintiff, damages 40*s*.

Godson now moved for a new trial, on the ground of misdirection. The act of the plaintiff in turning the donkey into the public highway was an illegal one, and, as the injury arose principally from that act, the plaintiff was not entitled to compensation for that injury which, but for his own unlawful act, would never have occurred. [PARKE, B. The declaration states that the ass was lawfully on the highway, and the defendant has not traversed that allegation; therefore it must be taken to be admitted.] The principle of law, as deducible from the cases is, that where an accident is the result of faults on both sides, neither party can maintain an action. Thus, in Butterfield *v.* Forrester, 11 East, 60, it was held that one who is injured by an obstruction on a highway, against which he fell, cannot maintain an action, if it appear that he was riding with great violence and want of ordinary care, without which he might have seen and avoided the obstruction. So, in Vennall *v.* Garner, 1 C. & M. 21, in case for running down a ship, it was held, that neither party can recover when both are in the wrong; and Bayley, B., there says, "I quite agree that if the mischief be the result of the combined negligence of the two, they must both remain in *statu quo*, and neither party can recover against the other." Here the plaintiff, by fettering the donkey, had prevented him from removing himself out of the way of accident; had his fore-feet been free no accident would probably have happened. Pluckwell *v.* Wilson, 5 Car. & P. 375; Luxford *v.* Large, Ibid. 421, and Lynch *v.* Nurdin, 1 Ad. & E. (N. S.) 29 [1]; 4 P. & D. 672, are to the same effect.

LORD ABINGER, C. B. I am of opinion that there ought to be no rule in this case. The defendant has not denied that the ass was lawfully in the highway, and therefore we must assume it to have been

[1] The usual mode of citation is 1 Q. B.

lawfully there; but even were it otherwise, it would have made no difference, for as the defendant might, by proper care, have avoided injuring the animal, and did not, he is liable for the consequences of his negligence, though the animal may have been improperly there.

PARKE, B. This subject was fully considered by this Court in the case of Bridge *v.* The Grand Junction Railway Company, 3 M. & W. 246, where, as appears to me, the correct rule is laid down concerning negligence, namely, that the negligence which is to preclude a plaintiff from recovering in an action of this nature, must be such as that he could, by ordinary care, have avoided the consequences of the defendant's negligence. I am reported to have said in that case, and I believe quite correctly, that "the rule of law is laid down with perfect correctness in the case of Butterfield *v.* Forrester, that, although there may have been negligence on the part of the plaintiff, yet unless he might, by the exercise of ordinary care, have avoided the consequences of the defendant's negligence, he is entitled to recover; if by ordinary care he might have avoided them, he is the author of his own wrong." In that case of Bridge *v.* Grand Junction Railway Company, there was a plea imputing negligence on both sides; here it is otherwise; and the judge simply told the jury, that the mere fact of negligence on the part of the plaintiff in leaving his donkey on the public highway, was no answer to the action, unless the donkey's being there was the immediate cause of the injury; and that, if they were of opinion that it was caused by the fault of the defendant's servant in driving too fast or, which is the same thing, at a smartish pace, the mere fact of putting the ass upon the road would not bar the plaintiff of his action. All that is perfectly correct; for, although the ass may have been wrongfully there, still the defendant was bound to go along the road at such a pace as would be likely to prevent mischief. Were this not so, a man might justify the driving over goods left on a public highway, or even over a man lying asleep there, or the purposely running against a carriage going on the wrong side of the road.

GURNEY, B., and ROLFE, B., concurred. *Rule refused.*[1]

[1] "The other instruction was in these words: 'There is another qualification of this rule of negligence, which it is proper I should mention. Although the rule is that, even if the defendant be shown to have been guilty of negligence, the plaintiff cannot recover if he himself be shown to have been guilty of contributory negligence which may have had something to do in causing the accident; yet the contributory negligence on his part would not exonerate the defendant, and disentitle the plaintiff from recovering, if it be shown that the defendant might, by the exercise of reasonable care and prudence, have avoided the consequences of the plaintiff's negligence.'

"The qualification of the general rule, as thus stated, is supported by decisions of high authority, and was applicable to the case on trial." Gray, J., in Inland Coasting Co. *v.* Tolson, 139 U. S. 551, 558.

"Although the defendant's negligence may have been the primary cause of the injury complained of, yet an action for such injury cannot be maintained if the proximate and immediate cause of the injury can be traced to the want of ordinary care and caution in the person injured; subject to this qualification, which has grown up in recent years (having been first enunciated in Davies *v.* Mann, 10 M.

NORTHERN PACIFIC RAILWAY COMPANY *v.* JONES

UNITED STATES CIRCUIT COURT OF APPEALS, NINTH CIRCUIT, FEBRUARY 5, 1906.

Reported in 144 *Federal Reporter,* 47.

GILBERT, J.[1] . . . The defendant in error was a miner of the age of 34 years, and was in the full possession of his senses. According to his own testimony, he walked upon the railroad track a distance of more than half a mile without once looking back or stopping to listen for an approaching train. In so doing, it must be held that he was guilty of gross negligence, which, irrespective of negligence in the failure of the engineer to discover him on the track, is sufficient to bar his right of recovery. It was no excuse for his failure to take such precautions that the wind was blowing in his face, or that the noise of a waterfall may have deadened the sound of an approaching train. Those circumstances only rendered the use of his senses the more imperative. It was his duty continually to exercise vigilance.

. . . .

On the authority of Inland & Seaboard Coasting Co. *v.* Tolson, 139 U. S. 551–558, 11 Sup. Ct. 653, 35 L. Ed. 270; Grand Trunk Ry. Co. *v.* Ives, 144 U. S. 408–429, 12 Sup. Ct. 679, 36 L. Ed. 485; and Bogan *v.* Carolina Central Ry. Co., 129 N. C. 154, 39 S. E. 808, 55 L. R. A. 418, the defendant in error invokes the doctrine that the contributory negligence of the party injured will not defeat the action, if it be shown that the defendant might, by the exercise of reasonable care and prudence, have avoided the consequences of the injured party's negligence. In the first of these decisions, the doctrine was applied in a case where the plaintiff, a wharfinger, was standing with his foot between the timbers of a wharf, to deliver freight to a vessel which was about to make a landing there, and which struck the wharf with such force as to crush his foot. But the court held that the doctrine was applicable, for the reason that the jury might well have been of opinion that, while there was some negligence on the plaintiff's part in standing where and as he did, yet the officers of the boat knew just where and how he stood, and might have avoided injuring him, if they had used reasonable care to prevent the steamboat from striking the wharf with unusual and unnecessary violence. In the Ives Case, the plaintiff's intestate was killed while attempting to cross a railroad track. There was evidence of negligence on the part of the railroad company. On the part of the plaintiff's intestate there was no evidence as to what precaution he took before placing himself in the place of danger, except that, at a distance of about seventy-six feet from the track, he stopped several minutes, presumably to listen for trains; that while there a train passed; and that, soon after it had passed, and while the noise caused by it was still quite distinct, he proceeded across the track and was struck by another train. The court held that the question of contributory negligence of the plaintiff's intestate was properly left to the jury, as one to be determined under all the circumstances of the

& W. 546) that the contributory negligence of the party injured will not defeat the action if it be shown that the defendant might, by the exercise of reasonable care and prudence, have avoided the consequences of the injured party's negligence." Lamar, J., in Grand Trunk R. Co. *v.* Ives, 144 U. S. 408, 429.

[1] The statement of facts and portions of the opinion are omitted.

case, but incidentally proceeded to affirm the rule above quoted, citing Davies v. Mann, 10 M. & W. 546; Inland & Seaboard Coasting Co. v. Tolson, and other cases. There was no evidence in the Ives Case that the plaintiff's intestate was seen by those who were managing the train in time to have avoided the accident. The court, in that case, however, reaffirmed the rule that a traveller, on going upon a railroad track, ought to make vigilant use of his senses of sight and hearing, and listen for signals, and look in the different directions from which a train might come, and said: —

"If by neglect of this duty he suffers injury from a passing train, he cannot recover of the company, although it may itself be chargeable with negligence, or have failed to give the signals required by statute, or be running at the time at a speed exceeding the legal rate."

It cannot be contended that in the Ives Case the Supreme Court intended to lay down the broad rule that no contributory negligence of the party injured will defeat his right to recover, if it be shown that the defendant might, by the exercise of reasonable care and prudence, have avoided the consequences of that negligence. To so hold would be to destroy the whole doctrine of contributory negligence. As applied to the present case, it would mean that the plaintiff in error was bound to know that the defendant in error was upon its track, and that he would not step aside in time to avoid the train. Such is not the doctrine of cases such as Northern Pacific Railroad v. Freeman [1] and the other decisions which we have cited above. The doctrine of "the last clear chance," so invoked by the defendant in error, originated in Davies v. Mann, in which it was held that the plaintiff's want of ordinary care in that case did not constitute contributory negligence, because it was a remote cause or mere condition of the injury, and did not proximately contribute to it, and because the negligence of the defendant arose subsequently to that of the plaintiff, and the latter's negligence was so obvious as to have been discoverable by the exercise of ordinary care. That doctrine has no application to a case where the plaintiff voluntarily places himself in a place of danger from which he has present means of escape, and continues there without exercising precautions which an ordinarily prudent man would exercise. We have nothing here to do with the law applicable to a case where the injured person is found in a place of danger, as upon a railroad trestle, from which he is powerless to extricate himself on the approach of a train, and where his situation is discovered, or ought to have been discovered, by those in charge of the train.

. . . .

JONES v. CHARLESTON & WESTERN CAROLINA RAILWAY COMPANY

SUPREME COURT, SOUTH CAROLINA, APRIL TERM, 1901.

Reported in 61 *South Carolina Reports*, 556.

ACTION under statute by administrator of Susan V. Jones to recover for her death. Mrs. Jones was killed by a train backing down upon her while she was walking on the railroad track. Plaintiff's evidence tended to show that the track at that place had been accustomed to be used by the public as a walkway with the knowledge and acquiescence of the defendant company. Mrs. Jones,

[1] 174 U. S. 379.

when killed, was on a trestle. The train was backing down behind her, at a speed of from five to ten miles an hour. There was evidence on plaintiff's part that no bell was rung, no whistle blown, no warning given of the approach of the train; also that there was no look-out on the train, and no rear-end lights.

Defendant requested the following instruction (No. 6): —

" Even if the defendant was guilty of negligence in the backing of its train, and such negligence was a proximate cause of the injury, if the jury also believe that the said Susan V. Jones showed a want of ordinary care in walking down the track that night, under all the circumstances, and such carelessness was a proximate cause of the injury, she was guilty of contributory negligence, and the plaintiff would not be entitled to recover."

The judge qualified this instruction by adding: —

" If the deceased, Mrs. Jones, was guilty of negligence in acting as you may find from the testimony that she acted, and if her conduct, her negligence, together with the negligence of the railroad company, contributed to her injury as the proximate cause, then the railroad company would not be responsible, unless the railroad company could have avoided injuring her notwithstanding her negligence."

The judge charged the jury, in accordance with plaintiff's ninth request, as follows: —

" Contributory negligence is a matter of defence, and must be proved by defendant by a preponderance of the evidence; but unless the contributory negligence was the proximate cause of the accident, and if in spite of such contributory negligence the accident could have been avoided by the use of ordinary care on the part of the defendant, then plaintiff is still entitled to recover."

Verdict for plaintiff and judgment thereon. Defendant appealed.[1]

Jones, J. . . . The testimony being undisputed that Mrs. Jones, plaintiff's intestate, was walking down the railroad track at the time of the injury, the defendant was entitled to have the sixth request to charge above mentioned in the tenth exception submitted to the jury as entirely correct. The remarks by the court down to the clause, " unless the railroad company could have avoided injuring her notwithstanding her negligence," were not improper nor inconsistent with the request, but the addition of such qualification was erroneous and wholly inconsistent with the well-settled principles governing contributory negligence. The same error was made in the charge excepted to in the eleventh exception above, when the court instructed the jury, " but unless the contributory negligence was the proximate cause of the accident, and if in spite of *such* contributory negligence (that is, negligence which contributed as a proximate cause), the accident could have been avoided by the use of ordinary care on the part of the defendant, then the plaintiff is still entitled to recover." The charge destroyed the defence of contributory negligence. In *every* case where there is contributory negligence the defendant could have avoided the injury by ordinary care, for the simple reason that there can be no such thing as contributory negligence unless the defendant be negligent. The error complained of is the same error which was condemned in Cooper v. Ry. Co., 56 S. C. 94. The law in this state is settled that contributory negligence as defined in Cooper's case, *supra*, to *any* extent, will *always* defeat plaintiff's

[1] The statement of facts is condensed, and the arguments of counsel and part of the opinion are omitted.

recovery, unless the injury is wantonly or wilfully inflicted; for the law cannot measure how much of the injury is due to the plaintiff's own fault, and will not recompense one for injury resulting to himself from his own misconduct. The objection to the charge is that it instructed the jury that although plaintiff's negligence contributed to her injury as a proximate cause, she could recover if the defendant by ordinary care could have avoided the injury. Is it not manifest that such a rule would abolish contributory negligence as a defence? The qualifying terms, "unless the railroad company could have avoided injuring her notwithstanding her negligence," would necessarily mislead a jury; for they would at once say the railroad company could have avoided the injury by not being negligent in the manner alleged in the complaint, by having suitable rear end lights, by a reasonable lookout, by loud warning of the train's approach, by running at such slow speed as to enable any one warned to get off the track; and then utterly ignore the defendant's plea and evidence of contributory negligence, because of the instruction that plaintiff, notwithstanding her negligence which proximately caused her injury, could still recover, if the defendant could have avoided the injury. The jury ought to have been instructed without qualification, that if plaintiff was negligent and that negligence contributed as a proximate cause to her injury, she could not recover, unless the injury was wantonly or wilfully inflicted.

The judgment of the Circuit Court is reversed, and the case remanded for a new trial.

CORDINER *v.* LOS ANGELES TRACTION COMPANY

District Court of Appeals, Second District, California, April 16, 1907.

Reported in 4 *California Appellate Decisions*, 480.

Shaw, J. Neither of the defendants questioned the right of plaintiff to recover such damages as she had sustained in the collision, but each contended that the other should be held responsible therefor; and with the view of having the jury pass upon the question, the Los Angeles Railway Company asked the court to instruct the jury, in effect, that notwithstanding the negligence of its motorman in driving his car upon the crossing, still if the traction motorman could, after he saw that it was beyond the power of the motorman of the Los Angeles Railway car to avoid the accident, have, by proper care, prevented the collision, then the negligence of the defendant Los Angeles Traction Company was the proximate cause of the injury. In other words, while admitting that plaintiff's injury resulted from the collison due to the joint or concurrent acts of negligence of defendants, she must be confined in her recovery for such damages to a judgment rendered against the defendant who had the "last clear chance" to avoid the collision and neglected to act upon it. Appellant seeks to apply the well-established principle that "he who last has a clear opportunity of avoiding the accident, by the exercise of proper care to avoid injuring another, must do so." Esrey *v.* S. Pacific Co., 103 Cal. 541. This rule is only applicable to cases where the defence is based upon the contributory negligence of plaintiff due to his want of care in placing himself in a position of danger, and where he may, notwithstanding his negligence, recover from a defendant, who by the exercise of proper care could have avoided the injury. We are unable to perceive why this rule should apply to plaintiff, who was in no way chargeable, by imputation or otherwise, with negligence; nor are we referred to any authority which supports the proposition. Indeed, all the authorities recognize the right of recovery against either or both of the defendants whose concurring acts of negligence united in producing the injury. 1 Shearman & Redfield on Neg. p. 122; 1 Thompson on Neg. p. 75; Doeg *v.* Cook, 126 Cal. 213; Tompkins *v.* Clay St. Ry. Co., 66 Cal. 163; Pastene *v.* Adams, 49 Cal. 87.[1]

STILES *v.* GEESEY

SUPREME COURT, PENNSYLVANIA, MAY 30, 1872.

Reported in 71 *Pennsylvania State Reports,* 439.

BEFORE THOMPSON, C. J., READ, AGNEW, SHARSWOOD and WILLIAMS, JJ.

Error to the Court of Common Pleas of York County.

Action on the case by Jacob B. Geesey against Thomas Stiles, for alleged injury by the negligence of William Stiles, son of defendant, by which plaintiff's horse and carriage were damaged.[2]

Plaintiff's wife, driving in a light carriage of plaintiff's, hitched her horse to a tree on the road, and went into a friend's house. The carriage projected into the travelled part of the road. Whilst the carriage was so left, the defendant's son, William Stiles, was driving his father's team with a loaded wagon along the road. He got off to do something to his wagon; and seeing an acquaintance in a neighboring barn, stopped a moment to exchange a few words with him, the team moving on slowly at the time with the load up the hill, keeping the travelled track of the road till the front horse was just behind plaintiff's carriage standing unattended where it was left. At this point of time William Stiles was behind his own wagon, at some distance from it; and did not see the obstruction in the road in time to avoid a collision. The wagon collided with the carriage. Stiles halloed "Whoa," and his horses stopped. In the collision, the plaintiff's horse was fatally injured.

The third point of the plaintiff, which was affirmed in the charge to the jury by Fisher, P. J., is as follows: —

"That Thomas Stiles cannot excuse the negligence of William Stiles by showing that the plaintiff's property was placed where it received the injury by want of ordinary care by Mrs. Geesey, if, in the opinion of the jury such want is imputable to her, should the jury believe that William Stiles was chargeable with negligence in leaving his team and permitting it to go along the highway unattended."

Verdict for plaintiff.

[1] Only a portion of the opinion is printed.

[2] The statement of facts is abridged from the statement in the opinion and from the statement made by the reporter. The citations of counsel are omitted.

READ, J. [After stating the facts.] We have taken in brief, the defendant's statement of his defence, which fairly raises the question of contributory negligence. " It is an incontestable principle that where the injury complained of is the product of mutual or concurring negligence, no action for damages will lie. The parties being mutually in fault there can be no apportionment of the damages. The law has no scales to determine in such cases whose wrong-doing weighed most in the compound that occasioned the mischief: " per Woodward, J., 12 Harris, 469.

" The question presented to the Court or the jury is never one of comparative negligence, as between the parties; nor does very great negligence on the part of a defendant so operate to strike a balance of negligence as to give a judgment to a plaintiff whose own negligence contributes in any degree to the injury." Wilds *v.* Hudson River Railroad Co., 24 N. Y. 432.

The third error assigned is that the Court erred in their charge to the jury on the plaintiff's third point, which was as follows: " That Thomas Stiles cannot excuse the negligence of William Stiles by showing that the plaintiff's property was placed where it received the injury, by want of ordinary care by Mrs. Geesey, if in the opinion of the jury such want is imputable to her, should the jury believe William Stiles was chargeable with negligence, in leaving his team and permitting it to go along the highway unattended," which point the Court affirmed, holding that although there was contributory negligence on the part of the plaintiff, he was entitled to recover from the defendant on account of his negligence. This was a binding instruction upon the jury, leaving nothing for them to inquire into practically, except the negligence of the defendant. In this the Court committed a clear error, and the judgment must be reversed, and *venire de novo* awarded.

RADLEY *v.* LONDON AND NORTH WESTERN RAILWAY COMPANY

IN THE HOUSE OF LORDS, DECEMBER 1, 1876.

Reported in Law Reports, 1 Appeal Cases, 754.

THIS was an appeal against a decision of the Court of Exchequer Chamber.

The appellants were the plaintiffs in an action brought in the Court of Exchequer, in which they claimed to recover damages for the destruction of a bridge occasioned, as they alleged, by the negligence of the defendants' servants. The plaintiffs were owners of the Sankey Brook Colliery, in the county of Lancaster, which was situated near a branch line of the defendants' railway. There was a siding belonging to the plaintiffs, which communicated with the railway, and the defendants' servants were in the habit of taking trucks loaded with coals from this siding, in order to run them on the railway to forward them to their destination, and also of bringing back empty trucks and running them from the railway on to the siding. On Saturday after working hours, when all the colliery men had gone away, the defendants' servants ran some of the plaintiffs' empty trucks from the railway upon the siding and there left them. In that position they remained. One of the watchmen employed by the plaintiffs knew that they were there, but nothing was done to remove them to a different place. In the first of these trucks had been placed a truck which had broken down, and the height of the two trucks combined was nearly eleven feet. There was, in advance of the spot where the trucks had been left, a bridge placed over a part of the siding, the span of which bridge was about eight feet from the ground. On Sunday afternoon the defendants' servants brought a long line of empty trucks belonging to the plaintiffs, and ran them on the line of the siding, pushing on the first set of trucks in front. Some resistance was perceived, and the pushing force of the engine employed was increased, and the result was, as the two trucks at the head of the line could not pass under the bridge, they struck with great force against it and broke it down.[1] For the damage thereby occasioned this action was brought. The defence was contributory negligence; it being insisted that the plaintiffs ought to have moved the first set of trucks to a safe place, or at all events, not to have left the truck with the disabled truck in it so as to be likely to occasion mischief. At the trial before Mr. Justice Brett, at the Summer Assizes at Liverpool, in 1873, the learned judge told the jury that "you must be satisfied that the plaintiffs' servants did not do anything which persons of ordinary care, under the circumstances, would not do, or that they omitted to do something which persons of ordinary care would do. . . . It is for you to say entirely as to both points; but the law is this, the plaintiffs must have satisfied you that this happened by the negligence of the defendants' servants, and without any contributory negligence of their own, in other words that it was solely by the negligence of the defendants' servants. If you think it was, then your verdict will be for the plaintiffs. If you think it was not solely by the negligence of the defendants' servants, your verdict must be for the defendants."[2] The jurors having, on this direction, stated that they thought there was contributory negligence on the part of the plaintiffs, the learned judge directed that the verdict should be entered for the defendants, but reserved leave for the plaintiffs to move.

[1] ". . . The wagon so loaded coming to the bridge and being unable to pass underneath it, the train stopped, and those who had charge of it, without looking to ascertain the cause of the stoppage, gave momentum to the engine to such an extent that the wagon with its load knocked the bridge down." Statement of facts in opinion of Bramwell, B., L. R. 9 Exch. 72. Compare statement in L. R. 10 Exch. 102.

[2] Printed papers in the case.

A rule having been obtained for a new trial, it was after argument before Barons Bramwell and Amphlett made absolute.[1] On appeal to the Exchequer Chamber the decision was, by Justices Blackburn, Mellor, Lush, Brett, and Archibald (*diss.* Justice Denman), reversed.[2] This appeal was then brought.[3]

LORD PENZANCE. My Lords, the action out of which this appeal arises is an action charging the defendants with negligence (through their servants) in so managing the shunting of some empty coal-wagons as to knock down a bridge and some staging and some colliery head-gearing, which stood upon it, and belonged to the plaintiffs.

The first question on the appeal is, whether the Court of Exchequer Chamber was right in holding that there was any evidence, proper to be submitted to the jury, tending to the conclusion that the plaintiffs themselves had been guilty of some negligence in the matter, and that such negligence had contributed to produce the accident and injury of which they complained.

The general facts of the case, the particular facts which gave rise to the imputation of negligence, and the contention of both sides as to the fair result of these facts, are stated in the judgment of the Court of Exchequer delivered by Baron Bramwell. His Lordship here read the statement from Mr. Baron Bramwell's judgment.[4]

It may be admitted that this is a fair and full statement of the arguments and considerations on the one side, and on the other, upon which the question of the plaintiffs' negligence had to be decided. But it had to be decided by the jurors, and not by the Court, and I am unable to perceive any reason why the learned judge did wrong in submitting these arguments and considerations to their decision accordingly. The bare statement of them is enough to show that there were in the case facts and circumstances sufficient at least to raise the question of negligence, whether they were a sufficient proof of negligence or not.

The decision, therefore, of the Exchequer Chamber upon this matter ought, I think, to be upheld.

The remaining question is whether the learned judge properly directed the jury in point of law. The law in these cases of negligence is, as was said in the Court of Exchequer Chamber, perfectly well settled and beyond dispute.

The first proposition is a general one, to this effect, that the plaintiff in an action for negligence cannot succeed if it is found by the jury that he has himself been guilty of any negligence or want of ordinary care which contributed to cause the accident.

But there is another proposition equally well established, and it is a qualification upon the first, namely, that though the plaintiff may have been guilty of negligence, and although that negligence may, in

[1] L. R. 9 Ex. 71.
[2] L. R. 10 Ex. 700.
[3] Arguments of counsel are omitted.
[4] L. R. 9 Ex. at 72.

fact, have contributed to the accident, yet if the defendant could in the result, by the exercise of ordinary care and diligence, have avoided the mischief which happened, the plaintiffs' negligence will not excuse him.

This proposition, as one of law, cannot be questioned. It was decided in the case of Davies *v.* Mann, 10 M. & W. 546, supported in that of Tuff *v.* Warman, 5 C. B. (N. S.) 573; 27 L. J. C. P. 322, and other cases, and has been universally applied in cases of this character without question.

The only point for consideration, therefore, is whether the learned judge properly presented it to the mind of the jury.

It seems impossible to say that he did so. At the beginning of his summing-up he laid down the following as the propositions of law which governed the case: It is for the plaintiffs to satisfy you that this accident happened through the negligence of the defendants' servants, and as between them and the defendants, that it was solely through the negligence of the defendants' servants. They must satisfy you that it was solely by the negligence of the defendants' servants, or, in other words, that there was no negligence on the part of their servants contributing to the accident; so that, if you think that both sides were negligent, so as to contribute to the accident, then the plaintiffs cannot recover.

This language is perfectly plain and perfectly unqualified, and in case the jurors thought there was any contributory negligence on the part of the plaintiffs' servants, they could not, without disregarding the direction of the learned judge, have found in the plaintiffs' favor, however negligent the defendants had been, or however easily they might with ordinary care have avoided any accident at all.

The learned judge then went on to describe to the jury what it was that might properly be considered to constitute negligence, first in the conduct of the defendants, and then in the conduct of the plaintiffs; and having done this, he again reverted to the governing propositions of law, as follows: " There seem to be two views. It is for you to say entirely as to both points. But the law is this, the plaintiff must have satisfied you that this happened by the negligence of the defendants' servants, and without any contributory negligence of their own; in other words, that it was solely by the negligence of the defendants' servants. If you think it was, then your verdict will be for the plaintiffs. If you think it was not solely by the negligence of the defendants' servants, your verdict must be for the defendants."

This, again, is entirely without qualification, and the undoubted meaning of it is, that if there was any contributory negligence on the part of the plaintiffs, they could in no case recover. Such a statement of the law is contrary to the doctrine established in the case of Davies *v.* Mann, 10 M. & W. 546, and the other cases above alluded to, and in no part of the summing-up is that doctrine anywhere to be found.

The learned counsel were unable to point out any passage addressed to it.

It is true that in part of his summing-up the learned judge pointed attention to the conduct of the engine-driver, in determining to force his way by violence through the obstruction, as fit to be considered by the jury on the question of negligence; but he failed to add that if they thought the engine-driver might at this stage of the matter by ordinary care have avoided all accident, any previous negligence of the plaintiffs would not preclude them from recovering.

In point of fact the evidence was strong to show that this was the immediate cause of the accident, and the jury might well think that ordinary care and diligence on the part of the engine-driver would, notwithstanding any previous negligence of the plaintiffs in leaving the loaded-up truck on the line, have made the accident impossible. This substantial defect of the learned judge's charge is that that question was never put to the jury.

On this point, therefore, I propose to move that your Lordships should reverse the decision of the Exchequer Chamber, and direct a new trial.

The Lord Chancellor (Lord Cairns). My Lords, I have had the advantage of considering the opinion which has just been expressed to your Lordships in this case by my noble and learned friend, and, concurring as I do with every word of it, I do not think it is necessary that I should do more than say that I hope your Lordships will agree to the motion which he has proposed.

Lord Blackburn. My Lords, I agree entirely with the noble Lord who has first spoken as to what were the proper questions for the jury in this case, and that they were not decided by the jury. I am inclined to think that the learned judge did in part of his summing-up sufficiently ask the proper questions, had they been answered, but unfortunately he failed to have an answer from the jury to those questions, it appearing by the case that the only finding was as to the plaintiffs' negligence.

I agree, therefore, in the result that there should be a new trial.

Lord Gordon. My Lords, I entirely concur in the motion which has been submitted to your Lordships by my noble and learned friend on the other side of the House. The question is one which has given rise to some difficulty in the courts of Scotland, but I think that it is very likely that the opinion which has been expressed in this case will be regarded as a very useful authority for guiding their decisions.[1]

Judgment of the Court of Exchequer Chamber reversed. Judgment of the Court of Exchequer restored, and a new trial ordered, with costs.

Lords' Journals, December 1, 1876.

[1] See also Cayzer *v.* Carron, 9 App. Cas. 873; McDermaid *v.* Edinburgh Tramways Co., 22 Sc. L. R. 13.

NASHUA IRON AND STEEL CO. *v.* WORCESTER & NASHUA RAILROAD CO.

SUPREME COURT, NEW HAMPSHIRE, JUNE, 1882.

Reported in 62 *New Hampshire Reports,* 159.

CASE. Demurrer to the declaration.

CARPENTER, J. The declaration alleges that by the defendants' careless management of their engine and cars, the plaintiffs' horse was frightened, and caused to run upon and injure Ursula Clapp, who was without fault; that Clapp brought her action therefor against the plaintiffs, and recovered judgment for damages, which they paid; that the defendants had notice of, and were requested to defend, the suit. The defendants demur. Inasmuch as Clapp could not have recovered against the plaintiffs unless they were in fault (Brown *v.* Collins, 53 N. H. 442; Lyons *v.* Child, 61 N. H. 72), it must be taken that their negligence co-operated with that of the defendants to produce the injury. If the plaintiffs were not liable in that action because their negligence was not, and the defendants' negligence was, the cause of the accident, the objection is not now open to the defendants. Littleton *v.* Richardson, 34 N. H. 179. In relation to Clapp, both parties were wrong-doers. She could pursue her remedy against either or both of them at her election. Burrows *v.* March Gas Co., L. R. 5 Ex. 67, 71.

One of several wrong-doers, who has been compelled to pay the damages caused by the wrong, has in general no remedy against the others. He cannot make his own misconduct the ground of an action in his favor. To this proposition there are, it has been said, so many exceptions, that it can hardly, with propriety, be called a general rule. Bailey *v.* Bussing, 28 Conn. 455. Its application is restricted to cases where the person seeking redress knew, or is presumed to have known, that the act for which he has been mulcted in damages was unlawful. Jacobs *v.* Pollard, 10 Cush. 287, 289; Coventry *v.* Barton, 17 Johns. 142. In many instances several parties may be liable in law to the person injured, while as between themselves some of them are not wrong-doers at all; and the equity of the guiltless to require the actual wrong-doer to respond for all the damages, and the equally innocent to contribute his proportion, is complete. Wooley *v.* Batte, 2 C. & P. 417; Pearson *v.* Skelton, 1 M. & W. 504; Betts *v.* Gibbins, 2 A. & E. 57; Adamson *v.* Jarvis, 4 Bing. 66; Avery *v.* Halsey, 14 Pick. 174; Gray *v.* Boston Gas Light Co., 114 Mass. 149; Churchill *v.* Holt, 127 Mass. 165, and 131 Mass. 67; Bailey *v.* Bussing, *supra;* Smith *v.* Foran, 43 Conn. 244. These cases, instead of being exceptions to the rule, seem rather not to fall within it. The right of recovery rests in the one case upon the principle that he who without fault on his part is injured by another's wrongful act is entitled to indemnity, and in the other upon the doctrine of contribution. One of two masters, who is compelled to pay damages by reason of his servant's negligence, may have contribution from the other because he has removed a burden common to both. They may recover indemnity of the servant, because as against him they are without fault, and are directly injured by his misconduct. One who is so far innocent that he can recover for an injury to his person or property, may also recover whatever sum he, by reason of his relation to the wrong, has been compelled to pay to a third person. If the plaintiffs could recover for an injury to their horse, caused by the accident, they may recover the sum which they paid to Clapp.

The declaration is general. It does not disclose the particulars of the plaintiffs' negligence, by reason of which Clapp recovered against them. Under it, cases differing widely in their facts and legal aspects may be proved. Among others possible, it may be shown that the horse was in the charge of the plaintiffs' servants, who might have prevented its fright or its running after the fright, or if they could do neither, that they might nevertheless have avoided the injury to Clapp; or it may appear that the plaintiffs' negligence consisted solely in permitting the horse, whether attended or unattended by their servants, to be at the place where it was at the time of the fright. The generality of the declaration does not render it bad in law. Corey *v.* Bath, 35 N. H. 531. If the plaintiffs are entitled to judgment upon any state of facts provable under it, the demurrer must be overruled. Whether the plaintiffs can recover in any case, and if so, in what cases, possible to be proved under the declaration, are speculative or hypothetical questions, of which none may, and all cannot, arise. They involve substantially the whole subject of the law relating to mutual negligence. The case might properly be discharged without considering them (Smith *v.* Cudworth, 24 Pick. 196), and the parties required to present by the pleadings, or by a verdict, the facts upon which their rights depend. A brief consideration, however, of the general questions involved, may, it is thought, facilitate a trial, and save expense to the parties.

Ordinary care is such care as persons of average prudence exercise under like circumstances. Tucker *v.* Henniker, 41 N. H. 317; Sleeper *v.* Sandown, 52 N. H. 244; Aldrich *v.* Monroe, 60 N. H. 118. Every one in the conduct of his lawful business is bound to act with this degree of care, and if he fails to do so is responsible for the consequences. It follows that a person injured by reason of his want of ordinary care, or (since the law makes no apportionment between actual wrongdoers) by the joint operation of his own and another's negligence, is remediless. This general rule of law justly applied to the facts determines, it is believed, the rights of the parties in all actions for negligence. In its application, the law, as in various other cases, deals with the immediate cause, — the cause as distinguished from the occasion,

— and looks at the natural and reasonably to be expected effects. Cowles *v.* Kidder, 24 N. H. 383; Hooksett *v.* Company, 44 N. H. 108; McIntire *v.* Plaisted, 57 N. H. 608; Solomon *v.* Chesley, 59 N. H. 243; China *v.* Southwick, 12 Me. 238; Lowery *v.* Western U. Tel. Co., 60 N. Y. 198; Rigby *v.* Hewitt, 5 Exch. 243; Blyth *v.* Birmingham Waterworks Co., 11 Exch. 781; Bank of Ireland *v.* Evans's Charities, 5 H. L. Ca. 389, 410, 411; Ionides *v.* Marine Ins. Co., 14 C. B. N. S. 259; Romney Marsh *v.* Trinity House, L. R. 5 Ex. 204; Holmes *v.* Mather, L. R. 10 Ex. 268; Sharp *v.* Powell, L. R. 7 C. P. 253; Pearson v. Cox, 2 C. P. Div. 369; Tutein *v.* Hurley, 98 Mass. 211; Bro. Leg. Max. 215.

Actions for negligence may, for convenience of consideration, be separated into four classes, namely, — where, upon the occasion of the injury complained of (1) the plaintiff, (2) the defendant, or (3) neither party was present, and (4) where both parties were present. In all of them it may happen that both parties were more or less negligent. Actions upon the statute of highways are a common example of the first class. The negligence of the defendant, however great, does not relieve the plaintiff from the duty of exercising ordinary care. If, notwithstanding the defective condition of the highway, this degree of care on the part of the plaintiff would prevent the accident, his and not the defendant's negligence, though but for the latter it could not happen, is, in the eye of the law, its sole cause. Farnum *v.* Concord, 2 N. H. 394; Butterfield *v.* Forrester, 11 East, 60. In this class of cases, an injury which the plaintiff's negligence contributes to produce could not happen without it. The not uncommon statement that the plaintiff cannot recover if his negligence contributes in any degree to cause the injury, is strictly correct, although the word "contribute" may be, as Crompton, J., in Tuff *v.* Warman, 5 C. B. N. S. 584, says it is, "a very unsafe word to use," and "much too loose." The result is the same whether the plaintiff acts with full knowledge of the danger, or, by reason of a want of proper care, fails to discover it seasonably. If he is not bound to anticipate, and in advance provide for, another's negligence, he may not wilfully or negligently shut his eyes against its possibility. He is bound to be informed of everything which ordinary care would disclose to him. He can no more recover for an injury caused by driving into a dangerous pit, of which he is ignorant, but of which ordinary care would have informed him, than for one caused by carelessly driving into a known pit. Norris *v.* Litchfield, 35 N. H. 271; Clark *v.* Barrington, 41 N. H. 44; Tucker *v.* Henniker, 41 N. H. 317; Winship *v.* Enfield, 42 N. H. 213, 214; Underhill *v.* Manchester, 45 N. H. 220.

The defendant's negligence being found or conceded, the remaining question is, whether the plaintiff, by the exercise of ordinary care, could have escaped the injury. If he could not, he is free from fault, and is entitled to recover. If he could, he not only cannot recover for his own injury, but is himself liable to the other party, if the latter is injured; and the case becomes one of the second class, of which Davies *v*. Mann, 10 M. & W. 546, is an instance. The defendant is liable here for the same reason that, as plaintiff, he could not recover, — that is to say, because ordinary care on his part would have prevented the injury. The fact that one has carelessly exposed his property in a dangerous situation does not absolve his neighbors from the obligation of conducting themselves in regard to it with ordinary care. An injury which that degree of care would prevent is caused by the want of it, and not by the owner's negligence in leaving his property in a perilous position. A surgeon, called to set a leg carelessly broken, cannot successfully urge, in answer to a suit for mal-practice, that the patient's negligence in breaking his leg caused the crooked or shortened limb. Lannen *v*. Albany Gas-light Co., 44 N. Y. 459, 463; Hibbard *v*. Thompson, 109 Mass. 286, 289. So far as the question of civil liability is concerned, there is no distinction, except it may be in the measure of damages (Fay *v*. Parker, 53 N. H. 342, Bixby *v*. Dunlap, 56 N. H. 456), between wilful and negligent wrongs. One who, without reasonable necessity, kills his neighbor's ox, found trespassing in his field, is equally liable whether he does it purposely or carelessly. Aldrich *v*. Wright, 53 N. H. 398; McIntire *v*. Plaisted, 57 N. H. 606; Cool. Torts, 688–694. Mann would be no more liable for wilfully shooting the fettered ass which Davies has carelessly left in the public highway, than he is for the running over it, which, by ordinary care, he could avoid. The owner's negligence, in permitting the ox to stray and in leaving the ass fettered in the street, although without it the injury would not happen, is no more the cause, in a legal sense, of the negligent than of the wilful wrong. In each case alike, — as in that of the broken leg, — it merely affords the wrong-doer an opportunity to do the mischief. Bartlett *v*. Boston Gas-light Co., 117 Mass. 533; Clayards *v*. Dethick, 12 Q. B. 439, 445.

Knowledge, or its equivalent, culpable ignorance, and ignorance without fault of the situation, are circumstances by which, among others, the requisite measure of vigilance is determined. Griffin *v*. Auburn, 58 N. H. 121, 124; Palmer *v*. Dearing, 93 N. Y. 7; Robinson *v*. Cone, 22 Vt. 213. The question of contributory negligence is not involved. The wrong, if any, is the negligent injury of property carelessly exposed to danger. The only question is, whether the defendant could have prevented it by ordinary care. If he could not, he is without fault, and not liable. If he could, his negligence is, in law, the sole cause of the injury. Davies *v*. Mann, 10 M. & W. 546; Radley *v*. London, &c. Railway, 1 App. Ca. 754; Mayor of Colchester *v*. Brooke, 7 Q. B. 377; Isbell *v*. N. Y. & N. H. Railroad, 27 Conn. 393; Trow *v*. Vt. Central Railroad, 24 Vt. 487; Harlan *v*. St. Louis, &c. Railroad, 64 Mo. 480; Kerwhacker *v*. Cleveland, &c. Railroad, 3 Ohio St. 172.

The law is not affected by the presence or the absence of the parties, nor by the difficulty of applying it to complicated facts. To warrant a recovery where both parties are present at the time of the injury, as well as in other cases, ability on the part of the defendant must concur with non-ability on the part of the plaintiff to prevent it by ordinary care. Their duty to exercise this degree of care is equal and reciprocal; neither is exonerated from his obligation by the present or previous misconduct of the other. The law no more holds one responsible for an unavoidable, or justifies an avoidable, injury to the person of one who carelessly exposes himself to danger, than to his property, similarly situated in his absence. He who cannot prevent an injury negligently inflicted upon his person or property by an intelligent agent, " present and acting at the time " (State *v.* Railroad, 52 N. H. 528, 557; White *v.* Winnisimmet Co., 7 Cush. 155, 157; Robinson *v.* Cone, 22 Vt. 213), is legally without fault, and it is immaterial whether his inability results from his absence, previous negligence, or other cause. On the other hand, his neglect to prevent it, if he can, is the sole or co-operating cause of the injury. No one can justly complain of another's negligence, which, but for his own wrongful interposition, would be harmless. Parker *v.* Adams, 12 Met. 415.

Cases of this class assume a great variety of aspects. While all are governed by the fundamental principle, that he only who by ordinary care can and does not prevent an injury, is responsible in damages, it is impossible to formulate a rule in language universally applicable. A statement of the law correct in its application to one state of facts may be inaccurate when applied to another. Instructions to the jury proper and sufficient in a case of the first class, would be not only inappropriate but incorrect in one of the second class. The doctrine laid down in Tuff *v.* Warman, 5 C. B. N. S. 573, 585, however just and well suited to the evidence in that case, was held erroneous as applied to the facts in Murphy *v.* Deane, 101 Mass. 455, 464–466, and, as a general proposition, seems indefensible.

An accident may result from a hazardous situation caused by the previous negligence of one or both parties. If, at the time of the injury, the defendant is unable to remove the danger which his negligence has created, the case becomes, in substance, one of the first class; the plaintiff can recover or not, according as, by ordinary care, he can or cannot protect himself from the natural consequences of the situation. If the plaintiff, in like manner, is unable to obviate the danger which his prior negligence has produced, the case becomes, substantially, one of the second class; he can recover or not, according as the defendant, by the same degree of care, can or cannot avoid the natural consequences of such negligence. If due care on the part of either at the time of the injury would prevent it, the antecedent negligence of one or both parties is immaterial, except it may be as one of the circumstances by which the requisite measure of care is to be determined. In such a case the law deals with their behavior in the situation in which it finds them at the time the mischief is done, regardless of their prior misconduct. The latter is *incuria*, but not *incuria dans locum injuriae*, — it is the cause of the danger; the former is the cause of the injury. Metropolitan Railway *v.* Jackson, 3 App. Ca. 193, 198; Dublin, &c. Railway *v.* Slattery, 3 App. Ca. 1155, 1166; Davey *v.* London, &c. Railway, 12 Q. B. Div. 70, 76; Churchill *v.* Rosebeck, 15 Conn. 359, 363–365.

If a person, who by his carelessness is put in a position perilous to himself and to others, while in that position does all that a person of average prudence could, he is guilty of no wrong towards another who embraces the opportunity negligently to injure him, or who receives an injury which proper care on his part would prevent. It would doubtless be esteemed gross carelessness to navigate the Atlantic in a vessel without a rudder, but if the owner, while sailing his rudderless ship with ordinary care, is negligently run down by a steamer, the latter must pay the damages, and can recover none if it is injured. Dowell *v.* Steam Navigation Co., 5 E. & B. 195; Haley *v.* Earle, 30 N. Y. 208; Hoffman *v.* Union Ferry Co., 47 N. Y. 176. If the vessel, by reason of its lack of a rudder, runs upon and injures the steamer, both being in the exercise of ordinary care at the time, the former must pay the damages. He who by his negligence has produced a dangerous situation is responsible for an injury resulting from it to one who is without fault.

If, at the time of the injury, each of the parties, or, in the absence of antecedent negligence, if neither of them could prevent it by ordinary care, there can be no recovery. The comparatively rare cases of simultaneous negligence will ordinarily fall under one or the other of these heads. If the accident results from the combined effect of the negligence of both parties, that of neither alone being sufficient to produce it, proof by the plaintiff that due care on the part of the defendant would have prevented it will not entitle him to recover, because like care on his own part would have had the same effect. If the misconduct of each party is an adequate cause of the injury, so that it would have occurred by reason of either's negligence without the co-operating fault of the other, proof by the plaintiff that by due care he could not have prevented it will not entitle him to recover, because no more could the defendant have prevented it by like care. Murphy *v.* Deane, 101 Mass. 464, 465; Churchill *v.* Holt, 131 Mass. 67. In each case alike they are equally in fault. To warrant a recovery, the plaintiff must establish both propositions, namely, that by ordinary care he could not, and the defendant could, have prevented the injury. State *v.* Railroad, 52 N. H. 528; Bridge *v.* Grand Junction Railway, 3 M. & W. 244; Dowell *v.* Steam Navigation Co., 5 E. & B. 195; Tuff *v.* Warman, 5 C. B. N. S. 573; Davey *v.* London, &c. Railway, 12 Q. B. Div. 70; Munroe *v.* Leach, 7 Met. 274; Lucas *v.* New Bedford,

&c. Railroad, 6 Gray, 64; Murphy *v.* Deane, 101 Mass. 455; Hall *v.* Ripley, 119 Mass. 135; Button *v.* Hudson, &c. Railroad, 18 N. Y. 248; Austin *v.* N. J. Steamboat Co., 43 N. Y. 75; Barker *v.* Savage, 45 N. Y. 194; Cool. Torts, 674, 675, and cases cited.

In the comparatively unfrequent cases of the third class, a negligent plaintiff can seldom, if ever, recover. Where both parties are careless, they are usually, if not always, equally in fault; ordinary care on the part of either would prevent the injury. Not being present on the occasion of the accident, neither can, in general, guard against the consequences of the other's negligence. Blyth *v.* Topham, Cro. Jac. 158; Sybray *v.* White, 1 M. & W. 435; Williams *v.* Groucott, 4 B. & S. 149; Lee *v.* Riley, 18 C. B. N. S. 722; Wilson *v.* Newberry, L. R. 7 Q. B. 31; Lawrence *v.* Jenkins, L. R. 8 Q. B. 274; Firth *v.* Bowling Iron Co., 3 C. P. Div. 254; Crowhurst *v.* Amersham Burial Board, 4 Ex. Div. 5; Bush *v.* Brainard, 1 Cow. 78; Lyons *v.* Merrick, 105 Mass. 71; Page *v.* Olcott, 13 N. H. 399.

If there are actions for negligence of such a character that the rights of the parties are not determinable by the application of these principles, the present case is not one of them. If, notwithstanding the defendants' negligence, the plaintiffs, by ordinary care, could have prevented the fright of the horse, or its running, after the fright, or, in the absence of ability to do either, if they could have avoided the running upon and injury to Clapp, their misconduct, and not that of the defendants, was the cause of the accident, and they cannot recover. On the other hand, if the plaintiffs' carelessness consisted solely in permitting the horse to be where it was at the time, and ordinary care by the defendants would have prevented its fright, or, if the plaintiffs, by proof of any state of facts competent to be shown under the declaration, can make it appear that at the time of the occurrence they could not, and the defendants could, by such care have prevented the accident, they are entitled to recover. *Demurrer overruled.*

OATES *v.* METROPOLITAN STREET RAILWAY COMPANY

SUPREME COURT, MISSOURI, MAY 21, 1902.

Reported in 168 *Missouri Reports*, 535, 547–549.

MARSHALL, J. . . . Instructions three and seven given for the defendant sharply drew a distinction between the negligence of the defendant and the contributory negligence of the plaintiff. Those instructions declared the law to be that the defendant was not liable unless its negligence was the direct cause of the injury, while the plaintiff was not entitled to recover if his negligence " but contributes to the injury." That is, that the defendant was liable only for direct negligence, while the plaintiff was cut off from recovery if he was guilty of any negligence, however slight or remote or indirect it may have been.

The law is that a defendant is liable if his negligence was the direct and proximate cause of the injury, unless the plaintiff has also been guilty of such negligence as directly contributed to the happening of the injury, and the defendant is not liable no matter how negligent he may have been if the plaintiff's negligence has thus contributed to the injury, for the doctrine of comparative negligence has never obtained in this State. Hurt *v.* Railroad, 94 Mo. 264. In each instance the negligence and the contributory negligence must be direct, that is, must have entered into and formed a part of the efficient cause of the accident. Hoepper *v.* Hotel Co., 142 Mo. 388; Beach on Contr. Neg. (2 ed.), sec. 24; Matthews *v.* Toledo, 21 Ohio Cir. Ct. Rep. 69; Dunkman *v.* Railroad, 16 Mo. App. 548; Corcoran *v.* Railroad, 105 Mo. 399; Murray *v.* Railroad, 101 Mo. 236; Kellny *v.* Railroad, 101 Mo. 67; Hicks *v.* Railroad, 46 Mo. App. 403; Pinnell *v.* Railroad, 49 Mo. App. 170; Meyers *v.* Railroad, 59 Mo. 223.

Mere negligence, without any resulting damage, no more bars a plaintiff's recovery than it creates a liability against a defendant. Dickson *v.* Railroad, 124 Mo. 140. Remote negligence which does not become an efficient cause, neither creates nor bars a liability. Kennedy *v.* Railroad, 36 Mo. 351; Meyers *v.* Railroad, 59 Mo. 223. It is only where the plaintiff's negligence contributes directly to his injury that it precludes his recovery therefor. Moore *v.* Railroad, 126 Mo. 265. And the plaintiff's contributory negligence must mingle with the defendant's negligence as a direct and proximate cause in order to bar a recovery. Nolan *v.* Shickle, 69 Mo. 336; Frick *v.* Railroad, 75 Mo. 542.

These instructions were, therefore, erroneous, and as the jury was misdirected and as the plaintiff had made out a *prima facie* case, he was entitled to have the law properly declared to the jury, and the trial court did right in granting a new trial.[1]

CARPENTER, J., IN NIEBOER *v.* DETROIT ELECTRIC RAILWAY

(1901) 128 *Michigan*, 486, 491, 492.[2]

CARPENTER, J. ". . . The law by which it is determined whether or not the contributory negligence of the plaintiff bars recovery is very uncertain. The adjudicated cases are by no means harmonious, and there is an irreconcilable conflict between the principles announced by eminent judges and the text-book writers. It has been stated that the plaintiff cannot recover if the injury complained of would not have occurred without his negligence. It has also been stated that plaintiff's negligence will not bar his recovery if due care on the part of the defendant would have prevented the injury. If the first statement is correct, contributory negligence always prevents a recovery; if the second statement is correct, contributory negligence never prevents recovery. The truth is that the first statement can be correctly applied only in cases of simultaneous negligence, as in the case of an injury to a person while crossing a railway in consequence of his own and the railway company's negligence. The second statement can be correctly applied only in cases of suc-

[1] Only a portion of the opinion is printed.

[2] This opinion of CARPENTER, J., was given in the Circuit Court; and was quoted by MOORE, J., in his dissenting opinion in the Supreme Court.

cessive negligence, as in the famous Donkey Case, of Davies *v.* Mann, 10 Mees. & W. 546, where defendant negligently ran into and injured the plaintiff's donkey, which plaintiff had negligently permitted to go unattended on the highway. The test almost universally approved is whether or not plaintiff's negligence is the proximate cause of his injury. If it is, he cannot recover; if it is not, he can. Even this test has been criticised on the ground that the term 'proximate' is misleading. I think this criticism just and important. The word 'proximate' is ordinarily used to indicate the relation between defendant's negligence and the plaintiff's injury. As so used, it has not the same meaning that it has when used to indicate the relation between plaintiff's negligence and plaintiff's injury. To illustrate, suppose in the case of Davies *v.* Mann, above referred to, that, as a result of the collision between the cart and the donkey, a third person had been injured; I think all will agree that the owner of the donkey, as well as the owner of the cart, would have been liable. See Lynch *v.* Nurdin, 1 Q. B. (N. S.) 29. And we have already seen that the negligence of the owner of the donkey was not so related to the collision as to preclude recovery in a suit by him against the owner of the cart. As used in relation to contributory negligence, the term 'proximate' simply means that in some way the relation between plaintiff's negligence and his injury is more remote than that between defendant's negligence and the injury." [1]

DROWN *v.* NORTHERN OHIO TRACTION COMPANY

SUPREME COURT, OHIO, MAY 7, 1907.

Reported in 76 *Ohio State Reports*, 234.

ACTION for damage done to plaintiff's buggy by an electric car which came up behind it and hit it. Answer: denying that defendant was negligent, and alleging negligence on plaintiff's part.

On the trial, it appeared that Hardy, plaintiff's driver, drove upon the track without looking behind to see if a car was coming.

Defendant requested the following instructions: —

(3) If the jury find from the evidence that the plaintiff, through his agent, Hardy, and the defendant were both negligent, and that the negligence of

[1] "We shall immediately see, moreover, that independent negligent acts of A and B may both be proximate in respect of harm suffered by Z, though either of them, if committed by Z himself, would have prevented him from having any remedy for the other. Thus it appears that the term 'proximate' is not used in precisely the same sense in fixing a negligent defendant's liability and a negligent plaintiff's disability." Pollock, *Torts*, 6th ed. 447.

". . . In determining whether the cause of the accident is proximate or remote, the same test must be applied to the conduct of the injured party as is to be applied to the defendant. The conduct of the latter cannot be judged by one rule and that of the former by some other rule." — O'BRIEN, J., in Rider *v.* Syracuse R. Co., 171 N. Y. 139, 154.

[An instruction as to the meaning of the word "proximately" intimates] "that there is a difference between the meaning of the word when applied to the defendant and when applied to the plaintiff. There is no such difference. Contributory negligence on the part of the plaintiff must bear the same proximate relation to the result as the actionable negligence of the defendant. It need not be the sole cause, and it may contribute but slightly, but it must be a proximate cause in the same sense that the defendant's negligence must be proximate." WINSLOW, J., in Boyce *v.* Wilbur Lumber Co., 119 Wis. 642, 649–650.

both directly contributed to cause the injury complained of in plaintiff's petition, then your verdict should be for the defendant.

(4) If the jury find that the negligence of both plaintiff's agent and the defendant combined so as to directly cause the injury complained of by plaintiff, then your verdict should be for the defendant.

These requests to instruct were refused.

The court, among other instructions, charged in substance as follows: —

If you find that the motorman could, by the exercise of ordinary care, have seen the plaintiff and stopped the car, and that by reason of the failure to stop the car Hardy's team was knocked down and injured, it would be such negligence on the part of the defendant as would entitle the plaintiff to recover, provided Hardy was free from contributory negligence on his part.

If Hardy was on this track driving south, and you find that he was negligent in being on it as he was, his failure to look or failure to watch to avoid injury, if he was negligent, would not prevent him from recovering in this suit, if the motorman, after discovering him in that position, could have, by the use of reasonable and ordinary care, avoided the injury by stopping the car. [This was a restatement in concrete form of an abstract proposition already stated in the charge.]

In the Common Pleas Court there was a verdict for plaintiff and judgment thereon. The Circuit Court reversed the judgment of the Common Pleas. Plaintiff brought error.[1]

DAVIS, J. Under the issues in this case, evidence was introduced tending to prove that the plaintiff's agent was guilty of negligence directly contributing to the injury to plaintiff's property. If the driver of the plaintiff's team, immediately upon entering Main Street, and without afterwards looking to the north, as he admits, drove southward upon the track until the car coming from the north overtook and collided with the buggy, he was negligent; because the street was open and unobstructed for from two hundred to two hundred and fifty feet from the point at which he entered upon it, and it was not necessary for him to go upon the street railway track, and because, the night being dark, he unnecessarily put himself in a place of obvious danger and continued therein until the moment of the accident, without looking out for an approaching car or doing anything whatever to avoid injury, apparently risking his life and the property of his principal upon the presumption that the defendant's employees would make no mistakes nor be guilty of any negligence. If, on the other hand, he drove along the street until he came to the obstruction and then turned out upon the track to go around it without again looking, as his own testimony shows that he did not, and was then almost in the same instant struck by the car, he was negligent. Upon either hypothesis, assuming that the defendant was negligent in not keeping a proper lookout, or was otherwise not exercising ordinary care to prevent collision with persons lawfully on its track, the plaintiff could not recover, if it should appear in the case that the negligence of both is contemporaneous and continuing until after the moment of the accident, because, in such case the negligence of each is a direct cause of the injury without which it would not have occurred, rendering it impracticable in all such instances, if not impossible, to apportion the responsibility and the damages. Suppose, for example, that not only the buggy and horses

[1] The statement has been abridged and the arguments and part of the opinion are omitted.

had been injured, but the defendant's car also, by what standard could the extent of liability of either party be determined? Timmons *v.* The Central Ohio Railroad Co., 6 Ohio St. 105; Village of Conneaut *v.* Naef, 54 Ohio St. 529, 531. In short, there can be no recovery in such a case unless the whole doctrine of contributory negligence, a doctrine founded in reason and justice, should be abolished.

Under these circumstances, therefore, it was not sufficient to say to the jury that if they should find that the motorman who had charge of the car which struck the team, could by the exercise of ordinary care have seen the team and could have stopped the car and that by reason of the failure to do so the team was injured, it would be such negligence by the defendant as would entitle the plaintiff to recover, provided that the plaintiff's driver was "free from contributory negligence." The defendant had the right to have the jury specifically instructed, as it requested, that if the jury should find from the evidence that both the plaintiff and the defendant, through their agents, were negligent, and that the negligence of both combined so as to directly cause the injury complained of, then the verdict should be for the defendant. The court refused to so instruct the jury, and the circuit court correctly held that the refusal to so charge was erroneous.

The error in refusing the defendant's request to charge, was extended and made much more prejudicial when the court, after giving instructions as to contributory negligence by the plaintiff in very general terms, proceeded to impress upon the jury, by repetition and with some emphasis, the doctrine known as "the last chance." This doctrine is logically irreconcilable with the doctrine of contributory negligence, and accordingly it has been vigorously criticised and warmy defended. Probably, as in many such controversies, the truth lies in middle ground; but it is certain that the rule is applicable only in exceptional cases, and the prevalent habit of incorporating it in almost every charge to the jury in negligence cases, in connection with, and often as a part of, instructions upon the subject of contributory negligence, is misleading and dangerous.

This confusion seems to arise either from misapprehension of the law or a want of definite thinking. The doctrine of the "last chance" has been clearly defined by a well-known text-writer as follows: "Although a person comes upon the track negligently, yet if the servants of the railway company, *after they see* his danger, can avoid injuring him, they are bound to do so. And, according to the better view with reference to injuries to travellers at highway crossings — as distinguished from injuries to *trespassers* and *bare licensees* upon railway tracks at places where they have no legal right to be — the servants of the railway company are bound to keep a vigilant lookout in front of advancing engines or trains, to the end of discovering persons exposed to danger on highway crossings; and the railway company will be liable for running over them if, by maintaining such a lookout and by using reasonable care and exertion to check or stop its train, it could avoid injury to them." 2 Thompson, Negligence, sec. 1629. The italics are the author's. Now, it must be apparent upon even a slight analysis of this rule that it can be applied only in cases where the negligence of the defendant is proximate and that of the plaintiff remote; for if the plaintiff and the defendant both be negligent and the negligence of both be concurrent and directly contributing to produce the accident, then the case is one of contributory negligence pure and simple. But if the plaintiff's negligence merely put him in the place of danger and stopped there, not actively continuing until the moment of the accident, and the defendant either knew of his danger, or by the exercise of such diligence as the law imposes on him would have known it, then, if the plaintiff's negligence did not concurrently combine with defendant's negligence to produce the injury, the defendant's negligence is the proximate cause of the injury and that of the plaintiff is a remote cause. This is all there is of the so-called doctrine of "the last clear chance." A good illustration is found in the case of Railroad Co. *v.* Kassen, 49 Ohio St. 230. Kassen walked through the rear car of the train on which he was a passenger to the rear platform, from which he either stepped off or fell off upon the track, where he lay for about two hours, when he was run over by another train. It was held that, although Kassen may have been negligent in going upon the rear platform and stepping or falling off, yet since the railroad company knew of his peril and had ample time to remove him or to notify the trainmen on the later train, its negligence in not doing so was the proximate cause of Kassen's death and the negligence of Kassen was remote. In that case the proximate cause and the remote cause were so clearly distinguishable, and it is so very evident from the opinion and the syllabus that this distinction was the real ground of the judgment of the court, that it is somewhat surprising that the doctrine of last chance as stated in that case should have been so often misinterpreted as a qualification of the doctrine of contributory negligence.

It is clear, then, that the last chance rule should not be given as a hit or miss rule in every case involving negligence. It should be given with discrimination. Since the plaintiff can recover only upon the allegations of his petition, if there is no charge in the petition that the defendant after having notice of the plaintiff's peril could have avoided the injury to plaintiff, and there is no testimony to support such charge, the giving of such a charge would be erroneous. There is no such allegation in the petition in this case. But further, there is testimony tending to prove that the plaintiff's team was driven upon the street railway track in the night time, ahead of the car, and that it continued on the track for a distance of two hundred and fifty feet until struck by the car, without taking any precaution to avoid accident. Assuming that the defendant was negligent in not seeing the buggy on the track and in not avoiding the accident, yet the plaintiff's negligence was continuous and was concurrent at the very moment of the collision. It proximately contributed to the collision, for without it the collision would not have occurred. There was no new act of negligence by the defendant, which was independent of the concurrent negligence and which made the latter remote. Therefore there was no place in the case for the doctrine of "the last clear chance."

[Remainder of opinion omitted.] *Judgment of Circuit Court affirmed.*

McLain, J., in FULLER *v.* ILLINOIS CENTRAL RAILROAD COMPANY

(1911) 100 *Mississippi*, 705, 716.

McLain, J. . . . The rule is settled beyond controversy or doubt, first that all that is required of the railroad company as against a trespasser is the abstention from wanton or willful injury, or that conduct which is characterized as gross negligence; second, although the injured party may be guilty of contributory negligence, yet this is no defense if the injury were willfully, wantonly, or recklessly done or the party inflicting the injury was guilty of such conduct as to characterize it as gross; and, third, that the contributory negligence of the party injured will not defeat the action if it is shown that the defendant might by the exercise of reasonable care and prudence have avoided the consequence of the injured party's negligence. This last principle is known as the doctrine of the "last clear chance." The origin of this doctrine is found in the celebrated case of Davies *v.* Mann, 10 Mees. & W. 545. . . . It is impossible to follow this case through its numerous citations in nearly every jurisdiction subject to Anglo-American jurisprudence. For the present it will be sufficient to say that the principle therein announced has met with practically almost universal favor. It has been severely criticised by some text-writers. . . . The law as enunciated in that case has come to stay. . . .

An analytical examination of the adjudged cases upon this subject will demonstrate the correctness of the above analysis, and, in addition, establish the soundness and technical accuracy announced in Davies *v.* Mann, *supra*. This case has been criticised most severely . . . by courts of high authority, but these courts have utterly and entirely failed to appreciate the base upon which the principle is bottomed, and in repudiating the principle do so upon the idea that Davies *v.* Mann establishes the much-abused comparative negligence doctrine, a doctrine repudiated by this court, but established in this state by Laws 1910, ch. 135, p. 125. (But this statute has no reference to the instant case because passed subsequent to the injuries complained of.) In order for the injured party's negligence to bar recovery, all of the authorities hold that it must be the proximate cause; otherwise, it is not contributory. Now, when it is fully understood that the negligence of the injured party must be the proximate cause in order to bar the remedy (and, as said above, all authorities everywhere, ancient and modern, so affirm), the principle announced in Davies *v.* Mann must, from necessity, be the correct and true rule. If the proximate and immediate cause of the injury — the *causa causans* — is the controlling and determining factor in ascertaining whether the injured party has the right to recover or whether the injuring party is not liable, then it must follow, as night the day, that the party who has the last opportunity to avoid the injury is the one upon whom the blame shall fall. To express the idea differently: If the injured party's negligence be remote, and not proximate, he can recover against the party who is guilty of negligence proximately contributing or causing the injury. The North Carolina courts have perhaps more satisfactorily and more clearly elucidated this question than have any opinions that have come under the writer's eye. In Smith *v.* N. & S. R.R. Co., 114 N. C. 728, 19 S. E. 863, 923, 25 L. R. A. 287, it is said that the rule in Davies *v.* Mann simply furnishes a means for ascertaining whether the plaintiff's negligence is a remote or proximate cause of the injury; that, before the introduction of this rule, any negligence on the part of the plaintiff, which in any degree contributes to the injury, was judicially treated as the proximate cause, and constituted contributory negligence which barred recovery. The same is clearly stated in Nashua Iron & Steel Co. *v.* W. & N. R. R. Co., 62 N. H. 159, 163, *et seq.* The antecedent negligence of the injured party, having been thus relegated to the position of a condition or remote cause of the accident, it cannot be regarded as contributory, since it is well established that negligence, in order to be contributory, must be at least one of the proximate causes.[1]

[1] Compare Rider *v.* Syracuse R. Co., 171 N. Y. 139.

Lord O'Brien, C. J., in BUTTERLY *v.* MAYOR OF DROGHEDA

[1907] 2 *Irish Reports*, 134, 137.

Lord O'Brien, L. C. J.: —

The facts which give rise to the controversy we have to determine, in this case, are comprised within a narrow compass. The plaintiff, on a Saturday morning, was coming into the town of Drogheda in a car driven by himself. Coming near the town he, as he alleged, was overtaken by the horse and car of Mrs. Morgan. She desired to pass. He says he made way for her, and, in doing so, ran against a heap of stones on the road, and his car was upset and he was injured. It appears that there were two heaps of stones on the road. They had been, immediately before the collision, thrown on the road in order that they might be spread on the road. The man who brought the load, and had thrown them on the road, was a servant of the defendants. The intention was to spread them immediately on the road. The man who brought them was in fact, at the time of the accident, engaged in spreading the heap next the town, some little distance from the heap where the accident occurred. Now the first heap, where the accident occurred, was placed on the road in such a position that there was between it and the right side of the road a space of 12 feet, and between this heap and the left side of the road, 6 feet. That is to say, on the right side there was a space sufficient for two cars to pass simultaneously, and on the left a space for one car to pass. The plaintiff's case was that, Mrs. Morgan overtaking him, he made room for her, pulled to the left, and without any default of his, his car ran upon the heap and was capsized. His case was that Mrs. Morgan caught him exactly where the heap was, and, in endeavoring to avoid her, and without any default or negligence on his part, the accident occurred. Now, three questions were left to the jury: —

1. Were the defendants, by their workmen, guilty of negligence? Yes.
2. Was the plaintiff guilty of negligence? Yes.

And if so —

3. Could the defendants, by the exercise of ordinary care, have avoided the consequence of the plaintiff's negligence? Yes.

I have invariably refused, in these negligence cases, to leave questions in this form to a jury. This formula appears to me calculated to perplex and embarrass a jury. No doubt this formula is used, and judges do their best to explain it, but I fear that when juries take up the questions in the jury-room, the explanation has not the desired effect. Chief Justice Monahan consistently refused to put the questions in this shape to the jury. I have always tried these cases on two questions: 1st, Were the defendants guilty of negligence? and, 2d, if so, was the defendant's negligence the real, direct, and immediate cause of the misfortune? Now, the jury in the present case answered the questions submitted to them in the way I have read. I am of opinion that the answer to the question finding that the plaintiff was guilty of negligence, determines the matter in favor of the defendants. It is quite plain, in my opinion, that his negligence was a direct contributory cause of the accident. It was a cause which brought him on the heap of stones. Assuming that there was negligence on the part of the defendants in having the stones there, still his negligence must have contributed to his running up against them. He either did not keep a sufficient look-out, or his unskilful driving brought him on the stones. Getting on the stones, through negligence, was at least a contributory cause of the accident. It directly contributed to the accident. If there be two causes directly contributing to the accident, one the negligence of the defendant and the other the negligence of the plaintiff, the result is a verdict for the defendant.

BRITISH COLUMBIA ELECTRIC RAILWAY COMPANY *v.* LOACH

In the Privy Council, July 26, 1915.

Reported in [1916] *Appeal Cases*, 719.

Lord Sumner. This is an appeal from a judgment of the Court of Appeal of British Columbia in favor of the administrator of the estate of Benjamin Sands, who was run down at a level crossing by a car of the appellant railway company and was killed. One Hall took Sands with him in a cart, and they drove together on to the level crossing, and neither heard nor saw the approaching car till they were close to the rails and the car was nearly on them. There was plenty of light and there was no other traffic about. The verdict, though rather curiously expressed, clearly finds Sands guilty of negligence in not looking out to see that the road was clear. It was not suggested in argument that he was not under a duty to exercise reasonable care, or that there was not evidence for the jury that he had disregarded it. Hall, who escaped, said that they went " right on to the track," when he heard Sands, who was sitting on his left, say " Oh," and looking up saw the car about fifty yards off. He says he could then do nothing, and with a loaded wagon and horses going two or three miles an hour he probably could not. It does not seem to have been suggested that Sands could have done any good by trying to jump off the cart and clear the rails. The car knocked cart, horses, and men over, and ran some distance beyond the crossing before it could be stopped. It approached the crossing at from thirty-five to forty-five miles an hour. The driver saw the horses as they came into view from behind a shed at the crossing of the road and the railway, when they would be ten or twelve feet from the nearest rail, and he at once applied his brake. He was then 400 feet from the crossing. If the brake had been in good order it should have stopped the car in 300 feet. Apart from the fact that the car did not stop in time, but overran the crossing, there was evidence for the jury that the brake was defective and inefficient and that the car had come out in the morning with the brake in that condition. The jury found that the car was approaching at an excessive speed and should have been brought under complete control, and although they gave as their reason for saying so the presence of possible passengers at the station by the crossing, and not the possibility of vehicles being on the road, there can be no mistake in the matter, and their finding stands. It cannot be restricted, as the trial judge and the appellants sought to restrict it, to a finding that the speed was excessive for an ill-braked car, but not for a properly-braked car, or to a finding that there was no negligence except the "original" negligence of sending the car out ill-equipped in the morning.

Clearly if the deceased had not got on to the line he would have suffered no harm, in spite of the excessive speed and the defective brake, and if he had kept his eyes about him he would have perceived the approach of the car and would have kept out of mischief. If the matter stopped there, his administrator's action must have failed, for he would certainly have been guilty of contributory negligence. He would have owed his death to his own fault, and whether his negligence was the sole cause or the cause jointly with the railway company's negligence would not have mattered.

It was for the jury to decide which portions of the evidence were true, and, under proper direction, to draw their own inferences of fact from such evidence as they accepted. No complaint was made against the summing-up, and there has been no attempt to argue before their Lordships that there was not evidence for the jury on all points. If the jury accepted the facts above stated, as certainly they well might do, there was no further negligence on the part of Sands after he looked up and saw the car, and then there was nothing that he could do. There he was, in a position of extreme peril and by his own fault, but after that he was guilty of no fresh fault. The driver of the car, however, had seen the horses some perceptible time earlier, had duly applied his brakes, and if they had been effective he could, as the jury found, have pulled up in time. Indeed, he would have had 100 feet to spare. If the car was 150 feet off when Sands looked up and said "Oh," then each had the other in view for fifty feet before the car reached the point at which it should have stopped. It was the motorman's duty, on seeing the peril of Sands, to make a reasonable use of his brakes in order to avoid injuring him, although it was by his own negligence that Sands was in danger. Apparently he did his best as things then were, but partly the bad brake and partly the excessive speed, for both of which the appellants were responsible, prevented him from stopping, as he could otherwise have done. On these facts, which the jury were entitled to accept and appear to have accepted, only one conclusion is possible. What actually killed Sands was the negligence of the railway company, and not his own, though it was a close thing.

Some of the judges in the Courts below appear to have thought that because the equipment of the car with a defective brake was the original cause of the collision, and could not have been remedied after Sands got on the line, no account should be taken of it in considering the motorman's failure to avoid the collision after he knew that Sands was in danger. "You cannot charge up the same negligence under different heads," said Murphy, J., at the trial; "you cannot charge it up twice." "On the question of ultimate negligence," he observed, "that negligence must arise on the conditions as existing at the time of the accident. It would, of course, be absurd to say the company had any opportunity between the time that this rig appeared upon the track and the collision to remedy any defect in the brake. If there was such a defect I think it was original negligence and not what may possibly be termed 'ultimate negligence.'"

In the Court of Appeal Macdonald, C. J. A., delivering a dissentient judgment in favor of the present appellants, said: "Where one party negligently approaches a point of danger, and the other party, with like obligation to take care, negligently approaches the same point of danger, if there arises a situation which could be saved by one and not by the other, and the former then negligently fail to use the means in his power to save it, and injury is caused to the latter, that failure is designated ultimate negligence, in the sense of being the proximate cause of the injury. In this case it is sought to carry forward, as it were, an anterior negligent omission of the defendants, though continuing, it is true, up to the time of the occurrence, and to assign to it the whole blame for the occurrence, although by no effort of the defendants or their servants could the situation at that stage have been saved."

So, too, McPhillips, J. A., also dissenting, said: "Upon the evidence, whether it was because of defective brakes or any of the acts of negligence found against the defendants, none of them were acts of negligence arising after the act of contributory negligence of the deceased, and cannot be held to be acts of negligence which, notwithstanding the later negligence of the deceased, warrant judgment going for the plaintiff. . . . The motorman after he saw the vehicle could not have stopped the car . . . therefore, as nothing could be then done by the motorman to remedy the ineffective brake, the want of care of the deceased was the direct and effective contributory cause of the accident resulting in his death."

These considerations were again urged at their Lordships' bar under somewhat different forms. It was said (1) that the negligence relied on as an answer to contributory negligence must be a new negligence, the initial negligence which founded the cause of action being spent and disposed of by the contributory negligence. Further, it was said (2) that if the defendants' negligence continued up to the moment of the collision, so did the deceased's contributory negligence, and that this series, so to speak, of replications and rebutters finally merged in the accident without the deceased ever having been freed from the legal consequence of his own negligence having contributed to it.

The last point fails because it does not correspond with the fact. The consequences of the deceased's contributory negligence continued, it is true, but, after he had looked, there was no more negligence, for there was nothing to be done, and, as it is put in the classic judgment in Tuff *v.* Warman, (1858) 5 C. B. (N. S.) 573, 585, his contributory negligence will not disentitle him to recover " if the defendant might by the exercise of care on his part have avoided the consequences of the neglect or carelessness of the plaintiff."

As to the former point, there seems to be some ambiguity in the statement. It may be convenient to use a phraseology which has been current for some time in the Canadian Courts, especially in Ontario, though it is not precise. The negligence which the plaintiff proves to launch his case is called " primary " or " original " negligence. The defendant may answer that by proving against the plaintiff "contributory negligence." If the defendant fails to avoid the consequences of that contributory negligence and so brings about the injury, which he could and ought to have avoided, this is called " ultimate " or " resultant " negligence. The opinion has been several times expressed, in various forms, that " original " negligence and " ultimate " negligence are mutually exclusive, and that conduct which has once been relied on to prove the first cannot in any shape constitute proof of the second.

Here lies the ambiguity. If the " primary " negligent act is done and over, if it is separated from the injury by the intervention of the plaintiff's own negligence, then no doubt it is not the " ultimate " negligence in the sense of directly causing the injury. If, however, the same conduct which constituted the primary negligence is repeated or continued, and is the reason why the defendant does not avoid the consequences of the plaintiff's negligence at and after the time when the duty to do so arises, why should it not be also the " ultimate " negligence which makes the defendant liable ?

This matter was much discussed in Brenner *v.* Toronto Ry. Co., 13 Ont. L. R. 423, when Anglin, J., delivered a very valuable judgment in the Divisional Court. The decision of the Divisional Court was reversed on appeal, 15 Ont. L. R. 195, (1908) 40 Can. S. C. R. 540, but on other grounds, and in their comments on the decision of the Divisional Court, Duff, J., in the Supreme Court, and also Chancellor Boyd in Rice *v.* Toronto Ry. Co., (1910) 22 Ont. L. R. 446, 450, and Hunter, C. J., in Snow *v.* Crow's Nest Pass Coal Co., (1907) 13 B. C. Rep. 145, 155, seem to have missed the point to which Anglin, J., had specially addressed himself.

The facts of that case were closely similar to those in the present appeal, and it was much relied on in argument in the court below. Anglin, J., following the decision in Scott *v.* Dublin and Wicklow Ry. Co., (1861) 11 Ir. C. L. Rep. 377, 394, observed as follows, 13 Ont. L. R. 437, 439, 440: " Again, the duty of the defendants to the plaintiff, breach of which would constitute 'ultimate' negligence, only arose when her danger was or should have been apparent. Prior to that moment there was an abstract obligation incumbent upon them to have their car equipped with efficient emergency appliances ready and in condition to meet the requirements of such an occasion. Had an occasion for the use of emergency appliances not arisen, failure to fulfil that obligation would have given rise to no cause of action. Upon the emergency arising, that abstract obligation became a concrete duty owing to the plaintiff to avoid the consequences of her negligence by the exercise of ordinary care. . . . Up to that moment there was no such breach of duty to the plaintiff. In that sense the failure of the defendants to avoid the mischief, though the result of an antecedent want of care, was negligence which occurred, in the sense of becoming operative, immediately after the duty, in the breach of which it consisted, arose. It effectively intervened between the negligence of the plaintiff and the happening of the casualty. But there is a class of cases where a situation of imminent peril has been created, either by the joint negligence of both plaintiff and defendant, or it may be, by that of the plaintiff alone, in which, after the danger is or should be apparent, there is a period of time, of some perceptible duration, during which both or either may endeavor to avert the impending catastrophe. . . . If, notwithstanding the difficulties of the situation, efforts to avoid injury duly made would have been successful, but for some self-created incapacity which rendered such efforts inefficacious, the negligence that produced such a state of disability is not merely part of the inducing causes — a remote cause or a cause merely *sine qua non* — it is, in very truth, the efficient, the proximate, the decisive cause of the incapacity, and therefore of the mischief. . . . Negligence of a defendant incapacitating him from taking due care to avoid the consequences of the plaintiff's negligence, may, in some cases, though anterior in point of time to the plaintiff's negligence, constitute 'ultimate' negligence, rendering the defendant liable notwithstanding a finding of contributory negligence of the plaintiff. . . ."

Their Lordships are of opinion that, on the facts of the presen case, the above observations apply and are correct. Were it otherwise the defendant company would be in a better position, when they had supplied a bad brake but a good motorman, than when the motorman was careless but the brake efficient. If the superintendent engineer sent out the car in the morning with a defective brake, which, on seeing Sands, the motorman strove to apply, they would not be liable, but if the motorman failed to apply the brake, which, if applied, would have averted the accident, they would be liable.

The whole law of negligence in accident cases is now very well settled, and, beyond the difficulty of explaining it to a jury in terms of the decided cases, its application is plain enough. Many persons are apt to think that, in a case of contributory negligence like the present, the injured man deserved to be hurt, but the question is not one of desert or the lack of it, but of the cause legally responsible for the injury. However, when once the steps are followed the jury can see what they have to do, for the good sense of the rules is apparent. The inquiry is a judicial inquiry. It does not always follow the historical method and begin at the beginning. Very often it is more convenient to begin at the end, that is at the accident, and work back along the line of events which led up to it. The object of the inquiry is to fix upon some wrong-doer the responsibility for the wrongful act which has caused the damage. It is in search not merely of a causal agency but of the responsible agent. When that has been done, it is not necessary to pursue the matter into its origins; for judicial purposes they are remote. Till that has been done there may be a considerable sequence of physical events, and even of acts of responsible human beings, between the damage done and the conduct which is tortious and is its cause. It is surprising how many epithets eminent judges have applied to the cause, which has to be ascertained for this judicial purpose of determining liability, and how many more to other acts and incidents, which for this purpose are not the cause at all. " Efficient or effective cause," " real cause," " proximate cause," " direct cause," " decisive cause," " immediate cause," " causa causans," on the one hand, as against, on the other, " causa sine qua non," " occasional cause," " remote cause," " contributory cause," " inducing cause," " condition," and so on. No doubt in the particular cases in which they occur they were thought to be useful or they would not have been used, but the repetition of terms without examination in other cases has often led to confusion, and it might be better, after pointing out that the inquiry is an investigation into responsibility, to be content with speaking of the cause of the injury simply and without qualification.

In the present case their Lordships are clearly of opinion that, under proper direction, it was for the jury to find the facts and to determine the responsibility, and that upon the answers which they returned, reasonably construed, the responsibility for the accident was upon the appellants solely, because, whether Sands got in the way of the car with or without negligence on his part, the appellants could and ought to have avoided the consequences of that negligence, and failed to do so, not by any combination of negligence on the part of Sands with their own, but solely by the negligence of their servants in sending out the car with a brake whose inefficiency operated to cause the collision at the last moment, and in running the car at an excessive speed, which required a perfectly efficient brake to arrest it. Their Lordships will accordingly humbly advise His Majesty that the appeal should be dismissed with costs.[1]

[1] The statement of facts and argument of counsel are omitted.

NEHRING v. THE CONNECTICUT COMPANY

SUPREME COURT, CONNECTICUT, JULY 19, 1912.

Reported in 86 *Connecticut Reports*, 109.

PRENTICE, J. It is clear and unquestioned that there was evidence, justifying its submission to the jury, tending to establish the defendant's negligence in the premises directly contributing to produce the fatal injury which the plaintiff's intestate suffered. The verdict for the defendant was directed upon the ground that the plaintiff had failed to present evidence, sufficient to go to the jury, tending to establish the intestate's freedom from contributory negligence. Plaintiff's counsel in his brief formally takes issue with this conclusion of the court, asserting that the evidence was such as entitled the plaintiff to go to the jury upon the question of the intestate's negligence. It is apparent, however, that little reliance is placed upon this particular claim, and that the contention that the court erred must fail unless the appeal which is made to the so-called doctrine of "the last clear chance," otherwise known as supervening or intervening negligence, is well made. This appeal is urged with vigor, so that the plaintiff's main contention, which alone calls for serious consideration, is that, notwithstanding the intestate's failure to use ordinary care, the defendant is liable through the operation of the doctrine referred to, which, it is said, the court disregarded.

. . . .

The notion appears to be more or less prevalent that this so-called doctrine is a discovery of recent years, that it embodies a new legal principle, and that this principle is one which invades the domain formerly assigned to contributory negligence, and sets limitations upon the operation of this latter doctrine so long and so deeply imbedded in English and American jurisprudence. This is by no means true as respects either the age or the character and scope of the principle which it embodies. The names by which it has come to be known are indeed of recent origin, and perhaps its present vogue and the misconception which prevails as to its true place in the law of negligence are due in part to its thus being given an independent status in the terminology of the law. In fact, the principle is no modern discovery. It runs back to the famous "Donkey Case" of Davies v. Mann, 10 Mees. & W. 546, decided in 1842. It was distinctly recognized by this court in 1858 in Isbell v. New York & N. H. R. Co., 27 Conn. 393. It was then not only recognized, but its true place in the law was assigned to it. It was shown to be no independent principle operating by the side of, and possibly overstepping the bounds of, other principles, but merely a logical and inevitable corollary of the long accepted doctrine of actionable negligence as affected by contributory negligence. The definition of its place, which was made in the clear-cut language of Judge Ellsworth, inexorably forbade that it could by possibility run counter in its application to the contributory negligence rule. This fundamental principle we have steadily adhered to. Smith *v.* Connecticut Ry. & Ltg. Co., 80 Conn. 268, 270, 67 Atl. 888; Elliott *v.* New York, N. H. & H. R. Co., 83 Conn. 320, 322, 76 Atl. 298, 84 Conn. 444, 447, 80 Atl. 283.

There are, indeed, cases which give countenance to a different view upon this latter subject. But their dicta, oftentimes, not to say generally, uttered without an apparent comprehension of their logical consequence, would create havoc with the law, and leave it guideless, or with two conflicting guides. A sober second thought is, however, fast correcting this mistake, so that there has already come to be a general concurrence of the well-considered authorities in the view which has been taken in this jurisdiction.

The contributory negligence rule has no practical application save in cases where the defendant has been guilty of actionable negligence. It proceeds upon the theory that whenever a person injured has contributed essentially to his injury by his own negligent conduct, the law will not give him redress, even against another who may have been directly instrumental in producing the result. To furnish a basis for its application there must have been a concurrence of negligent conduct. This negligent conduct, furthermore, must have been of such a character and so related to the result as to entitle it to be considered an efficient or proximate cause of it. If there is a failure to use due care on the part of either party at such a time, in such a way or in such a relation to the result that it cannot fairly be regarded as an efficient or proximate cause, the law will take no note of it. *Causa proxima, non remota, spectatur.*

It thus logically follows that, although a plaintiff may have failed to exercise reasonable care in creating a condition, or in some other way, which cannot be fairly said to have been the proximate cause of the injuries of which he complains, the contributory negligence rule cannot be invoked against him. The question with respect to negligent conduct on the part of a person injured through the negligence of another, as affecting the former's right to recover, thus becomes resolved in every case into one as to whether or not that conduct of his was a proximate cause of the injury. If it was, then the contributory negligence rule is applicable, and the plaintiff will by its operation be barred from recovery. If it was not, that rule has no pertinence to the situation, since there was no concurrence of negligence, without which there can be no contributory negligence in the legal sense. It is conduct of the latter kind — that is, conduct careless in itself, but not connected with the injury as a proximate cause of it — to which the so-called doctrine of "the last clear chance" relates, and that doctrine embraces within its purview such conduct only.

This being so, it may well be questioned whether the doctrine deserves a classification and a name as of an independent principle. But if, for convenience sake or other reason, it is to be dignified in that way, it is apparent that there is no manner of inconsistency between it and the contributory-negligence rule, and that the domain of the latter rule is in no way invaded or narrowed by a full recognition of it. It follows that the decisive question in each case, where a plaintiff injured is found to have been at fault in the premises from his failure to exercise the required degree of care, resolves itself into one as to whether that fault was or was not a proximate cause of the injury, and that the answer to that question will infallibly determine whether or not it will bar a recovery.

. . . .

Thus far we have had the way marked out for us by the clearly defined doctrine of former opinions. But the proposition just stated, which is thus supported, while sufficient for the determination of many cases and furnishing a helpful guide in most others, does not resolve all the difficulties which may be encountered. It leaves the question open as to when negligent conduct in a person injured in his person or property is to be regarded as a proximate cause of the injury. How close must be the causal connection between the negligence and the injury? It is at this point that any real uncertainty or trouble arises under the doctrine of this jurisdiction.

. . . .

The negligence referred to in the claimed rule is, of course, that which the law so denominates, to wit, want of due care which is a proximate cause of harm. The proposition is not dealing with a lack of due care which the law ignores. When it speaks of the negligence ceasing, negligence in the legal sense is meant. It may in a given sense cease in the sense that prudent conduct takes its place. It may for all legal purposes cease through the relegation of it, as events progress, to the domain of remote cause. In other words, it ceases when, and only when, the conditions of contributory negligence disappear. The claimed test thus solves no problems. It only brings one back, in doubtful cases, to the inquiry whether the plaintiff's conduct, lacking in due care, was of such a character, or so related to the injury, that it ought to be regarded as a proximate cause of it, as the real test which must be applied.

The impossibility of framing any general abstract statement which will suffice to resolve the difficulties which may be presented under varying conditions, or to anticipate all such conditions, is apparent. We shall undertake no such task. There are, however, certain sets of conditions, of not infrequent occurrence, concerning which general conclusions may be made safely and profitably.

There is, for instance, the occasional case where, after the plaintiff's peril, to which he has carelessly exposed himself or his property, becomes known to the defendant, the latter introduces into the situation a new and independent act of negligence without which there would have been no injury. Such was the case of Smith *v.* Connecticut Ry. & Ltg. Co., 80 Conn. 268, 270, 67 Atl. 888, and it was there held, in accordance with sound reason, that this new negligence was to be regarded as the sole proximate cause of the accident which ensued. The rule for that type of case is thus furnished.

Cases of another class occasionally arise, where it is disclosed that the plaintiff has by his lack of care placed himself in a position of danger from which he either cannot, or cannot reasonably, escape after the discovery of his danger. Here, again, there can be no hesitation in saying, that if the defendant, after his discovery that the plaintiff is in the situation described, fails to use reasonable care — and that is care proportioned to the danger — to save him from harm, and harm results from such failure, the defendant's want of care will be regarded as the sole proximate cause, and the plaintiff's a remote cause only.

The situation just stated is not infrequently changed, in that means of escape were open to the plaintiff by the exercise of reasonable care, but it was apparent to the defendant, in season to have avoided the doing of harm by the exercise of due care, that the plaintiff would not avail himself of them. Here it is assumed that the situation of exposure had been created and established by the plaintiff's action before the period of time began within which the defendant, acting reasonably, might have saved him, and that within that period the plaintiff did nothing to create or materially change that situation by active conduct which was not marked by reasonable care. Under the assumption he remains passive, in so far at least as negligent action is concerned, and can be regarded as careless only in this that he did not awake to his surroundings and do what he reasonably could to avoid the threatened consequences of a situation which he had already negligently brought about. In such cases the humane, and, to our mind, the better reason, all things considered, leads to the conclusion to which our former opinions, already cited, commit us, and which a large number of cases elsewhere approve, that the want of care on the part of the plaintiff will be regarded as a remote and not a proximate cause.

Another important variation is oftentimes introduced into the situation, in that the plaintiff continued as an active agent in producing the conditions under which his injury was received down to the time of its occurrence, or at least until it was too late for the defendant, with knowledge of his peril, to have saved him by the exercise of reasonable care under the circumstances. This variation imports into the situation an important factor. The plaintiff, during the period named, is not merely passively permitting an already fixed condition to remain unchanged. He is an actor upon the scene. He is, by acts of his volition, bringing into the situation which confronts the defendant changed conditions and, in the fullest sense, co-operating with the latter in bringing about the ultimate result. In such case his conduct must be regarded as a concurring efficient cause. It is, in the fullest sense, a proximate and not a remote one, making his negligence contributory.

It is said, however, that there are cases, and undoubtedly there are, where it is reasonably apparent to the one who inflicts the injury that the injured one is careless of his safety, and that, in continuance of his carelessness, he is about to place himself in a position of danger, which he subsequently does, and where the former thereafter, having a reasonable opportunity to save him from harm, fails to do so; and it is contended that in such cases the conduct of the injured person should be regarded as a remote cause only of the resulting harm. We are unable to discover any logical reason for such a conclusion, or any place at which a practical or certain line of division can be drawn between that careless conduct of a man, playing some part in an injury to him, which the law will regard as having that causal connection with the injury which makes it a proximate cause, and that careless conduct which will not be so regarded, if the contention under consideration is to be approved. The conduct of the man who inflicts the injury under such general conditions may indeed be such that it is open to the charge of wilfulness or wantonness. If so, the case is not one of negligence, and the defense of contributory negligence would not be available. Rowen *v.* New York, N. Y. & H. R. Co., 59 Conn. 364, 371, 21 Atl. 1073. If the conduct is not wilful or wanton, it is negligent only. Thus treated, it forms one factor of negligence in the situation. The plaintiff's want of care is another factor, and it certainly has something substantial to do in bringing about the result reached. Upon what theory or foundation in reason it can be said that, under the circumstances assumed, it is not an efficient cause of that result co-operating concurrently with the other cause to be found in the other party's negligence, we are unable to discover. The causal connection is plain to be seen, and the act of causation is that of a positive act of volition. The two actors upon the scene owe precisely the same duty to be reasonably careful. Dexter *v.* McCready, 54 Conn. 171, 174, 5 Atl. 855. Neither occupies in that regard a superior position, and the one who suffers can claim no precedence over his fellow actor or at the hands of the law. To say that no matter if one be negligent in going forward into danger, or in creating new conditions or complicating them, the law will protect him and cast upon the other party the responsibility for the result, is to ignore the fundamental principle of contributory negligence and bring the law upon that subject into hopeless confusion, and merit for it the condemnation which Thompson has so forcibly expressed. 1 Thompson on Negligence, §§ 230, 233. The well-considered cases which have directly dealt with this subject agree with us, we think, in our view that active continuing negligence of the kind assumed is to be regarded as contributory in the legal sense. Butler *v.* Rockland, T. & C. Street Ry. Co., 99 Me. 149, 160, 58 Atl. 775; Murphy *v.* Deane, 101 Mass. 455, 465; Dyerson *v.* Union Pacific R. Co., 74 Kan. 528, 87 Pac. 680; Little *v.* Superior Rapid Transit Ry. Co., 88 Wis. 402, 409, 60 N. W. 705; Green *v.* Los Angeles Terminal Ry. Co., 143 Cal. 31, 47, 76 Pac. 719; Olson *v.* Northern Pacific Ry. Co., 84 Minn. 258, 87 N. W. 843.

We have thus far dealt with cases in which actual knowledge on the part of the defendant of the plaintiff's peril enters into the assumption of facts. Suppose, however, that such knowledge is not established, but facts are shown from which it is claimed that the defendant ought in the exercise of due care to have known of it. What shall be said of such a situation?

In so far as imputed or constructive knowledge may be embraced in the assumption, the simple answer is to be found in the legal principle that full and adequate means of knowledge, present to a person when he acts, are, under ordinary circumstances, treated as the equivalent of knowledge. Post *v.* Clark, 35 Conn. 339, 342.

But our assumption reaches outside of the domain of knowledge, either actual or constructive. It suggests, in the use of the phrase "ought in the exercise of due care to have known," frequently met with in the books, the existence of a duty to exercise due care to acquire knowledge, and the query is, whether the law recognizes the existence of such a duty to the extent of making it a foundation for responsibility for conduct akin to that which flows from conduct with actual or constructive knowledge.

We have frequently held that the character of one's conduct in respect to care is to be determined in view of what he should have known as well as of what he did in fact know. Snow *v.* Coe Brass Mfg. Co., 80 Conn. 63, 66 Atl. 881. In these cases the question has been as to one's duty for his own self-protection. That duty, according to established principles, involves the making of reasonable use of one's senses under the penalty of forfeiture of all claim for redress in the event that harm results. Popke *v.* New York, N. H. & H. R. Co., 81 Conn. 724, 71 Atl. 1098.

But how about a duty of acquiring knowledge, owed to others for their safety, which, not being performed, will furnish a basis of liability? In Elliott *v.* New York, N. H. & H. R. Co., 83 Conn. 320, 76 Atl. 298, we recognized that such a duty might exist. That case involved the conduct of a locomotive engineer operating his engine at a grade-crossing, and we approved a charge which gave to the knowledge which the engineer, under the conditions, ought, in the use of due care, to have had, the same effect as actual knowledge. The duty imposed upon him was one to be watchful in order that needless harm might not come to persons who might be using the crossing, from the dangerous instrument of his calling. The duty was one toward others, which the circumstances and conditions must be regarded as fairly creating. For a like reason a similar duty rests upon other persons and under other conditions, in greater or lesser measure. Whether it exists, and the extent of it, depends upon the circumstances of each situation. A circumstance of chief significance, perhaps, is one which concerns the character of that about which the person is engaged in respect to its being calculated, under the conditions, to work injury to others. And so it is that a locomotive engineer, a motorman of a trolley-car running in a highway, or a chauffeur driving an automobile, is under a duty to be watchful for the protection of others which another man under other conditions would not owe to his fellows. Unreasonableness in one's conduct, as a foundation for responsibility to others, cannot justly be established upon the basis of knowledge not possessed. It can with propriety be predicated upon negligence in not having acquired more knowledge. Negligence in this respect, as in all others, implies the existence of a duty to make use of means of knowledge. This duty must be found in the circumstances, and caution must be exercised in order that it, with its consequences, be not raised where the circumstances do not fairly impose it, or be extended beyond the limits which the circumstances fairly justify.[1]

GEORGE W. WHEELER, J. (dissenting). Just prior to the accident the defendant's car was being negligently operated. Assuming the decedent walked either diagonally toward and upon the track, or close to it, without using his senses to learn of the approaching car, and that there was no excuse for his failure, he was negligent. If the accident occurred while decedent and defendant were negligent and decedent's negligence was a proximate cause of the accident, and there was nothing more to the case, there could be no recovery. But if the defendant's motorman saw, or could by the exercise of reasonable care have seen, the decedent either approaching the track and about to place himself in danger, or walking so near the track as to be in danger, apparently heedless and unconscious of his peril, he owed to the deceased the duty of warning him and of observing such precautions as might avoid running into him. This was the case before the jury. We hold knowledge and the means of knowledge of one having a duty to know equivalent. Elliott *v.* New York, N. H. & H. R. Co., 83 Conn. 320, 76 Atl. 298. This duty originated after the negligence of the motorman and of the deceased, and after the latter's peril and his unconsciousness of it might have been discovered by the motorman. If its performance would have avoided the injury to the deceased, its breach was the proximate cause of the accident, and his negligence in placing himself in the place of peril a condition, or the remote cause,

[1] The statement of facts, arguments and parts of the opinions are omitted.

of it. Of course, if he had not gone upon the track he would not have been injured; if he was negligent in going upon the track without using his senses, that was not the proximate cause of the accident, but the failure of the defendant to avoid the accident after it had the opportunity of avoidance and after it knew of the decedent's peril and his unconsciousness of it.

In each case of discovered peril caused by one's negligence the question is, did the defendant have the opportunity after such discovery, and was it his duty, to have avoided the accident? Whether the conduct of the motorman was gross negligence, or ordinary negligence, the breach of duty was the same in kind, though differing in degree. If one walks upon a railway track drunk, or in a reverie, or otherwise careless; or if one stands or lies on or so near the railway track as to be in danger and unconscious of it; or if one is in a position of peril through his own negligence from which he is unable to extricate himself, the person knowing or having the means and the duty to know of his presence owes him the duty of avoiding injuring him. One who is negligently in a position of danger and unconscious of it is in no different situation than if he were incapable of extricating himself from his peril.

The few authorities which hold the antecedent negligence of the deceased in getting into peril is concurrent with the defendant's negligence so as to bar a recovery, make meaningless the rule of duty compelling the defendant to use reasonable care to avoid the accident after discovery of the peril. A legal duty without a corresponding obligation is an anomaly. When we relieve the motorman of liability for failure to avoid an accident, he may operate his car at a negligent speed, without having it under control, without keeping an outlook, without giving warning of approach, and neither having nor using the ordinary instrumentalities of equipment for avoiding injury to travellers, and so long as his conduct is not gross negligence it carries with it no liability.

The opinion of the court classifies in five groups the several kinds of cases which have been thought to be within the "last clear chance" doctrine. In group one, the defendant, instead of doing his duty, does something which is a new act of negligence. In group two, the peril is one from which the plaintiff cannot, or cannot reasonably, extricate himself. Each group supports a recovery. In group three, means of escape were open to the plaintiff down to the accident, but he remained unconscious of his peril. The opinion holds that if the plaintiff remains passive after exposing himself to peril and does nothing to materially change that condition, there may be a recovery. But in group four, assuming the same facts as in group three, the court holds that if the plaintiff after exposing himself to peril, instead of permitting the fixed condition to remain unchanged continues as an active agent in producing the conditions under which the injury was received down to its occurrence, or until it was too late for the defendant to avoid the accident, there can be no recovery. In group five, the defendant knows, or ought to know, that the injured one is careless and is about to expose himself to danger of which he is unconscious, and after such knowledge has the opportunity to avoid injury to him, and in such case the court holds there can be no recovery.

We have attempted to show that the breach of duty of the defendant in each of these several groups is the same, and was a new act of negligence of the defendant, viz.: the failure of the defendant to avoid injuring the plaintiff after he knew of his peril when he was either unconscious of it or incapable of extricating himself from it, and that this breach was the proximate cause of the accident while the plaintiff's prior negligence was the remote cause.

The distinction between active and passive negligence made in groups three and four, is new to our law, as well as to the law of negligence generally prevailing in this country and in England. On analysis it does not seem logical. A is crossing a trolley track when hailed by a friend; he stops upon the track to talk and negligently fails to use his senses to discover an approaching car. The motorman could have seen A in his place of peril, unconscious of his danger, and in time, with the exercise of reasonable care to have avoided injuring him; instead he drives on his car and kills A. The opinion would hold A negligent in being upon the track without using his senses to keep out of the way of the oncoming car, but that as he remained passive and did nothing to change his situation of peril after the motorman had the opportunity to have avoided the accident, he may recover. But if A, instead of stopping on the track had gone on his way across or upon the track and been struck, his negligence would have been active and continued to the accident and would have been concurrent with that of the motorman. It must be conceded that the breach of the motorman's duty would have been the same in each case: a failure to use reasonable care to avoid the accident. We see no reason why it should be available in the one case and not in the other. In neither case has the plaintiff's negligence changed. It never became passive or nonexistent. It remained to the time of the accident. It ceased, in a legal sense, to be a proximate cause of the accident. A was relieved of its consequences because the negligence of the motorman in failing to avoid the accident intervened and became its proximate cause. If this distinction holds, and A be upon a trolley track intoxicated and asleep, his negligence is passive; if awake and walking his negligence is active.[1]

[1] See also Bruggeman *v.* Illinois R. Co., 147 Ia. 187, 204–214; Anderson *v.* Minneapolis R. Co., 103 Minn. 224; Cavanaugh *v.* Boston R. Co., 76 N. H. 68; Scholl *v.* Belcher, 63 Or. 310, 323; Underwood *v.* Old Colony R. Co., 33 R. I. 319. As to the requirement of a "new act of negligence" see Rider *v.* Syracuse R. Co., 171 N. Y. 139.

GAHAGAN *v.* BOSTON & MAINE RAILROAD

SUPREME COURT, NEW HAMPSHIRE, DECEMBER, 1900.

Reported in 70 *New Hampshire Reports*, 441.

PLAINTIFF was struck by a train while attempting to use a crossing provided by the Railroad Company for persons having business with a manufacturing company. From a point twenty-two feet from the nearest rails there was an unobstructed view of the track in the direction from which the train came. The accident happened near noon on a bright and clear day. Generally the engine bell was rung, while the whistle was sometimes sounded, for this crossing. Plaintiff knew it was usual to ring the bell. In this instance a danger whistle was sounded at, or immediately before, the time when plaintiff was struck; but there was evidence tending to prove that no other warning of the approach of the train was given. Plaintiff testified that he did not look or listen for an approaching train; and that he did not look because he expected to hear the bell or whistle if one was coming. The engineer testified that, when about one hundred and fifty to two hundred feet from the crossing, he saw plaintiff approaching the track; and that he kept watch of plaintiff until he got within a few feet of the track, when he whistled.[1]

A nonsuit was ordered, subject to exception.

PARSONS, J. . . . It is urged that the plaintiff relied upon the ringing of the bell, and that the failure to give the warning signals (of which there was some evidence which must here be taken to be true) excused him from the exercise of vigilance. Though the plaintiff testified that he did not look to see if a train was approaching because he expected to hear the whistle or bell if there was, it cannot be claimed that he was consciously at the time placing any reliance thereon, for he further testifies that he had no thought of a train coming and did not listen for the bell. As his counsel state in their brief, " There was no positive effort, no conscious ' harking ' or ' listening,' to ascertain if the train was coming." But assuming that it might be found as a fact that he did rely on the awakening of his consciousness by the performance of the railroad's duty of warning, the failure of the defendants to perform their duty did not release him from his. The obligation to use care was equally imposed upon each. If the defendants' negligence excused the plaintiff from his duty of care, the plaintiff's negligence with equal reason would excuse the defendants. If the plaintiff had the right to assume the defendants would perform their duty, and, relying thereon, approach the crossing without exercising care, the defendants had the right to assume that the plaintiff would perform his duty, and omit the warning of bell and whistle. The duty of care rested on each equally. If neither performed that

[1] Statement abridged. Only part of opinion is given.

duty both are in fault, and neither can recover of the other. The collision in this case resulted, it may be, because neither party performed their duty. If either had, there might and probably would have been no accident. The rights and liabilities of the parties consequent upon their acts resulting in the collision are not affected by the fact that subsequently one is plaintiff and the other defendant in a suit growing out of the collision. Their several responsibility is fixed at the time by their acts or failure to act. A suit by the engineer against Gahagan for personal injury resulting from the collision would present precisely the same legal question as that we now have. It would hardly be urged that the engineer was not guilty of contributory negligence in failing to ring the bell because he relied upon Gahagan's performance of his duty of stopping and allowing the train to go by. The negligence of neither is an excuse for concurrent want of care in the other, because for an injury resulting from the concurrent negligence of both neither can recover. Nashua Iron and Steel Co. *v.* Railroad, 62 N. H. 159, 163.

The rule is laid down in Railroad Co. *v.* Houston, 95 U. S. 697, 702, also a crossing case, as follows: "The failure of the engineer to sound the whistle or ring the bell, if such were the fact, did not relieve the deceased from the necessity of taking ordinary precautions for her safety. Negligence of the company's employees in these particulars was no excuse for negligence on her part."

. . . .

It is not claimed that after the plaintiff stepped upon the track almost immediately in front of the approaching train the defendants could have prevented the injury, or that the employees in charge of the train, when the danger thus became imminent, did not do all that could be done to prevent the collision. At any time before this the plaintiff could have avoided the collision. There was no moment when the defendants could, while the plaintiff could not, have prevented the injury. The plaintiff's act in stepping upon the track, without precaution to ascertain whether he could safely do so, was the last act in point of time in the causation producing the injury. As there was no evidence upon which it could reasonably be found that the plaintiff's action in this respect was the exercise of care, he cannot recover unless upon the evidence some negligent act or omission of the defendants' employees could be found to be the sole proximate cause of the injury.

. . . .

The plaintiff's negligent occupation of the track did not authorize the defendants to run upon and injure him, if by care they could have avoided it. Ordinarily, the negligent act or omission which fails to avoid the consequences of the plaintiff's negligence is the last act in time in the series leading to the injury. Such was the case in the cases cited; the negligent occupation of the track by the plaintiffs preceded the negligence of the defendants in failing to observe and guard against the danger so produced. But as ordinary care may require vigilance to guard against a dangerous situation reasonably to be apprehended, as well as actually imminent, it cannot always follow that the last negligent act in point of time is necessarily the proximate cause of the injury. If the engineer knew or ought to have known that the plaintiff's negligence would place him upon the crossing when the train reached it, the engineer was equally bound to avoid the collision as if he saw the plaintiff actually on the track. The question is one of evidence merely. The mere fact that the person when first seen is on the track is not decisive. If a person on foot is seen crossing the track at such distance ahead that it could not reasonably be apprehended that the train would reach him in this position, the engineer would not be in fault for not preparing to avoid a danger not reasonably to be expected. In the present case there is evidence that when the plaintiff was first seen by the engineer the collision could have been prevented. If the engineer knew or ought to have known then that the plaintiff would be upon the crossing when the train reached it, and could have avoided the collision, his failure to do so is the proximate cause of the injury.

As there was evidence the collision might then have been prevented by him, the sole remaining question is whether upon the evidence reasonable men might find the engineer ought then to have foreseen the plaintiff's negligence. The bare fact that the plaintiff was seen approaching the track is not sufficient to authorize such a finding. If it were, the rule heretofore laid down and found to be approved by the authorities and the reason of the case, that it is the duty of the highway traveller to stop and allow the train to pass, would be reversed. It would become the duty of the train to stop and wait for the person on foot to go by. This would be unreasonable, impracticable, and put an end to the modern system of rapid transportation demanded by the public, and to effectuate which railroads are authorized by the state.

" The company's servants may ordinarily presume that a person apparently of full age and capacity, who is walking on the track at some distance before the engine, will leave it in time to save himself from harm; or if approaching the track, that he will stop if it becomes dangerous for him to cross it. This presumption will not be justified under some circumstances, as when the person who is on the track appears to be intoxicated, asleep, or otherwise off his guard." Pierce R. R. 331; 2 Shearm. & Red. Neg. *s.* 483; Chicago, etc. R. R. *v.* Lee, 68 Ill. 576, 581; Terre Haute, etc. R. R. *v.* Graham, 46 Ind. 239, 245; Lake Shore, etc. R. R. *v.* Miller, 25 Mich. 274, 278, 280; Boyd *v.* Railway, 105 Mo. 371, 381, 382. The presumption is founded upon the general principle of right acting and the instinct of self-preservation. Huntress *v.* Railroad, 66 N. H. 185; Lyman *v.* Railroad, 66 N. H. 200; 2 Thomp. Neg. 1601.

The case discloses no evidence apparent to the engineer taking the present case out of the rule.

. . . .

Aside from the plaintiff's own statement and the fact of the subsequent collision, the case contains no evidence that the plaintiff, when seen by the engineer approaching the crossing, was not alert to the situation, or tending to produce a belief that he would voluntarily rush into danger without care. Until he stepped upon the track his only danger consisted in the fact of his mental obliviousness to his duty of taking care. So defining his danger, the claim of his counsel, that if the engineer knew the plaintiff's danger he could have avoided the injury and is in fault for not doing so, is sound; but to submit to the jury the question of fact whether the engineer ought to have known the *status* of the plaintiff's mind in season to have prevented the accident, not only in the absence of evidentiary facts tending to prove such knowledge but in the face of all the facts open only to a contrary inference, would be a violation of the familiar and elementary rule that in judicial trials facts are to be found upon evidence, not conjecture. Deschenes *v.* Railroad, 69 N. H. 285.

The evidence upon which counsel mainly rely, tending to show that when seen by the engineer Gahagan's face was not turned toward the train and that his appearance did not indicate whether he saw the train or not, does not tend to establish that he proposed to rush carelessly into known danger, or that he would go upon the track without care to ascertain if a train was approaching. That Gahagan knew the crossing, its danger, and his approach to it, was conceded. Hence, in the face of this admitted fact, although this evidence may have some tendency to prove the contrary, the jury could not find that Gahagan did not know he was approaching a place of danger, or that the engineer ought to have inferred a fact which it is conceded did not exist. As there is no evidence that the defendants ought to have known the plaintiff's danger in season to have avoided the results of his negligence, they cannot be found guilty of negligence for not doing so.

. . . .

Exceptions overruled.

KEITH, P., IN NORFOLK & W. R. CO. *v.* DEAN'S ADM'X

(1907) 107 *Virginia*, 505, 506, 507, 513.

KEITH, P. The Circuit Court . . . rests the case solely upon the second count in the declaration, in which the case presented is that, after it became apparent to the crew in charge of defendant company's train that intestate of plaintiff was on the track in front of the engine, that he was unconscious of his danger, and would take no measures to protect himself, the crew failed to use any measure to prevent the accident. Such being the issue to be determined, it is needless to consider so much of the evidence as relates to the use of the track as a public passway, or as to whether or not the person injured was a licensee or a trespasser. He was a human being, and when his dangerous position was seen and known, and that he himself was unconscious of his peril, and would take no measures for his own protection, it became the duty of the railroad company to do all that could be done consistent with its higher duties to others to save him from the consequences of his own act, regardless of whether he was guilty of contributory negligence or not. Seaboard & Roanoke R. Co. *v.* Joyner's Adm'r, 92 Va. 355, 23 S. E. 773.

This being the narrow issue to be decided, it becomes necessary to consider the evidence bearing upon it with care. . . .

[The learned judge then considered the testimony. He found that there was no failure of duty on the part of the train men; and he *held* that the demurrer to the evidence should have been sustained. He quoted, with approval, the following statements of the law.]

In N. & W. Ry. Co. *v.* Harman, 83 Va. 577, 8 S. E. 258, it is said that "if a person seen upon the track is an adult, and apparently in the possession of his or her faculties, the company has a right to presume that he will exercise his senses and remove himself from his dangerous position; and if he fails to do so, and is injured, the fault is his own, and there is, in the absence of wilful negligence on its part, no remedy against the company for the results of an injury brought upon him by his own recklessness."

. . . .

In Rangeley *v.* Southern Ry. Co., 95 Va. 715, 30 S. E. 386, it is said that a railroad company has the right to assume that a grown person seen on its track will get out of the way of an approaching train, and the company is not liable unless it is shown that after the company, in the exercise of ordinary care, could have discovered that he was not going to get off the track, it could have avoided the injury.

O'KEEFE, ADM'X, *v.* CHICAGO, ROCK ISLAND & PACIFIC RAILROAD COMPANY

SUPREME COURT, IOWA, OCTOBER 21, 1871.

Reported in 32 Iowa Reports, 467.

APPEAL from Polk District Court.

Action by an administratrix to recover damages for the death of her husband, Dennis O'Keefe, alleged to have been killed by being run over on the defendant's road, through the negligence of the defendant's agents and employees. Defence in denial, and also that the death was caused by the drunkenness and negligence of the plaintiff's intestate. There was a jury trial, resulting in a verdict and judgment for plaintiff for $1000. The defendant appeals.

COLE, J. [Omitting statement of evidence.] After the evidence was closed, the defendant asked the court to instruct the jury as follows: "If you are satisfied from the evidence that Dennis O'Keefe, plaintiff's intestate, was, a short time before the alleged injury, in a state of intoxication; that in such condition he went upon defendant's railroad and laid himself down upon the track, or fell down unable to support himself because of such intoxication; that remaining in that condition a passing train crushed one of his legs; that after the injury he was yet under the influence of intoxicating liquors drank before the injury; that the injured limb was amputated and death ensued, you will find for the defendant, unless you further find from a preponderance of the evidence that defendant or its agents had knowledge that he was thus lying in time to prevent the accident," to which the court added, and then gave it, "*or, could have known with the exercise of ordinary caution.*" This modification was excepted to at the time, and is now assigned as error.

The well-established law of this state is, that in an action to recover damages for the negligent act of the defendant, the plaintiff will not be entitled to recover if his own negligence contributed directly to the injury. In other words, this court recognizes and applies the doctrine of "contributory negligence," and not the doctrine of "comparative negligence." The latter doctrine obtains only in Illinois and Georgia, while the former obtains in the other states, and also in the Federal courts. The modification complained of ignored the doctrine of contributory negligence, and substantially told the jury that plaintiff might recover without regard to his negligence, if the defendant could have prevented the injury with the exercise of ordinary caution. The doctrine of the modification goes even farther than that of comparative negligence; for, by the latter, a plaintiff can only recover when he shows the defendant's negligence to have been greater, by comparison, than his, while by the modification the plaintiff might recover if the defendant did not exercise ordinary caution, although the plaintiff's intestate may have been guilty of a much greater negligence in laying himself down, in a condition of intoxication, near to or upon the track. A similar modification was made to the second instruction. In each there was error. *Reversed.*

PICKETT *v.* WILMINGTON & WELDON RAILROAD COMPANY

SUPREME COURT, NORTH CAROLINA, SEPTEMBER TERM, 1895.

Reported in 117 *North Carolina Reports,* 616.

AVERY, J.[1] The most important question presented by the appeal is whether the court erred in refusing to instruct the jury that if the plaintiff's intestate deliberately laid down upon the track and either carelessly or intentionally fell asleep there, the defendant was not liable, unless the engineer actually saw that he was lying there in time, by the reasonable use of appliances at his command, to have stopped the train before it reached him.

. . . .

[1] Statement omitted, also a large part of opinion.

In Gunter *v.* Wicker, 85 N. C. 310, this court gave its sanction to the principle first distinctly formulated in Davies *v.* Mann, 10 M. & W. (Ex.) 545, that " Notwithstanding the previous negligence of the plaintiff, if at the time the injury was done it might have been avoided by the exercise of reasonable care and prudence on the part of the defendant, an action will lie for damages." This doctrine was subsequently approved in Saulter *v.* Steamship Co., 88 N. C. 123; Turrentine *v.* Railroad, 92 N. C. 638; Meredith *v.* Iron Co., 99 N. C. 576; Roberts *v.* Railroad, 88 N. C. 560; Farmer *v.* Railroad, *Ibid.* 564; Bullock *v.* Railroad, 105 N. C. 180; Wilson *v.* Railroad, 90 N. C. 69; Snowden *v.* Railroad, 95 N. C. 93; Carlton *v.* Railroad, 104 N. C. 365; Randall *v.* Railroad, 104 N. C. 108; Bullock *v.* Railroad, 105 N. C. 180, and it was repeatedly declared in those cases that it was negligence on the part of the engineer of a railway company to fail to exercise reasonable care in keeping a lookout not only for stock and obstructions but for apparently helpless or infirm human beings on the track, and that the failure to do so supervening after the negligence of another, where persons or animals were exposed to danger, would be deemed the proximate cause of any resulting injury.

. . . .

[As to argument for defendant.] But the reasons and the authorities relied upon emanate generally from courts which hold that both persons and animals upon a track are trespassers and entitled to consideration only where actually seen in time to save them. . . .

It cannot be denied that, in a number of the states which have adopted the doctrine of Davies *v.* Mann, it has also been held that both man and beast were trespassers when they went upon a railway track and except at public crossings or in towns it was not the duty of the engineer to exercise care in looking to his front with a view to the protection of either. Where the law does not impose the duty of watchfulness it follows that the failure to watch is not an omission of duty intervening between the negligence of the plaintiff in exposing himself and the accident, unless he be actually seen in time to avert it. The negligence of the corporation grows out of omission of a legal duty and there can be no omission where there is no duty prescribed.

. . . .

We are of opinion that, when by the exercise of ordinary care an engineer can see that a human being is lying apparently helpless from any cause on the track in front of his engine in time to stop the train by the use of the appliances at his command and without peril to the safety of persons on the train, the company is liable for any injury resulting from his failure to perform his duty. If it is the settled law of North Carolina (as we have shown) that it is the duty of an engineer on a moving train to maintain a reasonably vigilant outlook along the track in his front, then the failure to do so is an omission of a legal duty. If by the performance of that duty an accident might have been averted, notwithstanding the previous negligence of another, then, under the doctrine of Davies *v.* Mann, and Gunter *v.* Wicker,[1] the breach of duty was the proximate cause of any injury growing out of such accident, and where it is a proximate cause the company is liable to respond in damages. Having adopted the principle that one whose duty it is to see does see, we must follow it to its logical results. The court committed no error of which the defendant could justly complain in stating the general rule which we have been discussing. . . . .

[1] 85 N. C. 310.

DYERSON *v.* UNION PACIFIC RAILROAD COMPANY

SUPREME COURT, KANSAS, NOVEMBER 10, 1906.

Reported in 74 *Kansas Reports*, 528.

PLAINTIFF sued for damages caused by being struck by the tender of an engine.

Plaintiff, an employee of the R. R. Co., had occasion to cross the track. As he was about to step upon the track, he was struck by the tender of a locomotive which was backing east at the rate of fifteen or twenty miles an hour without giving a signal of its approach and without keeping a lookout along the track. The track was straight for a quarter of a mile west. It was a clear day, and there was nothing to have prevented the plaintiff from seeing the engine and tender if he had looked.[1]

At the trial, the court rendered judgment against plaintiff upon his petition and preliminary statement to the jury which disclosed the above facts. Plaintiff brought error.

MASON, J.

. . . .

Finally it is contended in behalf of the plaintiff that, even admitting his own want of care to have been such as would ordinarily bar a recovery, still he had a right to submit to the jury the question whether the employees in charge of the engine by the use of reasonable diligence could have discovered his negligence in time to avert the accident, and that an affirmative answer would have entitled him to a verdict.

. . . .

In a number of cases it has been held that if the engineer by the exercise of reasonable diligence could have learned that danger was imminent but did not do so, the liability of the company will be determined in all respects as though he had in fact become aware of it, the constructive knowledge being apparently deemed the equivalent of actual knowledge. It is difficult or impossible to reconcile the decisions upon this and related questions, or to derive from them any generally accepted statement either of principle or result. Many of them are collected and discussed in chapter ix of volume i of Thompson's Commentaries on the Law of Negligence, especially in sections 222 to 247.

There seems, however, to be no sufficient reason why the mere fact that a defendant is negligent in failing to discover a plaintiff's negligence, or his danger, should in and of itself exclude all consideration of contributory negligence. Take the not unusual situation of a train being negligently operated, let us say by being run at too high a speed and without proper signals of warning being given. Now, any one injured as a result of such negligence has *prima facie* a right to recover. But, if his own negligence has contributed to his injury, then ordinarily his right is barred. How is the situation altered if the railroad employees add to their negligence in regard to speed and signals the negligence of failing to keep a sufficient lookout ? The negligence is of the same sort; and, if the contributory negligence of the person injured prevents a recovery when

[1] Statement abridged. Part of opinion omitted.

but the two elements of negligence are present, consistency requires that it should have the same effect although a third element is added. If in the present case the plaintiff was entitled to recover in spite of his own negligence it must be because the order of its occurrence with respect to that of the defendant made the latter the proximate cause of the injury. This indeed is his contention, and to support it reliance is placed upon the following text, which was quoted with approval in Railway Co. *v.* Arnold, 67 Kan. 260, 72 Pac. 857, and the substance of which is to be found also in volume xx of the American and English Encyclopædia of Law, at page 137: —

" And upon the principle that one will be charged with notice of that which by ordinary care he might have known, it is held that if either party to an action involving the questions of negligence and contributory negligence should, by the exercise of ordinary care, have discovered the negligence of the other, after its occurrence, in time to foresee and avoid its consequences, then such party is held to have notice; and his negligence in not discovering the negligence of the other, under such circumstances, is held the sole proximate cause of a following injury." (7 A. & E. Encycl. of L. 387.)

This may be accepted as a correct statement of a principle of universal application, according with both reason and authority, provided the words " after its occurrence " be interpreted to mean after the person concerned had ceased to be negligent. The rule that under the circumstances stated the neglect of one party to discover the omission of the other is to be held to be the sole proximate cause of a resulting injury is not an arbitrary but a reasonable one. The test is, What wrongful conduct occasioning an injury was in operation at the very moment it occurred or became inevitable ? If just before that climax only one party had the power to prevent the castastrophe, and he neglected to use it, the legal responsibility is his alone. If, however, each had such power, and each neglected to use it, then their negligence was concurrent and neither can recover against the other. As is said in the paragraph from which the foregoing quotation is made, " it is only when the negligence of one party is subsequent to that of the other that the rule can be invoked." In a note printed in volume ii of the supplement to the American and English Encyclopædia of Law, at page 64, many recent cases are cited bearing on the subject, and it is said: —

" This so-called exception to the rule of contributory negligence (*i. e.*, the doctrine of ' the last clear chance ') will not be extended to cases where the plaintiff's own negligence extended up to and actually contributed to the injury. To warrant its application there must have been some new breach of duty on the part of the defendant subsequent to the plaintiff's negligence."

In the present case it may be granted that the negligence of the plaintiff began when he walked between the track and the ice-box on the way to get the bucket, and that the employees in charge of the engine were themselves negligent in not discovering this negligence on his part and the peril to which it exposed him, and taking steps to protect him. But his negligence as well as theirs continued up to the moment of the accident, or until it could not possibly be averted. His opportunity to discover and avoid the danger was at least as good as theirs. His want of care existing as late as theirs was a concurring cause of his injury, and bars his recovery. This determination is entirely consistent with what Mr. Thompson in his work above cited has styled the " last clear chance " doctrine, as is obvious from a consideration of the terms in which it is stated. As originally announced it was thus phrased: —

"The party who has the last opportunity of avoiding accident is not excused by the negligence of any one else. His negligence, and not that of the one first in fault, is the sole proximate cause of the injury." (1 Shear. & Red. Law of Neg., 5th ed., § 99.)

Mr. Thompson rewords it as follows: —

"Where both parties are negligent, the one that had the last clear opportunity to avoid the accident, notwithstanding the negligence of the other, is solely responsible for it — his negligence being deemed the direct and proximate cause of it." (1 Thomp. Com. Law Neg. § 240.)

Expressions are to be found in the reports seemingly at variance with the conclusion here reached, but for the most part the decisions holding a defendant liable for failure to discover and act upon the plaintiff's negligence were made in cases which were in fact like Railway Co. v. Arnold, 67 Kan. 260, 72 Pac. 857, or were decided upon the theory that they fell within the same rule. There the plaintiff's decedent while riding a bicycle was through his own fault run into by a street car; he clung to the fender, was carried some seventy-five feet, then fell under the wheels, and was killed. A judgment against the street-car company was upheld only upon the theory that after he had reached a position of danger from which he could not extricate himself — that is, after his negligence had ceased — the defendant's employees were negligent in in failing to discover his peril and stop the car.

In Robinson v. Cone, 22 Vt. 213, 54 Am. Dec. 67, the writer of the opinion said: —

"I should hesitate to say that if it appeared that the want of ordinary care on the part of the plaintiff, *at the very time of the injury*, contributed either to produce or to enhance the injury, he could recover; because it seems to me that is equivalent to saying that the plaintiff, by the exercise of ordinary care at the time, could have escaped the injury." (Page 223.)

The principle thus intimated was embodied in a decision in French v. The Grand Trunk Railway Co., 76 Vt. 441, 58 Atl. 722, where it was said: —

It is true that when a traveller has reached a point where he cannot help himself, cannot extricate himself, and vigilance on his part will not avert the injury, his negligence in reaching that position becomes the condition and not the proximate cause of the injury, and will not preclude a recovery; but it is equally true that if a traveller, when he reaches the point of collision, is in a situation to help himself, and by a vigilant use of his eyes, ears, and physical strength to extricate himself and avoid injury, his negligence at that point will prevent a recovery, notwithstanding the fact that the trainmen could have stopped the train in season to have avoided injuring him. In such a case the negligence of the plaintiff is concurrent with the negligence of the defendant, and the negligence of each is operative at the time of the accident. When negligence is concurrent and operative at the time of the collision, and contributes to it, there can be no recovery." (Page 447.)

To the same effect are these extracts: —

. . . .

[As to the rule holding the defendant liable notwithstanding the contributory negligence of the plaintiff.]

Of the same rule it was said in O'Brien v. McGlinchy, 68 Me. 552:

"This rule applies usually in cases where the plaintiff or his property is in some position of danger from a threatened contact with some agency under the control of the defendant when the plaintiff cannot and the defendant can prevent an injury. . . . But this principle would not govern where both parties are contemporaneously and actively in fault, and by their mutual carelessness an injury ensues to one or both of them." (Pages 557, 558.)

In Smith *v.* Railroad, 114 N. C. 728, 19 S. E. 863, 25 L. R. A. 287, the general rule was thus concretely stated: —

" Applying the rule which we have stated to accidents upon railroad tracks, it may be illustrated as follows: First, there must be a duty imposed upon the engineer, as otherwise there can be no negligence to which the negligence of the injured party is to contribute. The duty under consideration is to keep a vigilant lookout . . . in order to discover and avoid injury to persons who may be on the track and who are apparently in unconscious or helpless peril. When such a person is on the track and the engineer fails to discover him in time to avoid a collision, when he could have done so by the exercise of ordinary care, the engineer is guilty of negligence. The decisive negligence of the engineer is when he has reached that point when no effort on his part can avert the collision. Hence, if A, being on the track and after this decisive negligence, fails to look and listen and is in consequence run over and injured, his negligence is not concurrent merely but really subsequent to that of the engineer, and he cannot recover, as he and not the engineer has ' the last clear opportunity of avoiding the accident.' If, however, A is on the track . . . and while there, and before the decisive negligence of the engineer, he by his own negligence becomes so entangled in the rails that he cannot extricate himself in time to avoid the collision, and his helpless condition could have been discovered had the engineer exercised ordinary care, then the negligence of A would be previous to that of the engineer, and the engineer's negligence would be the proximate cause, he, and not A, having the last clear opportunity of avoiding the injury. The same result would follow in the case of a wagon negligently stalled, when no effort of the owner could remove it, and there are other cases to which the principle is applicable." (Pages 755, 756.)

The principle running through these cases is reasonable and is consistent with the general rules that have met with practically universal acceptance. Applied to the facts of this case it requires an affirmance of the judgment.

All the Justices concurring.

BAKER, J., IN CLEVELAND R. CO. *v.* KLEE

(1900) 154 *Indiana*, 430, 434, 435.

BAKER, J. It is alleged in the fifth paragraph: " That on or about the 22d day of June, 1894, this plaintiff, a child nine years of age, was on the said crossing of Georgia and Helen streets and upon said track of said defendant in said Georgia Street; and while in said position and place, the defendant through and by its said employees and servants, ran said locomotive against this plaintiff and negligently dragged this plaintiff without fault or negligence on his part, a long distance, to wit, two hundred feet; that the defendant knew that it had run its locomotive against this plaintiff at said crossing; and knew that it had knocked this plaintiff down in front of its said locomotive upon its said track; and knew that this plaintiff was dragging in front of said locomotive on said track; but that this defendant negligently failed to stop said locomotive before this plaintiff was injured, although by the exercise of due care and caution it could have stopped said locomotive before this plaintiff was injured;

but negligently dragged this plaintiff as aforesaid, without fault or negligence on the part of this plaintiff, and negligently injured this plaintiff in his body, back, and limbs." The injury for which compensation is sought in this paragraph was not sustained in the collision at the crossing, but was wholly inflicted after appellant knew that appellee was being dragged along the track in front of the engine. By the exercise of due care appellant could have stopped the engine before appellee was injured, but failed to do so. Appellee, after being struck and while being dragged along the track, was free from fault contributing to his injury. These allegations constitute a cause of action. Though the paragraph confesses, by not denying, that appellee was guilty of negligence in being upon the track, that negligence was only the remote condition, not the proximate cause, of the injury complained of; for the injury resulted, after the collision, entirely from occurrences in which it is alleged that appellant was negligent and appellee was not.

HOLMES v. MISSOURI PACIFIC RAILWAY COMPANY

SUPREME COURT, MISSOURI, NOVEMBER 27, 1907.

Reported in 207 *Missouri Reports*, 149.

ACTION by C. W. Holmes and wife to recover for the death of their child, F. G. Holmes. The child, eight years old, was struck and killed by a locomotive engine at the crossing of an avenue. Two points in conflict were, whether defendant was negligent, and whether the child was contributorily negligent.

The following instruction was given at plaintiff's request: "(4) If the jury believe from the evidence that Freeborn G. Holmes was a boy of immature age, and had not the capacity of an adult, and that he exercised such care as ought reasonably to have been expected for one of his age and capacity, then he was not guilty of contributory negligence."

To this instruction defendant excepted.

An instruction given at the request of defendant was, that, if the child failed to exercise such care and caution as an ordinarily prudent boy of his age and capacity should have exercised under the circumstances, and by reason thereof contributed to his own death, then your verdict must be for the defendant, regardless of all other facts in the case.

Verdict for plaintiff. Judgment for plaintiff in Circuit Court. Defendant appealed.[1]

VALLIANT, J. . . . In the brief for defendant, pages 61 and 139, the idea is advanced that the only theory on which the plaintiffs' judgment could be sustained would be that the defendant is liable for the consequences of the reckless conduct of the deceased child. That is a misconception of the theory on which the defendant's liability rests. The defendant is liable only for its own negligence, and if its plea of contributory negligence is not sustained, still, it is not charged with the consequence of the child's negligence; but it is only not excused thereby for the result of its own negligence. It is not always essential to a plaintiff's recovery, in an action for tort, that the evidence should show that the accident was the result of the defendant's negligence alone. A de-

[1] The statement has been abridged and the arguments and part of the opinion are omitted.

fendant may be liable if his negligence contributes with that of a third person to produce the injury complained of; in such case he is not held liable for the negligence of the third person, but only for his own negligence, without the contributing force of which the negligence of the third person would not have caused the injury. But the policy of the law is such that ordinarily a defendant guilty of negligence is relieved from the liability for his own conduct if the person injured was himself guilty of negligence that contributed to the result. On that theory the defendant's act is none the less negligent, and he is none the less culpable, but the law will not allow a plaintiff to recover when he himself, or the person for whose injury he sues, was also guilty of negligence contributing with that of defendant to the result. There is reason and justice in that policy of the law; it is an admonition to every one to exercise due care for his own safety, and it authorizes another to presume that he will do so, and, so presuming, adjust his own conduct. But common experience tells us that a child may be too young and immature to observe the care necessary to his own preservation and therefore when a person comes in contact with such a child, if its youth and immaturity are obvious, he is chargeable with knowledge of that fact and he cannot indulge the presumption that the child will do what is necessary to avoid an impending danger. Therefore one seeing such a child in such a position is guilty of negligence if he does not take into account the fact that it is a child and regulate his own conduct accordingly.[1] An act in relation to a person of mature years might be free from the imputation of negligence while an act of like character in view of a child would be blameworthy. Therefore when the law says to the defendant although the act of the deceased child contributed with your act to produce the result, yet, because of his youth and immaturity, he is not adjudged guilty of negligence, it does not charge the defendant with the consequence of the child's conduct, but it only does not, for that reason, excuse him for its [his] own negligence.

If the defendant in such case had been guilty of no negligence there would have been no accident. *Judgment affirmed.*

GANTT, C. J., and BURGESS, LAMM, and WOODSON, JJ., concur. FOX and GRAVES, JJ., dissent.

CULBERTSON *v.* CRESCENT CITY RAILROAD CO.

SUPREME COURT, LOUISIANA, APRIL 6, 1896.

Reported in 48 Louisiana Annual Reports, Part 2, 1376.

PLAINTIFF sued for the killing of his son, 6 years and 11 months old, who was hit by a car at a street crossing.

In the District Court, there was a verdict for plaintiff, and judgment thereon. Defendant appealed.[2]

BREAUX, J. [After stating the claims of both parties, and reciting the testimony of plaintiff's witnesses and of part of defendant's witnesses.]

The motorman and the conductor substantially testify that everything was done to prevent the accident; that the boy darted in front of the car and, that the motorman quickly stopped the car.

[1] See also Weitzman *v.* Nassau R. Co., 33 App. Div. 585; Green *v.* Metropolitan R. Co., 42 App. Div. 160.
[2] Statement abridged.

After as careful and close an analysis of the evidence as it was possible for us to make, we think that the weight of the testimony is with the defendant.

Plaintiff's theory that the little boy was standing on the track, between the rails, and that the motorman ought to have seen him, is not sustained by the evidence of his own witnesses; they do not testify, with any degree of certainty, where he was just preceding the accident. The witnesses for the defendant agree in stating that he was not on the track, and that the accident was occasioned by the sudden act of the child.

Granted as contended by the plaintiff that the motorman did not see the child before he was knocked down by the fender: if the child had escaped his attention, because of his sudden and unanticipated act itself, it becomes evident that the defendant is not liable. Whether he was seen or was not seen by the motorman would not render the defendant responsible, if owing to thoughtless impulse of the child he brought about the accident by a sudden act which could not be foreseen or guarded against by the motorman or any one else in charge of the car.

This brings us to the question of contributory negligence. Courts are averse to finding children guilty of contributory negligence, and are readily and properly inclined to disregard the thoughtlessness natural to boyhood, but accidents may happen for which the unconscious agent may not be responsible.

The fact that a child may not be capable of contributory negligence does not always render a defendant liable upon the mere proof of the injury. The test is negligence *vel non*. If the defendant or the defendant's agent or employee was not negligent, it is not liable.

The only alternative, after the conclusion reached, is to set aside the verdict.

The verdict and judgment are reversed, annulled and avoided.

The demand of plaintiff is rejected and his action dismissed at his cost in both courts.[1]

HUTCHINSON *v.* ST. LOUIS & MERAMEC RIVER RAILROAD COMPANY

ST. LOUIS COURT OF APPEALS, MISSOURI, APRIL 9, 1901.

Reported in 88 *Missouri Appeal Reports*, 376.

APPEAL from St. Louis City Circuit Court.

Plaintiff (respondent) was injured while driving on the track of the street railroad at the crossing of two streets. The car collided with the rear of his wagon. Plaintiff testified that he had been driving for some three hundred yards with the left wheels of his wagon inside the north rail. Defendant's (appellant's) testimony tended to prove that plaintiff did not drive on the track until he had either reached or was near the crossing, and that he then turned and drove onto the track,

[1] In Kierzenkowski *v.* Philadelphia Traction Co., 184 Pa. St. 459, the plaintiff was a girl three years old, who had been knocked down by one of defendant's horse cars. The court (*inter alia*) instructed the jury, in substance, as follows: —

The law does not allow that children of this age can be guilty of contributory negligence; but you are obliged to consider the case as to the negligence alone of when the motor car coming up from behind collided with the rear of his wagon.

What is undisputed is, that he did not look back to see if a car was coming before attempting to cross, nor, according to his own testimony, after he drove onto the track three hundred yards or more to the east. He drove very slowly. There was testimony tending to show the motorneer in charge of the car was watching a train on the railroad just south of Manchester avenue, which inattention prevented him from observing plaintiff's perilous position until the car was within twenty or thirty feet of the wagon. He was required by a city ordinance, to be watching the track.

The evidence as to the warning of the car's approach was conflicting.

The plaintiff was entitled to the use of the entire street, and, therefore, was not a trespasser, while the defendant was entitled to the right of way.

Failure to signal the car's approach was omitted from the instructions. The only ground of recovery submitted to the jury was alleged negligence of the defendant's motorneer in not using ordinary care to avoid injuring plaintiff after he knew, or by the proper care might have known, the latter was in a dangerous position. One instruction was given that plaintiff was guilty of contributory negligence if he failed to look back at reasonable intervals to see if a car was coming and to get off the track if he saw one. This was practically telling them he was actually negligent, for he admitted he did not look back.

GOODE, J. The general principle on which the case was referred to the jury, commonly styled the humane doctrine, is well supported by authorities. It is accepted in some form in most of the state and federal jurisdictions. So far as this court is concerned, the rule is no longer debatable. All uncertainty about it being a substantive part of the law of torts has been set at rest by recent deliberate pronouncements of the Supreme Court. The authority of the rule is not impugned by the learned counsel for the appellant, who only insist that it is inapplicable to the cause in hand on account of the plaintiff's clear contributory negligence which continued to the moment of the collision. This contention requires a brief examination of some cases in which the doctrine has been applied. They divide into two classes and the disputation which has raged over it has been on the border line between the two. As enforced in one class, the rule has always

the defendant. If you were driving along the street with your horse and wagon, and a child runs under the feet of the horses and is killed, you are not responsible; not because the child is guilty of contributory negligence, but because you are not guilty of negligence. If it is an unavoidable accident, you are not responsible. If the jury believe from the evidence in this case that the child suddenly and unexpectedly appeared in the vicinity of the track under such circumstances that the driver of the car could not have discovered its presence in time to avoid the accident, the verdict must be for the defendant.

An exception to the charge was overruled.

seemed to the writer to be a phase of the doctrine of proximate cause, consistent with the theory of the entire law of negligence and without which the system would be incomplete. These instances are where the plaintiff's negligent act was detached from the injury so that the defendant's want of care was the sole active agency in inflicting it. When an accident happens under such circumstances, the plaintiff ought not to be refused a recovery because, though remiss, his fault does not contribute to the injury. Illustrations of this class of cases are numerous in the books, beginning with the one from which all the others proceeded. Davies *v.* Mann, 10 Mees. & W. 546, where the plaintiff had carelessly fettered his beast in the highway and the defendant's servant drove over him. It is manifest that the original negligence of the owner was separated from the injury, which was proximately caused solely by the defendant's tort. Another apt illustration is found in the Reardon case (114 Mo. 384), where the plaintiff carelessly went on the railway track and fell in endeavoring to get off when he saw a train coming. It was held that if the engineer failed to employ ordinary care to stop the train when he saw him prostrate, the company was liable. The same ruling has been made in actions where plaintiffs had fallen asleep on tracks or become fastened in cattle guards or switches or where the person hurt was a child or otherwise not of full legal capacity (Gabel *v.* Railway Co., 60 Mo. 475). The doctrine is exclusively met with, so far as our reading has shown, in controversies arising from injuries due to violent impacts and collisions. The above instances exemplify its use in such cases where properly expounded, it does not clash with the doctrine of contributory negligence, though some of the applications made have laid it open to that charge. The reconciliation and harmonious working of the two rules may be achieved by considering closely whether the defendant's carelessness was alone the proximate cause of the injury. If only the defendant's was the proximate cause, the plaintiff, while guilty of negligence, was not guilty of contributory negligence; his failure to use care did not proximately contribute to the mischief. Time elapsed between his wrongful act and the injury, during which the wrongful act of the defendant supervened or entered, as a separate agency, which, by its own independent action, wrought the unfortunate result. If, however, the plaintiff's want of care continues to the instant of the accident, or so near the instant as to be immediately influential in producing it, he is as much to blame as the defendant, and if the latter is compelled to compensate him, the theory of the law of negligence is thus far abandoned. When it is deemed expedient to allow a recovery under such circumstances, it must be done as a measure of public policy. The rule then becomes, in fact, an exception to the law of contributory negligence, as was said in Kelly *v.* Railway Co., 101 Mo. 67. The real basis of it, as it obtains in many jurisdictions in respect to injuries by cars and locomotives when the injured individual was negligent to the very instant of the collision, is to be sought, on an ultimate analysis, in its supposed necessity for the public security. The guilt of the plaintiff is excused, while that of the defendant is punished. In such instances, its administration in cases of injuries by cars and engines is attended with serious difficulty, viz.: determining when the employees of the railway company may be justly said to have had notice that the injured party was in a position of danger. Persons frequently remain on railway tracks when a car or train is approaching, until it would be impossible to stop it in time to avoid striking them, but easily get off themselves in time. Accustomed to take care of their safety where cars are constantly moving, they grow dexterous in avoiding them and run risks. Engineers and motormen have a right to presume an individual travelling on the track will leave it, and to act on that presumption until his situation becomes alarming. Riley *v.* Railway Company, 68 Mo. App. 661. Just when this happens must often be largely conjectural, which circumstance weighs heavily with many against the rule in question.

The doctrine in its wider scope prevails in this State. The plaintiff may recover, notwithstanding his negligence directly contributed to his hurt, if the defendant by ordinary care could have prevented the accident. In the Morgan case (60 S. W. Rep. 195), where a recovery was sustained, this language is spoken: "There can be no doubt, under the evidence, that the death of the plaintiff's husband resulted from the negligence of the defendant's servants in charge of the train, *and the negligence of the deceased himself contributing thereto.*" Similar expositions have been made in many other cases. Schmidt *v.* R'y Co., 50 S. W. 921; Klockenbrink *v.* Railway Co., 81 Mo. App. 351; Cooney *v.* Railway Co., 80 Mo. App. 226. They seem in conflict with the opinion in Hogan *v.* R'y Co., 150 Mo. 36. We must follow the latest controlling decision. The Morgan case was decided in banc.

In view of the strong utterances to be found in the foregoing authorities, it is useless to descant on the wisdom or fallacy of the rule, to explore its foundation, extol its justice, or regret its hardship. Our unmistakable duty is to enforce it as we would any other part of the law. The present case differs in no material respect, calling for its application, from the Morgan or Cooney cases, *supra,* which become therefore controlling precedents. The Morgan case is stronger because there the engineer did not see the deceased, who was flagrantly careless, to the time the engine struck him; here the motorman did not see the plaintiff. The court below did not err in refusing an instruction to find the issue for the defendant, but rightly submitted them. This practically disposes of the case.

. . . .

Judgment affirmed.[1]

[1] Birmingham R. Co. *v.* Brantley, 141 Ala. 614; Baltimore Traction Co. *v.* Wallace, 77 Md. 435; Lassiter *v.* Raleigh R. Co., 133 N. C. 244; Memphis R. Co. *v.* Haynes, 112 Tenn. 712 *Accord.*

"Let us view this subject in a more concrete form. The last railroad statistics

STEINMETZ *v.* KELLY

SUPREME COURT, INDIANA, NOVEMBER TERM, 1880.

Reported in 72 *Indiana Reports*, 442.

WORDEN, J. Action by the appellee against the appellant for assault and battery. The complaint consisted of three paragraphs, a demurrer to each of which, for want of sufficient facts, was overruled. The first, the only one to which any specific objection is made in this Court, alleged that the defendant, on, &c., "violently and unlawfully assaulted the plaintiff, and struck him, and also threw him, the plaintiff, from the house of the defendant on to the street pavement, in front of the defendant's house, with great violence, fracturing," &c.

The defendant answered: —

First. [That there was a justifiable occasion for his use of force, and that he used no more force than was necessary.]

Second. General denial.

The plaintiff replied by general denial to the first paragraph of the answer. Trial by jury, verdict and judgment for the plaintiff for $500.

The counsel for the appellant in their brief say: "We shall not stop now to discuss the merits of the complaint further than to say that the first paragraph of the complaint shows an eviction from the defendant's premises, and we have thought that the paragraph should aver

I have been able to find were issued by the Interstate Commerce Commission for the year 1906.

[The learned judge then copies a table from the report referred to and proceeds.]

It will be observed that while the road mileage and train mileage in Canada are each ten per cent of the entire road system and the entire train mileage, the number of trespassers injured or killed in that country was only three per cent of the total number; while in this State the road mileage is twenty-six per cent of the total road mileage and the train mileage twenty-five per cent of the total train mileage, forty-eight per cent of the total number of trespassers injured or killed were injured or killed in Missouri.

Illinois has thirty per cent of the road mileage and thirty-two per cent of the train mileage, and only twenty per cent of the total number of trespassers injured or killed were injured or killed in that State.

It is important to know both the train mileage and the road mileage, for the reason the greater number of trains that are run over a given road mileage the greater number of fatalities to trespassers will result. The train mileage, therefore, in the various States offers the most accurate basis for comparison.

A computation will show that one trespasser was killed for every eighty-one miles of road in Canada; for every seventeen miles in Michigan; for every forty-two miles in Ohio; for every thirty-one miles in Indiana; for every forty-six miles in Illinois; for every seventeen miles in Missouri; and for every forty-one miles in Iowa.

It will be observed that the number of miles for each trespasser killed in Missouri and Michigan is the same. This results, however, from the fact that the line from Chicago, St. Louis, and other points converging at Montpelier, Ohio, and thence all the traffic eastward goes over the one hundred and five miles of line located in the State of Michigan. The effect of this is also shown in the train mileage. Thus, while Michigan has only four per cent of road mileage, it has one-third or six per cent of the train mileage. The population along the Michigan that the injury occurred without the fault of the plaintiff." The paragraph does not charge an injury to the plaintiff arising out of the negligence of the defendant, but an unlawful assault upon, and battery of, the plaintiff's person. In such cases it is not necessary to allege that the plaintiff was without fault, or, in other words, was not guilty of contributory negligence. There remains nothing more to be considered except such questions as arise on a motion for a new trial.

[Omitting part of opinion.]

The defendant asked that the following interrogatory be answered by the jury, if they should return a general verdict, viz.: "Did the fault or negligence of the plaintiff contribute in any way to the injury of the plaintiff, received on the evening of the 3d of March, 1876 ?" The Court declined to direct the jury to answer the interrogatory, and in this we think no error was committed.

The right of the plaintiff to recover depended not upon any negligence of the defendant, but upon the assault and battery, which, if perpetrated at all by the defendant, was intentional and purposed. It may be that the defendant did not intend to inflict so severe an injury upon the plaintiff as seemed to result from the excess of force applied by him; but it does not therefore follow that he did not intend to apply that force.

The doctrine that contributory negligence on the part of the plaintiff will defeat his action has been generally applied in actions based on the negligence of the defendant, in short, in cases involving mutual negligence. But it has also been applied in some cases where the matter complained of was not negligence merely, but the commission of some act in itself unlawful, without reference to the manner of com-

mileage is very dense; about five miles of the line from Delray to Detroit run through a very densely populated district — practically a city.

It should also be noted that while Illinois has greater road and train mileage than Missouri, only sixteen trespassers were injured or killed while walking on tracks in that State, where thirty-nine persons were killed or injured while walking on the track in Missouri. If we also consider the more dense population of Illinois, the figures become more startling. And if we should extend these figures in the same proportion to all of the railroads of the State and country, we would then see the appalling number of trespassers killed and injured annually on account of this inhuman doctrine, which is approximately 7750.

In so far as I have been able to ascertain, the courts of all the other States than this hold that persons who walk upon railroad tracks do so at their peril, and I am thoroughly satisfied and convinced that this fact accounts for the small number of fatalities to track-walkers in those States as compared with Missouri; and by parity of reasoning I am also convinced that if said section 1105 was strictly enforced, as it should be, the contrast between those States and this would not be near so great as it is now; and that if we had a statute like that of Canada, making it a crime for persons to walk upon railroad tracks, then the percentage of fatalities to track-walkers in this State would fall still lower than what it is in any of the States mentioned. Such a policy and such a statute would exclude from the railroads all pedestrians, and thereby save this great sacrifice of life and limb, as well as the pecuniary loss incident thereto." WOODSON, J. (dissenting), in Murphy *v.* Wabash Railroad Company, 228 Mo. 56, 88, 108.

See also the observations of Professor Clark in University of Missouri Bulletin, Law Series, No. 12, 34–39.

mitting it, as the wilful and unauthorized obstruction of a highway, whereby a person is injured. Butterfield *v.* Forrester, 11 East, 60; Dygert *v.* Schenck, 23 Wend. 446.

The doctrine, however, can have no application to the case of an intentional and unlawful assault and battery, for the reason that the person thus assaulted is under no obligation to exercise any care to avoid the same by retreating or otherwise, and for the further reason that his want of care can in no just sense be said to contribute to the injury inflicted upon him by such assault and battery.

An intentional and unlawful assault and battery inflicted upon a person is an invasion of his right of personal security, for which the law gives him redress, and of this redress he cannot be deprived on the ground that he was negligent and took no care to avoid such invasion of his right.

The trespass was purposely committed by the defendant. If he could excuse it on the ground of the alleged misconduct of the plaintiff, and if he employed no more force than was necessary and reasonable, that was a complete defence. Otherwise the plaintiff, if he made out the trespass, was entitled to recover, and no negligence on his part, as before observed, could defeat his action. The case of Ruter *v.* Foy, 46 Iowa, 132, is in point. There the plaintiff alleged that the defendant had assaulted and beat her with a pitchfork. On the trial the defendant asked, but the Court refused, the following instruction: "If you find from the evidence that the plaintiff was injured, or contributed to her injury, by her own act or negligence, defendant would not be liable for assault and battery upon her, and plaintiff cannot recover." On appeal the Court said upon this point: "The doctrine of contributory negligence has no application in an action for assault and battery."

The case here is entirely unlike that of Brown *v.* Kendall, 6 Cush. 292. There the defendant's dog and another were fighting. The defendant was beating the dogs with a stick in order to separate them, in doing which he accidentally hit the plaintiff in the eye with the stick. It was held that trespass *vi et armis* was the proper form of action, because the injury to the plaintiff was immediate; but that as the parting of the dogs was a proper and lawful act, and as the hitting of the plaintiff was not intentional, but a mere accident or casualty, the plaintiff could not recover at all without showing a want of ordinary care on the part of the defendant; and then that contributory negligence on the part of the plaintiff would defeat the action.

Although, according to the common-law system of pleading, trespass *vi et armis* was the proper form of action in such case, the essential and only ground on which the action could rest was the negligence of the defendant in doing an act lawful in itself whereby the plaintiff was injured, and this is so as fully as if the plaintiff had framed his declaration in case for the negligence.

The difference between that case and the present is substantial and vital. In that case the battery was unintentional, and the defendant therein was guilty of no wrong save his negligence. Here the defendant intentionally perpetrated the battery, and the plaintiff's right to recover was not based upon the negligence of the defendant at all.

[Omitting part of opinion.]

We find no error in the record.

The judgment below is affirmed with costs.

Petition for a rehearing overruled. *Judgment affirmed.*[1]

AIKEN *v.* HOLYOKE STREET RAILWAY CO.

SUPREME JUDICIAL COURT, MASSACHUSETTS, OCTOBER 21, 1903.

Reported in 184 *Massachusetts Reports*, 269.

TORT by an infant against a street railway company for personal injuries. Writ dated July 6, 1898.

At a previous stage of this case, reported in 180 Mass. 8, the plaintiff's exceptions were sustained by this court after a verdict had been ordered in the Superior Court for the defendant. At the new trial in the Superior Court before Lawton, J., the jury returned a verdict for the plaintiff in the sum of $5000. The defendant alleged exceptions, raising the questions stated by the court.

KNOWLTON, C. J. The most important question in this case grows out of the instructions to the jury upon the third count. This count charges the defendant, by its servants, with having started up the car recklessly, wantonly and with gross disregard of the plaintiff's safety, while he was in a place of great peril upon the step of the car, and with having thrown him upon the ground and under the wheels of the car. There was evidence tending to show that the plaintiff, a boy six and one half years of age, ran near or against the car, and was upon the lower step at the forward end as the car was going around a curve from one street into another, and was clinging to the step trying to get into a stable position, and that he there cried out to the motorman, "Let me off"; that the motorman saw and heard him and knew that he was in a place of danger, and that he then turned on the power in a wanton and reckless way, with a view to start the car quickly, and that the plaintiff was thus thrown off and injured. This testimony was contradicted, but it was proper for the consideration of the jury. The judge instructed the jury that if they found the facts to be in accordance with this contention of the plaintiff, they would be warranted in finding that the conduct of the motorman was wanton and reckless, and in returning a verdict for the plaintiff. He also instructed them that to maintain the action on this ground, it must be proved that the

[1] Birmingham Light & Power Co. *v.* Jones, 146 Ala. 277; Indianapolis R. Co. *v.* Boettcher, 131 Ind. 82 *Accord.*

motorman wilfully and intentionally turned on the power, with a view to making the car start forward rapidly and go at full speed quickly, but that it was not necessary to prove that he did this with the intention of throwing the boy off and injuring him. He also told them that to warrant a recovery upon this state of facts, the plaintiff need not show that he was in the exercise of due care. The defendant excepted to that part of the instruction which relates to due care on the part of the plaintiff.

The defendant contends that while it was not necessary for the plaintiff to show due care anterior to the act of the motorman, he was bound to show due care which was concurrent with this act and immediately subsequent to it. This brings us to a consideration of the rules and principles applicable to this kind of liability. It is familiar law that in the absence of a statutory provision, mere negligence, whatever its degree, if it does not include culpability different in kind from that of ordinary negligence, does not create a liability in favor of one injured by it, if his own negligence contributes to his injury. It is equally true that one who wilfully and wantonly, in reckless disregard of the rights of others, by a positive act or careless omission exposes another to death or grave bodily injury, is liable for the consequences, even if the other was guilty of negligence or other fault in connection with the causes which led to the injury. The difference in rules applicable to the two classes of cases results from the difference in the nature of the conduct of the wrongdoers in the two kinds of cases. In the first case the wrongdoer is guilty of nothing worse than carelessness. In the last he is guilty of a wilful, intentional wrong. His conduct is criminal or *quasi* criminal. If it results in the death of the injured person, he is guilty of manslaughter. Commonwealth *v.* Pierce, 138 Mass. 165; Commonwealth *v.* Hartwell, 128 Mass. 415. The law is regardful of human life and personal safety, and if one is grossly and wantonly reckless in exposing others to danger, it holds him to have intended the natural consequences of his act, and treats him as guilty of a wilful and intentional wrong. It is no defence to a charge of manslaughter for the defendant to show that, while grossly reckless, he did not actually intend to cause the death of his victim. In these cases of personal injury there is a constructive intention as to the consequences, which, entering into the wilful, intentional act, the law imputes to the offender, and in this way a charge which otherwise would be mere negligence, becomes, by reason of a reckless disregard of probable consequences, a wilful wrong. That this constructive intention to do an injury in such cases will be imputed in the absence of an actual intent to harm a particular person, is recognized as an elementary principle in criminal law. It is also recognized in civil actions for recklessly and wantonly injuring others by carelessness. Palmer *v.* Chicago, St. Louis & Pittsburgh Railroad, 112 Ind. 250; Shumacher *v.* St. Louis & San Francisco

Railroad, 39 Fed. Rep. 174; Brannen *v.* Kokomo, Greentown & Jerome Gravel Road Co., 115 Ind. 115. In an action to recover damages for an assault and battery, it would be illogical and absurd to allow as a defence, proof that the plaintiff did not use proper care to avert the blow. See Sanford *v.* Eighth Avenue Railroad, 23 N. Y. 343, 346. It would be hardly less so to allow a similar defence where a different kind of injury was wantonly and recklessly inflicted. A reason for the rule is the fact that if a wilful, intentional wrong is shown to be the direct and proximate cause of an injury, it is hardly conceivable that any lack of care on the part of the injured person could so concur with the wrong as also to be a direct and proximate contributing cause to the injury. It might be a condition without which the injury could not be inflicted. See Newcomb *v.* Boston Protective Department, 146 Mass. 596. It might be a remote cause, but it hardly could be a cause acting directly and proximately with the intentional wrongful act of the offender. Judson *v.* Great Northern Railway, 63 Minn. 248, 255. The offence supposed is different in kind from the plaintiff's lack of ordinary care. It is criminal or *quasi* criminal. Not only is it difficult to conceive of a plaintiff's negligence as being another direct and proximate cause foreign to the first, yet acting directly with it, but it would be unjust to allow one to relieve himself from the direct consequences of a wilful wrong by showing that a mere lack of due care in another contributed to the result. The reasons for the rule as to the plaintiff's care in actions for ordinary negligence are wanting, and at the same time the facts make the rule impossible of application. The general rule that the plaintiff's failure to exercise ordinary care for his safety, is not a good defence to an action for wanton and wilful injury caused by a reckless omission of duty, has been recognized in many decisions, as well as by writers of text-books. Aiken *v.* Holyoke Street Railway, 180 Mass. 8, 14, 15; Wallace *v.* Merrimack River Navigation & Express Co., 134 Mass. 95; Banks *v.* Highland Street Railway, 136 Mass. 485, 486; Palmer *v.* Chicago, St. Louis & Pittsburgh Railroad, 112 Ind. 250; Brannen *v.* Kokomo, Greentown & Jerome Gravel Road Co., 115 Ind. 115; Florida Southern Railway *v.* Hirst, 30 Fla. 1; Shumacher *v.* St. Louis & San Francisco Railroad, 39 Fed. Rep. 174; 7 Am. & Eng. Encyc. of Law (2d ed.) 443 and note; Beach, Contr. Neg. (3d ed.) §§ 46, 50, 64, 65; Wood, Railroads (2d ed.), 1452; Elliott, Railroads, § 1175; Thompson, Neg. § 206; Cooley, Torts (2d ed.), 810. We have been referred to no case in which it is held that it makes any difference whether the plaintiff's lack of ordinary care is only previous to the defendant's wrong and continuing to the time of it, or whether there is such a lack after the wrong begins to take effect. It is difficult to see how there can be any difference in principle between the two cases. In this Commonwealth, as in most other jurisdictions, liability does not depend upon which of different causes contributing to an injury is latest in the time of its origin, but upon which is the direct, active, efficient cause, as distinguished from a remote cause, in producing the result.

There are expressions in some of the cases which imply the possibility of contributory negligence on the part of the plaintiff in a case of wanton and reckless injury by a defendant. If there is a conceivable case in which a plaintiff's want of due care may directly and proximately contribute as a cause of an injury inflicted directly and proximately by the wilful wrong of another, such a want of care must be something different from the mere want of ordinary care to avoid an injury coming in a usual way. There is nothing to indicate the existence of peculiar conditions of this kind in the present case. Conduct of a plaintiff which would be negligence precluding recovery if the injury were caused by ordinary negligence of a defendant, will not commonly preclude recovery if the injury is inflicted wilfully through wanton carelessness. This is illustrated by the former decision in this case and by many others. Aiken *v.* Holyoke Street Railway, 180 Mass. 8; McKeon *v.* New York, New Haven, & Hartford Railroad, 183 Mass. 271. As to this kind of liability of the defendant, it was certainly proper to instruct the jury that, in reference to ordinary kinds of care to avoid an injury from a car, the plaintiff need not show that he was in the exercise of due care if a lack of such care would have no tendency to cause the wilful and wanton injury. The fair interpretation of the instruction given is, that it referred to ordinary kinds of care to avoid an injury from an electric car. On this branch of the case there seems to have been no reason for an instruction in regard to any special care, and probably neither counsel nor the court had any care in mind except that, in reference to which, in any view of the law, the instruction was properly given. We are of opinion that the ruling excepted to was correct.

[Omitting opinion on other points.] *Exceptions overruled.*[1]

BANKS *v.* BRAMAN

SUPREME JUDICIAL COURT, MASSACHUSETTS, JUNE 20, 1905.

Reported in 188 *Massachusetts Reports*, 367.

TORT, for injuries from being struck by an automobile driven by the defendant on Mount Auburn Street in Cambridge near its intersection with Belmont Street shortly after eight o'clock on the evening of May 17, 1903. Writ dated November 18, 1903.

[1] Southern R. Co. *v.* Svendsen, 13 Ariz. 111; Kramm. *v.* Stockton R. Co., 10 Cal. App. 271; Nehring *v.* Connecticut Co., 86 Conn. 109; Central R. Co. *v.* Moore, 5 Ga. App. 562; Heidenreich *v.* Bremner, 260 Ill. 439; Kansas R. Co. *v.* Whipple, 39 Kan. 531; Schoolcraft *v.* Louisville R. Co., 92 Ky. 233; La Barge *v.* Pere Marquette R. Co., 134 Mich. 139; St. Louis R. Co. *v.* Ault, 101 Miss. 341; Brendle *v.* Spencer, 125 N. C. 474; Goodwin *v.* Atlantic R. Co., 82 S. C. 321; Bolin *v.* Chicago R. Co., 108 Wis. 333 *Accord.*

At the trial in the Superior Court before Aiken, C. J., the jury returned a verdict for the plaintiff in the sum of $3750; and the defendant alleged exceptions, raising the questions stated by the court.

KNOWLTON, C. J. This is an action to recover for injuries received from being struck by an automobile alleged to have been negligently run at an excessive rate of speed, and negligently managed by the defendant. The case was submitted to the jury on two alleged grounds of liability: one, that the defendant, with gross negligence, wantonly and recklessly injured the plaintiff, and the other that the plaintiff was in the exercise of due care, and that the injury was due to the defendant's negligence. On the first claim the judge instructed the jury as follows: " Gross negligence is great negligence. To make out the proposition of gross negligence, you must be satisfied that the way the machine was operated by Braman was reckless, was careless to the degree of recklessness; that it was run with a reckless disregard to the rights of Banks in this street. If that is established, namely, that there was a reckless disregard of the rights of Banks in the way this machine was run, then Banks is not required to show that he was himself in the exercise of due care. If the way — I repeat this for the purpose of plainness perhaps unnecessarily — if the manner in which the machine — the automobile, I mean by the machine — was run on the occasion of this accident was such that it was grossly negligent, that is, careless to such a degree that you can say it was reckless, using your common sense and judgment, and applying them to the evidence, then Banks is not required to show that he was in the exercise of due care; because if the defendant's carelessness was gross in the sense that has been defined to you, there is an obligation to pay damages independent of the matter of due care." The defendant excepted to this instruction. The jury were instructed as to the liability for a failure to exercise ordinary care, but there was no fuller statement of the law on this branch of the case.

The question is whether the difference between the two kinds of liability was sufficiently pointed out to give the jury an adequate understanding of it. The difference in culpability of the defendant, which distinguishes these different kinds of liability, is something more than a mere difference in the degree of inadvertence. In one case there need be nothing more than a lack of ordinary care, which causes an injury to another. In the other case there is wilful, intentional conduct whose tendency to injure is known, or ought to be known, accompanied by a wanton and reckless disregard of the probable harmful consequences from which others are likely to suffer, so that the whole conduct together, is of the nature of a wilful, intentional wrong.

[Here the learned judge quoted at length from Aiken *v.* Holyoke Street Railway, 184 Mass. 269, 271.]

In dealing with the same subject in Bjornquist *v.* Boston & Albany Railroad, 185 Mass. 130, 134, the court said: " The conduct which creates a liability to a trespasser in cases of this kind has been referred to in the books in a variety of ways. Sometimes it has been called gross negligence and sometimes wilful negligence. Plainly it is something more than is necessary to constitute the gross negligence referred to in our statutes and in decisions of this court. The term 'wilful negligence' is not a strictly accurate description of the wrong. But wanton and reckless negligence in this class of cases includes something more than ordinary inadvertence. In its essence it is like a wilful, intentional wrong. It is illustrated by an act which otherwise might be unobjectionable, but which is liable or likely to do great harm, and which is done in a wanton and reckless disregard of the probable injurious consequences." The ground on which it is held that, when an act of the defendant shows an injury inflicted in this way, the plaintiff need introduce no affirmative evidence of due care, is that such a wrong is a cause so independent of previous conduct of the plaintiff, which, in a general sense, may fall short of due care, that this previous conduct cannot be considered a directly contributing cause of the injury, and, in reference to such an injury, the plaintiff, without introducing evidence, is assumed to be in a position to claim his rights and to have compensation. So far as the cause of his injury is concerned, he is in the position of one who exercises due care. Aiken *v.* Holyoke Street Railway, *ubi supra.*

It is not easy to explain to a jury the nature of this liability. What was said by the judge in this case comes very near to a correct statement of the law. But it lacks something in fulness, and we think the jury may have understood that negligence somewhat greater in degree than a mere lack of ordinary care or a simple inadvertence, but not different from it in kind, would constitute the gross negligence referred to. We are of opinion that when there is an attempt to establish this peculiar kind of liability, which exists independently of a general exercise of due care by the plaintiff, the jury should be instructed with such fulness as to enable them to know that they are dealing with a wrong materially different in kind from ordinary negligence. Because we think the instruction may have left the jury with a misunderstanding of the law, the exceptions are sustained.

We are of opinion that there was evidence which justified the submission of the case to the jury on this ground, as well as on the ground that the plaintiff was in the exercise of due care.

Exceptions sustained.[1]

[1] Carrington *v.* Louisville R. Co., 88 Ala. 472; Wood *v.* Los Angeles R. Co., 172 Cal. 15; Rowen *v.* New York R. Co., 59 Conn. 364; Florida R. Co. *v.* Hirst, 30 Fla. 1; Louisville R. Co. *v.* McCoy, 81 Ky. 403; Davis *v.* Saginaw Bay R. Co., 191 Mich. 131 *Accord.* Compare Magar *v.* Hammond, 171 N. Y. 377.

"Mere negligence which gives a cause of action is the doing of an act, or the omission to act, which results in damage, but without intent to do wrong or cause damage. To constitute a wilful injury, there must be design, purpose, intent to do wrong and inflict the injury. Then there is that reckless indifference or disregard of the natural or probable consequence of doing an act, or omission of an act, desig-

GEORGIA PACIFIC RAILWAY CO. *v.* LEE

SUPREME COURT, ALABAMA, NOVEMBER TERM, 1890.

Reported in 92 *Alabama Reports*, 262.

McCLELLAN, J.[1] . . . Many of the rulings of the trial court in defining the gross negligence, recklessness or wantonness on the part of the defendant, which will authorize recovery, notwithstanding plaintiff's contributory negligence, are presented for review. The fault in the court's definitions in this regard lies, in our opinion, in the assumption that recklessness or wantonness implying wilful and intentional wrong-doing may be predicated of a mere omission of duty, under circumstances which do not, of themselves, impute to the person so failing to discharge the duty a sense of the probable consequences of the omission. The charges given by the court in this connection, and its rulings on charges requested by the defendant, proceed on the theory that a mere failure on the part of defendant's employees to see plaintiff's wagon and

nated whether accurately or not, in our decisions, as 'wanton negligence,' to which is imputed the same degree of culpability and held to be equivalent to wilful injury. A purpose or intent to injure is not an ingredient of wanton negligence. Where either of those exist, if damage ensues, the injury is wilful. In wanton negligence, the party doing the act, or failing to act, is conscious of his conduct, and without having the intent to injure, is conscious, from his knowledge of existing circumstances and conditions, that his conduct will likely or probably result in injury. These are the distinctions between simple negligence, wilful injury, and that wanton negligence which is the equivalent of wilful injury, drawn and applied in our decisions. A mere error of judgment as to the result of doing an act or the omission of an act, having no evil purpose or intent, or consciousness of probable injury, may constitute simple negligence, but cannot rise to the degree of wanton negligence or wilful wrong. . . ." Coleman, J., in Birmingham R. Co. *v.* Bowers, 110 Ala. 328, 331.

"The mere intentional omission to perform a duty or the intentional doing of an act contrary to duty, although such conduct be culpable and result in injury, without further averment, falls very far short of showing that the injury was intentionally or wantonly inflicted. Unless there was a purpose to inflict the injury, it cannot be said to have been intentionally done; and unless an act is done, or omitted to be done, under circumstances and conditions known to the person, that his conduct is likely to, or probably will result in injury, and through reckless indifference to consequences, he consciously and intentionally does a wrongful act, or omits an act, the injury cannot be said to be wantonly inflicted. These principles have been frequently declared by this court. . . ." Coleman, J., in Memphis R. Co. *v.* Martin, 117 Ala. 367, 382.

Central R. Co. *v.* Newman, 94 Ga. 560; Lafayette R. Co. *v.* Adams, 26 Ind. 76; Chicago R. Co. *v.* Bills, 118 Ind. 221; Alger *v.* Duluth-Superior Traction Co., 93 Minn. 314; Jensen *v.* Denver R. Co., 44 Utah, 100; Boggess *v.* Chesapeake R. Co., 37 W. Va. 297; Astin *v.* Chicago R. Co., 143 Wis. 477 *Contra.* But see Jaggard, J., dissenting, in Anderson *v.* Minneapolis R. Co., 103 Minn. 224, 230.

"For a motorman to be inattentive to the way ahead of him is so palpably negligent that it partakes of the nature of a reckless and wanton act. Therefore a defendant in an action of this character will not be heard to say that its motorman did not see the situation of the injured person where it was open to his view nor did not realize the peril where the indications would have disclosed it to any reasonable mind. Charged with the knowledge of the peril of another that could have been obtained by the use of ordinary care, a failure on the part of a motorman to make every reasonable effort to avoid injuring the endangered person would be in the highest degree wrongful, since it would be negligence committed with the knowl-

[1] Only a portion of the opinion is printed.

team as soon as they might have seen them by the exercise of due care was such recklessness or wantonness as implies a willingness or a purpose on their part to inflict the injury complained of. We do not think this proposition can be maintained either logically or upon the authorities. The failure to keep a lookout, which it was the duty of defendant's employees to maintain, and which would have sooner disclosed the peril of the driver and plaintiff's wagon and team — even conceding that such would have been the case — was, at the most, mere negligence, inattention, inadvertence; and it cannot be conceived, in the nature of things, how a purpose to accomplish a given result can be imputed to mental conditions, the very essence of which is the absence of all thought on the particular subject. To say that one intends a result which springs solely from his mind not addressing itself to the factors which conduce to it, to imply a purpose to do a thing from inadvertence in respect of it, are contradictions in terms. Wilful and intentional wrong, a willingness to inflict injury, cannot be imputed to one who is without consciousness, from whatever cause, that his conduct will inevitably or probably lead to wrong and injury. In the case at bar, this consciousness could not exist on the part of defendant's employees until they knew plaintiff's wagon and team were in a position of danger; and no degree of ignorance on their part of this state of things, however reprehensible in itself, could supply this element of conscious wrong, or reckless indifference to consequences, which, from their point of view, would probably or necessarily ensue.

The true doctrine, and that supported by many decisions of this court, as well as the great weight of authority in other jurisdictions, is that notwithstanding plaintiff's contributory negligence he may yet recover, if, in a case like this, the defendant's employees *discover the perilous situation in time to prevent disaster by the exercise of due care and diligence, and fail, after the peril of plaintiff's property becomes known to them as a fact* — and not merely after they should have known it — *to resort to all reasonable effort to avoid the injury.* Such failure, with such knowledge of the situation and the probable consequences of the omission to act upon the dictates of prudence and diligence to the end of neutralizing plaintiff's fault and averting disaster, notwithstand-

edge that another certainly and immediately would be injured thereby. The principles of right and justice do not tolerate the idea that the negligence of the person imperilled involved in his act of placing himself in position to be injured without giving proper heed to his own safety can coöperate with the negligence of one who comprehending his danger or being in a position to comprehend it by the use of ordinary care and having at hand the means and opportunity of avoiding it, fails to reasonably employ them and by such failure inflicts an injury. Such negligence engrosses the entire field of culpability and eliminates contributory negligence as a factor in the production of the injury. It logically follows from the principles stated that the issue of negligence in the performance of the humanitarian duty must be governed by the rules applicable to ordinary negligence. The determinative question in all such cases is, did the operators of the car use ordinary care to ascertain the peril of the plaintiff and to avoid the injury after they discovered it or should have discovered it ? In some of the decisions of the Supreme Court the idea appears to be expressed that in order to find a defendant guilty of a breach of the humanitarian rule the elements of wantonness and wilfulness must appear in its conduct, but as we have attempted to show the mere failure to observe ordinary care in situations of this character is of itself a wanton act since it is abhorrent not only to fundamental principles of law but to the dictates of common humanity. The views expressed are supported by the weight of authority in this state, including the most recent decisions of the Supreme and Appellate courts. . . ." Johnson, J., in Cole v. Metropolitan R. Co., 121 Mo. App. 605, 611.

ing his lack of care, is, strictly speaking, not *negligence* at all, though the term "gross negligence" has been so frequently used as defining it that it is perhaps too late, if otherwise desirable, to eradicate what is said to be an unscientific definition, if not indeed a misnomer; but it is more than any degree of negligence, inattention or inadvertence — which can never mean other than the omission of action without intent, existing or imputed, to commit wrong — it is that recklessness, or wantonness, or worse, which implies a willingness to inflict the impending injury, or a wilfulness in pursuing a course of conduct which will naturally or probably result in disaster, or an intent to perpetrate wrong. The theory of contributory negligence, as a defence, is that, conjointly with *negligence* on the part of the defendant, it conduces to the damnifying result, and defeats any action, the *gravamen* of which is such negligence. If defendant's conduct is not merely negligent, but worse, there is nothing for plaintiff's want of care to contribute to — there is no lack of mere prudence and diligence of like kind on the part of defendant to conjunctively constitute the efficient cause. Mere negligence on the one hand cannot be said to aid wilfulness on the other. And hence such negligence of a plaintiff is no defence against the consequences of the wilfulness of the defendant. But nothing short of the elements of actual knowledge of the situation on the part of defendant's employees, and their omission of preventive effort after that knowledge is brought home to them, when there is reasonable prospect that such effort will avail, will suffice to avoid the defence of contributory negligence on the part of, or imputable to, the plaintiff.

KELLOGG *v.* CHICAGO AND NORTHWESTERN RAILWAY COMPANY

SUPREME COURT, WISCONSIN, JUNE TERM, 1870.

Reported in 26 *Wisconsin Reports,* 223.

ACTION to recover damages for destruction of hay, sheds, stables, &c., by a fire alleged to have originated in the negligence of the railway company. Fire was communicated by sparks from railroad engine to dry grass, weeds, &c., which had been allowed to accumulate on defendant's land, on both sides of the track; and thence the fire passed upon plaintiff's land where dry grass and weeds had also been permitted to accumulate. A strong wind was blowing from the track toward plaintiff's buildings, about one hundred and forty rods distant. The dry and combustible matter on the railroad land and on plaintiff's land, together with the wind, served to carry the fire to plaintiff's building, &c., which were destroyed.

Trial; verdict and judgment for plaintiff. Defendant appealed.[1]

DIXON, C. J. All the authorities agree that the presence of dry grass and other inflammable material upon the way of a railroad, suffered to remain there by the company without cause, is a fact from

[1] Statement of facts abridged. Arguments omitted. Only such portion of the two opinions of Dixon, C. J., are given as relate to one question. The dissenting opinion of Paine, J., is omitted.

which the jury may find negligence against the company. The cases in Illinois, cited and relied upon by counsel for the defendant, hold this. They hold that it is proper evidence for the jury, who may find negligence from it, although it is not negligence *per se*. Railroad Co. *v.* Shanefelt, 47 Ill. 497; Illinois Central Railroad Co. *v.* Nunn, 51 id. 78; Railroad Co. *v.* Mills, 42 id. 407; Bass *v.* Railroad Co., 28 id. 9. The Court below ruled in the same way, and left it for the jury to say whether the suffering of the combustible material to accumulate upon the right of way and sides of the track, or the failure to remove the same, if the jury so found, was or was not, under the circumstances, negligence on the part of the company. No fault can be found with the instructions in this respect; and the next question is as to the charge of the Court, and its refusal to charge, respecting the alleged negligence of the plaintiff contributing, as it is said, to the loss or damage complained of. This is the leading and most important question in the case. It is a question upon which there is some conflict of authority.

The facts were, that the plaintiff had permitted the weeds, grass, and stubble, to remain upon his own land immediately adjoining the railway of the defendant. They were dry and combustible, the same as the weeds and grass upon the right of way, though less in quantity, because within the right of way no mowing had ever been done, and the growth was more luxuriant and heavy. The plaintiff had not cut and removed the grass and weeds from his own land, nor ploughed in or removed the stubble, so as to prevent the spread of fire in case the same should be communicated to the dry grass and weeds upon the railroad, from the engines operated by the defendant. The grass, weeds, and stubble, upon the plaintiff's land, together with the wind, which was blowing pretty strongly in that direction, served to carry the fire to the stacks, buildings, and other property of the plaintiff, which were destroyed by it, and which were situated some distance from the railroad. The fire originated within the line of the railroad, and near the track, upon the land of the defendant. It was communicated to the dry grass and other combustible material there, by coals of fire dropped from an engine of the defendant passing over the road. The evidence tends very clearly to establish these facts, and under the instructions the jury must have so found. The plaintiff is a farmer, and, in the particulars here in controversy, conducted his farming operations the same as other farmers throughout the country. It is not the custom anywhere for farmers to remove the grass or weeds from their waste lands, or to plough in or remove their stubble, in order to prevent the spread of the fire originating from such causes.

Upon this question, as upon the others, the Court charged the jury that it was for them to say whether the plaintiff was guilty of negligence, and, if they found he was, that then he could not recover. On the other hand, the defendant asked an instruction to the effect that it was negligence *per se* for the plaintiff to leave the grass, weeds, and stubble upon his own land, exposed to the fire which might be communicated to them from the burning grass and weeds on the defendant's right of way, and that for this reason there could be no recovery on the part of the plaintiff. The Court refused to give the instruction, and, I think, rightly. The charge upon this point, as well as upon the other, was quite as favorable to the defendant as the law will permit, and even more so than some of the authorities will justify. The authorities upon this point are, as I have said, somewhat in conflict. The two cases first above cited from Illinois hold that it is negligence on the part of the adjoining landowner not to remove the dry grass and combustible material from his own land under such circumstances, and that he cannot recover damages where the loss is by fire thus communicated. Those decisions were by a divided Court, by two only of the three judges composing it. They rest upon no satisfactory grounds, whilst the reasons found in the opinions of the dissenting judge are very strong to the contrary. Opposed to these are the unanimous decisions of the courts of New York, and of the English Court of Exchequer, upon the identical point. Cook *v.* Champlain Transportation Co., 1 Denio, 91; Vaughan *v.* Taff Vale Railway Co., 3 Hurl. and Nor. 743; Same *v.* Same, 5 id. 679. These decisions, though made many years before the Illinois cases arose, are not referred to in them. The last was the same case on appeal in the Exchequer Chamber, where, although the judgment was reversed, it was upon another point. This one was not questioned, but was affirmed, as will be seen from the opinions of the judges, particularly of Cockburn, C. J., and Willes, J. The reasoning of those cases is, in my judgment, unanswerable. I do not see that I can add anything to it. They show that the doctrine of contributory negligence is wholly inapplicable, — that no man is to be charged with negligence because he uses his own property or conducts his own affairs as other people do theirs, or because he does not change or abandon such use, and modify the management of his affairs, so as to accommodate himself to the negligent habits or gross misconduct of others, and in order that such others may escape the consequences of their own wrong, and continue in the practice of such negligence or misconduct. In other words, they show that no man is to be deprived of the free, ordinary, and proper use of his own property by reason of the negligent use which his neighbor may make of his. He is not his neighbor's guardian or keeper, and not to answer for his neglect. The case put by the Court of New York, of the owner of a lot who builds upon it in close proximity to the shop of a smith, is an apt illustration. Or let us suppose that A. and B. are proprietors of adjoining lands. A. has a dwelling-house, barns, and other buildings upon his, and cultivates some portion of it. B. has a planing mill, or other similar manufacturing establishment upon his, near the line of A., operated by steam. B. is a careless man, habitually so, and suffers shavings and other inflammable material to accumulate about his mills and up to the line of A., and so near to the fire in the mill that the same is liable at any time to be ignited. A. knows this, and remonstrates with B., but B. persists. Upon A.'s land, immediately adjoining the premises of B., it is unavoidable, in the ordinary course of husbandry, or of A.'s use of the land, that there should be at certain seasons of the year, unless A. removes them, dry grass and stubble, which, when set fire to, will endanger his dwelling-house and other property of a combustible nature, especially with the wind blowing in a particular direction at the time. It may be a very considerable annual expense and trouble to A. to remove them. It may require considerable time and labor, a useless expenditure to him, diverting his attention from other affairs and duties. The constant watching to guard against the carelessness and negligence of B. is a great tax upon his time and patience. The question is: Does the law require this of him, lest, in some unguarded moment, the fire should break out, his property be destroyed, and he be remediless ? If the law does so require, if it imposes on him the duty of guarding against B.'s negligence, and of seeing that no injury shall come from it, or, if it does come, that it shall be his fault and not B.'s, it is important to know upon what principle it is that the burden is thus shifted from B. to himself. I know of no such principle, and doubt whether any Court could be found deliberately to announce or affirm it. And yet such is the result of holding the doctrine of contributory negligence applicable to such a case. A. is compelled, all his lifetime, at much expense and trouble, to watch and guard against the negligence of B., and to prevent any injuries arising from it, and for what ? Simply that B. may continue to indulge in such negligence at his pleasure. And he does so with impunity. The law affords no redress against him. If the property is destroyed, it is because of the combustible material on A.'s land, which carries the fire, and which is A.'s fault, and A. is the loser. No loss can ever possibly overtake him. A. is responsible for the negligence, but not he himself. He kindles the fire, and A. stands guard over it. He sets the dangerous element in motion, and uses and operates it for his own benefit and advantage, negligently as he pleases, whilst A., with sleepless vigilance, sees to it that no damage is done, or if there is, that he will be the sufferer. This is the *reductio ad absurdum* of applying the doctrine of contributory negligence in such a case. And it is absurd, I care not by what Court or where applied.

Now the case of a railroad company is like the case of an individual. Both stand on the same footing with respect to their rights and liabilities. Both are engaged in the pursuit of a lawful business, and are alike liable for damage or injury caused by their negligence in the prosecution of it. Fire is an agent of an exceedingly dangerous and unruly kind, and, though applied to a lawful purpose, the law requires the utmost care in the use of all reasonable and proper means to prevent damage to the property of third persons. This obligation of care, the want of which constitutes negligence according to the circumstances, is imposed upon the party who uses the fire, and not upon those persons whose property is exposed to danger by reason of the negligence of such party. Third persons are merely passive, and have the right to remain so, using and enjoying their own property as they will, so far as responsibility for the negligence of the party setting the unruly and destructive agent in motion is concerned. If he is negligent, and damage ensues, it is his fault and cannot be theirs, unless they contribute to it by some unlawful or improper act. But the use of their own property as best suits their own convenience and purposes, or as other people use theirs, is not unlawful or improper. It is perfectly lawful and proper, and no blame can attach to them. He cannot, by his negligence, deprive them of such use, or say to them, "Do this or that with your property, or I will destroy it by the negligent and improper use of my fire." The fault, therefore, in both a legal and moral point of view, is with him, and it would be something strange should the law visit all the consequences of it upon them. The law does not do so, and it is an utter perversion of the maxim *sic utere tuo, etc.*, thus to apply it to the persons whose property is so destroyed by the negligence of another. It is changing it from "So use your own as not to injure another's property," to "So use your own that another shall not injure your property," by his carelessness and negligence. It would be a very great burden to lay upon all the farmers and proprietors of lands along our extensive lines of railway, were it to be held that they are bound to guard against the negligence of the companies in this way, — that the law imposes this duty upon them. Always burdensome and difficult, it would, in numerous instances, be attended with great expense and trouble. Changes would have to be made in the mode of use and occupation, and sometimes the use abandoned, or at least all profitable use. Houses and buildings would have to be removed, and valuable timber cut down and destroyed. These are, in general, very combustible, especially at particular seasons of the year. The presence of these along or near the line of the railroad would be negligence in the farmer or proprietor. In the event of their destruction by the negligence of the company, he would be remediless. He must remove them, therefore, for his own safety. His only security consists in that. He must remove everything combustible from his own land in order that the company may leave all things combustible on its land and exposed without fear of loss or danger to the company to being ignited at any moment by the fires from its own engines. If this duty is imposed upon the farmers and other proprietors of adjoining lands, why not require them to go at once to the railroad and remove the dry grass and other inflammable material there? There is the origin of the mischief, and there the place to provide securities against it. It is vastly easier, by a few slight measures and a little precaution, to prevent the conflagration in the first place than to stay its ravages when it has once begun, particularly if the wind be blowing at the time, as it generally is upon our open prairies. With comparatively little trouble and expense upon the road itself, a little labor bestowed for that purpose, the mischief might be remedied. And this is an additional reason why the burden ought not to be shifted from the company upon the proprietor of the adjoining land; although, if it were otherwise, it certainly would not change what ought to be the clear rule of law upon the subject.

And the following cases will be found in strict harmony with those above cited, and strongly to sustain the principles there laid down, and for which I contend: Martin *v.* Western Union Railroad Co., 23 Wis. 437; Piggott *v.* Eastern Counties R. R. Co., 54 E. C. L. 228; Smith *v.* London and Southwestern R. R. Co., Law Reports, 5 C. P. 98; Vaughan *v.* Menlove, 7 C. & P. 525 [32 E. C. L. 613]; Hewey *v.* Nourse, 54 Me. 256; Turberville *v.* Stampe, 1 Ld. Raym. 264; s. c. 1 Salk. 13; Pantam *v.* Isham, id. 19; Field *v.* N. Y. C. R. R., 32 N. Y. 339; Bachelder *v.* Heagan, 18 Maine, 32; Barnard *v.* Poor, 21 Pick. 378; Fero *v.* Buffalo and State Line R. R. Co., 22 N. Y. 209; Fremantle *v.* The London and Northwestern R. R. Co., 100 E. C. L. 88; Hart *v.* Western Railroad Co., 13 Met. 99; Ingersoll *v.* Stockbridge & Pittsfield R. R. Co., 8 Allen, 438; Perley *v.* Eastern Railroad Co., 98 Mass. 414; Hooksett *v.* Concord Railroad, 38 N. H. 242; McCready *v.* Railroad Co., 2 Strobh. Law R. 356; Cleveland *v.* Grand Trunk Railway Co., 42 Vt. 449; 1 Bl. Comm. 131; Com. Dig. Action for Negligence (A. 6).

It is true that some of these cases arose under statutes creating a liability on the part of railroad companies, but that does not affect the principle. Negligence in the plaintiff, contributing to the loss, is a defence to an action under the statutes, the same as to an action at common law. 8 Allen, 440; 6 id. 87.

COLE, J., concurred.

PAINE, J., delivered a dissenting opinion.

Judgment affirmed.

Defendants moved for a rehearing.

DIXON, C. J. (Sept. 21, 1871.) . . .

The learned counsel . . . argue that, if logically carried out, the doctrine would utterly abrogate the rule that a party cannot recover damages where, by the exercise of ordinary care, he could have avoided the injury; and so, in the present case, after discovering the fire, the plaintiff might have leaned on his plough-handles and watched its progress, without effort to stay it, where such effort would have been effectual, and yet have been free from culpable negligence. The distinction is between a known, present, or immediate danger, arising from the negligence of another, — that which is imminent and certain, unless the party does or omits to do some act by which it may be avoided, — and a danger arising in like manner, but which is remote and possible or probable only, or contingent and uncertain, depending on the course of future events, such as the future conduct of the negligent party, and other as yet unknown and fortuitous circumstances. The difference is that between realization and anticipation. A man in his senses, in face of what has been aptly termed a "seen danger" (Shearman and Redfield, § 34, note 1), that is, one which presently threatens and is known to him, is bound to realize it, and to use all proper care and make all reasonable efforts to avoid it, and if he does not, it is his own fault; and he having thus contributed to his own loss or injury, no damage can be recovered from the other party, however negligent the latter may have been. But, in case of a danger of the other kind, one which is not "seen," but exists in anticipation merely, and where the injury may or may not accrue, but is probable or possible only from the continued culpable negligence of another, there the law imposes no such duty upon the person who is or may be so exposed, and he is not obliged to change his conduct or the mode of transacting his affairs, which are otherwise prudent and proper, in order to avoid such anticipated injuries or prevent the mischiefs which may happen through another's default and culpable want of care.

Rehearing denied.[1]

[1] Vaughan *v.* Taff Vale R. Co., 3 H. & N. 743; Leroy Fibre Co. *v.* Chicago R. Co., 232 U. S. 340; Flynn *v.* San Francisco R. Co., 40 Cal. 14; Fitch *v.* Pacific R. Co., 45 Mo. 322; Salmon *v.* Delaware R. Co., 38 N. J. Law, 5; Philadelphia R. Co. *v.* Schultz, 93 Pa. St. 341 *Accord.* But see Collins *v.* New York R. Co., 5 Hun, 499.

In Leroy Fibre Co. *v.* Chicago R. Co., *supra,* Holmes, J., (concurring in the result) said:

"If a man stacked his flax so near to a railroad that it obviously was likely to be set fire to by a well-managed train, I should say that he could not throw the loss upon the road by the oscillating result of an inquiry by the jury whether the road had used due care. I should say that although of course he had a right to put his flax where he liked upon his own land the liability of the railroad for a fire was absolutely conditioned upon the stacks being at a reasonably safe distance from the train. I take it that probably many, certainly some, rules of law based on less than universal considerations are made absolute and universal in order to limit those over-refined speculations that we all deprecate, especially where such rules are based upon or affect the continuous physical relations of material things. The right that is given to inflict various inconveniences upon neighboring lands by building or digging, is given, I presume, because of the public interest in making improvement free, yet it generally is made absolute by the common law. It is not thought worth while to let the right to build or maintain a barn depend upon the speculations of a jury as to motives. A defect in the highway, declared a defect in the interest of the least competent travellers that can travel unattended without taking legal risks, or in the interest of the average man, I suppose to be a defect as to all. And as in this case the distinction between the inevitable and the negligent escape of sparks is one of the most refined in the world, I think that I must be right so far, as to the law in the case supposed.

If I am right so far, a very important element in determining the right to recover is whether the plaintiff's flax was so near to the track as to be in danger from even a prudently managed engine. Here certainly, except in a clear case, we should call

THE BERNINA

In the Court of Appeal, January 24, 1887.

Reported in Law Reports, 12 Probate Division, 58.

Appeal from a judgment of Butt, J. (in the Probate, Divorce, and Admiralty Division, reported in 11 Prob. Div. 31), on a special case stated for the opinion of the Court, in three actions brought *in personam* against the owners of the steamer Bernina.

Butt, J., held, on the authority of Thorogood *v.* Bryan, 8 C. B. 115, that the plaintiffs were unable to recover against the defendants, and dismissed the actions.

The plaintiffs appealed.[1]

Lindley, L. J. This was a special case. Three actions are brought in the Admiralty Division of the High Court by the respective legal personal representatives of three persons on board the Bushire against the owners of the Bernina. Those persons were killed by a collision between the two vessels, both of which were negligently navigated. One of the three persons (Toeg) was a passenger on the Bushire; one (Armstrong) was an engineer of the ship, though not to blame for the collision. The third (Owen) was her second officer, and was in charge of her, and was himself to blame for the collision. The ques-

in the jury. I do not suppose that any one would call it prudent to stack flax within five feet of the engines or imprudent to do it at a distance of half a mile, and it would not be absurd if the law ultimately should formulate an exact measure, as it has tended to in other instances; (Martin *v.* District of Columbia, 205 U. S. 135, 139) but at present I take it that if the question I suggest be material we should let the jury decide whether seventy feet was too near by the criterion that I have proposed. Therefore, while the majority answer the first question, No, on the ground that the railroad is liable upon the facts stated as matter of law, I should answer it Yes, with the proviso that it was to be answered No, in case the jury found that the flax, although near, was not near enough to the trains to endanger it if the engines were prudently managed, or else I should decline to answer the question because it fails to state the distance of the stacks.

I do not think we need trouble ourselves with the thought that my view depends upon differences of degree. The whole law does so as soon as it is civilized. See Nash *v.* United States, 229 U. S. 373, 376, 377. Negligence is all degree — that of the defendant here degree of the nicest sort; and between the variations according to distance that I suppose to exist and the simple universality of the rules in the Twelve Tables or the Leges Barbarorum, there lies the culture of two thousand years."

Where inflammable matter is brought upon land and kept near the track, see Erickson *v.* Pennsylvania R. Co., (C. C. A.) 170 Fed. 572; Southern R. Co. *v.* Wilson, 138 Ala. 510; Railway Co. *v.* Fire Ass'n, 55 Ark. 163; Cleveland R. Co. *v.* Scantland, 151 Ind. 488; Boston Excelsior Co. *v.* Bangor, 93 Me. 52; Peter *v.* Chicago R. Co., 121 Mich. 324; Kalbfleisch *v.* Long Island R. Co., 102 N. Y. 520; Southern R. Co. *v.* Patterson, 105 Va. 6, in accord with the principal case. See also Ross *v.* Boston R. Co., 6 All. 87.

Macon R. Co. *v.* McConnell, 27 Ga. 481; Coates *v.* Missouri R. Co., 61 Mo. 38 (but see Mo. Rev. St. 1909, § 3151); Murphy *v.* Chicago R. Co., 45 Wis. 222 *Contra.*

Compare Alabama R. Co. *v.* Fried, 81 Miss. 314; Louisville R. Co. *v.* Short, 110 Tenn. 713; San Antonio R. Co. *v.* Home I. Co., (Tex. Civ. App.) 70 S. W. 999.

[1] Statement of case abridged. Arguments omitted.

tions for decision are, whether any, and if any, which of these actions can be maintained ? and if any of them can, then whether the claims recoverable are to be awarded according to the principles which prevail at common law, or according to those which are adopted in the Court of Admiralty in cases of collision.

[The learned judge then decides that although actions under Lord Campbell's Act for causing death can now be brought in the Admiralty Division, yet the assessment of damages is to be governed by the rules prevailing in common-law actions.]

Having cleared the ground thus far, it is necessary to return to the statute and see under what circumstances an action upon it can be supported. The first matter to be considered is whether there has been any such wrongful act, neglect, or default of the defendants as would, if death had not ensued, have entitled the three deceased persons respectively to have sued the defendants. Now, as regards one of them, namely, Owen, the second officer, who was himself to blame for the collision, it is clear that, if death had not ensued, he could not have maintained an action against the defendants. There was negligence on his part contributing to the collision, and no evidence to show that, notwithstanding his negligence, the defendants could, by taking reasonable care, have avoided the collision. There was what is called such contributory negligence on his part as to render an action by him unsustainable. It follows, therefore, that his representatives can recover nothing under Lord Campbell's Act for his widow and children, and their action cannot be maintained. The other two actions are not so easily disposed of. They raise two questions: (1) Whether the passenger Toeg, if alive, could have successfully sued the defendants; and if he could, then (2) whether there is any difference between the case of the passenger and that of the engineer Armstrong. The learned judge whose decision is under review felt himself bound by authority to decide both actions against the plaintiffs. The authorities which the learned judge followed are Thorogood *v.* Bryan, 8 C. B. 115, and Armstrong *v.* Lancashire & Yorkshire Ry. Co., Law Rep. 10 Ex. 47; and the real question to be determined is whether they can be properly overruled or not. Thorogood *v.* Bryan, *supra*, was decided in 1849, and has been generally followed at Nisi Prius ever since when cases like it have arisen. But it is curious to see how reluctant the Courts have been to affirm its principle after argument, and how they have avoided doing so, preferring, where possible, to decide cases before them on other grounds. See, for example, Rigby *v.* Hewitt, 5 Ex. 240; Greenland *v.* Chaplin, 5 Ex. 243; Waite *v.* North Eastern Ry. Co., E. B. & E. 719. I am not aware that the principle on which Thorogood *v.* Bryan, *supra*, was decided has ever been approved by any Court which has had to consider it. On the other hand, that case has been criticised and said to be contrary to principle by persons of the highest eminence, not only in this country, but also in Scotland

and in America. And while it is true that Thorogood *v.* Bryan, *supra*, has never been overruled, it is also true that it has never been affirmed by any Court which could properly overrule it, and it cannot be yet said to have become indisputably settled law. I do not think, therefore, that it is too late for a Court of Appeal to reconsider it, or to overrule it if clearly contrary to well settled legal principles.

Thorogood *v.* Bryan, *supra*, was an action founded on Lord Campbell's Act. The facts were shortly as follows. The deceased was a passenger in an omnibus, and he had just got off out of it. He was knocked down and killed by another omnibus belonging to the defendants. There was negligence on the part of the drivers of both omnibuses, and it appears that there was also negligence on the part of the deceased himself. The jury found a verdict for the defendants, and there does not seem to have been any reason why the Court should have disallowed the verdict if not driven to do so on technical grounds. In those days, however, a misdirection by the judge to the jury compelled the Court to grant a new trial, whether any injustice had been done or not; and accordingly the plaintiff moved for a new trial on the ground of misdirection, and it is with reference to this point that the decision of the Court is of importance. The learned judge who tried the case told the jury in effect to find for the defendant if they thought that the deceased was killed either by reason of his own want of care or by reason of want of care on the part of the driver of the omnibus out of which he was getting. The last direction was complained of, but was upheld by the Court. The *ratio decidendi* was that if the death of the deceased was not occasioned by his own negligence it was occasioned by the joint negligence of both drivers, and that, if so, the negligence of the driver of the omnibus off which the deceased was getting was the negligence of the deceased; and the reason for so holding was that the deceased had voluntarily placed himself under the care of the driver. Maule, J., puts it thus: "The deceased must be considered as identified with the driver of the omnibus in which he voluntarily became a passenger, and the negligence of the driver was the negligence of the deceased." This theory of identification was quite new. No trace of it is to be found in any earlier decision, nor in any legal treatise, English or foreign, so far as I have been able to ascertain, nor has it ever been satisfactorily explained. It must be assumed, for the purpose of considering the grounds of the decision in question, that the passenger was not himself in fault. Assuming this to be so, then, if both drivers were negligent, and both caused the injury to the passenger, it is difficult to understand why both drivers or their masters should not be liable to him. The doctrine of identification laid down in Thorogood *v.* Bryan, *supra*, is, to me, quite unintelligible. It is, in truth, a fictitious extension of the principles of agency, but to say that the driver of a public conveyance is the agent of the passengers is to say that which is not true in fact.

Such a doctrine, if made the basis of further reasoning, leads to results which are wholly untenable, *e. g.*, to the result that the passengers would be liable for the negligence of the person driving them, which is obviously absurd, but which, of course, the Court never meant. All the Court meant to say was that for purposes of suing for negligence the passenger was in no better position than the man driving him. But why not? The driver of a public vehicle is not selected by the passenger otherwise than by being hailed by him as one of the public to take him up; and such selection, if selection it can be called, does not create the relation of principal and agent or master and servant between the passenger and the driver, the passenger knows nothing of the driver and has no control over him; nor is the driver in any proper sense employed by the passenger. The driver, if not his own master, is hired, paid, or employed by the owner of the vehicle he drives or by some other person who lets the vehicle to him. The orders he obeys are his employer's orders. These orders, in the case of an omnibus, are to drive from such a place to such a place and take up and put down passengers; and in the case of a cab the orders are to drive where the passenger for the time being may desire to go, within the limits expressly or impliedly set by the employer. If the passenger actively interferes with the driver by giving him orders as to what he is to do, I can understand the meaning of the expression that the passenger identifies himself with the driver, but no such interference was suggested in Thorogood *v.* Bryan, *supra.* The principles of the law of negligence, and in particular of what is called contributory negligence, have been discussed on many occasions since that case was decided, and are much better understood now than they were thirty years ago. Tuff *v.* Warman, 5 C. B. (N. S.) 573, in the Exchequer Chamber, and Radley *v.* London & North Western Ry. Co., 1 App. Cas. 754, in the House of Lords, show the true grounds on which a person himself guilty of negligence is unable to maintain an action against another for an injury occasioned by the combined negligence of both. If the proximate cause of the injury is the negligence of the plaintiff as well as that of the defendant, the plaintiff cannot recover anything. The reason for this is not easily discoverable. But I take it to be settled that an action at common law by A. against B. for injury directly caused to A. by the want of care of A. and B. will not lie. As Pollock, C. B., pointed out in Greenland *v.* Chaplin, *supra,* the jury cannot take the consequences and divide them in proportion according to the negligence of the one or the other party. But if the plaintiff can show that although he has himself been negligent, the real and proximate cause of the injury sustained by him was the negligence of the defendant, the plaintiff can maintain an action, as is shown not only by Tuff *v.* Warman, *supra,* and Radley *v.* London & North Western Ry. Co., *supra,* but also by the well-known case of Davies *v.* Mann, 10 M. & W. 546, and other cases of that class. The cases which give rise to actions for negligence are primarily reducible to three classes, as follows: —

1. A. without fault of his own is injured by the negligence of B., then B. is liable to A. 2. A. by his own fault is injured by B. without fault on his part, then B. is not liable to A. 3. A. is injured by B. by the fault more or less of both combined; then the following further distinctions have to be made: (*a*) if, notwithstanding B.'s negligence, A. with reasonable care could have avoided the injury, he cannot sue B.: Butterfield *v.* Forrester, 11 East, 60; Bridge *v.* Grand Junction Ry. Co., 3 M. & W. 244; Dowell *v.* General Steam Navigation Co., 5 E. & B. 195; (*b*) if, notwithstanding A.'s negligence, B. with reasonable care could have avoided injuring A., A. can sue B.: Tuff *v.* Warman, *supra;* Radley *v.* London & North Western Ry. Co., *supra;* Davies *v.* Mann, *supra;* (*c*) if there has been as much want of reasonable care on A.'s part as on B.'s or, in other words, if the proximate cause of the injury is the want of reasonable care on both sides, A. cannot sue B. In such a case A. cannot with truth say that he has been injured by B.'s negligence, he can only with truth say that he has been injured by his own carelessness and B.'s negligence, and the two combined give no cause of action at common law. This follows from the two sets of decisions already referred to. But why in such a case the damages should not be apportioned, I do not profess to understand. However, as already stated, the law on this point is settled, and not open to judicial discussion. If now another person is introduced the same principles will be found applicable. Substitute in the foregoing cases B. and C. for B., and unless C. is A.'s agent or servant there will be no difference in the result, except that A. will have two persons instead of one liable to him. A. may sue B. and C. in one action, and recover damages against them both; or he may sue them separately and recover the whole damage sustained against the one he sues: Clark *v.* Chambers, 3 Q. B. D. 327, where all the previous authorities were carefully examined by the late L. C. J. Cockburn. This is no doubt hard on the defendant, who is alone sued, and this hardship seems to have influenced the Court in deciding Thorogood *v.* Bryan, *supra.* In that case the Court appears to have thought it hard on the defendant to make him pay all the damages due to the plaintiff, and that it was no hardship to the plaintiff to exonerate the defendant from liability, as the plaintiff had a clear remedy against the master of the omnibus in which he was a passenger. But it is difficult to see the justice of exonerating the defendant from all liability in respect of his own wrong and of throwing the whole liability on some one who was no more to blame than he. The injustice to the defendant, which the Court sought to avoid, is common to all cases in which a wrong is done by two people and one of them alone is made to pay for it. The rule which does not allow of contribution among wrong-doers is what produces hardship in these cases, but the hardship produced by that rule (if

really applicable to such cases as these under discussion) does not justify the Court in exonerating one of the wrong-doers from all responsibility for his own misconduct or the misconduct of his servants. I can hardly believe that if the plaintiff in Thorogood *v.* Bryan, *supra,* had sued the proprietors of both omnibuses it would have been held that he had no right of action against one of them. Having given my reasons for my inability to concur in the doctrine laid down in Thorogood *v.* Bryan, *supra,* I proceed to consider how far that doctrine is supported by other authorities. [After commenting on various authorities]; Thorogood *v.* Bryan, *supra,* and Armstrong *v.* Lancashire & Yorkshire Ry. Co., *supra,* affirm that, although if A. is injured by the combined negligence of B. and C., A. can sue B. and C., or either of them, he cannot sue C. if he, A., is under the care of B. or in his employ. From this general doctrine I am compelled most respectfully to dissent, but if B. is A.'s agent or servant the doctrine is good. In Scotland the decision in Thorogood *v.* Bryan, *supra,* was discussed and held to be unsatisfactory in the case of Adams *v.* Glasgow & South Western Ry. Co., 3 Court Sess. Cas. 215. In America the subject was recently examined with great care by the Supreme Court of the United States in Little *v.* Hackett, 14 Am. Law Record, 577, 54 Am. Rep. 15,[1] in which the English and American cases were reviewed, and the doctrine laid down in Thorogood *v.* Bryan, *supra,* was distinctly repudiated as contrary to sound principles. In this case the plaintiff was driving in a hackney carriage and was injured by a collision between it and a railway train on a level crossing. There was negligence on the part of the driver of the carriage and on the part of the railway company's servants, but it was held that the plaintiff was not precluded from maintaining an action against the railway company. In this country Thorogood *v.* Bryan, *supra,* was distinctly disapproved by Dr. Lushington in The Milan, Lush. 388; and even Lord Bramwell, who has gone further than any other judge in upholding the decision, has expressed disapproval of the grounds on which it was based. No text-writer has approved of it, and the comments in Smith's Leading Cases are adverse to it (vol. i. p. 266, 6th ed.). For the reasons above stated, I am of opinion that the doctrines laid down in Thorogood *v.* Bryan, *supra,* and Armstrong *v.* Lancashire & Yorkshire Ry. Co., *supra,* are contrary to sound legal principles, and ought not to be regarded as law. Consequently, I am of opinion that the decision in Toeg's and Armstrong's case ought to be reversed.

Concurring opinions were delivered by LORD ESHER, M. R., and LOPES, L. J., the former elaborately reviewing the authorities.

Extract from opinion of LOPES, L. J.: —

If, again, the passenger is to be considered in the same position as the driver or owner, and their negligence is to be imputed to him, he would be liable to third parties; for instance, in case of a collision be-

[1] 116 U. S. 366.

tween two omnibuses, where the driver of one was entirely in fault, every passenger in the omnibus free from blame would have an action against every passenger in the other omnibus, because every such passenger would be identified with the driver, and is responsible for his negligence. Nor, again, in the case just put, could any passenger in the other omnibus bring an action against the owner of the omnibus in which he was carried, because the negligence of the driver is to be imputed to the passenger. If the negligence of the driver is to be attributed to the passenger for one purpose, it would be impossible to say he is not to be affected by it for others. Other cases might be put.

The more the decision in Thorogood *v.* Bryan, *supra,* is examined, the more anomalous and indefensible that decision appears.

The theory of the identification of the passengers with the negligent driver or owner is, in my opinion, a fallacy and a fiction, contrary to sound law and opposed to every principle of justice. A passenger in an omnibus whose injury is caused by the joint negligence of that omnibus and another, may, in my opinion, maintain an action, either against the owner of the omnibus in which he was carried or the other omnibus, or both. I am clearly of opinion Thorogood *v.* Bryan, *supra,* should be overruled.

Extract from opinion of LORD ESHER, M. R.: —

In Armstrong's action a point is suggested that he ought not to recover against the defendants, the owners of the Bernina, because he could not recover against the owners of the Bushire. He would, it is rightly said, in an action against the latter, be met by the doctrine of the accident being occasioned by the negligence of a fellow-servant. The suggestion would go too far. It would apply where passengers or goods are carried by railway, or in ship, under a notice limiting the liability of that railway company or shipowner. It would work manifest injustice by enabling a person to take advantage of a contract to which he was a stranger, and for the advantage of which he had given no consideration. The rule of law is, that a person injured by more than one wrong-doer may maintain an action for the whole damage done to him against any of them. There is no condition that he cannot do so unless he might, if he pleased, maintain an action against each of them. There is no disadvantage to the one sued, because there is no contribution between joint wrong-doers. The plaintiff Armstrong is therefore entitled to judgment for the whole of the damages he may be able to prove, according to the rule of damages laid down in Lord Campbell's Act. So in the case of the plaintiff Toeg. In the case of Owen, the deceased was personally negligent, so as that his negligence was partly directly a cause of the injury. He could not have recovered, neither can his administratrix. *Appeal allowed.*

Affirmed in the House of Lords under the name of Mills *v.* Armstrong; L. R. 13 App. Cases, 1.[1]

[1] Little *v.* Hackett, 116 U. S. 366; Baltimore R. Co. *v.* Friel, (C. C. A.) 77 Fed. 126; Georgia R. Co. *v.* Hughes, 87 Ala. 610; Little Rock R. Co. *v.* Harrell, 58

SHULTZ *v.* OLD COLONY STREET RAILWAY COMPANY

SUPREME JUDICIAL COURT, MASSACHUSETTS, JANUARY 1, 1907.

Reported in 193 *Massachusetts Reports*, 309.

TORT for personal injuries caused by the collision of an electric car of defendant with a carriage in which the plaintiff was being driven.

At the trial the evidence for plaintiff tended to show that plaintiff was being driven in a carriage by her friend B; that B owned the horse and carriage and was giving her a ride to her home; that plaintiff in no way interfered with B's driving, in no manner controlled him or directed how he should drive, but left the driving to him; and that the defendant's car from behind, without any warning, ran into the hind wheels of the carriage.

Defendant's evidence tended to show that the collision was due to B's negligently turning suddenly across the track.

The judge instructed the jury (*inter alia*) that if B was careless in driving and if his carelessness contributed to the injury, then plaintiff was bound by his carelessness and could not recover. To this instruction plaintiff excepted.

Verdict for defendant.[1]

RUGG, J. This case fairly raises the question as to whether the negligence of the driver of a vehicle is to be imputed to a guest, riding with him gratuitously, and personally in the exercise of all the care which ordinary caution requires.

[The learned judge then elaborately reviewed the authorities; and, both upon authority and principle, sustained the view reached in The Bernina, *ante*. He then continued:]

Ark. 454; Thompson *v.* Los Angeles R. Co., 165 Cal. 748; Fujise *v.* Los Angeles R. Co., 12 Cal. App. 207; Woodley *v.* Baltimore R. Co., 19 D. C. 542; Baltimore R. Co. *v.* Adams, 10 App. D. C. 97; Chicago R. Co. *v.* Hines, 183 Ill. 482; Chicago R. Co. *v.* Leach, 215 Ill. 184; Pittsburgh R. Co. *v.* Spencer, 98 Ind. 186; Miller *v.* Louisville R. Co., 128 Ind. 97; Chicago R. Co. *v.* Groves, 56 Kan. 601; Louisville R. Co. *v.* Case, 9 Bush, 728; Louisville R. Co. *v.* Molloy, 122 Ky. 219; Holzab *v.* New Orleans R. Co., 38 La. Ann. 185; Roby *v.* Kansas City R. Co., 130 La. 880; Consolidated Gas Co. *v.* Getty, 96 Md. 683; Cuddy *v.* Horn, 46 Mich. 596; Galloway *v.* Detroit Ry., 168 Mich. 343; Flaherty *v.* Minneapolis R. Co., 39 Minn. 328; Colton *v.* Willmar R. Co., 99 Minn. 366; Gulf R. Co. *v.* Barnes, 94 Miss. 484; Becke *v.* Missouri R. Co., 102 Mo. 544; Sluder *v.* St. Louis Transit Co., 189 Mo. 107; Bennett *v.* New Jersey R. Co., 36 N. J. Law, 225; New York R. Co. *v.* Steinbrenner, 47 N. J. Law, 161; Colegrove *v.* New York R. Co., 20 N. Y. 492; Webster *v.* Hudson R. Co., 38 N. Y. 260; Arctic Fire Ins. Co. *v.* Austin, 69 N. Y. 470; Lewis *v.* Long Island R. Co., 162 N. Y. 52; Ward *v.* International R. Co., 206 N. Y. 83; Crampton *v.* Ivie, 124 N. C. 591; Covington Transfer Co. *v.* Kelly, 36 Ohio St. 86; Chickasha R. Co. *v.* Marshall, 43 Okl. 192; Dean *v.* Pennsylvania R. Co., 129 Pa. St. 514; Bunting *v.* Hogsett, 139 Pa. St. 363; Markham *v.* Houston Navigation Co., 73 Tex. 247; Gulf R. Co. *v.* Pendry, 87 Tex. 553; New York R. Co. *v.* Cooper, 85 Va. 939; Croft *v.* Northwestern Steamship Co., 20 Wash. 175 *Accord.*

[1] Statement abridged. Greater part of opinion omitted.

The rule fairly deducible from our own cases, and supported by the great weight of authority by courts of other jurisdictions, is that where an adult person, possessing all his faculties and personally in the exercise of that degree of care, which common prudence requires under all the attending circumstances, is injured through the negligence of some third person and the concurring negligence of one with whom the plaintiff is riding as guest or companion, between whom and the plaintiff the relation of master and servant or principal and agent, or mutual responsibility in a common enterprise, does not in fact exist, the plaintiff being at the time in no position to exercise authority or control over the driver, then the negligence of the driver is not imputable to the injured person, but the latter is entitled to recover against the one through whose wrong his injuries were sustained. Disregarding the passenger's own due care, the test whether the negligence of the driver is to be imputed to the one riding depends upon the latter's control or right of control of the actions of the driver, so as to constitute in fact the relation of principal and agent or master and servant, or his voluntary, unconstrained, non-contractual surrender of all care for himself to the caution of the driver.[1]

Applying this statement of the law to the present case, the result is that the plaintiff would not be entitled to recover if in the exercise of common prudence she ought to have given some warning to the driver of carelessness on his part, which she observed or might have observed in exercising due care for her own safety,[2] nor if she negligently abandoned the exercise of her own faculties and trusted entirely to the vigi-

[1] Elyton Land Co. *v.* Mingea, 89 Ala. 521; Birmingham R. Co. *v.* Baker, 132 Ala. 507; Hot Springs R. Co. *v.* Hildreth, 72 Ark. 572; Farley *v.* Wilmington R. Co., 3 Pennewill 581; Porter *v.* Jacksonville Electric Co., 64 Fla. 409; Roach *v.* Western R. Co., 93 Ga. 785; West Chicago R. Co. *v.* Dougherty, 209 Ill. 241; Nonn *v.* Chicago R. Co., 232 Ill. 378; Yeates *v.* Illinois R. Co., 241 Ill. 205; Cincinnati R. Co. *v.* Cook, 44 Ind. App. 303; Larkin *v.* Burlington R. Co., 85 Ia. 492; Withey *v.* Fowler, 164 Ia. 377; City *v.* Hatch, 57 Kan. 57; Williams *v.* Withington, 88 Kan. 809; City *v.* Bott, 151 Ky. 578; State *v.* Boston R. Co., 80 Me. 430; Denis *v.* Lewiston R. Co., 104 Me. 39; Philadelphia R. Co. *v.* Hogeland, 66 Md. 149; United Railways *v.* Biedler, 98 Md. 564; Randolph *v.* O'Riordan, 155 Mass. 331; McKernan *v.* Detroit R. Co., 138 Mich. 519; Follman *v.* City, 35 Minn. 522; Dickson *v.* Missouri R. Co., 104 Mo. 491; Petersen *v.* St. Louis Transit Co., 199 Mo. 331; Farrar *v.* Metropolitan R. Co., 249 Mo. 210; Loso *v.* County, 77 Neb. 466; Noyes *v.* Town, 64 N. H. 361; Noonan *v.* Consolidated Traction Co., 64 N. J. Law, 579; Dyer *v.* Erie R. Co., 71 N. Y. 228; Geary *v.* Metropolitan R. Co., 84 App. Div. 514; Robinson *v.* Metropolitan R. Co., 91 App. Div. 158; Ward *v.* Brooklyn R. Co., 119 App. Div. 487; Morris *v.* Metropolitan R. Co., 63 App. Div. 78; Terwilliger *v.* Long Island R. Co., 152 App. Div. 168; Kammerdiener *v.* Rayburn, 233 Pa. St. 328; Sieb *v.* Central Traction Co., 47 Pa. Super. Ct. 228; Wilson *v.* Puget Sound R. Co., 52 Wash. 522 *Accord.*

See McLaughlin *v.* Pittsburgh R. Co., 252 Pa. St. 32.

[2] Davis *v.* Chicago R. Co., (C. C. A.) 159 Fed. 10; Rebillard *v.* Minneapolis R. Co., 216 Fed. 503; Ewans *v.* Wilmington R. Co., 7 Pennewill 458; Brannen *v.* Kokomo Road Co., 115 Ind. 115; Holden *v.* Missouri R. Co., 177 Mo. 456; Brickell *v.* New York R. Co., 120 N. Y. 290; Caminez *v.* Brooklyn R. Co., 127 App. Div. 138; Doctoroff *v.* Metropolitan R. Co., 55 Misc. 215; Southern R. Co. *v.* Jones, 118 Va. 685; Wilson *v.* Puget Sound R. Co., 52 Wash. 522; Warth *v.* Jackson County Court, 71 W. Va. 184 *Accord.*

See Atlantic R. Co. *v.* Ironmonger, 95 Va. 625.

lance and care of the driver.[1] She cannot hide behind the fact that another is driving the vehicle in which she is riding, and thus relieve herself of her own negligence. What degree of care she should have exercised, in accepting the invitation to ride, or in observing and calling to the attention of the driver perils unnoticed by him, depends upon the circumstances at the time of the injury. On the other hand, she would be permitted to recover if, in entering and continuing in the conveyance, she acted with reasonable caution, and had no ground to suspect incompetency and no cause to anticipate negligence on the part of the driver, and if the impending danger, although in part produced by the driver, was so sudden or of such a character as not to permit or require her to do any act for her own protection.

In view of the facts of the case the requests for rulings presented by the plaintiff were not correct propositions of law and were properly refused, but the portion of the charge excepted to failed to express with accuracy and fulness the rights of the plaintiff and the liability of the defendant to her. The jury were instructed to treat the plaintiff as identified with the driver, and burdened with his negligence. For the reasons we have stated and under the circumstances disclosed, this was not an accurate statement of the law.

Exceptions sustained.[2]

[1] City *v.* Thuis, 28 Ind. App. 523; Bush *v.* Union R. Co., 62 Kan. 709; Yarnold *v.* Bowers, 186 Mass. 396; Peabody *v.* Haverhill R. Co., 200 Mass. 277; Lundergan *v.* New York R. Co., 203 Mass. 460; Fogg *v.* New York R. Co., 223 Mass. 444; Marsh *v.* Kansas City R. Co., 104 Mo. App. 577; Meenagh *v.* Buckmaster, 26 App. Div. 451; Cunningham *v.* Erie R. Co., 137 App. Div. 506 *Accord.*

Driver known to be incompetent, see: Cahill *v.* Cincinnati R. Co., 92 Ky. 345.

Passenger unknown to driver, see: Cincinnati R. Co. *v.* Wright, 54 Ohio St. 181.

[2] Pyle *v.* Clark, (C. C. A.) 79 Fed. 744; Dale *v.* Denver Tramway Co., (C. C. A.) 173 Fed. 787; North Alabama Traction Co. *v.* Thomas, 164 Ala. 191; Lininger *v.* San Francisco R. Co., 18 Cal. App. 411; Tonsley *v.* Pacific Electric Co., 166 Cal. 457; Parmenter *v.* McDougall, 172 Cal. 306; Denver Tramway Co. *v.* Armstrong, 21 Col. App. 640; Sampson *v.* Wilson, 89 Conn. 707; Metropolitan R. Co. *v.* Powell, 89 Ga. 601; Southern R. Co. *v.* King, 128 Ga. 383; Chicago R. Co. *v.* Condon, 121 Ill. App. 440; Dudley *v.* Peoria R. Co., 153 Ill. App. 619; Town *v.* Musgrove, 116 Ind. 121; Lake Shore R. Co. *v.* Boyts, 16 Ind. App. 640; Nisbet *v.* Town, 75 Ia. 314; Hubbard *v.* Bartholomew, 163 Ia. 58; Corley *v.* Atchison R. Co., 90 Kan. 70; Bevis *v.* Vanceburg Tel. Co., 121 Ky. 177; Illinois R. Co. *v.* Wilkins, 149 Ky. 35; Sykes *v.* Maine R. Co., 111 Me. 182; United R. Co. *v.* Cram, 123 Md. 332; Chadbourne *v.* Springfield R. Co., 199 Mass. 574; Ingalls *v.* Lexington R. Co., 205 Mass. 73; Alabama R. Co. *v.* Davis, 69 Miss. 444; Mittelsdorfer *v.* West Jersey R. Co., 77 N. J. Law, 698; Weber *v.* Philadelphia R. Co., 88 N. J. Law, 398; Robinson *v.* New York R. Co., 66 N. Y. 11; Noakes *v.* New York R. Co., 121 App. Div. 716; Zimmerman *v.* Union R. Co., 28 App. Div. 445; Mack *v.* Town, 98 App. Div. 577; Jerome *v.* Hawley, 147 App. Div. 475; Duval *v.* Atlantic R. Co., 134 N. C. 331; Ouverson *v.* City, 5 N. D. 281; Toledo R. Co. *v.* Mayers, 93 Ohio St. 304; Tonseth *v.* Portland R. Co., 70 Or. 341; Little *v.* Central Tel. Co., 213 Pa. St. 229; Walsh *v.* Altoona R. Co., 232 Pa. St. 479; Wachsmith *v.* Baltimore R. Co., 233 Pa. St. 465; Trumbower *v.* Lehigh Transit Co., 235 Pa. St. 397; Hermann *v.* Rhode Island Co., 36 R. I. 447; Latimer *v.* County, 95 S. C. 187; Turnpike Co. *v.* Yates, 108 Tenn. 428; Missouri R. Co. *v.* Rogers, 91 Tex. 52; Lochhead *v.* Jensen, 42 Utah 99; Atwood *v.* Utah R. Co., 44 Utah 366 *Accord.*

Kneeshaw *v.* Detroit R. Co., 169 Mich. 697; Colborne *v.* United R. Co., 177 Mich. 139; Granger *v.* Farrant, 179 Mich. 19 (but compare Hampel *v.* Detroit R. Co., 138 Mich. 1); Whittaker *v.* City, 14 Mont. 124; Omaha R. Co. *v.* Talbot,

KOPLITZ *v.* CITY OF ST. PAUL

SUPREME COURT, MINNESOTA, JUNE 6, 1902.

Reported in 86 *Minnesota Reports*, 373.

ACTION in the District Court for Ramsey County to recover $2040 for personal injuries caused by a defective street in defendant city. The case was tried before Brill, J., and a jury, which rendered a general verdict in favor of plaintiff for $300. The jury also returned a special verdict, in answer to the specific question submitted by the court, that the driver of the vehicle from which plaintiff was thrown was guilty of negligence which contributed to the injury. From a judgment entered pursuant to the general verdict, defendant appealed.

48 Neb. 627; Prideaux *v.* City, 43 Wis. 513; Otis *v.* Town, 47 Wis. 422; Ritger *v.* City, 99 Wis. 190; Lightfoot *v.* Winnebago Traction Co., 123 Wis. 479; Lauson *v.* Town, 141 Wis. 57 *Contra.*

As to whether the negligence of an agent or servant will be imputed to a principal or employer not personally culpable, see also: Siegel *v.* Norton, 209 Ill. 201; Moore *v.* Stetson, 96 Me. 197; Bjbjian *v.* Woonsocket Rubber Co., 164 Mass. 214; Philip *v.* Heraty, 135 Mich. 446; Fero *v.* Buffalo R. Co., 22 N. Y. 209.

Contributory negligence of agent or servant in sole charge of the property injured, see: Kennedy *v.* Alton Traction Co., 180 Ill. App. 146; Toledo R. Co. *v.* Goddard, 25 Ind. 185; Louisville R. Co. *v.* Stommel, 126 Ind. 35; Young *v.* County, 137 Ia. 515; Dunn *v.* Old Colony R. Co., 186 Mass. 316; La Riviere *v.* Pemberton, 46 Minn. 5; Johnson *v.* Atchison R. Co., 117 Mo. App. 308; Page *v.* Hodge, 63 N. H. 610; Smith *v.* New York R. Co., 4 App. Div. 493; Puterbaugh *v.* Reasor, 9 Ohio St. 484; Hawley *v.* Sumpter R. Co., 49 Or. 509. Compare Gress *v.* Philadelphia R. Co., 228 Pa. St. 482 (care of injured child delegated to another child, whose negligence contributed).

As to when negligence of the servant is imputed to the master, see also: Sims *v.* Macon R. Co., 28 Ga. 93 (slave); Read *v.* City, 115 Ga. 366; Potter *v.* Ft. Wayne Traction Co., 43 Ind. App. 427; City *v.* Bott, 151 Ky. 578; Markowitz *v.* Metropolitan R. Co., 186 Mo. 350; Moon *v.* St. Louis Transit Co., 237 Mo. 425; Reed *v.* Metropolitan R. Co., 58 App. Div. 87; Wood *v.* Coney Island R. Co., 133 App. Div. 270; Crampton *v.* Ivie, 126 N. C. 894. Compare Snyder Ice Co. *v.* Bowron, (Tex. Civ. App.) 156 S. W. 550.

Whether husband's negligence will be imputed to the wife, see: McFadden *v.* Santa Ana R. Co., 87 Cal. 464; Basler *v.* Sacramento Gas Co., 158 Cal. 514; Joliet *v.* Seward, 86 Ill. 402; Yahn *v.* Ottumwa, 60 Ia. 429 (see also Nesbit *v.* Garner, 75 Ia. 314; Willfong *v.* Omaha R. Co., 116 Ia. 548); Denton *v.* Missouri R. Co., 90 Kan. 51; Livingston *v.* Philley, 155 Ky. 224; Ploetz *v.* Holt, 124 Minn. 169; Moon *v.* St. Louis Transit Co., 237 Mo. 425; Johnson *v.* Springfield Traction Co., 176 Mo. App. 174; Hajsek *v.* Chicago R. Co., 68 Neb. 539, 5 Neb. Unoff. 67; Pennsylvania R. Co. *v.* Goodenough, 55 N. J. Law, 577; Horandt *v.* Central R. Co., 78 N. J. Law, 190; Carlisle *v.* Sheldon, 38 Vt. 440.

Imputed negligence as between fellow servants, see: Nonn *v.* Chicago R. Co., 232 Ill. 378; Ford *v.* Hine, 237 Ill. 463; Paducah Traction Co. *v.* Sine, (Ky.) 111 S. W. 356; City *v.* Heitkemper, 169 Ky. 167; Earp *v.* Phelps, 120 Md. 282; Siever *v.* Pittsburgh R. Co., 252 Pa. St. 1; Landry *v.* Great Northern R. Co., 152 Wis. 379; Sommerfeld *v.* Chicago R. Co., 155 Wis. 102.

Whether bailor barred by contributory negligence of bailee, see: Svea Ins. Co. *v.* Vicksburgh R. Co., 153 Fed. 774; Henderson *v.* Chicago R. Co., 170 Ill. App. 616; Welty *v.* Indianapolis R. Co., 105 Ind. 55; Illinois R. Co. *v.* Sims, 77 Miss. 325; Spelman *v.* Delano, 177 Mo. App. 28; Forks Township *v.* King, 84 Pa. St. 230; Gibson *v.* Bessemer R. Co., 226 Pa. St. 198; Texas R. Co. *v.* Tankersley, 63 Tex. 57.

Consignor and consignee, see McCarthy *v.* Louisville R. Co., 102 Ala. 193.

Lessor and lessee, see Higgins *v.* Los Angeles Gas Co., 159 Cal. 651; Contos *v.* Jamison, 81 S. C. 488.

START, C. J. The plaintiff was one of a party of twenty-six young people who celebrated the Fourth of July last by a picnic at Lake Johanna, about twelve miles from St. Paul. The picnic was a mutual affair, in that the party consisted of about an equal number of young men and young women, each lady being invited and escorted by a gentleman, for whom and herself she furnished lunch; but at meal time the several lunches were merged, and became a common spread. The ladies had nothing to do with the matter of the transportation of the party to and from the lake. This was the exclusive business of the gentlemen, with which the ladies had no more to do than the young men had with the lunches. The gentlemen selected one of their number (Mr. Gibbons) to manage the transportation of the party. He hired for this purpose a long covered omnibus, drawn by four horses, and a driver and assistant, to drive the party to the lake and return. The party were driven to and from the lake in this conveyance, with the hiring of which, or the payment therefor, or the control thereof, the ladies, including the plaintiff, had nothing to do, other than may be inferred, if at all, from the fact that they were members of the picnic party. On the return trip, when the conveyance had reached Dale Street, in the city of St. Paul, it was tipped over, by reason of an embankment therein, whereby the plaintiff was injured.

At the time of the accident all of the party were riding inside of the omnibus, except Mr. Gibbons, who was outside, on the driver's seat, with the driver and his assistant, and was then driving the horses; but this fact was unknown to the plaintiff or any of the party inside of the conveyance. The negligence of the city in the care of the street was the proximate cause of the plaintiff's injury, but the negligence of Mr. Gibbons in driving the horses contributed thereto. The plaintiff was personally free from any negligence in the premises. This action was brought by the plaintiff to recover damages on account of such injuries, and the jury returned a verdict for $300, and a special verdict that Mr. Gibbons was guilty of contributory negligence in driving the conveyance. Thereupon the defendant moved for judgment in its favor upon the special verdict, notwithstanding the general verdict for the plaintiff. The motion was denied, and judgment entered for the plaintiff, from which the defendant appealed to this court.

The only question for our decision is whether the negligence of Mr. Gibbons must be imputed to the plaintiff, and a recovery denied her for that reason. The rule as to imputed negligence, as settled by this court in cases other than those where the parties stand in the relation of parent and child or guardian and ward, is that negligence in the conduct of another will not be imputed to a party if he neither authorized such conduct, nor participated therein, nor had the right or power to control it. If, however, two or more persons unite in the joint prosecution of a common purpose under such circumstances that each has authority, expressed or implied, to act for all in respect to the control of the means or agencies employed to execute such common purpose, the negligence of one in the management thereof will be imputed to all the others. Follman *v.* City of Mankato, 35 Minn. 522, 29 N. W. 317; Flaherty *v.* Minneapolis & St. L. Ry. Co., 39 Minn. 328, 40 N. W. 160; Howe *v.* Minneapolis, St. P. & S. Ste. M. Ry. Co., 62 Minn. 71, 64 N. W. 102; Johnson *v.* St. Paul City Ry. Co., 67 Minn. 260, 69 N. W. 900; Finley *v.* Chicago, M. & St. P. Ry. Co., 71 Minn., 471, 74 N. W. 174; Wosika *v.* St. Paul City Ry. Co., 80 Minn. 364, 83 N. W. 386; Lammers *v.* Great Northern Ry. Co., 82 Minn. 120, 84 N. W. 728.

It is too obvious to justify discussion that the plaintiff in this case neither expressly nor impliedly had any control over the drivers of the omnibus, or either of them, or of Mr. Gibbons, and that he and she were not engaged in a joint enterprise in any such sense as made her so far responsible for his negligence in driving the horses that it must be imputed to her. The claim of the defendant to the contrary is unsupported by the facts as disclosed by the record.

Judgment affirmed.[1]

FECHLEY *v.* SPRINGFIELD TRACTION COMPANY

St. Louis Court of Appeals, Missouri, May 8, 1906.

Reported in 119 *Missouri Appeal Reports*, 358.

Error to Circuit Court, Greene County. Verdict and judgment for defendant. Plaintiff appeals.

Appellant, Fechley, was damaged by the collision of a street car with a one-horse buggy in which he was riding. The buggy was owned and driven by Pierce, at whose invitation Fechley was riding. Pierce, upon his own statement, was negligent in not seasonably looking, or taking proper precautions, to ascertain if a car was approaching before he attempted to drive across two parallel railway tracks. The facts as to the alleged negligence of Fechley are sufficiently stated in the extracts from the opinion, given below.

One error assigned was the submission to the jury of the issue of appellant's contributory negligence.[2]

[1] See Alabama R. Co. *v.* Hanbury, 161 Ala. 358; Louisville R. Co. *v.* Armstrong, 127 Ky. 367; Beaucage *v.* Mercer, 206 Mass. 492; Ward *v.* Meads, 114 Minn. 18; Schron *v.* Staten Island R. Co., 16 App. Div. 11; Christopherson *v.* Minneapolis R. Co., 28 N. D. 128; Wentworth *v.* Town, 90 Vt. 60; Washington R. Co. *v.* Zell, 118 Va. 755.

According to the decision in Shindelus *v.* St. Paul City R. Co., 80 Minn. 364, if any of the young men of the party in the Koplitz case had sued the city, the negligence of Gibbons would have been imputed to them.

Compare Laurence *v.* Sioux City, 172 Ia. 320; Scheib *v.* New York R. Co., 115 App. Div. 578; Kansas City R. Co. *v.* Durrett, (Tex. Civ. App.) 187 S. W. 427.

[2] Statement abridged. Arguments omitted; also portions of opinion.

GOODE, J. [After stating the case; and holding that the negligence of Pierce would not bar Fechley from recovering against the company if the motorman's negligence was in part the proximate cause of the collision.]

Appellant himself must have been free from negligence proximately contributing to his injury or he is entitled to no damages, granting that Pierce's fault does not preclude a recovery and that the motorman's fault was a factor in bringing about the casualty. Few, if any, courts have held that an occupant of a vehicle may entrust his safety absolutely to the driver of a vehicle, regardless of the imminence of danger or the visible lack of ordinary caution on the part of the driver to avoid harm. The law in this state, and in most jurisdictions, is that if a passenger who is aware of the danger and that the driver is remiss in guarding against it, takes no care himself to avoid injury, he cannot recover for one he receives. This is the law not because the driver's negligence is imputable to the passenger, but because the latter's own negligence proximately contributed to his damage. Marsh *v.* Railroad, 104 Mo. App. 577, 78 S. W. 284; Dean *v.* Railroad, 129 Pa. St. 514; Township of Crescent *v.* Anderson, 114 Pa. St. 643; Koehler *v.* Railroad, 66 Hun, 566; Hoag *v.* Railroad, 111 N. Y. 179; Brickell *v.* Railroad, 120 N. Y. 290; 2 Thompson, Negligence, sec. 1620; Beach, Con. Neg., sec. 115; 3 Elliott, Railroads, sec. 1174.

[After discussing the pleadings.]

Therefore the question occurs whether, on the testimony for appellant, the court would have been justified in holding him guilty of contributory negligence; and we hold that such a ruling would have been proper. Appellant swore he knew cars were operated east and west on Commercial Street, but did not know there were double tracks on it. The two tracks were right before his eyes as he drove down Commercial Street and as Pierce turned the horse to cross them. He said he could have looked out of the buggy by merely pushing the curtain back with his hand. He was not bound to do this if Pierce's conduct was of such a character as to induce a reasonably prudent man to think there was no danger in driving across the tracks. But Fechley did not have the right to rely on the precaution taken by Pierce, unless, under the circumstances, a man of ordinary prudence would have relied on it. As we have pointed out, the testimony shows Pierce took no precaution which could be effective. He did not stop at all; nor did he look for a car until the horse was stepping over the south rail of the north track. The two tracks were less than five feet apart and the buggy moved but a few feet after Pierce looked, before the car struck it near the front of the rear wheels. Meanwhile Fechley was leaning back in the buggy, though he must have seen they had crossed the south track and were advancing diagonally on the north one, and, if he was paying any attention to the situation, must have known that a car was likely to come along on that track from the east. Pierce's behavior was so grossly careless, that Fechley was imprudent in doing nothing personally to insure his safety. The essential fact is that Pierce did not look in time, as Fechley knew, or, in reason, ought to have known. Therefore Fechley should have stopped Pierce or told him to look for a car, or have looked himself, before they had advanced so far into danger. It is palpable from appellant's own testimony that he was giving no heed to his safety, but either was relying blindly on Pierce, or, for some reason, was not aware of the proximity of the tracks.

[After stating authorities.]

On the testimony for appellant the case strikes us as one of concurrent negligence; for the buggy had not gone more than from six to twelve feet after Pierce looked for a car, until the collision occurred. There is an inconsistency in appellant's theory. He would have it that there was an appearance of danger of a collision which should have warned the motorman, as soon as the buggy was turned to go over the tracks and before Pierce looked for a car, but that appellant himself was not negligent in failing to guard against this apparent danger. That argument for appellant emphasizes and makes clear his own carelessness. The counsel in the case give several close calculations in support of their respective theories, and appellant's attorneys endeavor to demonstrate that the motorman could have stopped the car before it reached the buggy, if he had begun to get control of it when the horse turned to go over the south track. They insist that appellant, though he may have been guilty of contributory negligence, was entitled to a finding by the jury, under proper instructions, on the issue of whether or not the motorman could have prevented the accident after the turn, it being assumed that the danger of a collision then became apparent. The court submitted that issue by a charge which was extremely favorable to appellant.

[Omitting remainder of opinion.] *Judgment affirmed.*

NEWMAN *v.* PHILLIPSBURG HORSE CAR COMPANY

SUPREME COURT, NEW JERSEY, JULY TERM, 1890.

Reported in 52 New Jersey Law Reports, 446.

THE plaintiff was a child two years of age; she was in the custody of her sister, who was twenty-two; the former, being left by herself for a few minutes, got upon the railroad track of the defendant, and was hurt by the car. The occurrence took place in a public street of the village of Phillipsburg. The carelessness of the defendant was manifest, as at the time of the accident there was no one in charge of the horse drawing the car, the driver being in the car collecting fares.

The Circuit judge submitted the three following propositions to this Court for its advisory opinion, viz.: —

First. Whether the negligence of the persons in charge of the plaintiff, an infant minor, should be imputed to the said plaintiff.

Second. Whether the conduct of the persons in charge of the plaintiff at the time of the injury complained of, was not so demonstrably negligent that the said Circuit Court should have nonsuited the plaintiff, or that the Court should have directed the jury to find for the defendant.

Third. Whether a new trial ought not to be granted, on the ground that the damages awarded are excessive.

Argued at February term, 1890, before BEASLEY, C. J., and SCUDDER, DIXON and REED, JJ.

The opinion of the court was delivered by —

BEASLEY, C.J. There is but a single question presented by this case, and that question plainly stands among the vexed questions of the law.

The problem is, whether an infant of tender years can be vicariously negligent, so as to deprive itself of a remedy that it would otherwise be entitled to. In some of the American states this question has been answered by the Courts in the affirmative, and in others in the negative. To the former of these classes belongs the decision in Hartfield *v.* Roper & Newell, reported in 21 Wend. 615. This case appears to have been one of first impression on this subject, and it is to be regarded, not only as the precursor, but as the parent of all the cases of the same strain that have since appeared.

The inquiry with respect to the effect of the negligence of the custodian of the infant, too young to be intelligent of situations and circumstances, was directly presented for decision in the primary case thus referred to, for the facts were these: The plaintiff, a child of about two years of age, was standing or sitting in the snow in a public road, and in that situation was run over by a sleigh driven by the defendants. The opinion of the Court was, that as the child was permitted by its custodian to wander into a position of such danger it was without remedy for the hurts thus received, unless they were voluntarily inflicted, or were the product of gross carelessness on the part of the defendants. It is obvious that the judicial theory was, that the infant was, through the medium of its custodian, the doer, in part, of its own misfortune, and that, consequently, by force of the well-known rule, under such conditions, he had no right to an action. This, of course, was visiting the child for the neglect of the custodian, and such infliction is justified in the case cited in this wise: "The infant," says the Court, "is not *sui juris*. He belongs to another, to whom discretion in the care of his person is exclusively confided. That person is keeper and agent for this purpose; in respect to third persons his act must be deemed that of the infant; his neglects the infant's neglects."

It will be observed that the entire content of this quotation is the statement of a single fact, and a deduction from it; the premise being, that the child must be in the care and charge of an adult, and the inference being that, for that reason, the neglects of the adult are the neglects of the infant. But surely this is, conspicuously, a *non sequitur*. How does the custody of the infant justify, or lead to, the imputation of another's fault to him ? The law, natural and civil, puts the infant under the care of the adult, but how can this right to care for and protect be construed into a right to waive, or forfeit, any of the legal rights of the infant ? The capacity to make such waiver or forfeiture is not a necessary, or even convenient, incident of this office of the adult, but, on the contrary, is quite inconsistent with it, for the power to protect is the opposite of the power to harm, either by act or omission. In this case in Wendell it is evident that the rule of law enunciated by it is founded in the theory that the custodian of the infant is the agent of the infant; but this is a mere assumption without legal basis, for such custodian is the agent, not of the infant, but of the law. If such supposed agency existed, it would embrace many interests of the infant, and could not be confined to the single instance where an injury is inflicted by the coöperative tort of the guardian. And yet it seems certain that such custodian cannot surrender or impair a single right of any kind that is vested in the child, nor impose any legal burthen upon it. If a mother travelling with her child in her arms should agree with a railway company, that in case of an accident to such infant by reason of the joint negligence of herself and the company the latter should not be liable to a suit by the child, such an engagement would be plainly invalid on two grounds: *first*, the contract would be *contra bonos mores*, and *second*, because the mother was not the agent of the child authorized to enter into the agreement. Nevertheless, the position has been deemed defensible that the same evil consequences to the infant will follow from the negligence of the mother, in the absence of such supposed contract, as would have resulted if such contract should have been made and should have been held valid.

In fact, this doctrine of the imputability of the misfeasance of the keeper of a child to the child itself, is deemed to be a pure interpolation into the law, for until the case under criticism it was absolutely unknown; nor is it sustained by legal analogies. Infants have always been the particular objects of the favor and protection of the law. In the language of an ancient authority this doctrine is thus expressed: " The common principle is, that an infant in all things which sound in his benefit shall have favor and preferment in law as well as another man, but shall not be prejudiced by anything in his disadvantage." 9 Vin. Abr. 374. And it would appear to be plain that nothing could be more to the prejudice of an infant than to convert, by construction of law, the connection between himself and his custodian into an agency to which the harsh rule of *respondeat superior* should be applicable. The answerableness of the principal for the authorized acts of his agent is not so much the dictate of natural justice as of public policy, and has arisen, with some propriety, from the circumstances, that the creation of the agency is a voluntary act, and that it can be controlled and ended at the will of its creator. But in the relationship between the infant and its keeper, all these decisive characteristics are wholly wanting. The law imposes the keeper upon the child who, of course, can neither control or remove him, and the injustice, therefore, of making the latter responsible, in any measure whatever, for the torts of the former, would seem to be quite evident. Such subjectivity would be hostile, in every respect, to the natural rights of the infant, and, consequently, cannot, with any show of reason, be introduced into that provision which both necessity and law establish for his protection. Nor can it be said that its existence is necessary to give just enforcement to the rights of others. When it happens that both the infant and its custodian have been injured by the cooperative negligence of such custodian and a third party, it seems reasonable, at least in some degree, that the latter should be enabled to say to the custodian, "You and I, by our common carelessness, have done this wrong, and, therefore, neither can look to the other for redress;" but when such wrong-doer says to the infant, "Your guardian and I, by our joint misconduct, have brought this loss upon you, consequently you have no right of action against me, but you must look for indemnification to your guardian alone," a proposition is stated that appears to be without any basis either in good sense or law. The conversion of the infant, who is entirely free from fault, into a wrong-doer, by imputation, is a logical contrivance uncongenial with the spirit of jurisprudence. The sensible and legal doctrine is this: An infant of tender years cannot be charged with negligence; nor can he be so charged with the commission of such fault by substitution, for he is incapable of appointing an agent, the consequence being, that he can, in no case, be considered to be the blamable cause, either in whole or in part, of his own injury. There is no injustice, nor hardship, in requiring all wrong-doers to be answerable to a person who is incapable either of self-protection or of being a participator in their misfeasance.

Nor is it to be overlooked that the theory here repudiated, if it should be adopted, would go the length of making an infant in its nurse's arms answerable for all the negligences of such nurse while thus employed in its service. Every person so damaged by the careless custodian would be entitled to his action against the infant. If the neglects of the guardian are to be regarded as the neglects of the infant, as was asserted in the New York decision, it would, from logical necessity, follow, that the infant must indemnify those who should be harmed by such neglects. That such a doctrine has never prevailed is conclusively shown by the fact that in the reports there is no indication that such a suit has ever been brought.

It has already been observed that judicial opinion, touching the subject just discussed, is in a state of direct antagonism, and it would, therefore, serve no useful purpose to refer to any of them. It is sufficient to say, that the leading text-writers have concluded that the weight of such authority is adverse to the doctrine that an infant can become, in any wise, a tortfeasor by imputation. 1 Shearm. & R. Neg., § 75; Whart. Neg. § 311; 2 Wood Railw. L., p. 1284.

In our opinion, the weight of reason is in the same scale.

It remains to add that we do not think the damages so excessive as to place the verdict under judicial control.

Let the Circuit Court be advised to render judgment on the finding of the jury.[1]

BISAILLON v. BLOOD

SUPREME COURT, NEW HAMPSHIRE, JUNE, 1888.

Reported in 64 *New Hampshire Reports*, 565.

CASE, for the negligent injury of the plaintiff. Verdict for the defendant.

In October, 1886, the defendant, while driving a horse in a carriage on a public street of Manchester, ran over and injured the plaintiff, an infant then five years old, who had wandered from his home without an attendant or custodian, and was playing in the street with other children of about the same age.

The jury were instructed that the plaintiff being too young to exercise care for himself, it was the duty of his parents or natural

[1] Chicago R. Co. *v.* Kowalski, (C. C. A.) 92 Fed. 310; Pratt Coal Co. *v.* Brawley, 83 Ala. 371; St. Louis R. Co. *v.* Rexroad, 59 Ark. 180; Daley *v.* Norwich R. Co., 26 Conn. 591; Jacksonville Electric Co. *v.* Adams, 50 Fla. 429; Ferguson *v.* Columbus R. Co., 77 Ga. 102; Chicago R. Co. *v.* Wilcox, 138 Ill. 370; Evansville *v.* Senhenn, 151 Ind. 42 (overruling earlier cases *contra*); Ives *v.* Welden, 114 Ia. 476; Union R. Co. *v.* Young, 57 Kan. 168 (older cases *contra*); South Covington R. Co. *v.* Herrklotz, 104 Ky. 400; Westerfield *v.* Levis, 43 La. Ann. 63; Shippy *v.* Au Sable, 85 Mich. 280; Mattson *v.* Minnesota R. Co., 95 Minn. 477 (overruling older cases *contra*); Westbrook *v.* Mobile R. Co., 66 Miss. 560; Winters *v.* Kansas City R. Co., 99 Mo. 509; Neff *v.* City, 213 Mo. 350; Huff *v.* Ames, 16 Neb. 139; Warren *v.* Manchester R. Co., 70 N. H. 352; Bottoms *v.* Seaboard R. Co., 114 N. C. 699; Bellefontaine R. Co. *v.* Snyder, 18 Ohio St. 399; Erie R. Co. *v.* Schuster, 113 Pa. St. 412; Whirley *v.* Whiteman, 1 Head, 610; Galveston R. Co. *v.* Moore, 59 Tex. 64; Robinson *v.* Cone, 22 Vt. 213; Norfolk R. Co. *v.* Ormsby, 27 Grat. 455; Dicken *v.* Liverpool Coal Co., 41 W. Va. 511 *Accord.*

Meeks *v.* So. Pac. R. Co., 52 Cal. 602; O'Brien *v.* McGlinchy, 68 Me. 552; Baltimore R. Co. *v.* McDonnell, 43 Md. 534; Wright *v.* Malden R. Co., 4 All. 283; Cotter *v.* Lynn R. Co., 180 Mass. 145 (but see Mass. Acts 1914, c. 553); Hartfield *v.* Roper, 21 Wend. 615; Parishi *v.* Eden, 62 Wis. 272; Kuchler *v.* Milwaukee Electric Co., 157 Wis. 107 *Contra.*

As to the limits of the rule in the jurisdictions that follow Hartfield *v.* Roper, see McNeil *v.* Boston Ice Co., 173 Mass. 570; O'Brien *v.* McGlinchy, 68 Me. 552; Ihl *v.* Forty-Second Street Ferry, 47 N. Y. 317; McGarry *v.* Loomis, 63 N. Y. 104.

guardians to exercise care and prudence for him to prevent his being injured, and if they were negligent in this respect, and their neglect contributed to produce the injury complained of, he cannot recover. To these instructions the plaintiff excepted.

CARPENTER, J. The plaintiff would be entitled to damages for the defendant's negligent injury of his property similarly exposed to danger by the carelessness of his guardian. Davies *v.* Mann, 10 M. & W. 546; Smith *v.* Railroad, 35 N. H. 366, 367; Giles *v.* Railroad, 55 N. H. 555. An infant of such tender years as to be incapable of exercising care is not less under the protection of the law than his chattel. The previous negligence of the plaintiff's parents was immaterial. The only question for the jury was, whether the defendant by the exercise of ordinary care could have prevented the injury; if she could not, she was without fault, and is not liable; if she could, she is liable whether the plaintiff was in the street by reason of, or without, his parents' negligence. In cases of this character, where an irresponsible child or an idiot is, by the negligence of the parent or guardian, exposed to peril without an attendant, or where a chattel is in like manner placed by the owner in a dangerous position, and either is injured by the act of a "voluntary agent present and acting at the time" (State *v.* Railroad, 52 N. H. 528, 557), the question of contributory negligence is not involved. The only question is, whether the defendant by ordinary care could or could not have prevented the injury. Nashua Iron & S. Co. *v.* Nashua Railroad, 62 N. H. 159, and cases cited. *Exceptions sustained.*[1]

CONSOLIDATED TRACTION COMPANY *v.* HONE

SUPREME COURT, NEW JERSEY, NOVEMBER TERM, 1896.

Reported in 59 New Jersey Law Reports, 275.

BEASLEY, C. J. This is a suit brought by Henry Hone as the administrator of the estate of his deceased son, who was a minor and was killed by the carelessness of the servants of the plaintiff in error, the Consolidated Traction Company, in the management of one of their cars.

The statute lying at the basis of the suit provides "that whenever the death of a person shall be caused by wrongful act, neglect or default, and the act, neglect or default is such as would, if death had not ensued, have entitled the party injured to maintain an action and recover damages in respect thereof, then and in every such case the person who or the corporation which would have been liable if death had not ensued, shall be liable to an action of damages notwith-

[1] Savannah Electric Co. *v.* Dixon, (Ga.) 89 S. E. 373; Smith *v.* Marion Bottle Co., 84 Kan. 551 *Accord.*

standing the death of the person injured," etc. Gen. Stat., p. 1188, § 10.[1]

The following section directs "that the action shall be brought by and in the name of the personal representatives of the deceased person, and that the amount recovered shall be for the exclusive benefit of the widow and next of kin of such deceased person; and that in every such action the jury may give such damages as they shall deem fair and just, with reference to the pecuniary injury resulting from such death to the wife and next of kin of such deceased person," etc. Id., § 11.

From these extracts from the statute it will be at once perceived that in this suit founded upon it, as in all others of the same class, but two questions are raised, and but two can be raised upon the record, viz., first, could the deceased, if he had survived, have maintained an action ? and second, this being so, what pecuniary loss has fallen on his next of kin by reason of his death ?

These are the facts constituting the issue to be tried, and no subject for trial can be more clearly defined.

Notwithstanding this it is contended in this case by the counsel of this traction company that they have the right to defeat the action if they can show that the death in question was the result in part of the negligent conduct of the next of kin, although such negligent conduct is not to be imputed to the infant who is deceased. The plaintiff in the present case is not only the personal representative, but is likewise the next of kin, and it is insisted that as the damages that may be recovered will enure exclusively to his benefit, he should in justice not be allowed to recover them if he was in part the cause of their production.

[1] At common law, no civil action could be maintained for wrongfully causing the death of a human being. Following the English act of 1846, known as Lord Campbell's Act (9 & 10 Vict. c. 93) statutes in all jurisdictions now provide an action for the benefit of specified relatives of a deceased person against one who tortiously caused his death. In Tiffany, Death by Wrongful Act, 2 Edition, 1913, these statutes are printed in full in the appendix. The book also contains an analytical table of the statutes.

Sometimes the relatives are authorized to sue in person; while in other statutes it is provided that the action shall be brought by an administrator of the estate of the deceased. But, even under the latter class of statutes, the sum recovered does not usually become a part of the general assets of the estate available for the payment of creditors (unless, perhaps, in the absence of any relatives). In some instances the statute provides that an action can be brought only in case the person killed could have maintained an action if death had not ensued. But, even where the statute does not contain an explicit provision of the above nature, the courts generally hold that contributory negligence on the part of the deceased bars the statutory action. The question remains: Will the contributory negligence of the sole beneficiary bar the action, either where he is personally plaintiff, or where he is plaintiff in his capacity as administrator of the deceased, or where the plaintiff is a third person suing in the capacity of administrator ?

The statutes of a few states may, perhaps, be construed as proceeding upon the theory that a right of action is vested in the deceased, and that provision is now made for the survival of such right of action.

But it is to be remembered that the legal doctrine that bars a party injured by the unintentional misconduct of another by reason of his having himself been, in a measure, the occasion of the resulting damage, is rather an artificial rule of the law than a principle of justice, for its effect generally is to cast the entire loss ensuing from the joint fault upon one of the culpable parties, and oftentimes upon him who is but little to blame. Such a legal regulation has no claim to extension, and to apply it as is now insisted on would be to use it in a novel way. The question whether the deceased was negligent is within the issue formed by the pleading; while the question whether a third person who in his individual capacity has no connection with the suit was negligent has nothing whatever to do with such issue. In the legal practice of this state it is the established course to exclude everything that is not embraced in the issue as the parties have framed it and as it appears upon the record. On the trial of this case the inquiry whether the father of the deceased minor had, by his want of care, been instrumental in the production of the accident, was a matter utterly irrelevant to the subject then submitted to judicial inquiry.

The statute of Iowa, relating to this subject, and our own are similar, and in Wymor's case (78 Iowa, 396) [1] the court of that state expressed very distinctly what is deemed the correct view of this topic, in these words: "If," says the opinion, "his parents, by their negligence, contributed to his death, that does not seem to be a sufficient reason for denying his estate relief. Such negligence would prevent a recovery by the parents in their own right. . . . It is claimed that, . . . since they inherited his estate, the rule which would bar a negligent parent from recovering in such case in his own right ought to apply. But the plaintiff seeks to recover in right of the child and not of the parents. It may be that a recovery in this case will result in conferring an undeserved benefit upon the father, but that is a matter which we cannot investigate. If the facts are such that the child could have recovered had his injuries not been fatal, his administrator

[1] Wymore v. Mahaska County, 78 Ia. 396. The material provisions of the statute involved in that case were: —

Section 3730, McClain's Annotated Code of Iowa. All causes of action shall survive, and may be brought, notwithstanding the death of the person entitled or liable to the same.

Section 3731. . . . When a wrongful act produces death, the damages shall be disposed of as personal property belonging to the estate of the deceased, except that if the deceased leaves a husband, wife, child, or parent, it shall not be liable for the payment of debts.

Section 3732. The actions contemplated in the two preceding sections may be brought, or the court, on motion, may allow the action to be continued, by or against the legal representatives or successors in interest of the deceased. Such action shall be deemed a continuing one, and to have accrued to such representative or successor at the same time it did to the deceased if he had survived. . . .

Section 3761. A father, or, in case of his death or imprisonment or desertion of his family, the mother, may prosecute as plaintiff an action for the expenses and actual loss of service resulting from the injury or death of a minor child.

can recover the full amount of damages which the estate of the child sustained."

The subject will be found illustrated by a reference to many cases in 4 Am. & Eng. Encycl. L. 88.

My conclusion is that there is no fault to be found with the trial of this case in reference to this point.

[After overruling another objection.] *Judgment affirmed.*

[By writ of error to review the above judgment of the Supreme Court, the case was brought before the Court of Errors and Appeals. That court was equally divided upon the question whether contributory negligence on the part of the sole next of kin would defeat the action. No opinions on that question are reported. Consolidated Traction Co. *v.* Hone, 60 New Jersey Law, 444.] [1]

RICHMOND, FREDERICKSBURG & POTOMAC R. CO. *v.* MARTIN'S ADM'R

SUPREME COURT OF APPEALS, VIRGINIA, DECEMBER 9, 1903.

Reported in 102 *Virginia Reports,* 201.

WHITTLE, J. . . . This action was brought by the defendant in error, Patrick Martin, administrator of Alice Martin, deceased, against the plaintiff in error, the Richmond, Fredericksburg & Potomac Railroad Company, to recover damages for the negligent killing of his intestate, a daughter seven years of age, by a passenger train of the defendant company at a public crossing. The mother of the child was killed in the same collision, and the action was instituted for the sole benefit of the father, who, under the statute, is entitled to the recovery. At the trial there was a verdict for the plaintiff, upon which the judgment under review was rendered.

The defendant adduced evidence tending to prove that Patrick Martin, Jr., a minor eleven years old, and a son of the plaintiff, was put in charge of a two-horse Dayton wagon, as driver by his father, in which his mother and two younger sisters and a negro boy were to be driven from their home in the country to the city of Fredericksburg; that Patrick Martin, Jr., negligently drove upon and attempted to cross the railway track at Falmouth crossing, in plain view of a rapidly approaching train; and that in the collision which followed

[1] Southern R. Co. *v.* Shipp, 169 Ala. 327; Nashville Lumber Co. *v.* Busbee, 100 Ark. 76 *Accord.* See Macdonald *v.* O'Reilley, 45 Or. 589. In Warren *v.* Street R., 70 N. H. 352, 362, PIKE, J., said: "The child's cause of action survived by reason of the statute, and the money recovered in it will be assets in the hands of its administrator, to be distributed in accordance with the special provisions of the statute. If the father's negligence barred his right to recover in this action, there would seem to be no reason why it would not bar him from recovering any property of the child which he might inherit under the general provisions relating to descent and distribution, but this is not claimed to be and is not the law."

his mother and two sisters, who occupied a rear seat in the vehicle, were instantly killed. Thereupon the defendant moved the court to instruct the jury that if they believed from the evidence that Patrick Martin, Jr., the son and servant of the plaintiff, attempted to cross the track under the circumstances detailed, his conduct constituted such contributory negligence as to bar a recovery. The court refused to give the instruction, which ruling presents for decision the sole question in the case, namely, whether a father, whose negligence has contributed to the death of his minor child, can, under the statute, in an action instituted by him as administrator, suing for his own benefit, recover damages for the death of the child. The statute requires such actions to be brought by and in the name of the personal representative of the deceased person, and empowers the jury to award such damages as to it may seem fair and just, not exceeding ten thousand dollars.

The primary object of the statute in allowing an action to recover damages for death by wrongful act of another, like its prototype, Lord Campbell's act, was to compensate the family of the deceased, and was not in the interest of the general estate, the provision being that: " The amount recovered in any such action shall, after the payment of costs and reasonable attorneys' fees, be paid to the wife, husband, parent, and child of the deceased, in such proportion as the jury may have directed, or, if they have not directed, according to the statute of distributions, and shall be free from all debts and liabilities of the deceased; but if there be no wife, husband, parent, or child, the amount so received shall be assets in the hands of the personal representative, to be disposed of according to law." Code 1887, secs. 2903, 2905.

It will be observed that by the express language of the statute the damages awarded cannot become assets in the hands of the administrator, to be disposed of according to law, if the decedent is survived by a wife, husband, parent, or child; and the recovery is also made free from all debts of the decedent, thus leaving no doubt of the legislative intent to treat the recovery as wholly independent of the decedent and his estate in the event of the survival of any one of the enumerated kin, and making it enure directly and personally to such next of kin by force of the statute, and not derivatively from the decedent, to whom it never belonged either in fact or in contemplation of law.

The authorities all agree that there can be no recovery where the action is brought in the name and for the benefit of one whose negligence has contributed to the accident. Thus, if the child in this instance had been injured, instead of killed, and the father had brought a common-law action to recover damages for the injury, contributory negligence on his part, if established, would have constituted a bar to the action. But the contributory negligence of the father would interpose no defence to an action by the child for such injury. The rule is that the child's want of responsibility for negligence can no more be invoked to maintain the action of the negligent father than can the negligence of the latter be imputed to the child to defeat an action by him.

In this case both parties, at the time of the accident, were represented by agents — the defendant company by its employees, and the plaintiff, by his son, to whose care he had confided the custody of the younger sister — and both were responsible for the acts and omissions of their respective agents. Glassey *v.* Ry. Co., 57 Pa. 172.

In Bellefontaine Ry. Co. *v.* Snyder, 24 Ohio St. 670, the court said: "Where an infant intrusted to the care and custody of another by the father, is injured through the negligence of a railroad company, the custodian of the child also being guilty of negligence which contributed to the result, although the infant may maintain an action for such injury, the father cannot; the negligence of his agent, the custodian of the child, being in law 'the negligence of the father.'"

"When an action for negligent injury of an infant is brought by the parent, or for the parent's own benefit, it is very justly held that the contributory negligence of such parent may be shown in bar of the action, the negligence of his agent to whom he had intrusted the child having contributed to cause the injury; and such negligence, being, in contemplation of law, the parent's negligence, was held to bar the action." Beach on Con. Neg., sec. 131.

The doctrine of imputed negligence has no application to the case, but the rule that the negligent father cannot recover is founded upon the fundamental principle that no one can acquire a right of action by his own negligence. The principle involves a maxim of the law as old as the common law itself. The difference between an action by the father for injuries to the child where death does not ensue and an action by the father as administrator of his dead child, brought under the statute for his own benefit, is a difference in form merely, not in substance, and on principle there can be no more reason for permitting a recovery in the latter case than in the former. In both the father is the substantial plaintiff and the sole beneficiary. To allow a recovery in either would be a violation of the policy of the law, which forbids that one shall reap a benefit from his own misconduct. Accordingly the authorities are practically unanimous to the effect that the guiding principle in both classes of cases is identical, and the contributory negligence of the beneficial plaintiff will as effectually defeat a recovery in the one case as in the other.

In Kinkead's Com. on Torts, sec. 474, the author says the rule is well settled that the negligence of a parent of a minor is a bar to an action by him to recover damages for an injury to the minor, and adds: "It may, however, be contended with equal force that the fact that a parent is a beneficiary in case of death, that contributory negligence on his part should be a defence to an action brought under the statutes now being considered, as well as in an action in his own name for a personal injury. The policy of the law is not to allow a recovery for the benefit of a wrongdoer, and this should be applied as well to actions in the name of another for the benefit of those who may have contributed to the wrong. What shall constitute a defence to this class of actions is not prescribed in these statutes, but is governed by the same principles applicable to personal injuries. It is considered by the majority of cases that the administrator is only a trustee or a mere nominal party, and that the action will be defeated by the contributory negligence of the beneficiaries." [Remainder of opinion omitted.]

Judgment reversed. Case remanded for a new trial.[1]

WELCH *v.* WESSON

SUPREME JUDICIAL COURT, MASSACHUSETTS, SEPTEMBER TERM, 1856.

Reported in 6 *Gray*, 505.

ACTION OF TORT for running down the plaintiff while driving on the highway, and breaking his sleigh. Trial in the Court of Common Pleas, before Mellen, C. J., who signed a bill of exceptions, the substance of which is stated in the opinion.

MERRICK, J. It appears from the bill of exceptions to have been fully proved upon the trial that the defendant wilfully ran down the plaintiff and broke his sleigh, as is alleged in the declaration. No justification or legal excuse of this act was asserted or attempted to be shown by the defendant; but he was permitted, against the plaintiff's objection, to introduce evidence tending to prove that it was

[1] Lee *v.* New River Coal Co., (C. C. A.) 203 Fed. 644; Chicago R. Co. *v.* Logue, 158 Ill. 621; True *v.* Woda, 201 Ill. 315; Gibbons *v.* Williams, 135 Mass. 333; Tucker *v.* Draper, 62 Neb. 66; Davis *v.* Seaboard R. Co., 136 N. C. 115; Scherer *v.* Schlaberg, 18 N. D. 421; Bamberger *v.* Citizens' R. Co., 95 Tenn. 18; Palmer *v.* Oregon R. Co., 34 Utah, 466; Ploof *v.* Burlington Traction Co., 70 Vt. 509; Vinnette *v.* Northern R. Co., 47 Wash. 320; Gunn *v.* Ohio R. Co., 42 W. Va. 676 *Accord.*

"The right of recovery and measure of damages are different from what existed in the intestate. This right of recovery did not exist at common law. It is wholly given by the act. It is not an act to cause to survive a right of recovery which otherwise would be taken away by the death of the injured. . . . Hence the contention that the recovery is in the right of the intestate, and can be defeated only by his contributory negligence, cannot be sustained. . . . From a very early day the common law has denied a recovery, as unjust, to a party whose negligence has contributed to the accident causing the injury for which he demands damages. All statutes conferring a right of recovery of damages, especially when in terms they give such damages only as are *just*, must be read and considered with reference to this universal principle of the common law." Ross, C. J., in Ploof *v.* Burlington Traction Co., 70 Vt. 509, 516, 517.

"Shall the state say to the father, 'If you know that your child is in danger of injury from the negligence of others, you are under no legal obligation to protect it done while the parties were trotting horses in competition with each other for a purse of money, the ownership of which was to be determined by the issue of the race. And it was ruled by the presiding judge, that if this fact was established, no action could be maintained by the plaintiff to recover compensation for the damages he had sustained, even though the injury complained of was wilfully inflicted. Under such instructions, the jury returned a verdict for the defendant.

We presume it may be assumed as an undisputed principle of law, that no action will lie to recover a demand, or a supposed claim for damages, if, to establish it, the plaintiff requires aid from an illegal transaction, or is under the necessity of showing, and depending in any degree upon an illegal agreement, to which he himself had been a party. Gregg *v.* Wyman, 4 Cush. 322; Woodman *v.* Hubbard, 5 Foster, 67; Phalen *v.* Clark, 19 Conn. 421; Simpson *v.* Bloss, 7 Taunt. 246. But this principle will not sustain the ruling of the Court, which went far beyond it, and laid down a much broader and more comprehensive doctrine. Taken without qualification, and just as they were given to the jury, the instructions import that, if two persons are engaged in the same unlawful enterprise, each of them, during the continuance of such engagement, is irresponsible for wilful injuries done to the property of the other. No such proposition as this can be true. He who violates the law must suffer its penalties; but yet in all other respects he is under its protection, and entitled to the benefit of its remedies.

But in this case the plaintiff had no occasion to show, in order to maintain his action, that he was engaged, at the time his property was injured, in any unlawful pursuit, or that he had previously made any illegal contract. It is true that, when he suffered the injury, he was acting in violation of the law; for all horse trotting upon wagers for money is expressly declared by statute to be a misdemeanor punishable by fine and imprisonment. St. 1846, c. 200. But neither the contract nor the race had, as far as appears from the facts reported in the bill of exceptions, or from the intimations of the Court in its ruling, anything to do with the trespass committed upon the property of

from such injury, and if you allow the child to be killed, you may recover, from one who is equally at fault with yourself, for any pecuniary injury you may suffer by reason of the death?' No such meaning can be derived from the statute." SEDGWICK, C., in Tucker *v.* Draper, 62 Neb. 66, 67.

See Wigmore, Contributory Negligence of the Beneficiary as a Bar to an Administrator's Action for Death, 2 Illinois Law Rev. 487.

As to recovery where third person is administrator and there is negligence on the part of the sole beneficiary or all the beneficiaries, see: Toledo R. Co. *v.* Grable, 88 Ill. 441; Feldman *v.* Detroit R. Co., 162 Mich. 486; Davis *v.* Seaboard R. Co., 136 N. C. 115; Wolf *v.* Lake Erie R. Co., 55 Ohio St. 517; Gunn *v.* Ohio R. Co., 42 W. Va. 676. *Contra:* Wymore *v.* Mahaska County, 78 Ia. 396; McKay *v.* Syracuse R. Co., 208 N. Y. 359.

As to recovery where some of the beneficiaries are negligent and others not, see: Phillips *v.* Denver Tramway Co., 53 Col. 458; Love *v.* Detroit R. Co., 170 Mich. 1; Wolf *v.* Lake Erie R. Co., 55 Ohio St. 517; Darbrinsky *v.* Pennsylvania Co., 248 Pa. St. 503.

the plaintiff. That he had no occasion to show into what stipulations the parties had entered, or what were the rules or regulations by which they were to be governed in the race, or whether they were in fact engaged in any such business at all, is apparent from the course of the proceedings at the trial. The plaintiff introduced evidence tending to prove the wrongful acts complained of in the writ, and the damage done to his property, and there rested his case. If nothing more had been shown, he would clearly have been entitled to recover. He had not attempted to derive assistance either from an illegal contract or an illegal transaction. It was the defendant, and not the plaintiff, who had occasion to invoke assistance from proof of the illegal agreement and conduct in which both parties had equally participated. From such sources neither of the parties should have been permitted to derive a benefit. The plaintiff sought nothing of this kind, and the mutual misconduct of the parties in one particular cannot exempt the defendant from his obligation to respond for the injurious consequences of his own illegal misbehavior in another.

Exceptions sustained.[1]

BOSWORTH *v.* INHABITANTS OF SWANSEY

SUPREME JUDICIAL COURT, MASSACHUSETTS, OCTOBER TERM, 1845.

Reported in 10 *Metcalf,* 363.

THIS was an action on the Rev. Sts., c. 25, § 22, for an injury alleged to have been received by the plaintiff, by reason of a defect in a highway, in the town of Swansey, which said town was by law obliged to repair.

At the trial in the Court of Common Pleas, before Wells, C. J., it appeared that the injury set forth in the plaintiff's declaration was sustained by him, as therein alleged, on the 11th of June, 1843, being the Lord's day, in the forenoon of said day, as he was travelling from Warren (R. I.), where he resided, to Fall River, on business connected with the conduct of a cause then pending in the District Court of the United States in Rhode Island. The defendants admitted that they were by law bound to keep said highway in repair.

The judge instructed the jury, that the plaintiff would not be entitled to recover, unless he satisfied them that his travelling on the Lord's day was from necessity or for purposes of charity; that it being admitted that his business was of a secular character, the burden was upon him to show the necessity of transacting this business on the Lord's day.

The jury found a verdict for the defendants, and the plaintiff alleged exceptions to the judge's instructions.[2]

[1] See Broschart *v.* Tuttle, 59 Conn. 1; Dudley *v.* Northampton, 202 Mass. 443, 449.
[2] The arguments are omitted.

SHAW, C. J. This was an action to recover damages against a town for a defect in their highway, by means of which the plaintiff sustained a loss. It appeared that the accident occurred on the Lord's day.

It has been repeatedly decided that, to maintain this action, it must appear that the accident was occasioned exclusively by the defect of the highway; to establish which, it must appear that the plaintiff himself is free from all just imputation of negligence or fault. Smith *v.* Smith, 2 Pick. 621; Howard *v.* North Bridgewater, 16 Pick. 189. And in these and other cases, it has been held that the burden of proof is on the plaintiff, to prove affirmatively that he was so free from all fault. Adams *v.* Carlisle, 21 Pick. 146; Lane *v.* Crombie, 12 Pick. 177. The Court are of opinion that this case comes within this principle. The Rev. Sts., c. 50, § 2, provide that "no person shall travel on the Lord's day, except from necessity or charity," and that "every person so offending shall be punished by a fine, not exceeding ten dollars for every offence." The act of the plaintiff, therefore, in doing which the accident occurred, was plainly unlawful, unless he could bring himself within the excepted cases; and this would be a species of fault on his part, which would bring him within the principle of the cases cited. It would show that his own unlawful act concurred in causing the damage complained of. Then if he would bring himself within either of the exceptions, he must prove the fact which the statute makes an exception. In the case last above cited, Lane *v.* Crombie, the verdict was set aside, because the judge instructed the jury, that after the negligence of the defendants had been proved, if they relied on want of due care on the part of the plaintiff, the burden was upon them to prove it. This was held to be erroneous, and the burden was decided to be on the plaintiff to prove herself free from all fault. On this ground the verdict was set aside, although the evidence was such that probably the direction in regard to burden of proof had not much influence.

The Court are therefor of opinion that the instruction of the judge was right, that the burden of proof was on the plaintiff to show that his travelling on the Lord's day was from necessity or for purposes of charity.

What constitutes such necessity or purpose of charity, are questions not raised by the bill of exceptions. *Exceptions overruled.*[1]

[1] Hinckley *v.* Penobscot, 42 Me. 89; Smith *v.* Boston R. Co., 120 Mass. 490 (injury to passenger travelling on train in violation of Sunday law) *Accord.*

"The provisions of chapter ninety-eight of the Public Statutes relating to the observance of the Lord's day shall not constitute a defence to an action for a tort or injury suffered by a person on that day." Mass. Acts 1884, c. 57, § 1.

SUTTON v. TOWN OF WAUWATOSA

SUPREME COURT, WISCONSIN, JUNE TERM, 1871.

Reported in 29 Wisconsin Reports, 21.

APPEAL from County Court for Milwaukee County.

Action against a town to recover damages for injuries to plaintiff's cattle, caused by the breaking down of a defective bridge which they were crossing.

The plaintiff started from Columbus on a Friday morning with a drove of about fifty cattle, intending to take them to Milwaukee, and sell them. Stopping at Hartland over Saturday night, he resumed his journey on Sunday morning, and at about four o'clock, P. M., reached a public bridge of about seventy-two feet span, over the Menomonee River, in the town of Wauwatosa. The cattle were driven upon the bridge, and when the greater part of them were near the middle of the span the stringers broke, some twelve feet from the abutments at each end, and precipitated the structure, with the cattle upon it, into the river, causing the death of some, severely injuring others, and rendering the remainder for a time unsalable.

The complaint alleges, that the injury was caused by the dangerous, unsafe, and rotten condition of the bridge, and the neglect of the defendant to keep it in proper repair.

The answer denies the negligence charged to the defendant, and alleges that the cattle were driven upon the bridge in so careless and negligent a manner as to cause it to break; and, also, that they were so driven upon the bridge on Sunday.

After hearing the evidence on the part of the plaintiff, the Court granted a nonsuit, on the ground that the plaintiff, being in the act of violating the statute prohibiting the doing of secular business on Sunday, when the injury occurred, could not recover therefor. The plaintiff appealed.[1]

DIXON, C. J. It is very clear that the plaintiff, in driving his cattle along the road and over the bridge, to a market, on Sunday, was at the time of the accident in the act of violating the provisions of the statute of this State, which prohibits, under a penalty not exceeding two dollars for each offence, the doing of any manner of labor, business, or work on that day, except only works of necessity or charity, R. S., c. 183, § 5. It was upon this ground the nonsuit was directed by the Court below, and the point thus presented, that the unlawful act of the plaintiff was negligence, or a fault on his part contributing to the injury, and which will preclude a recovery against the town, is not a new one; nor is the law, as the Court below held it to be, without some adjudications directly in its favor, and those by a judicial tri-

[1] The arguments are omitted; also that part of the opinion which relates to the question of contributory negligence.

bunal as eminent and much respected for its learning and ability as any in this country. Bosworth *v.* Swansey, 10 Met. 363; Jones *v.* Andover, 10 Allen, 18. A similar, if not the very same principle has been maintained in other decisions of the same tribunal. Gregg *v.* Wyman, 4 Cush. 322; May *v.* Foster, 1 Allen, 408. But in others still, as we shall hereafter have occasion to observe, the same learned Court has, as it appears to us, held to a different and contradictory rule in a class of cases which it would seem ought obviously to be governed by the same principle. The two first above cases were in all material respects like the present, and it was held there could be no recovery against the towns. In the first, the opinion, delivered by Chief Justice Shaw, and which is very short, commences with a statement of the proposition, repeatedly decided by that Court, " that to maintain the action it must appear that the accident was occasioned exclusively by the defect of the highway; to establish which, it must appear that the plaintiff himself is free from all just imputation of negligence or fault." The authorities to this proposition are cited, and the statute against the pursuit of secular business and travel on the Lord's day then referred to, and the opinion proceeds: " The act of the plaintiff, therefore, in doing which the accident occurred, was plainly unlawful, unless he could bring himself within the excepted cases; and this would be a species of fault on his part which would bring him within the principle of the cases cited. It would show that his own unlawful act concurred in causing the damage complained of." This is all of the opinion touching the point under consideration.

In the next case there was a little, and but a little, more effort at reasoning upon the point. The illustrations on page 20, of negligence in a railway company in omitting to ring the bell of the engine, or to sound the whistle at the crossing of a highway, and of the traveller on the wrong side of the road with his vehicle at the time of the collision, and the language of the Court alluding to such " conduct of the party as contributing to the accident or injury which forms the groundwork of the action," very clearly indicate the true ground upon which the doctrine of contributory negligence, or want of due care in the plaintiff, rests, but it is not shown how or why the mere violation of a statute by the plaintiff constitutes such ground. Upon this point the Court only say: " It is true that no direct unlawful act of omission or commission by the plaintiff, done at the moment when the accident occurred, and tending immediately to produce it, is offered to be shown in evidence. But it is also true that, if the plaintiff had not been engaged in the doing of an unlawful act, the accident would not have happened, and the negligence of the defendants in omitting to keep the road in proper repair would not have contributed to produce an injury to the plaintiff. It is the disregard of the requirements of the statute by the plaintiff which constitutes the fault or want of due care, which is fatal to the action." It would seem from this language that the violation of the statute by the plaintiff is regarded only as a species of remote negligence, or want of proper care on his part contributing to the injury.

The two other cases above cited were actions of tort by the owners, to recover damages from the bailees for injuries to personal property loaned and used on Sunday, — horses loaned and immoderately driven on that day. They were decided against the plaintiffs, and chiefly on the ground of the unlawfulness of the act of loaning or letting on Sunday of the horses, to be driven on that day in violation of the statute, which the plaintiffs themselves were obliged to show, and the doctrine of *par delictum* was applied. It was in substance held in each case that the plaintiff, by the first wrong committed by him, had placed himself *in pari delicto* with the defendant, with respect to the subsequent and distinct wrong committed by the latter, and the actions were dismissed upon the principle that the law will not permit a party to prove his own illegal acts in order to establish his case.

In direct opposition to the above decisions are the numerous cases decided by the Courts of other States, the Supreme Court of the United States, and the Courts of Great Britain, which have been so diligently collected and ably and forcibly presented in the brief of the learned counsel for the present plaintiff. Of the cases thus cited, with some others, we make particular note of the following: Woodman *v.* Hubbard, 5 Foster, 67; Mohney *v.* Cook, 26 Penn. 342; Norris *v.* Litchfield, 35 N. H. 271; Corey *v.* Bath, id. 530; Merritt *v.* Earle, 29 N. Y. 115; Bigelow *v.* Reed, 51 Maine, 325; Hamilton *v.* Goding, 55 id. 428; Baker *v.* The City of Portland, 58 id. 199; Kerwhacker *v.* Railway Co., 3 Ohio St. 172; Phila., &c. Railway Co. *v.* Phila., &c. Tow Boat Co., 23 How. (U. S.) 209; Bird *v.* Holbrook, 4 Bing. 628; Barnes *v.* Ward, 9 M. G. & S. 420.

It seems quite unnecessary, if indeed it were possible, to add anything to the force or conclusiveness of the reasons assigned in some of these cases in support of the views taken and decisions made by the Courts. The cases may be summed up and the result stated generally to be the affirmance of two very just and plain principles of law as applicable to civil actions of this nature, namely: first, that one party to the action, when called upon to answer for the consequences of his own wrongful act done to the other, cannot allege or reply the separate or distinct wrongful act of the other, done not to himself nor to his injury, and not necessarily connected with, or leading to, or causing or producing the wrongful act complained of; and, secondly, that the fault, want of due care or negligence on the part of the plaintiff, which will preclude a recovery for the injury complained of, as contributing to it, must be some act or conduct of the plaintiff having the relation to that injury of a cause to the effect produced by it. Under the operation of the first principle, the defendant cannot exonerate himself or claim immunity from the consequences of his own tortious act, voluntarily or negligently done to the injury of the plaintiff, on the ground that the plaintiff has been guilty of some other and independent wrong or violation of law. Wrongs or offences cannot be set off against each other in this way. "But we should work a confusion of relations, and lend a very doubtful assistance to morality," say the Court in Mohney *v.* Cook, "if we should allow one offender against the law, to the injury of another, to set off against the plaintiff that he too is a public offender." Himself guilty of a wrong, not dependent on nor caused by that charged against the plaintiff, but arising from his own voluntary act or his neglect, the defendant cannot assume the championship of public rights, nor to prosecute the plaintiff as an offender against the laws of the State, and thus to impose upon him a penalty many times greater than what those laws prescribe. Neither justice nor sound morals require this, and it seems contrary to the dictates of both that such a defence should be allowed to prevail. It would extend the maxim, *ex turpi causa non oritur actio*, beyond the scope of its legitimate application, and violate the maxim, equally binding and wholesome, and more extensive in its operation, that no man shall be permitted to take advantage of his own wrong. To take advantage of his own wrong, and to visit unmerited and over-rigorous punishment upon the plaintiff, constitute the sole motive for such defence on the part of the person making it. In the cases of the horses let to be driven on Sunday, so far as the owners were obliged to resort to an action on the contract which was executory and illegal, of course there could be no recovery; but to an action of tort, founded not on the contract, but on the tort or wrong subsequently committed by the defendant, the illegality of the contract furnished no defence, as is clearly demonstrated in Woodman *v.* Hubbard, and the cases there cited. The decisions under the provision of the constitution of this State abolishing imprisonment for debt arising out of or founded on a contract express or implied, and some others in this Court strongly illustrate the same distinction. In re Mowry, 12 Wis. 52, 56, 57; Cotton *v.* Sharpstein, 14 Wis. 229, 230; Schennert *v.* Kœhler, 23 Wis. 523, 527.

And as to the other principle, that the act or conduct of the plaintiff which can be imputed to him as a fault, want of due care or negligence on his part contributing to the injury, must have some connection with the injury as cause to effect, this also seems almost too clear to require thought or elaboration. To make good the defence on this ground, it must appear that a relation existed between the act or violation of law on the part of the plaintiff, and the injury or accident of which he complains, and that relation must have been such as to have caused or helped to cause the injury or accident, not in a remote or speculative sense, but in the natural and ordinary course of events as one event is known to precede or follow another. It must have been some act, omission, or fault naturally and ordinarily calculated to produce the injury, or from which the injury or accident might naturally and reasonably have been anticipated under the circumstances. It is obvious that a violation of the Sunday law is not of itself an act, omission, or fault of this kind, with reference to a defect in the highway or in a bridge over which a traveller may be passing, unlawfully though it may be. The fact that the traveller may be violating this law of the State, has no natural or necessary tendency to cause the injury which may happen to him from the defect. All other conditions and circumstances remaining the same, the same accident or injury would have happened on any other day as well. The same natural causes would have produced the same result on any other day, and the time of the accident or injury, as that it was on Sunday, is wholly immaterial so far as the cause of it or the question of contributory negligence is concerned. In this respect it would be wholly immaterial also that the traveller was within the exceptions of the statute, and travelling on an errand of necessity or charity, and so was lawfully upon the highway.

The mere matter of time, when an injury like this takes place, is not in general an element which does or can enter at all into the consideration of the cause of it. Time and place are circumstances necessary in order that any event may happen or transpire, but they are not ordinarily, if they ever are, circumstances of cause in transactions of this nature. There may be concurrence or connection of time and place between two or three or more events, and yet one event not have the remotest influence in causing or producing either of the others. A traveller on the highway, contrary to the provisions of the statute, yet peaceably and quietly pursuing his course, might be assaulted and robbed by a highwayman. It would be difficult in such case to perceive how the highwayman could connect the unlawful act of the traveller with his assault and robbery so as to justify or excuse them, or how it could be said, that the former had any natural or legitimate tendency to cause or produce the latter. It is true, it might be said, if the traveller had not been present at that particular time or place, he would not have been assaulted and robbed, but that too might be said of any other assault or robbery committed upon him; for if his presence at one time and place be a fault or wrong on his part, contributing to the assault and robbery in the nature of cause to effect, it must be equally so at every other time and place, and so always a defence in the mouth of the highwayman. Every highwayman must have his opportunity by the passing of some traveller, and so some one must pass over a rotten and unsafe bridge or defective highway before any accident or injury can happen from that cause. Connection, therefore, merely in point of time, between the unlawful act or fault of the plaintiff, and the wrong or omission of the defendant, the same being in other respects disconnected and independent acts or events, does not suffice to establish contributory negligence or to defeat the plaintiff's action on that ground. As observed in Mohney *v.* Cook, such connection, if looked upon as in any sense a cause, whether sacred and mysterious or otherwise, clearly falls under the rule *causa proxima non remota spectatur.*

"The cause of an event," says Appleton, C. J., in Moulton *v.* Sanford, 51 Maine, 134, "is the sum total of the contingencies of every description, which, being realized, the event invariably follows. It is rare, if ever, that the invariable sequence of events subsists between one antecedent and one consequent. Ordinarily that condition is usually termed the cause, whose share in the matter is the most conspicuous and is the most immediately preceding and proximate to the event."

In the present case the weight of the same cattle, upon the same bridge, either the day before or the day after the event complained of, when the plaintiff would have been guilty of no violation of law in driving them, would most unquestionably have produced the same injurious result. And if, on that day even, the driving had been a work of necessity or charity, as if the city of Milwaukee had been in great part destroyed by fire, as Chicago recently was, and great numbers of her inhabitants in a condition of helplessness and starvation, and the plaintiff hurrying up his drove of beef cattle for their relief, no one doubts the same accident would then have happened, and the same injuries have ensued. The law of gravitation would not then have been suspended, nor would the rotten and defective stringers have refused to give way under the superincumbent weight, precisely as they did do on the present occasion. There are many other violations of law, which the traveller or other person passing along the highway may, at the time he receives an injury from a defect in it, be in the act of committing, and which are quite as closely connected with the injury, or the cause of it, as is the violation of which complaint is made against the present plaintiff. He may be engaged in cruelly beating or torturing his horse, or ox, or other animal; he may be in the pursuit of game, with intent to kill or destroy it, at a season of the year when this is prohibited; he may be exposing game for sale, or have it in his possession, when these are unlawful; he may be in the act of committing an assault, or resisting an officer; he may be fraudulently passing a toll gate, without paying his toll; and he may be unlawfully setting or using a net or seine, for the purpose of catching fish, in an inland lake or stream.

All of these are acts prohibited by the same chapter or statute in which we find the prohibition from work and labor on Sunday, and some of them under the same, but most under a greater penalty than is prescribed for that offence, thus showing the character or degree of culpability which was variously attached to them in the opinion of the legislature. And there are many other minor offences, *mala prohibita* merely, created by statute, which might be in like manner committed.

There are in Massachusetts, and doubtless in many of the States, statutes against blasphemy and profane cursing and swearing, the prevention of which seems to be equally if not more an object of solicitude and care on the part of the legislature, than the prevention of labor, travel, or other secular pursuits on Sunday, because more severely punished. It has not yet transpired, we believe, even in Massachusetts, that the action of any person to recover damages for an injury sustained by reason of defects in a highway, has been peremptorily dismissed because he was engaged at the time in profane cursing or swearing, or because he was in a state of voluntary intoxication, likewise prohibited under penalty by statute.

It is obvious that the breaking down of a bridge from the rottenness of the timbers, or their inability to sustain the weight of the person or of his horses and carriage, could not be affected by either of these circumstances, and yet, on the principle of the decisions above referred to in that State, it is not easy to see why the action must not be dismissed. On principle there could be no discrimination between the cases, and it could make no difference in what the unlawful act of the plaintiff consisted at the time of receiving the injury. We must reject the doctrine of those cases entirely and adopt that of the other cases cited, and which is well expressed by the Supreme Court of Maine, in Baker *v.* Portland, 58 Maine, 199, 204, as follows: "The defendant's counsel contends that the simple fact that the plaintiff is in the act of violating the law, at the time of the injury, is a bar to the right of recovery. Undoubtedly there are many cases where the contemporaneous violation of the law by the plaintiff is so connected with his claim for damages as to preclude his recovery: but to lay down such a rule as the counsel claims, and disregard the distinction in the ruling of which he complains, would be productive oftentimes of palpable injustice. The fact that a party plaintiff in an action of this description was at the time of the injury passing another wayfarer on the wrong side of the street, or without giving him half the road, or that he was travelling on runners without bells, in contravention of the statute, or that he was smoking a cigar in the street, in violation of municipal ordinance, while it might subject the offender to a penalty, will not excuse the town for a neglect to make its way safe and convenient for travellers, if the commission of the plaintiff's offence did not in any degree contribute to produce the injury of which he complains."

Strong analogy is afforded and much weight and force of reason bearing upon this question are found in some of the cases which have arisen upon life policies, and as to the meaning and effect to be given to the condition usually contained in them, exempting the company from liability in case the assured " shall die in the known violation of any law," &c., and it has been held that the violation must be such as is calculated to endanger life, by leading to acts of violence against, or to the bodily or personal injury or exposure of, the assured, and so to operate in producing his death in the connection of cause to effect. See opinions in Bradley *v.* Mutual Benefit Life Ins. Co., 45 N. Y. 422.

In the case of Clemens *v.* Clemens, recently decided by this Court, it became necessary to consider the same question, though under different circumstances, as to what violation of law on the part of the plaintiff would bar his action in a Court of justice and leave him remediless in the hands of an overreaching and dishonest antagonist, and the views there expressed are not without their relevancy and adaptation to the question as here presented. In that case, this Court adopted the rule of law as settled in Massachusetts, favoring the remedy of the plaintiff, against the opposite rule sustained by the adjudications in some of the other States, and consistency of decision seems now clearly to require that our action should be reserved with respect to the rule established by the cases here referred to. The inconsistency upon general principle between these decisions of the same learned Court and those there relied upon and adopted, will, we think, be readily perceived and conceded when carefully examined and considered in connection with each other.

. . . .

Judgment reversed, and a venire de novo awarded.[1]

STEELE *v.* BURKHARDT

SUPREME JUDICIAL COURT, MASSACHUSETTS, MARCH, 1870.

Reported in 104 *Massachusetts Reports*, 59.

TORT for injury alleged to have been caused to the plaintiffs' horse by the negligence of the defendant's servant; submitted to the judgment of the Superior Court, and, on appeal, of this Court, upon the following award of an arbitrator as upon a statement of agreed facts: —

"I find that the injury to the plaintiffs' horse, for which they seek to recover damages in this action, was occasioned by the negligence and want of due care of the defendant's servant, then in the employment of the defendant. At the time of the injury, the plaintiffs'

[1] Atlanta Steel Co. *v.* Hughes, 136 Ga. 511 (plaintiff working on Sunday); Black *v.* Lewiston, 2 Idaho, 276; Louisville R. Co. *v.* Buck, 116 Ind. 566 (plaintiff working on Sunday); Chicago R. Co. *v.* Graham, 3 Ind. App. 28; Schmid *v.* Humphrey, 48 Ia. 652; Taylor *v.* Star Coal Co., 110 Ia. 40 (plaintiff working on Sunday); City *v.* Orr, 62 Kan. 61; Illinois R. Co. *v.* Dick, 91 Ky. 434 (plaintiff working on Sunday); Opsahl *v.* Judd, 30 Minn. 126; Corey *v.* Bath, 35 N. H. 530; Delaware R. Co. *v.* Trautwein, 52 N. J. Law, 169; Platz *v.* City, 89 N. Y. 219; Mohney *v.* Cook, 26 Pa. St. 342; Baldwin *v.* Barney, 12 R. I. 392; Hoadley *v.* International Paper Co., 72 Vt. 79 (plaintiff working on Sunday) *Accord.*

In Johnson *v.* Town of Irasburgh, 47 Vt. 28, the Supreme Court of Vermont, while agreeing with the reasoning in Sutton *v.* Wauwatosa, on the question of causa-wagon, to which the injured horse was attached, was placed in Clinton Street in the city of Boston, by the plaintiffs' driver, having the care of the wagon for the loading of certain articles, the weight of which in each and every package thereof was less than five hundred pounds; and the wagon was then wholly or in part backed and placed across Clinton Street, and thereby the plaintiffs were guilty of a violation of an ordinance of the city, which provides as follows: 'And for the loading or unloading of any dirt, bricks, stones, sand, gravel, or of any articles, whether of the same description or not, the weight of which in any one package shall be less than five hundred pounds, no truck, cart, wagon, sleigh, sled, or other vehicle shall be wholly or in part backed or placed across any street, square, lane, or alley, or upon flag-stones or crossings of the same, but shall be placed lengthwise, and as near as possible to the abutting stone of the sidewalk or footway; and any owner or driver or other person having the care of any such vehicle, violating either of the provisions of this section, shall be liable to a fine of not less than five dollars, nor more than twenty dollars, for each offence.' It is in evidence that, at the time of the injury, there was sufficient room, with proper care, for the defendant's team to pass through Clinton Street (a greater degree of care being required by reason of the position of the plaintiffs' team as aforesaid, but not greater than the defendant was bound to use, in my judgment), but the defendant's servant, in passing between the plaintiffs' horse and the opposite curb-stone, ran over and upon the hoof of the plaintiff's horse, with a heavy team, and in so doing was guilty of the negligence which I report; and I further find, that the only fault upon the part of the plaintiffs is the fact of their horse and wagon having been placed against the curb in violation of the city ordinance above mentioned.

"In case the Court shall find, under the foregoing statement of facts, that the violation hereinbefore mentioned of said ordinance, on the part of the plaintiffs' driver, debarred the plaintiffs from maintaining their action for damages, my award would be judgment for the defendant for his costs of court, with the costs of this reference;

tion, nevertheless reached the same result as in Bosworth *v.* Swansey, holding that the plaintiff was not entitled to recover. This conclusion was arrived at upon grounds which were not discussed in the above Wisconsin and Massachusetts cases. The very able opinion of Ross, J., upon this point (47 Vt. 35–38), may be summarized as follows: —

The liability of the town for the insufficiency of the highway is purely statutory. The duty to travellers imposed by the statute is only a duty to that class of travellers who have the right to pass, to those who are legally travelling. The legislature did not intend to impose a duty upon towns "in behalf of a person who was forbidden to use all highways for the purposes of travel, and at a time when he was so forbidden to use them. Can he be a traveller within the purview of the statute who is forbidden to travel?" The duty and liability "are co-extensive with the purposes for which persons can legitimately use the highways, and no greater." "The plaintiff when injured was forbidden by law to use the highway, and by reason thereof the defendant town owed him no duty to provide any kind of a highway, and therefore was under no liability for any insufficiency in any highway."

otherwise, my award would be for the plaintiffs, for the sum of $225 and their costs of court."

CHAPMAN, C. J. The act complained of by the plaintiffs is, that while their horse was standing on Clinton Street, the defendant's servant, while driving a heavy team along the street, carelessly drove it upon the hoof of the plaintiffs' horse, and injured him. The award, which the parties have agreed to accept as a statement of facts, finds that the injury was occasioned by negligence and want of due care in the defendant's servant. The terms of this finding imply that there was no negligence on the part of the plaintiffs, which contributed to the injury. And it is further found that, though the plaintiffs' team was standing there in violation of a city ordinance, yet there was room for the defendant's team to pass by, using due care, and the only fault of the plaintiffs consisted in the violation of the city ordinance. It is not found that this violation contributed to the injury. It is said by Bigelow, C. J., in Jones *v.* Andover, 10 Allen, 20, that, " in case of a collision of two vehicles on a highway, evidence that the plaintiff was travelling on the left side of the road, in violation of the statute, when he met the defendant, would be admissible to show negligence." So the evidence that the plaintiffs' team was standing in the street in violation of a city ordinance was admissible to show negligence on their part. It did show negligence in respect to keeping the ordinance, but did not necessarily show negligence that contributed to the injury. And, notwithstanding this evidence, it was competent to the arbitrator to find, as a fact, that, towards the defendant, the plaintiffs were guilty of no negligence, but were careful to leave him ample room to pass. He did so find in substance; and his finding is agreed to as a fact.

A collision on the highway sometimes happens, when both parties are in motion, and both are active in producing it. In such cases, the plaintiff must prove that he was not moving carelessly. But the collision sometimes happens, as in this case, when the plaintiffs' team is standing still. In such a case, he must prove that his position was not so carelessly taken as to contribute to the collision. The fact is here found that it was not so taken, though it was in violation of the ordinance. There was therefore no such negligence on his part as to defeat the action.

Actions founded on negligence are governed by a plain principle. The plaintiffs' declaration alleges that the injury happened in consequence of the negligence of the defendant. This is held to imply that there was no negligence on the part of the plaintiff which contributed to the injury; and to throw upon him the burden of proving the truth of the allegation. It may depend upon care exercised by himself personally, or by his coachman, if he is riding; or by his teamster, in his absence; or by the person in charge of him, if he is an invalid, or an infant of tender years, or in any way so situated as to need the care of another person in respect to the matter. If there was want of care, either on the part of himself or the person acting for him, and the injury is partly attributable directly to that cause, he cannot recover, simply because he cannot prove what he has alleged. Among the numerous cases sustaining this view are, Parker *v.* Adams, 12 Met. 415; Horton *v.* Ipswich, 12 Cush. 488; Holly *v.* Boston Gas Light Co., 8 Gray, 131; Wright *v.* Malden & Melrose Railroad Co., 4 Allen, 283; Callahan *v.* Bean, 9 Allen, 401.

But it is further contended that these plaintiffs are compelled to prove their own violation of law in order to establish their case, and therefore the action cannot be maintained. The substance of the ordinance referred to is, that for loading and unloading packages weighing less than five hundred pounds, wagons shall stand lengthwise of streets, and not crosswise, under a prescribed penalty. The plaintiffs were loading packages of less weight, and their wagon was standing crosswise of the street. But proof of the weight of these packages was not necessary. In this respect the case is like that of Welch *v.* Wesson, 6 Gray, 505, where the plaintiff was injured while he was trotting his horse illegally. It is unlike the cases of Gregg *v.* Wyman, 4 Cush. 322, and Way *v.* Foster, 1 Allen, 408, which were decided in favor of the defendant upon the ground that the plaintiff was obliged to lay the foundation of his action in his own violation of law. Even in those cases, the violation of law by the plaintiffs would not have justified an assault and battery or a false imprisonment of the plaintiffs. In this case, if the packages had weighed more than five hundred pounds, the position of the team would have been the same. In Spofford *v.* Harlow, 3 Allen, 176, it was held that, though the plaintiff's sleigh was on the wrong side of the street, in violation of law, the defendant was liable, if his servant ran into the plaintiff carelessly and recklessly, the plaintiff's negligence not contributing to the injury. And it is true generally, that while no person can maintain an action to which he must trace his title through his own breach of the law, yet the fact that he is breaking the law does not leave him remediless for injuries wilfully or carelessly done to him, and to which his own conduct has not contributed. *Judgment for the plaintiffs.*

NEWCOMB *v.* BOSTON PROTECTIVE DEPARTMENT

SUPREME JUDICIAL COURT, MASSACHUSETTS, JANUARY 25, 1888.

Reported in 146 *Massachusetts Reports*, 596.

TORT for personal injuries occasioned to the plaintiff, a cab-driver, by a collision between the cab and a wagon of the defendant.

At the trial in the Superior Court, before Blodgett, J., evidence was introduced tending to show that the defendant was incorporated under the St. of 1874, c. 61,[1] for the protection of life and property at fires in the city of Boston, and that the collision occurred while one of its wagons, with its regular complement of men, was responding to a fire alarm; that the wagon was proceeding along Washington Street in a northerly direction; that the cab, upon which the plaintiff was sitting, was one of several cabs standing in a line upon the easterly side of Washington Street between the easterly track of a street railway and the curbstone; that the plaintiff's cab and horse were not drawn up lengthwise of the street and as near as possible to the curbstone, but that the horse was facing the sidewalk at an angle so that the body of the cab projected eighteen or twenty inches into the street beyond the line of the other cabs; and that the wagon of the defendant was driven negligently into the cab, causing the accident.

The defendant asked the judge to instruct the jury as follows: —

"1. If the plaintiff, at the time of the accident, was violating the ordinance of the city of Boston, to wit, 'Every owner, driver, or other person having the care and ordering of a vehicle shall, when stopping in a street, place his vehicle and the horse or horses connected therewith lengthwise with the street, as near as possible to the sidewalk,' that was an unlawful act, and he cannot recover in this action. 2. If that unlawful act contributed to cause the alleged injury, the plaintiff was not in the exercise of due care, and therefore he cannot maintain this action. 3. Under section 3, chapter 61, of the Acts of 1874, 'The officers and men of the Boston Protective Department, with their teams and apparatus, shall have the right of way, while going to a fire, through any street, lane, or alley in the city of Boston,' said defendant is not liable for an accident caused by the collision of one of its teams, while going to a fire, with a vehicle standing in the streets, in violation of either of the city ordinances. 4. If the plaintiff, at the time of the action, was violating the ordinance of the city of Boston, to wit, 'Every driver of a vehicle shall remain near it while it is unemployed or standing in a street, unless he is necessarily absent in the course of his duty and business, and he shall so keep his horse or horses and vehicle as not to obstruct the streets,' that was an unlawful act, and he cannot recover in this action. 5. If that unlawful act contributed to cause the alleged injury, the plaintiff was not in the exercise of due care, and therefore he cannot maintain this action."

The judge refused to give these instructions, but instructed the jury as to the effect of a violation of the ordinance as to the position of a

[1] Section 3 of this statute is as follows: —

"The officers and men of the Boston Protective Department, with their teams and apparatus, shall have the right of way, while going to a fire, through any street, lane, or alley in the city of Boston, subject to such rules and regulations as the city council and the fire commissioners may prescribe, and subject also to the rights of the Boston Fire Department; and any violation of the street rights of the Boston Protective Department shall be punished in the same manner as is provided for the punishment of violations of the rights of the Boston Fire Department in chapter three hundred and seventy-four of the acts of eighteen hundred and seventy-three."

vehicle and horse while standing in a street, stating that the rule was applicable to both ordinances as follows: —

"Bearing in mind the provision of the regulation as to the position of a vehicle when not in motion, I instruct you as to the law, that if, at the time of the injury to the plaintiff, he allowed his carriage to stand in the street in violation of this ordinance, such violation is evidence of negligence on his part; and, if such negligence directly contributed to the injury, the plaintiff cannot maintain the action. It cannot be said, as matter of law, that the fact that the plaintiff was violating a city ordinance necessarily shows negligence that contributed to the injury. Whether the position of the plaintiff's horse and carriage, in violation of an ordinance, did or did not contribute to the injury, is a question of fact for the jury; and in determining this question, the jury will take into consideration all the surrounding facts and circumstances. . . . The plaintiff must prove that his position was not so carelessly taken as to contribute to the collision; and the fact that his position was in violation of the ordinance is not conclusive proof of negligence which contributed to the injury. Or, stating the general rule in a somewhat different form, the fact that the plaintiff is engaged in violating the law does not prevent him from recovering damages of the defendant for an injury which the defendant could have avoided by the exercise of ordinary care, unless the unlawful act contributed proximately to produce the injury. . . . If, applying these rules, you are of the opinion that there was no negligence, in other words, no carelessness, on the part of the plaintiff, which directly contributed to the injury, then the plaintiff is entitled to maintain this action, if he proves another proposition; and as to that, the burden is upon him. And that proposition is, that the defendant's servants, in the care and management of this wagon, at the time the plaintiff was injured, were negligent."

The jury returned a verdict for the plaintiff; and the defendant alleged exceptions.

KNOWLTON, J. The plaintiff brought his action to recover for injuries received while sitting upon his cab, from the negligent driving of a wagon against it by a servant of the defendant corporation. There was evidence tending to show that, at the time of the accident, he was violating an ordinance of the city of Boston, by waiting in a street without placing his vehicle and horse lengthwise with the street, as near as possible to the sidewalk, and that this illegal conduct contributed to the injury. There was evidence applicable in like manner to another similar ordinance, which requires every driver of a vehicle standing in a street so to keep his horse or horses and vehicle as not to obstruct the streets.

As to the alleged violation of each of these ordinances, the defendant asked the Court to instruct the jury as follows: "If that unlawful act contributed to cause the alleged injury, the plaintiff was not in the exercise of due care, and therefore he cannot maintain this action." The presiding judge declined to give this instruction, and gave none which we deem to be equivalent to it. He instructed the jury in these words: "If, at the time of the injury to the plaintiff, he allowed his carriage to stand in the street in violation of this ordinance, such violation is evidence of negligence on his part; and, if such negligence directly contributed to the injury, the plaintiff cannot maintain the action. It cannot be said, as matter of law, that the fact that the plaintiff was violating a city ordinance necessarily shows negligence that contributed to the injury." In another part of the charge it was indirectly intimated that, if the plaintiff's unlawful act contributed proximately to produce the injury, he could not recover, but it was nowhere expressly stated.

The question before us then is, whether or not the defendant was entitled to this instruction, — in other words, whether, if the plaintiff's unlawful act contributed to cause his injury, it was a bar to his recovery, or merely evidence of negligence which might or might not bar him, according to the view which the jury should take of his conduct as a whole, in its relation to the accident.

It has often been held that a violation of law at the time of an accident, by one connected with it, is evidence of his negligence, but not conclusive. Hanlon *v.* South Boston Horse Railroad, 129 Mass. 310; Hall *v.* Ripley, 119 Mass. 135; Damon *v.* Scituate, 119 Mass. 66. In recent times a large number of penal statutes have been enacted, in which the legislature has seen fit to punish acts which are not *mala in se*, and sometimes when in a given case there is no actual criminal intent. On grounds of public policy, laws have been passed under which a person is bound to know the facts in regard to the subject with which he is dealing, when under possible circumstances ignorance would not be inconsistent with proper care. One who sells milk must know that it is not adulterated. An unlicensed person must know that what he sells is not intoxicating liquor. Commonwealth *v.* Boynton, 2 Allen, 160. And if in a possible case he trespasses in innocent ignorance, the law gives him no relief. He can only appeal to the sense of justice and the discretion of the public authorities to save him from the punishment which the law would inflict. It is obvious that in suits for negligence, if the contributing conduct of the plaintiff is to be considered as a whole, it may sometimes be found that he has not been guilty of actual negligence or fault, although he has violated the law. One element of his action may be neglect of a duty prescribed by a statute, when there are other concurring elements which show that his course was entirely justifiable.

As a general rule, in deciding a question in relation to negligence, each element which enters as a factor into one's act to give it character is to be considered in connection with every other, and the result is reached by considering all together. But, for reasons which will presently appear, illegal conduct of a plaintiff directly contributing to the occurrence on which his action is founded, is an exception to this rule. Such illegality may be viewed in either of two aspects: looking at the transaction to which it pertains as a whole, it may be considered as a circumstance bearing upon the question whether there was actual negligence; or looking at it simply in reference to the violated law, the act may be tried solely by the test of that law. In the latter aspect it wears a hostile garb, and an inquiry is at once suggested, whether the plaintiff, as a transgressor of the law, is in a position to obtain relief at the hand of the law. In the first view, the illegal conduct comes within the general rule just stated; in the second, it does not. This distinction has not always been observed. A plaintiff's violation of law has usually been discussed in connection with the subject of due care.

In Bosworth *v.* Swansey, 10 Met. 363, Chief Justice Shaw, after referring to the rule that a plaintiff must be free from " imputation of negligence or fault," says, in reference to unlawful travelling on the Lord's day, " This would be a species of fault on his part, which would bring him within the principle of the cases cited."

In Jones *v.* Andover, 10 Allen, 18, Chief Justice Bigelow says, " The term ' due care,' as usually understood, in cases where the gist of the action is the negligence of the defendant, implies not only that a party has not been negligent or careless, but that he has been guilty of no violation of law in relation to the subject-matter or transaction which constitutes the cause of action."

In Steele *v.* Burkhardt, 104 Mass. 59, an action for negligence in driving against the plaintiffs' horse, which was left standing in a street in violation of an ordinance, Chief Justice Chapman considers the general subject of the plaintiffs' due care, and then treats particularly the contention of the defendant that the plaintiffs were compelled to prove their violation of law in order to establish their case.

McGrath *v.* Merwin, 112 Mass. 467, was an action founded on the defendant's alleged negligence in starting the machinery of a mill, while the plaintiff was at work in the wheel-pit making repairs on the Lord's day, and Mr. Justice Morton, in delivering the opinion, deals with the case solely upon the principle that Courts will not aid a plaintiff whose action is founded upon his own illegal act, and says, " The decisions in this Commonwealth are numerous and uniform to the effect that the plaintiff, being engaged in a violation of law, cannot recover, if his own illegal act was an essential element of his case as disclosed upon all the evidence." He further states the rule in such cases to be, that, " if the illegal act of the plaintiff contributed to his injury, he cannot recover; but though the plaintiff at the time of the injury was acting in violation of law, if his illegal act did not contribute to the injury, but was independent of it, he is not precluded thereby from recovering."

In Davis *v.* Guarnieri, 45 Ohio St. 470, Owen, C. J., states, as the second of three considerations upon which the doctrine of contributory negligence is founded, " the principle which requires every suitor who seeks to enforce his rights or redress his wrongs to go into court with clean hands, and which will not permit him to recover for his own wrong."

No case has been brought to our attention, and upon careful investigation we have found none, in which a plaintiff whose violation of law contributed directly and proximately to cause him an injury has been permitted to recover for it; and the decisions are numerous to the contrary. Hall *v.* Ripley, 119 Mass. 135; Banks *v.* Highland Street Railway, 136 Mass. 485; Tuttle *v.* Lawrence, 119 Mass. 276, 278; Lyons *v.* Desotelle, 124 Mass. 387; Heland *v.* Lowell, 3 Allen, 407; Steele *v.* Burkhardt, 104 Mass. 59; Damon *v.* Scituate, 119 Mass. 66; Marble *v.* Ross, 124 Mass. 44; Smith *v.* Boston & Maine Railroad, 120 Mass. 490. And it is quite immaterial whether or not a plaintiff's unlawful act contributing to his injury is negligent or wrong when considered in all its relations. He is precluded from recovering on the ground that the Court will not lend its aid to one whose violation of law is the foundation of his claim. Hall *v.* Corcoran, 107 Mass. 251.

While this principle is universally recognized, there is great practical difficulty in applying it. The best minds often differ upon the question whether, in a given case, illegal conduct of a plaintiff was a direct and proximate cause contributing with others to his injury, or was a mere condition of it; or, to state the question in another way, appropriate to the reason of the rule, whether or not his own illegal act is an essential element of his case as disclosed upon all the evidence. Upon this point it is not easy to reconcile the cases. It has been unanimously decided that in Gregg *v.* Wyman, 4 Cush. 322, there was error in holding a plaintiff's illegal conduct to be an essential element of his case, when in fact it was merely incidental to it. Hall *v.* Corcoran, *ubi supra.* But whatever criticisms may have been made upon the decisions or the assumptions in certain cases, that illegal action of a plaintiff contributed to the result, or was to be treated as a concurring cause, or upon language in disregard of the distinction between a cause and a condition, there has been none upon the doctrine that, when a plaintiff's illegal conduct does directly contribute to his injury, it is fatal to his recovery of damages. Baker *v.* Portland, 58 Maine, 199; Norris *v.* Litchfield, 35 N. H. 271; Sutton *v.* Wauwatosa, 29 Wis. 21.

The plaintiff relies with great confidence upon the case of Hanlon *v.* South Boston Horse Railroad, 129 Mass. 310, in which the presiding judge at the trial refused to rule, that, " if the defendant was driving at a rate of speed prohibited by the ordinance of the city of Boston, and this speed contributed to the injury, this fact would itself constitute negligence on the part of the defendant, and would entitle the plaintiff to recover if he was in the exercise of due care," and his refusal was held right by this Court. In giving the opinion, after pointing out that driving at a rate of speed forbidden by the ordinance might have occurred without fault of the driver, and might have been justified by circumstances authorizing the jury to find that there was no negligence, Mr. Justice Colt said, " It is not true that, if an unlawful rate of speed contributed to the injury, that alone would give the plaintiff a right to recover, if he was without fault." There are intimations, without adjudication, to the same effect, in Wright *v.* Malden & Melrose Railroad, 4 Allen, 283, and in Lane *v.* Atlantic Works, 111 Mass. 136. See also Kirby *v.* Boylston Market Association, 14 Gray, 249; Heeney *v.* Sprague, 11 R. I. 456; Brown *v.* Buffalo & State Line Railroad, 22 N. Y. 191; Flynn *v.* Canton Co., 40 Md. 312.

But there is nothing in the language used in Hanlon *v.* South Boston Horse Railroad inconsistent with the principle which we have already stated. That decision related to the liability of a defendant. It may be, where a penal statute does not purport to create a civil liability, or to protect the rights of particular persons, that a violation of it will not subject the violator to an action for damages, unless his act, when viewed in connection with all the attendant circumstances, appears to be negligent or wrongful. And at the same time Courts may well hold that, in the sanctuary of the law, a violator of law imploring relief from the consequences of his own transgression will receive no favor.

The instruction requested in the case at bar would have become applicable only upon a finding by the jury that the plaintiff's unlawful act contributed to cause the injury. The jury may have so found; and we are of opinion that upon such a finding, irrespective of the question whether viewed in all its aspects his act was negligent or not, the Court could not properly permit him to recover. The instruction, therefore, should have been given.

The Court rightly refused the instruction requested, that the plaintiff could not recover if at the time of the accident he was violating the ordinance, and so doing an unlawful act. This request ignored the distinction between illegality which is a cause, and illegality which is a condition of a transaction relied on by a plaintiff, or between that which is an essential element of his case when all the facts appear, and that which is no part of it, but only an attendant circumstance. The position of a vehicle, which has been struck by another, may or may not have been one of the causes of the striking. Of course it could not have been struck if it had not been in the place where the blow came. But this is a statement of an essential condition, and not of a cause of the impact. The distinction is between that which directly and proximately produces, or helps to produce, a result as an efficient cause, and that which is a necessary condition or attendant circumstance of it. If the position of the plaintiff's vehicle was such as, in connection with ordinary and usual concurring causes, would naturally produce such an accident, that indicates that it contributed to it. But even in that case, external causes may have been so exclusive in their operation, and so free from any relation to the position of the vehicle, as to have left that a mere condition, without agency in producing the result. What is a contributing cause of an accident is usually a question for a jury, to be determined by the facts of the particular case; and such it has been held to be in many cases like the one before us. Damon *v.* Scituate, 119 Mass. 66; Hall *v.* Ripley, 119 Mass. 135; Welch *v.* Wesson, 6 Gray, 505; Spofford *v.* Harlow, 3 Allen, 176; White *v.* Lang, 128 Mass. 598; Baker *v.* Portland, 58 Maine, 199; Norris *v.* Litchfield, 35 N. H. 271; Sutton *v.* Wauwatosa, 29 Wis. 21.

The defendant's third request for an instruction was rightly refused, for reasons which have already been stated. The statute referred to does not relieve the defendant from liability for negligence to a plaintiff whose unlawful act or want of due care does not contribute to his injury. In the opinion of a majority of the Court the entry must be —

Exceptions sustained.[1]

HEMMING *v.* CITY OF NEW HAVEN

SUPREME COURT OF ERRORS, CONNECTICUT, JANUARY 4, 1910.

Reported in 82 Connecticut Reports, 661.

RORABACK, J. On September 21st, 1907, Ley & Company, electrical contractors, were constructing a conduit on Chapel Street in New Haven, under a contract with the United Illuminating Company, for the purpose of laying its underground system of wiring in said highway, and for that purpose had caused an excavation to be made on Chapel Street. On September 21st an automobile owned by the plaintiff, and driven by him personally, came through Temple Street in a southerly direction and ran into this excavation, causing the injuries described in the complaint. This automobile had been purchased by the plaintiff on July 27th, 1906, of one Holcombe. Prior thereto the plaintiff had owned another automobile, which was duly registered by the secretary of State, pursuant to the statute then in force. The plaintiff had not made application to the secretary of State for registration of the automobile last purchased, until September 21st, 1907, when he mailed his application, enclosing his check for registration fee, at the post-office in New Haven, to the secretary of State, by whom it was received on September 23d, 1907. On September 28th, 1907, a certificate of registration for the automobile driven by the plaintiff at the time of the accident was issued by the secretary of State, as provided for by law. The registration mark displayed by the plaintiff at the time of the accident bore the number which had been

[1] Monroe *v.* Hartford R. Co., 76 Conn. 201; Tackett *v.* Taylor, 123 Ia. 149; Baker *v.* Portland, 58 Me. 199; Bourne *v.* Whitman, 209 Mass. 155; Chesapeake R. Co. *v.* Jennings, 98 Va. 70 *Accord.*

assigned to him as the owner of another automobile owned by him, and which had been disposed of prior to the accident.

The reasons of appeal relied upon are that the court erred in refusing to charge as requested, and in the charge as given.

The defendant requested the court to instruct the jury as follows: "The burden of proof is on the plaintiff to prove by a preponderance of the evidence that at the time of the accident he had the authority of the State of Connecticut to use his machine on the highways of the State, and if the plaintiff does not prove that he had such authority and license, he cannot recover, and your verdict should be for the defendant. If at the time of the accident the plaintiff did not have the authority of the State of Connecticut to use his automobile described in the complaint on the highways of the State, he cannot recover and your verdict should be for the defendant."

The court declined to give these rulings, but instructed the jury that the plaintiff's failure to register would not of itself bar his right to recover, since the law does not provide that one who fails to register his automobile cannot make use of it upon the highway. "The failure of the plaintiff to register his automobile cannot be held to tend to prove contributory negligence on the part of the plaintiff, unless you find that such conduct was illegal, and that it directly contributed to the accident upon which this case is founded; that is, unless you find it to have been the cause, or one of the causes, of this accident; and no such claim, that is, that this did directly contribute to the accident, is made in this case as I understand the contention of counsel."

The statute relative to automobiles then in force (Public Acts of 1907, chap. 221, pp. 821 to 828), provides, in § 2, for the registering of automobiles and the placing of numbers on machines so registered. The penalty to any person having failed to register or display his number was not more than $100, or imprisonment not more than thirty days, or both.

The plaintiff was violating the statute relating to the registration of automobiles, but that fact does not relieve the defendant. This statute imposed an obligation upon the plaintiff to register his automobile, and for its violation prescribed a penalty. The statute goes no further, and it cannot be held that the right to maintain an action for damages resulting from the omission of the defendant to perform a public duty is taken away because the person injured was at the time his injuries were sustained disobeying a statute law which in no way contributed to the accident. A traveller with an unregistered and unnumbered automobile is not made a trespasser upon the street, neither does it necessarily follow that the property which he owns is outside of legal protection when injured by the unlawful acts of another. "There is some real and more apparent conflict of opinion in the many cases treating of the relation between an illegal act and a coincident injury. In doing an unlawful act a person does not necessarily put himself outside the protection of the law. He is not barred of redress for an injury suffered by himself, nor liable for an injury suffered by another, merely because he is a lawbreaker. In actions to recover for injuries not intentionally inflicted but resulting from a breach of duty which another owed to the party injured — commonly classed as actions for negligence — the fact that the plaintiff or defendant at the time of the injury was a lawbreaker may possibly be relevant as an incidental circumstance, but is otherwise immaterial unless the act of violating the law is in itself a breach of duty to the party injured in respect to the injury suffered." Monroe *v.* Hartford Street Ry. Co., 76 Conn. 201, 206, 56 Atl. 498.

The registration of the plaintiff's machine was of no consequence to the defendant. His failure to register and display his number in no way contributed to cause the injury. The accident would have happened if the law in this respect had been fully observed. The plaintiff's unlawful act was not the act of using the street, but in making a lawful use of it without having his automobile registered and marked as required by law. The statute contains no prohibition against using an unlicensed and unnumbered automobile upon the highways and streets of the State.

The defendant placed much reliance upon the authority of Dudley *v.* Northampton Street Ry. Co., 202 Mass. 443, 446, 89 N. E. 25. In that case the Supreme Court of Massachusetts was called upon to construe the effect of a statute which provided that no automobile should be operated upon any public highway unless it was registered, &c. Dudley, the plaintiff in that action, was a resident of Connecticut. He had fully complied with the laws of Connecticut, and had a right to operate his machine on the highways of Massachusetts for a period not exceeding fifteen days. After being in Massachusetts more than fifteen days, Dudley's automobile collided with the defendant's trolley-car. The Massachusetts court held that Dudley was a trespasser against the rights of all persons lawfully controlling or using the public highways of Massachusetts.

The difference between the Dudley case and the one now under consideration is that in Massachusetts there was a statutory prohibition against using upon the highways of that State an automobile unregistered and unmarked. As already stated, no such provisions appeared in the Connecticut statutes which were in force when the plaintiff's automobile was injured.

There is no error.

In this opinion the other judges concurred.[1]

[1] Atlantic R. Co. *v.* Weir, 63 Fla. 69; Lockridge *v.* Minneapolis R. Co., 161 Ia. 74 *Accord.* See Lindsay *v.* Cecchi, 3 Boyce, 133; Hyde *v.* McCreery, 145 App. Div. 729.

In Bourne *v.* Whitman, 209 Mass. 155, a duly licensed automobile was being driven by an unlicensed person. Knowlton, C. J., said:

"It is universally recognized that the violation of a criminal statute is evidence of negligence on the part of the violator, as to all consequences that the statute was intended to prevent. It has been said in a general way that such a violation is evidence of negligence of the violator, and it has sometimes been stated that this would show negligence that can be availed of as a ground of recovery by one who suffers any kind of an injury from him while this illegality continues; but it is now settled that it is not even evidence of negligence, except in reference to matters to which the statute relates. Davis *v.* John L. Whiting & Son Co., 201 Mass. 91, 96 and cases cited. A criminal statute in the usual form is enacted for the benefit of the public. It creates a duty to the public. Every member of the public is covered by the protecting influence of the obligation. If one suffers injury as an individual, in his person or his property, by a neglect of this duty, he has a remedy, not because our general criminal laws are divided in their operation, creating one duty to the public and a separate duty to individuals; but because as one of the public in a peculiar situation, he suffers a special injury, different in kind from that of the public generally, from the neglect of the public duty. . . .

If we consider the effect of such a violation of law by a plaintiff, upon his right to recover, the principles that have been recognized are instructive. They were considered long ago in connection with our Sunday law. It has been established from early times that one who is violating a criminal law cannot recover for an injury to which his criminality was a directly contributing cause. . . .

The only matter which seems to be left doubtful under our decisions in this class of cases, is what constitutes 'illegality,' which is sometimes a directly contributing cause of the injury. Some cases have been decided, which seem to imply that if there is an illegal element entering into a plaintiff's act or conduct, and this act or conduct directly contributes to his injury, he cannot recover, although the illegal element or the objectionable quality of the act had no tendency to produce the injury, and the consequences would have been the same under the other existing conditions, if the criminal element had been absent. In other cases the decision seems to turn upon whether the criminal element in the act or conduct, considered by itself alone, operated as a direct cause to produce a result that would not have been produced under the same conditions in other respects, if the criminal element had been absent. This latter seems to be the pivotal question in most cases decided in other States.

The fact that the number of punishable misdemeanors has multiplied many times in recent years, as the relations of men in business and society have grown complex with the increase of population, is a reason why the violation of a criminal statute of slight importance should not affect one's civil rights, except when this violation, viewed in reference to the element of criminality intended to be punished, has had a direct effect upon his cause of action. Our decisions seem to have been tending toward the adoption of such a rule. Welch *v.* Wesson, 6 Gray, 505. Spofford *v.* Harlow, 3 Allen, 176. Steele *v.* Burkhardt, 104 Mass. 59. Damon *v.* Scituate, 119 Mass. 66. Hall *v.* Ripley, 119 Mass. 135. Dudley *v.* Northampton Street Railway, 202 Mass. 443, 446. Moran *v.* Dickinson, 204 Mass. 559, 562. Chase *v.* New York Central & Hudson River Railroad, 208 Mass. 137, 157.

Under particular statutes, we are brought back to the question, what is the legal element which is the essence of the command or prohibition? In most cases, the effect of doing or failing to do that which the law forbids or requires under a penalty, when considered in reference to its relation to one's civil rights in collateral matters, ought to be limited pretty strictly. Take the case of driving without sleigh bells in violation of the law of the road. R. L., c. 54, § 3. Kidder *v.* Dunstable, 11 Gray, 342. Counter *v.* Couch, 8 Allen, 436, 437. The requirement of the law is that 'No person shall travel on a bridge or way with a sleigh or sled drawn by a horse, unless there are at least three bells attached to some part of the harness.' The wrong to be prevented is the failure to have bells while travelling in this way. The travelling in other respects is unobjectionable. The question arises whether the act should be deemed illegal as a whole, in reference to the rule that the courts will not aid one to obtain the fruits of his disobedience of law, or whether in this aspect its different qualities may be considered separately. It is possible to decide this question either way, but we think it is more consistent with justice and with the course of decision elsewhere, to hold that, in reference to the law of negligence and the rule as to rejection of causes of action that are founded on illegality, an act may be considered in its different aspects in its relation to the cause of action, and if only that part of it which is innocent affects the cause of action, the existence of an illegal element is immaterial. We do not think, under this statute, that one who drives in a sleigh without bells should be treated as a trespasser on the highway, although he is punishable criminally for the failure to have the bells attached to the harness, and is liable in damages to any member of the public who suffers a special injury by reason of this failure.

Consider the St. 1909, c. 514, § 74, which forbids, under a penalty, the regular operation of any elevator by a person under the age of sixteen years, and the regular operation of any rapidly running elevator by a person under the age of eighteen years. If a person under the prescribed age, while employed to operate an elevator, is injured through the negligence of the owner, in leaving it in an unsafe condition, shall his violation of the statute by entering this service before reaching the prescribed age, be treated as criminality, entering into every one of his acts in moving the elevator, so as to prevent his recovery for an injury from the joint effect of his employer's negligence and his own application of the power to raise or lower the elevator ? We think it better to hold, if his age and the degree of his competency, which might depend in part upon his age, had no causal connection with the injury, that his criminality was not a direct cause of the injury. In other words, that the punishable element in the act is only disobedience as to age, and although his act in applying the power to the elevator which brought him in contact with the defect, is punishable, and in a sense illegal because of the existence of that element, in determining the relation of his conduct to the cause of action, to see whether the court will aid him in the prosecution of it, we ought to limit the illegality to that part of his conduct towards which the statute is particularly directed. We are to consider the specific thing at which the statute is aimed, and the immediate effect that it was intended directly and proximately to accomplish by its command or prohibition. . . .

Take the provision in St. 1903, c. 473, § 5, that 'No person shall operate an automobile or motor cycle for hire, unless specially licensed by the commission so to do,' and the earlier provision in the same section that no person shall 'operate an automobile or motor cycle upon any public highway or private way laid out under authority of statute unless licensed so to do under the provisions of this act. The operating of the automobile in itself is unobjectionable. The illegal element in the act is the failure to have a license. The purpose of the requirement of a license is to secure competency in the operator. If in any case the failure to have a license, looking to those conditions that ordinarily accompany the failure to have it, is a cause contributing directly to an injury, a violator of the law would be legally responsible to another person injured by the failure; or, if he is injured himself, would be precluded from recovery against another person who negligently contributed to the injury. But we are of opinion that his failure in that respect is only evidence of negligence in reference to his fitness to operate a car, and to his skill in the actual management of it, unless in the case of the plaintiff, it is shown to be a contributing cause to the injury sued for, in which case it is a bar to recovery. We think that the operation of a car without a license, while it is a punishable act, does not render the operator a trespasser on the highway, but that the illegal element in the act is only the failure to have a license while operating it, so that if the operation and movement contributed to the accident with which the want of a license had no connection, except as a mere condition, they would not preclude the operator as a plaintiff from recovery. If the illegal quality of the act had no tendency to cause the accident, the fact that the act is punishable because of the illegality, ought not to preclude one from recovery for harmful results to which, without negligence, the innocent features of the act alone contributed.

The other part of this statute, relative to the licensing of automobiles, has been construed differently. In Dudley *v.* Northampton Street Railway, 202 Mass. 443, because of the peculiar provisions of the statute and the dangers and evils that it was intended to prevent, it was decided, after much consideration, that the having of such a machine in operation on a street, without a license, was the very essence of the illegality, and that the illegality was inseparable from the movement of the automobile upon the street at any time, for a single foot; that in such movement the machine was an outlaw, and any person on the street as an occupant of the automobile, participating in the movement of it, was for the time being a trespasser. Some of us were disinclined to lay down the law so broadly, and the opinion of the court was not unanimous; but the doctrine has been repeatedly reaffirmed and is now the established law of the Commonwealth. Feeley *v.* Melrose, 205 Mass. 329. Chase *v.* New York Central & Hudson River Railroad, 208 Mass. 137, 158. The difference between this provision of the statute and that involved in the present case is in part one of form, but in connection with the form, it is still more the seeming purpose and intent of the Legislature as to permitting such machines upon the public ways without adequate means of identifying them and ascertaining their owner, together with the requirement that the machine itself, as a thing of power, shall have its own registration and legalization, the evidence of which it shall always carry with it. . . .

We are of opinion that the law of these last cases should not be extended to the provision of the statute requiring every operator to have a personal license to operate the car. The jury should have been instructed that the defendant's failure to have a license was only evidence of his negligence as to the management of the car."

See also Holland *v.* Boston, 213 Mass. 560; Holden *v.* McGillicuddy, 213 Mass. 563; Conroy *v.* Mather, 217 Mass. 91.

In Taylor *v.* Stewart, 172 N. C. 203, Brown, J., (for the court) said:

" The plaintiff sues to recover for the death of his child, who was run over and killed by an automobile, belonging to the defendant J. W. Stewart. At the time the car was being operated by James Stewart, the son of the said J. W. Stewart, a lad of 13 years of age. A colored chauffeur, who had been sent out with the car by the owner, was sitting beside the lad.

His honor charged the jury that under the laws of North Carolina it was a misdemeanor for a person under the age of 16 to drive an automobile upon any highway or public street, and that it is a circumstance from which the jury may infer negligence, and that it does not necessarily follow that the jury shall conclude it was negligence, but that it is a circumstance to go to the jury. In this his honor erred. He should have instructed the jury that it is negligence *per se* for the defendant James Stewart to have driven the machine in violation of the statute law of the state. Zageir *v.* Southern Express Co., 89 S. E. 44; Paul *v.* Railroad, 170 N. C. 231, 87 S. E. 66, L. R. A. 1916B, 1079; Ledbetter *v.* English, 166 N. C. 125, 81 S. E. 1066."

See Davis, The Plaintiff's Illegal Act as a Defense in Actions of Tort, 18 Harvard Law Rev. 505; Thayer, Public Wrong and Private Action, 27 Harvard Law Rev. 317.

CHAPTER III

UNINTENDED NON-NEGLIGENT INTERFERENCE

Section I

Trespass on Land by Animals

NOYES *v.* COLBY

Supreme Court, New Hampshire, July Term, 1855.

Reported in 30 *New Hampshire Reports*, 143.

Trespass, for breaking and entering the plaintiff's close in Franklin. Plea, general issue.

The plaintiff proved that towards night, on June 27, the defendant's cow was upon his premises grazing, between his house and stable. There was no fence between his land and the highway.

The defendant then proposed to prove that, at that time he pastured his cow in a pasture, on the road to Salisbury, and that one Heath also pastured his cow in the same pasture. On the evening in question, when Heath drove home his own cow, he also let the defendant's cow out of the pasture. He did this without the knowledge or assent of the defendant, and without any authority, and had never done so before, and after this transaction was requested by the defendant not to do so again. He drove the cow down the road until she came to the point where it connects with the road through the village of Franklin, about two hundred feet from the plaintiff's land, when she strayed along the road and committed the trespass complained of.

The defendant contended that, under such circumstances he could not be held to be a trespasser merely from the fact that he owned the cow; that he had done no wrongful or improper act; that the act of Heath, being without his knowledge or assent, and without his authority, could not make him liable in trespass; that the action should not have been brought against him, but if any trespass had been committed, should have been brought against Heath.

There being no dispute about the facts, the Court ruled that the action could not be maintained; whereupon a verdict was taken for the defendant, upon which judgment was to be rendered, or it was to be set aside, and judgment rendered for the plaintiff for twenty-five cents damages, as this Court might order.[1]

WOODS, C. J. "A man is answerable for not only his own trespass, but that of his cattle also; for if by his negligent keeping they stray upon the land of another (and much more if he permits or drives them on), and they there tread down his neighbor's herbage, and spoil his corn or his trees, this is a trespass for which the owner must answer in damages." 3 Black. Com. 211. Such is the law as stated in the words of the author of the Commentaries, which are themselves very high authority on such subjects, and such has been the uniform practice and understanding of the law in all times, so far as the books show, and it is therefore too late to inquire whether the remedy by an action of trespass is founded upon the strictest logical propriety, where the cause of the damage is the negligence, and not the wilful act of the owner of the mischievous beasts.

It is hardly necessary to remark, but for the course of the defendant's argument, that the proposition quoted from Blackstone relates to the case in which the beasts "stray upon the land of another," and not to the case in which they are driven upon it by a stranger; for then the stranger is the author of the wrong, and the horse that he rides, or drives, is the mere passive instrument in his hands, and the owner of it, unless he have lent it for the purpose of the wrong, is as wholly guiltless as any other person. For in that case, the beast does not by the owner's negligent keeping stray upon the land of his neighbors.

It is substantially upon this ground that Tewksbury *v.* Bucklin, 7 N. H. Rep. 518, was decided; in which it was held that a party having the custody of the cattle was answerable for the trespass which they committed by straying upon another's inclosure.

The case finds that the cow "strayed along the road," and committed the act complained of. It would not be just to hold the party to the strict meaning of a single word, if it appeared by the context to have been used inaccurately; but it appears distinctly that the animal, although driven by Heath some distance from the pasture in the direction of the *locus in quo*, was not driven upon it so as to be in his hands a mere instrument for committing a trespass. Heath's trespass was upon the chattel of the defendant, but not upon the soil of the plaintiff. He abandoned the cow, and she being no longer in his custody, "strayed," and involved the owner in the consequences ordinarily incident to permitting beasts to stray into the inclosures of others.

When Heath abandoned the cow, she was about twelve rods from the lands of the plaintiff. From that period she was no longer under the control of Heath, but was again in the legal possession of the defendant, and under his general custody and control; and like other

[1] Part of case omitted; also arguments of counsel.

owners having the care and custody of their beasts at the time, he is answerable in trespass for her act in straying upon the close in question, and grazing there.

. . . .

For misdirection of the judge who tried the cause, the verdict must be set aside, and a *New trial granted.*[1]

BEARDSLEY, C. J., IN TONAWANDA R. CO. *v.* MUNGER

(1848) 5 *Denio,* 255, 267–268.

THE Court seem to have held that if the plaintiff's oxen escaped from his enclosure after the exercise of " ordinary care and prudence in taking care of " them, he was not responsible for their trespass on the defendants' land. This view of the law, we think, cannot be sustained. The plaintiff was bound at his peril to keep his cattle at home, or at all events to keep them out of the defendants' close, and no degree of " care and prudence," if the cattle found their way onto the defendants' land, would excuse the trespass. It would be a new feature in the law of trespass, if the owner of cattle could escape responsibility for their trespasses by showing he had used " ordinary," or even extraordinary " care and prudence " to keep them from doing mischief.[2]

TILLETT *v.* WARD

IN THE QUEEN'S BENCH DIVISION, NOVEMBER 27, 1882.

Reported in Law Reports, 10 *Queen's Bench Division,* 17.

APPEAL by special case from the decision of the judge of the County Court of Lincolnshire, holden at Stamford.

The action was to recover £1 for the damage done to goods in the plaintiff's shop.

[1] Williams *v.* New Albany R. Co., 5 Ind. 111; Vandalia R. *v.* Duling, 60 Ind. App. 332; Union R. Co. *v.* Rollins, 5 Kan. 167 (as to legislation, see Darling *v.* Rodgers, 7 Kan. 592; Missouri R. Co. *v.* Olden, 72 Kan. 110); Crawford *v.* Hughes, 3 J. J. Marsh. 433; Little *v.* Lathrop, 5 Me. 356; Richardson *v.* Milburn, 11 Md. 340; Eames *v.* Salem R. Co., 98 Mass. 560; Collins *v.* Lundquist, 154 Mich. 658; Vandegrift *v.* Rediker, 22 N. J. Law, 185; Munger *v.* Tonawanda R. Co., 4 N. Y. 349; Gregg *v.* Gregg, 55 Pa. St. 227; Hurd *v.* Rutland R. Co., 25 Vt. 116; Metropolitan Ins. Co. *v.* Clark, 145 Wis. 181 *Accord.*

As between adjoining owners, in absence of statutory duty as to division fence, see Bissell *v.* Southworth, 1 Root, 269; McNeer *v.* Boone, 52 Ill. App. 181; Myers *v.* Dodd, 9 Ind. 290; Stephenson *v.* Elliott, 2 Ind. App. 233; De Mers *v.* Rohan, 126 Ia. 488; Markin *v.* Priddy, 40 Kan. 684; Sturtevant *v.* Merrill, 33 Me. 62; Gillespie *v.* Hendren, 98 Mo. App. 622; Tewksbury *v.* Bucklin, 7 N. H. 518; Deyo *v.* Stewart, 4 Denio, 101; Angell *v.* Hill, 18 N. Y. Supp. 824; Kobayashi *v.* Strangeway, 64 Wash. 36.

As to liability of the owner for unauthorized entry of a dog on another's lands, see Brown *v.* Giles, 1 Carr. & P. 118; Read *v.* Edwards, 17 C. B. N. S. 245; Doyle *v.* Vance, 6 Vict. L. R. (Law) 87.

Trespass on unenclosed land by chickens, see Evans *v.* McLalin, 189 Mo. App. 310.

[2] Morgan *v.* Hudnell, 52 Ohio St. 552 *Accord.*

It appeared that on the 15th of May, 1882, an ox of the defendant was being driven from the live-stock market in Broad Street, Stamford, along a public street called Ironmonger Street, to the defendant's premises. Ironmonger Street has a paved carriage road with a foot pavement on either side, and the plaintiff was the occupier of an ironmonger's shop in the street. The ox, after having gone for some distance down the paved carriage road of Ironmonger Street, driven by the defendant's men, went for a short distance upon the foot pavement on the near or left-hand side, and was driven therefrom by one of the drovers in charge on to the carriage road, and after continuing for a farther distance upon such carriage road, turned again on the pavement about twelve yards from the plaintiff's shop, and continued upon the pavement until it came opposite the plaintiff's shop, when it passed through the open doorway into the shop and did damage to goods therein to the amount claimed. The ox was, as soon as possible after such entry and damage, driven by the defendant's men from the shop to the carriage road and to defendant's premises in another street; but they did not succeed in getting it out until about three-quarters of an hour from the time when it entered. No special act of negligence was proved on the part of the persons in charge of the ox, and there was no evidence that it was of a vicious or unruly nature, or that the defendant had any notice that there was anything exceptional in its temper or character, or that it would be unsafe to drive it through the public streets in the ordinary and usual way. It was proved that at the time the ox left the carriage-way the second time, one of the two men of the defendant in charge of the animal was walking by its side, having his hand upon it, and that the other man was walking about three yards in the rear of it. The two men in charge proved that they drove it unaccompanied by other cattle from the market, and they both declared that they did all they could under the circumstances to prevent it going on to the foot pavement and entering the open doorway of the plaintiff's shop, and they stated that the movement of the ox from the carriage-way on to the foot pavement was sudden and could not by any reasonable or available means have been prevented. It was alleged by the defendant's witnesses, and not contradicted, that it was a usual thing for several oxen to be driven from the Stamford market in charge of two men, and sometimes one man. It was admitted that it was not customary to drive oxen with halters, and that they would probably not go quietly if led by halters.

The County Court judge gave a verdict for the amount claimed, giving the defendant leave to appeal.

The question for the opinion of the Court was, whether upon the facts the plaintiff was entitled to the verdict.[1]

[1] Arguments omitted.

Lord Coleridge, C. J. In this action the County Court judge has found as a fact that there was no negligence on the part of the drivers of the ox, or, at all events, he has not found that there was negligence, and as it lies on the plaintiff to make out his case, the charge of negligence, so far as it has any bearing on the matter, must be taken to have failed.

Now, it is clear as a general rule that the owner of cattle and sheep is bound to keep them from trespassing on his neighbor's land, and if they so trespass an action for damages may be brought against him, irrespective of whether the trespass was or was not the result of his negligence. It is also tolerably clear that where both parties are upon the highway, where each of them has a right to be, and one of them is injured by the trespass of an animal belonging to the other, he must, in order to maintain his action, show that the trespass was owing to the negligence of the other or of his servant. It is also clear that where a man is injured by a fierce or vicious animal belonging to another, that *prima facie* no action can be brought without proof that the owner of the animal knew of its mischievous tendencies.

In the present case the trespass, if there was any, was committed off the highway upon the plaintiff's close, which immediately adjoined the highway, by an animal belonging to the defendant which was being driven on the highway. No negligence is proved, and it would seem to follow from the law that I have previously stated that the defendant is not responsible. We find it established as an exception upon the general law of trespass, that where cattle trespass upon unfenced land immediately adjoining a highway the owner of the land must bear the loss. This is shown by the judgment of Bramwell, B., in Goodwyn *v.* Cheveley, 28 L. J. (Ex.) 298. That learned judge goes into the question whether a reasonable time had or had not elapsed for the removal of cattle who had trespassed under similar circumstances, and this question would not have arisen if a mere momentary trespass had been by itself actionable. There is also the statement of Blackburn, J., in Fletcher *v.* Rylands, L. R. 1 Ex. 265, that persons who have property adjacent to a highway may be taken to hold it subject to the risk of injury from inevitable risk. I could not, therefore, if I were disposed, question law laid down by such eminent authorities, but I quite concur in their view, and I see no distinction for this purpose between a field in the country and a street in a market town. The accident to the plaintiff was one of the necessary and inevitable risks which arise from driving cattle in the streets in or out of town. No cause of action is shown, and the judgment of the County Court judge must be reversed.

Stephen, J. I am of the same opinion. As I understand the law, when a man has placed his cattle in a field it is his duty to keep them from trespassing on the land of his neighbors, but while he is driving them upon a highway he is not responsible, without proof of negligence on his part, for any injury they may do upon the highway, for they cannot then be said to be trespassing. The case of Goodwyn *v.* Cheveley, *supra*, seems to me to establish a further exception, that the owner of the cattle is not responsible without negligence when the injury is done to property adjoining the highway, — an exception which is absolutely necessary for the conduct of the common affairs of life. We have been invited to limit this exception to the case of high roads adjoining fields in the country, but I am very unwilling to multiply exceptions, and I can see no solid distinction between the case of an animal straying into a field which is unfenced or into an open shop in a town. I think the rule to be gathered from Goodwyn *v.* Cheveley, *supra*, a very reasonable one, for otherwise I cannot see how we could limit the liability of the owner of the cattle for any sort of injury which could be traced to them.

Judgment for defendant.[1]

COOLEY ON TORTS, 2D ED., 398–400.

The statutes which, under some circumstances, or for some purposes, require lands to be fenced by their owners, are so various in the several States that it is not easy even to classify them. Some of them provide merely that unless the owner shall cause his lands to be fenced with such a fence as is particularly described, he shall maintain no action for the trespasses of beasts upon them. These statutes are generally limited in their force to exterior fences, and are intended as a part of a system under which cattle are or may be allowed to depasture the highway. In some States, from the earliest days, beasts have been allowed to roam at large in the highways and unenclosed lands, either by general law or on a vote of the township or county to that effect; a futile permission, if owners of lands are not required to fence against them. A more common provision is one requiring the owners of adjoining premises to keep up, respectively, one-half the partition fence between them, this being apportioned for the purpose by agreement, by prescription, or by the order of fence-viewers. A neglect of duty under these statutes would not only preclude the party in fault from maintaining suit for injuries suffered by himself in consequence thereof, but it would seem that if the domestic animals of his neighbor should wander upon his lands, invited by his own neglect, and should there fall into pits, or otherwise receive injury, he would be responsible for this injury, as one occurring proximately from his own default. The statutes which require the construction of partition fences do so for the benefit exclusively of the adjoining proprietors. These proprietors may, at their option, by agreement, dispense with them, and even if they do not agree to do so, but fail to maintain them as the law contemplates, still, if the cattle of the

[1] Hartford *v.* Brady, 114 Mass. 466; Wood *v.* Snider, 187 N. Y. 28; Erdman *v.* Gottshall, 9 Pa. Super. Ct. 295; Metropolitan Ins. Co. *v.* Clark, 145 Wis. 181 *Accord.*

Cattle, while being driven on the highway, enter on the unfenced land of A adjoining the highway, and pass thence on to the unfenced land of B, adjoining the land of A, but not adjoining the highway. B has an action against the owner of the cattle. Wood *v.* Snider, 187 N. Y. 28. See also note in 12 L. R. A. N. S. 912.

third persons come wrongfully upon one man's lands, and from there enter the adjoining enclosure, it is no answer to an action of trespass brought by the owner of the latter that the partition fence provided for by the law was not maintained.[1]

WAGNER *v.* BISSELL

SUPREME COURT, IOWA, DECEMBER TERM, 1856.

Reported in 3 *Iowa Reports*, 396.

APPEAL from the Jones District Court.

This was an action of replevin for certain cattle. Defendant answered, denying the plaintiff's right to the possession, and also alleging as a special ground of defence, that said cattle (which he admits to be the property of plaintiff) did on the 17th day of August, 1856, trespass upon the uninclosed land of defendant, and while so trespassing, and after he had suffered damage to the amount of fifty dollars, he, said defendant, distrained the same, as he had a right to do; and while thus lawfully distrained, and while he thus rightfully had the possession, the said plaintiff replevied the said cattle, without paying, or offering to pay, for the damages sustained. To this answer the plaintiff demurred, which was sustained. Defendant refused to answer over, and judgment being against him, he appeals.[2]

WRIGHT, C. J. [After deciding a point of pleading.] There is then but one question in the case, and that is, whether the defendant, for the reasons stated in his answer, was entitled to the possession of the property, as against the plaintiff and owner. We are of opinion that he was not, and that the demurrer was therefore properly sustained.

That at common law, every man was bound to keep his cattle within his own close, under the penalty of answering in damage for all inju-

[1] As to the effect of statutes requiring lands to be fenced, see Northern R. Co. *v.* Cunningham, 89 Fed. 594; Comerford *v.* Dupuy, 17 Cal. 308 (as to later legislation see Hahn *v.* Garratt, 69 Cal. 146; Fisch *v.* Nice, 12 Cal. App. 60); Nuckolls *v.* Gaut, 12 Col. 361; Wright *v.* Wright, 21 Conn. 329; Frazier *v.* Nortinus, 34 Ia. 82 (but no application to cultivated land — Hallock *v.* Hughes, 42 Ia. 516); Louisville R. Co. *v.* Simmons, 85 Ky. 151; Gorman *v.* Pacific R. Co., 26 Mo. 441 (as to later legislation, see O'Riley *v.* Diss, 41 Mo. App. 184); Smith *v.* Williams, 2 Mont. 195; Randall *v.* Gross, 67 Neb. 255 (no application to cultivated lands); Jones *v.* Witherspoon, 52 N. C. 555; Kerwhaker *v.* Cleveland R. Co., 3 Ohio St. 172; Walker *v.* Bloomingcamp, 34 Or. 391; Gregg *v.* Gregg, 55 Pa. St. 227 (as to later legislation see Thompson *v.* Kyler, 9 Pa. Co. Ct. R. 205); Davis *v.* Davis, 70 Tex. 123; Poindexter *v.* May, 98 Va. 143; Walls *v.* Cunningham, 123 Wis. 346.

As to effect of statutes providing for division fences, see D'Arcy *v.* Miller, 86 Ill. 102; Duffees *v.* Judd, 48 Ia. 256; Wills *v.* Walters, 5 Bush, 351; Gooch *v.* Stephenson, 13 Me. 371; Shepherd *v.* Hees, 12 Johns. 433; Barber *v.* Mensch, 157 Pa. St. 390; Tower *v.* Providence R. Co., 2 R. I. 404.

Such statutes apply only as between adjoining owners: Aylesworth *v.* Herrington, 17 Mich. 417; Wilder *v.* Wilder, 38 Vt. 678; and as to cattle lawfully on the adjoining land: Lord *v.* Wormwood, 29 Me. 282; Vandegrift *v.* Rediker, 22 N. J. Law, 185; Melody *v.* Reab, 4 Mass. 471; Lawrence *v.* Combs, 37 N. H. 331.

[2] Arguments and portions of the opinion omitted.

ries arising from their being abroad, is admitted by all. And a part of the same rule is, that the owner of land is not bound to protect his premises from the intrusion of the cattle of a stranger, or third person; and that if such cattle shall intrude or trespass upon his premises, whether inclosed or not, he may, at his election, bring his action to recover the damages sustained, or distrain such trespassing animals, until compensated for such injury. We need not at present stop to ascertain the origin or reason of this rule. It is sufficient to say, that as a principle of the common law, it is well, and we believe universally settled. We are then led to inquire, whether, independent of any statutory provisions, this rule is applicable to our condition and circumstances as a people; and if it is, then whether it has or has not, been changed by legislative action.

Unlike many of the States, we have no statute declaring in express terms the common law to be in force in this State. That it is, however, has been frequently decided by this Court, and does not, perhaps, admit of controversy. But while this is true, it must be understood that it is adopted only so far as it is *applicable* to us as a people, and may be of a general nature. At this time we need only discuss the question whether the principle contended for is applicable; for there can be no fair ground for claiming that it is not of a general nature.

We have assumed that it is only so much of the common law as is *applicable* that can be said to be in force, or recognized as a rule of action in this State. To say that every principle of that law, however inapplicable to our wants or institutions, is to continue in force, until changed by some legislative rule, we believe has never been claimed, neither indeed could it be, with any degree of reason. What is meant however, by the term "applicable," has been thought to admit of some controversy. As stated by Catron, J., in the dissenting opinion in the case of Seely *v.* Peters, 5 Gilm. 130, "Does it mean applicable to the nature of our political institutions, and to the genius of our republican form of government, and to our Constitution, or to our domestic habits, our wants, and our necessities?" He then maintains that the former only is meant, and that to adopt the latter is a clear usurpation of legislative power by the courts. A majority of the Court held in that case, however, as had been previously decided in Boyer *v.* Sweet, 3 Scam. 121, "that in adopting the common law, it must be applicable to the habits and condition of our society, and in harmony with the genius, spirit, and objects of our institutions." And we can see no just or fair objection to this view of the subject. Indeed, there would seem to be much propriety in saying that the distinction attempted is more speculative than practical or real. For what is applicable to our wants, habits, and necessities as a community or state, must necessarily to some extent be determined from the nature and genius of our government and institutions. Or, in other words, to determine whether a particular principle harmonizes with the spirit of our institutions, we must look to the habits and condition of the society which has created and lived under these institutions. We have adopted a republican form of government, because we believe it to be better suited to our condition, as it is to that of all people, — and thereunder we believe our wants, rights, and necessities, as individuals and as a community, are more likely to be protected and provided for. And the conclusion would seem to fairly follow, that a principle or rule which tends to provide for, and protect our rights and wants, would harmonize with that form of government or those institutions which have grown up under it.

But, however this may be, we do not believe that in determining as a Court, whether a particular rule of the unwritten law is applicable, we are confined alone to its agreement or disagreement with our peculiar form of government. To make the true distinction between the rules which are, and are not, applicable, may be frequently embarrassing and difficult to courts.

Where the common law has been repealed or changed by the constitutions of either the States or national government, or by their legislative enactments, it is, of course, not binding. So also, it is safe to say, that where it has been varied by custom, not founded in reason, or not consonant to the genius and manners of the people, it ceases to have force. Bouvier's Law Dict., title Law, Common. And in accordance with this position, are the following authorities: "The common law of England is not to be taken in all respects to be that of America. Our ancestors brought with them its general principles, and claimed it as their birthright; but they brought with them and adopted only that portion which was applicable to their situation." Van Ness *v.* Packard, 2 Peters, 137. And see other remarks of the learned judge, in delivering the opinion in that case, page 143, which have a bearing upon the principal question involved in this.

In Goring *v.* Emery, 16 Pick. 107, in speaking of what parts of the common law and the statutes of England are to be taken as in force in Massachusetts, Shaw, C. J., says: "That what are to be deemed in force is often a question of difficulty, depending upon the nature of the subject, the difference between the character of our institutions, and our general course of policy, and those of the parent country, and upon fitness and usage." And in The Commonwealth *v.* Knowlton, 2 Mass. 534, it is said that "our ancestors, when they came into this new world, claimed the common law as their birthright, and brought it with them, except such parts as were adjudged inapplicable to their new state and condition."

In Ohio the rule is laid down as follows: "It has been repeatedly decided by the courts of this State that they will adopt the principles of the common law, as the rule of decision, so far only as those principles are adapted to our circumstances, state of society, and form of government." Lindsley *v.* Coats, 1 Ham. 243; see also Penny *v.* Little, 3 Scam. 301.

Is the rule of the common law, relied upon by the appellant in this case, applicable to our situation, condition, and usage, as a people? Is it in accordance with our habits, wants, and necessities? As applied to this State, is it founded in reason and the fitness of things? The legislature has certainly not so regarded it. On the contrary, we hope to be able to show that what legislation we have clearly recognizes the opposite rule. At present, we are considering the question without reference to any legislative interpretation or action.

These same inquiries were substantially discussed in the case of Seely *v.* Peters, above referred to; and as we could not hope to answer them more satisfactorily than is there done, we adopt the language used in that case, the appropriateness of which, as applied to this State, will be fully appreciated when we reflect that in their resources and necessities, Illinois and Iowa are almost twin sisters. Both alike are agricultural States — both alike have large and extensive prairies — and are alike destitute of timber, as compared with the eastern and older States of the Union.

Says Trumbull, J., in delivering that opinion: "However well adapted the rule of the common law may be to a densely populated country like England, it is surely but ill-adapted to a new country like ours. If this common-law rule prevails now, it must have prevailed from the time of the earliest settlement of the State, and can it be supposed that when the early settlers of this country located upon the borders of our extensive prairies, that they brought with them, and adopted as applicable to their condition, a rule of law requiring each one to fence up his cattle? that they designed the millions of fertile acres stretched out before them, to go ungrazed, except as each purchaser from the government was able to inclose his part with a fence? This State is unlike any of the eastern States in their early settlement, because, from the scarcity of timber, it must be many years yet before our extensive prairies can be fenced; and their luxuriant growth, sufficient for thousands of cattle, must be suffered to rot and decay where it grows, unless settlers upon their borders are permitted to turn their cattle upon them. Perhaps there is no principle of the common law so inapplicable to the condition of our country and the people as the one which is sought to be enforced now, for the first time, since the settlement of the State. It has been the custom of Illinois, so long that the memory of man runneth not to the contrary, for the owners of stock to suffer them to run at large. Settlers have located themselves contiguous to prairies, for the very purpose of getting the benefit of the range. The right of all to pasture their cattle upon uninclosed ground is universally conceded. No man has questioned this right, although hundreds of cases must have occurred where the owners of cattle have escaped the payment of damages on account of the insufficiency of the fences through which their stock have broken; and never till now has the common-law rule that the owner of cattle is bound to fence them up been suffered to prevail, or to be applicable to our condition. The universal understanding of all classes of community, upon which they have acted by inclosing their crops and letting their cattle run at large, is entitled to no little consideration in determining what the law is; and we should feel inclined to hold, independent of any statutes upon the subject, on account of the inapplicability of the common-law rule to the condition and circumstances of our people, that it does not, and never has, prevailed in Illinois."

The learned judge then proceeds to show that it is not necessary to assume that ground in the case before him, for the reason, as he says, that their entire legislation clearly shows that this rule of the common law never prevailed in that State. In like manner, we now propose to refer to some of our own legislation which, we think, will clearly show that it was never supposed to prevail in this State. [Here WRIGHT, C. J., stated, and commented upon, various statutes.]

This brief reference to these several acts must be sufficient, in our opinion, to satisfy any mind that the legislature never understood that the rule of the common law prevailed in this State. We do not maintain that these provisions expressly change the common-law rule. And did we believe that this principle had, at any time, been well established in this State, we should perhaps hold that it had not been changed by these different statutes. Where, however, it is, to say the least, doubtful whether the rule contended for is in accordance with our situation, condition, and wants as a people, where for a series of years there has been no legislation recognizing the existence of such a rule, and where custom and habit have uniformly negatived its existence, we feel entirely justified in giving force to these acts which, if they do not expressly, certainly do impliedly, change the unwritten law.

. . . .

Judgment affirmed.[1]

[1] Buford v. Houtz, 133 U. S. 320; Nashville R. Co. v. Peacock, 25 Ala. 229 (as to later legislation, see Phillips v. Bynum, 145 Ala. 549); Little Rock R. Co. v. Finley, 37 Ark. 562; Morris v. Fraker, 5 Col. 425; Studwell v. Ritch, 14 Conn. 292; Sprague v. Fremont R. Co., 6 Dak. 86; Savannah R. Co. v. Geiger, 21 Fla. 669; Macon R. Co. v. Lester, 30 Ga. 911 (but see later legislation, Puckett v. Young, 112 Ga. 578); Seeley v. Peters, 5 Gilm. 130 (but see Ill. Rev. St. c. 8, § 1); Bulpit v. Mathews, 145 Ill. 345; Vicksburgh R. Co. v. Patton, 31 Miss. 156; Gorman v. Pacific R. Co., 26 Mo. 441 (but see later legislation, Gumm v. Jones, 115 Mo. App. 597); Delaney v. Errickson, 10 Neb. 492; Laws v. North Carolina R. Co., 52 N. C. 468 (but see later legislation, State v. Mathis, 149 N. C. 546); Cleveland R. Co. v. Elliott, 4 Ohio St. 474 (but see later legislation, Marsh v. Koons, 78 Ohio St. 68); Murray v. South Carolina R. Co., 10 Rich. Law, 227; Hardman v. King, 14 Wyo. 503 *Accord.*

Turning or driving cattle on another's uninclosed, unimproved lands, where the common law is inapplicable or is abrogated by legislation: Lazarus v. Phelps, 152 U. S. 81; Bell v. Gonzales, 35 Col. 138; Bedden v. Clark, 76 Ill. 338; Dexter v.

BEINHORN *v.* GRISWOLD

SUPREME COURT, MONTANA, JULY 14, 1902.

Reported in 27 Montana Reports, 79.

PIGOTT, J.[1] Action to recover damages for injuries alleged to have been caused by the negligence of the defendant. The complaint states that the defendant negligently left exposed a vat containing poisonous liquid; that by reason of such negligence certain cattle of plaintiff and of one Holm drank from the vat some of the liquid, and died from the effects of the poison; and that Holm assigned his demand for damages to the plaintiff. The answer puts in issue the allegation of negligence, and avers that the death of the cattle was caused by the carelessness of the plaintiff and Holm. The plaintiff secured a judgment, and the defendant moved for a new trial on several grounds, one being the insufficiency of the evidence to prove negligence on the part of the defendant. From the order denying a new trial the defendant has appealed.

The facts upon which the plaintiff bases his allegations of negligence are substantially these: During the year 1898 the defendant was the lessee in possession of the Non-Such gold mine and mill site. The property was not inclosed by a legal fence. For the proper conduct of his mining operations he employed the cyanide process, using large quantities of poisonous chemicals, consisting principally of cyanide of potassium, which he diluted with water, and kept in suitable receptacles on the surface of the mining property, but not sufficiently covered to prevent easy access to the poisonous solution. In appearance it resembled water. Cattle of the plaintiff and of Holm, while ranging on the public domain, wandered over to and upon the defendant's mine and mill site, and there drank the poisonous liquid contained in the vats or tubs. The defendant knew that the cattle were in the habit of straying upon his uninclosed property, and he had driven them away whenever he saw them there.

The plaintiff insists there is but one question involved, which he states thus: Is a " landowner who negligently leaves exposed upon his uninclosed premises, where he knows stock are wont to stray, dangerous places or substances, whereby another's cattle, straying thereon, are injured, liable for such injury ? " He argues that, as the defend-

Heaghney, 47 Ill. App. 205; Harrison *v.* Adamson, 76 Ia. 337; Union R. Co. *v.* Rollins, 5 Kan. 167; Powers *v.* Kindt, 13 Kan. 74; Monroe *v.* Cannon, 24 Mont. 316; Musselshell Cattle Co. *v.* Woolfolk, 34 Mont. 126; Herrin *v.* Sieben, 46 Mont. 226; Delaney *v.* Errickson, 11 Neb. 533; Addington *v.* Canfield, 11 Okl. 204; Thomas *v.* Blythe, 44 Utah, 1; Cosgriff *v.* Miller, 10 Wyo. 190; Martin *v.* Platte Valley Sheep Co., 12 Wyo. 432; Healey *v.* Smith, 14 Wyo. 263. Compare Avery *v.* Maxwell, 4 N. H. 36.

Compare reasons given for the inapplicability of the common-law rule to Colorado. BECK, J., in Morris *v.* Fraker, 5 Col. 425, 428, 429.

[1] Arguments omitted.

ant's mining property was not inclosed by a legal fence, the cattle were not trespassing upon his property, but were rightfully thereon, and that therefore he owed to the plaintiff the duty so to use his property and conduct his business as not to injure the plaintiff's cattle; that, in failing to cover the poisonous solution so as to prevent the cattle from drinking of it, he violated this alleged duty, and as such negligence resulted in the death of the cattle, and consequent loss to the plaintiff, the defendant is liable in damages. In support of his contention the plaintiff cites Monroe *v.* Cannon, 24 Montana Reports, 316 (61 Pac. 863, 81 Am. St. Rep. 439), where the owner of pasture land was held entitled to recover the value of grass consumed by bands of sheep deliberately and intentionally driven on it by the herder in charge of them; the opinion containing the following language: "If in the case now under consideration the damage sustained by respondent had resulted from trespasses committed by cattle or sheep or other animals named in the statute, lawfully at large, and not under the direction and control of their owner, then appellant's position would be sound." Neither this language, nor anything said in the opinion, lends countenance to the contention of the plaintiff in the case at bar. The decision does not declare or define any duty owing by the landowner to the owner of straying cattle. These observations apply also to Section 3258 of the Political Code, which reads: "If any cattle, horse, mule, ass, hog, sheep, or other domestic animal break into any inclosure, the fence being legal, as hereinbefore provided, the owner of such animal is liable for all damages to the owner or occupant of the inclosure which may be sustained thereby. This section must not be construed so as to require a legal fence in order to maintain an action for injury done by animals running at large contrary to law." Even if it be conceded that the cattle of the plaintiff were not wrongfully upon defendant's property, no liability would be incurred from the fact that they were injured while there, unless it was the defendant's duty to protect from injury all cattle on his property whose trespass was not of such a nature as to render their owners liable for the trespass. Counsel for the plaintiff urge that, if these cattle were not wrongfully on the defendant's property, they must have been rightfully there; asserting that if there was no remedy by action, there could not be a trespass. To this we cannot yield assent.

The owner is entitled to the exclusive possession of his land, whether fenced or not; and it is beyond the power of the legislature to prescribe, or of custom to create, a right in another to occupy the land or enjoy its fruits. Either written law or custom may withhold from the owner who does not fence his land a remedy for loss suffered by reason of casual trespasses by cattle which stray upon it, and may give a remedy for such trespasses to those only who inclose their land. By custom as well as by statute the common law of England has been so modified in Montana. This is undoubtedly a legitimate exercise of the police power. It falls far short, however, of conferring a legal right to dispossess the nonfencing owner. He may at pleasure lawfully drive the intruding cattle from his land, and keep them away from it. This is his right, for the cattle are trespassing. The owners of domestic animals hold no servitude upon or interest, temporary or permanent, in the open land of another, merely because it is open. If the landowner fails to " fence out " cattle lawfully at large, he may not successfully complain of loss caused by such live stock straying upon his uninclosed land. For under these circumstances the trespass is condoned or excused, — the law refuses to award damages. While the landowner, by omitting to fence, disables himself from invoking the remedy which is given to those who inclose their property with a legal fence, and while the cattle owner is thereby relieved from liability for casual trespasses, it is nevertheless true that the cattle owner has no *right* to pasture his cattle on the land of another, and that cattle thus wandering over such lands are not rightfully there. They are there merely by the forbearance, sufferance, or tolerance of the nonfencing landowner; there they may remain only by his tolerance.

The cattle-owning plaintiff did not owe to the land-owning defendant the duty to fence his cattle in; the latter did not owe to the former the duty to fence them out; neither of them was under obligation to the other in that regard. The defendant is not liable in this action unless he was negligent. There cannot be negligence without breach of duty. Hence, manifestly, the defendant was not guilty of negligence in omitting to prevent the plaintiff's cattle from going upon his unfenced land.

As has just been said, the straying of the plaintiff's cattle upon the defendant's land did not involve the violation of any legal duty upon the part of the defendant. There would therefore seem to be no basis for the plaintiff's charge of negligence on the part of the defendant, unless it consists in the defendant's alleged failure to protect the cattle from injury while on his land. The damage resulted from a permissive, not an active, cause of injury. We are asked to hold that the law imposed upon the defendant, in addition to the duty of refraining from intentional or wanton injury to the cattle, the duty so to use his property and so to conduct his mining operations thereon as to avoid all dangers to which these trespassing beasts might expose themselves. Counsel invoke the provisions of Section 2296 of the Civil Code, which is declaratory of the common law: " Every one is responsible . . . for an injury occasioned to another by his want of ordinary care or skill in the management of his property. . . ." Giving to the principle thus expressed full recognition, and measuring the rights of the parties by the test of negligence thus furnished, we are unable to find in the record evidence of acts or omissions by the defendant constituting negligence in the management of his property. But the plaintiff contends that, irrespective of Section 2296, the defendant has been guilty of negligence in so using his property as to imperil, and in this case actually injure, the property of another. We think the principles which he invokes have no application to the facts disclosed by the record. To a naked trespasser or mere licensee by sufferance (if the expression may correctly be used) the landowner owes the duty to refrain from any wilful or wanton act causing injury to his person or chattels, and, after discovering that the trespasser is in imminent danger or immediate peril, to use reasonable care to avoid an active cause of injury. Egan *v.* Montana Central Railway Co., 24 Montana Reports, 569, 63 Pac. 831. The rule is different in respect of those who go upon property because of the owner's invitation, either express or implied. As to such persons he is bound, at his peril, to use reasonable care and diligence in keeping his property in safe condition. To a mere licensee or naked trespasser the landowner does not owe the active duty of being diligent or using care in providing against the danger of accident. The distinction is well expressed in Sweeny *v.* Old Colony & Newport Railroad Co., 10 Allen, 368, 87 Am. Dec. 644:

[A long quotation from the opinion in that case is omitted.]

The methods pursued by the defendant in the management and use of his property involved no danger to the plaintiff or his cattle, nor exposed either to risk, so long as he and they remained within the limits of the plaintiff's rights. The contention of the plaintiff rests upon the erroneous theory, heretofore considered, that the cattle owners hold a personal servitude upon, or the right of commons or profit in, all unfenced land, by virtue of which they are supposed to be entitled, as of right, to use for grazing and pasture all of the uninclosed lands of other persons. Such burden upon or easement in gross in open lands has not been granted, and does not exist. We have already decided that such use, while it does not constitute an actionable wrong, is not the exercise of a legal right; and as the cattle owner possessed no right to have his live stock upon the defendant's land, and the latter was clothed with the unquestioned right to drive them away because they were not rightfully there, clearly the defendant had no active duty in respect of them while there. He was, of course, bound to refrain from intentional or wanton injury; if he stood by and knowingly permitted them to drink of the poisonous solution, without making an effort to prevent them from doing so, he might, perhaps, be liable; but neither of these conditions is in the case at bar.

We think there is no proof in the record which justifies the application of the doctrine of invitation, enticement, allurement or attraction. Deane *v.* Clayton, 7 Taunt. 489, 531, 533; Jordin *v.* Crump, 8 Mees. & W. 782; Ponting *v.* Noakes, (1894) 2 Q. B. 281; Stendal *v.* Boyd, 67 Minn. 279, 69 N. W. 899; Twist *v.* Railroad Co., 39 Minn. 164, 39 N. W. 402, 12 Am. St. Rep. 626. The soundness of the principles upon which the so-called "turntable" and similar cases are supported is not presented for decision.

We have read the opinions which are opposed to the conclusions here announced. They need not be referred to or discussed. We are entirely satisfied that our conclusions are based upon correct fundamental principles.

The order refusing a new trial is reversed, with costs to the appellant, and the cause is remanded. *Reversed and remanded.*[1]

MR. CHIEF JUSTICE BRANTLY: I concur.

MR. JUSTICE MILBURN: Considering only the facts appearing in this case, I concur in the reversal of the order denying a new trial. I do not concur in all that is said in the opinion with reference to absence of duty owing by one person to another who is trespassing upon the premises of the former, or to the owner of live stock which wander upon such premises.

SECTION II

INJURIES BY ANIMALS

MAY v. BURDETT

IN THE QUEEN'S BENCH, JUNE 2, 1846.

Reported in 9 Queen's Bench Reports (Adolphus & Ellis, N. S.), 101.

CASE. The declaration stated that defendant, "before and at the time of the damage and injury hereinafter mentioned to the said Sophia, the wife of the said Stephen May, wrongfully, and injuriously kept a certain monkey, he the defendant well knowing that the said monkey was of a mischievous and ferocious nature, and was used and accustomed to attack and bite mankind, and that it was dangerous and improper to allow the monkey to be at large and unconfined; which said monkey, whilst the said defendant kept the same as aforesaid, heretofore and before the commencement of this suit, to wit, on the 2d of September, 1844, did attack, bite, wound, lacerate, and injure the said Sophia, then and still being the wife of said Stephen May, whereby the said Sophia became and was greatly terrified and alarmed, and became and was sick, sore, lame, and disordered, and so remained and continued for a long time, to wit, from the day and year last aforesaid to the time of the commencement of this suit; whereby,

[1] See Herold v. Meyers, 20 Ia. 378; Williams v. Michigan R. Co., 2 Mich. 259; Christy v. Hughes, 24 Mo. App. 275; Peek v. Western Tel. Co., 159 Mo. App. 148; Crandall v. Eldridge, 46 Hun, 411.

Whether there is a right of pasturage on uninclosed lands, where the common law rule is not in force, see Union R. Co. v. Rollins, 5 Kan. 167; Caulkins v. Mathews, 5 Kan. 191; Knight v. Abert, 6 Pa. St. 472.

and in consequence of the alarm and fright occasioned by the said monkey so attacking, biting, wounding, lacerating, and injuring her as aforesaid, the said Sophia has been greatly injured in her health," &c.

Plea, not guilty. Issue thereon.

On the trial, before Wightman, J., at the sittings in Middlesex, after Hilary term, 1845, a verdict was found for the plaintiff with £50 damages. Cockburn, in the ensuing term, obtained a rule to show cause why judgment should not be arrested.

[The cause was argued] before LORD DENMAN, C. J., PATTESON, J., COLERIDGE, J., and WIGHTMAN, J.[1]

LORD DENMAN, C. J., now delivered the judgment of the Court.

This was a motion to arrest the judgment in an action on the case for keeping a monkey which the defendant knew to be accustomed to bite people, and which bit the female plaintiff. The declaration stated that the defendant wrongfully kept a monkey, well knowing that it was of a mischievous and ferocious nature and used and accustomed to attack and bite mankind, and that it was dangerous to allow it to be at large; and that the monkey, whilst the defendant kept the same as aforesaid, did attack, bite, and injure the female plaintiff, whereby, &c.

It was objected on the part of the defendant that the declaration was bad for not alleging negligence or some default of the defendant in not properly or securely keeping the animal; and it was said that, consistently with this declaration, the monkey might have been kept with due and proper caution, and that the injury might have been entirely occasioned by the carelessness and want of caution of the plaintiff herself.

A great many cases and precedents were cited upon the argument; and the conclusion to be drawn from them appears to us to be that the declaration is good upon the face of it; and that whoever keeps an animal accustomed to attack and bite mankind, with knowledge that it is so accustomed, is *prima facie* liable in an action on the case at the suit of any person attacked and injured by the animal, without any averment of negligence or default in the securing or taking care of it. The gist of the action is the keeping the animal after knowledge of its mischievous propensities.

The precedents, both ancient and modern, with scarcely an exception, merely state the ferocity of the animal and the knowledge of the defendant, without any allegation of negligence or want of care. A great many were referred to upon the argument, commencing with the Register and ending with Thomas *v.* Morgan, 2 C. M. & R. 496; s. c. 5 Tyr. 1085; and all in the same form, or nearly so. In the Register, 110, 111, two precedents of writs are given, one for keeping a dog accustomed to bite sheep, and the other for keeping a boar accustomed to attack and wound other animals. The cause of action, as stated in

[1] The arguments are omitted.

both these precedents, is the propensity of the animals, the knowledge of the defendant, and the injury to the plaintiff; but there is no allegation of negligence or want of care. In the case of Mason *v.* Kneeling, reported in 1 Ld. Ray. and 12 Mod., and much relied upon on the part of the defendant, want of due care was alleged, but the scienter was omitted; and the question was, not whether the declaration would be good without the allegation of want of care, but whether it was good without the allegation of knowledge, which it was held that it was not. No case was cited in which it had been decided that a declaration stating the ferocity of the animal and the knowledge of the defendant was bad for not averring negligence also; but various *dicta* in the books were cited to show that this is an action founded on negligence, and therefore not maintainable unless some negligence or want of care is alleged.

In Comyns' Digest, tit. Action upon the Case for Negligence (A 5), it is said that " an action upon the case lies for a neglect in taking care of his cattle, dog, &c.; " and passages were cited from the older authorities, and also from some cases at *nisi prius*, in which expressions were used showing that, if persons suffered animals to go at large, knowing them to be disposed to do mischief, they were liable in case any mischief actually was done; and it was attempted to be inferred from this that the liability only attached in case they were suffered to go at large or to be otherwise ill secured. But the conclusion to be drawn from an examination of all the authorities appears to us to be this: that a person keeping a mischievous animal with knowledge of its propensities is bound to keep it secure at his peril, and that if it does mischief, negligence is presumed, without express averment. The precedents as well as the authorities fully warrant this conclusion. The negligence is in keeping such an animal after notice. The case of Smith *v.* Pelah, 2 Stra. 1264, and a passage in 1 Hale's Pleas of the Crown, 430,[1] put the liability on the true ground. It may be that if the injury was solely occasioned by the wilfulness of the plaintiff after warning, that may be a ground of defence, by plea in confession and avoidance; but it is unnecessary to give any opinion as to this; for

[1] After stating that " if a man have a beast, as a bull, cow, horse, or dog, used to hurt people, if the owner know not his quality, he is not punishable, &c.," Hale adds (citing authorities) that " these things seem to be agreeable to law.

" 1. If the owner have notice of the quality of his beast, and it doth anybody hurt, he is chargeable with an action for it.

" 2. Though he have no particular notice that he did any such thing before, yet if it be a beast that is *feræ naturæ*, as a lion, a bear, a wolf, yea an ape or monkey, if he get loose and do harm to any person, the owner is liable to an action for the damage, and so I knew it adjudged in Andrew Baker's Case, whose child was bit by a monkey that broke its chain and got loose.

" 3. And therefore in case of such a wild beast, or in case of a bull or cow, that doth damage, where the owner knows of it, he must at his peril keep him up safe from doing hurt, for though he use his diligence to keep him up, if he escape and do harm, the owner is liable to answer damages." 1 Hale's P. C. 430, Part I, c. 33. — Reporter's Note.

we think that the declaration is good upon the face of it, and shows a *prima facie* liability in the defendant.

It was said, indeed, further, on the part of the defendant, that, the monkey being an animal *feræ naturæ*, he would not be answerable for injuries committed by it if it escaped and went at large without any default on the part of the defendant, during the time it had so escaped and was at large, because at that time it would not be in his keeping nor under his control; but we cannot allow any weight to this objection; for, in the first place, there is no statement in the declaration that the monkey had escaped, and it is expressly averred that the injury occurred whilst the defendant kept it; we are besides of opinion, as already stated, that the defendant, if he would keep it, was bound to keep it secure at all events.

The rule therefore will be discharged. *Rule discharged.*[1]

FILBURN *v.* PEOPLE'S PALACE AND AQUARIUM COMPANY, LIMITED

In the Court of Appeal, June 30, 1890.

Reported in Law Reports, 25 Queen's Bench Division, 258.

Appeal from a judgment of Day, J.

The action was brought to recover damages for injuries sustained by the plaintiff by his being attacked by an elephant, which was the property of the defendants, and was being exhibited by them. The learned judge left three questions to the jury: whether the elephant was an animal dangerous to man; whether the defendant knew the elephant to be dangerous, and whether the plaintiff brought the attack on himself. The jury answered all three questions in the negative. The learned judge entered judgment for the plaintiff for a sum agreed upon in case the plaintiff should be entitled to recover.

The defendants appealed.

Lockwood, Q. C., and *Cyril Dodd,* Q. C., in support of the appeal. There are certain animals recognized as being of an untamable nature, and these a person keeps at his peril. In Hale's Pleas of the Crown (vol. i, p. 430), it is said: "Tho' he have no particular notice that he did any such thing before, yet if it be a beast, that is *ferae naturae,* as a lion, a bear, a wolf, yea an ape or a monkey, if he get

[1] Jackson *v.* Smithson, 15 M. & W. 563; Card *v.* Case, 5 C. B. 622; Strouse *v.* Leipf, 101 Ala. 433; Holt *v.* Leslie, 116 Ark. 433; Laverone *v.* Mangianti, 41 Cal. 138; Gooding *v.* Chutes Co., 155 Cal. 620; Woolf *v.* Chalker, 31 Conn. 121; Kightlinger *v.* Egan, 75 Ill. 141; Gordon *v.* Kaufman, 44 Ind. App. 603; Holt *v.* Myers, 47 Ind. App. 118; Kennett *v.* Engle, 105 Mich. 693; Hall *v.* Huber, 61 Mo. App. 384; O'Neill *v.* Blase, 94 Mo. App. 648; Muller *v.* McKesson, 73 N. Y. 195; People *v.* Shields, 142 App. Div. 194; Tubbs *v.* Shears, 55 Okl. 610; Mann *v.* Weiand, 81* Pa. St. 243; McCaskill *v.* Elliot, 5 Strob. 196; Missio *v.* Williams, 129 Tenn. 504; Harris *v.* Carstens Packing Co., 43 Wash. 647; Gunderson *v.* Bieren, 80 Wash. 459 *Accord.*

loose and do harm to any person, the owner is liable to an action for the damage." There is, however, no hard and fast line which prevents an animal *ferae naturae* ceasing to belong to that class and becoming domesticated. The distinction is drawn in Rex *v.* Huggins, 2 Ld. Raym. 1574, where it is said: "There is a difference between beasts that are *ferae naturae*, as lions and tygers, which a man must always keep up at his peril; and beasts that are *mansuetae naturae*, and break through the tameness of their nature, such as oxen and horses. In the latter case an action lies, if the owner has had notice of the quality of the beast; in the former case an action lies without such notice." All animals are wild by nature, and the reason for the distinction is, that some of them are treated as domesticated, because they have been tamed and are used in the service of man. Though there are wild elephants, just as there are wild oxen and horses, a great number have been tamed, and are used in the service of man; and the same ruling should apply to individuals of this class as to domesticated animals generally. The jury have negatived any knowledge on the part of the defendants of any dangerous character in this elephant, and they are, under these circumstances, entitled to the verdict.

LORD ESHER, M. R. The only difficulty I feel in the decision of this case is whether it is possible to enunciate any formula under which this and similar cases may be classified. The law of England recognizes two distinct classes of animals; and as to one of those classes, it cannot be doubted that a person who keeps an animal belonging to that class must prevent it from doing injury, and it is immaterial whether he knows it to be dangerous or not. As to another class, the law assumes that animals belonging to it are not of a dangerous nature, and any one who keeps an animal of this kind is not liable for the damage it may do, unless he knew that it was dangerous. What, then, is the best way of dealing generally with these different cases? I suppose there can be no dispute that there are some animals that every one must recognize as not being dangerous on account of their nature. Whether they are *ferae naturae* so far as rights of property are concerned is not the question; they certainly are not so in the sense that they are dangerous. There is another set of animals that the law has recognized in England as not being of a dangerous nature, such as sheep, horses, oxen, dogs, and others that I will not attempt to enumerate. I take it this recognition has come about from the fact that years ago, and continuously to the present time, the progeny of these classes has been found by experience to be harmless, and so the law assumes the result of this experience to be correct without further proof. Unless an animal is brought within one of these two descriptions, — that is, unless it is shown to be either harmless by its very nature, or to belong to a class that has become so by what may be called cultivation, — it falls within the class of animals as to which the rule is, that a man who keeps one must take the responsibility of keeping it safe. It cannot possibly be said that an elephant comes within the class of animals known to be harmless by nature, or within that shown by experience to be harmless in this country, and consequently it falls within the class of animals that a man keeps at his peril, and which he must prevent from doing injury under any circumstances, unless the person to whom the injury is done brings it on himself. It was, therefore, immaterial in this case whether the particular animal was a dangerous one, or whether the defendants had any knowledge that it was so. The judgment entered was in these circumstances right, and the appeal must be dismissed.

LINDLEY, L. J. I am of the same opinion. The last case of this kind discussed was May *v.* Burdett, 9 Q. B. 101, but there the monkey which did the mischief was said to be accustomed to attack mankind, to the knowledge of the person who kept it. That does not decide this case. We have had no case cited to us, nor any evidence, to show that elephants in this country are not as a class dangerous; nor are they commonly known here to belong to the class of domesticated animals. Therefore a person who keeps one is liable, though he does not know that the particular one that he keeps is mischievous. Applying that principle to this case, it appears that the judgment for the plaintiff was right, and this appeal must be dismissed.

BOWEN, L. J. I am of the same opinion. The broad principle that governs this case is that laid down in Fletcher *v.* Rylands, Law Rep. 1 Ex. 265; Law Rep. 3 H. L. 330, that a person who brings upon his land anything that would not naturally come upon it, and which is in itself dangerous, must take care that it is kept under proper control. The question of liability for damage done by mischievous animals is a branch of that law which has been applied in the same way from the times of Lord Holt [1] and of Hale until now. People must not be wiser than the experience of mankind. If from the experience of mankind a particular class of animals is dangerous, though individuals may be tamed, a person who keeps one of the class takes the risk of any damage it may do. If, on the other hand, the animal kept belongs to a class which, according to the experience of mankind, is not dangerous, and not likely to do mischief, and if the class is dealt with by mankind on that footing, a person may safely keep such an animal, unless he knows that the particular animal that he keeps is likely to do mischief. It cannot be doubted that elephants as a class have not been reduced to a state of subjection; they still remain wild and untamed, though individuals are brought to a degree of tameness which amounts to domestication. A person, therefore, who keeps an elephant, does so at his own risk, and an action can be maintained for any injury done by it, although the owner had no knowledge of its mischievous propensities. I agree, therefore, that the appeal must be dismissed.

Appeal dismissed.[2]

[1] See Mason *v.* Keeling, 12 Mod. 332.

[2] Besozzi *v.* Harris, 1 F. & F. 92; Texas R. Co. *v.* Juneman, 71 Fed. 939 (wild

MAUNG KYAW DUN *v.* MA KYIN

BEFORE THE JUDICIAL COMMISSIONER OF UPPER BURMA, MAY 7, 1900.

Reported in 2 *Upper Burma Rulings* (1897–1901), *Civil,* 570.

H. THIRKELL WHITE, ESQ., JUDICIAL COMMISSIONER.

The plaintiff-appellant sued to recover damages on account of the death of his elephant "Do," which died from the effect of wounds inflicted by the respondents' elephant, "Kya Gyi."

The issues which arise in a case of this kind have been stated in two cases of this court. In Maung Gyi *v.* Po To [same vol., p. 565] it was observed that the issue generally would no doubt be the usual issue as to the existence of negligence on the part of the owner of the animal doing the damage. In Maung Saw *v.* Maung Kyaw [same vol., p. 567], points which arise in a case very similar to the present were indicated. There has been some argument in this court on the application of the doctrine of *scienter*. It is said that "any one who keeps a wild animal, as a tiger or bear, which escapes and does damage, is liable without any proof of notice of the animal's ferocity; but where the damage is done by a domestic animal, the plaintiff must show that the defendant knew the animal was accustomed to do mischief." Collett on Torts, 7th edition, p. 100. Again, "a person keeping a mischievous animal with knowledge of its propensities is bound to keep it secure at his peril. If it escapes and does mischief, he is liable without proof of negligence, neither is proof required that he knew the animal to be mischievous, if it is of a notoriously fierce or mischievous species." Pollock on Torts, 3d edition, p. 442. In Smith's Leading Cases in the notes on Fletcher *v.* Rylands, 10th edition, vol. i, p. 827, it is said: "The law of England recognizes two distinct classes of animals. The first class consists of such animals as sheep, horses, oxen, and dogs, which the law assumes not to be of a dangerous nature, and a person who keeps an animal of this class is not liable for any damage it may do, when not trespassing, unless he knew that it was in fact dangerous. The other class consists of animals which have not

steer); Jackson *v.* Baker, 24 App. D. C. 100; Graham *v.* Payne, 122 Ind. 403 (ram); Marble *v.* Ross, 124 Mass. 44 (bull); Marquet *v.* La Duke, 96 Mich. 596; Phillips *v.* Garner, 106 Miss. 828; Manger *v.* Shipman, 30 Neb. 352; Van Leuven *v.* Lyke, 1 N. Y. 515; Mahoney *v.* Dwyer, 84 Hun, 348; Malloy *v.* Starin, 113 App. Div. 852 (reversed on other grounds, 191 N. Y. 21); Stamp *v.* Eighty-sixth St. Amusement Co., 95 Misc. 599 *Accord.*

Compare Hayes *v.* Miller, 150 Ala. 621, as to a wolf domesticated to such an extent that the owner believed it harmless.

As to the liability of the owner of bees, see O'Gorman *v.* O'Gorman, [1903] 2 I. R. 573; Parsons *v.* Manser, 119 Ia. 88; Petey Mfg. Co. *v.* Dryden, 5 Pennewill, 166; Lucas *v.* Pettit, 12 Ont. Law, 448; Notes in 97 Am. State Rep. 287, and 62 L. R. A. 132. Compare Earl *v.* Van Alstine, 8 Barb. 630; Olmsted *v.* Rich, 25 N. Y. St. Rep. 271; Arkadelphia *v.* Clark, 52 Ark. 23.

been shown by experience to be harmless by nature; and one who keeps animals of this class must prevent them from doing injury under any circumstances, unless the person to whom it is done brings it on himself." In the English case on which these remarks are based (Filburn *v.* People's Palace Company), it was held that an elephant "did not belong to a class which, according to the experience of mankind, is not dangerous to man, and therefore the owner kept such an animal at his own risk, and his liability for damage done by it was not affected by his ignorance of its dangerous character." Mew's Digest of English Case Law, p. 199.

I understand the remarks of my learned predecessor in Maung Gyi *v.* Po To above cited to go no further than to suggest that a man should be liable for injury caused by his animal, whether tame or wild, if it is proved that the injury was due to the owner's negligence. In that view, it would not be necessary to draw a distinction between wild and domestic animals. The point for decision would be whether the owner was guilty of negligence or whether he used such care as in the circumstances of the case was reasonable and ordinarily sufficient. The amount of care required would vary according to the class of the animal and according to its known disposition. It could not, I think, be laid down in this country that a man is liable for any damage done by his elephant without any proof of negligence or that he knew it to be of a vicious disposition. In view of the manner in, and extent to, which elephants are employed in this country such a proposition would be manifestly unjust.

In the present case, therefore, I think it was for the plaintiff to prove that the damage done to his elephant was caused, or rendered possible, by the defendant's negligence. In considering the question of negligence, the defendant's knowledge or want of knowledge that her elephant was of a vicious disposition would be an important point. In a suit of this kind, where an animal like an elephant is concerned, I think the burden of proving negligence is in the first place on the plaintiff who avers it. It might be otherwise if injury by a tiger or bear were concerned.

I agree with the Lower Courts in thinking that it is not proved that the defendant knew that the elephant "Kya Gyi" was of a vicious disposition. It was therefore not incumbent on her to take more than ordinary precautions with him. It does not seem to be shown that ordinary precautions were neglected. It is alleged that "Kya Gyi" twice gored the deceased elephant "Do," and the mahout called by the plaintiff declares that he had neither bell nor fetters. On the other hand, as pointed out in the judgment of the Court of First Instance, the plaintiff himself admitted that "Kya Gyi" had a bell and fetters on the second occasion. It is admitted that all the other elephants of the defendant had bells and fetters. There is direct evidence, at least as good as that for the plaintiff, that "Kya Gyi" was properly provided with them. In my opinion it has not been proved that there was any negligence on the part of the defendant, and any *prima facie* case made out by the plaintiff has been rebutted. I therefore hold that the Lower Courts have rightly decided that the defendants are not liable; and I dismiss this appeal with costs.[1]

BOSTOCK-FERARI AMUSEMENT COMPANY *v.* BROCKSMITH

APPELLATE COURT, INDIANA, FEBRUARY 14, 1895.

Reported in 34 *Indiana Appellate Court Reports*, 566.

ACTION by Otto Brocksmith against Bostock-Ferari Amusement Company. From a judgment for plaintiff, defendant appeals.

COMSTOCK, C. J. The complaint alleges that the plaintiff, while driving in his buggy, was injured in consequence of his horse taking fright from the sight of a bear walking along a public street in the city of Vincennes. The action was begun in the Circuit Court of Knox County, and, upon change of venue, tried in the Circuit Court of Sullivan County. The court rendered judgment upon the verdict of the jury in favor of appellee for $750. The complaint was in three paragraphs. The first was dismissed, and the cause was tried upon the amended second and third paragraphs, to which general denial was filed.

The errors relied upon are the action of the court in overruling demurrers to said second and third paragraphs, respectively, of the complaint, and overruling appellant's motion for a new trial. Some of the reasons set out in the motion for a new trial are that the verdict was contrary to the law, and was not sustained by sufficient evidence.

The question of the sufficiency of the second paragraph of the complaint is not entirely free from doubt, but we conclude that each of said paragraphs is sufficient to withstand a demurrer.

It is sought to maintain an action for damages resulting from the fright of a horse at the sight of a bear, which his keeper and owner was leading along a public street, for the purpose of transporting him from a railroad train, by which he had been carried to Vincennes, to the point in Vincennes at which the bear was to be an exhibit as a

[1] "Certain animals *ferae naturae* may doubtless be domesticated to such an extent as to be classed, in respect to the liability of the owner for injuries they commit, with the class known as tame or domestic animals; but inasmuch as they are liable to relapse into their wild habits and to become mischievous, the rule is that if they do so, and the owner becomes notified of their vicious habit, they are included in the same rule as if they had never been domesticated, the gist of the action in such a case, as in the case of untamed wild animals, being not merely the negligent keeping of the animal, but the keeping of the same with knowledge of the vicious and mischievous propensity of the animal." Clifford, J., in Spring Company *v.* Edgar, 99 U. S. 645, 653.

part of appellant's show. It is not claimed, either by allegation or proof, that the show was in itself unlawful; and there is no pretence that the transporting of the bear from one place to another for the purpose of exhibition was unlawful, or in itself negligence. The case is therefore one of the fright of a horse merely at the appearance of the bear while he was being led along the street, was making no noise or other demonstration, and was in the control of his keeper. It appears without contradiction from the evidence that when the horse took fright the bear was doing nothing except going with his keeper. He was muzzled. He had a ring in his nose to which a chain was attached. Said chain was strong enough to hold and control him. He had around his neck a collar about two inches wide and one-half inch thick, to which also was attached a chain. The keeper had both chains in his hand when the accident occurred. The chain connected with the ring in his nose was small. The one connected with his collar was large. It was for the purpose of chaining him at night when he was alone. The chains were strong enough to control the bear. The animal was characterized by the witnesses who knew him as " gentle," " kind," " docile." His keeper testified that he had never known him to be mean or to growl. He testified also that he never knew of a bear scaring a horse; that shortly before the accident the keeper met two ladies in a buggy, and their horse did not scare. He was described as of pretty good size and brown. One witness said he was a " large, ugly-looking, brown bear."

When a person is injured by an attack by an animal *ferae naturae*, the negligence of the owner is presumed, because the dangerous propensity of such an animal is known, and the law recognizes that safety lies only in keeping it secure. 2 Am. and Eng. Ency. Law (2d ed.), p. 351. In the case before us the injury did not result from any vicious propensity of the bear. He did nothing but walk in the charge of his owner and keeper, Peter Degeleih. He was being moved quietly upon a public thoroughfare for a lawful purpose.

We have given the facts that are not controverted. There is also evidence leading strongly to support the claim made by appellant that appellee was guilty of negligence, proximately contributing to his injury. Appellant also earnestly argues — supporting its argument with references to recognized authorities — that the owner and keeper of the bear was an independent contractor. But the disposition which we think should be made of the appeal makes it unnecessary to consider these questions. The liability of the appellant must rest on the doctrine of negligence. The gist of the action as claimed by appellee is the transportation of the bear, with knowledge that he was likely to frighten horses, without taking precaution to guard against fright.

1. An animal *ferae naturae*, reduced to captivity, is the property of its captor, 2 Blackstone's Comm., *391, *403; 4 Blackstone's Comm., *235, *236.

2. The owner of the bear had the right to transport him from one place to another for a lawful purpose, and it was not negligence *per se* for the owner or keeper to lead him along a public street for such purpose. Scribner *v.* Kelley, (1862) 38 Barb. 14; Macomber *v.* Nichols, (1876) 34 Mich. 212, 22 Am. Rep. 522; Ingham, Law of Animals, p. 230.

3. The conducting of shows for the exhibition of wild or strange animals is a lawful business. The mere fact that the appearance of a chattel, whether an animal or an inanimate object, is calculated to frighten a horse of ordinary gentleness, does not deprive the owner of such chattel of his lawful right to transport his property along a public highway. Macomber *v.* Nichols, *supra;* Holland *v.* Bartch, (1889) 120 Ind. 46, 16 Am. St. 307; Wabash, etc., R. Co. *v.* Farver, (1887) 111 Ind. 195, 60 Am. Rep. 696; Gilbert *v.* Flint, etc., R. Co., (1883) 51 Mich. 488, 16 N. W. 868, 47 Am. Rep. 592; Piolette *v.* Simers, (1894) 106 Pa. St. 95, 51 Am. Rep. 496. One must use his own so as not unnecessarily to injure another, but the measure of care to be employed in respect to animals and other property is the same. It is such care as an ordinarily prudent person would employ under similar circumstances. This is not inconsistent with the proposition that if an animal *ferae naturae* attacks and injures a person, the negligence of the owner or keeper is presumed. The evidence is that the horse was of ordinary gentleness, but this fact would not deprive the appellant of the right to make proper use of the street. If the bear had been carelessly managed, or permitted to make any unnecessary noise or demonstration, it would have been an act of negligence.

It is not uncommon for horses of ordinary gentleness to become frightened at unaccustomed sights on the public highway. The automobile, the bicycle, the traction-engine, the steam roller may each be frightful to some horses, but still they may be lawfully used on the public streets. King David said, " An horse is a vain thing for safety." Modern observation has fully justified the statement. A large dog, a great bull, a baby wagon may each frighten some horses, but their owners are not barred from using them upon the streets on that account. Nor under the decisions would the courts be warranted in holding that the owner of a bear, subjugated, gentle, docile, chained, would not, under the facts shown in the case at the bar, be permitted to conduct the homely brute along the public streets because of his previous condition of freedom.

In Scribner *v.* Kelley, *supra*, the court said: " It does not appear that the elephant was at large, but on the contrary that he was in the care, and apparently under the control, of a man who was riding beside him on a horse; and the occurrence happened before the passage of the act of April 2, 1862, regulating the use of public highways. There is nothing in the evidence to show that the plaintiff's horse was terrified because the object he saw was an elephant, but only that he was frightened because he suddenly saw moving upon a highway, crossing that upon which he was travelling, and fully one hundred feet from him, a large animate object to which he was unaccustomed — *non constat* that any other moving object of equal size and differing in appearance from such as he was accustomed to see might not have inspired him with similar terror. The injury which resulted from his fright is more fairly attributed to a lack of ordinary courage and discipline in himself, than to the fact that the object which he saw was an elephant."

4. It is alleged in the complaint that the bear was an object likely to frighten a horse of ordinary gentleness, which fact the appellant well knew. There is no evidence that the bear was an object likely to frighten horses of ordinary gentleness, nor that the appellant knew that the bear was an object likely to frighten horses of ordinary gentleness. The evidence shows, so far as the observation of the keeper and the appellant gave information, that the bear had not frightened horses.

. . . .

The facts upon the question of negligence are undisputed, and that question is therefore to be determined by the court as a matter of law.

Judgment is reversed, with instruction to sustain appellant's motion for a new trial.[1]

MARLOR *v.* BALL

IN THE COURT OF APPEAL, MARCH 1, 1900.

Reported in 16 *Times Law Reports*, 239.

THIS was an application by the defendant for judgment or a new trial in an action tried before Mr. Justice Phillimore and a special jury at Manchester. The action was brought to recover damages for personal injuries sustained by the plaintiff through being bitten by a zebra belonging to the defendant. The plaintiff was a working man. The defendant was the proprietor of the Chadderton-hall pleasure-grounds, at Oldham, where he kept an exhibition of wild animals. The plaintiff went with his wife and his brother-in-law to see the exhibition, and, having paid for admission, entered the gardens. While they were walking along they found the door of a stable standing open, and went in. There were four zebras inside the stable, each in a separate stall and properly tied up by a halter to the manger. The plaintiff went up to one of the zebras and stroked it. The animal kicked out, and the plaintiff being then standing against the partition, the animal pressed him through the partition, and he fell into the next stall, where another zebra bit his hand, which had to be ampu-

[1] See Bennet *v.* Bostock, 13 Scottish Sheriff Court Reports, 50; in the same direction with Scribner *v.* Kelley, 38 Barb. 14, cited in the foregoing opinion.

tated. At the trial the jury returned a verdict for the plaintiff for £175.

Mr. Montague Lush, for the defendant, in support of the application for judgment or a new trial, contended that there was no evidence on which the defendant could be held liable. The common law obligation of a person who kept animals *ferae naturae* was to keep them secure, or, in other words, to prevent them from getting loose. He was liable to an action, if, in consequence of a failure on his part to comply with that obligation, any other person was injured. In such a case it was not necessary for the plaintiff to allege negligence. But in this case there had been no failure to comply with that common law obligation. Here the animals were kept secure, they were not loose. The plaintiff, therefore, had to allege negligence, and the alleged negligence appeared to be this, that the defendant did not provide a keeper, or some physical barrier to prevent people from meddling with the animals. But this allegation did not show a cause of action at all. There was no authority for saying that an action lay for not preventing the plaintiff from bringing an injury on himself. It was not sufficient for the plaintiff here to show that the door was open. The door being open might be an invitation to go in, but it was not an invitation to meddle by stroking the zebras. The plaintiff failed to show any negligence on the part of the defendant, and he had no remedy. Counsel referred to Filburn *v.* The People's Palace and Aquarium Company (Limited), 25 Q. B. D. 258; and Memberz *v.* The Great Western Railway Company, 14 App. Cas. 179.

Mr. S. T. Evans, for the plaintiff, said the foundation of the action was that zebras were dangerous animals, and it was the duty of persons who kept dangerous animals to prevent them from doing injury. The leaving the door of the stable unlocked was a default on the part of the defendant. The plaintiff was not in any way warned that these zebras were wild animals. The evidence taken altogether showed that these zebras were kept in much the same way as horses would ordinarily be kept. He referred to May *v.* Burdett, 9 Q. B. 101.

The Court allowed the application and ordered judgment to be entered for the defendant.

LORD JUSTICE A. L. SMITH said it was conceded that a zebra was a dangerous animal, and that by law a man who kept a dangerous animal must do so at his peril, and that if any damage resulted, then, apart from any question of negligence, he was liable for the damage. But that was subject to this, that the person who complained of damage must not have brought the injury on himself. Where the plaintiff did something which he had no business to do, — *e. g.* by meddling, as the plaintiff in this case had done, — then the defendant was not liable. That was common law, and it was also common sense. In Filburn *v.* The People's Palace (Limited), Lord Esher expressly dealt with this point. He there said: "It cannot possibly be said that an elephant comes within the class of animals known to be harmless by nature, or within that shown by experience to be harmless in this country, and consequently it falls within the class of animals that a man keeps at his peril, and which he must prevent from doing injury under any circumstances, unless the person to whom the injury is done brings it on himself." The action, therefore, could not be maintained on the common law liability. The plaintiff then set up a claim for negligence, viz., that the door was not kept locked, and that there was no keeper at hand. The evidence showed that the door had been shut, but had got opened. If the plaintiff had been kicked while walking along the stable, an action might have lain, but the plaintiff went into the stall and meddled with the animal. Even if the fact of the door being open was an invitation to go into the stable, it was not an invitation to stroke the animals. In his opinion there was no evidence to go to the jury, and judgment must be entered for the defendant.

LORD JUSTICE COLLINS said the plaintiff's case was put on the footing of these zebras being wild animals. The duty of a person who owned a wild animal, as laid down in May *v.* Burdett, was to keep it secure at his peril. The evidence in this case all went to show that these animals were kept secure within the meaning of that case. In his opinion there was no evidence of any invitation to go and tamper with the animals.

LORD JUSTICE ROMER concurred.[1]

[1] Kelley *v.* Killourey, 81 Conn. 320; Keightlinger *v.* Egan, 65 Ill. 235; Feldman *v.* Sellig, 110 Ill. App. 130; Donahue *v.* Scott Transfer Co., 141 Ill. App. 174; Bush *v.* Wathen, 104 Ky. 548; Quimby *v.* Woodbury, 63 N. H. 370; Badali *v.* Smith, (Tex. Civ. App.) 37 S. W. 642 *Accord.*

"There are expressions in some of the cases indicating that the liability of the owner is not affected by the negligence of the person injured. . . . If a person with full knowledge of the evil propensities of an animal wantonly excites him or voluntarily and unnecessarily puts himself in the way of such an animal, he would be adjudged to have brought the injury upon himself, and ought not to be entitled to recover. In such a case it cannot be said, in a legal sense, that the keeping of the animal, which is the *gravamen* of the offence, produced the injury. . . . But as the owner is held to a rigorous rule of liability on account of the danger to human life and limb, by harboring and keeping such animals, it follows that he ought not to be relieved from it by slight negligence or want of ordinary care [on the part of the plaintiff]. . . . As negligence, in the ordinary sense, is not the ground of liability, so contributory negligence, in its ordinary meaning, is not a defence. These terms are not used in a strictly legal sense in this class of actions, but for convenience . . . I think . . . that the rule of liability before indicated is a reasonable one, and that the owner cannot be relieved from it by any act of the person injured, unless it be one from which it can be affirmed that he caused the injury himself, with a full knowledge of its probable consequences." CHURCH, C. J., in Muller *v.* McKesson, 73 N. Y. 195, 201, 202, 204.

So Woolf *v.* Chalker, 31 Conn. 121; Vredenberg *v.* Behan, 33 La. Ann. 627; Fake *v.* Addicks, 45 Minn. 37; Malloy *v.* Starin, 113 App. Div. 852.

Negligence of the person injured, see Graham *v.* Walsh, 14 Ga. App. 287; Buckley *v.* Gee, 55 Ill. App. 388; Milne *v.* Walker, 59 Ia. 186; Carpenter *v.* Latta, 29 Kan. 591; Tolin *v.* Terrell, 133 Ky. 210; Garland *v.* Hewes, 101 Me. 549; Twigg *v.* Ryland, 62 Md. 380; Spellman *v.* Dyer, 186 Mass. 176; Ryan *v.* Marren, 216 Mass. 556; Warrick *v.* Farley, 95 Neb. 565; Earhart *v.* Youngblood, 27 Pa. St. 331.

MASON *v.* KEELING

IN THE KING'S BENCH, MICHAELMAS TERM, 1699.

Reported in 12 *Modern Reports*, 332.

ACTION on the case, in which the plaintiff declared that on the twentieth of June, in the eleventh of the king, the defendant *quendam canem molossum valde ferocem* did keep, and let him go loose unmuzzled *per publica compita*, so that *pro defectu curæ* of the defendant the plaintiff was bit and worried by the said dog, as he was peaceably going about his business in such a street. There was another count, in which it was laid that the defendant knew the dog *ad mordend. assuet.* To the first count there was a demurrer, and to the second not guilty.[1]

GOULD, J. No doubt but in the case of sheep there ought to be a *sciens*, because that is an accidental quality, and not in the nature of a dog. And as to property of a dog, the Books distinguish; for a man has a property in a dog that is a mastiff or spaniel, for the one is for the guard of his house, the other for his pleasure; but this here is a mongrel, and laid to be *valde ferocem*, and that must be an innate fierceness, and not accidental; and if a dog be *assuet.* to bite cows, and the master know it, that will not be sufficient knowledge to make him liable for his biting sheep. Besides, this case is distinguishable in respect of the place, for the law takes notice of highway, and is a security for passengers; and it would be dangerous to keep such dogs near the highway, where all sorts of people pass at all hours; and to maintain this issue, they must give a natural fierceness in evidence.

HOLT, C. J. If it had been said that the defendant knew the dog to be *ferox*, I should think it enough. The difference is between things in which the party has a valuable property, for he shall answer for all damages done by them; but of things in which he has no valuable property, if they are such as are naturally mischievous in their kind, he shall answer for hurt done by them without any notice; but if they are of a tame nature, there must be notice of the ill quality; and the law takes notice that a dog is not of a fierce nature, but rather the contrary; and the presumption is against the plaintiff; for can it be imagined a man would keep a fierce dog in his family wittingly? If any beast in which I have a valuable property do damage in another's soil, in treading his grass, trespass will lie for it; but if my dog go into another man's soil, no action will lie. See the case of Millan *v.* Hawtree, 1 Jones, 131, Poph. 161, Latch, 13, 119, that *scienter* is the *gist* of the action; and so is 1 Cro., where it was doubted whether the *scienter* should go to the keeping or quality; nor does it appear here but it was an accidental fierceness, or suppose it were an innate one to this dog particularly; and it had been given to the owner but an hour

[1] Arguments omitted. Compare report of same case in 1 Ld. Raym. 606.

before, shall he take notice of all the qualities of his dog at his peril, or shall he have his action against the giver for bestowing him a naughty dog? In case a dog bites pigs, which almost all dogs will do, a *scienter* is necessary. 1 Cro. 255. And I do not doubt but if it be generally laid that a dog was used to bite *animalia*, and the defendant knew of it, it will be enough to charge him for biting of sheep, &c.; and by *animalia* shall not be intended frogs or mice, but such in which the plaintiff has property.

And judgment was given for the defendant by HOLT, Chief-Justice, and TURTON, Justice; GOULD, J., *mutante opinionem suam.*[1]

DE GRAY *v.* MURRAY

SUPREME COURT, NEW JERSEY, JUNE 8, 1903.

Reported in 69 *New Jersey Law Reports*, 458.

GUMMERE, C. J. This was an action to recover for injuries resulting to the plaintiff in error (the plaintiff below) from the bite of a dog, owned by the defendant in error, which attacked her while she was walking on the public street. At the close of the testimony the trial judge directed a verdict for the defendant, and the plaintiff seeks to review the judgment entered upon that verdict.

It is the settled law that the owner of a dog will not be held responsible for injuries resulting to another person from its bite unless it be shown that the dog had previously bitten some one else, or was vicious, to the knowledge of the owner. Smith *v.* Donohue, 20 Vroom, 548, and cases cited.

[After discussing the evidence, and holding that there was an utter failure to prove *scienter*.]

[1] *Sed quaere:* for in s. c. 1 Ld. Ray. 608, it is said that the case was adjourned, and that afterwards the parties agreed, and therefore no judgment was given. — Reporter's Note.

As to the requirement of *scienter* in case of injury by domestic animals, Shaw *v.* Craft, 37 Fed. 317; Kitchens *v.* Elliott, 114 Ala. 290; Finney *v.* Curtis, 78 Cal. 498; Warner *v.* Chamberlain, 7 Houst. 18; Reed *v.* Southern Express Co., 95 Ga. 108; Domm *v.* Hollenbeck, 259 Ill. 382; Indianapolis Abattoir Co. *v.* Bailey, 54 Ind. App. 370; Trumble *v.* Happy, 114 Ia. 624; Ballou *v.* Humphrey, 8 Kan. 219; Murray *v.* Young, 12 Bush. 337; Goode *v.* Martin, 57 Md. 606; Dix *v.* Somerset Coal Co., 217 Mass. 146; Durrell *v.* Johnson, 31 Neb. 796; Smith *v.* Donohue, 49 N. J. Law, 548; Vrooman *v.* Lawyer, 13 Johns. 339; Dufer *v.* Cully, 3 Or. 377; Robinson *v.* Marino, 3 Wash. 434; Johnston *v.* Mack Mfg. Co., 65 W. Va. 544; Kertschacke *v.* Ludwig, 28 Wis. 430 *Accord.*

Liability for injury to trespassers in case of scienter: Woolf *v.* Chalker, 31 Conn. 121; Conway *v.* Grant, 88 Ga. 40; Engebretson *v.* Bremer, 128 Minn. 232; Loomis *v.* Terry, 17 Wend. 496; Pierret *v.* Moller, 3 E. D. Smith, 574; Sherfey *v.* Bartley, 4 Sneed, 58.

Liability where dog runs at large unmuzzled in violation of ordinance: Buchanan *v.* Stout, 139 App. Div. 204.

Where vicious dog kills trespassing dog: Wiley *v.* Slater, 22 Barb. 506.

What constitutes knowledge, see: Shaw *v.* Craft, 37 Fed. 317; Barclay *v.* Hartman, 2 Marv. 351; Keightlinger *v.* Egan, 65 Ill. 235; Domm *v.* Hollenbeck, 259

But even if the evidence submitted would support the conclusion that the dog had a propensity to bite, and that what the defendant heard about its attack on the boy charged him with knowledge of that propensity, the direction of a verdict in his favor was not erroneous. In England, and in some of our sister states, it is held that the owner of an animal which has a propensity to attack and bite mankind, who keeps it with the knowledge that it has such a propensity, does so at his peril, and that his liability for injuries inflicted by it is absolute. A leading case is that of May *v.* Burdett, 9 Q. B. (N. S.) 112, in which it is stated that " the conclusion to be drawn from all the authorities appears to be this: that a person keeping a mischievous animal, with knowledge of its propensity, is bound to keep it secure at his peril, and that if it does mischief, negligence is presumed without express averment. The negligence is in keeping such an animal after notice." Subsequently, the Court of Exchequer Chamber, adopting as accurate the principle underlying the decision of May *v.* Burdett, and referring to the opinion in that case, among others, as an authority for its conclusion, declared, in the case of Fletcher *v.* Rylands, L. R. 1 Exch. 265, that " one who, for his own purposes, brings upon his land, and keeps there, anything likely to do mischief if it escapes, is *prima facie* answerable for all the damage which is the natural consequence of its escape." The application of this principle led the court to fix liability upon the owner of land, who had stored water in a reservoir built thereon, for injury done to adjoining property by water escaping from the reservoir, notwithstanding that such escape was not due to any negligence on the part of the owner. Ten years after the decision of Fletcher *v.* Rylands, the rule laid down in that case was applied in this state, at circuit, in the case of Marshall *v.* Welwood, 9 Vroom, 339, and the owner of a steam boiler, which blew up and wrecked adjacent property, was held liable for the damage done, notwithstanding the fact that the bursting of the boiler was not due to any negligence on his part. The case was subsequently reviewed here, on rule to show cause, and this court, in a masterly opinion by the late Chief Justice Beasley, expressly disapproved of the doctrine laid down in Fletcher *v.* Rylands (which, as I have already stated, is rested,

Ill. 382; Kolb *v.* Klages, 27 Ill. App. 531; Cameron *v.* Bryan, 89 Ia. 214; Holt *v.* Myers, 47 Ind. App. 118; Murray *v.* Young, 12 Bush, 337; Twigg *v.* Ryland, 62 Md. 380; Knowles *v.* Mulder, 74 Mich. 202; Slater *v.* Sorge, 166 Mich. 173; Rowe *v.* Ehrmanntraut, 92 Minn. 17; Reynolds *v.* Hussey, 64 N. H. 64; Emmons *v.* Stevane, 73 N. J. Law, 349, 77 N. J. Law, 570; Rider *v.* White, 65 N. Y. 54; Brice *v.* Bauer, 108 N. Y. 428; Martin *v.* Borden, 123 App. Div. 66; McGarry *v.* New York R. Co., 60 N. Y. Sup. Ct. 367; Hayes *v.* Smith, 62 Ohio St. 161; Holden *v.* Shattuck, 34 Vt. 336.

Knowledge of single vicious act: Eastman *v.* Scott, 182 Mass. 192; Kittredge *v.* Elliott, 16 N. H. 77; Keenan *v.* Gutta Percha Mfg. Co., 46 Hun, 544; Cockerham *v.* Nixon, 11 Ired. 269. Compare: Linck *v.* Scheffel, 32 Ill. App. 17; Cooper *v.* Cashman, 190 Mass. 75; Buckley *v.* Leonard, 4 Denio, 500.

Statutes making owners or keepers of dogs liable irrespective of *scienter* or of negligence in keeping are not uncommon, but vary greatly in detail.

among other decisions, on May *v.* Burdett), and declared that no man is, in law, an insurer that the acts which he does, such acts being lawful and done with care, shall not injuriously affect others; and that an injury which results from a lawful act, done in a lawful manner, and without negligence on the part of the person doing the act, will not support an action. Applying that principle to the case in hand, this court then held that the owner of a steam boiler, which he has in use on his own property, is not responsible, in the absence of negligence, for the damages done by its bursting. The principle laid down in Marshall *v.* Welwood was reiterated by this court in the case of Hill *v.* Ulshowski, 32 Id. 375.

The right of a man to keep a vicious dog for the protection of his home and property is conceded in the case of Roehers *v.* Remhoff, 26 Vroom, 475. He is, of course, bound to exercise a degree of care, commensurate with the danger to others which will follow the dog's escape from his control, to so secure it that it will not injure any one who does not unlawfully provoke or intermeddle with it. Worthen *v.* Love, 60 Vt. 285. But if the owner does use such care, and the dog nevertheless escapes and inflicts injury, he is not liable.

In the case now under consideration the undisputed evidence makes it clear that the defendant fully discharged the duty of using due care to prevent the escape of his dog from his premises, and that the plaintiff's injury was not due to any neglect in that regard upon his part. She was bitten in the early morning, between half-past six and seven o'clock. On the preceding evening the defendant shut the dog in his carpenter shop (which adjoined his dwelling) and locked him in. During the night the dog gnawed away the woodwork from around the lock of the door to such an extent that the lock became detached, thus permitting the door to open and the dog to escape. That a reasonably prudent man would not have anticipated any such occurrence must be admitted.

The judgment under review should be affirmed.[1]

[1] Worthen *v.* Love, 60 Vt. 285 *Accord.* Baker *v.* Snell, [1908] 2 K. B. 352, 825; Laverone *v.* Mangianti, 41 Cal. 138; Muller *v.* McKesson, 73 N. Y. 195; Dockerty *v.* Hudson, 125 Ind. 102 *Contra.*

Compare: The Lord Derby, 17 Fed. 265; Melsheimer *v.* Sullivan, 1 Col. App. 22; Woodbridge *v.* Marks, 17 App. Div. 139; Lloyd *v.* Bowen, 170 N. C. 216; Hayes *v.* Smith, 62 Ohio St. 161; Fallon *v.* O'Brien, 12 R. I. 518.

See also Vredenberg *v.* Behan, 33 La. Ann. 627 (bear teased by third person broke loose and injured plaintiff); Kinmouth *v.* McDougall, 19 N. Y. Supp. 771 (ram teased by children injured plaintiff).

See Bevan, The Responsibility at Common Law for the Keeping of Animals, 22 Harvard Law Rev. 465.

CROWLEY *v.* GROONELL

SUPREME COURT, VERMONT, FEBRUARY 9, 1901.

Reported in 73 *Vermont Reports,* 45.

CASE for an injury to the plaintiff by the defendant's dog. Plea, the general issue. Trial by jury, Rutland County, March Term, 1900, Rowell, J., presiding. Verdict and judgment for the plaintiff. The defendant excepted.

It appeared that the plaintiff, an old man, was a neighbor of the defendant and went one morning to the defendant's barn, where the latter was, to buy some potatoes of him; that when the plaintiff got near the barn, the defendant's dog, which was large, and was lying near the barn door, assaulted the plaintiff by jumping up and putting his feet upon him and throwing him down, breaking his hip. The testimony was conflicting as to whether this assault was vicious or playful and as to the propensities of the dog known to the plaintiff.

WATSON, J. The only exception upon which the defendant relies is the one to that part of the charge where the court said that a cross and savage disposition on the part of the dog was not necessary in order to impose liability; that a mischievous propensity to commit the kind of assault complained of was enough if the plaintiff's case was otherwise made out; and that in respect to imposing liability, it made no difference whether such assault proceeded from good nature or ill nature, from ugliness or playfulness.

The defendant contends that the duty of restraint attaches only when the owner or keeper has reason to apprehend that the dog may do damage by reason of its viciousness or ferocity, and that the acts of the dog, proceeding from good nature or playfulness, cannot render the defendant liable. If a man have a beast that is *ferae naturae* as a lion, a bear, a wolf, if he get loose and do harm to any person, the owner is liable to an action for damages, though he have no particular notice that he had done any such thing before. The same principle applies to damages done by domestic animals, except that as to them, the owner must have seen or heard enough to convince a man of ordinary prudence of the animal's inclination to commit the class of injuries complained of. With notice to the owner of such propensity in the animal, he is liable for whatever damages may be suffered by person or property therefrom. It makes no difference whether the animal was of cross and savage disposition and committed the injury by reason of its viciousness and ferocity, or whether such injury resulted from good nature and playfulness — the intent of the animal is not material. The owner or keeper having knowledge of its disposition to commit such injuries must restrain it at his peril, and it is no answer to say that the animal was not cross or savage and was in good nature and playfulness.

. . . .

In State v. McDermott, 6 Atl. Rep. 653 [49 N. J. Law, 163], at the close of the plaintiff's evidence, the defendant moved for a nonsuit on the ground that it did not appear that the dog had bitten McDermott maliciously, and also on the ground that there was no evidence that the dog had bitten other persons except in play, or that the defendant had knowledge of the propensity of the dog to bite. The motion was overruled. It was contended that although several persons had been bitten by the dog, of which the defendant had notice, yet it appeared that in every instance the biting occurred while the dog was in a playful mood; that damages could not be recovered where it was shown that the dog had a propensity to bite only in play; and that to justify a recovery, it must appear that the dog was in the habit of biting mankind while in an angry mood, actuated by a ferocious spirit. It was held that this was not the law, — that an action could be maintained against the owner by a party injured upon evidence that a dog, with the knowledge of the owner, had a mischievous propensity to bite mankind, whether in anger or not; for in either case, the person bitten would suffer injury, and that mischievous propensity, within the meaning of the law, was a propensity from which injury is the natural result.

. . . .

There was no error in the charge, and judgment is affirmed.[1]

Erle, C. J., in COX v. BURBIDGE

(1863) 13 *Common Bench, New Series*, 435–437.

I am of opinion that this rule must be made absolute, on the ground that there was a total absence of evidence to support the cause of action alleged. The facts I take to be these: The plaintiff, a child of tender age, was lawfully upon the highway, and a horse, the property of the defendant, was straying on the highway. As between the owner of the horse and the owner of the soil of the highway or of the herbage growing thereon, we may assume that the horse was trespassing; and, if the horse had done any damage to the soil, the owner of the soil might have had a right of action against his owner. So, it may be assumed, that if the place in question were a public highway, the owner of the horse might have been liable to be proceeded against under the Highway Act. But, in considering the claim of the plaintiff against the defendant for the injury sustained from the kick, the question whether the horse was a trespasser as against the owner of the soil, or whether his owner was amenable under the Highway Act, has nothing to do with the case of the plaintiff. I am also of opinion that so much of the argument which has been addressed to us

[1] Compare Merritt v. Matchett, 135 Mo. App. 176.

on the part of the plaintiff as assumes the action to be founded upon the negligence of the owner of the horse in allowing it to be upon the road unattended, is not tenable. To entitle the plaintiff to maintain the action, it is necessary to show a breach of some legal duty due from the defendant to the plaintiff; and it is enough to say that there is no evidence to support the affirmative of the issue that there was negligence on the part of the defendant for which an action would lie by the plaintiff. The simple fact found is, that the horse was on the highway. He may have been there without any negligence of the owner: he might have been put there by a stranger, or might have escaped from some enclosed place without the owner's knowledge. To entitle the plaintiff to recover, there must be some affirmative proof of negligence in the defendant in respect of a duty owing to the plaintiff. But, even if there was any negligence on the part of the owner of the horse, I do not see how that is at all connected with the damage of which the plaintiff complains. It appears that the horse was on the highway, and that, without anything to account for it, he struck out and injured the plaintiff. I take the well-known distinction to apply here, that the owner of an animal is answerable for any damage done by it, provided it be of such a nature as is likely to arise from such an animal, and the owner knows it. Thus, in the case of a dog, if he bites a man or worries sheep, and his owner knows that he is accustomed to bite men or to worry sheep, the owner is responsible; but the party injured has no remedy unless the *scienter* can be proved. This is very familiar doctrine; and it seems to me that there is much stronger reason for applying that rule in respect of the damage done here. The owner of a horse must be taken to know that the animal will stray if not properly secured, and may find its way into his neighbor's corn or pasture. For a trespass of that kind, the owner is of course responsible. But if the horse does something which is quite contrary to his ordinary nature, — something which his owner has no reason to expect he will do, he has the same sort of protection that the owner of a dog has; and everybody knows that it is not at all the ordinary habit of a horse to kick a child on a highway. I think the ground upon which the plaintiff's counsel rests his case fails. It reduces itself to the question whether the owner of a horse is liable for a sudden act of a fierce and violent nature which is altogether contrary to the usual habits of the horse, without more.[1]

[1] Hadwell *v.* Righton, [1907] 2 K. B. 345; Higgins *v.* Searle, 25 Times L. R. 301; Klenberg *v.* Russell, 125 Ind. 531; Dix *v.* Somerset Coal Co., 217 Mass. 146; Shipley *v.* Colclough, 81 Mich. 624; Smith *v.* Donahue, 49 N. J. Law, 548; Meegan *v.* McKay, 1 Okl. 59 *Accord.* But see Barnes *v.* Chapin, 4 All. 444.

DICKSON v. McCOY

COURT OF APPEALS, NEW YORK, JUNE TERM, 1868.

Reported in 39 *New York Reports*, 400.

THIS was an action for injury to the plaintiff by the horse of the defendant. The plaintiff, a child of ten years, was passing the stable of the defendant, upon the sidewalk of a populous street in the city of Troy, when the defendant's horse came out of the stable, going loose and unattended, and, in passing, kicked the plaintiff in the face. The complaint alleged that the horse was "of a malicious and mischievous disposition, and accustomed to attack and injure mankind;" also, that the defendant "wrongfully and negligently suffered the said horse to go at large in and upon the public streets," etc. The proof as to the disposition of the horse was only to the effect that he was young and playful, and, when loose in the street, was accustomed to run and kick in the air, but had never been seen to kick at any person. The defendant moved for a nonsuit, on the ground that there was no proof that the horse was vicious, which was refused. The defendant also requested the court to charge that there was no proof that the horse was possessed of any vicious propensity, or mischievous habit, which required the defendant to exercise special care over him; which the court declined to charge. The court did charge, that "it was for the jury to find, under the evidence, whether the defendant was or was not guilty of negligence in permitting the animal, which did the injury complained of, to run at large, as detailed by the witnesses on the part of the plaintiff," etc.

The jury found a verdict for the plaintiff for $500, which was affirmed, on appeal, at the General Term, and the defendant appeals to this court.

DWIGHT, J. I agree with the counsel for the defendant that there is no proof in the case to sustain the allegation in the complaint, that this horse was vicious and accustomed to attack and injure mankind. The fact that a horse is young and playful, that he kicks in the air, and runs and gambols when loose in the street, is no proof of a malicious or vicious disposition. But I regard the allegation as unnecessary, and the absence of proof on the point as not affecting the right to recover. The finding of the jury, under the charge of the court, was clearly to the effect that the defendant was guilty of negligence in suffering his horse to go at large upon the sidewalk, as shown in the case. And there was a sufficient allegation to that effect in the complaint. It is not necessary that a horse should be vicious to make the owner responsible for injury done by him through the owner's negligence. The vice of the animal is an essential fact only when, but for it, the conduct of the owner would be free from fault. If the most gentle horse be driven so negligently as to do injury to persons or property, the owner or driver will be responsible. Certainly, not less so if the horse be negligently turned loose in the street without restraint or control. The motion for a nonsuit was properly denied. The only question in the case was that propounded by the court to the jury, "was the defendant guilty of negligence in permitting the horse to go at large in the street?" The court, I think, might very properly have charged as requested by the defendant, that there was no proof to justify the jury in finding that the horse was possessed of any vicious propensity or mischievous habit. And, yet, it is, in one sense, a mischievous habit for a horse to run and play in the public streets. Though it is no proof of a mischievous disposition, it is liable to produce mischievous results. There was, therefore, no error in the refusal to charge as requested. The instructions of the court to the jury were correct, and the verdict is conclusive upon all the questions in the case. *The judgment must be affirmed.*

[The opinion of GROVER, J., is omitted.] [1]

DECKER v. GAMMON

SUPREME JUDICIAL COURT, MAINE, 1857.

Reported in 44 *Maine Reports*, 322.

THIS is an action on the case [2] to recover the value of a horse alleged to have been injured by the defendant's horse, and comes forward on exceptions to the rulings of Goodenow, J.

The plaintiff introduced evidence tending to prove that at night, on the 13th of September, 1855, he put his horse into his field well and uninjured. The next morning, September 14, his horse and the defendant's were together in his, the plaintiff's close, the defendant's horse, having, during the night, escaped from the defendant's enclosure, or from the highway, into the close of the plaintiff, and that the plaintiff's horse was severely injured by the defendant's horse, by

[1] Jewett v. Gage, 55 Me. 538 (hog) *Accord.*

Compare COULTER, J., in Goodman v. Gay, 15 Pa. St. 188, 193, 194; Corcoran v. Kelly, 61 Misc. 323.

A fortiori if one turns loose a vicious animal: McGuire v. Ringrose, 41 La. Ann. 1029.

Injuries by animals running at large contrary to statute, see: Williams v. Brennan, 213 Mass. 28; Low v. Barnes, 30 Okl. 15; Palmer v. Saccocia, 33 R. I. 476.

[2] In the argument for defendant the declaration is set out as follows: —

"In a plea of the case for that the said plaintiff, on the 14th day of September, 1855, was possessed of a valuable horse, of the value of $125.00, which was peaceably and of right depasturing in his own close, and the defendant was possessed of another horse, vicious and unruly, which was running at large where of right it ought not to be, and being so unlawfully at large, broke into the plaintiff's close, at the time aforesaid, and viciously and wantonly kicked, reared upon, and injured the plaintiff's horse, so that his death was caused thereby, which vicious habits and propensities were well known to the defendant at the time aforesaid. To the damage, &c."

kicking, biting, or striking with his fore feet, or in some other way, so that he died in a few days after.

The defendant requested the presiding judge to instruct the jury that to entitle the plaintiff to recover against the defendant he must prove, in addition to other necessary facts, that the defendant's horse was vicious, and that the defendant had knowledge of such viciousness prior to the time of the alleged injury.

The presiding judge declined giving these instructions, and directed the jury that if they should find that the defendant owned the horse alleged to have done the injury to the plaintiff's horse, and if, at the time of the injury, he had escaped into the plaintiff's close, and was wrongfully there, and while there occasioned the injury, and that the horse died in consequence, that the plaintiff would be entitled to recover the value of the horse so injured. That it was not necessary for the plaintiff to prove that the horse was vicious, or accustomed to acts of violence towards other animals or horses, or that the owner had notice of such viciousness or habits.

The jury returned a verdict for the plaintiff.[1]

DAVIS, J. There are three classes of cases in which the owners of animals are liable for injuries done by them to the persons or the property of others. And in suits of such injuries the allegations and proofs must be varied in each case, as the facts bring it within one or another of these classes.

1. The owner of wild beasts, or beasts that are in their nature vicious, is, under all circumstances, liable for injuries done by them. It is not necessary, in actions for injuries by such beasts, to allege or prove that the owner knew them to be mischievous, for he is conclusively presumed to have such knowledge; or that he was guilty of negligence in permitting them to be at large, for he is bound to keep them in at his peril.

"Though the owner have no particular notice that he did any such thing before, yet if he be a beast that is *ferae naturae* if he get loose and do harm to any person, the owner is liable to an action for the damage." 1 Hale, P. C. 430.

"If they are such as are naturally mischievous in their kind, in which the owner has no valuable property, he shall answer for hurt done by them, without any notice; but if they are of a tame nature, there must be notice of the ill quality." Holt, C. J. Mason *v.* Keeling, 12 Mod. R. 332.

"The owner of beasts that are *ferae naturae* must always keep them up, at his peril; and an action lies without notice of the quality of the beasts." Rex *v.* Huggins, 2 Lord Raym. 1583.

2. If domestic animals, such as oxen and horses, injure any one, in person or property, if they are rightfully in the place where they do the mischief, the owner of such animals is not liable for such injury

[1] The arguments are omitted.

unless he knew that they were accustomed to do mischief. And in suits for such injuries, such knowledge must be alleged, and proved. For unless the owner knew that the beast was vicious he is not liable. If the owner had such knowledge he is liable.

" The gist of the action is the keeping of the animal after knowledge of its vicious propensities." May *v.* Burdett, 58 Eng. C. L. 101.

" If the owner have knowledge of the quality of his beast, and it doth anybody hurt, he is chargeable in an action for it." 1 Hale P. C. 430.

" An action lies not unless the owner knows of this quality." Buxendin *v.* Sharp, 2 Salk. 662.

" If the owner puts a horse or an ox to grass in his field, and the horse or ox breaks the hedge and runs into the highway, and gores or kicks some passenger, an action will not lie against the owner unless he had notice that they had done such a thing before." Mason *v.* Keeling, 12 Modern R. 332.

" If damage be done by any domestic animal, kept for use or convenience, the owner is not liable to an action on the ground of negligence, without proof that he knew that the animal was accustomed to do mischief." Vrooman *v.* Sawyer, 13 Johns. R. 339.

3. The owner of domestic animals, if they are wrongfully in the place where they do any mischief, is liable for it, though he had no notice that they had been accustomed to do so before. In cases of this kind the ground of the action is that the animals were wrongfully in the place where the injury was done. And it is not necessary to allege or prove any knowledge on the part of the owner that they had previously been vicious.

" If a bull break into an enclosure of a neighbor, and there gore a horse so that he die, his owner is liable in an action of trespass *quare clausum fregit*, in which the value of the horse would be the just measure of damages." Dolph *v.* Ferris, 7 Watts & Serg. R. 367.

" If the owner of a horse suffers it to go at large in the streets of a populous city he is answerable in an action on the case for a personal injury done by it to an individual without proof that he knew that the horse was vicious. The owner had no right to turn the horse loose in the streets." Goodman *v.* Gay, 3 Harris R. 188. In this case the writ contained the allegation of knowledge on the part of the defendant; but the court held that it was not material and need not be proved.

The case before us is clearly within this class of cases last described. It is alleged in the writ that " the plaintiff had a valuable horse which was peaceably and of right depasturing in his own close, and the defendant was possessed of another horse, vicious and unruly, which was running at large where of right he ought not to be; and being so unlawfully at large, broke into the plaintiff's close, and injured the plaintiff's horse, &c." It is also alleged that " the vicious habits of the horse were well known to the defendant;" but this allegation was not necessary, and may well be treated as surplusage. If the defendant had had a right to turn his horse upon the plaintiff's close it would have been otherwise. But if the horse was wrongfully there the defendant was liable for any injury done by him, though he had no knowledge that the horse was vicious. The gravamen of the charge was that the horse was wrongfully upon the plaintiff's close; and this was what was put in issue by the plea of not guilty.

Nor are these principles in conflict with the decision in the case of Van Leuven *v.* Lyke, 1 Comstock, 515. In that case the action was not sustained because the declaration was not for trespass *quare clausum* with the other injuries alleged by way of aggravation. But in that case there was no allegation that the animal was wrongfully upon the plaintiff's close; or that the injury was committed upon the plaintiff's close. 4 Denio R. 127. And in the Court of Appeals it was expressly held that "if the plaintiff had stated in his declaration that the swine broke and entered his close, and there committed the injury complained of, and sustained his declaration by evidence, he would been entitled to recover all the damages thus sustained." 1 Coms. 515, 518.

In the case before us, though the declaration is not technically for trespass *quare clausum*, it is distinctly alleged that the defendant's horse, "being so unlawfully at large, broke and entered the plaintiff's close, and injured the plaintiff's horse," which was there peaceably and of right depasturing. This was sufficient; and the instruction given to the jury, "that if the defendant's horse, at the time of the injury, had escaped into the close, and was wrongfully there, and while there occasioned the injury, then the plaintiff would be entitled to recover," was correct. And this being so, the instruction requested "that the plaintiff must prove, in addition to other necessary facts, that the defendant's horse was vicious, and that the defendant had knowledge of such viciousness prior to the time of the injury," was properly refused.

CUTTING, J., did not concur. *Exceptions overruled.*[1]

[1] Angus *v.* Radin, 2 South. (N. J.) 815 *Accord.* The same result has often been reached in an action of trespass *quare clausum* in which the injury by the trespassing animal is set up in aggravation. Lee *v.* Riley, 17 C. B. N. S. 722; Theyer *v.* Purnell, [1918] 2 K. B. 333; Van Leuven *v.* Lyke, 1 N. Y. 515; Dolph *v.* Ferris, 7 Watts & Sergt. 367; Chunot *v.* Larson, 43 Wis. 536.

But see McDonald *v.* Jodrey, 8 Pa. Co. Ct. R. 142 (cat went on plaintiff's premises and killed canary).

DOYLE *v.* VANCE

Supreme Court, Victoria, April 16, 1880.

Reported in 6 *Victorian Law Reports, Cases at Law,* 87.

Stawell, C. J.[1] A dog belonging to the defendant got on land belonging to the plaintiff, how, does not appear, and barked at a horse of the plaintiff which was then grazing quietly in an inclosed field; the horse ran away, tried to leap over the fence, fell and broke its neck. The plaint was in the ordinary form, alleging a *scienter* in the defendant. At the trial, an application was made to add a count for trespass by the dog on the plaintiff's land. The application was granted, and though the amendment was not formally written on the plaint, it may now be considered as having been made. A verdict was given for the plaintiff, with £10 damages.

The defendant has appealed, and the question we have to consider is whether, as a matter of law, he is liable for the trespass committed by his dog. It would have been competent for the judge at the trial to have found that the dog was on the land, by the leave and license of the plaintiff; all the circumstances point to the probability of that being the case. But he has found that the dog was there as a trespasser. There are a number of cases in which judges have expressed *obiter dicta,* as to the non-liability of an owner for injuries done by his dog, and curious and singular reasons — that a dog was the companion of man (and the like) — have been assigned for those *dicta;* reasons which courts have treated as entitled to high respect, and which have not been dissented from. There is, however, a comparatively recent case, Read *v.* Edwards, *supra,*[2] in which an action was brought against the owner of a dog for having chased and destroyed game, the declaration alleging *scienter* by the defendant. All the *dicta* of the learned judges to which I have referred were cited in the argument, were commented on and received attention. The case was decided on another point, but Mr. Justice Willes, who delivered the judgment of the Court, said: —

" The question was much argued whether the owner of the dog is answerable in trespass for every unauthorized entry of the animal into the land of another, as in the case of an ox, and reasons were offered, which we need not now estimate, for a distinction in this respect between oxen, and dogs or cats, on account, first, of the difficulty or impossibility of keeping the latter under restraint; secondly, the slightness of the damage which their wandering ordinarily causes; thirdly, the common usage of mankind to allow them a wider liberty; and lastly, their not being considered in law so absolutely the chattels of the owner as to be the subject of larceny. It is not, however, necessary in the principal case to answer that question."

[1] Statement and arguments omitted. [2] 17 C. B. N. S. 260.

The legitimate inference from these observations is that the question, whether the *dicta* I have referred to are law, has not yet been decided, and that the subject is open for consideration. There may be very cogent reasons, socially, for exempting the owner from liability. But there is no reason which a court of law can recognize. Serious injury might be inflicted by a dog revelling in a highly-cultivated *parterre*, and can it with propriety be said that the owner of the garden can obtain no compensation ? It has been decided that a dog can be distrained for *damage feasant:* Bunch *v.* Kennington, 1 Q. B. 679. There can be no question, if an ox were substituted for a dog, as having done the mischief complained of in the present case, the owner would be liable. Cox *v.* Burbidge, *supra,*[1] which was cited, does not apply. There, the defendant's horse, being on the highway, kicked the plaintiff, a child who was playing there. The defendant was held not guilty of actionable negligence; but that was on the ground that the horse had a right to be on the highway, as well as the child, and was therefore not a trespasser.

In Lee *v.* Riley, *supra,*[2] through defect of fences which it was the defendant's duty to repair, the defendant's mare strayed in the night time from his close into an adjoining field, and so into a field of the plaintiff's, in which was a horse. From some unexplained cause the animals quarrelled, and the result was that the plaintiff's horse received a kick from the defendant's mare, which broke its leg, and it was necessarily killed. It was held that the defendant was answerable for the mare's trespass, and the damage was not too remote. The decision was based on the fact that the defendant's mare trespassed on the plaintiff's land, and that it was the duty of the owner of an animal to keep it from trespassing. In Ellis *v.* The Loftus Iron Co., *supra,*[3] the defendant's horse having injured the plaintiff's mare by biting and kicking her through the fence separating the plaintiff's land from the defendants', it was held that there was a trespass by the act of the defendants' horse, for which the defendants were liable, apart from any question of negligence on their part.

The owner of an animal is therefore responsible for any damage fairly resulting from a trespass by that animal. The damage here has resulted from the trespass, and the verdict will therefore stand.

The argument based upon " The Dog Act 1864 " (No. 229), sec. 15, enacting that the owner of a dog shall be liable for injury done to sheep, without proof of *scienter*, should be noticed; it was urged that the necessity for passing such an enactment implied that there was previously no liability. But that argument goes too far. One part of the enactment is declaratory, and the other is new.

Barry, J. I am of the same opinion. It is remarkable that this question should not have been settled until now, and, apparently from a desire to avoid overruling old cases which had been decided on the

[1] 13 C. B. n. s. 430. [2] 18 C. B. n. s. 732. [3] L. R. 10 C. P. 10.

most subtle reasons, the judges have abstained from considering the question in a broad aspect. The old reports abound with expressions of peculiar regard for dogs and cats; and Lord Tenterden does not think it beneath his dignity to quote, in his book on shipping, "if mice eat the cargo, and thereby occasion no small injury to the merchant, the master must make good the loss, because he is guilty of a fault; yet if he had cats on board his ship, he shall be excused." One reason given for the exemption of liability, so far as the dog is concerned, is on account of his familiarity with man. But we cannot regard these every day questions in the same subtle way as they were regarded three hundred years ago. The doctrine of trespass is considered on much more reasonable grounds in these days. Where sheep, oxen, or horses, commit a trespass, it has always been held that the owner is liable; and that liability has been extended to poultry, and poultry are as much domesticated as a dog or a cat. In Brown *v.* Giles, 1 C. & P. 118, Mr. Justice Park is reported to have said that he was decidedly of opinion that a dog jumping into a field without the consent of its master, not only was not a trespass, but was no trespass at all on which an action could be maintained. But that remark was merely *obiter;* the case was decided for the plaintiff on another point. The learned judge has found that there was a trespass. The dog was left to roam at its discretion, uncontrolled by its master.

STEPHEN, J. I also concur. It seems to have been considered, in old times, that there was a marked distinction between trespass by a dog, and trespass by an ox. Now, as a general rule, no such distinction is made. I cannot see why there should be any. This case illustrates how far the law ought to be altered, so as to preserve its accordance with change of time and place. Of course, the Court cannot alter the clearly-expressed language of an act of Parliament, though the reason for it may have ceased. And so also as to actual decisions of the Courts. If there is reason to alter the law, the legislature must do it. But on this question, there have been no more than *obiter dicta* based upon reasons which have no longer any existence. At one time a dog could not be the subject of a theft. The Court is at liberty, within reasonable limits, to meet the changed circumstances of the present day. I can see no sound reason why there should be a difference between the case of trespass by a dog, and one by an ox.

Appeal dismissed.[1]

[1] McClain *v.* Lewiston Driving Ass'n, 17 Idaho, 63; Green *v.* Doyle, 21 Ill. App. 205; Chunot *v.* Larson, 43 Wis. 536 *Accord.*

Buck *v.* Moore, 35 Hun, 338 (defendant's trespassing dog killed plaintiff's dog); Van Etten *v.* Noyes, 128 App. Div. 406 *Contra.*

TROTH *v.* WILLS

SUPERIOR COURT, PENNSYLVANIA, JULY 29, 1898.

Reported in 8 *Pennsylvania Superior Court Reports,* 1.

TRESPASS for personal injuries. Before Brégy, J.

It appears from the evidence that the plaintiff, a lady about fifty-five years of age, was temporarily living with her son, in a small country place, and the cow of the defendant strayed into the garden belonging to the son. The plaintiff, seeing the cow in the garden, came out of her son's house and attempted to drive the cow out of the garden back into the pasture field, from where she entered into the garden. The plaintiff alleges that while so driving the cow out of the garden back into the field, the cow deliberately went towards the field, and that she followed closely behind the cow, when the cow suddenly turned her head and butted the plaintiff in the abdomen, and hence her injuries.[1]

Defendant requested (Request No. 5) a ruling, that, under all the evidence, the verdict should be for the defendant. The court declined so to rule. Verdict and judgment for plaintiff. Defendant appealed.

SMITH, J. It is not necessary, in disposing of this case, to determine the liability of the owner of a domestic animal for all its acts while trespassing upon another's land. In such cases, the primary trespass is the entry of the animal upon the land; the attendant damage for which the owner may be held liable is matter of aggravation. The minimum liability of the owner is for acts arising from the natural propensities of the species, and from special characteristics and acquired habits of the individual of which the owner has notice. When the primary trespass is the wilful act of the owner, he may be held to a larger measure of responsibility; thus if he take a dog into a field where he is himself a trespasser, and the dog there kills or injures sheep, this, though its first offence, may be laid as an aggravation of the trespass: Beckwith *v.* Shordike, Burr. 2092; Michael *v.* Alestree, 2 Lev. 172, cited in Dolph *v.* Ferris, 7 W. & S. 367. Beyond this, the authorities appear unsettled, and principle and analogy form the only guide. Doubtless there may be mischief so far independent of the primary trespass, and unrelated to the propensity or habit leading to this, that it cannot be deemed matter of aggravation. In my view, however, the mischievous act, when incident to the primary trespass, in any of its aspects, or so closely associated with it as to form a substantive part or an immediate result of it, is a legitimate matter of aggravation, for which the owner should be held liable. In such case, the propensity or habit leading to the primary trespass may be regarded as the proximate cause of the resulting injury. If, for

[1] Statement condensed. Arguments and portions of opinions omitted.

example, trespassing cattle, in order to reach the vegetation in a hot-bed, break its glass covering, the owner must be held liable for this injury, though cattle are not by nature prone to break glass. Such breaking is incident to the primary trespass, and grows out of the propensity leading to this. If an animal injure a person lawfully trying to prevent it from trespassing, the owner should be held liable, though the injury be one which the animal is not prone to commit. In such case the mischievous act is closely associated with the primary trespass, and in fact grows directly out of it. The same principle must govern if a person be injured in trying to prevent the continuance of a trespass, or of acts forming an aggravation of it.

. . . .

In this view of the principles which should govern the determination of this case, the injury to the plaintiff must be deemed an aggravation of the trespass committed by the animal in entering the garden. This injury, indeed, is not such as a cow is ordinarily prone to commit; and there is no evidence that the defendant's cow had contracted the habit of making such assaults. But the act of the animal was one to which a creature of that kind is naturally disposed on being disturbed while feeding; and it was so directly associated with the primary trespass that, unless the plaintiff's right to prevent a continuance of this be denied, there can be no ground for questioning the liability of the owner. This right cannot be controverted, for under the circumstances the act of the plaintiff is to be regarded as that of the tenant of the premises. The act of the animal by which the plaintiff was injured, so far from being independent of the primary trespass, or unrelated to it, grew directly out of the propensity in which this originated, coupled with the plaintiff's attempt to prevent its continuance. The defendant's fifth point was therefore properly refused. The case was submitted to the jury with suitable instructions, and their finding on the questions involved was concurred in by the trial court. *The judgment is affirmed.*

WICKHAM, J. (dissenting.) . . . We are called on to determine whether the rule, so far as our authority goes, shall be established in Pennsylvania, that the owner of a useful, gentle, and domestic animal, belonging to a class recognized from the earliest times as harmless to man, watched, driven to and from the pasture fields, fed and milked by women and children the world over, shall be responsible for the conduct of the animal, foreign to its well-known nature and habits, if it happen that through any negligence of such owner, or his servant, it is permitted to trespass on the land of another, and there injures a third party.

The authorities on this subject are numerous and impossible to reconcile. Some of them rest on statutes or ordinances, not always adverted to in the text-books or digests, in which they are hastily cited. Others are based on the theory, that the right to recover exists because of the trespass to realty, and that any unusual and not to be expected injury caused by the animal to the person of the owner of the land, or his other property, must be alleged and proved by way of aggravation of damages. Another class of cases holds that all injuries committed by an animal, in a place where it has no right to be, must be compensated for by the owner. It is on the latter theory of the law that the plaintiff must recover, if she can sustain her action, as we do not deem it worth while to notice the few erratic and sporadic cases, seemingly decided on no discoverable reason, except an assumed natural equity, that any one injured by anything, animate or inanimate, belonging to another, should be compensated by the owner.

As has already been observed, the plaintiff was not the owner of the land trespassed upon, and it may be remarked that she is aided by no statute.

. . . .

It is argued that the appellant's cow was vicious. There is no evidence even suggesting such a tendency, and the learned trial judge so instructed the jury. Conceding that the animal was breachy, as alleged by the plaintiff, this indicated no ferocity or proneness to attack people. Any one, acquainted with the nature and habits of horses and cows, knows that usually the most intelligent and gentle animals of these species are the most cunning and successful in finding their way into forbidden inclosures and the readiest to run away when discovered. As was said in Keshan *v.* Gates, 2 Thomp. & C. (N. Y. Sup. Ct.) 288: "The vicious habits or propensities which the owner of an animal must, when known to him, guard against, are such as are directly dangerous, such as kicking and biting in horses, and hooking in horned animals, and biting in dogs. These habits or propensities may be indulged in at any moment and are inevitably dangerous."

The adoption of the rule, sanctioned by the decisions of many respectable tribunals in other states, that the owner of every trespassing domestic animal is liable merely because it is a trespasser for all injuries it may commit, however contrary to its usual nature and disposition, and regardless of his knowledge of its special viciousness, might often lead to strange and unthought-of consequences. For instance, suppose that a pet lamb, always regarded as a harmless playmate of children, is permitted to wander from its owner's premises into those of a neighbor (this as well as the next illustration is not a supposititious case), and there, in play or anger, butts a child from a high veranda, or a trespassing hatching hen, discovered on its nest by the little son of the owner of the premises, pecks out the eye of the boy as he is lawfully trying to drive it away, the unfortunate owner would be liable in each instance for all the resulting damages. In vain would he urge that the animal causing the injury belonged to a class ordinarily docile in its nature and harmless to man; that he had no reason to anticipate that it would do such unusual mischief; and that he was only responsible for the things hens, lambs, and milch cows usually do and may be expected to do when trespassing, that is, for the natural and probable consequences of their trespasses. The answer, under the rule we are considering, would be: "You were guilty of negligence in permitting your animal to trespass, and therefore you are liable for all its freaks, for the consequences of the wrong, near and remote, probable and improbable, for the things you had reason to anticipate, and those which no one would be likely to think could happen, save as a remote possibility." The results which might follow the application of such a rule demand its rejection, where it has not already been fully adopted.

The only negligence of the defendant revealed by the evidence was his failure to keep his cow out of the garden of the plaintiff's son. To the latter, the defendant would certainly be liable for the harm done to the realty, but as he had no notice or knowledge of any vicious or ferocious propensity on the part of the animal, we do not think that he should be mulcted in damages for the unfortunate injury suffered by the plaintiff, nor, for that matter, even to the owner of the land, had such owner been injured in like manner. The appellant's fifth point, asking the court to direct a verdict in his favor, should have been affirmed.

. . . .

PORTER, J., concurred in the dissenting opinion of WICKHAM, J.[1]

[1] But compare Bischoff *v.* Cheney, 89 Conn. 1 (trespassing cat).

In Pollock on Torts, 6th ed., 479, it is said that the owner of cattle and other live stock straying on the land of others is "liable only for natural and probable consequences, not for an unexpected event, such as a horse not previously known to be vicious kicking a human being." In 1 Beven on Negligence, 2d ed., 637, it is said, that if animals are trespassing and do injury not in accordance with the ordinary instinct of the animals, "the owner is not liable for the injury apart from the trespass (though he may be for the trespass), unless he knows of the particular vice which caused the injury."

See FISK, J., in Peterson *v.* Conlan, 18 N. D. 205, 212.

SECTION III

DANGEROUS USE OF LAND

FLETCHER v. RYLANDS

IN THE EXCHEQUER, MAY 5, 1865.

Reported in 3 Hurlstone & Coltman, 774.

FLETCHER v. RYLANDS

IN THE EXCHEQUER CHAMBER, MAY 14, 1866.

Reported in Law Reports, 1 Exchequer, 265.

RYLANDS v. FLETCHER

IN THE HOUSE OF LORDS, JULY 17, 1868.

Reported in Law Reports, 3 House of Lords, 330.

IN November, 1861, Fletcher brought an action against Rylands and Horrocks to recover damages for an injury caused to his mines by water flowing into them from a reservoir which defendants had constructed. The declaration (set out in L. R. 1 Exch. 265, 266) contained three counts, each count alleging negligence on the part of the defendants. The case came on for trial at the Liverpool Summer Assizes, 1862, when a verdict was entered for the plaintiff, subject to an award to be thereafter made by an arbitrator. Subsequently the arbitrator was directed, instead of making an award, to state a special case for the consideration of the Court of Exchequer.[1]

The material facts in the special case stated by the arbitrator were as follows: —

Fletcher, under a lease from Lord Wilton, and under arrangements with other landowners, was working coal mines under certain lands. He had worked the mines up to a spot where he came upon old horizontal passages of disused mines, and also upon vertical shafts which seemed filled with marl and rubbish.

Rylands and Horrocks owned a mill standing on land near that under which Fletcher's mines were worked. With permission of Lord Wilton, they constructed on Lord Wilton's land a reservoir to supply water to their mill. They employed a competent engineer and competent contractors to construct the reservoir. It was not known to Rylands and Horrocks, nor to any of the persons employed by them, that any coal had ever been worked under or near the site of the

[1] Statement abridged. Arguments in all the courts omitted; also opinions in Court of Exchequer.

reservoir; but in point of fact the coal under the site of the reservoir had been partially worked at some time or other beyond living memory, and there were old coal workings under the site of the reservoir communicating by means of other and intervening old underground workings with the recent workings of Fletcher.

In the course of constructing and excavating for the bed of the said reservoir, five old shafts, running vertically downwards, were met with in the portion of land selected for the site of the said reservoir. At the time they were so met with the sides or walls of at least three of them were constructed of timber, and were still in existence, but the shafts themselves were filled up with marl, or soil of the same kind as the marl or soil which immediately surrounded them, and it was not known to, or suspected by, the defendants, or any of the persons employed by them in or about the planning or constructing of the said reservoir, that they were (as they afterwards proved to be) shafts which had been made for the purpose of getting the coal under the land in which the said reservoir was made, or that they led down to coal workings under the site of the said reservoir.

For the selection of the site of the said reservoir, and for the planning and constructing thereof, it was necessary that the defendants should employ an engineer and contractors, and they did employ for those purposes a competent engineer and competent contractors, by and under whom the said site was selected and the said reservoir was planned and constructed, and on the part of the defendants themselves there was no personal negligence or default whatever in or about or in relation to the selection of the said site, or in or about the planning or construction of the said reservoir; but in point of fact reasonable and proper care and skill were not exercised by or on the part of the persons so employed by them, with reference to the shafts so met with as aforesaid, to provide for the sufficiency of the said reservoir to bear the pressure of water which, when filled to the height proposed, it would have to bear.

The said reservoir was completed about the beginning of December, 1860, when the defendants caused the same to be partially filled with water, and on the morning of the 11th December in the same year, whilst the reservoir was so partially filled, one of the shafts which had been so met with as aforesaid gave way and burst downwards; in consequence of which the water of the reservoir flowed into the old workings underneath, and by means of the underground communications so then existing between those old coal workings and the plaintiff's coal workings in the plaintiff's colliery, as above described, large quantities of the water so flowing from the said reservoir as aforesaid found their way into the said coal workings in the plaintiff's colliery, and by reason thereof the said colliery became and was flooded, and the working thereof was obliged to be and was for a time necessarily suspended.

The question for the opinion of the Court was whether the plaintiff was entitled to recover damages from the defendants by reason of the matters thus stated by the arbitrator.

The Court of Exchequer (POLLOCK, C. B., and MARTIN, B., concurring; BRAMWELL, B., dissenting) gave judgment for defendants.

Plaintiff brought error in the Exchequer Chamber.

May 14, 1866. The judgment of the Court (WILLES, BLACKBURN, KEATING, MELLOR, MONTAGUE SMITH, and LUSH, JJ.) was delivered by

BLACKBURN, J. This was a special case stated by an arbitrator, under an order of *nisi prius,* in which the question for the Court is stated to be, whether the plaintiff is entitled to recover any and, if any, what damages from the defendants by reason of the matters thereinbefore stated.

In the Court of Exchequer, the Chief Baron and Martin, B., were of opinion that the plaintiff was not entitled to recover at all, Bramwell, B., being of a different opinion. The judgment in the Exchequer was consequently given for the defendants, in conformity with the opinion of the majority of the Court. The only question argued before us was whether this judgment was right, nothing being said about the measure of damages in case the plaintiff should be held entitled to recover. We have come to the conclusion that the opinion of Bramwell, B., was right, and that the answer to the question should be that the plaintiff was entitled to recover damages from the defendants by reason of the matters stated in the case, and consequently that the judgment below should be reversed, but we cannot at present say to what damages the plaintiff is entitled.

It appears from the statement in the case that the plaintiff was damaged by his property being flooded by water which, without any fault on his part, broke out of a reservoir constructed on the defendants' land by the defendants' orders, and maintained by the defendants.

It appears from the statement in the case [see pp. 267–268], that the coal under the defendants' land had, at some remote period, been worked out; but this was unknown at the time when the defendants gave directions to erect the reservoir, and the water in the reservoir would not have escaped from the defendants' land, and no mischief would have been done to the plaintiff, but for this latent defect in the defendants' subsoil. And it further appears [see pp. 268–269] that the defendants selected competent engineers and contractors to make their reservoir, and themselves personally continued in total ignorance of what we have called the latent defect in the subsoil; but that these persons employed by them in the course of the work became aware of the existence of the ancient shafts filled up with soil, though they did not know or suspect that they were shafts communicating with old workings.

It is found that the defendants, personally, were free from all blame, but that in fact proper care and skill was not used by the persons employed by them to provide for the sufficiency of the reservoir with reference to these shafts. The consequence was that the reservoir when filled with water burst into the shafts, the water flowed down through them into the old workings, and thence into the plaintiff's mine, and there did the mischief.

The plaintiff, though free from all blame on his part, must bear the loss, unless he can establish that it was the consequence of some default for which the defendants are responsible. The question of law therefore arises, what is the obligation which the law casts on a person who, like the defendants, lawfully brings on his land something which, though harmless whilst it remains there, will naturally do mischief if it escape out of his land. It is agreed on all hands that he must take care to keep in that which he has brought on the land and keeps there, in order that it may not escape and damage his neighbors; but the question arises whether the duty which the law casts upon him, under such circumstances, is an absolute duty to keep it in at his peril, or is, as the majority of the Court of Exchequer have thought, merely a duty to take all reasonable and prudent precautions in order to keep it in, but no more. If the first be the law, the person who has brought on his land and kept there something dangerous, and failed to keep it in, is responsible for all the natural consequences of its escape. If the second be the limit of his duty, he would not be answerable except on proof of negligence, and consequently would not be answerable for escape arising from any latent defect which ordinary prudence and skill could not detect.

Supposing the second to be the correct view of the law, a further question arises subsidiary to the first, viz., whether the defendants are not so far identified with the contractors whom they employed as to be responsible for the consequences of their want of care and skill in making the reservoir in fact insufficient with reference to the old shafts, of the existence of which they were aware, though they had not ascertained where the shafts went to.

We think that the true rule of law is that the person who for his own purposes brings on his lands and collects and keeps there anything likely to do mischief if it escapes, must keep it in at his peril, and if he does not do so, is *prima facie* answerable for all the damage which is the natural consequence of its escape. He can excuse himself by showing that the escape was owing to the plaintiff's default; or perhaps that the escape was the consequence of *vis major*, or the act of God; but as nothing of this sort exists here, it is unnecessary to inquire what excuse would be sufficient. The general rule, as above stated, seems on principle just. The person whose grass or corn is eaten down by the escaping cattle of his neighbor, or whose mine is flooded by the water from his neighbor's reservoir, or whose cellar is invaded by the filth of his neighbor's privy, or whose habitation is made unhealthy by the fumes and noisome vapors of his neighbor's alkali works, is damnified without any fault of his own; and it seems but reasonable and just that the neighbor, who has brought something on his own property which was not naturally there, harmless to others so long as it is confined to his own property, but which he knows to be mischievous if it gets on his neighbor's, should be obliged to make good the damage which ensues if he does not succeed in confining it to his own property. But for his act in bringing it there no mischief could have accrued, and it seems but just that he should at his peril keep it there, so that no mischief may accrue, or answer for the natural and anticipated consequences. And upon authority, this we think is established to be the law, whether the things so brought be beasts, or water, or filth, or stenches.

The case that has most commonly occurred and which is most frequently to be found in the books is as to the obligation of the owner of cattle which he has brought on his land to prevent their escaping and doing mischief. The law as to them seems to be perfectly settled from early times; the owner must keep them in at his peril, or he will be answerable for the natural consequences of their escape; that is, with regard to tame beasts, for the grass they eat and trample upon, though not for any injury to the person of others, for our ancestors have settled that it is not the general nature of horses to kick, or bulls to gore; but if the owner knows that the beast has a vicious propensity to attack man, he will be answerable for that too.

As early as the Year Book, 20 Ed. 4, 11, placitum 10, Brian, C. J., lays down the doctrine in terms very much resembling those used by Lord Holt in Tenant *v.* Goldwin, 2 Ld. Raym. 1089, 1 Salk. 360, which will be referred to afterwards. It was trespass with cattle. Plea, that the defendant's land adjoined a place where defendant had common, that the cattle strayed from the common, and defendant drove them back as soon as he could. It was held a bad plea. Brian, C. J., says: "It behoves him to use his common so that he shall do no hurt to another man, and if the land in which he has common be not enclosed, it behoves him to keep the beasts in the common and out of the land of any other." He adds, when it was proposed to amend by pleading that they were driven out of the common by dogs, that although that might give a right of action against the master of the dogs, it was no defence to the action of trespass by the person on whose land the cattle went. In the recent case of Cox *v.* Burbidge, 13 C. B. N. S. 438, 32 L. J. C. P. 89, Williams, J., says: "I apprehend the general rule of law to be perfectly plain. If I am the owner of an animal in which by law the right of property can exist, I am bound to take care that it does not stray into the land of my neighbor, and I am liable for any trespass it may commit, and for the ordinary consequences of that trespass. Whether or not the escape of the animal is due to my negligence is altogether immaterial." So in May *v.* Burdett, 9 Q. B. 112, the Court, after an elaborate examination of the old precedents and authorities, came to the conclusion that "a person keeping a mischievous animal, with knowledge of its propensities, is bound to keep it secure at his peril." And in 1 Hale's Pleas of the Crown, 430, Lord Hale states that where one keeps a beast, knowing its nature or habits are such that the natural consequence of his being loose is that he will harm men, the owner "must at his peril keep him up safe from doing hurt; for though he use his diligence to keep him up, if he escape and do harm, the owner is liable to answer damages;" though, as he proceeds to show, he will not be liable criminally without proof of want of care. In these latter authorities the point under consideration was damage to the person, and what was decided was, that where it was known that hurt to the person was the natural consequence of the animal being loose, the owner should be responsible in damages for such hurt, though where it was not known to be so, the owner was not responsible for such damages; but where the damage is, like eating grass or other ordinary ingredients in damage feasant, the natural consequence of the escape, the rule as to keeping in the animal is the same. In Com. Dig. *Droit.* (M. 2), it is said that "if the owner of 200 acres in a common moor enfeoffs B. of 50 acres, B. ought to enclose at his peril, to prevent damage by his cattle to the other 150 acres. For if his cattle escape thither they may be distrained damage feasant. So the owner of the 150 acres ought to prevent his cattle from doing damage to the 50 acres at his peril." The authority cited is Dyer, 372 *b.*, where the decision was that the cattle might be distrained; the inference from that decision, that the owner was bound to keep in his cattle at his peril, is, we think, legitimate, and we have the high authority of Comyns for saying that such is the law. In the note to Fitzherbert, Nat. Brevium, 128, which is attributed to Lord Hale, it is said, "If A. and B. have lands adjoining, where there is no enclosure, the one shall have trespass against the other on an escape of their beasts respectively: Dyer, 372, Rastal Ent. 621, 20 Ed. 4, 10; although wild dogs, &c., drive the cattle of the one into the lands of the other." No case is known to us on which in replevin it has ever been attempted to plead in bar to an avowry for distress damage feasant, that the cattle had escaped without any negligence on the part of the plaintiff, and surely if that could have been a good plea in bar, the facts must often have been such as would have supported it. These authorities, and the absence of any authority to the contrary, justify Williams, J., in saying, as he does in Cox *v.* Burbidge, *supra,* that the law is clear that in actions for damage occasioned by animals that have not been kept in by their owners, it is quite immaterial whether the escape is by negligence or not.

As has been already said, there does not appear to be any difference in principle between the extent of the duty cast on him who brings cattle on his land to keep them in, and the extent of the duty imposed on him who brings on his land water, filth, or stenches, or any other thing which will, if it escape, naturally do damage, to prevent their escaping and injuring his neighbor; and the case of Tenant *v.* Goldwin, *supra*, is an express authority that the duty is the same, and is, to keep them in at his peril.

As Martin, B., in his judgment below, appears not to have understood that case in the same manner as we do, it is proper to examine it in some detail. It was a motion in arrest of judgment after judgment by default, and therefore all that was well pleaded in the declaration was admitted to be true. The declaration is set out at full length in the report in 6 Mod. p. 311. It alleged that the plaintiff had a cellar which lay contiguous to a messuage of the defendant, "and used (*solebat*) to be separated and fenced from a privy house of office, parcel of the said messuage of defendant, by a thick and close wall, which belongs to the said messuage of the defendant, and by the defendant of right ought to have been repaired (*jure debuit reparari*)." Yet he did not repair it, and for want of repair filth flowed into plaintiff's cellar. The case is reported by Salkeld, who argued it, in 6 Mod., and by Lord Raymond, whose report is the fullest. The objection taken was that there was nothing to show that the defendant was under any obligation to repair the wall, that, it was said, being a charge not of common right, and the allegation that the wall *de jure debuit reparari* by the defendant being an inference of law which did not arise from the facts alleged. Salkeld argued that this general mode of stating the right was sufficient in a declaration, and also that the duty alleged did of common right result from the facts stated. It is not now material to inquire whether he was or was not right on the pleading point. All three reports concur in saying that Lord Holt, during the argument, intimated an opinion against him on that, but that after consideration the Court gave judgment for him on the second ground. In the report of 6 Mod. 314, it is stated: "And at another day *per totam curiam*. The declaration is good; for there is a sufficient cause of action appearing in it; but not upon the word '*solebat*.' If the defendant has a house of office enclosed with a wall which is his, he is of common right bound to use it so as not to annoy another. . . . The reason here is, that one must use his own so as thereby not to hurt another, and as of common right one is bound to keep his cattle from trespassing on his neighbor, so he is bound to use anything that is his so as not to hurt another by such user. . . . Suppose one sells a piece of pasture lying open to another piece of pasture which the vendor has, the vendee is bound to keep his cattle from running into the vendor's piece; so of dung or anything else." There is here an evident allusion to the same case in Dyer, see *ante*, p. 334, as is referred to in Com. Dig. *Droit.* (M. 2). Lord Raymond in his report, 2 Ld. Raym. at p. 1092, says: " The last day of term, Holt, C. J., delivered the opinion of the Court that the declaration was sufficient. He said that upon the face of this declaration there appeared a sufficient cause of action to entitle the plaintiff to have his judgment; that they did not go upon the *solebat,* or the *jure debuit reparari,* as if it were enough to say that the plaintiff had a house and the defendant had a wall, and he ought to repair the wall; but if the defendant has a house of office, and the wall which separates the house of office from the plaintiff's house is all the defendant's, he is of common right bound to repair it. . . . The reason of this case is upon this account, that every one must so use his own as not to do damage to another; and as every man is bound so to look to his cattle as to keep them out of his neighbor's ground, that so he may receive no damage; so he must keep in the filth of his house of office that it may not flow in upon and damnify his neighbor. . . . So if a man has two pieces of pasture which lie open to one another, and sells one piece, the vendee must keep in his cattle so as they shall not trespass upon the vendor. So a man shall not lay his dung so high as to damage his neighbor, and the reason of these cases is because every man must so use his own as not to damnify another." Salkeld, who had been counsel in the case, reports the judgment much more concisely (1 Salk. 361), but to the same effect; he says: " The reason he gave for his judgment was because it was the defendant's wall and the defendant's filth, and he was bound of common right to keep his wall so as his filth might not damnify his neighbor, and that it was a trespass on his neighbor, as if his beasts should escape, or one should make a great heap on the border of his ground, and it should tumble and roll down upon his neighbor's, . . . he must repair the wall of his house of office, for he whose dirt it is must keep it that it may not trespass." It is worth noticing how completely the reason of Lord Holt corresponds with that of Brian, C. J., in the cases already cited in 20 Ed. 4. Martin, B., in the Court below says that he thinks this was a case without difficulty, because the defendant had, by letting judgment go by default, admitted his liability to repair the wall, and that he cannot see how it is an authority for any case in which no such liability is admitted. But a perusal of the report will show that it was because Lord Holt and his colleagues thought (no matter for this purpose whether rightly or wrongly) that the liability was not admitted, that they took so much trouble to consider what liability the law would raise from the admitted facts, and it does therefore seem to us to be a very weighty authority in support of the position that he who brings and keeps anything, no matter whether beasts, or filth, or clean water, or a heap of earth or dung on his premises, must at his peril prevent it from getting on his neighbor's, or make good all the damage which is the natural consequence of its doing so. No case has been found in which the question as to the liability for noxious vapors escaping from a man's works by inevitable accident has been discussed, but the following case will illustrate it. Some years ago several actions were brought against the occupiers of some alkali works at Liverpool for the damage alleged to be caused by the chlorine fumes of their works. The defendants proved that they at great expense erected contrivances by which the fumes of chlorine were condensed and sold as muriatic acid, and they called a great body of scientific evidence to prove that this apparatus was so perfect that no fumes possibly could escape from the defendants' chimneys. On this evidence it was pressed upon the jury that the plaintiff's damage must have been due to some of the numerous other chimneys in the neighborhood; the jury, however, being satisfied that the mischief was occasioned by chlorine, drew the conclusion that it had escaped from the defendants' works somehow, and in each case found for the plaintiff. No attempt was made to disturb these verdicts on the ground that the defendants had taken every precaution which prudence or skill could suggest to keep those fumes in, and that they could not be responsible unless negligence were shown; yet, if the law be as laid down by the majority of the Court of Exchequer, it would have been a very obvious defence. If it had been raised the answer would probably have been that the uniform course of pleading in actions on such nuisances is to say that the defendant caused the noisome vapors to arise on his premises, and suffered them to come on the plaintiff's, without stating that there was any want of care or skill in the defendant, and that the case of Tenant *v.* Goldwin, *supra*, showed that this was founded on the general rule of law, that he whose stuff it is must keep it that it may not trespass. There is no difference in this respect between chlorine and water; both will, if they escape, do damage, the one by scorching and the other by drowning, and he who brings them there must at his peril see that they do not escape and do that mischief. What is said by Gibbs, C. J., in Sutton *v.* Clarke, 6 Taunt. 44, though not necessary for the decision of the case, shows that that very learned judge took the same view of the law that was taken by Lord Holt. But it was further said by Martin, B., that when damage is done to personal property, or even to the person, by collision, either upon land or at sea, there must be negligence in the party doing the damage to render him legally responsible; and this is no doubt true, and as was pointed out by Mr. Mellish during his argument before us, this is not confined to cases of collision, for there are many cases in which proof of negligence is essential, as, for instance, where an unruly horse gets on the footpath of a public street and kills a passenger, Hammack *v.* White, 11 C. B. N. S. 588; 31 L. J. (C. P.) 129; or where a person in a dock is struck by the falling of a bale of cotton which the defendant's servants are lowering: Scott *v.* London Dock Company, 3 H. & C. 596; 35 L. J. (Ex.) 17, 220; and many other similar cases may be found. But we think these cases distinguishable from the present. Traffic on the highways, whether by land or sea, cannot be conducted without exposing those whose persons or property are near it to some inevitable risk; and that being so, those who go on the highway, or have their property adjacent to it, may well be held to do so subject to their taking upon themselves the risk of injury from that inevitable danger; and persons who by the license of the owner pass near to warehouses where goods are being raised or lowered, certainly do so subject to the inevitable risk of accident. In neither case, therefore, can they recover without proof of want of care or skill occasioning the accident; and it is believed that all the cases in which inevitable accident has been held an excuse for what *prima facie* was a trespass, can be explained on the same principle, viz., that the circumstances were such as to show that the plaintiff had taken that risk upon himself. But there is no ground for saying that the plaintiff here took upon himself any risk arising from the uses to which the defendants should choose to apply their land. He neither knew what these might be, nor could he in any way control the defendants, or hinder their building what reservoirs they liked, and storing up in them what water they pleased, so long as the defendants succeeded in preventing the water which they there brought from interfering with the plaintiff's property.

The view which we take of the first point renders it unnecessary to consider whether the defendants would or would not be responsible for the want of care and skill in the persons employed by them, under the circumstances stated in the case [pp. 268–269].

We are of opinion that the plaintiff is entitled to recover, but as we have not heard any argument as to the amount, we are not able to give judgment for what damages. The parties probably will empower their counsel to agree on the amount of damages; should they differ on the principle the case may be mentioned again.

Judgment for the plaintiff.

Rylands and Horrocks brought error in the House of Lords against the judgment of the Exchequer Chamber, which had reversed the judgment of the Court of Exchequer.

[Arguments omitted.]

THE LORD CHANCELLOR (Lord Cairns). My Lords, in this case the plaintiff (I may use the description of the parties in the action) is the occupier of a mine and works under a close of land. The defendants are the owners of a mill in his neighborhood, and they proposed to make a reservoir for the purpose of keeping and storing water to be used about their mill upon another close of land, which, for the purposes of this case, may be taken as being adjoining to the close of the plaintiff, although in point of fact some intervening land lay between the two. Underneath the close of land of the defendants on which they proposed to construct their reservoir there were certain old and disused mining passages and works. There were five vertical shafts and some horizontal shafts communicating with them. The vertical shafts had been filled up with soil and rubbish, and it does not appear that any person was aware of the existence either of the vertical shafts or of the horizontal works communicating with them. In the course of the working by the plaintiff of his mine he had gradually worked through the seams of coal underneath the close, and had come into contact with the old and disused works underneath the close of the defendants.

In that state of things the reservoir of the defendants was constructed. It was constructed by them through the agency and inspection of an engineer and contractor. Personally, the defendants appear to have taken no part in the works, or to have been aware of any want of security connected with them. As regards the engineer and the contractor, we must take it from the case that they did not exercise, as far as they were concerned, that reasonable care and caution which they might have exercised, taking notice, as they appear to have taken notice, of the vertical shafts filled up in the manner which I have mentioned. However, my Lords, when the reservoir was constructed and filled, or partly filled, with water, the weight of the water bearing upon the disused and imperfectly filled-up vertical shafts, broke through those shafts. The water passed down them and into the horizontal workings, and from the horizontal workings under the close of the defendants it passed on into the workings under the close of the plaintiff, and flooded his mine, causing considerable damage, for which this action was brought.

The Court of Exchequer, when the special case stating the facts to which I have referred was argued, was of opinion that the plaintiff had established no cause of action. The Court of Exchequer Chamber, before which an appeal from this judgment was argued, was of a contrary opinion, and the judges there unanimously arrived at the conclusion that there was a cause of action, and that the plaintiff was entitled to damages.

My Lords, the principles on which this case must be determined appear to me to be extremely simple. The defendants, treating them as the owners or occupiers of the close on which the reservoir was constructed, might lawfully have used that close for any purpose for which it might in the ordinary course of the enjoyment of land be used; and if, in what I may term the natural user of that land, there had been any accumulation of water, either on the surface or under ground, and if, by the operation of the laws of nature, that accumulation of water had passed off into the close occupied by the plaintiff, the plaintiff could not have complained that that result had taken place. If he had desired to guard himself against it, it would have lain upon him to have done so by leaving, or by interposing, some barrier between his close and the close of the defendants in order to have prevented that operation of the laws of nature.

As an illustration of that principle, I may refer to a case which was cited in the argument before your Lordships, the case of Smith v. Kenrick, in the Court of Common Pleas, 7 C. B. 515.

On the other hand, if the defendants, not stopping at the natural use of their close, had desired to use it for any purpose which I may term a non-natural use,[1] for the purpose of introducing into the close that which in its natural condition was not in or upon it, for the purpose of introducing water either above or below ground in quantities and in a manner not the result of any work or operation on or under the land; and if in consequence of their doing so, or in consequence of any imperfection in the mode of their doing so, the water came to escape and to pass off into the close of the plaintiff, then it appears to me that that which the defendants were doing they were doing at their own peril; and if in the course of their doing it the evil arose to which I have referred, the evil, namely, of the escape of the water and its passing away to the close of the plaintiff and injuring the plaintiff, then for the consequence of that, in my opinion, the defendants would be liable. As the case of Smith v. Kenrick is an illustration of the first principle to which I have referred, so also the second

[1] "It is not every use to which the land is put that brings into play that principle [Rylands v. Fletcher]. It must be some special use bringing with it increased danger to others, and must not merely be the ordinary use of the land or such a use as is proper for the general benefit of the community." Lord Moulton in Rickards v. Lothian, [1913] A. C. 263, 280.

"This was a case of the escape of water from lavatory pipes. It would appear, therefore, that the construction of distributing water-pipes in a building is an ordinary and natural use of land, but that the construction of the water-mains or reservoirs from which the water is obtained is not so. Such unreal and impracticable distinctions are not creditable to the development of English law." Salmond, Torts (4 ed.) § 61, n. 13.

See the remarks of Doe, C. J., in Brown v. Collins, *infra*, p. 482.

"This rule is rightly applicable only to such unusual and extraordinary uses of property in reference to the benefits to be derived from the use and the dangers or losses to which others are exposed, as should not be permitted except at the sole risk of the user. The standard of duty established by the courts in these cases is that every owner shall refrain from these unwarrantable and extremely dangerous uses of property unless he provides safeguards whose perfection he guarantees. . . . The principle applicable to the erection of common buildings whose fall might do damage to persons or property on the adjacent premises holds owners to a less strict duty. This principle is that where a certain lawful use of property will bring to pass wrongful consequences from the condition in which the property is put, if these are not guarded against, an owner who makes such a use is bound at his peril to see that proper care is taken in every particular to prevent the wrong. . . . The duty which the law imposes upon an owner of real estate in such a case, is to make the conditions safe so far as it can be done by the exercise of ordinary care on the part of all those engaged in the work. He is responsible for the negligence of independent contractors as well as for that of his servants. This rule is applicable to every one who builds an ordinary wall which is liable to do serious injury by falling outside of his own premises. . . . The uses of property governed by this rule are those that bring new conditions which involve risks to the persons or property of others, but which are ordinary and usual and in a sense natural, as incident to the ownership of the land. The rule first referred to applies to unusual and extraordinary uses which are so fraught with peril to others that the owner should not be permitted to adopt them for his own purposes without absolutely protecting his neighbors from injury or loss by reason of the use." Knowlton, J., in Ainsworth v. Lakin, 180 Mass. 397, 399–401.

principle to which I have referred is well illustrated by another case in the same Court, the case of Baird *v.* Williamson, 15 C. B. N. S. 317, which was also cited in the argument at the Bar.

My Lords, these simple principles, if they are well founded, as it appears to me they are, really dispose of this case.

The same result is arrived at on the principles referred to by Mr. Justice Blackburn in his judgment in the Court of Exchequer Chamber, where he states the opinion of that Court as to the law in these words: "We think that the true rule of law is that the person who, for his own purposes, brings on his land and collects and keeps there anything likely to do mischief if it escapes, must keep it in at his peril; and if he does not do so, is *prima facie* answerable for all the damage which is the natural consequence of its escape. He can excuse himself by showing that the escape was owing to the plaintiff's default; or, perhaps, that the escape was the consequence of *vis major*, or the act of God; but as nothing of this sort exists here, it is unnecessary to inquire what excuse would be sufficient. The general rule, as above stated, seems on principle just. The person whose grass or corn is eaten down by the escaping cattle of his neighbor, or whose mine is flooded by the water from his neighbor's reservoir, or whose cellar is invaded by the filth of his neighbor's privy, or whose habitation is made unhealthy by the fumes and noisome vapors of his neighbor's alkali works, is damnified without any fault of his own; and it seems but reasonable and just that the neighbor who has brought something on his own property (which was not naturally there), harmless to others so long as it is confined to his own property, but which he knows will be mischievous if it gets on his neighbor's, should be obliged to make good the damage which ensues if he does not succeed in confining it to his own property. But for his act in bringing it there no mischief could have accrued, and it seems but just that he should at his peril keep it there, so that no mischief may accrue, or answer for the natural and anticipated consequence. And upon authority this we think is established to be the law, whether the things so brought be beasts, or water, or filth, or stenches."

My Lords, in that opinion I must say I entirely concur. Therefore, I have to move your Lordships that the judgment of the Court of Exchequer Chamber be affirmed, and that the present appeal be dismissed with costs.

LORD CRANWORTH. My Lords, I concur with my noble and learned friend in thinking that the rule of law was correctly stated by Mr. Justice Blackburn in delivering the opinion of the Exchequer Chamber. If a person brings, or accumulates, on his land anything which, if it should escape, may cause damage to his neighbor, he does so at his peril. If it does escape and cause damage, he is responsible, however careful he may have been, and whatever precautions he may have taken to prevent the damage.

In considering whether a defendant is liable to a plaintiff for damage which the plaintiff may have sustained, the question in general is not whether the defendant has acted with due care and caution, but whether his acts have occasioned the damage. This is all well explained in the old case of Lambert *v.* Bessey, reported by Sir Thomas Raymond (Sir T. Raym. 421). And the doctrine is founded on good sense. For when one person, in managing his own affairs, causes, however innocently, damage to another, it is obviously only just that he should be the party to suffer. He is bound *sic uti suo ut non lædat alienum.* This is the principle of law applicable to cases like the present, and I do not discover in the authorities which were cited anything conflicting with it.

The doctrine appears to me to be well illustrated by the two modern cases in the Court of Common Pleas referred to by my noble and learned friend. I allude to the two cases of Smith *v.* Kenrick, *supra,* and Baird *v.* Williamson, *supra.* In the former the owner of a coal mine on the higher level worked out the whole of his coal, leaving no barrier between his mine and the mine on the lower level, so that the water percolating through the upper mine flowed into the lower mine, and obstructed the owner of it in getting his coal. It was held that the owner of the lower mine had no ground of complaint. The defendant, the owner of the upper mine, had a right to remove all his coal. The damage sustained by the plaintiff was occasioned by the natural flow or percolation of water from the upper strata. There was no obligation on the defendant to protect the plaintiff against this. It was his business to erect or leave a sufficient barrier to keep out the water, or to adopt proper means for so conducting the water as that it should not impede him in his workings. The water in that case was only left by the defendant to flow in its natural course.

But in the later case of Baird *v.* Williamson, the defendant, the owner of the upper mine, did not merely suffer the water to flow through his mine without leaving a barrier between it and the mine below, but in order to work in his own mine beneficially he pumped up quantities of water which passed into the plaintiff's mine in addition to that which would have naturally reached it, and so occasioned him damage. Though this was done without negligence and in the due working of his own mine, yet he was held to be responsible for the damage so occasioned. It was in consequence of his act, whether skilfully or unskilfully performed, that the plaintiff had been damaged, and he was therefore held liable for the consequences. The damage in the former case may be treated as having arisen from the act of God; in the latter, from the act of the defendant.

Applying the principle of these decisions to the case now before the House, I come without hesitation to the conclusion that the judgment of the Exchequer Chamber was right. The plaintiff had a right to work his coal through the lands of Mr. Whitehead and up to the old workings. If water naturally rising in the defendants' land (we may treat the land as the land of the defendants for the purpose of this case) had by percolation found its way down to the plaintiff's mine through the old workings, and so had impeded his operations, that would not have afforded him any ground of complaint. Even if all the old workings had been made by the plaintiff, he would have done no more than he was entitled to do; for, according to the principle acted on in Smith *v.* Kenrick, the person working the mine under the close in which the reservoir was made had a right to win and carry away all the coal without leaving any wall or barrier against Whitehead's land. But that is not the real state of the case. The defendants, in order to effect an object of their own, brought on to their land, or on to land which for this purpose may be treated as being theirs, a large accumulated mass of water, and stored it up in a reservoir. The consequence of this was damage to the plaintiff, and for that damage, however skilfully and carefully the accumulation was made, the defendants, according to the principles and authorities to which I have adverted, were certainly responsible.

I concur, therefore, with my noble and learned friend in thinking that the judgment below must be affirmed, and that there must be judgment for the defendant in error.

Judgment of the Court of Exchequer Chamber affirmed.[1]

[1] Eastern Tel. Co. *v.* Capetown Tramways Cos., [1902] A. C. 381; Midwood *v.* Manchester Corporation, [1905] 2 K. B. 597; Charing Cross Co. *v.* London Hydraulic Power Co., [1913] 3 K. B. 442, [1914] 3 K. B. 772; Brennan Construction Co. *v.* Cumberland, 29 App. D. C. 554 (crude petroleum in tank); Shipley *v.* Associates, 106 Mass. 194; Cahill *v.* Eastman, 18 Minn. 324; Wiltse *v.* Red Wing, 99 Minn. 255 (reservoir); French *v.* Carter Creek Mfg. Co., 173 Mo. App. 220 (stored nitroglycerine); Defiance Water Co. *v.* Olinger, 54 Ohio St. 532; Bradford Co. *v.* St. Mary's Co., 60 Ohio St. 560 (stored nitroglycerine); Langabaugh *v.* Anderson, 68 Ohio St. 131 (crude petroleum in tank); Texas R. Co. *v.* Frazer (Tex. Civ. App.) 182 S. W. 1161 (dam); Weaver Mercantile Co. *v.* Thurmond, 68 W. Va. 530 *Accord.* See Wing *v.* London General Omnibus Co., [1909] 2 K. B. 652.

"In every case of the kind which has been reported since Rylands *v.* Fletcher, that is, during the last 25 years, there has been a manifest inclination to discover something in the facts which took the case out of the rule. According to the English judicial system which has gone round the world with the English language and English or Anglicized institutions, the decisions of superior courts are not merely instructive and worthy of regard, but of binding authority in subsequent cases of the like sort. But there are some authorities which are followed and developed in the spirit, which become the starting-point of new chapters of the law; there are others that are followed only in the letter, and become slowly but surely choked and crippled by exceptions. This again, is independent of the considerations of local fitness which must always have weight when precedents are cited from a country remote both in place and in manners." Pollock, Law of Fraud in British India, 53–54 (1894).

"In August, 1908, Count Z. sent one of his dirigibles from Mainz to Friedericks-hafen. Some motor trouble happened, and the ship was landed in a field. Thousands of people rushed to the place, so ropes were run around it, and soldiers were ordered on guard. The ship was anchored, and in addition held by forty men with ropes at the stem, and by thirty at the stern. In the afternoon a sudden thunderstorm came up, struck the dirigible, tore it loose and sent it adrift for about a mile, when it caught fire and was destroyed.

Spectators had been around all the time, and were standing outside the ropes in rows several deep. Some unfortunate person standing in the outer row near the rear gondola, was caught by the ship's anchor, dragged into the air and carried for some distance; in the fall, one of his legs sustained such injuries that it had to be amputated.

He brought suit for damages, and was nonsuited; appealed; same result. Finally, he appealed to the Reichsgericht. It refused to interfere, for the following reasons: There being no special law governing damage by air-navigation, it becomes necessary to prove negligence on the part of the aviator or promoter. The idea that the mere undertaking of a business, acknowledged to be dangerous, carries with it responsibility for all damage caused thereby, is not law. The only duty which the hazardousness of the undertaking imposes upon the person engaged therein, is that of extra care. Otherwise, almost all kinds of transportation would be impossible.

In this case, the trip had commenced during exceptionally fine weather, which continued until after the time when the ship had been landed and anchored. Defendant had proved that on former occasions he had succeeded in landing, anchoring and holding his ship, even when the weather was unfavorable, and that the means he on such occasions had employed in keeping the ship at its moorings, were not any stronger than those employed on this occasion; in fact, they were weaker. It could not be demanded of the defendant that he should anticipate and provide against such an extraordinary violent gust of wind as tore his airship away." 75 Central Law Journ. 311 (1912).

In Charing Cross Co. *v.* London Hydraulic Power Co., [1914] 3 K. B. 772, hydraulic mains under the streets burst and injured plaintiff's cables, also laid in the streets. Lord Sumner said (pp. 779–780): " I think that this present case is also indistinguishable from Rylands *v.* Fletcher. Two grounds of distinction have been suggested. It is said that the doctrine of Rylands *v.* Fletcher is applicable between the owners of adjacent closes, which are adjacent whether there be any intermediate property or not; and that it is a doctrine depending upon the ownership of land and the rights attaching to the ownership of land, under which violations of that species of right can be prevented or punished. In the present case instead of having two adjacent owners of real property, you have only two neighboring owners, not strictly adjacent, of chattels, whose chattels are there under a permission which might have been obtained by the private license of the owners of the soil, though in fact obtained under parliamentary powers; hence the two companies are in the position of co-users of a highway, or at any rate of co-users of different rooms in one house, and Rylands *v.* Fletcher does not apply. The case depends on doctrines applicable to the highways, or to houses let out in tenements. I am unable to agree with any of these distinctions, though they have been pressed upon us by both learned counsel with great resource and command of the authorities. Midwood *v.* Manchester Corporation, [1905] 2 K. B. 597, is not decided as a case of a dispute arising between the owners of two adjacent closes. The case is treated as one between a corporation, whose business under the roadway is exactly similar to that of the defendant corporation here, and injured occupiers of the premises. If the distinction drawn between the present case and that of adjacent landowners in Rylands *v.* Fletcher be a good one, it either was not taken in Midwood *v.* Manchester Corporation or was taken and treated as of no importance. Further I am satisfied that Rylands *v.* Fletcher is not limited to the case of adjacent freeholders. I shall not attempt to show how far it extends. It extends as far as this case, and that is enough for the present purpose."

See Thayer, Liability Without Fault, 29 Harv. Law Rev. 801; Bohlen, The Rule in Rylands *v.* Fletcher, 59 University of Pennsylvania Law Rev. 298, 373, 423; Wigmore, Responsibility for Tortious Acts: Its History, 7 Harv. Law Rev. 315, 383, 442.

Liability in case of customary or statutory duty or authority to use land as defendant did, see Madras R. Co. *v.* Zemindar, L. R. 1 Ind. App. 364; Green *v.* Chelsea Waterworks Co., 70 L. T. 547; Price *v.* South Metropolitan Gas Co., 65 L. J. Q. B. N. S. 126; City *v.* Bridgeport Hydraulic Co., 81 Conn. 84.

NICHOLS *v.* MARSLAND

IN THE EXCHEQUER, JUNE 12, 1875.

Reported in Law Reports, 10 *Exchequer*, 255.

NICHOLS *v.* MARSLAND

IN THE COURT OF APPEAL, DECEMBER 1, 1876.

Reported in Law Reports, 2 *Exchequer Division*, 1.

THE plaintiff sued as the surveyor for the County of Chester of bridges repairable at the expense of the county.

The first count of the declaration alleged that the defendant was possessed of lands and of artificial pools constructed thereon for receiving and holding, and wherein were kept, large quantities of water, yet the defendant took so little and such bad care of the pools and the water therein that large quantities of water escaped from the pools and destroyed four county bridges, whereby the inhabitants of the county incurred expense in repairing and rebuilding them.

The second count alleged that the defendant was possessed of large quantities of water collected and contained in three artificial pools of the defendant near to four county bridges, and stated the breach as in the first count.

Plea, not guilty, and issue thereon.

At the trial before COCKBURN, C. J., at the Chester Summer Assizes, 1874, the plaintiff's witnesses gave evidence to the following effect: The defendant occupied a mansion-house and grounds at Henbury, in the County of Chester. A natural stream called Bagbrook, which rose in higher lands, ran through the defendant's grounds, and after leaving them flowed under the four county bridges in question. After entering the defendant's grounds the stream was diverted and dammed up by an artificial embankment into a pool of three acres in area called "the upper pool," from which it escaped over a weir in the embankment, and was again similarly dammed up by an artificial embankment into the "middle pool," which was between one and two acres in area. Escaping over a weir in the embankment, it was again dammed up into "the lower pool," which was between eight and nine acres in area, and from which the stream escaped into its natural and original course.

About five o'clock P.M. on the 18th of June, 1872, occurred a terrible thunder storm, accompanied by heavy rain, which continued till about three o'clock A.M. on the 19th. The rainfall was greater and more violent than any within the memory of the witnesses, and swelled the stream both above and in the defendant's grounds. On the morning of the 19th it was found that during the night the violence and volume of the water had carried away the artificial embankments of the three pools, the accumulated water in which, being thus suddenly let loose, had swelled the stream below the pools so that it carried away and destroyed the county bridges mentioned in the declaration. At the pools were paddles for letting off the water, but for several years they had been out of working order.

Some engineers and other witnesses gave evidence that in their opinion the weir in the upper pool was far too small for a pool of that size, and that the mischief happened through the insufficiency of the means for carrying off the water. It was not proved when these ornamental pools were constructed, but it appeared that they had existed before the defendant began to occupy the property, and that no similar accident had ever occurred within the knowledge of the witnesses.

After hearing the address of the defendant's counsel, the jury said they did not wish to hear his witnesses, and that in their opinion the accident was caused by *vis major*. In answer to Cockburn, C. J., they found that there was no negligence in the construction or maintenance of the works, and that the rain was most excessive. Cockburn, C. J., being of opinion that the rainfall, though extraordinary and unprecedented, did not amount to *vis major* or excuse the defendant from liability, entered the verdict for the plaintiff for 4092*l.*, the agreed amount, reserving leave to the defendant to move to enter it for her if the Court (who were to draw inferences of fact) should be of opinion that the rainfall amounted to *vis major*, and so distinguished the case from Rylands *v.* Fletcher, L. R. 3 H. L. 330.

A rule *nisi* having been accordingly obtained to enter the verdict for the defendant on the ground that there was no proof of liability, the plaintiff on showing cause to be at liberty to contend that a new trial should be granted on the ground that the finding of the jury was against the weight of evidence —

May 27. *McIntyre*, Q. C., and *Coxon*, for the plaintiff, showed cause. The defendant, having for her own purposes and advantage stored a dangerous element on her premises, is liable if that element escapes and injures the property of another, even though the escape be caused by an earthquake or any form of *vis major*.

[CLEASBY, B. Was not the flood brought on to the defendant's land by *vis major*?]

The pools were made by those through whom the defendant claims, and if there had been no pools the water of the natural stream would have escaped without doing injury. The case falls within the rule laid down by the judgment in Fletcher *v.* Rylands, L. R. 1 Ex. 265, 279, delivered by Blackburn, J.: "We think that the true rule of law is, that the person who for his own purposes brings on his lands, and collects and keeps there anything likely to do mischief if it escapes, must keep it in at his peril, and if he does not do so is *prima facie* answerable for all the damage which is the natural consequence of its escape.

He can excuse himself by showing that the escape was owing to the plaintiff's default, or perhaps that the escape was the consequence of *vis major*, or the act of God." This passage was cited with approval by Lord Cairns, C., and Lord Cranworth on appeal. L. R. 3 H. L. 330, 339, 340.

[CLEASBY, B. There the defendant brought the water on to his own land. Not so here.]

The intimation that *vis major* would perhaps be an excuse is not confirmed by any decision or any other *dictum*. But the facts here do not amount to *vis major*. If the weirs had been larger, or the banks stronger, the mischief would not have happened. *Vis major* means something which cannot be foreseen or resisted, as an earthquake or an act of the Queen's enemies.

Hughes and *Dunn* (*Sir J. Holker*, S. G., with them), in support of the rule, cited Broom's Legal Maxims, 5th ed. p. 230: "The act of God signifies in legal phraseology any inevitable accident occurring without the intervention of man, and may indeed be considered to mean something in opposition to the act of man, as storms, tempests, and lightning: *per* Mansfield, C. J., in Forward *v.* Pittard, 1 T. R. 33; Trent Navigation *v.* Wood, 3 Esp. 131; Rex *v.* Somerset, 8 T. R. 312." Also Amies *v.* Stevens, 1 Str. 127; Smith *v.* Fletcher, L. R. 9 Ex. 64; May *v.* Burdett, 9 Q. B. 101; and Jackson *v.* Smithson, 15 M. & W. 563.

[The question of the verdict being against the evidence was then argued.] *Cur. adv. vult.*

June 12. The judgment of the Court (KELLY, C. B., BRAMWELL, and CLEASBY, BB.) was read by

BRAMWELL, B. In this case I understand the jury to have found that all reasonable care had been taken by the defendant, that the banks were fit for all events to be anticipated, and the weirs broad enough; that the storm was of such violence as to be properly called the act of God, or *vis major*. No doubt, as was said by Mr. McIntyre, a shower is the act of God as much as a storm; so is an earthquake in this country: yet every one understands that a storm, supernatural in one sense, may properly, like an earthquake in this country, be called the act of God, or *vis major*. No doubt not the act of God or a *vis major* in the sense that it was physically impossible to resist it, but in the sense that it was practically impossible to do so. Had the banks been twice as strong, or if that would not do, ten times, and ten times as high, and the weir ten times as wide, the mischief might not have happened. But those are not practical conditions, they are such that to enforce them would prevent the reasonable use of property in the way most beneficial to the community.

So understanding the finding of the jury, I am of opinion the defendant is not liable. What has the defendant done wrong? What right of the plaintiff has she infringed? She has done nothing wrong, she has infringed no right. It is not the defendant who let loose the water and sent it to destroy the bridges. She did indeed store it, and store it in such quantities that, if it was let loose, it would do, as it did, mischief. But suppose a stranger let it loose, would the defendant be liable ? If so, then if a mischievous boy bored a hole in a cistern in any London house, and the water did mischief to a neighbor, the occupier of the house would be liable. That cannot be. Then why is the defendant liable if some agent over which she has no control lets the water out? Mr. McIntyre contended that she would be in all cases of the water being let out, whether by a stranger or the Queen's enemies, or by natural causes, as lightning or an earthquake. Why ? What is the difference between a reservoir and a stack of chimneys for such a question as this ? Here the defendant stored a lot of water for her own purposes; in the case of the chimneys some one has put a ton of bricks fifty feet high for his own purposes; both equally harmless if they stay where placed, and equally mischievous if they do not. The water is no more a wild or savage animal than the bricks while at rest, nor more so when in motion: both have the same property of obeying the law of gravitation. Could it be said that no one could have a stack of chimneys except on the terms of being liable for any damage done by their being overthrown by a hurricane or an earthquake ? If so, it would be dangerous to have a tree, for a wind might come so strong as to blow it out of the ground into a neighbor's land and cause it to do damage; or a field of ripe wheat, which might be fired by lightning and do mischief.

I admit that it is not a question of negligence. A man may use all care to keep the water in, or the stack of chimneys standing, but would be liable if through any defect, though latent, the water escaped or the bricks fell. But here the act is that of an agent he cannot control.

This case differs wholly from Fletcher *v.* Rylands, L. R. 1 Ex. 265, 279. There the defendant poured the water into the plaintiff's mine. He did not know he was doing so; but he did it as much as though he had poured it into an open channel which led to the mine without his knowing it. Here the defendant merely brought it to a place whence another agent let it loose. I am by no means sure that the likeness of a wild animal is exact. I am by no means sure that if a man kept a tiger, and lightning broke his chain, and he got loose and did mischief, that the man who kept him would not be liable. But this case and the case I put of the chimneys, are not cases of keeping a dangerous beast for amusement, but of a reasonable use of property in a way beneficial to the community. I think this analogy has made some of the difficulty in this case. Water stored in a reservoir may be the only practical mode of supplying a district and so adapting it for habitation. I refer to my judgment [3 H. & C. 788; 34 L. J. (Ex.) 181] in Fletcher *v.* Rylands, and I repeat that here the plaintiff had no right that has been infringed, and the defendant has done no wrong. The plaintiff's right is to say to the defendant, *Sic utere tuo ut alienum non lædas,* and that the defendant has done, and no more.

The CHIEF BARON and my brother CLEASBY agree in this judgment. As to the plaintiff's application for a new trial on the ground that the finding of the jury is against evidence, we have spoken to Cockburn, C. J.; he is not dissatisfied therewith, and we cannot see it is wrong. Consequently the rule will be absolute to enter a verdict for the defendant. *Rule absolute.*

In Court of Appeal.

Cotton, Q. C. (*McIntyre,* Q. C., and *Coxon* with him), for the plaintiff, appellant.[1]

Assuming the jury to be right in finding that the defendant was not guilty of negligence, and that the rainfall amounted to *vis major,* or the act of God, still the defendant is liable because she has, without necessity and voluntarily for her own pleasure, stored on her premises an element which was liable to be let loose, and which, if let loose, would be dangerous to her neighbors. Even if she be considered innocent of wrong-doing, why should the plaintiff suffer for the defendant's voluntary act of turning an otherwise harmless stream into a source of danger ? But for the defendant's embankments, the excessive rainfall would have escaped without doing injury.

Gorst, Q. C., and *Hughes* (*Dunn* with them), for defendant, cited Carstairs *v.* Taylor, L. R. 6 Ex. 217; McCoy *v.* Danbey, 20 Penn. State, 85; Tennent *v.* Earl of Glasgow, 1 Court of Session Cases, 3d series, 133.

The judgment of the Court (COCKBURN, C. J., JAMES, and MELLISH, L. JJ., and BAGGALLAY, J. A.) was read by

MELLISH, L. J. This was an action brought by the county surveyor [under 43 Geo. 3, c. 59, s. 4] of the County of Chester against the defendant to recover damages on account of the destruction of four county bridges which had been carried away by the bursting of some reservoirs. At the trial before Cockburn, C. J., it appeared that the defendant was the owner of a series of artificial ornamental lakes, which had existed for a great number of years, and had never, previous to the 18th day of June, 1872, caused any damage. On that day, however, after a most unusual fall of rain, the lakes overflowed, the dams at their end gave way, and the water out of the lakes carried away the county bridges lower down the stream. The jury found that there was no negligence either in the construction or the maintenance of the reservoirs, but that if the flood could have been anticipated, the effect might have been prevented.[2] Upon this finding the Lord Chief Jus-

[1] Argument abridged.

[2] The judgment of the Court below, read by BRAMWELL, B., states the finding thus: " In this case I understand the jury to have found that all reasonable care had been taken by the defendant, that the banks were fit for all events to be anticipated, and the weirs broad enough; that the storm was of such violence as to be properly called the act of God, or *vis major.*"

tice, acting on the decision in Rylands *v.* Fletcher, L. R. 3 H. L. 330, as the nearest authority applicable to the case, directed a verdict for the plaintiff, but gave leave to move to enter a verdict for the defendant. The Court of Exchequer have ordered the verdict to be entered for the defendant, and from their decision an appeal has been brought before us.

The appellant relied upon the decision in the case of Rylands *v.* Fletcher, *supra.* In that case the rule of law on which the case was decided was thus laid down by Mr. Justice Blackburn in the Exchequer Chamber [L. R. 1 Ex. 279]: "We think the true rule of law is that the person who for his own purposes brings on his lands and collects and keeps there anything likely to do mischief if it escapes, must keep it in at his peril, and if he does not do so, is *prima facie* answerable for all the damage which is the natural consequence of its escape. He can excuse himself by showing that the escape was owing to the plaintiff's default; or perhaps that the escape was the consequence of *vis major*, or the act of God; but as nothing of the sort exists here it is unnecessary to inquire what excuse would be sufficient." It appears to us that we have two questions to consider: First, the question of law, which was left undecided in Rylands *v.* Fletcher, *supra,* — Can the defendant excuse herself by showing that the escape of the water was owing to *vis major*, or, as it is termed in the law books, the "act of God?" And, secondly, if she can, did she in fact make out that the escape was so occasioned?

Now, with respect to the first question, the ordinary rule of law is that when the law creates a duty and the party is disabled from performing it without any default of his own, by the act of God, or the King's enemies, the law will excuse him; but when a party by his own contract creates a duty, he is bound to make it good notwithstanding any accident by inevitable necessity. We can see no good reason why that rule should not be applied to the case before us. The duty of keeping the water in and preventing its escape is a duty imposed by the law, and not one created by contract. If, indeed, the making a reservoir was a wrongful act in itself, it might be right to hold that a person could not escape from the consequences of his own wrongful act. But it seems to us absurd to hold that the making or the keeping a reservoir is a wrongful act in itself. The wrongful act is not the making or keeping the reservoir, but the allowing or causing the water to escape. If, indeed, the damages were occasioned by the act of the party without more — as where a man accumulates water on his own land, but, owing to the peculiar nature or condition of the soil, the water escapes and does damage to his neighbor — the case of Rylands *v.* Fletcher, *supra,* establishes that he must be held liable. The accumulation of water in a reservoir is not in itself wrongful; but the making it and suffering the water to escape, if damage ensue, constitute a wrong. But the present case is distinguished from that of Rylands *v.* Fletcher, *supra,* in this, that it is not the act of the defendant in keeping this reservoir, an act in itself lawful, which alone leads to the escape of the water, and so renders wrongful that which but for such escape would have been lawful. It is the supervening *vis major* of the water caused by the flood, which, superadded to the water in the reservoir (which of itself would have been innocuous), causes the disaster. A defendant cannot, in our opinion, be properly said to have caused or allowed the water to escape, if the act of God or the Queen's enemies was the real cause of its escaping without any fault on the part of the defendant. If a reservoir was destroyed by an earthquake, or the Queen's enemies destroyed it in conducting some warlike operation, it would be contrary to all reason and justice to hold the owner of the reservoir liable for any damage that might be done by the escape of the water. We are of opinion, therefore, that the defendant was entitled to excuse herself by proving that the water escaped through the act of God.

The remaining question is, did the defendant make out that the escape of the water was owing to the act of God? Now the jury have distinctly found, not only that there was no negligence in the construction or the maintenance of the reservoirs, but that the flood was so great that it could not reasonably have been anticipated, although, if it had been anticipated, the effect might have been prevented; and this seems to us in substance a finding that the escape of the water was owing to the act of God. However great the flood had been, if it had not been greater than floods that had happened before and might be expected to occur again, the defendant might not have made out that she was free from fault; but we think she ought not to be held liable because she did not prevent the effect of an extraordinary act of nature, which she could not anticipate. In the late case of Nugent *v.* Smith, 1 C. P. D. 423, we held that a carrier might be protected from liability for a loss occasioned by the act of God, if the loss by no reasonable precaution could be prevented, although it was not absolutely impossible to prevent it.

It was indeed ingeniously argued for the appellant that at any rate the escape of the water was not owing solely to the act of God, because the weight of the water originally in the reservoirs must have contributed to break down the dams, as well as the extraordinary water brought in by the flood. We think, however, that the extraordinary quantity of water brought in by the flood is in point of law the sole proximate cause of the escape of the water. It is the last drop which makes the cup overflow.

On the whole we are of opinion that the judgment of the Court of Exchequer ought to be affirmed. *Judgment affirmed.*[1]

[1] See Salmond, Torts (4 ed.) § 65.

BOX v. JUBB

In the Exchequer Division, February 25, 1879.

Reported in Law Reports, 4 Exchequer Division, 76.

Case stated in an action brought in the County Court of Yorkshire, holden at Bradford, to recover damages by reason of the overflowing of a reservoir of the defendants.

1. The defendants are the owners and occupiers of a woollen cloth-mill situate at Batley, in the county of York, and for the necessary supply of water to the mill is a reservoir, also belonging to the defendants. Such mill and reservoir have been built, and constructed, and used, as at the time of the overflowing of the reservoir hereinafter mentioned, for many years.

2. The plaintiff is the tenant of premises adjoining the reservoir.

3. The reservoir is supplied with water from a main drain or watercourse. The surplus water from the reservoir passes through an outlet into the main drain or watercourse. The inlet and outlet are furnished with proper doors or sluices, so as (when required) to close the communications between the reservoir and the main drain or watercourse.

4. The whole of the premises are within the borough of Batley, and the defendants have the right to use the main drain or watercourse by obtaining a supply of water therefrom and discharging their surplus water thereinto, as hereinbefore stated, but have otherwise no control over the drain or watercourse, which does not belong to them.

5. In the month of December, 1877, the plaintiff's premises were flooded by reason of the overflowing of the defendants' reservoir.

6. Such overflowing was caused by the emptying of a large quantity of water from a reservoir, the property of a third party, into the main drain or watercourse at a point considerably above the defendants' premises, and by an obstruction in the main drain or watercourse below the outlet of the defendants' reservoir, whereby the water from such main drain or watercourse was forced through the doors or sluices (which were closed at the time) into the defendants' reservoir.

7. Such obstruction was caused by circumstances over which the defendants had no control, and without their knowledge; and had it not been for such obstruction the overflowing of the reservoir would not have happened.

8. The defendants' reservoir, and the communications between it and the main drain or watercourse, and the doors or sluices, are constructed and maintained in a proper manner, so as to prevent the overflowing of the reservoir under all ordinary circumstances.

9. No negligence or wrongful act is attributable to either party.

Under the circumstances the judge of the County Court was of opinion that the defendants were liable for the damage sustained by the plaintiff, and accordingly gave judgment for the plaintiff.

The question for the opinion of the Court, having regard to the facts set out in the case, was whether the defendants were liable for the damage sustained by the plaintiff by reason of the flooding of his premises, such flooding being caused by water from a reservoir belonging to a third party, over which the defendants had no control, and without any knowledge or negligence on defendants' part, the overflowing of the defendants' reservoir being occasioned by the act of a third party, over whom the defendants had no control, and no wrongful act or negligence being attributable to the defendants, and the direct cause of the damage being the obstruction in the main drain or watercourse, which was caused by circumstances over which the defendants had no control and without their knowledge.[1]

KELLY, C. B. I think this judgment must be reversed. The case states that for many years the defendants have been possessed of a reservoir to which there are gates or sluices. There has been an overflow from the reservoir which has caused damage to the plaintiff. The question is, what was the cause of this overflow? Was it anything for which the defendants are responsible — did it proceed from their act or default, or from that of a stranger over which they had no control? The case is abundantly clear on this, proving beyond a doubt that the defendants had no control over the causes of the overflow, and no knowledge of the existence of the obstruction. The matters complained of took place through no default or breach of duty of the defendants, but were caused by a stranger over whom and at a spot where they had no control. It seems to me to be immaterial whether this is called *vis major* or the unlawful act of a stranger; it is sufficient to say that the defendants had no means of preventing the occurrence. I think the defendants could not possibly have been expected to anticipate that which happened here, and the law does not require them to construct their reservoir and the sluices and gates leading to it to meet any amount of pressure which the wrongful act of a third person may impose. The judgment must be entered for the defendants.

POLLOCK, B. I also think the defendants are entitled to judgment. Looking at the facts stated, that the defendants had no control over the main drain, and no knowledge of or control over the obstruction, apart from the cases, what wrong have the defendants done for which they should be held liable? The case of Rylands *v.* Fletcher, L. R. 3 H. L. 330, is quite distinguishable. The case of Nichols *v.* Marsland, L. R. 10 Ex. 255, 14 Eng. R. 538, is more in point. The illustrations put in that case clearly go to show that if the person who has collected the water has done all that skill and judgment can do he is not liable for damage by acts over which he has no control. In the judgment of the Court of Appeals, 2 Ex. D. 1, at p. 5, Mellish, L. J., adopts the principle laid down by this Court. He says: "If indeed the damages were occasioned by the act of the party without more — as where a

[1] Arguments omitted.

man accumulates water on his own land, but owing to the peculiar nature or condition of the soil the water escapes and does damage to his neighbor — the case of Rylands *v.* Fletcher, *supra*, establishes that he must be held liable." Here this water has not been accumulated by the defendants, but has come from elsewhere and added to that which was properly and safely there. For this the defendants, in my opinion, both on principle and authority, cannot be held liable.

Judgment for the defendants.[1]

MARSHALL *v.* WELWOOD

SUPREME COURT OF NEW JERSEY, JUNE TERM, 1876.

Reported in 38 *New Jersey Law Reports*, 339.

SUIT for damages done to the property of the plaintiff by the bursting of the boiler of a steam-engine on the adjoining property of the defendant Welwood. Garside, the other defendant, had sold this boiler to Welwood, and was experimenting with it at the time of the explosion.

The case came before the Court on a motion for a new trial, the verdict having gone for the plaintiff against both defendants.

Argued at February Term, 1876, before BEASLEY, C. J., and WOODHULL, VAN SYCKEL, and SCUDDER, JJ.

The opinion of the Court was delivered by

BEASLEY, C. J. The judge, at the trial of this cause, charged, among other matters, that as the evidence incontestably showed that one of the defendants. Welwood, was the owner of the boiler which caused the damage, he was liable in the action, unless it appeared that the same was not being run by him, or his agent, at the time of the explosion. The proposition propounded was, that a person is responsible for the immediate consequences of the bursting of a steam boiler, in use by him, irrespective of any question as to negligence or want of skill on his part.

This view of the law is in accordance with the principles maintained, with great learning and force of reasoning, in some of the late English decisions. In this class the leading case was that of Fletcher *v.* Rylands, L. R. 1 Exch. 265, which was a suit on account of damage done by water escaping on to the premises of the plaintiff from a reservoir which the defendant had constructed, with due care and skill, on his own land. The judgment was put on a general ground, for the Court said: " We think the true rule of law is, that the person who, for his own purposes, brings on his lands and collects and keeps there anything likely to do mischief, if it escapes, must keep it in at his peril, and if he does not do so, is *prima facie* answerable for all the damage

[1] See Carstairs *v.* Taylor, L. R. 6 Ex. 217; Wilson *v.* Newberry, L. R. 7 Q. B. 31; Rickards *v.* Lothian, [1913] A. C. 263.

which is the natural consequence of its escape." This result was deemed just, and was sought to be vindicated on the theory that it is but reasonable that a person who has brought something on his own property, which was not naturally there, harmless to others, so long as it is confined to his own property, but which he knows to be mischievous, if it gets on his neighbor's, should be obliged to make good the damage which ensues, if he does not succeed in confining it to his own property. This principle would evidently apply to, and rule, the present case: for water is no more likely to escape from a reservoir and do damage, than steam is from a boiler; and, therefore, if he who collects the former force upon his property, and seeks, with care and skill, to keep it there, is answerable for his want of success, so is he who, under similar conditions, endeavors to deal with the latter. There is nothing unlawful in introducing water into a properly constructed reservoir on a person's own land, nor raising steam in a boiler of proper quality; neither act, when performed, is a nuisance *per se;* and the inquiry consequently is, whether in the doing of such lawful act the party who does it is an insurer against all flaws in the apparatus employed, no matter how secret, or unascertainable by the use of every reasonable test, such flaws may be. This English adjudication takes the affirmative side of the question, conceding, however, that the subject is not controlled by any express decision, and that it is to be investigated with reference to the general grounds of jurisprudence. I have said the doctrine involved has been learnedly treated, and the decision is of great weight, and yet its reasoning has failed to convince me of the correctness of the result to which it leads, and such result is clearly opposed to the course which judicial opinion has taken in this country. The fallacy in the process of argument by which judgment is reached in this case of Fletcher *v.* Rylands, appears to me to consist in this: that the rule mainly applicable to a class of cases which, I think, should be regarded as, in a great degree, exceptional, is amplified and extended into a general, if not universal, principle. The principal instance upon which reliance is placed is the well-known obligation of the owner of cattle, to prevent them from escaping from his land and doing mischief. The law as to this point is perfectly settled, and has been settled from the earliest times, and is to the effect that the owner must take charge of his cattle at his peril, and if they evade his custody he is, in some measure, responsible for the consequences. This is the doctrine of the Year Books, but I do not find that it is grounded in any theoretical principle, making a man answerable for his acts or omissions, without regard to his culpability. That in this particular case of escaping cattle so stringent an obligation upon the owner should grow up, was not unnatural. That the beasts of the landowner should be successfully restrained, was a condition of considerable importance to the unmolested enjoyment of property, and the right to plead that the escape had occurred by inevitable accident would have seriously impaired, if it did not entirely frustrate, the process of distress damage feasant. Custom has had much to do in giving shape to the law, and what is highly convenient readily runs into usage, and is accepted as a rule. It would but rarely occur that cattle would escape from a vigilant owner, and in this instance such rare exceptions seem to have passed unnoticed, for there appears to be no example of the point having been presented for judicial consideration; for the conclusion of the liability of the unnegligent owner rests in *dicta*, and not in express decision. But waiving this, there is a consideration which seems to me to show that this obligation which is put upon the owner of errant cattle should not be taken to be a principle applicable, in a general way, to the use or ownership of property, which is this: that the owner of such cattle is, after all, liable only *sub modo* for the injury done by them, that is, he is responsible, with regard to tame beasts who have no exceptionally vicious disposition so far as is known, for the grass they eat, and such like injuries, but not for the hurt they may inflict upon the person of others, — a restriction on liability which is hardly consistent with the notion that this class of cases proceeds from a principle so wide as to embrace all persons whose lawful acts produce, without fault in them, and in an indirect manner, ill results which disastrously affect innocent persons. If the principle ruling these cases was so broad as this, conformity to it would require that the person being the cause of the mischief should stand as an indemnifier against the whole of the damage. It appears to me, therefoıe, that this rule, which applies to damage done by straying cattle, was carried beyond its true bounds, when it was appealed to [in] proof that a person in law is answerable for the natural consequences of his acts, such acts being lawful in themselves, and having been done with proper care and skill.

The only other cases which were referred to in support of the judgment under consideration were those of one who was sued for not keeping the wall of his privy in repair, to the detriment of his neighbor, being the case of Tenant v. Goulding, 1 Salk. 21, and several actions which it is said had been brought against the owners of some alkali works for damages alleged to have been caused by the chlorine fumes escaping from their works [which], the case showed, had been erected upon the best scientific principles. But I am compelled to think that these cases are but a slender basis for the large structure put upon it. The case of Tenant v. Goulding presented merely the question whether a landowner is bound in favor of his neighbor to keep the wall of his privy in repair, and the Court held that he was, and that he was responsible if, for want of such reparation, the filth escaped on the adjoining land. No question was mooted as to his liability in case the privy had been constructed with care and skill with a view to prevent the escape of its contents, and had been kept in a state of repair. Not to repair a receptacle of this kind when it was in want of repairs was, in itself, a *prima facie* case of negligence, and it seems to me that all the Court decided was to hold so.

But this consideration is also to be noticed, both with respect to this last case, and that of the injurious fumes from the alkali works, that in truth they stand somewhat by themselves, and having this peculiarity: that the things in their nature partake largely of the character of nuisances. Take the alkali works as an example. Placed in a town, under ordinary circumstances, they would be a nuisance. When the attempt is made by scientific methods to prevent the escape of the fumes, it is an attempt to legalize that which is illegal, and the consequence is, it may well be held that, failing in the attempt, the nuisance remains.

I cannot agree that, from these indications, the broad doctrine is to be drawn that a man in law is an insurer that the acts which he does, such acts being lawful and done with care, shall not injuriously affect others. The decisions cited are not so much examples of legal maxims as of exceptions to such maxims; for they stand opposed, and in contrast to principles, which it seems to me must be considered much more general in their operation and elementary in their nature.

The common rule, quite institutional in its character, is that, in order to sustain an action for a tort, the damage complained of must have come from a wrongful act. Mr. Addison, in his work on Torts, Vol. I, p. 3, very correctly states this rule. He says: "A man may, however, sustain grievous damage at the hands of another, and yet, if it be the result of inevitable accident, or a lawful act, done in a lawful manner, without any carelessness or negligence, there is no legal injury, and no tort giving rise to an action of damages." Among other examples, he refers to an act of force, done in necessary self-defence, causing injury to an innocent bystander, which he characterizes as *damnum sine injuria*, — "for no man does wrong or contracts guilt in defending himself against an aggressor." Other instances of a like kind are noted, such as the lawful obstruction of the view from the windows of dwelling-houses; or the turning aside, to the detriment of another, the current of the sea or river, by means of walls or dikes. Many illustrations, of the same bearing, are to be found scattered through the books of reports. Thus, Dyer, 25 b, says: "That if a man have a dog which has killed sheep, the master of the dog being ignorant of such quality and property of the dog, the master shall not be punished for that killing." This case belongs to a numerous, well-known class, where animals which are usually harmless do damage, the decisions being that, under such conditions, the owners of the animals are not responsible. Akin to these in principle are cases of injuries done to innocent persons by horses in the charge of their owners, becoming ungovernable by reason of unexpected causes; or where a person in a dock was struck by the falling of a bale of cotton which the defendants' servants were lowering, Scott *v.* London Dock Co., 3 H. &

C. 596; or in cases of collision, either on land or sea. Hammack *v.* White, 11 C. B. N. S. 588.

It is true that these cases of injury done to personal property, or to persons, are, in the case of Fletcher *v.* Rylands, sought to be distinguished from other damages, on the ground that they are done in the course of traffic on the highways, whether by land or sea, which cannot be conducted without exposing those whose persons or property are near it to some inevitable risk. But this explanation is not sufficiently comprehensive, for, if a frightened horse should, in his flight, break into an inclosure, no matter how far removed from the highway, the owner would not be answerable for the damage done. Nor is the reason upon which it rests satisfactory, for, if traffic cannot be carried on without some risk, why can it not be said with the same truth, that the other affairs of life, though they be transacted away from the highways, cannot be carried on without some risk; and if such risk is, in the one case, to be borne by innocent persons, why not in the other? Business done upon private property may be a part of traffic as well as that done by the means of the highway, and no reason is perceived why the same favor is not to be extended to it in both situations. But, besides this, the reason thus assigned for the immunity of him who is the unwilling producer of the damage has not been the ground on which the decisions illustrative of the rule have been put; that ground has been that the person sought to be charged had not done any unlawful act. Everywhere, in all the branches of the law, the general principle that blame must be imputable as a ground of responsibility for damage proceeding from a lawful act, is apparent. A passenger is injured by the breaking of an axle of a public conveyance; the carrier is not liable, unless negligence can be shown. A man's guest is hurt by the falling of a chandelier; a suit will not lie against the host, without proof that he knew, or ought to have known of the existence of the danger. If the steam-engine which did the mischief in the present case had been in use in driving a train of cars on a railroad, and had, in that situation, exploded, and had inflicted injuries on travellers or bystanders, it could not have been pretended that such damage was actionable, in the absence of the element of negligence or unskilfulness. By changing the place of the accident to private property, I cannot agree that a different rule obtains.

It seems to me, therefore, that in this case it was necessary to submit the matter, as a question of fact for the jury, whether the occurrence doing the damage complained of, was the product of pure accident, or the result of want of care or skill on the part of the defendant or his agents.

This view of the subject is taken in the American decisions. A case, in all respects in point, is that of Losee *v.* Buchanan, 51 N. Y. 476; S. C. 10 Am. Rep. 623. The facts were essentially the same with those of the principal case. It was an action growing out of the explosion of a steam boiler upon private property, and the ruling was that such action could not be sustained without proof of fault or negligence. In that report the line of cases is so fully set out that it is unnecessary here to repeat them.

The rule should be made absolute.[1]

BROWN *v.* COLLINS

SUPREME COURT, NEW HAMPSHIRE, JUNE, 1873.

Reported in 53 *New Hampshire Reports*, 442.

TRESPASS, by Albert H. Brown against Lester Collins, to recover the value of a stone post on which was a street lamp, situated in front of his place of business in the village of Tilton. The post stood upon the plaintiff's land, but near the southerly line of the main highway leading through the village and within four feet of said line. There was nothing to indicate the line of the highway, nor any fence or other obstruction between the highway, as travelled, and the post. The highway crosses the railroad near the place of accident, and the stone post stood about fifty feet from the railroad track at the crossing. The defendant was in the highway, at or near the railroad crossing, with a pair of horses loaded with grain, going to the grist-mill in Tilton village. The horses became frightened by an engine on the railroad near the crossing, and by reason thereof became unmanageable, and ran, striking the post with the end of the pole and breaking it off near the ground, destroying the lamp with the post. No other injury was done by the accident. The shock produced by the collision with the post threw the defendant from his seat in the wagon, and he struck on the ground between the horses, but suffered no injury except a slight concussion. The defendant was in the use of ordinary care and skill in managing his team, until they became frightened as aforesaid.

The foregoing facts were agreed upon for the purpose of raising the question of the right of the plaintiff to recover in this action.

[1] Actiesselskabet Ingrid *v.* Central R. Co., (C. C. A.) 216 Fed. 72 (explosives); Judson *v.* Giant Powder Co., 107 Cal. 549 (explosives); Lake Shore R. Co. *v.* Chicago R. Co., 48 Ind. App. 584 (semble); Owensboro *v.* Knox, 116 Ky. 451 (electricity); Murphy *v.* Gillum, 73 Mo. App. 478 (semble); Losee *v.* Buchanan, 51 N. Y. 476 (boiler); Cosulich *v.* Standard Oil Co., 122 N. Y. 118 (petroleum); Huff *v.* Austin, 46 Ohio St. 386 (boiler); Pennsylvania Coal Co. *v.* Sanderson, 113 Pa. St. 126 (semble); Sowers *v.* McManus, 214 Pa. St. 244 (explosives); Davis *v.* Charleston R. Co., 72 S. C. 112 (boiler) *Accord.*

Bursting of dam, see: Alabama Coal & Iron Co. *v.* Turner, 145 Ala. 639; Todd *v.* Cochell, 17 Cal. 97; Shrewsbury *v.* Smith, 12 Cush. 177; City Water Power Co. *v.* City, 113 Minn. 33; King *v.* Miles City Co., 16 Mont. 463; Livingston *v.* Adams, 8 Cow. 175; Lapham *v.* Curtis, 5 Vt. 371. Compare Pennock *v.* Central R. Co., 159 App. Div. 517.

As to constitutionality of legislation imposing liability without fault, see City *v.* Sturges, 222 U. S. 313, 322; Pittsburgh R. Co. *v.* Home Ins. Co., 183 Ind. 355; Daugherty *v.* Thomas, 174 Mich. 371; Ives *v.* South Buffalo R. Co., 201 N. Y. 271, 295–298.

DOE, J. It is agreed that the defendant was in the use of ordinary care and skill in managing his horses, until they were frightened; and that they then became unmanageable, and ran against and broke a post on the plaintiff's land. It is not explicitly stated that the defendant was without actual fault, — that he was not guilty of any malice, or unreasonable unskilfulness or negligence; but it is to be inferred that the fact was so; and we decide the case on that ground. We take the case as one where, without actual fault in the defendant, his horses broke from his control, ran away with him, went upon the plaintiff's land, and did damage there, against the will, intent, and desire of the defendant.

Sir Thomas Raymond's report of Lambert & Olliot *v.* Bessey, T. Raym. 421, and Bessey *v.* Olliot & Lambert, T. Raym. 467, is, " The question was this: A gaoler takes from the bailiff a prisoner arrested by him out of the bailiff's jurisdiction, Whether the gaoler be liable to an action of false imprisonment ? and the judges of the common pleas did all hold that he was; and of that opinion I am, for these reasons.

" 1. In all civil acts, the law doth not so much regard the intent of the actor, as the loss and damage of the party suffering; and therefore Mich. 6 E. 4, 7 *a. pl.* 18. *Trespass quare vi & armis clausum fregit & herbam suam pedibus conculcando consumpsit* in six acres. The defendant pleads that he hath an acre lying next the said six acres, and upon it a hedge of thorns, and he cut the thorns, and they, *ipso invito,* fell upon the plaintiff's land, and the defendant took them off as soon as he could, which is the same trespass; and the plaintiff demurred; and adjudged for the plaintiff; for though a man doth a lawful thing, yet if any damage do thereby befall another, he shall answer for it if he could have avoided it. As if a man lop a tree, and the boughs fall upon another, *ipso invito,* yet an action lies. If a man shoot at butts, and hurt another unawares, an action lies. I have land through which a river runs to your mill, and I lop the fallows growing upon the river side, which accidentally stop the water, so as your mill is hindered, an action lies. If I am building my own house, and a piece of timber falls on my neighbor's house, and breaks part of it, an action lies. If a man assault me, and I lift up my staff to defend myself, and, in lifting it up, hit another, an action lies by that person, and yet I did a lawful thing. And the reason of all these cases is, because he that is damaged ought to be recompensed. But otherwise it is in criminal cases, for there *actus non facit reum nisi mens sit rea.*

" Mich. 23. Car. 1. B. R. — Stile 72, Guilbert *versus* Stone. Trespass for entering his close, and taking away his horse. The defendant pleads, that he, for fear of his life, by threats of twelve men, went into the plaintiff's house, and took the horse. The plaintiff demurred; and adjudged for the plaintiff, because threats could not excuse the defendant, and make satisfaction to the plaintiff.

"Hob. 134, Weaver *versus* Ward. Trespass of assault and battery. The defendant pleads, that he was a trained soldier in London, and he and the plaintiff were skirmishing with their company, and the defendant, with his musket, *casualiter & per infortunium & contra voluntatem suam* in discharging of his gun hurt the plaintiff; and resolved no good plea. So here, though the defendant knew not of the wrongful taking of the plaintiff, yet that will not make any recompense for the wrong the plaintiff hath sustained. . . . But the three other judges resolved, that the defendant, the gaoler, could not be charged, because he could not have notice whether the prisoner was legally arrested or not."

In Fletcher *v.* Rylands,[1] L. R. 3 H. L. 330, Lord Cranworth said: "In considering whether a defendant is liable to a plaintiff for damage which the plaintiff may have sustained, the question in general is not whether the defendant has acted with due care and caution, but whether his acts have occasioned the damage. This is all well explained in the old case of Lambert *v.* Bessey, reported by Sir Thomas Raymond (Sir T. Raym. 421). And the doctrine is founded on good sense. For when one person, in managing his own affairs, causes, however innocently, damage to another, it is obviously only just that he should be the party to suffer."

The head-note of Weaver *v.* Ward. Hob. 134, is: "If one trained soldier wound another, in skirmishing for exercise, an action of trespass will lie, unless it shall appear from the defendant's plea that he was guilty of no negligence, and that the injury was inevitable." The reason of the decision, as reported, was this: "For though it were agreed, that if men tilt or tourney in the presence of the king, or if two masters of defence playing their prizes kill one another, that this shall be no felony; or if a lunatic kill a man, or the like; because felony must be done *animo felonico;* yet in trespass, which tends only to give damages according to hurt or loss, it is not so; and therefore if a lunatic hurt a man, he shall be answerable in trespass; and therefore no man shall be excused of a trespass (for this is the nature of an excuse, and not of a justification, *prout ei bene licuit*), except it may be judged utterly without his fault; as if a man by force take my hand and strike you; or if here the defendant had said that the plaintiff ran across his piece when it was discharging; or had set forth the case with the circumstances, so as it had appeared to the Court that it had been inevitable, and that the defendant had committed no negligence to give occasion to the hurt."

There may be some ground to argue that "utterly without his fault," "inevitable," and "no negligence," in the sense intended in that case, mean no more than the modern phrase "ordinary and reasonable care and prudence;" and that, in such a case, at the present

[1] See Cahill *v.* Eastman, 18 Minn. 324; Madras R. Co. *v.* Zemindar of Carvatenagarum, L. R. 1 Ind. App. 364. — Reporter's Note.

time, to hold a plea good that alleges the exercise of reasonable care, without setting forth all " the circumstances " or evidence sustaining the plea, would be substantially in compliance with the law of that case, due allowance being made for the difference of legal language used at different periods, and the difference in the forms of pleading. But the drift of the ancient English authorities on the law of torts seems to differ materially from the view now prevailing in this country. Formerly, in England, there seems to have been no well-defined test of an actionable tort. Defendants were often held liable "because," as Raymond says, "he that is damaged ought to be recompensed;" and not because, upon some clearly stated principle of law founded on actual culpability, public policy, or natural justice, he was entitled to compensation from the defendant. The law was supposed to regard " the loss and damage of the party suffering," more than the negligence and blameworthiness of the defendant: but how much more it regarded the former than the latter, was a question not settled, and very little investigated. " The loss and damage of the party suffering," if without relief, would be a hardship to him; relief compulsorily furnished by the other party would often be a hardship to him; when and why the " loss and damage " should, and when and why they should not, be transferred from one to the other, by process of law, were problems not solved in a philosophical manner. There were precedents, established upon superficial, crude, and undigested notions; but no application of the general system of legal reason to this subject.

Mr. Holmes says: " It may safely be stated that all the more ancient examples are traceable to conceptions of a much ruder sort (than actual fault), and in modern times to more or less definitely thought-out views of public policy. The old writs in trespass did not allege, nor was it necessary to show, anything savoring of culpability. It was enough that a certain event had happened, and it was not even necessary that the act should be done intentionally, though innocently. An accidental blow was as good a cause of action as an intentional one. On the other hand, when, as in Rylands v. Fletcher, modern courts hold a man liable for the escape of water from a reservoir which he has built upon his land, or for the escape of cattle, although he is not alleged to have been negligent, they do not proceed upon the ground that there is an element of culpability in making such a reservoir, or in keeping cattle, sufficient to charge the defendant as soon as a *damnum* occurs, but on the principle that it is politic to make those who go into extra-hazardous employments take the risk on their own shoulders." He alludes to the fact that " there is no certainty what will be thought extra-hazardous in a certain jurisdiction at a certain time," but suggests that many particular instances point to the general principle of liability for the consequences of extra-hazardous undertakings as the tacitly assumed ground of decision

7 Am. Law Rev. 652, 653, 662; 2 Kent Com. (12th ed.) 561, *n.* 1; 4 *id.* 110, n. 1. If the hazardous nature of things or of acts is adopted as the test, or one of the tests, and the English authorities are taken as the standard of what is to be regarded as hazardous, " it will be necessary to go the length of saying that an owner of real property is liable for all damage resulting to his neighbor's property from anything done upon his own land " (Mellish's argument in Fletcher *v.* Rylands, L. R. 1 Ex. 272), and that an individual is answerable " who, for his own benefit, makes an improvement on his own land, according to his best skill and diligence, and not foreseeing it will produce any injury to his neighbor, if he thereby unwittingly injure his neighbor " — Gibbs, C. J., in Sutton *v.* Clarke, 6 Taunt. 44, approved by Blackburn, J., in Fletcher *v.* Rylands, L. R. 1 Ex. 286. If danger is adopted as a test, and the English authorities are abandoned, the fact of danger, controverted in each case, will present a question for the jury, and expand the issue of tort or no tort into a question of reasonableness, in a form much broader than has been generally used; or courts will be left to devise tests of peril, under varying influences of time and place that may not immediately produce a uniform, consistent, and permanent rule.

It would seem that some of the early English decisions were based on a view as narrow as that which regards nothing but the hardship " of the party suffering; " disregards the question whether, by transferring the hardship to the other party, anything more will be done than substitute one suffering party for another; and does not consider what legal reason can be given for relieving the party who has suffered, by making another suffer the expense of his relief. For some of those decisions, better reasons may now be given than were thought of when the decisions were announced: but whether a satisfactory test of an actionable tort can be extracted from the ancient authorities, and whether the few modern cases that carry out the doctrine of those authorities as far as it is carried in Fletcher *v.* Rylands (3 H. & C. 774; L. R. 1 Ex. 265; L. R. 3 H. L. 330) can be sustained, is very doubtful. The current of American authority is very strongly against some of the leading English cases.

One of the strongest presentations of the extreme English view is by Blackburn, J., who says, in Fletcher *v.* Rylands, L. R. 1 Ex. 279, 280, 281, 282: " We think that the true rule of law is, that the person who for his own purposes brings on his lands, and collects and keeps there anything likely to do mischief if it escapes, must keep it in at his peril, and if he does not do so, is *prima facie* answerable for all the damage which is the natural consequence of its escape. He can excuse himself by showing that the escape was owing to the plaintiff's default; or perhaps that the escape was the consequence of *vis major*, or the act of God; but as nothing of this sort exists here, it is unnecessary to inquire what excuse would be sufficient. The general rule, as above stated, seems, on principle, just. The person whose grass or corn is eaten down by the escaping cattle of his neighbor, or whose mine is flooded by the water from his neighbor's reservoir, or whose cellar is invaded by the filth of his neighbor's privy, or whose habitation is made unhealthy by the fumes and noisome vapors of his neighbor's alkali works, is damnified without any fault of his own; and it seems but reasonable and just that the neighbor, who has brought something on his own property which was not naturally there, harmless to others so long as it is confined to his own property, but which he knows to be mischievous if it gets on his neighbor's, should be obliged to make good the damage which ensues if he does not succeed in confining it to his own property. But for his act in bringing it there no mischief could have accrued, and it seems but just that he should, at his peril, keep it there so that no mischief may accrue, or answer for the natural and anticipated consequences. And upon authority, this we think is established to be the law, whether the things so brought be beasts, or water, or filth, or stenches. The case that has most commonly occurred, and which is most frequently to be found in the books, is as to the obligation of the owner of cattle which he has brought on his land, to prevent their escaping and doing mischief. The law, as to them, seems to be perfectly settled from early times: the owner must keep them in at his peril, or he will be answerable for the natural consequences of their escape, — that is, with regard to tame beasts, for the grass they eat and trample upon, though not for any injury to the person of others, for our ancestors have settled that it is not the general nature of horses to kick, or bulls to gore [or he might have added, dogs to bite], — but if the owner knows that the beast has a vicious propensity to attack man, he will be answerable for that too. . . . In these latter authorities [relating to animals called mischievous or ferocious], the point under consideration was damage to the person; and what was decided was, that where it was known that hurt to the person was the natural consequence of the animal being loose, the owner should be responsible in damages for such hurt though where it was not known to be so, the owner was not responsible for such damages; but where the damage is, like eating grass or other ordinary ingredients in damage feasant, the natural consequence of the escape, the rule as to keeping in the animal is the same. . . . There does not appear to be any difference, in principle, between the extent of the duty cast on him who brings cattle on his land to keep them in, and the extent of the duty imposed on him who brings on his land water, filth, or stenches, or any other thing, which will, if it escape, naturally do damage, to prevent their escaping and injuring his neighbor."

This seems to be substantially an adoption of the early authorities, and an extension of the ancient practice of holding the defendant liable, in some cases, on the partial view that regarded the misfortune of the plaintiff upon whom a damage had fallen, and required no legal reason for transferring the damage to the defendant. The ancient rule was, that a person in whose house, or on whose land, a fire accidentally originated, which spread to his neighbor's property and destroyed it, must make good the loss. Filliter *v.* Phippard, 11 A. & E. N. S. 347, 354; Tubervil *v.* Stamp, 1 Comyns, 32; s. c. 1 Salk. 13; Com. Dig., Action upon the case for Negligence (A 6); 1 Arch. N. P. 539; Fletcher *v.* Rylands, 3 H. & C. 790, 793; Russell *v.* Fabyan, 34 N. H. 218, 225. No inquiry was made into the reason of putting upon him his neighbor's loss as well as his own. The rule of such cases is applied, by Blackburn, to everything which a man brings on his land, which will, if it escape, naturally do damage. One result of such a doctrine is, that every one building a fire on his own hearth, for necessary purposes, with the utmost care, does so at the peril, not only of losing his own house, but of being irretrievably ruined if a spark from his chimney starts a conflagration which lays waste the neighborhood. "In conflict with the rule, as laid down in the English cases, is a class of cases in reference to damage from fire communicated from the adjoining premises. Fire, like water or steam, is likely to produce mischief if it escapes and goes beyond control; and yet it has never been held in this country that one building a fire upon his own premises can be made liable if it escapes upon his neighbor's premises, and does him damage without proof of negligence." Losee *v.* Buchanan, 51 N. Y. 476, 487.

Everything that a man can bring on his land is capable of escaping, — against his will, and without his fault, with or without assistance, in some form, solid, liquid, or gaseous, changed or unchanged by the transforming processes of nature or art, — and of doing damage after its escape. Moreover, if there is a legal principle that makes a man liable for the natural consequences of the escape of things which he brings on his land, the application of such a principle cannot be limited to those things; it must be applied to all his acts that disturb the original order of creation; or, at least, to all things which he undertakes to possess or control anywhere, and which were not used and enjoyed in what is called the natural or primitive condition of mankind, whatever that may have been. This is going back a long way for a standard of legal rights, and adopting an arbitrary test of responsibility that confounds all degrees of danger, pays no heed to the essential elements of actual fault, puts a clog upon natural and reasonably necessary uses of matter, and tends to embarrass and obstruct much of the work which it seems to be man's duty carefully to do. The distinction made by Lord Cairns, Rylands *v.* Fletcher, L. R. 3 H. L. 330, between a natural and a non-natural use of land, if he meant anything more than the difference between a reasonable use and an unreasonable one, is not established in the law. Even if the arbitrary test were applied only to things which a man brings on his land, it would still recognize the peculiar rights of savage life in a wilderness, ignore the rights growing out of a civilized state of society, and make a distinction not warranted by the enlightened spirit of the common law: it would impose a penalty upon efforts, made in a reasonable, skilful, and careful manner, to rise above a condition of barbarism. It is impossible that legal principle can throw so serious an obstacle in the way of progress and improvement. Natural rights are, in general, legal rights; and the rights of civilization are, in a legal sense, as natural as any others. " Most of the rights of property, as well as of person, in the social state, are not absolute but relative," Losee *v.* Buchanan, 51 N. Y. 485; and, if men ever were in any other than the social state, it is neither necessary nor expedient that they should now govern themselves on the theory that they ought to live in some other state. The common law does not usually establish tests of responsibility on any other basis than the propriety of their living in the social state, and the relative and qualified character of the rights incident to that state.

In Fletcher *v.* Rylands, L. R. 1 Ex. 286, 287, Mr. Justice Blackburn, commenting upon the remark of Mr. Baron Martin, " that, when damage is done to personal property, or even to the person, by collision, either upon land or at sea, there must be negligence in the party doing the damage to render him legally responsible," says, — " This is no doubt true; and, as was pointed out by Mr. Mellish during his argument before us, this is not confined to cases of collision, for there are many cases in which proof of negligence is essential, as, for instance, where an unruly horse gets on the footpath of a public street and kills a passenger, Hammack *v.* White, 11 C. B. N. S. 588, 31 L. J. (C. P.) 129; or where a person in a dock is struck by the falling of a bale of cotton which the defendant's servants are lowering, Scott *v.* London Docks Company, 3 H. & C. 596, 35 L. J. (Ex.) 17, 220; and many other similar cases may be found. But we think these cases distinguishable from the present. Traffic on the highways, whether by land or sea, cannot be conducted without exposing those whose persons or property are near it to some inevitable risk; and that being so, those who go on the highway, or have their property adjacent to it, may well be held to do so subject to their taking upon themselves the risk of injury from that inevitable danger; and persons who, by the license of the owner, pass near to warehouses where goods are being raised or lowered, certainly do so subject to the inevitable risk of accident. In neither case, therefore, can they recover without proof of want of care or skill occasioning the accident; and it is believed that all the cases in which inevitable accident has been held an excuse for what, *prima facie*, was a trespass, can be explained on the same principle, viz., that the circumstances were such as to show that the plaintiff had taken that risk upon himself." This would be authority for holding, in the present case, that the plaintiff, by having his post near the street, took upon himself the risk of its being broken by an inevitable accident carrying a traveller off the street. But such a doctrine would open more questions, and more difficult ones, than it would settle. At what distance from a highway would an object be near it? What part of London is not near a street? And then, as the defendant had as good a right to be at home with his horses as to be in the highway, why might not his neighbor, by electing to live in an inhabited country, as well be held to take upon himself the risk of an inevitable accident happening by reason of the country being inhabited, as to assume a highway risk by living near a road? If neighborhood is the test, who are a man's neighbors but the whole human race? If a person, by remaining in England, is held to take upon himself one class of the inevitable dangers of that country because he could avoid that class by migrating to a region of solitude, why should he not, for a like reason, also be held to expose himself voluntarily to other classes of the inevitable dangers of that country? And where does this reasoning end?

It is not improbable that the rules of liability for damage done by brutes or by fire, found in the early English cases, were introduced by sacerdotal influence, from what was supposed to be the Roman or the Hebrew law. 7 Am. L. Rev. 652, note; 1 Domat Civil Law (Strahan's translation, 2d ed.), 304, 305, 306, 312, 313; Exodus xxi 28–32, 36; xxii. 5, 6, 9. It would not be singular if these rules should be spontaneously produced at a certain period in the life of any community. Where they first appeared is of little consequence in the present inquiry. They were certainly introduced in England at an immature stage of English jurisprudence, and an undeveloped state of agriculture, manufactures, and commerce, when the nation had not settled down to those modern, progressive, industrial pursuits which the spirit of the common law, adapted to all conditions of society, encourages and defends. They were introduced when the development of many of the rational rules now universally recognized as principles of the common law had not been demanded by the growth of intelligence, trade, and productive enterprise, — when the common law had not been set forth in the precedents, as a coherent and logical system on many subjects other than the tenures of real estate. At all events, whatever may be said of the origin of those rules, to extend them, as they were extended in Rylands *v.* Fletcher, seems to us contrary to the analogies and the general principles of the common law, as now established. To extend them to the present case would be contrary to American authority as well as to our understanding of legal principles.

The difficulty under which the plaintiff might labor in proving the culpability of the defendant, — which is sometimes given as a reason for imposing an absolute liability without evidence of negligence, — Rixford *v.* Smith, 52 N. H. 355, 359, or changing the burden of proof, Lisbon *v.* Lyman, 49 N. H. 553, 568, 569, 574, 575, seems not to have been given in the English cases relating to damage done by brutes or fire. And, however large or small the class of cases in which such a difficulty may be the foundation of a rule of law, since the difficulty has been so much reduced by the abolition of witness disabilities, the present case is not one of that class.

There are many cases where a man is held liable for taking, converting (C. R. Co. *v.* Foster, 51 N. H. 490) or destroying property, or doing something else, or causing it to be done, intentionally, under a claim of right, and without any actual fault. "Probably one half of the cases in which trespass *de bonis asportatis* is maintained, arise from a mere misapprehension of legal rights." Metcalf, J., in Stanley *v.* Gaylord, 1 Cush. 536, 551. When a defendant erroneously supposed, without any fault of either party, that he had a right to do what he did, and his act, done in the assertion of his supposed right, turns out to have been an interference with the plaintiff's property, he is generally held to have assumed the risk of maintaining the right which he asserted, and the responsibility of the natural consequences of his voluntary act. But when there was no fault on his part, and the damage was not caused by his voluntary and intended act; or by an act of which he knew, or ought to have known, the damage would be a necessary, probable, or natural consequence; or by an act which he knew or ought to have known, to be unlawful, — we understand the general rule to be, that he is not liable. Vincent *v.* Stinehour, 7 Vt. 62; Aaron *v.* State, 31 Ga. 167; Morris *v.* Platt, 32 Conn. 75; and Judge Redfield's note to that case in 4 Am. L. Reg. N. S. 532; Townshend on Slander, secs. 67, 88, p. 128, n. 1 (2d ed.). In Brown *v.* Kendall, 6 Cush. 292, the defendant, having interfered to part his dog and the plaintiff's which were fighting, in raising a stick for that purpose accidentally struck the plaintiff, and injured him. It was held, that parting the dogs was a lawful and proper act which the defendant might do by the use of proper and safe means; and that if the plaintiff's injury was caused by such an act done with due care and all proper precautions, the defendant was not liable. In the decision, there is the important suggestion that some of the apparent confusion in the authorities has arisen from discussions of the question whether a party's remedy is in trespass or case, and from the statement that when the injury comes from a direct act, trespass lies, and when the damage is consequential, case is the proper form of action, — the remark concerning the immediate effect of an act being made with reference to damage for which it is admitted there is a remedy of some kind, and on the question of the proper remedy, not on the general question of liability. Judge Shaw, delivering the opinion of the court, said: "We think, as the result of all the authorities, the rule is correctly stated by Mr. Greenleaf, that the plaintiff must come prepared with evidence to show either that the *intention* was unlawful, or that the defendant was *in fault;* for if the injury was unavoidable, and the conduct of the defendant was free from blame, he will not be liable. 2 Greenl. Ev., secs. 85 to 92; Wakeman *v.* Robinson, 1 Bing. 213. If, in the prosecution of a lawful act, a casualty purely accidental arises, no action can be supported for an injury arising therefrom. Davis *v.* Saunders, 2 Chit. R. 639; Com. Dig. Battery, A. (Day's ed.) and notes; Vincent *v.* Stinehour, 7 Vt. 62;" James *v.* Campbell, 5 C. & P. 372; Alderson *v.* Waistell, 1 C. & K. 358.

Whatever may be the rule or the exception, or the reason of it, in case of insanity, Weaver *v.* Ward, Hob. 134; Com. Dig. Battery, A. note *d*, Hammond's ed.; Dormay *v.* Borradaile, 5 M. G. & S. 380; Sedgwick on Damages, 455, 456, 2d ed.; Morse *v.* Crawford, 17 Vt. 499; Dickinson *v.* Barber, 9 Mass. 225; Krom *v.* Schoonmaker, 3 Barb. 647; Horner *v.* Marshall, 5 Munf. 466; Yeates *v.* Reed, 4 Blackf. 463, and whatever may be the full legal definitions of necessity, inevitable danger, and unavoidable accident, the occurrence complained of in this case was one for which the defendant is not liable, unless every one is liable for all damage done by superior force overpowering him, and using him or his property as an instrument of violence. The defendant, being without fault, was as innocent as if the pole of his wagon had been hurled on the plaintiff's land by a whirlwind, or he himself, by a stronger man, had been thrown through the plaintiff's window. Upon the facts stated, taken in the sense in which we understand them, the defendant is entitled to judgment. 1 Hilliard on Torts, ch. 3, 3d ed.; Losee *v.* Buchanan, 51 N. Y. 476; Parrot *v.* Wells, 15 Wall. 524, 537; Roche *v.* M. G. L. Co., 5 Wis. 55; Eastman *v.* Co., 44 N. H. 143, 156. *Case discharged.*

McCORD RUBBER CO. *v.* St. JOSEPH WATER CO.

SUPREME COURT, MISSOURI, MAY 25, 1904.

Reported in 181 *Missouri Reports*, 678.

APPEAL from Buchanan Circuit Court.

Action for damages for the flooding of plaintiff's cellar with water caused by defendant's negligence, whereby a large quantity of its goods stored in the cellar were damaged. Answer, a general denial.[1]

Defendant company supplied water distributed through pipes and mains from reservoirs. A service pipe from a main carried water to a building occupied by one August. There was a bursting in a " fish trap " used in connection with the service pipe. Water escaped on to the premises of August, and from thence to the adjoining premises of the plaintiff company. The jury found a verdict for the defendant. In view of the instructions given, this verdict must be regarded as negativing the allegations of negligence contained in the plaintiff's pleading.

Judgment having been rendered for defendant, the plaintiff appealed.

[Arguments and part of opinion omitted.]

[1] Only so much of the case is given as relates to a single point.

VALLIANT, J. . . . III. The plaintiff contends, however, that the defendants are liable regardless of whether they were guilty of any negligence directly causing the accident. This contention rests in the theory that one who brings into his premises anything that is liable to escape, and liable to inflict injury on his neighbors if it should escape, brings it there at his peril, and is responsible for any injury that it may cause.

That contention rests for its authority on the decision in Rylands *v.* Fletcher, L. R. 3 H. L. 330. In the briefs of the learned counsel for respondents, reference is made to a large number of authorities going to show that the doctrine of Rylands *v.* Fletcher has not been approved generally in America, and that it has been modified in England. Among the authorities so referred to are Griffith *v.* Lewis, 17 Mo. App. 605; Murphy *v.* Gillum, 73 Mo. App. 487; Cooley on Torts, 570; Losee *v.* Buchanan, 51 N. Y. 476; Brown *v.* Collins, 53 N. H. 442.

But in the facts, the case at bar is distinguished from Rylands *v.* Fletcher.

[After stating the facts of Rylands *v.* Fletcher, and quoting from the opinion of Lord Chancellor CAIRNS.] There is a wide difference between a great volume of water collected in a reservoir in dangerous proximity to the premises of another and water brought into a house through pipes in the manner usual in all cities, for the ordinary use of the occupants of the house. Whilst water so brought into a house cannot literally be said to have come in in the course of what might be called in the language above quoted of the Lord Chancellor "natural user" of the premises, yet it is brought in by the method universally in use in cities and is not to be treated as an unnatural gathering of a dangerous agent. The law applicable to the caging of ferocious animals is not applicable to water brought into a house by pipes in the usual manner.

The learned counsel for the plaintiff tried their case on the theory that the defendants were negligent, and that is the only theory on which they could have tried it.

. . . .

Judgment affirmed.[1]

GILES *v.* WALKER

IN THE QUEEN'S BENCH DIVISION, MARCH 27, 1890.

Reported in Law Reports, 24 *Queen's Bench Division,* 656.

APPEAL from the Leicester County Court.

The defendant, a farmer, occupied land which had originally been forest land, but which had some years prior to 1883, when the de-

[1] *Damage through escape of gas from pipes,* see: Gould *v.* Winona Gas Co., 100 Minn. 258; Taylor *v.* St. Joseph Gas Co., 185 Mo. App. 537; Morgan *v.* United Gas Co., 214 Pa. St. 109; Windish *v.* Peoples Gas Co., 248 Pa. St. 236.

fendant's occupation of it commenced, been brought into cultivation by the then occupier. The forest land prior to cultivation did not bear thistles; but immediately upon its being cultivated thistles sprang up all over it. The defendant neglected to mow the thistles periodically so as to prevent them from seeding, and in the years 1887 and 1888 there were thousands of thistles on his land in full seed. The consequence was that the thistle seeds were blown by the wind in large quantities on to the adjoining land of the plaintiff, where they took root and did damage. The plaintiff sued the defendant for such damage in the county court. The judge left to the jury the question whether the defendant in not cutting the thistles had been guilty of negligence. The jury found that he was negligent, and judgment was accordingly entered for the plaintiff. The defendant appealed.

Toller, for the defendant. The facts of this case do not establish any cause of action. The judge was wrong in leaving the question of negligence to the jury. Before a person can be charged with negligence, it must be shown that there is a duty on him to take care. But here there is no such duty. The defendant did not bring the thistles on to his land; they grew there naturally. [He was stopped by the court.]

R. Bray, for the plaintiff. If the defendant's predecessor had left the land in its original condition as forest land the thistles would never have grown. By bringing it into cultivation, and so disturbing the natural condition of things, he caused the thistles to grow, thereby creating a nuisance on the land just as much as if he had intentionally grown them. The defendant, by entering into occupation of the land with the nuisance on it, was under a duty to prevent damage from thereby accruing to his neighbor. The case resembles that of Crowhurst *v.* Amersham Burial Board, 4 Ex. D. 5, where the defendants were held responsible for allowing the branches of their yew trees to grow over their boundary, whereby a horse of the plaintiff, being placed at pasture in the adjoining field, ate some of the yew twigs and died.

LORD COLERIDGE, C. J. I never heard of such an action as this. There can be no duty as between adjoining occupiers to cut the thistles, which are the natural growth of the soil. The appeal must be allowed.

LORD ESHER, M. R. I am of the same opinion.

Appeal allowed.[1]

[1] Herndon *v.* Stultz, 124 Ia. 734 *Accord.* But see Indiana, Burns' Ann. Stat., 1914, §§ 5524–5525; Texas, McEachin's Civil Stat., arts. 6601–6602.
As to constitutionality of such legislation, see Ex parte Hodges, 87 Cal. 162.

GALVESTON, H. & S. A. R. CO. *v.* SPINKS

COURT OF CIVIL APPEALS, TEXAS, MAY 28, 1896.

Reported in 13 *Texas Civil Appeals,* 542.

WILLIAMS, Associate Justice. This case is submitted upon the facts found by the court below, upon an assignment which questions the correctness of the conclusion of law based upon them. In brief, those facts are, that appellant owns in fee a strip of land upon which its railroad is laid, and on each side of which lie cultivated lands owned by appellee. Upon the land owned by appellant there stands a natural growth of tall trees which shade and injure the crops upon appellee's adjacent land, and also saps such land of its fertility. For this injury to crops and land the judgment appealed from was rendered. No act of defendant is shown beyond the construction and maintenance of its road and its omission to cut down its trees, it having removed only such portion of them as was necessary to permit the repair of its road and the operation of its trains. We know of no principle of law which authorizes the judgment. The land and the trees are the property of appellant, and it has the same right to them that appellee has to his land and crops. The exercise of one right is not an invasion of the other. If the presence of the trees impairs the productiveness of appellee's land, or if the cultivation of the latter would injure the trees, these results would constitute no wrong by one owner to the other, but would only be the incidents of their ownership. No breach of any duty owed by appellant to appellee is shown. It is not stated that the roots or the branches of the trees penetrate or overhang appellee's land. If they did, appellee had the right to remove such roots or branches as entered or overhung his land, or if damage was caused by them, it may be true that he could maintain an action for such damage. Wood on Nuisances, 112, 113, 306.

But no such case is made here either in the statement of the cause of action or in the facts found by the court. It is not shown that appellee has not kept its right of way in proper condition for the safe and proper operation of its trains, but the contrary is inferable from the findings. Had it failed to do so, this might be a breach of the duty which it owed to those interested in the manner in which it conducted its road, but not of one due to appellee to protect his land and crops from such damage as that of which he complains. It is urged that as there is no statement of facts, we should presume that enough was shown to sustain the judgment. But the conclusions of the trial judge show affirmatively the facts upon which the judgment is rendered, and the conclusion of law based upon those facts was excepted to by appellant in the court below and is erroneous. It is not a case where there is an omission to find some fact, but one in which a ruling erroneous in law is grounded upon facts found.

Reversed and rendered.

BACHELDER *v.* HEAGAN

SUPREME JUDICIAL COURT, MAINE, JULY TERM, 1840.

Reported in 18 *Maine Reports*, 32.

THE action was trespass on the case, to recover damages, alleged to have been done to the plaintiffs' land, and to the fences and growth thereon, by the negligence of the defendant in setting a fire on his own land, near to the land of the plaintiffs, and in not carefully keeping the same.

At the trial before Emery, J., evidence was introduced by both parties. The counsel for the plaintiffs requested the judge to instruct the jury, that the plaintiffs were entitled to a verdict, if they were satisfied from the evidence, that the damage was occasioned by the defendant's fire, unless he satisfied them that it was not through negligence or mismanagement on his part. The judge instructed the jury, that the burthen of proof was upon the plaintiffs to satisfy them, beyond a reasonable doubt, that the damage was occasioned by the defendant's fire, and through the carelessness and negligence of the defendant in keeping the same; such carelessness and negligence being alleged in the plaintiffs' declaration, and it not being contended by the plaintiffs that the fire was wilfully and maliciously set by the defendant. On the return of a verdict for the defendant, the plaintiffs filed exceptions to the ruling of the judge.[1]

The opinion of the Court was by

WESTON, C. J. By the ancient common law, or custom of the realm, if a house took fire, the owner was held answerable for any injury thereby occasioned to others. This was probably founded upon some presumed negligence or carelessness, not susceptible of proof. The hardship of this rule was corrected by the statute of 6 Ann. c. 31, which exempted the owner from liability, where the fire was occasioned by accident. The rule does not appear to have been applied to the owner of a field, where a fire may have been kindled. It may frequently be necessary to burn stubble or other matter which encumbers the ground. It is a lawful act, unless kindled at an improper time or carelessly managed. Baron Comyns states, that an action of the case lies, at common law, against the owner of a house which takes fire, by which another is injured, and adds, "so if a fire be kindled in a yard or close, to burn stubble, and by negligence it burns corn in an adjoining close." Com. Dig. Action of the Case for Negligence, A. 6.

In Clark *v.* Foot, 8 Johns. R. 421, it was held, that if A. sets fire to his own fallow ground, as he may lawfully do, which communicates to and fires the woodland of B., his neighbor, no action lies against

[1] Argument omitted.

A., unless there was some negligence or misconduct in him or his servants. And this is a fair illustration of the common law, upon which the action depends. Negligence or misconduct is the gist of the action. And this must be proved. In certain cases, as in actions against innkeepers and common carriers, it is presumed, by the policy of the law, where property is lost which is confided to their care. But in ordinary cases, of which the one before us is not an exception, where the action depends on negligence, the burthen of proof is upon the plaintiff. This is common learning, and applies to all affirmative averments necessary to maintain an action. The defendant's fire was lawfully kindled on his own land. It is an element appropriated to many valuable and useful purposes; but which may become destructive from causes not subject to human control. Hence the fact, that an injury has been done to others, is not in itself evidence of negligence. The party who avers the fact is bound to satisfy the jury upon this point, before he can be entitled to a verdict. In our opinion, the direction of the presiding judge was correct as to the burthen of the proof. *Judgment on the verdict.*[1]

[1] Edwards *v.* Massingill, 3 Ala. App. 406; Kansas City R. Co. *v.* Wilson, (Ark.) 171 S. W. 484; Bullock *v.* Porter, 2 Boyce, 180; Talmadge *v.* Central R. Co., 125 Ga. 400; Beckham *v.* Seaboard Ry., 127 Ga. 550; Pittsburgh R. Co. *v.* Culver, 60 Ind. 469; Brummit *v.* Furness, 1 Ind. App. 401; Hanlon *v.* Ingram, 3 Ia. 81; Johnson *v.* Veneman, 75 Kan. 278; Needham *v.* King, 95 Mich. 303; Bolton *v.* Calkins, 102 Mich. 69; Steffens *v.* Fisher, 161 Mo. App. 386; Bock *v.* Grooms, 2 Neb. Unoff. 803; Read *v.* Pennsylvania R. Co., 44 N. J. Law, 280; Clark *v.* Foot, 8 Johns. 421; Stuart *v.* Hawley, 22 Barb. 619; Hitchcock *v.* Riley, 44 Misc. 260; McDermott *v.* Consolidated Ice Co., 44 Pa. Super. Ct. 445; Pfeiffer *v.* Aue, 53 Tex. Civ. App. 98; Waldy *v.* Preston Mill Co., 80 Wash. 25; Fahn *v.* Reichart, 8 Wis. 255 *Accord.*

Fires set by locomotives. As to liability for fires set by locomotives, there is a conflict. One view is that the plaintiff must establish negligence, as in other cases. Garrett *v.* Southern R. Co., (C. C. A.) 101 Fed. 102; Pittsburgh R. Co. *v.* Hixon, 110 Ind. 225 (changed by statute); Louisville R. Co. *v.* Haggard, 161 Ky. 317; Wallace *v.* New York R. Co., 208 Mass. 16 (*res ipsa loquitur* inapplicable); New England Box Co. *v.* New York R. Co., 210 Mass. 465; Fero *v.* Buffalo R. Co., 22 N. Y. 209; Peck *v.* New York R. Co., 165 N. Y. 347; Campbell *v.* Baltimore R. Co., 58 Pa. Super. Ct. 241.

Another view is that proof that the fire was due to sparks or coals from an engine makes a *prima facie* case of negligence or even casts upon the company the burden of disproving negligence. McCullen *v.* Chicago R. Co., (C. C. A.) 101 Fed. 66; Woodward *v.* Chicago R. Co., (C. C. A.) 145 Fed. 577 (statute); Erickson *v.* Pennsylvania R. Co., (C. C. A.) 170 Fed. 572 (statute); Alabama R. Co. *v.* Johnston, 128 Ala. 283; St. Louis R. Co. *v.* Trotter, 89 Ark. 273 (changed by statute); Florida R. Co. *v.* Welch, 53 Fla. 145 (statute); Southern R. Co. *v.* Thompson, 129 Ga. 367 (statute); Osburn *v.* Oregon R. Co., 15 Idaho, 478; American Strawboard Co. *v.* Chicago R. Co., 177 Ill. 513; Kennedy *v.* Iowa Ins. Co., 119 Ia. 29 (statute); Atchison R. Co. *v.* Geiser, 68 Kan. 281; Fuller *v.* Chicago R. Co., 137 La. 997; Dyer *v.* Maine R. Co., 99 Me. 195; Baltimore R. Co. *v.* Dorsey, 37 Md. 19; Continental Ins. Co. *v.* Chicago R. Co., 97 Minn. 467; Alabama R. Co. *v.* Barrett, 78 Miss. 432; Miller *v.* St. Louis R. Co., 90 Mo. 389; Rogers *v.* Kansas City R. Co., 52 Neb. 86; Laird *v.* Connecticut R. Co., 62 N. H. 254 (statute); Goodman *v.* Lehigh R. Co., 78 N. J. Law, 317 (statute); North Fork Lumber Co. *v.* Southern R. Co., 143 N. C. 324; Missouri R. Co. *v.* Gentry, 31 Okl. 579 (but changed by statute); Anderson *v.* Oregon R. Co., 45 Or. 211; Hutto *v.* Seaboard Ry., 81 S. C. 567; Gulf R. Co. *v.* Johnson, 92 Tex. 591; Ide *v.* Boston R. Co., 83 Vt. 66 (statute); Norfolk R. Co. *v.* Thomas, 110 Va. 622; Thorgrimson *v.* Northern R. Co.,

HEEG *v.* LICHT

COURT OF APPEALS, NEW YORK, APRIL 6, 1880.

Reported in 80 *New York Reports*, 579.

APPEAL from judgment of the General Term of the Supreme Court in the Second Judicial Department, affirming a judgment in favor of defendant, entered upon a verdict. (Reported below, 16 Hun, 257.)

This action was brought to recover damages for injuries to plaintiff's buildings, alleged to have been caused by the explosion of a powder magazine on the premises of defendant; also to restrain the defendant from manufacturing and storing upon his premises fire-works or other explosive substances.

The facts are sufficiently stated in the opinion.

MILLER, J. This action is sought to be maintained upon the ground that the manufacturing and storing of fire-works, and the use and keeping of materials of a dangerous and explosive character for that purpose, constituted a private nuisance for which the defendant was liable to respond in damages, without regard to the question whether he was chargeable with carelessness or negligence. The defendant had constructed a powder magazine upon his premises, with the usual safeguards, in which he kept stored a quantity of powder which, without any apparent cause, exploded and caused the injury complained of. The judge upon the trial charged the jury that they must find for the defendant, unless they found that the defendant carelessly and negligently kept the gunpowder upon his premises. The judge refused to charge that the powder magazine was dangerous in itself to plaintiff and his property, and was a private nuisance, and the defendant was liable to the plaintiff whether it was carelessly kept or not; and the plaintiff duly excepted to the charge and the refusal to charge.

We think that the charge made was erroneous and not warranted by the facts presented upon the trial. The defendant had erected a building and stored materials therein, which from their character were liable to and actually did explode, causing injury to the plaintiff. The fact that the explosion took place tends to establish that the magazine was dangerous and liable to cause damage to the property of persons residing in the vicinity. The locality [legality ?] of works of this

64 Wash. 500; Jacobs *v.* Baltimore R. Co., 68 W. Va. 618; Moore *v.* Chicago R. Co., 78 Wis. 120.

In other jurisdictions there is a statutory absolute liability for such fires. St. Louis R. Co. *v.* Cooper, 120 Ark. 595; British Assur. Co. *v.* Colorado R. Co., 52 Col. 589; Martin *v.* New York R. Co., 62 Conn. 331; Pittsburgh R. Co. *v.* Chappell, 183 Ind. 141; Stewart *v.* Iowa R. Co., 136 Ia. 182; Murphy *v.* St. Louis R. Co., 248 Mo. 28; Baltimore R. Co. *v.* Kreager, 61 Ohio St. 312; Midland R. Co. *v.* Lynn, 38 Okl. 695; MacDonald *v.* New York R. Co., 23 R. I. 558; Peoples Oil Co. *v.* Charleston R. Co., 83 S. C. 530; Jensen *v.* South Dakota R. Co., 25 S. D. 506.

description must depend upon the neighborhood in which they are situated. In a city, with buildings immediately contiguous and persons constantly passing, there could be no question that such an erection would be unlawful and unauthorized. An explosion under such circumstances, independent of any municipal regulations, would render the owner amenable for all damages arising therefrom. That the defendant's establishment was outside of the territorial limits of a city does not relieve the owner from responsibility or alter the case, if the dangerous erection was in close contiguity with dwelling-houses or buildings which might be injured or destroyed in case of an explosion. The fact that the magazine was liable to such a contingency, which could not be guarded against or averted by the greatest degree of care and vigilance, evinces its dangerous character, and might in some localities render it a private nuisance. In such a case the rule which exonerates a party engaged in a lawful business, when free from negligence, has no application. The keeping or manufacturing of gunpowder or of fire-works does not necessarily constitute a nuisance *per se*. That depends upon the locality, the quantity, and the surrounding circumstances, and not entirely upon the degree of care used. In the case at bar it should have been left for the jury to determine whether from the dangerous character of the defendant's business, the proximity to other buildings, and all the facts proved upon the trial, the defendant was chargeable with maintaining a private nuisance and answerable for the damages arising from the explosion.

A private nuisance is defined to be anything done to the hurt or annoyance of the lands, tenements, or hereditaments of another. 3 Bl. Com. 216. Any unwarrantable, unreasonable, or unlawful use by a person of his own property, real or personal, to the injury of another, comes within the definition stated, and renders the owner or possessor liable for all damages arising from such use. Wood's Law of Nuis., § 1, and authorities cited. The cases which are regarded as private nuisances are numerous, and the books are full of decisions holding the parties answerable for the injuries which result from their being maintained. The rule is of universal application that while a man may prosecute such business as he chooses on his own premises, he has no right to erect and maintain a nuisance to the injury of an adjoining proprietor or of his neighbors, even in the pursuit of a lawful trade. Aldred's Case, 9 Coke, 58; Brady *v.* Weeks, 3 Barb. 159; Dubois *v.* Budlong, 15 Abb. 445; Wier's Appeal, 74 Penn. St. 230.

While a class of the reported cases relates to the prosecution of a legitimate business, which of itself produces inconvenience and injury to others, another class refers to acts done on the premises of the owner which are of themselves dangerous to the property and the persons of others who may reside in the vicinity, or who may by chance be passing along or in the neighborhood of the same. Of the former class are cases of slaughter-houses, fat and offal boiling establishments, hog-styes or tallow manufactories, in or near a city, which are offensive to the senses and render the enjoyment of life and property uncomfortable. Catlin *v.* Valentine, 9 Pai. 575; Brady *v.* Weeks, 3 Barb. 157; Dubois *v.* Budlong, 15 Abb. 445; Rex *v.* White, 1 Burr. 337; 2 Bl. Com. 215; Farrand *v.* Marshall, 21 Barb. 421. It is not necessary in these cases that the noxious trade or business should endanger the health of the neighborhood. So also the use of premises in a manner which causes a noise so continuous and excessive as to produce serious annoyance, or vapors or noxious smells; Tipping *v.* St. Helen's Smelting Co., 4 B. & S. (Q. B.) 608; Brill *v.* Flagler, 23 Wend. 354; Pickard *v.* Collins, 23 Barb. 444; Wood's Law of Nuis., § 5; or the burning of a brick kiln, from which gases escape which injure the trees of persons in the neighborhood. Campbell *v.* Seaman, 63 N. Y. 568; s. c., 20 Am. Rep. 567. Of the latter class also are those where the owner blasts rocks with gunpowder, and the fragments are liable to be thrown on the premises and injure the adjoining dwelling-houses, or the owner or persons there being, or where persons travelling may be injured by such use. Hay *v.* Cohoes Co., 3 Barb. 42; s. c., 2 N. Y. 159; Tremain *v.* Cohoes Co., 2 N. Y. 163; Pixley *v.* Clark, 35 id. 523.

Most of the cases cited rest upon the maxim *sic utere tuo,* etc., and where the right to the undisturbed possession and enjoyment of property comes in conflict with the rights of others, that it is better, as a matter of public policy, that a single individual should surrender the use of his land for especial purposes injurious to his neighbor or to others, than that the latter should be deprived of the use of their property altogether, or be subjected to great danger, loss, and injury, which might result if the rights of the former were without any restriction or restraint.

The keeping of gunpowder or other materials in a place, or under circumstances, where it would be liable, in case of explosion, to injure the dwelling-houses or the persons of those residing in close proximity, we think, rests upon the same principle, and is governed by the same general rules. An individual has no more right to keep a magazine of powder upon his premises, which is dangerous, to the detriment of his neighbor, than he is authorized to engage in any other business which may occasion serious consequences.

The counsel for the defendant relies upon the case of People *v.* Sands, 1 Johns. 78; 3 Am. Dec. 296, to sustain the position that the defendant's business was neither a public nor a private nuisance. That was an indictment for keeping a quantity of gunpowder near dwelling-houses and near a public street; and it was held (Spencer, J., dissenting), that the fact as charged did not amount to a nuisance, and that it should have been alleged to have been negligently and improvidently kept. It will be seen that the case was disposed of upon the form of the indictment, and while it may well be that an allegation of negligence is necessary where an indictment is for a public nuisance, it by no means follows that negligence is essential in a private action to recover damages for an alleged nuisance. In Myers *v.* Malcolm, 6 Hill, 292, it was held that the act of keeping a large quantity of gunpowder insufficiently secured near other buildings, thereby endangering the lives of persons residing in the vicinity, amounted to a public nuisance, and an action would lie for damages where an explosion occurred causing injury. Nelson, C. J., citing People *v.* Sands, *supra*, says: "Upon the principle that nothing will be intended or inferred to support an indictment, the Court said, for aught they could see, the house may have been one built and secured for the purpose of keeping powder in such a way as not to expose the neighborhood;" and he cites several authorities which uphold the doctrine that where gunpowder is kept in such a place as is dangerous to the inhabitants or passengers, it will be regarded as a nuisance. The case of People *v.* Sands is not therefore controlling upon the question of negligence.

Fillo *v.* Jones, 2 Abb. Ct. Ap. Dec. 121, is also relied upon, but does not sustain the doctrine contended for; and it is there held that an action for damages caused by the explosion of fire-works may be maintained upon the theory that the defendant was guilty of a wrongful and unlawful act, or of default, in keeping them at the place they were kept, because they were liable to spontaneous combustion and explosion, and thus endangered the lives of persons in their vicinity, and that the injury was occasioned by such spontaneous combustion and explosion.

It is apparent that negligence alone in the keeping of gunpowder is not controlling, and that the danger arising from the locality where the fire-works or gunpowder are kept, is to be taken into consideration in maintaining an action of this character. We think that the request to charge was too broad, and properly refused. The charge however should have been in conformity with the rule herein laid down, and for the error of the judge in the charge, the judgment should be reversed and a new trial granted, with costs to abide the event.

All concur. *Judgment reversed.*[1]

[1] State *v.* General Stevedoring Co., 213 Fed. 51; Kinney *v.* Koopman, 116 Ala. 310; Kleebauer *v.* Western Fuse Co., 138 Cal. 497; Simpson *v.* Du Pont Powder Co., 143 Ga. 465; Barnes *v.* Zettlemoyer, 25 Tex. Civ. App. 468 *Accord.*

French *v.* Center Creek Powder Co., 173 Mo. App. 220 *Contra.*

Compare Sloss-Sheffield Steel Co. *v.* Prosch, 190 Ala. 290; Flynn *v.* Butler, 189 Mass. 377; Reilly *v.* Erie R. Co., 72 App. Div. 476.

DILWORTH'S APPEAL

SUPREME COURT, PENNSYLVANIA, OCTOBER 9, 1879.

Reported in 91 *Pennsylvania State Reports,* 247.

APPEAL from Court of Common Pleas, No. 2, of Allegheny County.

Bill in equity by Robinson and forty-seven others against Dilworth, to restrain Dilworth from erecting a powder magazine upon his lot in Penn Township, Allegheny County. The case was referred to a master, who recommended that an injunction should be refused and the bill dismissed. The facts are set forth in the opinion of this court. The court below thought that the public interest would be subserved by refusing the injunction; but in deference to the authority of Wier's Appeal, 24 P. F. Smith, 230, a majority of the court entered a *pro forma* decree for an injunction. Appeal was taken to the Supreme Court.[1]

TRUNKEY, J. [After stating general principles and quoting from the statement of the facts in Wier's Appeal.]

After a careful revision of the master's report by the court below, the facts found in this case, and which are well sustained by proof, are as follows: This magazine has been located so as to endanger as few persons and as little property as possible, and yet be reasonably accessible as a point of supply and distribution; it is more remote from population than the magazines generally in use throughout the United States, and it is doubtful if a better location could be made in Allegheny County. It is situated about two miles from East Liberty, the nearest closely built-up district, and is separated therefrom by intervening hills and ravines. It is in a sparsely settled locality, for the vicinity of a city, and land near it has not been, nor is it likely to be for some years, in demand for building purposes. That portion of Lincoln Avenue which terminates at a point five hundred feet from the magazine is very little travelled, very few people travel it within considerable distance of its terminus, having no occasion to do so; it was the wildest of the many absurd enterprises undertaken in Pittsburgh to carry city improvements into wild rural regions, expecting population to rapidly follow. The other public road, passing within twenty-two feet of the magazine, has for some time been almost abandoned by the people in the vicinity, and is used by about three farmers. The magazine is so situated that the force of an explosion would be down the ravine and away from the road. The greater distance of this magazine from a borough, or closely built-up district, the absence of demand of land for building purposes, and the unlikelihood of such demand in the vicinity, the little travel on the public road which passes near it, and the ravine opening from the road, are

[1] Only part of case is given. Argument omitted.

the chief points wherein this case differs from Wier's Appeal. The dwellings and families near the magazine number about the same in one as the other. None will deny that the law protects the small and cheap home as it does the large and costly mansion, and the rights of a tenant are as sacred as those of his landlord. But it is equally undeniable that if a tenant hold by lease at will, or by month, and his landlord grants that a lawful and necessary, yet offensive or dangerous factory or magazine may be erected, the tenant has not a right of action for its prevention. If such structure were placed near tenant houses occupied by miners, where the mines are likely to be worked for considerable time, it would be a material fact to be weighed with others — almost of like weight as if the houses were owned by the occupants. Here the mine is nearly exhausted, a fact to be considered in reference to the probable increase of population in the neighborhood.

It was urged that the location being only two hundred and fifty-five feet from the boundary line of Pittsburgh, and five hundred feet from the end of Lincoln Avenue, is dangerous to life and property in the city. The facts, as we have seen, are that that end of the avenue is very little travelled, and is remote from the population of the city; and, without question, " the region of country in which the magazine is located is wild and broken as to its general surface, it is traversed by numerous ravines and hills, and altogether possesses a romantic and secluded aspect." It is the real character of the location, with its surroundings, which determines its fitness, and not a city line two miles from city life, nor the unused and useless part of a graded and paved street extended beyond the visible city.

Confessedly, the demand for and consumption of powder in Pittsburgh and vicinity are very great, and it is indispensable in carrying on important branches of industry, and it would be inimical to the business interests of the community to trammel the sale of it with unnecessary restrictions and burdens. Besides the magazine at the United States Arsenal there are no others in Allegheny County, except those of a single company, and the Dilworth. In view of the whole case the master, and one of the judges of the Common Pleas, thought the injunction should be refused. The majority of the court, in a considerate opinion, concluded that the public interest would be subserved by refusing the injunction, and that the complainants were not entitled to an injunction, but for the ruling in Wier's Appeal, on the authority of which they felt constrained to grant it. A decree was entered, with direction that it would not be enforced until the defendant could be heard on appeal. We fully agree with the court below, except that we do not think the principles in Wier's Appeal, applied to the facts in this case, require an injunction to be granted.

Decree reversed. Bill dismissed.

SECTION IV
VIOLATION OF STATUTORY DUTY

KNUPFLE v. KNICKERBOCKER ICE CO.

COURT OF APPEALS, NEW YORK, MARCH 15, 1881.

Reported in 84 New York Reports, 488.

PER CURIAM.[1] One of the principal questions litigated upon the trial of this action related to the alleged negligence of the driver of the defendant's team in leaving the horses untied in the street, which, it was claimed, was the cause of the death of the intestate. Among other evidence to establish such negligence, the plaintiff offered and introduced in evidence, against the objection of the defendant, an ordinance of the city of Brooklyn, prohibiting the leaving of any horse or horses attached to a vehicle standing in any street without a person in charge, or without being secured to a tying post. We think there is no question as to the admissibility of such testimony under the decisions of this court, and the exception taken to the ruling in this respect cannot be upheld.

A more serious question arises as to the effect to be given to the evidence referred to. At the close of the charge the plaintiff's counsel requested the judge to charge the jury that a violation of an ordinance of the city is necessarily negligence; and the judge replied: "it is; I have so told the jury; it is negligence;" and the defendant's counsel excepted. We think there was error in the charge thus made, and that the judge went too far in holding that a violation of the ordinance was negligence of itself.

The question presented has been the subject of consideration in this court, as will be seen by reference to the reported cases. In Brown *v.* B. & State Line R. R. Co., 22 N. Y. 191, the court charged the jury that if the injury occurred while defendant's train was running in violation of a city ordinance and at a rate of speed forbidden by it, and was occasioned by or would not have occurred except for such violation, the defendant was liable, and this direction was held to be error. This doctrine is, however, repudiated in Jetter *v.* N. Y. & H. R. R. Co., 2 Abb. Ct. App. Dec. 458, as well as in subsequent cases. In the last case cited it was held that a party in doing a lawful act, where there is no present danger, or appearance of danger, has a right to assume that others will conform their conduct to the express requirements of the law and not bring injury upon him by its violation. It is also strongly intimated that a violator of such an ordinance is a wrong-doer and necessarily negligent, and a person injured thereby is

[1] Statement and arguments omitted.

entitled to a civil remedy. The distinct point now raised was not, however, fairly presented by the charge to which exception was taken, which was not otherwise erroneous. In Beisegel *v.* N. Y. C. R. R. Co., 14 Abb. Pr. [N. S.] 29, it was held that it was some evidence of negligence to show that an ordinance was violated, and the charge of the judge upon the trial to that effect was upheld. In McGrath *v.* N. Y. C. & H. R. R. R. Co., 63 N. Y. 522, it was laid down that the violation or disregard of an ordinance, while not conclusive evidence of negligence, is some evidence for the consideration of the jury. In Massoth *v.* D. & H. Canal Co., 64 N. Y. 524, the cases are reviewed, and it was said to be an open question in this court whether the violation of a municipal ordinance was negligence *per se;* and it was held that the city ordinance being submitted to the jury with the other evidence as bearing upon the question, but not as conclusive, there was no error in the parts of the charge excepted to. The result of the decisions, therefore, is, that the violation of the ordinance is some evidence of negligence, but not necessarily negligence. The judge not only assented unqualifiedly to the request made, but he also said that it was negligence; and thus went further than to hold, within the cases cited, that it was evidence of negligence.

The counsel for the plaintiff urges that even if erroneous, the charge worked defendant no injury. This position is based upon the theory that as the question was submitted to the jury as one of fact, whether the team was left loose and unattended, and as the judge had charged that the ordinance adds very little to what would have been the rule without it, and that it was negligence to leave a horse untied or not in charge of some one, in a public street, whether there is an ordinance or not, they must have found that they were so left, and, therefore, the plaintiff was entitled to a verdict. The difficulty about this position is, that the question, whether leaving the horses untied was negligence, was one of fact depending upon the circumstances attending the case, and while the jury may have found in favor of the defendant as to this, their verdict may have resulted from the charge made as to the effect of the ordinance. It cannot, therefore, be said that by the portion of the charge which has been considered the defendant was not prejudiced.

For the error in the charge, without considering the other questions raised, the judgment should be reversed and a new trial granted, costs to abide event.

All concur, except MILLER and DANFORTH, JJ., dissenting, and RAPALLO, J., absent. *Judgment reversed.*[1]

[1] Wright *v.* Malden R. Co., 4 All. 283; Nelson *v.* Burnham & Morrill Co., 114 Me. 213; Fluker *v.* Ziegele Brewing Co., 201 N. Y. 40; Beck *v.* Vancouver R. Co., 25 Or. 32 *Accord.* See also Newcomb *v.* Boston Protective Department, *ante*, p. 391; Bourne *v.* Whitman, *ante*, p. 400, note 1.

Platte & Denver Canal Co. *v.* Dowell, 17 Col. 376; Richardson *v.* El Paso Min. Co., 51 Col. 440; Lindsay *v.* Cecchi, 3 Boyce, 133; Toledo R. Co. *v.* O'Connor, 77

HOLMAN *v.* CHICAGO, ROCK ISLAND & PACIFIC R. CO.

SUPREME COURT, MISSOURI, MAY TERM, 1876.

Reported in 62 *Missouri Reports*, 562.

HOUGH, J.[1] This was an action to recover damages for the killing of a cow, belonging to the plaintiff, by a train on defendant's railroad in a street of the town of Cameron.

The evidence given at the trial is stated in the bill of exceptions in the following language: "The plaintiff, to maintain the issues on his

Ill. 391; United States Brewing Co. *v.* Stoltenberg, 211 Ill. 531; Presto-Lite Co. *v.* Skeel, 182 Ind. 593; Correll *v.* Burlington R. Co., 38 Ia. 120; Schlereth *v.* Missouri R. Co., 96 Mo. 509; Brannock *v.* Elmore, 114 Mo. 55; Olson *v.* Nebraska Tel. Co., 83 Neb. 735; Texas R. Co. *v.* Brown, 11 Tex. Civ. App. 503; Smith *v.* Milwaukee Builders' Exchange, 91 Wis. 360 *Contra.*

In Evers *v.* Davis, 86 N. J. Law, 196, 202, GARRISON, J., says:

"The question then is, What is, upon common law principles, the effect of statutes such as the one we are considering upon the action of negligence? The familiar expressions that the breach of such a statute is 'negligence *per se*' or is '*prima facie* evidence of negligence' seem to me to postpone elucidation rather than to contribute to it, while the implication that proof of a breach of a public statute will support a private recovery is positively misleading.

A fact constantly to be borne in mind in tracing the legal effect of such statutes is that the negligence that is essential to the action of negligence is not solely in the overt act that produced the injury complained of, but may lie in the failure to foresee the danger likely to result from the doing of such act. 'Danger, reasonably to be foreseen at the time of acting, is the established test of negligence' says the writer already cited. Of negligence of this sort it may be said that it is common to all phases of the action, which cannot be said of the mere overt act, which may not be an act of neglect or omission at all, but, on the contrary, one of affirmative commission, e. g., the blowing of a locomotive whistle (Bittle *v.* Camden and Atlantic Railroad Co., 55 N. J. L. 615), the discharge of steam (Mumma *v.* Easton and Amboy Railroad Co., 73 Id. 653) or the extraordinary lurching of a train (Burr *v.* Pennsylvania Railroad Co., 64 Id. 30). But whether the overt act be one of omission or of commission, and whether the conduct of the defendant be stated in terms of 'duty' or of 'fault,' the one common denominator, so to speak, of the action of negligence is this element of what we may call discoverable danger; that is to say, a danger that is susceptible of being discovered in advance of action or inaction by the exercise of that degree of care which if a man fails to exercise he becomes civilly liable for the consequences of his conduct. Now, it is precisely upon this element of discoverable danger that public statutes or ordinances act, and they do this not by giving to the plaintiff a right of action he did not have before, but by their operation upon what we may call the common law conscience of the defendant, better known to us in its personified form of 'the ordinary prudent man,' the familiar fiction designed by the common law to aid juries, when deciding what was the proper thing for a man to do, to lose sight of the personal point of view of that particular man and to base their judgment upon a general standard which in the final assize is what the jury itself thinks was the proper thing to do.

Now this ordinary prudent man of common law creation must in the nature of things be regarded as a law-abiding citizen to whom, as is pointed out by Dean Thayer in the article referred to, it would be an unjust reproach to suppose that, knowing the statute — for upon familiar principles he can claim no benefit from his ignorance of it — he would break it, *reasonably* believing that it was a prudent thing for him to do, and that in all probability no harm would come of it.

In other words, it is inconsistent with ordinary prudence for an individual to set up his private judgment against that of the lawfully constituted public authority. We must assume, therefore, that the ordinary prudent man would not do such

[1] Arguments omitted.

part, introduced evidence tending to show, that the bell was not rung, nor the whistle sounded on the train mentioned in his statement, as it

a thing since to do so would be to change his entire nature and to forego the very traits that brought him into existence. He would, in fine, cease to be the pattern man he must continue to be in order to be at all.

Upon common law principles, therefore, when the legislature has by public statute established a certain standard of conduct in order to prevent a danger that it foresaw, it has in this regard forewarned the 'ordinary prudent man' and through him the defendant in a civil action, whose conduct must always coincide with this common law criterion. Such danger, therefore, does not have to be proved by the plaintiff, since there is no longer room for a reasonable difference of opinion, for by his breach of the statute the defendant, through his common law conscience, is charged with knowledge that if injury ensues he will have acted at his peril.

The court therefore should so instruct the jury, whether such instruction be couched in the terms of the defendant's duty to perform or of his culpability for neglect, or of his liability for the result of his action or inaction, as the case may be; and thus upon common law principles the plaintiff in an action of negligence obtains the benefit of the statute if he be one of the class for whose protection it was enacted and the breach of such statute was the efficient cause of the injury of which he complains."

In Smith *v.* Mine & Smelter Co., 32 Utah, 21, 30, Frick, J., says:

"The court instructed the jury in substance that, if they found from the evidence that the appellant had violated the city ordinance in respect to keeping or storing explosives, such violation constituted negligence *per se*. Counsel insist that such is not the law; that it would be *prima facie* negligence at most. As to whether a violation of a law or ordinance constitutes negligence *per se* depends in a large measure upon the nature of the law or ordinance. When a standard of duty or care is fixed by law or ordinance, and such law or ordinance has reference to the safety of life, limb, or property, then, as a matter of necessity, a violation of such law or ordinance constitutes negligence. In any case the standard is usually defined as that degree of care that men of ordinary care and prudence usually exercise. But, when the standard is fixed by law or ordinance, how can one be heard to say that he exercised care in exceeding, or in refraining to comply with, the standard fixed? There is, in such cases, no comparison to be made. Care and prudence alone cannot excuse. Exceeding or disregarding the standard of care imposed must be held to be negligence, if it is anything. If it is held not to be such *per se*, it simply amounts to this: That it is for the jury to say whether, in violating a law or ordinance fixing a standard of care to be observed the law was carefully or negligently violated. The violation, thus in and of itself, would mean nothing, and one would be permitted to violate the law with impunity, provided the jury find it to have been carefully done. Neither is it an answer to say that the violation may have been caused by the act of God or unavoidable accident. If such be the case, then the act constituted no violation in law, and when there is no violation there would be no negligence arising out of such act or acts alone, and the jury would be required to find whether the act or acts complained of constituted a violation, as above indicated, or not. If they found that the law was disregarded, but that it was occasioned by a higher power or through unavoidable accident, then there would be no violation by the person charged, and hence no negligence imputable to him from that act alone. But if they found that he had violated the law by his own act, or by the acts of others chargeable to him, then there would be negligence *per se*. This negligence, however, standing alone, is not civilly actionable. The negligence must in all cases be found to be the proximate cause of the injury. The court instructed the jury that unless they found that the negligence, if they found negligence as above stated, was the proximate cause of the injury complained of, the respondent could not recover. This, we think, is a correct statement of the law pertaining to ordinances such as the one in question here. We do not hold that a violation of all laws or ordinances constitutes negligence *per se*, but we do hold that the violation of ordinances designed for the safety of life, limb, or property, does constitute negligence *per se*, and this, we think, is supported by the clear weight of authority."

It is sometimes said that violation of a duty so imposed is "*prima facie* evidence of negligence;" Giles *v.* Diamond State Iron Co., 7 Houst. 453; True *v.* Woda, approached and ran over the cow in controversy; that the cow was killed on defendant's railroad on a public travelled street of the town

104 Ill. App. 15; Wabash R. Co. *v.* Kamradt, 109 Ill. App. 203; Mize *v.* Rocky Mountain Tel. Co., 38 Mont. 521; Briggs *v.* New York R. Co., 72 N. Y. 26; Acton *v.* Reed, 104 App. Div. 507.

A distinction between a statute and a municipal ordinance has been urged. Philadelphia R. Co. *v.* Ervin, 89 Pa. St. 71; Lederman *v.* Pennsylvania R. Co., 165 Pa. St. 118; Riegert *v.* Thackery, 212 Pa. St. 86.

In Ubelmann *v.* American Ice Co., 209 Pa. St. 398, 400, Brown, J., says:

"When negligence is charged it must be proved. Proof of the violation of an ordinance regulating or relating to conduct alleged to have been negligent is not in itself conclusive proof of the negligence charged. The ordinance and its violation are matters of evidence, to be considered with all other evidence in the case: Lane *v.* Atlantic Works, 111 Mass. 136. But this rule is limited to cases in which the ordinance relates to the alleged negligent act under investigation. Here, as stated, it was the use of an alleged defective shifting rod in the elevator. Ordinances and their violation are admissible, not as substantive and sufficient proof of the negligence of the defendant, but as evidence of municipal expression of opinion, on a matter as to which the municipal authorities had acted, that the defendant was negligent, and are to be taken into consideration with all the other facts in the case. Illustrations of this are found in several of our later cases. In Lederman *v.* Pennsylvania Railroad Co., 165 Pa. 118, one of the questions was the undue rate of speed at which the defendant company was running its cars through the city of Lancaster, and we held that the ordinance in relation to the speed of railway trains within the city limits had been properly admitted. An ordinance of the city of Philadelphia requires all vehicles, including bicycles, to keep to the right, and, in Foote *v.* American Product Co., 195 Pa. 190, where the rider of the bicycle had conformed to this ordinance, and the driver of the wagon that ran into him had not, we said, through our Brother Mestrezat: 'While the ordinance in itself was not evidence of negligence, it may be considered with other evidence in ascertaining whether the defendant was guilty of negligence.' When the suit is against the municipality itself, and it is charged with negligence, due to the dereliction of its employees, their violation or disregard of its own regulations and ordinances relating to the matter under investigation are proof of such dereliction, though not necessarily of the specific negligence charged, which, as in all other cases, must be proved by proper and satisfactory evidence. The dereliction of the municipal employees is to be taken into consideration with the other facts in the case, upon proof of which the plaintiff relies to sustain his allegation of negligence. An illustration of this is Herron *v.* The City of Pittsburg, 204 Pa. 509, which was an action against the city to recover damages for personal injuries sustained by a boy from contact with a live, naked telephone wire used in the police service of the city, and it appeared that the break in the wire was known to the police officials within an hour after it had occurred, and that it was also known to them to be in close proximity to other wires, some of which carried strong and dangerous currents of electricity. We regarded as proper the admission of the ordinance of the city and the rules of the police department relating to the inspection and use of the city wires.

The ordinance of April 10, 1894, provides for the inspection of elevators by inspectors duly appointed by the city of Philadelphia, and makes it the duty of the owner or operator of an elevator, after its inspection, to procure from the inspector a certificate that it is in condition to be operated, and to expose the certificate to public view as near as possible to the elevator car. This ordinance does not make it the duty of one owning or operating an elevator to demand an inspection, and it is only after the inspector has inspected that he must procure and expose the certificate. But, even if there had been an inspection here, and the defendant company had not procured and exposed the proper certificate, its failure to do so is not the negligence charged against it that resulted in the plaintiff's injury, and the ordinance clearly had no proper place in his evidence."

Breach of rules of a private corporation, see Hoffman *v.* Cedar Rapids R. Co., 157 Ia. 655; Stevens *v.* Boston R. Co., 184 Mass. 476; Virginia R. Co. *v.* Godsey, 117 Va. 167.

See Thayer, Public Wrong and Private Action, 27 Harvard Law Rev. 317.

of Cameron, in Shoal township, by a train on said railroad, and that said cow was worth thirty-five dollars. The defendant introduced one Kiley, who testified that he was the conductor on said train, and that the bell was rung and the whistle sounded. This was all the evidence offered."

It will not be necessary to notice the instructions given and refused. There was a verdict and judgment for the plaintiff, and the defendant has brought the case here by appeal.

The statute in relation to railroad corporations, which requires the bell on the locomotive to be rung, or the steam whistle to be sounded, before reaching and while crossing any travelled public road or street, provides a penalty for the neglect of such requirement, and further declares that the corporation shall be liable for all damages which shall be sustained by any person by reason of such neglect. Conceding that the servants of the defendant neglected to ring the bell or sound the whistle, the question is whether there is any evidence tending to show that the cow was killed by reason of such neglect.

In the case of Stoneman *v.* Atl. & Pac. R. R. Co., 58 Mo. 503, it was said, on the point in judgment, that " the court had no right to declare as a matter of law, that the jury had nothing to find but the killing of the animal at the crossing of a public highway, and the failure of the company to have the bell rung or the whistle sounded. There may have been no connection, whatever, between the negligent omission and the damage; and the very terms of the statute, under which the suit is brought, clearly indicate that the damage must be the result of the negligence."

The foregoing extract clearly asserts, that there is no necessary connection between the failure to ring the bell or sound the whistle, and the killing; that both may concur in point of time, and the latter not be the result of the former. How, then, must the connection be shown? By evidence, undoubtedly. Who must produce such evidence? The party who asserts that such connection exists. The damage must be shown to be the result of the negligence; that is, the negligence must first be shown, and this fact must be supplemented by testimony tending to show that the negligence occasioned the damage. This testimony should consist of all the facts and circumstances attending the killing, so that the jury could fairly and rationally conclude whether it resulted from the failure to ring the bell or sound the whistle, or from other causes. In the case at bar no such testimony was offered; but two facts were shown to fix the defendant's liability, the failure to give the required signal at the crossing, and the killing. No fact was shown tending to connect the two. If the plaintiff can recover on the evidence embodied in the bill of exceptions, it must be, because it is only necessary for the jury to find the killing of the animal on the highway, and the failure to ring the bell or sound the whistle, for there is no testimony from which they can find more. But this, we have seen, is not sufficient. Upon the case made, it was the duty of the court to declare as a matter of law that the plaintiff was not entitled to recover.

This conclusion has been reached after a careful consideration of the case of Owens *v.* Hann. & St. Jo. R. R., 58 Mo. 386; and Howenstein *v.* Pac. R. R., 55 Mo. 33.

The judgment must be reversed and the cause remanded. All the judges concur, except Judge Vories, who is absent.[1]

BRATTLEBORO *v.* WAIT

SUPREME COURT, VERMONT, FEBRUARY TERM, 1872.

Reported in 44 *Vermont Reports*, 459.

ACTION ON THE CASE, to recover damages sustained by reason of the defendant's neglect and refusal to comply with the requirements of § 39, ch. 83 of the General Statutes, and § 1 of No. 6 of the acts of the legislature of 1865. Demurrer to the declaration by the defendant.

The court, September term, 1870, BARRETT, J., presiding, sustained the demurrer, and rendered judgment for the defendant. Exceptions by the plaintiff.

The opinion of the court was delivered by —

ROSS, J. The question in this case is whether the defendant as cashier of the Windham County Bank for the years commencing April 1, 1864, and April 1, 1865, and of the First National Bank of Brattleboro for the years commencing April 1, 1866, and April 1, 1867, is liable for any loss that may have resulted to the town, by his neglect to return to the town clerk of the plaintiff, for the first two years named, the names of the stockholders in the Windham County Bank, agreeably to the requirements of § 39, ch. 83 of the General Statutes, and for the last two years the names of the stockholders of the First National Bank of Brattleboro, agreeably to the requirements of § 1, of No. 6 of the acts of 1865; or whether the penalties imposed by § 47 of ch. 83, and by § 5 of the act of 1865, are the only remedies given for the neglect of the defendant to perform the duties imposed by the two sections first above named.

These duties are created solely by the statutes named, and by them are superimposed upon the defendant in addition to those duties which

[1] Steel Car Forge Co. *v.* Chec, (C. C. A.) 184 Fed. 868; Great Southern R. Co. *v.* Chapman, 80 Ala. 615; Lindsay *v.* Cecchi, 3 Boyce, 133; Gibson *v.* Leonard, 143 Ill. 182; Browne *v.* Siegel, 90 Ill. App. 49 (aff'd on another ground, 191 Ill. 226); Presto-Lite Co. *v.* Skeel, 182 Ind. 593; Kidder *v.* Dunstable, 11 Gray, 342; Curwen *v.* Bofferding, 133 Minn. 28; Koch *v.* Fox, 71 App. Div. 288; Kuhnen *v.* White, 102 App. Div. 36; Ledbetter *v.* English, 166 N. C. 125; Dobbins *v.* Missouri R. Co., 91 Tex. 60; Stacy *v.* Knickerbocker Ice Co., 84 Wis. 614; Derouso *v.* International Harvester Co., 157 Wis. 32 *Accord.*

Compare Hartnett *v.* Boston Store, 265 Ill. 331, with Pizzo *v.* Wiemann, 149 Wis. 235; Beauchamp *v.* Burn Mfg. Co., 250 Ill. 303, with Berdos *v.* Tremont Mills, 209 Mass. 489.

were incumbent on him by reason of his acceptance of the office of cashier. The principle, that the law will furnish a remedy to a party injured by the neglect or non-performance of a duty imposed on an individual by statute, where the statute itself furnishes no remedy, is too familiar and well established to need the support of authorities. If the statute which imposes a new duty also provides a particular remedy, that remedy is usually the only remedy the injured party has. In Regina *v.* Wigg, 2 Salk. 460, the court says: " Where a new penalty is applied for a matter which at common law was an indictable offence, either remedy may be pursued; but where the statute makes the offence, that remedy must be taken which the statute gives." Lord MANSFIELD, in Rex *v.* Robinson, 2 Bur. 799, stating the doctrine more fully, says: " The true rule of distinction seems to be, that where the offence intended to be guarded against was punishable before the making of such statute, prescribing a particular method of punishing it, there such particular remedy is cumulative, and does not take away the former remedy; but where the statute only enacts ' that the doing any act not punishable before, shall for the future be punishable in such and such a particular manner there,' it is necessary that such particular method, by such act prescribed, must be specifically pursued, and not the common law method of an indictment." The doctrine stated in these early leading cases is as applicable to civil as to criminal prosecutions. The question then is, was the penalty or forfeiture of $100 provided for by § 47, ch. 83 of the General Statutes, and of $500 provided for in § 5 of the act of 1865, intended for the remedies to the plaintiff for the non-performance by the defendant of the duties imposed by § 39, and by § 1. We think they were. The penalties under these statutes are given to the town, as the party injured or aggrieved by the failure of the defendant to perform the duties imposed, as has been held in Newman, Treasurer of Brattleboro, *v.* this defendant, 43 Vt. 587, in which the plaintiff through its treasurer sought to recover the penalty imposed by § 5 of the act of 1865, for the defendant's failure to comply with § 1 of that act during the years 1866 and 1867. It is unnecessary to repeat what has been said in that case. It would be inconsistent with the principle we have already stated, to hold that the plaintiff can recover the penalty as the party aggrieved, and also all damages it has sustained by the defendant's failure to perform a duty wholly imposed upon him by the statute. Such holding would give the plaintiff a double remedy for the same failure by the defendant to perform a duty imposed by statute, and due to the plaintiff only by the force of the statute; the penalty prescribed, and an amercement in damages for all the plaintiff can show he has suffered from such failure. The penalty cannot be held to be a cumulative remedy; for before the passage of the act no duty was due from the defendant as cashier to the plaintiff, and, therefore, there could be no remedy, and nothing for the penalty to be cumulative to. Such holding would interpret one and the same act as giving a double remedy, which is contrary to all rules of interpretation, and only allowable when it is given in express terms by the statute. *The judgment of the county court is affirmed.*[1]

[1] In Cowley *v.* Newmarket Local Board, [1892] A. C. 345, 351, Lord Herschell said:

"My Lords, the question which arises in this action is whether the defendants are liable in respect of an accident which happened to the plaintiff, owing to the existence of a drop of eighteen inches in the level of a footway vested in the defendants, in consequence of which the plaintiff fell and sustained considerable injury. The difference of level in the footway arose from a carriageway having been made for the purpose of access to Captain Machell's stable, the yard of which adjoined the footway. This work was executed by Captain Machell in the year 1873. The plaintiff in his statement of claim asserted that the defendants had wrongfully suffered and permitted the footway to be out of repair and in a condition dangerous to passengers. It appeared clearly at the trial that there had been no misfeasance on the part of the defendants. The utmost that could be charged against them was non-feasance. It was strongly urged at the bar that the highway including the footway being vested in the defendants, they were responsible if it was not kept in proper condition and repair to any one who was injured by reason of its not being so kept. In support of their contention they relied mainly on the 144th and 149th sections of the Public Health Act, 1875. By the former of those sections every urban authority is to execute the office of surveyor of highways, and to exercise and be subject to all the powers, duties, and liabilities of surveyors. By the latter it is provided that the urban sanitary authority shall from time to time cause all streets vested in them to be levelled, paved, metalled, flagged, channelled, altered, and repaired as occasion may require. Amongst the duties thus imposed upon the urban authority was undoubtedly the duty of keeping this highway in repair, and it is said that any person injured by the non-performance of a statutory duty is entitled to recover against the person on whom that duty rests. I entertain very grave doubts whether the proposition thus broadly stated can be maintained. The principal authority in support of it is the decision of the Court of Queen's Bench in the case of Couch *v.* Steel, 3 E. & B. 402. But in the case of Atkinson *v.* Newcastle Waterworks Company, 2 Ex. D. 441, the late Lord Cairns and Cockburn, C. J., and the present Master of the Rolls all expressed serious doubts whether the case of Couch *v.* Steel was rightly decided, and whether the broad general proposition could be supported, that whenever a statutory duty is created any person who can show he has sustained injury from the non-performance of that duty can maintain an action for damages against the person on whom the duty is imposed. I share the doubt expressed by these learned judges and the opinion expressed by Lord Cairns that much must 'depend on the purview of the Legislature in the particular statute and the language which they have there employed.' In the case of Glossop *v.* Heston and Isleworth Local Board, 12 Ch. D. 102, 109, James, L. J., made some observations bearing on this point, which seem to me to be of great weight. In that case the plaintiff claimed an injunction to restrain a nuisance on the ground that the defendants had neglected to perform the statutory duty cast on them as the sanitary authority of a particular district. The learned Lord Justice said: 'It appears to me that if this action could be sustained it would be a very serious matter indeed for every rate-payer in England in any district in which there is any local authority upon whom duties are cast for the benefit of the locality. If this action could be maintained, I do not see why it could not, in a similar manner, be maintained by every owner of land in that district who could allege that if there had been a proper system of sewage his property would have been very much improved.' And he expressed the opinion that such a contention was not supported either by principle or authority. It is to be observed that the Highway Act, which defines the duties of surveyors of highways, prescribes the mode of proceeding when the duty of repairing the highway is unfulfilled and the liability which is then to attach to the surveyor. By sect. 94 he may be summoned before the justices, and if it appears either upon the report of a person appointed by them to view, or on their own view, that the highway is not in a state of thorough and perfect repair, they are to convict the sur-

OSBORNE v. McMASTERS

SUPREME COURT, MINNESOTA, JANUARY 30, 1889.

Reported in 40 *Minnesota Reports,* 103.

APPEAL by defendant from a judgment of the District Court for Ramsey County, where the action was tried before Kelly, J., and a jury, and a verdict rendered for plaintiff.

MITCHELL, J. Upon the record in this case it must be taken as the facts that defendant's clerk in his drug-store, in the course of his employment as such, sold to plaintiff's intestate a deadly poison without labelling it "Poison," as required by statute; that she, in ignorance of its deadly qualities, partook of the poison, which caused her death. Except for the ability of counsel and the earnestness with which they have argued the case, we would not have supposed that there could be any serious doubt of defendant's liability on this state of facts. It is immaterial for present purposes whether section 329 of the Penal Code or section 14, c. 147, Laws 1885, or both, are still in force, and constitute the law governing this case.[1] The requirements of both statutes are substantially the same, and the sole object of both is to protect the public against the dangerous qualities of poison. It is now well settled, certainly in this state, that where a statute or municipal ordinance imposes upon any person a specific duty for the protection or benefit of others, if he neglects to perform that duty he is liable to those for whose protection or benefit it was imposed for any injuries of the character which the statute or ordi-

veyor in a penalty, and to make an order on the surveyor to repair it within a limited time; and if the repairs are not made within the time so limited the surveyor is to forfeit and pay to a person to be named and appointed in a second order a sum of money equal to the cost of repairing the highway. I think it, to say the least, doubtful whether, apart from the reason to which I am about to refer, the contention that an action lies against the local board for a breach of their statutory duty to repair the highways can be maintained."

Sydney Municipal Council v. Bourke, [1895] A. C. 433; Maguire v. Liverpool Corporation, [1905] 1 K. B. 767 *Accord.* But compare Dawson v. Bingley Urban District Council, [1911] 2 K. B. 149.

Statutory duty to repair street or sidewalk, see Manchester v. Hartford, 30 Conn. 118; Kirby v. Boylston Market, 14 Gray, 249; Rochester v. Campbell, 123 N. Y. 405.

[1] "A person who sells, gives away, or disposes of, any poison, or poisonous substance, without attaching to the vial, box, or parcel containing such poisonous substance, a label, with the name and residence of such person, the word 'poison,' and the name of such poison, all written or printed thereon, in plain and legible characters, is guilty of a misdemeanor." — Minnesota Penal Code, section 329.

"No person shall sell at retail any poisonous commodity recognized as such, and especially" [here enumerating various poisons], "without affixing to the box, bottle, vessel or package containing the same, and to the wrapper or cover thereof, a label bearing the name 'poison' distinctly shown, together with the name and place of business of the seller. . . . Any person failing to comply with the requirements of this section shall be deemed guilty of a misdemeanor, and shall be liable to a fine of not less than five (5) dollars for each and every such omission." — Minnesota Laws, 1885, chap. 147, section 14.

nance was designed to prevent, and which were proximately produced by such neglect. In support of this we need only cite our own decision in Bott *v.* Pratt, 33 Minn. 323 (23 N. W. Rep. 237).

Defendant contends that this is only true where a right of action for the alleged negligent act existed at common law; that no liability existed at common law for selling poison without labelling it, and therefore none exists under this statute, no right of civil action being given by it. Without stopping to consider the correctness of the assumption that selling poison without labelling it might not be actionable negligence at common law, it is sufficient to say that, in our opinion, defendant's contention proceeds upon an entire misapprehension of the nature and gist of a cause of action of this kind. The common law gives a right of action to every one sustaining injuries caused proximately by the negligence of another. The present is a common-law action, the gist of which is defendant's negligence, resulting in the death of plaintiff's intestate. Negligence is the breach of legal duty. It is immaterial whether the duty is one imposed by the rule of common law requiring the exercise of ordinary care not to injure another, or is imposed by a statute designed for the protection of others. In either case the failure to perform the duty constitutes negligence, and renders the party liable for injuries resulting from it. The only difference is that in the one case the measure of legal duty is to be determined upon common-law principles, while in the other the statute fixes it, so that the violation of the statute constitutes conclusive evidence of negligence, or, in other words, negligence *per se.* The action in the latter case is not a statutory one, nor does the statute give the right of action in any other sense except that it makes an act negligent which otherwise might not be such, or at least only evidence of negligence. All that the statute does is to establish a fixed standard by which the fact of negligence may be determined. The gist of the action is still negligence, or the non-performance of a legal duty to the person injured.

What has been already said suggests the answer to the further contention that if any civil liability exists it is only against the clerk who sold the poison, and who alone is criminally liable. Whether the act constituting the actionable negligence was such on common-law principles, or is made such by statute, the doctrine of agency applies, to wit, that the master is civilly liable for the negligence of his servant committed in the course of his employment, and resulting in injuries to third persons. *Judgment affirmed.*[1]

[1] Couch *v.* Steel, 3 E. & B. 402; Salisbury *v.* Herchenroder, 106 Mass. 458; Parker *v.* Barnard, 135 Mass. 116; Marino *v.* Lehmaier, 173 N. Y. 530; Westervelt *v.* Dives, 220 Pa. St. 617 *Accord.* Compare Nugent *v.* Vanderveer, 38 Hun, 487.

See also Great Northern Fishing Co. *v.* Edgehill, 11 Q. B. D. 225.

WILLY *v.* MULLEDY

COURT OF APPEALS, NEW YORK, SEPTEMBER 30, 1879.

Reported in 78 *New York Reports*, 310.

EARL, J.[1] This is an action to recover damages for the death of plaintiff's wife, alleged to have been caused by the fault of the defendant. Prior to the 1st day of November, 1877, the plaintiff hired of the defendant certain apartments in the rear of the third story of a tenement house in the city of Brooklyn, and with his wife and infant child moved into them on that day. On the fifth day in the same month, in the day-time, a fire took place, originating in the lower story of the house, and plaintiff's wife and child were smothered to death.

It is claimed that the defendant was in fault because he had not constructed for the house a fire-escape, and because he had not placed in the house a ladder for access to the scuttle.

Section 36 of title 13 of chapter 863 of the Laws of 1873 provides that every building in the city of Brooklyn shall have a scuttle or place of egress in the roof thereof of proper size, and "shall have ladders or stairways leading to the same; and all such scuttles and stairways or ladders leading to the roof shall be kept in readiness for use at all times." It also provides that houses like that occupied by the plaintiff "shall be provided with such fire-escapes and doors as shall be directed and approved by the commissioners (of the department of fire and buildings); and the owner or owners of any building upon which any fire-escapes may now or hereafter be erected, shall keep the same in good repair and well painted, and no person shall at any time place any incumbrance of any kind whatsoever upon said fire-escapes now erected or that may hereafter be erected in the city. Any person, after being notified by said commissioners, who shall neglect to place upon any such building the fire-escape herein provided for, shall forfeit the sum of $500, and shall be deemed guilty of a misdemeanor."

Under this statute the defendant was bound to provide this house with a fire-escape. He was not permitted to wait until he should be directed to provide one by the commissioners. He was bound to do it in such way as they should direct and approve, and it was for him to procure their direction and approval. No penalty is imposed for the simple omission to provide one. The penalty can be incurred only for the neglect to provide one after notification by the commissioners.

Here was, then, an absolute duty imposed upon the defendant by statute to provide a fire-escape, and the duty was imposed for the sole benefit of the tenants of the house, so that they would have a mode of escape in the case of a fire. For a breach of this duty causing damage, it cannot be doubted that the tenants have a remedy. It is a general

[1] Arguments omitted. Only so much of the opinion is given as relates to a single point.

rule, that whenever one owes another a duty, whether such duty be imposed by voluntary contract or by statute, a breach of such duty causing damage gives a cause of action. Duty and right are correlative; and where a duty is imposed, there must be a right to have it performed. When a statute imposes a duty upon a public officer, it is well settled that any person having a special interest in the performance thereof may sue for a breach thereof causing him damage, and the same is true of a duty imposed by statute upon any citizen: (Cooley on Torts, 654; Hover *v.* Barkhoff, 44 N. Y. 113; Jetter *v.* N. Y. C. and H. R. R. R. Co., 2 Abb. Ct. of App. Dec. 458; Heeney *v.* Sprague, 11 R. I. 456; Couch *v.* Steele, 3 Ell. & Bl. 402). In Comyn's Digest, Action upon Statute (F.), it is laid down as the rule that "in every case where a statute enacts or prohibits a thing for the benefit of a person, he shall have a remedy upon the same statute for the thing enacted for his advantage, or for the recompense of a wrong done to him contrary to the said law."

[Remainder of opinion omitted.]

Judgment for plaintiff affirmed.[1]

GORRIS *v.* SCOTT

In the Exchequer, April 22, 1874.

Reported in Law Reports, 9 Exchequer, 125.

Declaration, first count: that after the passing of the Contagious Diseases (Animals) Act, 1869, the Privy Council, in exercise of the powers and authorities vested in them by the Act (s. 75), made an order (called the Animals Order of 1871) with reference to animals brought by sea to ports in Great Britain, and to the places used and occupied by such animals on board any vessel in which the same should be so brought to such ports; and thereby, amongst other things, ordered (1) that every such place should be divided into pens by substantial divisions; (2) that each such pen should not exceed nine feet in breadth and fifteen feet in length; that afterwards and whilst the order was in force the plaintiffs delivered on board a vessel called the Hastings, to the defendant as owner of the vessel, certain sheep of the plaintiffs, to be carried by the defendant for reward on board the said vessel from Hamburg to Newcastle, and there delivered to the plaintiffs; and the defendant, as such owner, received and started on the said voyage with the sheep for the purposes and on the terms aforesaid; that all conditions were fulfilled, &c., yet the place in and on board the said vessel which was used and occupied by the

[1] Groves *v.* Wimborne, [1898] 2 Q. B. 402; Cowen *v.* Story & Clark Co., 170 Ill. App. 92; Andersen *v.* Settergren, 100 Minn. 294; Schaar *v.* Conforth, 128 Minn. 460 *Accord.* Compare Stehle *v.* Jaeger Machine Co., 220 Pa. St. 617; Drake *v.* Fenton, 237 Pa. St. 8.

sheep during the voyage was not, during the said voyage or any part thereof, divided into pens by substantial or other divisions, by reason whereof divers of the sheep were washed and swept away by the sea from off the said ship, and were drowned and wholly lost to the plaintiffs.

Second count, similar to the first, but setting out a third regulation: "that the floor of each such pen should have proper battens or other foot-hold thereon," and alleging the loss of the sheep as aforesaid to have been caused by the want of such battens.

Demurrer and joinder.

[The preamble of the Contagious Diseases (Animals) Act of 1869, 32 & 33 Vict. chapter 70, recited in a note to the report, is as follows:

"Whereas it is expedient to confer on Her Majesty's most honourable Privy Council powers to take such measures as may appear from time to time necessary to prevent the introduction into Great Britain of contagious or infectious diseases among cattle, sheep, and other animals, by prohibiting or regulating the importation of foreign animals; and it is further expedient to provide against the spreading of such diseases in Great Britain, and to consolidate and make perpetual the Acts relating thereto, and to make such other provisions as are contained in this Act."

Sect. 75 of said Act: "The Privy Council may from time to time make such orders as they think expedient for all or any of the following purposes: —

"For insuring for animals brought by sea to ports in Great Britain a proper supply of food and water during the passage and on landing;

"For protecting such animals from unnecessary suffering during the passage and on landing;

(Then follow certain inland purposes.)

"And generally any orders whatsoever which they think it expedient to make for the better execution of this Act, or for the purpose of in any manner preventing the introduction or spreading of contagious or infectious disease among animals in Great Britain."] [1]

KELLY, C. B. This is an action to recover damages for the loss of a number of sheep which the defendant, a shipowner, had contracted to carry, and which were washed overboard and lost by reason (as we must take it to be truly alleged) of the neglect to comply with a certain order made by the Privy Council, in pursuance of the Contagious Diseases (Animals) Act, 1869. The Act was passed merely for sanitary purposes, in order to prevent animals in a state of infectious disease from communicating it to other animals with which they might come in contact. Under the authority of that Act certain orders were made; amongst others, an order by which any ship bringing sheep or cattle from any foreign port to ports in Great Britain is to have the place occupied by such animals divided into pens of certain dimen-

[1] Arguments of counsel omitted.

sions, and the floor of such pens furnished with battens or foot-holds. The object of this order is to prevent animals from being overcrowded, and so brought into a condition in which the disease guarded against would be likely to be developed. This regulation has been neglected, and the question is, whether the loss, which we must assume to have been caused by that neglect, entitles the plaintiffs to maintain an action.

The argument of the defendant is, that the Act has imposed penalties to secure the observance of its provisions, and that, according to the general rule, the remedy prescribed by the statute must be pursued; that although, when penalties are imposed for the violation of a statutory duty, a person aggrieved by its violation may sometimes maintain an action for the damage so caused, that must be in cases where the object of the statute is to confer a benefit on individuals, and to protect them against the evil consequences which the statute was designed to prevent, and which have in fact ensued; but that if the object is not to protect individuals against the consequences which have in fact ensued, it is otherwise; that if, therefore, by reason of the precautions in question not having been taken, the plaintiffs had sustained that damage against which it was intended to secure them, an action would lie, but that when the damage is of such a nature as was not contemplated at all by the statute, and as to which it was not intended to confer any benefit on the plaintiffs, they cannot maintain an action founded on the neglect. The principle may be well illustrated by the case put in argument of a breach by a railway company of its duty to erect a gate on a level crossing, and to keep the gate closed except when the crossing is being actually and properly used. The object of the precaution is to prevent injury from being sustained through animals or vehicles being upon the line at unseasonable times; and if by reason of such a breach of duty, either in not erecting the gate, or in not keeping it closed, a person attempts to cross with a carriage at an improper time, and injury ensues to a passenger, no doubt an action would lie against the railway company, because the intention of the legislature was that, by the erection of the gates and by their being kept closed individuals should be protected against accidents of this description. And if we could see that it was the object, or among the objects of this Act, that the owners of sheep and cattle coming from a foreign port should be protected by the means described against the danger of their property being washed overboard, or lost by the perils of the sea, the present action would be within the principle.

But, looking at the Act, it is perfectly clear that its provisions were all enacted with a totally different view; there was no purpose, direct or indirect, to protect against such damage; but, as is recited in the preamble, the Act is directed against the possibility of sheep or cattle being exposed to disease on their way to this country. The preamble recites that "it is expedient to confer on Her Majesty's most honourable Privy Council power to take such measures as may appear from time to time necessary to prevent the introduction into Great Britain of contagious or infectious diseases among cattle, sheep, or other animals, by prohibiting or regulating the importation of foreign animals," and also to provide against the "spreading" of such diseases in Great Britain. Then follow numerous sections directed entirely to this object. Then comes sect. 75 which enacts that "the Privy Council may from time to time make such orders as they think expedient for all or any of the following purposes." What, then, are these purposes? They are "for securing for animals brought by sea to ports in Great Britain a proper supply of food and water during the passage and on landing," "for protecting such animals from unnecessary suffering during the passage and on landing," and so forth; all the purposes enumerated being calculated and directed to the prevention of disease, and none of them having any relation whatever to the danger of loss by the perils of the sea. That being so, if by reason of the default in question the plaintiffs' sheep had been overcrowded, or had been caused unnecessary suffering, and so had arrived in this country in a state of disease, I do not say that they might not have maintained this action. But the damage complained of here is something totally apart from the object of the Act of Parliament, and it is in accordance with all the authorities to say that the action is not maintainable.

PIGOTT, B. For the reasons which have been so exhaustively stated by the Lord Chief Baron, I am of opinion that the declaration shows no cause of action. It is necessary to see what was the object of the legislature in this enactment, and it is set forth clearly in the preamble as being "to prevent the introduction into Great Britain of contagious or infectious diseases among cattle, sheep, or other animals," and the "spread of such diseases in Great Britain." The purposes enumerated in sect. 75 are in harmony with this preamble, and it is in furtherance of that section that the order in question was made. The object, then, of the regulations which have been broken was, not to prevent cattle from being washed overboard, but to protect them against contagious disease. The legislature never contemplated altering the relations between the owners and carriers of cattle, except for the purposes pointed out in the Act; and if the Privy Council had gone out of their way and made provisions to prevent cattle from being washed overboard, their act would have been *ultra vires*. If, indeed, by reason of the neglect complained of, the cattle had contracted a contagious disease, the case would have been different. But as the case stands on this declaration, the answer to the action is this: Admit there has been a breach of duty; admit there has been a consequent injury; still the legislature was not legislating to protect against such an injury, but for an altogether different purpose; its object was not to regulate the duty of the carrier for all purposes, but only for one particular purpose.

[POLLOCK, B., delivered a concurring opinion. AMPHLETT, B., concurred.] *Judgment for the defendant.*[1]

[1] Bischof *v.* Illinois R. Co., 232 Ill. 446; Frontier Steam Laundry Co. *v.* Connolly, 72 Neb. 767; Hocking R. Co. *v.* Phillips, 81 Ohio St. 453 *Accord.*

Breach of statutory duty toward third person, see Gibson *v.* Leonard, 143 Ill. 182; Woodruff *v.* Bowen, 136 Ind. 431; Bott *v.* Pratt, 33 Minn. 323; Kelly *v.* Muhs, 71 N. J. Law, 348; Beehler *v.* Daniels, 19 R. I. 49. Compare Racine *v.* Morris, 201 N. Y. 240.

In Stanley *v.* Atchison R. Co., 88 Kan. 84, MASON, J., says:

"The evidence tended to show these facts: Stanley kept a number of cattle in a feed lot one side of which was formed by the right-of-way fence. Employees of the company who were engaged in its repair removed a part of it, as well as a part of Stanley's fence which connected with it, and as a temporary protection strung two wires across the gap. The protection was insufficient and the cattle escaped. None of them was injured upon the right of way, but a number strayed and were not recovered, and others suffered injury, in some cases fatal.

The defendant maintains that in any view of the findings the judgment ought not to be reversed, for the reason that the petition does not state a cause of action, because the company was under no obligation to maintain the fence, except for the purpose of avoiding liability for animals killed or injured by its trains, and therefore cannot be held accountable for any other kind of loss occasioned by the want of a sufficient fence. The original statute upon the subject does not in terms require a railroad right of way to be fenced. It makes the company responsible for animals killed or injured by the operation of its railway irrespective of negligence, except where the road is enclosed with a lawful fence. . . . The later statute imposed a duty on the railroad company to maintain the fence, and it is liable for any injury of which its neglect of such duty is the proximate cause. . . .

The defendant urges that the purpose of the statute referred to is to promote safety in the running of trains; that in this purpose is found the only warrant for imposing upon the railroad company the obligation to fence its right of way; and that therefore the company's liability must be limited to injuries resulting from the operation of the road, and the state has no power to make it liable for losses occasioned by the escape of animals which do not meet with any injury upon the right of way. Assuming that the right of the legislature to require a railroad company to fence its tracks is based solely upon the consideration that such fencing may be deemed necessary to diminish the danger of injury to animals from the operation of trains, and to persons and property resulting from trains colliding with animals, it is competent as a means of enforcing such requirement to make the company liable for losses occasioned to the landowner by the escape of his cattle through a defective fence, although they pass from the right of way without injury."

Liability to licensee in case of breach of statutory duty as to condition of premises, see Sheyer *v.* Lowell, 134 Cal. 357.

Liability to trespassers, see Nelson *v.* Burnham & Morrill Co., 114 Me. 213; Flanagan *v.* Sanders, 138 Mich. 253; Hamilton *v.* Minneapolis Desk Co., 78 Minn. 3; Bennett *v.* Odell Mfg. Co., 76 N. H. 180. Compare Butz *v.* Cavanaugh, 137 Mo. 503.

See Thayer, Public Wrong and Private Action, 27 Harvard Law Rev. 313, 336.

PART II

INTERFERENCE WITH GENERAL SUBSTANCE OR INTERESTS IN INTANGIBLE THINGS

CHAPTER IV

DECEIT

PASLEY *v.* FREEMAN

IN THE KING'S BENCH, HILARY TERM, 1789.

Reported in 3 *Term Reports* (*Durnford & East*), 51.

THIS was an action in the nature of a writ of deceit, to which the defendant pleaded the general issue. And after a verdict for the plaintiffs on the third count, a motion was made in arrest of judgment.

The third count was as follows: "And whereas, also, the said Joseph Freeman afterwards, to wit, on the twenty-first day of February, in the year of our Lord 1787, at London aforesaid, in the parish and ward aforesaid, further intending to deceive and defraud the said John Pasley and Edward, did wrongfully and deceitfully encourage and persuade the said John Pasley and Edward to sell and deliver to the said John Christopher Falch divers other goods, wares, and merchandises, to wit, sixteen other bags of cochineal of great value, to wit, of the value of £2,634 16*s.* 1*d.* upon trust and credit; and did for that purpose then and there falsely, deceitfully, and fraudulently assert and affirm to the said John Pasley and Edward that the said John Christopher then and there was a person safely to be trusted and given credit to in that respect, and did thereby falsely, fraudulently, and deceitfully cause and procure the said John Pasley and Edward to sell and deliver the said last-mentioned goods, wares, and merchandises upon trust and credit to the said John Christopher; and, in fact, they the said John Pasley and Edward, confiding in, and giving credit to, the said last-mentioned assertion and affirmation of the said Joseph, and believing the same to be true, and not knowing the contrary thereof, did afterwards, to wit, on the twenty-eighth day of February, in the year of our Lord 1787, at London aforesaid, in the parish and ward aforesaid, sell and deliver the said last-mentioned goods, wares, and merchandises upon trust and credit to the said John Christopher; whereas in truth and fact, at the time of the said Joseph's making his said last-mentioned assertion and affirmation, the said John Christopher was not then and there a person safely to be trusted and given credit to in that respect, and the said Joseph well knew the same, to wit, at London aforesaid, in the parish and ward aforesaid. And the said John Pasley and Edward further say, that the said John Christopher hath not, nor hath any other person on his behalf, paid to the said John Pasley and Edward, or either of them, the said sum of £2,634 16*s.* 1*d.* last mentioned, or any part thereof, for the said last-mentioned goods, wares, and merchandises; but, on the contrary, the said John Christopher then was and still is wholly unable to pay the said sum of money last mentioned, or any part thereof, to the said John and Edward, to wit, at London aforesaid, in the parish and ward aforesaid; and the said John Pasley and Edward aver that the said Joseph falsely and fraudulently deceived them in this, that at the time of his making his said last-mentioned assertion and affirmation the said John Christopher was not a person safely to be trusted or given credit to in that respect, as aforesaid, and the said Joseph then well knew the same, to wit, at London aforesaid, in the parish and ward aforesaid; by reason of which said last-mentioned false, fraudulent, and deceitful assertion and affirmation of the said Joseph, the said John Pasley and Edward have been deceived and imposed upon, and have wholly lost the said last-mentioned goods, wares, and merchandises, and the value thereof, to wit, at London aforesaid, in the parish and ward aforesaid, to the damage," &c.

Application was first made for a new trial, which after argument was refused, and then this motion in arrest of judgment. *Wood* argued for the plaintiffs, and *Russell* for the defendant, in the last term; but as the Court went so fully into this subject in giving their opinions, it is unnecessary to give the arguments at the bar.

The Court took time to consider of this matter, and now delivered their opinions *seriatim.*

Grose, J. Upon the face of this count in the declaration no privity of contract is stated between the parties. No consideration arises to the defendant; and he is in no situation in which the law considers him in any trust, or in which it demands from him any account of the credit of Falch. He appears not to be interested in any transaction between the plaintiffs and Falch, nor to have colluded with them; but he knowingly asserted a falsehood, by saying that Falch might be safely intrusted with the goods, and given credit to, for the purpose of inducing the plaintiffs to trust him with them, by which the plaintiffs lost the value of the goods. Then this is an action against the defendant for making a false affirmation, or telling a lie, respecting the credit of a third person, with intent to deceive, by which the third person was damnified; and for the damages suffered, the plaintiffs contend that the defendant is answerable in an action upon the case. It is admitted that the action is new in point of precedent; but it is insisted that the law recognizes principles on which it may be supported. The principle upon which it is contended to lie is that, wherever deceit or falsehood is practised to the detriment of another, the law will give redress. This proposition I controvert, and shall endeavor to show that, in every case where deceit or falsehood is practised to the detriment of another, the law will not give redress; and I say that by the law, as it now stands, no action lies against any person standing in the predicament of this defendant for the false affirmation stated in the declaration. If the action can be supported, it must be upon the ground that there exists in this case what the law deems *damnum cum injuria.* If it does, I admit that the action lies; and I admit that upon the verdict found the plaintiffs appear to have been damnified. But whether there has been *injuria,* a wrong, a tort, for which an action lies, is a matter of law. The tort complained of is the false affirmation made with intent to deceive; and it is said to be an action upon the case analogous to the old writ of deceit. When this was first argued at the bar, on the motion for a new trial, I confess I thought it reasonable that the action should lie; but, on looking into the old books for cases in which the old action of deceit has been maintained upon the false affirmation of the defendant, I have changed my opinion. The cases on this head are brought together in Bro. tit. Deceit, pl. 29, and in Fitz. Abr. I have likewise looked into Danvers, Kitchins, and Comyns, and I have not met with any case of an action upon a false affirmation, except against a party to a contract, and where there is a promise, either express or implied, that the fact is true, which is misrepresented; and no other case has been cited at the bar. Then if no such case has ever existed, it furnishes a strong objection against the action, which is brought for the first time for a supposed injury, which has been daily committed for centuries past. For I believe there has been no time when men have not been constantly damnified by the fraudulent misrepresentations of others; and if such an action would have lain, there certainly has been, and will be, a plentiful source of litigation, of which the public are not hitherto aware. A variety of cases may be put. Suppose a man recommends an estate to another, as knowing it to be of greater value than it is; when the purchaser has bought it he discovers the defect, and sells the estate for less than he gave; why may not an action be brought for the loss upon any principle that will support this action? And yet such an action has never been attempted. Or suppose a person present at the sale of a horse asserts that he was his horse, and that he knows him to be sound and surefooted, when in fact the horse is neither the one nor the other; according to the principle contended for by the plaintiffs, an action lies against the person present as well as the seller, and the purchaser has two securities. And even in this very case, if the action lies, the plaintiffs will stand in a peculiarly fortunate predicament, for they will then have the responsibility both of Falch and the defendant. And they will be in a better situation than they would have been if, in the conversation that passed between them and the defendant, instead of asserting that Falch might safely be trusted, the defendant had said, "If he do not pay for the goods, I will;" for then undoubtedly an action would not have lain against the defendant. Other and stronger cases may be put of actions that must necessarily spring out of any principle upon which this can be supported, and yet which were never thought of till the present action was brought. Upon what principle is this act said to be an injury? The plaintiffs say, on the ground that, when the question was asked, the defendant was bound to tell the truth. There are cases, I admit, where a man is bound not to misrepresent, but to tell the truth; but no such case has been cited, except in the case of contracts; and all the cases of deceit for misinformation may, it seems to me, be turned into actions of assumpsit. And so far from a person being bound in a case like the present to tell the truth, the books supply me with a variety of cases, in which even the contracting party is not liable for a misrepresentation. There are cases of two sorts in which, though a man is deceived, he can maintain no action. The first class of cases (though not analogous to the present) is where the affirmation is that the thing sold has not a defect which is a visible one; there the imposition, the fraudulent intent, is admitted, but it is no tort. The second head of cases is where the affirmation is (what is called in some of the books) a nude assertion, such as the party deceived may exercise his own judgment upon; as where it is matter of opinion, where he may make inquiries into the truth of the assertion, and it becomes his own fault from laches that he is deceived. 1 Roll. Abr. 101; Yelv. 20; 1 Sid. 146; Cro. Jac. 386; Bayly *v.* Merrel. In Harvey *v.* Young, Yelv. 20, J. S., who had a term for years, affirmed to J. D. that the term was worth £150 to be sold, upon which J. D. gave £150, and afterwards could not get more than £100 for it, and then brought his action; and it was alleged that this matter did not prove any fraud, for it was only a naked assertion that the term was worth so much, and it was the plaintiff's folly to give credit to such assertion. But if the defendant had warranted the term to be of such a value to be sold, and upon that the plaintiff had bought it, it would have been otherwise; for the warranty given by the defendant is a matter to induce confidence and trust in the plaintiff. This case, and the passage in 1 Roll. Abr. 101, are recognized in 1 Sid. 146. How, then, are the cases? None exist in which such an action as the present has been brought; none, in which any principle applicable to the present case has been laid down to prove that it will lie; not even a *dictum*. But from the cases cited some principles may be extracted to show that it cannot be sustained: 1st. That what is fraud, which will support an action, is matter of law. 2d. That in every case of a fraudulent misrepresentation, attended with damage, an action will not lie even between contracting parties. 3d. That if the assertion be a nude assertion, it is that sort of misrepresentation the truth of which does not lie merely in the knowledge of the defendant, but may be inquired into, and the plaintiff is bound so to do; and he cannot recover a damage which he has suffered by his laches. Then let us consider how far the facts of the case come within the last of these principles. The misrepresentation stated in the declaration is respecting the credit of Falch; the defendant asserted that the plaintiffs might safely give him credit; but credit to which a man is entitled is matter of judgment and opinion, on which different men might form different opinions, and upon which the plaintiffs might form their own, to mislead which no fact to prove the good credit of Falch is falsely asserted. It seems to me, therefore, that any assertion relative to credit, especially where the party making it has no interest, nor is in any collusion with the person respecting whose credit the assertion is made, is like the case in Yelverton respecting the value of the term. But at any rate, it is not an assertion of a fact peculiarly in the knowledge of the defendant. Whether Falch deserved credit depended on the opinion of many; for credit exists on the good opinion of many. Respecting this the plaintiffs might have inquired of others who knew as much as the defendant; it was their fault that they did not, and they have suffered damage by their own laches. It was owing to their own gross negligence that they gave credence to the assertion of the defendant, without taking pains to satisfy themselves that that assertion was founded in fact, as in the case of Bayly *v.* Merrel. I am, therefore, of opinion that this action is as novel in principle as it is in precedent, that it is against the principles to be collected from analogous cases, and consequently that it cannot be maintained.

BULLER, J. The foundation of this action is fraud and deceit in the defendant, and damage to the plaintiffs. And a question is, whether an action thus founded can be sustained in a court of law. Fraud without damage, or damage without fraud, gives no cause of action; but where these two concur, an action lies. Per Croke, J., 3 Bulst. 95. But it is contended that this was a bare, naked lie; that, as no collusion with Falch is charged, it does not amount to a fraud; and, if there were any fraud, the nature of it is not stated. And it was supposed by the counsel, who originally made the motion, that no action could be maintained unless the defendant, who made this false assertion, had an interest in so doing. I agree that an action cannot be supported for telling a bare, naked lie; but that I define to be, saying a thing which is false, knowing or not knowing it to be so, and without any design to injure, cheat, or deceive another person. Every deceit comprehends a lie; but a deceit is more than a lie, on account of the view with which it is practised, its being coupled with some dealing, and the injury which it is calculated to occasion, and does occasion, to another person. Deceit is a very extensive head in the law; and it will be proper to take a short view of some of the cases which have existed on the subject, to see how far the Courts have gone, and what are the principles upon which they have decided. I lay out of the question the case in 2 Cro. 196, and all other cases which relate to freehold interests in lands; for they go on the special reason that the seller cannot have them without title, and the buyer is at his peril to see it. But the cases cited on the part of the defendant deserving notice are Yelv. 20, Carth. 90, Salk. 210. The first of these has been fully stated by my brother Grose; but it is to be observed that the book does not affect to give the reasons on which the Court delivered their judgment; but it is a case quoted by counsel at the bar, who mentions what was alleged by counsel in the other case. If the Court went on a distinction between the words "warranty" and "affirmation," the case is not law; for it was rightly held by Holt, C. J., in the subsequent cases, and has been uniformly adopted ever since, that an affirmation at the time of a sale is a warranty, provided it appear on evidence to have been so intended. But the true ground of that determination was that the assertion was of mere matter of judgment and opinion; of a matter of which the defendant had no particular knowledge, but of which many men will be of many minds, and which is often governed by whim and caprice. Judgment, or opinion, in such case implies no knowledge. And here this case differs materially from that in Yelverton; my brother Grose considers this assertion as mere matter of opinion only, but I differ from him in that respect. For it is stated on this record that the defendant knew that the fact was false. The case in Yelverton admits that, if there had been fraud, it would have been otherwise. The case of Crosse *v.* Gardner, Carth. 90, was upon an affirmation that oxen which the defendant had in his possession and sold to the plaintiff were his, when in truth they belonged to another person. The objection against the action was that the declaration neither stated that the defendant deceitfully sold them, or that he knew them to be the property of another person; and a man may be mistaken in his property and right to a thing without any fraud or ill intent. *Ex concessis* therefore if there were fraud or deceit, the action would lie; and knowledge of the falsehood of the thing asserted is fraud and deceit. But, notwithstanding these objections, the Court held that the action lay, because the plaintiff had no means of knowing to whom the property belonged but only by the possession. And in Cro. Jac. 474, it was held that affirming them to be his, knowing them to be a stranger's, is the offence and cause of action. The case of Medina *v.* Stoughton, Salk. 210, in the point of decision, is the same as Crosse *v.* Gardner; but there is an *obiter dictum* of Holt, C. J., that where the seller of a personal thing is out of possession, it is otherwise; for there may be room to question the seller's title, and *caveat emptor* in such case to have an express warranty or a good title. This distinction by Holt is not mentioned by Lord Raym. 593, who reports the same case; and if an affirmation at the time of sale be a warranty, I cannot feel a distinction between the vendor's being in or out of possession. The thing is bought of him, and in consequence of his assertion; and if there be any difference, it seems to me that the case is strongest against the vendor when he is out of possession, because then the vendee has nothing but the warranty to rely on. These cases, then, are so far from being authorities against the present action, that they show that if there be fraud or deceit, the action will lie; and that knowledge of the falsehood of the thing asserted is fraud and deceit. Collusion, then, is not necessary to constitute fraud. In the case of a conspiracy, there must be a collusion between two or more to support an indictment; but if one man alone be guilty of an offence which, if practised by two, would be the subject of an indictment for a conspiracy, he is civilly liable in an action for reparation of damages at the suit of the person injured. That knowledge of the falsehood of the thing asserted constitutes fraud, though there be no collusion, is further proved by the case of Risney *v.* Selby, Salk. 211, where, upon a treaty for the purchase of a house, the defendant fraudulently affirmed that the rent was £30 per annum, when it was only £20 per annum, and the plaintiff had his judgment; for the value of the rent is a matter which lies in the private knowledge of the landlord and tenant; and if they affirm the rent to be more than it is, the purchaser is cheated, and ought to have a remedy for it. No collusion was there stated; nor does it appear that the tenant was ever asked a question about the rent, and yet the purchaser might have applied to him for information; but the judgment proceeded wholly upon the ground that the defendant knew that what he asserted was false. And, by the words of the book, it seems that if the tenant had said the same thing he also would have been liable to an action. If so, that would be an answer to the objection that the defendant in this case had no interest in the assertion which he made. But I shall not leave this point on the *dictum* or inference which may be collected from that case. If A., by fraud and deceit, cheat B. out of £1,000, it makes no difference to B. whether A. or any other person pockets that £1,000. He has lost his money; and if he can fix fraud upon A., reason seems to say that he has a right to seek satisfaction against him. Authorities are not wanting on this point. 1 Roll. Abr. 91, pl. 7. If the vendor affirm that the goods are the goods of a stranger, his friend, and that he had authority from him to sell them, and upon that B. buys them, when in truth they are the goods of another, yet, if he sell them fraudulently and falsely on this pretence of authority, though he do not warrant them, and though it be not averred that he sold them knowing them to be the goods of the stranger, yet B. shall have an action for this deceit. It is not clear from this case whether the fraud consisted in having no authority from his friend, or in knowing that the goods belonged to another person; what is said at the end of the case only proves that "falsely" and "fraudulently" are equivalent to "knowingly." If the first were the fact in the case, namely, that he had no authority, the case does not apply to this point; but if he had an authority from his friend, whatever the goods were sold for his friend was entitled to, and he had no interest in them. But, however that might be, the next case admits of no doubt. For in 1 Roll. Abr. 100, pl. 1, it was held that if a man acknowledge a fine in my name, or acknowledge a judgment in an action in my name of my land, this shall bind me forever; and therefore I may have a writ of deceit against him who acknowledged it. So if a man acknowledge a recognizance, statute-merchant or staple, there is no foundation for supposing that in that case the person acknowledging the fine or judgment was the same person to whom it was so acknowledged. If that had been necessary it would have been so stated; but if it were not so, he who acknowledged the fine had no interest in it. Again, in 1 Roll. Abr. 95, l. 25, it is said, "If my servant lease my land to another for years, reserving a rent for me, and, to persuade the lessee to accept it, he promise that he shall enjoy the land without incumbrances, if the land be incumbered, &c., the lessee may have an action on the case against my servant, because he made an express warranty." Here, then, is a case in which the party had no interest whatever. The same case is reported in Cro. Jac. 425; but no notice is taken of this point, probably because the reporter thought it immaterial whether the warranty be by the master or servant. And if the warranty be made at the time of the sale, or before the sale, and the sale is upon the faith of the warranty, I can see no distinction between the cases. The gist of the action is fraud and deceit; and if that fraud and deceit can be fixed by evidence on one who had no interest in his iniquity, it proves his malice to be the greater. But it was objected to this declaration that if there were any fraud, the nature of it is not stated. To this the declaration itself is so direct an answer that the case admits of no other. The fraud is that the defendant procured the plaintiffs to sell goods on credit to one whom they would not otherwise have trusted, by asserting that which he knew to be false. Here, then, is the fraud and the means by which it was committed; and it was done with a view to enrich Falch by impoverishing the plaintiffs, or, in other words, by cheating the plaintiffs out of their goods. The cases which I have stated, and Sid. 146, and 1 Keb. 522, prove that the declaration states more than is necessary; for *fraudulenter* without *sciens*, or *sciens* without *fraudulenter*, would be sufficient to support the action. But, as Mr. J. Twisden said in that case, the fraud must be proved. The assertion alone will not maintain the action; but the plaintiff must go on to prove that it was false, and that the defendant knew it to be so; by what means that proof is to be made out in evidence need not be stated in the declaration. Some general arguments were urged at the bar to show that mischiefs and inconveniences would arise if this action were sustained; for if a man who is asked a question respecting another's responsibility hesitate or is silent, he blasts the character of the tradesman; and if he say that he is insolvent, he may not be able to prove it. But let us see what is contended for: it is nothing less than that a man may assert that which he knows to be false, and thereby do an everlasting injury to his neighbor, and yet not be answerable for it. This is as repugnant to law as it is to morality. Then it is said that the plaintiffs had no right to ask the question of the defendant. But I do not agree in that; for the plaintiffs had an interest in knowing what the credit of Falch was. It was not the inquiry of idle curisoity, but it was to govern a very extensive concern. The defendant undoubtedly had his option to give an answer to the question or not; but if he gave none, or said he did not know, it is impossible for any court of justice to adopt the possible inferences of a suspicious mind as a ground for grave judgment. All that is required of a person in the defendant's situation is that he shall give no answer, or that, if he do, he shall answer according to the truth as far as he knows. The reasoning in the case of Coggs *v.* Barnard, which was cited by the plaintiff's counsel, is, I think, very applicable to this part of the case. If the answer import insolvency, it is not necessary that the defendant should be able to prove that insolvency to a jury; for the law protects a man in giving that answer, if he does it in confidence and without malice. No action can be maintained against him for giving such an answer, unless express malice can be proved. From the circumstance of the law giving that protection, it seems to follow, as a necessary consequence, that the law not only gives sanction to the question, but requires that, if it be answered at all, it shall be answered honestly. There is a case in the books which, though not much to be relied on, yet serves to show that this kind of conduct has never been thought innocent in Westminster Hall. In R. *v.* Gunston, 1 Str. 589, the defendant was indicted for pretending that a person of no reputation was Sir J. Thornycraft, whereby the prosecutor was induced to trust him; and the Court refused to grant a *certiorari*, unless a special ground were laid for it. If the assertion in that case had been wholly innocent the Court would not have hesitated a moment. How, indeed, an indictment could be maintained for that I do not well understand; nor have I learnt what became of it. The objection to the indictment is that it was merely a private injury: but that is no answer to an action. And if a man will wickedly assert that which he knows to be false, and thereby draws his neighbor into a heavy loss, even though it be under the specious pretence of serving his friend, I say *ausis talibus istis non jura subserviunt.*

Ashhurst, J. The objection in this case, which is to the third count in the declaration, is that it contains only a bare assertion, and does not state that the defendant had any interest, or that he colluded with the other party who had. But I am of opinion that the action lies notwithstanding this objection. It seems to me that the rule laid down by Croke, J., in Bayly *v.* Merrel, 3 Bulstr. 95, is a sound and solid principle, namely, that fraud without damage, or damage without fraud, will not found an action; but where both concur an action will lie. The principle is not denied by the other judges, but only the application of it, because the party injured there, who was the carrier, had the means of attaining certain knowledge in his own power, namely, by weighing the goods; and therefore it was a foolish credulity, against which the law will not relieve. But that is not the case here, for it is expressly charged that the defendant knew the falsity of the allegation, and which the jury have found to be true; but *non constat* that the plaintiffs knew it, or had any means of knowing it, but trusted to the veracity of the defendant. And many reasons may occur why the defendant might know that fact better than the plaintiffs; as if there had before this event subsisted a partnership between him and Falch which had been dissolved; but at any rate it is stated as a fact that he knew it. It is admitted that a fraudulent affirmation, when the party making it has an interest, is a ground of action, as in Risney *v.* Selby, which was a false affirmation made to a purchaser as to the rent of a farm which the defendant was in treaty to sell to him. But it was argued that the action lies not unless where the party making it has an interest, or colludes with one who has. I do not recollect that any case was cited which proves such a position; but if there were any such to be found, I should not hesitate to say that it could not be law, for I have so great a veneration for the law as to suppose that nothing can be law which is not founded in common sense or common honesty. For the gist of the action is the injury done to the plaintiff, and not whether the defendant meant to be a gainer by it; what is it to the plaintiff whether the defendant was or was not to gain by it? the injury to him is the same. And it should seem that it ought more emphatically to lie against him, as the malice is more diabolical if he had not the temptation of gain. For the same reason, it cannot be necessary that the defendant should collude with one who has an interest. But if collusion were necessary, there seems all the reason in the world to suppose both interest and collusion from the nature of the act; for it is to be hoped that there is not to be found a disposition so diabolical as to prompt any man to injure another without benefiting himself. But it is said that if this be determined to be law, any man may have an action brought against him for telling a lie, by the crediting of which another happens eventually to be injured. But this consequence by no means follows; for in order to make it actionable it must be accompanied with the circumstances averred in this count, namely, that the defendant, "intending to deceive and defraud the plaintiffs, did deceitfully encourage and persuade them to do the act, and for that purpose made the false affirmation, in consequence of which they did the act." Any lie accompanied with those circumstances I should clearly hold to be the subject of an action; but not a mere lie thrown out at random without any intention of hurting anybody, but which some person was foolish enough to act upon; for the *quo animo* is a great part of the gist of the action. Another argument which has been made use of is, that this is a new case, and that there is no precedent of such an action. Where cases are new in their principle, there I admit that it is necessary to have recourse to legislative interposition in order to remedy the grievance; but where the case is only new in the instance, and the only question is upon the application of a principle recognized in the law to such new case, it will be just as competent to courts of justice to apply the principle to any case which may arise two centuries hence, as it was two centuries ago; if it were not, we ought to blot out of our law-books one fourth part of the cases that are to be found in them. The same objection might, in my opinion, have been made with much greater reason in the case of Coggs *v.* Barnard; for there the defendant, so far from meaning an injury, meant a kindness, though he was not so careful as he should have been in the execution of what he undertook. And indeed the principle of the case does not, in my opinion, seem so clear as that of the case now before us, and yet that case has always been received as law. Indeed, one great reason, perhaps, why this action has never occurred may be that it is not likely that such a species of fraud should be practised unless the party is in some way interested. Therefore I think the rule for arresting the judgment ought to be discharged.

LORD KENYON, C. J. I am not desirous of entering very fully into the discussion of this subject, as the argument comes to me quite exhausted by what has been said by my brothers. But still I will say a few words as to the grounds upon which my opinion is formed. All laws stand on the best and broadest basis which go to enforce moral and social duties. Though, indeed, it is not every moral and social duty the neglect of which is the ground of an action. For there are, which are called in the civil law, duties of imperfect obligation, for the enforcing of which no action lies. There are many cases where the pure effusion of a good mind may induce the performance of particular duties, which yet cannot be enforced by municipal laws. But there are certain duties, the non-performance of which the jurisprudence of this country has made the subject of a civil action. And I find it laid down by the Lord Ch. B. Comyns (Com. Dig. tit. Action upon the Case for a Deceit, A. 1), that "an action upon the case for a deceit lies when a man does any deceit to the damage of another." He has not, indeed, cited any authority for his opinion; but his opinion alone is of great authority, since he was considered by his contemporaries as the most able lawyer in Westminster Hall. Let us, however, consider whether that proposition is not supported by the invariable principle in all the cases on this subject. In 3 Bulstr. 95, it was held by Croke, J., that "fraud without damage, or damage without fraud, gives no cause of action; but where these two do concur, there an action lieth." It is true, as has been already observed, that the judges were of opinion in that case that the action did not lie on other grounds. But consider what those grounds were. Dodderidge, J., said: "If we shall give way to this, then every carrier would have an action upon the case; but he shall not have any action for this, because it is merely his own default that he did not weigh it." Undoubtedly, where the common prudence and caution of man are sufficient to guard him, the law will not protect him in his negligence. And in that case, as reported in Cro. Jac. 386, the negligence of the plaintiff himself was the cause for which the Court held that the action was not maintainable. Then, how does the principle of that case apply to the present? There are many situations in life, and particularly in the commercial world, where a man cannot by any diligence inform himself of the degree of credit which ought to be given to the persons with whom he deals; in which cases he must apply to those whose sources of intelligence enable them to give that information. The law of prudence leads him to apply to them; and the law of morality ought to induce them to give the information required. In the case of Bulstrode, the carrier might have weighed the goods himself; but in this case the plaintiffs had no means of knowing the state of Falch's credit but by an application to his neighbors. The same observation may be made to the cases cited by the defendant's counsel respecting titles to real property. For a person does not have recourse to common conversation to know the title of an estate which he is about to purchase; but he may inspect the title-deeds; and he does not use common prudence if he rely on any other security. In the case of Bulstrode, the Court seemed to consider that *damnum* and *injuria* are the grounds of this action; and they all admitted that, if they had existed in that case, the action would have lain there; for the rest of the judges did not controvert the opinion of Croke, J., but denied the application of it to that particular case. Then it was contended here that the action cannot be maintained for telling a naked lie; but that proposition is to be taken *sub modo*. If, indeed, no injury is occasioned by the lie it is not actionable; but if it be attended with a damage, it then becomes the subject of an action. As calling a woman a whore, if she sustain no damage by it, is not actionable; but if she lose her marriage by it, then she may recover satisfaction in damages. But in this case the two grounds of the action concur; here are both the *damnum et injuria*. The plaintiffs applied to the defendant, telling him that they were going to deal with Falch, and desiring to be informed of his credit, when the defendant fraudulently, and knowing it to be otherwise, and with a design to deceive the plaintiffs, made the false assertion which is stated on the record, by which they sustained a considerable damage. Then, can a doubt be entertained for a moment but that this is injurious to the plaintiffs? If this be not an injury, I do not know how to define the word. Then, as to the loss; this is stated in the declaration, and found by the verdict. Several of the words stated in this declaration, and particularly *fraudulenter*, did not occur in several of the cases cited. It is admitted that the defendant's conduct was highly immoral and detrimental to society. And I am of opinion that the action is maintainable on the grounds of deceit in the defendant, and injury and loss to the plaintiffs.

Rule for arresting the judgment discharged.[1]

WORK *v.* CAMPBELL

Supreme Court, California, December 13, 1912.

Reported in 164 *California Reports,* 343.

Angellotti, J.[2] The action is one to recover of defendant fifteen thousand dollars' damages alleged to have been caused plaintiff by reason of the fact that she has become finally separated from her husband, L. B. Work, and has thereby suffered and will continue to suffer great distress of mind and mental anguish, and has lost and will continue to lose forever his society, comfort, love, and affection, as well as the support and maintenance which he would give her. On or about February 15, 1910, the husband "separated from plaintiff, and from their said children, and departed from the said county of Kings, and has gone to parts unknown to plaintiff with intent to desert and abandon plaintiff." It is not alleged that defendant, who is the husband of an aunt of plaintiff, ever said or did anything to influence the husband to leave plaintiff, or to cause any change of feeling on his part toward her. It is frankly alleged that his departure was caused solely by the fact that she became very angry with him, refused to see him, refused to speak or talk with him, sent him a letter in which she told him that she would hold no further communication with him, but would sue him for a divorce and that she hoped she might never see or speak to him again. Her complaint characterizes her conduct toward her husband, alleged to be the sole inducement for his departure, as "harsh and cruel treatment" of him. The claim of any liability on the part of defendant to her on account of the separation is based on allegations to the effect that her attitude and conduct toward her husband, which caused the separation, were wholly induced by certain false statements knowingly made to her by defendant concerning her husband, which, owing to her confidence and trust in defendant, she fully believed and relied upon, and certain advice and counsel given to her by defendant in the matter, all of which statements and advice were wilfully made and given by defendant with the intent and design on his part to cause a separation between plaintiff and her husband. The complaint alleges in detail the alleged statements and advice of defendant in this behalf, and also the object sought to be obtained by him in causing a separation of the husband and wife, but no useful purpose can be subserved by stating these things here. It further alleges that when she discovered the falsity of the representations and the intent and purpose

[1] By "Lord Tenterden's Act," 9 Geo. IV. ch. 14, s. 6, it is provided, that no action shall be brought to charge any person upon any representation made concerning the character, conduct, credit, ability, trade, or dealings of any other person, to the intent that such other person may obtain credit, money, or goods, unless such representation "be made in writing, signed by the party to be charged therewith." Statutes of a similar nature have been enacted in some of the United States.

[2] Only part of the opinion is printed.

of defendant in making them, she at once instituted diligent search for her husband, but has been unable to ascertain his whereabouts. It is further alleged " that by reason of the premises hereinabove stated, defendant has unlawfully, fraudulently and wrongfully abducted and enticed from the plaintiff her said husband, and that by reason of the said abduction, this plaintiff has suffered," &c., to her great damage in the sum of fifteen thousand dollars.

Under our statutes, a wife may maintain an action for damages suffered by her by reason of the abduction or enticement from her of her husband, as may a husband for the damages suffered by him for the abduction or enticement from him of his wife, and in such an action by the wife her husband is not a necessary party plaintiff. (See Civ. Code, sec. 49, subds. 1 and 2; Humphrey *v.* Pope, 122 Cal. 253 [54 Pac. 847].) It may be assumed, purely for the purposes of this decision, that no cause of action for the abduction or enticement of her husband from her is stated by the wife in her complaint. . . .

We can see no reason why, regardless of the question we have just referred to, the matters alleged in the complaint do not show a cause of action in behalf of plaintiff against defendant. According to the complaint, the sole cause of the conduct of plaintiff causing the separation of the husband and wife, with the same injurious consequences to her that would have followed the abduction or enticement of her husband from her, was the action of defendant in making to her the wilfully false representations concerning her husband, for the very purpose and with the design on his part to so influence her as to bring about such a separation. His deception in the matter was the sole cause of such conduct on her part, and such conduct on her part was tantamount to a refusal by her to continue the relation between her husband and herself of husband and wife. It is declared in section 1708 of the Civil Code that " every person is bound, without contract, to abstain from injuring the person or property of another, or infringing upon any of his rights," and in section 1709, " one who wilfully deceives another with intent to induce him to alter his position to his injury or risk, is liable for any damage which he thereby suffers." These are but statements of the well settled law independent of statute. It is substantially said in 20 Cyc. at page 10, and the statement is well supported by the authorities, that as a general rule, an action for damages for deceit will lie wherever a party has made a false representation of a material fact susceptible of knowledge knowing it to be false or not having sufficient knowledge on the subject to warrant the representation, with the intent to induce the person to whom it is made, in reliance upon it, to do or refrain from doing something to his pecuniary hurt, when such person, acting with reasonable prudence, is thereby deceived and induced to so do or refrain, to his damage. No reason is apparent to us why the alleged facts set forth in the complaint should not be held to bring the case within the operation of this rule.

It is no answer to such an action that the action or conduct of the plaintiff is the direct cause of the result occasioning damages. Such is the situation wherever such an action is allowed. The whole basis of the action is that such act or conduct is fraudulently induced by the defendant. A is wilfully deceived by B into selling goods to C upon credit, by false representations as to C's solvency wilfully and knowingly made by B to A for the very purpose of inducing him to so do and thereby suffers a pecuniary injury. The direct and immediate cause of the injury is, of course, the sale by A to C on credit.

But B is held liable to A for the damage thereby suffered because by fraud he induced A to make such sale on credit.

It may be urged that a person fraudulently misled cannot found his claim on conduct violative of sound morals or public policy, or of a criminal statute. Here the conduct and attitude of the wife causing the separation was her harsh and cruel conduct toward her husband, her refusal to live with him or to see him, her refusal to further continue the relationship of husband and wife, &c. Of course, all her conduct would have been fully justified if the representations made to her by defendant had been true in point of fact, as the complaint sufficiently alleges that plaintiff believed to be the situation. It has been held that where the fraudulent representation is intended to create and actually does create in the mind of the party a belief that under the circumstances represented the act which he is induced to do is neither illegal nor immoral, he may recover the damages he has sustained even though a statute makes the act a criminal offence. (See 20 Cyc. 80; Burrows *v.* Rhodes, [1899] 1 Q. B. 816; Prescott *v.* Norris, 32 N. H. 101; Morrill *v.* Palmer, 68 Vt. 1 [33 L. R. A. 411, 33 Atl. 829].) We are not called upon to go as far as this in this case. The complaint indicates no criminal offence on plaintiff's part. Certainly, however, under the circumstances stated, it cannot fairly be said that plaintiff did not believe her conduct toward her husband to be in full accord with good morals and public policy, or was not justified in so believing. It is not claimed that the complaint does not sufficiently show that plaintiff acted with reasonable prudence in accepting as true and relying on defendant's statements. In view of the circumstances alleged as to her relationship to defendant, and her confidence and trust in him, we think the complaint is not fatally defective in this regard, although it must be conceded to be somewhat remarkable that a wife having any affection for or confidence in her husband should be willing to accept as true such statements as are here alleged to have been made to her, without making some further inquiry.

We have not found any case in which the remedy of action for damages for deceit has been invoked under such circumstances as appear here. The fact that the case presented is unique in its circumstances is not, however, any warrant for a refusal to apply a rule that appears, on principle, to be applicable. We think the facts confessed by the demurrer show a liability on the part of defendant to plaintiff for any damage caused her by the loss of her husband.[1]

STATE *v.* GORDON

Supreme Court, Kansas, July Term, 1895.

Reported in 56 *Kansas Reports*, 64.

Gordon was convicted and sentenced in the District Court upon a charge of obtaining money from Trenier on false pretences. He appealed from the judgment.

The facts alleged and proved were, in brief, as follows: —

Gordon represented to Trenier that Gordon and a certain Indian owned and possessed a gold brick of the value of $10,000; that they

[1] Cf. Lillegren *v.* Burns, 135 Minn. 60.

were about to take the brick to the United States Mint at Philadelphia to be coined into money; that the Indian would not allow the brick to be taken to the mint unless he received a certain sum of money on his interest in the brick. Gordon told Trenier that, if Trenier would give Gordon money to pay the Indian on his share in the brick, he (Gordon) would deliver said brick to Trenier to be by Trenier taken to the mint, and that Trenier should have a third interest in the money coined from the brick. Relying on these statements, Trenier gave Gordon money to pay the Indian.

It appeared that Gordon and the Indian did not own or possess a gold brick; that the representations were all known by Gordon to be false; and that they were made for the purpose of defrauding Trenier.[1]

JOHNSTON, J. . . . The substantial features of the charge were representations and assurances of present existing facts, viz., that Gordon and the Indian were then the owners and possessors of a valuable gold brick, which they then had in Shawnee County, and that they were then on their road to take the gold brick to the United States Mint at Philadelphia to be coined. It is alleged that on the faith of these representations and the assurance of those facts the money was obtained from Trenier. The mere fact that a false pretence of an existing or past fact is accompanied by a future promise will not relieve the defendant or take the case out of the operation of the statute. Besides,

"It is not necessary, to constitute the offence of obtaining goods by false pretences, that the owner has been induced to part with his property solely and entirely by pretences which are false; nor need the pretences be the paramount cause of the delivery to the prisoner. It is sufficient if they are a part of the moving cause, and without them the defrauded party would not have parted with the property." (In re Snyder, 17 Kan. 542.)

[Remainder of opinion omitted.]

Judgment affirmed.[2]

[1] Statement abridged. Only part of opinion is given.

[2] In Aaron's Reefs Ltd. *v.* Twiss, [1896] A. C. 273, 280–281, Lord Halsbury, L. C., says: "I must protest against it being supposed that in order to prove a case of this character of fraud, and that a certain course of conduct was induced by it, a person is bound to be able to explain with exact precision what was the mental process by which he was induced to act. It is a question for the jury. If a man said he was induced by such and such an inducement held out in the prospectus, I should not think that conclusive. It must be for the jury to say what they believed upon the evidence. Looking at the evidence in this case, I should say if I were a juryman that this was a very fascinating prospectus, and was calculated to induce any one who believed the statements in it to invest his money in the concern."

In Mathews *v.* Bliss, 22 Pick. 48, Shaw, C. J., says: "The judge further instructed the jury, that in order to maintain this action, they must be satisfied that the defendants had made the false representation, and that the sale was produced by means of it; that it was not necessary that it should be the sole and only motive inducing the sale, but it must have been a predominant one. In this par-

EDGINGTON *v.* FITZMAURICE

IN THE COURT OF APPEAL, MARCH 7, 1885.

Reported in Law Reports, 29 *Chancery Division*, 459.

ACTION against Fitzmaurice *et als.*, directors of the Army and Navy Provision Market (Limited), and against Hunt, the secretary, and Hanley, the manager, asking for the repayment by them of a sum of £1500 advanced by the plaintiff on debentures of the company, on the ground that he was induced to advance the money by the fraudulent misrepresentations of the defendants.

Plaintiff, who was a shareholder in the company, received a prospectus issued by order of the directors, inviting subscription for debenture bonds. This prospectus contained the following statement as to the objects for which the issue of debentures was made: —

"1. To enable the society to complete the present alterations and additions to the buildings, and to purchase their own horses and vans, whereby a large saving will be effected in the cost of transport.

"2. To further develop the arrangements at present existing for the direct supply of cheap fish from the coast, which are still in their infancy."

Plaintiff took debenture bonds to the amount of £1500; and testified that he relied, as one inducement, on the fact that the company wanted the money for the objects stated in the prospectus.

At the hearing before Denman, J., the plaintiff contended and offered evidence tending to show that the real object of the directors in issuing the debentures was to pay off pressing liabilities of the company, and not to complete the buildings or to purchase horses and vans, or to develop the business of the company.[1]

Davey, Q. C., *W. W. Karslake*, Q. C., and *J. Kaye*, for Fitzmaurice.

ticular, the Court are of opinion, that the direction, as it may have been and probably was understood by the jury, was not strictly correct; though it may have been so qualified and illustrated as to prevent the jury from being misled by it.

The term 'predominant,' in its natural and ordinary signification, is understood to be something greater or superior in power and influence to others, with which it is connected or compared. So understood, a predominant motive, when several motives may have operated, is one of greater force and effect, in producing the given result, than any other motive. But the Court are of opinion, that if the false and fraudulent representation was a motive at all, inducing to the act, if it was one of several motives, acting together, and by their combined force producing the result, it should have been left to the jury so to find it. If the false suggestion had no influence, if the plaintiff's agent would have done the same thing and made the sale if such representation had not been made, then it was not a motive to the act, and the plaintiff's agent was not induced to sell by means of it. On the whole, considering that the ordinary and natural meaning of the term 'predominant,' when applied to one among several motives, is such as has been stated, that the jury may have so understood it, and if they did so understand it, they may have come to a verdict not warranted by law, upon the evidence before them, the Court are of opinion, that the verdict ought to be set aside, and a new trial granted."

[1] The case has been much abridged, and the greater part of the report omitted.

There was no misrepresentation of any fact, and the directors merely stated their intention as to the money, which of course they might alter. There is every difference between the two: Maddison *v.* Alderson, 8 App. Cases, 467. Unless it amounts to a contract, a mere statement that you will do something is of no effect: Jordan *v.* Money, 5 H. L. C. 185; and if it was a contract then it was with the company, and the directors cannot be sued: Ferguson *v.* Wilson, L. R. 2 Chan. 77.

Sir F. Herschell, in reply. An allegation of intention may be fraudulent: Ex parte Whittaker, L. R. 10 Chan. 446.

[Denman, J., delivered an elaborate opinion, substantially sustaining the plaintiff's contention. He gave judgment against the directors.]

From this judgment, Fitzmaurice and the four other directors appealed.

Bowen, L. J. [After stating the requisites of an action for deceit, and commenting upon other alleged misrepresentations.] But when we come to the third alleged misstatement I feel that the plaintiff's case is made out. I mean the statement of the objects for which the money was to be raised. These were stated to be to complete the alterations and additions to the buildings, to purchase horses and vans, and to develop the supply of fish. A mere suggestion of possible purposes to which a portion of the money might be applied would not have formed a basis for an action of deceit. There must be a misstatement of an existing fact; but the state of a man's mind is as much a fact as the state of his digestion. It is true that it is very difficult to prove what the state of a man's mind at a particular time is, but if it can be ascertained it is as much a fact as anything else. A misrepresentation as to the state of a man's mind is, therefore, a misstatement of fact. Having applied as careful consideration to the evidence as I could, I have reluctantly come to the conclusion that the true objects of the defendants in raising the money were not those stated in the circular. I will not go through the evidence, but looking only to the cross-examination of the defendants, I am satisfied that the objects for which the loan was wanted were misstated by the defendants, I will not say knowingly, but so recklessly as to be fraudulent in the eye of the law.

Then the question remains: Did this misstatement contribute to induce the plaintiff to advance his money. Mr. Davey's argument has not convinced me that they did not. He contended that the plaintiff admits that he would not have taken the debentures unless he had thought they would give him a charge on the property, and therefore he was induced to take them by his own mistake, and the misstatement in the circular was not material. But such misstatement was material if it was actively present to his mind when he decided to advance his money. The real question is, what was the state of the plaintiff's mind, and if his mind was disturbed by the misstatement of the defendants, and such disturbance was in part the cause of what he did, the mere fact of his also making a mistake himself could make no difference. It resolves itself into a mere question of fact. I have felt some difficulty about the pleadings, because in the statement of claim this point is not clearly put forward, and I had some doubt whether this contention as to the third misstatement was not an afterthought. But the balance of my judgment is weighed down by the probability of the case. What is the first question which a man asks when he advances money? It is, what is it wanted for? Therefore I think that the statement is material, and that the plaintiff would be unlike the rest of his race if he was not influenced by the statement of the objects for which the loan was required. The learned judge in the Court below came to the conclusion that the misstatement did influence him, and I think he came to a right conclusion. *Appeal dismissed.*[1]

GALLAGHER *v.* BRUNEL

SUPREME COURT, NEW YORK, AUGUST, 1826.

Reported in 6 *Cowen,* 347.

ON demurrer to the declaration. The first count stated, that on the 9th of April, 1823, Castro & Henriques proposed to purchase of the plaintiffs a quantity of cotton, at a certain price; part to be paid in cash, and part to be secured by the promissory note of the purchasers endorsed by the defendant, at four months; that C. & H. were then unable to pay for the cotton; and the plaintiffs therefore unwilling to sell all, or any part, on their sole credit; and the defendant knew this. Yet, contriving and intending to injure and defraud the plaintiffs; and to induce them to sell and deliver the cotton to C. & H.; and thereby subject the plaintiffs to the loss of the balance due after the cash payment, the defendant falsely and deceitfully represented and held out to the plaintiffs, that he, the defendant, was willing to endorse the proposed note; and with the like intent, &c., falsely, fraudulently, and deceitfully encouraged and induced the plaintiffs to sell and deliver the cotton. That they did sell and deliver it, in confidence of such false, fraudulent and deceitful representation, &c., when, in

[1] Cockrill *v.* Hall, 65 Cal. 326; United States Home Co. *v.* O'Connor, 48 Col. 354; Lynch *v.* Hall, 41 Conn. 238; Jones *v.* Crawford, 107 Ga. 318; Hinchey *v.* Starrett, 91 Kan. 181; Oldham *v.* Bentley, 6 B. Mon. 428; Price *v.* Read, 2 Har. & G. 291; Adams *v.* Anderson, 4 Har. & J. 558; Sweet *v.* Kimball, 166 Mass. 332; Garry *v.* Garry, 187 Mass. 62; McElrath *v.* Electric Investment Co., 114 Minn. 358; Holmes *v.* Wilkes, 130 Minn. 170; Cerny *v.* Paxton Co., 78 Neb. 134; Gabriel *v.* Graham, 168 App. Div. 847; American Hosiery Co. *v.* Baker, 18 Ohio Cir. Ct. R. 604; Standard Elevator Co. *v.* Wilson, 218 Pa. St. 280; Bowe *v.* Gage, 127 Wis. 245 *Accord.* See also Wilson *v.* Yocum, 77 Ia. 569.

truth, the defendant was then not willing, and did not mean or intend to endorse the note, or make himself responsible; nor did he then, nor had he at any time since endorsed, or made himself legally responsible. By means whereof the plaintiffs lost the cotton and the price.

The second count averred, that C. & H. were in bad credit and unfit to be trusted, at the time of the sale. But the defendant, well knowing this; and contriving and intending to defraud and injure the plaintiffs, and wrongfully and deceitfully to enable C. & H. to obtain the possession of the cotton, and convert it to their own use, without paying the plaintiffs for it; falsely, fraudulently and deceitfully represented to the plaintiffs, and gave them to understand and believe, that, in case they would sell the cotton to C. & H., the defendant would become answerable to the plaintiffs, for so much as should be unpaid, by endorsing the note or notes of C. & H., &c.; that without such representation, they would not have sold the cotton, &c. (*In other respects, this count was substantially the same as the first.*)

General demurrer and joinder.[1]

WOODWORTH, J. . . . The attempt here is, to sustain the action, not on a contract, which, if in writing, might perhaps be obligatory; but on a deceitful representation. If the promise was in writing, I perceive no objection to its validity, inasmuch as a good consideration is stated, viz., that if the plaintiffs would sell and deliver, the defendant would endorse. If, then, there is a binding contract existing between the parties, and on which the defendant is liable, I apprehend it is not competent for the plaintiffs to say they have an election to turn this into an action for deceit, and recover in that form, unless the case is such as to render the party liable, not only on the contract; but in addition, contains facts sufficient to sustain an action for deceit. For example, suppose A represents B to be solvent, knowing it to be false, whereby B obtains credit; but notwithstanding this representation, the seller takes from A his written stipulation to guaranty the payment. In this case, I perceive no objection to a creditor's election of the remedy. The fraudulent representation of solvency would sustain the action for deceit. The written guaranty would support an action on the contract. It seems, therefore, immaterial here, whether the plaintiffs have or have not a demand which may be enforced in a different form. The question is, will the facts stated sustain an action for deceit ?

After attentive consideration, I am inclined to think the plaintiffs are not entitled to recover. However reprehensible the conduct of the defendant may appear in a moral point of view, we cannot deny to him the protection of the common law; which does not reach cases of imperfect obligation. If this be an attempt on the part of the plaintiffs to get rid of the statute of frauds, I can only say, the occasion justified the experiment, and calls for a patient and critical examination.

[1] Arguments and part of opinion omitted.

If this case is stripped of the general allegations in the declaration, of fraud and deceit, it appears to me that the gravamen is nothing more than that the defendant encouraged the plaintiffs to sell to Castro and Henriques; and, as surety, promised to endorse their notes. The intention of the party not to fulfil, has not, I believe, ever been considered among the fraudulent acts, which, in judgment of law, render a party liable. The maker of a promissory note may not, at the time, intend to make payment. On this note, the plaintiff may declare that the defendant intended to deceive and defraud; but it is mere matter of form, sanctioned by precedent in pleading. The maker may go farther, and on the strength of assurances to pay punctually, never intended to be performed, induce the lender to part with his money, and accept the borrower's note. All this is immoral. Still the remedy is on the contract. The law has not recognized it as the substantive ground of fraud. That no cases are to be met with in the books going the length contended for, is good evidence that the doctrine is novel, and has never been acted upon.

. . . .

It is evident what must be the species of fraud, for which the law gives redress; falsehood as to an existing fact. If, as Buller, J., observes, every deceit includes a lie, it follows, that the representation, and promise of the defendant are not comprised within the legal acceptation of that term. The test of a lie is, that the fact asserted is not true at the time; which cannot be predicated of the facts in this case; for, although the defendant promised with the intent not to perform, it was not then false, nor could it be. It referred to an act to be done *in futuro*. Until the defendant had refused to endorse, it could not be said he had violated his promise.

. . . .

Judgment for defendant.[1]

[1] Harriage *v.* Daley, 121 Ark. 23; Dickinson *v.* Atkins, 100 Ill. App. 401; McAllister *v.* Indianapolis R. Co., 15 Ind. 11; Welshbillig *v.* Dienhart, 65 Ind. 94; Long *v.* Woodman, 58 Me. 49; Davis *v.* Reynolds, 107 Me. 61; Bullock *v.* Wooldridge, 42 Mo. App. 356; Wolters *v.* Fidelity Trust Co., 73 N. J. Law, 57 *Accord.* See also Bennett *v.* McIntire, 121 Ind. 231.

In Adams *v.* Gillig, 199 N. Y. 314, plaintiff sued in equity for cancellation of a conveyance procured by falsely representing that defendant intended to build a dwelling on the land, when his real intention was to build a garage. Chase, J., said (pp. 320–322): "A promise as such to be enforceable must be based upon a consideration, and it must be put in such form as to be available under the rules relating to contracts and the admission of evidence relating thereto. It may include a present intention, but as it also relates to the future it can only be enforced as a promise under the general rules relating to contracts.

A mere statement of intention is a different thing. It is not the basis of an action on contract. It may in good faith be changed without affecting the obligations of the parties. A statement of intention does not relate to a fact that has a corporal and physical existence, but to a material and existing fact nevertheless not amounting to a promise but which as in the case under discussion affects and determines important transactions. The question here under discussion is not affected by the rules relating to the admission of testimony. As it was not promissory and contractual in its nature there is nothing in the rules of evidence to prevent oral

SWIFT v. ROUNDS

SUPREME COURT, RHODE ISLAND, JULY 6, 1896.

Reported in 19 *Rhode Island Reports*, 527.

TRESPASS ON THE CASE for deceit. Certified from the Common Pleas Division on demurrer to the declaration.

TILLINGHAST, J. This is trespass on the case for deceit. The first count in the declaration alleges that the defendant, intending to deceive and defraud the plaintiffs, did buy of them on credit certain goods and chattels of the value of $400, the said defendant not then and there intending to pay for the same, but intending wickedly and fraudulently to cheat the plaintiffs out of the value of said goods and chattels, which said sum of $400 the defendant refuses to pay, to the plaintiffs' damage, &c. The second count, after setting out the fraudulent conduct aforesaid, alleges that the defendant thereby then and there represented that he intended to pay for said goods, but that he did not then and there intend to pay for the same, but wickedly and fraudulently intended to cheat the plaintiffs out of the value of said goods and chattels, &c.

To this declaration the defendant has demurred, and for grounds of demurrer to the first count thereof, he says, (1) that the plaintiffs do not allege any false representation by the defendant; (2) that the plaintiffs do not allege that they have acted upon any false representation of the defendant; and (3) that the plaintiffs do not allege any damage suffered by them in acting upon any false representation of the defendant.

proof of the representations made by the defendant to the plaintiff. In an action brought expressly upon a fraud, oral evidence of facts to show the fraud is admissible. (Pomeroy's Equity Jurisprudence, Sec. 889.)

This case stands exactly as it would have stood if the plaintiff and defendant before the execution and delivery of the deed had entered into a writing by which the defendant had stated therein his intention as found by the court on the trial and the plaintiff had stated her acceptance of his offer based upon her belief and faith in his statement of intention, and it further appeared that the statement was so made by the defendant for the purpose of inducing the plaintiff to sell to him the lot, and that such statement was so made by him falsely, fraudulently and purposely for the purpose of bringing about such sale.

Intent is of vital importance in very many transactions. In the criminal courts it is necessary in many cases for jurors to determine as a question of fact the intent of the person charged with the crime. Frequently the life or liberty of the prisoner at the bar depends upon the determination of such question of fact. In civil actions relating to wrongs, the intent of the party charged with the wrong is frequently of controlling effect upon the conclusion to be reached in the action. The intent of a person is sometimes difficult to prove, but it is nevertheless a fact and a material and existing fact that must be ascertained in many cases, and when ascertained determines the rights of the parties to controversies. The intent of Gillig was a material existing fact in this case, and the plaintiff's reliance upon such fact induced her to enter into a contract that she would not otherwise have entered into. The effect of such false statement by the defendant of his intention cannot be cast aside as immaterial simply because it was possible for him in good faith to have changed his mind or to have sold the property to another who might

The grounds of demurrer to the second count are, (1) that the plaintiffs do not allege any false representation by the defendant as to any fact present or past, but only as to something that would happen in the future, which, if in the future it proved not to be true, would not be the subject matter of a false representation, but simply a promise broken, and therefore not a ground of an action of deceit; (2) that the plaintiffs do not allege that they acted upon any false representation made by the defendant; and (3) that the plaintiffs do not allege that they suffered any damage by acting upon any false representation made by the defendant to the plaintiffs.

We are inclined to the opinion, after some hesitation, that the declaration states a case of deceit. Any fraudulent misrepresentation or device whereby one person deceives another, who has no means of detecting the fraud, to his injury and damage, is a sufficient ground for an action of deceit. Deceit is a species of fraud, and consists of any false representation or contrivance whereby one person overreaches and misleads another, to his hurt. And, while the fraudulent misrepresentation relied upon usually consists of statements made as to material facts, either verbally or in writing, yet it may be made by conduct as well. Grinnell on Law of Deceit, p. 35. A man may not only deceive another, to his hurt, by deliberately asserting a falsehood, as, for instance, by stating that A. is an honest man when he knows him to be a rogue, or that a horse is sound and kind when he knows him to be unsound and vicious, but also by any act or demeanor which would naturally impress the mind of a careful man with a mistaken belief, and form the basis of some change of position by him. 1 Story, Eq. Jur. § 192. In Ex parte Whittaker, In re Shackleton, L. R. 10 Ch. 449, Mellish, L. J., says: "It is true, in-

have a different purpose relating thereto. As the defendant's intention was subject to change in good faith at any time it was of uncertain value. It was, however, of some value. It was of sufficient value so that the plaintiff was willing to stand upon it and make the conveyance in reliance upon it.

The use of property in a particular manner changes from time to time and restrictive covenants of great value at one time may become a source of serious embarrassment at a later date. The fact that restrictive covenants cannot ordinarily be drawn to bend to changed conditions has made many purchasers disinclined to accept conveyances with such covenants. A restrictive covenant in a deed may be of sufficient importance to justify a refusal by a contractee to accept a conveyance subject to such conditions. A person in selling property may be quite willing to execute and deliver a deed thereof without putting restrictive covenants therein and in reliance upon the good faith of express, unqualified assurances of the present intention of the prospective purchaser. In such case the intention is material and the statement of such intention is the statement of an existing fact.

Unless the court affirms this judgment, it must acknowledge that although a defendant deliberately and intentionally, by false statements, obtained from a plaintiff his property to his great damage it is wholly incapable of righting the wrong, notwithstanding the fact that by so doing it does in no way interfere with the rules that have grown up after years of experience to protect written contracts from collateral promises and conditions not inserted in the contract.

We are of the opinion that the false statements made by the defendant of his intention should, under the circumstances of this case, be deemed to be a statement of a material, existing fact of which the court will lay hold for the purpose of defeating the wrong that would otherwise be consummated thereby."

deed, that a party must not make any misrepresentation, express or *implied*, and as at present advised I think Shackleton when he went for the goods must be taken to have made an implied representation that he intended to pay for them, and if it were clearly made out that at that time he did not intend to pay for them, I should consider that a case of fraudulent misrepresentation was shown." See also Lobdell *v.* Baker, 1 Met. 201; 1 Benjamin on Sales, ed. of 1888, § 524.

In the case at bar, the declaration alleges that the defendant bought the goods in question upon credit, fraudulently intending not to pay for them but to cheat the plaintiffs out of the value thereof. By the act of buying the goods of the plaintiffs the defendant impliedly promised to pay for the same, which promise was equally as strong and binding as though it had been made in words, or even in writing. The plaintiffs had the right to rely on this promise, and to presume that it was made in good faith. It turns out, however, according to the allegations aforesaid, that it was not made in good faith, but, on the contrary, was made for the purpose of deceiving the plaintiffs into the act of parting with their goods, the defendant intending by the transaction to cheat them out of the value thereof. The fraud, then, consisted in the making of the promise, in the manner aforesaid, with intent not to perform it. By the act of purchasing the goods on credit, the defendant impliedly represented that he intended to pay for them. The plaintiffs relied on this representation, which was material and fraudulent, and were damaged thereby. All the necessary elements of fraud or deceit therefore were present in the transaction. See Upton *v.* Vail, 6 Johns. 181; Bartholomew *v.* Bentley, 15 Ohio, 666; Bishop, Non-Contract Law, §§ 314–318; Burrill *v.* Stevens, 73 Me. 400; Barney *v.* Dewey, 13 Johns. 226; Hubbel *v.* Meigs, 50 N. Y. 491. The general doctrine which controls this action is fully reviewed by Mr. Wallace in a note to Pasley *v.* Freeman, 2 Smith's Lead. Cas. 101. As said by Bigelow on Fraud, page 484, " to profess an intent to do or not to do when a party intends the contrary, is as clear a case of misrepresentation and of fraud as could be made." See also p. 466 as to what constitutes a representation. In Goodwin *v.* Horne, 60 N. H. 486, the court say: " Ordinarily false promises are not fraudulent, nor evidence of fraud, and only false representations of past or existing facts are actionable or can be made the ground of defence. . . . But when a promise is made with no intention of performance, and for the very purpose of accomplishing a fraud, it is a most apt and effectual means to that end, and the victim has a remedy by action or defence. Such are cases of concealed insolvency and purchases of goods with no intention to pay for them." In Byrd *v.* Hall, 1 Abb. A. D. 286, it was held that, although a purchase of goods on credit by one who knows himself to be insolvent is not fraudulent, yet where it is made with a preconceived design not to pay, it is fraudulent. See also Milliken *v.* Miller, 12 R. I. 296; Thompson *v.* Rose, 16 Conn. 81; Hennequin *v.*

Naylor, 24 N. Y. 129; Devoe *v.* Brandt, 53 N. Y. 465; Story on Sales, 2d ed. § 176, and cases in note 2; Douthitt *v.* Applegate, 33 Kans. 395; Morrill *v.* Blackman, 42 Conn. 324; Skinner *v.* Flint, 105 Mass. 528; Earl of Bristol *v.* Wilsmore, 2 Dow. & Ry. 760; Lobdell *v.* Baker, 1 Met. 193; Cooley on Torts, 2d ed. 559; Load *v.* Green, 15 M. & W. 215. In short, the making of one state of things to appear, to those with whom you deal, to be the true state of things, while you are acting on the knowledge of a different state of things — among the oldest definitions of fraud in contracts — is exemplified in this case. See Lee *v.* Jones, 17 C. B. N. S. 494. The defendant made it to appear, by the act of buying on credit, that he intended to pay for the goods in question, while in fact he intended to cheat the plaintiffs out of them. And to hold that such a transaction does not amount to fraud, would be to make it easy for cheats and swindlers to escape the just consequence of their unrighteous acts.

We have hesitated somewhat in arriving at the conclusion that an action of deceit will lie, upon the facts set out in the declaration, for the reason that, amongst the numerous cases of fraud and deceit to be found in the books, we have not been referred to any, nor have we been able to find any, where the action of deceit was based simply on the act of buying goods on credit, intending not to pay for them. In Lyons *v.* Briggs, 14 R. I. 224, which was an action of deceit, Durfee, C. J., intimates, however, that deceit would lie in a case like the one before us, by the use of the following language: "It is not alleged that the buyer did not intend to pay when he bought, but only that he falsely and fraudulently asserted that he could be safely trusted." But the authorities are overwhelming to the effect that it is fraud to purchase goods intending not to pay for them, and that the vendor, upon discovering the fraud, may repudiate the sale and reclaim the property, or may sue in trover, or in some other action of tort, for the damages sustained by the fraud. And this being so, we fail to see why an action of deceit, which is an action of tort, based on fraud, may not lie as well. For to obtain goods on credit, intending not to pay for them, is as much a trick or device as it would be falsely to represent in words any material fact whereby the vendor should be induced to part therewith.

But defendant's counsel contends that the alleged representation was not as to any fact present or past, but merely as to what the defendant would do in the future with reference to paying for the goods, and that to say what one intends to do is identical to saying what one will do in the future, which amounts simply to a promise; and, furthermore, that a representation of what will happen in the future, even if not realized, is not such a representation as will support this action. We do not assent to this method of reasoning. The state of a man's mind at a given time is as much a fact as is the state of his digestion. Intention is a fact; Clift *v.* White, 12 N. Y. 538;

hence a witness may be asked with what intent he did a given act. Seymour *v.* Wilson, 14 N. Y. 567. A man who buys and obtains possession of goods on credit, intending not to pay for them, is then and there guilty of fraud. The wrong is fully completed and no longer exists in intention merely, and a cause of action instantly accrues thereon in favor of the vendor to recover for the wrong and injury sustained. It is true the purchaser may afterwards repent of the wrong and pay for the goods, and the vendor may never know of the wrongful intent. But this does not alter the case at all as to the original wrong and the liability incurred thereby. Of course a mere intention to commit a crime or to do a wrong is no offence. But when the intention is coupled with the doing or accomplishment of the act intended, that moment the wrong is perpetrated and the corresponding liability incurred. See Oswego Starch Factory *v.* Lendrum, 57 Iowa, 573.

In Stewart *v.* Emerson, 52 N. H. 301, where it was alleged, in reply to the defendant's plea of discharge in bankruptcy, that the debt in question was created by the fraud of the defendant, Doe, J., in the course of a long and vigorous opinion, used the following language, which is so apt and pertinent that we quote it. He said: "When the intent not to pay is concealed, the intent to defraud is acted out. The mere omission of A. to disclose his insolvency might not be satisfactory proof of a fraudulent intent in all cases. He might expect to become solvent. He might intend to pay all his creditors. He might intend to pay B. though unable to pay others. His fixed purpose *never* to pay B. is a very different thing from his present inability to pay all or any of his creditors. A man may buy goods, with time for trying to pay for them, on the strength of his known or inferred disposition to pay his debts, his habits, character, business capacity, and financial prospects, without his present solvency being thought of, and even when his present insolvency is known to the vendor. But who could obtain goods on credit, with an unconcealed determination that they should never be paid for ? The concealment of such a determination is conduct which reasonably involves a false representation of an existing fact, is not less material than a misrepresentation of ability to pay (Bradley *v.* Obear, 10 N. H. 477), and is an actual artifice, intended and fitted to deceive."

"An application for or acceptance of credit, by a purchaser, is a representation of the existence of an intent to pay at a future time, and a representation of the non-existence of an intent not to pay. What principle of law requires a false and fraudulent representation to be express, or forbids it to be fairly inferred from the act of purchase ? A representation of a material fact, implied from the act of purchase, and inducing the owner of goods to sell them, is as effective for the vendee's purpose as if it had been previously and expressly made. If it is false, and known to the pretended purchaser to be false, and is intended and used by him as a means of converting another's goods to his own use without compensation, under the false pretence of a purchase, why does it not render such a purchase fraudulent? When the intent is to pay, it is necessarily understood by both parties, and need not be expressly represented as existing. When the intent is not to pay, it is of course concealed. Whether the deceit is called a false and fraudulent representation of the existence of an intent to pay, or a fraudulent concealment of the existence of an intent not to pay, the fraud described is, in fact, one and the same fraud."

Demurrer overruled, and case remitted to the Common Pleas Division for further proceedings.[1]

[1] Butler *v.* Watkins, 13 Wall. 456; Rogers *v.* Virginia-Carolina Chemical Co., (C. C. A.) 149 Fed. 1; Sallies *v.* Johnson, 85 Conn. 77; McLaughlin *v.* Thomas, 86 Conn. 252; Olson *v.* Smith, 116 Minn. 430; Herndon *v.* Durham R. Co., 161 N. C. 650; Blackburn *v.* Morrison, 29 Okl. 510 *Accord.*

Grubb *v.* Milan, 249 Ill. 456; Murray *v.* Smith, 42 Ill. App. 548; Chambers *v.* Mitchell, 123 Ill. App. 595; Younger *v.* Hoge, 211 Mo. 444 *Contra.*

In Commonwealth *v.* Althause, 207 Mass. 32, 47–49, Loring, J., says: "As a general proposition of law apart from statutes making it a crime to obtain property by a false pretence, it would seem that a man's present intention as to a future act is a fact. Edgington *v.* Fitzmaurice, 29 Ch. D. 459. Swift *v.* Rounds, 19 R. I. 527. In the first of these two cases (Edgington *v.* Fitzmaurice) Bowen, L. J., said, at p. 483: 'The state of a man's mind is as much a fact as the state of his digestion.' And Chapman, C. J., in Commonwealth *v.* Walker, 108 Mass. 309, 312, said: 'A man's intention is a matter of fact, and may be proved as such. . . .'

But in the case at bar the presiding judge went beyond any decided case in the explanation which he gave of the difference between the representation of a person's present intention as to a future act and an assurance or promise that the future act shall be done. For the purpose of illustrating the essential difference between the two he put as an example of obtaining property by a false pretence a case which is not obtaining property by a false pretence. In effect he told the jury that if A buys property intending not to pay for it he obtains that property by a false pretence. In that case A makes no representation at all. All that he does is to make a promise, and a promise is not a representation of a fact. It has been sought to make out that in legal contemplation a promise with an intention not to perform is a false pretence because a promise to do a thing of necessity implies a present intention to do it, and therefore whenever you have a promise coupled with an intent not to perform you have an implied false representation of an intention to do the act which the defendant promised to do and so a false pretence. And this finds some apparent support in Swift *v.* Rounds, 19 R. I. 527. In that case it was held that where a defendant buys property intending not to pay for it he is liable in an action of deceit because he impliedly represents that he intends to pay for it by the act of buying. It may be doubted whether the making of a promise implies of necessity in all cases a present intention to perform that promise. Upon that question we do not find it necessary to express an opinion. For however that may be, the fraud of obtaining property by buying it intending not to pay for it is not, as matter of construction of the statute creating it, the crime of obtaining property by a false pretence. . . . It is evident that the fraud (which by enacting that statute the Legislature intended to make a crime) was obtaining the property of another by a false statement of a fact; and it is equally evident that in enacting it the Legislature did not have in mind the fraud of buying goods not intending to pay for them. Both are frauds but they are not the same fraud. In our opinion it was the former alone which the Legislature had in mind in making it a crime to obtain property by a false pretence."

As to whether intention at the time of the contract or at the time of delivery of the goods is to be regarded, see *In re* Levi, 148 Fed. 654; Whitten *v.* Fitzwater, 129 N. Y. 626.

PETERS, J., IN BURRILL *v.* STEVENS

(1882) 73 *Maine*, 395, 398–400.

THE instructions to the jury upon that point present the question, whether getting property by a purchase upon credit, with an intention of the purchaser never to pay for the same, constitutes such a fraud as will entitle the seller to avoid the sale, although there are no fraudulent misrepresentations or false pretences.

The question has never been fairly before this Court before this time, so as to require a deliberate decision. The plaintiff contends that the question was settled in the negative in the case of Long *v.* Woodman, 58 Maine, 49. But that case falls short of meeting the question presented in the present case. The gist of the charge against the purchaser in that case seems to have been that he fraudulently refused to do after the contract what he agreed to do at the time of the contract, the alleged fraud being an intention formed after the contract rather than contemporaneously with it; and that was an action of deceit based upon a broken promise to convey real estate. Of late years, *nisi prius* rulings in our own Courts have frequently been in accordance with the law as delivered to the jury by the presiding judge in the case at bar, and we think the doctrine may safely be accepted and approved, both upon authority and principle.

It is the admitted doctrine of the English cases, and is sustained by most of the courts in the United States. In Benj. on Sales (2d Amer. ed.), § 440, note e, very numerous cases are cited to the proposition. Stewart *v.* Emerson, 52 N. H. 301, discusses the question at length, and reviews many authorities.

The plaintiff relies upon the objection that it is not an indictable fraud, an argument which seems to have inclined the Pennsylvania Court against admitting the principle into the jurisprudence of that State. Smith *v.* Smith, 21 Pa. St. 367; Backentoss *v.* Speicher, 31 Pa. St. 324. It has been held by some Courts to be an indictable cheat, the false pretence being in the vendee's pretendingly making a purchase, while his only purpose is to cheat the vendor out of his goods. It is more often considered, however, as not a matter for indictment. Bish. Crim. Law, § 419. But the objection taken by the plaintiff has generally been considered as insufficient to override the rule.

But the doctrine governing the case before us should not be misunderstood. To constitute the fraud, there must be a preconceived design never to pay for the goods. A mere intent not to pay for the goods when the debt becomes due, is not enough; that falls short of the idea. A design not to pay according to the contract is not equivalent to an intention never to pay for the goods, and does not amount to an intention to defraud the seller outright, although it may be evidence of such a contemplated fraud.

Nor is it enough to constitute the fraud that the buyer is insolvent, and knows himself to be so, at the time of the purchase, and conceals the fact from the seller, and has not reasonable expectations that he can ever pay the debt.[1] Some Courts have gone so far as to denominate that a fraud which will avoid the sale. And it may have been so held in bankruptcy Courts, in some instances, as between a vendor and the assignee of the vendee. But it would

[1] See Gardner *v.* State, 4 Ala. App. 131; Syracuse Knitting Co. *v.* Blanchard, 69 N. H. 447.

not, generally, be enough to prove the fraud. The inquiry is not whether the vendee had reasonable grounds to believe he could pay the debt at some time and in some way, but whether he intended in point of fact not to pay it.

Nor is it enough that after the purchase the vendee conceives a design and forms a purpose not to pay for the goods, and successfully avoids paying for them. The only intent that renders the sale fraudulent is a positive and predetermined intention, entertained and acted upon at the time of going through the forms of an apparent sale, never to pay for the goods. Cross *v.* Peters, 1 Greenl. 378; Biggs *v.* Barry, 2 Curtis, (C. C. R.) 259; Parker *v.* Byrnes, 1 Low. 539; Rowley *v.* Bigelow, 12 Pick. 306.

RIDDICK, J., IN BUGG *v.* WERTHEIMER-SCHWARTZ SHOE COMPANY

(1897) 64 *Arkansas*, 12, 17, 18.

NOR can we sustain the contention of appellant that to entitle the vendor to avoid a sale after delivery it must in all cases be shown that the vendee did not intend to pay for the goods. That is, as above stated, one ground on which the sale may be avoided, but not the only one. If the vendee knowingly makes false representations concerning material facts, and thus induces the seller to part with his goods, the seller may elect to avoid the sale, and this without regard to whether the buyer intended to pay for the goods or not. The fraud in such a case consists in inducing the vendor to part with his goods by false statements of the buyer, known to be false when made, or made by him when he has no reasonable ground to believe that they are true. If a vendor parts with his goods on the faith of such false statements made by the buyer, it would be strange if the law permitted the buyer to reap the fruits of such conduct, and retain the goods against the will of the vendor. To illustrate, let us suppose a case. A man with no property, but with great faith in his ability as a merchant, goes to a city and calls on a wholesale merchant for the purpose of buying a stock of goods. He believes that if he can obtain a stock of goods, his experience and ability will soon enable him to pay off the purchase price, but, fearing that the merchant may refuse to sell if he learns that he has no property, he thereupon, for the purpose of obtaining the goods, states to the merchant that he has money in the bank, and owns a large amount of both real and personal property. The merchant, ignorant of the facts, and relying on the truth of these statements, parts with his goods. He afterwards discovers the fraud, and brings an action to recover the goods. In such a case would it be a valid defence for the buyer to say that, although he had secured the goods by misrepresentation, yet he did honestly intend to pay for them ? Clearly it would not. The courts would answer such a question substantially as it was answered by the Supreme Court of Connecticut when it said that the intent of the buyer to pay "may have lessened the moral turpitude of his act, but it will not suffice to antidote and neutralize an intentionally false statement which had accomplished its object of benefiting himself and of misleading the plaintiffs to their injury." Judd *v.* Weber, 55 Conn. 267; Reid *v.* Cowduroy, 79 Iowa, 169; s. c. 18 Am. St. Rep. 359, and note; Strayhorn *v.* Giles, 22 Ark. 517.

McCOMB v. BREWER LUMBER COMPANY

SUPREME JUDICIAL COURT, MASSACHUSETTS, OCTOBER 21, 1903.

Reported in 184 *Massachusetts Reports*, 276.

THE third count in the declaration is tort for deceit in the sale of certain stock by the defendant to the plaintiff.

The allegations, so far as material here, are in substance as follows: —

Plaintiff says that the defendant, by its agent, with intent to deceive and defraud the plaintiff, falsely and fraudulently represented to him [here specifying certain representations], and that, if the plaintiff would purchase a certain number of shares of stock in the defendant corporation and pay therefor the sum of $9000, . . . the $9000 paid by the plaintiff should be put in the treasury of said corporation to be used as a working capital. And plaintiff says that, relying upon the representations, he bought the shares and paid therefor $9000; and plaintiff says that said representations were false and untrue to the knowledge of the defendant in this: [specifying certain particulars], and the $9000 paid by plaintiff was not put in its treasury and used as working capital, but was, with the approval of the defendant, its directors and manager, used for other purposes than the business of the defendant.

Verdict for plaintiff for $1.00 damages. Plaintiff alleged exceptions as to the ruling at the trial in reference to this count.[1]

HAMMOND, J. . . . The exceptions relate only to the third count, and since the verdict was for the plaintiff on this, they are material only so far as they respect the question of damages. The principal difference between the instructions given by the judge and those requested by the plaintiff is that the judge declined to permit the jury to consider the allegation with reference to the promised use of the $9000 paid by the plaintiff for the stock. As to this it is contended by the plaintiff that at the time the defendant promised to use the money as working capital it did not intend to keep the promise, and that a representation of a present intention is a representation of an existing fact and therefore may be false and fraudulent. But, without implying that the plaintiff's contention would be true under any circumstances, the difficulty with his case is that the question is not raised upon the record. The ruling that the jury should not consider the allegation with reference to the promised use of the money appears to have been made with reference to the third count, and, as applied to that, it was correct. An examination of the count will show that it does not contain any allegation that at the time the defendant said that the money should be used for working capital it had not the intention to perform that promise. It first sets out the representations which induced the plaintiff to purchase the stock,

[1] Statement abridged. Part of opinion omitted.

then proceeds to state in what respects they were false and fraudulent and the defendant's knowledge of the falsity, and then follows the only allegation respecting the representation as to the promised use of the money: "And the nine thousand dollars paid by the plaintiff to the defendant was not put in its treasury and used as working capital, but was, with the approval of the defendant, its directors and manager, used for other purposes than the business of the defendant." This is an allegation that the defendant failed to carry out its promise, and falls far short of an allegation that the defendant at the time it was made did not intend to carry it out. There is no allegation whatever as to the intent of the defendant at the time the promise was made. Indeed it is difficult to read that count, either by itself or in connection with the other counts, without feeling that the pleader studiously avoided alleging anything as to that intent. While the evidence as to the promised use and the actual use of this money may have been admissible upon the second count, the object of which was to recover damages for breach of the promise, it was not material upon the third count, even upon the question of damages, for the reasons above stated.

. . . .

Exceptions overruled.[1]

DORR *v.* CORY

SUPREME COURT, IOWA, APRIL 5, 1899.

Reported in 108 *Iowa Reports*, 725.

APPEAL from Polk District Court.

Action at law on contracts in writing for the purchase of interests in real estate. Answer alleges (*inter alia*) that the contracts were obtained by fraud.

Verdict for plaintiff, and judgment.

ROBINSON, C. J.[2] . . . The only statement purporting to be of fact which is shown to have been false is that relating to the cost of the land. Would that statement have authorized the jury to find for the defendant? It was said in Hemmer *v.* Cooper, 8 Allen, 334, that "the representations of a vendor of real estate, to the vendee, as to the price he paid for it, are to be regarded in the same light as representations respecting its value. A purchaser ought not to rely upon them; for it is settled that even when they are false, and uttered with a view to deceive, they furnish no ground of action." That rule was followed in Cooper *v.* Lovering, 106 Mass. 77, and it is the rule of

[1] As to "promissory representations," see also Sawyer *v.* Prickett, 19 Wall. 146; Sallies *v.* Johnson, 85 Conn. 77; Carter *v.* Orne, 112 Me. 365; Pedrick *v.* Porter, 5 All. 324; Pile *v.* Bright, 156 Mo. App. 301.

Known impossible prophecy by one having superior knowledge, see Murray *v.* Tolman, 162 Ill. 417; French *v.* Ryan, 104 Mich. 625; Hedin *v.* Minneapolis Institute, 62 Minn. 146.

[2] Only part of the case is given.

Tuck *v.* Downing, 76 Ill. 71, and Banta *v.* Palmer, 47 Ill. 99. In Holbrook *v.* Connor, 60 Me. 578, it was said: "The statement of the vendor that he paid a certain price for the land, if true, can be no more than an indication of his opinion of its value; and when we consider the various motives which may, and often do, actuate men in making their purchases, and especially when it is done for speculation, it is but the slightest proof of such opinion." As a general rule, a vendee has no right to rely upon the statements of the vendor respecting the value of the property sold, but must act upon his own judgment, or seek information for himself. But to that rule there are exceptions. It was said in Simar *v.* Canaday, 53 N. Y. 306, that where statements as to the value are mere matter of opinion and belief, no liability is created by uttering them, but that such statements "may be, under certain circumstances, affirmations of fact. When known to the utterer to be untrue, if made with the intention of misleading the vendee, if he does rely upon them, and is misled to his injury, they avoid the contract." The fraud which vitiates a contract must be material, affecting the very essence of the contract; but ordinarily, "if the fraud be such that, had it not been practiced, the contract would not have been made, then it is material to it." 2 Parsons, Contract, 770. See, also, 2 Pomeroy Equity Jurisprudence, section 878, and notes. That rule was applied in Smith *v.* Countryman, 30 N. Y. 656, which was an action upon a contract for the sale of hops. It was held that a false representation made by the vendee as to the price at which he had purchased hops of another person, which was relied upon by the vendor, and induced him to enter into the contract of sale, was material, and constituted a defence to an action on the contract. This rule appears to us to be in harmony with reason and the principles of justice. The price at which property actually sells in the open market is very satisfactory evidence of its value at the time of the sale. We cannot assent to the proposition that the statement of a vendor that he paid a specified price for the property he sells is a mere expression of opinion, upon which the purchaser has no right to rely. On the contrary, we think it is a statement of fact; and if the purchaser, without knowing or having reason to know what price was paid, relies upon the false statement, to his injury, he is entitled to relief. The cases of Teachout *v.* Van Hoesen, 76 Iowa, 113; Iler *v.* Griswold, 83 Iowa, 442, and Coles *v.* Kennedy, 81 Iowa, 360, although not precisely in point, tend to sustain our conclusion. See French *v.* Ryan, 104 Mich. 625 (62 N. W. Rep. 1016); Moon *v.* McKinstry, 107 Mich. 668 (65 N. W. Rep. 546), and Woolen Co. *v.* Smalley, 111 Mich. 321 (69 N. W. Rep. 722).

. . . .

Judgment reversed.[1]

[1] But see Davis *v.* Reynolds, 107 Me. 61.

In Van Epps *v.* Harrison, 5 Hill, 63, 70–71, Bronson, J., says: "If an affirmation concerning the cost of the property was of any consequence, I think the defendant

DEMING *v.* DARLING

SUPREME JUDICIAL COURT, MASSACHUSETTS, FEBRUARY 27, 1889.

Reported in 148 *Massachusetts Reports,* 504.

HOLMES, J. This is an action for fraudulent representations alleged to have been made to one Dr. Jordan, the plaintiff's agent, for the purpose of inducing the plaintiff to purchase a railroad bond from the defendant. . . .[1]

Among the representations relied on, one was that the railroad mortgaged, which was situated in Ohio, was good security for the bonds; and another was that the bond was of the very best and safest, and was an A No. 1 bond. With regard to these and the like, the defendant asked the Court to instruct the jury "that no representations which the defendant might have made or did make to Dr. Jordan in relation to the value of the bond in question, or of the railroad, its terminals, and other property which were mortgaged to secure it, with other bonds, even though false, were representations upon which Dr. Jordan ought to have relied, and are not sufficient to furnish any grounds for this action;" and also, "that each of the expressions 'and that the same' (meaning said railroad and all the property covered by the mortgage) 'was good security for said bonds,' 'that said bond was of the very best and safest, and was an A No. 1 bond,' are expressions of

should have taken the trouble to inquire and satisfy himself. But I cannot think it a matter of any legal importance. It was only another mode of asserting that the property was of the value of $32,000; and all the books agree that no action will lie if such an affirmation prove false. It is the folly of the purchaser to trust to it. Indeed, the representation here amounts to less than a direct affirmation of value, for it only asserts that the plaintiff and another man agreed that such was the value. It would lead to great mischief to allow men to annul contracts upon such a ground. If the defendant could make out that the plaintiff was his agent in purchasing from Van Rensselaer, then what the plaintiffs said about the price he paid might be material; but not in any other point of view.

Such are my views upon this branch of the case; but my brethren are of opinion that the false affirmation concerning the price paid for the land furnishes a good ground of action. There must, therefore, be a new trial upon this point, as well as the one relating to the condition of the land."

As to "puffing," see: Mumford *v.* Tolman, 157 Ill. 258; Miller *v.* Craig, 36 Ill. 109; Wightman *v.* Tucker, 50 Ill. App. 75; Woods *v.* Nicholas, 92 Kan. 258; Buckingham *v.* Thompson, 135 S. W. 652.

But see Pratt *v.* Judge, 177 Mich. 558; Adams *v.* Soule, 33 Vt. 538.

Statements as to value, see: Harvey *v.* Young, Yelverton, 21; Lake *v.* Loan Assn., 72 Ala. 207; Stevens *v.* Alabama Land Co., 121 Ala. 450; Kincaid *v.* Price, 82 Ark. 20; Williams *v.* McFadden, 23 Fla. 143; Noetling *v.* Wright, 72 Ill. 390; Cagney *v.* Cuson, 77 Ind. 494; Bossingham *v.* Syck, 118 Ia. 192; Else *v.* Freeman, 72 Kan. 666; Reynolds *v.* Evans, 123 Md. 365; Picard *v.* McCormick, 11 Mich. 68; Doran *v.* Eaton, 40 Minn. 35; Boasberg *v.* Walker, 111 Minn. 445; Union Bank *v.* Hunt, 76 Mo. 439; Dalrymple *v.* Craig, 149 Mo. 345; Dresher *v.* Becker, 88 Neb. 619; Sandford *v.* Handy, 23 Wend. 260; Ellis *v.* Andrews, 56 N. Y. 83; Van Slochem *v.* Villard, 207 N. Y. 587; Mecum *v.* Becker, 166 App. Div. 793; Campbell *v.* Zion's Real Estate Co., 46 Utah, 1; Shanks *v.* Whitney, 66 Vt. 405.

Compare Moon *v.* Benton, 13 Ala. App. 473; Pate *v.* Blades, 163 N. C. 267; Crompton *v.* Beedle, 83 Vt. 287.

[1] Portions of the opinion are omitted.

opinion of value, and even though false, are not such representations as Dr. Jordan had a right to rely upon, and are not enough to furnish any grounds for this action."

The Court declined to give these instructions, and instead instructed the jury that "an expression of opinion, judgment, or estimate, or a statement of a promissory nature relating to what would be in the future, so far as they were expressions of opinion, if made in good faith, however strong as expressions of belief, would not support an action of deceit."

It will be seen that the fundamental difference between the instructions given and those asked is that the former require good faith. The language of some cases certainly seems to suggest that bad faith might make a seller liable for what are known as seller's statements, apart from any other conduct by which the buyer is fraudulently induced to forbear inquiries. Pike *v.* Fay, 101 Mass. 134. But this is a mistake. It is settled that the law does not exact good faith from a seller in those vague commendations of his wares which manifestly are open to difference of opinion, which do not imply untrue assertions concerning matters of direct observation (Teague *v.* Irwin, 127 Mass. 217), and as to which it always has been "understood, the world over, that such statements are to be distrusted." Brown *v.* Castles, 11 Cush. 348, 350; Gordon *v.* Parmelee, 2 Allen, 212; Parker *v.* Moulton, 114 Mass. 99; Poland *v.* Brownell, 131 Mass. 138, 142; Burns *v.* Lane, 138 Mass. 350, 356. Parker *v.* Moulton also shows that the rule is not changed by the mere fact that the property is at a distance, and is not seen by the buyer. Moreover, in this case, market prices at least were easily accessible to the plaintiff.

The defendant was known by the plaintiff's agent to stand in the position of a seller. If he went no further than to say that the bond was an A No. 1 bond, which we understand to mean simply that it was a first rate bond, or that the railroad was good security for the bonds, we are constrained to hold that he is not liable under the circumstances of this case, even if he made the statement in bad faith. See, further, Veasey *v.* Doton, 3 Allen, 380; Belcher *v.* Costello, 122 Mass. 189. The rule of law is hardly to be regretted, when it is considered how easily and insensibly words of hope or expectation are converted by an interested memory into statements of quality and value when the expectation has been disappointed.

. . . .

Exceptions sustained.[1]

[1] Gordon *v.* Butler, 105 U. S. 553; Kimber *v.* Young, (C. C. A.) 137 Fed. 744; Pittsburgh Life & Trust Co. *v.* Northern Ins. Co., 140 Fed. 888, 148 Fed. 674; Dotson *v.* Kirk, (C. C. A.) 180 Fed. 14; Rendell *v.* Scott, 70 Cal. 514; Wrenn *v.* Truitt, 116 Ga. 708; Dowden *v.* Wilson, 108 Ill. 257; Curry *v.* Keyser, 30 Ind. 214; Conant *v.* Nat'l State Bank, 121 Ind. 323; Scroggin *v.* Wood, 87 Ia. 497; Vokes *v.* Eaton, 119 Ky. 913; Holbrook *v.* Connor, 60 Me. 578; Bishop *v.* Small, 63 Me. 12; Donnelly *v.* Baltimore Trust Co., 102 Md. 1; Mooney *v.* Miller, 102 Mass. 217; Nash *v.* Minnesota Title & Trust Co., 159 Mass. 437; Lynch *v.* Murphy,

ANDREWS *v.* JACKSON

SUPREME JUDICIAL COURT, MASSACHUSETTS, MAY 18, 1897.

Reported in 168 *Massachusetts Reports,* 266.

TORT for deceit. The declaration alleged that the plaintiff sold and conveyed to the defendant certain real estate situate in Medford "for the sum of nineteen hundred dollars, and received in payment thereof fourteen hundred dollars in cash and four certain promissory notes all signed by one H. Joseph, amounting together to the sum of six hundred and fourteen hundredths dollars; that the defendant, to induce the plaintiff to convey said real estate to him, falsely represented to the plaintiff that the maker of said notes was a man of property, and that said notes were as 'good as gold'; that your plaintiff, believing said representations to be true, was thereby induced to convey said real estate to the defendant; that said representations were false and were known to the defendant to be false, and by reason thereof the plaintiff suffered great damage."

Trial in the Superior Court, without a jury, before Hammond, J., who found for the plaintiff; and the defendant alleged exceptions, the nature of which appears in the opinion.

The case was submitted on briefs to all the justices.

KNOWLTON, J. The principal question in this case is whether there was any evidence to warrant a finding that the false representations made by the defendant in regard to the notes were actionable. This finding is in these words: "I find that the defendant represented these notes to be as good as gold, and that that representation was intended by him and understood by the plaintiff, not to be an expression of opinion, but a statement of a fact of his own knowledge. I find that the notes were worthless." It is contended by the defendant that such a representation is necessarily, and as a matter of law, a mere expression of opinion, for which, however wilfully false, and however damaging in the reliance placed upon it, no action can be maintained.

It is true that such a representation may be, and often is, a mere expression of opinion. But we think that it may be made under such

171 Mass. 307; Nowlin *v.* Snow, 40 Mich. 699; Myers *v.* Alpena Loan Ass'n, 117 Mich. 389; Getchell *v.* Dusenbury, 145 Mich. 197; Perkins *v.* Trinka, 30 Minn. 241; Brown *v.* South Joplin Min. Co., 194 Mo. 681; Ray County Bank *v.* Hutton, 224 Mo. 42; Fisher *v.* Seitz, 172 Mo. App. 162; Duffany *v.* Ferguson, 66 N. Y. 482; Hatton *v.* Cook, 166 App. Div. 257; Pritchard *v.* Dailey, 168 N. C. 330; Martin *v.* Eagle Creek Development Co., 41 Or. 448; Watts *v.* Cummins, 59 Pa. St. 84; Horrigan *v.* First Nat. Bank, 9 Baxt. 137; Jude *v.* Woodburn, 27 Vt. 415; Randall *v.* Farnum, 52 Vt. 539; Romaine *v.* Excelsior Machine Co., 54 Wash. 41; Crislip *v.* Cain, 19 W. Va. 438 *Accord.*

Compare Wall *v.* Graham, 192 Ala. 396; Barron Estate Co. *v.* Woodruff Co., 163 Cal. 561; Phelps *v.* Grady, 168 Cal. 73; Sleeper *v.* Smith, 77 N. H. 337; Olston *v.* Oregon R. Co., 52 Or. 343.

Opinion of third person, see Adams *v.* Collins, 196 Mass. 422.

circumstances and in such a way as properly to be understood as a statement of fact upon which one may well rely.

In Stubbs *v.* Johnson, 127 Mass. 219, one of the representations in regard to a note was that it was " as good as gold," and the jury were instructed that, if this was intended as a representation of the financial ability of the maker of the note, it was a statement of a material fact, for which the defendant was liable. This instruction was held erroneous " because a representation as to a man's financial ability to pay a debt may be made either as a matter of opinion, or as a matter of fact; the subject of the statement does not necessarily determine which it is. . . . It is often impossible," says Mr. Justice Colt further in the opinion, " to determine, as matter of law, whether a statement is a representation of a fact, which the defendant intended should be understood as true of his own knowledge, or an expression of opinion. That will depend upon the nature of the representation, the meaning of the language used, as applied to the subject matter, and as interpreted by the surrounding circumstances, in each case. The question is generally to be submitted to the jury." The opinion plainly implies that, if the jury had been left to determine whether there was a representation of the maker's financial ability to pay made as matter of fact and not as mere matter of opinion, they might have found against the defendant on his false representation that the note was " as good as gold." In Belcher *v.* Costello, 122 Mass. 189, there is also a strong intimation that the rule is as above stated. In Safford *v.* Grout, 120 Mass. 20, the representation set out in the declaration was that the maker of the note " was a person of ample means and ability to pay said note, and that the note was good." The plaintiff was allowed to recover. The court says of the representations, " We must presume that they were legally sufficient to support the action; that is to say, that they were statements of facts susceptible of knowledge, as distinguished from matters of mere opinion or belief." See also Morse *v.* Shaw, 124 Mass. 59; Teague *v.* Irwin, 127 Mass. 217.

In two recent cases, Way *v.* Ryther, 165 Mass. 226, and Kilgore *v.* Bruce, 166 Mass. 136, 138, this court has expressed a disinclination to extend the rule which permits dealers to indulge with impunity in false representations of opinion.

In the case now before us the notes were turned over to the plaintiff in part payment of the agreed price for land sold to the defendant. He professed to know, and probably did know, all about the financial standing of the maker of them, who lived in Boston. The plaintiff lived in a suburban town and knew nothing of the maker. She was obliged to take the defendant's representations or to decline to deal with him until she could go to Boston and make an investigation for herself.[1] He told her that he had lent money to the maker, and said,

[1] Jarratt *v.* Langston, 99 Ark. 438; Baum *v.* Holton, 4 Col. App. 406; Shelton *v.* Healy, 74 Conn. 265; Kenner *v.* Harding, 85 Ill. 264; Dwight *v.* Chase, 3 Ill.

"Do you suppose I would lend my money to any one that was not good?"

A representation that a note is as good as gold may be founded on absolute personal knowledge of the validity of the note, and upon an equally certain knowledge of the maker's financial ability. The known facts upon which financial ability depends may be so clear and cogent as to make the consequent conclusion, which ordinarily would be a mere matter of opinion, a matter of moral certainty which can properly be called knowledge. We cannot say, as matter of law, that this representation was not intended to be, and properly understood to be, a representation of facts within the defendant's knowledge.

The case of Deming *v.* Darling, 148 Mass. 504, differs materially from this at bar. The property to which the representation related was one of many mortgage bonds issued by a railroad company, of which, in the language of the opinion, the "market prices at least were easily accessible to the plaintiff." The representations which were held to be insufficient on which to found an action were "in relation to the value of the bond in question, or of the railroad, its terminals, and other property which were mortgaged to secure it." The value of articles sold in market, and especially of railroad property and of railroad bonds payable in the distant future, is ordinarily only a matter of opinion. A statement of the value of such property is very different from a statement that a promissory note which is almost due is known to be valid, and that the maker of it is a person of such known integrity and financial ability that his promise to pay is as good as that of the state or nation. A statement that a note is as good as gold may be intended to represent facts of this kind.

. . . .

Exceptions overruled.[1]

App. 67; Wightman *v.* Tucker, 50 Ill. App. 75; Coulter *v.* Clark, 160 Ind. 311; Stauffer *v.* Hulwick, 176 Ind. 410; Beck *v.* Goar, 180 Ind. 81; Automobile Co. *v.* Crowell, 149 N. W. 861; Hetland *v.* Bilstad, 140 Ia. 411; Picard *v.* McCormick, 11 Mich. 68; Nowlin *v.* Snow, 40 Mich. 699; McDonald *v.* Smith, 139 Mich. 211; Conlan *v.* Roemer, 52 N. J. Law, 53; Bacon *v.* Frisbie, 15 Hun, 26; Marshall *v.* Seelig, 49 App. Div. 433; Ganow *v.* Ashton, 32 S. D. 458; Rodee *v.* Seaman, 33 S. D. 184; Rorer Iron Co. *v.* Trout, 83 Va. 397; Fitzgerald *v.* Frankel, 109 Va. 603; Grant *v.* Huschke, 74 Wash. 257 *Accord.*

[1] Winkler *v.* Jerrue, 20 Cal. App. 555; Hodgkins *v.* Dunham, 10 Cal. App. 690; Olvey *v.* Jackson, 106 Ind. 286; Crane *v.* Elder, 48 Kan. 259; Gurney *v.* Tenney, 197 Mass. 457; Van de Wiele *v.* Garbade, 60 Or. 585; Corey *v.* Boynton, 82 Vt. 257; Simons *v.* Cissna, 52 Wash. 115 *Accord.* Compare Foster *v.* Kennedy, 38 Ala. 359; Sheer *v.* Hoyt, 13 Cal. App. 662; Judy *v.* Jester, 53 Ind. App. 74; Burr *v.* Willson, 22 Minn. 206; Adan *v.* Steinbrecher, 116 Minn. 174.

WILLIAMS v. STATE

SUPREME COURT, OHIO, FEBRUARY 11, 1908.

Reported in 77 Ohio State Reports, 468.

ERROR to the Circuit Court of Montgomery County.

The plaintiff in error was indicted for obtaining money and property by certain false pretences, to wit: that certain real estate situate in Benton township, Pike County, being one hundred and ten acres in quantity, was then and there of the value of $11,000, and that one Martha M. Williams, then and there believing said representation of value to be true, and relying and acting upon that belief, was induced to and did purchase from the plaintiff in error, the said real estate, and accepted his deed therefor, and gave to him and one Neal Overholser in payment therefor, money and property to the amount and value of $7700, whereas, in fact, the said real estate was not then and there of the value of $11,000, and was of the value not to exceed three dollars per acre, that is, $330 in all; and that the plaintiff in error then and there knew that the value of said real estate did not exceed the sum of $330, and knew at the time he so falsely represented the value of said real estate that the same was false. To this indictment the plaintiff in error filed a motion to quash and also a demurrer, which were both overruled; and the case coming on for trial, at the close of the evidence introduced by the state, a motion was made by the defendant to instruct the jury to return a verdict of acquittal, which was overruled; and the court thereupon charged the jury, among other things, as follows: "But where the buyer relies entirely upon the representations of the seller and the seller knows that the property he is describing is of such small value as to be practically worthless, and nevertheless represents it to be worth a specified sum of great amount, and the discrepancy between the real and the represented value is so enormous as to shock the conscience; when the representation is so grossly untrue that it could not be made upon any possible foundation of belief; and when it appears that the seller was plainly seeking by means of such statement to obtain the property of the buyer and practically return no equivalent therefor, the court takes the responsibility of saying to you that you have the right, if your judgment of evidence so convinces you, to regard such representations as one of fact rather than mere opinion." The jury found the defendant guilty and judgment was rendered accordingly, which judgment was affirmed by the Circuit Court, and this proceeding in error is to reverse that judgment.[1]

DAVIS, J. A statement of value may be given either as an opinion or as a statement of fact. All the authorities agree that if a statement of value is given as an opinion merely it cannot be regarded as a foundation for an indictment. But if the statement is made as an existing fact, when the accused knows it to be false and intends it to be an inducement to the other party, and it is so understood and relied upon by the other party, then it becomes a false representation of a material fact for which the party making the representation is indictable. Whether the representation of value is intended as an expression of opinion, or whether it was made as a statement of an existing fact

[1] Arguments omitted.

which the speaker intends to be an inducement to the other party, is therefore a material question of fact to be determined by the jury.

There is no novelty in this view of the law. In Reg. *v.* Evans, 8 Cox, C. C. 257, it was said by Pollock, C. B.: "As my brother, Crowder, J., has suggested, if the prisoner had represented the note to be of the value of £5 when she knew it was not of that value, she might have been guilty of false pretences." In People *v.* Peckens, 153 N. Y. 576, 591, the court say: "It is insisted that many of the representations to the complainant and her husband, which induced the making and delivery of her deed, were expressions of opinion, and although false and known to be so, no liability resulted. As a general rule, the mere expression of an opinion, which is understood to be only an opinion, does not render a person expressing it liable for fraud. But where the statements are as to value or quality, and are made by a person knowing them to be untrue, with an intent to deceive and mislead the one to whom they are made, and he is thus induced to forbear making inquiries which he otherwise would, that may amount to an affirmation of fact rendering him liable therefor. In such a case, whether a representation is an expression of an opinion or an affirmation of a fact is a question for the jury. The rule that no one is liable for an expression of an opinion is applicable only when the opinion stands by itself as a distinct thing. If it is given in bad faith, with knowledge of its untruthfulness, to defraud others, the person making it is liable, especially when it is as to a fact affecting quality or value and is peculiarly within the knowledge of the person making it. Watson *v.* People, 87 N. Y. 561; Simar *v.* Canaday, 53 N. Y. 298; Hickey *v.* Morrell, 102 N. Y. 454, 463; Schumacher *v.* Mather, 133 N. Y. 590, 595." The same view of the question is presented in Holton *v.* State, 109 Ga. 127, 130; and also in People *v.* Jordan, 66 Cal. 10, 13, 14.

Simar *v.* Canaday, 53 N. Y. 298, was a civil action for damages for an alleged fraud in inducing the plaintiffs to convey certain premises. The court, at page 306, said: "The defendant contends that the representations alleged to have been made by the defendant were not such as to afford a ground for an action. It is first insisted that the statements as to the value of the lands and of the mortgages thereon were mere matter of opinion and belief, and that no action could be maintained upon them if false. If they were such, no liability is created by the utterance of them; but all statements as to the value of property sold are not such. They may be, under certain circumstances, affirmation of fact. When known to the utterer to be untrue, if made with the intention of misleading the vendee, if he does rely upon them and is misled to his injury, they avoid the contract. Stebbins *v.* Eddy, 4 Mason, 414–423. And where they are fraudulently made of particulars in relation to the estate which the vendee has not equal means of knowing, and where he is induced to forbear inquiries which he would otherwise have made, and damage ensues, the party guilty of the fraud should be liable for the damage sustained. Medbury *v.* Watson, 6 Metc. 246, per Hubbard, J.; and see McClellan *v.* Scott, 24 Wis. 81." More recently the cases of Coulter *v.* Minion, 139 Mich. 200, and Scott *v.* Burnight, 131 Ia. 507, are to the same effect.

These considerations determine every question raised upon the record and therefore the judgment of the Circuit Court is *Affirmed.*

PRICE, CREW, SUMMERS and SPEAR, JJ., concur.

BOWEN, L. J., IN SMITH *v.* LAND CORPORATION

(1884) *Law Reports*, 28 *Chancery Division*, 15–16.

IN considering whether there was a misrepresentation, I will first deal with the argument that the particulars only contain a statement of opinion about the tenant. It is material to observe that it is often fallaciously assumed that a statement of opinion cannot involve the statement of a fact. In a case where the facts are equally well known to both parties, what one of them says to the other is frequently nothing but an expression of opinion. The statement of such opinion is in a sense a statement of a fact, about the condition of the man's own mind, but only of an irrelevant fact, for it is of no consequence what the opinion is. But if the facts are not equally known to both sides, then a statement of opinion by the one who knows the facts best involves very often a statement of a material fact, for he impliedly states that he knows facts which justify his opinion. Now a landlord knows the relations between himself and his tenant; other persons either do not know them at all or do not know them equally well, and if the landlord says that he considers that the relations between himself and his tenant are satisfactory, he really avers that the facts peculiarly within his knowledge are such as to render that opinion reasonable. Now are the statements here statements which involve such a representation of material facts ? They are statements on a subject as to which *prima facie* the vendors know everything and the purchasers nothing. The vendors state that the property is let to a most desirable tenant; what does that mean ? I agree that it is not a guarantee that the tenant will go on paying his rent, but it is to my mind a guarantee of a different sort, and amounts at least to an assertion that nothing has occurred in the relations between the landlords and the tenant which can be considered to make the tenant an unsatisfactory one. This is an assertion of a specific fact. Was it a true assertion ? Having regard to what took place between Lady Day and Midsummer, I think that it was not. On the 25th of March, a quarter's rent became due. On the 1st of May, it was wholly unpaid and a distress was threatened. The tenant wrote to ask for time. The plaintiffs replied that the rent could not be allowed to remain over Whitsuntide. The tenant paid on the 6th of May £30, on the 13th of June £40, and the remaining £30 shortly before the auction. Now could it, at the time of the auction, be said that nothing had occurred to make Fleck an undesirable tenant ? In my opinion a tenant who had paid his last quarter's rent by driblets under pressure must be regarded as an undesirable tenant.[1]

[1] See also Nevada Bank *v.* Portland Nat. Bank, 59 Fed. 338.

In Aaron's Reefs *v.* Twiss, [1896] A. C. 273, Lord Halsbury, L. C., said (pp. 283–284): " I do not think any particular form of words is necessary to convey a false impression. Supposing a person goes to a bank where the people are foolish enough

KIDNEY *v.* STODDARD

SUPREME JUDICIAL COURT, MASSACHUSETTS, OCTOBER TERM, 1843.

Reported in 7 *Metcalf*, 252.

TRESPASS upon the case for an alleged fraudulent representation by the defendant as to the credit of his son, Alden D. Stoddard, Jr., in the following letter to F. Delano of New York: "Fairhaven, 9 mo. 27, 1841. Franklin Delano, Esq. My dear Sir: The bearer, my son, A. D. Stoddard, Jr., wishes to purchase a bill of goods in your city. Any assistance you can render him, by a recommendation or otherwise, will be gratefully received by him, and much oblige your obedient servant, who will take the liberty to say that A. D. S. Jr.'s contracts, of whatever nature, will unquestionably be punctually attended to. Very respectfully your friend, A. D. Stoddard."

At the trial before Wilde, J., one Ammidon testified that he was agent of the plaintiffs; that Stoddard, Jr., called on him in New York, about the 1st of October, 1841, to purchase some goods, and referred him to Delano; that the witness called on Delano, who showed said letter to him, and made statements concerning Stoddard, Senior. The witness sold the son goods which he would not have sold him, if it had not been for the letter and the statements of Delano. No part of the debt was ever paid. After the sale the plaintiff discovered that the son was a minor at the time the letter was written.

The judge instructed the jury that when a party intentionally conceals a material fact, in giving a letter of recommendation, it amounts to a false representation; that the defendant, giving a letter in this case to an unlimited amount, was bound to communicate every ma-

to believe his words, and says, 'I want a mortgage upon my house, and my house is not completed, but in the course of next week I expect to have it fully completed.' Suppose there was not a house upon his land at all, and no possibility, therefore, that it could be fully completed next week, can anybody say that that was not an affirmative representation that there was a house which was so near to completion that it only required another week's work upon it to complete it? Could anybody defend himself if he was charged upon an indictment for obtaining money under false pretences, the allegation in the indictment being that he pretended that there was a house so near completion that it only required a week's work upon it, by saying that he never represented that there was a house there at all? So here, when I look at the language in which this prospectus is couched, and see that it speaks of a property which requires only the erection of machinery to be either at once or shortly in a condition to do work so as to obtain all this valuable metal from the mine, it seems to me that, although it is put in ambidextrous language, it means as plainly as can be that this is now the condition of the mine, that such and such additions to it will enable it shortly to produce all those great results, and that that is a representation of an actually existing fact. I should quite agree with the proposition that the Lord Chancellor of Ireland and the Master of the Rolls put forward — if you are looking to the language as only the language of hope, expectation, and confident belief, that is one thing; but it does not seem to have been in the minds of the learned judges that you may use language in such a way as, although in the form of hope and expectation, it may become a representation as to existing facts; and if so, and if it is brought to your knowledge that these facts are false, it is a fraud."

terial fact; that if he concealed the fact that the son was a minor, with the view to give him a credit, knowing or believing that he would not get a credit if that fact was known, it was a fraud, and the plaintiff was entitled to recover; that it was immaterial whether there was any moral fraud; and that every man was presumed to know the consequences of his own acts.

The defendant's counsel requested the judge to instruct the jury, that if the defendant gave his opinion merely, he was not bound to communicate any facts; and that if he gave an honest opinion, he was not liable. But the judge refused so to instruct the jury. It was also contended by the defendant's counsel that the plaintiffs should have made an effort to recover the debt of the son.

The jury found a verdict for the plaintiffs for the amount of the goods sold, and the defendant moved for a new trial, on the ground that the jury were misdirected in matter of law.[1]

HUBBARD, J.

. . . .

It is very certain, as has been maintained by the defendant's counsel, that a mistaken opinion, honestly given, can never be taken as a fraudulent representation. This is true in principle, and supported abundantly by authorities. But the misfortune of the defendant's case is, that the verdict of the jury rests not on the honest mistake of the defendant, but upon the ground of material concealment of a fact especially within his knowledge; a fact important to be known, as it regarded the credit of the son; a fact designedly concealed, and with the view of obtaining that credit for the son, which he, the father, knew or believed he could not obtain if that fact were known.

It needs no lengthened argument to establish the materiality of the fact. The result of this case is a sufficient witness of it. The plaintiffs were induced by the letter, from which this fact was carefully excluded, to give a credit to the son, which they would not otherwise have given; and as the direct consequence of it, they have sustained the loss set out in the declaration. Here then are proved fraud and deceit on the part of the defendant, and damage to the plaintiffs; and these facts have long been held to constitute a substantial cause of action. From the time of the judgment in the great case of Pasley *v.* Freeman, 3 T. R. 51, to the present day, through the long line of decisions both in England and America, the principle of that case, though with some statute modifications, remains unshaken and unimpaired.

[Remainder of opinion omitted.] *Judgment on the verdict.*[2]

[1] The statement has been abridged.

[2] Loewer *v.* Harris, (C. C. A.) 57 Fed. 368; King *v.* White, 119 Ala. 429; Christy *v.* Campbell, 36 Col. 261; Kronfeld *v.* Missal, 87 Conn. 491; James *v.* Crosthwait, 97 Ga. 673; Gordon *v.* Irvine, 105 Ga. 144; Aortson *v.* Ridgway, 18 Ill. 23; Dayton *v.* Kidder, 105 Ill. App. 107; Craig *v.* Hamilton, 118 Ind. 565; Firestone *v.* Werner, 1 Ind. App. 293; Coles *v.* Kennedy, 81 Ia. 360; Howerton *v.* Augustine,

DERRY *v.* PEEK

In the House of Lords, July 1, 1889

Reported in Law Reports, 14 *Appeal Cases*, 337.

THE action in this case was brought by Sir H. Peek against Mr. W. Derry, the chairman, and Messrs. J. C. Wakefield, M. M. Moore, J. Pethick, and S. J. Wilde, four of the directors of the Plymouth, Devonport, and District Tramways Company, claiming damages for the

130 Ia. 389; Nairn *v.* Ewalt, 51 Kan. 355; Faris *v.* Lewis, 2 B. Mon. 375; Weikel *v.* Sterns, 142 Ky. 513; Prentiss *v.* Russ, 16 Me. 30; Barrett *v.* Lewiston R. Co., 110 Me. 24; Johnston *v.* Cope, 3 Har. & J. 89; Burns *v.* Dockray, 156 Mass. 135; Batty *v.* Greene, 206 Mass. 561; Kenyon *v.* Woodruff, 33 Mich. 310; Tompkins *v.* Hollister, 60 Mich. 470; Busch *v.* Wilcox, 82 Mich. 315; Marsh *v.* Webber, 13 Minn. 109; Thomas *v.* Murphy, 87 Minn. 358; McAdams *v.* Cates, 24 Mo. 223; Morley *v.* Harrah, 167 Mo. 74; Manter *v.* Truesdale, 57 Mo. App. 435; Stevens *v.* Fuller, 8 N. H. 463; Fleming *v.* Slocum, 18 Johns. 403; Allen *v.* Addington, 7 Wend. 9; March *v.* First National Bank, 4 Hun, 466; Brown *v.* Gray, 6 Jones Law, 103; Lunn *v.* Shermer, 93 N. C. 164; Gidney *v.* Chappell, 26 Okl. 737; Fitzhugh *v.* Nirschl, 77 Or. 514; Rheen *v.* Naugatuck Wheel Co., 33 Pa. St. 356; Cardwell *v.* McClelland, 3 Sneed, 150; Allison *v.* Tyson, 5 Humph. 449; Graham *v.* Stiles, 38 Vt. 578; Maynard *v.* Maynard, 49 Vt. 297; Crompton *v.* Beedle, 83 Vt. 287; Jarrett *v.* Goodnow, 39 W. Va. 602; Morgan *v.* Hodge, 145 Wis. 143 *Accord.* Compare: Randolph *v.* Allen, (C. C. A.) 73 Fed. 23; Ball *v.* Farley, 81 Ala. 288; Cherry *v.* Brizzolara, 89 Ark. 309; Roper *v.* Sangamon Lodge, 91 Ill. 518; Potts *v.* Chapin, 133 Mass. 276; Cochrane *v.* Halsey, 25 Minn. 52; Crowell *v.* Jackson, 53 N. J. Law, 656; Babcock *v.* Libbey, 82 N. Y. 144; Jones *v.* Stewart, 62 Neb. 207; Wicker *v.* Worthy, 51 N. C. 500; Harris *v.* Tyson, 24 Pa. St. 347; Iron Bank *v.* Anderson, 194 Pa. St. 205; Bishop *v.* Buckley, 33 Pa. Super. Ct. 123; Campbell *v.* Kinlock, 9 Rich. Law, 300.

In Wiser *v.* Lawler, 189 U. S. 260, Brown, J., said (pp. 264–65): "Attached to these prospectuses was a map entitled 'Map of the group of mines belonging to the Seven Stars Gold Mining Company.' It is true that there is neither in the prospectuses nor in the map a distinct assertion that the legal title to the properties mentioned was vested in the Seven Stars Company; but we think that no one can read them without inferring and believing that the Seven Stars was the owner of these properties, and that the net proceeds of their operation would be distributed in dividends to stockholders. As they were circulated as an inducement to take stock in the enterprises, we are bound to interpret them by the effect they would produce upon an ordinary mind. Andrews *v.* Mockford, (1896) 1 Q. B. D. 372. They were, however, even more damaging in their omissions than in their statements. No mention was made of the fact that the title to these properties stood in the names of Lawler and Wells; no allusion to the Cowland agreement, with its provisions for forfeiture, nor to the fact that the only interest of the company was an equitable right to the properties after the sum of $450,000 had been realized from the profits and paid to defendants. In estimating the probability of subscribers being misled by these prospectuses we may take into consideration not only the facts stated, but the facts suppressed. New Brunswick Co. *v.* Muggeridge, 1 Drewey & Smale, 363. They are entitled to know the *cons* as well as the *pros*. Gluckstein *v.* Barnes, (1900) App. Cas. 240; Hubbard *v.* Weare, 79 Iowa, 678; Hayward *v.* Leeson, 175 Mass. 310; In re Leeds and Hanley Theatres, (1902) 2 Ch. Div. 809."

In Peek *v.* Gurney, L. R. 6 H. L. 377, Lord Cairns said (p. 403): "Mere non-disclosure of material facts, however morally censurable, however that non-disclosure might be a ground in a proper proceeding at a proper time for setting aside an allotment or a purchase of shares, would in my opinion form no ground for an action in the nature of an action for misrepresentation. There must, in my opinion, be some active misstatement of fact, or, at all events, such a partial and fragfraudulent misrepresentations of the defendants whereby the plaintiff was induced to take shares in the company.[1]

The company was incorporated in the year 1882 for making and maintaining tramways in Plymouth, Devonport, and Stonehouse. The nominal capital was £125,000 in shares of £10 each.

The Plymouth, Devonport, and District Tramways Act, 1882 (45 & 46 Vict. c. clix.), by which the company was incorporated, contained the following clause (sect. 35): —

"The carriages used on the tramways may, subject to the provisions of this Act, be moved by animal power, and, with the consent of the Board of Trade, during a period of seven years after the opening of the same for public traffic, and with the like consent during such further periods not exceeding seven years as the said board may from time to time specify in any order to be signed by a secretary or an assistant secretary of the said board, by steam-power or any mechanical power: Provided always, that the exercise of the powers hereby conferred with respect to the use of steam or any mechanical power shall be subject to the regulations set forth in the Schedule A. to this Act annexed, and to any regulations which may be added thereto or substituted therefor by any order which the Board of Trade may and which they are hereby empowered to make from time to time, as and when they may think fit, for securing to the public all reasonable protection against danger in the exercise of the powers by this Act conferred with respect to the use of steam or any mechanical power on the tramways: Provided also,

mentary statement of fact, as that the withholding of that which is not stated makes that which is stated absolutely false."

Compare Mitchell, J., in Newell *v.* Randall, 32 Minn. 171, 172–73: "It is doubtless the general rule that a purchaser, when buying on credit, is not bound to disclose the facts of his financial condition. If he makes no actual misrepresentations, if he is not asked any questions, and does not give any untrue, evasive, or partial answers, his mere silence as to his general bad pecuniary condition, or his indebtedness, will not constitute a fraudulent concealment. 2 Pom. Eq. Jur. § 906; Bigelow on Fraud, 36, 37. But this was not a case of mere passive non-disclosure. The object of De Laittre's inquiry clearly was to ascertain Bauman's financial condition and ability to pay. Bauman's statement was in response to that inquiry, and, when he undertook to answer, he was bound to tell the whole truth, and was not at liberty to give an evasive or misleading answer, which, although literally true, was partial, containing only half the truth, and calculated to convey a false impression. The natural construction which would, under the circumstances, be put on this statement is that he had $3,300 capital in his business. It was couched in language calculated to negative the idea that this was merely the gross amount of his assets, and that he owed debts to the extent of two-thirds or the whole of that amount. Such a statement, made under the circumstances it was, might fairly and reasonably be understood as amounting to a representation that he had that amount of capital which was and would remain available, out of which to collect any debt which he might contract with plaintiff. We think this is the way in which men would ordinarily have understood it. It is immaterial that more explicit inquiries by plaintiff would have disclosed the fact of his indebtedness. It does not lie in Bauman's mouth to say that plaintiff relied too implicitly on this general statement. To tell half a truth only is to conceal the other half. Concealment of this kind, under the circumstances, amounts to a false representation."

[1] The statement is taken from 37 Ch. D. 541, omitting the last part. Arguments are omitted. None of the opinions are given except portions of Lord Herschell's.

that the company shall not use steam-power or any mechanical power on the said tramways unless and until they shall have obtained the previous consent in writing of the corporations [Plymouth and Devonport] therefor, and then for such terms only and subject to such conditions and regulations as the corporations may from time to time prescribe."

By sect. 64 it was provided that the company should not open any of the tramways for public traffic without the consent of the corporations.

In October, 1882, the directors issued a prospectus which contained the following paragraph: "As by sect. 35 of the Plymouth and Devonport District Tramways Act, 1882, power is given to use either animal, steam, or mechanical means of locomotion, the directors will adopt that motive power which experience may demonstrate to be at once the most economical and effective." It did not appear that the plaintiff ever received a copy of this prospectus.

On the 1st of February, 1883, the directors of the company issued a second prospectus, which contained a heading in large type as follows: "Incorporated by special Act of Parliament 45 & 46 Vict. authorizing the use of steam or other mechanical motive power." The prospectus contained the following paragraphs: —

"One great feature of this undertaking, to which considerable importance should be attached, is, that by the special Act of Parliament obtained, the company has the right to use steam or mechanical motive power instead of horses, and it is fully expected that by means of this a considerable saving will result in the working expenses of the line, as compared with other tramways worked by horses."

"Looking to the exceptional advantages offered by this undertaking from the dense population of the towns it traverses, the unusually favorable conditions as to motive power open to the company, and the annual dividends earned by other companies which do not enjoy such special privileges, the directors have reason to believe that the enterprise will prove highly remunerative, and the shares now for subscription offer a very favorable opportunity for a sound and progressive investment."

The defendants at the same time issued a circular letter, which was sent with the prospectus, in which it was stated that "the company by its Act enjoys the special privilege of the right to use steam-power instead of horse-power, from which it is expected considerable savings will result in the working expenses."

The plaintiff received copies of this prospectus and circular, and believing, as he alleged, that the company had an absolute right to use steam and other mechanical power, and relying upon the representations and statements in the prospectus and circular, applied on the 7th of February for 400 shares, for which he paid £4000.

About £40,000 only of the capital was subscribed; but the directors completed part of their tramway in Plymouth. The corporation of

Devonport refused their consent to the company opening the completed part until the remaining portion was ready, and on the 14th of November, 1884, obtained an injunction restraining the company from so doing. When the Board of Trade were applied to, they refused to sanction the use of steam-power except over a small portion of the tramways.

The result was that the company was unable to carry out its proposed undertaking, and a petition for winding-up was presented, which was followed by a winding-up order on the 2d of May, 1885.

The writ in this action was issued on the 4th of February, 1885, a few days after the petition for winding-up, by Sir H. Peek, against the chairman and directors named above, claiming in the first instance a rescission of the contract for shares and repayment of the money paid by him, and damages; but the writ was afterwards amended, and claimed only damages for the misrepresentations in the prospectus and circular.

The defence pleaded by the defendants was that they did not represent, or intend to represent, in the prospectus and circular, that the company had an absolute right to use steam or other mechanical power; that the plaintiff knew that the use of steam-power was never, or seldom, given unconditionally to a tramway company, and that he was acquainted, or might have made himself acquainted, with the provisions of the company's special Act, which was referred to in the prospectus, and might be seen at the company's office; and they denied that the plaintiff was induced to take the shares by the representations complained of. They also pleaded that if the statements complained of were untrue, they were made by the defendants in good faith, and that they had reasonable grounds for believing them to be true: that in fact the consent of the corporation of Plymouth to the use of steam was given in June, 1883, and the consent of the Board of Trade to its being used in a portion of the tramways had also been given.

The action came on for hearing before Mr. Justice STIRLING. At this hearing the parties testified.

STIRLING, J., came to the conclusion that the directors all believed that the company had the right stated in the prospectus; and that their belief was not unreasonable, and their proceedings so reckless or careless, that they ought to be fixed with the consequences of deceit. He ordered the action to be dismissed.[1]

On appeal by plaintiff to the Court of Appeal, the judgment of STIRLING, J., was reversed by COTTON, HANNEN, and LOPES, L.JJ. They held the directors liable in this action for deceit, on the ground that they made the statement without any reasonable ground for believing it to be true. L. R. 37 Ch. Div. 541.

The defendants, Derry, *et al.*, appealed from the decision of the Court of Appeal to the House of Lords.

[1] The opinion of STIRLING, J., is reported in 37 Ch. D. 550. See especially 556–558.

The House of Lords unanimously reversed the judgment of the Court of Appeal, and restored the order of STIRLING, J. Opinions were delivered by LORDS HALSBURY, WATSON, BRAMWELL, FITZGERALD, and HERSCHEL.

Portions of the opinion of LORD HERSCHELL are as follows: —

LORD HERSCHELL. My Lords, in the statement of claim in this action the respondent, who is the plaintiff, alleges that the appellants made in a prospectus issued by them certain statements which were untrue, that they well knew that the facts were not as stated in the prospectus, and made the representations fraudulently, and with the view to induce the plaintiff to take shares in the company.

"This action is one which is commonly called an action of deceit, a mere common-law action." This is the description of it given by Cotton, L. J., in delivering judgment. I think it important that it should be borne in mind that such an action differs essentially from one brought to obtain rescission of a contract on the ground of misrepresentation of a material fact. The principles which govern the two actions differ widely. Where rescission is claimed it is only necessary to prove that there was misrepresentation; then, however honestly it may have been made, however free from blame the person who made it, the contract, having been obtained by misrepresentation, cannot stand. In an action of deceit, on the contrary, it is not enough to establish misrepresentation alone; it is conceded on all hands that something more must be proved to cast liability upon the defendant, though it has been a matter of controversy what additional elements are requisite. I lay stress upon this because observations made by learned judges in actions for rescission have been cited and much relied upon at the bar by counsel for the respondent. Care must obviously be observed in applying the language used in relation to such actions to an action of deceit. Even if the scope of the language used extend beyond the particular action which was being dealt with, it must be remembered that the learned judges were not engaged in determining what is necessary to support an action of deceit, or in discriminating with nicety the elements which enter into it.

There is another class of actions which I must refer to also for the purpose of putting it aside. I mean those cases where a person within whose special province it lay to know a particular fact, has given an erroneous answer to an inquiry made with regard to it by a person desirous of ascertaining the fact for the purpose of determining his course accordingly, and has been held bound to make good the assurance he has given. Burrowes v. Lock, 10 Ves. 470, may be cited as an example, where a trustee had been asked by an intended lender, upon the security of a trust fund, whether notice of any prior incumbrance upon the fund had been given to him. In cases like this it has been said that the circumstance that the answer was honestly made in the belief that it was true affords no defence to the action. Lord Selborne pointed out in Brownlie *v.* Campbell, 5 App. Cas. p. 935, that these cases were in an altogether different category from actions to recover damages for false representation, such as we are now dealing with.

One other observation I have to make before proceeding to consider the law which has been laid down by the learned judges in the Court of Appeal in the case before your Lordships. "An action of deceit is a common-law action, and must be decided on the same principles, whether it be brought in the Chancery Division or any of the Common Law Divisions, there being, in my opinion, no such thing as an equitable action for deceit." This was the language of Cotton, L. J., in Arkwright *v.* Newbould, 17 Ch. D. 320. It was adopted by Lord Blackburn in Smith *v.* Chadwick, 9 App. Cas. 193, and is not, I think, open to dispute.

In the Court below Cotton, L. J., said: "What in my opinion is a correct statement of the law is this, that where a man makes a statement to be acted upon by others which is false, and which is known by him to be false, or is made by him recklessly, or without care whether it is true or false, that is, without any reasonable ground for believing it to be true, he is liable in an action of deceit at the suit of any one to whom it was addressed, or any one of the class to whom it was addressed, and who was materially induced by the misstatement to do an act to his prejudice." About much that is here stated there cannot, I think, be two opinions. But when the learned Lord Justice speaks of a statement made recklessly or without care whether it is true or false, that is, without any reasonable ground for believing it to be true, I find myself, with all respect, unable to agree that these are convertible expressions. To make a statement, careless whether it be true or false, and therefore without any real belief in its truth, appears to me to be an essentially different thing from making, through want of care, a false statement, which is nevertheless honestly believed to be true. And it is surely conceivable that a man may believe that what he states is the fact, though he has been so wanting in care that the Court may think that there were no sufficient grounds to warrant his belief. I shall have to consider hereafter whether the want of reasonable ground for believing the statement made is sufficient to support an action of deceit. I am only concerned for the moment to point out that it does not follow that it is so, because there is authority for saying that a statement made recklessly, without caring whether it be true or false, affords sufficient foundation for such an action.

. . . .

It will thus be seen that all the learned judges [in the Court of Appeal] concurred in thinking that it was sufficient to prove that the representations made were not in accordance with fact, and that the person making them had no reasonable ground for believing them. They did not treat the absence of such reasonable ground as evidence merely that the statements were made recklessly, careless whether they were true or false, and without belief that they were true, but they adopted as the test of liability, not the existence of belief in the truth of the assertions made, but whether the belief in them was founded upon any reasonable grounds. It will be seen, further, that the Court did not purport to be establishing any new doctrine. They deemed that they were only following the cases already decided, and that the proposition which they concurred in laying down was established by prior authorities. Indeed, Lopes, L. J., expressly states the law in this respect to be well settled. This renders a close and critical examination of the earlier authorities necessary.

. . . .

Having now drawn attention, I believe, to all the cases having a material bearing upon the question under consideration, I proceed to state briefly the conclusions to which I have been led. I think the authorities establish the following propositions: First, in order to sustain an action of deceit there must be proof of fraud, and nothing short of that will suffice. Secondly, fraud is proved when it is shown that a false representation has been made (1) knowingly, or (2) without belief in its truth, or (3) recklessly, careless whether it be true or false. Although I have treated the second and third as distinct cases, I think the third is but an instance of the second, for one who makes a statement under such circumstances can have no real belief in the truth of what he states. To prevent a false statement being fraudulent there must, I think, always be an honest belief in its truth. And this probably covers the whole ground, for one who knowingly alleges that which is false has obviously no such honest belief.[1] Thirdly, if fraud be proved, the motive of the person guilty of it is immaterial. It matters not that there was no intention to cheat or injure the person to whom the statement was made.

I think these propositions embrace all that can be supported by decided cases from the time of Pasley *v.* Freeman, 2 Smith's L. C. 74, down to Western Bank of Scotland *v.* Addie, Law Rep. 1 H. L. Sc. 145, in 1867, when the first suggestion is to be found that belief in the truth of what he has stated will not suffice to absolve the defendant if his belief be based on no reasonable grounds. I have shown that this view was at once dissented from by Lord Cranworth, so that there was at the outset as much authority against it as for it. And I have met with no further assertion of Lord Chelmsford's view until the case of Weir *v.* Bell, 3 Ex. D. 238, where it seems to be involved in Lord Justice Cotton's enunciation of the law of deceit. But no reason is there

[1] "Want of honest belief in the truth of what one asserts, not positive knowledge that it is false, is the essence of the wrong. A man who knows that he is making a reckless assertion about things of which he really knows nothing may not be speaking against his own belief, but he is not speaking according to it, and therefore his conduct is dishonest, and is esteemed fraud by the law." Pollock, Law of Fraud in British India, 43.

given in support of the view, it is treated as established law. The *dictum* of the late Master of the Rolls, that a false statement made through carelessness, which the person making it ought to have known to be untrue, would sustain an action of deceit, carried the matter still further. But that such an action could be maintained notwithstanding an honest belief that the statement made was true, if there were no reasonable grounds for the belief, was, I think, for the first time decided in the case now under appeal.

In my opinion making a false statement through want of care falls far short of, and is a very different thing from, fraud, and the same may be said of a false representation honestly believed though on insufficient grounds. Indeed Cotton, L. J., himself indicated, in the words I have already quoted, that he should not call it fraud. But the whole current of authorities, with which I have so long detained your Lordships, shows to my mind conclusively that fraud is essential to found an action of deceit, and that it cannot be maintained where the acts proved cannot properly be so termed. And the case of Taylor *v.* Ashton, 11 M. & W. 401, appears to me to be in direct conflict with the *dictum* of Sir George Jessel, and inconsistent with the view taken by the learned judges in the Court below. I observe that Sir Frederick Pollock, in his able work on Torts (p. 243, note), referring, I presume, to the *dicta* of Cotton, L. J., and Sir George Jessel, M. R., says that the actual decision in Taylor *v.* Ashton, 11 M. & W. 401, is not consistent with the modern cases on the duty of directors of companies. I think he is right. But for the reasons I have given I am unable to hold that anything less than fraud will render directors or any other persons liable to an action of deceit.

At the same time I desire to say distinctly that when a false statement has been made the questions whether there were reasonable grounds for believing it, and what were the means of knowledge in the possession of the person making it, are most weighty matters for consideration. The ground upon which an alleged belief was founded is a most important test of its reality. I can conceive many cases where the fact that an alleged belief was destitute of all reasonable foundation would suffice of itself to convince the Court that it was not really entertained, and that the representation was a fraudulent one. So, too, although means of knowledge are, as was pointed out by Lord Blackburn in Brownlie *v.* Campbell, 5 App. Cas. p. 952, a very different thing from knowledge, if I thought that a person making a false statement had shut his eyes to the facts, or purposely abstained from inquiring into them I should hold that honest belief was absent, and that he was just as fraudulent as if he had knowingly stated that which was false.

I have arrived with some reluctance at the conclusion to which I have felt myself compelled, for I think those who put before the public a prospectus to induce them to embark their money in a commercial enterprise ought to be vigilant to see that it contains such representations only as are in strict acordance with fact, and I should be very unwilling to give any countenance to the contrary idea. I think there is much to be said for the view that this moral duty ought to some extent to be converted into a legal obligation, and that the want of reasonable care to see that statements made under such circumstances are true should be made an actionable wrong. But this is not a matter fit for discussion on the present occasion. If it is to be done the legislature must intervene and expressly give a right of action in respect of such a departure from duty. It ought not, I think, to be done by straining the law, and holding that to be fraudulent which the tribunal feels cannot properly be so described. I think mischief is likely to result from blurring the distinction between carelessness and fraud, and equally holding a man fraudulent whether his acts can or cannot be justly so designated.

It now remains for me to apply what I believe to be the law to the facts of the present case. [After reviewing the evidence of each defendant.] I cannot hold it proved as to any one of them that he knowingly made a false statement, or one which he did not believe to be true, or was careless whether what he stated was true or false. In short, I think they honestly believed that what they asserted was true,[1] and I am of opinion that the charge of fraud made against them has not been established. [Remainder of opinion omitted.][2]

[1] For a criticism of the view that the directors all believed the statement, see 6 Law Quarterly Rev. 73; 5 Law Quarterly Rev. 420–422.

[2] Schuchardt *v.* Allens, 1 Wall. 359; Union R. Co. *v.* Barnes, (C. C. A.) 64 Fed. 80; Pittsburgh Life & Trust Co. *v.* Northern Life Ins. Co., (C. C. A.) 148 Fed. 674; Foster *v.* Kennedy, 38 Ala. 359; Morton *v.* Scull, 23 Ark. 289; Hutchinson *v.* Gorman, 71 Ark. 305; Davidson *v.* Jordan, 47 Cal. 351; Bartholomew *v.* Bushnell, 20 Conn. 271; Fooks *v.* Waples, 1 Har. (Del.) 131; Manes *v.* Kenyon, 18 Ga. 291; Cooley *v.* King, 113 Ga. 1163; Wheeler *v.* Randall, 48 Ill. 182; Holdom *v.* Ayer, 110 Ill. 448; Herman *v.* Foster, 185 Ill. App. 97; Holmes *v.* Clark, 10 Ia. 423; Scroggin *v.* Wood, 87 Ia. 497; Boddy *v.* Henry, 113 Ia. 462; Farmers' Stock Breeding Ass'n *v.* Scott, 53 Kan. 534; Campbell *v.* Hillman, 15 B. Mon. 508; Haynes *v.* Gould, 83 Me. 344; Cahill *v.* Applegarth, 98 Md. 493; Emerson *v.* Brigham, 10 Mass. 197; Pike *v.* Fay, 101 Mass. 134; Cole *v.* Cassidy, 138 Mass. 437; Holst *v.* Stewart, 154 Mass. 445; Lillegren *v.* Burns, 135 Minn. 60; Taylor *v.* Frost, 39 Miss. 328; Utley *v.* Hill, 155 Mo. 232; Allen *v.* Wanamaker, 31 N. J. Law, 370; Williams *v.* Wood, 14 Wend. 126; Marsh *v.* Folker, 40 N. Y. 562; Wakeman *v.* Dalley, 51 N. Y. 27; Kountze *v.* Kennedy, 147 N. Y. 124; Hamrick *v.* Hogg, 1 Dev. 350; Taylor *v.* Leith, 26 Ohio St. 428; Staines *v.* Shore, 16 Pa. St. 200; Erie Iron Works *v.* Barber, 106 Pa. St. 125; Lamberton *v.* Dunham, 165 Pa. St. 129; Deppen *v.* Light, 228 Pa. St. 79; Gibbs *v.* Odell, 2 Cold. 132; Weeks *v.* Burton, 7 Vt. 67 *Accord.*

In Heilbut *v.* Buckleton, [1913] A. C. 30, Lord Moulton said (p. 48): "In the history of English law we find many attempts to make persons responsible in damages by reason of innocent misrepresentations, and at times it has seemed as though the attempts would succeed. On the Chancery side of the Court the decisions favoring this view usually took the form of extending the scope of the action for deceit. There was a tendency to recognize the existence of what was sometimes called 'legal fraud,' i. e., that the making of an incorrect statement of fact without reasonable grounds, or of one which was inconsistent with information which the person had received or had the means of obtaining, entailed the same legal consequences as making it fraudulently. Such a doctrine would make a man liable for

HOLMES, J., DISSENTING IN NASH *v.* MINNESOTA TITLE & TRUST COMPANY

(1895) 163 *Massachusetts* 574, 586–587.

IF I were making the law, I should not hold a man answerable for representations made in the common affairs of life without bad faith in some sense, if no consideration was given for them, although it would be hard to reconcile even that proposition with some of our cases. But the proposition, even if accepted, seems to me not to apply to this case. The proper meaning of the

forgetfulness or mistake or even for honestly interpreting the facts known to him or drawing conclusions from them in a way which the Court did not think to be legally warranted. The high-water mark of these decisions is to be found in the judgment pronounced by the Court of Appeal in the case of Peek *v.* Derry, (1887) 37 Ch. D. 541; (1889) 14 App. Cas. 337, when they laid down that where a defendant has made a misstatement of fact and the Court is of opinion that he had no reasonable grounds for believing that it was true he may be made liable in an action of deceit if it has materially tended to induce the plaintiff to do an act by which he has incurred damage. But on appeal to your Lordships' House this decision was unanimously reversed, and it was definitely laid down that, in order to establish a cause of action sounding in damages for misrepresentation, the statement must be fraudulent or, what is equivalent thereto, must be made recklessly, not caring whether it be true or not. The opinions pronounced in your Lordships' House in that case show that both in substance and in form the decision was, and was intended to be, a reaffirmation of the old common law doctrine that actual fraud was essential to an action for deceit, and it finally settled the law that an innocent misrepresentation gives no right of action sounding in damages.

"On the Common Law side of the Court the attempts to make a person liable for an innocent misrepresentation have usually taken the form of attempts to extend the doctrine of warranty beyond its just limits and to find that a warranty existed in cases where there was nothing more than an innocent misrepresentation. The present case is, in my opinion, an instance of this. But in respect of the question of the existence of a warranty the Courts have had the advantage of an admirable enunciation of the true principle of law which was made in very early days by Holt, C. J., with respect to the contract of sale. He says: 'An affirmation at the time of the sale is a warranty, provided it appear on evidence to be so intended.' So far as decisions are concerned, this has, on the whole, been consistently followed in the Courts of Common Law. But from time to time there have been dicta inconsistent with it which have, unfortunately, found their way into text-books and have given rise to confusion and uncertainty in this branch of the law. For example, one often sees quoted the dictum of Bayley, J., in Cave *v.* Coleman, 3 Man. & Ry. 2, where, in respect of a representation made verbally during the sale of a horse, he says that 'being made in the course of a dealing, and before the bargain was complete, it amounted to a warranty' — a proposition that is far too sweeping and cannot be supported. A still more serious deviation from the correct principle is to be found in a passage in the judgment of the Court of Appeal in DeLassalle *v.* Guildford, [1901] 2 K. B. 215, at p. 221, which was cited to us in the argument in the present case. In discussing the question whether a representation amounts to a warranty or not the judgment says: 'In determining whether it was so intended, a decisive test is whether the vendor assumes to assert a fact of which the buyer is ignorant, or merely states an opinion or judgment upon a matter of which the vendor has no special knowledge, and on which the buyer may be expected also to have an opinion and to exercise his judgment.'

"With all deference to the authority of the Court that decided that case, the proposition which it thus formulates cannot be supported. It is clear that the Court did not intend to depart from the law laid down by Holt, C. J., and cited above, for in the same judgment that dictum is referred to and accepted as a correct statement of the law. It is, therefore, evident that the use of the phrase 'decisive test' cannot be defended. Otherwise it would be the duty of a judge to direct a jury that if a vendor states a fact of which the buyer is ignorant, they must, as a matter of law, find the existence of a warranty, whether or not the totality of the evidence shows that the parties intended the affirmation to form words used by the defendant has been settled by this court already. 159 Mass. 437. The representation was not made in casual talk, but in a business matter, for the very purpose of inducing others to lay out their money on the faith of it. When a man makes such a representation, he knows that others will understand his words according to their usual and proper meaning, and not by the accident of what he happens to have in his head, and it seems to

part of the contract; and this would be inconsistent with the law as laid down by Holt, C. J. It may well be that the features thus referred to in the judgment of the Court of Appeal in that case may be criteria of value in guiding a jury in coming to a decision whether or not a warranty was intended; but they cannot be said to furnish decisive tests, because it cannot be said as a matter of law that the presence or absence of those features is conclusive of the intention of the parties. The intention of the parties can only be deduced from the totality of the evidence, and no secondary principles of such a kind can be universally true.

"It is, my Lords, of the greatest importance, in my opinion, that this House should maintain in its full integrity the principle that a person is not liable in damages for an innocent misrepresentation, no matter in what way or under what form the attack is made. In the present case the statement was made in answer to an inquiry for information. There is nothing which can by any possibility be taken as evidence of an intention on the part of either or both of the parties that there should be a contractual liability in respect of the accuracy of the statement. It is a representation as to a specific thing and nothing more. The judge, therefore, ought not to have left the question of warranty to the jury, and if, as a matter of prudence, he did so in order to obtain their opinion in case of appeal he ought then to have entered judgment for the defendants notwithstanding the verdict."

But compare Kirkpatrick *v.* Reeves, 121 Ind. 280; Mendenhall *v.* Stewart, 18 Ind. App. 262; McLeod *v.* Tutt, 2 Miss. 288; Searing *v.* Lum, 2 South, 683; Indianapolis R. Co. *v.* Tyng, 63 N. Y. 653; Cobb *v.* Fogalman, 1 Ired. 440; Mason *v.* Moore, 73 Ohio St. 275; Loper *v.* Robinson, 54 Tex. 510; Magill *v.* Coffmann, (Tex. Civ. App.) 129 S. W. 1146; Smith *v.* Columbus Buggy Co., 40 Utah, 580; Ogden Resort Co. *v.* Lewis, 41 Utah, 183; Cameron *v.* Mount, 86 Wis. 477; Palmer *v.* Goldberg, 128 Wis. 103; Knudson *v.* George, 157 Wis. 520.

As to whether an action ought not to be allowed for negligence in the use of language, see Smith, Liability for Negligent Language, 14 Harvard Law Rev. 184; Cunningham *v.* Pease, 74 N. H. 435; Conway National Bank *v.* Pease, 76 N. H. 319. The English Directors' Liability Act (1890), 53 & 54 Vict. c. 64, makes directors and others who issue prospectuses liable in certain cases to compensate persons sustaining loss by reason of any untrue statement in the prospectus, unless it is proved that the persons issuing the prospectus had reasonable ground to believe and did believe that the prospectus was true. See also the statute of Oklahoma, Howe *v.* Martin, 23 Okl. 561, 567.

Liability for statement made recklessly not knowing whether true or not, see: Cooper *v.* Schlesinger, 111 U. S. 148; Hindman *v.* First National Bank, (C. C. A.) 112 Fed. 931; Mueller Furnace Co. *v.* Cascade Foundry Co., 145 Fed. 596; Einstein *v.* Marshall, 58 Ala. 153; McCoy *v.* Prince, 11 Ala. App. 388; Stimson *v.* Helps, 9 Col. 33; Scholfield Gear Co. *v.* Scholfield, 71 Conn. 1; Upchurch *v.* Mizell, 50 Fla. 456; Corbett *v.* Gilbert, 24 Ga. 454; Miller *v.* John, 208 Ill. 173; Snively *v.* Meixsell, 97 Ill. App. 365; West *v.* Wright, 98 Ind. 335; Graves *v.* Lebanon Bank, 10 Bush, 23; Stone *v.* Denny, 4 Met. 151; Fisher *v.* Mellen, 103 Mass. 503; Beebe *v.* Knapp, 28 Mich. 53; Stone *v.* Covell, 29 Mich. 359; Bullitt *v.* Farrar, 42 Minn. 8; Hamlin *v.* Abell, 120 Mo. 188; Chase *v.* Rusk, 90 Mo. App. 25; Ruddy *v.* Gunby, (Mo.) 180 S. W. 1043; Rowell *v.* Chase, 61 N. H. 135; Shackett *v.* Bickford, 74 N. H. 57; Zabriskie *v.* Smith, 13 N. Y. 322; Bennett *v.* Judson, 21 N. Y. 238; Taylor *v.* Commercial Bank, 174 N. Y. 181; Bell *v.* James, 128 App. Div. 241; Whitehurst *v.* Life Ins. Co., 149 N. C. 273; Cawston *v.* Sturgis, 29 Or. 331; Robertson *v.* Frey, 72 Or. 599; Thompson *v.* Chambers, 13 Pa. Super. Ct. 213; Mitchell *v.* Zimmerman, 4 Tex. 75; Katzenstein *v.* Reid, Murdock & Co., 41 Tex. Civ. App. 106; Benton *v.* Kuykendall, (Tex. Civ. App.) 160 S. W. 438; Wheeler *v.* Wheelock, 34 Vt. 553; Agnew *v.* Hackett, 80 Wash. 236; Cotzhausen *v.* Simon, 47 Wis. 103.

Compare Ray County Bank *v.* Hutton, 224 Mo. 42; Ramsey *v.* Wallace, 100 N. C. 75.

me one of the first principles of social intercourse that he is bound at his peril to know what that meaning is. In this respect it seems to me that there is no difference between the law of fraud and that of other torts, or of contract or estoppel. If the language of fiction be preferred, a man is conclusively presumed in all parts of the law to contemplate the natural consequences of his act, as well in the conduct of others as in mechanical results. I can see no difference in principle between an invitation by words and an invitation by other acts, such as opening the gates of a railroad crossing (Brow *v.* Boston & Albany Railroad, 157 Mass. 399), or an intentional gesture, having as its manifest consequence, according to common experience, a start and a fall on the part of the person toward whom it is directed, in either of which cases I suppose no one would say that a defendant could get off by proving that he did not anticipate the natural interpretation of the sign. Of course, if the words used are technical, or have a peculiar meaning in the place where they were used, this can be shown; if by the context, or the subject matter, or the circumstances, the customary meaning of the words is modified, this can be shown by proof of the circumstances, the subject matter, and the context; but when none of these things appears, a defendant cannot be heard to say that for some undisclosed reason he had in his mind, and intended to express by the words, something different from what the words appear to mean, and were understood by the plaintiff to mean, and are interpreted by the court to mean, whether the action be in tort or contract.

Neither, in my opinion, are there any peculiar safeguards set up about the action for deceit. That action was given by the common law for any false statement of present facts of which the defendant took the risk, and which was followed by damage. He might take the risk at different points in different cases. A false warranty used to be laid as a deceit in tort for a false and fraudulent representation. Clift, Entries, 932, pl. 40. Liber Placitandi, 40, pl. 54, 55. Y. B. 11 Ed. IV. pl. 10. So even an implied warranty. Brown *v.* Edgington, 2 Man. & G. 279. See Y. B. 11 Ed. IV. 6 b; Keilw. 91, pl. 16. Yet it was not necessary to lay the scienter, or if you laid it, to prove it, for the plain reason, as Shaw, C. J., puts it, in substance, that the defendant is answerable for the facts, however honest he may have been. Norton *v.* Doherty, 3 Gray, 372, 373. Schuchardt *v.* Allens, 1 Wall. 359, 368. Williamson *v.* Allison, 2 East, 446. Gresham *v.* Postan, 2 C. & P. 540. Denison *v.* Ralphson, 1 Vent. 365, 366. In the last century an alternative form in assumpsit was introduced (Stuart *v.* Wilkins, 1 Doug. 18, 21, Lawrence, J., and Williamson *v.* Allison, 2 East, 446, 451), and it may be that now we should require the warranty to be alleged, which has the advantage of telling the defendant more exactly what the case is against him. Cooper *v.* Landon, 102 Mass. 58. But there is no doubt about the common law. I am of opinion, as I have stated, that in a case like the present a man takes the risk of the interpretation of his words as it may afterwards be settled by the court.

Hand, J., in SLATER TRUST COMPANY *v.* GARDINER

(1910) 183 *Federal Reporter*, 268, 270–271.

At the outset the character of the mistake must be observed. Gardiner knew the facts, but he did not know the meaning of the words. Although the great weight of authority is to the contrary (Derry *v.* Peek, 14 App. Cas.

337), I may assume for the purposes of this case that a man may be responsible for his uttered false words, even when he believes them to be true.

Such authorities as hold to this rule regard the uttered word as the cause of the damage, which, of course, it is, and they hold that a man, by speaking or writing words on which he knows others will rely, must be held to their truth quite as much as though he made a promise (Mr. Justice Holmes, dissentiente, Nash *v.* Minnesota Title Co., 163 Mass. 574, 40 N. E. 1039, 28 L. R. A. 753, 47 Am. St. Rep. 489; Pollock on Torts, [6th Ed.] page 283). But these authorities, which regard the word as the tortious act, certainly should not, in analogy with the other law of torts, be supposed to mean that a man should be responsible for the remote results of his words. The extent of his responsibility, indeed, ought to be limited, as it is in other torts, to those matters which would come within the foresight of the hypothetical reasonable man. With remoter damage it is as unjust to charge the words of his mouth as the movements of his legs or arms. Although they do not in these words indicate the distinction, I think that this is the explanation of such of the cases as make negligence the test, and of these there are a number.

If Gardiner was responsible for the words he uttered, regardless of *scienter*, at least he was not responsible for such consequences as no man could avoid with the use of reasonable care. What happened in spite of the exercise of such care was remote, within all the analogies of the law of torts. "Causa proxima non remota spectatur." Nor does it make any difference that it was in respect of the meaning of his words that he was mistaken. The utterance of a word is one thing; its eventual interpretation by a reader is another, and is as much the external consequence of its utterance as anything else. A given interpretation, even a legal one, may be, from the point of view of the original utterer, so remote a consequence that no one ought in justice to be held accountable for it. For example, in the case at bar, if Gardiner did all a layman could do to get the facts set down correctly, the interpretation that J. T. Woodward put on the words Gardiner was not bound to anticipate, not even if it was the right one.

The authorities do not make any distinction between the discrepancy of the statement with the facts stated and the discrepancy of the statement with its subsequent interpretation. Thus in Derry *v.* Peek, 14 App. Cas. 337, it appeared that the directors who issued the prospectus knew all the facts and trusted their solicitors to prepare the statement correctly (see Lord Bramwell's judgment, page 348); their misstatement was in calling the franchise absolute which was in fact conditional. This statement they successfully justified, because they regarded the condition attached to the franchise as practically certain of fulfilment and the statement really truthful (Lord Herschell's Judgment, pages 378, 379). The point is that the error was in supposing that the facts which they knew were correctly set forth in the statement. A similar case, where the exact point was passed on by the Supreme Court of Massachusetts, is Nash *v.* Minnesota Title Co., 163 Mass. 574, 40 N. E. 1039, 28 L. R. A. 753, 47 Am. St. Rep. 489, the dissent in which I have already mentioned. But that dissent proceeds upon the theory that no scienter is ever necessary in an action for deceit.

CARPENTER, J., IN ALDRICH *v.* SCRIBNER

(1908) 154 *Michigan*, 23.

Holcomb *v.* Noble, 69 Mich. 396, 37 N. W. 497, is also in point. There defendant and plaintiff exchanged lands. In making this exchange plaintiff relied on certain representations of fact respecting the pine on the land transferred to him by defendant. These representations were based — and this was understood by plaintiff — upon the reports of a land looker, and defendant told plaintiff "that all he knew about the land was what he learned from the land looker." Defendant believed these representations to be true. They were in fact false, and plaintiff sustained damages by his reliance thereon. An action of fraud was brought, and it was held that plaintiff could recover. There were two opinions in the case, one written by Justice Campbell and concurred in by Justice Champlin, one written by Justice Morse and concurred in by Chief Justice Sherwood. In the opinion of Justice Campbell it is said: "It is admitted that in equity an actual design to mislead is not necessary if a party is actually misled by another in a bargain. There was abundant evidence in this case to authorize the jury to find that defendant, whether honestly or dishonestly, expected plaintiff to act on his representations of the reliableness of the reports which he produced, and that plaintiff did rely on them. There is no reason for a difference in action, in such cases, between courts of law and courts of equity. Where an equitable cause of grievance exists, it in no way differs from a legal one, unless a different remedy is needed. A court of law cannot cancel a contract, and for such a purpose the equitable remedy must be sought. But where the relief desired is compensation for the wrong, the equitable remedy is much less appropriate, and an action in equity for mere damages will generally be denied, but denied only because the legal remedy is better. If there could be no legal remedy, there can be no doubt that equity would act. If the fraud is such that it creates a right of action anywhere, an action must lie on the case where a money judgment is needed." I now quote from the opinion of Justice Morse, concurred in by Chief Justice Sherwood: "I was strongly impressed, upon the argument of this case, with the theory of the defendant, supported by abundant authority outside of our own state, that unless the jury found that the representations relied upon by the plaintiff as false were made by the defendant, Noble, knowing them to be false, or he made the statements as facts within his own knowledge, when he was ignorant of the truth or falsity of them, he could not be held liable in this action; that if he told plaintiff that he had never seen the lands, but that he had had the same examined by a competent land looker, who said that there were 5,000,000 feet of pine on the land, and made no representations as of his own knowledge, the plaintiff could not recover. A subsequent careful examination of the case and the authorities cited by defendant's counsel has but confirmed me in the correctness and justness of his claim. I am satisfied that the law ought not to make a different contract for the seller than he sees fit to make for himself, and hold him in effect, for warranties that he never made. But an equally careful examination of the cases adjudicated in this state satisfies me that the doctrine is settled here, by a long line of cases, that if there was in fact a misrepresentation, though made innocently, and its deceptive influence was effective, the consequences to the plaintiff being as serious as though it had proceeded from a vicious purpose, he would have a right of action for the damages caused thereby either at law or in equity. Baughman *v.* Gould, 45 Mich. 483, 8 N. W. 73; Converse *v.* Blumrich, 14 Mich. 109, 90 Am. Dec. 230; Steinbach *v.* Hill, 25 Mich. 78; Webster *v.* Bailey, 31 Mich. 36; Starkweather *v.* Benjamin, 32 Mich. 305; Beebe *v.* Knapp, 28 Mich. 53." I think these decisions are indistinguishable from the case at bar, and require us to say that the trial court erred in directing a verdict for the defendant. The Busch Case and the Holcomb Case cannot be distinguished from the case under consideration by saying that in them " the principal adopted the agent's estimate as his own." For in this case, as heretofore stated, defendant asserted to plaintiff " that those representations Barnard had made were true." It might therefore be said in this case, then, the principal adopted the agent's estimate as his own.

Our attention is called to Krause *v.* Cook, 144 Mich. 365, 108 N. W. 81. There defendant, acting for one Parker, sold mining stock to the plaintiff. Certain false representations were made, and an action to recover damages for fraud was brought. It was held that the trial court should have given the following instruction: " If a person received information from others, and believes it, repeats it, explaining that he has no personal knowledge, he is not guilty of fraud. Therefore, if you find that the defendant received information from others, and repeated that information to plaintiff, and explained to plaintiff the sources of his information, he is not guilty of any fraud, if he acts honestly and in good faith." At first blush it would seem, that this principle is opposed to the decisions of Holcomb *v.* Noble and Busch *v.* Wilcox, *supra*. And it must be admitted, I think, that if this principle had been applied in those cases, a different conclusion would there have been reached. If there was no difference in the facts, it might be said that Krause *v.* Cook, *supra*, is opposed to the principle announced in the Busch and Holcomb Cases. But there is a difference in the cases, and, in my judgment, such a difference as to require a different rule of law. In the Holcomb and Busch Cases the defendant himself obtained what plaintiff lost by means of the false representations. In the Krause Case the defendant was an agent, who at most received only 10 per cent of the damages caused by the false representations. This difference, in my judgment, places the Krause Case outside the rule of the Holcomb and Busch Cases. That rule is peculiarly a Michigan rule. Elsewhere in order to create liability for deceit, it must be shown that " the person making the statement, or the person responsible for it, either knows it to be untrue, or is culpably ignorant (that is, recklessly and consciously ignorant) whether it be true or not." See Webb's Pollock on Torts, p. 355. In Michigan we have held (see cases cited in the opinion of Justice Morse in the Holcomb Case, *supra*) that in order to constitute a fraud it is not necessary that the person making the statement should either know that it is untrue or be recklessly and consciously ignorant whether it be true or not. It is sufficient if it be false in fact. It must be said, however, that in the cases in which this principle has been applied the defendant obtained what the false representations caused the plaintiff to lose. Applied in such cases, the principle is a just and salutary one. This may be illustrated by the Holcomb Case — which is a typical case. There, because plaintiff Holcomb credited a certain false statement of fact, he paid defendant Noble more for land purchased than otherwise he would have paid. The false statement of fact was an agency whereby the property of the plaintiff was transferred to defendant. The law would be justly subject to reproach if it afforded no redress in such case. In

Michigan the law does give redress in such a case, and that redress may be obtained in an action for fraud. It may seem somewhat unjust to characterize such conduct as fraudulent, but the court was apparently placed in the dilemma of either so characterizing it or of altogether denying compensation, and it chose the least objectionable of these two alternatives. This principle, which is altogether just in its application to cases where the loss of the plaintiff has inured to the profit of the defendant, would be most unjust if applied to cases where the defendant has obtained no such profit. This may be illustrated by taking a concrete case, and I take a case even plainer in its facts than the Krause Case. Let us suppose that, with commendable motives and in the best of faith, one friend communicates to another with all amplitude of detail certain information he has received respecting a mine, which it is known that neither of them has ever visited. The object of this communication is to induce the one to whom it is made to purchase stock, but not from the one making the communication, but from a third person having no relation to him. The stock is purchased accordingly, without any profit resulting to the friend making the communication; the information proves to be false and the stock worthless. Did the friend who communicated the information which proved to be false commit a fraud ? He did no moral wrong. Indeed, from a moral point of view his conduct was commendable, and, unless compelled to do so, the court should not announce a rule of law which penalizes commendable conduct. Are we compelled to declare that there exists a rule of law which makes such conduct fraudulent ? Manifestly not unless we are bound to declare that the doctrine of the Holcomb and Busch Cases applies. Must we so declare ? As already pointed out, the case differs materially from the Holcomb and Busch Cases, and this difference is such that the doctrine of those cases has no just application. That doctrine was designed to accomplish justice: as applied in the Holcomb and Busch Cases and in similar cases it does accomplish justice. As applied to cases where the loss of the plaintiff has not inured to the profit of the defendant it accomplishes an injustice, and it therefore has no application to such cases.

LORD HALDANE, L. C., IN NOCTON *v.* LORD ASHBURTON

(1914) *Appeal Cases,* 932, 945–946, 951–954.

I HAVE read the evidence of the appellant, and, although it is obviously unreliable evidence, it leaves on my mind the same impression that it left on that of the learned judge who heard it, that the solicitor did not consciously intend to defraud his client, but, largely owing to a confused state of mind, believed that he was properly joining with him and guiding him in a good speculation.

I cannot, therefore, treat the case, so far as based on intention to deceive, as made out. But where I differ from the learned judges in the Courts below is as to their view that, if they did not regard deceit as proved, the only alternative was to treat the action as one of mere negligence at law unconnected with misconduct. This alternative they thought was precluded by the way the case had been conducted. I am not sure that, on the pleadings and on the facts proved, they were right even in this. The question might well have been treated as in their discretion and as properly one of costs only, having regard to the unsatisfactory evidence of the appellant. But I do not take the view that they were shut up within the dilemma they supposed. There is a third form of procedure to which the statement of claim approximated very closely, and that is the old bill in Chancery to enforce compensation for breach of a fiduciary obligation. There appears to have been an impression that the necessity which recent authorities have established of proving moral fraud in order to succeed in an action of deceit has narrowed the scope of this remedy. For the reasons which I am about to offer to your Lordships, I do not think that this is so. . . .

My Lords, it is known that in cases of actual fraud the Courts of Chancery and of Common Law exercised a concurrent jurisdiction from the earliest times. For some of these cases the greater freedom which, in early days, the Court of Chancery exercised in admitting the testimony of parties to the proceedings made it a more suitable tribunal. Moreover, its remedies were more elastic. Operating *in personam* as a Court of conscience it could order the defendant, not, indeed, in those days, to pay damages as such, but to make restitution, or to compensate the plaintiff by putting him in as good a position pecuniarily as that in which he was before the injury.

But in addition to this concurrent jurisdiction, the Court of Chancery exercised an exclusive jurisdiction in cases which, although classified in that Court as cases of fraud, yet did not necessarily import the element of *dolus malus*. The Court took upon itself to prevent a man from acting against the dictates of conscience as defined by the Court, and to grant injunctions in anticipation of injury, as well as relief where injury had been done. Common instances of this exclusive jurisdiction are cases arising out of breach of duty by persons standing in a fiduciary relation, such as the solicitor to the client, illustrated by Lord Hardwicke's judgment in Chesterfield *v.* Janssen, 2 Ves. Sen. 125. I can hardly imagine that those who took part in the decision of Derry *v.* Peek, 14 App. Cas. 337, imagined that they could be supposed to have cast doubt on the principle of any cases arising under the exclusive jurisdiction of the Court of Chancery. No such case was before the House, which was dealing only with a case of actual fraud as to which the jurisdiction in equity was concurrent. . . .

So far as the equity jurisdiction in cases of what is called fraud is concurrent only and exercised in actions for mere deceit apart from breach of special duty, an actual intention to cheat has now to be proved. But there are cases of other classes to which, as I have already said, the Court of Chancery undoubtedly did apply the term fraud, although I think unfortunately.

Fraud in such cases is, as James, L. J., said in Torrance *v.* Bolton, L. R. 8 Ch. 118, at p. 124, "*nomen generalissimum*, and it must not be construed so as to mislead persons into the notion that contracts for the sale and purchase of lands are in any respect privileged, so as to be free from the ordinary jurisdiction of the Court to deal with them as it deals with any instrument, or any other transactions, in which the Court is of opinion that it is unconscientious for a person to avail himself of the legal advantage which he has obtained. Indeed, the books are full of cases in which the Court has dealt with contracts of that kind — contracts obtained by persons from others over whom they have dominion, contracts obtained by persons in a fiduciary position, contracts for the sale of shares obtained by directors through misrepresentation contained in the prospectus, in respect of which it was never necessary to allege or prove that the directors were wilfully guilty of moral fraud in what they had done." In Chancery the term "fraud" thus came to be used to describe what fell short of deceit, but imported breach of a duty to which equity had attached its sanction. What was laid down by Lord Eldon in this House in Bulkely *v.* Wilford, 2 Cl. & F. 102, at p. 177, explains the nature of the duty.

My Lords, I have dealt thus fully with this distinction because I think that confusion has arisen from overlooking it. It must now be taken to be settled that nothing short of proof of a fraudulent intention in the strict sense will suffice for an action of deceit. This is so whether a Court of Law or a court of equity in the exercise of concurrent jurisdiction is dealing with the claim, and in this strict sense it was quite natural that Lord Bramwell and Lord Herschell should say that there was no such thing as legal as distinguished from moral fraud. But when fraud is referred to in the wider sense in which the books are full of the expression, used in Chancery in describing cases which were within its exclusive jurisdiction, it is a mistake to suppose that an actual intention to cheat must always be proved. A man may misconceive the extent of the obligation which a Court of Equity imposes on him. His fault is that he has violated, however innocently because of his ignorance, an obligation which he must be taken by the Court to have known, and his conduct has in that sense always been called fraudulent, even in such a case as a technical fraud on a power. It was thus that the expression "constructive fraud" came into existence. The trustee who purchases the trust estate, the solicitor who makes a bargain with his client that cannot stand, have all for several centuries run the risk of the word fraudulent being applied to them. What it really means in this connection is, not moral fraud in the ordinary sense, but breach of the sort of obligation which is enforced by a Court that from the beginning regarded itself as a Court of conscience.

KAY, L. J., IN LOW *v.* BOUVERIE

(1891) 3 *Chancery*, 82, 111–113.

THE result of the authorities seems to be as follows: —

1. There has been from ancient time a jurisdiction in Courts of Equity in certain cases to enforce a personal demand against one who made an untrue representation upon which he knew that the person to whom it was made intended to act, if such person did act upon the faith of it and suffered loss by so acting.

2. This was readily done where the representation was fraudulently made, in which case an action of deceit would lie at law.

3. Relief will also be given at Law and in Equity, even though the representation was innocently made without fraud, in all cases where the suit will be effective if the defendant is estopped from denying the truth of his representation.

4. Where there is no estoppel, an innocent misrepresentation will not support an action at law for damages occasioned thereby.

5. Estoppel is effective where an action must succeed or fail if the defendant or plaintiff is prevented from disputing a particular fact alleged: for example, if an assign of A. sues A.'s trustee to recover the fund assigned, and the trustee is prevented from denying its existence in his hands; or at law, if the

assign of a debt should sue the alleged debtor and he was prevented from denying that the debt was due. Or, in the converse case, an estoppel may be a defence; as if a joint stock company were to sue a shareholder for calls and they were estopped from denying that the shares were paid up, their action would fail.

It is obvious that this rule does not apply to an action for deceit. In such an action the plaintiff relies, not on the truth of the statement, but upon its falsehood; and he is bound to prove, not only that the representation was untrue, but also that it was made fraudulently. Derry *v.* Peek, 14 App. Cas. 337, very well illustrates the difference. It was an action by a person who had been induced to take shares in a joint stock company by an untrue statement in a prospectus. The action was not against the company, but against the directors who had issued the prospectus. The representation was not fraudulently made. Preventing the defendants from denying the truth of their representation would not enable the plaintiff to succeed in such an action; so that the plaintiff could not rely on estoppel. That could only be if the defence had been that the statement was inaccurate, and the defendants were estopped from denying the accuracy of their own statement. The plaintiff's case was not that the statement must be treated as accurate: on that supposition he could not have had any relief against the defendants. The plaintiff sued the defendants upon the ground that the statement was false, and false to their knowledge — that is, fraudulent; and the defence that prevailed was that, if it was inaccurate, it was not fraudulent.

6. I am not satisfied that relief in the nature of a personal demand against the defendant has been given in Equity in cases which did not involve fraud or to which this doctrine of estoppel would not apply. Slim *v.* Croucher, 1 D. F. & J. 518, is the only instance I know of; and, as Lord Campbell said that there might be relief at law in that case, he probably considered, either that it was a case of estoppel, or that an action of deceit would lie — which latter view is not consistent with Derry *v.* Peek, 14 App. Cas. 337.

FARWELL, L. J., IN FRY *v.* SMELLIE

(1912) 3 *King's Bench Division*, 282, 294–295.

I CAN only say that certificates and a blank transfer are in everyday use as securities for raising money, and that every man who lends money to A. on documents which show a title in B. is of course put on inquiry. This does not mean that he must refuse to deal with the agent at all but must refer to the principal, but that he must make such inquiry as is reasonable under the circumstances. If he is foolish enough to lend to A. without inquiry, and A. has no right or authority to deal with the documents, he loses his money, and it is perfectly immaterial whether the security is a deposit of title deeds to real estate or certificates of shares with a blank transfer. Such a question as arises in the present case can only arise when the owner of the property has authorized such a dealing with the property as is corroborated by the possession of the indicia of title. If no authority at all has in fact been given it is quite immaterial whether the lender inquires and is given an untrue answer or does not inquire at all; in either case he loses his money. But if the owner has in fact given the borrower authority to deal with the property by way of loan or by way of sale, and has entrusted him with the indicia of title, enabling him so to deal, then the owner cannot be heard to say that there is any limit on the authority so given. If the indicia of title are apparently co-extensive with the authority claimed there is nothing to suggest any limit. The estoppel arises out of the conduct of the owner of the property. Estoppel is merely a rule of evidence which prevents the person estopped from giving certain facts in evidence. If A.'s conduct amounts to an invitation to B. to advance money to C. without limit on the title deeds of A.'s property, he cannot be heard to say that he had imposed on C. a limit, any more than if he had written or said to B. that he had given C. authority to borrow money and had not mentioned any limit. If he has simply deposited his deeds with C. such deposit involves no such representation, and there is therefore no such estoppel. In speaking of estoppel, I am referring to the doctrine of estoppel by representation which Lord Macnaghten, in Whitechurch *v.* Cavanagh, [1902] A. C. 117, at p. 130, says " is a very old head of equity." (See Low *v.* Bouverie, [1891] 3 Ch. 82.) It is sometimes called equitable estoppel or a rule of equity, and has been expressed in some of the cases as the rule which compels a man to make good his representations of fact, in reliance on which the person to whom they have been made for the purpose of inducing him to act on them has so acted. Indeed equitable estoppel is the only way in which this doctrine of making good representations has survived the decision in Derry *v.* Peek, 14 App. Cas. 337. The circumstances must necessarily be such as to show a duty to some one to disclose fully on the person making the representation, but it is not a quesion of negligence in the sense that an action for damages would lie at common law, and no bill in equity would ever have been filed for damages.[1]

CARTER, J., IN WATSON *v.* JONES

(1899) 41 *Florida*, 241, 253–255.

[After citing Wheeler *v.* Baars, 33 Florida, 696.]

It is there said that the *scienter* may be proved by showing, first, actual knowledge of the falsity of the representation by defendant; second, that defendant made the statement as of his own knowledge, or in such absolute unqualified and positive terms as to imply his personal knowledge of the fact, when in truth defendant had no knowledge whether the statement was true or false; or, third, that the party's special situation or means of knowledge were such as to make it his duty to know as to the truth or falsity of the representation. Under each phase the proof must show that the statement was in fact

[1] " The doctrine seems to be well established by authority that the conduct and admissions of a party operate against him in the nature of an estoppel, wherever, in good conscience and honest dealing, he ought not to be permitted to gainsay them. Thus, negligence becomes constructive fraud, — although, strictly speaking, the actual intention to mislead or deceive may be wanting, and the party may be innocent, if innocence and gross negligence may be deemed compatible; and in such cases the maxim is justly applied to him, that where one of two innocent persons must suffer, he shall suffer who by his own acts occasioned the confidence and loss. The application of the maxim to the case before us is obvious. The principle involved in it is kindred to that of an equitable estoppel, the difference being that the application of the estoppel, instead of the maxim, avoids the loss to the innocent party who has been misled by the conduct of another. See 1 Story's Eq. Jur.,

false, and in addition, under the first, that defendant had actual knowledge that it was false; under the second, that defendant made the statement as of his own knowledge, when in fact he had no knowledge whether it was true or false, which seems to bear a close resemblance to the English rule, "without belief in its truth, or recklessly careless whether it be true or false"; and under the third, that defendant's special situation or means of knowledge were such as made it his duty to know as to the truth or falsity of the representation. From this statement it is quite evident that proof sufficient to sustain the third phase tends very strongly to sustain the idea that the defendant had actual knowledge of the falsity of his statement; for when it is shown that the statement was material and false, and that the defendant's situation or means of knowledge were such as to make it incumbent upon him as a matter of duty to know whether the statement was true or false, the conclusion is almost irresistible that he did know that which his duty required him to know. For this reason the law conclusively presumes from the existence of these facts that defendant had actual knowledge of the falsity of his statement, or, more properly speaking, proof of these facts is sufficient to sustain a charge of actual knowledge, dispensing with further proof upon that subject, and admitting no proof to rebut the fact of actual knowledge, but only proof to rebut the existence of the facts from which such actual knowledge is inferred. We are therefore of opinion that proof of *scienter* in the third phase does not give another or different right or ground of action from that given by proof under the first phase, but that it simply establishes the same ultimate fact, viz., knowledge, by a different class of evidence, and consequently that an allegation that defendant "knew" his representation to be false is provable by evidence embraced in the third phase. In other words, an averment that defendant's situation or means of knowledge were such as made it his duty to know whether his statement was true or false, and an averment that defendant well knew his statements to be untrue, are but different methods of stating the same ultimate fact, viz., knowledge.[1]

secs. 387, 389; Lucas *v.* Hart, 5 Iowa, 415; Commonwealth *v.* Moltz, 10 Pa. St. 527, 531; Smith *v.* McNeal, 68 Pa. St. 164." Foster, J., in Stevens *v.* Dennett, 51 N. H. 324, 335.

"The usual form of expressing the situation which founds an estoppel *in pais* has been that followed in the rulings given, in which, as in many of the older decisions, it is said that an intent to deceive is a necessary element. But under this formula the jury were not prohibited from finding the intention and the estoppel, if, without more, the plaintiff spoke or acted falsely, knowing or having cause to believe that his words or conduct reasonably might influence the defendant's action. The more modern statement, that one is responsible for the word or act which he knows, or ought to know, will be acted upon by another, includes the older statement that the estoppel comes from an intention to mislead. White *v.* Duggan, 140 Mass. 18, 20. Tracy *v.* Lincoln, 145 Mass. 357, 359. O'Donnell *v.* Clinton, 145 Mass. 461, 463. Washburn *v.* Hammond, 151 Mass. 132, 141." Barker, J., in Stiff *v.* Ashton, 155 Mass. 130, 133.

[1] Milson *v.* Gerstenberg, 43 App. D. C. 165; Ballard *v.* Thibodeau, 109 Me. 559; Kiefer *v.* Rogers, 19 Minn. 32; Hedin *v.* Minneapolis Medical Institute, 62 Minn. 146; Flaherty *v.* Till, 119 Minn. 191; Devero *v.* Sparks, 189 Mo. App. 500; Craig

CABOT *v.* CHRISTIE

SUPREME COURT, VERMONT, FEBRUARY TERM, 1869.

Reported in 42 *Vermont Reports*, 121.

CASE for false warranty in the sale of a farm. Plea, not guilty. Trial by jury, May term, 1868, Barrett, J., presiding.

The plaintiff gave evidence tending to show that he bought the farm at the time and for the price stated in the declaration, and that the defendant made representations in respect to the number of acres, as of his own knowledge, designedly intending to induce the plaintiff to suppose and believe, and thereby the plaintiff was induced to and did suppose and believe, that the farm contained at least one hundred and thirty acres of land, and relying thereupon, the plaintiff made the purchase; that the defendant knew that there was not one hundred and thirty acres, or he didn't know that there was that quantity; that in fact there was only one hundred and seventeen acres and a few rods in the farm; that the plaintiff had no knowledge of the quantity except from the defendant's representation.

The defendant gave evidence tending to show that he supposed there was one hundred and thirty acres and a little more in the farm, derived from what he had heard said, and from various deeds in his possession of various grantors and of various parcels, but that he did not know, and did not profess or represent to the plaintiff that he knew how many acres there were in fact; that he gave the plaintiff all the information and sources of information he had on the subject, neither making any false representation, nor fraudulent concealment, nor any undertaking as to the number of acres in the farm. There was no evidence or claim that the farm was sold by the acre; but it appeared that it was sold in lump, or as a farm entire.

The plaintiff requested the Court to charge the jury: —

First, That under the declaration the plaintiff is entitled to recover if he proves a warranty of the number of acres in the farm, or if he proves a fraudulent representation of the number of acres.

Second, That the fraudulent representation may be proved either by evidence of false representations, known to the defendant to be false, and relied upon by the plaintiff, or by proof of an absolute representation of the number of acres, which representation was made with

v. Ward, 1 Abb. Dec. 454; Garvin *v.* Harrell, 27 Okl. 373; Wells *v.* Driskell, (Tex. Civ. App.) 149 S. W. 205 *Accord.*

See Water Com'rs *v.* Robbins, 82 Conn. 623; Auman *v.* McKibben, 179 Ill. App. 425; Huntress *v.* Blodgett, 206 Mass. 318; Bank *v.* Wood, 189 Mo. App. 62.

As to the fiction of "presumption of knowledge," see: Hicks *v.* Stevens, 121 Ill. 186; Ward *v.* Trimble, 103 Ky. 153; Reynolds *v.* Evans, 123 Md. 365; Unitype Co. *v.* Ashcraft, 155 N. C. 63; Collins *v.* Chipman, 41 Tex. Civ. App. 563. Compare Brooks *v.* Hamilton, 15 Minn. 26.

intent that the plaintiff should rely upon it, and was made upon professed knowledge, but without actual knowledge, and which was in fact false, but was relied upon by the plaintiff as true.

The Court complied with said requests only so far as is shown by the charge, and charged as follows: —

In order to entitle the plaintiff to recover he must satisfy the jury that the defendant knew the farm did not contain one hundred and thirty acres, or that he did not believe it contained one hundred and thirty acres; and that in order to induce the plaintiff to buy the farm he falsely represented it to contain one hundred and thirty acres; and that the plaintiff was by such false representation induced to make the purchase, believing it to contain that quantity.

If he honestly believed it contained one hundred and thirty acres, the plaintiff cannot recover, though the defendant was in error about it. Honest mistake is not fraud. Incorrect is not the same as false. You must find that he represented the quantity different from what he knew or believed to be true, with the fraudulent intent. Also, that the plaintiff was thus induced to make the purchase. That is, that the plaintiff would not have made the purchase if the defendant had not represented it to be one hundred and thirty acres. Inquire as to these several points. Fraud is not presumed, but must be proved.

The jury returned a verdict for the defendant. The plaintiff excepted to the charge in the respects in which it failed to comply with, or was against said requests. In other respects the charge was satisfactory.

The declaration counted both upon a false warranty of the defendant in regard to the number of acres contained in the farm, and a warranty in regard to said quantity.

The opinion of the Court was delivered by

STEELE, J. 1. The plaintiff cannot recover upon the ground of a parol warranty of the quantity of the land. If the quantity was warranted it should be provable by the deed. It is true that a deed of conveyance need not contain all the stipulations of the parties. For example, the agreements as to consideration and mode of payment need not be embraced in the deed, for the instrument purports to be the deed of but one of the parties. But it does purport to contain the convenants of the grantor with respect to the property conveyed. To add a new covenant by parol proof would be a palpable violation of the familiar rule that written contracts are not to be varied by oral testimony. Such a parol stipulation, it has been held, could not be proved in respect to an ordinary bill of sale of personal property.

Nor is the plaintiff entitled to recover in this action upon the ground of mistake. A mutual and material mistake, by which the purchaser was misled as to the quantity of land, would be a more appropriate ground for relief in a court of chancery than in a court of law.

If, then, the plaintiff was entitled to recover at all in this case, it was by reason of some fraud on the part of the defendant by which the bargain was induced.

2. The plaintiff complains of the ruling of the County Court upon the subject of fraud. It is conceded that the quantity of land was represented incorrectly. The Court properly told the jury that this, in itself, would not amount to fraud. To entitle the plaintiff to a recovery upon that ground, the defendant must have made some representation upon the subject that he did not believe to be true. The plaintiff claims, and his evidence tended to prove, that the defendant did make such a representation by stating the quantity of land as a matter within his own knowledge, when, in fact, as the defendant concedes, it was a matter upon which he had only a belief. We think it very clear that a party may be guilty of fraud by stating his belief as knowledge. Upon a statement of the defendant's mere belief, judgment, or information, the plaintiff might have regarded it prudent to procure a measurement of the land before completing his purchase. A statement, as of knowledge, if believed, would make a survey or measurement seem unnecessary. A representation of a fact, as of the party's own knowledge, if it prove false, is, unless explained, inferred to be wilfully false and made with an intent to deceive, at least in respect to the knowledge which is professed. A sufficient explanation however sometimes arises from the nature of the subject itself, or from the situation of the parties being such that the statement of knowledge could only be understood as an expression of strong belief or opinion. But the quantity of land in a farm is a matter upon which accurate or approximately accurate knowledge is not at all impossible or unusual. If the defendant had only a belief or opinion as to the quantity of land, it was an imposition upon the plaintiff to pass off such belief as knowledge. So, too, if he made an absolute representation as to the quantity, which was understood and intended to be understood as a statement upon knowledge, it is precisely the same as if he had distinctly and in terms professed to have knowledge as to the fact. It is often said that a representation is not fraudulent if the party who makes it believes it to be true. But a party who is aware that he has only an opinion how a fact is, and represents that opinion as knowledge, does not believe his representation to be true. As is well said in a note to the report of the case of Taylor *v.* Ashton, 11 Mees. & Wels. 418 (Phila. Ed.), the belief of a party to be an excuse for a false representation must be " a belief in the representation as made. The *scienter* will therefore be sufficiently established by showing that the assertion was made as of the defendant's own knowledge, and not as mere matter of opinion, with regard to facts of which he was aware that he had no such knowledge." The same principle of law has been repeatedly recognized. Hammatt *v.* Emerson, 27 Maine, 308, 326; Bennett *v.* Judson, 21 N. Y. 238; Stone *v.* Denny, 4 Met. 151; Hazard *v.* Irwin, 18 Pick. 95.

In the case before us the plaintiff, under the charge of the Court, was denied the benefit of this rule of law, although there was evidence tending to show every necessary element of a fraud of the nature we have been considering. The plaintiff's request was refused, and the jury were instructed that the plaintiff could only recover in case they found "that the defendant represented the quantity of land different from what he knew or believed to be true." Under these instructions it would be immaterial whether he made the representation as a matter of knowledge or as a matter of opinion so long as he kept within his belief as to the quantity of land. In this we think there was error. The Court properly instructed the jury that the representation, to warrant a recovery, must have been relied on and have been an inducement to the purchase. The subsequent remark that the jury, to hold the defendant, must find that the plaintiff would not have made the purchase but for the representation, we regard as probably inadvertent.

What the plaintiff would have done but for the false representation is often a mere speculative inquiry, and is not the test of the plaintiff's right. If the false representations were material and relied upon, and were intended to operate and did operate as one of the inducements to the trade, it is not necessary to inquire whether the plaintiff would or would not have made the purchase without this inducement.

The judgment of the County Court is reversed and the cause is remanded.[1]

[1] O'Neill *v.* Conway, 88 Conn. 651; Bethell *v.* Bethell, 92 Ind. 318; Riley *v.* Bell, 120 Ia. 618; Gund Brewing Co. *v.* Peterson, 130 Ia. 301; Davis *v.* Central Land Co., 162 Ia. 269; Altoona State Bank *v.* Hart, 82 Kan. 398; Braley *v.* Powers, 92 Me. 203; Litchfield *v.* Hutchinson, 117 Mass. 195; Savage *v.* Stevens, 126 Mass. 207; Teague *v.* Irwin, 127 Mass. 217; Adams *v.* Collins, 196 Mass. 422; Huntress *v.* Blodgett, 206 Mass. 318; Chatham Furnace Co. *v.* Moffatt, 147 Mass. 403; Riggs *v.* Thorpe, 67 Minn. 217; Vincent *v.* Corbitt, 94 Miss. 46; Western Cattle Co. *v.* Gates, 190 Mo. 391; Paretti *v.* Rebenack, 81 Mo. App. 494; Leicher *v.* Keeney, 98 Mo. App. 394, 110 Mo. App. 292; Leach *v.* Bond, 129 Mo. App. 315; Crosby *v.* Wells, 73 N. J. Law, 790; Thompson *v.* Koewing, 79 N. J. Law, 246; Hadcock *v.* Osmer, 153 N. Y. 604; Modlin *v.* Roanoke Navigation Co., 145 N. C. 218; Pate *v.* Blades, 163 N. C. 267; Joines *v.* Combs, 38 Okl. 380; Gibbens *v.* Bourland, (Tex. Civ. App.) 145 S. W. 274; Grant *v.* Huschke, 74 Wash. 257; Tolly *v.* Poteet, 62 W. Va. 231; Rogers *v.* Rosenfeld, 158 Wis. 285 *Accord.* See Roberts *v.* Anheuser Busch Ass'n, 211 Mass. 449.

In Brownlie *v.* Campbell, 5 App. Cas. 925, Lord Blackburn said (pp. 952–53): "The Courts of Law had to refer fraud, in which knowledge was an essential ingredient, to a jury. A Court of Equity had to find it for itself, and consequently the judges in Courts of Equity were not driven to be so precisely accurate in stating exactly whether they were going upon the ground that there was a contract or warranty that the thing was so, or whether they were going upon the ground that the party, knowing it was not, and representing that it was, had committed a fraud in doing that. Most of the cases (the leading one is Burrowes *v.* Loch, 10 Ves. 470, and it is sufficient to mention that, though there were others) when looked at, if they do not absolutely amount to contract, come uncommonly near it. In Burrowes *v.* Loch a man proposing to lend money on the security of an equitable assignment of a share of what remained due on account of the residue of a testator's estate, went to the trustee who held the fund and asked him, telling him the facts, 'I am going to lend money upon the security of this share, has any prior loan upon this been communicated to you so as to make you have prior notice, so as to make

FOSTER *v.* CHARLES

IN THE COMMON PLEAS, NOVEMBER 10, 1830.

Reported in 7 *Bingham*, 105.

CASE for deceit; the declaration alleging that certain false representations were made by the defendant to the plaintiffs, merchants in London, in order to induce them to engage one Jacque as their agent at Manchester.[1]

Plea, the general issue.

At the trial before Tindal, C. J., London sittings after Michaelmas term, it appeared that in November or December, 1824, the defendant, a soap manufacturer, called on the plaintiffs, wholesale tea dealers, with whom he was on terms of intimacy, and after asking them if they did business at Manchester, said "he had a young friend for whom he was anxious to procure a commission in the tea trade at Manchester; a nice young man, who had an excellent connection there, and would be a great acquisition to any person who wanted to do business there; the defendant being on such terms with the plaintiffs, he had offered it to them before he proposed it to Smith and Co., — a respectable house in the same line of business; that Smith and Co. would jump at the offer; that his friend was so excellent a young man, that he would rather trust him without security than most men with; that this young man had been doing business at Manchester for a London tea house, who could no longer execute his extensive orders; that he had an uncle at Manchester, a clergyman of the Scotch Church, who would

that other loan come in before me and cut me out, tell me that, in order that I may know whether I will lend the money or not.' The party on the other side answered, 'There has been none such.' To say that that is not warranty or contract that he has received no such notice is, I think, going very near the wind; if it was not that it was so uncommonly like it, that I cannot make the distinction myself. That would have been sufficient for the Master of the Rolls to say, 'You have warranted this.' He also had considerable ground for doubting whether the man had really *bona fide* forgotten. The man, he seems to have thought, had thought this, 'I will not take the trouble of a search,' the fact being that he really knew nothing about this and would not take the trouble of looking, but he boldly made the assertion, 'I know there is none,' saying as a fact, 'I know there is none,' when the real truth could not be more than 'I am pretty sure there is none.' If, when a man thinks it is highly probable that a thing exists, he chooses to say he knows the thing exists, that is really asserting what is false — it is positive fraud. That has been repeatedly laid down, and I think the more it is considered the more clear it becomes. If you choose to say, and say without inquiry, 'I warrant that,' that is a contract. If you say, 'I know it,' and if you say that in order to save the trouble of inquiring, that is a false representation — you are saying what is false to induce them to act upon it. I think all the cases which have been cited come round to pointing to that, but none of them, as far as I am aware, are in contradiction with that which I have cited from Chief Justice Tindal, and I think there are a good many other authorities to the same effect."

As to liability where defendant had no reasonable ground to believe what he stated, see Mayer *v.* Salazar, 84 Cal. 646; McCabe *v.* Desnoyers, 20 S. D. 581.

Statement as to matter of which obviously defendant could not have personal knowledge, see: Krause *v.* Cook, 144 Mich. 365; Spead *v.* Tomlinson, 73 N. H. 46.

[1] Part of the statement is an abridgment of the report in 6 Bingham, 396.

afford him great facilities in the way of business, and knew all the Scotch travellers in the trade; that defendant would like him to sell soap for defendant and his partner, but feared his other connections would not allow him time."

The plaintiffs said they had an objection to giving commissions; but the very strong recommendation defendant had given of his friend would induce them to think of it.

Accordingly, in the beginning of 1825, the plaintiffs employed James Jacque, the defendant's young friend, to do business for them on commission at Manchester. But by the middle of 1827, after repeatedly sending incorrect statements of the amount of his receipts on their behalf, he contrived to be a defaulter to them to the extent of £900 and upwards, and to involve them in bad debts to a much greater amount.

He then took the benefit of the insolvent debtors' act.

Instead of having been employed in the Manchester commission tea trade in the year 1824, as the defendant had stated to the plaintiffs, it appeared that he had, at the recommendation of the defendant, been taken into partnership without any capital by Mr. R. C. Stewart, a warehouseman in London, in July, 1823; but great losses having been incurred in that concern, aggravated by a robbery to some amount, Mr. Stewart closed the concern and dissolved the partnership in October, 1824.

Jacque was then indebted to Stewart in the sum of £800, which he undertook by deed, dated November 13, 1824, to pay by instalments, in two, three, and four years; but nothing was ever paid.

All this was known to the defendant, who had acted throughout for Jacque, and had negotiated the terms of the dissolution of partnership.

Letters were also put in, written by the defendant to Jacque, after the exposure of the Manchester transactions, in which the defendant exhorted Jacque to write various falsehoods to the plaintiffs with a view to the exculpation of the defendant, and to conceal from the plaintiffs his knowledge of some of the transactions at Manchester.

When the defendant was first applied to on the subject by the plaintiffs, he expressed his regret that his house should have been the means of introducing an unworthy agent to the plaintiffs; but that as they had been instrumental in bringing the loss on the plaintiffs, he would see his partner on the subject, and see what could be done towards relieving them from it. No step of that kind having been taken, the present action was commenced.

Tindal, C. J., told the jury to consider whether the representation complained of by the plaintiffs had ever been made, and if made, whether it was false within the knowledge of the defendant; for unless it were false within his knowledge, the action did not lie.

The jury returned a verdict for the defendant, which was set aside by the Court. [6 Bingham, 396.]

Upon a new trial, Tindal, C. J., told the jury that if the defendant made representations concerning Jacque, the tendency of which was to occasion loss to the plaintiff, knowing such representations to be false, and intending thereby to benefit himself, he was guilty of fraud in the common acceptation of the term; if he made such representations, knowing them to be false, without proposing thereby any advantage to himself, but proposing, perhaps, to benefit a third person, he was guilty of fraud in the legal acceptation of the term, and responsible to the plaintiff for any injury resulting from such representations.

The jury thereupon found for the plaintiff, damages £800; but added: "We consider there was no actual fraud on the part of the defendant, and that he had no fraudulent intention, although what he has done constituted a fraud in the legal acceptation of the term."

Jones, Serjt., now contended that this amounted to a verdict for the defendant; and therefore moved that the verdict might be entered for him, instead of the plaintiff.

He urged, at some length, nearly the same arguments as he had advanced on a former occasion, and adverted to the same authorities (see 6 Bing. 402); contending that this action was substituted for the ancient writ of deceit; that the gist of the action was a fraudulent intent on the part of the defendant to injure the plaintiff by deceiving him; that a defendant was not responsible for the consequences of a statement, merely because he knew it to be false; he was not responsible for the consequences of a bare lie; in order to render him responsible, it ought to be shown that he intended to defraud the plaintiff of something by the deceit he had practised. That if a party were responsible for the consequences of a lie told without any intention to defraud the hearer of something, no line could be drawn, and parties might be called on to answer for those excusable untruths, which were sometimes told for the purpose of avoiding a greater mischief.

TINDAL, C. J. No sufficient ground has been laid to induce us to disturb the verdict which has been found for the plaintiff. The application arises on a misconception of what the jury have found. They first deliver a verdict for the plaintiff, with damages, and then add, that in point of fact they consider the defendant had no fraudulent intention, although he had been guilty of fraud in the legal acceptation of the term.

Their attention had been drawn by me to two classes of motives possible on the part of the defendant; first, a desire to benefit himself by making a statement which he knew to be false; secondly, a desire to benefit some third person; and I stated that, although there might be no intention on his part to obtain an advantage for himself, it would still be a fraud, for which he was responsible in law, if he made representations productive of loss to another, knowing such representations to be false.

The jury in finding that he had no intention to defraud mean only that he was not actuated by the baser motive of obtaining an advantage for himself, but that he was guilty of fraud in law by stating that which he knew to be false, and which was the cause of loss to the plaintiff.

The question, therefore, is, whether, if a party makes representations which he knows to be false, and occasions injury thereby, he is not liable for the consequences of his falsehood.

It would be most dangerous to hold that he is not.

The confusion seems to have arisen from not distinguishing between what is fraud in law and the motives for actual fraud. It is fraud in law if a party makes representations which he knows to be false, and injury ensues, although the motive from which the representations proceeded may not have been bad; the person who makes such representations is responsible for the consequences; and the verdict, therefore, in this case ought not to be disturbed.

PARK, J. I am of the same opinion. In what fell from this Court in the case of Tapp *v.* Lee, and upon the former decision of the present case, the doctrine has been laid down most accurately. It would be unfair to take the expressions of the jury, without connecting them with what the Chief Justice had just presented for their consideration. It is clear that the jury meant to draw the distinction between the sordid motive of personal advantage and the legal fraud which might be committed by a representation false within the knowledge of the speaker, although made without any view to his own advantage. For such a representation the defendant is responsible if mischief ensues, whatever may have been his motive; and as to its being necessary to prove the motive by which he was actuated: when the case was last before the Court, Tindal, C. J., said, "I am not aware of any authority for such a position, nor that it can be material what the motive was; the law will infer an improper motive, if what the defendant says is false within his own knowledge, and is the occasion of damage to the plaintiff."

Here the defendant said "That his friend was so excellent a young man, that he would rather trust him without security than most men with;" when he knew the contrary to be the fact, he was guilty of a fraud in law in making such a representation; and fraud in law is sufficient to support this action.

GASELEE, J. When this verdict is taken in connection with the direction of the Chief Justice, there is an end to all doubt as to the meaning of the jury, and the finding is a perfect finding. What the jury meant by actual fraud was a sordid regard to self-interest; but the legal fraud, which is sufficient to sustain the action, was complete when the intention to mislead was followed by actual injury.

BOSANQUET, J. There seems to me to be no reason for disturbing this verdict. In the course of the trial, it is probable that improper motives had been ascribed to the defendant. The Chief Justice, therefore, stated to the jury, and stated correctly, that motives of that description in the defendant were not essential to the plaintiff's action. If a person tells a falsehood, the natural and obvious consequence of which, if acted on, is injury to another, that is fraud in law. Coupling that with what the Chief Justice addressed to the jury, their verdict only means that the defendant did not propose to benefit himself, perhaps intended to benefit another; but that what he said, intending to benefit another, was false within his own knowledge, injurious to the party who received the communication, and, consequently, a fraud in the legal acceptation of the term. *Rule refused.*[1]

POLHILL v. WALTER

IN THE KING'S BENCH, JANUARY 20, 1832.

Reported in 3 *Barnewall & Adolphus*, 114.

LORD TENTERDEN, C. J.[2] In this case, in which the defendant obtained a verdict on the trial before me at the sittings after Hilary Term, a rule *nisi* was obtained to enter a verdict for the plaintiff, and cause was shown during the last term. The declaration contained two counts: the first stated, that a foreign bill of exchange was drawn on a person of the name of Hancorne, and that the defendant falsely, fraudulently, and deceitfully did represent and pretend that he was duly authorized to accept the bill by the procuration, and on behalf of Hancorne, and did falsely and fraudulently pretend to accept the same by the procuration of Hancorne. It then proceeded to allege several indorsements of the bill, and that the plaintiff, relying on the pretended acceptance, and believing that the defendant had authority from Hancorne to accept, received the bill from the last indorsee in discharge of a debt; that the bill was dishonored, and that the plaintiff brought an unsuccessful action against Hancorne. The second count contained a similar statement of the false representation by the defendant, and that he accepted the bill in writing under pretence of the procuration from Hancorne; and then proceeded to describe the indorsements to the plaintiff, and the dishonor of the bill, and alleged, that thereupon it became and was the duty of the defendant to pay the bill as the acceptor thereof, but that he had not done so.

[1] Hindman v. First Nat. Bank, (C. C. A.) 112 Fed. 931; Hart v. Tallmadge, 2 Day, 381; Young v. Hall, 4 Ga. 95; Endsley v. Johns, 120 Ill. 469; Leonard v. Springer, 197 Ill. 532; Skeels v. Porter, 165 Ia. 255; Carpenter v. Wright, 52 Kan. 221; Bean v. Herrick, 12 Me. 262; Page v. Bent, 2 Met. 371; Stoney Creek Woolen Co. v. Smalley, 111 Mich. 321; Busterud v. Farrington, 36 Minn. 320; Brownlee v. Hewitt, 1 Mo. App. 360; Bingham v. Fish, 86 N. J. Law, 316; White v. Merritt, 7 N. Y. 352; Hubbard v. Briggs, 31 N. Y. 518; Carpenter v. Lee, 5 Yerg. 265; Paddock v. Fletcher, 42 Vt. 389 *Accord.*

[2] Statement of facts and arguments of counsel omitted.

On the trial it appeared, that when the bill was presented for acceptance by a person named Armfield, who was one of the payees of the bill, Hancorne was absent; and that the defendant, who lived in the same house with him, was induced to write on the bill an acceptance as by the procuration of Hancorne, Armfield assuring him that the bill was perfectly regular, and the defendant fully believing that the acceptance would be sanctioned, and the bill paid at maturity, by the drawee. It was afterwards passed into the plaintiff's hands, and being dishonored when due an action was brought against Hancorne; the defendant was called as a witness on the trial of that action, and he negativing any authority from Hancorne, the plaintiff was nonsuited. I left to the jury the question of deceit and fraud in the defendant, as a question of fact on the evidence, and the jury having negatived all fraud, the defendant had a verdict, liberty being reserved to the plaintiff to move to enter a verdict, if the Court should think the action maintainable notwithstanding that finding.

On the argument, two points were made by the plaintiff's counsel. It was contended, in the first place, that although the defendant was not guilty of any fraud or deceit, he might be made liable as acceptor of the bill; that the second count was applicable to that view of the case; and that, after rejecting the allegations of fraud and falsehood in that count, it contained a sufficient statement of a cause of action against him, as acceptor. But we are clearly of opinion that the defendant cannot be made responsible in that character. It is enough to say that no one can be liable as acceptor but the person to whom the bill is addressed, unless he be an acceptor for honor, which the defendant certainly was not.

This distinguishes the present case from that of a pretended agent making a promissory note (referred to in Mr. Roscoe's Digest of the Law of Bills of Exchange, note 9, p. 47), or purchasing goods in the name of a supposed principal. And, indeed, it may well be doubted if the defendant, by writing this acceptance, entered into any contract or warranty at all, that he had authority to do so; and if he did, it would be an insuperable objection to an action as on a contract by this plaintiff, that at all events there was no contract with, or warranty to him.

It was in the next place contended that the allegation of falsehood and fraud in the first count was supported by the evidence; and that, in order to maintain this species of action, it is not necessary to prove that the false representation was made from a corrupt motive of gain to the defendant, or a wicked motive of injury to the plaintiff; it was said to be enough if a representation is made which the party making it knows to be untrue, and which is intended by him, or which, from the mode in which it is made, is calculated to induce another to act on the faith of it, in such a way as that he may incur damage, and that damage is actually incurred. A wilful falsehood of such a nature was contended to be, in the legal sense of the word, a fraud; and for this position was cited the case of Foster *v.* Charles, 6 Bing. 396; 7 Bing. 105, which was twice under the consideration of the Court of Common Pleas, and to which may be added the recent case of Corbet *v.* Brown, 8 Bing. 33. The principle of these cases appears to us to be well founded, and to apply to the present.

It is true that there the representation was made immediately to the plaintiff, and was intended by the defendant to induce the plaintiff to do the act which caused him damage. Here, the representation is made to all to whom the bill may be offered in the course of circulation, and is, in fact, intended to be made to all, and the plaintiff is one of those; and the defendant must be taken to have intended, that all such persons should give credit to the acceptance, and thereby act upon the faith of that representation, because that, in the ordinary course of business, is its natural and necessary result.

If, then, the defendant, when he wrote the acceptance, and thereby, in substance, represented that he had authority from the drawee to make it, knew that he had no such authority (and upon the evidence there can be no doubt that he did), the representation was untrue to his knowledge, and we think that an action will lie against him by the plaintiff for the damage sustained in consequence.

If the defendant had had good reason to believe his representation to be true, as, for instance, if he had acted upon a power of attorney which he supposed to be genuine, but which was, in fact, a forgery, he would have incurred no liability, for he would have made no statement which he knew to be false: a case very different from the present, in which it is clear that he stated what he knew to be untrue, though with no corrupt motive.

It is of the greatest importance in all transactions that the truth should be strictly adhered to. In the present case, the defendant no doubt believed that the acceptance would be ratified, and the bill paid when due, and if he had done no more than to make a statement of that belief, according to the strict truth, by a memorandum appended to the bill, he would have been blameless. But then the bill would never have circulated as an accepted bill, and it was only in consequence of the false statement of the defendant that he actually had authority to accept, that the bill gained its credit, and the plaintiff sustained a loss. For these reasons we are of opinion that the rule should be made absolute to enter a verdict for the plaintiff.

Rule absolute.[1]

[1] See West London Bank *v.* Kitson, 13 Q. B. D. 360; National Bank *v.* Kershaw Oil Mill, (C. C. A.) 202 Fed. 90. Compare Tackey *v.* McBain, [1912] A. C. 186.

BUTTERFIELD *v.* BARBER

SUPREME COURT, RHODE ISLAND, MAY 15, 1897.

Reported in 20 *Rhode Island Reports,* 99.

CASE for deceitful representations by a debtor to his creditor, the plaintiff having subsequently purchased the claim from the latter in the form of a promissory note. Heard on defendant's petition for new trial.

PER CURIAM. Assuming that the representations testified to by the plaintiff were made by the defendant, the testimony shows that they were made for the purpose of being communicated to Murphy, to procure an extension of time for the payment of his claim against the defendant. At the time they were made the defendant had no expectation that the note, which was subsequently made, was to be taken by the plaintiff, who, in the meantime, had purchased the claim from Murphy. We do not think that in these circumstances the plaintiff had the right to rely on the representations, if they were made, because they were not made with the intention of inducing his action, and consequently that he has no ground to maintain an action for deceit.

Case remitted to the Common Pleas Division, with direction to enter judgment for the defendant for costs.[1]

ALDEN *v.* WRIGHT

SUPREME COURT, MINNESOTA, SEPTEMBER 30, 1891.

Reported in 47 *Minnesota Reports,* 225.

ACTION for deceit in the exchange of real property for shares of corporate stock. Plaintiff alleged fraudulent representations on the part of defendants as to the value of the shares, whereby he was induced to make the exchange. Trial. Verdict for defendants. Plaintiff appealed from an order denying a new trial.[2]

[1] Iasigi *v.* Brown, 17 How. 183; Bank of Montreal *v.* Thayer, 7 Fed. 622; Merchants Nat. Bank *v.* Armstrong, 65 Fed. 932; Hindman *v.* First Nat. Bank, (C. C. A.) 98 Fed. 562, 112 Fed. 931; Western Tel. Co. *v.* Schriver, 141 Fed. 538; Harrison *v.* Savage, 19 Ga. 310; Slade *v.* Little, 20 Ga. 371; Hunnewell *v.* Duxbury, 154 Mass. 286; Nash *v.* Minnesota Title & Trust Co., 159 Mass. 437; Rawlings *v.* Bean, 80 Mo. 614; Lembeck *v.* Gerken, 88 N. J. Law, 329; McCracken *v.* West, 17 Ohio, 16; Wells *v.* Cook, 16 Ohio St. 67 *Accord.* But see Merchants Nat. Bank *v.* Robison, 8 Utah, 256.

Person or member of a class to whom defendant expected the representation to be passed on, see Shrewsbury *v.* Blount, 2 Man. & Gr. 475; Gerhard *v.* Bates, 2 E. & B. 476; Bedford *v.* Bagshaw, 4 H. & N. 538; Scott *v.* Brown, [1892] 2 Q. B. 724; Andrews *v.* Mockford, [1896] 1 Q. B. 372; Warfield *v.* Clark, 118 Ia. 69; Wells *v.* Western Tel. Co., 144 Ia. 605; Henry *v.* Dennis, 95 Me. 24; Chubbuck *v.* Cleveland, 37 Minn. 466; Baker *v.* Crandall, 78 Mo. 584; Stuart *v.* Bank of Staplehurst, 57 Neb. 569; Addington *v.* Allen, 11 Wend. 374; Hadcock *v.* Osmer, 153 N. Y. 604; Cazeaux *v.* Mali, 25 Barb. 578; Converse *v.* Sickles, 16 App. Div. 49.

[2] Statement abridged. Part of opinion omitted.

COLLINS, J. . . .

2. At defendants' request the court charged the jury, in substance, that they must find for defendants, unless it appeared by a preponderance of testimony that the property conveyed by plaintiff in exchange for the shares of stock was worth more than the latter; and to this plaintiff excepted, on the ground that it prevented the jury from returning a verdict in his favor for nominal damages; that, even if the jury should fail to find that the property conveyed by plaintiff was of greater value than the shares of stock transferred to him, — passing on all other questions in his favor, — they might award him nominal damages at least; and that the possibility of such an award was excluded by the charge. But, at plaintiff's request, the jury was instructed that, if they found for him, the amount he would be entitled to recover would be the amount of the difference between the actual value of the property which he conveyed and the actual value of the stock received by him. The rule as to the measure of damages in the case was stated in better form in plaintiff's than in defendants' request, but one was, in effect, a repetition of the other. The rule was correctly stated in each, and the same proposition of law was elsewhere in the charge laid down by the court in very concise and proper, but different, language. The essential elements which constitute a cause of action for deceit are well stated in Busterud *v.* Farrington, 36 Minn. 320 (31 N. W. Rep. 360), and one is that the party induced to act has been damaged. He must have acted on the faith of the false representations *to his damage.* A party cannot sustain an action of this character where no harm has come to him. Deceit and injury must concur, — Doran *v.* Eaton, 40 Minn. 35 (41 N. W. Rep. 244); — or, as it has frequently been put by the courts, fraud without damage or damage without fraud will not sustain the action for deceit. Taylor *v.* Guest, 58 N. Y. 262; Nye *v.* Merriam, 35 Vt. 438; Freeman *v.* McDaniel, 23 Ga. 354; Byard *v.* Holmes, 34 N. J. Law, 296; 3 Suth. Dam. 594; Cooley, Torts, 474; Bailey, Onus Probandi, 770. If, therefore, the shares of stock were worth what plaintiff gave for them, were of equal value with the property exchanged, the plaintiff was not damaged, and was not entitled to recover; for the proper measure of damages was the difference in value between the shares of stock and the property conveyed by plaintiff for them. Redding *v.* Godwin, 44 Minn. 355 (46 N. W. Rep. 563), and cases cited. The plaintiff, under such a rule, would not be permitted to recover nominal damages even without proof of loss or injury, and there is nothing said in Potter *v.* Mellen, 36 Minn. 122 (30 N. W. Rep. 438), as counsel has contended, indicating a contrary view. Damage is of the essence of the action of deceit; an essential element to the right of action, and not merely a consequence flowing from it. *Order affirmed.*[1]

[1] In Allaire *v.* Whitney, 1 Hill, 484, 487, Cowen, J., says that actual damage is not necessary to an action for fraud; and see also Ingraham, J., in Isman *v.* Loring, 130 App. Div. 845. The same doctrine is stated in Northrop *v.* Hill, 57

FREEMAN *v.* VENNER

SUPREME JUDICIAL COURT, MASSACHUSETTS, JUNE 23, 1876.

Reported in 120 *Massachusetts Reports*, 424.

ACTION of tort. Writ dated Dec. 22, 1873. Plaintiff held the negotiable promissory note of J. W. and J. H. Cox, dated July 16, 1873, payable to plaintiff or order in two years from date; and he also held a mortgage conditioned to secure the note. In consideration of land to be conveyed to him by the defendant, plaintiff agreed to assign to defendant the mortgage and note; but he did not agree to make an unrestricted indorsement of the note, and the defendant was not entitled to have the personal liability of the plaintiff as indorser of the note. Plaintiff, through ignorance of the law, and by reason of the false and fraudulent representations of defendant, on Dec. 1, 1873, indorsed the note in blank without any qualification. As soon as the plaintiff became aware of the obligation he had thus assumed, and before defendant had negotiated the note or altered his position in any way, plaintiff demanded to be allowed to qualify his indorsement so that it should merely transfer the title according to the agreement. Defendant refused to allow this. Thereupon plaintiff forbade defendant to negotiate the note; but defendant, notwithstanding, negotiated the note before maturity to one Tenney, a *bona fide* holder for value.

Upon a trial by a judge, without a jury, the foregoing facts were found, substantially as alleged in the declaration.

It also appeared, that, before commencing his action, or at any time before said trial, the plaintiff had made no payment on account or by reason of the indorsement; that, before the commencement of this action and before the maturity of the note, the makers thereof had become bankrupts; that since the commencement a semi-annual instalment of interest had become due; that Tenney had caused the real estate to be sold by virtue of the power contained in the mortgage, had applied a part of the proceeds of the sale in liquidation of that interest, and, since the maturity of the note, had applied the balance of the proceeds in part payment of the note, and had commenced an action against the plaintiff to recover the balance of said note (due demand having been made and notice given), which action is now pending.

N. Y. 351; and in Van Velsor *v.* Seaberger, 35 Ill. App. 598; but neither case was one of merely nominal damages. Leadbetter *v.* Morris, 3 Jones, Law, 543, sustains the view of Cowen, J. The doctrine of Cowen, J., in Allaire *v.* Whitney is also cited approvingly in 1 Sedgwick on Damages, 8th ed., § 101, and in 1 Sutherland on Damages, 3d ed., § 10.

But the great weight of authority is against this doctrine, and accords with the view taken by the Minnesota court in the above case of Alden *v.* Wright: viz., that an action of deceit cannot be maintained in the absence of actual damage. See Pollock, Torts, 9 ed., 190, 291; Pollock, Law of Fraud in British India, 22, 23; 1 Jaggard, Torts, 600, 601; Pigott, Torts, 270, 271; McCarrel *v.* Hayes, 186 Ala. 323; Winkler *v.* Jerrue, 20 Cal. App. 555; Morrison *v.* Martin, 84 Conn. 628; Wesselhoeft *v.* Schanze, 153 Ill. App. 443; Bailey *v.* Oatis, 85 Kan. 339; Barnard *v.* Napier, 167 Ky. 824; Reynolds *v.* Evans, 123 Md. 365; Brackett *v.* Perry, 201 Mass. 502; Tregner *v.* Hazen, 116 App. Div. 829; Badger *v.* Pond, 120 App. Div. 619.

Compare Skowhegan Bank *v.* Maxfield, 83 Me. 576 (fraudulently inducing plaintiff to pay debts); Garry *v.* Garry, 187 Mass. 62 (inducing release of inchoate right of dower); Urtz *v.* New York R. Co., 202 N. Y. 170 (release of disputed claim).

Defendant requested the judge to rule that, upon the foregoing facts the plaintiff could not maintain his action, but, if he could, that he was entitled to recover only nominal damages. The judge declined so to rule, and held that defendant was liable for the conversion of the note, and that the measure of the plaintiff's damages was the amount which the plaintiff was legally compellable to pay to the holder of the note, namely, the face of the note and interest, less the amount realized from the sale under the mortgage, treating the same as a partial payment. Defendant excepted.[1]

COLT, J. [After deciding that there was no conversion of the note.] The further objection is, that treating this as an action to recover damages for an alleged fraud, the plaintiff shows no damages sustained at the time his action was commenced. It was then uncertain and contingent whether he would ever be called on to pay the note. It was payable to the plaintiff or order in two years, and was dated in July, 1873, shortly before its transfer by his indorsement to the defendant. The liability of the plaintiff depended on the failure of the makers to pay and the giving of due notice to him as indorser. No payment has in fact ever been made by him. If the holder receives his pay from the makers through the mortgage security or otherwise, the plaintiff will have suffered no actionable wrong. There will have been no concurrence of damage with fraud, within the rule on which such actions are founded. And as there has been no invasion of the plaintiff's rights, no breach of promise, and no interference with his property, there can be no recovery of even nominal damages in this action. Pasley v. Freeman, 3 T. R. 51; 2 Smith Lead. Cas. (6th Am. ed.) 157, and notes. *Exceptions sustained.*[2]

LUETZKE v. ROBERTS

SUPREME COURT, WISCONSIN, DECEMBER 4, 1906.

Reported in 130 *Wisconsin Reports*, 97, 106.

[PLAINTIFFS, by fraudulent representations of defendants, were induced to execute promissory notes to defendants. Upon a proceeding to cancel and annul the notes, it appeared that the notes had been transferred to, and were then held by, *bona fide* purchasers for value; and hence could not be decreed to be cancelled. It was *held*, that the court having jurisdiction of the defendants personally, had power to render judgment for damages. The opinion then proceeds as follows: —] [3]

SIEBECKER, J. It is urged that compensatory damages cannot be awarded because they are not ascertainable under the facts found, and that plaintiffs must wait until they have made actual payment of the notes. This contention cannot be sustained. The court properly held that these notes in the hands of *bona fide* purchasers for value established a liability according to their terms against these plaintiffs, and that such liability was measured by the amount

[1] Statement abridged. Part of opinion omitted.

[2] In re Pennewell, 119 Fed. 139; Kimmans v. Chandler, 13 Ia. 327; Dunn v. Bishop, (R. I.) 90 Atl. 1073 *Accord.* Compare Van Vliet Automobile Co. v. Crowell, (Ia.) 149 N. W. 861.

[3] A new statement has been made covering but one point and only the portion of the opinion relating to that point is given.

they call for on their face with interest. We deem this the correct measure of damages in the case, and within the principle of the case of Lyle *v.* McCormick H. M. Co., 108 Wisc. 81, 84 N. W. 18.[1]

FOTTLER *v.* MOSELEY

SUPREME JUDICIAL COURT, MASSACHUSETTS, JUNE 18, 1901.

Reported in 179 *Massachusetts Reports*, 295.

TORT for deceit, alleging that, relying upon the false and fraudulent representations of the defendant, a broker, that certain sales of the stock of the Franklin Park Land Improvement Company in the Boston Stock Exchange from January 1, to March 27, 1893, were genuine transactions, the plaintiff revoked an order for the sale of certain shares of that stock held for him by the defendant, whereby the plaintiff suffered loss. Writ dated February 17, 1896.[2]

At the trial in the Superior Court, Hopkins, J., at the close of the evidence, directed the jury to return a verdict for the defendant. The verdict was returned as directed; and the plaintiff alleged exceptions. The findings warranted by the evidence are stated in the opinion of the court.

. . . .

HAMMOND, J. The parties to this action testified in flat contradiction of each other on many of the material issues, but the evidence in behalf of the plaintiff would warrant a finding by the jury, that on March 25, 1893, the plaintiff, being then the owner of certain shares of stock in the Franklin Park Land and Improvement Company, gave an order to the defendant, a broker who was carrying the stock for him on a margin, to sell it at a price not less than $28.50 per share; that on March 27 the defendant, for the purpose of inducing the plaintiff to withdraw the order and refrain from selling, represented to the plaintiff that the sales which had been made of said stock in the market had all been made in good faith and had been "actual true sales throughout"; that these statements were made as of the personal knowledge of the defendant, and that the plaintiff, believing them to be true and relying upon them, was thereby induced to and did cancel his oral order to the defendant to sell, and did refrain from selling; and that the statements were not true, as to some of the sales in the open market, of which the last was in December, 1892, and that the defendant knew it at the time he made the representations. The evidence would warrant a further finding that in continuous reliance upon such representations the plaintiff kept his stock, when he otherwise would have sold it, until the following July, when its market value depreciated, and he thereby suffered loss. The defendant, protesting that he made no such representation and that the jury would not be justified in finding that he had, says that even upon such a finding the plaintiff would have no case. He contends that the representation was not material, that a false representation to be material must not only induce action but must be adequate to induce it by

[1] Ely *v.* Stannard, 46 Conn. 124; Goring *v.* Fitzgerald, 105 Ia. 507; Briggs *v.* Brushaber, 43 Mich. 330; Currier *v.* Poor, 155 N. Y. 344; Hoffman *v.* Toft, 70 Or. 488 *Accord.*

See Conway Bank *v.* Pease, 76 N. H. 319.

[2] Statement abridged.

offering a motive sufficient to influence the conduct of a man of average intelligence and prudence, and that in this case the representation complained of, so far as it was false, was not adequate to induce action because the fictitious sales were so few and distant in time, and that therefore it was not material.

It may be assumed that the plaintiff desired to handle his stock in the manner most advantageous to himself, and that the question whether he would withdraw his order to sell was dependent, somewhat, at least, upon his view of the present or future market value of the stock; and upon that question a man of ordinary intelligence and prudence would consider whether the reported sales in the market were "true sales throughout" or were fictitious, and what was the extent of each. It is true that a corporation may be of so long standing and of such a nature, and the number of the shares so great and the daily sales of the stock in the open market so many and heavy, that the knowledge that a certain percentage of the sales reported are not actual business transactions would have no effect upon the conduct of an ordinary man. On the other hand a corporation may be so small and of such a nature and have so slight a hold upon the public, and the number of its shares may be so small and the buyers so few, that the question whether certain reported sales are fictitious may have a very important bearing upon the action of such a man. Upon the evidence in this case, we cannot say, as matter of law, that the representation so far as false was not material. This question is for the jury, who are to consider it in the light of the nature of the corporation and its standing in the market, and of other matters, including such as those of which we have spoken.

It is further urged by the defendant that one of the fundamental principles in a suit like this is that the representation should have been acted upon by the complaining party and to his injury; that at most the plaintiff simply refrained from action, and that "refraining from action is not acting upon representation" within the meaning of the rule; and further that it is not shown that the damages, if any, suffered by the plaintiff are the direct result of the deceit.

Fraud is sometimes defined as the "deception practised in order to induce another to part with property or to surrender some legal right," Cooley, Torts (2d ed.), 555, and sometimes as the deception which leads "a man into damage by wilfully or recklessly causing him to believe and act on a falsehood." Pollock, Torts (Webb's ed.), 348, 349. The second definition seems to be more comprehensive than the first (see for instance Barley *v.* Walford, 9 Q. B. 197, and Butler *v.* Watkins, 13 Wall. 456), and while the authorities establishing what is a cause of action for deceit are to a large extent convertible with those which define the right to rescind a contract for fraud or misrepresentation and the two classes of cases are generally cited without any express discrimination, still discrimination is sometimes needful in the comparison of the two classes of cases. Pollock, Torts (Webb's ed.), 352.

It is true that it must appear that the fraud should have been acted upon. It is a little difficult to see precisely what is meant by the contention that "refraining from action is not acting upon representation." If by refraining from action it is meant simply that the person defrauded makes no change but goes on as he has been going and would go whether the fraud had been committed or not, then the proposition is doubtless true. Such a person has been in no way influenced, nor has his conduct been in any way changed by the fraud. He has not acted in reliance upon it. If, however, it is meant to include the case where the person defrauded does not do what he had intended and started to do and would have done save for the fraud practised upon him, the proposition cannot be true. So far as respects the owner of property, his change of conduct between keeping the property on the one hand and selling it on the other, is equally great, whether the first intended action be to keep or to sell; and if by reason of fraud practised upon him the plaintiff was induced to recall his order to sell, and, being continuously under the influence of this fraud, kept his stock when, save for such fraud, he would have sold it, then with reference to this property he acted upon the representation within the meaning of the rule as applicable to cases like this. Barley *v.* Walford, 9 Q. B. 197; Butler *v.* Watkins, 13 Wall. 456.

The cases of Lamb *v.* Stone, 11 Pick. 527; Wellington *v.* Small, 3 Cush. 145; and Bradley *v.* Fuller, 118 Mass. 239, upon which the defendant relies, are not authorities for the proposition that " refraining from action is not acting upon representation."

As to whether the loss suffered by the plaintiff is legally attributable to the fraud, much can be said in favor of the defendant, and a verdict in his favor on this as well as on other material points might be the one most reasonably to be expected upon the evidence, especially when it is considered that during the years 1892 and 1893 the plaintiff was a director in the company; but we cannot decide the question as a matter of law. If the fraud operated on the plaintiff's mind continuously, up to the time of the depreciation of the stock in June, 1893, so that he kept his stock when otherwise he would have sold it, and such was the direct, natural and intended result, then we think the causal relation between the fraud and the loss is sufficiently made out. See Reeve *v.* Dennett, 145 Mass. 23, 29. *Exceptions sustained.*[1]

FOTTLER *v.* MOSELEY

Supreme Judicial Court, Massachusetts, May 19, 1904.

Reported in 185 *Massachusetts Reports*, 563.

Tort for deceït, alleging, that, relying upon the false and fraudulent representations of the defendant, a broker, that certain sales of the stock of the Franklin Park Land Improvement Company in the Boston Stock Exchange from January 1 to March 27, 1893, were genuine transactions, the plaintiff revoked an order for the sale of certain shares of that stock held for him by the defendant, whereby the plaintiff suffered loss. Writ dated February 17, 1896.

At the first trial of the case in the Superior Court a verdict was ordered for the defendant, and the exceptions of the plaintiff were sustained by this court in a decision reported in 179 Mass. 295. At the new trial in the Superior Court before Sherman, J., it appeared that one Moody Merrill, a director and officer of the Franklin Park Land Improvement Company, absconded late in May or early in June of 1893, and that immediately upon his departure it was discovered that he had embezzled nearly $100,000 of the funds of that company, the result of which was that the market price of the stock immediately

[1] See Graham *v.* Peale, (C. C. A.) 173 Fed. 9 (delay in asserting claim); Spreckels *v.* Gorrill, 152 Cal. 383; Barron Estate Co. *v.* Woodruff Co., 163 Cal. 561 (preparations for building); Williams Crusher & Pulverizer Co. *v.* Lyth Tile Co., 150 N. Y. Suppl. 6 (expensive investigation preliminary to contract not made).

fell and the stock could not be sold; that the plaintiff from the time of the discovery of the defendant's alleged fraud did his best to sell his stock, but was unable to do so at more than $3 a share, at which price he sold it after bringing this action.

The plaintiff among other requests asked the judge to rule, "That it is of no consequence so far as the defendant's liability is concerned that an outside intervening cause has been the sole or contributing cause of the decline in price to which the plaintiff's loss is due."

The judge refused this and other rulings requested by the plaintiff, and instructed the jury, among other things, as follows: —

"If you find the fair market value of that stock was always above what it was fictitiously quoted, or equal to it, and that it was so on the 25th of March, 1893, and remained so and would have remained so, except for the embezzlement and absconding of Moody Merrill, then the plaintiff is not entitled to recover.

"If you find that Moody Merrill's going away did destroy the value of the stock, practically destroy its value, then the plaintiff is not entitled to recover anything.

"You may take all the evidence on this subject, the fact of what Moody Merrill did, and what effect it had upon the market value of this stock, and if that destroyed the market value, then, as I have told you, the plaintiff is not entitled to recover anything. If his going away and embezzlement did not affect the market value of this stock, then the plaintiff may recover the full value of it."

The judge submitted to the jury the following questions, which the jury answered as stated below: —

"1. Did the defendant make a representation to the plaintiff on or about March 25, 1893, that the quotations in the Boston Stock Exchange of Franklin Park Land and Improvement Company stock were quotations of actual and true sales?" The jury answered "Yes."

"2. Were such quotations at or about the same sum as the quotations of actual sales and the sales at public auction?" The jury answered "Yes."

"3. What was the fair market value of said stock on or about March 25, 1893?" The jury answered "$28.50 per share."

"4. What was the fair market value of said stock on the last day of May, or immediately prior to June, 1893, the day before Moody Merrill's absconding?" The jury answered "$27.75 per share."

The jury returned a verdict for the defendant; and the plaintiff alleged exceptions.

KNOWLTON, C. J. The parties and the court seem to have assumed that the evidence was such as to warrant a verdict for the plaintiff under the law stated at the previous decision in this case, reported in 179 Mass. 295, if the diminution in the selling price of the stock came from common causes. The defendant's contention is that the embezzlement of an officer of a corporation, being an unlawful act of a third person, should be treated as a new and independent cause of the loss, not contemplated by the defendant, for which he is not liable.

To create a liability, it never is necessary that a wrongdoer should contemplate the particulars of the injury from his wrongful act, nor the precise way in which the damages will be inflicted. He need not even expect that damage will result at all, if he does that which is unlawful and which involves a risk of injury. An embezzler is criminally liable, notwithstanding that he expects to return the money appropriated after having used it. If the defendant fraudulently induced the plaintiff to refrain from selling his stock when he was about to sell it, he did him a wrong, and a natural consequence of the wrong for which he was liable was the possibility of loss from diminution in the value of the stock, from any one of numerous causes. Most, if not all, of the causes which would be likely to affect the value of the stock, would be acts of third persons, or at least conditions for which neither the plaintiff nor the defendant would be primarily responsible. Acts of the officers, honest or dishonest, in the management of the corporation, would be among the most common causes of a change in value. The defendant, if he fraudulently induced the plaintiff to keep his stock, took the risk of all such changes. The loss to the plaintiff from the fraud is as direct and proximate, if he was induced to hold his stock until an embezzlement was discovered, as if the value had been diminished by a fire which destroyed a large part of the property of the corporation, or by the unexpected bankruptcy of a debtor who owed the corporation a large sum. Neither the plaintiff nor the defendant would be presumed to have contemplated all the particulars of the risk of diminution in value for which the defendant made himself liable by his fraudulent representations. It would be unjust to the plaintiff in such a case, and impracticable, to enter upon an inquiry as to the cause of the fall in value, if the plaintiff suffered from the fall wholly by reason of the defendant's fraud. The risk of a fall, from whatever cause, is presumed to have been contemplated by the defendant when he falsely and fraudulently induced the plaintiff to retain his stock.

We do not intimate that these circumstances, as well as others, may not properly be considered in determining whether the plaintiff was acting under the inducement of the fraudulent representations in continuing to hold the stock up to the time of the discovery of the embezzlement. The false representations may or may not have ceased to operate as an inducement as to the disposition of his stock before that time. Of course there can be no recovery, except for the direct results of the fraud. But if the case is so far established that the plaintiff, immediately upon the discovery of the embezzlement, was entitled to recover on the ground that he was then holding the stock in reliance upon the fraudulent statements, and if the great diminution in value came while he was holding it, the fact that this diminution was brought about by the embezzlement of an officer leaves the plaintiff's right no less than if it had come from an ordinary loss. *Exceptions sustained.*[1]

[1] " But there is one thing which intervenes between the *injuria* and the *damnum* and that is the plaintiff's *action* which results in damage. It is clear that a misrepresentation cannot of itself directly produce damage. It requires a means of conveyance, and that is the action which it produces, and which results in damage."

" . . . It is the action of the plaintiff, and not the damage, which must be materially induced by the misrepresentation."

" The fallacy is in regarding the damage, and the action resulting in damage, as the same thing." Moncrieff, Law of Fraud and Misrepresentation, 187.

MORSE v. HUTCHINS

SUPREME JUDICIAL COURT, MASSACHUSETTS, OCTOBER TERM, 1869.

Reported in 102 *Massachusetts Reports*, 439.

TORT for deceit in making false and fraudulent representations to the plaintiff touching the business and profits of a firm of which the defendant was a member, and thereby inducing the plaintiff to buy the interest of the defendant in the stock and good will of the firm. A count in contract for the same cause of action was joined. Answer, a general denial and a plea of a discharge in bankruptcy.

At the trial in the Superior Court, Brigham, C. J., ruled that the discharge in bankruptcy was a defence to the second count, but not to the first count; and the plaintiff relied on the first count only.

The judge instructed the jury that "the measure of damages would be the difference between the actual value of the stock and good will purchased at the time of the purchase and the value of the same had the representation been true."

The jury returned a verdict for the plaintiff, and the defendant alleged exceptions.

GRAY, J. The objections that either the joinder of a count in contract with the count in tort, or the certificate of discharge in bankruptcy, would defeat the plaintiff's right of action in tort for the defendant's false and fraudulent representations, were hardly relied on at the argument, and are groundless. Gen. Sts. c. 129, § 2, cl. 5. Crafts v. Belden, 99 Mass. 535. U. S. St. 1867, c. 176, § 33.

The rule of damages was rightly stated to the jury. It is now well settled that, in actions for deceit or breach of warranty, the measure of damages is the difference between the actual value of the property at the time of the purchase and its value if the property had been what it was represented or warranted to be. Stiles v. White, 11 Met. 356; Tuttle v. Brown, 4 Gray, 457; Whitemore v. South Boston Iron Co., 2 Allen, 52; Fisk v. Hicks, 11 Foster, 535; Woodward v. Thacher, 21 Verm. 580; Muller v. Eno, 4 Kernan, 597; Sherwood v. Sutton, 5 Mason, 1; Loder v. Kekulé, 3 C. B. N. S. 128; Dingle v. Hare, 7 C. B. N. S. 145; Jones v. Just, Law Rep. 3 Q. B. 197. This is the only rule which will give the purchaser adequate damages for not having the thing which the defendant undertook to sell him. To allow to the plaintiff (as the learned counsel for the defendant argued in this case) only the difference between the real value of the property and the price which he was induced to pay for it would be to make any advantage lawfully secured to the innocent purchaser in the original bargain inure to the benefit of the wrongdoer; and, in proportion as the original price was low, would afford a protection to the party who had broken, at the expense of the party who was ready to abide by, the terms of the contract. The fact that the property sold was of such a character as to make it difficult to ascertain with exactness what its value would have been if it had conformed to the contract affords no reason for exempting the defendant from any part of the direct consequences of his fraud. And the value may be estimated as easily in this action as in an action against him for an entire refusal to perform his contract. *Exceptions overruled.*

SMITH *v.* BOLLES

SUPREME COURT OF THE UNITED STATES, NOVEMBER 11, 1889.

Reported in 132 *United States Reports*, 125.

ERROR to the United States Circuit Court for the Northern District of Ohio.

Action to recover damages for fraudulent representations in the sale of shares of mining stock.

The amended petition alleged (*inter alia*) that plaintiff was induced by defendant's fraudulent representations to buy of defendant four thousand shares of mining stock at $1.50 per share, amounting to $6000; that "said stock and mining property was then, and still is, wholly worthless; and that had the same been as represented by defendant it would have been worth at least ten dollars per share; and so plaintiff says that by reason of the premises he has sustained damages to the amount of forty thousand dollars."

Answer, denying plaintiff's material allegations. Trial by jury. The instructions given as to damages are stated in the opinion. Verdict for plaintiff. Motion for new trial overruled. Judgment for plaintiff. Defendant brought error.[1]

FULLER, C. J. The bill of exceptions states that the court charged the jury "as to the law by which the jury were to be governed in the assessment of damages under the issues made in the case," that "the measure of recovery is generally the difference between the contract price and the reasonable market value, if the property had been as represented to be, or in case the property or stock is entirely worthless, then its value is what it would have been worth if it had been as represented by the defendant, and as may be shown in the evidence before you."

In this there was error. The measure of damages was not the difference between the contract price and the reasonable market value if the property had been as represented to be, even if the stock had been worth the price paid for it; nor if the stock were worthless, could the plaintiff have recovered the value it would have had if the property had been equal to the representations. What the plaintiff might have gained is not the question, but what he had lost by being deceived into the purchase. The suit was not brought for breach of contract. The gist of the action was that the plaintiff was fraudulently induced by the defendant to purchase stock upon the faith of certain false and fraudulent representations, and so as to the other persons on whose claims the plaintiff sought to recover. If the jury believed from the evidence that the defendant was guilty of the fraudulent and false representations alleged, and that the purchase of stock had been made in reliance thereon, then the defendant was liable to respond in such damages as naturally and proximately resulted from the fraud. He was bound to make good the loss sustained, such as the moneys the plaintiff had paid out and interest, and any other outlay legitimately attributable to defendant's fraudulent conduct; but this liability did not include the expected fruits of an unrealized speculation. The reasonable market value, if the property had been as represented, afforded, therefore, no proper element of recovery.

[1] Statement abridged and arguments omitted.

Nor had the contract price the bearing given to it by the court. What the plaintiff paid for the stock was properly put in evidence, not as the basis of the application of the rule in relation to the difference between the contract price and the market or actual value, but as establishing the loss he had sustained in that particular. If the stock had a value in fact, that would necessarily be applied in reduction of the damages. "The damage to be recovered must always be the *natural and proximate consequence* of the act complained of," says Mr. Greenleaf, vol. ii, § 256; and "the test is," adds Chief Justice Beasley in Crater *v.* Binninger, 33 N. J. Law (4 Vroom), 513, 518, "that those results are proximate which the wrong-doer from his position must have contemplated as the probable consequence of his fraud or breach of contract." In that case, the plaintiff had been induced by the deceit of the defendant to enter into an oil speculation, and the defendant was held responsible for the moneys put into the scheme by the plaintiff in the ordinary course of the business, which moneys were lost, less the value of the interest which the plaintiff retained in the property held by those associated in the speculation.

[Remainder of opinion omitted.]

Judgment reversed. Cause remanded with a direction to grant a new trial.[1]

SCHWABACKER *v.* RIDDLE

SUPREME COURT, ILLINOIS, JUNE 20, 1891.

Reported in 99 *Illinois Reports*, 343.

ACTION for deceit, brought by Riddle against Schwabacker *et als.*, alleging that, in the purchase of property to be taken at the invoice price, Riddle was cheated out of the sum of $2677.09 by fraudulent representations made by defendants in regard to the amount the goods purchased inventoried. On trial there was a verdict for plaintiff. Some of the instructions are stated in the opinion. Judgment in favor of Riddle. Schwabacker *et als.* appealed.[2]

CRAIG, C. J. . . . Instruction No. 2 reads as follows: —

"If a party misrepresents a fact within his own knowledge, to the injury of a third party, an action will lie for damages, if any, for such misrepresentation."

This instruction is liable to several serious objections. In the first place, a misrepresentation, to be actionable, must be a material one, or no action will lie. In the second place, in an action for deceit no recovery can be had unless the plaintiff himself exercised ordinary prudence to guard against the deception and fraud practised upon him, unless he has been thrown off his guard by the other party. These two principles were entirely ignored by the instruction, and the

[1] Reaffirmed in Sigafus *v.* Porter, 179 U. S. 116. The authorities on each side of this controverted question are collected in a note to George *v.* Hesse, (100 Tex. 44) 8 L. R. A. N. S. 804. For later cases, see: Harris *v.* Neil, 144 Ga. 519 (*accord*); Trayne *v.* Boardman, 207 Mass. 581; Crawford *v.* Armacost, 85 Wash. 622 (*contra*).

[2] Statement abridged; arguments omitted; also part of opinion.

jury, under this direction of the court, was at liberty to find against the defendants if they misrepresented any immaterial fact, however remote, and the plaintiff exercised no precaution whatever to guard against imposition. This is not a sound rule to be adopted, and as the instruction was calculated to mislead the jury, it ought not to have been given.

. . . .

Instruction No. 13, given for the plaintiff, reads as follows: —

"It is not necessary, in this case, that the plaintiff should show any prior conspiracy or combination between the defendants to defraud the plaintiff; it is enough if the evidence shows that a sale was made to Riddle, or Riddle and Fosbender, and that the agreed price was for the value of the property, as shown by a certain invoice, and that notes were to be taken for the amount, and that the defendants had notes drawn for $2677.09 more than the value of the property as shown by such invoice; and if the plaintiff, before signing the notes, asked if they were for the amount of the invoice, and Fosbender said they were, in the presence and hearing of the other defendants, and if Riddle relied upon such statement in signing the notes, which was known to the defendants, then such conduct and representations would amount to a fraud in the other defendants, if they resulted in damages to the plaintiff."

[After stating an objection to this instruction.]

Again, under this instruction a recovery may be had although the plaintiff was deceived from a total want of reasonable care on his part. At the time the notes were signed, as we understand the evidence of plaintiff himself, the invoice, which showed the correct amount of the goods, was present, and in the hands of one of the defendants. If that be true, and it could have been obtained and inspected by the plaintiff, and he failed and neglected to do so, but relied upon a statement made by Fosbender at the time, it was for the jury to determine whether, under the evidence, he had exercised proper diligence to guard against deception, and if he did not, he could not recover. But this principle was ignored in this and other instructions given for the plaintiff. Indeed, this principle is not stated, but seems to be ignored in all of the instructions given for the plaintiff. This last instruction, in our judgment, was calculated to mislead the jury.

. . . .

Judgment reversed.[1]

[1] Henderson *v.* Henshall, (C. C. A.) 54 Fed. 320; Tooker *v.* Alston, 159 Fed. 599; Jordan *v.* Pickett, 78 Ala. 331; Dingle *v.* Trask, 7 Col. App. 16; Carondelet Iron Works *v.* Moore, 78 Ill. 65; Jones *v.* Foster, 175 Ill. 459; Press *v.* Hair, 133 Ill. App. 528; Anderson Foundry *v.* Myers, 15 Ind. App. 385; Moore *v.* Turbeville, 2 Bibb, 602; Weaver *v.* Shriver, 79 Md. 530; Silver *v.* Frazier, 3 All. 382; Parker *v.* Moulton, 114 Mass. 99; Poland *v.* Brownell, 131 Mass. 138; Thompson *v.* Pentecost, 206 Mass. 505; Anderson *v.* McPike, 86 Mo. 293; Brown *v.* Kansas City R. Co., 187 Mo. App. 104; Morrill *v.* Madden, 35 Minn. 493; Grindrod *v.* Anglo-American Bond Co., 34 Mont. 169; Power *v.* Turner, 37 Mont. 521; Osborne *v.*

FARGO GAS & COKE COMPANY *v.* FARGO GAS & ELECTRIC COMPANY

SUPREME COURT, NORTH DAKOTA, JULY 23, 1894.

Reported in 4 North Dakota Reports, 219.

CORLISS, J.[1] The plaintiff has recovered judgment for the balance of the purchase price of a gas and electric plant located in the City of Fargo, N. D., sold by plaintiff to the defendant. A portion of the consideration was paid, and, upon being sued for the unpaid portion of the purchase price, defendant set up as a defence a partial failure of consideration from the nondelivery of some of the property purchased, and also a counterclaim for damages arising out of the alleged deceit of the plaintiff in making the sale. The view we take of the case renders a more particular reference to the defence of partial failure of consideration unnecessary. We will confine ourselves to the single question of fraud. The property purchased consisted of a gas plant, with mains and all the other classes of property which go to make up such a plant, and also an arc electric light plant, with poles, wires, and other fixtures distributed over different parts of the City of Fargo. These two plants were used by the plaintiff at the time of making the sale thereof to defendant, to light the public streets of the City of Fargo, its public buildings, stores, hotels, and dwelling houses, and had been so used for some time prior to such sale. The alleged fraudulent representations were of two classes, — one class relating to the physical condition of the plant, embracing statements as to the number of miles of wire, the number of poles, the gas mains, and as to the condition of the plant in other respects; and the other

Missouri R. Co., 71 Neb. 180; Saunders *v.* Hatterman, 2 Ired. 32; Mulholland *v.* Washington Match Co., 35 Wash. 315; Mosher *v.* Post, 89 Wis. 602; Farr *v.* Peterson, 91 Wis. 182; Kaiser *v.* Nummerdor, 120 Wis. 234; Jacobsen *v.* Whitely, 138 Wis. 434 *Accord.*

But see Wilson *v.* Higbee, 62 Fed. 723; King *v.* Livingston Mfg. Co., 180 Ala. 118; Mason *v.* Thornton, 74 Ark. 46; Linington *v.* Strong, 107 Ill. 295; Robinson *v.* Reinhart, 137 Ind. 674; Hanks *v.* McKee, 2 Litt. 227; Bowen *v.* Carter, 124 Mass. 426; Arnold *v.* Teele, 182 Mass. 1; Light *v.* Jacobs, 183 Mass. 206; Bachman *v.* Travelers Ins. Co., (N. H.) 97 Atl. 223; Fox *v.* Duffy, 95 App. Div. 202.

"The doctrine . . . is not to be extended. It relates merely to seller's talk." Sheldon, J., in Townsend *v.* Niles, 210 Mass. 524, 531.

Equal means of knowledge, see Hill *v.* Bush, 19 Ark. 522; Strong *v.* Peters, 2 Root, 93; McDaniell *v.* Strohecker, 19 Ga. 432; Knight *v.* Gaultney, 23 Ill. App. 376; Foley *v.* Cowgill, 5 Blackf. 18; Boddy *v.* Henry, 113 Ia. 462; Hinchman *v.* Weeks, 85 Mich. 535; Bradford *v.* Wright, 145 Mo. App. 623; Conway Nat. Bank *v.* Pease, 76 N. H. 319; Long *v.* Warren, 68 N. Y. 426; Crislip *v.* Cain, 19 W. Va. 438.

Execution of instrument without reading it, see Dunham Lumber Co. *v.* Holt, 123 Ala. 336; Robinson *v.* Glass, 94 Ind. 211; Porter *v.* United Railways, 165 Mo. App. 619; Muller *v.* Rosenblath, 157 App. Div. 513; Griffin *v.* Roanoke Lumber Co., 140 N. C. 514.

Reliance on friendship, see Gray *v.* Reeves, 69 Wash. 374.

[1] Arguments omitted; also part of opinion.

class related to the net earnings of the plant for the previous year, and the prices charged customers for gas and electric light. It appears that defendant relied chiefly upon the earning capacity of the plant in making the purchase, and was induced to believe that its net annual earnings would equal 10 per cent of the purchase price ($85,-300), because of the statements of the plaintiff's officers that its net earnings during the past year had been $8913. There was evidence tending to show that this statement was false, and that it must have been known to be false by plaintiff's officers who negotiated the sale. Having in this brief manner set forth the general character of the property sold, and the general nature of the fraudulent representations upon which defendant's counterclaim for deceit was founded, we can now intelligently turn to what we regard as a fatal error in the case.

In the course of his charge to the jury, the learned trial judge instructed them as follows: "If the means were at the defendant's hands to discover the truth or untruth of the plaintiff's statements with regard to the amount and character of the property, defendant must be presumed to have had a knowledge of the actual facts." This instruction must be considered in the light of the refusal of the court to charge the jury as follows, at the request of defendant's counsel: "If you find that, during the negotiations, statements were made by the plaintiff as to the earnings of the plant, the defendant had a right to rely upon these statements; and if they were so relied on, and were false, and the defendant suffered injury thereby, the defendant would be entitled to recover the damages which it suffered in consequence thereof." It is apparent from this refusal to charge, and from the charge as cited given, that the court told the jury that, as a matter of law, defendant did not have the right implicitly to rely upon the representations of the plaintiff touching the character of the plant, but must make inquiries concerning them, and must make investigation as to their truth or falsity. It is true that the word "investigate" is not used; but, when we consider the nature of the property and the character of the representations made, it is obvious that something more than a mere inspection of an object present before a purchaser was necessary in order to enable the purchaser in this case to "discover" the truth or falsity of plaintiff's statements. Such an instruction to a jury might be appropriate in an action in which fraud in the sale of a horse was set up, the seller having represented the horse to be perfectly sound, and it appearing that the horse stood before the purchaser at the time the representation was made, and that the only defect consisted in the absence of a leg, easily discernible by the ordinary use of eyesight. But in the case at bar the means of discovering the truth or untruth of these false statements were not at hand in the sense that they must have been employed before the seller could be held responsible for his fraudulent representations; and, when this language was used, the jury must have drawn the inference from the fact that this plant was in the same city, and could be investigated with respect to its condition and its earnings, and the prices charged customers for gas and electric light, and with reference to the other features embraced in the statements made by plaintiff on the sale, that therefore the means were at hand, within the rule laid down by the court requiring the purchaser to discover at its peril the truth or falsity of the statements made. Such a rule of law would be unjust and intolerable. When parties deal at arm's length, the doctrine of *caveat emptor* applies; but the moment the vendor makes a false statement of fact, and its falsity is not palpable to the purchaser, he has an undoubted right implicitly to rely upon it. That would, indeed, be a strange rule of law which, when the seller had successfully entrapped his victim by false statements, and was called to account in a court of justice for his deceit, would permit him to escape by urging the folly of his dupe for not suspecting that he, the seller, was a knave. In the absence of such a suspicion, it is entirely reasonable for one to put faith in the deliberate representations of another. The jury must have understood that the means were at hand to discover the claim, because the defendant might have measured the wire, counted the poles, examined the gas mains, ascertained how much customers were paying for gas and electric light, and might have hired an expert to examine into the earnings and expenses of the plaintiff in running the plant, with a view to discovering whether a business man had told the truth. It should not have been left to the jury to determine whether the means were at hand to discover the falsity of the statements made, in view of the character of such statements and the nature of the property sold. The defendant, as a matter of law, had a right to rely implicitly upon the statements made by plaintiff touching the character of this plant. So long as defendant did not actually know the representations to be false, it was under no obligation to investigate to determine their truth or falsity. In Mead *v*. Bunn, 32 N. Y. 280, the court say: "Every contracting party has an absolute right to rely on the express statements of an existing fact, the truth of which is known to the opposite party and unknown to him, as a basis of mutual engagement, and he is under no obligation to investigate and verify statements, to the truth of which the other party to the contract, with full means of knowledge, has deliberately pledged his faith." In Redding *v*. Wright, (Minn.) 51 N. W. 1056 (a case very much in point), the court say: "If the representations were fraudulently made with the intent to induce the plaintiff to rely upon the fact being as represented, and to act upon the belief thus induced, the wrongdoer who succeeds in such a purpose is not to be shielded from responsibility by the plea that the defrauded party would have discovered the falsity of the representation if he had pursued such means of information as were available to him." While the rule has been in some cases stated in terms more favorable to plaintiff, yet no decision can be found which establishes a doctrine under which defendant would be bound, under the circumstances of this case, to make any investigation or inquiry touching the truth or falsity of the statements made in connection with the sale. There are many well considered cases which sustain our view that defendant had a right implicitly to rely upon the representations made by plaintiff with respect to the character of the property to be purchased by defendant. In addition to the cases already cited, we refer to Maxfield *v.* Schwartz, 45 Minn. 150, 47 N. W. 448; Gardner *v.* Trenary, 65 Iowa, 646, 22 N. W. 912; Schumaker *v.* Mather, 133 N. Y. 590, 30 N. E. 755; McClellan *v.* Scott, 24 Wis. 81; Caldwell *v.* Henry, 76 Mo. 254; Oswald *v.* McGehee, 28 Miss. 340; Cottrill *v.* Krum, 100 Mo. 397, 13 S. W. 753; Campbell *v.* Frankern, 65 Ind. 591; Kerr, Fraud & M. 77, 80, 81; Erickson *v.* Fisher, (Minn.) 53 N. W. 638; Alfred Shrimpton & Sons *v.* Philbrik, (Minn.) 55 N. W. 551; Barndt *v.* Frederick, (Wis.) 47 N. W. 6; Bigelow, Fraud, 522, 528. We are aware that cases can be found which exact from the buyer more care in ascertaining the truth or falsity of representations than the decisions just cited. These cases appear to us to have been rightfully decided, in view of the facts. In determining what the courts in such cases intended to hold, the language of each opinion must be read, in the light of the facts of the particular case. The unmistakable drift is towards the just doctrine that the wrong-doer cannot shield himself from liability by asking the law to condemn the credulity of his victim. The falsity of the statement may be apparent because the thing misrepresented is before the buyer, and the most casual look will suffice to discover the falsehood, no artifice being used to divert his attention; or the statement may carry its own refutation upon its face, — may be so absurd or monstrous that it is palpably false, as a statement by a person carrying on a business known to the purchaser to be very small that the receipts of the business are a million dollars a year. In these and other similar cases the law will not allow a person to assert that he was deceived. But the general rule is, and, upon principle, must be, that the question is one of reliance by the buyer upon the false statement of the seller. Whether it was wise for him to rely upon it, whether he was prudent in so doing, whether he is not chargeable with negligence in a certain sense in not investigating, — these inquiries are, in general, immaterial, provided the purchaser has in fact been deceived. The circumstances under which fraud is accomplished are so varied, the nature of the property and the character of the misrepresentations are so widely different, in different cases, that it is unwise to attempt to enunciate with precision a general rule by which all cases shall be governed. It is better to decide the cases as they arise, keeping in view the general principle that courts will not readily listen to the plea that the defrauded party was too easily deceived. For this error in the charge, the judgment will be reversed, and a new trial granted.

[Omitting opinion on another point.]

Judgment reversed. New trial ordered.[1]

STARKWEATHER *v.* BENJAMIN

SUPREME COURT, MICHIGAN, JUNE TERM, 1875.

Reported in 32 *Michigan Reports*, 305.

ERROR to Macomb Circuit.

CAMPBELL, J. This action was brought to recover damages arising from alleged misrepresentations made by Starkweather to Benjamin concerning the quantity of land in a parcel purchased from Starkweather and others, for whom he acted, and which was bought by the acre.

The defence rested mainly on the ground that the purchaser saw the land, and was as able to judge of its size as Starkweather.

[1] Martin *v.* Burford, (C. C. A.) 181 Fed. 922; Hutchinson *v.* Gorman, 71 Ark. 305; Scott *v.* Moore, 89 Ark. 321; Montgomery *v.* McLaury, 143 Cal. 83; Teague *v.* Hall, 171 Cal. 668; Eames *v.* Morgan, 37 Ill. 260; Ladd *v.* Pigott, 114 Ill. 647; Kehl *v.* Abram, 210 Ill. 218 (public records); Backer *v.* Pyne, 130 Ind. 288 (records); McGibbons *v.* Wilder, 78 Ia. 531; Faust *v.* Hosford, 119 Ia. 97 (records); Scott *v.* Burnight, 131 Ia. 507; McKee *v.* Eaton, 26 Kan. 226 (records of patent office); Davis *v.* Jenkins, 46 Kan. 19 (records of land office); Carpenter *v.* Wright. 52 Kan. 221 (deed records); Trimble *v.* Ward, 97 Ky. 748; Martin *v.* Jordan, 60 Me. 531; Braley *v.* Powers, 92 Me. 203; Harlow *v.* Perry, 113 Me. 239; David *v.* Park, 103 Mass. 501 (records of patent office); Holst *v.* Stewart, 161 Mass. 516; Rollins *v.* Quimby, 200 Mass. 162 (mortgage records); Jackson *v.* Armstrong, 50 Mich. 65; Smith *v.* Werkheiser, 152 Mich. 177; Faribault *v.* Sater, 13 Minn. 223; Redding *v.* Wright, 49 Minn. 322; Union Bank *v.* Hunt, 76 Mo. 439; Cottrill *v.* Krum, 100 Mo. 397; Stonemets *v.* Head, 248 Mo. 243; Shearer *v.* Hill, 125 Mo. App. 375; Gerner *v.* Mosher, 58 Neb. 135 (books of corporation); Perry *v.* Rogers, 62 Neb. 898; Martin *v.* Hutton, 90 Neb. 34; Bradbury *v.* Haines, 60 N. H. 123; Blossom *v.* Barrett, 37 N. Y. 434 (records of court); Gage *v.* Peetsch, 16 Misc. 291 (mortgage records); Blumenfield *v.* Stine, 42 Misc. 411 (records); Blacknall *v.* Rowland, 108 N. C. 554; Bank of North America *v.* Sturdy, 7 R. I. 109; Handy *v.* Waldron, 19 R. I. 618 (failure to inquire of references); Hunt *v.* Barker, 22 R. I. 18 (deed records); Wright *v.* United States Mfg. Co., (Tex. Civ. App.) 42 S. W. 789 (tax records); Chamberlain *v.* Rankin, 49 Vt. 133; Morrill *v.* Palmer, 68 Vt. 1; Jordan *v.* Walker, 115 Va. 109; City *v.* Tacoma Light Co., 17 Wash. 458; Simons *v.* Cissna, 52 Wash. 115; Borde *v.* Kingsley, 76 Wash. 613; Hall *v.* Bank, 143 Wis. 303 (records); Woteshek *v.* Neuman, 151 Wis. 365; Rogers *v.* Rosenfeld, 158 Wis. 285 *Accord.*

See Henry *v.* Allen, 93 Ala. 197; Hanger *v.* Evins, 38 Ark. 334; Wheeler *v.* Baars, 33 Fla. 696 (records); Forbes *v.* Thorpe, 209 Mass. 570. Compare Campbell *v.* Frankem, 65 Ind. 591.

Assertion of title, see: Crandall *v.* Parks, 152 Cal. 772; Hale *v.* Philbrick, 42 Ia. 81; Young *v.* Hopkins, 6 T. B. Mon. 18; Cobb *v.* Wright, 43 Minn. 83; Manley *v.* Johnson, 85 Vt. 262.

Statements as to boundaries, see: Roberts *v.* Plaisted, 63 Me. 335; Olson *v.* Orton, 28 Minn. 36; Clark *v.* Baird, Seld. Notes, 187; Schwenk *v.* Naylor, 102 N. Y. 683; Roberts *v.* Holliday, 10 S. D. 576.

Plaintiff informed of truth by third person, see: Moncrief *v.* Wilkinson, 93 Ala. 373; Haight *v.* Hayt, 19 N. Y. 464; Grosjean *v.* Galloway, 82 App. Div. 380.

Refusal of defendant to put representation in writing, Ettlinger *v.* Weil, 184 N. Y. 179.

We do not think the doctrine that where both parties have equal means of judging there is no fraud applies to such a case. The maxim is equally valid, that one who dissuades another from inquiry and deceives him to his prejudice is responsible. It cannot be generally true that persons can judge of the contents of a parcel of land by the eye. When any approach to accuracy is needed, there must be measurement. When a positive assurance of the area of a parcel of land is made by the vendor to the vendee with the design of making the vendee believe it, that assurance is very material, and equivalent to an assurance of measurement. In this case the testimony goes very far, and shows that the assertions and representations, which the jury must have found to be true, were of such a nature that if believed, as they were, a re-survey must have been an idle ceremony. They were calculated to deceive, and as the jury have found, they did deceive Benjamin, and he had a clear right of action for the fraud.

[Omitting remainder of opinion.] *Judgment affirmed.*[1]

MABARDY v. McHUGH

Supreme Judicial Court, Massachusetts, May 21, 1909.

Reported in 202 *Massachusetts Reports*, 148.

Tort for deceit in the sale of land. Writ in the Superior Court for the county of Middlesex dated January 18, 1906.

The case was tried before Stevens, J. The facts are stated in the opinion. The jury found for the defendants; and the plaintiffs alleged exceptions.

Rugg, J. This is an action of tort sounding in deceit. There was evidence tending to show that the plaintiffs went upon a certain irregularly shaped tract of land (for false representations inducing the purchase of which this action was brought) with one of the defendants, who pointed out the true boundaries and fraudulently stated that the tract contained sixty-five acres, when in fact it contained forty and three-fourths acres. Upon this aspect of the evidence, the trial judge instructed the jury that " if the plaintiffs . . . were taken over the farm by the defendants . . . or [and] were shown the bounds so that the plaintiffs knew where the farm was and what was comprised within the bounds, it would not be of any consequence that representations may have been made by the defendant in relation to the acreage." The evidence being conflicting as to whether the boundaries were shown, the jury were further instructed that if the defendant, who talked with the plaintiffs, " knew that there were not sixty-five or nearly sixty-five acres, or if he did not know anything about it and stated it as a fact within his personal knowledge, then it would be a false representation for which he would be liable provided " the other elements essential to a recovery were found to exist.

The correctness of the first of these instructions is challenged. It is in exact accordance with the law as laid down in Gordon v. Parmelee, 2 Allen,

[1] O'Neill v. Conway, 88 Conn. 651; Antle v. Sexton, 137 Ill. 410; Ledbetter v. Davis, 121 Ind. 119; Speed v. Hollingsworth, 54 Kan. 436; Judd v. Walker, 215 Mo. 312; Miller v. Wissert, 38 Okl. 808; Farris v. Gilder, (Tex. Civ. App.) 115 S. W. 645 *Accord.*

Compare Cawston v. Sturgis, 29 Or. 331. And see Disney v. Lang, 90 Kan. 309.

212, and Mooney *v.* Miller, 102 Mass. 217. The facts in the case at bar are similar in all material respects to these cases. An attempt is made to distinguish them on the ground that the present plaintiffs were Syrians, ignorant of our language, and that hence a trust relation existed between them and the defendant. But whatever else may be said of this contention, it fails because they were accompanied by two of their own countrymen, who were thoroughly familiar with our language and acted as interpreters for them. In effect, the contention of the plaintiffs amounts to a request to overrule these two cases. They have been cited with approval in Roberts *v.* French, 153 Mass. 60, and as supporting authorities, without criticism, in other opinions. The court, however, has refused to apply the rule of those decisions to other facts closely analogous. See Lewis *v.* Jewell, 151 Mass. 345; Holst *v.* Stewart, 161 Mass. 516; Whiting *v.* Price, 172 Mass. 240; Kilgore *v.* Bruce, 166 Mass. 136. This court in recent years, by pointed language and by conclusions reached, has indicated a plain disposition not to extend legal immunity for the falsehood of vendors in the course of negotiations for sales beyond the bounds already established. . . .

This judicial attitude perhaps reflects an increasingly pervasive moral sense in some of the common transactions of trade. While the science of jurisprudence is not, and under present conditions cannot be, coextensive with the domain of morality, nor generally undertake to differentiate between motives which mark acts as good or bad, yet it is true, as was said by Mr. Justice Brett, in Robinson *v.* Mollett, L. R. 7 H. L. 802, 817, that "The courts have applied to the mercantile business brought before them what have been called legal principles, which have almost always been the fundamental ethical rules of right and wrong." This is only a concrete expression of the broader generalization that law is the manifestation of the conscience of the Commonwealth.

In many other jurisdictions the rule of Gordon *v.* Parmelee and Mooney *v.* Miller has not been followed and false representations as to area of land, even though true boundaries were pointed out, have been held actionable. McGhee *v.* Bell, 170 Mo. 121, 135, 150. May *v.* Loomis, 140 N. C. 350. Boddy *v.* Henry, 113 Iowa, 462, 465; s. c. 126 Iowa, 31. Antle *v.* Sexton, 137 Ill. 410. Estes *v.* Odom, 91 Ga. 600, 609. Lovejoy *v.* Isbell, 73 Conn. 368, 375. Cawston *v.* Sturgis, 20 Ore. 331. Starkweather *v.* Benjamin, 32 Mich. 305. Paine *v.* Upton, 87 N. Y. 327. Mitchell *v.* Zimmerman, 4 Texas, 75. Walling *v.* Kinnard, 10 Texas, 508. Speed *v.* Hollingsworth, 54 Kans. 436. See also Fairchild *v.* McMahon, 139 N. Y. 290; Schumaker *v.* Mather, 133 N. Y. 590.

Other cases apparently opposed to the Massachusetts rule, on examination prove to go no further than to decide that misrepresentations as to area, when there is no evidence that boundaries were shown, constitute deceit. Griswold *v.* Gebbie, 126 Penn. St. 353. Cabot *v.* Christie, 42 Vt. 121. Coon *v.* Atwell, 46 N. H. 510. Ledbetter *v.* Davis, 121 Ind. 119. Perkins Manuf. Co. *v.* Williams, 98 Ga. 388. Sears *v.* Stinson, 3 Wash. 615. Hill *v.* Brower, 76 N. C. 124. Stearns *v.* Kennedy, 94 Minn. 439. This is the substance of the latter part of the instruction given in the Superior Court, and is the law of this Commonwealth.

The rule of Mooney *v.* Miller seemingly has been approved or followed in Lynch *v.* Mercantile Trust Co., 18 Fed. Rep. 486; Crown *v.* Carriger, 66 Ala. 590; and Mires *v.* Summerville, 85 Mo. App. 183, although the last case has been overruled in Judd *v.* Walker, 114 Mo. App. 128, 135.

If the point were now presented for the first time, it is possible that we might be convinced by the argument of the plaintiffs and the great weight of persuasive authority in its support, especially in view of Lewis *v.* Jewell, 151 Mass. 345. But there is something to be said in support of the two earlier decisions now questioned. A purchase and a sale of real estate is a transaction of importance and cannot be treated as entered into lightly. People must use their own faculties for their protection and information, and cannot assume that the law will relieve them from the natural effects of their heedlessness or take better care of their interests than they themselves do. Thrift, foresight and self-reliance would be undermined if it was the policy of the law to attempt to afford relief for mere want of sagacity. It is an ancient and widely, if not universally, accepted principle of the law of deceit that, where representations are made respecting a subject as to which the complaining party has at hand reasonably available means for ascertaining the truth and the matter is open to inspection, if, without being fraudulently diverted therefrom, he does not take advantage of this opportunity, he cannot be heard to impeach the transaction on the ground of the falsehoods of the other party. Salem India Rubber Co. *v.* Adams, 23 Pick. 256, 265. Slaughter *v.* Gerson, 13 Wall. 379, 383. Long *v.* Warren, 68 N. Y. 426, 432. Baily *v.* Merrell, 3 Bulstr. 94. This rule in its general statement applies to such a case as that before us. It is easy for one disappointed in the fruits of a trade to imagine, and perhaps persuade himself, that the cause of his loss is the deceit of the other party, rather than his own want of judgment.

It is highly desirable that laws for conduct in ordinary affairs, in themselves easy of comprehension and memory, when once established, should remain fast. The doctrine of *stare decisis* is as salutary as it is well recognized. . . . While perhaps it is more important as to far-reaching juridical principles that the court should be right, in the light of higher civilization, later and more careful examination of authorities, wider and more thorough discussion and more mature reflection upon the policy of the law, than merely in harmony with previous decisions (Barden *v.* Northern Pacific Railroad, 154 U. S. 288, 322), it nevertheless is vital that there be stability in the courts in adhering to decisions deliberately made after ample consideration. Parties should not be encouraged to seek re-examination of determined principles and speculate on a fluctuation of the law with every change in the expounders of it. As to many matters of frequent occurrence, the establishment of some certain guide is of more significance than the precise form of the rule. It is likely that no positive rule of law can be laid down that will not at some time impinge with great apparent severity upon a morally innocent person. The law of gravitation acts indifferently upon the just and the unjust. A renewed declaration of law that is already in force, supported by sound reason and not plainly wrong, in the long run probably works out substantial justice, although it may seem harsh in its application to some particular case. These considerations are regarded as so weighty by the House of Lords that it cannot overrule any of its own decisions. London Tramways Co. *v.* London County Council, [1898] A. C. 375.

The conclusion is that we do not overrule the decisions whose soundness has been debated at the bar, although we do not extend their scope, but confine them strictly to their precise point, namely, that where the seller of real estate shows upon the face of the earth its true boundaries to the purchaser and does not fraudulently dissuade him from making full examination and measurement and the estate is not so extensive or of such character as to be reasonably incapable of inspection and estimate, and there is no relation of trust between the parties, the purchaser has no remedy for a misrepresentation as to the area alone. . . . *Exceptions overruled.*[1]

EASTERN TRUST & BANKING COMPANY *v.* CUNNINGHAM

SUPREME COURT, MAINE, FEBRUARY 20, 1908.

Reported in 103 *Maine Reports,* 455.

SAVAGE, J. But the defendant contends further, that, if the plaintiff did not know, it ought to have known, and would have known but for its own negligence. We think this defence cannot avail. There are cases which hold that where one carelessly relies upon a pretence of inherent absurdity and incredibility upon mere idle talk, or upon a device so shadowy as not to be capable of imposing upon any one, he must bear his misfortune, if injured. He must not shut his eyes to what is palpably before him. But that doctrine, if sound, is not applicable here. We think the well-settled rule to be applied here is that if one intentionally misrepresents to another facts particularly within his own knowledge, with an intent that the other shall act upon them, and he does so act, he cannot afterwards excuse himself by saying, "You were foolish to believe me." It does not lie in his mouth to say that the one trusting him was negligent. In this case the fact whether or not there were funds in the Gardiner bank to meet the checks was peculiarly within the knowledge of the defendant. The rule is stated in Pollock on Torts, § 252, as follows: "It is now settled law that one who chooses to make positive assertions without warrant shall not excuse himself by saying that the other party need not have relied upon them. He must show that his representation was not in fact relied upon. In short, nothing will excuse a culpable misrepresentation short of proof that it was not relied upon, either because the other party knew the truth, or because he relied wholly on his own investigations, or because the alleged fact did not influence his action at all." In Linington *v.* Strong, 107 Ill. 295, we find this language: "The doctrine is well settled that as a rule a party guilty of fraudulent conduct shall not be allowed to cry 'negligence' as against his own deliberate fraud. . . . While the law does require of all parties the exercise of reasonable prudence in the business

[1] Credle *v.* Swindell, 63 N. C. 305; Wamsley *v.* Currence, 25 W. Va. 543 *Accord.* See Cagney *v.* Cuson, 77 Ind. 494. Compare Lewis *v.* Jewell, 151 Mass. 345.

Representations as to matter of law, see Eaglesfield *v.* Londonderry, 4 Ch. D. 693, 702–703; Mutual Life Ins. Co. *v.* Phinney, 178 U. S. 327; Martin *v.* Wharton, 38 Ala. 637; Lehman *v.* Shackleford, 50 Ala. 437; McDonald *v.* Smith, 95 Ark. 523; Kehl *v.* Abram, 210 Ill. 218; Hill *v.* Coates, 127 Ill. App. 196; Clodfelter *v.* Hulett, 72 Ind. 137; Kinney *v.* Dodge, 101 Ind. 573; Whitman *v.* Atchison R. Co., 85 Kan. 150; Thompson *v.* Phoenix Ins. Co., 75 Me. 55; Stevens *v.* Odlin, 109 Me. 417; Bilafsky *v.* Conveyancers Ins. Co., 192 Mass. 504; Kerr *v.* Shurtleff, 218 Mass. 167; Rose *v.* Saunders, 38 Hun, 575; Unckles *v.* Hentz, 18 Misc. 644; Moreland *v.* Atchison, 19 Tex. 303; Texas Cotton Co. *v.* Denny, (Tex. Civ. App.) 78 S. W. 557; Gormely *v.* Gymnastic Ass'n, 55 Wis. 350.

Law of another state, see Travelers Protective Ass'n *v.* Smith, 183 Ind. 59; Schneider *v.* Schneider, 125 Ia. 1; Anderson *v.* Heasley, 95 Kan. 572; Wood *v.* Roeder, 50 Neb. 476.

of life, and does not permit one to rest indifferent in reliance upon the interested representations of an adverse party, still, as before suggested, there is a certain limitation to this rule; and, as between the original parties to the transaction we consider that, when it appears that one party has been guilty of an intentional and deliberate fraud by which to his knowledge the other party has been misled or influenced in his action, he cannot escape the legal consequences of his fraudulent conduct by saying that the fraud might have been discovered had the party whom he deceived exercised reasonable diligence and care." See Griffin *v.* Roanoke R. & Lumber Co., 140 N. C. 514, 53 S. E. 307, 6 L. R. A. (N. S.) 463.[1]

S. PEARSON & SON, LIMITED, *v.* LORD MAYOR OF DUBLIN

IN THE HOUSE OF LORDS, MAY 30, 1907.

Reported in [1907] *Appeal Cases*, 351.

THE Dublin Corporation having by their agents furnished the appellants with plans, drawings, and specifications, the appellants contracted to execute certain sewage outfall works according to the plans, &c. In the plans, &c., representations were made as to the existence and position of a certain wall. In the contract (clauses 43, 46, 47, 48) it was stipulated that the contractor should satisfy himself as to the dimensions, levels and nature of all existing works and other things connected with the contract works; that the corporation did not hold itself responsible for the accuracy of the information as to the sections or foundations of existing walls and works; and that no charges for extra work or otherwise would be allowed in consequence of incorrect information or inaccuracies in the drawings or specifications. The appellants performed the contract, and brought an action of deceit against the corporation, claiming damages for false representations as to the position, dimensions and foundations of the wall, whereby the appellants were compelled to execute more costly works than would otherwise have been required. The plans, drawings and specifications were prepared by engineers employed by the corporation.[2]

[At the trial before PALLES, C. B., the plaintiffs offered evidence tending to show that the aforesaid representations were not sincerely believed by the engineers to be true.] PALLES, C. B., refused to leave any question to the jury, and entered judgment for the respondents on the ground that the contractors were bound by their contract to verify for themselves all the information given in the plans, &c.

The King's Bench Division (Wright, Boyd, and Gibson, JJ., Lord O'Brien, C. J., dissenting) reversed the decision of Palles, C. B., and entered judgment for the appellants on the ground that there was a question of fact for the jury upon the allegation of fraud.

[1] "This contention assumes that the defrauded party owes to the party who defrauded him a duty to use diligence to discover the fraud. There is no such obligation. One who perpetrates a fraud cannot complain because his victim continues to have a confidence which a more vigilant person could not have." Carpenter, J., in Smith *v.* McDonald, 139 Mich. 225, 229. See Barley *v.* Walford, 9 Q. B. 197, 209. Compare Thaler *v.* Neidermeyer, 185 Mo. App. 257.

[2] The statement has been redrawn and only parts of the opinion are printed.

The Court of Appeal (Sir Samuel Walker, L. C., Fitzgibbon and Holmes, L. JJ.) reversed that decision, and restored the decision of Palles, C. B.

Plaintiff appealed to the House of Lords.

The House of Lords (LORDS LOREBURN, HALSBURY, ASHBOURNE, MACNAGHTEN, JAMES OF HEREFORD, ROBERTSON, ATKINSON, and COLLINS) reversed the order of the Court of Appeal, and restored the judgment of the King's Bench Division. Portions of the opinions are as follows: —

LORD LOREBURN, L. C. . . . Now it seems clear that no one can escape liability for his own fraudulent statements by inserting in a contract a clause that the other party shall not rely upon them. I will not say that a man himself innocent may not under any circumstances, however peculiar, guard himself by apt and express clauses from liability for the fraud of his own agents. It suffices to say that in my opinion the clauses before us do not admit of such a construction. They contemplate honesty on both sides and protect only against honest mistakes. The principal and the agent are one, and it does not signify which of them made the incriminated statement or which of them possessed the guilty knowledge.

. . . .

EARL OF HALSBURY. . . . The action is based on the allegation of fraud, and no subtilty of language, no craft or machinery in the form of contract, can estop a person who complains that he has been defrauded from having that question of fact submitted to a jury. . . .

LORD ASHBOURNE. . . . [As to clause 43.] Such a clause might in some cases be part of a fraud, and might advance and disguise a fraud, and I cannot think that on the facts and circumstances of this case it can have such a wide and perilous application as was contended for. Such a clause may be appropriate and fairly apply to errors, inaccuracies, and mistakes, but not to cases like the present. . . .

LORD JAMES OF HEREFORD. . . . Now the learned Chief Baron in respect of this clause expressed the opinion that the contractor was not entitled in point of law to say he acted upon the statement contained in the plans. He was told to act upon his own judgment, and ought to have done so.

If this dictum be read as general in its terms, and so applied, it may be read as conferring considerable advantage upon the designers of fraud. At any rate, by inserting such a clause those who framed it would run a fair chance of the contractor saying, "I assume that those with whom I deal are honest and honorable men. I scout the idea of their being guilty of fraud. An inquiry testing the plan will be expensive and difficult, and so I will not make it." The protecting clause might be inserted fraudulently, with the purpose and hope that, notwithstanding its terms, no test would take place. When the fraud succeeds, surely those who designed the fraudulent protection cannot take advantage of it. Such a clause would be good protection against any mistake or miscalculation, but fraud vitiates every contract and every clause in it. As a general principle I incline to the view that an express term that fraud shall not vitiate a contract would be bad in law, but it is unnecessary in this case to determine whether special circumstances may not create an exception to that rule.

. . . .

LORD ATKINSON. . . . If, therefore, the *direction* given to the jury is to be upheld on the grounds upon which it was purported to be based, it must, in my opinion, be because these several articles of the contract, on their true construction, are to be held to embody a contract by the plaintiffs that they in effect are not, under any circumstances, to have a remedy by action for deceit for any fraud which may be practised upon them by the defendants or by those acting on their behalf in the nature of a false representation, that is a contract to submit to a fraud.

As at present advised I am inclined to think, on the authority of Tullis *v.* Jacson, [1892] 3 Ch. 441, and Brownlie *v.* Campbell, (1880) 5 App. Cas. 925, 937, 956, that such a contract would be illegal in point of law. And, with the most profound respect for the Chief Baron, I do not think that the articles of the contract relied upon can, on their true construction, be held to have had fraud, whether conscious or unconscious, within their purview or contemplation, or to apply at all to such a case of fraud as the present is alleged to be. They were, I think, intended to apply, and do apply, to inaccuracies, errors, and mistakes, or matters of that sort, but not to fraud, whether of principal or agent, or of both combined.[1]

. . . .

[1] See Hicks *v.* Stevens, 121 Ill. 186.

CHAPTER V

MALICIOUS PROSECUTION AND ABUSE OF PROCESS

HALBERSTADT *v.* NEW YORK LIFE INSURANCE CO.

COURT OF APPEALS, NEW YORK, JANUARY 5, 1909.

Reported in 194 *New York Reports,* 1.

THE action is brought to recover damages for an alleged malicious prosecution claimed to have been instituted by the respondent against the appellant in Mexico. It is in the complaint, amongst other things, alleged that the respondent through its agent in the Criminal Court of the city of Mexico charged the appellant with the crime of embezzlement "and thereupon and in and by virtue of said charge and the institution of said criminal proceedings a warrant was issued by said court for the arrest of the plaintiff (in this action)," and that thereafter "the said criminal proceedings for the punishment of said plaintiff were dismissed and extinguished and the said prosecution was thereby wholly determined . . . in favor of the plaintiff."

The respondent, by its second defence, which is challenged here for insufficiency, alleged, in substance, that before the warrant referred to in the complaint could be served upon the appellant and before he could be apprehended, "he left the Republic of Mexico and thereafter continuously remained absent . . . and by such absence avoided being arrested under such warrant, or being tried . . . but remained absent from said Republic of Mexico for a sufficient period of time to enable him to procure the dismissal of said proceedings under the law of Mexico on account solely of the lapse of time," and, conversely, that said criminal proceedings "were not dismissed on account of a determination of the case in favor of the plaintiff on the trial thereof on the merits, nor was it dismissed for failure to prosecute said case except as above set forth, nor was it dismissed on account of any withdrawal of the complaint."

The plaintiff demurred to this defence and also to the third defence which was not materially different from the second. The demurrer was sustained at Special Term. This judgment was reversed by the General Term, and the plaintiff now appeals.[1]

HISCOCK, J. The respondent's first reply to the appellant's attack upon its answer is of the *tu quoque* nature, it insisting that the complaint is as deficient in the statement of a good cause of action as the

[1] The statement of the case has been abridged and only a part of the opinion is given.

answer is alleged to be in the statement of a good defence. This contention is based upon the fact that the complaint does not allege any act subsequent or in addition to the mere issuance of a warrant in the criminal proceeding complained of; does not allege that the warrant was ever executed in any way whatever, or that the appellant was ever actually brought into said proceedings either by force of process or voluntary appearance. Therefore, the question is presented whether the mere application for and issuance to a proper officer for execution of a warrant on a criminal charge may institute and constitute such a prosecution as may be made the basis of a subsequent civil action by the party claimed to have been injured. In considering this question we must keep in mind that the facts alleged in the complaint, and in the light of which it is to be determined, do not show, as the answer does, that the defendant in those proceedings was beyond the jurisdiction of the court.

This question does not seem to have been settled by any decision which we regard as controlling on us.

The respondent cites the following authorities deciding it in the negative: Newfield *v.* Copperman, 15 Abb. Pr., N. S., 360; Lawyer *v.* Loomis, 3 T. & C. 393; Cooper *v.* Armour, 42 Fed. 215; Heyward *v.* Cuthbert, 4 McCord, 354; O'Driscoll *v.* M'Burney, 2 Nott & McCord, 54; Bartlett *v.* Cristliff, 14 Atl. R. 518; Gregory *v.* Derby, 8 C. & P. 749; Paul *v.* Fargo, 84 App. Div. 9.

The case last cited was concerned with an alleged malicious prosecution by means of civil process and what was there said must be interpreted with reference to that fact, and thus interpreted it is not applicable here. Of the other cases, only two, Heyward *v.* Cuthbert and Cooper *v.* Armour, considered the question here involved with sufficient thoroughness to require brief comment. An examination will show that the decision in each of them rested in whole or part on a principle not, as I believe, adopted in this state. In the former it was said that "The foundation of this sort of action is the wrong done to the plaintiff by the direct detention or imprisonment of his person." As I think we shall see hereafter, that is not a correct statement of the law in this state. In the other case it was stated, "The only injury sustained by the person accused, when he is not taken into custody, and no process has been issued against him, is to his reputation; and for such an injury the action of libel or slander is the appropriate remedy, and would seem to be the only remedy." I think that this doctrine, which if correct would provide an adequate remedy outside of an action for malicious prosecution for an injured party in a case where no warrant had been executed, also is opposed to the weight of authority both in this state and elsewhere hereafter to be referred to.

The authorities holding to the contrary on the question above stated, and that the execution of the warrant is not necessary to lay the foundation for an action of malicious prosecution, are: Addison on Torts, vol. 2 [4th Eng. ed.], p. 478; Newell on Malicious Prosecution, sect. 30; Stephens on Malicious Prosecution, Am. ed., sect. 8; Stapp *v.* Partlow, Dudley's Repts., (Ga.) 176; Clarke *v.* Postan, 6 C. & P. 423; Fezale *v.* Simpson, 2 Ill. 30; Britton *v.* Granger, 13 Ohio Cir. Ct. Repts. 281, 291; Holmes *v.* Johnson, Busbee's L. R. 44; Coffey *v.* Myers, 84 Ind. 105.

And to the like effect in the absence of special statutory provisions in Swift *v.* Witchard, 103 Ga. 193.

Thus it is apparent, as before stated, that there is no controlling decision on this question and we are remitted to a search for some general considerations which may be decisive. It seems to me that these may be found and that they favor the view that a prosecution may be regarded as having been instituted even though a warrant has not been executed.

The first one of these considerations is found in the rule applied in civil actions and proceedings to an analogous situation. There it has many times been held that the mere issue of various forms of civil process for service or other execution is sufficient independent of statute to effect the commencement of a case or proceeding. Carpenter *v.* Butterfield, 3 Johns. Cases, 146; Cheetham *v.* Lewis, 3 Johns. 42; Bronson *v.* Earl, 17 Johns. 63; Ross *v.* Luther, 4 Cowen, 158; Mills *v.* Corbett, 8 How. Pr. 500; Hancock *v.* Ritchie, 11 Ind. 48, 52; Howell *v.* Shepard, 48 Mich. 472; Webster *v.* Sharpe, 116 N. C. 466, 471.

I see no reason why a similar rule should not be applied to criminal proceedings, at least for the purposes of such an action as this.

Then there is another reason resting on justice which seems to me to lead us to adopt this conclusion. In opposition to what was said in the South Carolina case already referred to, the sole foundation for an action of malicious prosecution is not "the wrong done to the plaintiff by the direct detention or imprisonment of his person." In an action for false imprisonment that would be so. But in an action of the present type, the substantial injury for which damages are recovered and which serves as a basis for the action may be that inflicted upon the feelings, reputation and character by a false accusation as well as that caused by arrest and imprisonment. This element "indeed is in many cases the gravamen of the action." Sheldon *v.* Carpenter, 4 N. Y. 579, 580; Woods *v.* Finnell, 13 Bush Repts. 628; Townsend on Slander, sec. 420; Wheeler *v.* Hanson, 161 Mass. 370; Gundermann *v.* Buschner, 73 Ill. App. 180; Lawrence *v.* Hagerman, 56 Ill. 68; Davis *v.* Seeley, 91 Iowa, 583.

But no matter how false and damaging the charge may be in a criminal proceeding upon which a warrant may be issued, damages for the injury caused thereby cannot under any ordinary circumstances be recovered in an action for libel or slander. Howard *v.* Thompson, 21 Wend. 319, 324; Woods *v.* Wiman, 47 Hun, 362, 364; Sheldon *v.*

Carpenter, *supra;* Dale *v.* Harris, 109 Mass. 193; Gabriel *v.* McMullin, 127 Iowa, 427; Hamilton *v.* Eno, 81 N. Y. 116; Newell on Malicious Prosecution, sec. 10.

Therefore, it follows that a person who has most grievously injured another by falsely making a serious criminal accusation against him whereon a warrant has been actually issued, may escape all liability by procuring the warrant at that point to be withheld unless an action for malicious prosecution will lie. It seems to me that under such circumstances we should hold that such action will lie, if for no other reason than to satisfy that principle of law which demands an adequate remedy for every legal wrong.[1] . . .

VANN, J. I concur in the result because there was merely an attempt to prosecute with no actual prosecution. The Mexican court did not acquire jurisdiction of the person of the plaintiff, for he was not arrested, nor was process or notice of any kind served upon him. He was not brought into court and the prosecution could not end because it was never begun. He could not be a party defendant until he was notified or voluntarily appeared. He was threatened with prosecution, but neither his person nor his property was touched. There can be no prosecution unless knowledge thereof is brought home to the alleged defendant in some way. If there had been a prosecution commenced the crime could not have outlawed during the defendant's absence, as is admitted of record. While in civil actions, in order to arrest the Statute of Limitations, "an attempt to commence an action, in a court of record, is equivalent to the commencement thereof," still the attempt goes for naught unless followed by service, actual or constructive, within sixty days. (Code Civil Proc. § 399.) The rule was similar at common law. Although, in order to prevent injustice, an action was deemed to be commenced by the delivery of process for service, it was never treated as effectual for any purpose unless actual service was subsequently made. The authorities cited in the prevailing opinion illustrate this proposition.

In the absence of controlling authority, which it is conceded does not exist, I favor restricting rather than enlarging the scope of the action. This accords with the general position of the court upon the subject.

GRAY, HAIGHT and CHASE, JJ., concur with HISCOCK, J.; CULLEN, Ch. J., and WILLARD BARTLETT, J., concur with VANN, J.

Order affirmed.[2]

[1] The court decided that the answer was good.

[2] In accordance with the opinion of the majority of the court see Clarke *v.* Postan, 6 Car. & P. 423; Stapp *v.* Partlow, Dudley, (Ga.) 176; Feazle *v.* Simpson, 2 Ill. 30 (*semble*); Holmes *v.* Johnson, Busbee, 44; Britton *v.* Granger, 13 Ohio Cir. Ct. Rep. 281, 291.

In accordance with the opinion of the minority see Gregory *v.* Derby, 8 Car. & P. 749, 750 (*semble*); Cooper *v.* Armour, 42 Fed. 215, 217; Sheppard *v.* Furniss, 19 Ala. 760 (*semble*); Davis *v.* Sanders, 133 Ala. 275, 278 (*semble*); Newfield *v.* Copperman, 15 Abb. Pr. N. S. 360 (*semble*); Lawyer *v.* Loomis, 3 Th. & C. 393,

CHAMBERS v. ROBINSON

At Nisi Prius, Coram Raymond, C. J., Hilary Term, 1726.

Reported in 2 *Strange*, 691.

An action for a malicious prosecution of an indictment for perjury.

Upon the trial it appeared, the perjury was ill-assigned, so that the now plaintiff could not have been convicted; and that exception was taken to it by the judge, and he was acquitted without any examination of witnesses. But the Chief Justice held the action lay, though it was a faulty indictment, relying upon the case of Jones v. Gwynn, where the distinction in Salk. 13 was denied, and held by the whole court that the action would lie, though the indictment was bad; a bad indictment serving all the purposes of malice, by putting the party to expense, and exposing him, but it serves no purpose of justice in bringing the party to punishment if he be guilty.[1]

BYNE v. MOORE

In the Common Pleas, November 13, 1813.

Reported in 5 *Taunton*, 187.[2]

This was an action for a malicious prosecution in indicting the plaintiff for an assault and battery. The only evidence on the part of the plaintiff being, that the bill was preferred and not found, Lord Chief Baron Macdonald who tried the cause, nonsuited him.[3]

395; Mitchell v. Donanski, 28 R. I. 94; O'Driscoll v. McBurney, 2 N. & McC. 54 (*semble*); Heyward v. Cuthbert, 4 McC. 354 (*semble*).

Compare Swift v. Witchard, 103 Ga. 193.

Arrest without warrant, not followed by prosecution, see Auerbach v. Freeman, 43 App. D. C. 176; McDonald v. National Art Co., 69 Misc. 325.

Search warrant issued but no arrest or seizure of property, see Gulsby v. Louisville R. Co., 167 Ala. 122; Hardin v. Hight, 106 Ark. 190; Chicago R. Co. v. Holliday, 30 Okl. 680; Olson v. Haggerty, 69 Wash. 48.

Application for a warrant, none issued, see Schneider v. Schlang, 159 App. Div. 385. But see Kashare v. Robbins, 135 N. Y. Supp. 1041.

Some jurisdictions, however, require legal process of at least *prima facie* validity. See Strain v. Irwin, 195 Ala. 414; Smith v. Brown, 119 Md. 236; Tiede v. Fuhr, 264 Mo. 622; Segusky v. Williams, 89 S. C. 414.

Cf. Grissom v. Lawler, 10 Ala. App. 540 (plaintiff gave bond after complaint, so no process issued).

[1] Pippet v. Hearn, 5 B. & Al. 634; Rutherford v. Dyer, 146 Ala. 665; Peterson v. Hoyt, 4 Alaska, 713; Harrington v. Tibbet, 143 Cal. 78; Streight v. Bell, 37 Ind. 550; Shaul v. Brown, 28 Ia. 37; Bell v. Keepers, 37 Kan. 64; Potter v. Gjertsen, 37 Minn. 386; Stocking v. Howard, 73 Mo. 25; Hackler v. Miller, 79 Neb. 209; Dennis v. Ryan, 65 N. Y. 385; Kline v. Shuler, 8 Ired. 484; Chicago R. Co. v. Holliday, 30 Okl. 680; Ward v. Sutor, 70 Tex. 343; Strehlow v. Pettit, 96 Wis. 22; McIntosh v. Wales, 21 Wyo. 397 *Accord.*

Alexander v. West, 6 Ga. App. 72 *Contra.*

Prosecution under unconstitutional statute: Murten v. Garbe, 91 Neb. 439.

Court without jurisdiction: Calhoun v. Bell, 136 La. 149. Compare Grorud v. Lossl, 48 Mont. 274.

[2] 1 Marsh. 12, s. c.

[3] The statement of the case has been taken from 1 Marsh. 12; the arguments of counsel are omitted.

Best, Serjt., had obtained a rule *nisi* to set aside that nonsuit and have a new trial; against which

Shepherd, Serjt., showed cause.

Mansfield, C. J. I feel a difficulty to understand how the plaintiff could recover in the present action, wherein he could recover no damages, because he clearly has not proved that he has sustained any: I can understand the ground upon which an action shall be maintained for an indictment which contains scandal, but this contains none, nor does any danger of imprisonment result from it: this bill was a piece of mere waste paper. All the cases in Buller's Nisi Prius, 13, are directly against this action, for the author speaks of putting the plaintiff to expense, and affecting his good fame, neither of which could be done here. If this action could be maintained, every bill which the grand jury threw out would be the ground of an action. The judge too might certify in this cause against the costs, if the damages had been under 40*s*.

Heath, J., concurred.

Chambre, J. It would be a very mischievous precedent if the action could be supported on this evidence. *Rule discharged.*[1]

STEWARD *v.* GROMETT

In the Common Pleas, November 11, 1859.

Reported in 7 Common Bench Reports, New Series, 191.

Erle, C. J.[2] I am of opinion that our judgment in this case must be for the plaintiff. It is an action against the defendant for falsely and maliciously, and without reasonable or probable cause, making information on oath before a magistrate that the plaintiff had used threatening language to him, whereby he went in fear of bodily harm, and so procuring a warrant under which the plaintiff was incarcerated in the castle at Swaffham, for want of sureties, for a period of six months. It is admitted on the pleadings that the defendant did falsely and maliciously, and without reasonable or probable cause, procure that wrong to be done to the plaintiff; and the question is whether the declaration shows enough to entitle the plaintiff to maintain an action for that wrong. This is in some sort an action for a malicious prosecution; and it has been contended by Mr. Couch, for the defendant, that the case falls within the ordinary rule applicable to such actions, that the plaintiff must show that the proceeding terminated in his favor, and that no action lies where they are shown to have terminated against the accused. But I am of opinion that the distinction taken by Mr. Keane removes that objection, and shows that that rule does not apply to this case, because the proceeding before the magistrate being founded upon a statement which the party charged is not at liberty to controvert, is an *ex parte* proceeding, and, although it attains the result which is sought, it is not a judgment, but is in the nature of a writ

[1] See Saville *v.* Roberts, 1 Ld. Ray. 374; 12 Mod. 208, s. c.

"It is difficult to see on what grounds it can be maintained that a charge of breaking the peace conveys no imputation on the character of the person charged, and it may be doubted whether the authority of the cases above mentioned (Byne *v.* Moore and Saville *v.* Roberts) would now be recognized on this point." Clerk & Lindsell, Torts, (5 ed.) 663.

[2] Only the opinion of Erle, C. J., is given.

of process. It is not like the case of an application to a magistrate upon a matter on which he is to exercise his discretion: there, the injury sustained by the party is the act of the law, and therefore no action lies unless the person who sets the magistrate in motion is actuated by malice. But here the law was directly put in motion by the defendant against the plaintiff, and, it must be assumed, falsely and maliciously and without reasonable or probable cause. If a party goes before a judge, under the 1 & 2 Vict. c. 110, with an affidavit of debt for the purpose of procuring a capias to arrest his debtor, upon a suggestion that he is going abroad, and that is done falsely and maliciously, and without reasonable or probable cause, an action lies. So, if a party go to the Court of Queen's Bench, and maliciously exhibit articles of the peace against another, supported by a false oath that such other had used threats against him, his statement being incontrovertible, it is clear to my mind that an action would lie. Can it make any difference that here the proceeding took place before a magistrate? It seems to me that the two proceedings are quite analogous: the same remedy is sought, only by a different mode. As in the one case the truth of the articles cannot be controverted, so in the other the statement made before the magistrate upon oath cannot be contradicted by the accused. There is not the least sign of authority to show that the magistrate had any discretion, so that the plaintiff might have had a decision in his favor. In Burn's Justice, sureties of the peace are treated as being subject to precisely the same rule as articles of the peace at the sessions or in the Court of Queen's Bench, in respect of their truth being incontrovertible. And there is strong reason for assuming that to be the true state of the law; the fact of there being no authority exactly in point as to sureties of the peace, may well be accounted for by supposing that no one has entertained doubt enough upon it to take the opinion of any court. But as far as authority goes, The King *v.* Doherty, 13 East, 171, and Venafra *v.* Johnson, 10 Bing. 301, 3 M. & Sc. 807, are in favor of the plaintiff. In the latter case, Johnson made precisely the same application to the justices as was made here, and they exercised a precisely analogous jurisdiction, the only difference being that there the magistrates held the plaintiff to bail for his appearance at the sessions, whereas here the magistrate at once committed the plaintiff to jail until he should find the required sureties: and it was there decided by implication that the proceeding before the magistrate was incontrovertible; for, the court held that the judge was wrong in not leaving it to the jury to say whether or not the defendant believed the menaces when he put the law in motion against the plaintiff. If Mr. Couch's argument to-day is right, the counsel and the court in that case were all wrong. Upon principle, therefore, and upon authority, it seems to me that the argument for the plaintiff in this case ought to prevail. *Judgment for the plaintiff.*[1]

[1] Hyde *v.* Greuch, 62 Md. 577; Pixley *v.* Reed, 26 Minn. 80 (*semble*); Apgar *v.* Woolston, 43 N. J. Law, 57, 65 (*semble*); Bump *v.* Betts, 19 Wend. 421; Fortman *v.* Rottier, 8 Ohio St. 548 *Accord.*

See Brinkley *v.* Knight, 163 N. C. 194 (release by constable without a hearing).

FISHER *v.* BRISTOW

IN THE KING'S BENCH, JUNE 15, 1779.

Reported in 1 *Douglas*, 215.

ACTION for a malicious presentment (for incest), in the ecclesiastical court of the archdeaconery of Huntingdon. Demurrer to the declaration and cause assigned, that it was not stated how the prosecution was disposed of, or that it was not still depending. The court were clearly of opinion, that the objection was fatal, and said it was settled, that the plaintiff in such an action, must show the original suit, wherever instituted, to be at an end; otherwise he might recover in the action, and yet be afterwards convicted on the original prosecution. *Judgment for the defendants.*[1]

BROWN *v.* RANDALL

SUPREME COURT, CONNECTICUT, MARCH TERM, 1869.

Reported in 36 *Connecticut Reports*, 56.

CARPENTER, J.[2] The defendants complained to a grandjuror of the town of Norwich against the plaintiff, charging him with a breach of the peace, and induced the grandjuror to enter a complaint to a magistrate in due form, whereupon a warrant was issued, and the plaintiff arrested and held to answer the complaint. After remaining in custody several hours, the magistrate informed the defendants and their counsel, who acted for the grandjuror, that he was ready to proceed with the trial. The defendants sent word to the court that they should prosecute the complaint no further, and thereupon the plaintiff was discharged. It is alleged in the declaration that this proceeding was

[1] Parker *v.* Langley, 10 Mod. 209; Whitworth *v.* Hall, 2 B. & Ad. 695; Mellor *v.* Baddeley, 2 Cr. & M. 675; Watkins *v.* Lee, 5 M. & W. 270; McCann *v.* Preneveau, 10 Ont. 573; Poitras *v.* LeBeau, 14 Can. S. C. 742; Stewart *v.* Sonneborn, 98 U. S. 187; Steel *v.* Williams, 18 Ind. 161; West *v.* Hayes, 104 Ind. 251; Olson *v.* Neal, 63 Ia. 214; Wood *v.* Laycock, 3 Met. (Ky.) 192; Smith *v.* Brown, 119 Md. 236; Hamilburgh *v.* Shepard, 119 Mass. 30; Wilson *v.* Hale, 178 Mass. 111; Pixley *v.* Reed, 26 Minn. 80; Lowe *v.* Wartman, 47 N. J. Law, 413; Clark *v.* Cleveland, 6 Hill, 344; Searll *v.* McCracken, 16 How. Pr. 262; Swartwout *v.* Dickelman, 12 Hun, 358; Johnson *v.* Finch, 93 N. C. 205; Forster *v.* Orr. 17 Or. 447; Scheibler *v.* Steinburg, 129 Tenn. 614; Luby *v.* Bennett, 111 Wis. 613 *Accord.*

Consequently, the Statute of Limitations does not run until the prosecution is terminated. Mayor *v.* Hall, 12 Can. S. C. 74; Printup *v.* Smith, 74 Ga. 157; Rider *v.* Kite, 61 N. J. Law, 8.

Also although discharged by a magistrate, plaintiff can not sue if the grand jury afterwards indict. Hartshorn *v.* Smith, 104 Ga. 235; Weglein *v.* Trow Directory Co., 152 App. Div. 705. See Schippel *v.* Norton, 38 Kan. 567; Knott *v.* Sargent, 125 Mass. 95. Compare Simmons *v.* Sullivan, 42 App. D. C. 523 (amended or substitute information, altering the charge); Mistich *v.* Collette, 136 La. 294 (second prosecution instituted after termination of first and still pending).

[2] Everything is omitted, except the opinion of the court on the question of the termination of the prosecution.

malicious and without probable cause, and the jury have found that allegation to be true.

The important question in this case is whether, upon the facts alleged and proved, the plaintiff is entitled to recover. All the material averments seem to have been proved except the allegation of acquittal. That was not proved, and the court charged the jury that it was not necessary. The defendants complain of this, as they rely upon the non-existence of that fact as a complete defence to the action. Decisions of courts of the highest respectability, both in England and in this country, justify this claim. It does not appear that this question has ever been directly determined by this court. We are referred to the case of Monroe *v.* Maples, 1 Root, 553. But no such question arose in that case. It simply decided that a person convicted of the crime charged against him could not maintain the action. We are therefore at liberty to determine the question upon principle.

The grounds of this action are, the malice of the defendant, the want of probable cause, and an injury sustained by the plaintiff. 1 Swift's Digest, 491. The conviction of the plaintiff is justly considered as conclusive evidence of probable cause. The authorities referred to virtually decide — without sufficient reason as it seems to us — that the termination of the prosecution by a *nolle prosequi*, or abandonment, was equally conclusive upon that question.

One reason given for this is, that no termination of the prosecution in favor of the accused short of an acquittal will discharge the crime or be a bar to a new indictment. This reasoning is not satisfactory. The possibility that the plaintiff may be again prosecuted for the same alleged offence is not inconsistent with an entire want of probable cause in the first prosecution. This reason seems to have been disregarded in Sayles *v.* Briggs, 4 Met. 421. The complainant abandoned the prosecution against the plaintiff after a trial, and the magistrate, who could only bind over or discharge the person accused, discharged him. The court held that the action could be maintained. Yet such a discharge could be no bar to a subsequent prosecution.

Another reason given is, that the common law will not favor actions in behalf of a party criminally prosecuted against one who has acted as complainant in behalf of the public, and ostensibly for the public good; it therefore requires that the plaintiff in such an action shall begin by offering the verdict of a jury who have considered the cause on its merits. This may be a very proper caution to a jury, and a matter which ought to be considered by them in weighing evidence, but we see no sufficient reason for adopting it as an absolute rule of law, the effect of which is, in some cases at least, to shut out the truth. No such rule has been adopted in this State, and we think it is contrary to the prevailing notions of the profession. Judge Swift, in his Digest, vol. 1, p. 491, states five different modes of terminating a prosecution in favor of the accused which will lay the foundation for this action, and one of them is, "when the prosecution has been abandoned and given up."

In Parker *v.* Farley, 10 Cush. 279, Shaw, C. J., in speaking of the rule under consideration, says: "Were this a new and original question, to be decided upon principle, it might be doubted whether it would be just and wise to establish this as an inflexible rule of practice."

On the whole we think it wise and safe, when a prosecution has been abandoned, as this was, without any arrangement with the accused, and without any request from him that it should be so abandoned, to leave the question of probable cause to the jury.

The charge of the court was in harmony with these views, and we do not advise a new trial.

In this opinion the other judges concurred.[1]

[1] Cotton *v.* Wilson, Minor, 203; Hurgren *v.* Union Co., 141 Cal. 585; Chapman *v.* Woods, 6 Blackf. 504; Richter *v.* Koster, 45 Ind. 440; Coffey *v.* Myers, 84 Ind. 105; Kelley *v.* Sage, 12 Kan. 109; Bell *v.* Matthews, 37 Kan. 686; Yocum *v.* Polly, 1 B. Mon. 358; Stanton *v.* Hart, 27 Mich. 539; Swensgaard *v.* Davis, 33 Minn. 368 (*semble*); Kennedy *v.* Holladay, 25 Mo. App. 503; Casebeer *v.* Drahoble, 13 Neb. 465; Casebeer *v.* Rice, 18 Neb. 203; Apgar *v.* Woolston, 43 N. J. Law, 57; Lowe *v.* Wartman, 47 N. J. Law, 413; Clark *v.* Cleveland, 6 Hill, 344 (*semble*); Moulton *v.* Beecher, 8 Hun, 100; Fay *v.* O'Neill, 36 N. Y. 11 (*semble*); Murray *v.* Lackey, 2 Murph. 368; Rice *v.* Ponder, 7 Ired. 390; Hatch *v.* Cohen, 84 N. C. 602; Marcus *v.* Bernstein, 117 N. C. 31; Douglas *v.* Allen, 56 Ohio St. 156; Murphy *v.* Moore, (Pa.) 11 Atl. 665; Driggs *v.* Burton, 44 Vt. 124; Woodworth *v.* Mills, 61 Wis. 44; Manz *v.* Klippel, 158 Wis. 557; McCrosson *v.* Cummings, 5 Hawn, 391 *Accord.*

Massachusetts formerly held to the contrary. Parker *v.* Farley, 10 Cush. 279. But see Graves *v.* Dawson, 130 Mass. 78, 133 Mass. 419; Langford *v.* Boston R. Co., 144 Mass. 431; Briggs *v.* Shepard Mfg. Co., 217 Mass. 446.

Indictment quashed, see Simmons *v.* Sullivan, 42 App. D. C. 523; Wilkerson *v.* McGee, 265 Mo. 574; Reit *v.* Meyer, 160 App. Div. 752.

Case stricken from docket because sent to wrong court, Sandlin *v.* Anders, 187 Ala. 473.

Termination of a previous civil action. — If a party sues for a malicious arrest or seizure of property in a civil action, a voluntary abandonment of the latter action by the plaintiff therein is equivalent to its termination in favor of his adversary. Arundell *v.* White, 14 East, 216; Nicholson *v.* Coghill, 4 B. & C. 21; Pierce *v.* Street, 3 B. & Ad. 397; Watkins *v.* Lee, 5 M. & W. 270; Ross *v.* Norman, 5 Ex. 359; Emery *v.* Ginnan, 24 Ill. App. 65; Cardival *v.* Smith, 109 Mass. 158; Ludwick *v.* Penny, 158 N. C. 104; Mayer *v.* Walter, 64 Pa. St. 283. Compare Hales *v.* Raines, 162 Mo. App. 46 (action recommenced after voluntary nonsuit).

The rule is the same as to malicious prosecutions of civil actions without arrest or attachment in jurisdictions where one is allowed to sue for malicious prosecution of a civil action, without more. Wall *v.* Toomey, 52 Conn. 35; Marbourg *v.* Smith, 11 Kan. 554; Mitchell *v.* Sullivan, 30 Kan. 231. See also Wilson *v.* Hale, 178 Mass. 111; Luby *v.* Bennett, 111 Wis. 613.

But an abandonment of the previous proceeding, brought about as a compromise, is not a termination in favor of the original defendant. Wilkinson *v.* Howel, M. & M. 495; Kinsey *v.* Wallace, 36 Cal. 462 (*semble*); Waters *v.* Winn, 142 Ga. 138; Emery *v.* Ginnan, 24 Ill. App. 65; Fadner *v.* Filer, 27 Ill. App. 506; Ruehl Brewing Co. *v.* Atlas Brewing Co., 187 Ill. App. 392; Singer Machine Co. *v.* Dyer, 156 Ky. 156; Marks *v.* Gray, 42 Me. 86; Sartwell *v.* Parker, 141 Mass. 405; Langford *v.* Boston R. Co., 144 Mass. 431; Rachelman *v.* Skinner, 46 Minn. 196; McCormick *v.* Sisson, 7 Cow. 715; Gallagher *v.* Stoddard, 47 Hun, 101; Atwood *v.* Beirne, 73 Hun, 547 (but see Reit *v.* Meyer, 160 App. Div. 752); Welch *v.* Cheek, 115 N. C. 310; Clark *v.* Everett, 2 Grant, (Pa.) 416; Mayer *v.* Walter, 64 Pa. St.

FOSHAY *v.* FERGUSON

SUPREME COURT, NEW YORK, MAY, 1846.

Reported in 2 *Denio,* 617.

By the Court, BRONSON, C. J.[1] There was evidence enough in the case to warrant the jury in finding, that the defendant set the prosecution in motion from a bad motive. But all the books agree, that proof of express malice is not enough, without showing also the want of probable cause. Probable cause has been defined, a reasonable ground of suspicion, supported by circumstances sufficiently strong in themselves to warrant a cautious man in the belief, that the person accused is guilty of the offence with which he is charged. Munns *v.* Nemours, 3 Wash. C. C. 37. However innocent the plaintiff may have been of the crime laid to his charge, it is enough for the defendant to show, that he had reasonable grounds for believing him guilty at the time the charge was made. In Swain *v.* Stafford, 3 Iredell, N. C. 289, and 4 id. 392, the action was brought against the defendant, who was a merchant, for charging the plaintiff with stealing a piece of ribbon from his store. At the time the complaint was made, the defendant had received such information as induced a belief of the plaintiff's guilt; and although it afterwards turned out that the property had not been taken by any one, and was never out of the defendant's possession, it was held that an action for malicious prosecution could not be supported. The doctrine that probable cause depends on the knowledge or information which the prosecutor had at the time the charge was made, has been carried to a great length. In Delegal *v.* Highley, 3 Bing. N. C. 950, which was an action for maliciously, and without probable cause, procuring a third person to charge the plaintiff with a criminal offence, the defendant pleaded specially, showing that the plaintiff was guilty of the offence which had been laid to his charge; and the plea was held bad in substance, because it did not show that the defendant, at the time the charge was made, had been informed, or knew the facts on which the charge rested. The question of probable cause does not turn on the actual guilt or innocence of the accused; but upon the belief of the prosecutor concerning such guilt or innocence. Seibert *v.* Price, 5 Watts & Serg. 438.

Without going into a particular examination of the evidence in this case, it is enough to say that the defendant, at the time he went before the grand jury had strong grounds for believing that the plaintiff had stolen the cattle: and, so far as appears, not a single fact had then come to his knowledge which was calculated to induce a different

283, 287; Rounds *v.* Humes, 7 R. I. 535; Russell *v.* Morgan, 24 R. I. 134. Unless the settlement was obtained by duress of the person or the goods of the original defendant. Morton *v.* Young, 55 Me. 24; White *v.* International Textbook Co., 156 Ia. 210.

[1] Only the opinion of the court is given.

opinion. Although the plaintiff was in fact innocent, there would be no color for this action, if it were not for the fact that the defendant settled the matter with the plaintiff, instead of proceeding against him for the supposed offence. If the parties intended the settlement should extend so far as to cover up and prevent a criminal prosecution, the defendant was guilty of compounding a felony. And the fact that he made no complaint until the plaintiff commenced the two suits against him, goes far to show that he was obnoxious to that charge; and that he was governed more by his own interest, than by a proper regard to the cause of public justice. But however culpable the defendant may have been for neglecting his duty to the public, that cannot be made the foundation of a private action by the plaintiff. Although the defendant may have agreed not to prosecute, and the complaint may have been afterwards made from a malicious feeling towards the plaintiff, still the fact of probable cause remains; and so long as it exists, it is a complete defence. There is enough in the defendant's conduct to induce a rigid scrutiny of the defence. But if upon such scrutiny it appear, that he had reasonable grounds for believing the plaintiff guilty, and there is nothing to show that he did not actually entertain that belief, there is no principle upon which the action can be supported.

On a careful examination of the case, I am of opinion that the verdict was clearly wrong. But as the charge of the judge is not given, we must presume that the case was properly submitted to the jury; and a new trial can therefore only be had on payment of costs.

Ordered accordingly.[1]

[1] Anon., 6 Mod. 73; Turner *v.* Ambler, 10 Q. B. 252; Hailes *v.* Marks, 7 H. & N. 56; Wheeler *v.* Nesbitt, 24 How. 544, 550; Stewart *v.* Sonneborn, 98 U. S. 187; Sanders *v.* Palmer, 55 Fed. 217; Jordan *v.* Alabama Co., 81 Ala. 220; Price *v.* Morris, 122 Ark. 382; Mark *v.* Rich, 43 App. D. C. 182; Marable *v.* Mayer, 78 Ga. 710; Joiner *v.* Ocean Co., 86 Ga. 238; Ames *v.* Snider, 69 Ill. 376; Barrett *v.* Spaids, 70 Ill. 408; Leyenberger *v.* Paul, 12 Ill. App. 635; Morrell *v.* Martin, 17 Ill. App. 336; Adams *v.* Lisher, 3 Blackf. 241; Green *v.* Cochran, 43 Ia. 544; Yocum *v.* Polly, 1 B. Mon. 358; Medcalfe *v.* Brooklyn Co., 45 Md. 198; Flickinger *v.* Wagner, 46 Md. 580; Stone *v.* Crocker, 24 Pick. 81; Coupal *v.* Ward, 106 Mass. 289; Hamilton *v.* Smith, 39 Mich. 222; Smith *v.* Austin, 49 Mich. 286; Webster *v.* Fowler, 89 Mich. 303; Cox *v.* Lauritsen, 126 Minn. 128; Burris *v.* North, 64 Mo. 426; Renfro *v.* Prior, 22 Mo. App. 403; Kennedy *v.* Holladay, 25 Mo. App. 503, 519; Harris *v.* Quincy R. Co., 172 Mo. App. 261; McDonald *v.* Goddard Grocery Co., 184 Mo. App. 432; Woodman *v.* Prescott, 65 N. H. 224; Heyne *v.* Blair, 62 N. Y. 19; Miller *v.* Milligan, 48 Barb. 30; Linitzky *v.* Gorman, 146 N. Y. Supp. 313; Dietz *v.* Langfitt, 63 Pa. St. 234; Emerson *v.* Cochran, 111 Pa. St. 619; Bartlett *v.* Brown, 6 R. I. 37; Welch *v.* Boston R. Corp., 14 R. I. 609; Stoddard *v.* Roland, 31 S. C. 342; Kelton *v.* Bevins, Cooke, (Tenn.) 90; Evans *v.* Thompson, 12 Heisk. 534; Johnson *v.* State, 32 Tex. Cr. 58; South Bank *v.* Suffolk Bank, 27 Vt. 505; Waring *v.* Hudspeth, 75 Wash. 534; Bailey *v.* Gollehon, 76 W. Va. 322; Reicher *v.* Neacy, 158 Wis. 657 *Accord.*

Definitions of probable cause, see Gulsby *v.* Louisville R. Co., 167 Ala. 122; Hanchey *v.* Brunson, 175 Ala. 236; Runo *v.* Williams, 162 Cal. 444; Redgate *v.* Southern R. Co., 24 Cal. App. 573; Mark *v.* Rich, 43 App. D. C. 182; Pianco *v.* Joseph, 188 Ill. App. 555; Schwartz *v.* Boswell, 156 Ky. 103; Indianapolis Traction Co. *v.* Henby, 178 Ind. 239; Banken *v.* Locke, 136 La. 155; Chapman *v.* Nash, 121 Md. 608; Gilecki *v.* Dolemba, 189 Mich. 107; Cox *v.* Lauritsen, 126 Minn.

CLOON v. GERRY

SUPREME JUDICIAL COURT, MASSACHUSETTS, JUNE, 1859.

Reported in 13 *Gray*, 201.

SHAW, C. J.[1] In an action for a malicious prosecution against one, in the name of the Commonwealth, the averment on the part of the plaintiff, that the complaint was made without reasonable cause, lies at the foundation of the suit; and although it is in form a negative proposition, it is incumbent on the plaintiff to establish it by satisfactory proof. This kind of suit, by which the complainant in a criminal prosecution is made liable to an action for damages, at the suit of the person complained of, is not to be favored; it has a tendency to deter men who know of breaches of the law, from prosecuting offenders, thereby endangering the order and peace of the community. Absence of probable cause is essential; from want of probable cause, malice may be inferred; but from malice, even if express, want of probable cause cannot be inferred.

An ultimate acquittal of the offence charged, though necessary to be proved, is but a short step towards the maintenance of an action for malicious prosecution. Malice, and absence of any reasonable and probable cause, must also concur with an acquittal.

In the present case, the prosecution complained of was a complaint before a justice of the peace by whom the plaintiff was convicted; from this judgment he appealed, and on trial in the Court of Common Pleas was acquitted.

On the trial, it appeared from the pleadings and evidence, and was admitted, that the complaint was for an offence which the magistrate had, by law, jurisdiction to hear, decide and render a judgment in; also, that neither in the trial before the magistrate, nor in the trial in the Common Pleas, was the defendant a witness. On this case, the court ruled that such a conviction was proof of probable cause; or, to state the proposition with more precision, it negatived the plaintiff's leading and essential averment that the complaint was made without reasonable and probable cause, and that, for this reason, the action could not be maintained, and thereupon ordered a nonsuit.

The court are of opinion that this direction was right. The question of reasonable and probable cause, when the facts are not contested, is a question of law. And when the plaintiff had been convicted by a tribunal, constituted by law, with authority to render a judgment, which, if not appealed from, would have been conclusive of his guilt, and such judgment is not impeached on the ground of fraud,

128; Lammers v. Mason, 123 Minn. 204; Wilkerson v. McGhee, 163 Mo. App. 356, 153 Mo. App. 343; Humphries v. Edwards, 164 N. C. 154; Cole v. Reece, 47 Pa. Super. Ct. 212; Waring v. Hudspeth, 75 Wash. 534; Bailey v. Gollehon, 76 W. Va. 322.

[1] Only the opinion of the court is given.

conspiracy or subornation in its procurement, although afterwards reversed on another trial, it constitutes sufficient proof that the prosecution was not groundless, and to defeat an action for malicious prosecution. The case of Whitney v. Peckham, 15 Mass. 243, is directly in point, and we think it is well sustained by authorities.

It is said that the question of probable cause is a mixed question of law and fact, and that the facts should have been left to the jury. Here no fact material to the question was controverted, and then there was nothing to leave to a jury. *Exceptions overruled.*[1]

[1] *Conviction reversed.* — It is generally agreed that a conviction of the defendant in the criminal proceeding, although subsequently reversed, negatives the absence of probable cause, unless it is also made to appear that the conviction was procured by the fraud of the instigator of the criminal proceeding. Accordingly, a declaration alleging the conviction and its reversal, but not alleging any such fraud, is bad on demurrer. Reynolds v. Kennedy, 1 Wils. 232; Crescent Co. v. Butcher's Co., 120 U. S. 141; Knight v. Internat. R. Co., 61 Fed. 87; Blackman v. West Co., 126 Fed. 252; Casey v. Dorr, 94 Ark. 433; Carpenter v. Sibley, 153 Cal. 215; Goodrich v. Warner, 21 Conn. 432 (*semble*); McElroy v. Catholic Press Co., 254 Ill. 290; Dahlberg v. Grace, 178 Ill. App. 97; Adams v. Bicknell, 126 Ind. 210; Moffatt v. Fisher, 47 Ia. 473; Bowman v. Brown, 52 Ia. 437; Olson v. Neal, 63 Ia. 214; Barber v. Scott, 92 Ia. 52; White v. International Text Book Co., 156 Ia. 210; Ross v. Hixon, 46 Kan. 550, 555; Spring v. Besore, 12 B. Mon. 551; Kaye v. Kean, 18 B. Mon. 839; Duerr v. Ky. Co., 132 Ky. 228; Witham v. Gowen, 14 Me. 362; Payson v. Caswell, 22 Me. 212; Sidelinger v. Trowbridge, 113 Me. 537; Whitney v. Peckham, 15 Mass. 243; Dennehey v. Woodsum, 100 Mass. 195, 197; Phillips v. Kalamazoo, 53 Mich. 33 (see Spalding v. Lowe, 56 Mich. 366); Boogher v. Hough, 99 Mo. 183; Nehr v. Dobbs, 47 Neb. 863; Burt v. Place, 4 Wend. 591; Palmer v. Avery, 41 Barb. 290; Francisco v. Schmeelk, 156 App. Div. 335; Root v. Rose, 6 N. D. 575; Thienes v. Francis, 69 Or. 165; Herman v. Brookerhoff, 8 Watts, 240 (*semble*); Welch v. Boston R. Co., 14 R. I. 609; Hull v. Sprague, 23 R. I. 188; Memphis Co. v. Williamson, 9 Heisk. 314; Saunders v. Baldwin, 112 Va. 431; Topolewski v. Plankinton Packing Co., 143 Wis. 52. Compare Carpenter v. Hood, 172 Mich. 533; Platt v. Bonsall, 136 App. Div. 397.

As to fraudulently procured plea of guilty, see Johnson v. Girdwood, 7 Misc. 651; Holtman v. Bullock, 142 Ky. 335.

In a few jurisdictions the conviction, although set aside, is treated as conclusive evidence of probable cause, proof of fraud in its procurement being inadmissible. Hartshorn v. Smith, 104 Ga. 235; Clements v. Odorless Co., 67 Md. 461, 605 (Bryan, J., diss.); Parker v. Huntington, 7 Gray, 36; Griffis v. Sellars, 4 Dev. & B. 176.

In Virginia, on the contrary, a count alleging a conviction and its reversal is sufficient without any allegation in regard to fraud. Jones v. Finch, 84 Va. 204 (*semble*); Blanks v. Robinson, 1 Va. Dec. 600; Va. L. J. (1886) 398 (overruling Womack v. Circle, 32 Grat. 324). See Hale v. Boylen, 22 W. Va. 234.

Commitment for grand jury. — The holding of the defendant for the grand jury is *prima facie* evidence of probable cause. Miller v. Chicago Co., 41 Fed. 898; Ewing v. Sanford, 19 Ala. 605; Price Mercantile Co. v. Cuilla, 100 Ark. 316; Ganea v. Southern Co., 51 Cal. 140; Diemer v. Herber, 75 Cal. 287; Ritchey v. Davis, 11 Ia. 124; Ross v. Hixon, 46 Kan. 550; Danzer v. Nathan, 145 App. Div. 448; Giesener v. Healy, 86 Misc. 16; Ricord v. Central Co., 15 Nev. 167; Ash v. Marlow, 20 Ohio, 119; Raleigh v. Cook, 60 Tex. 438; Hale v. Boylen, 22 W. Va. 234.

Finding of indictment. — The finding of an indictment is *prima facie* evidence of probable cause. Garrard v. Willet, 4 J. J. Marsh. 628; Sharpe v. Johnston, 76 Mo. 660; Peck v. Chouteau, 91 Mo. 138; Wilkerson v. McGhee, 153 Mo. App. 343, 163 Mo. App. 356.

Failure of the prosecution. — The failure of the original prosecution is in some jurisdictions regarded as *prima facie* evidence of want of probable cause. Miller v. Chicago R. Co., 41 Fed. 898; Hanchey v. Brunson, 175 Ala. 236; Tucker v. Bart-

RAVENGA *v.* MACKINTOSH

IN THE KING'S BENCH, MAY 8, 1824.

Reported in 2 Barnewall & Cresswell, 693.

THIS was an action for a malicious arrest: plea not guilty. At the trial before Abbott, C. J., at the London sittings after last Hilary term, the jury was directed to find a verdict for the defendant, if they were of opinion that, at the time when the arrest was made, Mackintosh acted truly and sincerely upon the faith of the opinion given by his professional adviser, actually believing that Ravenga was personally liable, and that he might be lawfully arrested, and that he (Mackintosh) could recover in that action; but to find for the plaintiff, if they were of opinion that Mackintosh believed that he must fail in the action, and that he intended to use the opinion as a protection, in case the proceedings were afterwards called in question; and that he made the arrest, not with a view of obtaining his debt, but to compel the plaintiff to sanction the debentures. The jury found a verdict for the plaintiff, with £250 damages.[1]

The *Attorney-General* now moved for a new trial.

BAYLEY, J. I have no doubt that in this case there was a want of probable cause. I accede to the proposition, that if a party lays all the facts of his case fairly before counsel, and acts *bona fide* upon the opinion given by that counsel (however erroneous that opinion may be), he is not liable to an action of this description.[2] A party, how-

lett, 97 Kan. 163; Straus *v.* Young, 36 Md. 246; Whitfield *v.* Westbrook, 40 Miss. 311; Bostick *v.* Rutherford, 4 Hawks, 83; Downing *v.* Stone, 152 N. C. 525; Barhigh *v.* Tammany, 158 Pa. St. 545; McKenzie *v.* Canning, 42 Utah, 529 (but compare Smith *v.* Clark, 37 Utah, 116); Jones *v.* Finch, 84 Va. 204; Waring *v.* Hudspeth, 75 Wash. 534; Saunders *v.* First Nat. Bank, 85 Wash. 125; Brady *v.* Stiltner, 40 W. Va. 289; Fetty *v.* Huntington Loan Co., 70 W. Va. 688; Winn *v.* Peckham, 42 Wis. 493; Lawrence *v.* Cleary, 88 Wis. 473; Manz *v.* Klippel, 158 Wis. 557. In others there is no such presumption. Incledon *v.* Berry, 1 Camp. 203 n; Stewart *v.* Sonneborn, 98 U. S. 187, 195; Thompson *v.* Beacon Co., 56 Conn. 493; Plummer *v.* Collins, 1 Boyce, 281; Skidmore *v.* Bricker, 77 Ill. 164; Bitting *v.* Ten Eyck, 82 Ind. 421; Prine *v.* Singer Machine Co., 176 Mich. 300; Williams *v.* Vanmeter, 8 Mo. 339; Boeger *v.* Langenberg, 97 Mo. 390; Eckerle *v.* Higgins, 159 Mo. App. 177 (distinguishing nol. pros. and discharge on preliminary examination — see also Smith *v.* Glynn, (Mo.) 144 S. W. 149); Harris *v.* Quincy R. Co., 172 Mo. App. 261; Scott *v.* Simpson, 1 Sandf. 601; Central Light Co. *v.* Tyron, 42 Okl. 86; Eastman *v.* Monastes, 32 Or. 291; Bekkeland *v.* Lyons, 96 Tex. 255; McIntosh *v.* Wales, 21 Wyo. 397. See also Grorud *v.* Lossl, 48 Mont. 274.

Order vacating attachment as *prima facie* evidence of want of probable cause in action for malicious attachment, see Petruschke *v.* Kamerer, 131 Minn. 320.

[1] The statement of the evidence, the argument for the defendant, and the concurring opinion of HOLROYD, J., are omitted.

[2] Snow *v.* Allen, 1 Stark. 502; Abrath *v.* North Eastern Co., 11 Q. B. Div. 440, 11 App. Cas. 247; Scougall *v.* Stapleton, 12 Ont. 206; Stewart *v.* Sonneborn, 98 U. S. 187; Blunt *v.* Little, 3 Mason, 102; Cuthbert *v.* Galloway, 35 Fed. 466 (*semble*); Miller *v.* Chicago Co., 41 Fed. 898; Coggswell *v.* Bohn, 43 Fed. 411; Staunton *v.* Goshorn, 94 Fed. 52; McLeod *v.* McLeod, 73 Ala. 42; Jordan *v.* Alabama Co., 81 Ala. 220; Lemay *v.* Williams, 32 Ark. 166; Bliss *v.* Wyman, 7 Cal. 257; Jones *v.* Jones, 71 Cal. 89; Brooks *v.* Bradford, 4 Col. App. 410; Mark *v.*

ever, may take the opinions of six different persons, of which three are one way and three another. It is therefore a question for the jury, whether he acted *bona fide* on the opinion, believing that he had a cause of action. The jury in this case have found, and there was abundant evidence to justify them in drawing the conclusion, that the defendant did not act *bona fide*, and that he did not believe that he had any cause of action whatever. Assuming that the defendant's belief that he had a cause of action would amount to a probable cause, still, after the jury have found that he did not believe that he had any cause of action whatever, the judge would have been bound to say, that he had not reasonable or probable cause of action.

Rule refused.[1]

Rich, 43 App. D. C. 182; Joiner *v.* Ocean Co., 86 Ga. 238; Baker *v.* Langley, 3 Ga. App. 751; Ross *v.* Innis, 26 Ill. 259; Ames *v.* Snider, 69 Ill. 376; Barrett *v.* Spaids, 70 Ill. 408; Brown *v.* Smith, 83 Ill. 291; Roy *v.* Goings, 112 Ill. 656; Aldridge *v.* Churchill, 28 Ind. 62; Paddock *v.* Watts, 116 Ind. 146; Adams *v.* Bicknell, 126 Ind. 210; Mesher *v.* Iddings, 72 Ia. 553; Schippel *v.* Norton, 38 Kan. 567; Dyer *v.* Singer Machine Co., 164 Ky. 538; Carrigan *v.* Graham, 166 Ky. 333; Stevens *v.* Fassett, 27 Me. 266; Soule *v.* Winslow, 66 Me. 447; Cooper *v.* Utterbach, 37 Md. 282; Hyde *v.* Greuch, 62 Md. 577; Torsch *v.* Dell, 88 Md. 459; Stone *v.* Swift, 4 Pick. 389; Monaghan *v.* Cox, 155 Mass. 487; Stanton *v.* Hart, 27 Mich. 539; Perry *v.* Sulier, 92 Mich. 72; Moore *v.* Northern Co., 37 Minn. 147; Boyd *v.* Mendenhall, 53 Minn. 274; Alexander *v.* Harrison, 38 Mo. 258; Burris *v.* North, 64 Mo. 426; Whitfield *v.* Westbrook, 40 Miss. 311; Grorud *v.* Lossl, 48 Mont. 274; Jonasen *v.* Kennedy, 39 Neb. 313; Magowan *v.* Rickey, 64 N. J. Law, 402; Hall *v.* Suydam, 6 Barb. 83; Richardson *v.* Virtue, 2 Hun, 208; Turner *v.* Dinnegar, 20 Hun, 465; Beal *v.* Robeson, 8 Ired. 276; Ash *v.* Marlow, 20 Ohio, 119; El Reno Gas Co. *v.* Spurgeon, 30 Okl. 88; Sims *v.* Jay, 53 Okl. 183; Walter *v.* Sample, 25 Pa. St. 275; Smith *v.* Walter, 125 Pa. St. 453; Bartlett *v.* Brown, 6 R. I. 37; Jackson *v.* Bell, 5 S. D. 257; Kendrick *v.* Cypert, 10 Humph. 291; St. Johnsbury Co. *v.* Hunt, 59 Vt. 294; Forbes *v.* Hagman, 75 Va. 168; Saunders *v.* Baldwin, 112 Va. 431; Hightower *v.* Union Trust Co., 88 Wash. 179; Sutton *v.* McConnell, 46 Wis. 269; Manz *v.* Klippel, 158 Wis. 557 *Accord.*

But see Brewer *v.* Jacobs, 22 Fed. 217; Stewart *v.* Mulligan, 11 Ga. App. 660; Smith *v.* Glynn, (Mo.) 144 S. W. 149; Downing *v.* Stone, 152 N. C. 525; Ramsey *v.* Arrott, 64 Tex. 320; Glasgow *v.* Owen, 69 Tex. 167; Shannon *v.* Jones, 76 Tex. 141; Tiedeman's Note, 21 Am. L. Reg. N. S. 582.

The advice must be that of a lawyer, and not a layman. Murphy *v.* Larson, 77 Ill. 172; McCullough *v.* Rice, 59 Ind. 580; Olmstead *v.* Partridge, 16 Gray, 381; Beal *v.* Robeson, 8 Ired. 276. Even though the layman be a justice of the peace. Stephens *v.* Gravit, 136 Ky. 479; Coleman *v.* Heurich, 2 Mack. 189; Straus *v.* Young, 36 Md. 246; Monaghan *v.* Cox, 155 Mass. 487 (*semble*); Gee *v.* Culver, 12 Or. 228; Brobst *v.* Ruff, 100 Pa. St. 91; Sutton *v.* McConnell, 46 Wis. 269. But see Ball *v.* Rawles, 93 Cal. 222; Sisk *v.* Hurst, 1 W. Va. 53. Compare Marks *v.* Hastings, 101 Ala. 165.

The lawyer must have no personal interest in the controversy. Smith *v.* King, 62 Conn. 515; White *v.* Carr, 71 Me. 555.

In Hazzard *v.* Flury, 120 N. Y. 223, the Court of Appeals held that mistaken advice of counsel upon a point of law would not justify the client, since every one is presumed to know the law. Surely that much-abused fiction has seldom been so glaringly perverted in behalf of injustice. See Singer Machine Co. *v.* Dyer, 156 Ky. 156.

[1] Vann *v.* McCreary, 77 Cal. 434; Boyd *v.* Mendenhall, 53 Minn. 274; Acton *v.* Coffman, 74 Ia. 17; Johnson *v.* Miller, 82 Ia. 693; Sharpe *v.* Johnston, 76 Mo. 660; Ames *v.* Rathbun, 37 How. Pr. 289; Laird *v.* Taylor, 66 Barb. 139; Davenport *v.* Lynch, 6 Jones, (N. C.) 545; Powell *v.* Woodbury, 85 Vt. 504 *Accord.*

Withholding facts from or unfair statement to counsel. Fowlkes *v.* Lewis, 10 Ala. App. 543; Rothschach *v.* Diven, 97 Kan. 38; Indianapolis Traction Co. *v.* Henby,

MITCHELL *v.* JENKINS

In the King's Bench, November 11, 1833.

Reported in 5 *Barnewall & Adolphus,* 588.

This was an action on the case for a malicious arrest.

At the trial, before Taunton, J., at the last Summer Assizes for the county of Devon, it appeared, that the plaintiff was indebted to the defendant in the sum of £45, for one year's composition of tithe; and that the sum of £16 5*s*. was due to the plaintiff from the defendant; that the defendant, under the advice of his attorney, arrested the plaintiff for the whole sum of £45, instead of for the balance, after deducting the sum of £16 5*s*. The defendant, on finding out that he was mistaken in point of law, and that he should only have arrested for the balance, discontinued the action.

There was no evidence at all of malice in fact; but the learned judge told the jury, that, as the plaintiff ought not, by law, to have been arrested for more than the balance, the law implied malice; and that the only question for their consideration was, the amount of damages; upon which a verdict was found for the plaintiff for £20.

A rule had been obtained, in a former term, calling on the plaintiff to show cause why that verdict should not be set aside, and a new trial had; [1] against which —

Follett now showed cause.

Coleridge, Serjt., and *Bere*, contra.

Denman, C. J. Every arrest by a creditor for more than is due, is, in some sense, a wrongful act. By statute, if it be made without reasonable or probable cause, though with an entire absence of malice, the party arresting may be deprived of his costs, and at common law, if the party arrested has suffered damage to a greater extent than those costs, he may, if the arrest was also made maliciously, bring his action on the case. In that action, however, it is still incumbent on the plaintiff to allege and to prove malice as an independent fact; though it may in some instances be fairly inferred by the jury from the arrest itself, and the circumstances under which it is made, without any other proof. They, however, are to decide, as a matter of fact, whether there be malice or not. I have always understood the question of reasonable or probable cause on the facts found to be a question for the opinion

178 Ind. 239; Lammers *v.* Mason, 123 Minn. 204; Bowers *v.* Walker, 192 Mo. App. 230; Lathrop *v.* Mathers, 143 App. Div. 376; Baer *v.* Chambers, 67 Wash. 357; Rogers *v.* Van Eps, 143 Wis. 396; Boyer *v.* Bugher, 19 Wyo. 463.

Must state facts which might have been ascertained with reasonable diligence. Weddington *v.* White, 148 Ky. 671; Virtue *v.* Creamery Mfg. Co., 123 Minn. 17; Duffy *v.* Scheerger, 91 Neb. 511. *Contra* — enough to make full and fair disclosure of known facts, Roby *v.* Smith, 40 Okl. 280.

[1] The statement of facts is taken from 3 L. J. K. B. n. s. 35. The arguments of counsel and the concurring opinions of Patteson and Taunton, JJ., are omitted.

of the court, and malice to be altogether a question for the jury.[1] Here, the question of malice having been wholly withdrawn from the consideration of the jury, there ought to be a new trial.

PARKE, J. I am also of opinion that there ought to be a new trial, on the ground that the learned judge withdrew altogether from the consideration of the jury the question of malice. I have always understood, since the case of Johnstone *v.* Sutton, 1 T. R. 510, which was decided long before I was in the profession, that no point of law was more clearly settled than that in every action for a malicious prosecution or arrest, the plaintiff must prove what is averred in the declaration, viz. that the prosecution or arrest was malicious and without reasonable or probable cause: if there be reasonable or probable cause, no malice, however distinctly proved, will make the defendant liable; but when there is no reasonable or probable cause, it is for the jury to infer malice from the facts proved. That is a question in all cases for their consideration, and it having in this instance been withdrawn from them, it is impossible to say whether they might or might not have come to the conclusion that the arrest was malicious. It was for them to decide it, and not for the judge. I can conceive a case where there are mutual accounts between parties, and where an arrest for the whole sum claimed by the plaintiff would not be malicious; for example, the plaintiff might know that the set-off was open to dispute, and that there was reasonable ground for disputing it. In that case, though it might afterwards appear that the set-off did exist, the arrest would not be malicious. The term "malice" in this form of action is not to be considered in the sense of spite or hatred against an individual, but of *malus animus*, and as denoting that the party is actu-

[1] Willans *v.* Taylor, 6 Bing. 183; Busst *v.* Gibbons, 30 L. J. Ex. N. S. 75; Brown *v.* Hawkes, [1891] 2 Q. B. 718; Stewart *v.* Sonneborn, 98 U. S. 187; Brown *v.* Selfridge, 224 U. S. 189; Sanders *v.* Palmer, 55 Fed. 217; Staunton *v.* Goshorn, 94 Fed. 52; Gulsby *v.* Louisville R. Co., 167 Ala. 122; Louisville R. Co. *v.* Stephenson, 6 Ala. App. 578; Ball *v.* Rawles, 93 Cal. 222; Johnson *v.* Southern R. Co., 157 Cal. 333; Smith *v.* King, 62 Conn. 515; Carroll *v.* Perry, 43 App. D. C. 363; Boyd *v.* Mendenhall, 53 Minn. 274; Helwig *v.* Beckner, 149 Ind. 131; Indianapolis Traction Co. *v.* Henby, 178 Ind. 239; Lawrence *v.* Leathers, 31 Ind. App. 414; Henderson *v.* McGruder, 49 Ind. App. 682; Atchison Co. *v.* Allen, 70 Kan. 743; Michael *v.* Matson, 81 Kan. 360; Metrop. Co. *v.* Miller, 114 Ky. 754; Moser *v.* Fable, 164 Ky. 517; Medcalfe *v.* Brooklyn Co., 45 Md. 198; Thelin *v.* Dorsey, 59 Md. 539; Campbell *v.* Baltimore R. Co., 97 Md. 341; Bishop *v.* Frantz, 125 Md. 183; Good *v.* French, 115 Mass. 201; Bartlett *v.* Hawley, 38 Minn. 308; Shafer *v.* Hertzig, 92 Minn. 171; Williams *v.* Pullman Co., 129 Minn. 97; Harris *v.* Quincy R. Co., 172 Mo. App. 261; McNulty *v.* Walker, 64 Miss. 198; Cohn *v.* Saidel, 71 N. H. 558; Magowan *v.* Rickey, 64 N. J. Law, 402; Hartdorn *v.* Webb Mfg. Co., (N. J.) 75 Atl. 893; Heyne *v.* Blair, 62 N. Y. 19; Fagnan *v.* Knox, 66 N. Y. 525; Anderson *v.* How, 116 N. Y. 336; L. I. Union *v.* Seitz, 180 N. Y. 243; Viele *v.* Gray, 10 Abb. Pr. 1; McCarthy *v.* Barrett, 144 App. Div. 727; Galley *v.* Brennan, 156 App. Div. 443; Stanford *v.* Grocery Co., 143 N. C. 419; Humphries *v.* Edwards, 164 N. C. 154; Dunnington *v.* Loeser, (Okl.) 149 Pac. 1161; Leahey *v.* March, 155 Pa. St. 458; Roessing *v.* Pittsburgh R. Co., 226 Pa. St. 523; McCoy *v.* Kalbach, 242 Pa. St. 123; Cooper *v.* Flemming, 114 Tenn. 40; Landa *v.* Obert, 45 Tex. 539; Finigan *v.* Sullivan, 65 Wash. 625; Bailey *v.* Gollehon, 76 W. Va. 322 *Accord.* But see Wilson *v.* Thurlow, 156 Ia. 656; Griffin *v.* Dearborn, 210 Mass. 308.

ated by improper and indirect motives.[1] That would not be the case where, there being an unsettled account, with items on both sides, one of the parties, believing *bona fide* that a certain sum was due to him, arrested his debtor for that sum, though it afterwards appeared that a less sum was due; nor where a party made such an arrest, acting *bona fide* under a wrong notion of the law and pursuant to legal advice. The question of malice having in this case been wholly withdrawn from the jury, I think the rule for a new trial must be made absolute. *Rule absolute.*[2]

[1] Abrath *v.* North Eastern Co., 11 Q. B. Div. 440, 448, 455; Wiggin *v.* Coffin, 3 Story, 1; Johnson *v.* Ebberts, 11 Fed. 129, 6 Sawy. 538, s. c.; Brewer *v.* Jacobs, 22 Fed. 217; Gulsby *v.* Louisville R. Co., 167 Ala. 122; Hammond *v.* Rowley, 86 Conn. 6; Coleman *v.* Allen, 79 Ga. 637; South Western Co. *v.* Mitchell, 80 Ga. 438; Stewart *v.* Mulligan, 11 Ga. App. 660; McElroy *v.* Catholic Press Co., 254 Ill. 290; White *v.* International Text Book Co., 156 Ia. 210; Foltz *v.* Buck, 89 Kan. 381; Metrop. Co. *v.* Miller, 114 Ky. 754; Pullen *v.* Glidden, 66 Me. 202; Wills *v.* Noyes, 12 Pick. 324; Mitchell *v.* Wall, 111 Mass. 492; Ross *v.* Langworthy, 13 Neb. 492; Callahan *v.* Kelso, 170 Mo. App. 338; Gee *v.* Culver, 13 Or. 598; Squires *v.* Job, 50 Pa. Super. Ct. 289; Culberston *v.* Cabeen, 29 Tex. 247, 256; Sebastian *v.* Cheney, (Texas) 24 S. W. 970; Barron *v.* Mason, 31 Vt. 189, 198; Forbes *v.* Hagman, 75 Va. 168; Spear *v.* Hiles, 67 Wis. 350; Boyer *v.* Bugher, 19 Wyo. 463 *Accord.*

In Abrath *v.* North Eastern Co., *supra*, malice was defined by Brett, M. R., p. 448, as "a malicious intention in the mind of the defendant, that is, not with the mere intention of carrying the law into effect," and by Bowen, L. J., as "a malicious spirit, that is, an indirect and improper motive, and not in furtherance of justice." See also especially Pullen *v.* Glidden, and Johnson *v.* Ebberts, cited *supra* in this note; Magowan *v.* Rickey, 64 N. J. Law, 402; Peterson *v.* Reisdorph, 49 Neb. 529; Nobb *v.* White, 103 Ia. 352; Brooks *v.* Bradford, 4 Col. App. 410; Jackson *v.* Bell, 5 S. D. 257.

Definitions of "malice" in this connection, see Fowlkes *v.* Lewis, 10 Ala. App. 543; Redgate *v.* Southern R. Co., 24 Cal. App. 573; Cincinnati R. Co. *v.* Cecil, 164 Ky. 377; Lammers *v.* Mason, 123 Minn. 204; Downing *v.* Stone, 152 N. C. 525; Wright *v.* Harris, 160 N. C. 542.

[2] Farmer *v.* Darling, 4 Burr. 1971; Busst *v.* Gibbons, 30 L. J. Ex. N. S. 75; Coulter *v.* Dublin Co., 60 L. T. 180; Hicks *v.* Faulkner, 46 L. T. Rep. 127 (affirming s. c. 8 Q. B. D. 167); Wheeler *v.* Nesbitt, 24 How. 544; Stewart *v.* Sonneborn, 98 U. S. 191; Wiggin *v.* Coffin, 3 Story, 1; Burnap *v.* Albert, Taney, 244; Benson *v.* McCoy, 36 Ala. 710; Lunsford *v.* Dietrich, 93 Ala. 565; Bozeman *v.* Shaw, 37 Ark. 160; Levy *v.* Brannan, 39 Cal. 485; Harkrader *v.* Moore, 44 Cal. 144; Porter *v.* White, 5 Mackey, 180; Harpham *v.* Whitney, 77 Ill. 32; Krug *v.* Ward, 77 Ill. 603; Boyd *v.* Mendenhall, 53 Minn. 274; Frankfurter *v.* Bryan, 12 Ill. App. 549; Gardiner *v.* Mays, 24 Ill. App. 286; Newell *v.* Downs, 8 Blackf. 523; Oliver *v.* Pate, 43 Ind. 132; Ritchey *v.* Davis, 11 Ia. 124; Atchison Co. *v.* Watson, 37 Kan. 773; Gourgues *v.* Howard, 27 La. Ann. 339; Humphries *v.* Parker, 52 Me. 502; Medcalfe *v.* Brooklyn Co., 45 Md. 198; Mitchell *v.* Wall, 111 Mass. 492; Bartlett *v.* Hawley, 38 Minn. 308; Greenwade *v.* Mills, 31 Miss. 464; Sharpe *v.* Johnston, 59 Mo. 557; Finley *v.* St. Louis Co., 99 Mo. 559; March *v.* Vandiver, 181 Mo. App. 281; McKown *v.* Hunter, 30 N. Y. 625; Farnam *v.* Feeley, 56 N. Y. 451; Heyne *v.* Blair, 62 N. Y. 19; Thompson *v.* Lumley, 50 How. Pr. 105; Voorhes *v.* Leonard, 1 Th. & C. 148; Johnson *v.* Chambers, 10 Ired. 287; Gee *v.* Culver, 12 Or. 228, 13 Or. 598; Schofield *v.* Ferrers, 47 Pa. St. 194; Dietz *v.* Langfitt, 63 Pa. St. 234; Gilliford *v.* Windel, 108 Pa. St. 142; Bell *v.* Graham, 1 N. & M'C. 278; Campbell *v.* O'Bryan, 9 Rich. 204; Willis *v.* Knox, 5 S. C. 474; Caldwell *v.* Bennett, 22 S. C. 1; Evans *v.* Thompson, 12 Heisk. 534; Stansell *v.* Cleveland, 64 Tex. 660; Shannon *v.* Jones, 76 Tex. 141; Barron *v.* Mason, 31 Vt. 189; Carleton *v.* Taylor, 50 Vt. 220; Scott *v.* Shelor, 28 Grat. 891; Forbes *v.* Hagman, 75 Va. 168 *Accord.*

But see, *contra*, Wilson *v.* Bowen, 64 Mich. 133.

HADDRICK *v.* HESLOP

IN THE QUEEN'S BENCH, TRINITY TERM, 1848.

Reported in 12 Queen's Bench Reports, 267.

CASE for maliciously and without reasonable and probable cause indicting the plaintiff for perjury. Averment that the plaintiff was tried and acquitted, and judgment given that he should depart without day, as by record appeared, &c.

Plea, by Heslop: Not guilty. Issue thereon.

On the trial, before Wightman, J., at the Durham Summer Assizes, 1847, it was shown, on the part of the plaintiff, that the now defendant Heslop received the account of Haddrick's evidence from another party, and then stated that he would indict Haddrick for perjury; and that his informant thereupon expressed an opinion that there was no ground for such indictment; on which Heslop said that, even if there were not sufficient grounds for the indictment, it would tie up the mouths of Hinde and Haddrick for a time, and that he would move for a new trial. No witnesses were called for the defence. The learned judge asked the jury whether Heslop believed that there was reasonable ground for indicting, and whether he had indicted from malice. The jury answered that Heslop did not so believe; and, as to the malice, they said that they thought that the word "malice" was strong, but that they thought the defendant had indicted from an improper motive. The learned judge then decided that the indictment was without reasonable or probable cause, and told the jury that they might infer malice from the improper motive. Verdict for the plaintiff.

In Michaelmas term (November 5th), 1847,

Bliss moved for a new trial, on the grounds of misdirection.[1]

First: the question of the defendant's belief ought not to have been left to the jury. It is for the judge to decide whether there was reasonable and probable cause. It is true that he may, in order to decide this, obtain the opinion of the jury upon facts which, when found, he himself is to act upon in deciding as to the reasonableness and probability. But belief is not such a fact: it is material as to the malice, but there may well exist reasonable and probable cause constituted by facts from which the defendant has wrongly drawn an inference of want of cause. It is otherwise where the belief becomes material as an ingredient in the question of *mala fides:* that was the case in Ravenga *v.* Mackintosh, where the defendant rested his defence upon the ground that he had acted *bona fide* on a legal opinion, and the jury found that he had not so acted. Nothing should be left to the jury but "the truth of the facts proved, and the justice of the inferences to be drawn from such facts;" and it is only as affecting those questions that the belief of the party is material.

[1] The statement of facts and the argument for the defendant are abridged; the concurring opinions of Coleridge, Wightman, and Erle, JJ., are omitted.

Next: the jury were misdirected as to malice. The mere fact that the defendant had an indirect motive, however improper, in instituting the prosecution does not show malice. The malice required in this action is express malice in fact, not mere malice in law. In the judgment of Lords Mansfield and Loughborough, in Johnstone *v.* Sutton,[1] it is said:[2] "From the want of probable cause, malice may be, and most commonly is, implied. The knowledge of the defendant is also implied." The jury ought therefore to have been told that the indirect motive was quite consistent with absence of malice, unless the defendant knew (not simply believed) that there was no probable cause, or unless there was some evidence of express malice towards the plaintiff.

LORD DENMAN, C. J. It would be quite outrageous if, where a party is proved to believe that a charge is unfounded, it were to be held that he could have reasonable and probable cause. Reference has been made to Turner *v.* Ambler, 10 Q. B. 252, where there was an allusion to a decision of my Brother Maule, upheld afterwards in the Common Pleas,[3] to the effect that reasonable and probable cause cannot exist without belief. There may possibly be some difficulty in distinguishing the case last mentioned from some others: but I think that belief is essential to the existence of reasonable and probable cause: I do not mean abstract belief, but a belief upon which a party acts. Where there is no such belief, to hold that the party had reasonable and probable cause would be destructive of common sense.[4] Proof of the absence of belief is almost always involved in the proof of malice. In Turner *v.* Ambler there was no point directly made at the trial as to want of belief: the only question was whether the facts of themselves bore out the probability and reasonableness. But, where a plaintiff takes upon himself to prove that, assuming the facts to be as the defendant contends, still the defendant did not believe them, we ought

[1] In Exch. Ch. 1 T. R. 510, reversing the judgment of the Court of Exchequer in Sutton *v.* Johnstone, 1 T. R. 493. Judgment of Exch. Ch. affirmed on error, in Dom. Proc. 1 T. R. 784. S. C. 1 Bro. P. C. 76 (2d ed.).

[2] 1 T. R. 545.

[3] The case alluded to is perhaps Broad *v.* Ham, 5 B. N. C. 722. By the report of S. C. in 8 Scott, 40, the cause appears to have been tried before Maule, B. (Reporter's note.)

[4] Broad *v.* Ham, 5 B. N. C. 722; Turner *v.* Ambler, 10 Q. B. 252; Roret *v.* Lewis, 5 D. & L. 371; Hinton *v.* Heather, 14 M. & W. 131; Williams *v.* Banks, 1 F. & F. 557; Chatfield *v.* Comerford, 4 F. & F. 1008; Shrosbery *v.* Osmaston, 37 L. T. Rep. 792; Steed *v.* Knowles, 79 Ala. 446; Harkrader *v.* Moore, 44 Cal. 144; Ball *v.* Rawles, 93 Cal. 222; Galloway *v.* Stewart, 49 Ind. 156; Donnelly *v.* Burkett, 75 Ia. 613; Humphries *v.* Parker, 52 Me. 502, 505; Mitchell *v.* Wall, 111 Mass. 492; Bartlett *v.* Hawley, 38 Minn. 308; Peck *v.* Chouteau, 91 Mo. 138; Chicago Co. *v.* Kriski, 30 Neb. 215; Howard *v.* Thompson, 21 Wend. 319; Burlingame *v.* Burlingame, 8 Cow. 141; Fagnan *v.* Knox, 66 N. Y. 525; Anderson *v.* How, 116 N. Y. 336; Wass *v.* Stephens, 128 N. Y. 123; Wilson *v.* King, 39 N.Y. Super. Ct. 384; Linitzky *v.* Gorman, 146 N. Y. Supp. 313; Thienes *v.* Francis, 69 Or. 165; King *v.* Colvin, 11 R. I. 582; Scott *v.* Shelor, 28 Grat. 891; Forbes *v.* Hagman, 75 Va. 168; Spear *v.* Hiles, 67 Wis. 350; Baker *v*, Kilpatrick, 7 Br. Col. L. R. 150; Harcourt *v.* Aiken, 22 N. Zeal. L. R. 389; Clift *v.* Birmingham, 4 W. Aust. L. R. 20 *Accord.*

not to entertain any doubt that it is proper to leave the question of belief as a fact to the jury. It is not absolutely necessary that this belief should be the motive on which he acted: he may act from malice, and yet, if there was reasonable and probable cause in which he believed, the case against him must fail.

Rule refused as to misdirection.

VANDERBILT *v.* MATHIS

SUPREME COURT, CITY OF NEW YORK, FEBRUARY, 1856.

Reported in 5 *Duer*, 304.

By the Court, BOSWORTH, J.[1] — To maintain an action for malicious prosecution, three facts, if controverted, must be established:

1. That the prosecution is at an end, and was determined in favor of the plaintiff.
2. The want of probable cause.
3. Malice.

In such an action, it is necessary to give some evidence of the want of probable cause. It is insufficient to prove a mere acquittal; that, alone, is not *prima facie* evidence of the want of probable cause. Gorton *v.* De Angelis, 6 Wend. 418.

It is equally essential, that the former prosecution should appear to have been maliciously instituted. Malice may be inferred from the want of probable cause, but such an inference is one which a jury is not required to make, at all events, merely because they may find the absence of probable cause.

Unless the evidence, in relation to the circumstances under which the prosecution was ended, and that given to establish the want of probable cause, justify the inference of malice, other evidence, in support of it, must be given.

Evidence as to the conduct of the defendant, in the course of the transaction, his declarations on the subject, and any forwardness and activity in exposing the plaintiff by a publication, are properly admitted to prove malice. Such evidence must be given as will justify a jury in finding the existence of malice.

The rule is uniformly stated, that, to maintain an action, for a former prosecution, it must be shown to have been without probable cause, and malicious. Vanduzer *v.* Linderman, 10 J. R. 110; Murray *v.* Long, 1 Wend. 140; 2d Stark. Ev. 494; Willans *v.* Taylor, 6 Bing. 183.

The judge, at the trial, charged, that the fact, that the plaintiff was discharged before the magistrate showed, *prima facie*, that there was no probable cause for the arrest, and shifted the burden of proof from

[1] Only the opinion of the court is given.

the plaintiff to the defendant, who was bound to show, affirmatively, that there was probable cause.

He was requested to charge, "that the discharge of Vanderbilt was not *prima facie* evidence of the want of probable cause." This he refused to do. To this refusal to charge, and to the charge as made, the defendant excepted.

He also charged, "that, if probable cause is made out, the question of malice becomes immaterial, except as bearing on the question of damages."

"This question of malice, in fact, supposing that probable cause did not exist, is material only as affecting the question of damages."

He was requested to charge, "that the jury could not find a verdict for the plaintiff, unless he has proved that there was no probable cause for the complaint, and not even then, unless they believed, from the evidence, that, in making the complaint, the defendant acted from malicious motives." This the judge declined to do, and to his refusal to so charge the defendant excepted.

Although the evidence which establishes the want of probable cause may be, and generally is, such as to justify the inference of malice, yet we understand the rule to be, that when it is a just and proper inference from all the facts and circumstances of the case, upon all the evidence given in the cause, "that the defendant was not actuated by any improper motives, but only from an honest desire to being a supposed offender to justice, the action will not lie, because such facts and circumstances disprove that which is of the essence of the action, viz., the malice of the defendant in pressing the charge."

In Bulkley *v.* Smith, 2 Duer, 271, the court stated the rule to be, "that, in order to maintain a suit for a malicious prosecution, the plaintiff is bound to prove the entire want of a probable cause for the accusation, and the actual malice of the defendant in making it. Malice is a question of fact, which, when the case turns upon it, must be decided by the jury."

Story, J., in Wiggin *v.* Coffin, instructed the jury that two things must concur, to entitle a plaintiff to recover in such an action: "The first is, the want of probable cause for the prosecution; the second is, malice in the defendant in carrying on the prosecution. If either ground fail, there is an end of the suit."

In Vanduzer *v.* Linderman, 10 J. R. 110, the court said: "No action lies, merely for bringing a suit against a person without sufficient ground. To maintain a suit for a former prosecution, it must appear to have been without cause, and malicious."

If the charge must be understood to mean, that if the want of probable cause was established, the plaintiff was entitled to recover, although the jury should believe, from the whole evidence, that, in making the complaint, the defendant did not act from malicious motives, then we deem it to be erroneous. This construction is the only one, of which the language of the instruction appears to be susceptible;

for the judge, in charging the jury stated that the "question of malice in fact, supposing that probable cause did not exist, is material only as affecting the question of damages."

Malice in fact, is that kind of malice which is to be proved. When malice may be, and is inferred, from the want of probable cause, it is actual malice which is thus proved.

There is no theoretical malice which can satisfy this rule, and which can coexist with the established fact, that the prosecution was instituted in an honest belief of the plaintiff's guilt, and with no other motives than to bring a supposed offender to justice.

The question of malice may be a turning-point of the controversy, in an action of this nature.

The want of probable cause may be shown, and yet upon the whole evidence, in any given case, it may be a fair question for the determination of a jury, whether the defendant was actuated by malice. If the whole evidence is such, that a jury cannot properly doubt the honesty and purity of the motive which induced the former prosecution, and if they fully believe that it was instituted from good motives, and in the sincere conviction that the plaintiff was guilty of the offence charged, and without malice, the defendant would be entitled to a verdict.

The charge made, and which was excepted to, must be deemed to have been made, to give the jury a rule of action, in disposing of the case upon the whole evidence. We think it was not only calculated to mislead, but was erroneous.

A new trial must be granted, with costs to abide the event.[1]

[1] Brown *v.* Hawkes, [1891] 2 Q. B. 718; Grant *v.* Book, 25 Nova Scotia, 266 *Accord.*

Malice may be inferred from want of probable cause. Hanchey *v.* Brunson, 175 Ala. 236; Hawkins *v.* Collins, 5 Ala. App. 522; Fowlkes *v.* Lewis, 10 Ala. App. 543; Price *v.* Morris, 122 Ark. 382; Redgate *v.* Southern R. Co., 24 Cal. App. 573; Stewart *v.* Mulligan, 11 Ga. App. 660; Holliday *v.* Coleman, 12 Ga. App. 779; McElroy *v.* Catholic Press Co., 254 Ill. 290; Pontius *v.* Kimball, 56 Ind. App. 144; Singer Machine Co. *v.* Dyer, 156 Ky. 156; Mertens *v.* Mueller, 119 Md. 525; Griffin *v.* Dearborn, 210 Mass. 308; Moscob *v.* Frank Ridlon Co., 216 Mass. 193; Krzyszke *v.* Kamin, 163 Mich. 290; Bowers *v.* Walker, 192 Mo. App. 230; Grorud *v.* Lossl, 48 Mont. 274; Galley *v.* Brennan, 156 App. Div. 443; Kellogg *v.* Ford, 70 Or. 213; Cole *v.* Reece, 47 Pa. Super. Ct. 212; Keener *v.* Jeffries, 54 Pa. Super. Ct. 553; Tufshinsky *v.* Pittsburgh R. Co., 61 Pa. Super. Ct. 121; Fetty *v.* Huntington Loan Co., 70 W. Va. 688.

It is not a necessary inference. Hanowitz *v.* Great Northern R. Co., 122 Minn. 241; Smith *v.* Glynn, (Mo.) 144 S. W. 149; Chicago R. Co. *v.* Holliday, 30 Okl. 680; Boyer *v.* Bugher, 19 Wyo. 463.

It is not inferred from failure to prosecute, Malloy *v.* Chicago R. Co., 34 S. D. 330, nor from discharge or acquittal. Waring *v.* Hudspeth, 75 Wash. 534.

Want of probable cause is not to be inferred from malice. Runo *v.* Williams, 162 Cal. 444; Redgate *v.* Southern R. Co., 24 Cal. App. 573; Plummer *v.* Collins, 1 Boyce, 281; McElroy *v.* Catholic Press Co., 254 Ill. 290; Shadden *v.* Butler, 164 Ia. 1; Hudson *v.* Nolen, 142 Ky. 824; Chapman *v.* Nash, 121 Md. 608; Griffin *v.* Dearborn, 210 Mass. 308; Callahan *v.* Kelso, 170 Mo. App. 338; Motsinger *v.* Sink, 168 N. C. 548; Kellogg *v.* Ford, 70 Or. 213; McCoy *v.* Kalbach, 242 Pa. St. 123; Boyer *v.* Bugher, 19 Wyo. 463; McIntosh *v.* Wales, 21 Wyo. 397. But see Squires *v.* Job, 50 Pa. Super. Ct. 289.

MACK *v.* SHARP

SUPREME COURT, MICHIGAN, DECEMBER 14, 1904.

Reported in 138 *Michigan Reports*, 448.

MONTGOMERY, J.[1] The court also ruled throughout the case that in this action the defendant was not at liberty to prove that the plaintiff was in fact guilty of the criminal offence imputed to him in the prosecution instituted by the defendant. It is well established by authority that in an action for malicious prosecution it is a complete defence to show that the plaintiff was in fact guilty of the offence charged against him by defendant, and this though the proof of guilt is furnished by evidence not known to defendant when the prosecution against the plaintiff was instituted. This testimony is not in such case offered in support of probable cause, but to show that the plaintiff has suffered no wrong by his arrest. The law considers that, if a criminal is fortunate enough to escape conviction, he should rest content with his good luck, and not belabor one who suspected his guilt and acted accordingly. As was said in Newton *v.* Weaver, 13 R. I. 617: —

" The action for malicious prosecution was designed for the benefit of the innocent, and not of the guilty. It matters not whether there was proper cause for the prosecution, or how malicious may have been the motives of the prosecutor, if the accused is guilty he has no legal cause for complaint."

See, also, Threefoot *v.* Nuckols, 68 Miss. 123; Whitehurst *v.* Ward, 12 Ala. 264; Parkhurst *v.* Masteller, 57 Iowa, 478; Turner *v.* Dinnegar, 20 Hun, 465; Lancaster *v.* McKay, 103 Ky. 616.

The judgment is reversed, and a new trial ordered.

The other Justices concurred.[2]

CHAPMAN *v.* PICKERSGILL

IN THE COMMON PLEAS, MICHAELMAS TERM, 1762.

Reported in 2 *Wilson*, 145.

ACTION upon the case for falsely and maliciously suing out a commission of bankrupt against the plaintiff, who declared upon three counts; in the first, having stated his honesty, he alleges that the de-

[1] Only a portion of the opinion is given.

[2] Whitehurst *v.* Ward, 12 Ala. 264; Shannon *v.* Simms, 146 Ala. 673; Whipple *v.* Gorsuch, 82 Ark. 252; Adams *v.* Lisher, 3 Blackf. 241; Bruley *v.* Rose, 57 Ia. 651; Parkhurst *v.* Masteller, 57 Ia. 474; White *v.* International Text Book Co., 156 Ia. 210; Lancaster *v.* McKay, 103 Ky. 616, 624; Bacon *v.* Towne, 4 Cush. 217, 241; Threefoot *v.* Nuckols, 68 Miss. 116; Morris *v.* Corson, 7 Cow. 281; Turner *v.* Dinnegar, 20 Hun, 465; Bell *v.* Pearcy, 5 Ired. 83; Johnson *v.* Chambers, 10 Ired. 287; Thurber *v.* Eastern Ass'n, 118 N. C. 129 *Accord.* See Indianapolis Traction Co. *v.* Henby, 178 Ind. 239.

fendant did falsely and maliciously exhibit a petition to the Lord Chancellor that the plaintiff was indebted to him in £200, and had committed an act of bankruptcy, that the commission thereupon issued, and the plaintiff was declared a bankrupt, and that afterwards the commission was superseded; and the plaintiff avers that he never committed any act of bankruptcy; the second count is much the same, with the like averment; the third count is much the same, but without such averment. To this the defendant pleaded the general issue, and there was a general verdict and damages for the plaintiff taken, upon all the three counts; whereupon it was moved that the judgment might be arrested.

This case was argued twice at the bar, in two former terms by Serjeant *Hewitt* and Serjeant *Burland* for the defendant, and by Serjeant *Whitaker* and Serjeant *Nares* for the plaintiff; and in this term the Lord Chief Justice gave the opinion of the whole court, that judgment must be for the plaintiff.

LORD CHIEF JUSTICE. Upon the arguing of this case, the first objection was, that this action will not lie, there being a remedy given by statute, that a proceeding on a commission of bankruptcy, was a proceeding in nature of a civil suit; and that no action of this sort was ever brought: but we are all of opinion that this action is maintainable.[1]

The general grounds of this action are, that the commission was falsely and maliciously sued out, that the plaintiff has been greatly damaged thereby, scandalized upon record, and put to great charges in obtaining a *supersedeas* to the commission; here is falsehood and malice in the defendant, and great wrong and damage done to the plaintiff thereby. Now, wherever there is an injury done to a man's property by a false and malicious prosecution, it is most reasonable he should have an action to repair himself. See 5 Mod. 407, 8; 10 Mod. 218; 12 Mod. 210. I take these to be two leading cases, and it is dangerous to alter the law. See also 12 Mod. 273; 7 Rep. Bulwer's case, 1. 2 Leon. —— 1 Ro. Abr. 101; 1 Ven. 86; 1 Sid. 464.

[1] Watson *v.* Norbury, Sty. 3, 201; Brown *v.* Chapman, 1 W. Bl. 427; Cotton *v.* James, 1 B. & Ad. 128; Whitworth *v.* Hall, 2 B. & Ad. 695; Hay *v.* Weakley, 5 Car. & P. 361; Farley *v.* Danks, 4 E. & B. 493; Johnson *v.* Emerson, L. R. 6 Ex. 329; Metropolitan Bank *v.* Pooley, 10 App. Cas. 210; Stewart *v.* Sonneborn, 98 U. S. 187; Wilkinson *v.* Goodfellow Co., 141 Fed. 218; McDonald *v.* Goddard Grocery Co., 184 Mo. App. 432; Lawton *v.* Green, 5 Hun, 157; Cohen *v.* Nathaniel Fisher & Co., 135 App. Div. 238; King *v.* Sullivan, (Tex. Civ. App.) 92 S. W. 51; Carleton *v.* Taylor, 50 Vt. 220 (*semble*) *Accord.*

Similarly an action will lie without proof of special damage for a malicious and unfounded presentation of a petition to wind up a trading company. Quartz Co. *v.* Eyre, 11 Q. B. Div. 674; Wyatt *v.* Palmer, [1899] 2 Q. B. 106 (*semble*).

Malicious inquisition of lunacy, see Lockenour *v.* Sides, 57 Ind. 360; Dordoni *v.* Smith, 82 N. J. Law, 525.

Malicious proceeding for suspension or removal of an officer. Fulton *v.* Ingalls, 165 App. Div. 323.

Malicious prosecution of unfounded claim for a patent. Strelitzer *v.* Schnaier, 135 App. Div. 384.

But it is said this action was never brought; and so it was said in Ashby and White; I wish never to hear this objection again. This action is for a tort; torts are infinitely various, not limited or confined, for there is nothing in nature but may be an instrument of mischief, and this of suing out a commission of bankruptcy falsely and maliciously, is of the most injurious consequence in a trading country.

It is further said the stat. 5 Geo. 2, has given a remedy, and therefore this action will not lie; but we are all of opinion, that in this case the plaintiff would have been entitled to this remedy by action at common law, if this Act had never been made, and that the statute being in the affirmative, hath not taken away the remedy at law. 2 Raym. 163. And this is a universal rule, that an affirmative statute is hardly ever repealed by a subsequent affirmative statute, for if it is possible to reconcile two statutes they shall both stand together; if they cannot be reconciled, the last shall be a repeal of the first; but the most decisive answer is, that this statute-remedy is a most inadequate and uncertain remedy; for though there be the most outrageous malice and perjury, and the party injured suffer to the amount of ten or twenty thousand pounds, yet the Chancellor has no power to give him more than the penalty of £200; besides, the method of applying to the Chancellor, is more tedious, expensive, and inconvenient than this common law remedy, and this case in its nature is more properly the province of a jury, than of any judge whatever.

It is further objected, that in the third count there is no averment that the plaintiff was not indebted to the defendant, or ever committed an act of bankruptcy; but no case was cited to show such averment to be necessary; the ground and substance of the declaration is falsehood and malice; there are no instances of such averments in conspiracy, that the party was innocent, or did not do the fact on which he was indicted, but the precedents are the other way. In an action for words, as for saying a man is a thief, the plaintiff has no occasion to aver he is not a thief, and this case is analogous; for after the plaintiff has alleged that the commission was false and malicious, it would be tautology, to make such averment that he was not indebted, &c., and this declaration would have been good on a demurrer; more clearly it is so, after a verdict. *Judgment for the plaintiff.*

TOMLINSON *v.* WARNER

SUPREME COURT, OHIO, DECEMBER, 1839.

Reported in 9 *Ohio Reports*, 104.

MALICIOUS prosecution. From Licking. The plaintiffs declared that they were residents of the town of Newark, and possessed of a large amount of personal property, deposited in a warehouse to be forwarded to New York, for a market; and that the defendant well knowing the premises, and that the plaintiffs had not absconded, but contriving and maliciously intending wrongfully to injure them, made oath before a justice of the peace, that they had absconded to the injury of their creditors, as he verily believed, and thereupon sued out of the Court of Common Pleas, a writ of attachment, and caused the said property to be seized by the sheriff, and held for a long time, whereby the same was injured, the plaintiffs deprived of the opportunity of forwarding their goods to a market, and greatly injured. Plea, not guilty.

Upon trial to the jury, the counsel for the plaintiffs admitted that the plaintiffs were indebted to the defendant at the time of his affidavit, as sworn to in it; whereupon the court directed a nonsuit, with leave to move to open it, and for a new trial, which is now made.[1]

By the Court, WOOD, J. The only question presented in this motion, is, do the facts set forth in the declaration constitute a legal cause of action, provided the plaintiffs were indebted to the defendant, when he sued out the writ of attachment?

In Connecticut, there is a statute which provides, that where a plaintiff shall "willingly and wittingly" wrong any defendant by prosecuting any action against him with intent wrongfully to trouble and vex him, such plaintiff shall pay treble damages for the first offence, be liable to a fine for the second, and for the third, may be proceeded against as a common barrator. Judge Swift thinks the act founded in the clearest principles of justice. Swift Dig. 493. At common law, it seems well settled, that no action will lie for a malicious prosecution of a civil suit, without cause, where there is no arrest. I Salk. R. 14. The costs allowed in all other cases are supposed to be a sufficient compensation for the injury, however malicious. The rule itself may perhaps be admitted, but the reason on which it is said to be founded cannot be so readily admitted, for at common law no costs were allowed. If the plaintiff failed, he was amerced for his false clamor, and if he succeeded, the defendant was at the mercy of the King. But at common law, whenever there was an arrest, holding to bail, or imprisonment, where no debt was due, or for a greater sum than was due, with a malicious intention to injure, the action lay for a malicious arrest. 1 Saund. R. 228. The action for a malicious prosecution, which technically only applies to cases of malicious prosecution of criminal complaints, lies as well where there is not, as where there is an arrest; and the grounds of the action are the malice of the defendant, want of probable cause, and injury to the plaintiff's person by imprisonment, his reputation by scandal, or to his property by expense. 1 Swift Dig. 491. Having no direct adjudication on the question before us, we may look to the analogies of the law. The counsel for the defendant insist that because the plaintiffs' indebtedness to the defendant in the former suit is admitted, there was probable cause for suing out the writ of attachment. This does not seem to us to follow. To constitute probable cause for suing out a writ of attachment, the law requires an affidavit of indebtedness, and also that the debtor has absconded, or is non-resident. The absence of either is absence of probable cause for the writ, and the false affirmation of either fact, knowingly, as a means of procuring the writ, shows express malice, whilst the taking of property without cause is a sufficient injury to sustain the action.

In the Supreme Court of New York, it has been decided, that case would lie against both plaintiff and defendant, for fraudulently setting up the judgment as unsatisfied, when in fact paid, and causing an execution and sale of

[1] The arguments of counsel are omitted.

land once held by it as a lien, but which had been afterwards conveyed by the defendant to a third person. The court in that case say, "If it appear that the unlawful acts of the defendant occasioned trouble, inconvenience, or expense to the plaintiff, this action lies." The general rule is, that for every injury the law gives redress; and it would be a reproach to the administration of justice, if one, by perjury, could take from another the control of his property, under form of law, and the law afford no remedy. Nice technicalities are sometimes applied to get rid of a hard case; but when, under form of law, opportunity is sought to gratify malice, to the injury of another, courts will not be astute to avoid, but rather seek ground to sustain an action. We have no facts in this case, before us, but the statement in the declaration, and the admission of indebtedness; but these show a sufficient *prima facie* cause of action, and cause for opening up the nonsuit.

New trial granted.[1]

[1] *Malicious arrest on civil process.* Stribler *v.* Jones, 1 Lev. 276; Daw *v.* Swain, 1 Sid. 424; Parker *v.* Langley, Gilb. 163, 10 Mod. 209, s. c.; Goslin *v.* Wilcock, 2 Wils. 302; Sinclair *v.* Eldred, 4 Taunt. 7; Pierce *v.* Street, 3 B. & Ad. 397; Cozer *v.* Pilling, 4 B. & C. 26; Saxon *v.* Castle, 6 A. & E. 652; Roret *v.* Lewis, 5 D. & L. 371; Medina *v.* Grove, 10 Q. B. 152; Daniels *v.* Fielding, 16 M. & W. 200 (*semble*, see Clerk & Lindsell, Torts, 5 ed. 683); Moore *v.* Guardner, 16 M. & W. 595 (*semble*); Ross *v.* Norman, 5 Ex. 359; Ventress *v.* Rosser, 73 Ga. 534; Joiner *v.* Ocean Co., 86 Ga. 238; Cardival *v.* Smith, 109 Mass. 158; Hamilburgh *v.* Shepard, 119 Mass. 30; Cotter *v.* Nathan & Hurst Co., 218 Mass. 315; Stanfield *v.* Phillips, 78 Pa. St. 73; Emerson *v.* Cochran, 111 Pa. St. 619; Ward *v.* Sutor, 70 Tex. 343.

Malicious holding to bail. Steer *v.* Scoble, Cro. Jac. 667; Berry *v.* Adamson, 6 B. & C. 528; Small *v.* Gray, 2 Car. & P. 605.

Malicious seizure of property on civil process. Sanders *v.* Powell, 1 Lev. 129, 1 Sid. 183, 1 Keb. 603, s. c.; Craig *v.* Hasell, 4 Q. B. 481; Medina *v.* Grove, 10 Q. B. 152; Redway *v.* McAndrew, L. R. 9 Q. B. 74; Kirksey *v.* Jones, 7 Ala. 622; Vesper *v.* Crane Co., 165 Cal. 36; Juchter *v.* Boehm, 67 Ga. 534; Wilcox *v.* McKenzie, 75 Ga. 73; Lawrence *v.* Hagerman, 56 Ill. 68; Spaids *v.* Barrett, 57 Ill. 289; Western Co. *v.* Wilmarth, 33 Kan. 510; Wills *v.* Noyes, 12 Pick. 324; Savage *v.* Brewer, 16 Pick. 453; O'Brien *v.* Barry, 106 Mass. 300; Bobsin *v.* Kingsbury, 138 Mass. 538; Grant *v.* Reinhart, 33 Mo. App. 74; Smith *v.* Smith, 56 How. Pr. 316; Jaksich *v.* Guisti, 36 Nev. 104; Tyler *v.* Mahoney, 166 N. C. 509; Fortman *v.* Rottier, 8 Ohio St. 548; Sommer *v.* Wilt, 4 S. & R. 19; Mayer *v.* Walter, 64 Pa. St. 283.

Malicious replevin. O'Brien *v.* Barry, 106 Mass. 300; McPherson *v.* Runyon, 41 Minn. 524; Martin *v.* Rexford, 170 N. C. 540.

Malicious issue of an injunction. Munce *v.* Black, 7 Ir. C. L. R. 475; McFarlane *v.* Garrett, 3 Pennewill, 36; Landis *v.* Wolf, 206 Ill. 392; Krzyszke *v.* Kamin, 163 Mich. 290; Manlove *v.* Vick, 55 Miss. 567; Burt *v.* Smith, 84 App. Div. 47; Coal Co. *v.* Upson, 40 Ohio St. 17; Hess *v.* German Co., 37 Or. 297; Batson *v.* Paris Co., 73 S. C. 368; Powell *v.* Woodbury, 85 Vt. 504; Williams *v.* Ainsworth, 121 Wis. 600 (*semble*).

Malicious procurement of the execution of a search warrant. Cooper *v.* Booth, 3 Esp. 135, s. c. 1 T. R. 535 (*cited*); Elsee *v.* Smith, 2 Chit. R. 304, 1 D. & R. 97, s. c.; Wyatt *v.* White, 29 L. J. Ex. 193; Carey *v.* Sheets, 60 Ind. 17, 67 Ind. 375; Whitson *v.* May, 71 Ind. 269; Olson *v.* Tvete, 46 Minn. 225; Miller *v.* Brown, 3 Mo. 94; Boeger *v.* Langenberg, 97 Mo. 390.

Malicious garnishment. King *v.* Yarbray, 136 Ga. 212; Lopes *v.* Connolly, 210 Mass. 487.

Levy of execution under fraudulent judgment. Atlanta Ice Co. *v.* Reeves, 136 Ga. 294.

See also Hope *v.* Evered, 17 Q. B. Div. 338; Lea *v.* Charrington, 23 Q. B. Div. 45; Utting *v.* Berney, 5 T. L. Rep. 39.

WETMORE *v.* MELLINGER

SUPREME COURT, IOWA, APRIL 9, 1884.

Reported in 64 *Iowa Reports*, 741.

BECK, J.[1] The petition alleges that defendants brought an action against plaintiff and his wife, charging in the petition that they two conspired and confederated together to defraud defendants, by representing to defendants, under the assumed name of Baker, that they were the owners of certain lands in Poweshiek County, which defendants were induced to purchase of plaintiff and his wife, who, in such assumed name, executed to defendants a warranty deed therefor; that, in an action by one Woodward, a deed, purporting to be executed by him to the Bakers, under which they claimed title to the lands, was declared to be void, for the reason that it was forged and fraudulent, and that plaintiff herein and his wife well knew the condition of their title, and representing that they were the owners thereof, for the purpose of cheating defendants, and of obtaining money by false and fraudulent pretences, and did, in that manner, obtain the sum of $3,000 from defendants. It is further alleged that defendants herein served out a writ of attachment in the suit brought by them, which was levied upon real estate owned by plaintiff's wife, and that defendants for a time prosecuted their action, but finally dismissed it at their own costs. Plaintiff, in his petition in this case, alleges that he was not indebted to defendants in any sum at the time their action was brought against him; that he was not guilty of the frauds therein charged, and that the action was commenced and prosecuted by defendants maliciously and without probable cause. The defendants, in their answer, admit the commencement of the suit, the issuing of the attachment, and that it was levied upon real estate owned by plaintiff's wife. There was no evidence showing, or tending to show, that the writ of attachment was levied upon any property owned by plaintiff. The wife of plaintiff does not join in this action.

We think the doctrine is well established by the great preponderance of authority that no action will lie for the institution and prosecution of a civil action with malice and without probable cause, where there has been no arrest of the person or seizure of the property of defendant, and no special injury sustained, which would not necessarily result in all suits prosecuted to recover for like causes of action.

See 1 Am. Leading Cases, p. 218, note to Munn *v.* Dupont *et al.*, and cases there cited; Mayer *v.* Walter, 64 Pa. St. 289; Kramer *v.* Stock, 10 Watts, 115; Bitz *v.* Meyer, 11 Vroom, 252, s. c. 29 Am. Rep. 233; Eberly *v.* Rupp, 90 Pa. St. 259; Gorton *v.* Brown, 27 Ill. 489; Woodmansie *v.* Logan, 2 N. J. L. 93 (1 Pen.); Parker's Adm'rs *v.* Frambes, Id. 156; Potts *v.* Imlay, 4 N. J. L. 330 (1 South.)

[1] Only the opinion of the court on this point is given.

This doctrine is supported by the following considerations: The courts are open and free to all who have grievances and seek remedies therefor, and there should be no restraint upon a suitor, through fear of liability resulting from failure in his action, which would keep him from the courts. He ought not, in ordinary cases, to be subject to a suit for bringing an action, and be required to defend against the charge of malice and the want of probable cause. If an action may be maintained against a plaintiff for the malicious prosecution of a suit without probable cause, why should not a right of action accrue against a defendant who defends without probable cause and with malice? The doctrine surely tends to discourage vexatious litigation, rather than to promote it.

It will be observed that the statement of the doctrine we have made extends it no farther than to cases prosecuted in the usual manner, where defendants suffer no special damages or grievance other than is endured by all defendants in suits brought upon like causes of action. If the bringing of the action operates to disturb the peace, to impose care and expense, or even to cast discredit and suspicion upon the defendant, the same results follow all actions of like character, whether they be meritorious, or prosecuted maliciously and without probable cause. They are incidents of litigation. But if an action is so prosecuted as to entail unusual hardship upon the defendant, and subject him to special loss of property or of reputation, he ought to be compensated. So, if his property be seized, or if he be subjected to arrest by an action maliciously prosecuted, the law secures to him a remedy. In the case at bar, the pleadings and evidence show no such special damages. No action could be prosecuted to recover money fraudulently obtained, in which the defendant would not suffer the very things for which plaintiff in this case seeks compensation in damages.

Counsel for plaintiff, in support of their position that the action may be maintained, though no arrest of defendant or seizure of property be had in the proceeding alleged to have been maliciously prosecuted, cite Green *v.* Cochran, 43 Iowa, 544, and Moffatt *et al. v.* Fisher, 47 Id. 473. In the first case, the action alleged to be malicious was a proceeding for bastardy, which, under the statute, operated as a lien upon defendant's lands from the commencement. In the other case, the action which was the foundation of plaintiff's claim was forcible entry and detainer, and, before final disposition thereof, the defendant was ousted of possession of the land, whereon was a coal mine. In both instances the property of the respective defendants was reached by the proceedings. The facts of these cases are not within the rule we have stated, and do not support counsel's position.

Affirmed.[1]

[1] Savile *v.* Roberts, 1 Ld. Ray. 374; Purton *v.* Honnor, 1 B. & P. 205; Cotterell *v.* Jones, 11 C. B. 713; Quartz Co. *v.* Eyre, 11 Q. B. Div. 674; Ray *v.* Law, Pet. C. C. 207; Tamblyn *v.* Johnston, 126 Fed. 267, 270; Mitchell *v.* South Western

FLIGHT *v.* LEMAN

IN THE QUEEN'S BENCH, JUNE 9, 1843.

Reported in 4 Queen's Bench Reports, 883.

CASE. The second count of the declaration alleged that the defendant heretofore, to wit 1st January, 1838, and on divers &c. between that day and 22d November, 1838, contriving and maliciously intending to injure, harass and damnify plaintiff, and to put him to great vexation, unlawfully and maliciously did advise, procure, instigate and stir up John Thomas to commence and prosecute an action of trespass on the case in the court &c. (Queen's Bench) against the now plaintiff; that by and through such advice, procurement, instigation and stirring-up, John Thomas did in fact afterwards, to wit 4th January, 1838, commence and prosecute the last-mentioned action. The present declaration then set out three counts of a declaration in case at the

Co., 75 Ga. 398 (but see Slater *v.* Kimbro, 91 Ga. 217); Smith *v.* Mich. Co., 175 Ill. 619; Bonney *v.* King, 201 Ill. 47; McCormick *v.* Weber, 187 Ill. App. 290; Smith *v.* Hintrager, 67 Ia. 109; Cattle Co. *v.* Nat. Bank, 127 Ia. 153, 158; White *v.* International Text Book Co., 156 Ia. 310; Cade *v.* Yocum, 8 La. Ann. 477; McNamee *v.* Mink, 49 Md. 122; Sup. Lodge *v.* Unverzagt, 76 Md. 104 (see Clements *v.* Odorless Co., 67 Md. 461); Woodmansie *v.* Logan, 1 Penningt. 93; Potts *v.* Imlay, 1 South. 330; State *v.* Meyer, 40 N. J. Law, 252; Ely *v.* Davis, 111 N. C. 24 (*semble*); Terry *v.* Davis, 114 N. C. 31; Carpenter *v.* Hanes, 167 N. C. 551; Cincinnati Co. *v.* Bruck, 61 Ohio St. 489 (explaining Pope *v.* Pollock, 46 Ohio St. 367); Kramer *v.* Stock, 10 Watts, 115; Mayer *v.* Walter, 64 Pa. St. 283; Muldoon *v.* Rickey, 103 Pa. St. 110; Emerson *v.* Cochran, 111 Pa. St. 619, 622; Michell *v.* Donanski, 28 R. I. 94, 97 (*semble*); Smith *v.* Adams, 27 Tex. 28; Johnson *v.* King, 64 Tex. 226; Nowotny *v.* Grona, 44 Tex. Civ. App. 325; J. Calisher Co. *v.* Bloch, (Tex. Civ. App.) 147 S. W. 683; Abbott *v.* Thorne, 34 Wash. 692; Luby *v.* Bennett, 111 Wis. 613 (*semble*); Cross *v.* Comm. Agency, 18 N. Zeal. L. R. 153 *Accord.*

Burnap *v.* Albert, Taney, 244; Cooper *v.* Armour, 42 Fed. 215, 217; Wade *v.* Nat. Bank, 114 Fed. 377; Eastin *v.* Stockton Bank, 66 Cal. 123; Berson *v.* Ewing, 84 Cal. 89; Hoyt *v.* Macon, 2 Col. 113 (*semble*); Whipple *v.* Fuller, 11 Conn. 582; Wall *v.* Toomey, 52 Conn. 35; Payne *v.* Donegan, 9 Ill. App. 566 (*semble*); Lockenour *v.* Sides, 57 Ind. 360; McCardle *v.* McGinley, 86 Ind. 538; Whitesell *v.* Study, 37 Ind. App. 429; Marbourg *v.* Smith, 11 Kan. 554; Cox *v.* Taylor, 10 B. Mon. 17; Woods *v.* Finnell, 13 Bush. 628; Johnson *v.* Meyer, 36 La. Ann. 333 (*semble*); Allen *v.* Codman, 139 Mass. 136 (*semble*); Wilson *v.* Hale, 178 Mass. 111; Brand *v.* Hinchman, 68 Mich. 590; Antcliff *v.* June, 81 Mich. 477; McPherson *v.* Runyon, 41 Minn. 524; O'Neill *v.* Johnson, 53 Minn. 439; Eickhoff *v.* Fidelity Co., 74 Minn. 139; Virtue *v.* Creamery Mfg. Co., 123 Minn. 17; Brown *v.* City, 90 Mo. 377 (*semble*); Smith *v.* Burrus, 106 Mo. 94; McCormick Co. *v.* Willan, 63 Neb. 391; Pangburn *v.* Bull, 1 Wend. 345; Dempsey *v.* Lepp, 52 How. Pr. 11; Smith *v.* Smith, 20 Hun, 555 (*semble*); Willard *v.* Holmes, 21 N. Y. Supp. 998 (*semble*); (but see Willard *v.* Holmes, 142 N. Y. 492; Paul *v.* Fargo, 84 App. Div. 9); Kolka *v.* Jones, 6 N. D. 461; Sawyer *v.* Shick, 30 Okl. 353; Lipscomb *v.* Shofner, 96 Tenn. 112; Swepson *v.* Davis, 109 Tenn. 99; Closson *v.* Staples, 42 Vt. 209 *Contra.*

In Eastin *v.* Stockton Bank, *supra*, the court said: "The English cases which deny the right to maintain the action, stand upon the ground that the successful defendant is adequately compensated for the damages he sustains by the costs allowed him by the statute. Those costs, it seems, include the attorney's charges for preparing the case for trial in all its parts, the fees of the witnesses and the court officials, and even the *honorarium* of the barrister who conducted the case in court. The reason upon which the English rule rests would not, therefore, seem to apply here, where the costs recoverable under the statute are confined to much narrower limits. . . .

"Two other objections made to the maintenance of the action, — first, the claim that if such suits are allowed, litigation will become interminable, because suit of John Thomas against the defendant, averment of a trial at *nisi prius* at Dorchester, on 18th July, 1838, and that the defendant was then and there acquitted of the premises mentioned to be charged against him by John Thomas. And thereupon afterwards, to wit 22d November, 1838, it was considered, in and by the said court &c., amongst other things, that the said John Thomas be in mercy for his false claim against the now plaintiff defendant in the said last-mentioned action as aforesaid. Whereby the now plaintiff was not only put to great trouble and vexation, but was also obliged to pay, and did in fact pay, a large &c., to wit £800, in and about the defence of the said action.

The defendant pleaded, in effect, that the advice given by him was given in the character of an attorney.

Replication *de injuria.*

Special demurrer. Joinder.[1]

LORD DENMAN, C. J. The case of Pechell *v.* Watson, 8 M. & W. 691, proceeded on the principle that to maintain an action already commenced was unlawful. That is not here charged; and therefore the count ought to show the ingredients which make the instigation to a suit actionable. The plaintiff has not done this; for, beyond all doubt, the absence of reasonable or probable cause is one such ingredient, in the absence of which it does not appear that the plaintiff has been unlawfully disturbed.

PATTESON, J. I think this declaration is bad, for the reason already given. The case is analogous to that of a complaint of malicious prosecution or arrest; and here, as there, the want of reasonable or probable cause ought to be alleged.

every successful action will be followed by another, alleging malice in the prosecution of the former; and second, that if the defendant may sue for damages sustained by an unfounded prosecution, the plaintiff may equally bring an action when the defendant makes a groundless defence, — are well answered in the article already alluded to [Mr. Lawson's note, 21 A. L. Reg. N. S. 281, 353]: 'To the first objection, it is enough to say that the action will never lie for an unsuccessful prosecution, unless begun and carried on with malice and without probable cause. With the burden of this difficult proof upon him, the litigant will need a very clear case before he will be willing to begin a suit of this character. The second argument fails to distinguish between the position of the parties, plaintiff and defendant, in an action at law. The plaintiff sets the law in motion; if he does so groundlessly and maliciously he is the cause of the defendant's damage. But the defendant stands only on his legal rights — the plaintiff having taken his case to court, the defendant has the privilege of calling upon him to prove it to the satisfaction of the judge or jury, and he is guilty of no wrong in exercising this privilege.'"

In Doane *v.* Hescock, 155 N. Y. Supp. 210, the court (Appellate Term, First Department) says: "It clearly appears that the complaint does not state facts sufficient to constitute a cause of action for abuse of process, nor are the allegations sufficient to support an action for malicious prosecution of a civil action in this state. There is no allegation that the action resulted in damages to the business or reputation of the defendant or that in any way his personal or property rights were interfered with. The sole allegation as to damage is the trouble, inconvenience, and expense of defending the action. This is not sufficient. Paul *v.* Fargo, 84 App. Div. 9, 11, 13 (dissenting opinion, 21), 82 N. Y. Supp. 369; Fulton *v.* Ingalls, 165 App. Div. 323, 326, 151 N. Y. Supp. 130."

Malicious excessive attachment. Tamblyn *v.* Johnston, (C. C. A.) 126 Fed. 267; Mills *v.* Larrance, 217 Ill. 446; Savage *v.* Brewer, 16 Pick. 453; Paul *v.* Fargo, 84 App. Div. 9; Sommer *v.* Wilt, 4 S. & R. 19.

[1] The averments of the count are abridged and the arguments of counsel are omitted.

WILLIAMS, J. The averments in this declaration might be sustained by proof that the defendant, not being an attorney, had held a conversation with Thomas, and had said, "If your story is correct, you might sue Flight." No action could be maintained on that, unless it further appeared that the now defendant knew that there was no right to sue the now plaintiff.

COLERIDGE, J. It is not asserted here that the suit maintained was without reasonable or probable cause: there are only general words, imputing an instigation and a stirring-up. There should be added to these, in strict analogy with actions for malicious prosecution or arrest, as my Brother Patteson has pointed out, an averment of want of reasonable or probable cause: and without such averment this declaration shows no right of action.

Judgment for defendant.[1]

GRAINGER *v.* HILL

IN THE COMMON PLEAS, JANUARY 20, 1838.

Reported in 4 *Bingham, New Cases*, 212.

TINDAL, C. J.[2] This is a special action on the case, in which the plaintiff declares that he was the master and owner of a vessel which, in September, 1836, he mortgaged to the defendant for the sum of £80, with a covenant for repayment in September, 1837, and under a stipulation that, in the mean time, the plaintiff should retain the command of the vessel, and prosecute voyages therein for his own profit; that the defendants, in order to compel the plaintiff through duress to give up the register of the vessel, without which he could not go to sea before the money lent on mortgage became due, threatened to arrest him for the same unless he immediately paid the amount; that, upon the plaintiff refusing to pay it, the defendants, knowing he could not provide bail, arrested him under a *capias*, indorsed to levy £95, 17*s*. 6d., and kept him imprisoned, until, by duress, he was compelled to give up the register, which the defendants then unlawfully detained; by means whereof the plaintiff lost four voyages from London to Caen. There is also a count in trover for the register. The defendants pleaded the general issue; and, after a verdict for the plaintiff, the case comes before us on a double ground, under an application for a nonsuit, and in arrest of judgment.

[1] Fivaz *v.* Nicholls, 2 C. B. 501, 514 (*semble*); Grove *v.* Brandenburg, 7 Blackf. 234 *Accord.*

"Pechell *v.* Watson came to be considered in Flight *v.* Leman. Its authority was recognized, but the latter case was decided against the plaintiff, who sued for maintenance, on the ground, I own I should have thought the narrow ground, that to instigate a suit was not maintenance, though to support one already instituted was." *Per* Coleridge, C. J., in Bradlaugh *v.* Newdegate, 11 Q. B. Div. 1, 8.

See also Alabaster *v.* Harness, [1894] 2 Q. B. 897, [1895] 1 Q. B. 339; Grieg *v.* National Union, 22 T. L. Rep. 274; Goodyear Co. *v.* White, 2 N. J. Law Journ. 150, 10 Fed. Cas. 752, no. 5602; Breeden *v.* Frankford Ins. Co., 220 Mo. 327, 373, 378–420, 424–443. Compare Metropolitan Bank *v.* Pooley, 10 App. Cas. 210, 217–218.

[2] Only the opinion of the Chief Justice upon the point of abuse of legal process is given.

The second ground urged for a nonsuit is, that there was no proof of the suit commenced by the defendants having been terminated. But the anwser to this, and to the objection urged in arrest of judgment, namely, the omission to allege want of reasonable and probable cause for the defendants' proceeding, is the same, — that this is an action for abusing the process of the law, by applying it to extort property from the plaintiff, and not an action for a malicious arrest or malicious prosecution, in order to support which action the termination of the previous proceeding must be proved, and the absence of reasonable and probable cause be alleged as well as proved. In the case of a malicious arrest, the sheriff at least is instructed to pursue the exigency of the writ; here the directions given, to compel the plaintiff to yield up the register, were no part of the duty enjoined by the writ. If the course pursued by the defendants is such that there is no precedent of a similar transaction, the plaintiff's remedy is by an action on the case, applicable to such new and special circumstances; and his complaint being that the process of the law has been abused, to effect an object not within the scope of the process, it is immaterial whether the suit which that process commenced has been determined or not, or whether or not it was founded on reasonable and probable cause.[1]

[1] Heywood *v.* Collinge, 9 A. & E. 268; King *v.* Yarbray, 136 Ga. 212; Wicker *v.* Hotchkiss, 62 Ill. 107 (*semble*); Emery *v.* Ginnan, 24 Ill. App. 65 (*semble*); Whitesell *v.* Study, 37 Ind. App. 429 (*semble*); Page *v.* Cushing, 38 Me. 523; Wood *v.* Graves, 144 Mass. 365; White *v.* Apsley Co., 181 Mass. 339; White *v.* Apsley Co., 194 Mass. 97; Malone *v.* Belcher, 216 Mass. 209; Pixley *v.* Reed, 26 Minn. 80 (*semble*); Rossiter *v.* Minn. Co., 37 Minn. 296; Bebinger *v.* Sweet, 6 Hun, 478; Buffalo Co. *v.* Everest, 30 Hun, 586 (*semble*); Hazard *v.* Harding, 63 How. Pr. 326; Prough *v.* Entriken, 11 Pa. St. 81; Mayer *v.* Walter, 64 Pa. St. 283; Lauzon *v.* Charroux, 18 R. I. 467 *Accord.*

As to the distinction between malicious prosecution and abuse of process, see Waters *v.* Winn, 142 Ga. 138; Wright *v.* Harris, 160 N. C. 542; Cooper *v.* Southern R. Co., 165 N. C. 578.

In Wood *v.* Graves, 144 Mass. 365, Allen, J., said, p. 366: "There is no doubt that an action lies for the malicious abuse of lawful process, civil or criminal. It is to be assumed, in such a case, that the process was lawfully issued for a just cause, and is valid in form, and that the arrest or other proceeding upon the process was justifiable and proper in its inception. Perhaps the most frequent form of such abuse is by working upon the fears of the person under arrest for the purpose of extorting money or other property, or of compelling him to sign some paper, to give up some claim, or to do some other act, in accordance with the wishes of those who have control of the prosecution. The leading case upon this subject is Grainger *v.* Hill, 4 Bing. N. C. 212, where the owner of a vessel was arrested on civil process, and the officer, acting under the directions of the plaintiffs in the suit, used the process to compel the defendant therein to give up his ship's register, to which they had no right. He was held entitled to recover damages, not for maliciously putting the process in force, but for maliciously abusing it, to effect an object not within its proper scope."

In Mayer *v.* Walter, 64 Pa. St. 283, Sharswood, J., said: "There is a distinction between a malicious use and a malicious abuse of legal process. An abuse is where the party employs it for some unlawful object, not the purpose which it is intended by the law to effect; in other words, a perversion of it. Thus, if a man is arrested, or his goods seized in order to extort money from him, even though it be to pay a just claim other than that in suit, or to compel him to give up possession of a deed or other thing of value, not the legal object of the process, it is settled that in an action for such malicious abuse it is not necessary to prove that the action in which

BOND v. CHAPIN

SUPREME JUDICIAL COURT, MASSACHUSETTS, SEPTEMBER, 1844.

Reported in 8 *Metcalf*, 31.

HUBBARD, J.[1] In the present suit, which is an action on the case against the defendant for prosecuting a suit in the name of Thomas Bond against the plaintiff, the plaintiff avers, in his declaration, (which accompanies the exceptions) that the defendant, without authority from said Thomas, and having no reasonable ground for believing that anything was due from the plaintiff to him, attached the plaintiff's property, and prosecuted said suit against him, from November term, 1840, to November term, 1841, when he became nonsuit; and evidence was offered tending to prove these allegations. The instructions to the jury were, that " the plaintiff must prove the former action to have been commenced and prosecuted maliciously, that is to say, with some improper motive, or without due care to ascertain his rights, as well as without authority, and without probable cause." The error complained of may have arisen from not distinguishing, during the trial, between an action on the case for malicious prosecution, and an action on the case for prosecuting a suit in the name of a third person, without authority, by reason of which the defendant sustains injury.

In a suit for malicious prosecution, the gist of the action is malice; but there must also exist the want of probable cause. And without the proof of both facts, the action cannot be maintained, though the existence of malice may often be inferred from the want of probable cause. But in an action on the case for damages for prosecuting a suit against the plaintiff without authority, in the name of a third person, the gist of the action is not a want of probable cause, — for there may be a good cause of action, — but for the improper liberty of using the name of another person in prosecuting a suit, by which the defendant in the action is injured. Nor is the proof of malice essential to the maintenance of such action. If the party supposes he has authority to commence a suit, when in fact he has none, and the nominal plaintiff does not adopt it, the action fails for want of such authority. In

the process issued has been determined, or to aver that it was sued out without reasonable or probable cause: Grainger v. Hill, 4 Bing. N. C. 212. It is evident that when such a wrong has been perpetrated, it is entirely immaterial whether the proceeding itself was baseless or otherwise. We know that the law is good, but only if a man use it lawfully.

" On the other hand, legal process, civil or criminal, may be maliciously used so as to give rise to a cause of action where no object is contemplated to be gained by it other than its proper effect and execution. As every man has a legal power to prosecute his claims in a court of law and justice, no matter by what motives of malice he may be actuated in doing so, it is necessary in this class of cases to aver and prove that he has acted not only maliciously, but without reasonable or probable cause. It is clearly settled also, that the proceeding must be determined finally before any action lies for the injury; because, as it is said in Arundell v. Tregono, Yelv. 117, the plaintiff will clear himself too soon, viz., before the fact tried, which will be inconvenient; besides, the two determinations might be contrary and inconsistent."

To proceed unfairly and oppressively but without seeking to compel another to do what he is not obliged to do, e. g., to enter up judgment on a note after 10 P. M. and to bring immediate execution, is not a ground of action according to Docter v. Riedel, 96 Wis. 158. But see dissenting opinion of Marshall, J.

[1] Only the opinion of the court is given.

such case, though the party supposed he had authority, and acted upon that supposition, without malice, still if the defendant suffers injury by reason of the prosecution of the unauthorized suit against him, he may maintain an action for the actual damages sustained by him, in the loss of time, and for money paid to procure the discontinuance of the suit, but nothing more. Where, however, in addition to a want of authority, the suit commenced was altogether groundless, and was prosecuted with malicious motives — which may be inferred from there existing no right of action, as well as proved in other ways — then, in addition to the actual loss of time and money, the party may recover damages for the injury inflicted on his feelings and reputation.

In this case, the learned judge having instructed the jury that a want of probable cause and malice must concur with the want of authority to commence the suit in the name of a third person, to enable the plaintiff to maintain the action, we think there was error in the instruction, and that though the damages might be enhanced by showing malice and a want of probable cause, yet that the proof of them is not essential to the maintenance of the action. *New trial granted.*[1]

[1] Y. B. 7 Hen. VI. 43; 1 Roll. Ab. 101, pl. 1, s. c.; Holliday *v.* Sterling, 62 Mo. 321 *Accord.*

CHAPTER VI

DEFAMATION

CLUTTERBUCK *v.* CHAFFERS

AT NISI PRIUS, CORAM LORD ELLENBOROUGH, C. J.,
DECEMBER 14, 1816.

Reported in 1 *Starkie,* 471.

THIS was an action for the publication of a libel.

The witness who was called to prove the publication of the libel (which was contained in a letter written by the defendant to the plaintiff) stated on cross-examination that the letter had been delivered to him folded up, but unsealed, and that without reading it, or allowing any other person to read it, he had delivered it to the plaintiff himself, as he had been directed.

LORD ELLENBOROUGH held that this did not amount to a publication which would support an action, although it would have sustained an indictment,[1] since a publication to the party himself tends to a breach of the peace. *Verdict for the defendant.*[2]

[1] Edwards *v.* Wooton, 12 Rep. 35; Peacock *v.* Raynell, 2 Brownl. 151; Barrow *v.* Lewellin, Hob. 152; Hick's Case, Hob. 375; Rex *v.* Burdett, 4 B. & Ald. 95 *Accord.*

[2] Phillips *v.* Jansen, 2 Esp. 624; Ward *v.* Smith, 4 Car. & P. 302; Sharp *v.* Skues, (C. A.) 25 T. L. Rep. 336; Warnock *v.* Mitchell, 43 Fed. 428; Western Co. *v.* Cashman, 149 Fed. 367; Spaits *v.* Poundstone, 87 Ind. 522; Yousling *v.* Dare, 122 Ia. 539; Lyon *v.* Lash, 74 Kan. 745; Buckwalter *v.* Gossow, 75 Kan. 147; McIntosh *v.* Matherly, 9 B. Mon. 119; Roberts *v.* English Co., 155 Ala. 414; Dickinson *v.* Hathaway, 122 La. 644; Gambrill *v.* Schooley, 93 Md. 48; Rumney *v.* Worthley, 186 Mass. 144, 145; Youmans *v.* Smith, 153 N. Y. 214, 218; Lyle *v.* Clason, 1 Caines, 581; Waistel *v.* Holman, 2 Hall, 172; Prescott *v.* Tousey, 50 N. Y. Super. Ct. 12; Shepard *v.* Lamphier, 84 Misc. 498; Fonville *v.* McNease, Dudley, 303; State *v.* Syphrett, 27 S. C. 29; Fry *v.* McCord, 95 Tenn. 678; Sylvis *v.* Miller, 96 Tenn. 94; Wilcox *v.* Moon, 63 Vt. 481; Wilcox *v.* Moon, 64 Vt. 450 *Accord.*

See Ahern *v.* Maguire, A. M. & O. 39.

If two persons combine in sending a libel to the plaintiff, each is guilty of a publication to the other. Spaits *v.* Poundstone, 87 Ind. 522, 524, 525.

In Virginia, by statute, an action lies for insulting words written or spoken, although not read or heard by a third person. Rolland *v.* Batchelder, 84 Va. 664; Strode *v.* Clement, 90 Va. 553.

SNYDER *v.* ANDREWS

SUPREME COURT, NEW YORK, MARCH 5, 1849.

Reported in 6 *Barbour*, 43.

THIS was an action on the case for a libel. The defendant pleaded the general issue, and gave notice of special matter.[1]

The cause was tried at the Saratoga circuit in November, 1847, before Justice Paige. On the trial the defendant admitted that he wrote the letter containing the alleged libel, sealed the same, and put it into the post-office at Saratoga Springs, directed to the plaintiff at his residence. The plaintiff proved by John R. Brown that the letter was read to the witness by the defendant at his office in the presence of a young man who was a clerk of the defendant. The defendant's counsel then moved for a nonsuit, on the ground that a publication of the libel had not been proved. The judge denied the motion.

The jury found a verdict for the plaintiff of $250. And the defendant, upon a bill of exceptions, moved for a new trial.

WILLARD, J. The fact that the defendant read the letter to a stranger, before it was sent to the plaintiff, was not questioned on the trial, and is assumed to be true by the form of the objection; but it is insisted that such reading did not amount to a publication of the libel. No man incurs any civil responsibility by what he thinks or even writes, unless he divulges his thoughts to the temporal prejudice of another. Hence, a sealed letter containing libellous matter, if communicated to no one but to the party libelled, is not the foundation for a civil action, although it may be of an indictment. Lyle *v.* Clason, 1 Caines, 581; Hodges *v.* The State, 5 Humphrey, 112; 1 Wms. Saund. 132, *n.* 2; Phillips *v.* Jansen, 2 Esp. 626; 2 Starkie on Slander (Wend. ed.), 14. But where the defendant, knowing that letters addressed to the plaintiff were usually opened by and read by his clerk, wrote a libellous letter and directed it to the plaintiff and his clerk received and read it, it was held there was a sufficient publication to support the action. Delacroix *v.* Thevenot, 2 Stark. 63. And in Schenck *v.* Schenck, 1 Spencer, 208, a sealed letter addressed and delivered to the wife containing a libel on her husband was held a publication sufficient to enable the latter to sustain an action.[2] Reading or singing the contents of a libel in the presence of others has been

[1] Part of the case, not relating to publication, is omitted.

[2] Wenman *v.* Ash, 13 C. B. 836; Jones *v.* Williams, 1 T. L. Rep. 572; Sesler *v.* Montgomery, 78 Cal. 486, 489 (*semble*); Luick *v.* Driscoll, 13 Ind. App. 279; Wilcox *v.* Moon, 63 Vt. 481; Wilcox *v.* Moon, 64 Vt. 450 *Accord.*

But a communication by the libeller to his own wife is said not to be a publication. Wennhak *v.* Morgan, 20 Q. B. D. 635; Sesler *v.* Montgomery, 78 Cal. 486; Trumbull *v.* Gibbons, 3 City H. Rec. 97. But see State *v.* Shoemaker, 101 N. C. 690. See also Central R. Co. *v.* Jones, 18 Ga. App. 414 (dictation by officer of corporation to co-employee); Kirschenbaum *v.* Kaufman (N. Y. City Ct.), 50 N. Y. Law Journ. 406 (defamatory matter uttered to business partner in course of adjudged a publication. 2 Starkie on Slander, 16; 5 Rep. 125; 9 Id. 59 *b*; 1 Saund. 132, *n*. 2. The reading of the letter in question by the defendant in the presence of Brown was a sufficient publication to sustain this action. *New trial denied.*[1]

DELACROIX *v.* THEVENOT

AT NISI PRIUS, CORAM LORD ELLENBOROUGH, C. J., MARCH 4, 1817.

Reported in 2 Starkie, 63.

THIS was an action for a libel and slanderous words. The libel was contained in a letter directed to plaintiff.

A clerk of the plaintiff proved that he had received the letter; that it was in the handwriting of the defendant; and that in the absence of the plaintiff he was in the habit of opening letters directed to him which were not marked " private." He further stated that defendant, who was well acquainted with the plaintiff, was aware of the nature of his (the clerk's) employment, and that he believed defendant knew that witness was in the habit of opening plaintiff's letters.

LORD ELLENBOROUGH said that there was sufficient evidence for the jury to consider whether defendant did not intend the letter to come to the hands of a third person, which would be a publication.

Verdict for plaintiff. Damages, £100.[2]

SHEFFILL *v.* VAN DEUSEN

SUPREME JUDICIAL COURT, MASSACHUSETTS, SEPTEMBER TERM, 1859.

Reported in 13 *Gray,* 304.

ACTION of tort for slander.

BIGELOW, J.[3] Proof of the publication of the defamatory words alleged in the declaration was essential to the maintenance of this action. Slander consists in uttering words to the injury of a person's reputation. No such injury is done when the words are uttered only

business). It would be more accurate to say that the communication in such cases is privileged. In Powell *v.* Gelston, [1916] 2 K. B. 615, a libellous letter, privileged as a communication to A, was sent to B, who asked for the information in his own name at A's request. The letter was opened and read by A only.

[1] M'Coombs *v.* Tuttle, 5 Blackf. 431; Van Cleef *v.* Lawrence, 2 City H. Rec. 41 *Accord.*

[2] Wyatt *v.* Gore, Holt, 299; Wenman *v.* Ash, 13 C. B. 836; Kiene *v.* Ruff, 1 Ia. 482; Allen *v.* Wortham, 89 Ky. 485; Rumney *v.* Worthley, 186 Mass. 144; Schenck *v.* Schenck, Spencer, 208; State *v.* McIntire, 115 N. C. 769; Wilcox *v.* Moon, 64 Vt. 540; Adams *v.* Lawson, 17 Gratt. 250 *Accord.*

See Fox *v.* Broderick, 14 Ir. C. L. R. 453; Callan *v.* Gaylord, 3 Watts, 321.

Slanderous statements to plaintiff in presence of his counsel, Massee *v.* Williams, 207 Fed. 222.

Sending libellous letter to plaintiff's attorney, Brown *v.* Elm City Lumber Co., 167 N. C. 9.

[3] Only the opinion of the court is given.

to the person concerning whom they are spoken, no one else being present or within hearing. It is damage done to character in the opinion of other men, and not in a party's self-estimation, which constitutes the material element in an action for verbal slander. Even in a civil action for libel, evidence that the defendant wrote and sent a sealed letter to the plaintiff, containing defamatory matter, was held insufficient proof of publication; although it would be otherwise in an indictment for libel, because such writings tend directly to a breach of the peace. So, too, it must be shown that the words were spoken in the presence of some one who understood them. If spoken in a foreign language, which no one present understood, no action will lie therefor.[1] Edwards v. Wooton, 12 Co. 35; Hick's Case, Pop. 139, Hob. 215; Wheeler & Appleton's Case, Godb. 340; Phillips v. Jansen, 2 Esp. 624; Lyle v. Clason, 1 Caines, 581; Hammond N. P. 287.

It is quite immaterial in the present case that the words were spoken in a public place. The real question for the jury was, were they so spoken as to have been heard by third persons? The defendants were therefore entitled to the instructions for which they asked.

Exceptions sustained.[2]

[1] Jones *v.* Davers, Cro. Eliz. 496; Price *v.* Jenkings, Cro. Eliz. 865; Amann *v.* Damm, 8 C. B. N. S. 597; Kiene *v.* Ruff, 1 Ia. 42; Hurtert *v.* Weines, 27 Ia. 134; Mielenz *v.* Quasdorf, 68 Ia. 726; Economopoulos *v.* A. G. Pollard Co., 218 Mass. 294; Wormouth *v.* Cramer, 3 Wend. 394 *Accord.*

See Bechtell *v.* Shatler, Wright, (Ohio) 107. Conf. Anon., Moore, 182; Gibs *v.* Jenkins, Hob. 335; Zenobio *v.* Axtell, 6 T. R. 162; Jenkins *v.* Phillips, 9 Car. & P. 766; Hickley *v.* Grosjean, 6 Blackf. 351; Keenholts *v.* Becker, 3 Den. 346; Rahauser *v.* Barth, 3 Watts, 28; Zeig *v.* Ort, 3 Chandl. 26; K. *v.* H., 20 Wis. 239; Filber *v.* Dautermann, 26 Wis. 518; Simonsen *v.* Herald Co., 61 Wis. 626; Pelzer *v.* Benishy, 67 Wis. 291.

[2] Anon., Sty. 70; Force *v.* Warren, 15 C. B. N. S. 806; Desmond *v.* Brown, 33 Ia. 13; Marble *v.* Chapin, 132 Mass. 225, 226; Cameron *v.* Cameron, 162 Mo. App. 110; Traylor *v.* White, 185 Mo. App. 325; Broderick *v.* James, 3 Daly, 481 *Accord.*

Mailing of post card. Three views have been expressed as to whether the mailing of a post card is a publication.

(1) The mailing is a publication. Sadgrove *v.* Hole, [1901] 2 K.B. 1, 4, 5 (*semble*); Logan *v.* Hodges, 146 N. C. 38; Spence *v.* Burt, 18 Lanc. L. Rev. 251; Robinson *v.* Jones, L. R. 4 Ir. 391 (*semble*); McCann *v.* Edinburgh Co., L. R. 28 Ir. 24, 28 per Palles, C. B.

(2) The mailing is *prima facie* a publication. Odgers, Libel and Slander (4 ed.), 153, 281.

(3) The mailing is *prima facie* not a publication, i. e., is not a publication unless evidence is given that the post card was read *in transitu.* Steele *v.* Edwards, 15 Ohio Cir. Ct. 52, 58.

Publication in ignorance of the libel. The dissemination of a libel by a carrier or newsvender or a public library, who neither knew nor ought to have known of the libel and who had no reason to suppose that the newspaper was likely to contain libellous matters, gives no cause of action. Emmens *v.* Pottle, 16 Q. B. D. 354; Martin *v.* Trustees of British Museum, 10 T. L. Rep. 338. But the proprietor of a circulating library was held liable for giving out a book containing defamatory statements, because his freedom from negligence did not appear. Vizetelly *v.* Mudie's Library, [1900] 2 Q. B. 170. See also Morris *v.* Ritchie, Court of Sess., March 12, 1902, 4 F. 645.

HANKINSON *v.* BILBY

In the Exchequer, January 28, 1847.

Reported in 16 *Meeson & Welsby,* 442.

Case. The declaration stated that the defendant, in the presence and hearing of divers subjects, falsely and maliciously charged the plaintiff, a gardener, with being a thief. Plea: Not guilty. At the trial, before Rolfe, B., it appeared that the words were uttered by the defendant, a toll collector, to the plaintiff, as he passed the Kingsland turnpike-gate, in the presence of several persons as well as the witness. The nature of the previous conversation between the plaintiff and defendant did not appear. The learned Baron told the jury that it was immaterial whether the defendant intended to convey a charge of felony against the plaintiff by the words used, the question being, whether the bystanders would understand that charge to be conveyed by them. Verdict for the plaintiff for £5.

Humfrey now moved for a new trial, on the ground of misdirection.[1]

Alderson, B. In this case, had there been no by-standers who could understand the words as imputing felony, or who knew all about the affair respecting which they were uttered, the judge's direction would have been wrong, for it would then be *damnum absque injuria,* the *injuria* being the having no lawful occasion to impute felony.

Parke, B. The witness appears to have been well acquainted with the affair to which the words related. If the by-standers were equally cognizant of it, the defendant would have been entitled to a verdict; but here the only question is, whether the private intention of a man who utters injurious words is material, if by-standers may fairly understand them in a sense and manner injurious to the party to whom they relate, *e. g.,* that he was a felon.

Some doubt being suggested as to the facts proved, the court conferred with Rolfe, B.; and the next day,

Pollock, C. B., said, We find from my Brother Rolfe that there were several by-standers who not only might but must have heard the expressions which form the subject of this action. That disposes of the case as to the matter of law. Words uttered must be construed in the sense which hearers of common and reasonable understanding would ascribe to them, even though particular individuals better informed on the matter alluded to might form a different judgment on the subject. *Rule refused.*[2]

[1] The case has been much abridged.

[2] Phillips *v.* Bradshaw, 167 Ala. 199; Allen *v.* Fincher, 187 Ala. 599; Pouchan *v.* Godeau, 167 Cal. 692; United Mine Workers *v.* Cromer, 159 Ky. 605; Tawney *v.* Simonson, 109 Minn. 341; Sweaas *v.* Evenson, 110 Minn. 304; Vanloon *v.* Vanloon, 159 Mo. App. 255; Jones *v.* Banner, 172 Mo. App. 132; Bigley *v.* National Fidelity Co., 94 Neb. 813; Phillips *v.* Barber, 7 Wend. 439; Church *v.* New York Tribune Ass'n, 135 App. Div. 30; Rossiter *v.* New York Press Co., 141 App. Div.

BROMAGE *v.* PROSSER

IN THE KING'S BENCH, EASTER TERM, 1825.

Reported in 4 Barnewall & Cresswell, 247.

BAYLEY, J., now delivered the judgment of the court.[1] This was an action for slander. The plaintiffs were bankers at Monmouth, and the charge was, that in answer to a question from one Lewis Watkins, whether he, the defendant, had said that the plaintiff's bank had stopped, the defendant's answer was, "It was true, he had been told so." The evidence was, that Watkins met defendant and said, "I hear that you say the bank of Bromage and Snead, at Monmouth, has stopped. Is it true?" Defendant said, "Yes, it is; I was told so." He added, "It was so reported at Crickhowell, and nobody would take their bills, and that he had come to town in consequence of it himself." Watkins said, "You had better take care what you say; you first brought the news to town, and told Mr. John Thomas of it." Defendant repeated, "I was told so." Defendant had been told, at Crickhowell, there was a run upon plaintiff's bank, but not that it had stopped, or that nobody would take their bills, and what he said went greatly beyond what he had heard. The learned judge considered the words as proved, and he does not appear to have treated it as a case of privileged communication; but as the defendant did not appear to be actuated by any ill will against the plaintiffs, he told the jury that if they thought the words were not spoken maliciously, though they might unfortunately have produced injury to the plaintiffs, the defendant ought to have their verdict; but if they thought them spoken maliciously, they should find for the plaintiff: and the jury having found for the defendant, the question upon a motion for a new trial was upon the propriety of this direction. If in an ordinary case of slander (not a case of privileged communication), want of malice

339; Spencer *v.* Minnick, 41 Okl. 613; McGeary *v.* Leader Pub. Co., 52 Pa. Super. Ct. 35; Lehmann *v.* Medack, (Tex. Civ. App.) 152 S. W. 438 *Accord.* Compare Marshall *v.* Chicago Herald Co., 185 Ill. App. 224; Willfred Coal Co. *v.* Sapp, 193 Ill. App. 400; Sweet *v.* Post Pub. Co., 215 Mass. 450; Corr *v.* Sun Printing & Pub. Ass'n, 177 N. Y. 131. But see M. *v.* J., 164 Wis. 39.

A lunatic is liable for torts generally and also for a libel. Mordaunt *v.* Mordaunt, 39 L. J. Pr. & M. 57, 59. But it is another illustration of the rule of the principal case that defamatory words spoken by a lunatic whose insanity was obvious or known to all the hearers, are not actionable. Yeates *v.* Reed, 4 Blackf. 463; Irvine *v.* Gibson, 117 Ky. 306; Dickinson *v.* Barber, 9 Mass. 225, 227; Bryant *v.* Jackson, 6 Humph. 199. So also of words spoken and understood as a jest. Donoghue *v.* Hayes, Hayes, 265. Drunkenness is no defence. Kendrick *v.* Hopkins, Cary, 133; Gates *v.* Meredith, 7 Ind. 440.

The old rule of construing defamatory statements *in mitiori sensu* was long ago exploded. See Odgers, Libel & Slander (5 ed.), 111–113.

Explanation of words by context, see Deitchman *v.* Bowles, 166 Ky. 285; McCurda *v.* Lewiston Journal Co., 109 Me. 53; Wing *v.* Wing, 66 Me. 62; Larsen *v.* Brooklyn Eagle, 165 App. Div. 4; Guenther *v.* Ridgway Co., 170 App. Div. 725; Eddy *v.* Cunningham, 69 Wash. 544; Leuch *v.* Berger, 161 Wis. 564.

[1] Only the opinion of the court is given.

is a question of fact for the consideration of a jury, the direction was right; but if in such a case the law implies such malice as is necessary to maintain the action, it is the duty of the judge to withdraw the question of malice from the consideration of the jury: and it appears to us that the direction in this case was wrong. That malice, in some sense, is the gist of the action, and that therefore the manner and occasion of speaking the words is admissible in evidence to show they were not spoken with malice, is said to have been agreed (either by all the judges, or at least by the four who thought the truth might be given in evidence on the general issue) in Smith *v.* Richardson, Willes, 24; and it is laid down in 1 Com. Dig. action upon the case for defamation, G 5, that the declaration must show a malicious intent in the defendant, and there are some other very useful elementary books in which it is said that malice is the gist of the action, but in what sense the words malice or malicious intent are here to be understood, whether in the popular sense, or in the sense the law puts upon those expressions, none of these authorities state. Malice in common acceptation means ill-will against a person, but in its legal sense it means a wrongful act, done intentionally, without just cause or excuse. If I give a perfect stranger a blow likely to produce death, I do it of malice, because I do it intentionally and without just cause or excuse. If I maim cattle, without knowing whose they are; if I poison a fishery, without knowing the owner, I do it of malice, because it is a wrongful act, and done intentionally. If I am arraigned of felony, and wilfully stand mute, I am said to do it of malice, because it is intentional and without just cause or excuse. Russell on Crimes, 614, N. 1. And if I traduce a man, whether I know him or not, and whether I intend to do him an injury or not, I apprehend the law considers it as done of malice, because it is wrongful and intentional. It equally works an injury, whether I meant to produce an injury or not, and if I had no legal excuse for the slander, why is he not to have a remedy against me for the injury it produces? And I apprehend the law recognizes the distinction between these two descriptions of malice, malice in fact and malice in law, in actions of slander. In an ordinary action for words, it is sufficient to charge that the defendant spoke them falsely, it is not necessary to state that they were spoken maliciously. This is so laid down in Style, 392, and was adjudged upon error in Mercer *v.* Sparks, Owen, 51; Noy, 35. The objection there was, that the words were not charged to have been spoken maliciously, but the court answered, that the words were themselves malicious and slanderous, and, therefore, the judgment was affirmed. But in actions for such slander as is *prima facie* excusable on account of the cause of speaking or writing it, as in the case of servant's characters, confidential advice, or communications to persons who ask it, or have a right to expect it, malice in fact must be proved by the plaintiff, and in Edmonson *v.* Stevenson, 1 Term Rep.

110, Lord Mansfield takes the distinction between these and ordinary actions of slander. In Weatherstone *v.* Hawkins, Bull. N. P. 8, where a master who had given a servant a character, which prevented his being hired, gave his brother-in-law, who applied to him upon the subject, a detail by letter of certain instances in which the servant had defrauded him; Wood, who argued for the plaintiff, insisted that this case did not differ from the case of common libels, that it had the two essential ingredients, slander and falsehood; that it was not necessary to prove express malice; if the matter is slanderous, malice is implied, it is sufficient to prove publication; the motives of the party publishing are never gone into, and that the same doctrine held in actions for words, no express malice need be proved. Lord Mansfield said the general rules are laid down as Mr. Wood has stated, but to every libel there may be an implied justification from the occasion. So as to the words, instead of the plaintiff's showing it to be false and malicious, it appears to be incidental to the application by the intended master for the character; and Buller, J., said, this is an exception to the general rule, on account of the occasion of writing. In actions of this kind, the plaintiff must prove the words "malicious" as well as false. Buller, J., repeats in Pasley *v.* Freeman, 3 T. R. 61, that for words spoken confidentially upon advice asked, no action lies, unless express malice can be proved. So in Hargrave *v.* Le Breton, 3 Burr. 2425, Lord Mansfield states that no action can be maintained against a master for the character he gives a servant, unless there are extraordinary circumstances of express malice. But in an ordinary action for a libel or for words, though evidence of malice may be given to increase the damages, it never is considered as essential, nor is there any instance of a verdict for a defendant on the ground of want of malice. Numberless occasions must have occurred (particularly in cases where a defendant only repeated what he had heard before, but without naming the author), upon which, if that were a tenable ground, verdicts would have been sought for and obtained, and the absence of any such instance is a proof of what has been the general and universal opinion upon the point. Had it been noticed to the jury how the defendant came to speak the words, and had it been left to them as a previous question, whether the defendant understood Watkins as asking for information for his own guidance, and that the defendant spoke what he did to Watkins, merely by way of honest advice to regulate his conduct, the question of malice in fact would have been proper as a second question to the jury, if their minds were in favor of the defendant upon the first; but as the previous question I have mentioned was never put to the jury, but this was treated as an ordinary case of slander, we are of opinion that the question of malice ought not to have been left to the jury. It was, however, pressed upon us with considerable force, that we ought not to grant a new trial, on the ground that the evidence did not support any of the counts in the declaration, but upon carefully attending to the declaration and the evidence, we think we are not warranted in saying that there was no evidence to go to the jury to support the declaration; and had the learned judge intimated an opinion that there was no such evidence, the plaintiff might have attempted to supply the defect. We, therefore, think that we cannot properly refuse a new trial, upon the ground that the result upon the trial might have been doubtful. In granting a new trial, however, the court does not mean to say that it may not be proper to put the question of malice as a question of fact for the consideration of the jury; for if the jury should think that when Watkins asked his question the defendant understood it as asked in order to obtain information to regulate his own conduct, it will range under the cases of privileged communication, and the question of malice, in fact, will then be a necessary part of the jury's inquiry; but it does not appear that it was left to the jury in this case, to consider whether this was understood by the defendant as an application to him for advice, and if not, the question of malice was improperly left to their consideration. We are, therefore, of opinion, that the rule for a new trial must be absolute. *Rule absolute.*[1]

HANSON *v.* GLOBE NEWSPAPER COMPANY

SUPREME JUDICIAL COURT, MASSACHUSETTS, JUNE 20, 1893.

Reported in 159 *Massachusetts Reports*, 293.

KNOWLTON, J.[2] The defendant published in its newspaper an article describing the conduct of a prisoner brought before the Municipal Court of Boston, and the proceedings of the court in the case, designating him as " H. P. Hanson, a real estate and insurance broker of South Boston." He was, in fact, a real estate and insurance broker of South Boston, and the article was substantially true, except that he should have been called A. P. H. Hanson instead of H. P. Hanson. The plaintiff, H. P. Hanson, is also a real estate and insurance broker in South Boston, and in writing the article the reporter used his name by mistake.[3] The justice of the Superior Court, before whom the case was tried, without a jury, " found as a fact that the alleged libel

[1] Massee *v.* Williams, (C. C. A.) 207 Fed. 222; Ivie *v.* King, 167 N. C. 174; Olympia Waterworks *v.* Mottman, 88 Wash. 694 *Accord.* See *Ex parte* Nelson, 251 Mo. 63.

[2] A portion of the opinion is omitted.

[3] The article was as follows: " He Waxed Eloquent. H. P. Hanson fined ten dollars for refusing payment of car fare. . . . H. P. Hanson, a real estate and insurance broker of South Boston, emerged from the seething mass of humanity that filled the dock and indulged in a wordy bout with policeman Hogan, who claimed to have arrested Hanson on the charge of evading car fare and being drunk at the same time. The judge agreed that the prisoner was sober, but on the charge of evasion of car fare the evidence warranted the fining of the eloquent occupant of the dock ten dollars without costs, which he paid."

declared on by the plaintiff was not published by the defendant of or concerning the plaintiff," and the only question in the case is whether this finding was erroneous as matter of law.

In every action of this kind the fundamental question is, What is the meaning of the author of the alleged libel or slander, conveyed by the words used interpreted in the light of all the circumstances? The reason of this is obvious. Defamatory language is harmful only as it purports to be the expression of the thought of him who uses it. In determining the effect of a slander the questions involved are, What is the thought intended to be expressed, and how much credit should be given to him who expresses it? The essence of the wrong is the expression of what purports to be the knowledge or opinion of him who utters the defamatory words, or of some one else whose language he repeats. His meaning, to be ascertained in a proper way, is what gives character to his act, and makes it innocent or wrongful. The damages depend chiefly upon the weight which is to be given to his expression of his meaning, and all the questions relate back to the ascertainment of his meaning.

In the present case we are concerned only with the meaning of the defendant in regard to the person to whom the language of the published article was to be applied, and the question to be decided is, How may his meaning legitimately be ascertained? Obviously, in the first place, from the language used; and in construing and applying the language, the circumstances under which it was written and the facts to which it relates are to be considered, so far as they can readily be ascertained by those who read the words, and who attempt to find out the meaning of the author in regard to the person of whom they were written. It has often been said that the meaning of the language is not necessarily that which it may seem to have to those who read it as strangers, without knowledge of facts and circumstances which give it color and aid in its interpretation, but that which it has when read in the light of events which have relation to the utterance or publication of it.

For the purposes of this case it may be assumed, in favor of the plaintiff, that if the language used in a particular case, interpreted in the light of such events and circumstances attending the publication of it as could readily be ascertained by the public, is free from ambiguity in regard to the person referred to, and points clearly to a well known person, it would be held to have been published concerning that person, although the defendant should show that through some mistake of fact, not easily discoverable by the public, he had designated in his publication a person other than the one whom he intended to designate. It may well be held that where the language, read in connection with all the facts and circumstances which can be used in its interpretation, is free from ambiguity, the defendant will not be permitted to show that through ignorance or mistake he said something, either by way of designating the person, or making assertions about him, different from that which he intended to say; but his true meaning should be ascertained, if it can be, with the aid of such facts and circumstances attending the publication as may easily be known by those of the public who wish to discover it.

Whether the defendant should ever be permitted to state his undisclosed intention in regard to the person of whom the words are used, may be doubtful. If language purporting to be used of only one person would refer equally to either of two different persons of the same name, and if there were nothing to indicate that one was meant rather than the other, there is good reason for holding that the defendant's testimony in regard to his secret intention might be received, but perhaps such a case is hardly supposable. Odgers, in his book on Libel and Slander, at page 129, says: "So, if the words spoken or written, though plain in themselves, apply equally well to more persons than one, evidence may be given both of the cause and occasion of publication, and of all the surrounding circumstances affecting the relation between the parties, and also any statement or declaration made by the defendant as to the person referred to." In Regina *v.* Barnard, 43 J. P. 127, when it was uncertain whether the libel referred to the complainant or not, and when the language was applicable to him, Lord Chief Justice Cockburn held the affidavit of the writer that he did not mean him, but some one else, to be a sufficient reason for refusing process. In De Armond *v.* Armstrong, 37 Ind. 35, evidence was received of what the witnesses understood in regard to the person referred to. In Smart *v.* Blanchard, 42 N. H. 137, it is stated that extrinsic evidence is to be received "to show that the defendant intended to apply his remarks to the plaintiff," when his meaning is doubtful. Goodrich *v.* Davis, 11 Met. 473, 480, 484, 485, and Miller *v.* Butler, 6 Cush. 71, are of similar purport. See also Barwell *v.* Adkins, 1 M. & G. 807; Knapp *v.* Fuller, 55 Vt. 311; Commonwealth *v.* Morgan, 107 Mass. 199, 201.

If the defendant's article had contained anything libellous against A. P. H. Hanson, there can be no doubt that he could have maintained an action against the defendant for this publication. The name used is not conclusive in determining the meaning of the libel in respect to the person referred to; it is but one fact to be considered with other facts upon that subject. Fictitious names are often used in libels, and names similar to that of the person intended, but differing somewhat from it. A. P. H. Hanson could have shown that the description of him by name, residence, and occupation was perfect, except in the use of the initials "H. P." instead of "A. P. H.," that the article referred to an occasion on which he was present, and gave a description of conduct of a prisoner, and of proceedings in court, which was correct in its application to him and to no one else. The internal evidence when applied to facts well known to the public would have been ample to show that the language referred to him, and not to the person whose name was used.

So, in the present suit, the court had no occasion to rely on the testimony of the writer as to the person to whom the language was intended to apply. The language itself, in connection with the publicly known circumstances under which it was written, showed at once that the article referred to A. P. H. Hanson, and that the name H. P. Hanson was used by mistake. As the evidence showed that the words were published of and concerning A. P. H. Hanson, the finding that they were not published of the plaintiff followed of necessity. The article was of such a kind that it referred, and could refer, to one person only; when that person was ascertained, it might appear that the publication as against him was or was not libellous, and his rights, if he brought a suit, would depend upon the finding in respect to that. No one else would have a cause of action, even if, by reason of identity of name with that used in the publication, he might suffer some harm. For illustration, suppose a libel is written concerning a person described as John Smith of Springfield. Suppose there are five persons in Springfield of that name. The language refers to but one. When we ascertain by legitimate evidence to which one the words are intended to apply, he can maintain an action. The other persons of the same name cannot recover damages for a libel merely because of their misfortune in having a name like that of the person libelled. Or, if the defendant can justify by proving that the words were true, and published without malice, he is not guilty of a libel, even if, written of other persons of the same name of whose existence very likely he was ignorant, the words would be libellous; otherwise, one who has published that which by its terms can refer to but one person, and be a libel on him only, might be responsible for half a dozen libels on as many different persons, and one who has justifiably published the truth of a person might be liable to several persons of the same name of whom the language would be untrue. The law of libel has never been extended, and should not be extended, to include such cases.

Whether there should be a liability founded on negligence in any case when the truth is published of one to whom the words, interpreted in the light of accompanying circumstances easily ascertainable by those who read them, plainly apply; and where, by reason of identity of names, or similarity of names and description, a part of the public might think them applicable to another person of whom they would be libellous, is a question which does not arise on the pleadings in this case. So far as we are aware, no action for such a cause has ever been maintained. It is ordinarily to be presumed, although it may not always be the fact, that those who are enough interested in a person to be affected by what is said about him, will ascertain, if they easily can, whether libellous words which purport to refer to one of his name were intended to be applied to him or to some one else.

The question in this case, whether the words were published of and concerning the plaintiff, was one of fact on all the evidence. Unless it appears that the matters stated in the report would not warrant a finding for the defendant, there must be judgment for him, even if the finding of fact might have been the other way. We are of opinion that the finding was well warranted, and there must be,

Judgment on the finding.

HOLMES, J. I am unable to agree with the decision of the majority of the court, and as the question is of some importance in its bearing on legal principles, and as I am not alone in my views, I think it proper to state the considerations which have occurred to me.

Those words [H. P. Hanson, a real estate and insurance broker of South Boston] describe the plaintiff, and no one else. The only ground, then, on which the matters alleged of and concerning that subject can be found not to be alleged of and concerning the plaintiff, is that the defendant did not intend them to apply to him, and the question is narrowed to whether such a want of intention is enough to warrant the finding, or to constitute a defence, when the inevitable consequence of the defendant's acts is that the public, or that part of it which knows the plaintiff, will suppose that the defendant did use its language about him.

On general principles of tort, the private intent of the defendant would not exonerate it. It knew that it was publishing statements purporting to be serious, which would be hurtful to a man if applied to him. It knew that it was using as the subject of those statements words which purported to designate a particular man, and would be understood by its readers to designate one. In fact, the words purported to designate, and would be understood by its readers to designate, the plaintiff. If the defendant had supposed that there was no such person, and had intended simply to write an amusing fiction, that would not be a defence, at least unless its belief was justifiable. Without special reason, it would have no right to assume that there was no one within the sphere of its influence to whom the description answered. So, when the description which points out the plaintiff is supposed by the defendant to point out another man whom in fact it does not describe, the defendant is equally liable as when the description is supposed to point out nobody. On the general principles of tort, the publication is so manifestly detrimental that the defendant publishes it at the peril of being able to justify it in the sense in which the public will understand it.

A man may be liable civilly, and formerly, at least by the common law of England, even criminally, for publishing a libel without knowing it. Curtis *v.* Mussey, 6 Gray, 261; Commonwealth *v.* Morgan,

107 Mass. 199; Dunn *v.* Hall, 1 Ind. 344; Rex *v.* Walter, 3 Esp. 21; Rex *v.* Gutch, Mood. & Malk. 433. See also Rex *v.* Cuthell, 27 St. Tr. 642. And it seems he might be liable civilly for publishing it by mistake, intending to publish another paper. Mayne *v.* Fletcher, 4 Man. & Ry. 311, 312, note. Odgers, Libel and Slander, (2d ed.) 5. So, when by mistake the name of the plaintiff's firm was inserted under the head " First Meetings under the Bankruptcy Act," instead of under " Dissolution of Partnerships." Shepheard *v.* Whitaker, L. R. 10 C. P. 502. So a man will be liable for a slander spoken in jest, if the bystanders reasonably understand it to be a serious charge. Donoghue *v.* Hayes, Hayes, 265. Of course it does not matter that the defendant did not intend to injure the plaintiff, if that was the manifest tendency of his words. Curtis *v.* Mussey, 6 Gray, 261, 273; Haire *v.* Wilson, 9 B. & C. 643. And to prove a publication concerning the plaintiff, it lies upon him " only to show that this construction, which they 've put upon the paper, is such as the generality of readers must take it in, according to the obvious and natural sense of it." The King *v.* Clerk, 1 Barnard. 304, 305. See further Fox *v.* Broderick, 14 Ir. C. L. 453; Odgers, Libel and Slander, (2d ed.) 155, 269, 435, 638. In Smith *v.* Ashley, 11 Met. 367, the jury were instructed that the publisher of a newspaper article written by another, and supposed and still asserted by the defendant to be a fiction, was not liable if he believed it to be so. Under the circumstances of the case, " believed " meant " reasonably believed." Even so qualified, it is questioned by Mr. Odgers if the ruling would be followed in England. Odgers, Libel and Slander, (1st Am. ed.) 387, (2d ed.) 638. But it has no application to this case, as here the defendant's agent wrote the article, and there is no evidence that he or the defendant had any reason to believe that H. P. Hanson meant any one but the plaintiff.

The foregoing decisions show that slander and libel now, as in the beginning, are governed by the general principles of the law of tort, and, if that be so, the defendant's ignorance that the words which it published identified the plaintiff is no more an excuse, than ignorance of any other fact about which the defendant has been put on inquiry. To hold that a man publishes such words at his peril, when they are supposed to describe a different man, is hardly a severer application of the law, than when they are uttered about a man believed on the strongest grounds to be dead, and thus not capable of being the subject of a tort. It has been seen that by the common law of England such a belief would not be an excuse. Hearne *v.* Stowell, 12 A. & E. 719, 726, denying Parson Prick's case.

I feel some difficulty in putting my finger on the precise point of difference between the minority and majority of the court. I understand, however, that a somewhat unwilling assent is yielded to the general views which I have endeavored to justify, and I should gather that the exact issue was to be found in the statement that the article was one describing the conduct of a prisoner brought before the Municipal Court of Boston, coupled with the later statement that the language, taken in connection with the publicly known circumstances under which it was written, showed at once that the article referred to A. P. H. Hanson, and that the name of H. P. Hanson was used by mistake. I have shown why it seems to me that these statements are misleading. I only will add on this point, that I do not know what the publicly known circumstances are. I think it is a mistake of fact to suppose that the public generally know who was before the Municipal Criminal Court on a given day. I think it is a mistake of law to say that, because a small part of the public have that knowledge, the plaintiff cannot recover for the harm done him in the eyes of the greater part of the public, probably including all his acquaintances who are ignorant about the matter, and I also think it no sufficient answer to say that they might consult the criminal records, and find out that probably there was some error. Blake *v.* Stevens, 4 F. & F. 232, 240. If the case should proceed further on the facts, it might appear that, in view of the plaintiff's character and circumstances, all who knew him would assume that there was a mistake, that the harm to him was merely nominal, and that he had been too hasty in resorting to an action to vindicate himself. But that question is not before us.

With reference to the suggestion that, if the article, in addition to what was true concerning A. P. H. Hanson, had contained matter which was false and libellous as to him, he might have maintained an action, it is unnecessary to express an opinion. I think the proposition less obvious than that the plaintiff can maintain one. If an article should describe the subject of its statements by two sets of marks, one of which identified one man and one of which identified another, and a part of the public naturally and reasonably were led by the one set to apply the statements to one plaintiff, and another part were led in the same way by the other set to apply them to another, I see no absurdity in allowing two actions to be maintained. But that is not this case.

Even if the plaintiff and A. P. H. Hanson had borne the same name, and the article identified its subject only by a proper name, very possibly that would not be enough to raise the question. For, as every one knows, a proper name always purports to designate one person and no other, and although, through the imperfection of our system of naming, the same combination of letters and sounds may be applied to two or more, the name of each, in theory of law, is distinct, although there is no way of finding out which person was named but by inquiring which was meant. "*Licet idem sit nomen, tamen diversum est propter diversitatem personæ.*" Bract. fol. 190 a. Commonwealth *v.* Bacon, 135 Mass. 521, 525. Cocker *v.* Crompton, 1 B.

& C. 489. In re Cooper, 20 Ch. D. 611. Mead *v.* Phenix Ins. Co., 158 Mass. 124, 125. Kyle *v.* Kavanagh, 103 Mass. 356. Raffles *v.* Wichelhaus, 2 H. & C. 906.

Mr. Justice Morton and Mr. Justice Barker agree with this opinion.[1]

PECK *v.* TRIBUNE COMPANY

SUPREME COURT OF THE UNITED STATES, MAY 17, 1909.

Reported in 214 *United States Reports,* 185.

MR. JUSTICE HOLMES delivered the opinion of the court.

This is an action on the case for a libel. The libel alleged is found in an advertisement printed in the defendant's newspaper, *The Chicago Sunday Tribune*, and so far as is material is as follows: "Nurse and Patients Praise Duffy's—Mrs. A. Schuman, One of Chicago's Most Capable and Experienced Nurses, Pays an Eloquent Tribute to the Great Invigorating, Life-Giving and Curative Properties of Duffy's Pure Malt Whiskey. . . ." Then followed a portrait of the plaintiff, with the words "Mrs. A. Schuman" under it. Then, in quotation marks, "After years of constant use of your Pure Malt Whiskey, both by myself and as given to patients in my capacity as nurse, I have no hesitation in recommending it as the very best tonic and stimulant for all weak and rundown conditions," &c., &c., with the words "Mrs. A. Schuman, 1576 Mozart St., Chicago, Ill.," at the end, not in quotation marks, but conveying the notion of a signature, or at least that the words were hers. The declaration alleged that the plaintiff was not Mrs. Schuman, was not a nurse, and was a total abstainer from whiskey and all spirituous liquors. There was also a count for publishing the plaintiff's likeness without leave. The defendant pleaded not guilty. At the trial, subject to exceptions, the judge excluded the plaintiff's testimony in support of her allegations just stated, and directed a verdict for the defendant. His action was sustained by the Circuit Court of Appeals, 154 Fed. Rep. 330; S. C., 83 C. C. A. 202.

Of course the insertion of the plaintiff's picture in the place and with the concomitants that we have described imported that she was the nurse and made the statements set forth, as rightly was decided in Wandt *v.* Hearst's Chicago American, 129 Wisconsin, 419, 421. Morrison *v.* Smith, 177 N. Y. 366. Therefore the publication was of and concerning the plaintiff, notwithstanding the presence of another fact, the name of the real signer of the certificate, if that was Mrs. Schu-

[1] The opinion of the dissenting judges is supported by the decisions and *dicta* in other jurisdictions. Butler *v.* Barret, 130 Fed. 944 (*semble*); Every Evening Co. *v.* Butler, 144 Fed. 916; Taylor *v.* Hearst, 107 Cal. 262; Hulbert *v.* New Co., 111 Ia. 490; Davis *v.* Marxhausen, 86 Mich. 281, 103 Mich. 315 (*semble*); Clark *v.* North American Co., 203 Pa. St. 346 (*semble*); Hutchinson *v.* Robinson, 21 N. S. W. L. R. (Law) 130 (*semble*). Compare Newton *v.* Grubbs, 155 Ky. 479; Ellis *v.* Brockton Pub. Co., 198 Mass. 538; Dunlop *v.* Sundberg, 55 Wash. 609.

man, that was inconsistent, when all the facts were known, with the plaintiff's having signed or adopted it. Many might recognize the plaintiff's face without knowing her name, and those who did know it might be led to infer that she had sanctioned the publication under an alias. There was some suggestion that the defendant published the portrait by mistake, and without knowledge that it was the plaintiff's portrait or was not what it purported to be. But the fact, if it was one, was no excuse. If the publication was libellous the defendant took the risk. As was said of such matters by Lord Mansfield, "Whatever a man publishes he publishes at his peril." The King *v.* Woodfall, Lofft, 776, 781. See further Hearne *v.* Stowell, 12 A. & E. 719, 726; Shepheard *v.* Whitaker, L. R. 10 C. P. 502; Clark *v.* North American Co., 203 Pa. St. 346, 351, 352. The reason is plain. A libel is harmful on its face. If a man sees fit to publish manifestly hurtful statements concerning an individual, without other justification than exists for an advertisement or a piece of news, the usual principles of tort will make him liable, if the statements are false or are true only of some one else. See Morasse *v.* Brochu, 151 Massachusetts, 567, 575.

The question, then, is whether the publication was a libel. It was held by the Circuit Court of Appeals not to be, or at most to entitle the plaintiff only to nominal damages, no special damage being alleged. It was pointed out that there was no general consensus of opinion that to drink whiskey is wrong or that to be a nurse is discreditable. It might have been added that very possibly giving a certificate and the use of one's portrait in aid of an advertisement would be regarded with irony, or a stronger feeling, only by a few. But it appears to us that such inquiries are beside the point. It may be that the action for libel is of little use, but while it is maintained it should be governed by the general principles of tort. If the advertisement obviously would hurt the plaintiff in the estimation of an important and respectable part of the community, liability is not a question of a majority vote.

We know of no decision in which this matter is discussed upon principle. But obviously an unprivileged falsehood need not entail universal hatred to constitute a cause of action. No falsehood is thought about or even known by all the world. No conduct is hated by all. That it will be known by a large number and will lead an appreciable fraction of that number to regard the plaintiff with contempt is enough to do her practical harm. Thus if a doctor were represented as advertising, the fact that it would affect his standing with others of his profession might make the representation actionable, although advertising is not reputed dishonest and even seems to be regarded by many with pride. See Martin *v.* The Picayune, 115 Louisiana, 979. It seems to us impossible to say that the obvious tendency of what is imputed to the plaintiff by this advertisement is not seriously to hurt her standing with a considerable and respectable class in the community. Therefore it was the plaintiff's right to prove her case and go to the jury, and the defendant would have got all that it could ask if [it] had been permitted to persuade them, if it could, to take a contrary view. Culmer *v.* Canby, 101 Fed. Rep. 195, 197; Twombly *v.* Monroe, 136 Massachusetts, 464, 469. See Gates *v.* New York Recorder Co., 155 N. Y. 228.

It is unnecessary to consider the question whether the publication of the plaintiff's likeness was a tort *per se.* It is enough for the present case that the law should at least be prompt to recognize the injuries that may arise from an unauthorized use in connection with other facts, even if more subtilty is needed to state the wrong than is needed here. In this instance we feel no doubt.

Judgment reversed.[1]

E. HULTON AND COMPANY *v.* JONES

IN THE HOUSE OF LORDS, DECEMBER 6, 1909.

Reported in [1909] *Appeal Cases,* 20.

THE following statement is taken from the opinion of Lord Alverstone, C. J., in the Court of Appeal.[2]

" The action was brought by the plaintiff, a member of the Bar, in respect of a libel published in the *Sunday Chronicle* on July 12, 1908 (the passages complained of are set out in the statement of claim), which appeared in an article in the defendants' paper purporting to describe what the Paris correspondent of the paper had witnessed at Dieppe, and the particular passage on which the question really turns was in these words: ' " Whist! there is Artemus Jones with a woman who is not his wife, who must be, you know — the other thing! " whispers a fair neighbor of mine excitedly into her bosom friend's ear. Really, is it not surprising how certain of our fellow-countrymen behave when they come abroad ? ' It was alleged by the plaintiff that this passage was a libel upon him.

" The material facts which were proved in evidence at the trial were as follows. The plaintiff, whose real name is Thomas Jones, is thirty-seven years old, and since the year 1901 has been a member of the Bar, practising on the North Wales Circuit. His baptismal name was Thomas Jones, but ever since he was at school he has been known by

[1] Compare Gandia *v.* Pettingill, 222 U. S. 452; Van Wiginton *v.* Pulitzer Pub. Co., (C. C. A.) 218 Fed. 795; Jones *v.* R. L. Polk & Co., 190 Ala. 243 (publishing of white woman that she is colored); Ball *v.* Evening American Co., 237 Ill. 592; MacIntyre *v.* Fruchter, 148 N. Y. Suppl. 786 (" fit only for negroes to associate with "); Spencer *v.* Looney, 116 Va. 767 (assertion of white person that he was colored); Galveston Tribune *v.* Guisti, (Tex. Civ. App.) 134 S. W. 239.

[2] This abridged statement has been substituted. The arguments and all but one of the opinions have been omitted.

the name of Artemus Jones or Thomas Artemus Jones. He was confirmed in the latter name in the year 1886, and it appears to have been given him by his father in order to distinguish him from other persons of the name of Jones. The defendants alleged that the name was used as a fictitious name adopted by the writer of the article without any knowledge of the existence of the plaintiff or of any person named Artemus Jones; and both the writer and the editor, who were called as witnesses by the defendants under circumstances to which I shall have to refer, stated that they had no knowledge whatever of the plaintiff, and had no intention to refer to him, and that so far as they were concerned the name was entirely an imaginary name. The counsel for the plaintiff accepted the explanation given by the writer, Mr. Dawbarn, and the editor, Mr. Woodbridge, and expressly stated that he did not, after their evidence, allege that they or either of them were in fact actuated by malice, or intended to refer to the plaintiff in their article. Some question was raised both at the trial and on the appeal before us as to the possibility of there being other individuals in the employment of the defendant company who were actuated by express malice towards the plaintiff, but for the purpose of my judgment I assume that there was no proof of malice in fact on the part of any agent or servant of the defendants. The plaintiff called five witnesses who stated that upon reading the article they thought that it referred to the plaintiff, and the plaintiff was prepared to call further witnesses to give evidence to the same effect, but, at the suggestion of the learned judge, he abstained from calling them. . . .

"At the conclusion of the plaintiff's case, Mr. Langdon, who was then the leading counsel for the defendants, submitted that, as the name Artemus Jones was a fictitious name, coined by the writer of the article, and not intended to refer to any particular individual at all, it was not a libel on anybody, and *a fortiori* not on the plaintiff himself. In support of this contention the case of Harrison *v.* Smith, 20 L. T. (N. S.) 713, was at that stage of the proceedings cited to the learned judge. He ruled that, if a person chooses to publish a thing of this description, the question is not whether the man really intended it, but whether it would be understood by readers to apply to a particular person, adding that, if sensible readers would see at once that it was only an imaginary thing, if any one reading it would see that it did not refer to a gentleman who happened to bear the name of Artemus Jones, it would not be a libel, but if he would think the contrary, that it did not refer to an imaginary person, but to a real individual, the action might be maintained."

It also appeared that up to the year 1901 plaintiff had contributed signed articles to defendants' newspaper.

At the trial before Channell, J., the plaintiff had a verdict for £1750, upon which judgment was rendered. Defendants appealed.

The Court of Appeal (Lord Alverstone, C. J., and Farwell, L. J., — Fletcher Moulton, L. J., dissenting) dismissed the appeal. Jones *v.* E. Hulton & Co., [1909] 2 K. B. 444.

Defendants then appealed to the House of Lords.

LORD LOREBURN, L. C. My Lords, I think this appeal must be dismissed. A question in regard to the law of libel has been raised which does not seem to me to be entitled to the support of your Lordships. Libel is a tortious act. What does the tort consist in ? It consists in using language which others knowing the circumstances would reasonably think to be defamatory of the person complaining of and injured by it. A person charged with libel cannot defend himself by showing that he intended in his own breast not to defame, or that he intended not to defame the plaintiff, if in fact he did both. He has none the less imputed something disgraceful and has none the less injured the plaintiff. A man in good faith may publish a libel believing it to be true, and it may be found by the jury that he acted in good faith believing it to be true, and reasonably believing it to be true, but that in fact the statement was false. Under those circumstances he has no defence to the action, however excellent his intention. If the intention of the writer be immaterial in considering whether the matter written is defamatory, I do not see why it need be relevant in considering whether it is defamatory of the plaintiff. The writing, according to the old form, must be malicious, and it must be of and concerning the plaintiff. Just as the defendant could not excuse himself from malice by proving that he wrote it in the most benevolent spirit, so he cannot show that the libel was not of and concerning the plaintiff by proving that he never heard of the plaintiff. His intention in both respects equally is inferred from what he did. His remedy is to abstain from defamatory words.

It is suggested that there was a misdirection by the learned judge in this case. I see none. He lays down in his summing up the law as follows: " The real point upon which your verdict must turn is, ought or ought not sensible and reasonable people reading this article to think that it was a mere imaginary person such as I have said — Tom Jones, Mr. Pecksniff as a humbug, Mr. Stiggins, or any of that sort of names that one reads of in literature used as types ? If you think any reasonable person would think that, it is not actionable at all. If, on the other hand, you do not think that, but think that people would suppose it to mean some real person — those who did not know the plaintiff of course would not know who the real person was, but those who did know of the existence of the plaintiff would think that it was the plaintiff — then the action is maintainable, subject to such damages as you think under all the circumstances are fair and right to give to the plaintiff."

I see no objection in law to that passage. The damages are certainly heavy, but I think your Lordships ought to remember two things. The first is that the jury were entitled to think, in the absence of proof satisfactory to them (and they were the judges of it), that some ingredient of recklessness, or more than recklessness, entered into the writing and the publication of this article, especially as Mr. Jones, the plaintiff, had been employed on this very newspaper, and his name was well known in the paper and also well known in the district in which the paper circulated. In the second place the jury were entitled to say this kind of article is to be condemned. There is no tribunal more fitted to decide in regard to publication, especially publications in the newspaper Press, whether they bear a stamp and character which ought to enlist sympathy and to secure protection. If they think that the license is not fairly used and that the tone and style of the libel is reprehensible and ought to be checked, it is for the jury to say so; and for my part, although I think the damages are certainly high, I am not prepared to advise your Lordships to interfere, especially as the Court of Appeal have not thought it right to interfere, with the verdict.

Lords Atkinson, Gorell, and Shaw of Dunfermline concurred.

Appeal dismissed.[1]

McPHERSON *v.* DANIELS

In the King's Bench, Michaelmas Term, 1829.

Reported in 10 *Barnewall & Cresswell*, 263.

Slander for an imputation of insolvency. The defendant pleaded that at the time of uttering the said words he declared that he had heard and been told the same from and by one T. W. Woor. General demurrer.[2]

Littledale, J. For the reasons already given by my Brother Bayley, I think that the plea is bad; but with reference to the resolution in Lord Northampton's case, I will say a few words. That resolution has been frequently referred to within the last thirty years, and though not expressly overruled has been generally disapproved of. The latter part of that resolution is extra-judicial, for it was not necessary to come to any resolution respecting private slander in the Star Chamber. It is somewhat inconsistent with the third resolution, where it is laid down, "that if one hear false and horrible rumors, either of the king or of any of the grandees, it is not lawful for him to relate to others that he heard J. S. say such false and horrible words, for if it should be lawful, by this means *they may be published gener-*

[1] Compare Northrop *v.* Tibbles, (C. C. A.) 215 Fed. 99. See Smith, Jones *v.* Hulton, Three Conflicting Views as to a Question of Defamation, 60 University of Pennsylvania Law Rev. 365, 461.

[2] The statement of the pleadings is abridged, and only the opinion of Littledale, J., is given. Bayley and Parke, JJ., concurred.

ally." It was resolved then, that in the case of *scandalum magnatum* it was not lawful to repeat slander, because, if it was, it might circulate generally. Now the same inconvenience, viz. the general publication of slander, though differing in degree, would follow from the repetition of slander in either case. The fourth resolution, however, in terms, perhaps does not go the length of saying that a defendant may justify the repetition of slander generally, but only that he may justify under certain circumstances. Assuming that it imports that a defendant may justify the repetition of slander generally, by showing that he named his original author, I think that it is not law.

The declaration, which contains a technical statement of the facts necessary to support the action, alleges that the defendant falsely and maliciously published the slander to the plaintiff's damage. In order to maintain such an action, there must be malice in the defendant and a damage to the plaintiff, and the words must be untrue. Where words, falsely and maliciously spoken, as in this case, are actionable in themselves, the law *prima facie* presumes a consequent damage without proof. In other cases actual damage must be proved. To constitute a good defence, therefore, to such an action, where the publication of the slander is not intended to be denied, the defendant must negative the charge of malice (which in its legal sense denotes a wrongful act done intentionally without just cause or excuse), or show that the plaintiff is not entitled to recover damages. It is competent to a defendant, upon the general issue, to show that the words were not spoken maliciously; by proving that they were spoken on an occasion, or under circumstances which the law, on grounds of public policy, allows, as in the course of a parliamentary or judicial proceeding, or in giving the character of a servant. But if the defendant relies upon the truth as an answer to the action, he must plead that matter specially; because the truth is an answer to the action, not because it negatives the charge of malice (for a person may wrongfully or maliciously utter slanderous matter though true, and thereby subject himself to an indictment), but because it shows that the plaintiff is not entitled to recover damages. For the law will not permit a man to recover damages in respect of an injury to a character which he either does not, or ought not, to possess. Now, a defendant, by showing that he stated at the time when he published slanderous matter of a plaintiff, that he heard it from a third person does not negative the charge of malice, for a man may wrongfully and maliciously repeat that which another person may have uttered upon a justifiable occasion. Such a plea does not show that the slander was published on an occasion, or under circumstances which the law, on grounds of public policy, allows. Nor does it show that the plaintiff has not sustained, or is not entitled in a court of law to recover, damages. As great an injury may accrue from the wrongful repetition, as from the first publication of slander, the first utterer may have been a person insane, or of bad character. The person who repeats it gives greater weight to the slander. A party is not the less entitled to recover damages in a court of law for injurious matter published concerning him, because another person previously published it. That shows not that the plaintiff has been guilty of any misconduct which renders it unfit that he should recover damages in a court of law, but that he has been wronged by another person as well as the defendant; and may, consequently if the slander was not published by the first utterer on a lawful occasion, have an action for damages against that person as well as the defendant. It seems to me, therefore, that such a plea is not an answer to an action for slander, because it does not negative the charge of malice, nor does it show that the plaintiff is not entitled to recover damages. *Judgment for plaintiff.*[1]

THORLEY v. LORD KERRY

IN THE EXCHEQUER CHAMBER, MAY 9, 1812.

Reported in 4 *Taunton*, 355.

THIS was a writ of error brought to reverse a judgment of the Court of King's Bench. "This was an action for a libel contained in a letter addressed to Lord Kerry, and sent open by one of his servants, who became acquainted with its contents. The libel charged his Lordship with being a hypocrite, and using the cloak of religion for unworthy purposes."[2] Upon not guilty pleaded, the cause was tried at the Surrey spring assizes, 1809, when the writing of the letter by the defendant was proved, and that he delivered it unsealed to a servant to carry, who opened and read it; a verdict was found for the plaintiff with £20 damages, and judgment passed for the plaintiff without

[1] That the defendant repeated a defamation, giving the name of the author, seems originally to have been a justification. Northampton's Case, 12 Rep. 134 (Fourth Resolution). But the name of the author was to be given at the time of repetition, and not for the first time in the plea. Davis v. Lewis, 7 T. R. 17. The words, furthermore, had to be given with sufficient exactness to ground an action against the author. Maitland v. Goldney, 2 East, 426. Doubts were thrown upon the validity of this justification in Lewis v. Walter, 4 B. & Al. 605. The whole doctrine was repudiated, as to libel, in De Crespigny v. Wellesley, 5 Bing. 392, and Tidman v. Ainslie, 10 Ex. 63; and as to slander, in McPherson v. Daniels; Watkin v. Hall, L. R. 3 Q. B. 396.

See to same effect Age-Herald Pub. Co. v. Waterman, 188 Ala. 272; Washington Herald Co. v. Berry, 41 App. D. C. 322; Brewer v. Chase, 121 Mich. 526; Hagener v. Pulitzer Pub. Co., 172 Mo. App. 436; Vallery v. State, 42 Neb. 123; Walling v. Commercial Advertiser, 165 App. Div. 26; Galveston Tribune v. Johnson, (Tex. Civ. App.) 141 S. W. 302. See also Whitney v. Moignard, 24 Q. B. D. 630.

In Speight v. Gosnay, 60 L. J. Q. B. 231, the words were not actionable without special damage and the special damage resulted only from unauthorized repetition by a third person.

[2] This short statement of the case, taken from 3 Camp. 214, has been substituted for the declaration which is set out at considerable length in the original report.

argument in the court below. The plaintiff in error assigned the general errors.

MANSFIELD, C. J., delivered the opinion of the court.

This is a writ of error, brought to reverse a judgment of the Court of King's Bench, in which there was no argument. It was an action on a libel published in a letter which the bearer of the letter happened to open. The declaration has certainly some very curious recitals. It recites that the plaintiff was tenant to Archibald Lord Douglas of a messuage in Petersham; that, being desirous to become a parishioner and to attend the vestry, he agreed to pay the taxes of the said house, that the plaintiff in error was churchwarden, and that the defendant in error gave him notice of his agreement with Lord Douglas; and that the plaintiff in error, intending to have it believed that the said earl was guilty of the offences and misconducts thereinafter mentioned (offences there are none, misconduct there may be), wrote the letter to the said earl which is set forth in the pleadings. There is no doubt that this was a libel, for which the plaintiff in error might have been indicted and punished; because, though the words impute no punishable crimes, they contain that sort of imputation which is calculated to vilify a man, and bring him, as the books say, into hatred, contempt, and ridicule; for all words of that description an indictment lies; and I should have thought that the peace and good name of individuals was sufficiently guarded by the terror of this criminal proceeding in such cases. The words, if merely spoken, would not be of themselves sufficient to support an action. But the question now is, whether an action will lie for these words so written, notwithstanding such an action would not lie for them if spoken; and I am very sorry it was not discussed in the Court of King's Bench, that we might have had the opinion of all the twelve judges on the point, whether there be any distinction as to the right of action between written and parol scandal; for myself, after having heard it extremely well argued, and especially, in this case, by Mr. Barnewall, I cannot, upon principle, make any difference between words written and words spoken, as to the right which arises on them of bringing an action. For the plaintiff in error it has been truly urged, that in the old books and abridgments no distinction is taken between words written and spoken. But the distinction has been made between written and spoken slander as far back as Charles the Second's time, and the difference has been recognized by the courts for at least a century back. It does not appear to me that the rights of parties to a good character are insufficiently defended by the criminal remedies which the law gives, and the law gives a very ample field for retribution by action for words spoken in the cases of special damage, of words spoken of a man in his trade or profession, of a man in office, of a magistrate or officer; for all these an action lies. But for mere general abuse spoken, no action lies. In the arguments both of the judges and counsel, in almost all the cases in which the question has been, whether what is contained in a writing is the subject of an action or not, it has been considered whether the words, if spoken, would maintain an action. It is curious that they have also adverted to the question, whether it tends to produce a breach of the peace; but that is wholly irrelevant, and is no ground for recovering damages. So it has been argued that writing shows more deliberate malignity; but the same answer suffices, that the action is not maintainable upon the ground of the malignity, but for the damage sustained. So it is argued that written scandal is more generally diffused than words spoken, and is, therefore, actionable; but an assertion made in a public place, as upon the Royal Exchange, concerning a merchant in London, may be much more extensively diffused than a few printed papers dispersed, or a private letter; it is true that a newspaper may be very generally read, but that is all casual. These are the arguments which prevail on my mind to repudiate the distinction between written and spoken scandal; but that distinction has been established by some of the greatest names known to the law, Lord Hardwicke, Hale, I believe Holt, C. J., and others. Lord Hardwicke, C. J., especially has laid it down that an action for a libel may be brought on words written, when the words, if spoken, would not sustain it. Com. Dig. tit. Libel, referring to the case in Fitzg. 122, 253, says there is a distinction between written and spoken scandal; by his putting it down there as he does, as being the law, without making any query or doubt upon it, we are led to suppose that he was of the same opinion. I do not now recapitulate the cases, but we cannot, in opposition to them, venture to lay down at this day that no action can be maintained for any words written, for which an action could not be maintained if they were spoken; upon these grounds we think the judgment of the Court of King's Bench must be affirmed. The purpose of this action is to recover a compensation for some damage supposed to be sustained by the plaintiff by reason of the libel. The tendency of the libel to provoke a breach of the peace, or the degree of malignity which actuates the writer, has nothing to do with the question. If the matter were for the first time to be decided at this day, I should have no hesitation in saying that no action could be maintained for written scandal which could not be maintained for the words if they had been spoken.

Judgment affirmed.[1]

[1] "When our ancestors years ago drew the distinction between libel and slander, they exercised that kind of wise discretion which they always exercised over the whole field of the common law. It would to my mind be very dangerous for us nowadays to relax in any way the rule of law which confines actions for spoken words, in the absence of proof of special damage, to a very limited number of cases." Vaughan Williams, L. J., in Dauncey v. Holloway, [1901] 2 K. B. 441, 448. See also A. L. Smith, L. J., Id. 447. But compare Colby v. Reynolds, 6 Vt. 489, 493; Tillson v. Robbins, 68 Me. 295.

The distinction sanctioned in the principal case between oral and written scandal still obtains in England and the United States. The definition of a libel as

WEBB v. BEAVAN

IN THE QUEEN'S BENCH DIVISION, MAY 10, 1883.

Reported in 11 *Queen's Bench Division*, 609.

DEMURRER to a statement of claim which alleged that the defendant falsely and maliciously spoke and published of the plaintiff the words following: "I will lock you" (meaning the plaintiff) "up in Gloucester Gaol next week. I know enough to put you" (meaning the plaintiff) "there," meaning thereby that the plaintiff had been and was guilty of having committed some criminal offence or offences. The plaintiff claimed £500 damages.

Demurrer, on the ground that the statement of claim did not allege circumstances showing that the defendant had spoken or published of the plaintiff any actionable language, and that no cause of action was disclosed. Joinder in demurrer.

W. H. Nash, in support of the demurrer, contended that, in order to make the words actionable, the innuendo should have alleged that they imputed an offence for which the plaintiff could have been indicted, and that it was not sufficient to allege that they imputed a criminal offence merely. He referred to Odgers on Libel and Slander, p. 54.

Hammond Chambers, contra, contended that, according to the earlier authorities, the test, in ascertaining whether words were actionable *per se*, was whether the offence imputed was punishable corporally or by fine, and that it was not necessary to allege that the words imputed an indictable offence. He cited Com. Dig. tit. Action on the Case for Defamation, D. 5 and 9; Curtis v. Curtis, 10 Bing. 477.

POLLOCK, B. I am of opinion that the demurrer should be overruled. The expression "indictable offence" seems to have crept into the text-books, but I think the passages in Comyns' Digest are conclusive to show that words which impute any criminal offence are actionable *per se*. The distinction seems a natural one, that words imputing that the plaintiff has rendered himself liable to the mere infliction of a fine are not slanderous, but that it is slanderous to say that he has done something for which he can be made to suffer corporally.

a written publication calculated to bring another into hatred, ridicule, or contempt, is also universally recognized in English-speaking countries. As it is a pure question of fact for the jury whether the publication in a given case comes within this definition, it has not seemed advisable to bring together in this book the multitudinous instances which have been passed upon. A full collection of the cases may be found in Odgers, Libel and Slander, (5 ed.) 18–38; Townshend, Slander and Libel, (4 ed.) 203–221; 25 Cyc. 255–264.

An action for a libel made in the course of judicial proceedings cannot be maintained until the proceedings have terminated in favor of the person defamed, Masterson v. Brown, 72 Fed. 136.

LOPES, J. I am of the same opinion. I think it is enough to allege that the words complained of impute a criminal offence. A great number of offences which were dealt with by indictment twenty years ago are now disposed of summarily, but the effect cannot be to alter the law with respect to actions for slander. *Demurrer overruled.*[1]

BROOKER *v.* COFFIN

SUPREME COURT, NEW YORK, NOVEMBER, 1809.

Reported in 5 *Johnson*, 188.

SPENCER, J., delivered the opinion of the court.[2] The first count is for these words, " She is a common prostitute, and I can prove it; " and the question arises, whether speaking these words gives an action

[1] There is great diversity of opinion as to what words, imputing the commission of a crime, are actionable *per se*. The authorities may be classified as follows: —

I. Words imputing a criminal offence punishable corporally.

In Hawes's Case, March, 113 (speaking against common prayer); Heake *v.* Moulton, Yelv. 90; Walden *v.* Mitchell, 2 Ventr. 265; Scoble *v.* Lee, 2 Show. 32 (regrating); McCabe *v.* Foot, 15 L. T. Rep. 115; Elliott *v.* Ailsberry, 2 Bibb, 473 (fornication); M'Gee *v.* Wilson, Litt. S. C. 187 (unchastity); Mills *v.* Wimp, 10 B. Mon. 417 (*semble*); Buck *v.* Hersey, 31 Me. 558 (drunkenness); Wagaman *v.* Byers, 17 Md. 183 (adultery); Birch *v.* Benton, 26 Mo. 153 (whipping one's wife); Speaker *v.* McKenzie, 26 Mo. 255 (whipping one's mother); Billings *v.* Wing, 7 Vt. 439 (" he snaked his mother out of doors by the hair of her head; it was the day before she died "), the words uttered were held not to give a right of action, since they imputed crimes punishable only by fine, or by imprisonment merely as a consequence of the non-payment of the fine.

II. Words imputing a criminal offence and involving moral turpitude. Sipp *v.* Coleman, 179 Fed. 997; Taylor *v.* Gumpert, 96 Ark. 354; Frisbie *v.* Fowler, 2 Conn. 707; Hoag *v.* Hatch, 23 Conn. 585; Page *v.* Merwin, 54 Conn. 426; Kennenberg *v.* Neff, 74 Conn. 62; Yakavicze *v.* Valentukevicious, 84 Conn. 350; Reitan *v.* Goebel, 33 Minn. 151.

III. Words imputing a criminal offence, involving moral turpitude and punishable corporally. Redway *v.* Gray, 31 Vt. 292 (qualifying Billings *v.* Wing, 7 Vt. 439); Murray *v.* McAllister, 38 Vt. 167.

IV. Words imputing a criminal offence involving disgrace. Miller *v.* Parish, 8 Pick. 384; Brown *v.* Nickerson, 5 Gray, 1; Kenney *v.* McLaughlin, 5 Gray, 3; Ranger *v.* Goodrich, 17 Wis. 78; Mayer *v.* Schleichter, 29 Wis. 646; Gibson *v.* Gibson, 43 Wis. 23; Geary *v.* Bennett, 53 Wis. 444.

V. Words imputing a criminal offence subjecting the offender to infamous punishment. Shipp *v.* McCraw, 3 Murph. 463; Brady *v.* Wilson, 4 Hawks. 93; Skinner *v.* White, 1 Dev. & Bat. 471; Wall *v.* Hoskins, 5 Ired. 177; Wilson *v.* Tatum, 8 Jones, (N.C.) 300; McKee *v.* Wilson, 87 N. C. 300; Harris *v.* Terry, 98 N. C. 131.

VI. Words imputing an *indictable* offence involving moral turpitude, or subjecting the offender to an infamous punishment. See Brooker *v.* Coffin, *infra*, and cases cited.

VII. Words imputing an *indictable* offence punishable corporally. Griffin *v.* Moore, 43 Md. 246; Shafer *v.* Ahalt, 48 Md. 171; Birch *v.* Benton, 26 Mo. 153; Curry *v.* Collins, 37 Mo. 324; Bundy *v.* Hart, 46 Mo. 460; Lewis *v.* McDaniel, 82 Mo. 577; Houston *v.* Woolley, 37 Mo. App. 15, 24; Parsons *v.* Henry, 177 Mo. App. 329.

As to defamation of a corporation, see Oram *v.* Hutt, [1913] 1 Ch. 259; Axton Tobacco Co. *v.* Evening Post Co., 169 Ky. 64; Stone *v.* Textile Employers Ass'n, 137 App. Div. 655.

[2] Only the opinion of the court is given.

without alleging special damage.[1] By the statute (1 R. L. 124), common prostitutes are adjudged disorderly persons, and are liable to commitment by any justice of the peace, upon conviction, to the bridewell or house of correction, to be kept at hard labor for a period not exceeding sixty days, or until the next general sessions of the peace. It has been supposed that, therefore, to charge a woman with being a common prostitute, was charging her with such an offence as would give an action for the slander. The same statute which authorizes the infliction of imprisonment on common prostitutes, as disorderly persons, inflicts the same punishment for a great variety of acts, the commission of which renders persons liable to be considered disorderly; and to sustain this action would be going the whole length of saying, that every one charged with any of the acts prohibited by that statute, would be entitled to maintain an action for defamation. Among others, to charge a person with pretending to have skill in physiognomy, palmistry, or pretending to tell fortunes, would, if this action is sustained, be actionable. Upon the fullest consideration, we are inclined to adopt this as the safest rule, and one which, as we think, is warranted by the cases. In case the charge, if true, will subject the party charged to an indictment for a crime involving moral turpitude, or subject him to an infamous punishment, then the words will be in themselves actionable;[2] and Baron Comyns considers the test to be, whether the crime is indictable or not. 1 Com. tit. Action on the Case for Defamation, F, 20. There is not, perhaps, so much uncertainty in the law upon any subject as when words shall be in themselves actionable. From the contradiction of cases, and the uncertainty prevailing on this head, the court think they may, without overleaping the bounds of their duty, lay down a rule which will conduce to cer-

[1] By 54 & 55 Vict. c. 51, words which impute unchastity or adultery to any woman or girl are actionable, without special damage.

[2] This rule has been approved in the following cases: Pollard *v.* Lyon, 91 U. S. 225; Perdue *v.* Burnett, Minor, 138; Dudley *v.* Horn, 21 Ala. 379; Hillhouse *v.* Peck, 2 St. & P. 395; Heath *v.* Devaughn, 37 Ala. 677; Kinney *v.* Hosea, 3 Harring, 77; Pleasanton *v.* Kronemeier, 29 Del. 81; Pledger *v.* Hathcock, 1 Ga. 550; Giddens *v.* Mirk, 4 Ga. 364; Richardson *v.* Roberts, 23 Ga. 215; Burton *v.* Burton, 3 Greene, 316; Halley *v.* Gregg, 74 Ia. 563; Wooten *v.* Martin, 140 Ky. 781; St. Martin *v.* Desnoyer, 1 Minn. 156; West *v.* Hanrahan, 28 Minn. 385; Chaplin *v.* Lee, 18 Neb. 440; Hendrickson *v.* Sullivan, 28 Neb. 329; McCuen *v.* Ludlum, 2 Harr. 12; Johnson *v.* Shields, 25 N. J. Law, 116; Widrig *v.* Oyer, 13 Johns. 124; Martin *v.* Stilwell, 13 Johns. 275; Alexander *v.* Alexander, 9 Wend. 141; Case *v.* Buckley, 15 Wend. 327; Bissell *v.* Cornell, 24 Wend. 354; Demarest *v.* Haring, 6 Cow. 76; Young *v.* Miller, 3 Hill, 21; Wright *v.* Paige, 3 Keyes, 581, 3 Trans. App. 134, s. c.; Crawford *v.* Wilson, 4 Barb. 504; Johnson *v.* Brown, 57 Barb. 118; Quinn *v.* O'Gara, 2 E. D. Sm. 388; Torres *v.* Huner, 150 App. Div. 798; Dial *v.* Holter, 6 Ohio St. 228; Alfele *v.* Wright, 17 Ohio St. 238; Hollingsworth *v.* Shaw, 19 Ohio St. 430; Davis *v.* Brown, 27 Ohio St. 326; Davis *v.* Sladden, 17 Or. 259; Andres *v.* Koppenheafer, 3 S. & R. 255; Davis *v.* Carey, 141 Pa. St. 314; Lodge *v.* O'Toole, 20 R. I. 405; Gage *v.* Shelton, 3 Rich. 242; Smith *v.* Brown, 97 S. C. 239; Smith *v.* Smith, 2 Sneed, 473; McAnally *v.* Williams, 3 Sneed, 26; Poe *v.* Grever, 3 Sneed, 664; Payne *v.* Tancil, 98 Va. 262. See Moore *v.* Francis, 121 N. Y. 199.

tainty, and they therefore adopt the rule I have mentioned as the criterion. In our opinion, therefore, the first count in the declaration is defective. *The defendant must, therefore, have judgment.*[1]

COOPER *v.* SEAVERNS

SUPREME COURT, KANSAS, DECEMBER 11, 1909.

Reported in 81 *Kansas Reports*, 267.

BURCH, J.[2] The common law of England was that verbal imputations of unchaste conduct on the part of a female were not actionable, in the absence of special damages, unless they related to a person in some office or employment for which morality and virtue were qualifications (Folkhard, Law Slan. & Lib. 7th ed., p. 43), and except in the local courts of the city of London, the borough of Southwark and the city of Bristol, where it was the custom to whip strumpets at cart's tail, tingling a basin before them (Odgers, Lib. & Slan., p. *84). This rule has been accounted for on the supposition that in the early, formative days of the common law social relations were rude, manners were unrefined, and the people were accustomed to hearing gross and vulgar epithets freely tossed about without regarding them seriously. (Odgers, Lib. & Slan., p. *86.) The case of Oxford & ux. *v.* Cross, in the king's bench, Trinity term, 41 Elizabeth (1599), Coke's Reports (vol. 2, p. 307; part 4, p. 18a), is cited in support of this view, wherein it was said that a custom " to maintain actions for such brabling words is against law." Pollock and Maitland discover a better state of civilization from the early records than the view indicated takes for granted:

" We should be much mistaken, however, if we believed that the temporal law of the middle ages gave no action to the defamed. Nothing could be less true than that our ancestors in the days of their barbarism could only feel blows and treated hard words as of no account. Even the rude *lex Salica* decrees that if one calls a man ' wolf ' or ' hare ' one must pay him three shillings, while if one calls a woman ' harlot ' and cannot prove the truth of the charge, one must pay her forty-five shillings. The oldest English laws exact *bot* and *wite* if one gives another bad names. . . ."

This being true, a reason for the rule must be found elsewhere than in any essential brutality of the early Englishman. The doctrine appears to be

[1] Hence it is not actionable (without special damage) to call a man a " bastard," Paysse *v.* Paysse, 86 Wash. 349, or a " blackleg and swindler," McIntyre *v.* Fruchter, 148 N. Y. Supp. 786; or a " rascal," Massee *v.* Williams, 207 Mass. 222, or to call a woman a "bitch." Craver *v.* Norton, 114 Ia. 46; Sturdivant *v.* Duke, 155 Ky. 100; Kerone *v.* Block, 144 Mo. App. 575; Blake *v.* Smith, 19 R. I. 476.

But in Fowler *v.* Dowdney, 2 Moody & R. 119, the words " he is a returned convict " were held actionable, Lord Denman, C. J., saying that though the punishment had been suffered, " still the obloquy remains." Gainford *v.* Tuke, Cro. Jac. 536; Boston *v.* Tatam, Cro. Jac. 623; Beavor *v.* Hides, 2 Wils. 300; Stewart *v.* Howe, 17 Ill. 71; Wiley *v.* Campbell, 5 T. B. Monr. 396; Krebs *v.* Oliver, 12 Gray, 239; Johnson *v.* Dicken, 25 Mo. 580; Van Ankin *v.* Westfall, 14 Johns. 233; Ship *v.* McCraw, 3 Murphy, 463; Smith *v.* Stewart, 5 Pa. St. 372; Beck *v.* Stitzel, 21 Pa. St. 522; Poe *v.* Grever, 3 Sneed, (Tenn.) 664 *Accord.*

Compare Carpenter *v.* Tarrant, C. t. Hardw. 339; French *v.* Creath, Breese, 12; Barclay *v.* Thompson, 2 Pen. & W. 148.

[2] Only portions of the opinion are given.

fully accounted for through the partition of authority in England between the spiritual and the temporal courts. (Odgers, Lib. & Slan., p. *86.) It is familiar history that in the middle ages, for reasons and by means which need not be sketched here, the all-powerful ecclesiastics acquired jurisdiction over a large portion of the most important concerns of life — testaments, matrimony, and among innumerable others, defamation. This breach of the social order was regarded as a sin and was punishable in the spiritual courts as such. . . .

The struggle to limit and define the authority of the ecclesiastical courts was long and bitter, and frequently exhibited some striking features. In the progress of the duel the common-law courts used as their principal weapon the king's writ of prohibition to restrain the exercise of jurisdiction over causes which they desired to adjudicate. The ecclesiastics returned the fire by excommunicating those who sued out such writs. By and by an increasing number of pecuniary matters came to be regarded as pertaining to things of this world, and the civil courts finally succeeded in maintaining their right to administer relief in an action on the case where specific damages were occasioned by slanderous words.

[After discussing the jurisdiction of the ecclesiastical courts, the opinion proceeds:]

Although the English judges felt constrained to follow the common-law rule until it was superseded by act of parliament, it did not satisfy their consciences. In 1759, in the case of Jones *v.* Herne, in the Court of King's Bench (2 Wil. 87, 95 Eng. Rep., Full Reprint, 701), Chief Justice Willes, after holding it actionable to say a man is a forger, added that if it were *res integra* he would hold that calling a man a rogue or a woman a whore in public company is actionable.

Very near the time when this state entered upon its separate constitutional existence the common-law rule fell under the censure of some of the ablest exponents of English justice.

[The opinion then sets forth a number of judicial criticisms of the common-law doctrine and proceeds:]

From the foregoing it appears that the rule under consideration resulted solely from the early seizure of jurisdiction over slander by the ecclesiastical courts, which could not award damages at all, and the inability of the temporal courts to strip that jurisdiction from their rivals except in cases involving special damages. It never did rest upon any principle of right or justice or any decent regard for character. It was unsuited to the true genius and real needs of the people over whom it tyrannized, even from the earliest times. It created anomalies in the law of defamation which rendered that law absurd and grotesque. For example, words "touching" some disreputable good-for-nothing in his work or trade were actionable. The most sensitive, cultivated, high-bred woman could be foully slandered with impunity. Written ridicule of the style of her hat gave ground for exemplary damages. She had no redress for spoken words inflicting one of the deepest wounds her sex can suffer. The rule was not merely insufferably wrong; it was wrong in a matter of so precious a nature that it was shocking. It was suppressed because it had long been reprobated as odious and was universally detested. The question now to be decided is, Does that rule obtain in this state? . . . .

This is not the case of a principle which commands considerable approval, is founded upon fair reason, is merely of questionable wisdom, and which therefore ought to be followed until abrogated by the legislature. It is the case of an outlawed rule of negation whose sole function has always been to thwart natúral justice in one of the dearest and tenderest of human interests. Therefore its rejection is justified by Duncan *v.* Baker (21 Kan. 99) and Whitaker *v.* Hawley (25 Kan. 674), *supra.*

The world is censorious, and a woman's or a maiden's reputation for modesty and chastity is an asset of inestimable value. Its loss renders her poor indeed. Injury in fact is the necessary result of such a deprivation, whether or not the sufferer can point to specific damage in a few paltry dollars or to liability to a trifling fine if the charge were true. Therefore the pleading of special damages as a basis for relief ought to be treated as a useless fiction, like the one condemned in Anthony *v.* Norton (60 Kan. 341), *supra.*

Taking into consideration the origin and history of the rule, the reason supporting it, its character, its consequences, and the degree of its appositeness to our constitution and system of laws, it does not apply to the conditions or meet the needs of the people of this state, and consequently it is not a part of the law of this state.

This problem has been met and solved by different states of the American Union in different ways. In some the rule is obediently observed. In some it is followed under protest — is characterized as a disgrace to the state — but still is followed. In some statutes have relieved from its iniquity in whole or in part. In some it is frankly repudiated by the courts because it lacks the sanction of reason and justice. This court has no legislative functions. As Lord Campbell said, it is here only to declare the law. Under the statute of 1868 it must determine whether a rule of the common law invoked in a judicial proceeding contravenes the constitution or statutes of the state, or has been modified by judicial decision, and whether it is adapted to the conditions and is suitable to the needs of the people of the state. This duty has been discharged in the present case.[1]

LUMBY *v.* ALLDAY

IN THE EXCHEQUER, HILARY TERM, 1831.

Reported in 1 *Crompton & Jervis,* 301.

ACTION for words.

The judgment of the court was now delivered by

BAYLEY, B.[2] This case came before the court upon a rule *nisi* to enter a nonsuit. The ground of motion was that the words (in slander) proved upon the trial were not actionable.

Two points were discussed upon the motion: one, whether the words were actionable or not; and the other, whether this was properly a ground of nonsuit.

The declaration stated that the plaintiff was clerk to an incorporated company, called the Birmingham and Staffordshire Gas Light

[1] See also Keck *v.* Shepard, (Ark.) 180 S. W. 501 (statutory); Craver *v.* Norton, 114 Ia. 46; Hahn *v.* Lumpa, 158 Ia. 560; Traylor *v.* White, 185 Mo. App. 325 (statutory); Culver *v.* Marx, 157 Wis. 320. On the whole subject, see Veeder, History and Theory of the Law of Defamation, 4 Columbia Law Rev. 33, 52.

[2] Only the opinion of the court is given.

Company, and had behaved himself as such with great propriety, and thereby acquired, and was daily acquiring, great gains; but that the defendant, to cause it to be believed that he was unfit to hold his situation, and an improper person to be employed by the company, and to cause him to be deprived of his situation, spoke the words complained of in the declaration, viz.: "You are a fellow, a disgrace to the town, unfit to hold your situation, for your conduct with whores. I will have you in the 'Argus.' You have bought up all the copies of the 'Argus,' knowing you have been exposed. You may drown yourself, for you are not fit to live, and are a disgrace to the situation you hold."

The objection to maintaining an action upon these words is, that it is only on the ground of the plaintiff being clerk to the company that they can be actionable; that it is not alleged that they are spoken of him in reference to his character or conduct as clerk; that they do not, from their tenor, import that they were spoken with any such reference; that they do not impute to him the want of any qualification such as a clerk ought to have, or any misconduct which would make him unfit to discharge faithfully and correctly all the duties of such a clerk.

The plaintiff relied on the rule laid down by De Grey, C. J., in Onslow v. Horne, 3 Wils. 177, "that words are actionable when spoken of one in an office of profit, which may probably occasion the loss of his office; or when spoken of persons touching their respective professions, trades, and business, and do or may probably tend to their damage." The same case occurs in Sir Wm. Bl. Rep. 753, and there the rule is expressed to be, "if the words be of probable ill consequence to a person in a trade or profession, or an office." [1]

The objection to the rule, as expressed in both reports, appears to me to be, that the words "probably" and "probable" are too indefinite and loose, and unless they are considered as equivalent to "having a natural tendency to," and are confined within the limits, I have expressed in stating the defendant's objections, of showing the want of some necessary qualification, or some misconduct in the office, it goes beyond what the authorities warrant.

Every authority which I have been able to find, either shows the want of some general requisite, as honesty, capacity, fidelity, &c., or connects the imputation with the plaintiff's office, trade, or business. As at present advised, therefore, I am of opinion that the charge proved in this case is not actionable, because the imputation it contains does not imply the want of any of those qualities which a clerk ought to possess, and because the imputation has no reference to his

[1] "We think that the rule as to words spoken of a man in his office or trade is not necessarily confined to offices and trades of the nature and duties of which the court can take judicial notice. The only limitation of which we are aware is, that it does not apply to illegal callings." Channel, B., in Foulger v. Newcomb, L. R. 2 Ex. 327, 330.

conduct as clerk. I say as at present advised, for the reason which I am about to state.

The next question is, whether this is properly a ground of nonsuit; and I am of opinion that, under the circumstances of this case, it is not. The words proved are nearly all the words which the first count contains; and if the words proved are not actionable, none of the other words contained in that count are. When the general issue is pleaded to a count, it puts in issue to be tried by the jury the question, whether the facts stated in that count exist. The legal effect of those facts, whether they constitute a cause of action or not, is not properly in question. The proper mode to bring that legal effect into consideration is, before trial, to demur; after trial, to move in arrest of judgment. The duty of the judge, under whose direction the jury try questions of fact, is not to consider whether the facts charged give a ground of action, but to assist the jury in matters of law, which may arise upon the trial of those facts.

As the defendant, therefore, in this case puts in issue the allegations in the declaration, and those allegations were proved upon the trial, we are of opinion that the rule for a nonsuit ought to be discharged; and, notwithstanding the lapse of time, that there ought to be a rule *nisi* to arrest the judgment, if the defendant be advised to take such rule. *Rule discharged.*[1]

[1] Alexander *v.* Angle, 1 Cr. & J. 143; Sibley *v.* Tomlins, 4 Tyrwh. 90; Doyley *v.* Roberts, 3 B. N. C. 835; Brayne *v.* Cooper, 5 M. & W. 249; James *v.* Brook, 9 Q. B. 7; Dauncey *v.* Holloway, [1901] 2 K. B. 441; Hogg *v.* Dorrah, 2 Porter, (Ala.) 212; Oram *v.* Franklin, 5 Blackf. 42; Buck *v.* Hersey, 31 Me. 558; Oakley *v.* Farrington, 1 Johns. Cas. 129; Van Tassel *v.* Capron, 1 Den. 250; Ireland *v.* McGarvish, 1 Sandf. 155; Chomley *v.* Watson, [1907] Vict. L. R. 502 *Accord.*

Compare Ware *v.* Clowney, 24 Ala. 707; Butler *v.* Howes, 7 Cal. 87; Fowles *v.* Bowen, 30 N. Y. 20.

"Some of the cases have proceeded to a length which can hardly fail to excite surprise: a clergyman having failed to obtain redress for the imputation of adultery; and a school-mistress having been declared incompetent to maintain an action for a charge of prostitution. Such words were undeniably calculated to injure the success of the plaintiffs in their several professions, but, not being applicable to their conduct therein, no action lay." Lord Denman, C. J., in Ayre *v.* Craven, 2 A. & E. 2. See Morasse *v.* Brooks, 151 Mass. 567, 568.

Imputation of misconduct to a clergyman, see Bishop of Norwich *v.* Pricket, Cro. Eliz. 1 (heterodoxy in religion); Payne *v.* Bewmorris, 1 Lev. 248 (incontinence); Pope *v.* Ramsey, 1 Keb. 542 (knave, &c); Chaddock *v.* Briggs, 13 Mass. 248 (drunkenness); Ritchie *v.* Widdemer, 59 N. J. Law, 290; Demarest *v.* Haring, 6 Cow. 76 (incontinence); Potter *v.* N. Y. Journal, 68 App. Div. 95; Hayner *v.* Cowden, 27 Ohio St. 292 (drunkenness); McMillan *v.* Birch, 1 Binney, 178 (drunkenness); Starr *v.* Gardner, 6 Up. Can. Q. B. O. S. 512 (incontinence; but see, *contra,* Breeze *v.* Sails, 23 Up. Can. Q. B. 94, incontinence), holding the words actionable.

Parrat *v.* Carpenter, Cro. El. 502; Nicholson *v.* Lyne, Cro. El. 94; Anon., Sty. 49 *Contra.* Compare Gallwey *v.* Marshall, 9 Ex. 294, 568.

Imputation to teacher of discreditable conduct with pupils. Spears *v.* McCoy, 155 Ky. 1. Compare Nicholson *v.* Dillard, 137 Ga. 225.

Imputation to an officer of drunkenness while on duty. Reilly *v.* Curtis, 83 N. J. Law, 77.

JONES *v.* LITTLER

IN THE EXCHEQUER, JANUARY 16, 1841.

Reported in 7 Meeson & Welsby, 423.

SLANDER. The declaration stated that the plaintiff was a brewer, and that the defendant falsely and maliciously spoke and published of and concerning him in the way of his trade as a brewer the false, scandalous, malicious, and defamatory words following: "I'll" (meaning that he, the defendant, would) "bet £5 to £1, that Mr. Jones" (meaning the plaintiff) "was in a sponging-house for debt within the last fortnight, and I can produce the man who locked him up; the man told me so himself." Whereupon the said Henry Pye then asked the defendant, "Do you mean to say that Mr. Jones, brewer, of Rose Hill" (meaning and describing the plaintiff), "has been in a sponging-house within this last fortnight for debt?" and thereupon the defendant then replied to the said Henry Pye, and the said other persons then present, "Yes, I do."

The jury having returned a verdict for the plaintiff, the court granted a rule to show cause why there should not be a new trial, on a suggestion that the learned judge ought to have left it as a question to the jury whether the words were spoken of the plaintiff in the way of his trade, and did not.

PARKE, B. It is quite clear that this rule ought to be discharged, for the only ground on which it was granted has failed, inasmuch as the learned judge did leave the question to the jury, whether the words were spoken of the plaintiff in his trade; and, indeed, it is plain that the words were so used, from the fact that in the conversation in question the plaintiff was spoken of as a brewer. Independently of that, however, and even if they were spoken of him in his private character, I think the case of Stanton *v.* Smith, 2 Ld. Raym. 1480, is an authority to show that the words would have been actionable, because they must necessarily affect him in his trade. It is there said, "We were all of opinion that such words spoken of a tradesman must greatly lessen the credit of a tradesman, and be very prejudicial to him, and therefore that they were actionable." That case is distinguishable from Ayre *v.* Craven, 2 A. & E. 2, and Doyley *v.* Roberts, 1 Bing. N. C. 135. In the latter of those cases the words were not spoken of the plaintiff in his business of an attorney; and in the former it did not appear in what manner the immorality was connected with the plaintiff's profession of a physician; and it was possible that such imputations of incorrect conduct, out of the line of their respective professions, might not injure their professional characters. But this case is distinguishable, because here the imputation is that of insolvency, which must be injurious; for if a tradesman be incapable of paying all his debts, whether in or out of trade, his credit as a tradesman, which depends on his general solvency, must be injured. The case of Stanton *v.* Smith, as it appears to me, is good law, notwithstanding the observations of Coltman, J., in Doyley *v.* Roberts.

ALDERSON and ROLFE, BB., concurred. *Rule discharged.*[1]

SECOR *v.* HARRIS

SUPREME COURT, NEW YORK, SEPTEMBER, 1854.

Reported in 18 *Barbour*, 425.

MOTION by the plaintiff for a new trial, upon a bill of exceptions.

MASON, J. This is an action for slander. Upon the trial of the cause the plaintiff proved the following words, which were also alleged in the complaint: "Doctor Secor killed my children." "He gave them teaspoonful doses of calomel, and they died." "Dr. Secor gave them teaspoonful doses of calomel, and it killed them; they did not live long after they took it. They died right off, — the same day." The plaintiff was proved to be a practising physician, and the evidence shows that he had practised in the defendant's family, and had prescribed for the defendant's children, and that the words were spoken of him in his character of a physician. The plaintiff claimed that the words were actionable, and that he was entitled to have this branch of the case, upon the words, submitted to the jury. The judge at the circuit held that the words were not actionable, and took them from the consideration of the jury. These words, spoken of the plaintiff as a physician, are actionable *per se*, whatever may be said upon the question, whether they impute a criminal offence. They do not impute a criminal offence, unless there is evidence, arising from the quantity of the calomel which the defendant alleged that the plaintiff gave these children, from which a jury would be justified in finding an intention to kill them. One of them was three years of age, and the other one year and a half. If the natural result, which should reasonably be expected from feeding children of such tender years full teaspoon doses of calomel, would be certain death, then it is not a forced construction of the words to say that the defendant intended to charge the plaintiff with an intention to kill these children, in giving them such doses. It is not necessary, however, to say that the judge should have submitted this case to the jury upon the question, whether the defendant did not intend to impute to the plaintiff, by these words, a criminal offence. I am quite inclined to think, however, that had the judge submitted the case to the jury upon the imputation of a criminal intent in these words, and had the jury found that such intent was imputed, we should not be justified in setting aside their verdict. It is not necessary, however, to place the case upon this ground; for it is certainly slanderous to say of a physician that

[1] Kempe's Case, Dy. 72, pl. 6; Stanton *v.* Smith, 2 Ld. Ray. 1480; Brown *v.* Smith, 13 C. B. 596; Pacific Packing Co. *v.* Bradstreet, 25 Idaho, 696; Simons *v.* Burnham, 102 Mich. 189; Traynor *v.* Sielaff, 62 Minn. 420; Hynds *v.* Fourteenth Street Store, 159 App. Div. 766; Davis *v.* Ruff, Cheeves, 17 *Accord.*

Barnes *v.* Trundy, 31 Me. 321; Redway *v.* Gray, 31 Vt. 292 *Contra.*

See Bell *v.* Thatcher, Freem. 276; Bryant *v.* Loxton, 11 Moore, 344; Marino *v.* Di Marco, 41 App. D. C. 76 ("sells rotten goods"); Taylor *v.* Church, 1 E. D. Smith, 287; Fowles *v.* Bowen, 30 N. Y. 20; Bilgrien *v.* Ulrich, 150 Wis. 532 (habitual cheating).

he killed these children of such tender years, by giving them teaspoonful doses of calomel. The charge, to say the least, imports such a total ignorance of his profession as to destroy all confidence in the physician. It is a disgrace to a physician to have it believed that he is so ignorant of this most familiar and common medicine, as to give such quantities thereof to such young children. The law is well settled that words published of a physician, falsely imputing to him general ignorance or want of skill in his profession, are actionable, in themselves, on the ground of presumed damage. Starkie on Slander, 100, 110, 115, 10, 12; Martyn *v.* Burlings, Cro. Eliz. 589; Bacon's Abr. title Slander, B; Watson *v.* Van Derlash, Hetl. 69; Tutler *v.* Alwin, 11 Mod. R. 221; Smith *v.* Taylor, 1 New R. 196; Sumner *v.* Utley, 7 Conn. R. 257. I am aware that it was held, in the case of Poe *v.* Mondford, Cro. El. 620, that it is not actionable to say of a physician, " He hath killed a patient with physic; " and that, upon the strength of the authority of that case, it was decided in this court in Foot *v.* Brown, 8 Johns. 64, that it was not actionable to say of an attorney or counsellor, when speaking of a particular suit. " He knows nothing about the suit; he will lead you on until he has undone you." These cases are not sound. The case of Poe *v.* Mondford is repudiated in Bacon's Abr. as authority, and cases are referred to as holding a contrary doctrine (vol. ix. pages 49, 50). The cases of Poe *v.* Mondford, and of Foot *v.* Brown, were reviewed by the Supreme Court of Connecticut, in the case of Sumner *v.* Utley, 7 Conn. R. 257, with most distinguished ability, and the doctrine of those cases repudiated. In the latter case it is distinctly held, that words are actionable in themselves, which charge a physician with ignorance or want of skill in his treatment of a particular patient, if the charge be such as imports gross ignorance or unskilfulness. To the same effect is the case of Johnson *v.* Robertson, 8 Porter's R. 486, where it was held that the following words spoken of a physician in regard to his treatment of a particular case, " He killed the child by giving it too much calomel," are actionable in themselves; and such is the case of Tutler *v.* Alwin, 11 Mod. R. 221, where it was held to be actionable to say of an apothecary, that " he killed a patient with physic." See also 3 Wilson's R. 186; Bacon's Abr. title Slander, letter B, 2, vol. ix. page 49 (Bouv. ed.). The cases of Poe *v.* Mondford and Foot *v.* Brown have been repudiated by the highest judicial tribunal in two of the American States, while the case of Poe *v.* Mondford seems to have been repudiated in England; and I agree with Clinch, J., that the reason upon which that case is decided is not apparent. I do not go the length to say that falsehood may not be spoken of a physician's practice, in a particular case, without subjecting the party to this action. A physician may mistake the symptoms of a patient, or may misjudge as to the nature of his disease, and even as to the powers of medicine, and yet his error may be of that pardonable kind that will do him no essential prejudice, because it is rather a proof of human imperfection than of culpable ignorance or unskilfulness; and where charges are made against a physician that fall within this class of cases, they are not actionable, without proof of special damages.[1] 7 Conn. R. 257. It is equally true, that a single act of a physician may evince gross ignorance, and such a total want of skill, as will not fail to injure his reputation, and deprive him of general confidence. When such a charge is made against a physician, the words are actionable *per se.* 7 Conn. R. 257. The rule may be laid

[1] Sumner *v.* Utley, 7 Conn. 257; Garr *v.* Selden, 6 Barb. 416; Rodgers *v.* Kline, 56 Miss. 808; Lynde *v.* Johnson, 39 Hun. 5 *Accord.*

down as a general one that, when the charge implies gross ignorance and unskilfulness in his profession, the words are actionable *per se*. This is upon the ground that the law presumes damage to result, from the very nature of the charge. The law in such a case lays aside its usual strictness; for when the presumption of damage is violent, and the difficulty of proving it is considerable, the law supplies the defect, and, by converting presumption into proof secures the character of the sufferer from the misery of delay, and enables him at once to face the calumny in open court. Starkie on Slander, 581. It was well said by the learned Chief Justice Hosmer, in Sumner *v.* Utley, 7 Conn. 257, that, " As a general principle, it can never be admitted that the practice of a physician or surgeon in a particular case may be calumniated with impunity, unless special damage is shown. By confining the slander to particulars, a man may thus be ruined in detail. A calumniator might follow the track of the plaintiff, and begin by falsely ascribing to a physician the killing of three persons by mismanagement, and then, the mistaking of an artery for a vein, and thus might proceed to misrepresent every single case of his practice, until his reputation should be blasted beyond remedy. Instead of murdering character by one stroke, the victim would be cut successively in pieces, and the only difference would consist in the manner of effecting the same result." It is true, as was said by the learned Chief Justice Hosmer in that case, the redress proposed, on the proof of special damage, is inadequate to such a case. Much time may elapse before the fact of damage admits of any evidence; and then the proof will always fall short of the mischief. In the mean time the reputation of the calumniated person languishes and dies; and hence, as we have before said, the presumption of damage being violent, and the difficulty of proving it considerable, the law supplies the defect by converting presumption of damage into proof: Starkie on Slander, 581; in other words, the law presumes that damages result from the speaking of the words. In the case under consideration, the words proved impute to the plaintiff such gross ignorance of his profession, if nothing more, as would be calculated to destroy his character wherever the charge should be credited. It would be calculated to make all men speak out and say, as did the witness Richard Morris, " that it was outrageous, and the plaintiff ought not to be permitted to practise." The law will therefore presume damages to result from the speaking of the words, and consequently hold the words actionable in themselves. The judge at the circuit erred in taking this branch of the case from the consideration of the jury, and a new trial must be granted; costs to abide the event of the action.

CRIPPEN, J., concurred. SHANKLAND, J., dissented. *New trial granted.*[1]

[1] Johnson *v.* Robertson, 8 Port. (Ala.) 486; Sumner *v.* Utley, 7 Conn. 257; Lovejoy *v.* Whitcomb, 174 Mass. 586; Freisinger *v.* Moore, 65 N. J. Law, 286; Mattice *v.* Wilcox, 147 N. Y. 624; Krug *v.* Pitass, 162 N. Y. 154, 163 N. Y. 600; Lynde *v.* Johnson, 39 Hun, 12; Hollingsworth *v.* Spectator Co., 49 App. Div. 16; McIntyre *v.* Weinert, 195 Pa. St. 52; Holland *v.* Flick, 212 Pa. St. 201; Gauvreau *v.* Superior Co., 62 Wis. 403 *Accord.* See Watson *v.* Vanderlash, Hetl. 69; Edsall *v.* Russell, 4 M. & Gr. 1090. Compare Twiggar *v.* Ossining Printing Co., 161 App. Div. 718; Larsen *v.* Brooklyn Eagle, 165 App. Div. 4.

Foot *v.* Brown, 8 Johns. 64 *Contra.* See Camp *v.* Martin, 23 Conn. 86; Pratt *v.* Pioneer Co., 35 Minn. 251.

The imputation of misconduct in an office of honor but not of profit is actionable *per se*, Booth *v.* Arnold, [1895] 1 Q. B. 571; Livingston *v.* McCartin, [1907] Vict. L. R. 48. But the rule is otherwise, according to Alexander *v.* Jenkins, [1892] 1 Q. B. 797, as to the imputation of unfitness for such an office.

SMITH v. HOBSON

In the King's Bench, Trinity Term, 1647.

Reported in Style, 112.

Smith, an innkeeper in Warwick, brought an action upon the case against Hobson for speaking these words: "Colonel Egerton had the French pox, and hath set it in the house" (meaning the plaintiff's house), "and William Smith and his wife" (meaning the plaintiff and his wife) "have it, and all you." The plaintiff hath a verdict. The defendant moves in arrest of judgment, and for cause shows, that the words are not actionable; for the words are, that Colonel Egerton hath set the French pox in the house, which is impossible; for the house could not have the pox, and the words, "William Smith and his wife have it," shall not be meant that they have the pox, but the house, for that is the next antecedent to the words, to which they shall refer. Roll, J., held the words here actionable, and bid the plaintiff take his judgment, if cause were not shown to the contrary Saturday following. Judgment was afterwards given accordingly.[1]

JOANNES v. BURT

Supreme Judicial Court, Massachusetts, January Term, 1863.

Reported in 6 *Allen*, 336.

Hoar, J.[2] The declaration is in tort for slander, by orally imputing insanity to the plaintiff. We are aware of no authority for maintaining such an action, without the averment of special damage. The authorities upon which the plaintiff relies are both cases of libel. The King v. Harvey, 2 B. & C. 257; Southwick v. Stevens, 10 Johns. 443. An action for oral slander, in charging the plaintiff with disease, has been confined to the imputation of such loathsome and infectious

[1] Brook v. Wife, Cro. El. 878; Davis v. Taylor, Cro. El. 648; Garford v. Clerk, Cro. El. 857; Miller's Case, Cro. Jac. 430; Crittal v. Horner, Hob. 219 *b*; Elyott v. Blague, Sty. 283; Marshall v. Chickall, 1 Sid. 50; Comming's Case, 2 Sid. 5; Lymbe v. Hockly, 1 Lev. 205; Grimes v. Lovel, 12 Mod. 242; Clifton v. Wells, 12 Mod. 634; Whitfield v. Powel, 12 Mod. 248; Bloodworth v. Gray, 7 M. & G. 334; Watson v. McCarthy, 2 Ga. 57; Nichols v. Guy, 2 Ind. 82; McDonald v. Nugent, 122 Ia. 651; Meteye v. Times Co., 47 La. Ann. 824; Golderman v. Stearns, 7 Gray, 181; Williams v. Holdredge, 22 Barb. 396; Hewitt v. Mason, 24 How. Pr. 366; Upton v. Upton, 51 Hun, 184; Simpson v. Press Co., 33 Misc. 228; Kaucher v. Blinn, 29 Ohio St. 62; Irons v. Field, 9 R. I. 216 *Accord.*

Bury v. Chappel, Golds. 135; James v. Rutlech, 4 Rep. 17 *a*; Hunt v. Jones, Cro. Jac. 499; Califord v. Knight, Cro. Jac. 514 *Contra.*

In Taylor v. Hall, 2 Strange, 1189, it was held not actionable to say that plaintiff had had the pox. Smith's Case, Noy, 151; Dutton v. Eaton, Al. 30; Carslake v. Mapledoram, 2 T. R. 473; Nichols v. Guy, 2 Ind. 82; Pike v. Van Wormer, 5 How. Pr. 171; Irons v. Field, 9 R. I. 216 *Accord.* Austin v. White, Cro. El. 214; Anon. Ow. 34; Hobson v. Hudson, Sty. 199, 219 *Contra.*

[2] Only the opinion of the court is given.

maladies as would make him an object of disgust and aversion, and banish him from human society. We believe the only examples which adjudged cases furnish are of the plague, leprosy, and venereal disorders.

In addition to this vital objection in matter of substance, the declaration fails to set forth the supposed cause of action in substantial conformity with the requirements of the statute; and contains many superfluous allegations, which are manifestly irrelevant, impertinent, and scandalous. *Appeal dismissed.*[1]

FOSS *v.* HILDRETH

SUPREME JUDICIAL COURT, MASSACHUSETTS, JANUARY, 1865

Reported in 10 *Allen*, 76.

CHAPMAN, J. The defendant's counsel requested the court to give certain instructions to the jury, as stated in the bill of exceptions. One of the instructions prayed for was, that the truth is not a defence to an action of slander, if the words were spoken maliciously or without any reason on the part of the defendant to believe they were true.[2] But in respect to verbal slander the law has always been otherwise. A special plea in justification sets forth the truth of the words merely. 3 Chit. Pl. 1031. *Exceptions overruled.*[3]

SCOTT *v.* STANSFIELD

IN THE EXCHEQUER, JUNE 3, 1868.

Reported in Law Reports, 3 *Exchequer*, 220.

DECLARATION that the defendant published of the plaintiff in relation to his business as a scrivener these words: "You are a harpy, preying on the vitals of the poor."

[1] But see Fitzgerald *v.* Young, 89 Neb. 693 (imputation of insanity to a teacher).

[2] Only the opinion of the court upon this point is given.

[3] Lucas *v.* Cotton, Moore, 79; Underwood *v.* Parks, 2 Stra. 1200; Ellis *v.* Buzzell, 60 Me. 209; Baum *v.* Clause, 5 Hill, 196 *Accord.*

The rule is the same as to actions for a libel. Leyman *v.* Latimer, 3 Ex. D. 15, 352; Grand Union Tea Co. *v.* Lorch, (C. C. A.) 231 Fed. 390; Schuler *v.* Fischer, 167 Ala. 184; Children *v.* Shinn, 168 Ia. 531; Castle *v.* Hunston, 19 Kan. 417; Hanson *v.* Bristow, 87 Kan. 72; Herald Pub. Co. *v.* Feltner, 158 Ky. 35; Cook *v.* Pulitzer Pub. Co., 241 Mo. 326; Merrey *v.* Guardian Pub. Co., 79 N. J. Law, 177; Willetts *v.* Scudder, 72 Or. 535. Unless modified by statute, as in Delaware, Florida, Illinois, Maine, Massachusetts, Nebraska, New York, Rhode Island and West Virginia. Delaware Co. *v.* Croasdale, 6 Houst. 181; Jones *v.* Townsend, 21 Fla. 431; Palmer *v.* Adams, 137 Ind. 72; Perry *v.* Porter, 124 Mass. 338; Fordyce *v.* Richmond, 78 Neb. 752; McClaugherty *v.* Cooper, 39 W. Va. 313. In New Hampshire and Pennsylvania, however, the mere truth of the libel is not always a defence, although there is no such statute. Hutchins *v.* Page, 75 N. H. 215; Burkhart *v.* N. Am. Co., 214 Pa. St. 39.

Plea: That the defendant uttered the said words while acting as a judge in the trial of a cause wherein the now plaintiff was defendant.

Replication: That the words were spoken falsely and without reasonable cause, and were wholly irrelevant and impertinent to the cause before the defendant as the latter then well knew.

Demurrer.[1]

KELLY, C. B. I am of opinion that our judgment must be for the defendant. The question raised upon this record is whether an action is maintainable against the judge of a county court, which is a court of record, for words spoken by him in his judicial character and in the exercise of his functions as judge in the court over which he presides, where such words would as against an ordinary individual constitute a cause of action, and where they are alleged to have been spoken maliciously and without probable cause, and to have been irrelevant to the matter before him. The question arises, perhaps, for the first time with reference to a county court judge, but a series of decisions uniformly to the same effect, extending from the time of Lord Coke to the present time, establish the general proposition that no action will lie against a judge for any acts done or words spoken in his judicial capacity in a court of justice. This doctrine has been applied not only to the Superior Courts, but to the court of a coroner and to a court martial, which is not a court of record. It is essential in all courts that the judges who are appointed to administer the law should be permitted to administer it under the protection of the law independently and freely, without favor and without fear. This provision of the law is not for the protection or benefit of a malicious or corrupt judge, but for the benefit of the public, whose interest it is that the judges should be at liberty to exercise their functions with independence and without fear of consequences. How could a judge so exercise his office if he were in daily and hourly fear of an action being brought against him, and of having the question submitted to a jury whether a matter on which he had commented judicially was or was not relevant to the case before him? Again, if a question arose as to the *bona fides* of the judge it would have, if the analogy of similar cases is to be followed, to be submitted to the jury. Thus, if we were to hold that an action is maintainable against a judge for words spoken by him in his judicial capacity, under such circumstances as those appearing on these pleadings, we should expose him to constant danger of having questions such as that of good faith or relevancy raised against him before a jury, and of having the mode in which he might administer justice in his court submitted to their determination. It is impossible to overestimate the inconvenience of such a result. For these reasons I am most strongly of opinion that no such action as this can, under any circumstances, be maintainable. *Judgment for the defendant.*[2]

[1] The statement of the pleadings is abridged; the arguments of counsel and the concurring opinions of Martin, Channell, and Bramwell, BB., are omitted.

[2] Rex v. Skinner, Lofft, 55; Thomas v. Churton, 2 B. & S. 475; Dawkins v.

MUNSTER *v.* LAMB

In the Court of Appeal, July 5, 1883.

Reported in 11 *Queen's Bench Division*, 588.

Brett, M. R.[1] This action is brought against a solicitor for words spoken by him before a court of justice, whilst he was acting as the advocate for a person charged in that court with an offence against the law. For the purposes of my judgment, I shall assume that the words complained of were uttered by the solicitor maliciously, that is to say, not with the object of doing something useful towards the defence of his client: I shall assume that the words were uttered without any justification or even excuse, and from the indirect motive of personal ill-will or anger towards the prosecutor arising out of some previously existing cause; and I shall assume that the words were irrelevant to every issue of fact which was contested in the court where they were uttered; nevertheless, inasmuch as the words were uttered with reference to, and in the course of, the judicial inquiry which was going on, no action will lie against the defendant, however improper his behavior may have been.

It has been contended that as a person defamed has, *prima facie*, a cause of action, the person defaming must produce either some statute or some previous decision directly in point which will justify his conduct. I cannot agree with that argument. The common law does not consist of particular cases decided upon particular facts: it consists of a number of principles, which are recognized as having existed during the whole time and course of the common law. The judges cannot make new law by new decisions; they do not assume a power of that kind: they only endeavor to declare what the common law is and has been from the time when it first existed. But inasmuch as new circumstances, and new complications of fact, and even new facts, are constantly arising, the judges are obliged to apply to them what they consider to have been the common law during the whole course of its existence, and therefore they seem to be laying down a new law,

Paulet, L. R. 5 Q. B. 94; Dawkins *v.* Prince Edward, 1 Q. B. D. 499; Law *v.* Llewellyn, [1906] 1 K. B. 487 (judge of inferior court — Scotch case Allardice *v.* Robertson, 1 Dow & Cl. 495 not followed); Bottomley *v.* Brougham, [1908] 1 K. B. 584 (official receiver); Miller *v.* Hope, 2 Shaw, App. Cas. 125; Yates *v.* Lansing, 5 Johns. 282, 9 Johns. 395 (but see Aylesworth *v.* St. John, 25 Hun, 156); Allen *v.* Earnest, (Tex. Civ. App.) 145 S. W. 1101 *Accord.*

Kendillon *v.* Maltby, Car. & M. 402, 2 M. & Rob. 438, s. c., lays down too restricted a rule.

"The publication of defamatory words may be under an absolute or under a qualified or conditional privilege. Under the former there is no liability, although the defamatory words are falsely and maliciously published. The class of absolutely privileged communications is narrow and practically limited to legislative and judicial proceedings and acts of state." Hall, C. J., in Hassett *v.* Carroll, 85 Conn. 23, 35.

See Tanner *v.* Stevenson, 138 Ky. 578; Peterson *v.* Steenerson, 113 Minn. 87.

[1] Only the opinion of Brett, M. R., is given.

whereas they are merely applying old principles to a new state of facts. Therefore, with regard to the present case, we have to find out whether there is a principle of the common law, which although it has existed from the beginning, is now to be applied for the first time. I cannot find that there has been a decision of a court of law with reference to such facts as are now before us, that is, with regard to a person acting in the capacity of counsel: but there have been decisions upon analogous facts; and if we can find out what principle was applied in these decisions upon the analogous facts, we must consider how far it governs the case before us.

Actions for libel and slander have always been subject to one principle: defamatory statements, although they may be actionable on ordinary occasions, nevertheless are not actionable libel and slander when they are made upon certain occasions. It is not that these statements are libel or slander subject to a defence, but the principle is that defamatory statements, if they are made on a privileged occasion, from the very moment when they are made, are not libel or slander of which the law takes notice. Many privileged occasions have been recognized. The occasion, with which we now have to deal, is that a defamatory statement has been made either in words or by writing in the course of an inquiry regarding the administration of the law. It is beyond dispute that statements made under these circumstances are privileged as to some persons, and it has been admitted by the plaintiff's counsel that one set of these persons are advocates: it could not be denied that advocates are privileged in respect of at least some defamatory statements made by them in the course of an inquiry as to the administration of the law. It was admitted that so long as an advocate acts *bona fide* and says what is relevant, owing to the privileged occasion, defamatory statements made by him do not amount to libel or slander, although they would have been actionable if they had not been made whilst he was discharging his duty as an advocate. But it was contended that an advocate cannot claim the benefit of the privilege unless he acts *bona fide,* that is, for the purpose of doing his duty as an advocate, and unless what he says is relevant. That is the question which we now have to determine. Certain persons can claim the benefit of the privilege which arises as to everything said or written in the course of an inquiry as to the administration of the law, and without making an exhaustive enumeration I may say that those persons are judges, advocates, parties, and witnesses. There have been decisions with regard to three of these classes, namely, judges, parties, and witnesses, and it has been held that whatever they may have said in the course of an inquiry as to the administration of the law, has been said upon a privileged occasion, and that they are not liable to any action for libel or slander. But it has been suggested that only some of these classes of persons can successfully claim the privilege of the occasion, and those are judges, parties, and witnesses, who make statements without malice and relevantly; and that those judges, parties, and witnesses, who either speak or write without relevancy and with malice, cannot successfully claim the privilege of the occasion. I am inclined to think that with regard to these classes of persons the law has not always been stated in the same manner by the judges, and some judges have a strong objection to carry the privilege beyond the point to which they are obliged by authority to carry it; they are disinclined to admit the existence of the privilege. Other judges are inclined to carry the privilege to its full extent, and we must see what is the doctrine which has been finally adopted. With regard to witnesses, the chief cases are, Revis *v.* Smith, 18 C. B. 126, 25 L. J. C. P. 195, and Henderson *v.* Broomhead, 4 H. & N. 569, and with regard to witnesses, the general conclusion is that all witnesses speaking with reference to the matter which is before the court — whether what they say is relevant or irrelevant, whether what they say is malicious or not — are exempt from liability to any action in respect of what they state, whether the statement has been made in words, that is, on *viva voce* examination, or whether it has been made upon affidavit. It was at one time suggested that although witnesses could not be held liable to actions upon the case for defamation, that is, for actions for libel and slander, nevertheless they might be held liable in another and different form of action on the case, namely, an action analogous to an action for malicious prosecution, in which it would be alleged that the statement complained of was false to the knowledge of the witness, and was made maliciously and without reasonable or probable cause. This view has been supported by high authority; but it seems to me wholly untenable. If an action for libel or slander cannot be maintained, how can such an action as I have mentioned be maintained, it being in truth an action for defamation in an altered form ? Every objection and every reason, which can be urged against an action for libel or slander, will equally apply against the suggested form of action. Therefore, to my mind, the best way to deal with the suggested form of action is to dispose of it in the words of Crompton, J., in Henderson *v.* Broomhead, where he said: " The attempts to obtain redress for defamation having failed, an effort was made in Revis *v.* Smith, 18 C. B. 126, 25 L. J. C. P. 195, to sustain an action analogous to an action for malicious prosecution. That seems to have been done in despair." Nothing could be more strong, nothing could show more clearly his entire disbelief in the possibility of supporting that new form of action. The answer to the suggested form of action was that during the hundreds of years which had elapsed such an action never had been sustained. No reported case from the time of the commencement of the common law until the present day can be found in which the suggested form of action has been maintained, and yet it is impossible to suppose that opportunities for bringing actions of that kind and of carrying them to a conclusion have not occurred again and again. However, the question is not as to the form of the action, but whether an action of any kind will lie for defamation uttered in the course of a judicial proceeding. Crompton, J., in Henderson *v.* Broomhead, also said: "No action will lie for words spoken or written in the course of any judicial proceeding. In spite of all that can be said against it, we find the rule acted upon from the earliest times. The mischief would be immense if the person aggrieved, instead of preferring an indictment for perjury, could turn his complaint into a civil action. By universal assent it appears that in this country no such action lies. Cresswell, J., pointed out in Revis *v.* Smith, 18 C. B. 126, that the inconvenience is much less than it would be if the rule were otherwise. The origin of the rule was the great mischief that would result, if witnesses in courts of justice were not at liberty to speak freely, subject only to the animadversion of the court." It is there laid down that the reason for the rule with regard to witnesses is public policy. In Scott *v.* Stansfield it was held that all judges, inferior as well as superior, are privileged for words spoken in the course of a judicial proceeding, although they are uttered falsely and maliciously and without reasonable or probable cause. The ground of the decision was that the privilege existed for the public benefit: of course it is not for the public benefit that persons should be slandered without having a remedy; but upon striking a balance between convenience and inconvenience, between benefit and mischief to the public, it is thought better that a judge should not be subject to fear for the consequences of anything which he may say in the course of his judicial duty. Therefore the cases of both witnesses and judges fall within the rule as to privileged occasions, notwithstanding it may be proved that any defamatory words spoken by them were uttered from an indirect motive and to gratify their own malice. In Dawkins *v.* Lord Rokeby, Law Rep. 8 Q. B. 255, it was assumed for the purposes of the decision, that the defendant had been guilty of both falsehood and malice; nevertheless it was held that no action would lie against him for statements made by him as a witness. The ground of the decision was no doubt that a witness in giving his evidence should not be afraid of being sued for anything that he might say. A similar view of the law was taken in Seaman *v.* Netherclift; and the same rule has been applied to the parties. If upon the grounds of public policy and free administration of the law the privilege be extended to judges and witnesses, although they speak maliciously and without reasonable or probable cause, is it not for the benefit of the administration of the law that counsel also should have an entirely free mind? Of the three classes — judge, witness, and counsel — it seems to me that a counsel has a special need to have his mind clear from all anxiety. A counsel's position is one of the utmost difficulty. He is not to speak of that which he knows: he is not called upon to consider, whether the facts with which he is dealing are true or false. What he has to do, is to argue as best he can, without degrading himself, in order to maintain the proposition which will carry with it either the protection or the remedy which he desires for his client. If amidst the difficulties of his position he were to be called upon during the heat of his argument to consider whether what he says is true or false, whether what he says is relevant or irrelevant, he would have his mind so embarrassed that he could not do the duty which he is called upon to perform. For, more than a judge, infinitely more than a witness, he wants protection on the ground of benefit to the public. The rule of law is that what is said in the course of the administration of the law, is privileged; and the reason of that rule covers a counsel even more than a judge or a witness. To my mind it is illogical to argue that the protection of privilege ought not to exist for a counsel, who deliberately and maliciously slanders another person. The reason of the rule is, that a counsel, who is not malicious and who is acting *bona fide*, may not be in danger of having actions brought against him. If the rule of law were otherwise, the most innocent of counsel might be unrighteously harrassed with suits, and therefore it is better to make the rule of law so large that an innocent counsel shall never be troubled, although by making it so large counsel are included who have been guilty of malice and misconduct. In Rex *v.* Skinner, Lofft, 55, Lord Mansfield, a judge most skilful in enunciating the principles of the law, treated a counsel as standing in the same position as a judge or a witness. In Dawkins *v.* Lord Rokeby, Law Rep. 8 Q. B. 255, at pp. 263, 264, 268, a most careful judgment was delivered on behalf of all the judges in the Exchequer Chamber, and the opinion of Lord Mansfield was cited and adopted. If the authority of these two cases is to be followed, counsel are equally protected with judges and witnesses. I will refer to Kennedy *v.* Hilliard, 10 Ir. C. L. Rep. N. S. 195, and in that case Pigott, C. B., delivered a most learned judgment, in the course of which he said: "I take this to be a rule of law, not founded (as is the protection in other cases of privileged statements) on the absence of malice in the party sued, but founded on public policy, which requires that a judge, in dealing with the matter before him, a party in preferring or resisting a legal proceeding, and a witness in giving evidence, oral or written, in a court of justice, shall do so with his mind uninfluenced by the fear of an action for defamation or a prosecution for libel." 10 Ir. C. L. Rep., at p. 209. Into the rule thus stated the word "counsel" must be introduced, and the rule may be taken to be the rule of the common law. That rule is founded upon public policy. With regard to counsel, the questions of malice, *bona fides*, and relevancy, cannot be raised; the only question is, whether what is complained of has been said in the course of the administration of the law. If that be so, the case against a counsel must be stopped at once. No action of any kind, no criminal prosecution, can be maintained against a defendant, when it is established that the words complained of were uttered by him as counsel in the course of a judicial inquiry, that is, an inquiry before any court of justice into any matter concerning the administration of the law.

I am of opinion that the rule of law is such as I have pointed out, that it ought to be applied in the present case, and therefore that this action cannot be maintained.

From our judgments it is obvious that we dissent from the opinion of Lord Denman, C. J., expressed by him at Nisi Prius in Kendillon *v.* Maltby, Car. & M. 402; 2 M. & R. 438. *Appeal dismissed.*[1]

[1] Pedley *v.* Morris, 61 L. J. Q. B. 21 *Accord.*

See Buckley *v.* Wood, 4 Rep. 14 *b*; Hodgson *v.* Scarlett, 1 B. & Ald. 232; Mackay *v.* Ford, 5 H. & N. 792; Smallwood *v.* York, 163 Ky. 139; Rudin *v.* Fauver, 33 Ohio Cir. Ct. R. 315; Kruegel *v.* Cockrell (Tex. Civ. App.) 151 S. W. 352.

"We cannot accept the absolute and unqualified privilege laid down in Munster *v.* Lamb. . . . We cannot agree with Brett, M. R., that in a suit against counsel for slander the only inquiry is whether the words were spoken in a judicial proceeding, and if so, the case must be stopped. We quite agree however, with Bramwell, J. A., in Seaman *v.* Netherclift, that 'relevant' and 'pertinent' are not the best words that could be used. These words have in a measure a technical meaning, and we all know the difficulty in determining in some cases what is relevant or pertinent. With Lord Chancellor Cairns we prefer the words 'having reference' or 'made with reference,' or in the language of Shaw, C. J., 'having relation to the cause or subject-matter.' And if counsel in the trial of a cause maliciously slanders a party, or witness or any other person in regard to a matter that has no reference or relation to, or connection with, the case before the Court, he is and ought to be answerable in an action by the party injured. This qualification of his privilege in no manner impairs the freedom of discussion so necessary to the proper administration of the law, nor does it subject counsel to actions for slander except in cases in which upon reason and sound public policy he ought to be held answerable. We cannot agree that for the abuse of his privilege he is amenable only to the authority of the Court. Mere punishment by the Court is no recompense to one who has thus been maliciously and wantonly slandered." Robinson, J., in Maulsby *v.* Reifsnider, 69 Md. 143, 162. La Porta *v.* Leonard, 88 N. J. Law, 663; Andrews *v.* Gardiner, 165 App. Div. 595 *Accord.*

Defamatory statements in brief of counsel. Brooks *v.* Bank of Acadia, 138 La. 657.

Pleadings. Nalle *v.* Oyster, 230 U. S. 165; Carpenter *v.* Grimes Min. Co., 19 Idaho, 384; Hess *v.* McKee, 150 Ia. 409; Lebovitch *v.* Levy, 128 La. 518; Flynn *v.* Boglarsky, 164 Mich. 513; Rosenberg *v.* Dworetsky, 139 App. Div. 517; Harris *v.* Santa Fé Townsite Co., (Tex. Civ. App.) 125 S. W. 77.

In England, statements in a pleading are absolutely privileged, though not relevant. Hodson *v.* Pare, [1899] 1 Q. B. 455.

In the United States, statements in a pleading not pertinent to the action are not privileged. Union Ins. Co. *v.* Thomas, 83 Fed. 803; King *v.* McKissick, 126 Fed. 215; Potter *v.* Troy, 175 Fed. 128; Myers *v.* Hodges, 53 Fla. 197; Gaines *v.* Aetna Ins. Co., 104 Ky. 695; Jones *v.* Brownlee, 161 Mo. 258; Gilbert *v.* People, 1 Denio, 41; Kemper *v.* Fort, 219 Pa. St. 85; Crockett *v.* McLanahan, 109 Tenn. 517; Miller *v.* Gust, 71 Wash. 139.

Charges in disbarment proceedings, see Preusser *v.* Faulhaber, 33 Ohio Cir. Ct. R. 312.

Statements in a petition for pardon. Connollee *v.* Blanton, (Tex. Civ. App.) 163 S. W. 404 (held absolutely privileged).

Statement by defendant on trial for crime. Nelson *v.* Davis, 9 Ga. App. 131.

In Louisiana the statements of parties in judicial proceedings are not absolutely privileged. Lescale *v.* Joseph Schwartz Co., 116 La. 293, 118 La. 718; Dunn *v.* Southern Co., 116 La. 431.

SEAMAN *v.* NETHERCLIFT

IN THE COURT OF APPEAL, DECEMBER 15, 1876.

Reported in 2 Common Pleas Division, 53.

APPEAL from the decision of the Common Pleas Division, ordering judgment to be entered for the defendant. 1 C. P. D. 540.

Claim: That defendant said of a will, to the signature of which the plaintiff was a witness, "I believe the signature to the will to be a rank forgery, and I shall believe so to the day of my death," meaning that the plaintiff had been guilty of forging the signature of the testator, or of aiding and abetting in the forgery.

Defence: That defendant spoke the words in the course of giving his evidence as a witness on a charge of forgery before a magistrate.

Reply: That the words were not *bona fide* spoken by defendant as a witness, or in answer to any question put to him as a witness, and he was a mere volunteer in speaking them for his own purposes otherwise than as a witness and maliciously and out of the course of his examination.[1]

COCKBURN, C. J. The case is, to my mind, so abundantly clear, and I believe to the minds of my learned brothers, that I think we ought not to hesitate to at once pronounce our decision.

The plaintiff brings his action against the defendant for slander, alleged to have been uttered on the occasion of a prosecution for forgery before a magistrate of the city of London. The defence set up is: "True, I did utter the words imputed to me, but I spoke them when I was a witness in a case in which I was called as a witness." The plaintiff's answer to that is, "Yes, you were called as a witness, but you spoke these words when you were no longer giving evidence, and not only knowing them to be false, but also not in the inquiry, and dehors altogether the subject-matter of the inquiry, for your own purpose of maliciously defaming me." At the trial before Lord Coleridge it appeared that in the Probate suit of Davies *v.* May the defendant had been examined, as an adept, to express his opinion as to the genuineness of a signature to a will, and he gave it as his opinion that the signature was a forgery. The president of the court, in addressing the jury, made some very strong observations on the rashness of the defendant in expressing so confident an opinion in the face of the direct evidence. Soon afterwards, on a prosecution for forgery before the magistrate, the defendant was called as an adept by the person charged, when he expressed an opinion favorable to the genuineness of the document. He was then asked by the counsel for the prosecution whether he had been a witness in the suit of Davies *v.* May. He answered. "Yes." And he was then asked, "Did you read a report of the observations which the presiding judge made on your evidence?" He again said, "Yes." And then the counsel stopped. I presume the circumstances of the trial were well known, and the counsel thought he had done enough. The defendant, the witness, expressed a desire to make a statement. The magistrate told him he could not hear it. Nevertheless the defendant persisted and made the statement, the subject-matter of this action of slander.

On the proof of these facts Lord Coleridge reserved leave to the defendant to move to enter judgment, if the court should be of opinion that there was no

[1] The arguments and the opinion of Amphlett, J. A., are omitted.

evidence on behalf of the plaintiff which ought to be left to the jury. It occurred to him, however, that it would be as well to take the opinion of the jury, and they found that the replication was true, viz., that the words were spoken, not as a witness in the course of the inquiry, but maliciously for his own purpose, that is, with intent to injure the plaintiff. Upon these findings judgment was entered for the plaintiff, leave being again reserved to enter judgment for the defendant, and the Court of Common Pleas gave judgment for the defendant.

Now, if the findings of the jury had been founded upon evidence by which they could have been supported, I might have had some hesitation about the decision. But they were not; and we are asked to come to a conclusion contrary to what has been established law for nearly three centuries.

If there is anything as to which the authority is overwhelming it is that a witness is privileged to the extent of what he says in course of his examination. Neither is that privilege affected by the relevancy or irrelevancy of what he says; for then he would be obliged to judge of what is relevant or irrelevant, and questions might be, and are, constantly asked which are not strictly relevant to the issue. But that, beyond all question, this unqualified privilege extends to a witness is established by a long series of cases, the last of which is Dawkins *v.* Lord Rokeby, Law Rep. 7 H. L. 744, after which to contend to the contrary is hopeless. It was there expressly decided that the evidence of a witness with reference to the inquiry is privileged, notwithstanding it may be malicious; and to ask us to decide to the contrary is to ask what is beyond our power. But I agree that if in this case, beyond being spoken maliciously, the words had not been spoken in the character of a witness or not while he was giving evidence in the case, the result might have been different. For I am very far from desiring to be considered as laying down as law that what a witness states altogether out of the character and sphere of a witness, or what he may say dehors the matter in hand, is necessarily protected. I quite agree that what he says before he enters or after he has left the witness-box is not privileged, which was the question in the case before Lord Ellenborough. Trotman *v.* Dunn, 4 Camp. 211. Or if a man when in the witness-box were to take advantage of his position to utter something having no reference to the cause or matter of inquiry in order to assail the character of another, as if he were asked, " Were you at York on a certain day ? " and he were to answer, " Yes, and A. B. picked my pocket there; " it certainly might well be said in such a case that the statement was altogether dehors the character of witness, and not within the privilege.

If, therefore, the findings of the jury, that the defendant had ceased to be a witness when he spoke the words, were justified by the evidence, I should hesitate before I decided in his favor. But I think the defendant was entitled to judgment on the first reservation. There was no evidence to go to the jury upon the plaintiff's case. What the defendant said was said in his character of witness; for there can be no doubt that the words were spoken in consequence of the question put to him by counsel for the prosecution, the object and effect of the cross-examination having been to damage his credibility as a witness before the magistrate, and of this the witness was conscious. The counsel, having put the question, stops; and if there had been counsel present for the prisoner who had re-examined the witness, he would have put the proper questions to rehabilitate him to the degree of credit to which he was entitled. That such questions would have been relevant I cannot bring myself for a moment to doubt, relating as they do to the credibility of the witness, which is part of the matter of which the magistrate has to take cognizance. That being so, the witness himself, who is sworn to speak the whole truth, is properly entitled, not only with a view to his own vindication, but in the interest of justice, to make such an observation in explanation of his former answer as is just and fair under the circumstances. That is what the defendant did. The sitting magistrate having allowed the disparaging question to be put and answered, ought not to have interfered to prevent the defendant from giving an explanation. I think the statement, coming immediately after the damaging question had been put to him, must be taken to be part of his testimony touching the matter in question, as it affects his credibility as a witness in the matter as to which he was called. It was given as part of his evidence before he had become divested of his character of witness; and but for the question of the opposite counsel he never would have made the statement at all.

As to the finding of malice, it is true that what the defendant said might possibly have the effect of damaging the plaintiff's character; but can any one suppose that the defendant had this in his mind when he spoke, or that he intended to injure the plaintiff? He thought only of his own credit as a witness, which had been attacked. He spoke, on the impulse of the moment, no doubt very foolishly; and it was probably his foolish persistence in maintaining the same attitude and setting up his own opinion against the positive testimony of the other witnesses that prejudiced the jury against him, and led them to return the findings they did, founded, in reality, upon no evidence at all. In my opinion, the Lord Chief Justice should have nonsuited the plaintiff, which is the conclusion at which the Court of Common Pleas ultimately arrived; for there really was no evidence that the defendant was speaking otherwise than as a witness and relevantly to the matters in issue, because relevantly to his own character and credibility as a witness in the matter. That being so, even if express malice could have been properly inferred from the circumstances, the case of Dawkins *v.* Lord Rokeby, Law Rep. 7 H. L. 744, conclusively decides that malice has ceased to be an element in the consideration of such cases, unless it can be shown that the statement was made not in the course of giving evidence, and therefore not in the character of a witness. A long series of authorities, from the time of Elizabeth to the present time, has established that the privilege of a witness while giving evidence is absolute and unqualified. Allardice *v.* Robertson, 1 Dow, N. S. 495, 515, was relied upon by Mr. Chambers. That was the case of an action against a magistrate for words spoken on the bench, and Lord Wynford expressly distinguishes the two cases, and says that the privilege of a judge of the superior courts does not apply to the judge of an inferior court; and that in the case of the latter the privilege is not absolute and unqualified, and that a "subordinate judge" would be liable to an action if malice were proved. It does not, therefore, touch the present case; and as to a witness speaking with reference to the subject-matter of the issue, it is clear that the privilege is unqualified.

The judgment of the Common Pleas Division must, therefore, be affirmed.

BRAMWELL, J. A. I am of the same opinion. The judgment of the Common Pleas affirmed two propositions. First, that what the defendant said was said as a witness, and was relevant to the inquiry before the magistrate; secondly, that, that being so, the Lord Chief Justice should have stopped the trial of the action by nonsuiting the plaintiff.

As to the first proposition, I am by no means sure that the word "relevant" is the best word that could be used; the phrases used by the Lord Chief Baron and the Lord Chancellor in Dawkins *v.* Lord Rokeby, Law Rep. 7 H. L., at p. 744, would seem preferable, "having reference," or "made with reference to the inquiry." Now, were the judges of the Common Pleas Division right in holding that this statement of the defendant had reference to the inquiry? I think that they were. There can be no doubt that the question put by the cross-examining counsel ought not to have been allowed: "Have you read what Sir James Hannen is reported to have said as to your evidence in Davies *v.* May?" What Sir James Hannen had said in a former case was not evidence. It was, therefore, an improper question, and the answer to it, if untrue, would not have subjected the witness to an indictment for perjury. But the question having been put, and the answer having been in the affirmative — and the question being, as Lord Coleridge observed, "ingeniously suggestive," viz., that the way the defendant had been dealt with on the former occasion did not redound to his credit as a witness — the defendant insisted on making in addition the statement complained of. He did so, in my opinion, very foolishly. It would have been better to have been satisfied with retaining his own opinion without setting it up in direct opposition to the positive testimony of eye-witnesses. But he foolishly, as I think, and coarsely exclaimed, "I believe that will to be a rank forgery, and shall believe so to the day of my death." Suppose after he had said "yes," he had added in a decent and becoming manner, "and I am sorry Sir James Hannen said what he did, for I took great pains to form my own opinion, and I shall always retain it, as I still think it right." Would not that have had reference to the inquiry before the magistrate? And would it not have been reasonable and right that the witness should have added that statement in justification of himself? Surely, yes. Mr. Clarke said he was prepared to maintain that as long as a witness spoke as a witness in the witness-box, he was protected, whether the matter had reference to the inquiry or not. I am reluctant to affirm so extreme a proposition. Suppose while the witness is in the box, a man were to come in at the door, and the witness were to exclaim, "That man picked my pocket." I can hardly think that would be privileged. I can scarcely think a witness would be protected for anything he might say in the witness-box, wantonly and without reference to the inquiry. I do not say he would not be protected. It might be held that it was better that everything a witness said as a witness should be protected, than that witnesses should be under the impression that what they said in the witness-box might subject them to an action. I certainly should pause before I affirmed so extreme a proposition, but without affirming that, I think the words "having reference to the inquiry" ought to have a very wide and comprehensive application, and ought not to be limited to statements for which, if not true, a witness might be indicted for perjury, or the exclusion of which by the judge would give ground for a new trial; but ought to extend to that which a witness might naturally and reasonably say when giving evidence with reference to the inquiry as to which he had been called as a witness. Taking that view, I think the first proposition is established, that the statement of the defendant was made as witness and had reference to the inquiry.

As to the second proposition, that, if the first be made out, no inquiry can be gone into as to whether the statement was false or malicious or as a volunteer, we are bound by authority. The case of Dawkins *v.* Lord Rokeby, Law

Rep. 7 H. L. 744, is directly in point, and binding upon us even if we disliked the decision. Mr. Chambers has not attempted to distinguish that case except on the ground that the inquiry in that case was before a military court. But it is clearly not distinguishable on that ground. The learned Lords determined that what is true of a civil tribunal is true of a military court of inquiry; and they affirmed most distinctly the proposition that if the evidence has reference to the inquiry, the witness is absolutely privileged. There is also the case in the Court of Error of Henderson v. Broomhead, 4 H. & N. 569, which is precisely to the same effect, and undistinguishable from the present case.

I am, therefore, of opinion that the judgment of the Common Pleas Division was right, and must be affirmed. *Judgment affirmed.*[1]

WHITE v. CARROLL

Court of Appeals, New York, March 18, 1870.

Reported in 42 New York Reports, 161.

Sutherland, J.[2] On the trial of this action, before Mr. Justice Potter and a jury at the circuit, it appeared, that in 1858 and 1859, a proceeding was going on before the surrogate of Montgomery county

[1] Revis v. Smith, 18 C. B. 126; Henderson v. Broomhead, 4 H. & N. 569; Dawkins v. Rokeby, L. R. 7 H. L. 744, L. R. 8 Q. B. 255 (military court of inquiry); Goffin v. Donnelly, 6 Q. B. D. 307 (select committee of House of Commons); Gompas v. White, 6 T. L. R. 20; Watson v. Jones, [1905] A. C. 480 (privilege extends to statement to client and solicitor in preparation of case for trial); Terry v. Fellows, 21 La. Ann. 375; Hunckle v. Voneiff, 69 Md. 173; Dodge v. Gilman, 122 Minn. 177; Runge v. Franklin, 72 Tex. 585; Kennedy v. Hilliard, 10 Ir. C. L. R. 195 *Accord*. But the English courts do not extend the doctrine to hearings before an administrative board. Atwood v. Chapman, 111 L. T. 726.

See also Hutchinson v. Lewis, 75 Ind. 55; Liles v. Gaster, 42 Ohio St. 631.

In Dawkins v. Lord Rokeby, *supra*, Lord Penzance said: "It is said that a statement of fact of a libellous nature which is palpably untrue — known to be untrue by him who made it, and dictated by malice — ought to be the subject of a civil remedy, though made in the course of a purely military inquiry. This mode of stating the question assumes the untruth and assumes the malice. If by any process of demonstration, free from the defects of human judgment, the untruth and malice could be set above and beyond all question or doubt, there might be ground for contending that the law of the land should give damages to the injured man.

"But this is not the state of things under which this question of law has to be determined. Whether the statements were, in fact, untrue, and whether they were dictated by malice, are, and always will be, open questions, upon which opinions may differ, and which can only be resolved by the exercise of human judgment. And the real question is, whether it is proper on grounds of public policy to remit such questions to the judgment of a jury. The reasons against doing so are simple and obvious. A witness may be utterly free from malice, and may yet in the eyes of a jury be open to that imputation; or, again, the witness may be cleared by the jury of the imputation, and may yet have to encounter the expenses and distress of a harassing litigation. With such possibilities hanging over his head, a witness cannot be expected to speak with that free and open mind which the administration of justice demands.

"These considerations have long since led to the legal doctrine that a witness in the courts of law is free from any action; and I fail to perceive any reason why the same considerations should not be applied to an inquiry such as the present, and with the same result."

[2] The statement, arguments of counsel and parts of the opinion are omitted.

in which the contested point or question was the testamentary capacity of one Jay Phillips; that the plaintiff and the defendant were both at the time, and for some years previously had been, practising as physicians at Amsterdam, Montgomery county, the plaintiff as a homœopathic physician, and the defendant as an allopathic physician; that both had been sworn as witnesses, and testified in the proceedings before the surrogate, the defendant some time after the plaintiff; that on the examination of the defendant as such witness, he was asked whether any other physician was in attendance on Jay Phillips, at the time he was attending him, and that he answered: " Not as I know of." That he was then asked: " Did not any physician attend him at the time he was at Mrs. Moore's, when you did not ? " That to this question, the defendant answered: " Not as I know of; I understand he had a quack, I would not call him a physician; I understood that Dr. White, as he is called, had been there." That this evidence was reduced to writing by the surrogate, and filed in the surrogates' office; and thereupon this action was brought, the complaint in which contains two counts, one for libel, or for words written; and the other for slander, or for words spoken.

No point was made on the trial of the action, that the words alleged in the complaint had not been proved to have been spoken by the defendant, but a motion was made on his part to dismiss the complaint, substantially upon the ground that the words spoken by the defendant were not actionable, because they were spoken on his examination as a witness, and were spoken as pertinent and responsive to the questions asked him.

Justice Potter denied the motion to dismiss the complaint, and the defendant excepted.

In submitting to the jury the question, " whether the defendant, at the time he so testified and used the words in question, believed the words so used by him were relevant or pertinent to the question then on trial," Justice Potter charged the jury as follows: " That if the jury believed, from all the circumstances proved, from the questions put to him, and from his manner of answering, and from the answers themselves, that he testified in good faith, or in the belief that his answers were pertinent and relevant, then the law protected him in what he said; it was privileged, and their verdict should be for the defendant. That if, on the contrary, they should believe from this evidence, that the defendant, though testifying at the time as a witness, and as such entitled to the protection of the law, in so using the words proved, was actuated by malice; that he used the words for the mere purpose of defaming the plaintiff, then the law withdrew the protection it would otherwise have afforded him, and he became amenable to the consequences of uttering the slander, or of publishing the libel."

There is certainly some doubt whether the defendant's exception which he claims applies to this part of the charge, was sufficiently specific or definite to raise the question as to its correctness; but I shall assume that it was; and I shall also assume, in view of what I have said preliminarily, as the counsel for the defendant assumed on the argument, and assumes in his points, that the only material questions presented by this appeal, are those presented by the two exceptions referred to.

Now, as to the first, it is perfectly clear, that the question, whether the defendant was protected under the circumstances, was not a question of law for the court, but was a question of fact for the jury. It was really a question of conduct, of motive, of good faith and honest purpose, or of bad faith and malicious purpose.

The question was, whether the defendant did, or did not, avail himself of the occasion to maliciously answer the questions put to him as a witness, in the way he did.

This question was most emphatically a question for the jury; and, I think it was submitted to the jury as favorably for the defendant as he had a right to expect or ask.

It is true, that in submitting it to the jury, Justice Potter assumed that the defendant, when he answered the questions as he did, knew what the question in the proceeding before the surrogate was; but Justice Potter had a right to assume this under the circumstances.

I think the judgment should be affirmed, with costs.

All concur for affirmance. *Judgment affirmed.*[1]

[1] "White *v.* Carroll, rightly understood, is in harmony with the other cases. The case shows that the court held that the answer given to the question put to the defendant as a witness before the surrogate was not material and pertinent to the inquiry; and further held it was privileged if the defendant, when he gave it, in good faith believed that it was; and whether he so believed, was a question of fact to be determined by the jury. Had the evidence proved that the answer was material and pertinent, the court must have held it privileged, irrespective of the defendant's belief upon the subject." Grover, J., in Marsh *v.* Ellsworth, 50 N. Y. 309, 313.

"It seems to be settled by the English authorities that judges, counsel, parties, and witnesses are absolutely exempted from liability to an action for defamatory words published in the course of judicial proceedings; and that the same doctrine is generally held in the American courts, with the qualification, as to parties, counsel, and witnesses, that their statements made in the course of an action must be pertinent and material to the case." Lord, J., in McLaughlin *v.* Cowley, 127 Mass. 316, 319.

"The examination of witnesses is regulated by the tribunal before which they testify, and if witnesses answer pertinently questions asked them by counsel which are not excluded by the tribunal, or answer pertinently questions asked them by the tribunal, they ought to be absolutely protected. It is not the duty of a witness to decide for himself whether the questions asked him under the direction of the tribunal are relevant. As the witness is sworn to tell the whole truth relating to the matter concerning which his testimony is taken, he ought also to be absolutely protected in testifying to any matter which is relevant to the inquiry, or which he reasonably believes to be relevant to it. But a witness ought not to be permitted with impunity to volunteer defamatory statements which are irrelevant to the matter of inquiry, and which he does not believe to be relevant. This statement of the law

RICE *v.* COOLIDGE

SUPREME JUDICIAL COURT, MASSACHUSETTS, DECEMBER 1, 1876.

Reported in 121 *Massachusetts Reports*, 393.

MORTON, J. This is an action of tort. The principal question raised by the demurrer is, whether the plaintiff's declaration states any legal cause of action. Each count alleges, in substance, that a proceeding for a divorce was pending in the courts of the State of Iowa, between Joseph S. Coolidge and Mary L. Coolidge, in which the latter alleged that the said Joseph S. Coolidge had been guilty of adultery with the plaintiff; that the defendants conspired together and with the

we think, is supported by the decisions in this Commonwealth. The English decisions, perhaps, go somewhat further than this in favor of a witness; certainly they apply the rule liberally for his protection." Field, J., in Wright *v.* Lothrop, 149 Mass. 385, 389.

The principal case and the preceding extracts in this note represent the views of the American courts in general.

King *v.* McKissick, 126 Fed. 215; Lawson *v.* Hicks, 38 Ala. 279; Wyatt *v.* Buell, 47 Cal. 624; Hollis *v.* Meux, 69 Cal. 625; People *v.* Green, 9 Col. 506; Lester *v.* Thurmond, 51 Ga. 118; Buschbaum *v.* Heriot, 5 Ga. App. 521; Spaids *v.* Barrett, 57 Ill. 289; Fagan *v.* Fries, 30 Ill. App. 236; Smith *v.* Howard, 28 Ia. 51; Hawk *v.* Evans, 76 Ia. 593; Forbes *v.* Johnson, 11 B. Mon. 48; Morgan *v.* Booth, 13 Bush, 480; Stewart *v.* Hall, 83 Ky. 375; Sebree *v.* Thompson, 126 Ky. 223; Kelly *v.* Lafitte, 28 La. Ann. 435; Gardemal *v.* McWilliams, 43 La. Ann. 454; Barnes *v.* McCrate, 32 Me. 442; Hoar *v.* Wood, 3 Met. 193; Kidder *v.* Parkhurst, 3 All. 393; McLaughlin *v.* Cowley, 127 Mass. 316; Wright *v.* Lothrop, 149 Mass. 385; Wheaton *v.* Beecher, 49 Mich. 348; Acre *v.* Starkweather, 118 Mich. 214; Hastings *v.* Lusk, 22 Wend. 410; Ring *v.* Wheeler, 7 Cow. 725; Garr *v.* Selden, 4 N. Y. 91; Marsh *v.* Ellsworth, 50 N. Y. 309; Moore *v.* Manufacturers' Bank, 123 N. Y. 420, 136 N. Y. 666; Newfield *v.* Copperman, 15 Abb. Pr. N. S. 360; Perkins *v.* Mitchell, 31 Barb. 461; Dada *v.* Piper, 41 Hun, 254; McLaughlin *v.* Charles, 60 Hun, 239; Beggs *v.* McCrea, 62 App. Div. 39 (*semble*); Suydam *v.* Moffat, 1 Sandf. 459; Perzel *v.* Tousey, 52 N. Y. Super. Ct. 79; Cooper *v.* Phipps, 24 Or. 357; Shadden *v.* McElwee, 86 Tenn. 146; Mower *v.* Watson, 11 Vt. 536; Dunham *v.* Powers, 42 Vt. 1; Johnson *v.* Brown, 13 W. Va. 71; Jennings *v.* Paine, 4 Wis. 358; Calkins *v.* Sumner, 13 Wis. 193; Larkin *v.* Noonan, 19 Wis. 82.

Statements volunteered by witness. Viss *v.* Calligan, 91 Wash. 673.

Statements in affidavit. Perry *v.* Perry, 153 N. C. 266; Baggett *v.* Grady, 154 N. C. 342; Keeley *v.* Great Northern R. Co., 156 Wis. 181. But see Ritschy *v.* Garrels, 195 Mo. App. 670.

Affidavit in legislative investigation. Tuohy *v.* Hassell, 35 Okl. 61.

Defamatory statements at creditors' meeting. Smith *v.* Agee, 178 Ala. 627.

Statements in notice of foreclosure sale. Tierney *v.* Ruppert, 150 App. Div. 863.

Report of grand jury without indictment. Rich *v.* Eason, (Tex. Civ. App.) 180 S. W. 303.

Statement of guardian as to person making claim against ward's estate. Marney *v.* Joseph, 94 Kan. 18.

Letter from one attorney to another, not confined to the matters in litigation. Savage *v.* Stover, 86 N. J. Law, 478.

Message of a mayor. A communication from the mayor of a city to the common council is absolutely privileged. Trebilcock *v.* Anderson, 117 Mich. 39.

Official statements of officers of state are absolutely privileged. Chatterton *v.* Secretary of State, [1895] 2 Q. B. 189; Spalding *v.* Vilas, 161 U. S. 483.

Statements of administrative officers. Farr *v.* Valentine, 38 App. D. C. 413; Haskell *v.* Perkins, 165 Ill. App. 144; Tanner *v.* Stevenson, 138 Ky. 578; Peterson *v.* Steenerson, 113 Minn. 87; Johnson *v.* Marsh, 82 N. J. Law, 4 (notice not to sell liquor to alleged drunkard); Bingham *v.* Gaynor, 203 N. Y. 27.

said Mary L. Coolidge to procure and suborn witnesses to falsely testify in support of said charges of adultery; and that the defendants, in pursuance and execution of said conspiracy, did procure and suborn certain witnesses named, to testify in said divorce suit, and to falsely swear to criminal sexual intercourse between the plaintiff and said Joseph S. Coolidge, and between the plaintiff and other persons, and to various other acts and things which, if believed, would tend to bring disgrace and infamy upon the plaintiff.

Three of the counts also allege that the defendants, in pursuance and execution of the conspiracy, published or caused to be published a printed pamphlet in which the false testimony of such witnesses was repeated, and made the pretext for false and malicious charges upon the plaintiff's character and good name.

The gist of the plaintiff's case is that the defendants have suborned witnesses to falsely swear to defamatory statements concerning her, and have done other connected acts in pursuance of a scheme or plan to defame her. The alleged conspiracy or combination is not one of the elements of the cause of action. That is not created by the conspiracy, but by the wrongful acts done by the defendants to the injury of the plaintiff. If the acts charged, when done by one alone, are not actionable, they are not made actionable by being done by several in pursuance of a conspiracy. Wellington *v.* Small, 3 Cush. 145; Parker *v.* Huntington, 2 Gray, 124; Bowen *v.* Matheson, 14 Allen, 499.

The question is presented, therefore, whether the plaintiff can maintain an action of tort, in the nature of the common-law action on the case, against the defendants for suborning witnesses to falsely swear to defamatory statements concerning the plaintiff in a suit in which neither of the parties to this suit was a party.

It requires no argument to show that the acts charged as done by the defendants, if proved, are a great wrong upon the plaintiff. It is a general rule of the common law that a man shall have a remedy for every injury. The plaintiff should have a remedy for the injury done to her by the defendants, unless there are some other rules of law, or some controlling considerations of public policy, which take the case out of this rule.

The defendants contend that the witnesses who uttered the defamatory statements are protected from an action, because they were statements made in the course of judicial proceedings, and that therefore a person, who procured and suborned them to make the statements, is not liable to an action.

It seems to be settled by the English authorities that judges, counsel, parties, and witnesses are absolutely exempted from liability to an action for defamatory words published in the course of judicial proceedings. Henderson *v.* Broomhead, 4 H. & N. 569; Revis *v.* Smith, 18 C. B. 126; Dawkins *v.* Rokeby, L. R. 8 Q. B. 255, and cases cited; affirmed, L. R. 7 H. L. 744; Seaman *v.* Netherclift. The same doctrine is generally held in the American courts, with the qualification, as to parties, counsel, and witnesses, that, in order to be privileged, their statements made in the course of an action must be pertinent and material to the case. White *v.* Carroll, Smith *v.* Howard, 28 Iowa, 51; Barnes *v.* McCrate, 32 Maine, 442; Kidder *v.* Parkhurst, 3 Allen 393; Hoar *v.* Wood, 3 Met. 193. In the last-cited case, Chief Justice Shaw says: "We take the rule to be well settled by the authorities, that words spoken in the course of judicial proceedings, though they are such as impute crime to another, and therefore, if spoken elsewhere, would import malice and be actionable in themselves, are not actionable if they are applicable and pertinent to the subject of inquiry."

We assume, therefore, for the purposes of this case, that the plaintiff cannot maintain an action against the witnesses in the suit in Iowa, for their defamatory statements, though they were false. But it does not follow that she may not maintain an action against those who, with malice and intent to injure her, procured and suborned those witnesses to testify falsely.

The reasons why the testimony of witnesses is privileged are that it is given upon compulsion and not voluntarily, and that, in order to promote the most thorough investigation in courts of justice, public policy requires that witnesses shall not be restrained by the fear of being vexed by actions at the instance of those who are dissatisfied with their testimony.[1] But these reasons do not apply to a stranger to the suit, who procures and suborns false witnesses, and the rule should not be extended beyond those cases which are within its reasons.

The argument, that an accessory cannot be held civilly liable for an act for which no remedy can be had against the principal, is not satisfactory to our minds. The perjured witness and the one who suborns him are joint tort-feasors, acting in conspiracy or combination to injure the party defamed. The fact that one of them is protected from a civil suit by a personal privilege does not exempt the other joint tort-feasor from such suit. A similar argument was disregarded by the court in Emery *v.* Hapgood, 7 Gray, 55, where it was held that the defendant, who instigated and procured an officer to arrest the plaintiff upon a void warrant, was liable to an action of tort therefor, although the officer who served the warrant was protected from an action, for reasons of public policy.

[1] It is well settled that no action is allowed against a witness for damage caused by his perjury. Damport *v.* Sympson, Cro. El. 520, Ow. 158, 2 And. 47, s. c.; Eyres *v.* Sedgewicke, Cro. Jac. 601; Yelv. 142, 2 Roll. R. 197, s. c.; Wimberly *v.* Thompson, Noy, 6; Harding *v.* Bodman, Hutt. 11; Coxe *v.* Smithe, 1 Lev. 119; Taylor *v.* Bidwell, 65 Cal. 489; Bostwick *v.* Lewis, 2 Day, 447; Grove *v.* Brandenburg, 7 Blackf. 239; Dunlap *v.* Glidden, 31 Me. 435; Severance *v.* Judkins, 73 Me. 376, 379; Garing *v.* Fraser, 76 Me. 37; Phelps *v.* Stearns, 4 Gray, 105; Curtis *v.* Fairbanks, 16 N. H. 542; Smith *v.* Lewis, 3 Johns. 157; Cunningham *v.* Brown, 18 Vt. 123.

See Bell *v.* Senneff, 83 Ill. 122. Compare Schaub *v.* O'Ferrell, 116 Md. 131.

The defendants rely upon the cases of Bostwick *v.* Lewis, 2 Day, 447, and Smith *v.* Lewis, 3 Johns. 157. But those cases turn upon a principle which does not apply in the case at bar. The facts in those cases were as follows: Lewis brought an action in Connecticut against several defendants, in which he prevailed. Afterwards Bostwick, one of the defendants in the original action, brought an action in Connecticut against Lewis, for suborning a witness in that action; and Smith, another of the defendants, brought a similar action in New York. It was held in each case that the action could not be maintained, because, in the language of Mr. Justice Kent, it was "an attempt to overhaul the merits" of a former suit. The case of Dunlap *v.* Glidden, 31 Maine, 435, is to the same effect. Although the parties to a former action cannot retry its merits, while a judgment therein is in force and unreversed, yet any person who was not a party to the action, or in privity with a party, may in a collateral action impeach the judgment and overhaul the merits of the former action. Those cases, therefore, are not decisive of the case at bar.[1]

The defendants argue that an action of this nature ought not to be maintained, because the plaintiff therein might, by the testimony of a single witness, prove that a witness in another action had committed perjury. The rule of law, that a man cannot be convicted of perjury upon the unaided testimony of one witness, is a rule applicable only to criminal proceedings. The argument may go to show that the rule ought to be extended to civil cases in which perjury is charged against a witness, but it does not furnish a satisfactory reason why a plaintiff should be altogether deprived of a remedy for an injury inflicted upon him.

It is also urged, as an argument against the maintenance of this action, that it is a novelty. The fact that an action is without a precedent would call upon the court to consider with care the question whether it is justified by correct principles of law; but if this is found, it is without weight. In answer to the same argument, Lord Chief Justice Willes said: "A special action on the case was introduced for this reason, that the law will never suffer an injury and a damage without a remedy, but there must be new facts, in every special action on the case." Winsmore *v.* Greenbank, Willes, 577.

Upon a careful consideration of the case, we are of opinion that there are no rules of law and no reasons of public policy which deprive the plaintiff of her remedy for the wrong done her by the defendants by suborning witnesses to defame her character.[2]

Demurrer overruled.

[1] See also Taylor *v.* Bidwell, 65 Cal. 489; Curtis *v.* Fairbanks, 16 N. H. 542; Stevens *v.* Rowe, 59 N. H. 578.

[2] A part of the opinion relating to points of pleading is omitted.

RYALLS *v.* LEADER

IN THE EXCHEQUER, MAY 26, 1866.

Reported in Law Reports, 1 *Exchequer,* 296.

DECLARATION on a libel published of the plaintiff by the defendants, in a newspaper called the "Sheffield and Rotherham Independent."

Plea. Not guilty. Issue thereon.

The libel complained of was contained in a report of an examination of a debtor in custody, held in York Castle, before the registrar of the Leeds Bankruptcy Court, pursuant to the provisions of the Bankruptcy Act, 1861 (24 & 25 Vict. c. 134), ss. 101, 102; and it conveyed an imputation on the solvency of the plaintiff, who had been the debtor's partner. The cause was tried at the last Leeds spring assizes before Keating, J., when, the publication of the defamatory matter having been proved, the learned judge told the jury that "the libel was a privileged communication, and that the defendants were entitled to the verdict if the jury thought that the libel was a fair report of the proceedings before the registrar of the Court of Bankruptcy, and published without malice." The report contained no original comment on what passed. The jury found a verdict for the defendants.

In Easter Term last, a rule *nisi* was obtained for a new trial.[1]

POLLOCK, C. B. I am of opinion that my Brother Keating was right in his ruling. The complaint here made is that certain proceedings held by a registrar in bankruptcy in York Castle, and published by the defendant, were libellous on the plaintiff. The defence is, that the alleged libel was contained in a fair, correct, and *bona fide* report of what took place; and if these proceedings were in a public court, and the publication was fair, there is no foundation for this action.[2] The

[1] The arguments and the concurring opinions of Martin and Channell, BB., are omitted.

[2] Risk Allah Bey *v.* Whitehurst, 18 L. T. Rep. 615; Hope *v.* Leng, 23 T. L. R. 243; Furniss *v.* Cambridge News, 23 T. L. R. 705; Todd *v.* Every Evening Co., (Del.) 62 Atl. 1089 (*semble*); Blodgett *v.* Des Moines Co., (Ia.) 113 N. W. 821; Billet *v.* Publishing Co., 107 La. 751 (*semble*); McBee *v.* Fulton, 47 Md. 403; Cowley *v.* Pulsifer, 137 Mass. 392; Conner *v.* Standard Co., 183 Mass. 474; Nixon *v.* Dispatch Co., 101 Minn. 309; Hawkins *v.* Globe Co., 10 Mo. App. 174; Boogher *v.* Knapp, 97 Mo. 122; Brown *v.* Knapp, 213 Mo. 655 (*semble*); Brown *v.* Globe Co., 213 Mo. 611; Thompson *v.* Powning, 15 Nev. 195; Edsall *v.* Brooks, 17 Abb. Pr. 221; N. Y. Code Civ. Proc., § 1907; Ackerman *v.* Jones, 37 N. Y. Super. Ct. 42; Salisbury *v.* Union Co., 45 Hun, 120; Hart *v.* Sun Co., 79 Hun, 358; Cincinnati Co. *v.* Timberlake, 10 Ohio St. 548; Metcalf *v.* Times Co., 20 R. I. 674; Saunders *v.* Baxter, 6 Heisk. 369; American Co. *v.* Gamble, 115 Tenn. 663; People *v.* Glassman, 12 Utah, 238 *Accord.*

So publication of copies from the register of judgments is privileged. Searles *v.* Scarlett, [1892] 2 Q. B. 56.

Publication of papers filed in the clerk's office, but not produced in open court, is not privileged. Meeker *v.* Post Pub. Co., 45 Col. 355; Cowley *v.* Pulsifer, 137 Mass. 392; Lundin *v.* Post Pub. Co., 217 Mass. 213; Park *v.* Detroit Co., 72 Mich. 560; Barber *v.* St. Louis Co., 3 Mo. App. 377; Stuart *v.* Press Co., 83 App. Div.

only question then is, whether the registrar's court was under the circumstances a public court. I think that it was. We ought, in my opinion, to make as wide as possible the right of the public to know what takes place in any court of justice, and to protect a fair *bona fide* statement of proceedings there. The jury found that the publication of this report was *bona fide*, and the verdict, therefore, ought not to be set aside.

BRAMWELL, B. I am of the same opinion. I think that this court was a public court. That is shown from the terms of ss. 101 and 102. And even if it were not so, yet if the officer who holds it chooses to make it public, it would be public for this purpose. Then as to the point made, that nothing ought to be published affecting a third party, even when relevant to the inquiry, I think there is no such restriction. Those who are present hear all the evidence, relevant or irrelevant, and those who are absent, may, as far as I can see, have all that is said reported to them. The doctrine contended for is an entire novelty, because, if sound, every witness might bring an action against the newspaper publisher reporting his evidence, and call upon that publisher to prove all the libellous statements which might be contained in his examination or cross-examination. I do not think that there is any such qualification as that suggested, nor do I concur in the other suggestion made to us, viz., that what is *irrelevant* and libellous on a third person is not protected. There are cases where an individual must suffer for the public good, and it is difficult to draw the line between relevancy and irrelevancy. My opinion is, that when once you establish that a court is a public court, a fair *bona fide* report of all that passes there may be published. Possibly this privilege is applied to courts of justice, because needless scandals are usually avoided in them. I am therefore of opinion that this rule should be discharged.

Rule discharged.

467; Byers *v.* Meridian Printing Co., 84 Ohio St. 408; American Co. *v.* Gamble, 115 Tenn. 663; Houston Pub. Co. *v.* McDavid, (Tex. Civ. App.) 173 S. W. 467; Ilsley *v.* Sentinel Co., 133 Wis. 20.

Report of criminal proceeding before magistrate with no jurisdiction. Lee *v.* Brooklyn Pub. Co., 209 N. Y. 245.

Report of investigation before grand jury. Poston *v.* Washington R. Co., 36 App. D. C. 359; Sweet *v.* Post Publishing Co., 215 Mass. 450.

Report in advance of judicial proceeding as to evidence to be adduced. Houston Pub. Co. *v.* Tiernan, (Tex. Civ. App.) 171 S. W. 542. See Kelly *v.* Independent Pub. Co., 45 Mont. 127.

Humorous report. Bresslin *v.* Star Co., 85 Misc. 609.

Matter added to the report. Smith *v.* New Yorker Staats Zeitung, 154 App. Div. 458.

USILL *v.* HALES

IN THE COMMON PLEAS DIVISION, JANUARY 30, 1878.

Reported in 3 Common Pleas Division, 319.

LORD COLERIDGE, C. J.[1] I am of opinion that this rule must be discharged.

This was an action against the proprietor of a newspaper for publishing a *bona fide* and fair report of proceedings before a magistrate. Three persons, surveyors, who had been employed by a civil engineer to assist in the construction of a railway in Ireland, hearing that their employer had been paid, and conceiving that the money due to them had been improperly withheld by him, went before a police magistrate in London, and (I must take it for the purpose of my judgment, and do so take it) applied to him for a summons or order under the Masters and Workman's Act. In the result, the magistrate thought that the facts stated by the complainants showed no ground for a summons against the plaintiff under the Act; and therefore in the result it turned out that, in a certain sense, an application had been made to the magistrate with regard to a matter as to which he had no jurisdiction. I say in a certain sense: but it has been long held, and I think most properly held, that it is not the result but the nature of the application made to the magistrate which founds his jurisdiction: and that, wherever an application is made to a magistrate as to a matter over which, supposing the facts to bear out the statement, he has jurisdiction, he then has jurisdiction to ascertain whether the facts make out a case for the exercise of that jurisdiction which, if the facts make out the case, undoubtedly he has.

It has been laid down again and again in broad terms that the publication of the proceedings in courts of justice is privileged if the report of such proceedings be fair and honest; and this is so found to be. An attempt however has been made (and Mr. Shortt will allow me to say that, if it were possible to have succeeded, I think his argument would have succeeded, because he has said everything that could be said, and has said it well) to distinguish this case and take it out of the general proposition, by bringing it within an undoubted qualification which has been grafted upon that general proposition, viz., that the application to the magistrate here was what may be called an *ex parte* or a preliminary proceeding. Now, there is no doubt that, in many cases to which Mr. Shortt has referred, the term "*ex parte* proceeding" has been over and over again used by judges of great eminence, sometimes affirmatively to say that an *ex parte* proceeding is not privileged, and sometimes negatively to say, this, being a proceeding not *ex parte*, is privileged; and I do not doubt for my own part

[1] Only the opinion of Lord Coleridge, and that, too, slightly abridged, is given. Lopes, J., concurred.

that, if this argument had been addressed to a court some sixty or seventy years ago, it might have met with a different result from that which it is about to meet with to-day. Speaking frankly, — and it is useless, if a case has made a certain impression upon your mind after you have done the best you can to understand it, to say it has not made that impression, — it seems to me quite plain that in such cases as Rex *v.* Fleet, 1 B. & A. 379, judgments of great judges do lay down the rule that an *ex parte* or preliminary proceeding is not privileged on the ground, good or bad, that it is very hard upon an individual to have a matter stated against him behind his back which he has no means of answering; and that oftentimes an accused person will come to trial, if he be tried, with a heavy weight of prejudice; where the case against him has been reported in the public newspapers, and his own answer, if he has one, from the necessities of the case has not been similarly made known. No doubt there are very strong observations in those cases adopted in Duncan *v.* Thwaites, 3 B. & C. 556, which go very far to maintain that proposition. There is also a *dictum* of one of the greatest authorities in our law, Lord Eldon, than whom few greater lawyers have ever sat in Westminster Hall, who is reported, by Mr. Starkie, Starkie on Libel, 4th ed., p. 191 (9), to have once observed that he recollected the time when it would have been matter of surprise to every lawyer in Westminster Hall to learn that the publication of *ex parte* proceedings was legal.

But we are not now living, so to say, within the shadow of those cases: and it is idle to deny that there are cases since that time, in which the decisions I have just now referred to have been brought to the attention of the learned judges, where the courts have been pressed with the authority of those decisions, and have come to conclusions which it is not for me to say are inconsistent, but which I am perfectly unable to reconcile with those earlier cases: and I find what I think is excellent good sense in the judgment of the Court of Queen's Bench in the case of Wason *v.* Walter, which explains how that is. It is a passage which one of the learned counsel read to us, and it is a passage which upon the whole I should desire to adopt and adhere to: "Whatever disadvantages attach to a system of unwritten law, — and of this we are fully sensible,—it has at least this advantage, that its elasticity enables those who administer it to adapt it to the varying conditions of society and to the requirements and habits of the age in which we live, so as to avoid the inconveniences and injustice which arise where the law is no longer in harmony with the wants and usages and interests of the generation to which it is immediately applied. Our law of libel has in many respects only gradually developed itself into anything like satisfactory and settled form. The full liberty of public writers to comment on the conduct and motives of public men has only in very recent times been recognized." And then the passage goes on, — "Even in quite recent days judges, in holding the publication of the proceedings of courts of justice lawful, have thought it necessary to distinguish what we call *ex parte* proceedings as a probable exception from the operation of the rule. Yet *ex parte* proceedings before magistrates, and even before this court, as, for instance, on applications for criminal informations, are published every day; but such a thing as an action or indictment founded on a report of such an *ex parte* proceeding is unheard of; and, if any such action or indictment should be brought, it would probably be held that the true criterion of the privilege is not whether the report was or was not *ex parte*, but whether it was a fair and honest report of what had taken place, published simply with a view to the honest publication, and innocent of all intention to do injury to the reputation of the party affected." Now, to the general line of argument in that passage, and to the accuracy of the statement in the last sentence I have read, I entirely adhere; and it is familiar that not only are unimportant cases and *ex parte* proceedings published, but a particular class of inquiries which in some of the earlier cases I find actually by name excluded from the privilege, — I mean inquiries before a coroner, — are in cases which may be supposed to interest the public reported in all the newspapers in the kingdom; and yet no one ever heard, at least since I have known Westminster Hall, of an action being brought by a person injuriously affected by such publication, where the report is honest and *bona fide*, and published without intention to injure. That, therefore, seems to introduce this element into the determination of these cases, that there is a certain elasticity in the rules which apply to questions of privilege (development is perhaps the more correct expression), and that the courts have from time to time applied as best they may what they think is the good sense of the rules which exist to cases which have not been positively decided to come within them. If there had been a case directly in point in which a proceeding such as this, where the matter was at an end, and where the publication had been found by the jury to have been *bona fide*, honest, and fair, had been held by a court of co-ordinate jurisdiction not to be privileged, I do not hesitate to say for my own part that I should have gladly acted upon it, because I do not disguise that my own judgment is not at all satisfied with the enormous advantage to the public of having every small personal matter reported day by day, often to the extreme pain and injury of individuals, which is supposed to form its justification. Nevertheless, I feel it to be the duty of a judge not to declare what he considers the law ought to be, but to decide according to what to the best of his judgment he finds it is: and, if he finds a principle laid down upon competent authority, it is far better to accept and apply it broadly and honestly, even if he is not in his own mind satisfied with the foundation of the rule, than to attempt to fritter it away in its application to cases which manifestly come within it.

I come therefore to the consideration of this case feeling that the general tendency of the law has been to hold such a publication as this to be within the protection of the privilege. Now, I do find one case which to the best of my judgment appears to cover this case, and from which I am unable, according to the principle laid down in it, to distinguish the case now before us. It is a case to which much reference has been made, and which Mr. Shortt has dealt with at considerable length, viz., Lewis *v.* Levy; and it has no doubt a most important bearing upon this question. I do not propose to read the elaborate judgment delivered by Lord Campbell in that case: it is well summed up in these words: "The rule, that the publication of a fair and correct report of proceedings taking place in a public court of justice is privileged, extends to proceedings taking place publicly before a magistrate on the preliminary investigation of a criminal charge terminating in the discharge by the magistrate of the party charged." I am perfectly aware that there may be subtle distinctions, — distinctions which I will not say are merely shadowy, but which are subtle, — between the facts of that case and those of the case now before us: but I cannot disguise from myself that the *ratio decidendi* and the argument by which the court was there led to hold such proceedings to be privileged, do in effect cover this case. I am of opinion that this is a case in which there was a judicial proceeding terminating, not in the discharge of the party accused, because there was no such person before the magistrate, but terminating in a refusal to proceed with the charge and to set the criminal process in motion. I am unable to distinguish the principle of Lewis *v.* Levy from that involved in the present case; and I adopt what is said there of the old, — and I may say great case, because it was decided by judges of high authority, — of Curry *v.* Walter, so far back as the year 1796. That case is adopted by the Court of Queen's Bench in a written judgment in the year 1858, as a ground of their decision; and, whatever may have been said about it in some of the intermediate cases, and the doubts that have been thrown upon it by some eminent judges, it must I think be considered to be completely rehabilitated by the judgment of the Court of Queen's Bench in Lewis *v.* Levy, E. B. & E. 537. I am content, therefore, to rest my judgment in this case upon the principles laid down in Curry *v.* Walter, 1 B. & P. 525, and deliberately reaffirmed in Lewis *v.* Levy, E. B. & E., at p. 559, and to say that, upon the principles there laid down, I am of opinion that this rule must be discharged.

Rule discharged.[1]

[1] Curry *v.* Walter, 1 Esp. 456, 1 B. & P. 525; Lewis *v.* Levy, E. B. & E. 537; Kimber *v.* Press Association, [1893] 1 Q. B. 65; McBee *v.* Fulton, 47 Md. 403; Salisbury *v.* Union Co., 45 Hun, 120 (*semble*); Metcalf *v.* Times Co., 20 R. I. 674 (*semble*); Brown *v.* Providence Co., 25 R. I. 117 (*semble*) *Accord.*

See Duncan *v.* Thwaites, 3 B. & C. 556; Parsons *v.* Age Herald Pub. Co., 181 Ala. 439; Todd *v.* Every Evening Co., (Del.) 62 Atl. 1089; Flues *v.* New Nonpareil

WASON *v.* WALKER

IN THE QUEEN'S BENCH, NOVEMBER 25, 1868.

Reported in Law Reports, 4 Queen's Bench, 73.

THE judgment of the court was delivered by

COCKBURN, C. J.[1] This case was argued a few days since before my Brothers LUSH, HANNEN, and HAYES, and myself, and we took time, not to consider what our judgment should be, for as to that our minds were made up at the close of the argument, but because, owing to the importance and novelty of the point involved, we thought it desirable that our judgment should be reduced to writing before it was delivered.

The main question for our decision is, whether a faithful report in a public newspaper of a debate in either house of parliament, containing matter disparaging to the character of an individual, as having been spoken in the course of the debate, is actionable at the suit of the party whose character has thus been called in question. We are of opinion that it is not.

Important as the question is, it comes now for the first time before a court of law for decision. Numerous as are the instances in which the conduct and character of individuals have been called in question in parliament during the many years that parliamentary debates have been reported in the public journals, this is the first instance in which an action of libel founded on a report of a parliamentary debate has come before a court of law. There is, therefore, a total absence of direct authority to guide us. There are, indeed, *dicta* of learned judges having reference to the point in question, but they are conflicting and inconclusive, and, having been unnecessary to the decision of the cases in which they were pronounced, may be said to be extrajudicial.

. . . .

The case of Stockdale *v.* Hansard, 9 Ad. & E. 1, which was much pressed upon us by the counsel for the defendant, is . . . beside the question. In that case a report from the inspectors of prisons relative to the jail of Newgate, in which a work published by the plaintiff, a bookseller, and which had been permitted to be introduced into the prison, had been described as "of a most disgusting nature," and as containing, "plates obscene and indecent in the extreme," had been presented to the House in conformity with the Act of 5 & 6 Wm. 4, c. 38. In another report, being a reply to a report of the court of aldermen on the same subject, the inspectors had reiterated their charges as to the character of the book, adding that it had been described by medical booksellers, to whom they (the inspectors) had applied for information as to its character, as "one of Stockdale's obscene books." These papers the House had ordered to be printed, not only for the use of members, but also, in conformity with a modern practice, for public sale, the proceeds to be applied to the general expenses of printing by the House. An action of libel having been

Co., 155 Ia. 290; Cowley *v.* Pulsifer, 137 Mass. 392; Jones *v.* Pulitzer Pub. Co., 240 Mo. 200; Stanley *v.* Webb, 4 Sandf. 21; Matthews *v.* Beach, 5 Sandf. 256; Cincinnati Co. *v.* Timberlake, 10 Ohio St. 548; Mengel *v.* Reading Eagle Co., 241 Pa. St. 367.

The report of *ex parte* proceedings may be published before their termination, if of such a character that there will be a final decision. Kimber *v.* Press Association, [1893] 1 Q. B. 65.

[1] Only the opinion of the court is given.

brought by Stockdale against the defendants, the printers of the House of Commons, for publishing these papers, the defence as raised by the plea which this court had to consider was, first, that the papers in question had been published by order of the House of Commons; secondly, that the House having resolved (as it had done with a view to such an action) that the power of publishing such of its reports, votes, and proceedings, as it should deem necessary, was an essential incident to the functions of parliament, the question became one of privilege, as to which the decision of the House was conclusive, and could not be questioned in a court of law.

From the doctrines involved in this defence, namely, that the House of Commons could by their order authorize the violation of private rights, and, by declaring the power thus exercised to be matter of privilege, preclude a court of law from inquiring into the existence of the privilege, — doctrines which would have placed the rights and liberties of the subject at the mercy of a single branch of the Legislature,—Lord Denman and his colleagues, in a series of masterly judgments which will secure to the judges who pronounced them admiration and reverence so long as the law of England and a regard for the rights and liberties of the subject shall endure, vindicated at once the majesty of the law and the rights which it is the purpose of the law to uphold.

To the decision of this court in that memorable case we give our unhesitating and unqualified adhesion. But the decision in that case has no application to the present. The position, that an order of the House of Commons cannot render lawful that which is contrary to law, still less that a resolution of the House can supersede the jurisdiction of a court of law by clothing an unwarranted exercise of power with the garb of privilege, can have no application where the question is, not whether the act complained of, being unlawful at law, is rendered lawful by the order of the House or protected by the assertion of its privilege, but whether it is, independently of such order or assertion of privilege, in itself privileged and lawful.

Decided cases thus leaving us without authority on which to proceed in the present instance, we must have recourse to principle in order to arrive at a solution of the question before us, and fortunately we have not far to seek before we find principles in our opinion applicable to the case, and which will afford a safe and sure foundation for our judgment.

It is now well established that faithful and fair reports of the proceedings of courts of justice, though the character of individuals may incidentally suffer, are privileged, and that for the publication of such reports the publishers are neither criminally nor civilly responsible.

The immunity thus afforded in respect of the publication of the proceedings of courts of justice rests upon a twofold ground. In the English law of libel, malice is said to be the gist of an action for defamation. And though it is true that by malice, as necessary to give a cause of action in respect of a defamatory statement, legal, and not actual malice, is meant, while by legal malice, as explained by Bayley, J., in Bromage *v.* Prosser, is meant no more than the wrongful intention which the law always presumes as accompanying a wrongful act without any proof of malice in fact, yet the presumption of law may be rebutted by the circumstances under which the defamatory matter has been uttered or published, and, if this should be the case, though the character of the party concerned may have suffered, no right of action will arise. "The rule," says Lord Campbell, C. J., in the case of Taylor *v.* Hawkins, 16 Q. B., at p. 321, "is that, if the occasion be such as repels the presumption of malice, the communication is privileged, and the plaintiff must then, if he can, give evidence of malice."

It is thus that in the case of reports of proceedings of courts of justice, though individuals may occasionally suffer from them, yet, as they are published without any reference to the individuals concerned, but solely to afford information to the public and for the benefit of society, the presumption of malice is rebutted, and such publications are held to be privileged.

The other and the broader principle on which this exception to the general law of libel is founded is, that the advantage to the community from publicity being given to the proceedings of courts of justice is so great, that the occasional inconvenience to individuals arising from it must yield to the general good. It is true that with a view to distinguish the publication of proceedings in parliament from that of proceedings of courts of justice, it has been said that the immunity accorded to the reports of the proceedings of courts of justice is grounded on the fact of the courts being open to the public, while the houses of parliament are not; as also that by the publication of the proceeding of the courts the people obtain a knowledge of the law by which their dealings and conduct are to be regulated. But in our opinion the true ground is that given by Lawrence, J., in Rex *v.* Wright, 8 T. R., at p. 298, namely, that " though the publication of such proceedings may be to the disadvantage of the particular individual concerned, yet it is of vast importance to the public that the proceedings of courts of justice should be universally known. The general advantage to the country in having these proceedings made public, more than counterbalances the inconvenience to the private persons whose conduct may be the subject of such proceedings." In Davison *v.* Duncan, 7 E. & B., at p. 231, Lord Campbell says: " A fair account of what takes place in a court of justice is privileged. The reason is, that the balance of public benefit from publicity is great. It is of great consequence that the public should know what takes place in court; and the proceedings are under the control of the judges. The inconvenience, therefore, arising from the chance of injury to private character is infinitesimally small as compared to the convenience of publicity." And Wightman, J., says: " The only foundation for the exception is the superior benefit of the publicity of judicial proceedings which counterbalances the injury to individuals, though that at times may be great."

Both the principles, on which the exemption from legal consequences is thus extended to the publication of the proceedings of courts of justice, appear to us to be applicable to the case before us. The presumption of malice is negatived in the one case as in the other by the fact that the publication has in view the instruction and advantage of the public, and has no particular reference to the party concerned. There is also in the one case as in the other a preponderance of general good over partial and occasional evil. We entirely concur with Lawrence, J., in Rex *v.* Wright, 8 T. R., at p. 298, that the same reasons which apply to the reports of the proceedings in courts of justice apply also to proceedings in parliament. It seems to us impossible to doubt that it is of paramount public and national importance that the proceedings of the houses of parliament shall be communicated to the public, who have the deepest interest in knowing what passes within their walls, seeing that on what is there said and done, the welfare of the community depends. Where would be our confidence in the government of the country or in the Legislature by which our laws are framed, and to whose charge the great interests of the country are committed, — where would be our attachment to the constitution under which we live, — if the proceedings of the great council of the realm were shrouded in secrecy and concealed from the knowledge of the nation? How could the communications between the representatives of the people and their constituents, which are so essential to the working of the representative system, be usefully carried on, if the constituencies were kept in ignorance of what their representatives are doing? What would become of the right of petitioning on all measures pending in parliament, the undoubted right of the subject, if the people are to be kept in ignorance of what is passing in either house? Can any man bring himself to doubt that the publicity given in modern times to what passes in parliament is essential to the maintenance of the relations subsisting between the government, the Legislature, and the country at large? It may, no doubt, be said that, while it may be necessary as a matter of national interest that the proceedings of parliament should in general be made public, yet that debates in which the character of individuals is brought into question ought to be suppressed. But to this, in addition to the difficulty in which parties publishing parliamentary reports would be placed, if this distinction were to be enforced and every debate had to be critically scanned to see whether it contained defamatory matter, it may be further answered that there is perhaps no subject in which the public have a deeper interest than in all that relates to the conduct of public servants of the state, — no subject of parliamentary discussion which more requires to be made known than an inquiry relating to it. Of this no better illustration could possibly be given than is afforded by the case before us. A distinguished counsel, whose qualification for the judicial bench had been abundantly tested by a long career of forensic eminence, is promoted to a high judicial office, and the profession and the public are satisfied that in a most important post the services of a most competent and valuable public servant have been secured. An individual comes forward and calls upon the House of Lords to take measures for removing the judge, in all other respects so well qualified for his office, by reason that on an important occasion he had exhibited so total a disregard of truth as to render him unfit to fill an office for which a sense of the solemn obligations of truth and honor is an essential qualification. Can it be said that such a subject is not one in which the public has a deep interest, and as to which it ought not to be informed of what passes in debate? Lastly, what greater anomaly or more flagrant injustice could present itself than that, while from a sense of the importance of giving publicity to their proceedings, the houses of parliament not only sanction the reporting of their debates, but also take measures for giving facility to those who report them, while every member of the educated portion of the community from the highest to the lowest looks with eager interest to the debates of either house, and considers it a part of the duty of the public journals to furnish an account of what passes there, we were to hold that a party publishing a parliamentary debate is to be held liable to legal proceedings because the conduct of a particular individual may happen to be called in question?

The learned counsel for the plaintiff scarcely ventured as of his own assertion to deny that the benefit to the public from having the debates in parliament published was as great as that which arose from the publishing of the proceedings of courts of justice, but he relied on the *dicta* of Littledale, J., and Patteson, J., in Stockdale *v.* Hansard, 9 Ad. & E. 1, and on the opinions of certain noble and learned lords in the course of debates in the House of Lords on bills introduced by Lord Campbell for the purpose of amending the law of libel.[1] There is no doubt that in delivering their opinions in Stockdale *v.* Hansard, the two learned judges referred to denied the necessity and in effect the public advantage of the proceedings in parliament being made public. The counsel for the defendant in that case having insisted, as a reason why the power to order papers to be printed and published should be considered within the privileges of the House of Commons, on the advantage which resulted from the proceedings of parliament being made known, the two learned judges, not satisfied with demonstrating, as they did, by conclusive arguments, that the House had not the power to order papers of a libellous character and forming no part of the proceedings of the House to be published, still less to conclude the legality of such a proceeding by the assertion of privilege, thought it necessary to follow the counsel into the question of policy and convenience, and in so doing took what we cannot but think a very short-sighted view of the subject. This is the more to be regretted, as their observations apply not only to the printing of papers by order of the House, the only question before them, but also to the publication of parliamentary proceedings in general, the consideration of which was not before them, and therefore was unnecessary. Lord Denman, in his admirable judgment, than which a finer never was delivered within these walls, and in which the spirit of Holt is combined with the luminous reasoning of a Mansfield, while overthrowing by irresistible arguments the positions of the Attorney-General, was content to answer the argument as to the policy of allowing papers to be published by order of either of the houses of parliament, not by denying the policy of giving power to the House to order the printing and publishing of papers, but by saying that such power must be provided for by legislation. On the subject of the publication of parliamentary debates he said nothing, nor was he called upon to say anything. That the Legislature did not concur with the two judges in their view of the policy is manifest from the Act of 3 Vict. c. 9, passed in consequence of the decision in Stockdale *v.* Hansard, 9 Ad. & E. 1, the preamble of which statute recites that "it is essential to the due and effectual exercise and discharge of the functions and duties of parliament and to the promotion of wise legislation that no obstructions or impediments should exist to the publication of such of the reports, papers, votes, or proceedings of either house of parliament as such house of parliament may deem fit or necessary to be published." After which the Act proceeds to provide for the prevention of actions being brought in respect of papers published by order of either house of parliament.

As regards the attempt of Lord Campbell to fix the legality of the publication of parliamentary debates on the sure foundation of statutory enactment,[2] we think it may be as well accounted for by the apprehension, as to the result of any proceeding at law in which the legality of such publication should come in question, produced in his mind by the language of the judges in Stockdale *v.* Hansard, as by any conviction of the defectiveness of the law. . . .

We, however, are glad to think that, on closer inquiry, the law turns out not to be as on some occasions it has been assumed to be. To us it seems clear that the principles on which the publication of reports of the proceedings of courts of justice have been held to be privileged apply to the reports of par-

[1] In 1843, see Hansard's Parliamentary Debates, 3d series, vol. lxx. pp. 1254–8; and in 1858, see vol. cxlix. pp. 947–82. — Reporter's Note.

[2] See Hansard's Parliamentary Debates, 3d series, vol. lxx. p. 1254; and vol. cxlix. p. 947. — Reporter's Note.

liamentary proceedings. The analogy between the two cases is in every respect complete. If the rule has never been applied to the reports of parliamentary proceedings till now, we must assume that it is only because the occasion has never before arisen. If the principles which are the foundation of the privilege in the one case are applicable to the other, we must not hesitate to apply them, more especially when by so doing we avoid the glaring anomaly and injustice to which we have before adverted. Whatever disadvantages attach to a system of unwritten law, and of these we are fully sensible, it has at least this advantage, that its elasticity enables those who administer it to adapt it to the varying conditions of society, and to the requirements and habits of the age in which we live, so as to avoid the inconsistencies and injustice which arise when the law is no longer in harmony with the wants and usages and interests of the generation to which it is immediately applied. Our law of libel has, in many respects, only gradually developed itself into anything like a satisfactory and settled form. The full liberty of public writers to comment on the conduct and motives of public men has only in very recent times been recognized. Comments on government, on ministers and officers of state, on members of both houses of parliament, on judges and other public functionaries, are now made every day, which half a century ago would have been the subject of actions or *ex officio* informations, and would have brought down fine and imprisonment on publishers and authors. Yet who can doubt that the public are gainers by the change, and that, though injustice may often be done, and though public men may often have to smart under the keen sense of wrong inflicted by hostile criticism, the nation profits by public opinion being thus freely brought to bear on the discharge of public duties ? Again, the recognition of the right to publish the proceedings of courts of justice has been of modern growth. Till a comparatively recent time the sanction of the judges was thought necessary even for the publication of the decisions of the courts upon points of law. Even in quite recent days, judges in holding publication of the proceedings of courts of justice lawful, have thought it necessary to distinguish what are called *ex parte* proceedings as a probable exception from the operation of the rule. Yet *ex parte* proceedings before magistrates, and even before this court, as, for instance, on applications for criminal informations, are published every day, but such a thing as an action or indictment founded on a report of such an *ex parte* proceeding is unheard of, and, if any such action or indictment should be brought, it would probably be held that the true criterion of the privilege is, not whether the report was or was not *ex parte*, but whether it was a fair and honest report of what had taken place, published simply with a view to the information of the public, and innocent of all intention to do injury to the reputation of the party affected.

It is to be observed that the analogy between the case of reports of proceedings of courts of justice and those of proceedings in parliament being complete, all the limitations placed on the one to prevent injustice to individuals will necessarily attach on the other: a garbled or partial report, or of detached parts of proceedings, published with intent to injure individuals, will equally be disentitled to protection. Our judgment will in no way interfere with the decisions that the publication of a single speech for the purpose or with the effect of injuring an individual will be unlawful, as was held in the cases of Rex *v.* Lord Abingdon, 1 Esp. 226, and Rex *v.* Creevey, 1 M. & S. 273. At the same time it may be as well to observe that we are disposed to agree with what was said in Davidson *v.* Duncan, 7 E. & B., at p. 233, as to such a speech being privileged if *bona fide* published by a member for the information of his constituents. But whatever would deprive a report of the proceedings in a court of justice of immunity will equally apply to a report of proceedings in parliament.

It only remains to advert to an argument urged against the legality of the publication of parliamentary proceedings, namely, that such publication is illegal as being in contravention of the standing orders of both houses of parliament. The fact, no doubt, is, that each house of parliament does, by its standing orders, prohibit the publication of its debates. But, practically, each house not only permits, but also sanctions and encourages, the publication of its proceedings, and actually gives every facility to those who report them. Individual members correct their speeches for publication in Hansard or the public journals, and in every debate reports of former speeches contained therein are constantly referred to. Collectively, as well as individually, the members of both houses would deplore as a national misfortune the withholding their debates from the country at large. Practically speaking, therefore, it is idle to say that the publication of parliamentary proceedings is prohibited by parliament. The standing orders which prohibit it are obviously maintained only to give to each house the control over the publication of its proceedings, and the power of preventing or correcting any abuse of the facility afforded. Independently of the orders of the houses, there is nothing unlawful in publishing reports of parliamentary proceedings. Practically, such publication is sanctioned by parliament; it is essential to the working of our parliamentary system, and to the welfare of the nation. Any argument founded on its alleged illegality appears to us, therefore, entirely to fail. Should either house of parliament ever be so ill-advised as to prevent its proceedings from being made known to the country — which certainly never will be the case — any publication of its debates made in contravention of its orders would be a matter between the house and the publisher. For the present purpose, we must treat such publication as in every respect lawful, and hold that, while honestly and faithfully carried on, those who publish them will be free from legal responsibility, though the character of individuals may incidentally be injuriously affected.

So much for the great question involved in this case. We pass on to the second branch of this rule, which has reference to alleged misdirection in respect of the second count of the declaration, which is founded on the article in the "Times" commenting on the debate in the House of Lords, and the conduct of the plaintiff in preferring the petition which gave rise to it. We are of opinion that the direction given to the jury was perfectly correct. The publication of the debate having been justifiable, the jury were properly told the subject was, for the reasons we have already adverted to, pre-eminently one of public interest, and therefore one on which public comment and observation might properly be made, and that consequently the occasion was privileged in the absence of malice. As to the latter, the jury were told that they must be satisfied that the article was an honest and fair comment on the facts, — in other words, that, in the first place, they must be satisfied that the comments had been made with an honest belief in their justice, but that this was not enough, inasmuch as such belief might originate in the blindness of party zeal, or in personal or political aversion; that a person taking upon himself publicly to criticise and to condemn the conduct or motives of another, must bring to the task, not only an honest sense of justice, but also a reasonable degree of judgment and moderation, so that the result may be what a jury shall deem, under the circumstances of the case, a fair and legitimate criticism on the conduct and motives of the party who is the object of censure.

Considering the direction thus given to have been perfectly correct, we are of opinion that in respect of the alleged misdirection as also on the former point, the ruling at *nisi prius* was right, and that consequently this rule must be discharged. *Rule discharged.*[1]

PURCELL *v.* SOWLER

IN THE COURT OF APPEAL, FEBRUARY 3, 1877.

Reported in 2 Common Pleas Division Reports, 215.

ACTION for libel.

The libel was contained in a report, published in a Manchester newspaper, by the defendants, the proprietors, of the proceedings at a meeting of the board of guardians for the Altrincham poor-law union, at which *ex parte* charges were made against the plaintiff, the medical officer of the union workhouse at Knutsford, of neglect in not attending the pauper patients when sent for.

At the trial it appeared that the charges were unfounded in fact, but it was admitted that the report was accurate and *bona fide.* A verdict was taken by consent for the plaintiff, with nominal damages and costs, judgment to be entered accordingly, with leave to move to enter judgment for the defendants, if the court should be of opinion that the publication was privileged.

The Common Pleas Division refused the motion, ordering judgment to stand for the plaintiff. 1 C. P. D. 781.

The libel, &c., are set out at length in the report in the court below.

The defendants appealed.

MELLISH, L. J.[2] I am of the same opinion. We are asked to extend the law of privilege as to the report of proceedings of a public body to an extent beyond what it has as yet been carried. In Lord Campbell's time it was supposed that the privilege only extended to the proceedings in a court of law. A report of such proceedings has always been held privileged, because all her Majesty's subjects have a right to be present, and there would, therefore, be nothing wrong in putting the rest of the public in the position of those who were actually present. The privilege has been extended to the publication of debates in parliament, and properly extended, as they stand on the same principle as the proceedings in courts of law. There is no doubt this distinction: that as to courts of law the public have a right to be present, but they are only admitted to the debates in either House of Parliament when the House chooses to permit them to be present. The House has a discretion, but when the debates are held in public, it is clear that a newspaper ought not to be held to commit an offence by putting those who were not present in the same position as those who were. It is argued that this privilege ought to be extended as to a variety

[1] Garby *v.* Bennett, 57 N. Y. Sup. Ct. 853; Buckstaff *v.* Hicks, 94 Wis. 34 (*semble* — report of proceedings of common council of a city not privileged); Dillon *v.* Balfour, L. R. 20 Ir. 600 *Accord.*

The publication must purport to be a report. Lewis *v.* Hayes, 165 Cal. 527.

[2] The concurring opinions of Cockburn, C. J., and Baggallay and Bramwell, JJ. A., and the arguments of counsel are omitted.

of other public bodies. I express no decided opinion, and I desire, with the Lord Chief Justice, to be understood as expressing no opinion; but at the same time I am clearly of opinion that the privilege ought not to be extended to such a case as the present. A board of guardians have a discretion whether or not they will admit the public to their meetings; and whether they choose to exclude or choose to admit, the public have no right to complain. But I cannot think that the courts of law are to be bound by the mode in which the guardians exercise their discretion in admitting or excluding strangers. Although they admit the public on an occasion when *ex parte* charges are made against a public officer, which may affect his character and injure his private rights, it is most material that there should be no further publication; there is no reason why the charges should be made public before the person charged has been told of the charges, and has had an opportunity of meeting them; and I cannot see any inconvenience in holding that the publication is not privileged; in holding otherwise we should be depriving the individual of his rights without any commensurate advantage. The law on the subject of privilege is clearly defined by the authorities. Such a communication as the present ought to be confined in the first instance to those whose duty it is to investigate the charges. If one of the guardians had met a person not a ratepayer or parishioner, and had told him the charge against the plaintiff, surely he would have been liable to an action of slander. I do not mean to say that the matter was not of such public interest as that comments would not be privileged if the facts had been ascertained. If the neglect charged against the plaintiff had been proved, then fair comments on his conduct might have been justified. But that is a very different thing from publishing *ex parte* statements, which not only are not proved, but turn out to be unfounded in fact. I am, therefore, clearly of opinion that the occasion of the publication was not privileged, and that the judgment for the plaintiff ought to be affirmed.

Judgment affirmed.[1]

[1] See Charlton *v.* Watton, 6 Car. & P. 385; Davison *v.* Duncan, 7. E. & B. 229, 233; Popham *v.* Pickburn, 7 H. & N. 891; Davis *v.* Duncan, L. R. 9 C. P. 396; Allbutt *v.* General Council, 23 Q. B. D. 400, 411.

By St. 51 & 52 Vict. c. 64, §§ 3 and 4, " § 3. A fair and accurate report in any newspaper of proceedings publicly heard before any court exercising judicial authority shall, if published contemporaneously with such proceedings, be privileged: Provided that nothing in this section shall authorize the publication of any blasphemous or indecent matter.

" § 4. A fair and accurate report published in any newspaper of the proceedings of a public meeting, or (except where neither the public nor any newspaper reporter is admitted) of any meeting of a vestry, town council, school board, board of guardians, board or local authority formed or constituted under the provisions of any Act of Parliament, or of any committee appointed by any of the above-mentioned bodies, or of any meeting of any commissioners authorized to act by letters patent, Act of Parliament, warrant under the Royal Sign Manual, or other lawful warrant or authority, select committees of either House of Parliament, justices of the peace in quarter sessions assembled for administrative or deliberative purposes, and the publication at the request of any Government office or department, officer of state, commissioner of police, or chief constable of any notice or report issued by them for the information of the public, shall be privileged, unless it shall be proved that such report or publication was published or made maliciously: Provided that nothing in this section shall authorize the publication of any blasphemous or indecent matter: Provided also, that the protection intended to be afforded by this section shall not be available as a defence in any proceedings if it shall be proved that the defendant has been requested to insert in the newspaper in which the report or other publication complained of appeared a reasonable letter or statement by way of contradic-

BARROWS *v.* BELL

SUPREME JUDICIAL COURT, MASSACHUSETTS, OCTOBER, 1856.

Reported in 7 *Gray*, 301.

SHAW, C. J.[1] The present is an action of tort, brought to recover damage for a publication alleged to be a libel upon the plaintiff, consisting of an article published in the Boston Medical and Surgical Journal, under the direction of the defendant.

The article alleged to be libellous is headed, "The suits against the Massachusetts Medical Society," and it proceeds to give a brief account of the proceedings of the medical society, which resulted in the expulsion of the plaintiff from his membership, for misconduct.

Whatever may be the rule as adopted and practised on in England, we think that a somewhat larger liberty may be claimed in this country and in this Commonwealth, both for the proceedings before all public bodies, and for the publication of those proceedings for the necessary information of the people. So many municipal, parochial and other public corporations, and so many large voluntary associations formed for almost every lawful purpose of benevolence, business or interest, are constantly holding meetings, in their nature public, and so usual is it that their proceedings are published for general use and information, that the law, to adapt itself to this necessary condition of society, must of necessity admit of these public proceedings, and a just and proper publication of them, as far as it can be done consistently with private rights. This view of the law of libel in Massachusetts is recognized, and to some extent sanctioned, by the case of Commonwealth *v.* Clapp, 4 Mass. 163, and many other cases.

The Massachusetts Medical Society were not a private association; they were a public corporation, chartered by one of the earliest Acts under the Constitution, which was amended and their powers confirmed by several subsequent Acts. Sts. 1781, c. 15; 1788, c. 49; 1802, c. 123; 1818, c. 113.

The charter invested the society, their members and licentiates, with large powers and privileges, in regulating the important public interest of the practice of medicine and surgery, enabled them to prescribe a course of studies, to examine candidates in regard to their qualifications for practice, and give letters testimonial to those who might be found duly qualified. They were authorized to elect fellows, and vested with power to suspend, expel or dis-

tion or explanation of such report or other publication, and has refused or neglected to insert the same: Provided further, that nothing in this section contained shall be deemed or construed to limit or abridge any privilege now by law existing, or to protect the publication of any matter not of public concern and the publication of which is not for the public benefit.

"For the purposes of this section 'public meeting' shall mean any meeting *bona fide* and lawfully held for a lawful purpose, and for the furtherance or discussion of any matter of public concern, whether the admission thereto be general or restricted." Kelly *v.* O'Malley, 6 T. L. R. 62, was decided under this statute.

Newspaper publication of reports of administrative officers. Tilles *v.* Pulitzer Pub. Co., 241 Mo. 609; Schwarz *v.* Evening News Co., 84 N. J. Law, 486; Bingham *v.* Gaynor, 203 N. Y. 27. *Contra,* Madill *v.* Currie, 168 Mich. 546. See Morasca *v.* Item Co., 126 La. 426.

Report of investigation by administrative officers. Williams *v.* Black, 24 S. D. 501.

[1] The case has been much abridged.

franchise any fellow or member, and to make rules and by-laws for their government. No person could be a member, but by his own act in accepting the appointment.

This society was regarded by these legislative Acts as a public institution, by the action of which the public would be deeply affected in one of its important public interests, the health of the people. The plaintiff, by accepting his appointment as a fellow, voluntarily submitted himself to the government and jurisdiction of the society in his professional relations, so long as they acted within the scope of their authority.

The *status* or condition of being a member of this society was one of a permanent character and recognized by law — one in which each member has a valuable interest; and that it was so regarded by the plaintiff is manifest from his effort to obtain a restoration to it by a judgment of this court, by a writ of mandamus.

We think it obvious that the subject-matter of the complaint — dishonorable conduct, a fraudulent transaction between the plaintiff and another member of the profession and of the same society — was within the scope of the authority conferred by law on the society; and that the direction of the court, that their action was conclusive upon the plaintiff, was correct. As to the legal proceedings set forth in the supposed libel, it was admitted by the plaintiff's counsel that the account there given of those proceedings was substantially true.

If then this charge of dishonorable or fraudulent conduct by the plaintiff, in his dealings with Dr. Carpenter, was within the jurisdiction of the medical society, and proceedings were instituted and carried on to their final determination in the expulsion of the plaintiff from his fellowship, then the proceedings might be rightly characterized, as in the case of Farnsworth *v.* Storrs, as *quasi* judicial; and then the only remaining question of fact was, whether the publication was a true and correct narrative of such proceedings and determination. This question the judge did leave, or proposed to leave, to the jury; with the direction, that if they should find upon the evidence that that part of the publication was true, the defendant would be entitled to a verdict. We are of opinion that this direction was right. As the verdict was for the defendant, we are to assume that it was found by them; or, if the verdict was taken by consent, it would have been found under the instruction that the publication did present a true and correct narrative of the proceedings before the society, and their determination thereon.

The fact, that these proceedings were considered closed and finished, takes away from this publication the objection, that it would have a tendency to prejudice the public mind and prevent the party affected from having a fair trial. *Judgment on the verdict for the defendant.*[1]

[1] Allbutt *v.* General Council, 23 Q. B. D. 400 *Accord.* But see Kimball *v.* Post Pub. Co., 199 Mass. 248; Peoples Bank *v.* Goodwin, 148 Mo. App. 364.

Report of proceedings of a church commission. Bass *v.* Mathews, 69 Wash. 214.

MILISSICH *v.* LLOYD'S

IN THE COURT OF APPEAL, FEBRUARY 10, 1877.

Reported in 13 *Cox, Criminal Cases,* 575.

MELLISH, L. J.[1] In this case the defendants have appealed from a decision of the Common Pleas Division, ordering a new trial on the ground that the verdict given for the plaintiff was against the weight of evidence. They are not satisfied with that order, but they come before us to have judgment entered for themselves. The question for us is an important one, as to the power of the court to enter judgment under the Judicature Acts. Now, although the Judicature Acts do undoubtedly give very general powers to the court as to entering of judgment, it is clearly not intended by the Legislature that the court should take advantage of that general rule to remove questions from the consideration of the jury which are questions of fact properly for their consideration. The action was brought by the plaintiff against Lloyd's for an alleged libel published by Lloyd's in a pamphlet. At the trial, no doubt, the defence of privileged communication was raised and Lord Coleridge expressed an opinion that Lloyd's would not have the same privilege as an ordinary newspaper; and he also expressed an opinion that, inasmuch as only the speech of the prosecuting counsel and the summing up of the judge, and not the speech of the counsel for the defence, at the criminal trial, was published, the report could not be a fair one of the trial. I cannot agree with either of these doubts. I cannot think there is any difference between the privilege attaching to a report in a newspaper or in a pamphlet, unless some question of malice is raised. Of course, if actual malice is alleged, the fact that the libel was published in a pamphlet and not in a newspaper might be very material, but when no such allegation is made I cannot conceive there is any difference. I also cannot agree that the mere fact that the publisher did not publish the evidence in full, but only the summing up of the judge and the speech of the prosecuting counsel, made the report of the trial an unfair one. I think that proposition implies that proceedings at trials cannot be reported at all unless they are reported in full. It must, therefore, be sufficient to publish a fair abstract of the evidence. Now, I do not know how the reporter could do better than take the judge's summing up to get that fair abstract, although I do not, of course, lay down as a matter of law that the summing up of a judge is necessarily a correct summary for the report. I think this report may be fair or it may be unfair; but then, is it a question of fact or law whether the report is fair or unfair? I think that it is a question of fact, and should be left to the jury to determine. Then the argument is that the evidence is all one way and that it is useless sending the case down to a new trial because no

[1] Only the opinion of Mellish, L. J., is given.

jury could reasonably find the other way. In my opinion, the court must be very cautious not to take upon itself the functions of a jury. Notwithstanding the great powers given by the Judicature Acts, it is still, of course, the province of the jury to determine between the credibility of witnesses on either side. Here, however, the question is more what is the inference to be drawn from the facts proved in evidence. The general inference to be drawn from all the facts, as in Lewis *v.* Levy, E. B. & E. 537, is for the jury. There the whole proceedings before the magistrates were put in evidence, in order to judge of the fairness of the report. Here a full shorthand note is produced, and, being placed in the hands of the jury, they are to draw the inference, and not the court. Now, although I think that persons might draw very unfair inferences against a man who, like the plaintiff, did not appear at the trial himself and could not defend himself from the charges which were made against him on both sides, still, if the report is a fair one of what took place the defendants will be privileged. The question for the jury will be at the new trial — was the report a fair one, and would it give a fair notion to people who were not there of what took place? That question is one for the jury, and I think the case should, therefore, be sent for a new trial.

Judgment below affirmed.[1]

BARNES *v.* CAMPBELL

SUPREME COURT, NEW HAMPSHIRE, JUNE, 1879.

Reported in 59 *New Hampshire Reports*, 128.

CASE, for libel in accusing the plaintiff of crime. Plea, the general issue, with a brief statement alleging that the defendants are conductors and publishers of a newspaper published at, &c., and as such it was part of their duty to give to their readers such items of news as they might properly judge to be of interest and value to the community, and that, as such conductors and publishers, they published the article complained of, in good faith, without malice, believing and having good reason to believe the same to be true.

Motion by the plaintiff to reject the brief statement.

SMITH, J. Matter in justification must be pleaded. But according to some decisions, matter in excuse may be given in evidence under the general issue, or be pleaded. State *v.* Burnham, 9 N. H. 34, 43, and authorities cited; Carpenter *v.* Bailey, 53 N. H. 590. In this view of the case, it is, perhaps, immaterial whether or not the brief statement is defective. But, treating the brief statement and the motion to reject it as intended to raise the question whether the brief statement

[1] Macdougall *v.* Knight, 14 App. Cas. 194 (explaining s. c. 17 Q. B. Div. 636); Salisbury *v.* Union Co., 45 Hun, 120 *Accord.*
See Annaly *v.* Trade Co., L. R. 26 Ir. 394.

sets forth a defence, we are of opinion that it does not. The defendants probably intended to set out the excuse of a lawful occasion, good faith, proper purpose, and belief and probable cause to believe that the publication was true. They laid stress upon their business of publishing a newspaper. But professional publishers of news are not exempt, as a privileged class, from the consequences of damage done by their false news. Their communications are not privileged merely because made in a public journal. They have the same right to give information that others have, and no more. Smart *v.* Blanchard, 42 N. H. 137, 151; Palmer *v.* Concord, 48 N. H. 211, 216; Sheckell *v.* Jackson, 10 Cush. 25. The occasion of the defendants' publishing a false charge of crime against the plaintiff was not lawful, if the end to be attained was not to give useful information to the community of a fact of which the community had a right to be and ought to be informed, in order that they might act upon such information. State *v.* Burnham, 9 N. H. 34, 41, 42; Palmer *v.* Concord, 48 N. H. 211, 217; Carpenter *v.* Bailey, 53 N. H. 590; s. c. 56 N. H. 283. The defendants do not state facts that would constitute a lawful occasion. They make a loose averment of their general duty to give their readers such news as they (the defendants) might properly judge to be of interest and value to the community. This should be struck out of the record as insufficient and misleading. It is, in effect, an intimation that they published the libel in the usual course of their business, and is calculated to give the jury the erroneous impression that the defendants' judgment of the propriety of the publication is evidence of the lawfulness of the occasion. The defendants' general business of publishing interesting and valuable news was not, of itself, a lawful occasion for publishing this particular, false, and criminal charge against the plaintiff. It will be for the jury to say what weight the defendants' business has as evidence on the question of malice. But however high the defendants' vocation, and however interesting and valuable the truth which they undertake to give their readers, their ordinary and habitual calling is no excuse for assailing the plaintiff's character with this false charge of crime. They must show specific facts constituting a lawful occasion in this particular instance, as if this false charge had been the only thing they ever published. They allege nothing of that kind. They do not state that the community had any interest which would have been protected or promoted by the publication complained of if it had been true, or had a right to be or ought to be informed of the subject-matter of it in order that they might act upon correct information of it, or that the information given would have been practically useful to anybody if it had been true. This is the substance of a lawful occasion. The brief statement contains no specification on this point. *Motion granted.*[1]

[1] Parsons *v.* Age Herald Pub. Co., 181 Ala. 439; Washington Herald Co. *v.* Berry, 41 App. D. C. 322; Lundin *v.* Post Pub. Co., 217 Mass. 213; Schwarz *v.*

LAWLESS v. THE ANGLO-EGYPTIAN COTTON CO.

IN THE QUEEN'S BENCH, FEBRUARY 11, 1869.

Reported in Law Reports, 4 Queen's Bench, 262.

LIBEL. The declaration charged that the defendants falsely and maliciously published of the plaintiff, their manager, in a certain report of the affairs of the company, these words: "The shareholders will observe that there is a charge of £1,306 1*s.* 7*d.* for deficiency of stock, which the manager is responsible for; his accounts as such manager in the company have been badly kept, and have been rendered to us very irregularly."

Plea: Not guilty. Issue thereon.[1]

It was objected on behalf of the defendants that there was no evidence of a publication of the libel, and that it was a privileged communication. The Chief Baron overruled the objections, but reserved leave to the defendants to move to enter a nonsuit on both points. The plaintiff having proved his special damage, the jury found a verdict for £500.

A rule having been obtained to enter a nonsuit pursuant to the leave reserved,

Holker, Q. C., and *Gorst*, showed cause.

Manisty, Q. C. (*R. C. Fisher* with him), in support of the rule.

MELLOR, J. I am of opinion that the rule should be made absolute to enter a nonsuit. Had I been able to perceive that any substantial injustice might have been done by not leaving any question to the jury, I should have been disposed to send the case down for a new trial. But I think there was no evidence of express malice which ought to have been left to the jury.

As I understand the facts of the case, the plaintiff was employed as the agent of the defendants in Egypt, and his transactions were necessarily brought under the notice of the auditors, who are appointed by

Evening News Co., 84 N. J. Law, 486; Williams v. Black, 24 S. D. 501; Williams Printing Co. v. Saunders, 113 Va. 156 *Accord.*

But see U. S. v. Journal Co., 197 Fed. 415; Tilles v. Pulitzer Pub. Co., 241 Mo. 609.

"Their Lordships regret to find that there appeared on the one side of this case the time-worn fallacy that some kind of privilege attaches to the profession of the Press as distinguished from the members of the public. The freedom of the journalist is an ordinary part of the freedom of the subject, and to whatever lengths the subject in general may go so also may the journalist, but, apart from statute law, his privilege is no other and no higher. The responsibilities which attach to his power in the dissemination of printed matter may, and in the case of a conscientious journalist do, make him more careful; but the range of his assertions, his criticisms, or his comments is as wide as, and no wider than, that of any other subject. No privilege attaches to his position." Lord Shaw in Arnold v. King-Emperor, 111 L. T. 324, 325.

[1] The statement has been condensed, the facts sufficiently appearing in the opinion of Mellor, J. The arguments of counsel and the concurring opinion of Hannen, J., are omitted.

Act of Parliament, or at all events by the articles of association of the company, and who are fit persons to investigate the accounts of the company. The auditors considered that a deficiency in the stock of the company was owing in some sense to the plaintiff's default, and they expressed that opinion in their report. It seems they did this after having received such explanations as Mr. Bell could offer, but it must be observed that those explanations were offered to the auditors and not to the directors. What the directors did was this, in their report to a meeting of the shareholders they appended the statement which had been made to them by the auditors. There is nothing whatever to show that the directors had any reason to doubt the truth of that statement, and there was no evidence of any act on their part from which malice could be inferred, and therefore I think the Chief Baron was right in not putting the question of malice to the jury. As to the question of intrinsic or extrinsic evidence, the report was one which the directors were fully warranted in believing was correct; and there is nothing to show that the directors acted otherwise than *bona fide* in communicating it to the shareholders. No doubt the directors are to make their report to a meeting of the shareholders, to be called for that purpose, and it is clear that those who are absent are bound by the acts of those who are present, but the absent shareholders are interested in the prosperity or adversity of the company, and in knowing all the circumstances upon which the welfare of the company depends. It seems to me, therefore, that to print the report was a necessary and reasonable mode of communicating it to all the shareholders, who must be more or less numerous.

This case does not fall within the rule in Cooke *v.* Wildes, 5 E. & B. 328; 24 L. J. Q. B. 367. There the question of malice was properly left to the jury, because the letter contained defamatory expressions which were unnecessary; the defendant was not content with stating the facts that he had heard, but he made a calumnious observation of his own and put a gloss on the plaintiff's conduct which was libellous. There was therefore intrinsic evidence of malice, and that the defendant had not acted *bona fide*, and these questions were properly left to the jury. I think we are bound by the cases of Somerville *v.* Hawkins and Taylor *v.* Hawkins, 16 Q. B. 308; 20 L. J. Q. B. 313. The principle there laid down is, that where there is no evidence of malice the judge ought not to leave any question to the jury. Here I think the conduct of the directors negatives malice on their part, and it is clear that they acted *bona fide*. I think we should be going against what I may call progress, if we were to hold that the delivery of the manuscript of the report to the printer, for the purpose of having it printed, is a publication which prevents the communication from being privileged. I also think that it was the duty of the directors to communicate the report not only to the shareholders present at the meeting, but to all the shareholders, and that they had an interest in receiving it. I am glad that Mr. Holker called our attention to the American authority, for it supports the judgment of the court. In Philadelphia, Wilmington, and Baltimore Railroad Company *v.* Quigley, 21 Howard (Rep. Sup. Court, U. S.), 202, it was held that it was within the course of business and employment of the president and directors for them to investigate the conduct of their officers and agents, and to report the result to the stockholders. It was also held, in the absence of malice and bad faith, that the report to the shareholders was privileged; therefore, to this extent, that case appears to me to be an express authority. But, independently of any authority, I am quite prepared to hold that a company, having a great number of shareholders all interested in knowing how their officers conduct themselves, are justified in making a communication in a printed report, relating to the conduct of their officers, to all the shareholders, whether present or absent, if the communication be made without malice and *bona fide*. The communication in this case is *prima facie* privileged, and there being no evidence intrinsic or extrinsic of malice, that question was very properly not left to the jury. I think the conclusion at which the Chief Baron arrived at *nisi prius* without hearing any argument erroneous, and with great deference to that eminent and learned judge, I am of opinion this rule to enter a nonsuit should be made absolute. *Rule absolute.*[1]

PADMORE *v.* LAWRENCE

IN THE QUEEN'S BENCH, JANUARY 18, 1840.

Reported in 11 *Adolphus & Ellis*, 380.

CASE for slander. The words charged to have been spoken by the defendant imputed that the plaintiff had stolen a brooch belonging to the defendant's wife; and they were said to have been uttered in a discourse, &c., and in the hearing of one Jane Cole and divers, &c.

Pleas. 1. Not guilty. 2. A traverse of part of the inducement not material here.

On the trial before Parke, B., at the Hampshire summer assizes, 1838, it appeared that the plaintiff had called at the defendant's house, and that soon afterwards the brooch was missed; that defendant then went to an inn, where

[1] Barbaud *v.* Hookham, 5 Esp. 109; McDougall *v.* Claridge, 1 Camp. 267; Dunman *v.* Bigg, 1 Camp, 269 *n.*; Todd *v.* Hawkins, 2 M. & R. 20, 8 Car. & P. 88; Shipley *v.* Todhunter, 7 Car. & P. 680; Harris *v.* Thompson, 13 C. B. 333; Maitland *v.* Bramwell, 2 F. & F. 623; Scarll *v.* Dixon, 4 F. & F. 250; Cooke *v.* Wildes, 5 E. & B. 328; Croft *v.* Stevens, 7 H. & N. 570; Whiteley *v.* Adams, 15 C. B. N. S. 392; Spill *v.* Maule, L. R. 4 Ex. 232; Laughton *v.* Bishop, L. R. 4 P. C. 495; Davies *v.* Snead, L. R. 5 Q. B. 608; Waller *v.* Loch, 7 Q. B. D. 619; Cowles *v.* Potts, 34 L. J. Q. B. 247; Quartz Co. *v.* Beall, 20 Ch. Div. 501; Royal Aquarium *v.* Parkinson, [1892] 1 Q. B. 431; Pittard *v.* Oliver, [1891] 1 Q. B. 474; Phila. Co. *v.* Quigley, 21 How. 202; Broughton *v.* McGrew, 39 Fed. 672; Haight *v.* Cornell, 15 Conn. 74; Etchison *v.* Pergerson, 88 Ga. 620; Wharton *v.* Wright, 30 Ill. App. 343; Coombs *v.* Rose, 8 Blackf. 155; Kirkpatrick *v.* Eagle Lodge, 26 Kan. 384; Lynch *v.* Febiger, 39 La. Ann. 336; Remington *v.* Congdon, 2 Pick. 310; Bradley *v.*

the plaintiff was, and stated to her his suspicions, in the presence of a third person; and that the plaintiff, with her own concurrence, was afterwards searched by Jane Cole and another female, who were called in for the purpose and to whom the defendant at the time repeated the charge. The brooch was not found on the plaintiff, but was afterwards discovered to have been left by the defendant's wife at another place. The defendant's counsel first applied for a nonsuit, which the learned judge refused. The defendant's counsel then, in his address to the jury, contended that the words were spoken without malice, under circumstances which privileged them. The learned judge told the jury that the verdict must be for the plaintiff, if they thought that the words imputed felony, for that it was clear they were not privileged. Verdict for the plaintiff.

In Michaelmas term, 1838, Erle obtained a rule for a new trial, on the ground of misdirection.

Crowder and *Butt* now showed cause.

Erle and *Barstow*, contra.[1]

Heath, 12 Pick. 163; Farnsworth *v.* Storrs, 5 Cush. 412; York *v.* Pease, 2 Gray, 282; Gassett *v.* Gilbert, 6 Gray, 94; Shurtleff *v.* Parker, 130 Mass. 293 (*semble*); Howland *v.* Flood, 160 Mass. 509; Landis *v.* Campbell, 79 Mo. 433; Rothholz *v.* Dunkle, 53 N. J. Law, 438; Jarvis *v.* Hatheway, 3 Johns, 180; O'Donaghue *v.* McGovern, 23 Wend. 26; Streety *v.* Wood, 15 Barb. 105; Fowles *v.* Bowen, 30 N. Y. 20; Kilinck *v.* Colby, 46 N. Y. 427; McKnight *v.* Hasbrouck, 17 R. I. 70; Tillinghast *v.* McLeod, 17 R. I. 208; Holt *v.* Parsons, 23 Tex. 9; Shurtleff *v.* Stevens, 51 Vt. 501 (*semble*) *Accord.*

See also Dickeson *v.* Hilliard, L. R. 9 Ex. 79; Lyman *v.* Gowing, L. R. 6 Ir. 259 (where the communication was made to unsuitable persons); Phillips *v.* Bradshaw, 181 Ala. 541; Bohlinger *v.* Germania Ins. Co., 100 Ark. 477.

Communication by promoter of an enterprise to one whose assistance is sought. Cook *v.* Gust, 155 Wis. 594.

Communication from superintendent of railroad to express company as to employee who serves both. International R. Co. *v.* Edmundson, (Tex. Civ. App.) 185 S. W. 402.

Communication by insurance adjuster to insurers. Richardson *v.* Cooke, 129 La. 365.

Indorsement of officer on recommendation for promotion. Gray *v.* Mossman, 88 Conn. 247.

Communication between stockholders as to manager of a corporation. Ashcroft *v.* Hammond, 197 N. Y. 488.

Communication by person immediately interested made honestly to protect his own interest. Delany *v.* Jones, 4 Esp. 190 (but see Lay *v.* Lawson, 4 A. & E. 798); Fairman *v.* Ives, 5 B. & A. 642; Coward *v.* Wellington, 7 Car. & P. 531; Tuson *v.* Evans, 12 A. & E. 733 (*semble*); Blackham *v.* Pugh, 2 C. B. 611; Wenman *v.* Ash, 13 C. B. 836 (*semble*, communication to unsuitable person); Manby *v.* Witt, 18 C. B. 544; Taylor *v.* Hawkins, 16 Q. B. 308; Amann *v.* Damm, 8 C. B. N. S. 597; Force *v.* Warren, 15 C. B. N. S. 806; Oddy *v.* Paulet, 4 F. & F. 1009 (*semble*); Cooke *v.* Wildes, 5 E. & B. 328; Regina *v.* Perry, 15 Cox C. C. 169; Bank *v.* Strong, 1 App. Cas. 307; Hunt *v.* Great Northern Co., [1891] 2 Q. B. 189; Baker *v.* Carrick, [1894] 1 Q. B. 838; Hobbs *v.* Bryers, L. R. 2 Ir. 496; Lang *v.* Gilbert, 4 All. (N. B.) 445; Gasley *v.* Moss, 9 Ala. 266; Butterworth *v.* Conrow, 1 Marv. 361; Henry *v.* Moberly, 23 Ind. App. 305; Nichols *v.* Eaton, 110 Ia. 509; Caldwell *v.* Story, 107 Ky. 10; Baysett *v.* Hire, 49 La. Ann. 904; Dickinson *v.* Hathaway, 122 La. Ann. 644; Beeler *v.* Jackson, 64 Md. 589; Brow *v.* Hathaway, 13 All. 239; Bacon *v.* Mich. Co., 66 Mich. 166; Howard *v.* Dickie, 120 Mich. 238; Alabama Co. *v.* Brooks, 69 Miss. 168; Lovell Co. *v.* Houghton, 116 N. Y. 520; Lent *v.* Underhill, 54 App. Div. 609; Reynolds *v.* Plumbers' Ass'n, 30 Misc. 709; Behee *v.* Missouri R. Co., 71 Tex. 424; Missouri R. Co. *v.* Richmond, 73 Tex. 568; Missouri Co. *v.* Behee, 2 Tex. Civ. App. 107; Miller *v.* Armstrong, 24 N. Zeal. 968.

[1] The arguments of counsel are omitted.

LORD DENMAN, C. J. The question ought to have gone to the jury, whether this charge was made *bona fide.* Unless Toogood *v.* Spyring is to be overruled, it is clear that the judge was not warranted in withdrawing that question from their consideration.

LITTLEDALE, J. The jury were to say whether the defendant believed that the brooch was stolen by the plaintiff, and for that reason charged her with having stolen it, and whether his language was stronger than necessary, or whether the charge was made before more persons than was necessary. The law has been laid down so over and over again.

COLERIDGE, J. For the sake of public justice, charges and communications, which would otherwise be slanderous, are protected if *bona fide* made in the prosecution of an inquiry into a suspected crime. Then had not the defendant a right to make out that case ? The facts were for the jury. It is argued that the charge ought to be true, or ought to be made only before an officer of justice. But the exigencies of society could never permit such a restriction. If I stop a party suspected, must not I say why I do so? Supposing it unjustifiable to search a person against his will, here the plaintiff agreed to be searched. The presence of other parties would not do away with the privilege. When the two females were desired to make the search, were they not to be told for what they were to look ? The question was clearly for the jury.

Rule absolute.[1]

CHILD *v.* AFFLECK

IN THE KING'S BENCH, MAY 13, 1829.

Reported in 9 *Barnewall & Cresswell,* 403.

CASE for a libel. Plea, the general issue. At the trial before Lord Tenterden, C. J., at the Westminster sittings after Hilary term, it appeared in evidence that the plaintiff had been in the service of the defendants, Mrs. Affleck having before she hired her made inquiries of two persons, who gave her a good character. The plaintiff remained in that service a few months, and was afterwards hired by another person, who wrote to Mrs. Affleck for her character, and received the following answer, which was the alleged libel: " Mrs. A.'s compliments to Mrs. S., and is sorry that in reply to her inquiries respecting E. Child, nothing can be in justice said in her favor. She lived with Mrs.

[1] Johnson *v.* Evans, 3 Esp. 32; Fowler *v.* Homer, 3 Camp. 294; Jones *v.* Thomas, 34 W. R. 104; Lightbody *v.* Gordon, 9 Scotch Sess. Cas. (4th series) 934; Dale *v.* Harris, 109 Mass. 193 *Accord.*

See to the same effect Flanagan *v.* McLane, 87 Conn. 220; Wall *v.* Seaboard Ry., 18 Ga. App. 457; Cristman *v.* Cristman, 36 Ill. App. 567; Harper *v.* Harper, 10 Bush, 447; Hyatt *v.* Lindner, 133 La. 614; Bavington *v.* Robinson, 127 Md. 46, 124 Md. 85; Eames *v.* Whittaker, 123 Mass. 342; Wells *v.* Toogood, 165 Mich. 677; Lally *v.* Emery, 59 Hun, 237; Hayden *v.* Hasbrouck, 34 R. I. 556; Viss *v.* Calligan, 91 Wash. 673. Compare Hansen *v.* Hansen, 126 Minn. 426; Hooper *v.* Truscott, 2 B. N. C. 457; Harrison *v.* Fraser, 29 W. R. 652.

But see Peak *v.* Taubman, 251 Mo. 390; Vanloon *v.* Vanloon, 159 Mo. App. 255; Hagener *v.* Pulitzer Pub. Co., 172 Mo. App. 436.

Relevant statement in course of dispute as to property. Alderson *v.* Kahle, 73 W. Va. 690.

A. but for a few weeks, in which short time she frequently conducted herself disgracefully; and Mrs. A. is concerned to add she has, since her dismissal, been credibly informed she has been and now is a prostitute in Bury." In consequence of this letter the plaintiff was dismissed from her situation. It further appeared that after that letter was written, Mrs. Affleck went to the persons who had recommended the plaintiff to her, and made a similar statement to them. Upon this evidence it was contended, for the defendants, that there was no proof of malice, and that consequently the plaintiff must be nonsuited. On the other hand, it was urged that Mrs. Affleck's statement of what the plaintiff's conduct had been after she left her service was not privileged, and that, at all events, that part of the letter and the statement that she voluntarily made to other persons, and not in answer to any inquiries, were evidence of malice. Lord Tenterden, C. J., was of opinion that the latter part of the letter was privileged, and that the other communications being made to persons who had recommended the plaintiff, were not evidence of malice, and he directed a nonsuit.

F. Kelly now moved for a rule *nisi* for a new trial.[1]

PARKE, J. The rule laid down by Lord Mansfield, in Edmondson *v.* Stevenson, Bull. N. P. 8, has been followed ever since. It is, that in an action for defamation in giving a character of a servant, " the gist of it must be malice, which is not implied from the occasion of speaking, but should be directly proved." The question then is, whether the plaintiff in this case adduced evidence, which, if laid before a jury, could properly lead them to find express malice. That does not appear upon the face of the letter. *Prima facie* it is fair, and undoubtedly a person asked as to the character of a servant may communicate all that is stated in that letter. Independently of the letter, there was no evidence except of the two persons that had recommended the plaintiff. The communication to them, therefore, was not officious, and Mrs. Affleck was justified in making it. In Rogers *v.* Clifton, 3 B. & P. 587, evidence of the good conduct of the servant was given, and the communication also appeared to be officious. In Blackburn *v.* Blackburn, 4 Bing. 395, the occasion of writing the alleged libel did not distinctly appear, it was therefore properly left to the jury to say, whether it was confidential and privileged or not, and they found that it was not. Here the letter was undoubtedly *prima facie* privileged, the plaintiff, therefore, was bound to prove express malice in order to take away the privilege. *Rule refused.*[2]

[1] The argument for the plaintiff and the opinions of Lord Tenterden, C. J., Bayley, and Littledale, JJ., are omitted.

[2] *Servant cases.* Edmondson *v.* Stevenson, Bull. N. P. 8; Weatherston *v.* Hawkins, 1 T. R. 110; Rogers *v.* Clifton, 3 B. & P. 587; Pattison *v.* Jones, 8 B. & C. 578; Gardner *v.* Slade, 13 Q. B. 796; Murdoch *v.* Funduklian, 2 T. L. R. 614 (reversing s. c. 2 T. L. R. 215); Doane *v.* Grew, 220 Mass. 171; Carroll *v.* Owen, 178 Mich. 551 *Accord.*

Commercial agency cases. Lemay *v.* Chamberlain, 10 Ont. 638; Todd *v.* Dun, 12 Ont. 791; Erber *v.* Dun, 12 Fed. 526; Johnson *v.* Bradstreet Co., 77 Ga. 172; Pol-

COXHEAD *v.* RICHARDS

IN THE COMMON PLEAS, JANUARY 31, 1846.

Reported in 2 Common Bench Reports, 569.

TINDAL, C. J.[1] This was an action upon the case for the publication of a false and malicious libel, in the form of a letter written by one John Cass, the first mate of a ship called The England, to the defendant; the letter stating that the plaintiff, who was the captain of the ship, and then in command of her, had been in a state of constant drunkenness during part of the voyage, whereby the ship and crew had been exposed to continual danger: and the publication by the defendant was, the communication by him of this letter to the owner of the ship, by reason whereof — which was the special damage alleged in the declaration — the plaintiff was dismissed from the ship, and lost his employment.

The defendant pleaded — first, not guilty; secondly, that the charges made by the mate against the plaintiff in his letter were true;

lasky *v.* Minchener, 81 Mich. 280; Mitchell *v.* Bradstreet Co., 116 Mo. 226; King *v.* Patterson, 49 N. J. Law, 417; Taylor *v.* Church, 8 N. Y. 452; Sunderlin *v.* Bradstreet, 46 N. Y. 188; Bradstreet Co. *v.* Gill, 72 Texas, 115 *Accord.*

Macintosh *v.* Dun, [1908] A. C. 390 *Contra.* *Aliter* in case of credit association not for profit. London Ass'n for Protection of Trade *v.* Greenlands, [1916] 2 A. C. 15.

But information given to persons having no interest in the mercantile standing of the plaintiff — for example, reports sent by a commercial agency to its subscribers generally — is not privileged. Erber *v.* Dun, 12 Fed. 526; Trussell *v.* Scarlett, 18 Fed. 214 (criticising Beardsley *v.* Tappan, 5 Blatchford, 497); Locke *v.* Bradstreet Co., 22 Fed. 771; Pacific Packing Co. *v.* Bradstreet, 25 Idaho, 696; Pollasky *v.* Minchener, 81 Mich. 280; Ormsby *v.* Douglass, 37 N. Y. 477; State *v.* Lonsdale, 48 Wis. 348.

For other cases of communications privileged because made in answer to proper inquiries, see Cockayne *v.* Hodgkisson, 5 Car. & P. 543; Storey *v.* Challands, 8 Car. & P. 234; Kline *v.* Sewell, 3 M. & W. 297; Hopwood *v.* Thorn, 8 C. B. 293; Robshaw *v.* Smith, 38 L. T. Rep. 423; Weldon *v.* Winslow, Odgers, Lib. & Sl. (5th ed.) 255; Melcher *v.* Beeler, 48 Col. 233; Zuckerman *v.* Sonnenschein, 62 Ill. 115; Richardson *v.* Gunby, 88 Kan. 47; Atwill *v.* Mackintosh, 120 Mass. 177; Howland *v.* Blake Co., 156 Mass. 543; Froslee *v.* Lund's State Bank, 131 Minn. 435; Fahr *v.* Hayes, 50 N. J. Law, 275; Posnett *v.* Marble, 62 Vt. 481; Rude *v.* Nass, 79 Wis. 321.

Advice by attorney to client as to person with whom client has business. Kruse *v.* Rabe, 80 N. J. Law, 378.

Fiduciary relations. Communications made in the line of a business duty, for example, by an agent or employee to his principal or employer are privileged. Wright *v.* Woodgate, 2 C. M. & R. 573; Scarll *v.* Dixon, 4 F. & F. 250; Stace *v.* Griffith, L. R. 2 P. C. 420; Hume *v.* Marshall, 42 J. P. 136; Washburn *v.* Cooke, 3 Den. 110; Lewis *v.* Chapman, 16 N. Y. 369.

Family relations. A *bona fide* communication by a brother to his sister reflecting on the character of her suitor is privileged. Anon., 2 Smith, 4, cited; Adams *v.* Coleridge, 1 T. L. R. 4. So is a similar communication by a son-in-law to his mother-in-law. Todd *v.* Hawkins, 2 M. & Rob. 20, 8 C. & P. 88.

Inquiry as to character of candidate for admission to a society. Cadle *v.* McIntosh, 51 Ind. App. 365.

[1] Only this opinion and the dissenting opinion of Creswell, J., are given. Erle, J., concurred with the Lord Chief Justice; Coltman, J., agreed with Cresswell, J.

and, lastly, that the shipowner did not dismiss the captain by reason, and in consequence, of the communication of the letter to him.

Upon the last two issues a verdict was found for the plaintiff; but, upon the first issue, for the defendant.

I told the jury at the trial, that the occasion and circumstances under which the communication of this letter took place, were such, as, in my opinion, to furnish a legal excuse for making the communication; and that the inference of malice, — which the law *prima facie* draws from the bare act of publishing any statements false in fact, containing matter to the reproach and prejudice of another, — was thereby rebutted; and that the plaintiff, to entitle himself to a verdict, must show malice in fact: concluding by telling them that they should find their verdict for the defendant, if they thought the communication was strictly honest on his part, and made solely in the execution of what he believed to be a duty; but, for the plaintiff, if they thought the communication was made from any indirect motive whatever, or from any malice against the plaintiff. And the only question now before us, is, whether, upon the evidence given at the trial, such direction was right.

There was no evidence whatever that the defendant was actuated by any sinister motive in communicating the letter to Mr. Ward, the shipowner: on the contrary, all the evidence went to prove that what he did he did under the full belief that he was performing a duty, however mistaken he might be as to the existence of such duty, or in his mode of performing it. The writer of the letter was no stranger to the defendant: on the contrary, both were proved to have been on terms of friendship with each other for some years; and, from the tenor of the letter itself, it must be inferred the defendant was a person upon whose judgment the writer of the letter placed great reliance, the letter itself being written for the professed purpose of obtaining his advice how to act, under a very pressing difficulty. The letter was framed in very artful terms, such as were calculated to induce the most wary and prudent man (knowing the writer) to place reliance on the truth of its details: and there can be no doubt but that the defendant did in fact thoroughly believe the contents to be true, amongst other things, that the ship, of which Mr. Ward was the owner, and the crew and cargo on board the same, had been exposed to very imminent risk, by the continued intoxication of the captain on the voyage from the French coast to Llanelly, where the ship then was, and that the voyage to the Eastern Seas, for which the ship was chartered, would be continually exposed to the same hazard, if the vessel should continue under his command. In this state of facts, after the letter had been a few days in his hands, the defendant considered it to be his duty to communicate its contents to Mr. Ward, whose interests were so nearly concerned in the information; not communicating it to the public, but to Mr. Ward; and not accompanying such disclosure with any directions or advice, but merely putting him in possession of the facts stated in the letter, that he might be in a condition to investigate the truth, and take such steps as prudence and justice to the parties concerned required: in making which disclosure he did not act hastily or unadvisedly, but consulted two persons well qualified to give good advice on such an emergency — the one, an Elder Brother of the Trinity House — the other, one of the most eminent ship-owners in London: in conformity with whose advice he gave up the letter to the owner of the ship. At the same time, if the defendant took a course which was not justifiable in point of law, although it proceeded from an error in judgment only, not of intention, still it is undoubtedly he, and not the plaintiff, who must suffer for such error.

The only question is, whether the case does or does not fall within the principle, well recognized and established in the law, relating to privileged or confidential communications; and, in determining this question, two points may, as I conceive, be considered as settled — first, that if the defendant had had any personal interest in the subject-matter to which the letter related, as, if he had been a part-owner of the ship, or an underwriter on the ship, or had had any property on board, the communication of such a letter to Mr. Ward would have fallen clearly within the rule relating to excusable publications — and, secondly, that if the danger disclosed by the letter, either to the ship or the cargo, or the ship's company, had been so immediate as that the disclosure to the shipowner was necessary to avert such danger, then, upon the ground of social duty, by which every man is bound to his neighbor, the defendant would have been not only justified in making the disclosure, but would have been *bound* to make it. A man who received a letter informing him that his neighbor's house would be plundered or burnt on the night following by A. and B., and which he himself believed, and had reason to believe, to be true, would be justified in showing that letter to the owner of the house, though it should turn out to be a false accusation of A. and B. The question before us appears, therefore, to be narrowed to the consideration of the facts which bear upon these two particular qualifications and restrictions of the general principle.

As to the first, I do not find the rule of law is so narrowed and restricted by any authority, that a person having information materially affecting the interests of another, and honestly communicating it, in the full belief, and with reasonable grounds for the belief, that it is true, will not be excused, though he has no personal interest in the subject-matter. Such a restriction would surely operate as a great restraint upon the performance of the various social duties by which men are bound to each other, and by which society is kept up. In Pattison *v.* Jones, 8 B. & C. 578, the defendant, who had discharged the plaintiff from his service, wrote a letter to the person who was about to engage him, unsolicited; he was therefore a volunteer in the matter; and might be considered as a stranger, having no interest in the business; but, neither at the trial, nor on the motion before the court, was it suggested that the letter was, on that account, an unprivileged communication; but it was left to the jury to say whether the communication was honest or malicious. Again, in Child *v.* Affleck and Wife, the statement, by the former mistress, of the conduct of her servant, not only during her service, but after she had left it, was held to be privileged. The rule appears to have been correctly laid down by the Court of Exchequer, that, "if fairly warranted by any reasonable occasion or exigency, and honestly made, such communications are protected, for the common convenience and welfare of society; and the law has not restricted the right to make them, within any narrow limits." 1 C. M. & R. 181. In the present case, the defendant stood in a different situation from any other person; he was the only person in the world who had received the letter, or was acquainted with the information contained in it. He cannot, therefore, properly be treated as a complete stranger to the subject-matter of inquiry, even if the rule excluded strangers from the privilege.

Upon the second ground of qualification — was the danger sufficiently imminent to justify the communication — it is true, that the letter, which came to the defendant's hands about the 14th of December, contains within it the information that the ship cannot get out of harbor before the end of the month. It was urged that the defendant, instead of communicating the letter to the owner, might have instituted some inquiry himself. But it is to be observed that every day the ship remained under the command of such a person as the plaintiff was described to be, the ship and crew continued exposed to hazard, though not so great hazard as when at sea; not to mention the immediate injury to the shipowner which must necessarily follow from want of discipline of the crew, and the bad example of such a master. And, after all, it would be too much to say, that, even if the thing had been practicable, any duty was cast upon *the defendant*, to lay out his time or money in the investigation of the charge.

Upon the consideration of the case, I think it was the duty of the defendant not to keep the knowledge he gained by this letter himself, and thereby make himself responsible, in conscience, if his neglect of the warnings of the letter brought destruction upon the ship or crew — that a prudent and reasonable man would have done the same; that the disclosure was made, not publicly, but privately to the owner, that is, to the person who of all the world was the best qualified, both from his interest in the subject-matter, and his knowledge of his own officers, to form the most just conclusion as to its truth, and to adopt the most proper and effective measures to avert the danger; after which disclosure, not the defendant, but the owner, became liable to the plaintiff, if the owner took steps which were not justifiable; as, by unjustly dismissing him from his employment, if the letter was untrue. And, as all this was done with entire honesty of purpose, and in the full belief of the truth of the information, — and that, a reasonable belief, — I am still of the same opinion which I entertained at the trial, that this case ranges itself within the pale of privileged communication, and that the action is not maintainable.

I therefore think the rule for setting aside the verdict and for a new trial, should be discharged.

CRESWELL, J. I cannot, without much regret, express an opinion in this case at variance with that which is entertained by my lord and one of my learned brothers. But, having given full consideration to the arguments urged at the bar, and the cases cited, and not being able to shake off the impression which they made in favor of the plaintiff, I am bound to act upon the opinion that I have formed. I will not repeat the facts of the case, which have been already stated, but proceed shortly to explain the grounds upon which my opinion rests.

There is no doubt that the letter published by the defendant of the plaintiff was defamatory; and the truth of its contents could not be proved. The plaintiff was, therefore, entitled to maintain an action against the publisher of that letter, unless the occasion on which it was published made the publication of such letter a lawful act, as far as the plaintiff was concerned, if done in good faith, and without actual malice. To sustain an action for a libel or slander, the plaintiff must show that it was malicious; but every unauthorized publication of defamatory matter is, in point of law, to be considered as malicious. The law, however, on a principle of policy and convenience, authorizes many communications, although they affect the characters of individuals; and I take it to be a question of law, whether the communication is authorized or not. If it be authorized, the legal presumption of malice arising from the unauthorized publication of defamatory matter, fails, and the plaintiff, to sustain his action, must prove actual malice, or, as it is usually expressed, malice in fact. In the present case, the existence of malice in fact was negatived by the jury; and if my lord was right in telling them, that, in the absence of malice in fact, the publication of the letter was privileged, this rule should be discharged. It therefore becomes necessary to inquire within what limits and boundaries the law authorizes the publication of defamatory matter. Perhaps the best description of those limits and boundaries that can be given in few words, is to be found in the judgment of Parke, B., in Toogood *v.* Spyring: "The law considers such publication as malicious, unless it is fairly made by a person in the discharge of some public or private duty, whether legal or moral, or in the conduct of his own affairs in matters where his interest is concerned." It was not contended in this case that any *legal* duty bound the defendant to communicate to the shipowner the contents of the letter he had received, nor was the communication made in the conduct of his own affairs, nor was his interest concerned: the authority for the publication, if any, must therefore be derived from some *moral* duty, public or private, which it was incumbent upon him to discharge. I think it impossible to say that the defendant was called upon by any *public duty* to make the communication; neither his own situation nor that of any of the parties concerned, nor the interests at stake were such as to affect the public weal. Was there then any *private* duty? There was no relation of principal and agent between the shipowner and the defendant, nor was any trust or confidence reposed by the former in the latter; there was no relationship or intimacy between them; no inquiries had been made; they were, until the time in question, strangers: the duty, if it existed at all as between them, must, therefore, have arisen from the mere circumstance of their being fellow-subjects of the realm. But the same relation existed between the defendant and the plaintiff. If the property of the shipowner on the one hand was at stake, the character of the captain was at stake on the other; and I cannot but think that the moral duty not to publish of the latter defamatory matter which he did not *know* to be true, was quite as strong as the duty to communicate to the shipowner that which he *believed* to be true. Was, then, the defendant bound by any moral duty towards the writer of the letter, to make the communication? Surely not. If the captain had misconducted himself, the mate was capable of observing it, and was as capable of communicating it to the owner as to the defendant. The crew were, in like manner, capable of observing and acting for themselves. The mate (if he really believed that which he wrote to be true) might, indeed, be under a moral duty to communicate it to his owner: but the defendant had no right to take that vicarious duty upon himself: he was not requested by the mate to do so, but was, on the contrary, enjoined *not* to make the communication.

I will not attempt to comment upon the very numerous cases that were quoted at the bar on the one side and on the other, but will advert to one or two which tend to explain the term "moral duty," and see whether it has ever been held to authorize the publication of defamatory matter under circumstances similar to those which exist in the present case. In Bromage *v.* Prosser, Bayley, J., in his very elaborate judgment, speaks of slander as "*prima facie* excusable on account of the cause of speaking or writing it, in the case of servants' characters, confidential advice, or communications to those who ask it or have a right to expect it." With regard to the characters of servants and agents, it is so manifestly for the advantage of society that those who are about to employ them should be enabled to learn what their previous conduct has been, that it may be well deemed the moral duty of former employers to answer inquiries to the best of their belief. But, according to the opinion of the same learned judge, intimated in Pattison *v.* Jones, 8 B. & C. 578, it is necessary that *inquiry* should be made, in order to render lawful the communication of defamatory matter, although he was also of opinion that such inquiry may be invited by the former master. And in Rogers *v.* Clifton, Chambre, J., quoted a similar opinion of Lord Mansfield's, expressed in Lowry *v.* Aikenhead, Mich. 8 G. 3, 3 B. & P. 594.

It was contended during the argument of this case, that the protection given to masters when speaking of the conduct of servants, was more extensive, and applied also to communications made to former employers; and Child *v.* Affleck was mentioned as an instance. But the communication to the former master was not made a ground of action in that case, and was introduced only as evidence that the statement made in answer to the inquiry of the new master was malicious. The same observation applies to Rogers *v.* Clifton; and it may be collected from that report that Chambre, J., was of opinion, that, where statements are made which are not in answer to inquiries, the defendant must plead, and prove, a justification.

Again, where a party asks advice or information upon a subject on which he is interested; or where the relative position of two parties is such that the one has a right to expect confidential information and advice from the other; it may be a moral duty to answer such inquiries and give such information and advice; and the statements made may be rendered lawful by the occasion, although defamatory of some third person, as in Dunman *v.* Bigg, 1 Campb. 269, and Todd *v.* Hawkins, 2 M. & Rob. 20, 8 C. & P. 88.

Two cases — Herver *v.* Dowson, Bull. N. P. 8, and Cleaver *v.* Sarraude, reported in M'Dougall *v.* Claridge, 1 Campb. 268 — were quoted as authorities for giving a more extended meaning to the term "moral duty," and making it include all cases where one man had information, which, if true, it would be important for another to know. But the notes of those cases are very short: in the former the precise circumstances under which the statement was made — see King *v.* Watts, 8 C. & P. 614, that such a statement made *without inquiry* is not lawful — and in the latter, the position of the defendant with reference to the Bishop of Durham, to whom it was made, are left unexplained. I cannot, therefore, consider them as satisfactory authorities for the position to establish which they were quoted: and, in the absence of any clear and precise authority in favor of it, I cannot persuade myself that it is correct, as, if established at all, it must be at the expense of another moral duty, viz., not to publish defamatory matter unless you *know* it to be true.

For these reasons, I am of opinion, that the rule for a new trial should be made absolute.

The court being thus divided in opinion, the rule for a new trial fell to the ground, and the defendant retained his verdict.[1]

[1] "If it had been necessary, I should have been fully prepared to go the whole length of the doctrine laid down by Tindal, C. J., in the case of Coxhead *v.* Richards," *per* Willes, J., in Amann *v.* Damm, 8 C. B. N. S. 592, 602. Blackburn, J.,

JOANNES *v.* BENNETT

SUPREME JUDICIAL COURT, MASSACHUSETTS, OCTOBER, 1862.

Reported in 5 *Allen*, 169.

TORT brought on the 12th of June, 1860, in the name of "The Count Joannes (born 'George Jones')"[1] for two libels upon him contained in letters to a woman to whom he was then a suitor, and was afterwards married, endeavoring to dissuade her from entering into the marriage.

At the trial in this court, before Merrick, J., it appeared that the defendant had for several years held the relation of pastor to the parents of the woman, as members of his church, and to the daughter, as a member of his choir; and there was evidence tending to show that he was on the most intimate terms of friendship with the parents, and that, on the 18th of May, 1860, being on a visit from his present residence in Lockport, New York, he called upon the father at his place of business in Boston, and was urged by him to accompany him to his residence in South Boston, the father stating that both he and his wife were in great distress of mind and anxiety about their daughter, and that they feared she would engage herself in marriage to the plaintiff. On their way to South Boston, the father stated to the defendant what he and his wife had heard and apprehended about the plaintiff, and their views with regard to his being an unsuitable match for their daughter, who, with a young child by a former husband, was living with them. On reaching the house, it was found that the daughter had gone out; and it was then arranged that the defendant should write a letter, and materials for that purpose were furnished, and the letter set forth in the first count[2] was written, addressed to the daugh-

in Davies *v.* Snead, L. R. 5 Q. B. 605, 611, and Lindley, J., in Stuart *v.* Bell, [1891] 2 Q. B. 341, 347, expressed similar approval of the opinion of Tindal, C. J.

Vanspike *v.* Cleyson, Cro. El. 541; Peacock *v.* Reynal, 2 Br. & Gold. 151, 15 C. B. N. S. 418, cited; Herver *v.* Dowson, Bull. N. P. 8; Cleaver *v.* Sarraude, 1 Camp. 268, cited; Picton *v.* Jackman, 4 Car. & P. 257; Dixon *v.* Smith, 29 L. J. Ex. 125, 126; Masters *v.* Burgess, 3 T. L. R. 96; Stuart *v.* Bell, [1891] 2 Q. B. 341; Hart *v.* Reed, 1 B. Mon. 166; Fresh *v.* Cutter, 73 Md. 87; Noonan *v.* Orton, 32 Wis. 106 *Accord.*

Cockayne *v.* Hodgkisson, 5 Car. & P. 543 (*semble*); King *v.* Watts, 8 Car. & P. 614; Brown *v.* Vannaman, 85 Wis. 451 *Contra.* But see Hocks *v.* Sprangers, 113 Wis. 123.

In Bennett *v.* Deacon, 2 C. B. 628, a creditor of a buyer volunteered a warning to the seller as to the buyer's credit. The court was evenly divided as to whether the communication was privileged.

Compare Irion *v.* Knapp, 132 La. 60 (letter to a public board as to a candidate for an appointment).

INDIAN PENAL CODE, § 499, exception 9. It is not defamation to make an imputation on the character of another, provided that the imputation be made in good faith for the protection of the interests of the person making it, or of any other person, or for the public good.

[1] As to this remarkable litigant, see the article by Irving Browne, "Count Joannes," 8 Green Bag. 435.

[2] Only what relates to this count is given.

ter, and left open and unsealed with the mother, after the principal portion of it had been read aloud at the tea-table in the presence of the parents and a confidential friend of the family. On leaving, the defendant was further requested to do what he thought best to induce the daughter to break up the match.

The judge ruled that the letter was not a privileged communication; and a verdict was returned for the plaintiff. The defendant alleged exceptions.

BIGELOW, C. J. The doctrine, that the cause or occasion of a publication of defamatory matter may afford a sufficient justification in an action for damages, has been stated in the form of a legal rule or canon, which has been sanctioned by high judicial authority. The statement is this: A communication made *bona fide* upon any subject-matter in which the party communicating has an interest, or in reference to which he has a duty to perform, is privileged, if made to a person having a corresponding interest or duty, although it contains defamatory matter, which without such privilege would be libellous and actionable. It would be difficult to state the result of judicial decisions on this subject, and of the principles on which they rest, in a more concise, accurate and intelligible form. Harrison *v.* Bush, 5 E. & B. 344; Gassett *v.* Gilbert, 6 Gray, 94, and cases cited. It seems to us very clear that the defendant in the present case fails to show any facts or circumstances in his own relation to the parties, or in the motives or inducements by which he was led to write the letter set out in the first count of the declaration, which bring the publication within the first branch of this rule. He certainly had no interest of his own to serve or protect in making a communication concerning the character, occupation and conduct of the plaintiff, containing defamatory or libellous matter. It does not appear that the proposed marriage which the letter written by the defendant was intended to discountenance and prevent, could in any way interfere with or disturb his personal or social relations. It did not even involve any sacrifice of his feelings or injury to his affections. The person to whom the letter was addressed was not connected with him by the ties of consanguinity or kindred. It is not shown that he had any peculiar interest in her welfare. Under such circumstances, without indicating the state of facts which might afford a justification for the use of defamatory words, it is plain that the defendant held no such relation towards the parties as to give him any interest in the subject-matter to which his communication concerning the plaintiff related. Todd *v.* Hawkins, 2 M. & Rob. 20; s. c. 8 C. & P. 88. No doubt, he acted from laudable motives in writing it. But these do not of themselves afford a legal justification for holding up the character of a person to contempt and ridicule. Good intentions do not furnish a valid excuse for violating another's rights, or give impunity to those who cast unjust imputations on private character.

It is equally clear that the defendant did not write and publish the alleged libellous communications in the exercise of any legal or moral duty. He stood in no such relation towards the parties as to confer on him a right or impose on him an obligation to write a letter containing calumnious statements concerning the plaintiff's character. Whatever may be the rule which would have been applicable under similar circumstances while he retained his relation of religious teacher and pastor towards the person to whom this letter in question was addressed, and towards her parents, he certainly had no duty resting upon him after that relation had terminated. He then stood in no other attitude towards the parties than as a friend. His duty to render them a service was no greater or more obligatory than was his duty to refrain from uttering and publishing slanderous or libellous statements concerning another. It is obvious that if such communications could be protected merely on the ground that the party making them held friendly relations with those to whom they were written or spoken, a wide door would be left open by which indiscriminate aspersion of private character could escape with impunity. Indeed, it would rarely be difficult for a party to shelter himself from the consequences of uttering or publishing a slander or libel under a privilege which could be readily made to embrace almost every species of communication. The law does not tolerate any such license of speech or pen. The duty of avoiding the use of defamatory words cannot be set aside except when it is essential to the protection of some substantial private interest, or to the discharge of some other paramount and urgent duty. It seems to us, therefore, that on the question of justification set up by the defendant under a supposed privilege which authorized him to write the letter set out in the first count, the instructions of the court were correct.[1]

BEALS v. THOMPSON

SUPREME JUDICIAL COURT, MASSACHUSETTS, JUNE 20, 1889.

Reported in 149 *Massachusetts Reports*, 405.

TORT for a libel contained in letters written by the defendant to the plaintiff's husband, and charging her with having been guilty of dishonorable conduct, deception, and ingratitude and dishonesty towards the defendant, whereby she lost the comfort and society of her husband, who refused to live longer with her.[2]

The jury returned a verdict for the plaintiff in the sum of $30,000; and the defendant alleged exceptions.

[1] Krebs *v.* Oliver, 12 Gray, 239; Byam *v.* Collins, 111 N. Y. 143 *Accord.*
Anon., 15 C. B. N. S. 410 (cited); Adcock *v.* Marsh, 8 Ired. 360 *Contra.* See Dobbin *v.* Chicago R. Co., 157 Mo. App. 689.

[2] The statement of the case has been condensed.

FIELD, J. The exceptions also state, that the court refused "to instruct the jury that each of the letters mentioned in plaintiff's declaration was a privileged communication, and that this action could not therefore be maintained," and "instructed the jury that no privilege was shown." No facts are recited in the bill of exceptions which tend to show that the occasion was privileged, except such as may be inferred from the relation of the parties to each other, and from the contents of the letters. Taking the case most favorably for the defendant, it is that the plaintiff owed a debt to the defendant for money lent to her before her marriage, which, after her marriage with a rich man, she refused to pay, under circumstances which showed ingratitude on her part, and that the defendant wrote a letter to the husband defamatory of the plaintiff, for the purpose of compelling him or her to pay the debt. This is not a lawful method of collecting a debt, or of compelling another person than the debtor to pay it. The defendant owed no duty to the husband to inform him of the bad conduct of his wife before her marriage, and the husband was under no obligation to pay the debts of his wife contracted before her marriage. There is no evidence that the defendant in sending the letter to the husband was acting in the discharge of any duty, social, moral, or legal. The ruling was right. Gassett *v.* Gilbert, 6 Gray, 94; Krebs *v.* Oliver, 12 Gray, 239; Joannes *v.* Bennett, 5 All. 169; Shurtleff *v.* Parker, 130 Mass. 293; White *v.* Nicholls, 3 How. 266. *Exceptions overruled.*[1]

TOOGOOD *v.* SPYRING

IN THE EXCHEQUER, TRINITY TERM, 1834.

Reported in 1 *Crompton, Meeson & Roscoe,* 181.

THE judgment of the court was delivered by

PARKE, B.[2] In this case, which was argued before my Brothers BOLLAND, ALDERSON, GURNEY, and myself, a motion was made for a nonsuit, or a new trial, on the ground of misdirection. It was an action of slander, for words alleged to be spoken of the plaintiff as a journeyman carpenter, on three different occasions. It appeared that the defendant, who was a tenant of the Earl of Devon, required some work to be done on the premises occupied by him under the earl, and the plaintiff, who was generally employed by Brinsdon, the earl's agent, as a journeyman, was sent by him to do the work. He did it, but in a negligent manner; and, during the progress of the work, got drunk; and some circumstances occurred which induced the defendant to believe that he

[1] In Simmonds *v.* Dunne, Ir. R. 5 C. L. 358; Over *v.* Schiffling, 102 Ind. 191; York *v.* Johnson, 116 Mass. 482, the communications were not privileged for want of a legitimate interest or duty on the part of the defendant.
See Whiteley *v.* Newman, 9 Ga. App. 89.

[2] Only the opinion of the court is given.

had broken open the cellar door, and so obtained access to his cider. The defendant a day or two afterwards met the plaintiff in the presence of a person named Taylor, and charged him with having broken open his cellar door with a chisel, and also with having got drunk. The plaintiff denied the charges. The defendant then said he would have it cleared up, and went to look for Brinsdon; he afterwards returned and spoke to Taylor, in the absence of the plaintiff; and, in answer to a question of Taylor's, said he was confident that the plaintiff had broken open the door. On the same day the defendant saw Brinsdon, and complained to him that the plaintiff had been negligent in his work, had got drunk, and he thought he had broken open the door, and requested him to go with him in order to examine it. Upon the trial it was objected, that these were what are usually termed "privileged communications." The learned judge thought that the statement to Brinsdon might be so, but not the charge made in the presence of Taylor; and in respect of that charge, and of what was afterwards said to Taylor, both which statements formed the subject of the action, the plaintiff had a verdict. We agree in his opinion, that the communication to Brinsdon was protected, and that the statement, upon the second meeting, to Taylor, in the plaintiff's absence, was not; but we think, upon consideration, that the statement made to the plaintiff, though in the presence of Taylor, falls within the class of communications ordinarily called privileged; that is, cases where the occasion of the publication affords a defence in the absence of express malice. In general, an action lies for the malicious publication of statements which are false in fact, and injurious to the character of another (within the well-known limits as to verbal slander), and the law considers such publication as malicious, unless it is fairly made by a person in the discharge of some public or private duty, whether legal or moral, or in the conduct of his own affairs, in matters where his interest is concerned. In such cases, the occasion prevents the inference of malice, which the law draws from unauthorized communications, and affords a qualified defence depending upon the absence of actual malice. If *fairly* warranted by any reasonable occasion or exigency, and honestly made, such communications are protected for the common convenience and welfare of society; and the law has not restricted the right to make them within any narrow limits.

Among the many cases which have been reported on this subject, one precisely in point has not, I believe, occurred; but one of the most ordinary and common instances in which the principle has been applied in practice is that of a former master giving the character of a discharged servant; and I am not aware that it was ever deemed essential to the protection of such a communication that it should be made to some person interested in the inquiry, *alone*, and not in the presence of a third person. If made with honesty of purpose to a party who has any interest in the inquiry (and that has been very liberally construed, Child *v.* Affleck, 4 Man. & Ryl. 590; 9 B. & C. 403), the simple fact that there has been some casual bystander cannot alter the nature of the transaction. The business of life could not be well carried on if such restraints were imposed upon this and similar communications, and if, on every occasion in which they were made, they were not protected unless strictly private. In this class of communications is, no doubt, comprehended the right of a master *bona fide* to charge his servant for any supposed misconduct in his service, and to give him admonition and blame; and we think that the simple circumstance of the master exercising that right in the presence of another, does by no means *of necessity* take away from it the protection which the law would otherwise afford. Where, indeed, an opportunity is *sought* for making such a charge before third persons, which might have been made in private, it would afford strong evidence of a malicious intention, and thus deprive it of that immunity which the law allows to such a statement, when made with honesty of purpose; but the mere fact of a third person being present does not render the communication absolutely unauthorized, though it may be a circumstance to be left with others, including the style and character of the language used, to the consideration of the jury, who are to determine whether the defendant has acted *bona fide* in making the charge, or been influenced by malicious motives.[1] In the present case, the defendant stood in such a relation with respect to the plaintiff, though not strictly that of master, as to authorize him to impute blame to him, provided it was done fairly and honestly, for any supposed misconduct in the course of his employment; and we think that the fact, that the imputation was made in Taylor's presence, does not, *of itself*, render the communication unwarranted and officious, but at most is a circumstance to be left to the consideration of the jury. We agree with the learned judge, that the statement to Taylor, in the plaintiff's absence, was unauthorized and officious, and therefore not protected, although made in the belief of its truth, if it were, in point of fact, false; but, inasmuch as no damages have been separately given upon this part of the charge alone, to which the fourth count is adapted, we cannot support a general verdict, if the learned judge was wrong in his opinion as to the statement to the plaintiff in Taylor's presence; and, as we think that at all events it should have been left to the jury whether the defendant acted maliciously or not on that occasion, there must be a new trial. *Rule absolute for a new trial.*[2]

[1] Jones *v.* Thomas, 34 W. R. 104; Pittard *v.* Oliver, [1891] 1 Q. B. 474; Broughton *v.* McGrew, 39 Fed. 672; Brow *v.* Hathaway, 13 All. 239; Billings *v.* Fairbanks, 136 Mass. 177, 139 Mass. 66; Keane *v.* Sprague (N. Y. City Court), 30 Alb. L. J. 283 *Accord.*

Webber *v.* Vincent, 9 N. Y. Supp. 101 *Contra.*

Defamatory letter after termination of employment. National Cash Register Co. *v.* Salling, 173 Fed. 22.

[2] In Christopher *v.* Akin, 214 Mass. 332, the plaintiff was a journeyman painter in the employ of the defendant, and was at work on the house of one Tillinghast.

WILLIAMSON *v.* FREER

IN THE COMMON PLEAS, APRIL 20, 1874.

Reported in Law Reports, 9 *Common Pleas,* 393.

THIS was an action for a libel, tried before Brett, J., at the last assizes for Leicester. The facts were as follows: The plaintiff was employed as assistant in the shop of the defendant, a shoemaker, at Leicester. The defendant having accused the plaintiff of robbing him of money, sent two post-office telegrams to her father, who resided in London, to inform him of his suspicions. The first telegram was to this effect: " Come at once to Leicester, if you wish to save your child from appearing before a magistrate." The second was as follows: " Your child will be given in charge of the police unless you reply and come to-day. She has taken money out of the till."

The charge was persisted in down to the trial; but there was no evidence to support it. It did not appear that, beyond the officials of the post-office, through whose hands the telegrams passed, they had come to the knowledge of any other persons than the father, mother, and brother of the plaintiff.

The learned judge left it to the jury to say whether the statements were libellous, and whether it was reasonable to transmit them by telegraph rather than by post.

The jury found that the statements were libellous, and that it was not reasonable to send them by telegraph, and they returned a verdict for the plaintiff, damages £100.

Tillinghast complained to the defendant that some of his men had stolen a putty knife and other property belonging to him. The defendant recompensed Tillinghast for the property and testified that he was told by one of his men that the plaintiff had admitted to him that he took the putty knife. The men were paid off by the defendant at his shop on Saturday night, — their time being made up to Wednesday. Their pay was handed to them in envelopes. When a man was discharged his envelope contained his pay up to Saturday night. The plaintiff's envelope contained his pay in full, less what the defendant had paid Tillinghast for the property, with a bill for it. There were four or five men in the shop waiting to be paid off when it came the plaintiff's turn to be paid. The plaintiff opened his envelope and counted the money and found the bill. The plaintiff asked the defendant what that meant, and the defendant said in response, " Do you want to know in front of all these men ? " and he said " Yes," whereupon the defendant said, " That is the stuff you stole from the Tillinghast job." Morton, J., said: " Whether a communication is or is not privileged does not depend so much on the manner or form in which crime is imputed, where the alleged slander consists as here of a charge of crime, as on the occasion and circumstances under which the charge is made. If made in good faith in reference to a matter in which the person making it is immediately interested, and for the purpose of protecting his interest and in the belief that it is true and without any malicious motive, the communication is what is termed privileged; that is, the occasion and the circumstances under which it is made are held to be such as, if nothing more appears, to excuse or justify the statements that are made."

See Madill *v.* Currie, 168 Mich. 546.

Compare Adam *v.* Ward, [1917] A. C. 309 (statement given to the press by the army board in reply to a speech in Parliament regarding an army officer).

O'Malley, Q. C. (with him *Merewether*), pursuant to leave, moved to enter a verdict for the defendant.[1]

BRETT, J. I reserved the point because I thought it was a very important one. It is whether, where a communication is to be made to a relative of a person against whom a charge is preferred, which communication would be privileged if sent by letter in the ordinary way the privilege is not lost by sending it in the form of a telegram, — whether a communication in that form can be said to be made to one person, when in point of fact it passes through several hands before it reaches its ultimate destination. Privilege is not wanted unless the publication is libellous. The question then is whether the character of an innocent person is to be destroyed because the libeller thinks fit to send the libel in this shape rather than in a sealed letter. I do not mean to say that there was malice in fact here. But I agree with my Lord that sending the messages by telegraph when they might have been sent by letter was evidence of malice. I desire, however, to put this higher. I think that a communication which would be privileged if made by letter becomes unprivileged if sent through the telegraph office, because it is necessarily communicated to all the clerks through whose hands it passes. It is like the case of a libel contained on the back of a post card.[2] It was never meant by the Legislature that these facilities for postal and telegraphic communication should be used for the purpose of more easily disseminating libels. Where there is such a publication, it avoids the privilege, because it is communicated through unprivileged persons. As to the damages, I am not at all disposed to think them excessive. The charge against the plaintiff was of a very grave character. It was made with considerable severity, and it was insisted upon even down to the trial. *Rule refused.*[3]

[1] The statement of the case is abridged; the arguments of counsel and the concurring opinions of Lord Coleridge, C. J., and Denman, J., are omitted.

[2] Robinson *v.* Jones, L. R. 4 Ir. 391 *Accord.*

[3] Robinson *v.* Jones, L. R. 4 Ir. 391 *Accord.* See also Smith *v.* Crocker, 5 T. L. R. 441; Muetze *v.* Tuteur, 77 Wis. 236.

Statement in presence of third persons not interested. Fowlie *v.* Cruse, 52 Mont. 222; Fields *v.* Bynum, 156 N. C. 413.

Notice of discharge of employee posted on the premises. Ramsdell *v.* Pennsylvania Co., 79 N. J. Law, 379.

Notice to customers in a local newspaper. Hatch *v.* Lane, 105 Mass. 394. See Delany *v.* Jones, 4 Esp. 190 (but see Ley *v.* Lawson, 4 A. & E. 798); Commonwealth *v.* Featherston, 9 Phila. 594; Holliday *v.* Ontario Co., 33 Up. Can. Q. B. 558.

General publicity with respect to candidate for local office. Duncombe *v.* Daniel, 1 Willmore, W. & H. 101, 8 Car. & P. 222; Jones *v.* Varnum, 21 Fla. 431; State *v.* Haskins, 109 Ia. 656; Coleman *v.* MacLennan, 78 Kan. 711; Bronson *v.* Bruce, 59 Mich. 467; Wheaton *v.* Beecher, 66 Mich. 307; Belknap *v.* Ball, 83 Mich. 583; Aldrich *v.* Press Co., 9 Minn. 133 (but see, *contra*, Marks *v.* Baker, 28 Minn. 162); Bigner *v.* Hodges, 82 Miss. 215; Lewis *v.* Few, 5 Johns. 1; Root *v.* King, 7 Cow. 613; Hunt *v.* Bennett, 19 N. Y. 173; Seely *v.* Blair, Wright, (Ohio) 358, 683; Knapp *v.* Campbell, 14 Tex. Civ. App. 199; Sweeney *v.* Baker, 13 W. Va. 158. Compare Flynn *v.* Boglarsky, 164 Mich. 513.

But a communication to the electors alone is privileged, if made in good faith. Wisdom *v.* Brown, 1 T. L. R. 412; Pankhurst *v.* Hamilton, 3 T. L. R. 500; Burke

MARKS *v.* BAKER

SUPREME COURT, MINNESOTA, JULY 25, 1881.

Reported in 28 *Minnesota Reports*, 162.

BERRY, J. This is an action for libel. The plaintiff was, at the times hereinafter mentioned, treasurer of the city of Mankato, and, as such, custodian of the moneys, and from April 1 to 6, 1880, a candidate for re-election to the same office, at an election fixed for the latter day. The defendants were residents and tax-payers of the city, and publishers thereat of the Mankato Free Press, a weekly newspaper, and as such they published therein, on April 2, 1880, the article complained of, in which, as the plaintiff claims in his complaint, they charged and intended to charge the defendant as treasurer with embezzling city funds. It is alleged in the complaint that the matter charged as libellous was of and concerning the plaintiff in his office — that it was false and defamatory, and that the publication was malicious. The answer denies malice, all intent to injure or defame plaintiff, any intention on defendants' part to charge him with embezzlement, and alleges that defendants published the article complained of, as a communication, solely for the purpose of calling the attention of the public to the matter therein referred to, viz., to a discrepancy in certain official reports tending to show that the plaintiff had failed to charge himself with the full amount of city funds which he had received from the county treasury, and with the view of obtaining an inquiry as to the cause of such discrepancy. The answer further alleges that " the publication was made in good faith; . . . that defendants believed that there was reasonable cause for the publication; " and " that they were then and there discharging a sacred and moral obligation as . . . editors and publishers." The reply puts these allegations of the answer in issue. Upon the trial it was admitted that, notwithstanding the discrepancy, (which in fact, existed) the plaintiff had accounted for the full sum received by him as city treasurer from the county treasurer, so that the defendants' charge or insinuation to the contrary was false.

Defendant, Baker, having been called for the defence, was asked the questions following, to which he made answers as follows, all against the objection and exception of the plaintiff:

(1) " Did you believe the report of the city recorder to be true ? *Answer.* I did believe it to be true. (This report was that from which, as defendants in the alleged libel charged or insinuated, it appeared that plaintiff had failed to account for all the money received by him from the county treasurer.)

(2) " What was your object in publishing the article? *Answer.* I published it for the general public interest.

(3) " Did you have any other object in publishing the article ? *Answer.* I did not.

v. Mascarich, 81 Cal. 302 (*semble*); Mott *v.* Dawson, 46 Ia. 533; Bays *v.* Hunt, 60 Ia. 251; State *v.* Balch, 31 Kan. 465; Commonwealth *v.* Wardwell, 136 Mass. 164; Briggs *v.* Garrett, 111 Pa. St. 404.

But see, *contra*, Smith *v.* Burrus, 106 Mo. 94, where the distinction between fair comment and qualified privilege was overlooked. See also Estelle *v.* Daily News Pub. Co., 99 Neb. 397; Arnold *v.* Ingram, 151 Wis. 438; Putnam *v.* Browne, 162 Wis. 524.

(4) "You have stated that you had no other purpose than doing a public duty in publishing the article. I want to know what your object was, — to charge somebody with a crime, or whether you had some other object? *Answer.* To draw attention to the discrepancy of the two reports. I had seen what purported to be the official report of the county auditor, and I had seen the city recorder's; and the county auditor's showed that Marks, as city treasurer, had received from the county, during the fiscal year, $115.02 more than the city recorder's report showed that he had received from the county for the same time. (These are the two reports between which the discrepancy was charged to exist.)

(5) "Did you, by publishing the article, intend to charge the plaintiff with embezzling any sum whatever? *Answer.* I did not."

The defence set up in the answer is, in effect, that the publication complained of is a privileged communication.

The rule is that a communication made in good faith upon any subject-matter in which the party communicating has an interest, or in reference to which he has a duty, public or private, either legal, moral, or social, if made to a person having a corresponding interest or duty, is privileged; that in such case the inference of malice which the law draws from defamatory words is rebutted, and the *onus* of proving actual malice is cast upon the person claiming to have been defamed. Toogood *v.* Spyring, 1 Cr. M. & R. 181; 2 Addison on Torts, § 1091; Harrison *v.* Bush, 5 E. & B. 544; Moak's Underhill on Torts, 146; Quinn *v.* Scott, 22 Minn. 456. That the subject-matter of the communication is one of public interest in the community of which the parties to the communication are members, is sufficient, as respects interest, to confer the privilege. Purcell *v.* Sowler, 2 C. P. D. 215; Palmer *v.* City of Concord, 48 N. H. 211; Cooley on Torts, 217. The subject-matter of the communication in the case at bar was one of public interest in the city of Mankato, where the publication was made, and one in which the defendants had an interest as residents and tax-payers of the city. It was, therefore, a privileged communication, within the rule mentioned, if made in good faith.[1]

Judgment affirmed.[2]

[1] The court found that the defendant acted in good faith.

[2] Ashford *v.* Evening Star Co., 41 App. D. C. 395; Addington *v.* Times Pub. Co., 138 La. 731; Briggs *v.* Garrett, 111 Pa. St. 404 (*semble*); Express Co. *v.* Copeland, 64 Tex. 354 *Accord.* Compare Bingham *v.* Gaynor, 141 App. Div. 301; Ivie *v.* Minton, 75 Or. 483.

Statement at a meeting to oppose a candidate for public office. Baker *v.* Warner, 231 U. S. 588.

Criticism of minister in a church convention. Dickson *v.* Lights, (Tex. Civ. App.) 170 S. W. 834.

Criticism of member of association at a meeting to discuss the affairs of the association. Caldwell *v.* Hayden, 42 App. D. C. 166.

Reply to defamatory statements. Adam *v.* Ward [1917] A. C. 309; Preston *v.* Hobbs, 161 App. Div. 363; Smith *v.* Kemp, 132 La. 943.

CARTER *v.* PAPINEAU

SUPREME JUDICIAL COURT, MASSACHUSETTS, JANUARY 27, 1916.

Reported in 222 *Massachusetts Reports*, 464.

BRALEY, J.[1] The evidence would have amply warranted the jury in finding that the defendant Papineau as priest in charge declined to administer to the plaintiff the rite of " Holy Communion " or to permit her to partake thereof, and that by his authority and order she had been refused admission on the Lord's Day to the building in which religious services were being held. It is contended that for these acts he and the defendant Lawrence, bishop of the diocese, are responsible in damages, and that the verdicts in their favor were ordered wrongly.

The record shows that the Protestant Episcopal Church of America, of which the parties are members, has a body of canons or ecclesiastical law of its own, by which the plaintiff upon baptism and confirmation agreed to be bound, and under which her rights of worship must be determined. Fitzgerald *v.* Robinson, 112 Mass. 371. Grosvenor *v.* United Society of Believers, 118 Mass. 78. By the " Rubric in the Order for the Administration of the Lord's Supper, or Holy Communion " the " minister " is given authority to refuse the rite to any one whom he knows " to be an open and notorious evil liver, or to have done any wrong to his neighbors by word or deed." By " Canon 40. Of Regulations Respecting the Laity," Section II, " When a person to whom the Sacraments of the Church have been refused, or who has been repelled from the Holy Communion under the Rubrics, shall lodge a complaint with the Bishop, it shall be the duty of the Bishop, unless he see fit to require the person to be admitted or restored because of the insufficiency of the cause assigned by the Minister, to institute such an inquiry as may be directed by the Canons of the Diocese or Missionary District, and should no such Canon exist, the Bishop shall proceed according to such principles of law and equity as will insure an impartial decision, but no Minister of this Church shall be required to admit to the Sacraments a person so refused or repelled, without the written direction of the Bishop."

The plaintiff has not availed herself of this right of appeal to the only personage having the requisite ecclesiastical authority to review her standing as a member and communicant or to pass upon her ceremonial rights in accordance with the principles of " law and equity." Grosvenor *v.* United Society of Believers, 118 Mass. 78, 91. The letter of her counsel to the bishop, to which no reply appears to have been made, cannot be considered as an appeal which had been denied. It contains only recitals of all her grievances, for the rectification of which his friendly intercession is requested.

[1] Only part of the opinion is given.

But if an appeal had been taken properly and the decision had been adverse, the plaintiff would have been remediless, for in this Commonwealth her religious rights as a communicant are not enforceable in the civil courts. Fitzgerald *v.* Robinson, 112 Mass. 371, 379. Canadian Religious Association *v.* Parmenter, 180 Mass. 415, 420, 421. For the same reason it is unnecessary to decide whether at common law, as the plaintiff contends, a member of the Church of England could sue if unjustifiably denied participation in the communion. See Rex *v.* Dibdin, [1910] P. D. 57; Thompson *v.* Dibdin, [1912] A. C. 533.

Nor can the action be maintained for defamation. Undoubtedly she suffered mental distress, and the omission was in the presence of the other communicants. The plaintiff, however, was not publicly declared to be "an open and notorious evil liver," or to be a person who had done wrong to her neighbors by word or deed. The act of "passing her by" without comment was within the discipline or ecclesiastical polity of the church and does not constitute actionable defamation of character. Farnsworth *v.* Storrs, 5 Cush. 412, 415. Fitzgerald *v.* Robinson, 112 Mass. 371. Morasse *v.* Brochu, 151 Mass. 567. See R. L. c. 36, §§ 2, 3.

The action for exclusion from the church building also must fail. It appears that upon being informed by the constable employed for the purpose that she could not enter the plaintiff made no attempt to pass, but acquiesced and obeyed the order. The elements of an assault are absent. No intimidation was used, or unjustifiable coercion exercised. By Canon 16, to which the plaintiff subjected herself, control of the worship and spiritual jurisdiction of the mission, including the use of the building for religious services, was in Papineau as the minister in charge, "subject to the authority of the Bishop." [1]

PULLMAN *v.* WALTER HILL & COMPANY

IN THE COURT OF APPEAL, DECEMBER 19, 1890.

Reported in [1891] 1 *Queen's Bench*, 524.

MOTION by the plaintiffs for a new trial.

At the trial before Day, J., with a jury, it appeared that the plaintiffs were members of a partnership firm of R. & J. Pullman, in which there were three other partners. The place of business of the firm was No. 17, Greek Street, Soho. The plaintiffs were the owners of some property in the Borough Road, which they had contracted in 1887 to sell to Messrs. Day & Martin. The plaintiffs remained in possession of the property for some time, and agreed to let a hoarding, which was erected upon the property, at a rent to the defendants, who

[1] *Criticism of member of congregation in a sermon.* Hassett *v.* Carroll, 85 Conn. 23. *Statement by clergyman to congregation as to conduct of a trustee.* Everett *v.* DeLong, 144 Ill. App. 496.

were advertising agents, for the display of advertisements. In 1889 a dispute arose between the plaintiffs and Day & Martin, who were building upon the land, as to which of the two were entitled to the rent of the hoarding; and on September 14, 1889, the defendants, after some prior correspondence, wrote the following letter: —

"Messrs. Pullman & Co., 17, Greek Street, Soho.
"*Re* Boro' Road.

"Dear Sirs, — We must call your serious attention to this matter. The builders state distinctly that you had no right to this money whatever; consequently it has been obtained from us under false pretences. We await your reply by return of post.

"Yours faithfully,
" (Signed) Walter Hill & Co., Limited."

This letter was dictated by the defendants' managing director to a short-hand clerk, who transcribed it by a type-writing machine. This type-written letter was then signed by the managing director, and, having been press-copied by an office-boy, was sent by post in an envelope addressed to Messrs. Pullman & Co., 17, Greek Street, Soho. The defendants did not know that there were any other partners in the firm besides the plaintiffs. The letter was opened by a clerk of the firm in the ordinary course of business, and was read by two other clerks. The plaintiffs brought this action for libel. The defendants contended that there was no publication, and that, if there were, the occasion was privileged. The learned judge held that there was no publication, that the occasion was privileged, and that there was no evidence of malice. He therefore nonsuited the plaintiffs.[1]

LORD ESHER, M. R. Two points were decided by the learned judge: (1) that there had been no publication of the letter which is alleged to be a libel; (2) that, if there had been publication, the occasion was privileged. The question whether the letter is or is not a libel is for the jury, if it is capable of being considered an imputation on the character of the plaintiffs. If there is a new trial, it will be open to the jury to consider whether there is a libel, and what the damages are. The learned judge withdrew the case from the jury.

The first question is, whether, assuming the letter to contain defamatory matter, there has been a publication of it. What is the meaning of "publication"? The making known the defamatory matter after it has been written to some person other than the person of whom it is written. If the statement is sent straight to the person of whom it is written, there is no publication of it; for you cannot publish a libel of a man to himself. If there was no publication, the question whether the occasion was privileged does not arise. If a letter is not communicated to any one but the person to whom it is written,

[1] The arguments of counsel and the concurring opinions of Lopes and Kay, L.JJ., are omitted.

there is no publication of it. And, if the writer of a letter locks it up in his own desk, and a thief comes and breaks open the desk and takes away the letter and makes its contents known, I should say that would not be a publication. If the writer of a letter shows it to his own clerk in order that the clerk may copy it for him, is that a publication of the letter? Certainly it is showing it to a third person; the writer cannot say to the person to whom the letter is addressed, "I have shown it to you and to no one else." I cannot, therefore, feel any doubt that, if the writer of a letter shows it to any person other than the person to whom it is written, he publishes it. If he wishes not to publish it, he must, so far as he possibly can, keep it to himself, or he must send it himself straight to the person to whom it is written. There was, therefore, in this case a publication to the type-writer.

Then arises the question of privilege, and that is, whether the occasion on which the letter was published was a privileged occasion. An occasion is privileged when the person who makes the communication has a moral duty to make it to the person to whom he does make it, and the person who receives it has an interest in hearing it. Both these conditions must exist in order that the occasion may be privileged. An ordinary instance of a privileged occasion is in the giving a character of a servant. It is not the legal duty of the master to give a character to the servant, but it is his moral duty to do so; and the person who receives the character has an interest in having it. Therefore, the occasion is privileged, because the one person has a duty and the other has an interest. The privilege exists as against the person who is libelled; it is not a question of privilege as between the person who makes and the person who receives the communication; the privilege is as against the person who is libelled. Can the communication of the libel by the defendants in the present case to the type-writer be brought within the rule of privilege as against the plaintiffs — the persons libelled? What interest had the type-writer in hearing or seeing the communication? Clearly, she had none. Therefore, the case does not fall within the rule.

Then again, as to the publication at the other end — I mean when the letter was delivered. The letter was not directed to the plaintiffs in their individual capacity; it was directed to a firm of which they were members. The senders of the letter no doubt believed that it would go to the plaintiffs; but it was directed to a firm. When the letter arrived it was opened by a clerk in the employment of the plaintiffs' firm, and was seen by three of the clerks in their office. If the letter had been directed to the plaintiffs in their private capacity, in all probability it would not have been opened by a clerk. But mercantile firms and large tradesmen generally depute some clerk to open business letters addressed to them. The sender of the letter had put it out of his own control, and he had directed it in such a manner that it might possibly be opened by a clerk of the firm to which it was addressed. I agree that under such circumstances there was a publication of the letter by the sender of it, and in this case also the occasion was not privileged for the same reasons as in the former case. There were, therefore, two publications of the letter, and neither of them was privileged. And, there being no privilege, no evidence of express malice was required; the publication of itself implied malice. I think the learned judge was misled. I do not think that the necessities or the luxuries of business can alter the law of England. If a merchant wishes to write a letter containing defamatory matter, and to keep a copy of the letter, he had better make the copy himself. If a company have deputed a person to write a letter containing libellous matter on their behalf, they will be liable for his acts. He ought to write such a letter himself, and to copy it himself, and, if he copies it into a book, he ought to keep the book in his own custody.[1]

I think there ought to be a new trial. *Order for new trial.*

STEVENS v. SAMPSON

In the Court of Appeal, November 15, 1879.

Reported in 5 *Exchequer Division Reports*, 53.

Claim for falsely and maliciously printing and publishing of the plaintiff certain words in certain newspapers. The libel set out in the claim was a report, published by the defendant, of certain proceedings in a plaint of Nettlefold v. Fulcher, tried at the Marylebone county court, and brought to recover damages and costs sustained by Nettlefold in setting aside certain proceedings instituted by Fulcher against Nettlefold to recover the possession of certain premises. It alleged that at the county court the defendant in the present action appeared for Nettlefold, and made statements regarding the conduct of the

[1] Bohlinger v. Germania Ins. Co., 100 Ark. 477; Gambrill v. Schooley, 93 Md. 48 *Accord.* See Central R. Co. v. Jones, 18 Ga. App. 414. But the dictation of a defamatory letter by a lawyer to his clerk and the copying of it by another clerk in the regular course of serving his clients, although a publication, is, nevertheless, privileged. Boxsius v. Goblet, [1894] 1 Q. B. 842. And the authority of Pullman v. Hill is greatly weakened by Edmonson v. Birch, [1907] 1 K. B. 371, which treats as privileged the dictation of a defamatory letter by a company through one of its officers to a stenographer, and Roff v. British Chemical Co., [1918] 2 K. B. 277 (letter passed through the hands of two clerks of addressee). See to the same effect Owen v. Ogilvie Co., 32 App. Div. 465.

Exchange of letters by mistake whereby privileged letter goes to wrong person. See Tompson v. Dashwood, 11 Q. B. D. 43; Hebditch v. McIlwaine, [1894] 2 Q. B. 54, 61.

A defamatory statement true of A. but published concerning B., by mistake, will support an action by B. Shepheard v. Whitaker, L. R. 10 C. P. 502; Taylor v. Hearst, 107 Cal. 262; Griebel v. Rochester Co., 60 Hun, 319. But see, *contra*, Hanson v. Globe Co., *supra*, 665 (Holmes, Morton, and Barker, JJ., dissenting).

Compare Brett v. Watson, 20 W. R. 723; Fox v. Broderick, 14 Ir. C. L. R. 453, 459; Loibl v. Breidenbach, 78 Wis, 49.

plaintiff in the present action, who was a debt collector and employed by Fulcher as agent to recover possession of the premises.

Statement of defence: That the words alleged to have been published were a true and correct account and report of a certain trial in a court of justice having jurisdiction in that behalf, and of certain words spoken during the sitting of the court in the course of the trial, and published for the public benefit, and without malice. Issue thereon.

At the trial before Cockburn, C. J., at the Hilary Sittings, 1879, at Westminster, it was proved that the defendant, who was a solicitor, had sent the report set out in the claim of the trial of Nettlefold *v.* Fulcher, before the Judge of the Marylebone county court, to the local newspapers. Cockburn, C. J., left two questions to the jury: 1. Was the report a fair one? 2. Was it sent honestly, or with a desire to injure the plaintiff? The jury answered these questions: 1. That it was in substance a fair report; 2. That it was sent with a certain amount of malice; and found a verdict for the plaintiff with 40*s.* damages. Cockburn, C. J., directed judgment to be entered for the plaintiff for that amount.

The defendant appealed on the ground that the judgment entered upon the findings of the jury was wrong.

LORD COLERIDGE, C. J.[1] The question before us is whether, on the findings of the jury, the entry of the judgment for the plaintiff is right. I am of opinion that it was rightly entered for the plaintiff. The principle which governs this case is plain. It is like that which governs most other cases of privilege. In order, in cases of libel, to establish that the communication is privileged, two elements must exist: not only must the occasion create the privilege, but the occasion must be made use of *bona fide* and without malice; if either of these is absent, the privilege does not attach; here the second element is absent, for *bona fides* is wanting, and malice exists. There are certain cases in which the privilege is absolute. Words spoken in the course of a legal proceeding by a witness or by counsel, and words used in an affidavit in the course of a legal proceeding, are absolutely privileged. It is considered advantageous for the public interests that such persons should not in any way be fettered in their statements. This is the first time that a report of proceedings in a court of justice has been sought to be brought within this same class of privilege. I am not disposed to extend the bounds of privilege beyond the principles already laid down, and I find no authority for its extension.

Judgment affirmed.[2]

[1] The concurring opinions of Bramwell and Brett, L.JJ., and the argument for defendant are omitted.

[2] Salmon *v.* Isaac, 20 L. T. Rep. 885; Lawyers Pub. Co. *v.* West Pub. Co., 32 App. Div. 585; Saunders *v.* Baxter, 6 Heisk. 369 *Accord.*

CLARK *v.* MOLYNEUX

IN THE COURT OF APPEAL, DECEMBER 4, 1877.

Reported in 47 *Law Journal Reports, Common Law,* 230.[1]

THE action was for slander and libel. The plaintiff, a clergyman of the Church of England, had been formerly in the army, but left it in the year 1863; and, after taking his degree at Cambridge, was ordained by the Bishop of Exeter, and subsequently became curate at Assington, to the Rev. H. L. Maud.

In March, 1876, the defendant, the Rev. Canon Molyneux, the Rector of Sudbury, which is in the neighborhood of Assington, when calling on a Mr. G. Bevan, a banker, with whom he had been intimate for twenty-four years, was informed by Mr. Bevan that the plaintiff was going to preach one of a course of Lenten sermons at Newton Church, in the neighborhood, and that he was sure that if Mr. Charles Smith, the rector, knew what sort of a person the plaintiff was, he would never permit him to preach in his church. Mr. Bevan then desired the defendant, as an old friend of Mr. Smith's, to let him know what the plaintiff's character was. In answer to the defendant's inquiry as to what was the nature of the charges against the plaintiff, Mr. Bevan said that he had been obliged to leave the army through cheating with cards, had lived an irregular life at Cambridge, had been guilty of gross immorality when curate at Horringer, and had boasted of it. The defendant, placing implicit reliance on Mr. Bevan, and thinking that it was his duty to acquaint Mr. Charles Smith with the matter, at once rode to his house, and, finding that he was ill in bed, communicated his information to the Rev. H. Smith, his son, who was in the house.

At the end of the same month the defendant consulted the Rev. J. C. Martyn, his rural dean, as to whether he should not speak to Mr. Maud, the plaintiff's rector. Mr. Martyn said he thought the defendant ought to do so. As Mr. Maud was abroad, the defendant spoke to his solicitor on the subject; and on Mr. Maud's return he received a letter from him, asking for information. The defendant wrote an answer detailing the facts substantially as communicated to him by Mr. Bevan; but some of the expressions in the letter were stronger than those used by Mr. Bevan. "Profligate" was used instead of "irregular," and "expelled the army," instead of "obliged to leave the army."

The defendant also consulted Mr. Green, his curate, who was announced to preach one of the same course of sermons as the plaintiff. Mr. Green had been with the plaintiff for twenty years, and was consulted by him on every ecclesiastical matter that came before him.

[1] 3 Q. B. Div. 237, s. c.

The communications made to Mr. Green, Mr. H. Smith and Mr. Martyn were the slanders complained of, and the letter to Mr. Maud was the libel.

The defendant relied solely on the privilege of the occasions and the *bona fides* of his statements.

The action was tried before Baron Huddleston and a special jury at Bury St. Edmunds, at the Summer Assizes, 1876.

The learned judge ruled that all the occasions were privileged, and the case went to the jury on the question of express malice.

In the course of his summing up the learned judge said: "Now in law if a man says what is not true, or writes what is libellous, or says what is slanderous of another, it is presumed that it is malicious. But where the occasion is privileged, then you require something more, and you require what the law calls express malice. I must tell you what express malice means."

And again, at the close of the summing up: —

"What you have to consider, then, is really and substantially this — assuming that these occasions were privileged, do you think that the defendant made those statements and wrote that letter *bona fide*, and in the honest belief that they were true — not merely that he believed them himself, but honestly believed them, which means that he had good grounds for believing them to be true. I do not mean to say pig-headedly, pertinaciously and obstinately perhaps persuaded himself of the matter for which he had no reasonable grounds, and of which you twelve gentlemen would say they were perfectly unjustified. If you think that under these circumstances Mr. Molyneux has taken himself out of the privilege in consequence of the statements not being made *bona fide* and in the honest belief they were true, and that therefore there is what in law is called malice in fact, which I have explained to you, then your verdict will be for the plaintiff." [1]

The jury found a verdict for the plaintiff, with £200 damages.

These passages and the general tenor of the summing up, which was to the same effect, constituted the misdirection complained of.

The defendant moved for a new trial in the Queen's Bench Division, on the ground of misdirection, and that the verdict was against evidence; but the court refused the rule. The defendant appealed.

Brett, L. J. I am of the same opinion; I think that there was, what amounts in law to a misdirection; that the verdict was against the evidence; and, further, that there was no evidence to go to the jury.

With regard to the alleged misdirection, I do not think that we differ from the Queen's Bench Division in our view of the law, but I think that, whatever the idea Baron Huddleston intended to convey to the jury in his careful, elaborate, and, if I may say so, able summing up,

[1] The charge of the learned baron is abridged; the arguments of counsel and the concurring opinions of Bramwell and Cotton, L.JJ., are omitted.

really was, it may have materially misled them, and if it may, that is in law a misdirection.

The summing up is founded on the assumption that the occasions of the alleged slanders and libel were privileged, and that the defendant was therefore excused in that which would otherwise have been actionable, if he used the occasions fairly. Now it is right before criticising the summing up of the learned judge to state, as clearly as one can, what the law relating to excuse by reason of privilege in cases of libel and slander really is. It is, I apprehend, this: When a defendant claims that the occasion of a libel or slander is privileged, and when it is held by the judge, whose duty it is to decide the matter, that the occasion is privileged, the question arises, — under what conditions can the defendant take advantage of the privilege ? If the occasion is privileged, it is so for some reason, and the defendant is entitled to the protection of the privilege if he uses the occasion for that reason, but not otherwise. If he uses the occasion for an indirect reason or motive, he uses it, not for the reason which makes it privileged, but for another. One, but by no means the only, indirect motive which can be alleged, is the gratification of some anger or malice of his own. By malice here I mean, not a pleading expression, but actual malice, or what is termed malice in fact, *i. e.*, a wrong feeling in the defendant's mind. If this malice be the indirect and wrong motive suggested in a particular case, there are certain tests by which its existence may be investigated. Two such tests are these: If a man is proved to have stated what he knew to be false, no one inquires further, everybody assumes thenceforth that he was malicious, that he did so wrong a thing from some wrong motive. Again, if it be proved that out of anger or from some other wrong motive the defendant has stated something as a truth or as true, without knowing or inquiring whether it was true or not, therefore reckless, by reason of his anger or other motive, whether it is true or not, the jury may infer, and generally will infer, that he used the occasion for the gratification of his anger or malice, or other indirect motive, and not for the reason or motive which occasions or justifies the privilege.

These tests have been suggested before, and they were approved by the whole Court of Common Pleas in a case tried before me at Leeds, and I apprehend they are correct.

That being so, I think that Baron Huddleston did not follow these rules and tests, but others. Take his summing up as a whole, as I think we ought, he left the case as if the burden of proving there was no malice lay on the defendant, but if the occasion be privileged, the *onus* of showing malice is at once thrown on the plaintiff. Further, in order to guide the jury as to what malice was, he read the passage in Bromage *v.* Prosser; what he read there is not a definition of malice in fact, at all, but of that malice which is a technical term in certain pleadings, where it simply means " wilfully." It has been held, that in such pleadings the absence of the word maliciously is immaterial if the word wilfully is present — because they are in such pleadings synonymous terms. Then, I think the passage at the end of the summing up is really a recapitulation of the sense of the whole summing up, and might lead the jury to believe that, although they were of opinion that the defendant did believe what he stated, he would not be protected unless his belief was a reasonable one, as distinguished from a pig-headed, obstinate, and insensible one. But the real question, as I have stated, is, whether the defendant did, in fact, believe his statement,[1] or whether being angry or moved by some other indirect motive, did not know, and did not care, whether his statement was true or false. Questions of pig-headedness and obstinacy may be tests as to whether a man really did honestly believe or not, but Baron Huddleston left them as if they were of the essence of the definition of malice.

The direction was therefore wrong if the occasions were privileged. That they were I have a very strong opinion. The only occasion disputed is that of the communication to Mr. Green the curate. I am clearly of opinion that that was privileged. I think that where a clergyman consults his curate as to his conduct in an ecclesiastical matter, the occasion is a privileged one.

As to the other points, I think that at least the verdict was against the evidence. But I think more, I think there was no evidence fit to be submitted to a jury, and, therefore, if on a new trial the facts remain the same, the judge's duty will be to direct the jury that there is no case. In this matter, therefore, there has been a miscarriage. But I think that the case is not one in which to apply Order XL., rule 10, and enter the verdict for the defendant, as it does not follow that on a new trial further evidence may not be forthcoming.

Appeal allowed.

CARPENTER v. BAILEY

SUPREME COURT, NEW HAMPSHIRE, DECEMBER, 1873.

Reported in 53 *New Hampshire Reports*, 590.

THIS is an action on the case for a libel, by J. N. Carpenter against J. H. Bailey, the writ bearing date September 21, 1869.[2] The declaration alleges, that, on April 20, 1869, the plaintiff was a paymaster in the navy, stationed as purchasing agent at Portsmouth; that, by the rules of the navy department, he was entitled to remain on that station three years; and that the defendant, contriving, &c., published of him the following libel: " To the Honorable the Senators and Members of

[1] Barry v. McCollom, 81 Conn. 293; Bays v. Hunt, 60 Ia. 251, 255–6; Hemmens v. Nelson, 138 N. Y. 517; Haft v. First Bank, 19 App. Div. 423 *Accord.*

[2] The case is materially abridged.

the House of Representatives in Congress from New Hampshire: The undersigned, after much patience has been exhausted, beg to remonstrate against the further continuance at this station of Paymaster J. N. Carpenter as purchasing agent. In all our struggles, Paymaster Carpenter has always voted against us, carrying the straight Democratic ticket, throwing his patronage adversely to the friends of General Grant, and always filling the requirements of a tool sent here by ex-Secretary Welles to carry out the interests of Andrew Johnson. May we hope for relief from such a burden? Let the rebel sympathizer be exchanged for a man who will have office hours of a convenient kind, and will be found there *at least once a day* to attend to those having business there, and officers and citizens will alike be grateful. Portsmouth, N. H., April 20, 1869. E. G. Peirce, Jr., Chas. Robinson, Aaron Young, Daniel J. Vaughan, E. A. Stevens, W. H. Hackett, John H. Bailey, Paine Durkee."

The defendant pleaded in substance that he was informed and believed that the plaintiff had done the things charged in the petition and that he believed that "the public good, and the welfare of said administration of General Grant, required that the said plaintiff should be removed from said office at said station, and that a suitable officer should be put there in his stead, and that the senators and members of the House of Representatives in Congress from the State of New Hampshire were the proper persons and officers to be petitioned in order to procure the removal of the said plaintiff from said office at said naval station, the defendant, in good faith, and without malice or ill-will to the said plaintiff, but in order to procure the removal of the plaintiff for the causes aforesaid from the said office, signed said petition to said senators and representatives containing said supposed libellous words in the plaintiff's declaration mentioned, as he lawfully might have done, for the cause aforesaid, and this he is ready to verify." Wherefore, &c.

To this plea the plaintiff demurred generally.

Sargent, C. J. If the defendant cannot justify by showing the truth of the matter charged, he may excuse the publication by showing that it was made upon a lawful occasion, upon probable cause, and from good motives.

It is also said that matter in excuse in a prosecution for libel is where the defendant, upon a lawful occasion, proceeded with good motives upon probable grounds, — that is, upon reasons that were apparently good, but upon a supposition which turns out to be unfounded. This is a very different thing from showing the actual truth of the allegations: where that is proved with a proper occasion, it is a justification without regard to motives; but where the statements made prove false, the defendant needs to show not only a proper occasion, but a good motive also, — for, if the matter be untrue and the motive bad, how could the end be justified or even excused? But when the occasion is proper, one may be excused for stating what proves to be untrue, if he had probable cause to believe it true, and spoke it from good motives; see authorities, 9 N. H. 45.

So, in Palmer *v.* Concord, 48 N. H. 217, it is said, by Smith, J., that most of what are called "privileged communications" are conditionally, not absolutely, privileged. The question is one of good faith, or motive, and can be settled only by a jury. A court cannot rule that a communication is privileged, without assuming the conditions on which it is held to be privileged, namely, that it was made in good faith, for a justifiable purpose, and with a belief, founded on reasonable grounds, of its truth; — and see cases cited.

In the case before us, the occasion would be a lawful one, provided the motive was good, and there was probable cause. And the question is, whether the mere fact, that the defendant had been informed and believed that a fact was so, is equivalent to having probable cause to believe it to be so. And we think it could not be assumed that it was so. A person might be informed of a fact by one in whom he might, for some special reason, have confidence, but to whom no one else would give the slightest credence; and a jury would readily find that a belief in that case was founded upon information which would not amount to probable cause for the belief of any man of ordinary capacity. The question for the jury would be, not whether the defendant believed it, but had he probable cause to believe it? There might be belief without probable cause for it; and hence it would not be sufficient to allege merely information and belief, because that might not, in a given case, amount to probable cause. The fourth plea is substantially correct in form, and goes as far as the rule thus laid down will warrant; and we think this third plea is insufficient.

Demurrer sustained.[1]

[1] Ranson *v.* West, 125 Ky. 457 (*semble*); Toothaker *v.* Conant, 91 Me. 438; Briggs *v.* Garrett, 111 Pa. St. 404; Conroy *v.* Pittsburgh Times, 139 Pa. St. 334; Mulderig *v.* Wilkes Barre Times, 215 Pa. St. 470; Egan *v.* Dotson, 36 S. D. 459 *Accord.*

See also, Douglass *v.* Daisley, 114 Fed. 628.

Compare Glisson *v.* Biggio, 139 La. 23; Estelle *v.* Daily News Pub. Co., 99 Neb. 397; Wiese *v.* Riley, 146 Wis. 640.

Petition or memorial for removal of public officer privileged. Blake *v.* Pilfold, 1 M. & Rob. 198; Woodward *v.* Lander, 6 Car. & P. 548; James *v.* Boston, 2 Car. & K. 4; Spackman *v.* Gibney, Odgers, Lib. & Sl. (5th ed.) 278; Beatson *v.* Skene, 5 H. & N. 838; Harrison *v.* Bush, 5 E. & B. 344; Hart *v.* Von Gumpach, L. R. 4 P. C. 439; Stanton *v.* Andrews, 5 Up. Can. Q. B. O. S. 211; Corbett *v.* Jackson, 1 Up. Can. Q. B. 128; Rogers *v.* Spalding, 1 Up. Can. Q. B. 258; McIntire *v.* McBean, 13 Up. Can. Q. B. 534; Bell *v.* Parke, 10 Ir. C. L. R. 279 (*semble*); White *v.* Nichols, 3 How. 266; Vogel *v.* Gruaz, 110 U. S. 311; Pearce *v.* Brower, 72 Ga. 243; Young *v.* Richardson, 4 Ill. App. 364; Rainbow *v.* Benson, 71 Ia. 301; Rabb *v.* Trevelyan, 122 La. 174; Bodwell *v.* Osgood, 3 Pick. 379; Wieman *v.* Mabee, 45 Mich. 484; Greenwood *v.* Cobbey, 26 Neb. 449; State *v.* Burnham, 9 N. H. 34; Thorn *v.* Blanchard, 5 Johns. 508; Vanderzee *v.* McGregor, 12 Wend. 545; Howard *v.* Thompson, 21 Wend. 319; Halstead *v.* Nelson, 24 Hun, 395; Decker *v.* Gaylord, 35 Hun, 584; Woods *v.* Wiman, 122 N. Y. 445, 47 Hun, 362; Cook *v.* Hill, 3 Sandf. 341; Van Wyck *v.* Aspinwall, 17 N. Y. 190; Harwood *v.* Keech, 6 Th. & C. 665; Logan *v.* Hodges, 146 N. C. 38; Gray *v.* Pentland, 2 S. & R. 23;

CAMPBELL v. SPOTTISWOODE

In the Queen's Bench, April 18, 1863.

Reported in 3 Best & Smith, 769.

Cockburn, C. J.[1] I am of opinion that there ought to be no rule. The article on which this action is brought is undoubtedly libellous. It imputes to the plaintiff that, in putting forth to the public the sacred cause of the dissemination of religious truth among the heathen, he was acting as an impostor, and that his purpose was to put money into his own pocket by obtaining contributions to his newspaper. The article also charges that, in furtherance of that base and sordid purpose, he published in his newspaper the name of a fictitious person as the authority for his statements, and still further that, with a view to induce persons to contribute towards his professed cause, he published a fictitious subscription list. These are serious imputations upon the plaintiff's moral as well as public character.

It is said, on behalf of the defendant, that, as the plaintiff addressed himself to the public in a matter, not only of public, but of universal interest, his conduct in that matter was open to public criticism, and I entirely concur in that proposition. If the proposed scheme were defective, or utterly disproportionate to the result aimed at, it might be assailed with hostile critisicm. But then a line must be drawn between criticism upon public conduct and the imputation of motives by which that conduct may be supposed to be actuated; one man has no right to impute to another, whose conduct may be fairly open to ridicule or disapprobation, base, sordid, and wicked motives, unless there is so much ground for the imputation that a jury shall find, not only that he had an honest belief in the truth of his statements, but that his belief was not without foundation.

In the present case, the charges made against the plaintiff were unquestionably without foundation. It may be that, in addition to the motive of religious zeal, the plaintiff was not wholly insensible to the collateral object of promoting the circulation of his newspaper, but there was no evidence that he had resorted to false devices to induce persons to contribute to his scheme. That being so, Mr. Bovill is obliged to say that, because the writer of this article had a *bona fide* belief that the statements he made were true, he was privileged. I cannot assent to that doctrine. It was competent to the writer to have attacked the plaintiff's scheme; and perhaps he might have suggested, that the effect of the subscriptions which the plaintiff was asking the public to contribute would be only to put money into his pocket. But to say that he was actuated only by the desire of putting money into his pocket, and that he resorted to fraudulent expedients for that purpose, is charging him with dishonesty: and that is going further than the law allows.

Kent v. Bongartz, 15 R. I. 72; Reid v. Delorme, 2 Brev. 76; Harris v. Huntington, 2 Tyler, 129 *Accord.*

But not absolutely privileged, where the proceeding is not judicial. Dickson v. Wilton, 1 F. & F. 419; Proctor v. Webster, 16 Q. B. D. 112; Woods v. Wiman, 122 N. Y. 445; Morah v. Steele, 157 App. Div. 109; Fulton v. Ingalls, 165 App. Div. 323.

Compare McKee v. Hughes, 133 Tenn. 455 (petition to revoke merchant's license).

[1] The statement of the case, the arguments of counsel, the judgment of Mellor, J., and portions of the judgments of Crompton and Blackburn, JJ., are omitted.

It is said that it is for the interests of society that the public conduct of men should be criticised without any other limit than that the writer should have an honest belief that what he writes is true. But it seems to me that the public have an equal interest in the maintenance of the public character of public men; and public affairs could not be conducted by men of honor with a view to the welfare of the country, if we were to sanction attacks upon them, destructive of their honor and character, and made without any foundation. I think the fair position in which the law may be settled is this: that where the public conduct of a public man is open to animadversion, and the writer who is commenting upon it makes imputations on his motives which arise fairly and legitimately out of his conduct so that a jury shall say that the criticism was not only honest, but also well founded, an action is not maintainable.[1] But it is not because a public writer fancies that the conduct of a public man is open to the suspicion of dishonesty, he is therefore justified in assailing his character as dishonest.[2]

The cases cited do not warrant us in going that length. In Paris *v.* Levy, 2 F. & F. 71, there may have been an honest and well-founded belief that the man who published the handbill which was commented upon could only have had a bad motive in publishing it, and if the jury were of that opinion, the writer who attacked him in the public press would be protected. We cannot go farther than that.

Crompton, J. I am of the same opinion. . . . The first question is, whether the article on which this action is brought is a libel or no libel, — not whether it is privileged or not. It is no libel, if it is within the range of fair comment, that is, if a person might fairly and *bona fide* write the article; otherwise it is. It is said that there is a privilege, not to writers in newspapers only but to the public in general, to comment on the public acts of public men, provided the writer believes that what he writes is true; in other words, that this belongs to the class of privileged communications, in which the malice of the writer becomes a question for the jury; that is, where, from the particular circumstances or position in which a person is placed, there is a legal or social duty in the nature of a private or peculiar right, as opposed to the rights possessed by the community at large, to assert what he believes. In these cases of privilege there is an exemption from legal liability in the absence of malice; and it is necessary to prove actual malice. But there is no such privilege here. It is the right of all the Queen's subjects to discuss public matters; but no person can have a right on that ground to publish what is defamatory merely because he believes it to be true. If this were so, a public man might have base motives imputed to him without having an opportunity of righting himself.

[1] Hibbs *v.* Wilkinson, 1 F. & F. 608; Turnbull *v.* Bird, 2 F. & F. 508; Hunter *v.* Sharpe, 4 F. & F. 983; Hunt *v.* Star Co., [1908] 2 K. B. 309; Walker *v.* Hodgson, [1909] 1 K. B. 239, 253; De Mestre *v.* Syme, 9 Vict. L. R. (L) 10; Davis *v.* Duncan, L. R. 9 C. P. 396; Queen *v.* Carden, 5 Q. B. D. 1, 8; Crane *v.* Waters, 10 Fed. 619; Kinyon *v.* Palmer, 18 Ia. 377; Bradford *v.* Clark, 90 Me. 298; People *v.* Glassman, 12 Utah, 238 *Accord.*

[2] Stuart *v.* Lovell, 2 Stark. 93; Macleod *v.* Wakley, 3 Car. & P. 311; Green *v.* Chapman, 4 Bing. N. C. 92; Parmiter *v.* Coupland, 6 M. & W. 105; Whistler *v.* Ruskin, Odgers, Lib. & Sl., (5th ed.) 196; Wilson *v.* Reed, 2 F. & F. 149; Morrison *v.* Belcher, 3 F. & F. 614; Hedley *v.* Barlow, 4 F. & F. 224; Risk Allah Bey *v.* Whitehurst, 18 L. T. Rep. 615; Joynt *v.* Cycle Co., [1904] 2 K. B. 292; Massie *v.* Toronto Co., 11 Ont. 362; Burt *v.* Advertiser Co., 154 Mass. 238; Cooper *v.* Stone, 24 Wend. 434; Reade *v.* Sweetzer, 6 Abb. Pr. N. S. 9, n.; Ullrich *v.* N. Y. Co., 23 Misc. 168 *Accord.*

Therefore it is necessary to confine privilege, as the law has always confined it, to cases of real necessity or duty, as that of a master giving a servant a character, or of a person who had been robbed charging another with robbing him. Though the word " privilege " is used loosely in some of the cases as applied to the right which every person has to comment on public matters, I think that in all the cases cited the real question was whether the alleged libel was a fair comment such as every person might make upon a public matter, and if not, there was no privilege.

BLACKBURN, J. I also think that the law governing this case is so clearly settled that we ought not to grant a rule. It is important to bear in mind that the question is, not whether the publication is privileged, but whether it is a libel. The word " privilege " is often used loosely, and in a popular sense, when applied to matters which are not, properly speaking, privileged. But, for the present purpose, the meaning of the word is that a person stands in such a relation to the facts of the case that he is justified in saying or writing what would be slanderous or libellous in any one else. For instance, a master giving a character of a servant stands in a privileged relation; and the cases of a memorial to the Lord Chancellor or the Home Secretary on the conduct of a justice of the peace, Harrison *v.* Bush, and of a statement to a public functionary, reflecting upon some public officer, Beatson *v.* Skene, 5 H. & N. 538, rank themselves under that class. In these cases no action lies unless there is proof of express malice. If it could be shown that the editor or publisher of a newspaper stands in a privileged position, it would be necessary to prove actual malice. But no authority has been cited for that proposition;[1] and I take it to be certain that he has only the general right which belongs to the public to comment upon public matters, for example, the acts of a minister of state; or, according to modern authorities somewhat extending the doctrine, where a person has done or published anything which may fairly be said to invite comment, as in the case of a handbill or advertisement; Paris *v.* Levy, 2 F. & F. 71. In such cases every one has a right to make fair and proper comment; and, so long as it is within that limit, it is no libel.

The question of libel or no libel, at least since Fox's Act (32 G. 3, c. 60), is for the jury; and in the present case, as the article published by the defendant obviously imputed base and sordid motives to the plaintiff, that question depended upon another, — whether the article exceeded the limits of a fair and proper comment on the plaintiff's prospectus; and this last question was therefore rightly left to the jury. Then Mr. Bovill asked that a further question should be left to them, viz., whether the writer of the article honestly believed that it was true; and the jury have found that he did. We have to say whether that prevents an action being maintained. I think not. *Bona fide* belief in the truth of what is written is no defence to an action; it may mitigate the amount, but it cannot disentitle the plaintiff to damages.

Rule refused.[2]

[1] See *contra,* Williams *v.* Spowers, 8 Vict. L. R. (Law) 82.

[2] Honest belief is no defense apart from privilege. Van Wiginton *v.* Pulitzer Pub. Co., (C. C. A.) 218 Fed. 483; Brandt *v.* Story, 161 Ia. 451; Tanner *v.* Stevenson, 138 Ky. 578; Reid *v.* Nichols, 166 Ky. 423; Sweet *v.* Post Pub. Co., 215 Mass. 450; Clair *v.* Battle Creek Journal Co., 168 Mich. 467; Ivie *v.* King, 167 N. C. 174; Spencer *v.* Minnick, 41 Okl. 613; Williams *v.* Hicks Printing Co., 159 Wis. 90

Fair comment on public affairs and public officers. See Gandia *v.* Pettingill, 222 U. S. 452; Lowe *v.* News Pub. Co., 9 Ga. App. 103; Diener *v.* Star Chronicle Pub.

CARR v. HOOD

BEFORE LORD ELLENBOROUGH, C. J., LONDON SITTINGS AFTER TRINITY TERM, 1808.

Reported in 1 *Campbell,* 355, *n.*

THE declaration stated, that the plaintiff, before the publishing of any of the false, scandalous, malicious, and defamatory libels thereinafter mentioned, was the author of, and had sold for divers large sums of money, the respective copyrights of divers books of him the said Sir John, to wit a certain book entitled "The Stranger in France," a certain other book, entitled "A Northern Summer," a certain other book, entitled "The Stranger in Ireland," &c. which said books had been respectively published in 4to, yet that defendant intending to expose him to, and to bring upon him great contempt, laughter, and ridicule, falsely and maliciously published a certain false, scandalous, malicious, and defamatory libel, in the form of a book, of and concerning the said Sir John, and of and concerning the said books, of which the said Sir John was the author as aforesaid, which same libel was entitled "My Pocket Book, or Hints for a Ryghte Merrie and conceited Tour, in quarto, to be called The Stranger in Ireland in 1805, (thereby alluding to the said book of the said Sir John, thirdly above mentioned,) by a knight errant (thereby alluding to the said Sir John)," and which same libel contained therein a certain false, scandalous, malicious, and defamatory print, of and concerning the said Sir John, and of and concerning the said books of the said Sir John, 1st and 2dly above mentioned, therein called, "Frontispiece," and entitled "The Knight (meaning the said Sir John) leaving Ireland with Regret," and containing and representing in the said print, a certain false, scandalous and malicious, defamatory, and ridiculous representation of the said Sir John, in the form of a man of ludicrous and ridiculous appearance, holding a pocket-handkerchief to his face, and appearing to be weeping, and also containing therein a certain false, malicious, and ridiculous representation of a man of ludicrous and ridiculous appearance, following the said representation of the said Sir John, and representing a man loaded with, and bending under the weight of three large books, one of them having the word "Baltic," printed on the back thereof, &c., and a pocket-handkerchief appearing to be held in one of the hands of the said representation of a man, and the corners thereof appearing to be held or tied together, as if containing something therein, with the printed word "wardrobe" depending there-

Co., 230 Mo. 613; Cook v. Globe Printing Co., 227 Mo. 471; Merrey v. Guardian Pub. Co., 79 N. J. Law, 177; Bingham v. Gaynor, 203 N. Y. 27.

Fair comment on candidates. Walsh v. Pulitzer Pub. Co., 250 Mo. 142; Schull v. Hopkins, 26 S. D. 21; Ingalls v. Morrissey, 154 Wis. 632.

Fair comment on persons seeking public patronage. Ott v. Murphy, 160 Ia. 730.

from, (thereby falsely, scandalously, and maliciously, meaning and intending to represent, for the purpose of rendering the said Sir John ridiculous, and exposing him to laughter, ridicule, and contempt, that one copy of the said 1st mentioned book of the said Sir John, and two copies of the said book of the said Sir John 2dly above mentioned, were so heavy as to cause a man to bend under the weight thereof, and that his the said Sir John's wardrobe was very small, and capable of being contained in a pocket-handkerchief,) and which said libel also contained, &c. &c. The declaration concluded by laying as special damage, that the said Sir John had been prevented and hindered from selling to Sir Richard Philips Knt. for a large sum of money to wit £600, the copyright of a certain book or work of him the said Sir John, of which the said Sir John was the author, containing an account of a tour of him the said Sir John through part of Scotland, which but for the publishing of the said false, scandalous, malicious, and defamatory libels, he the said Sir John would, could, and might have sold to the said Sir Richard Philips for the said last mentioned sum of money, and the same remained wholly unsold and undisposed of, and was greatly depreciated and lessened in value to the said Sir John. — Plea, not guilty.

LORD ELLENBOROUGH, as the trial was proceeding, intimated an opinion, that if the book published by the defendants only ridiculed the plaintiff as an author, the action could not be maintained.

Garrow, for the plaintiff, allowed, that when his client came forward as an author, he subjected himself to the criticism of all who might be disposed to discuss the merits of his works; but that criticism must be fair and liberal; its object ought to be to enlighten the public, and to guard them against the supposed bad tendency of a particular publication presented to them, not to wound the feelings and to ruin the prospects of an individual. If ridicule was employed, it should have some bounds. While a liberty was granted of analyzing literary productions, and pointing out their defects, still he must be considered as a libeller, whose only object was to hold up an author to the laughter and contempt of mankind. A man with a wen upon his neck perhaps could not complain if a surgeon in a scientific work should minutely describe it, and consider its nature and the means of dispersing it; but surely he might support an action for damages against any one who should publish a book to make him ridiculous on account of this infirmity, with a caricature print as a frontispiece. The object of the book published by the defendants clearly was, by means of immoderate ridicule to prevent the sale of the plaintiff's works, and entirely to destroy him as an author. In the late case of Tipper *v.* Tabbart, 1 Camp. 350, his lordship had held that a publication by no means so offensive or prejudicial to the object of it, was libellous and actionable.

LORD ELLENBOROUGH. In that case the defendant had falsely accused the plaintiff of publishing what he had never published. Here the supposed libel has only attacked those works of which Sir John Carr is the avowed author; and one writer in exposing the follies and errors of another may make use of ridicule however poignant. Ridicule is often the fittest weapon that can be employed for such a purpose. If the reputation or pecuniary interests of the person ridiculed suffer, it is *damnum absque injuria.* Where is the liberty of the press if an action can be maintained on such principles ? Perhaps the plaintiff's " Tour through Scotland " is now unsaleable; but is he to be indemnified by receiving a compensation in damages from the person who may have opened the eyes of the public to the bad taste and inanity of his compositions ? Who would have bought the works of Sir Robert Filmer after he had been refuted by Mr. Locke ? but shall it be said that he might have sustained an action for defamation against that great philosopher, who was laboring to enlighten and ameliorate mankind ? We really must not cramp observations upon authors and their works. They should be liable to criticism, to exposure, and even to ridicule, if their compositions be ridiculous; otherwise the first who writes a book on any subject will maintain a monopoly of sentiment and opinion respecting it. This would tend to the perpetuity of error. — Reflection on personal character is another thing. Show me an attack on the moral character of this plaintiff, or any attack upon his character unconnected with his authorship, and I shall be as ready as any judge who ever sat here to protect him; but I cannot hear of malice on account of turning his works into ridicule.

The counsel for the plaintiff still complaining of the unfairness of this publication, and particularly of the print affixed to it, the trial proceeded.

The *Attorney-General* having addressed the jury on behalf of the defendants —

LORD ELLENBOROUGH said, Every man who publishes a book commits himself to the judgment of the public, and any one may comment upon his performance. If the commentator does not step aside from the work, or introduce fiction for the purpose of condemnation, he exercises a fair and legitimate right. In the present case, had the party writing the criticism followed the plaintiff into domestic life for the purposes of slander, that would have been libellous; but no passage of this sort has been produced, and even the caricature does not affect the plaintiff, except as the author of the book which is ridiculed. The works of this gentleman may be, for ought I know, very valuable; but whatever their merits, others have a right to pass their judgment upon them, — to censure them if they be censurable, and to turn them into ridicule if they be ridiculous. The critic does a great service to the public, who writes down any vapid or useless publication, such as ought never to have appeared. He checks the dissemination of bad taste, and prevents people from wasting both their time and money upon trash.—I speak of fair and candid criticism; and this every one has a right to publish, although the author may suffer a loss from it. Such a loss the law does not consider as an injury; because it is a loss which the party ought to sustain. It is in short the loss of fame and profits to which he was never entitled. Nothing can be conceived more threatening to the liberty of the press than the species of action before the court. We ought to resist an attempt against free and liberal criticism at the threshold. — The CHIEF JUSTICE concluded by directing the jury, that if the writer of the publication complained of had not travelled out of the work he criticised for the purpose of slander, the action would not lie; but if they could discover in it anything personally slanderous against the plaintiff, unconnected with the works he had given to the public, in that case he had a good cause of action, and they would award him damages accordingly.

Verdict for the defendants.[1]

MERIVALE *v.* CARSON

IN THE COURT OF APPEAL, DECEMBER 2, 1887.

Reported in 20 *Queen's Bench Division*, 275.

APPEAL by the defendant against the refusal of a divisional court (Mathew and Grantham, JJ.) to allow a new trial of the action, or to enter judgment for the defendant.

The action was brought to recover damages in respect of an alleged libel. At the trial before Field, J., it appeared that the plaintiff and his wife were the joint authors of a play called "The Whip Hand."

[1] Dibdin *v.* Swan, 1 Esp. 28; Heriot *v.* Stuart, 1 Esp. 437; Stuart *v.* Lovell 2 Stark. 93 (*semble*); Tabart *v.* Tipper, 1 Camp. 350 (*semble*); Dunne *v.* Anderson, Ry. & M. 287, 3 Bing. 88; Soane *v.* Knight, M. & M. 74; Thompson *v.* Shackell, M. & M. 187; Macleod *v.* Wakley, 3 Car. & P. 311; Fraser *v.* Berkeley, 7 Car. & P. 621; Evans *v.* Harlow, Dav. & M. 507; Paris *v.* Levy, 9 C. B. N. S. 342; Eastwood *v.* Holmes, 1 F. & F. 347; Hibbs *v.* Wilkinson, 1 F. & F. 608; Turnbull *v.* Bird, 2 F. & F. 508; Strauss *v.* Francis, 4 F. & F. 939, 1107, 15 L. T. Rep. 674; Henwood *v.* Harrison, L. R. 7 C. P. 606; Jenner *v.* A'Beckett, L. R. 7 Q. B. 11; Mulkern *v.* Ward, 13 Eq. 619, 622; Whistler *v.* Ruskin, Odgers, Lib. & Sl., (5 ed.) 196; Duplany *v.* Davis, 3 T. L. R. 184; McQuire *v.* Western Co., [1903] 2 K. B. 100; Crane *v.* Waters, 10 Fed. 619; Snyder *v.* Fulton, 34 Md. 128, 137; Gott *v.* Pulsifer, 122 Mass. 235; O'Connor *v.* Sill, 60 Mich. 175; Dowling *v.* Livingstone, 108 Mich. 321; Cooper *v.* Stone, 24 Wend. 434 (*semble*); Reade *v.* Sweetzer, 6 Abb. Pr. N. S. 9, *n.* (*semble*); Adolf Philipp Co. *v.* New Yorker Staatszeitung, 165 App. Div. 377; Press Co. *v.* Stewart, 119 Pa. St. 584 *Accord.*

"The defendant was, in my opinion, entitled to have the jury's decision, as to the plea of fair comment, whether or not, in all the circumstances proved, the libel went beyond a fair comment on the plaintiff and on the system of medical enterprise with which he associated himself, as a matter of public interest treated by the defendant honestly and without malice. The plea of fair comment does not arise if the plea of justification is made good, nor can it arise unless there is an imputation on a plaintiff. It is precisely where the criticism would otherwise be actionable as a libel that the defence of fair comment comes in. But the learned judge put aside that defence, and told the jury that unless a justification was proved they were bound to find a verdict for the plaintiff, and that, unless justified, the libel is not fair comment and cannot come within the region of fair comment." Lord Loreburn, L. C., in Dakhyl *v.* Labouchere, [1908] 2 K. B. 325, 326–27.

The defendant was the editor of a theatrical newspaper called "The Stage." Early in May, 1886, the play was performed at a theatre in Liverpool. On May 7 a criticism of the play was published in the defendant's newspaper. The part of the article charged in the statement of claim as libellous was as follows: "'The Whip Hand,' the joint production of Mr. and Mrs. Herman Merivale, gives us nothing but a hash-up of ingredients which have been used *ad nauseam*, until one rises in protestation against the loving, confiding, fatuous husband with the naughty wife and her double existence, the good male genius, the limp aristocrat, and the villainous foreigner. And why dramatic authors will insist that in modern society comedies the villain must be a foreigner, and the foreigner must be a villain, is only explicable on the ground, we suppose, that there is more or less of romance about such gentry. It is more in consonance with accepted notions that your Continental croupier would make a much better fictitious prince, marquis, or count than would, say, an English billiard-marker or stable-lout. And so the Marquis Colonna in 'The Whip Hand' is offered up by the authors upon the altar of tradition and sacrificed in the usual manner when he gets too troublesome to permit of the reconciliation of husband and wife, and lover and maiden, and is proved, also much as usual, to be nothing more than a kicked-out croupier." The innuendo suggested was that the article implied that the play was of an immoral tendency.

It was admitted that there was no adulterous wife in the play.

Field, J., in the course of his summing-up to the jury, said: "The question is, first, whether this criticism bears the meaning which the plaintiffs put upon it. If it is a fair temperate criticism, and does not bear that meaning, or is not fairly to be read as having that meaning, then your verdict will be for the defendants. . . . It is not for a moment suggested by any one that the defendant is animated by the smallest possible malice towards the plaintiffs. There is no ground for saying so, and no one has said so. . . . The malice which is necessary in this action is one, which, if it existed at all, will be because the defendant has exceeded his right of criticism upon the play. You have the play before you, you must judge for yourselves. If it is no more than fair, honest, independent, bold, even exaggerated, criticism, then your verdict will be for the defendant. It is for the plaintiffs to make out their case. They have to satisfy you that it is more than that, otherwise they cannot complain. If you are satisfied upon the evidence that it is more than that, then you will give your verdict for the plaintiffs."

The jury found a verdict for the plaintiffs with one shilling damages, and the judge entered judgment for the plaintiffs accordingly, and declined to deprive them of costs.

The defendant appealed.[1]

[1] The arguments are omitted.

LORD ESHER, M. R. This action is brought in respect of an alleged libel contained in a criticism by the defendant upon a play written by the plaintiffs. The first thing to be considered is, what are the questions which in such a case ought to be left to the jury? The first question to be left to them is, what is the meaning of the alleged libel? The jury must look at the criticism, and say what in their opinion any reasonable man would understand by it. I am not prepared to say that in coming to their conclusion they would not also have to look at the work criticised. That, however, is not very material for us to consider now. The proper question was put to the jury in the present case. Two interpretations of the defendant's article were placed before them. One was that it meant that the play is founded upon adultery, without containing any stigma on the fact that it is so founded. The defendant's article is alleged to be libellous in that it attributed to the plaintiffs that they had written a play founded upon adultery, without any objection to it on their part, in other words, that they had written an immoral play. On behalf of the defendant it was said that the article had no such meaning, that the expression "naughty wife" does not mean "adulterous wife." It would not have that meaning in every case, but the question is whether, looking at the context of the article, it has that meaning. If the court should come to the conclusion that the expression could not by any reasonable man be thought to have that meaning, they could overrule the verdict of the jury; otherwise the question is for the jury.

What is the next question to be put to the jury? Are they to be told that the criticism of a play is a privileged occasion, within the well-settled meaning of the word "privilege," and that their verdict must go for the defendant, unless the plaintiff can prove malice in fact, that is, that the writer of the article was actuated by an indirect or malicious motive? I think it is clear that that is not the law, and that it was so decided in Campbell *v.* Spottiswoode, which has never been overruled. All the judges, both before and ever since that case, have acted upon the view there expressed, that a criticism upon a written published work is not a privileged occasion. Blackburn, J., in his judgment, shows why it is not a privileged occasion. A privileged occasion is one on which the privileged person is entitled to do something which no one who is not within the privilege is entitled to do on that occasion. A person in such a position may say or write about another person things which no other person in the kingdom can be allowed to say or write. But, in the case of a criticism upon a published work, every person in the kingdom is entitled to do, and is forbidden to do exactly the same things, and therefore the occasion is not privileged. Therefore the second question to be put to the jury is, whether the alleged libel is or is not a libel. The form in which that question should be put is, I think, best expressed by Crompton, J., in Campbell *v.* Spottiswoode. He says: "Nothing is more important than that fair and full latitude of discussion should be allowed to writers upon any public matter, whether it be the conduct of public men, or the proceedings in courts of justice, or in Parliament, or the publication of a scheme, or a literary work. But it is always to be left to a jury to say whether the publication has gone beyond the limits of a fair comment on the subject-matter discussed. A writer is not entitled to overstep those limits, and impute base and sordid motives which are not warranted by the facts, and I cannot for a moment think, because he has a *bona fide* belief that he is publishing what is true, that is any answer to an action for libel." He says that upon the answer to the question there stated it depends whether the article upon which the action is brought is or is not a libel. The question is not whether the article is privileged, but whether it is a libel. What is the meaning of a "fair comment"? I think the meaning is this: is the article in the opinion of the jury beyond that which any fair man, however prejudiced or however strong his opinion may be, would say of the work in question? Every latitude must be given to opinion and to prejudice, and then an ordinary set of men with ordinary judgment must say whether any fair man would have made such a comment on the work. It is very easy to say what would be clearly beyond that limit; if, for instance, the writer attacked the private character of the author. But it is much more difficult to say what is within the limit. That must depend upon the circumstances of the particular case. I think the right question was really left by Field, J., to the jury in the present case. No doubt you can find in the course of his summing up some phrases which, if taken alone, may seem to limit too much the question put to the jury. But, when you look at the summing up as a whole, I think it comes in substance to the final question which was put by the judge to the jury: "If it is no more than fair, honest, independent, bold, even exaggerated, criticism, then your verdict will be for the defendants." He gives a very wide limit, and, I think, rightly. Mere exaggeration, or even gross exaggeration, would not make the comment unfair. However wrong the opinion expressed may be in point of truth, or however prejudiced the writer, it may still be within the prescribed limit. The question which the jury must consider is this: Would any fair man, however prejudiced he may be, however exaggerated or obstinate his view, have said that which this criticism has said of the work which is criticised? If it goes beyond that, then you must find for the plaintiff; if you are not satisfied that it does, then it falls within the allowed limit, and there is no libel at all. I cannot doubt that the jury were justified in coming to the conclusion to which they did come, when once they had made up their minds as to the meaning of the words used in the article, viz. that the plaintiffs had written an obscene play; and no fair man could have said that. There was therefore a complete misdescription of the plaintiffs' work, and the inevitable conclusion was that an imputation was cast upon the characters of the authors. Even if I had thought that the right direction had not been given to the jury, I should have declined to grant a new trial, for the same verdict must inevitably have been found if the jury had been rightly directed.

Another point which has been discussed is this: It is said that if in some other case the alleged libel would not be beyond the limits of fair criticism, and it could be shown that the defendant was not really criticising the work, but was writing with an indirect and dishonest intention to injure the plaintiffs, still the motive would not make the criticism a libel. I am inclined to think that it would, and for this reason, that the comment would not then really be a criticism of the work. The mind of the writer would not be that of a critic, but he would be actuated by an intention to injure the author.

In my opinion this appeal must be dismissed.

Bowen, L. J. We must begin with asking ourselves, what is the true meaning of the words used in the alleged libel? We have the benefit of the machinery which the law gives — the verdict of a jury — for ascertaining the meaning, and it must now be taken to have been conclusively settled, that the writer of the criticism has imputed to the plaintiffs that the story of their play turns in its main incident upon an adulterous wife, and in such a way as not to lead any one to suppose that the plaintiffs objected to the adultery, but, on the contrary, that they had treated the adultery as a spicy incident in the play, without expressing any opinion as to its morality. It has been admitted by the defendant that the play does not in fact contain any adulterous wife, that there is no incident of adultery in it, and therefore it is not open to the suggestion that the plaintiffs have treated adultery lightly in such a way as to tend to immorality. These are the facts.

What then is the law applicable to them? We must see, first, what is the question which ought to have been left to the jury on this assumption of the meaning of the article, and then whether it was in fact left to them, and whether there was any miscarriage on their part. I take precisely the same view as the Master of the Rolls with regard to the way in which the word "privilege" ought to be used. The present case is not, strictly speaking, one of "privileged occasion." In a legal sense that term is used with reference to a case in which one or more members of the public are clothed with a greater immunity than the rest. But in the present case we are dealing with a common right of public criticism which every subject of the realm equally enjoys, — the right of publishing a written criticism upon a literary work which is offered to public criticism.

It is true that a different metaphysical exposition of this common right is to be found in the judgment of Willes, J., in Henwood *v.* Harrison, Law Rep. 7 C. P. 606. That learned judge and the majority of the Court of Common Pleas seem to have treated this right as a branch of the general law of privilege, and to have found a justification for the use of the word "privilege" in the subject matter of the criticism, although there is no limit of the number of the persons entitled to make the criticism. With great respect to Willes, J., I agree with the Master of the Rolls that this is not so good an exposition of the right as that which is given by Blackburn, J., and Crompton, J., in Campbell *v.* Spottiswoode. But the question is rather academical than practical, for I do not think it would make any substantial difference in the present case which view was the right one. But, among other reasons, why I prefer the view of Blackburn, J., and Crompton, J., is this, that it leaves undisturbed the mode of directing the jury in cases of this class which has been ordinarily adopted, viz., to begin by asking them whether they think the limits of fair criticism have been passed. That implies that there is no libel if those limits are not passed. It is only when the writer goes beyond the limits of fair criticism that his criticism passes into the region of libel at all. This leaves unsettled the inquiry, and perhaps it was intended in Campbell *v.* Spottiswoode (a case which has never been questioned) to leave it unsettled, what is the standard for the jury of "fair criticism"? The criticism is to be "fair," that is, the expression of it is to be fair. The only limitation is upon the mode of expression. In this country a man has a right to hold any opinion he pleases, and to express his opinion, provided that he does not go beyond the limits which the law calls "fair," and, although we cannot find in any decided case an exact and rigid definition of the word "fair," this is because the judges have always preferred to leave the question what is "fair" to the jury. The nearest approach, I think, to an exact definition of the word "fair" is contained in the judgment of Lord Tenterden, C. J., in Macleod *v.* Wakley, 3 C. & P., at p. 313, where he said, "Whatever is fair, and can be reasonably said of the works of authors or of themselves, as connected with their works, is not actionable, unless it appears that, under the pretext of criticising the works, the defendant takes an opportunity of attacking the character of the author: then it will be a libel." It must be assumed that a man is entitled to entertain any opinion he pleases, however wrong, exaggerated, or violent it may be, and it must be left to the jury to say whether the mode of expression exceeds the reasonable limits of fair criticism.

In the case of literary criticism it is not easy to conceive what would be outside that region, unless the writer went out of his way to make a personal attack on the character of the author of the work which he was criticising. In such a case the writer would be going beyond the limits of criticism altogether, and therefore beyond the limits of fair criticism. Campbell *v.* Spottiswoode was a case of that kind, and there the jury were asked whether the criticism was fair, and they were told that, if it attacked the private character of the author, it would be going beyond the limits of fair criticism. Still there is another class of cases in which, as it seems to me, the writer would be travelling out of the region of fair criticism, — I mean if he imputes to the author that he has written something which in fact he has not written. That would be a misdescription of the work. There is all the difference in the world between saying that you disapprove of the character of a work, and that you think it has an evil tendency, and saying that a work treats adultery cavalierly, when in fact there is no adultery at all in the story. A jury would have a right to consider the latter beyond the limits of fair criticism.

Applying the law to the present case, we have to see whether the learned judge misdirected the jury, having regard to their finding as to the true construction of the article. Their construction of the words of the article could not have been affected by what he said to them about the meaning of "fair criticism." The alleged libel stated that the story of the plaintiffs' play turned upon adultery. In a case of manifest misdescription such as this the judge is not bound to go into all the minutiæ as if the libel had been of a different character, and his summing-up must be read with reference to this fact. I have read through the summing-up of Field, J., and, though I do not think that his language was altogether exact, yet what possible harm could it have done having regard to the facts of the case? The jury had to deal with a case of positive misdescription, a question not of opinion, but of fact. Did not that fall clearly beyond the limits of fair criticism? Could this court since the Judicature Act set aside the verdict of the jury, merely because the language of the learned judge was not exactly that which he would have used if he had written his summing-up? Assuming the interpretation the jury put on the meaning of the words to be correct, as we must assume, I entertain no doubt as to the correctness of the remainder of the verdict. And, even if the view of the law as to privilege which I do not adopt were the right view, I do not think it would make any difference in the present case, because, the misrepresentation being clear, the writer having not merely said that the play had an evil tendency, but having imputed to the authors that it was founded on adultery when there is no adultery at all in it, the jury would have inferred, if the question had been left sufficiently to them, that the writer was actuated by a malicious motive; that is to say, by some motive other than that of a pure expression of a critic's real opinion. *Appeal dismissed.*

THOMAS *v.* BRADBURY, AGNEW & CO.

IN THE COURT OF APPEAL, JUNE 25, 1906.

Reported in [1906] 2 *King's Bench*, 627.

APPLICATION by the defendants for a new trial or that judgment should be entered for them in an action for libel tried before Darling, J., with a jury.

The alleged libel was the following review in *Punch* of the plaintiff's book: —

" MANGLED REMAINS.

" *Extract from the Recess Diary of Toby, M. P.*

" Been reading ' Fifty Years of Fleet Street ' just issued by Macmillan. Purports to be the ' Life and Recollections of Sir John Robinson,' the man who made, and for a quarter of a century maintained at high level, the *Daily News*. The story is written by Mr. F. M. Thomas, who has added a new terror to death. There are biographies of sorts ranging in value with the personality of the subject and the skill of the compiler. The former occasionally suffers from the incapacity of the latter. But at least his individuality is scrupulously observed. Like Don José, what he has said he has said, his observations and written memoranda not being mixed up with what his biographer thinks he himself thought, uttered, and recorded. Mr. Thomas goes about the biographer's business in fresh fashion, complacently announced by way of introduction to the volume. ' I have not thought it necessary or desirable,' he writes, ' to indicate in all cases what is his (Sir John Robinson's) and what is my own. If there is anything amusing or entertaining in these pages, I am quite content that my dear old chief should have the credit of it. The dulness I take upon myself.' Here be generosity! Here magnanimity! It is true that in the performance of his task Mr. Thomas occasionally falls from this high estate. More than once he airily alludes to ' our diary ' and ' our notes,' as if he had prepared them in collaboration with his chief. Possibly conscious for a moment of this indiscretion, and reverting to more generous mood, he, approaching a particular narrative, introduces it with the remark, ' the incident may be given in the diarist's own words.' The procedure is perhaps not unusual with earlier biographers. With Mr. Thomas the relapse is rare. When he does let the hapless subject speak for himself, he is relegated to small type. For the rest, it is Mr. Thomas who *loquitur*, retelling poor Robinson's cherished stories as if they were his own, sometimes with heavy hand brushing off the bloom. Even in these depressing circumstances there is no mistaking Robinson's sly humour, his gift of graphic characterization. The worst of it is that, happening in the very same page upon some banal remark, some pompous platitude, the alarmed reader, recognizing Mr. Thomas, hastily turns over half-a-dozen pages, and possibly misses a handful of the genuine ore. These are hard lines, unjust to Robinson, unfair to the public. It is plain to see, from the few unmutilated extracts from Robinson's manuscript which illuminate the book, that the materials at hand for a delightful biography were abundant. For nearly forty years the manager of the *Daily News* lived in the very heart of things. He was behind most scenes of public life, was more or less intimately acquainted with the principal personages figuring in it. His sympathies were bountifully wide, his observation alert, his sense of humour keen. He loved his newspaper work with almost passionate affection. For him fifty years of Fleet Street were worth a cycle of Cathay. That he habitually made notes of what he saw and heard with the view to publication in biographical form is undoubted. Mr. Thomas, impregnable in the chain armour of complacency, positively admits it. 'Robinson,' he says, 'did leave some diaries — our diaries — more or less fragmentary, and a number of thick, closely-written volumes of jottings in his own handwriting, descriptive of events of which he had been an eye-witness and people he had seen and known.' Where is this treasure trove ? Presumably portions the biographer was good enough to regard as worth adapting are filtered through the wordy pages of larger type. Happily the material is so good, its original literary form so excellent, that even this unparalleled atrocity cannot quite spoil the book. We who knew Robinson on his throne in Bouverie Street and at the well-known table in the dining-room of the Reform Club, rich in recollections of William Black, Payn, and Sala; who watched him enjoying himself like a boy at theatre first nights; who recognized his rare capacity as a newspaper man; who knew the kind heart hidden behind a studiously cultured severity of manner in business relations — we, perhaps jealously, cherish his memory, and regret the surprising chance that has made possible this slight upon it."

The defence admitted that the defendant Lucy wrote, and that the other defendants published, the words complained of, and pleaded that the words were incapable of a defamatory meaning; and further, that they were written for publication and were published as a criticism and fair comment upon the plaintiff's book without any malice towards the plaintiff, and were a fair and *bona fide* criticism and comment upon the book which was a matter of public interest.

At the trial the plaintiff's case was, first, that the language of the review itself was such as to furnish evidence that the writer was not in truth criticising the book, but was maliciously attacking the author; and, secondly, that there was evidence outside the review that the defendant Lucy, in writing the criticism, was actuated by malice towards the plaintiff. As extrinsic evidence of malice the plaintiff relied upon the strained relations between Lucy and himself before the criticism was published; on the fact that the criticism was published as a separate article under the heading " Mangled Remains," and was not included in that part of the journal usually devoted to reviews of books under the heading " Our Booking Office "; and on the answers and demeanor of Lucy in the witness-box at the trial. At the close of the plaintiff's case counsel for the defendants submitted that there was no case to go to the jury, upon the grounds that the article was incapable of a defamatory meaning, and that there was no evidence that it exceeded the limits of fair comment.

The learned judge declined to withdraw the case from the jury, who found a verdict for the plaintiff with 300*l.* damages.

The defendants appealed.[1] *Cur. adv. vult.*

June 25. COLLINS, M. R., read the following judgment: This is an appeal by the defendants from the verdict and judgment for the plaintiff in an action of libel, tried before Darling, J., and a special jury, based on a critique of a book written by the plaintiff. The critique was written by the defendant Lucy, and appeared in *Punch*, of which the first defendants are the publishers. The defence was fair comment. The learned judge refused to withdraw the case from the jury, who found for the plaintiff, with 300*l.* damages. The defendants do not complain of misdirection other than that involved in holding that there was any evidence fit for the consideration of a jury. They ask for judgment on the ground that there was nothing in the article which any reasonable jury could find to fall outside the limits of fair comment, or in the alternative they ask for a new trial on the ground that the verdict was against the weight of evidence.

The defendants pressed us strongly with the case of McQuire *v.* Western Morning News Co., [1903] 2 K. B. 100, a decision of this court in an action for libel in respect of an article criticising adversely a play of which the plaintiff was the author, where the court set aside a verdict and judgment for the plaintiff on the ground that there was no evidence on which a rational verdict for the plaintiff could be founded. There were, however, two distinctions between that case and the present. There was admittedly in that case no evidence of actual malice unless it could be inferred from the terms of the article itself, and there was some reason for supposing that the direction was misleading. In the present case the plaintiff's counsel strenuously contended that there was extrinsic evidence of malice in the proved relations of the parties before the action; the special manner in which the particular article appeared in *Punch;* and in the expressions which fell from the defendant Lucy, coupled with his demeanor in the witness-box, and they relied also on the terms of an apology subsequently printed as fortifying their contention. They urged besides that the language of the article itself raised a question for the jury as to its

[1] The statement has been abridged, and the arguments of counsel together with a small portion of the judgment are omitted.

meaning, and that upon their view of its meaning would depend the question whether it exceeded the bounds of fair comment or not. The question, therefore, for our decision is whether there was any evidence upon which a rational verdict for the plaintiff could be founded. If so, the learned judge was bound to leave it to the jury. I have already said that extrinsic evidence of malice, which I have attempted to summarize, was allowed to go to the jury. The defendants contended that this evidence amounted to nothing, and that no reasonable jury could act upon it, but they also raised a contention which alone, as it seems to me, gives any importance to this case. Their point was that if the article itself, apart from the extrinsic evidence, did not raise a case for the jury that the bounds of fair comment had been overstepped, proof of actual malice on the part of the writer could not affect the question or disturb his immunity. This is a formidable contention. It involves the assertion that fair comment is absolute, not relative, and must be measured by an abstract standard; that it is a thing quite apart from the opinions and motives of its author and his personal relations towards the writer of the thing criticised. It involves the position also that an action based on a criticism is wholly outside the ordinary law of libel, of which malice, express or implied, has always been considered to be the gist.

The basis of this contention, such as it is, appears to be a misconception of the effect of the gloss, if I may so phrase it, first put upon the law of libel in relation to fair comment in the dicta of Crompton, J., and Blackburn, J., in Campbell *v.* Spottiswoode, decided in 1863, and subsequently approved in Merivale *v.* Carson, decided in 1887. I have already had occasion to examine the effect of these views upon the law of libel in McQuire *v.* Western Morning News Co., [1903] 2 K. B. 100. In my opinion the substance of the matter remains unchanged and malice remains exactly where it did. The dicta no doubt assert the etymological inexactitude of the word " privilege " as connoting a right common to the public at large, and the limits of the right itself are pointed out which, whether it be called privilege or by any other name, does not extend to cover misstatements of fact however *bona fide;* [1] but they in no degree affect the standard by which the fair-

[1] Merivale *v.* Carson, *supra,* 775; McQuire *v.* Western Co., [1903] 2 K. B. 100, 110; Joynt *v.* Cycle Co., [1904] 2 K. B. 292; Digby *v.* Financial News, [1907] 1 K. B. 502; Hunt *v.* Star Co., [1908] 2 K. B. 309, 317; Walker *v.* Hodgson, [1909] 1 K. B. 239; Starks *v.* Comer, 190 Ala. 245; Com. *v.* Pratt, 208 Mass. 553; Williams *v.* Hicks Printing Co., 159 Wis. 90; Putnam *v.* Browne, 162 Wis. 524 *Accord.*

In Walker *v.* Hodgson, Kennedy, L. J., said, p. 256: " Now it is true that there may be comment of an injurious nature in which there is no statement of facts, or which refers to facts which are admitted or are indisputable. In such a case the fairness of the comment depends upon the character of the criticisms, or the inferences of which it is composed, that is, whether it is a comment made honestly and *bona fide,* or a comment made *mala fide* and maliciously. . . . But where the words which are alleged to be defamatory allege, or assume as true, facts concerning the plaintiff which the plaintiff denies, and which either involve a slanderous imputation in themselves, or upon which the comment bases imputations or in-ness of the comment is to be judged or relieve the commentator from liability, if the comment be malicious, if, indeed, it can then be described as comment at all. The right, though shared by the public, is the right of every individual who asserts it, and is, qua him, an individual right whatever name it be called by, and comment by him which is colored by malice cannot from his standpoint be deemed fair. He, and he only, is the person in whose motives the plaintiff in the libel action is concerned, and if he, the person sued, is proved to have allowed his view to be distorted by malice, it is quite immaterial that somebody else might without malice have written an equally damnatory criticism. The defendant, and not that other person, is the party sued. This seems to me quite clear in point of principle; but, as already pointed out in McQuire *v.* Western Morning News Co., [1903] 2 K. B. 100, the law continued to be administered after Campbell *v.* Spottiswoode, just as it always had been before, down to and since Merivale *v.* Carson. That case decided nothing inconsistent with the law of libel as thus administered, though each of the learned judges expressed an opinion in favor of the view taken in the dicta I have referred to of Crompton, J., and Blackburn, J., in preference to that of Willes, J., in Henwood *v.* Harrison, L. R. 7 C. P. 600. But, as already pointed out in McQuire *v.* Western Morning News Co., [1903] 2 K. B. 100, the difference between the two views is, in the language of Bowen, L. J., in Merivale *v.* Carson, a difference in the "metaphysical exposition" of the right and " is rather academical than practical." I think the head-note in the last-mentioned case is to some extent the cause of what seems to me an erroneous impression as to the effect of the decision. The words of that note seem to suggest a difference of right, under the general law of libel, in respect of communications made on a privileged occasion and communications made in the shape of criticism on a matter of public interest. In cases of privilege, properly so called, nothing that falls outside the privilege is protected by it, and if defamatory it must be otherwise justified. The occasion being privileged, the extent of the privilege may vary according to the na-

ferences injurious to the plaintiff, it is, I think, settled law that the defence of fair comment fails, unless the comment is truthful in regard to its allegation or assumption of such facts." See also the remarks of Buckley, L. J., in the same case, p. 253.

In Hubbard *v.* Allyn, 200 Mass. 167, Rugg, J., said (p. 170): " The right of the defendant was not to make false statements of fact because the subject matter was of public interest, but only to criticise, discuss and comment upon the real acts of the plaintiff and the consequences likely to follow from them, or upon any other aspect of the case in a reasonable way. This may be done with severity. Ridicule, sarcasm and invective may be employed. But the basis must be a fact, and not a falsehood."

Nor does it cover violent attacks and insulting statements. Press Pub. Co. *v.* Gillette, (C. C. A.) 229 Fed. 108; Jozsa *v.* Moroney, 125 La. 813; Hines *v.* Shumaker, 97 Miss. 669; Patten *v.* Harpers Weekly Corp., 158 N. Y. Supp. 70; Hayden *v.* Hasbrouck, 34 R. I. 556; Spencer *v.* Looney, 116 Va. 767; Williams *v.* Hicks Printing Co., 159 Wis. 90; Putnam *v.* Browne, 162 Wis. 524; Compare Dickson *v.* Lights, (Tex. Civ. App.) 170 S. W. 834. And see Phillips *v.* Bradshaw, 167 Ala. 199.

ture of the case and the limits of the right or duty which is the basis of the privilege. But this is precisely the position in the case where the right exercised is one shared by the rest of the public, and not one limited to an individual or a class. The extent of the right has to be ascertained, and in respect of any communication which falls within it the immunity, if it be not absolute, can be displaced only by proof of malice. In the case of comment on literary works the occasion is created by the publication, and a right then arises to criticise honestly, however adversely. No such occasion would arise in respect of a private unpublished letter. If a writer were to get hold of a private letter of a well-known author and publish a damnatory article on the author's literary style and taste, as evidenced by the letter, it seems to me that he would have no immunity from the ordinary law in respect of defamatory writings. The only difference, then, in the legal incidents of ordinary privilege, limited to individuals on the one hand and the right in the public to criticise on the other, would seem to be that the one might, with somewhat less latitude than the other, though not, perhaps, with perfect accuracy, be described as "privilege." Now, the head-note might possibly suggest, at first sight at all events, particularly when it adds "Henwood *v.* Harrison, L. R. 7 C. P. 606, dissented from," that not merely an academical difference in the analysis of rights had been expressed, but that there was a difference of substance in the bearing of malice in the two cases in respect of communications or criticisms falling *prima facie* within the right or privilege. The limits of the right, as I have already pointed out, may be, and are, different, but the law with respect to communications that *prima facie* fall within them is the same. Proof of malice may take a criticism *prima facie* fair outside the right of fair comment, just as it takes a communication *prima facie* privileged outside the privilege. The particular allegation which was unprotected in Merivale *v.* Carson was never within the "right" when the facts were ascertained by the jury in interpreting the passage impugned. Proof of *bona fide* belief was therefore irrelevant; nothing but proof of the truth could justify the allegation. If the analysis be strictly carried out it will be found that the two rights, whatever name they are called by, are governed by precisely the same rules. The only practical difference is that in an action based on a criticism of a published work the transaction begins by the admission, on the part of the plaintiff, implied from the averment by him of publication of the work criticised, that the comment came into existence on a protected occasion. He is placed, therefore, in precisely the same position as he would have been in had he sued in respect of a defamatory writing *prima facie* unprotected and therefore actionable, but had gone on to aver facts which created a privilege strictly so called. Beginning thus at this stage in the transaction, he would have accepted the onus of proving malice in fact. If he had veiled the fact that the writing criticised had become matter of public interest by publication it would have been *prima facie* libellous, and the defendant would have had to plead such a publication as would let in the right to comment on a matter of public interest in order to bring himself within the protection. This shows that acceptance of the dicta under discussion does not in the slightest degree affect the place of malice in the law of libel, and that it is only by leaving out one step in the analysis that the public right, as distinguished from the privilege, may appear to carry with it different incidents. There is not even any decision that the word privilege, as used in Henwood *v.* Harrison, to which Lord Esher was himself a party, is not as good a word as any substitute that can be suggested to express the right by which, in certain circumstances, writing defamatory of another person may be published with impunity, because the presumption of malice is negatived. For the reasons I have given the difference is one of words only, and could not be a matter of legal decision.

I have thought it worth while to sift this contention somewhat elaborately, as it is apparently based upon a misconception which seems to have a tendency to repeat itself as to the effect of Merivale *v.* Carson, on the law of libel. But the contention of the defendants can be met, not by reference to principle only, but also by direct authority. To go back to the source itself of the supposed new departure, Campbell *v.* Spottiswoode, Blackburn, J., says: "Honest belief may be an ingredient to be taken into consideration by the jury in determining whether the publication is a libel, that is, whether it exceeds the limits of a fair and proper comment." In Merivale *v.* Carson itself Lord Esher, M. R., deals with the question. He says: "It is said that if in some other case the alleged libel would not be beyond the limits of fair criticism, and it could be shown that the defendant was not really criticising the work, but was writing with an indirect and dishonest intention to injure the plaintiffs still the motive would not make the criticism a libel. I am inclined to think that it would, and for this reason, that the comment would not then really be a criticism of the work. The mind of the writer would not be that of a critic, but he would be actuated by an intention to injure the author." Though the learned judge in this passage expresses only an inclination of opinion, the reason given seems to me to be conclusive. But in a very recent case in this court, the point is actually decided: Plymouth Mutual Coöperative and Industrial Society *v.* Traders' Publishing Association, [1906] 1 K. B. 403. The question there was whether an interrogatory addressed to the state of mind of the defendant, who had pleaded fair comment in an action of libel, was admissible. The court decided that it was, following a previous decision of this court in a case of privilege strictly so called. Vaughan Williams, L. J., referring to White & Co. *v.* Credit Reform Association and Credit Index, [1905] 1 K. B. 653, says at page 413 of the report: "It seems to me that that case shows that an interrogatory of this kind is just as relevant and admissible in a case where the defence is fair comment as in one where it is privilege. In either case the question raised is really as to the state of mind of the defendant when he published the alleged libel, the question being in the one case whether he published it in the spirit of malice, in the other whether he published it in the spirit of unfairness. In either case, I think such an interrogatory as the one now in question is admissible." Fletcher Moulton, L. J., says at page 418 of the report: "I am clear that, both in cases in which the defence of privilege and in those in which the defence of fair comment is set up, the state of mind of the defendant when he published the alleged libel is a matter directly in issue."

It is, of course, possible for a person to have a spite against another and yet to bring a perfectly dispassionate judgment to bear upon his literary merits; but, given the existence of malice, it must be for the jury to say whether it has warped his judgment. Comment distorted by malice cannot in my opinion be fair on the part of the person who makes it. I am of opinion, therefore, that evidence of malice actuating the defendant was admissible, and that the learned judge was right in letting the evidence in this case go to the jury. But I am also of opinion on a close examination of the alleged libel that, apart from the extrinsic evidence of malice, the learned judge could not have withdrawn the case from the jury. One point made by the plaintiff would, I think, of itself suffice to establish this position. The defendant Lucy says in the alleged libel "it is plain to see from the few unmutilated extracts . . . that the materials at hand for a delightful biography were abundant." This statement was described by the plaintiff in a letter to the editor of *Punch* as "simply untrue." A short statement was thereupon published in the issue of December 7, in which the defendant, while accepting the plaintiff's statement as to the paucity of materials, quotes a passage from the preface to the book dealing with the existence of materials, and concludes thus: "Toby, M. P., had at the time of writing no knowledge of the subject beyond the definite statements quoted in the biographer's own words. He regrets that, accepting them in their ordinary sense, he received and conveyed an impression of Mr. Thomas's literary methods which turns out to have been erroneous." He is thus in the difficulty of having to admit a misstatement of fact in respect of which, to put it at the lowest, a question must arise for the jury whether the passage he relied upon justifies the statement. I think also that the learned judge could not have properly held that there was no evidence fit for the consideration of the jury as to some of the innuendoes averring imputations of discreditable motives. I am of opinion, therefore, that we could not direct judgment for the defendants without usurping the functions of the jury. Neither can we say that the evidence is so slight as to justify us in ordering a new trial on the ground that the verdict is against the weight of the evidence.

COZENS-HARDY, L. J. I agree.

SIR GORELL BARNES, PRESIDENT. I have had an opportunity of reading the judgment of the Master of the Rolls, and I agree with it.

Appeal dismissed.[1]

JACKSON *v.* HOPPERTON

IN THE COMMON PLEAS, MAY 25, 1864.

Reported in 12 *Weekly Reporter*, 913.[2]

THIS case was tried before Williams, J., at Guildhall, in the sittings after last Easter Term.

The declaration stated that, " before the speaking, &c., the defendant had been a man-milliner, and the plaintiff had been in his service and employ as a saleswoman and assistant, and the defendant falsely, &c., spoke, &c., of the plaintiff the words ' Miss Jackson ' (thereby meaning the plaintiff) ' is dishonest,' thereby meaning that the plaintiff was a thief and a dishonest servant, and had been guilty of fraudulent conduct in her capacity as such saleswoman, &c., whereby, &c., the plaintiff was injured in credit and reputation, and certain persons trading under the name and style of ' Capper, Son, & Co.' refused to employ the plaintiff as saleswoman and servant in their employ, as they otherwise would have done, and the plaintiff lost and was deprived of her said situation in the employ of the said ' Capper, Son, & Co.,' and has been for a long space of time unable to obtain employment, &c."

[1] Robinson *v.* Coulter, 215 Mass. 566; Tawney *v.* Simonson, 109 Minn. 341 *Accord.*

The burden is on the plaintiff to show malice, not on the defendant to show good faith. Jenoure *v.* Delmege, [1891] A. C. 73; Davis *v.* Hearst, 160 Cal. 143; Locke *v.* Bradstreet Co., 22 Fed. 771; Hemmens *v.* Nelson, 138 N. Y. 517; Haft *v.* Newcastle Bank, 19 App. Div. 423; Strode *v.* Clement, 90 Va. 553.

Definitions of " malice." Doane *v.* Grew, 220 Mass. 171; Peake *v.* Taubman, 251 Mo. 390. See Marney *v.* Joseph, 94 Kan. 18.

" If proof of a malevolent motive would rebut the privilege, which we do not decide, nothing less than that would do, so far as malice is concerned. It is true, as is said in the very careful brief for the plaintiff, that in most connections malice means only knowledge of facts sufficient to show that the contemplated act is very likely to have injurious consequences. Apart from statute it generally means no more when the question is what is sufficient *prima facie* to charge a defendant. Burt *v.* Advertiser Newspaper Co., 154 Mass. 238, 245. But sometimes the defence is not that the damage was not to be foreseen, but rests on what in substance is a privilege, whether of a kind usually pleaded as such or not, that is to say, on a right to inflict the damage even knowingly. In such cases, if malice in any sense makes a difference, as distinguished from excess over what was reasonable or needful to do or say under the circumstances, which often is included under the same word, Gott *v.* Pulsifer, 122 Mass. 235, 239, it means that the defendant is not within the privilege because he was not acting in *bona fide* answer to the needs of the occasion, but outside of it from a wish to do harm. See Wren *v.* Weild, L. R. 4 Q. B. 730, 735, 736; Clark *v.* Molyneux, 3 Q. B. D. 237, 246, 247." Holmes, C. J., in Squires *v.* Wason Mfg. Co., 182 Mass. 137, 141.

See Advertiser Co. *v.* Jones, 169 Ala. 196, 670; Davis *v.* Hearst, 160 Cal. 143.

Reckless republication without inquiry. Houston Chronicle Pub. Co. *v.* Wegner, (Tex. Civ. App.) 182 S. W. 45.

" Malice " on the face of publication. Ashford *v.* Evening Star Co., 41 App. D. C. 395; Dickson *v.* Lights, (Tex. Civ. App.) 170 S. W. 834.

[2] 16 C. B. N. S. 829, S. C.

Plea — Not guilty.

The plaintiff entered the defendant's service on December 1st, 1862, and remained in his employ till October, 1863, when she left, he having accused her of taking some money, and a few other things. Shortly after she left, she returned for her boxes, and asked him for her wages, and he then accused her of taking £3 10s., but said, " if you had come back, I should have said nothing about it." A few days after he paid her her wages. Two or three days after this, she applied to the Messrs. Capper, Son & Co., for a situation; and she informed the defendant that a young lady was coming to him for a reference, and he then said, " I will give you no reference, but if you own that you took the money I will give you a reference." The lady from Messrs. Capper, Son, & Co. called at the defendant's and asked him for the plaintiff's character, when he spoke the words in the declaration, and said he would not give her a character, she was dishonest, and that he had money and goods which he could prove she had taken. The plaintiff did not get the situation, the wages for which were £50 a year and board. The jury found a verdict for the plaintiff for £60.

Mr. Chambers, Q. C. (*Hance* with him), now moved for a rule calling on the plaintiff to show cause why this verdict should not be set aside, and instead thereof a nonsuit entered, on the ground that there was no evidence of express malice; or for a new trial, on the grounds that the verdict was against the evidence, and that the damages were excessive.

ERLE, C. J. I am of opinion that there should be no rule in this case. This was an action for defamation of character, and evidence was adduced on the part of the defendant to show that the defamatory words were uttered on an occasion which justified the use of them. The question left to the jury was, whether the defendant believed the imputation of dishonesty, which he made against the plaintiff, was true or not, and they found he did not believe it to be so, and the judge is satisfied with their answer. I think this was a necessary question to be left to them. Then, as to the damages being excessive, the plaintiff lost a situation for which she would have received £50 a year, and it cannot be said that £60 is too large a sum as compensation for that loss. Mr. Chambers also moved on the ground that it was the judge's duty to nonsuit the plaintiff at the close of the plaintiff's case; but she tried to get another situation, and a lady called on the defendant for her character, and he then spoke to the lady the words complained of; where words are spoken on such an occasion as that, if the person uttering them believe them to be true, and there be no further evidence to show a probability that they were spoken maliciously, it is the duty of the judge to nonsuit the plaintiff. The cases of Taylor *v.* Hawkins, 16 Q. B. 308, and Somerville *v.* Hawkins, 10 C. B. 583, show what is the law under such circumstances, and lay down that, if the plaintiff give evidence from which the jury might infer malice, such as, that the defendant made the imputations not believing them to be true, or that at the time when he spoke the words he did not believe he was in the discharge of a duty, the question of malice ought to be left to the jury; and it appears from the old cases, and also the two cases above cited, that defamation carries with it a presumption of malice, and that it is *prima facie* evidence of malice, but the occasion on which the defamatory words are spoken may rebut the *prima facie* inference of malice, and then additional evidence may be given to show that there was malice, and the jury are to find on that evidence and on the libel itself whether there be malice. In the case of Wright *v.* Woodgate, 2 C. M. &

R. 573, it is thus laid down by Parke, B., at p. 577: "The proper meaning of a privileged communication is only this, that the occasion on which the communication was made rebuts the inference *prima facie* arising from a statement prejudicial to the character of the plaintiff, and puts it upon him to prove that there was malice; in fact, that the defendant was actuated by motives of personal spite or ill-will, independent of the occasion on which the communication was made. In the present case, it became, in my opinion, incumbent upon the plaintiff to show malice in fact. This he might have made out, either from the language of the letter itself, or by extrinsic evidence, as by proof of the conduct or expressions of the defendant, showing that he was actuated by a motive of personal ill-will." And in Taylor *v.* Hawkins, Lord Campbell lays it down at p. 321 thus: "The rule is, that, if the occasion be such as repels the presumption of malice, the communication is privileged, and the plaintiff must then, if he can, give evidence of malice." I think that the fact of his charging her with stealing the £3 10*s*., and, not making that charge till after she had threatened to leave, and then the fact of his telling her that if she had come back he should have said nothing about it, and that if she owned she took it he would give her a reference, were sufficient facts to justify the jury in inferring that he was not performing the important duty between man and man, of stating what he believed to be the plaintiff's true character, when he spoke the words which are the subject of this action.

WILLIAMS, WILLES, and BYLES, JJ., concurred. *Rule refused.*[1]

DAVIS *v.* SHEPSTONE

IN THE PRIVY COUNCIL, MARCH 5, 1886.

Reported in 11 *Appeal Cases,* 187.

THE judgment of their lordships was delivered by

LORD HERSCHELL, L. C.[2] This is an appeal from a judgment of the Supreme Court of the Colony of Natal refusing a new trial in an action brought against the appellants in which the respondent obtained a verdict for £500 damages.

The action was brought to recover damages for alleged libels published by the appellants in the "Natal Witness" newspaper in the months of March and May, 1883.

The respondent was, in December, 1882, appointed Resident Commissioner in Zululand, and proceeded in the discharge of his duties to the Zulu reserve territory. In the month of March, 1883, the appellants published in an issue of their newspaper serious allegations with reference to the conduct of the respondent whilst in the execution of his office in the reserve territory. They stated that he had not only

[1] Nevill *v.* Fine Arts Co., [1895] 2 Q. B. 156; Hollenbeck *v.* Ristine, 105 Ia 488; Children *v.* Shinn, 168 Ia. 531; Atwill *v.* Mackintosh, 120 Mass. 177; Wagner *v.* Scott, 164 Mo. 289; McGaw *v.* Hamilton, 184 Pa. St. 108; Hellstern *v.* Katzer, 103 Wis. 391 *Accord.* Compare Davis *v.* New England Pub. Co., 203 Mass. 470; Doane *v.* Grew, 220 Mass. 171.

[2] Only the opinion of the court is given.

himself violently assaulted a Zulu chief, but had set on his native policemen to assault others. Upon the assumption that these statements were true, they commented upon his conduct in terms of great severity, observing, " We have always regarded Mr. Shepstone as a most unfit man to send to Zululand, if for no other reason than this, that the Zulus entertain towards him neither respect nor confidence. To these disqualifications he has now, if our information is correct, added another which is far more damnatory. Such an act as he has now been guilty of cannot be passed over, if any kind of friendly relations are to be maintained between the colony and Zululand. There are difficulties enough in that direction without need for them to be increased by the headstrong and almost insane imprudence and want of self-respect of the official who unworthily represents the government of the Queen."

In the same issue, under the heading " Zululand," there appeared a statement that four messengers had come from Natal to Zululand, from whom details had been obtained of the respondent's treatment of certain chiefs of the reserved territory who had visited Cetewayo, and, what purported to be the account derived from these messengers of the assault and abusive language of which the respondent had been guilty, was given in detail.

On the 16th of May, 1883, the appellants published a further article, relating to the respondent, which commenced as follows: — " Some time ago we stated in these columns that Mr. John Shepstone, whilst in Zululand, had committed a most unprovoked and altogether incomprehensible assault upon certain Zulu chiefs. At the time the statement was made, a good deal of doubt was thrown upon the truth of the story. We are now in a position to make public full details of the affair, which the closest investigation will prove to be correct. A representative of this journal, learning that a deputation had come to Natal to complain of the attack, met five of the number, and in the presence of the competent interpreters took down the stories of each man."

The article then gave at length the statements so taken down, which disclosed, if true, the grossest misconduct on the part of the respondent. It was in respect of these publications of the appellants that the action was brought by the respondent.

The appellants by their defence averred that the conduct of the plaintiff as British Resident Commissioner was a matter of general public interest affecting the territory of Natal, and that the alleged libels constituted a fair and accurate report of the information brought to the Governor of Natal, and published in the colony by messengers from Zululand and its king as to the conduct of the plaintiff in the discharge of the duties of his office, and a fair and impartial comment upon the conduct of the plaintiff in his public capacity published *bona fide* and without malice.

The case came on for trial before Mr. Justice Wragg and a jury on the 4th of September, 1883, when it was proved that the allegations of misconduct made against Mr. Shepstone were absolutely without foundation, and no attempt was made to support them by evidence. It appeared that the messengers from whom the statements contained in the issue in March were derived had come from Zululand to see the Bishop of Natal, and that their statements had been conveyed to the editor of a newspaper by a letter from the bishop. The statements contained in the issue of May were communicated by a Mr. Watson, who was connected with the staff of the newspaper, and who had sought and obtained an interview with certain Zulus when on their way to convey a message from the king to the Governor of Natal.

At the close of the evidence the learned judge summed up the case to the jury, who returned a verdict for the plaintiff, the present respondent, for £500.

Application was afterwards made to the Supreme Court to grant a new trial, but this application was refused, and the present appeal was then brought. The appellants rested their appeal upon two grounds, first, that the learned judge misdirected the jury in leaving to them the question of privilege and in not telling them that the occasion was a privileged one. The second ground insisted upon was that the damages were excessive. Their Lordships are of opinion that the contention that the learned judge ought to have told the jury that the occasion was a privileged one, and that the plaintiff could only succeed on proof of express malice, is not well founded.

There is no doubt that the public acts of a public man may lawfully be made the subject of fair comment or criticism, not only by the press, but by all members of the public. But the distinction cannot be too clearly borne in mind between comment or criticism and allegations of fact, such as that disgraceful acts have been committed, or discreditable language used. It is one thing to comment upon or criticise, even with severity, the acknowledged or proved acts of a public man, and quite another to assert that he has been guilty of particular acts of misconduct.[1]

[1] Parmiter *v.* Coupland, 6 M. & W. 105; Odger *v.* Mortimer, 28 L. T. Rep. 472; Queen *v.* Carden, 5 Q. B. Div. 1, 8; Bryce *v.* Rusden, 2 T. L. R. 435; Duplany *v.* Davis, 3 T. L. R. 184; R. *v.* Flowers, 44 J. P. 377, *per* Field, J.; LeFroy *v.* Burnside, L. R. 4 Ir. 556, 565, 566; Stewart *v.* McKinley, 11 Vict. L. R. 802; Browne *v.* McKinley, 12 Vict. L. R. 240; Smith *v.* Tribune Co., 4 Biss. 477; McDonald *v.* Woodruff, 2 Dill. 244; Hallam *v.* Post Co., 55 Fed. 456, 59 Fed. 530; Parsons *v.* Age Herald Pub. Co., 181 Ala. 439; Jarman *v.* Rea, 137 Cal. 339; Dauphiny *v.* Buhne, 153 Cal. 757; Star Co. *v.* Donahoe, (Del.) 58 Atl. 513; Jones *v.* Townsend, 21 Fla. 431; Rearick *v.* Wilcox, 81 Ill. 77; Klos *v.* Zahorik, 113 Ia. 161; Ott *v.* Murphy, 160 Ia. 730; Bearce *v.* Bass, 88 Me. 521; Negley *v.* Farrow, 60 Md. 158; Commonwealth *v.* Clap, 4 Mass. 163, 169 (*semble*); Curtis *v.* Mussey, 6 Gray, 261; Burt *v.* Advertiser Co., 154 Mass. 238 (compare Sillars *v.* Collier, 151 Mass. 50); Hubbard *v.* Allyn, 200 Mass. 166; Foster *v.* Scripps, 39 Mich. 376; Bronson *v.* Bruce, 59 Mich. 467; Bourreseau *v.* Detroit Co., 63 Mich. 425; Wheaton *v.* Beecher, 66 Mich. 307; Belknap *v.* Ball, 83 Mich. 583; Hay *v.* Reid, 85 Mich. 296; Smurthwaite *v.* News Co., 124 Mich. 377; Aldrich *v.* Press Co., 9 Minn. 133 (but

In the present case the appellants, in the passages which were complained of as libellous, charged the respondent, as now appears without foundation, with having been guilty of specific acts of misconduct, and then proceeded, on the assumption that the charges were true, to comment upon his proceedings in language in the highest degree offen-

see, *contra*, Marks *v.* Baker, 28 Minn. 162); Smith *v.* Burrus, 106 Mo. 94; State *v.* Schmitt, 49 N. J. Law, 579; Lewis *v.* Few, 5 Johns. 1; Root *v.* King, 7 Cow. 613; Littlejohn *v.* Greeley, 13 Abb. Pr. 41; Hamilton *v.* Eno, 81 N. Y. 116; Mattice *v.* Wilcox, 147 N. Y. 624; Hoey *v.* New York Times Co., 138 App. Div. 149; Ullrich *v.* N. Y. Co., 23 Misc. 168; Seely *v.* Blair, Wright, (Ohio) 358, 683; Post Co. *v.* Moloney, 50 Ohio St. 71; Upton *v.* Hume, 24 Or. 420; Barr *v.* Moore, 87 Pa. St. 385; Brewer *v.* Weakley, 2 Overt. 99; Banner Co. *v.* State, 16 Lea, 176; Democrat Co. *v.* Jones, 83 Tex. 302; Sweeney *v.* Baker, 13 W. Va. 158; Spiering *v.* Andrae, 45 Wis. 330; Eviston *v.* Cramer, 57 Wis. 570; Gagen *v.* Dawley, 162 Wis. 152; D. Ward *v.* Derrington, 14 S. Aust. L. R. 35; Haselgrove *v.* King, 14 S. Aust. L. R. 192 *Accord.*

Mott *v.* Dawson, 46 Ia. 533; Bays *v.* Hunt, 60 Ia. 251 (but see State *v.* Haskins, 109 Ia. 656, 658, and Morse *v.* Printing Co., 124 Ia. 707, 723); State *v.* Balch, 31 Kan. 465; Coleman *v.* McLennan, 78 Kan. 711; Marks *v.* Baker, 28 Minn. 162; State *v.* Burnham, 9 N. H. 34; Neeb *v.* Hope, 111 Pa. St. 145; Briggs *v.* Garrett, 111 Pa. St. 404; Press Co. *v.* Stewart, 119 Pa. St. 584; Jackson *v.* Pittsburgh Times, 152 Pa. St. 406; Ross *v.* Ward, 14 S. D. 240; Boucher *v.* Clark Co., 14 S. D. 72 *Contra.*

See Palmer *v.* Concord, 48 N. H. 211.

In Burt *v.* Advertiser Co., 154 Mass. 238, Holmes, J., said: "But there is an important distinction to be noticed between the so-called privilege of fair criticism upon matters of public interest, and the privilege existing in the case, for instance, of answers to inquiries about the character of a servant. In the latter case, a *bona fide* statement not in excess of the occasion is privileged, although it turns out to be false. In the former, what is privileged, if that is the proper term, is criticism, not statement, and however it might be if a person merely quoted or referred to a statement as made by others, and gave it no new sanction, if he takes upon himself in his own person to allege facts otherwise libellous, he will not be privileged if those facts are not true. The reason for the distinction lies in the different nature and degree of the exigency and of the damage in the two cases. In these, as in many other instances, the law has to draw a line between conflicting interests, both intrinsically meritorious. When private inquiries are made about a private person, a servant, for example, it is often impossible to answer them properly without stating facts, and those who settled the law thought it more important to preserve a reasonable freedom in giving necessary information than to insure people against occasional unintended injustice, confined as it generally is to one or two persons. But what the interest of private citizens in public matters requires is freedom of discussion rather than of statement. Moreover, the statements about such matters which come before the courts are generally public statements, where the harm done by a falsehood is much greater than in the other case. If one private citizen wrote to another that a high official had taken a bribe, no one would think good faith a sufficient answer to an action. He stands no better, certainly, when he publishes his writing to the world through a newspaper, and the newspaper itself stands no better than the writer. Sheckell *v.* Jackson, 10 Cush. 25, 26."

Participants in legal proceedings are legitimate subjects for comment if restricted to their conduct therein. Rex *v.* White, 1 Camp. 359; Seymour *v.* Butterworth, 3 F. & F. 372; Hedley *v.* Barlow, 4 F. & F. 224; Woodgate *v.* Ridout, 4 F. & F. 202; Hibbins *v.* Lee, 4 F. & F. 243; Risk Allah Bey *v.* Whitehurst, 18 L. T. Rep. 615; Reg. *v.* Sullivan, 11 Cox C. C. 44, 57; Kane *v.* Mulvany, Ir. R. 2 C. L. 402; Miner *v.* Detroit Co., 49 Mich. 358. See also Kelly *v.* Tinling, L. R. 1 Q. B. 699 (churchwarden); Harle *v.* Catherall, 14 L. T. Rep. 801 (waywarden).

Matters not of public interest. The right of comment was denied in Latimer *v.* Western Co., 25 L. T. Rep. 44; Hogan *v.* Sutton, 16 W. R. 127; Wilson *v.* Fitch, 41 Cal. 363.

See also Hearne *v.* Stowell, 12 A. & E. 719; Gathercole *v.* Miall, 15 M. & W. 319; Walker *v.* Brogden, 19 C. B. N. S. 65; Booth *v.* Briscoe, 2 Q. B. Div. 496.

sive and injurious; not only so, but they themselves vouched for the statements by asserting that though some doubt had been thrown upon the truth of the story, the closest investigation would prove it to be correct. In their Lordships' opinion there is no warrant for the doctrine that defamatory matter thus published is regarded by the law as the subject of any privilege.

It was insisted by the counsel for the appellants that the publications were privileged, as being a fair and accurate report of the statements made by certain messengers from King Cetewayo upon a subject of public importance. It has, indeed, been held that fair and accurate reports of proceedings in parliament and in courts of justice are privileged, even though they contain defamatory matter affecting the character of individuals.

But in the case of Purcell *v.* Sowler the Court of Appeal expressly refused to extend the privilege even to the report of a meeting of poor law guardians, at which accusations of misconduct were made against their medical officer. And in their Lordships' opinion it is clear that it cannot be extended to a report of statements made to the Bishop of Natal, and by him transmitted to the appellants, or to statements made to a reporter in the employ of the appellants, who for the purposes of the newspaper, sought an interview with messengers on their way to lay a complaint before the governor.

The language used by the learned judge in summing up the present case to the jury is open to some criticism, and does not contain so clear and complete an exposition of the law as might be desired. But in their Lordships' opinion, so far as it erred, it erred in being too favorable to the appellants, and it is not open to any complaint on their part.

The only question that remains is as to the amount of damages. The assessment of these is peculiarly the province of the jury in an action of libel. The damages in such an action are not limited to the amount of pecuniary loss which the plaintiff is able to prove. And their Lordships see no reason for saying that the damages awarded were excessive or for interfering with the finding of the jury in this respect.

They will, therefore, humbly advise Her Majesty that the judgment appealed against should be affirmed and the appeal dismissed with costs.

CHAPTER VII

INTERFERENCE WITH PRIVACY

ROBERSON *v.* ROCHESTER FOLDING BOX COMPANY

COURT OF APPEALS, NEW YORK, JUNE 27, 1902.

Reported in 171 *New York Reports*, 538.

PARKER, C. J.[1] The Appellate Division [2] has certified that the following questions of law have arisen in this case, and ought to be reviewed by this court: 1. Does the complaint herein state a cause of action at law against the defendants or either of them ? 2. Does the complaint herein state a cause of action in equity against the defendants or either of them ? These questions are presented by a demurrer to the complaint, which is put upon the ground that the complaint does not state facts sufficient to constitute a cause of action.

As a demurrer admits not only those facts which are expressly alleged in the complaint, but everything which can be implied by fair and reasonable intendment from its allegations (Marie *v.* Garrison, 83 N. Y. 14, 23), we are to inquire whether the complaint, regarded from the standpoint of this rule, can be said to show any right to relief either in law or in equity.

The complaint alleges that the Franklin Mills Co., one of the defendants, was engaged in a general milling business and in the manufacture and sale of flour; that before the commencement of the action, without the knowledge or consent of plaintiff, defendants, knowing that they had no right or authority so to do, had obtained made, printed, sold, and circulated about 25,000 lithographic prints, photographs and likenesses of plaintiff, made in a manner particularly set up in the complaint; that upon the paper upon which the likenesses were printed and above the portrait there were printed, in large, plain letters, the words, " Flour of the Family," and below the portrait in large capital letters, "Franklin Mills Flour," and in the lower right-hand corner in smaller capital letters, " Rochester Folding Box Co., Rochester, N. Y."; that upon the same sheet were other advertisements of the flour of the Franklin Mills Co.; that those 25,000 likenesses of the plaintiff thus ornamented have been conspicuously posted and displayed in stores, warehouses, saloons, and other public places; that they have been recognized by friends of the plaintiff and other

[1] Arguments omitted.

[2] The decision of the Appellate Division, overruling demurrer to complaint, is reported in 64 App. Div. 30.

people, with the result that plaintiff has been greatly humiliated by the scoffs and jeers of persons who have recognized her face and picture on this advertisement and her good name has been attacked, causing her great distress and suffering both in body and mind; that she was made sick and suffered a severe nervous shock, was confined to her bed and compelled to employ a physician, because of these facts; that defendants had continued to print, make, use, sell, and circulate the said lithographs, and that by reason of the foregoing facts plaintiff had suffered damages in the sum of $15,000. The complaint prays that defendants be enjoined from making, printing, publishing, circulating, or using in any manner any likenesses of plaintiff in any form whatever, for further relief (which it is not necessary to consider here) and for damages.

It will be observed that there is no complaint made that plaintiff was libelled by this publication of her portrait. The likeness is said to be a very good one, and one that her friends and acquaintances were able to recognize: indeed, her grievance is that a good portrait of her, and, therefore, one easily recognized, has been used to attract attention toward the paper upon which defendant mill company's advertisements appear. Such publicity, which some find agreeable, is to plaintiff very distasteful, and thus, because of defendants' impertinence in using her picture without her consent for their own business purposes, she has been caused to suffer mental distress where others would have appreciated the compliment to their beauty implied in the selection of the picture for such purposes; but as it is distasteful to her, she seeks the aid of the courts to enjoin a further circulation of the lithographic prints containing her portrait made as alleged in the complaint, and as an incident thereto, to reimburse her for the damages to her feelings, which the complaint fixes at the sum of $15,000.

There is no precedent for such an action to be found in the decisions of this court; indeed, the learned judge who wrote the very able and interesting opinion in the Appellate Division said, while upon the threshold of the discussion of the question: " It may be said in the first place that the theory upon which this action is predicated is new, at least in instance if not in principle, and that few precedents can be found to sustain the claim made by the plaintiff, if indeed it can be said that there are any authoritative cases establishing her right to recover in this action." Nevertheless, that court reached the conclusion that plaintiff had a good cause of action against defendants, in that defendants had invaded what is called a " right of privacy " — in other words, the right to be let alone. Mention of such a right is not to be found in Blackstone, Kent, or any other of the great commentators upon the law, nor so far as the learning of counsel or the courts in this case have been able to discover, does its existence seem to have been asserted prior to about the year 1890, when it was presented with attractiveness and no inconsiderable ability in the Harvard Law

Review (Vol. IV, page 193) in an article entitled "The Right of Privacy."

The so-called right of privacy is, as the phrase suggests, founded upon the claim that a man has the right to pass through this world, if he wills, without having his picture published, his business enterprises discussed, his successful experiments written up for the benefit of others, or his eccentricities commented upon either in handbills, circulars, catalogues, periodicals, or newspapers, and, necessarily, that the things which may not be written and published of him must not be spoken of him by his neighbors, whether the comment be favorable or otherwise. While most persons would much prefer to have a good likeness of themselves appear in a responsible periodical or leading newspaper rather than upon an advertising card or sheet, the doctrine which the courts are asked to create for this case would apply as well to the one publication as to the other, for the principle which a court of equity is asked to assert in support of a recovery in this action is that the right of privacy exists and is enforceable in equity, and that the publication of that which purports to be a portrait of another person, even if obtained upon the street by an impertinent individual with a camera, will be restrained in equity, on the ground that an individual has the right to prevent his features from becoming known to those outside of his circle of friends and acquaintances.

If such a principle be incorporated into the body of the law through the instrumentality of a court of equity, the attempts to logically apply the principle will necessarily result, not only in a vast amount of litigation, but in litigation bordering upon the absurd, for the right of privacy, once established as a legal doctrine, cannot be confined to the restraint of the publication of a likeness, but must necessarily embrace as well the publication of a word-picture, a comment upon one's looks, conduct, domestic relations, or habits. And were the right of privacy once legally asserted, it would necessarily be held to include the same things if spoken instead of printed, for one, as well as the other, invades the right to be absolutely let alone. An insult would certainly be in violation of such a right, and with many persons would more seriously wound the feelings than would the publication of their picture. And so we might add to the list of things that are spoken and done day by day which seriously offend the sensibilities of good people, to which the principle which the plaintiff seeks to have imbedded in the doctrine of the law would seem to apply. I have gone only far enough to barely suggest the vast field of litigation which would necessarily be opened up should this court hold that privacy exists as a legal right enforceable in equity by injunction, and by damages where they seem necessary to give complete relief.

The legislative body could very well interfere and arbitrarily provide that no one should be permitted for his own selfish purpose to use the picture or the name of another for advertising purposes without his consent. In such event no embarrassment would result to the general body of the law, for the rule would be applicable only to cases provided for by the statute. The courts, however, being without authority to legislate, are required to decide cases upon principle, and so are necessarily embarrassed by precedents created by an extreme, and, therefore, unjustifiable application of an old principle.

The court below properly said that " while it may be true that the fact that no precedent can be found to sustain an action in any given case is cogent evidence that a principle does not exist upon which the right may be based, it is not the rule that the want of a precedent is a sufficient reason for turning the plaintiff out of court," provided — I think should be added — there can be found a clear and unequivocal principle of the common law which either directly or mediately governs it or which by analogy or parity of reasoning ought to govern it.

It is undoubtedly true that in the early days of chancery jurisdiction in England the chancellors were accustomed to deliver their judgments without regard to principles or precedents, and in that way the process of building up the system of equity went on, the chancellor disregarding absolutely many established principles of the common law. " In no other way," says Pomeroy, " could the system of equity jurisprudence have been commenced and continued so as to arrive at its present proportions." (Pomeroy's Eq. Jur. sect. 48.) In their work the chancellors were guided not only by what they regarded as the eternal principles of absolute right, but also by their individual consciences; but after a time when " the period of infancy was passed and an orderly system of equitable principles, doctrines, and rules began to be developed out of the increasing mass of precedents, this theory of a personal conscience was abandoned; and ' the conscience,' which is an element of the equitable jurisdiction, came to be regarded, and has so continued to the present day, as a metaphorical term, designating the common standard of civil right and expediency combined, based upon general principles and limited by established doctrines to which the court appeals, and by which it tests the conduct and rights of suitors — a juridical and not a personal conscience." (Pomeroy's Eq. Jur. sect. 57.)

The importance of observing the spirit of this rule cannot be overestimated, for, while justice in a given case may be worked out by a decision of the court according to the notions of right which govern the individual judge or body of judges comprising the court, the mischief which will finally result may be almost incalculable under our system which makes a decision in one case a precedent for decisions in all future cases which are akin to it in the essential facts.

So in a case like the one before us, which is concededly new to this court, it is important that the court should have in mind the effect upon future litigation and upon the development of the law which would necessarily result from a step so far outside of the beaten paths of both common law and equity, assuming — what I shall attempt to show in a moment — that the right of privacy as a legal doctrine enforceable in equity has not, down to this time, been established by decisions.

The history of the phrase " right of privacy " in this country seems to have begun in 1890 in a clever article in the Harvard Law Review — already referred to — in which a number of English cases were analyzed, and, reasoning by analogy, the conclusion was reached that — notwithstanding the unanimity of the courts in resting their decisions upon property rights in cases where publication is prevented by injunction — in reality such prevention was due to the necessity of affording protection to thoughts and sentiments expressed through the medium of writing, printing, and the arts, which is like the right not to be assaulted or beaten; in other words, that the principle actually involved though not always appreciated, was that of an inviolate personality, not that of private property.

This article brought forth a reply from the Northwestern Review (Vol. III, page 1) urging that equity has no concern with the feelings of an individual or with considerations of moral fitness, except as the inconvenience or discomfort which the person may suffer is connected with the possession or enjoyment of property, and that the English authorities cited are consistent with such view. Those authorities are now to be examined in order that we may see whether they were intended to and did mark a departure from the established rule which had been enforced for generations; or, on the other hand, are entirely consistent with it.

[The learned judge then commented upon various English cases; also upon several American cases, especially Schuyler *v.* Curtis, 147 N. Y. 434; Atkinson *v.* Doherty, 121 Mich. 372; and Corliss *v.* E. W. Walker Co., 57 Fed. Rep. 434. The point *actually decided* in 147 N. Y. 434 and in 121 Mich. 372 was that the widow or relatives of a deceased person cannot restrain the erection of his statue or the publication of his picture. In the Corliss case, the court declined to grant the request of a widow that the publication of a biography of her deceased husband should be enjoined; and finally (64 Fed. Rep. 280) declined to restrain the publication of his picture. The latter decision proceeded upon the ground that Mr. Corliss was a public character.]

This dictinction between public and private characters cannot possibly be drawn. On what principle does an author or artist forfeit his right of privacy and a great orator, a great preacher, or a great advocate retain his ? Who can draw a line of demarcation between public characters and private characters, let that line be as wavering and irregular as you please ? In the very case then before the judge, what had Mr. Corliss done by which he surrendered his right of privacy? In what respect did he by his inventions "ask for and desire public recognition" any more than a banker or merchant who prosecutes his calling? Or is the right of privacy the possession of mediocrity alone, which a person forfeits by giving rein to his ability, spurs to his industry, or grandeur to his character? A lady may pass her life in domestic privacy when, by some act of heroism or self-sacrifice, her name and fame fill the public ear. Is she to forfeit by her good deed the right of privacy she previously possessed? These considerations suggest the answer we would make to the position of the learned judge and at the same time serve to make more clear what we have elsewhere attempted to point out, namely, the absolute impossibility of dealing with this subject save by legislative enactment, by which may be drawn arbitrary distinctions which no court should promulgate as a part of general jurisprudence.

. . . .

An examination of the authorities leads us to the conclusion that the so-called "right of privacy" has not as yet found an abiding place in our jurisprudence, and, as we view it, the doctrine cannot now be incorporated without doing violence to settled principles of law by which the profession and the public have long been guided.

I do not say that, even under the existing law, in every case of the character of the one before us, or indeed in this case, a party whose likeness is circulated against his will is without remedy. By section 245 of the Penal Code any malicious publication by picture, effigy, or sign which exposes a person to contempt, ridicule, or obloquy is a libel, and it would constitute such at common law. Malicious in this definition means simply intentional and wilful. There are many articles, especially of medicine, whose character is such that using the picture of a person, particularly that of a woman, in connection with the advertisement of those articles might justly be found by a jury to cast ridicule or obloquy on the person whose picture was thus published. The manner or posture in which the person is portrayed might readily have a like effect. In such cases both a civil action and a criminal prosecution could be maintained. But there is no allegation in the complaint before us that this was the tendency of the publication complained of, and the absence of such an allegation is fatal to the maintenance of the action, treating it as one of libel. This case differs from an action brought for libellous words. In such case the alleged libel is stated in the complaint, and if the words are libellous *per se*, it is unnecessary to charge that their effect exposes the plaintiff to disgrace, ridicule, or obloquy. The law attributes to them that result. But where the libel is a picture which does not appear in the record, to make it libellous there must be a proper allegation as to its character.

The judgment of the Appellate Division and of the Special Term should be reversed and questions certified answered in the negative without costs, and with leave to the plaintiff to serve an amended complaint within twenty days, also without costs.

GRAY, J. (dissenting).

. . . .

In the present case, we may not say that the plaintiff's complaint is fanciful, or that her alleged injury is, purely, a sentimental one. Her objection to the defendants' acts is not one born of caprice; nor is it based upon the defendants' act being merely "distasteful" to her. We are bound to assume, and I find no difficulty in doing so, that the conspicuous display of her likeness, in various public places, has so humiliated her by the notoriety and by the public comments it has provoked, as to cause her distress and suffering, in body and in mind, and to confine her to her bed with illness.

If it were necessary, to be entitled to equitable relief, that the plaintiff's sufferings, by reason of the defendants' acts, should be serious, and appreciable by a pecuniary standard, clearly, we might well say, under the allegations of the complaint, that they were of such degree of gravity. However, I am not of the opinion that the gravity of the injury need be such as to be capable of being estimated by such a standard. If the right of privacy exists and this complaint makes out a case of its substantial violation, I think that the award of equitable relief, by way of an injunction, preventing the continuance of its invasion by the defendants, will not depend upon the complainant's ability to prove substantial pecuniary damages and, if the court finds the defendants' act to be without justification and for selfish gain and purposes, and to be of such a character, as is reasonably calculated to wound the feelings and to subject the plaintiff to the ridicule, or to the contempt of others, that her right to the preventive relief of equity will follow; without considering how far her sufferings may be measurable by a pecuniary standard.

The right of privacy, or the right of the individual to be let alone, is a personal right, which is not without judicial recognition. It is the complement of the right to the immunity of one's person. The individual has always been entitled to be protected in the exclusive use and enjoyment of that which is his own. The common law regarded his person and property as inviolate, and he has the absolute right to be let alone. (Cooley on Torts, page 29.) The principle is fundamental and essential in organized society that every one, in exercising a personal right and in the use of his property, shall respect the rights and properties of others. He must so conduct himself, in the enjoyment of the rights and privileges which belong to him as a member of society, as that he shall prejudice no one in the possession and enjoyment of those which are exclusively his. When, as here, there is an alleged invasion of some personal right, or privilege, the absence of exact precedent and the fact that early commentators upon the common law have no discussion upon the subject are of no material importance in awarding equitable relief. That the exercise of the preventive power of a court of equity is demanded in a novel case, is not a fatal objection.

. . . .

In an article in the Harvard Law Review, of December 15, 1890, which contains an impressive argument upon the subject of the "right of privacy," it was well said by the authors "that the individual shall have full protection in person and in property is a principle as old as the common law; but it has been found necessary from time to time to define anew the exact nature and extent of such protection. . . . The right to life had come to mean the right to enjoy life — the right to be let alone; the right to liberty secures the exercise of extensive civil privileges; and the term 'property' has grown to comprise every form of possession — intangible as well as tangible."

Instantaneous photography is a modern invention and affords the means of securing a portraiture of an individual's face and form *in invitum* their owner. While, so far forth as it merely does that, although a species of aggression, I concede it to be an irremediable and irrepressible feature of the social evolution. But, if it is to be permitted that the portraiture may be put to commercial or other uses for gain, by the publication of prints therefrom, then an act of invasion of the individual's privacy results, possibly more formidable and more painful in its consequences than an actual bodily assault might be. Security of person is as necessary as the security of property; and for that complete personal security, which will result in the peaceful and wholesome enjoyment of one's privileges as a member of society, there should be afforded protection, not only against the scandalous portraiture and display of one's features and person, but against the display and use thereof for another's commercial purposes or gain. The proposition is, to me, an inconceivable one that these defendants may, unauthorizedly, use the likeness of this young woman upon their advertisement, as a method of attracting widespread public attention to their wares, and that she must submit to the mortifying notoriety, without right to invoke the exercise of the preventive power of a court of equity.

Such a view, as it seems to me, must have been unduly influenced by a failure to find precedents in analogous cases, or some declaration by the great commentators upon the law of a common-law principle which would, precisely, apply to and govern the action; without taking into consideration that, in the existing state of society, new conditions affecting the relations of persons demand the broader extension of those legal principles, which underlie the immunity of one's person from attack. I think that such a view is unduly restricted, too, by a search for some property, which has been invaded by the defendants' act. Property is not, necessarily, the thing itself, which is owned; it is the right of the owner in relation to it. The right to be protected in one's possession of a thing, or in one's privileges, belonging to him as an individual, or secured to him as a member of the commonwealth, is property, and as such entitled to the protection of the law. The protective power of equity is not exercised upon the tangible thing, but upon the right to enjoy it; and, so, it is called forth for the protection of the right to that which is one's exclusive possession, as a property right. It seems to me that the principle, which is applicable, is analogous to that upon which courts of equity have interfered to protect the right of privacy, in cases of private writings, or of other unpublished products of the mind. The writer, or the lecturer, has been protected in his right to a literary property in a letter, or a lecture, against its unauthorized publication; because it is property, to which the right of privacy attaches. (Woolsey *v.* Judd, 4 Duer, 399; Gee *v.* Pritchard, 2 Swanst. 402; Abernathy *v.* Hutchinson, 3 L. J. Ch. 209; Folsom *v.* March, 2 Story, 100.) I think that this plaintiff has the same property in the right to be protected against the use of her face for defendant's commercial purposes, as she would have if they were publishing her literary compositions. The right would be conceded, if she had sat for her photograph; but if her face, or her portraiture, has a value, the value is hers exclusively until the use be granted away to the public. Any other principle of decision, in my opinion, is as repugnant to equity as it is shocking to reason. Judge Colt, of the United States Court, in Corliss *v.* Walker Co., 64 Fed. Rep. 280–285, a case involving the same question of an invasion of the right of privacy, with respect to the publication of a printed likeness of Mr. Corliss, expressed the opinion that "independently of the question of contract, I believe the law to be that a private individual has a right to be protected in the representation of his portrait in any form; that this is a property as well as a personal right; and that it belongs to the same class of rights which forbids the reproduction of a private manuscript or painting, or the publication of private letters, or of oral lectures delivered by a teacher to his class, or the revelation of the contents of a merchant's books by a clerk." The case itself is not in point in its facts; because the complainant was the widow of Mr. Corliss, and thus it came within the limitations of Schuyler *v.* Curtis.

The right to grant the injunction does not depend upon the existence of property, which one has in some contractual form. It depends upon the existence of property in any right which belongs to a person.

. . . .

It would be, in my opinion, an extraordinary view which, while conceding the right of a person to be protected against the unauthorized circulation of an unpublished lecture, letter, drawing, or other ideal property, yet would deny the same protection to a person whose portrait was unauthorizedly obtained, and made use of, for commercial purposes. The injury to the plaintiff is irreparable; because she cannot be wholly compensated in damages for the various consequences entailed by defendants' acts. The only complete relief is an injunction restraining their continuance. Whether, as incidental to that equitable relief, she should be able to recover only nominal damages is not material; for the issuance of the injunction does not, in such a case, depend upon the amount of the damages in dollars and cents.

A careful consideration of the question presented upon this appeal leads me to the conclusion that the judgment appealed from should be affirmed.

O'BRIEN, CULLEN, and WERNER, JJ., concur with PARKER, Ch. J.; BARTLETT and HAIGHT, JJ., concur with GRAY, J.

Judgment reversed, etc.[1]

[1] Corelli *v.* Wall, 22 Times L. R. 532 (post cards depicting imaginary incidents of an author's life); Atkinson *v.* Doherty, 121 Mich. 372 (picture of plaintiff's dead husband on cigar label); Henry *v.* Cherry, 30 R. I. 13 (picture as advertisement); Hillman *v.* Star Pub. Co., 64 Wash. 691 (picture of plaintiff in connection with report of arrest of her father for crime) *Accord.* Compare Chappell *v.* Stewart, 82 Md. 323 (shadowing).

Corliss *v.* Walker, 57 Fed. 434 (*semble*); Von Theodorovich *v.* Josef Beneficiary Ass'n, 154 Fed. 911 (*semble*); Pavesich *v.* New England Ins. Co., 122 Ga. 190 (picture as advertisement); Foster-Milburn Co. *v.* Chinn, 134 Ky. 424 (picture as advertisement); Douglas *v.* Stokes, 149 Ky. 506 (publishing photograph of deceased deformed child of plaintiff); Itzkovitch *v.* Whitaker, 115 La. 479, 117 La. 708 (photograph in rogues' gallery); Schulman *v.* Whitaker, 117 La. 704; Munden *v.* Harris, 153 Mo. App. 652 (picture as advertisement); Edison *v.* Edison Polyform & Mfg. Co., 73 N. J. Eq. 136 (picture — but here there was chiefly an interest of substance) *Contra.*

See also Dill, J. in Vanderbilt *v.* Mitchell, 72 N. J. Eq. 910, 919.

As to photographing persons arrested on charges of crime, see Hodgman *v.* Olsen, 86 Wash. 615.

NEW YORK, CIVIL RIGHTS LAW, §§ 50, 51 (Laws of 1903, ch. 132, §§ 1, 2).

§ 50. A person, firm, or corporation that uses for advertising purposes, or for the purposes of trade, the name, portrait, or picture of any living person without having first obtained the written consent of such person, or if a minor of his or her parent or guardian, is guilty of a misdemeanor.

§ 51. Any person whose name, portrait, or picture is used within this state for advertising purposes or for the purposes of trade without the written consent first obtained as above provided may maintain an equitable action in the supreme court of this state against the person, firm, or corporation so using his name, portrait, or picture, to prevent and restrain the use thereof; and may also sue and recover damages for any injuries maintained by reason of such use, and if the defendant shall have knowingly used such person's name, portrait, or picture in such manner as is forbidden or declared to be unlawful by this act, the jury, in its discretion, may award exemplary damages.

See Binns *v.* Vitagraph Co., 210 N. Y. 51.

On the whole subject, see Warren and Brandeis, The Right to Privacy, 4 Harvard Law Rev. 193; Pound, Interests of Personality, 28 Harvard Law Rev. 343, 362–364.

CHAPTER VIII

INTERFERENCE WITH ADVANTAGEOUS RELATIONS

DAVIES *v.* GARDINER

IN THE COMMON PLEAS, TRINITY TERM, 1593.

Reported in Popham, 36.[1]

AN action upon the case for a slander was brought by Anne Davies against John Gardiner; That whereas there was a communication of a marriage to be had between the plaintiff and one Anthony Elcock, the defendant, to the intent to hinder the said marriage, said and published that there was a grocer in London that did get her with child, and that she had the child by the said grocer, whereby she lost her marriage. To which the defendant pleaded not guilty, and was found guilty at the assizes at Aylesbury, to the damage of 200 marks. And now it was alleged, in arrest of judgment, that this matter appeareth to be merely spiritual, and therefore not determinable at common law, but to be prosecuted in the spiritual court. But *per Curiam* the action lies here, for a woman not married cannot by intendment have so great advancement as by her marriage, whereby she is sure of maintenance for her life, or during her marriage, and dower and other benefits which the temporal law gives by reason of her marriage; and therefore by this slander she is greatly prejudiced in that which is to be her temporal advancement, for which it is reason to give her remedy by way of action at common law. As if a woman keep a victualling house, to which divers of great credit repair, whereby she hath her livelihood, and one will say to her guests, that as they respect their credits, they take care how they use such a house, for there the woman is known to be a bawd, whereby the guests avoid her house, to the loss of her husband, shall not she in this case have an action at common law for such a slander? It is clear that she will. So, if one saith that a woman is a common strumpet, and that it is a slander to them to come to her house, whereby she loseth the advantage which she was wont to have by her guests, she shall have her action for this at common law.

So here upon these collateral circumstances, whereby it may appear that she hath more prejudice than can be by calling of one harlot, and the like. *And judgment was given for the plaintiff.*[2]

[1] 4 Rep. 16 *b*, s. c.

[2] Dame Morrison's Case, Jenk. 316; Matthew *v.* Crasse, 2 Bulst. 89; Sell *v.* Facy, 2 Bulst. 276, 3 Bulst. 48; Nelson *v.* Staff, Cro. Jac. 422; Thomson's Case,

ALLSOP *v.* ALLSOP

In the Exchequer, April 25, 1860.

Reported in 5 Hurlstone & Norman, 534.

Declaration. — That, before the committing of the grievances, the said Hannah was the wife of the plaintiff, William Allsop; and the defendant, on divers occasions, falsely and maliciously spoke and published of the plaintiff Hannah the words following (to the effect that he had had carnal connection with her whilst she was the wife of the plaintiff, William Allsop): "Whereby the plaintiff Hannah lost the society of her friends and neighbors, and they refused to, and did not, associate with her as they otherwise would have done, and she was much injured in her credit and reputation, and brought into public scandal and disgrace; and, by reason of the committing of the grievances, the said Hannah became and was ill and unwell for a long time and unable to attend to her necessary affairs and business, and the plaintiff, William Allsop, was put to and incurred much expense in and about the endeavoring to cure her of the illness which she labored under as aforesaid by reason of the committing of the said grievances; and the said William Allsop lost the society and association of his said wife for a long time in his domestic affairs, which he otherwise would have had."

Demurrer and joinder.[1]

Pollock, C. B. We are all of opinion that the defendant is entitled to judgment. There is no precedent for any such special damage as that laid in this declaration being made a ground of action, so as to render words actionable which otherwise would not be so. We ought to be careful not to introduce a new element of damage, recollecting to what a large class of actions it would apply, and what a dangerous use might be made of it. In actions for making false charges before magistrates, for giving false characters, and for torts of all kinds, illness might be said to have arisen from the wrong sustained by the plaintiff. The case of Ford *v.* Monroe, 20 Wendell, 210, is the only authority that has any tendency to throw light on the argument; but we ought not to act upon the authority of that case, opposed as it is to the universal practice of the law in this country. The courts here have always taken care that parties shall not be responsible for fanciful or remote damages, or, in fact, any that do not fairly and naturally result

Bendl. 148; Countess of Salop's Case, Bendl. 155; Taylor *v.* Tolwin, Latch, 218; Wicks *v.* Shepherd, Cro. Car. 155; Southold *v.* Daunston, Cro. Car. 269 *Accord.*

See Bridge *v.* Langton, Litt. 193; Norman *v.* Simons, 1 Vin. Abr. Act. Words, D, *a*, 12.

In Felty *v.* Felty, 164 Ky. 355, plaintiff's husband left her as a result of the defamatory words.

[1] The arguments of counsel are omitted, together with the concurring opinions of Martin, Bramwell, and Wilde, BB.

from the wrongful act itself. It is only lately that a clear and distinct view of the subject of damages was taken, in Hadley *v.* Baxendale, 9 Exch. 341, in which it was held that a person whose duty it is to deliver goods to another is not responsible for any damages resulting from the non-delivery, unless they are the damages which would result immediately and naturally, that is, according to the usual course of things, from the breach of contract itself, or such as may reasonably be supposed to have been in the contemplation of both parties at the time they made contract. Slander may be repeated, and the repetition may cause mischief. In one sense nothing is more natural than that such should be the case. So there are many other consequences which may follow in libel and slander in respect of which there is no remedy. This particular damage depends on the temperament of the party affected, and it may be laid down that illness arising from the excitement which the slanderous language may produce is not that sort of damage which forms a ground of action.

Judgment for the defendant.[1]

DAVIES *v.* SOLOMON

IN THE QUEEN'S BENCH, NOVEMBER 29, 1871.

Reported in Law Reports, 7 *Queen's Bench,* 112.

BLACKBURN, J.[2] The sole difficulty in deciding the case is caused by the opinion of Lord Wensleydale in Lynch *v.* Knight, 9 H. L. C. 577. He held that no action would lie for slander of a wife when the

[1] Guy *v.* Gregory, 9 Car. & P. 584; Adams *v.* Smith, 58 Ill. 417; Woodbury *v.* Thompson, 3 N. H. 194; Butler *v.* Hoboken Co., 73 N. J. Law, 45; Beach *v.* Ranney, 2 Hill, 309; Terwilliger *v.* Wands, 17 N. Y. 54 (overruling Bradt *v.* Towsley, 13 Wend. 253; Olmsted *v.* Brown, 12 Barb. 657; Fuller *v.* Fenner, 16 Barb. 333); Wilson *v.* Goit, 17 N. Y. 442; Bassell *v.* Elmore, 48 N. Y. 561; Shepherd *v.* Lamphier, 84 Misc. 498; Clark *v.* Morrison, 80 Or. 240 *Accord.* But see Garrison *v.* Sun Publishing Ass'n, 207 N. Y. 1 (defendant published a libel on plaintiff's wife resulting in illness and loss of her services).

McQueen *v.* Fulgham, 27 Tex. 463; Underhill *v.* Welton, 32 Vt. 40 *Contra.*

Damage caused by another person's repetition of the defendant's words is too remote. Holwood *v.* Hopkins, Cro. El. 787; Ward *v.* Weeks, 7 Bing. 211 (but see Riding *v.* Smith, 1 Ex. D. 91); Rutherford *v.* Evans, 4 Car. & P. 74; Tunnicliff *v.* Moss, 3 Car. & K. 83; Kendillon *v.* Maltby, 1 Car. & M. 402; Parkins *v.* Scott, 1 H. & C. 153; Dixon *v.* Smith, 5 H. & N. 450; Clarke *v.* Morgan, 38 L. T. Rep. 354; Bree *v.* Marescaux, 7 Q. B. Div. 434; Cates *v.* Kellogg, 9 Ind. 506; Stevens *v.* Hartwell, 11 Met. 542; Hastings *v.* Stetson, 126 Mass. 329; Hastings *v.* Palmer, 20 Wend. 225; Hallock *v.* Miller, 2 Barb. 630; Olmsted *v.* Brown, 12 Barb. 657; Terwilliger *v.* Wands, 17 N. Y. 54; Fowles *v.* Bowen, 30 N. Y. 20; Bassell *v.* Elmore, 48 N. Y. 561 (but see Sewell *v.* Catlin, 3 Wend. 295; Keenholts *v.* Becker, 3 Den. 346).

See also Whitney *v.* Moignard, 24 Q. B. Div. 630; Speight *v.* Gosnay, 60 L. J. Q. B. 231; Adams *v.* Cameron, 27 Cal. App. 625; Mills *v.* Flynn, 157 Ia. 477; Fitzgerald *v.* Young, 89 Neb. 693.

The rule is otherwise where the repetition is made as a privileged communication. Gillett *v.* Bullivant, 7 L. T. 490; Derry *v.* Handley, 16 L. T. Rep. 263; Fowles *v.* Bowen, 30 N. Y. 20.

[2] Only the opinion of the court is given.

only special damage alleged was the loss to the plaintiff of the consortium of her husband. In the present case, however, it is unnecessary to decide this question, for the declaration, after alleging the loss of cohabitation by the wife, proceeds to aver that "she lost, and was deprived of the companionship, and ceased to receive the hospitality of divers friends." Now, first, was that consequence such as might reasonably and naturally be expected to follow from the speaking of the slanderous words? Judging from the habits and manners of society, of all the consequences that might be expected to result from a statement that a woman had committed adultery, or had been guilty of unchastity, the most natural would be that those who had invited her and given her hospitality would thenceforth cease to do so. Then Moore *v.* Meagher, 1 Taunt. 39, decides that the loss of the hospitality of friends is sufficient special damage to sustain an action like the present, and the hospitality, as the word is there used, means simply that persons receive another into their houses, and give him meat and drink gratis. Perhaps such a definition may rather extend the signification of the word, but it is true in effect — for if they do not receive him, or if they make him pay for his entertainment, that is not hospitality. In Roberts *v.* Roberts, 5 B. & S. 384, 33 L. J. Q. B. 249, it is to be observed, that the loss suffered by the plaintiff in being excluded from a religious society was not temporal, and was therefore held not to be enough. But in the present case there is a matter of temporal damage — small though it be — laid in the declaration. It is also argued, that inasmuch as this action is brought by the wife, the husband being merely joined for conformity, the damage necessary to give a right to recover must be damage to her alone, and that the loss of hospitality which she has hitherto enjoyed is only pecuniary loss to her husband, and not to her. That certainly is a plausible argument, as the husband is of course bound to maintain his wife and to supply her with food, although her friends cease to do so. I am, however, unwilling to agree with such artificial reasoning, and I think that the real damage in this case is to the wife herself. Notwithstanding that it is the husband's duty to support his wife, he is only bound to provide her with necessaries suitable to his station in life; and she might, by visiting friends in a higher position than himself, enjoy luxuries which he either could not or might not choose to afford her. But I should be sorry to say that we must enter into a nice inquiry as to whether such hospitality would save the purse of the husband or of the wife. I am therefore of opinion that the declaration is good; and the demurrer must be overruled.

MELLOR and HANNEN, JJ., concurred.

Judgment for the plaintiffs.

CORCORAN v. CORCORAN

IN THE EXCHEQUER, IRELAND, NOVEMBER 17, 1857.

Reported in 7 Irish Common Law Reports, 272.

DEFAMATION. — The summons and plaint stated the speaking of words imputing prostitution to the plaintiff Anne, and calling her a vagabond, with an innuendo that this word imputed that she was a vagrant without a fixed place of abode. By means of the committing of which several grievances, the said plaintiff Anne hath been injured in her credit and reputation, and brought into disgrace with her acquaintances, in so much that her brother K. Dooley, who had promised to supply the said Anne with means to enable her to emigrate to Australia to join her husband, has now, in consequence of the imputations cast upon her character by the said defendant, retracted his promise until the truth or falsehood of the said charges shall have been first ascertained and established; whereby, &c.

Demurrer.

PENNEFATHER, B.[1] It certainly does strike me that this summons and plaint would not be good without the allegation of special damage.

Then, as to the special damage laid. I certainly agree that mere apprehension of damage would not be a sufficient statement; but here a promise has been laid. It is argued that no averment of the promisor's intention to perform it has been made, but I think it must be taken that he intended to perform it, until the contrary be shown. In cases of actions for breach of promise, as, for instance, of marriage, there is never any allegation contained to that effect, nor could it be maintained that, without such an averment, the pleading would not be sufficient.

Then follows an allegation here that, by reason of the speaking of the words, the promisor retracted his promise, and broke off his treaty of giving the plaintiff funds to enable her to emigrate. Now, if the words stopped there, I think there is no question whatever but there was special damage sustained by the breach of a promise which must have been beneficial to the plaintiff. The demurrer must be overruled.

MILLER v. DAVID

IN THE COMMON PLEAS, JANUARY 20, 1874.

Reported in Law Reports, 9 Common Pleas, 1187.

THE first count stated that the defendant falsely and maliciously published of the plaintiff, a stone-mason, and employed as such in certain works carried on by one Mayberry, these words: "He was the ringleader of the nine-hours system," whereby and by means of which

[1] The case is materially abridged.

premises the plaintiff was injured in his occupation of a stone-mason, and was discharged from his said employment at the said works, to wit, the Old Castle Iron and Tin Plate Works, and was without and could not obtain employment for a considerable time, and could get no employment but one of less value to the plaintiff, the place of employment being distant from his place of abode, and his necesary meals thereby becoming more costly, and such place of employment being exposed to wet weather.

The second count was similar, except that the words spoken were: "He has ruined the town by bringing about the nine hours system, and he has stopped several good jobs from being carried out, by being the ringleader of the system at Llanelly."

Demurrer, on the ground that the words were not in themselves defamatory, and that special damage consequent thereon, therefore, gave no action. Joinder in demurrer.[1]

Jan. 20. The judgment of the court (LORD COLERIDGE, C. J., and KEATING, BRETT, and DENMAN, JJ.) was delivered by

LORD COLERIDGE, C. J. In this case time was taken to consider our judgment, from the wish entertained by at least one member of the court to hold, if there were authority for the proposition, that a statement false and malicious made by one person in regard to another, whereby that other might probably, under some circumstances, and at the hands of some persons, suffer damage, would, if the damage resulted in fact, support an action for defamation. No proposition less wide in its terms than this would support the present declaration; for to call a man "the ringleader of the nine hours system," and to say of him that he "had ruined a place by bringing about that system," could not under many circumstances and at the hands of many people do the subject of such statement any damage at all. But we are unable to find any authority for a proposition so wide and general in its terms as would alone support this action.[2]

The rule, as laid down by De Grey, C. J., in Onslow *v.* Horne, that words are actionable if they be of probable ill consequence to a person in a trade or profession, or an office, is expressly disapproved of by the Court of Exchequer in Lumby *v.* Allday. Bayley, B., there says: "Every authority which I have been able to find either shows the want of some general requisite, as honesty, capacity, fidelity, or the like, or connects the imputation with the plaintiff's office, trade, or business." In that case, the words proved were a very strong imputation on the morality of the plaintiff, who was a clerk to a gas company. But the court held them not actionable, because the imputation con-

[1] The statement of the counts is abridged, and the arguments of counsel are omitted.

[2] But see now Paterson *v.* Welch, (Court of Sess. May 31, 1893) 20 R. 744. See also Odgers, Lib. & Sl. (1st ed.) 87, 91; Odgers, Outlines of Law of Libel, 17, 18; Clerk & Lindsell, Torts, (1st ed.) 497–98; Salmond, Torts, 426–27; Bower's Code of Actionable Defamation, 338–39, 443–45.

veyed by them did not imply the want of any of those qualities which a clerk ought to possess, and because the imputation had no reference to his conduct as clerk. That case and the language of Bayley, B., in delivering the judgment of the court, have since been repeatedly approved of, and are really decisive of this case.

The words before us are not actionable in themselves. No expression in them was argued to be so except the word "ringleader;" and, as to that, it is sufficient perhaps to say that Dr. Johnson points out the mistake of supposing that the word is by any means necessarily a word of bad import; for, amongst other authorities, he cites Barrow as calling St. Peter the "ringleader" of the Apostles.[1] Neither are the words connected with the trade or profession of the plaintiff, either by averment or by implication; so that, on neither ground can the declaration be supported. There is no averment here that the consequence which followed was intended by the defendant as the result of his words; and therefore it is not necessary to consider the question which was suggested on the argument, whether words not in themselves actionable or defamatory spoken under circumstances and to persons likely to create damage to the subject of the words, are, when the damage follows, ground of action. The judgment of Lord Wensleydale in Lynch v. Knight, 9 H. L. C., at p. 600, appears in favor of the affirmative of this question. But it is not necessary for us, for the reasons given, to express any opinion upon it; and upon this demurrer there must be judgment for the defendant.

Judgment for the defendant.

HATCHARD v. MÈGE

IN THE QUEEN'S BENCH DIVISION, APRIL 1, 1887.

Reported in 18 *Queen's Bench Division Reports*, 771.

DAY, J.[2] This is an application to set aside a nonsuit, which was directed by the Lord Chief Justice on the opening statement of counsel, and the question is whether the nonsuit was properly entered.

The statement of claim alleged that the defendants wrote and published "of and concerning the plaintiff and his said trade as a wine-merchant and importer the following false and malicious libel, that is to say: —

"'Caution: Delmonico Champagne. Messrs. Delbeck & Co., finding that wine stated to be Delmonico champagne is being advertised

[1] "It may be reasonable to allow St. Peter a primacy of order, such a one as the ringleader hath in a dance." — Barrow's Treatise of the Pope's Supremacy, Oxford edition of Works, 1830, vol. vii. p. 70. In Fox's Preface to Tyndall's Works, "these three learned fathers of blessed memory, William Tyndall, John Frith, and Robert Barons," are styled "chief ringleaders in these latter tymes of thys Church of England." — Reporter's Note.

[2] Only the opinion of Day, J., is given. Wills, J., concurred.

for sale in Great Britain, hereby give notice that such wine cannot be the wine it is represented to be, as no champagne shipped under that name can be genuine unless it has their names on their labels. Messrs. Delbeck & Co. further give notice that if such wine be shipped from France they will take proceedings to stop such shipments, and such other proceedings in England as they may be advised,' thereby meaning that the plaintiff had no right to use his said registered trade-mark or brand for champagne imported or sold by him, and that in using such trade-mark or brand he was acting fraudulently, and endeavoring to pass off an inferior champagne as being of the manufacture of Messrs. Delbeck & Co., and that the champagne imported and sold by the plaintiff was not genuine wine, and that no person other than the defendants had the right to use the word 'Delmonico' as a trade-mark or brand, or part of a trade-mark or brand, of champagne in the United Kingdom."

The publication there set out is complained of as a libel on the plaintiff in relation to his trade. It is substantially a warning not to buy Delmonico champagne because it is not genuine. The statement of claim alleges that the publication is false and malicious; that would be a question for the jury; it is not for us to consider the facts of the case; we can only look at what was opened by the plaintiff's counsel and what appears on the pleadings. The innuendo charges that the defendants intended to convey the meaning that the plaintiff had no right to use his trade-mark or brand, and that the wine he sold was not genuine. It may be that the publication bears that meaning, and that the words used import dishonesty. The plaintiff has died, and the question to be decided is how much, if any part, of the cause of action survives. The statute 4 Edw. 3, c. 7, and the course of practice, make it clear that a civil action for libel dies with the death of the person libelled. It does not come within the spirit, and certainly not within the letter of the statute. There is, however, a further question whether a right of action can survive because injury to the plaintiff's trade-mark is alleged. Injury to trade is constantly alleged in actions for libel, and therefore that does not affect the question of survivorship. In the present case the second part of the statement of claim may be subdivided into two separate and distinct claims. The first is for ordinary defamation, either independently of the plaintiff's trade, affecting his character by charging him with being a dishonest man, or defamation of him in his trade by charging him with being a dishonest wine-merchant. That claim would not survive, for it is nothing more than a claim in respect of a libel on an individual. But this publication may be construed to mean that the plaintiff had no right to use his trade-mark. This is not properly a libel, but is rather in the nature of slander of title, which is well defined in Odgers on Libel and Slander, c. v. p. 137, in the following passage: "But wholly apart from these cases there is a branch of the law (generally known by the inapproriate but convenient name — slander of title) which permits an action to be brought against any one who maliciously decries the plaintiff's goods or some other thing belonging to him, and thereby produces special damage to the plaintiff. This is obviously no part of the law of defamation, for the plaintiff's reputation remains uninjured; it is really an action on the case for maliciously acting in such a way as to inflict loss upon the plaintiff. All the preceding rules dispensing with proof of malice and special damage are therefore wholly inapplicable to cases of this kind. Here, as in all other actions on the case, there must be *et damnum et injuria.* The *injuria* consists in the unlawful words maliciously spoken, and the *damnum* is the consequent money loss to the plaintiff."

It appears, therefore, that the first and last parts of the innuendo in the present case suggest slander of title. As appears from the passage I have read, an action for slander of title is not an action for libel, but is rather in the nature of an action on the case for maliciously injuring a person in respect of his estate by asserting that he has no title to it. The action differs from an action for libel in this, that malice is not implied from the fact of publication, but must be proved, and that the falsehood of the statement complained of, and the existence of special damage, must also be proved in order to entitle the plaintiff to recover. The question whether the publication is false and malicious is for the jury. Here, I think, special damage is alleged by the statement of claim, and if the plaintiff could have shown injury to the sale of the wine which he sold under his trade-mark, he would have been entitled to recover, and that is a cause of action which survives.

For these reasons I am of opinion that the nonsuit was right so far as it related to the claim in respect of a personal libel, but was wrong as to the claim in respect of so much of the publication as impugned the plaintiff's right to sell under his trade-mark or brand.

There will, therefore, be an order for a new trial, but it will be limited to this latter part of the claim. *Order for a new trial.*[1]

[1] *Slander of title.* Mildmay's Case, 1 Rep. 175; Marvin *v.* Maynard, Cro. El. 419; Pennyman *v.* Rabanks, Cro. Eliz. 427; Newman *v.* Zachary, Al. 3; Rowe *v.* Roach, 1 M. & S. 304; Bignell *v.* Buzzard, 3 H. & N. 217; Webb *v.* Cecil, 9 B. Mon. 198; Ross *v.* Pynes, Wythe, 71, 3 Call, 490.

In Rowe *v.* Roach, *supra*, Lord Ellenborough said, p. 310: "The law makes no allowance for the slander of strangers, whatever it may do in behalf of those who have a real title, or a claim of title. *Rei immiscet se alienæ* is the good sense which must govern this case. Here the defendant is a stranger himself, and shows no authority from those who are parties in interest."

Where defendant has some interest, it is enough if he actually believes what he says against plaintiff's title.

Gerard *v.* Dickenson, 4 Rep. 18 a, Cro. El. 196; Lovett *v.* Weller, 1 Rolle R. 409; Anon., Sty. 414; Pitt *v.* Donovan, 1 M. & S. 639; Smith *v.* Spooner, 3 Taunt. 246; Green *v.* Button, 2 C. M. & R. 707; Pater *v.* Baker, 3 C. B. 831; Watson *v.* Reynolds, M. & M. 1; Carr *v.* Duckett, 5 H. & N. 783; Atkins *v.* Perrin, 3 F. & F. 179; Brook *v.* Rawl, 4 Ex. 521; Burnett *v.* Tak, 45 L. T. Rep. 743; Steward *v.* Young, L. R. 5 C. P. 122; Wren *v.* Weild, L. R. 4 Q. B. 730; Hart *v.* Wall, 2 C. P. D. 146 (*semble*); Baker *v.* Piper, 2 T. L. R. 733; Dicks *v.* Brooks, 15

MALACHY *v.* SOPER

In the Common Pleas, November 25, 1836.

Reported in 3 *Bingham, New Cases,* 371.

Tindal, C. J.[1] In this case a verdict having been found for the plaintiff at the trial of the cause with £5 damages, a motion has been made to arrest the judgment on the ground that the declaration does not state any legal cause of action. And we are of opinion that this objection is well founded; and that the judgment must be arrested.

This is not an ordinary action for defamation of the person, by the publication of slander either oral or written; in which form of action no special damage need either be alleged or proved; the law presuming that the uttering of the slanderous words, or the publishing of the libel, have of themselves a natural and necessary tendency to injure the plaintiff. But this is an action to recover damages by reason of the publication of a paragraph in a newspaper, which contains no other charge than that the "petition in a bill filed in the Court of Chancery against the plaintiff, and certain other persons as share-owners in a certain mine, for an account and an injunction, had been granted by the Vice-Chancellor, and that persons duly authorized had arrived in the workings." The publication therefore is one which slanders not the person or character of the plaintiff, but his title as one of the shareholders to the undisputed possession and enjoyment of his shares of the mine. And the objection taken is, that the plaintiff, in order to maintain this action, must show a special damage to have happened from the publication, and that this declaration shows none.

The first question therefore is, does the law require in such an action an allegation of special damage? And looking at the authorities we think they all point the same way. The law is clearly laid down in Sir W. Jones, 196 (Lowe *v.* Harewood): "of slander of title, the plaintiff

Ch. D. 22; Halsey *v.* Brotherhood, 19 Ch. D. 386; Royal Co. *v.* Wright, 18 Pat. Cas. Rep. 95; Dunlop Co. *v.* Talbot, 20 T. L. R. 579; Boulton *v.* Shields, 3 Up. Can. Q. B. 21; Hill *v.* Ward, 13 Ala. 310; McDaniel *v.* Baca, 2 Cal. 326; Thompson *v.* White, 70 Cal. 135; Reid *v.* McLendon, 44 Ga. 156; Van Tuyl *v.* Riner, 3 Ill. App. 556; Stark *v.* Chitwood, 5 Kan. 141; Gent *v.* Lynch, 23 Md. 58; Swan *v.* Tappan, 5 Cush. 104; Walkley *v.* Bostwick, 49 Mich. 374; Chesebro *v.* Powers, 78 Mich. 472; Meyrose *v.* Adams, 12 Mo. App. 329; Butts *v.* Long, 106 Mo. App. 313; Andrew *v.* Deshler, 45 N. J. Law, 167; Kendall *v.* Stone, 5 N. Y. 14; Like *v.* McKinstry, 4 Keyes, 397, 3 Abb. App. 62, 41 Barb. 186; Hovey *v.* Rubber Co., 57 N. Y. 119; Dodge *v.* Colby, 37 Hun, 515, 108 N. Y. 445; Lovell Co. *v.* Houghton, 116 N. Y. 520; Hastings *v.* Giles Co., 51 Hun, 364, 121 N. Y. 674; Cornwell *v.* Parke, 52 Hun, 596, 123 N. Y. 657; McElwee *v.* Blackwell, 94 N. C. 261; Harriss *v.* Sneeden, 101 N. C. 273.

Compare Virtue *v.* Creamery Mfg. Co., 123 Minn. 17.

As to the requirement of "malice," see Coffman *v.* Henderson, 9 Ala. App. 553; Fearon *v.* Fodera, 169 Cal. 370; Long *v.* Rucker, 166 Mo. App. 572; Potosi Zinc Co. *v.* Mahoney, 36 Nev. 390; Fant *v.* Sullivan, (Tex. Civ. App.) 152 S. W. 515.

See Smith, Disparagement of Property, 13 Columbia Law Rev. 13, 121.

[1] Only the opinion of the court is given.

shall not maintain action, unless it was *re vera* a damage; *scil.*, that he was hindered in sale of his land; so there the particular damage ought to be alleged." And in addition to the cases cited at the bar, viz., Sir John Tasborough *v.* Day, Cro. Jac. 484, and Manning *v.* Avery, Keb. 153, the case of Cane *v.* Goulding, Style's Rep. 169, 176, furnishes a strong authority. That was an action on the case for slandering the plaintiff's title, by speaking these words, viz., "his right and title thereunto is nought, and I have a better title than he." The words were alleged to be spoken *falso et malitiose,* and that he was likely to sell, and was injured by the words; and that by reason of speaking the words, he could not recover his tithes. After verdict for the plaintiff, there was a motion in arrest of judgment; and Rolle, C. J., said, "there ought to be a scandal and a particular damage set forth, and there is not here;" and upon its being moved again and argued by the judges, Rolle, C. J., held that the action did not lie, although it was alleged that the words were spoken *falso et malitiose* for "the plaintiff ought to have a special cause; but that, the verdict might supply; but the plaintiff ought also to have showed a special damage which he hath not done, and this the verdict cannot supply: the declaration here is too general, and upon which no good issue can be joined; and he ought to have alleged, that there was a communication had before the words spoken touching the sale of the lands whereof the title was slandered, and that by speaking of them the sale was hindered;" and cited several cases to that effect.

We hold, therefore, on the authority of these cases, that an action for slander of title is not properly an action for words spoken, or for libel written and published, but an action on the case for special damage sustained by reason of the speaking or publication of the slander of the plaintiff's title. This action is ranged under that division of actions in the Digests, and other writers on the text law, and such we feel bound to hold it to remain at the present day.

The next question is, has there been such a special damage alleged in this case, as will satisfy the rule laid down by the authorities above referred to? The doctrine of the older cases is, that the plaintiff ought to aver that, by the speaking, he could not sell or lease (Cro. Eliz. 197, Cro. Car. 140); and that it will not be sufficient to say only, that he had an intent to sell, without alleging a communication for sale (R. 1 Roll. 244). Admitting, however, that these may be put as instances only, and that there may be many more cases in which a particular damage may be equally apparent without such allegation, they establish at least this, that in the action for slander of title, there must be an express allegation of some particular damage resulting to the plaintiff from such slander. Now the allegation upon this record is only this, "that the plaintiff is injured in his rights; and the shares so possessed by him, and in which he is interested, have been and are much depreciated and lessened in value; and divers persons have believed and do believe that he has little or no right to the shares, and that the mine cannot be lawfully worked or used for his benefit; and that he hath been hindered and prevented from selling or disposing of his said shares in the said mine, and from working and using the same in so ample and beneficial a manner as he otherwise would have done." And we are of opinion that this is not such an allegation of special damage as the authorities above referred to require, where the action is not founded on the words spoken or written, but upon the special damage sustained.

It has been argued in support of the present action, that it is not so much an action for slander of title as an action for a libel on the plaintiff in the course of his business, and in the way of gaining his livelihood, and that such an action is strictly and properly an action for defamation, and so classed and held by all the authorities. But we think it sufficient to advert to the declaration, to be convinced that the publication complained of was really and strictly a slander of the plaintiff's title to his shares, and nothing else. The bill in Chancery, out of which the publication arose, is filed by Tollervy, who disputed the plaintiff's right to the whole of the shares, and claimed in himself a right to part of the same, and prayed that he might be declared to be entitled to some of them and the only mention made as to the working of the mines, was with reference to the appointment of a receiver to the profits thereof. And we think it would be doing violence to the natural meaning of the terms of the publication, if we were to hold it to be published of the plaintiff in the course of his business or occupation, or mode of acquiring his livelihood, and not as referring to the disputed title of the shares of the mine.

It has been urged, secondly, that however necessary it may be, according to the ancient authorities, to allege some particular damage in cases of unwritten slander of title, the case of written slander stands on different grounds; and that an action may be maintained without an allegation of damage actually sustained, if the plaintiff's right be impeached by a written publication, which of itself, it is contended, affords presumption of injury to the plaintiff. No authority whatever has been cited in support of this distinction. And we are of opinion that the necessity for an allegation of actual damage in the case of slander of title, cannot depend upon the medium through which that slander is conveyed, that is, whether it be through words, or writing, or print; but that it rests on the nature of the action itself, namely, that it is an action for special damage actually sustained, and not an action for slander. The circumstance of the slander of title being conveyed in a letter or other publication appears to us to make no other difference than that it is more widely and permanently disseminated, and the damages in consequence more likely to be serious than where the slander of title is by words only; but that it makes no difference whatever in the legal ground of action.

For these reasons we are of opinion, that the action is not maintainable, and that the judgment must be arrested; and, consequently, it becomes unnecessary to inquire whether the *innuendo* laid in the declaration is more large than it ought to have been.

We therefore make the rule for arresting the judgment,

Absolute.[1]

WHITE *v.* MELLIN

IN THE HOUSE OF LORDS, FEBRUARY 14, 1895.

Reported in [1895] *Appeal Cases*, 154.

THE respondent was the proprietor of Mellin's food for infants, which he sold in bottles enclosed in wrappers bearing the words "Mellin's Infants' Food." The respondent was in the habit of supplying the appellant with these bottles, which the appellant sold again to the public after affixing on the respondent's wrappers a label as follows: —

"Notice.

"The public are recommended to try Dr. Vance's prepared food for infants and invalids, it being far more nutritious and healthful than any other preparation yet offered. Sold in barrels, each containing 1 lb. nett weight, at 7½*d.* each, or in 7 lb. packets 3*s.* 9*d.* each. Local agent, Timothy White, chemist, Portsmouth."

The appellant was the proprietor of Vance's food. Discovering this practice, the respondent brought an action against the appellant, claiming an injunction to restrain him and damages.

At the trial before Romer, J., the plaintiff proved the above facts, and called two analysts and a physician, the result of whose evidence is stated in Lord Herschell's judgment. Briefly, they testified that in their opinion Mellin's food was suitable for infants, especially up to the age of six months, and persons who could not digest starchy mat-

[1] Tasburgh *v.* Day, Cro. Jac. 484; Gresham *v.* Grinsley, Yelv. 88; Sneade *v.* Badley, 3 Bulst. 74, 1 Roll. 244; Law *v.* Harwood, Cro. Car. 140, W. Jones, 196; Cane *v.* Golding, Sty. 169, 176; Manning *v.* Avery, 3 Keb. 153; Haddan *v.* Lott, 15 C. B. 411; Evans *v.* Harlow, 5 Q. B. 624; Ashford *v.* Choate, 20 Up. Can; C. P. 471; Collins *v.* Whitehead, 34 Fed. 121; Ebersole *v.* Fields, 181 Ala. 421; Stark *v.* Chitwood, 5 Kan. 141; Continental Co. *v.* Little, 135 Ky. 618; Swan *v.* Tappan, 5 Cush. 104; Gott *v.* Pulsifer, 122 Mass. 235; Dooling *v.* Budget Co., 144 Mass. 258; Boynton *v.* Shaw Co., 146 Mass. 219; Wilson *v.* Dubois, 35 Minn. 471; Tobias *v.* Harland, 4 Wend. 537; Madison Church *v.* Madison Church, 26 How. Pr. 72; Linden *v.* Graham, 1 Duer, 670; Bailey *v.* Dean, 5 Barb. 297; Kendall *v.* Stone, 5 N. Y. 14; Kennedy *v.* Press Co., 41 Hun, 422; Childs *v.* Tuttle, 48 Hun, 228; Maglio *v.* N. Y. Co., 93 App. Div. 546; Felt *v.* Germania Life Ins. Co., 149 App. Div. 14; Witteman Bros. *v.* Witteman Co., 88 Misc. 266; McGuinness *v.* Hargiss, 56 Wash. 162 *Accord.*

Compare Fleming *v.* McDonald, 230 Pa. St. 75.

The breach of a contract by a third person is special damage. Green *v.* Button, 2 C. M. & R. 707. But see *contra*, Kendall *v.* Stone, 5 N. Y. 14; Brentman *v.* Note, 3 N. Y. Sup. 420 (N. Y. City Court).

ters, and that Vance's food was unsuitable for such beings, nay pernicious and dangerous for very young infants. At the close of the plaintiff's case Romer, J., being of opinion that the label was merely the puff of a rival trader and that no cause of action was disclosed, dismissed the action with costs. The Court of Appeal (Lindley, Lopes, and Kay, L.JJ.) being of opinion that the cause ought to have been heard out, discharged that judgment and ordered a new trial, [1894] 3 Ch. 276.[1]

LORD HERSCHELL, L. C. (after stating the facts): —

My Lords, in the Court of Appeal Lindley, L. J., stated the law thus: "If upon hearing the whole of the evidence to be adduced before him the result should be that the statement contained in the label complained of is a false statement about the plaintiff's goods to the disparagement of them, and if that statement has caused injury to or is calculated to injure the plaintiff, this action will lie." Lopes, L. J., said: "All I desire to say is that, in my opinion, it is actionable to publish maliciously without lawful occasion a false statement disparaging the goods of another person and causing such other person damage, or likely to cause such other person damage."

None of the learned judges in the Court of Appeal dealt with the evidence which had been adduced on behalf of the plaintiff; but I think it must be taken that they had arrived at the conclusion that that evidence did bring the case within those statements of the law. Of course, if the plaintiff, on his evidence, had made out no case, he could not complain that the learned judge decided against him and did not hear the witnesses for the defendant; the action was in that case properly dismissed. I take it, therefore, that although the learned judges did not analyse the evidence or make any reference to it, they must have concluded that it established a case coming within the law as they laid it down. My Lords, as I understand, in the view of those learned judges, or in the view of Lindley, L. J., to take his statement of the law in the first place, it was necessary in order to the maintenance of the action that three things should be proved: that the defendant had disparaged the plaintiff's goods, that such disparagement was false, and that damage had resulted or was likely to result. Now, my Lords, the only statement made by the defendant by means of the advertisement is this: that Vance's food was the most healthful and nutritious for infants and invalids that had been offered to the public. The statement was perfectly general, and would apply in its terms not only to the respondent's infants' food but to all others that were offered to the public. I will take it as sufficiently pointed at the plaintiff's food by reason of its being affixed to a bottle of the plaintiff's food when sold, and that it does disparage the plaintiff's goods by asserting that they are not as healthful and as nutri-

[1] The arguments and the concurring opinions of Lords Watson, Macnaghten, Morris, and Shand are omitted.

tious as those recommended by the defendant. The question then arises, Has it been proved on the plaintiff's own evidence that that was a false disparagement of the plaintiff's goods ?

I will state what I understand to be the result of the plaintiff's evidence. Mellin's food for infants and invalids is a preparation of such a nature that the food is said to be predigested, and therefore not to make that call upon the digestion which food ordinarily does; that as regards children under six months of age Mellin's food is the only one which could be suitably used in the place of the ordinary means of nourishment, the mother's milk, and that any farinaceous food would at that age be not only not nutritious but prejudicial. And so far, accepting the plaintiff's evidence for this purpose, there being no evidence to the contrary, the plaintiff, I think, establishes that his food was specially meritorious for that class of cases, and that it would not be correct to say that as regards these children of very tender age Vance's food or any other farinaceous food would be not only more healthful and nutritious, but as healthful and nutritious. But then it appears that when a child has passed the age up to which nutrition at the breast may ordinarily be said to continue, the use of some farinaceous food is not only not prejudicial but desirable, and that if the child were to be always brought up upon a food which would be suitable during the very earliest weeks or months, its digestion would be likely to suffer rather than benefit, and there would be not more, but less nourishment. After twelve months, as I understand the evidence, the farinaceous food would be distinctly better for the purposes of nutrition and health than this pre-digested food. That, my Lords, I take to be a fair statement of the result of the evidence. Can it be said, under those circumstances, that it is a false disparagement of the plaintiff's goods to say that this other preparation — Vance's — is more nutritious and healthful for infants and invalids ? I put aside the question of invalids: upon that there was no evidence at all. The plaintiff did not say that his was more healthful, or that the defendant's was not more healthful. It is therefore unnecessary to consider the case of invalids, and it is enough to confine one's attention to the case of infants.

The word " infants " is not in ordinary parlance confined to children of very tender age. If one looks at its derivation etymologically it would apply to children so long as they are not able to articulate distinctly — not able to speak — and nobody would hesitate to refer to children, I should say, at least under two years of age as infants, just as much as they would to children under six months of age. Therefore, if you look at the class of infants as a whole, it is by no means shown that the statement that Vance's food is more nutritious and healthful than the plaintiff's food is false. If the reference had been specially to that very early period of life during which Mellin's food would be beneficial and the other prejudicial, no doubt a statement of that description might well be said to be a false statement; but looking fairly at the language used and the meaning to be attributed to it, I am not satisfied that it has been shown that by means of this advertisement the defendant falsely disparaged the plaintiff's goods. But, my Lords, assuming that he did so, the Court of Appeal regarded it as requisite for the maintenance of the action that something further should be proved, and that is that the disparaging statement has caused injury to or is calculated to injure the plaintiff. Upon that there is a complete absence of evidence. The plaintiff was called, but he did not state that he had sustained any injury, nor did he even say that it was calculated to injure him, and I own it seems to me impossible, in the absence of any such statement or evidence, to say that it is a case in which such must be the necessary consequence; on the contrary, speaking for myself, I should doubt very much whether it was likely to be the consequence. After all, the advertisement is of a very common description, puffing, it may be, extremely and in an exaggerated fashion, these particular goods, Vance's food. That advertisement was outside the wrapper; inside was found an advertisement of Mellin's food, in which Mellin's food was stated to be recommended by the faculty as best for infants and invalids. Why is it to be supposed that any one buying this bottle at the chemist's would be led to believe that Mellin's food which he had bought was not a good article or not as good an article as another, merely because a person who obviously was seeking to push a rival article said that his article was better? My Lords, why should people give such a special weight to this anonymous puff of Vance's food, obviously the work of some one who wanted to sell it, as that it should lead him to determine to buy it instead of Mellin's food, which was said to be recommended by the faculty as the best for infants and invalids? I confess I do not wonder that the plaintiff did not insist that he had sustained injury by what the defendant had done. There is an entire absence of any evidence that the statement complained of either had injured or was calculated to injure the plaintiff. If so, then the case is not brought even within the definition of the law which Lindley, L. J., gives.

Lopes, L. J., adds the word "maliciously," that "it is actionable to publish maliciously without lawful occasion a false statement disparaging the goods of another person." By that it may be intended to indicate that the object of the publication must be to injure another person, and that the advertisement is not published *bona fide* merely to sell the advertiser's own goods, or at all events, that he published it with a knowledge of its falsity. One or other of those elements, it seems to me, must be intended by the addition of the word "maliciously." Both those are certainly absent here. There is nothing to show that the object of the defendant was other than to puff his own goods and so sell them, nor is there anything to show that he did not believe that his food was better than any other.

The only case which the learned counsel for the respondent was able to rely upon as at all approaching the present is the case of the Western Counties Manure Company *v.* Lawes Chemical Manure Company, L. R. 9 Ex. 218, in which case a declaration was held good which alleged the disparagement of the plaintiff's goods by stating that they were inferior to those sold by the defendants.[1] In that case special damage was alleged in the declaration, and I think that that allegation was regarded by both the learned judges who were parties to the decision as material and essential. In the earlier case of Evans *v.* Harlow, 5 Q. B. 624, a statement was complained of which distinctly disparaged the plaintiff's goods. It cautioned the public against them, it pointed out to the public that they were not likely to realize the purpose for which they were designed, and the allegation was that "the defendant published a libel of and concerning the plaintiff and of and concerning him in his said trade and of and concerning his design as follows." In that case there was no allegation of special damage; there was a demurrer to the declaration, and the declaration was held bad. Now, the only distinction that I can see between that case and the case of the Western Counties Manure Company *v.* Lawes Chemical Manure Company is that in the latter case special damage was alleged, whereas in the former it was not. Bramwell, B., does not call specific attention to the differentia between the case before him and the case of Evans *v.* Harlow, but he says that there is nothing in any of the cases inconsistent with the judgment which he is pronouncing. Pollock, B., who was the other judge, pointed out that in Evans *v.* Harlow there was no allegation of special damage. Therefore, my Lords, the utmost that the Western Counties Manure Company *v.* Lawes Chemical Manure Company, L. R. 9 Ex. 218, can be claimed as an authority for is this, that an action will lie for falsely disparaging another's goods where special damage results. Evans *v.* Harlow, 5 Q. B. 624, is a distinct authority that it will not lie where special damage does not result. In the present case it cannot be pretended that any special damage was either alleged or proved.

Mr. Moulton sought to extricate himself from that difficulty in this way: he said that if this were an action for damages that might be a well-founded objection to it, but that it is not an action for damages but a claim for an injunction, and that although it may be that to support an action for damages it would be necessary to allege and prove special damage, that is not necessary where an injunction is claimed — that it is enough if a false statement is made and is likely to be repeated.

[1] *Disparagement of goods.* In the case cited it was held actionable to say falsely that plaintiffs' manure was inferior to defendants' if done without legal excuse. Young *v.* Macrae, 3 B. & S. 264; Alcott *v.* Millar, 21 T. L. R. 30; Dooling *v.* Budget Co., 144 Mass. 258 (*semble*); Boynton *v.* Shaw Co., 146 Mass. 219; Wilson *v.* Dubois, 35 Minn. 471; Wier *v.* Allen, 51 N. H. 177; Snow *v.* Judson, 38 Barb. 210; Kennedy *v.* Press Co., 41 Hun, 422 (*semble*); Paull *v.* Halferty, 63 Pa. St. 46; Young *v.* Geiske, 209 Pa. St. 515 *Accord.*

Now my Lords, no authority was cited to show that a Court of Equity under any of the branches of its jurisdiction had ever granted or would grant an injunction in such a case. Certainly there is no rule of equity under which it may be said generally that a Court of Equity would restrain every publication of a false statement. In the case of Canham *v.* Jones, 2 V. & B. 218, the bill stated that a certain Mr. Swainson had been the sole proprietor of a secret for preparing the medicine called " Velno's Vegetable Syrup," and that the plaintiff had obtained title to it under his will and had sold the medicine. Then the complaint was that the defendant, who had been a servant of Swainson, was employed in the preparation of the syrup but was not acquainted with the complete preparation, certain essential ingredients being introduced only by Swainson himself and only in the presence of the plaintiff. Then it alleged " that the defendant being discharged from his service had made and advertised for sale a spurious preparation under the name of Velno's Vegetable Syrup, stated by him to be the same medicine in composition and quality as that made by Swainson and the plaintiff, the defendant's advertisement certifying that the medicine prepared by him at his residence under the name of Velno's Vegetable Syrup is precisely the same with that made and sold by the late Mr. Swainson." It was alleged that that was untrue, and that it was a spurious preparation pretending to be the same when it really was not. To that bill the defendant put in a general demurrer for want of equity. That demurrer was sustained by the Vice-Chancellor, Sir Thomas Plumer, although for the purposes of that demurrer it was taken that the defendant selling this article was falsely stating that it was the same as the plaintiff's.

My Lords, the learned counsel relied upon recent cases in which an injunction has been granted to restrain the publication of a libel, and he suggested that there had been a growth of equity jurisprudence which had brought within its ambit a class of cases which were previously not regarded as within it. But when the case in which the Court of Appeal laid down that an injunction might be granted to restrain the publication of a libel is looked at, it will be seen that the decision was not founded upon any principle or rule of equity jurisprudence, but upon the fact that a Court of Common Law could have granted such an injunction in an action of libel, and that since the Judicature Act the power which a Court of Common Law possessed in that respect is now possessed also by the Court of Chancery. That was distinctly the ground upon which the judgment was founded, that " the 79th and 82d sections of the Common Law Procedure Act 1854 undoubtedly conferred on the Courts of Common Law the power, if a fit case should arise, to grant injunctions at any stage of a cause in all personal actions of contract or tort, with no limitation as to defamation; " and then, inasmuch as those powers are now possessed by the

Chancery Division, it was held that they likewise could in such cases grant an injunction. That was the decision in Bonnard *v.* Perryman, [1891] 2 Ch. 269.

My Lords, obviously to call for the exercise of that power it would be necessary to show that there was an actionable wrong well laid, and if the statement only showed a part of that which was necessary to make up a cause of action — that is to say, if special damage was necessary to the maintenance of the action, and that special damage was not shown — a tort in the eye of the law would not be disclosed, the case would not be within those provisions, and no injunction would be granted. I think, therefore, for these reasons, that the plaintiff would not be entitled to an injunction, any more than he would be entitled to maintain an action unless he established all that was necessary to make out that a tort had been committed; and for the reasons which I have given, taking the Western Counties Manure Company *v.* Lawes Chemical Manure Company, L. R. 9 Ex. 218, to be good law, he has not brought himself within it.

But, my Lords, I cannot help saying that I entertain very grave doubts whether any action could be maintained for an alleged disparagement of another's goods, merely on the allegation that the goods sold by the party who is alleged to have disparaged his competitor's goods are better either generally or in this or that particular respect than his competitor's are. Of course, I put aside the question (it is not necessary to consider it) whether where a person intending to injure another, and not in the exercise of his own trade and vaunting his own goods, has maliciously and falsely disparaged the goods of another, an action will lie; I am dealing with the class of cases which is now before us, where the only disparagement consists in vaunting the superiority of the defendant's own goods. In Evans *v.* Harlow Lord Denman expressed himself thus: "The gist of the complaint is the defendant's telling the world that the lubricators sold by the plaintiff were not good for their purpose, but wasted the tallow. A tradesman offering goods for sale exposes himself to observations of this kind, and it is not by averring them to be 'false, scandalous, malicious, and defamatory' that the plaintiff can found a charge of libel upon them. To decide so would open a very wide door to litigation, and might expose every man who said his goods were better than another's to the risk of an action." My Lords, those observations seem to me to be replete with good sense. It is to be observed that Evans *v.* Harlow, 5 Q. B. 624, does not appear to have been decided on the ground merely that there was no allegation of special damage. The only judge who alludes to the absence of such an allegation is Patteson, J. No reference to it is to be found either in the judgment of Lord Denman or in the judgment of Wightman, J., the other two judges who took part in that decision; and I think it is impossible not to see that, as Lord Denman says, a very wide door indeed would be opened to litigation, and that the courts might be constantly employed in trying the relative merits of rival productions, if an action of this kind were allowed.

Mr. Moulton sought to distinguish the present case by saying that all that Lord Denman referred to was one tradesman saying that his goods were better than his rival's. That, he said, is a matter of opinion, but whether they are more healthful and more nutritious is a question of fact. My Lords, I do not think it is possible to draw such a distinction. The allegation of a tradesman that his goods are better than his neighbor's very often involves only the consideration whether they possess one or two qualities superior to the other. Of course "better" means better as regards the purpose for which they are intended, and the question of better or worse in many cases depends simply upon one or two or three issues of fact. If an action will not lie because a man says that his goods are better than his neighbor's, it seems to me impossible to say that it will lie because he says that they are better in this or that or the other respect. Just consider what a door would be opened if this were permitted. That this sort of puffing advertisement is in use is notorious; and we see rival cures advertised for particular ailments. The Court would then be bound to inquire, in an action brought, whether this ointment or this pill better cured the disease which it was alleged to cure — whether a particular article of food was in this respect or that better than another. Indeed, the courts of law would be turned into a machinery for advertising rival productions by obtaining a judicial determination which of the two was the better. As I said, advertisements and announcements of that description have been common enough; but the case of Evans *v.* Harlow, 5. Q. B. 624, was decided in the year 1844, somewhat over half a century ago, and the fact that no such action — unless it be Western Counties Manure Co. *v.* Lawes Chemical Manure Co., L. R. 9 Ex. 218 — has ever been maintained in the Courts of Justice is very strong indeed to show that it is not maintainable. It is, indeed, unnecessary to decide the point in order to dispose of the present appeal.

For the reasons which I have given I have come to the conclusion that the judgment of the court below cannot be sustained, even assuming the law to be as stated by the learned judges; but inasmuch as the case is one of great importance, and some additional color would be lent to the idea that an action of this description was maintainable by the observations in the court below, I have thought it only right to express my grave doubts whether any such action could be maintained even if the facts brought the case within the law there laid down.

Upon the whole, therefore, I think that the judgment of Romer, J., was right and ought to be restored and that this appeal should be allowed, with the usual result as to costs; and I so move your Lordships.

Order of the Court of Appeal reversed; Judgment of Romer, J., restored, with costs here and in the Court of Appeal; Cause remitted to the Chancery Division.[1]

STONE *v.* CARLAN

SUPERIOR COURT, NEW YORK, 1850.

Reported in 13 *Law Reporter*, 360.

THE important facts of this case appear in the opinion of the court.

CAMPBELL, J. A motion is made for an injunction restraining the defendants from using the names "Irving Hotel," "Irving House," "Irving," &c., upon their coaches and upon certain badges worn by defendants upon their arms and hats. The complainants have an agreement with the proprietors of the Irving House, in this city, under which they are permitted to use the name of such proprietors, and the name of their hotel, upon their coaches and the badges of their servants; the complainants paying therefor a stipulated sum, and having also entered into bonds for the faithful discharge of these duties. All the porters are engaged in carrying passengers and their baggage to and from the hotels, boats, railroad depots, &c.

It was well remarked by the Master of the Rolls, in Croft *v.* Day, 7 Bevan, 84, that "No man has a right to dress himself in colors, or adopt and bear symbols, to which he has no peculiar or exclusive right, and thereby personate another person, for the purpose of inducing the public to suppose, either that he is that other person, or that he is connected with and selling the manufacture of such other person, while he is really selling his own. It is perfectly manifest that to do these things is to commit a fraud, and a very gross fraud. I stated upon a former occasion, that, in my opinion, the right which any person may have to the protection of this court does not depend upon any exclusive right which he may be supposed to have to a particular name, or to a particular form of words. His right is to be protected against fraud; and fraud may be practised against him by means of a name, though the person practising it may have a perfect right to use that name, provided he does not accompany the use of it with such other circumstances as to effect a fraud upon others." I entirely concur in the foregoing views. The question is, whether the defendants have committed a fraud. I cannot doubt that their intention was to mislead, and to induce travellers to believe that they were servants of the proprietors of the Irving House. This is a large and popular hotel,

[1] Lyne *v.* Nicholls, 23 T. L. R. 86; Barrett *v.* Associated Newspapers, 23 T. L. R. 666; Burkett *v.* Griffith, 90 Cal. 532 *Accord.*
Compare Marlin Fire Arms Co. *v.* Shields, 171 N. Y. 384.

well known in the country, and many a traveller may wish to resort to it on his arrival in this city, who, at the same time, may not know whether the carriages of the proprietors are painted red or white, or whether the exact designation is that of the Irving House or Irving Hotel. Such traveller may wish to intrust himself and his baggage to the servants of the hotel, feeling that, in doing so, he would be protected against loss or damage by the responsibility of the proprietors. Now, in this case, it can hardly be doubted but that the object of the defendant was to induce the belief on the part of the travellers that they were the servants of this hotel. To induce such belief, it was not necessary that the resemblance of all carriages and badges should be complete. From the very circumstances of the case, it would not be necessary to have a perfect resemblance, in order to commit even a gross fraud. It is not necessary to go, in this case, the length of the ordinary cases of trade-marks, though this case might come within the rules of those cases. (See Coates *v.* Holluck, 2 Sanford Ch. R., and Notes, and cases there cited.) The false pretences of the defendants would, I think, necessarily tend to mislead. The defendants have a perfect right to engage in a spirited competition in conveyance of passengers and their baggage. They may employ better carriages than the plaintiffs. They may carry for less fare. They may be more active, energetic, and attentive. The employment is open to them, but " they must not dress themselves in colors, and adopt and bear symbols," which belong to others. I had some doubt, at the time of the argument, whether the complaint should not have been made by the proprietors of the Irving House; but, on further reflection, think that the suit is well brought. The plaintiffs are the real parties in interest. It is possible that, owing to the general liability of the proprietors, as innkeepers, for the loss of the property of guests, the proprietors might also be entitled to an injunction restraining the defendants from holding themselves out as the servants of the hotel.

An injunction must issue, as prayed for, against all the defendants.[1]

[1] Prestolite Co. *v.* Heiden, (C. C. A.) 219 Fed. 845; Zittlosen Mfg. Co. *v.* Boss, (C. C. A.) 219 Fed. 887; Coca-Cola Co. *v.* Butler, 229 Fed. 224; Hartzler *v.* Goshen Ladder Co., 55 Ind. App. 455; National Biscuit Co. *v.* Pacific Coast Biscuit Co., 83 N. J. Eq. 369; Sanford Iron Works *v.* Enterprise Machine Works, 130 Tenn. 669; Pacific Coast Milk Co. *v.* Frye, 85 Wash. 133 *Accord.* Iu March *v.* Billings, 7 Cush. 322, under similar circumstances, the plaintiff recovered in an action at law.

See also Coffin, Fraud as an Element of Unfair Competition, 16 Harvard Law Rev. 272; Wyman, Competition and the Law, 15 Harvard Law Rev. 427; Cox, The Prevention of Unfair Competition in Business, 5 Harvard Law Rev. 139; Cushing, On Certain Cases Analogous to Trade Marks, 4 Harvard Law Rev. 321.

Misleading similarity. Hanover Milling Co. *v.* Metcalf, 240 U. S. 403; McDonald Mfg. Co. *v.* Mueller Mfg. Co., 183 Fed. 972; British American Tobacco Co. *v.* British American Cigar Stores Co., (C. C. A.) 211 Fed. 933; Hiram Walker & Sons *v.* Grubman, 224 Fed. 725; Jenkins *v.* Kelly & Jones Co., (C. C. A.) 227 Fed. 211; Jacoway *v.* Young, (C. C. A.) 228 Fed. 630; Van Zile *v.* Norub Mfg. Co., 228 Fed. 829; Moline Plow Co. *v.* Omaha Stores Co., (C. C. A.) 235 Fed. 519; Boston Shoe Shop *v.* McBroom Shoe Shop, 196 Ala. 262; Italian Swiss Colony

HUGHES *v.* McDONOUGH

SUPREME COURT OF JUDICATURE, NEW JERSEY, NOVEMBER, 1881.

Reported in 43 *New Jersey Law Reports*, 459.

ON writ of error.

The substance of the declaration was, that the plaintiff was a blacksmith and horseshoer by trade, of good character, &c.; that he had obtained the patronage of one Peter Van Riper, and that on a certain occasion he shod a certain mare of the said Van Riper in a good and workmanlike manner; that the defendant, maliciously intending to injure the plaintiff in his said trade, &c., "did wilfully and maliciously mutilate, impair and destroy the work done and performed by the said plaintiff upon the mare of the said Van Riper, without the knowledge of the said Van Riper, by loosing a shoe which was recently put on by the said plaintiff, so that if the mare was driven, the shoe would come off easily, and thus make it appear that the said plaintiff was an unskilful and careless horseshoer and blacksmith, and that the said mare was not shod in a good and workmanlike manner, and thus deprive the said plaintiff of the patronage and custom of the said Van Riper."

The second count charges the defendant with driving a nail in the foot of the horse of Van Riper, after it had been shod by the plaintiff, with the same design as specified in the first count.

The special damage laid was the loss of Van Riper as a customer.

Argued at June term, 1881, before Beasley, Chief Justice, and Justices Scudder, Knapp and Reed.

v. Italian Vineyard Co., 158 Cal. 252; Dunston *v.* Los Angeles Van & Storage Co., 165 Cal. 89; Modesto Creamery *v.* Stanislaus Creamery Co., 168 Cal. 289; Motor Accessories Co. *v.* Marshalltown Mfg. Co., 167 Ia. 202; Bonnie & Co. *v.* Bonnie Bros., 160 Ky. 487; Crutcher *v.* Starks, 161 Ky. 690; George G. Fox Co. *v.* Best Baking Co., 209 Mass. 251; C. A. Briggs & Co. *v.* National Wafer Co., 215 Mass. 100; Grocers' Supply Co. *v.* Dupuis, 219 Mass. 576; Rodseth *v.* Northwestern Marble Works, 129 Minn. 472; Rubber & Celluloid Co. *v.* Rubber Bound Brush Co., 81 N. J. Eq. 419, 519; Westcott Chuck Co. *v.* Oneida Chuck Co., 199 N. Y. 247; World's Dispensary Ass'n *v.* Pierce, 203 N. Y. 419; Material Men's Ass'n *v.* New York Material Men's Ass'n, 169 App. Div. 843; German American Button Co. *v.* Heymsfeld, 170 App. Div. 416; Collier *v.* Jones, 66 Misc. 97; Frohman *v.* William Morris, 68 Misc. 461; Elbs *v.* Rochester Egg Carrier Co., 134 N. Y. Supp. 979; Columbia Engineering Works *v.* Mallory, 75 Or. 542; Rosenburg *v.* Fremont Undertaking Co., 63 Wash. 52; J. I. Case Plow Works *v.* J. I. Case Machine Co., 162 Wis. 185.

Use of one's own name, see L. E. Waterman Co. *v.* Modern Pen Co., 235 U. S. 88; Borden Ice Cream Co. *v.* Borden's Consolidated Milk Co., (C. C. A.) 201 Fed. 510; Deister Concentrator Co. *v.* Deister Machine Co., 63 Ind. App. 412; C. H. Batchelder Co. *v.* Batchelder, 220 Mass. 42; Zagier *v.* Zagier, 167 N. C. 616.

Where defendant passes off his product as plaintiff's, recovery is allowed without proof of actual damage. Blofeld *v.* Payne, 4 B. & A. 410; Singleton *v.* Bolton, 3 Doug. 293 (*semble*); Sykes *v.* Sykes, 3 B. & C. 541; Morison *v.* Salmon, 2 M. & G. 385; Crawshay *v.* Thompson, 4 M. & G. 357 (*semble*); Rodgers *v.* Nowill, 5 C. B. 109; Forster Co. *v.* Cutter Co., 211 Mass. 219. Compare Glendon Co. *v.* Uhler, 75 Pa. St. 467.

The opinion of the court was delivered by

BEASLEY, C. J. The single exception taken to this record is, that the wrongful act alleged to have been done by the defendant does not appear to have been so closely connected with the damages resulting to the plaintiff as to constitute an actionable tort. The contention was, that the wrong was done to Van Riper; that it was his horse whose shoe was loosened, and whose foot was pricked, and that the immediate injury and damage were to him, and that, consequently, the damages of the plaintiff were too remote to be made the basis of a legal claim.

But this contention involves a misapplication of the legal principle, and cannot be sustained. The illegal act of the defendant had a close causal connection with the hurt done to the plaintiff, and such hurt was the natural and almost direct product of such cause. Such harmful result was sure to follow, in the usual course of things, from the specified malfeasance. The defendant is conclusively chargeable with the knowledge of this injurious effect of his conduct, for such effect was almost certain to follow from such conduct, without the occurrence of any extraordinary event, or the help of any extraneous cause. The act had a twofold injurious aspect: it was calculated to injure both Van Riper and the plaintiff; and as each was directly damnified, I can perceive no reason why each could not repair his losses by an action.

The facts here involved do not, with respect to their legal significance, resemble the juncture that gave rise to the doctrine established in the case of Vicars *v.* Wilcocks, 8 East, 1. In that instance the action was for a slander that required the existence of special damage as one of its necessary constituents, and it was decided that such constituent was not shown by proof of the fact that as a result of the defamation the plaintiff had been discharged from his service by his employer before the end of the term for which he had contracted. The ground of this decision was that this discharge of the plaintiff from his employment was illegal, and was the act of a third party, for which the defendant was not responsible, and that, as the wrong of the slander became detrimental only by reason of an independent wrongful act of another, the injury was to be imputed to the last wrong, and not to that which was farther distant one remove. In his elucidation of the law in this case, Lord Ellenborough says, alluding to the discharge of the plaintiff from his employment, that it "was a mere wrongful act of the master, for which the defendant was no more answerable, than if, in consequence of the words, other persons had afterwards assembled and seized the plaintiff and thrown him into a horse-pond by way of punishment for his supposed transgression." The class of cases to which this authority belongs, rests upon the principle that a man is responsible only for the natural consequences of his own misdeeds, and that he is not answerable for detriments that ensue from the misdeeds of others. But this doctrine, it is to be remembered, does not exclude responsibility when the damage results to the party injured through the intervention of the legal and innocent acts of third parties; for, in such instances, damage is regarded as occasioned by the wrongful cause, and not at all by those which are not wrongful. Where the effect was reasonably to have been foreseen, and where, in the usual course of events, it was likely to follow from the cause, the person putting such cause in motion will be responsible, even though there may have been many concurring events or agencies between such cause and its consequences. This principle is stated, and is illustrated by a reference to a multitude of decisions in Cooley on Torts, 70, *et seq.* . . .[1]

The principles thus propounded must have a controlling effect in the decision of the question now before this court, as they decisively show that the damage of which the plaintiff complained was not, in a legal sense, remote from the wrongful act. What, in point of substance, was done by the defendant, was this: he defamed, by the medium of a fraudulent device, the plaintiff in his trade, and by means of which defamation, the latter sustained special detriment. If this defamation had been accomplished by word spoken or written, or by signs or pictures, it is plain the wrong could have been remedied, in the usual form, by an action on the case for the slander; and, plainly, no reason exists why the law should not afford a similar redress when the same injury has been inflicted by disreputable craft. It is admitted upon the record that the plaintiff has sustained a loss by the fraudulent misconduct of the defendant; that such loss was not only likely, in the natural order of events, to proceed from such misconduct, but that it was the design of the defendant to produce such result by his act. Under such circumstances it would be strange indeed if the party thus wronged could not obtain indemnification by an appeal to the judicial tribunals.

HUGHES v. SAMUELS BROTHERS

SUPREME COURT, IOWA, OCTOBER 17, 1916.

Reported in 179 *Iowa Reports*, 1077.

GAYNOR, J. Plaintiff and defendant both reside in the city of Storm Lake, and each is and was engaged in the retail furniture business, and, as an incident thereto, carried on a business of undertaking. Defendants are a copartnership.

The plaintiff claims: That on the 6th day of October, 1914, the

[1] The learned judge here discussed McDonald *v.* Snelling, 14 All. 290, and Rigby *v.* Hewitt, 5 Ex. 240, and cited 2 Pars. Cont. 456; Dixon *v.* Fawcus, 30 L. J. Q. B. 137; Tarleton *v.* McGawley, Peake, 270; Bell *v.* Midland Co., 10 C. B. N. S. 307 Keeble *v.* Hickeringill, 11 East, 574, *n.*

defendants falsely and maliciously composed and published of and concerning the plaintiff the following:

"Bear in mind our Undertaking Department. Satisfaction guaranteed. (Signed) H. L. Hughes."

That the defendants caused the same to be printed upon a card and mailed to the address of one Albert Cattermole, a citizen and resident of Storm Lake. That at the time the card was mailed the wife of the said Cattermole was lying critically ill in a hospital in Storm Lake. That of this fact the defendants had full knowledge at the time they composed and published said statement. That they composed and published it for the malicious purpose of injuring the plaintiff in his reputation and business as aforesaid. That the same as so published tended to provoke plaintiff to wrath, and expose him to public hatred, contempt, and ridicule, and to deprive him of public confidence and esteem and social intercourse. That the same was further published for the malicious and wicked purpose of causing the said Albert Cattermole and members of his family, and others to whom the said card or letter might become known, to believe that plaintiff sent the card, and for the further purpose of inducing the said Cattermole to refrain from patronizing the business of the plaintiff. That the publication was further made for the purpose of inciting indignation and hatred in the minds of said Cattermole and the members of his family towards the plaintiff and his business as an undertaker, and that it did this. That similar cards were sent to other persons under similar circumstances, and for the purposes aforesaid.

To this petition defendants filed a demurrer, the substance of which is, that the plaintiff's petition stated no cause of action; that the words published were not libellous *per se*, and no special damages are alleged to have been suffered by the plaintiff on account of its publication. This demurrer was sustained by the court. Plaintiff elected to stand on his pleading and not to plead further, and his petition was thereupon dismissed, and from the action of the court in the premises plaintiff has appealed to this court. . . .

It appears that Cattermole's wife was sick unto death at the time this card was composed by defendants and sent to him. The defendants knew this fact at the time they composed and mailed the card. We take judicial notice of the fact that the city in which the parties resided was not so populous that the active business men of the city were not known to each other and to the general public. The card was so framed and mailed by the defendants as to lead the receiver to believe that the plaintiff had composed and mailed it, and this was their purpose in mailing it. What possible reason could they have in preparing and publishing this card? Was it to help a rival? Was it to exploit the business of a rival? Was it intended as a letter of credit to the public by and through which he would be better installed in its confidence and esteem? Is this the usual and ordinary course of procedure on the part of rival business firms? With the largest charity, we cannot think this was the purpose of the publication. What, then, was the purpose in the minds of these defendants when they composed and sent these cards to the sick and dying in the community? Was it not rather, as the petition says, to deprive him of public confidence and esteem? Was it not rather to expose him to public contempt and ridicule? Was it not rather to divert business through this means from the plaintiff, and to injure him by such diversion?

Cattermole's wife was sick unto death at the time he received this card; confined in the hospital. What impression would this card make upon his mind? Would it not bring before him the spectacle of a vulture waiting to prey upon the dead? A man without sympathy for the living because he found more revenue in the dead? What is it these defendants meant by this thing that they have done? What end had they in view? We think, surely, that which the petition charges, to wit, to injure the plaintiff in his reputation and business, to expose him to public contempt or ridicule, to deprive him of public confidence and esteem. What, then, would be the natural and ordinary effect of such a card upon the mind of one to whom it was sent, under the conditions attending Cattermole? Surely it would bring the sender of such a card, under the conditions then existing, into contempt and hatred, and deprive him of public confidence and esteem. Can the thought be entertained for a moment that after the receipt of a card like this under those circumstances, that the receiver would patronize the sender in the event the stricken wife had died? Was it to secure this for the plaintiff that the card was sent?

Published words which directly tend to the prejudice or injury of a person in his office, profession, or business are actionable. Williams *v.* Davenport, 42 Minn. 393, 44 N. W. 311, 118 Am. St. Rep. 519.

Any publication calculated to expose one to public hatred, contempt, or ridicule is libellous *per se.* Dressel *v.* Shipman, 57 Minn. 23, 58 N. W. 684.

The general rule is, that when language is published concerning a person or his affairs, which, from its nature, necessarily must, or presumably will as its natural and proximate consequence, occasion him pecuniary loss, its publication is libellous *per se.* See Townsend on Slander and Libel, (4th ed.) §§ 146 and 147; Fry *v.* McCord, 95 Tenn. 680, 33 S. W. 568.

Peculiar damages are required to be alleged only when the publication, with its attending facts and circumstances, is such that damages do not naturally arise from the publication. If the publication, with its attending facts and circumstances, is such that the court can legally presume that injury followed as a natural and inevitable consequence of the act complained of, then there is no occasion, in order to maintain an action, that the plaintiff allege or prove peculiar damages. If the nature and character of the publication, with its attending facts and circumstances, are such as to injuriously affect or detract from the reputation and standing of another, and as a natural and proximate result, tend to bring him into public contempt, hatred, or ridicule, then it is libellous *per se*. If such injury can be said to be a natural proximate result or consequence of its publication, then the plaintiff is presumed to have been damaged, and there is no need of any allegation of peculiar damages. The extent of the damages is for the jury.

It is the venom of poisoned speech that constitutes the libel. In tracing the wrong that flows from the publication, we come first to the mind of the reader, and inquire what effect it would naturally have upon the ordinary thinking mind. We first consider the facts published, and the circumstances under which they were published, and the persons to whom a knowledge of the publication was brought. An inquiry arises, would such a publication, under such circumstances, naturally tend to poison the mind against the person concerning whom the matter was published? If the matter published can be said, in its natural effect upon the mind, to produce hurt to the good name, fame, and reputation of the person about whom the publication is made, then we say the matter is defamatory, and the person necessarily has suffered not only wrong, but damages, as a proximate result of the wrong — damage to his good name, fame, and reputation in the community. If the words in and of themselves, when published, do not tend to this effect naturally and of their own force and vitality, the mind naturally inquires into the circumstances under which they were published, the manner of their publication, and the persons to whom a knowledge of the publication was brought. This inquiry is pursued to ascertain the effect which the publication, under the circumstances, would naturally have upon the mind of the person to whom a knowledge of the publication was brought. If the words and the circumstances attending their publication would not naturally affect the mind prejudicially against the person concerning whom the publication is made, it must be alleged and shown, not only that they were used in a defamatory sense, but that they were so understood by the hearers. When words, innocent in themselves, are charged to have been intended and used in a defamatory sense, it must be alleged and proven that they were intended in a defamatory sense and were so understood by the persons to whom they were addressed. If they do not themselves convey a defamatory meaning, or an imputation that is defamatory, something must be alleged which shows, or tends to show, that the user of the words intended them in a defamatory sense, and that the persons to whom a knowledge of the publication came were affected in their mental attitude towards the person, to the injury of his good name, fame, and reputation. The publication may be so worded that this could not be gathered from the publication itself. It may be innocent and even commendatory in itself, yet the facts and circumstances attending the publication, the relationship of the parties — the defamer and the defamed — to the public may be such, considered in the light of the subject-matter concerning which the publication is made, that it is apparent that there was not only an intent to defame, but that a defamatory imputation was so exposed, that the ordinary mind easily grasped the purpose of the publication and its injurious consequences to the good name, fame, and reputation of the defamed.

Men receive impressions of and concerning others from what they hear others say about them. Libel is a tort. It consists in a wrong done to the good name, fame, and reputation of another. It is in the nature of an assault upon the good name, fame, and reputation of another. The law protects a man in the possession of his good name, and denies to others the right, wrongfully and wickedly, to make an assault upon it. It is often the only asset a man has. Rob him of this, and you rob him of all that he has in life that makes life worth living.

A physical assault is clearly understood and easily defined. One may be punished criminally or mulcted in damages civilly for physical assault. Libel is an assault upon that invisible and intangible thing known as reputation. Though invisible and intangible, it exists among men and is prized, and the law protects it. As has been said by this court, libel rests upon the thought that a public wrong has been committed; an act has been done in violation of the statute, to the hurt of the complaining citizen. A citizen's right to remain secure in his good name and reputation among his fellows, and to enjoy their confidence and esteem, has been violated. A libel is that which tends to take from him one of his most valuable rights — his right to the confidence, esteem, and respect of his fellow men. One who, by right living and right conduct, has built up for himself an enviable name among his fellows, and has drawn to him their confidence and esteem, is entitled to retain and enjoy the same, and one who wrongfully and maliciously, and without just cause, makes an assault thereon, and impairs or injures the same, does a grievous wrong for which he is answerable in damages.

It is true that the wrong must be found in the publication, not merely in the wording of the thing published. The injury must flow from the publication. The damage must be the natural and proximate result of the publication; a result that usually, naturally, and ordinarily follows as a result of the wrong done.

Though the article itself conveys no wrong impression concerning the complainant, and in and of itself could do no harm, it may become most injurious, most hurtful; it may become a direct assault upon the good name, fame, and reputation, because of the manner and the circumstances under which it was published. The publication must be libellous, not necessarily that the article in and of itself is libellous. "A libel is the malicious defamation of a person made public by any writing," &c. It is the malicious defamation against which the inhibition of the statute is raised; malicious defamation made public by writing. A writing made public which is intended to and does, because of its publication, tend to provoke to wrath, to expose to public hatred, contempt, or ridicule, or which deprives one of the benefits of public confidence and social intercourse, is libellous *per se.*

Every written publication, maliciously made, defamatory of another, which tends to any of the consequences set out in the statute, is a violation of the inhibitions of the statute. It is therefore a wrong done to a citizen in violation of the statute. It is therefore actionable *per se.* The fact that it is a violation of the inhibition of the statute makes it actionable *per se.*

In contemplation of law, reputation is a delicate plant, withered by the breath of scandal. Any publication which imputes to another conduct which right-thinking men condemn, whether the conduct involve a crime, moral turpitude, or any conduct in life, purpose, or manner of living which the common sense of right-thinking men condemns, is presumed in law to have injuriously affected the reputation of the person so assailed, and, by such injury, to have caused him some damage.

It follows, therefore, that libel is an assault upon character resulting in some injury to reputation. The injury must be traceable to the assault, and the damage must be the proximate result of the injury. Every one recognizes the blighting effect of scandalous utterances directed against the character, conduct, or reputation of men. Every one recognizes that such assaults, publicly made, tend injuriously to affect the reputation and standing of the one so assailed among his fellows. It is from the recognition of this that the law implies damages, without allegation or proof of special damages.

Defamation consists in maliciously poisoning the minds of others against the party assaulted by printing, writing, &c., thereby bringing on them some of the consequences provided against in the statute. The statute is intended to, and does, prohibit the malicious poisoning of the minds of others against a citizen, under the protection of the law, by the use of public printing, &c., and this inhibition attaches whether done directly by the wording of the thing complained of, or indirectly by insinuation, imputation, or suggestion. The statute is intended to protect one in a right, and to deny to others the liberty to invade that right.

With no explanation from the defendants, we may rightly assume that they prepared and mailed this card for the purpose hereinbefore indicated, and that the consequences charged in the petition were the consequences that naturally flowed from the thing done. We think the pleading was sufficient to present the question to the jury. As supporting what we have said, see Call *v.* Larabee, 60 Iowa, 212, 14 N. W. 237; Hollenbeck *v.* Ristine, 105 Iowa, 488, 75 N. W. 355, 67 Am. St. Rep. 306; Halley *v.* Gregg, 74 Iowa, 564, 38 N. W. 416. In the latter case it is said, in substance, that if the act charged constitutes a libel, as defined by the statute, it is actionable *per se.* See Zier *v.* Hofflin, 33 Minn. 66, 21 N. W. 862, 53 Am. Rep. 9, in which it is said:

"Words which may be innocent of themselves may be rendered libellous by the place and circumstances of their publication, for such place and circumstances may impress on them a meaning and suggestion which, standing alone, they do not have. Thus, though the words here do not of themselves impute wrong, they might be published in such a place or under such circumstances as to make them capable of naturally conveying the impression that plaintiff had been guilty of dishonest practices, either in contracting the debt or in withholding payment of it. . . . What meaning they would naturally convey was for the jury to determine in view of the circumstances of their publication." State of Missouri *v.* Armstrong, 106 Mo. 395, 16 S. W. 604, reported in 13 L. R. A. 419, 27 Am. St. Rep. 361, together with citations and annotations; Nichols *v.* Daily, 30 Utah, 74, 83 Pac. 573, 3 L. R. A. N. S. 339, 116 Am. St. Rep. 296, 8 Ann. Cas. 841.

We find no case directly in point on the questions here considered. We think, however, the plaintiff presented a fair question for the jury, and the court erred in sustaining the demurrer, and the cause is therefore reversed. *Reversed.*

Evans, C. J., and Ladd, J., concur. Salinger, J., special concurrence.

Salinger, J. There is language in the opinion which indicates there may be libel which is not libel *per se.* I do not wish to be bound by it. I think it is settled by our cases that whatever is libellous is libellous *per se;* that the action for libel rests on the fact that a "crime has been committed," and that, therefore, the law presumes damage if a libel is established.[1]

[1] Defendant put out an envelope, with the word "telegram" conspicuously printed thereon, similar to that used by plaintiff, a telegraph company, to be used for advertising circulars. Plaintiff claimed that it tended to make its patrons think plaintiff was imposing on them by allowing advertisers to use its facilities in order to gain their attention and so injured its business. An injunction was denied. Postal Telegraph Co. *v.* Livermore & Knight Co., 188 Fed. 696.

In Riding *v.* Smith, 1 Ex. D. 91, plaintiff sued for injury to his business due to defendant's charging his wife with adultery, by reason whereof customers ceased to deal with him.

In Hamon *v.* Falle, 4 App. Cas. 247, an officer of an insurance company notified a shipowner that the company would not insure the ship if plaintiff was employed as master. Defendant set up that he honestly believed plaintiff unfit. See also Bowen *v.* Matheson, 14 All. 499.

In Morasse *v.* Brochu, 151 Mass. 567, defendant in a sermon warned his congregation against a physician who had been excommunicated for remarrying after divorce.

WESTMINISTER LAUNDRY CO. v. HESSE ENVELOPE CO.

ST. LOUIS COURT OF APPEALS, MISSOURI, MAY 6, 1913.

Reported in 174 Missouri Appeal Reports, 238.

NORTONI, J. This is a suit for damages, in which plaintiff recovered a verdict for one dollar. On this verdict, judgment was given, and defendant prosecutes an appeal therefrom.

All of the relevant facts appear from the face of the petition, and the question of liability is to be determined thereon. It appears that the plaintiff, the defendant and the D'Arcy Advertising Company are each corporations engaged in their respective callings in the city of St. Louis. Plaintiff owns and is engaged in the business of operating a steam laundry. Defendant is engaged in the business of manufacturing envelopes. The D'Arcy Advertising Company is engaged in the advertising business — that is to say, it places advertisement in St. Louis for those who choose to patronize it. The plaintiff laundry company engaged the D'Arcy Advertising Company to do certain advertising for it by running what is known as a " blind " advertisement. Such " blind " advertisement is described in the petition as follows:

" The fundamental idea of same (the ' blind ' advertisement) being the use of some striking device well adapted to attract public attention, but unaccompanied, upon its first appearance, by the name of the advertiser using it, other matter being added later and the name of the advertiser, also, being given when the curiosity of the public has been sufficiently piqued and the attention of the public has been excited by the ' blind ' nature of the advertisement."

The striking device referred to in the quotation from the petition and that contemplated in the instant case is the word " Stopurkicken." The petition avers that plaintiff entered into a contract with the D'Arcy Advertising Company whereby it was to have the exclusive use of the word " Stopurkicken; " that the D'Arcy Advertising Company, in pursuance of plaintiff's plan, had the word " Stopurkicken " published upon signboards and by way of printed cards. After the word " Stopurkicken " had been so used and before plaintiff had time to determine upon a proper supplement to such advertisement to disclose its own name and identity, the defendant, Hesse Envelope Company, well knowing the word " Stopurkicken " was being used in the manner mentioned and desiring to take advantage of the word " Stopurkicken," as above described, printed and distributed throughout the city of St. Louis a large number of cards bearing the word " Stopurkicken " and followed by the name of the Hesse Envelope Company. Because of this use of the word by defendant, Hesse Envelope Company, plaintiff avers it is damaged and prays a recovery therefor.

It is said the word " Stopurkicken " is an attractive misspelling and contraction of the phrase " Stop your kicking," designed to excite public curiosity. It is obvious the petition states no cause of action against defendant unless the word " Stopurkicken " is either a trade-mark in which plaintiff enjoys a proprietary right, or is possessed of a secondary meaning, which, by user, has become a part of the good will of plaintiff's business, otherwise the word is *publici juris* and available to every person desiring to employ it identically as is the original phrase of which it is a contraction. From the affirmative averments of the petition, it is entirely clear plaintiff enjoyed no trade-mark in the word under consideration. Indeed, the cause does not proceed upon that theory. Plaintiff is engaged in the laundry business, which, of course, is that of washing and ironing for others. There is no suggestion in the petition that the word " Stopurkicken " was in any manner annexed to plaintiff's wares or the output of its laundry. Infringement of a trade-mark consists in the unauthorized use or colorable imitation of it upon substituted goods of the same class as those for which the mark has been appropriated. (38 Cyc. 741.) The petition reveals that plaintiff has not yet employed the word in any manner so as to identify it with its business, for it says, though a contract had been entered into between plaintiff and the D'Arcy Advertising Company for the use of the word and it had been employed in blank space on signboards and on cards, plaintiff had not yet revealed its identity in connection therewith. Defendant is engaged in the manufacture and sale of envelopes and used the word on an advertising card followed immediately by the name Hesse Envelope Company. These facts appearing as they do in the petition, sufficiently disclose that no proprietary right as in trade-mark existed in the plaintiff in respect of the word " Stopurkicken." Not only must an exclusive proprietary right appear in the trade-mark but the actual use of the trade-mark is essential as a means of identifying the origin, ownership or manufacture of the goods of its proprietor, and, furthermore, such trade-mark must be annexed to and accompany the goods into the market to the end of their identification. (See Grocers Journal Co. *v.* Midland Publishing Co., 127 Mo. App. 356, 366, 105 S. W. 310; 38 Cyc. 691, 693.) Unless the word or insignia relied upon is in some manner attached or affixed to the article in trade or stamped or inscribed thereon, it is not a trade-mark and the maker of such article is without trade-mark rights concerning it. (See Oakes *v.* St. Louis Candy Co., 146 Mo. 391, 48 S. W. 467; St. Louis Piano Mfg. Co. *v.* Merkel, 1 Mo. App. 305.) It is entirely clear that defendant in using the word " Stopurkicken " in connection with advertising its envelopes, was not infringing upon plaintiff's laundry business, for the wares or commodities of the two companies are entirely dissimilar. But aside from this, it appears affirmatively that the plaintiff had never used the word in connection with the output of its laundry. It had, therefore, obtained no proprietary right thereto by continued use through affixing it to the workmanship of its laundry turned out into the market.

For the same reasons, in part at least, no secondary right to the use of the phrase appears in plaintiff by user such as is essential to render it a portion of the good will of its laundry business as if reputation obtained thereon. It is certain that the case may not be sustained as one for unfair competition. Unfair competition consists in passing off or attempting to pass off upon the public the goods or business of one person as and for the goods or business of another. (See Cyc. 756.) Nothing less than conduct tending to pass off one man's goods or business as that of another will constitute unfair competition, for such is the very essence of the wrong on which the law affords redress to the injured party. (See Elgin National Watch Co. *v.* Illinois Watch Co., 179 U. S. 665, 674, 21 S. Ct. 270, 45 L. Ed. 365; 38 Cyc. 762, 763; 38 Cyc. 758; see, also, Grocers Journal Co. *v.* Midland Pub. Co., 127 Mo. App. 356, 367, 105 S. W. 310.) The relief, in cases of unfair competition, proceeds upon the theory that the words or phrase employed as by long use in connection with the goods or business of a particular trade come to be understood by the public as designating the goods or business of that particular trader. Because of such user, the word or phrase becomes identified with the business of him who employs it and constitutes a part of its good will. Such meaning of the words or phrase, it is said, is the genesis of the law of unfair competition as distinguished from technical trade-mark, and, therefore, relief against unfair competition is afforded upon the ground that one who has built up a good will and reputation for his goods or business under a particular designation is entitled to the benefits therefrom. And secondary to this, the theory is that the deception of the public injures the proprietor of the business by diverting his customers and filching his trade. (Grocers Journal Co. *v.* Midland Pub. Co., 127 Mo. App. 356, 367, 105 S. W. 310; 38 Cyc. 760, 761, 763, 769.)

It is to be observed that, though the right to complain as for unfair competition does not in every instance require that the complainant shall have a proprietary right in the phrase, it does require that he shall have used it in his business as a means of identifying his goods as his product and for a sufficient length of time to establish a repute therefor in the market as pointing his product. (Grocers Journal Co. *v.* Midland Pub. Co., 127 Mo. App. 356, 367, 105 S. W. 310; Reach Co. *v.* Simmons Hardware Co., 155 Mo. App. 412, 135 S. W. 503; 38 Cyc. 769, 763.) Unless the word or phrase involved has become a parcel of the good will of his business by continued user in connection with the product of the proprietor, it is entirely clear that the use of the same word by another does not reveal an unfair competition. (Shelley *v.* Sperry, 121 Mo. App. 429, 99 S. W. 488.)

The petition shows on its face that plaintiff had never used the word " Stopurkicken " in connection with the output of its laundry, but on the contrary only employed it on billboards and cards otherwise blank, as an attraction to arouse the curiosity of the public with a view of revealing the name of the advertiser (plaintiff) thereafter. It is clear enough that, though defendant interposed and used the same word on cards bearing its name, as it did, no unfair competition appears when considered in the sense of the law on the subject and until plaintiff had obtained a right thereto by actual user in connection with the product of its laundry, the phrase " Stopurkicken " must be regarded as *publici juris* and available to all who desired to employ it identically as was the original phrase " Stop your kicking." It is certain the D'Arcy Advertising Company had no superior right to either the phrase or the contracted word and that it could confer none upon plaintiff by its contract to employ it as a means of arousing the curiosity of the public for plaintiff's benefit. (Reach *v.* Simmons Hardware Co., 155 Mo. App. 412, 135 S. W. 503.) Though persons who have acquired a right in respect of words and phrases by user as above indicated, may assign or contract such right to another in conjunction with the good will of the commodity, the identity of which they point, it is obvious that an advertising agent may not appropriate any word or phrase he chooses by merely seizing it out of our vocabulary, and confer an exclusive right thereto on another by a contract to employ it in aid of his business. We are advised of no principle of our jurisprudence on which the judgment in this case may be sustained, and the counsel for plaintiff have omitted to file a brief suggesting one. The judgment should be reversed. It is so ordered. Reynolds, P. J., and Allen, J., concur.

THE MIDLAND INSURANCE CO. *v.* SMITH

IN THE QUEEN'S BENCH DIVISION, MARCH 23, 1881.

Reported in Law Reports, 6 *Queen's Bench Division,* 561.

WATKIN WILLIAMS, J.[1] This action is one of an extraordinary, and so far as I am aware of an unprecedented, character. The questions of law involved in the case, which was argued before me yesterday, arise upon demurrer to the statement of claim, and I now proceed to give judgment.

The facts, which for the purposes of the argument are assumed to be true, are as follows: The plaintiffs, an insurance company, granted to the defendant, Charles Smith, a policy of fire insurance, dated the 26th of June, 1880, by which they agreed with him that if certain property in a certain house should be destroyed or damaged by fire

[1] Only the opinion of the court is given.

they would pay or make good all such loss or damage during the currency of the policy. The defendant Mary, the wife of the defendant Charles Smith, having been left by him in charge of the house and property insured did, with the malicious intention of destroying the insured property and of injuring the insurance company and of creating a claim upon the policy, wilfully set fire to and destroy the house and the insured property. Charles Smith, the assured, then made a claim upon the policy against the company. The company thereupon brought this present action against Smith and his wife, to recover damages for the loss which the company alleged they had sustained or might sustain through the wrongful and felonious act of the defendant Mary, if the defendant Charles made good his claim upon his policy.

I was informed in the course of the argument, although these facts do not appear formally before me, that the defendant Charles had, before this present action, brought an action against the company upon the policy to recover the amount of his loss, and that in that action the company disputed their liability on the ground that the loss, having been caused by the arson of the wife, was not covered by the policy, and that they had also set up a counter-claim for damages against Smith and his wife, who was brought in as a party to the action upon the same ground; that that action went down to trial, and that the learned judge, before whom the cause came on for trial, adjourned the proceedings in order to enable the company to test the validity in law of their contention in a separate and distinct manner before proceeding to try the question of arson. The present action was then commenced. The questions, however, for determination in this action must depend exclusively upon the facts set forth in the statement of claim, and the issues of law raised by the demurrer.

The company in support of their case started with the general principle that " every husband is liable for the wrongful acts of his wife," and that as the defendant Mary had wrongfully injured and destroyed the insured property, and had caused the damage upon which a claim upon the policy had been based, they, as the insurers of the property, had a right to sue her and her husband for the damage and injury so done by her, and not the less so because the husband happened to be himself the assured whom they had agreed to indemnify. In substance, the contention of the company came to this, that they ought not to be called upon to pay the assured the amount claimed, without being entitled concurrently to claim damages from him for the loss caused by the act of his wife, for which he is answerable.

The defendants, by their demurrer to this claim, raised two main issues of law. In the first place they said that the company were not in a position to maintain any action for the alleged damage done to the goods, because they were not the owners of the goods, nor had they sufficient interest therein to entitle them to maintain an action; that their only right as insurers would be to avail themselves of such rights and remedies as were vested in their assured, after they had admitted his claim and been subrogated to his rights in relation to the subject of insurance; and that, even if they had been subrogated to the rights of the assured, they could only sue in his name and could not maintain an action in their own name, and therefore that no such action could be maintained in the present case, because the assured had no right of action against his own wife.

In the next place the defendants contended that this action being based upon an act, which on the face of the statement of claim amounted to a felony, could not be maintained, because it was not shown that the rights of the public law had been vindicated by a prosecution of the felon.[1]

Upon the first ground of demurrer the defendants are, in my judgment, clearly entitled to judgment both upon principle and upon authority. It appears to me that the insurance company have no right of action under the circumstances for the damage done to the goods by the defendant Mary. At the time when the damage was done to the goods the company had no property or interest in the goods sufficient to sustain any action for damage done to them; no right or interest in the goods could accrue to the insurance company, until they had acknowledged the claim under the policy, and by so doing entitled themselves to the benefit of any claims and causes of action vested in the assured; but it seems that even up to this moment the insurance company dispute the claim and deny the right of the assured to demand an indemnity under the policy. But, further, it seems to me equally clear that, if they had done everything to entitle themselves to the benefit of such a claim, it could only be enforced in the name of the assured and for the purpose of enforcing his rights, and inasmuch as he could have no such claim or right against his wife, it follows that in no possible view of the case is the plaintiffs' claim sustainable. The case of Simpson *v.* Burrell, 3 App. Cas. 279, is in point upon this question. In that case Burrell was the owner of two ships, one of which negligently ran down and sank the other with a valuable cargo. Burrell's underwriters upon the sunken ship paid him for a total loss, and were so subrogated to all his rights. A claim was made by the owners of the cargo in the sunken ship against Burrell, as the owner of the ship in fault, for the value of their goods, and Burrell, as the owner of the ship in fault, paid into court the whole value of that ship at £8 per ton, as the limit of his liability under the Merchant Shipping Acts, to be ratably divided among all who had sustained loss and damage by the ship being negligently run down and sunk; thereupon Burrell's underwriters upon the sunken ship who had paid for a total loss claimed to come in and share with

[1] The opinion of the court on this point is omitted. The defendant's contention was not sustained.

the rest the money paid in by the ship in fault; but the House of Lords, reversing the decision of the Lords of Session in Scotland, decided that they had no such right, and the reasoning in that case is directly applicable to the present. The Lord Chancellor Cairns said, "The view of the Lord President therefore appears to be that, after payment by the underwriters as on a total loss, there is effected by some independent operation of law a transfer of whatever, if anything, can be recovered in specie of the thing insured — and by reason of the transfer of the thing insured an independent right in the underwriters to maintain in their own name, and without reference to the person assured, an action for the damage to the thing insured which was the cause of the loss. I am not aware of any authority for the view of the case thus taken. I know of no foundation for the right of the underwriters, except the well-known principle of law that where one person has agreed to indemnify another he will, on making good the indemnity, be entitled to succeed to all the ways and means by which the person indemnified might have protected himself against or reimbursed himself for the loss."

Lord Penzance said: "The learned counsel for the underwriters contended that they, by virtue of the policy which they entered into in respect of this ship, had an interest of their own in her welfare and protection, inasmuch as any injury or loss sustained by her would indirectly fall upon them as a consequence of their contract, and that this interest was such as would support an action by them in their own names and behalf against a wrongdoer. This proposition virtually affirms a principle which I think your Lordships will do well to consider with some care, as it will be found to have a much wider application and signification than any which may be involved in the incidents of a contract of insurance. The principle involved seems to me to be this, — that where damage is done by a wrongdoer to a chattel, not only the owner of the chattel, but all those who by contract with the owner have bound themselves to obligations which are rendered more onerous, or have secured to themselves advantages which are rendered less beneficial by the damage done to the chattel, have a right of action against the wrongdoer, although they have no immediate or reversionary property in the chattel, and no possessory right by reason of any contract attaching to the chattel itself, such as by lien or hypothecation. This, I say, is the principle involved in the respondent's contention. If it be a sound one, it would seem to follow that if by the negligence of a wrongdoer goods are destroyed, which the owner of them had bound himself by contract to supply to a third person, this person, as well as the owner, has a right of action for any loss inflicted upon him by their destruction. But if this be true as to injuries done to chattels, it would seem to be equally so as to injuries to the person. An individual injured by a negligently driven carriage has an action against the owner of it. Would a doctor, it may be asked, who had contracted to attend him and provide medicines for a fixed sum by the year, also have a right of action in respect of the additional cost of the attendance and medicine cast upon him by the accident ? And yet it cannot be denied that the doctor had an interest in his patient's safety. In like manner an actor or singer, bound for a term to a manager of a theatre, is disabled by the wrongful act of a third person to the serious loss of the manager; can the manager recover damages for that loss from the wrongdoer ? Such instances might be indefinitely multiplied, giving rise to rights of action which in modern communities, where every complexity of mutual relations is daily created by contract, might be both numerous and novel." See, also, the cases of Randal *v.* Cockran, 1 Ves. Sen. 97; North of England Insurance Association *v.* Armstrong, Law Rep. 5 Q. B. 244; Stewart *v.* Greenock Marine Insurance Co., 2 H. L. C. 159; Davidson *v.* Case, 8 Price, 542; Mason *v.* Sainsbury, 3 Douglas, 61; Yates *v.* Whyte, 4 Bing. N. C. 272.

This action cannot therefore in my judgment be maintained, nor is there any substantial injustice in such a result, because, as it seems to me, the insurance company are in this dilemma; the loss and damage caused by the wrongful act of the wife either is or is not a loss which the company have agreed to indemnify the husband against; now, if it is such a loss, an attempt by the company to enforce against the husband a return indemnity or reimbursement is at variance with the very substance of their undertaking to indemnify him; if, on the other hand, the loss, by reason of its having arisen from the act of the wife, is not within the risks and losses covered by the policy, then this action is as wholly misconceived, unnecessary, and unfounded, as if the loss had been caused by any other risk not covered by the policy. The truth is that the real and substantial contention on the part of the insurance company is, that the loss in question having been caused by the wilful act of the wife of the assured, although acting without the privity of her husband, is not a loss covered or insured against by the policy. That question might be raised in the action brought by the assured against the company upon the policy, but it does not arise, and indeed could not be raised, so as to receive a binding and judicial determination, in such an action as the present. As however the question has been fully and ably argued before me, and as the parties have expressed a desire to elicit an opinion upon the point, I have no hesitation in saying that it appears to me to be upon principle perfectly clear and free from doubt that such a loss would be covered by an ordinary policy against loss caused by fire; under such a policy the company would be liable for every loss caused by fire, unless the fire itself were caused and procured by the wilful act of the assured himself or some one acting with his privity and consent. In order to escape from responsibility for such a loss as the present the company ought to introduce into their policy an express exception.

Judgment for the defendants.

KLOUS v. HENNESSEY

SUPREME COURT, RHODE ISLAND, JUNE 14, 1881.

Reported in 13 Rhode Island Reports, 332.

DURFEE, C. J.[1] This is an action on the case for conspiracy. The declaration charges in effect that the defendants and one Patrick Kenney, said Kenney being then a debtor of the plaintiffs, conspired together to prevent the plaintiffs and the other creditors of said Kenney from getting payment of their claims out of his property, and that, in pursuance of the conspiracy, Kenney made fictitious mortgages of his real and personal property to the defendants, under cover of which the defendants removed the personal property out of the possession of Kenney, and secreted it so that the plaintiffs were prevented from attaching it, and thus lost their claims. At the trial, after the plaintiffs had introduced their testimony in proof of the declaration, the court, on motion of the defendants, it having appeared that the plaintiffs were merely creditors at large of Kenney, without any interest in his property or lien upon it by attachment, levy, or otherwise, ruled that the action, in respect of the charges aforesaid, was not maintainable. The plaintiffs excepted to the ruling for error, and now petition for a new trial.

There is some conflict of authority on the question thus raised, but the more numerous and, we think, the better-reasoned and stronger cases are against the action. The principal ground of decision in these cases is that the damage, which is the gist of the action, is too remote, uncertain, and contingent, inasmuch as the creditor has, not an assured right, but simply a *chance* of securing his claim by attachment or levy, which he may or may not succeed in improving.[2] It is im-

[1] Only the opinion is given.

[2] "It is contended that the amount of the plaintiff's loss is so entirely a matter of pure chance as to be incapable of assessment. I cannot for this purpose draw any distinction between a chance and a probability. In the Oxford English Dictionary one of the definitions of 'chance' is 'a possibility or probability of anything happening, as distinct from a certainty,' and a citation is given from Reid's Intellectual Powers, 'The doctrine of chances is a branch of mathematics little more than an hundred years old.' The two words 'chance' and 'probability' may be treated as being practically interchangeable, though it may be that the one is somewhat less definite than the other. . . . It is obvious, of course, that the chance or probability may in a given case be so slender that a jury could not properly give more than nominal damages, say one shilling; if they had done so in the present case, it would have been entirely a question for them, and this Court could not have interfered. But in the present competition we find chance upon chance, two of which the plaintiff had succeeded in passing. From being one of six thousand she had become a member of a class of fifty, and, as I understand it, was first in her particular division by the votes of readers of the paper; out of those fifty there were to be selected twelve prize-winners; it is obvious that her chances were then far greater and more easily assessable than when she was only one of the original six thousand. If the plaintiff had never been selected at all, the case would have been very different; but that was not the case. In my opinion the existence of a contingency, which is dependent on the volition of a third person, is not enough to justify us in saying that the damages are incapable of assessment." Farwell, L. J., in Chaplin v. Hicks, [1911] 2 K. B. 786, 798.

possible to find any measure of damages for the loss of such a mere chance or possibility. Another ground, added in some of the cases, is that no action would lie in favor of such a creditor against the debtor for putting his property beyond the reach of legal process, if the debtor were to do it by himself alone, and that what would not be actionable if done by himself alone cannot be actionable any the more when done by him with the assistance of others. The first of these grounds, which is the fundamental one and has been chiefly relied on, has been so exhaustively analyzed and discussed in the cases that it is impossible for us to add anything to the reasons adduced in support of it; and therefore, without reproducing them, we deem it sufficient simply to cite the cases themselves, all of which are accessible and can be readily consulted. Lamb *v.* Stone, 11 Pick. 527; Wellington *v.* Small, 3 Cush. 145; Moody *v.* Burton, 27 Me. 427, 431; Adler *v.* Fenton, 24 How. U. S. 407; Austin *v.* Barrows, 41 Conn. 287, 296; Kimball *v.* Harman & Burch, 34 Md. 407, 410; Bradley *v.* Fuller, 118 Mass. 239. See also Bump on Fraudulent Conveyances, 505, 506; Cooley on Torts, 124, 586. *Petition dismissed.*[1]

HUTCHINS *v.* HUTCHINS

SUPREME COURT, NEW YORK, JANUARY, 1845.

Reported in 7 *Hill*, 104.

By the Court, NELSON, C. J.[2] The case is substantially this: — The father of the plaintiff devised to him, in due form of law, a farm consisting of one hundred and fifty-one acres of land. The defendant, being aware of the fact, and intending to deprive the plaintiff of the benefit and advantage of the devise, and of his expected estate and interest in the farm, falsely and maliciously represented to the father, that, after his decease, the plaintiff intended to set up a large demand against the estate, which would absorb the greater part of it, and thus deprive the other children of their just share; at the same time defaming and calumniating the character of the plaintiff in several par-

[1] Adler *v.* Fenton, 24 How. 407; Findlay *v.* McAllister, 113 U. S. 104 (*semble*); Austin *v.* Barrows, 41 Conn. 287; Green *v.* Kimble, 6 Blackf. 552; Moody *v.* Burton, 27 Me. 427; Lamb *v.* Stone, 11 Pick. 527; Wellington *v.* Small, 3 Cush. 145; Security Bank *v.* Reger, (Okl.) 151 Pac. 1170; LeGierse *v.* Kellum, 66 Tex. 242 *Accord.*

Penrod *v.* Mitchell, 8 S. & R. 522; Penrod *v.* Morrison, 2 Pen. & W. 126; Mott *v.* Danforth, 6 Watts, 305; Hopkins *v.* Beebe, 26 Pa. St. 85, 87; Kelsey *v.* Murphy, 26 Pa. St. 78, 84; Collins *v.* Cronin, 117 Pa. St. 35, 45 *Contra.* See note in 47 L. R. A. 433–440.

In Smith *v.* Tonstall, Carthew, 3, defendant was held liable for conspiracy with plaintiff's debtor on *scire facias* to procure a false judgment and anticipate plaintiff by execution thereon and carrying off of all the debtor's property. Findlay *v.* McAllister, 113 U. S. 104 (*semble*); Adams *v.* Paige, 7 Pick. 541 *Accord.* See Pullen *v.* Headberg, 53 Col. 502.

[2] Only the opinion is given, and it is somewhat abridged.

ticulars. By these fraudulent means the defendant prevailed upon the father to revoke and cancel the will, and to make and execute a new one, by which the plaintiff was excluded from all participation in his father's estate.

This is the substance of the case, in its strongest aspect, as presented by the pleadings; and the question arises whether any actual damage, in contemplation of law, is shown to have been sustained by the plaintiff?

Fraud without damage, or damage without fraud, gives no cause of action; but where both concur, an action lies. Damage, in the sense of the law, may arise out of injuries to the person or to the property of the party; as any wrongful invasion of either is a violation of his legal rights, which it is the object of the law to protect. Thus, for injuries to his health, liberty and reputation, or to his rights of property, personal or real, the law has furnished the appropriate remedies. The former are violations of the absolute rights of the person, from which damage results as a legal consequence. As to the latter, the party aggrieved must not only establish that the alleged tort or trespass has been committed, but must aver and prove his right or interest in the property or thing affected, before he can be deemed to have sustained damages for which an action will lie.

Now, testing the plaintiff's declaration by these principles, has he made out a case from which it can be said that damage has resulted to him? I think not. In respect to the farm devised to him by the first will, he fails to show that he had any such interest in it as the law will recognize. The only foundation of his claim rests upon the mere unexecuted intention of his father to make a gift of the property; and this cannot be said to have conferred a right of any kind. To hold otherwise, and sanction the doctrine contended for by the plaintiff, would be next to saying that every voluntary courtesy was matter of legal obligation; that private thoughts and intentions, concerning benevolent or charitable distributions of property, might be seized upon as the foundation of a right which the law would deal with and protect.

I have not overlooked the cases referred to on the argument, of actions of slander, where special damage must be shown in order to make the words actionable; and where the deprivation of any present substantial advantage, even though gratuitous, such as the loss of customers, of a permanent home at a friend's, or advancement in life, and such like, if the immediate and direct consequence of the words, will sustain the action. 1 Starkie on Slander, 158 to 186, Ed. of 1843. If this description of special damage is to be regarded as the gist and foundation of the action, I rather think the principle should be regarded as peculiar to that species of injury. I am not aware of any class of remedies given for a violation of the rights of property, where so remote and contingent a damage has been allowed as a substantial ground of action.

But the law applicable to the cases referred to proceeds upon the ground that the plaintiff, by the wrongful act complained of, has been deprived of the present, actual enjoyment of some pecuniary advantage. No such damage can be pretended here. At best, the contemplated gift was not to be realized till after the death of the testator, which might not happen until after the death of the plaintiff; or the testator might change his mind, or lose his property.

In short, the plaintiff had no interest in the property of which he says he has been deprived by the fraudulent interference of the defendant, beyond a mere naked possibility; an interest which might indeed influence his hopes and expectations, but which is altogether too shadowy and evanescent to be dealt with by courts of law.

I am of opinion that the defendant is entitled to judgment.

Ordered accordingly.[1]

LEWIS *v.* CORBIN

SUPREME JUDICIAL COURT, MASSACHUSETTS, MAY 15, 1907.

Reported in 195 *Massachusetts Reports*, 520.

ACTION OF TORT. Demurrer to declaration.

KNOWLTON, C. J.[2] This is an action of tort in which the defendant is charged with having deprived the plaintiff of a legacy, through his fraud in inducing a testatrix to execute the codicil by which the legacy purported to be given with only one witness, whereby the codicil was rendered invalid. The legatee named in the codicil was the plaintiff's father, who had deceased before the codicil was made, although neither the testatrix nor the defendant then knew of his death.

One question is whether this legacy, which would be void at common law (see Maybank *v.* Brooks, 1 Brown Ch. 76; Dildine *v.* Dildine, 32 N. J. Eq. 78, 80; Moss *v.* Helsley, 60 Tex. 426, 436), is within the R. L. chap. 135, sec. 21, which provides that when a devise or legacy is made to a child or other relation of the testator who dies before the testator, leaving issue surviving the testator, such issue shall take the gift unless the will requires a different disposition of it.

. . . .

We are of opinion that the purpose of the Legislature is best accomplished by holding the statute applicable to devises and legacies given to relations who died before the making of the will, as well as legacies and devises to those who died after the making of the will.

. . . .

The defendant contends that the plaintiff's declaration fails to aver damage suffered by him on account of the defendant's misconduct.

[1] In Randall *v.* Hazelton, 12 All. 412, plaintiff, a mortgagor, had a gratuitous promise from the mortgagee not to foreclose without notice. In order to obtain the property, defendant falsely told the mortgagee that plaintiff wished the mortgage assigned to defendant and obtained an assignment and foreclosed without plaintiff's knowledge.

[2] Statement, and part of opinion, omitted.

It is true, as he argues, that in order to create a liability of this kind, there must be, not only a wrong inflicted by the defendant, but damage to the plaintiff resulting directly therefrom. Lamb *v.* Stone, 11 Pick. 527, 534, 535; Wellington *v.* Small, 3 Cush. 145, 149; Bradley *v.* Fuller, 118 Mass. 239, 241. See also Jenks *v.* Hoag, 179 Mass. 583, 585; Freeman *v.* Venner, 120 Mass. 424, 426, 427; Adler *v.* Fenton, 24 How. 408, 410.

In this case the averments are, in substance, that the defendant was the executor and residuary legatee named in a will of one Jane V. Corbin, and that she formed a purpose to give a legacy of $5000 to Henry G. Lewis, the plaintiff's father, who was her second cousin, that she was over eighty years of age, and, for advice and assistance in matters of business, was dependent upon the defendant, who occupied a confidential relation towards her, that, wrongfully and fraudulently intending and contriving to defeat her will and intention, and to deprive and defraud Henry G. Lewis and his heirs of the sum of $5000, he advised and procured the testatrix to execute a codicil to her will in the presence of only one witness, namely, the defendant, whereas the law of Rhode Island required the execution of the codicil in the presence of more than one witness, as the defendant well knew. It is then averred that the estate of the testatrix was large, and that, if the codicil had not failed for want of due attestation owing to the fraud practised by the defendant, the plaintiff would have received about $1650.

Whether a person named as legatee has a remedy, in a case like this, is a question which, so far as we know, has never been decided in this Commonwealth. See Melanefy *v.* Morrison, 152 Mass. 473, 476. The testatrix, desiring to give the legacy and intending to express her desire in a way that would be effectual after her death, unless in the meantime she should change her purpose, was fraudulently induced to express it ineffectually, when she supposed that she had made a legal and valid codicil. Plainly such fraudulent conduct was a wrong upon the plaintiff as well as upon the testatrix. The question in the case is whether the plaintiff has averred sufficient facts to show that damage resulted to him directly as a consequence of the wrong. The defendant relies strongly upon Hutchins *v.* Hutchins, 7 Hill, 104, decided by the Supreme Court of New York. The declaration in that case charged that the plaintiff's father had made a will devising a farm to the plaintiff, and that the defendants, who were interested in the testator's estate, he being a feeble man, advanced in years, and incapable of transacting business, fraudulently induced him to make another will in which the devise to the plaintiff was omitted. The case was heard on a demurrer. The court said "Fraud without damage, or damage without fraud gives no cause of action; but where both concur, an action lies. . . . The only foundation of his claim rests upon the mere unexecuted intention of his father to make a gift of the property, and this cannot be said to have conferred a right of any kind. To hold otherwise and sanction the doctrine contended for by the plaintiff would be next to saying that every voluntary courtesy was matter of legal obligation, and that private thoughts and intentions concerning benevolent or charitable distributions of property might be seized upon as the foundation of a right which the law would deal with and protect. . . . But the law applicable to the cases referred to proceeds upon the ground that the plaintiff, by the wrongful act complained of, has been deprived of the present actual enjoyment of some pecuniary advantage. No such damage can be pretended here. At best the contemplated gift was not to be received until after the death of the plaintiff, or the testator might change his mind, or lose his property." This case has been cited with approval in this Commonwealth and elsewhere. Randall *v.* Hazelton, 12 Allen, 412, 416; Emmons *v.* Alvord, 177 Mass. 466, 471; Adler *v.* Fenton, 24 How. 408, 410. We have been referred to no other decision upon similar facts, and we have found no other. It seems pretty plain that, if a suit were brought in the lifetime of the testator, immediately after the practice of the fraud, no substantial damage could be recovered. Very likely the court was right in deciding that no action could be maintained. The plaintiff's relation to the subject to which the fraud was directed was not close enough to cause him pecuniary loss, apart from the happening of subsequent events. Even if there were no fraud the legacy might never take effect. The testator might lose his property, or destroy his will, or make a different one. But the fraud put the plaintiff in a less advantageous position than he otherwise would have occupied in reference to the probability of receiving property under the will, and this change of position, accomplished by a fraud, naturally and probably might deprive him of that which, with fair dealing, he would receive. It seems to us that, while the fraud does not cause substantial damage apart from the happening of subsequent events which reasonably may be expected to happen, if these do happen, the defendant is chargeable with the natural consequences of his act. Suppose, in the present case, that the testatrix did not change her purpose to give the legacy of $5000 to Henry G. Lewis, and that for the rest of her life she desired and intended that this legacy should take effect, and thought that it would take effect. The fraud then would be operative up to the time of her death, and would accomplish the result intended by its author, by depriving the legatee of that which otherwise he would have received. It is averred that the testatrix left an estate sufficient to pay all or nearly all of this legacy, with the others. If the facts supposed above are proved, does it not follow that the fraud directly and proximately caused the plaintiff's loss of his legacy? The defendant cannot complain that these supposed facts followed as conditions concurring with his fraud to cause the damage. His fraud was planned in reference to the probability that these events would follow. In Hutchins *v.* Hutchins, *supra*, there was no averment to show that the fraud was operative up to the time when the title to the property was changed by the death of the testator. The court treated the case as if the testator might have changed his purpose as to the disposition of his estate, for reasons of his own independently of the fraud.

While the declaration in the present case declares a result which might justify an inference that the loss was caused by the fraud alone, the averment seems hardly more than a statement of a conclusion of law from the facts given previously. Upon demurrer we think the pleading is defective in not averring facts which exclude the possibility that the testatrix changed her purpose in regard to this legacy, and which show that the fraud continued operative to the time of her death, and thus caused the loss to the plaintiff.

We think the charge of fraud is a sufficient statement of an actionable wrong. It charges much more than an expression of opinion by which the testatrix was misled. The defendant is accused of having dealt with a matter of fact, and with having fraudulently procured the making of the codicil without sufficient attestation of it.

We infer from the record that the testatrix was domiciled in Massachusetts, and that the construction of the will is governed by the law of this State. Welch *v.* Adams, 152 Mass. 74, 79; Sewall *v.* Wilmer, 132 Mass. 131, 136. *Demurrer sustained.*[1]

DULIN *v.* BAILEY

Supreme Court, North Carolina, November 29, 1916.

Reported in 172 *North Carolina Reports*, 608.

Clark, C. J. The complaint alleges that after the death of W. A. Bailey the defendants conspired to deprive the plaintiff and others of the benefits of his last will by removing from the paper writing to which the sheet of paper containing the alleged signature of the deceased was attached, that part providing for the legacy to the plaintiff and others and substituting other provisions therefor. The plaintiff contends that thereby a previous will has been admitted to probate. In the course of the proceeding the plaintiff asked for the appointment of a commissioner to take the examination of the defendants in the nature of a bill of discovery. The defendants demurred that the complaint did not state a cause of action. The court sustained the demurrer, and held that unless the will that had been proven in common form was attacked and set aside by caveat, the plaintiff could

[1] In Rice *v.* Manley, 66 N. Y. 82, plaintiff had a contract with a third person for a cheese. By means of a forged telegram defendant procured the third person to sell to him instead. The contract was within the Statute of Frauds, but it was found that the third person would have performed but for defendant's act.

not maintain the cause of action set out in the complaint. This put an end to the plaintiff's further progress in the cause, and she took a nonsuit and appealed.

The plaintiff is not seeking to attack the will on record, nor to probate what she alleges was a subsequent will. She is not seeking to recover anything out of the estate, but is bringing an action of tort against the parties who, as she alleges, conspired and injured her by removing the clause of, and the signature to, what was a subsequent will by which she would have received a legacy. It is an action of spoliation by which she alleges the defendants have prevented her receiving the sum of money which was due her if they had not fraudulently altered and defaced the subsequent will. She alleges that she does not attempt to set up the second will because the evidence accessible to her would not prove its entire contents. She prefers, therefore, to bring this action against the defendants for their wrongdoing in fraudulently destroying the part of the will which was beneficial to herself.

Though this action seems to be of the first impression in this state, and is doubtless a very unusual one, there is foundation and reason for the action upon well-settled principles of law, and we are not entirely without precedent. In Tucker *v.* Phipps, 3 Atkins, 359; cited in Barnesly *v.* Powel, 1 Ves. Sr. 284, it was held that, the spoliation being clearly proven, the plaintiff could maintain his action without setting up the will by a probate. It was held that:

"Where a will is destroyed or concealed, while the general rule is to probate the alleged will by proof in the Ecclesiastical Court [which was there the court for probate wills], yet the legatee might bring his action for the damage sustained by spoliation and suppression."

In that case the spoliation was alleged to have been a destruction or concealment of the will by the executor. Such action against a stranger is even more appropriate than an independent action against the executor. Tucker *v.* Phipps is to be found in 26 English Reports (Reprinted) 1008. Another case very much in point is Barnesley *v.* Powell, 1 Ves. 119, 27 English Reports (Reprinted) 1034, in which Tucker *v.* Phipps is cited as authority and the court also refers with approval to

"A late case where the defendant burned a will, in which was a legacy to the plaintiff, so that it could not be proven in the Ecclesiastical Court [which cannot prove a will on loose parts of the contents of it], yet on the evidence of there being such a will, and the defendants destroying it, the court decreed the legacy to the plaintiff, as the defendant by his own iniquity had prevented the plaintiff from coming at it."

There may be other precedents, but the instances must have been rare. Even if there had been no precedent, it would seem that, upon the principle of justice that there is "no wrong without a remedy," the plaintiff is entitled to maintain this action, if, as she alleges, the defendants conspired and destroyed the subsequent will in which the legacy was left her. If she cannot prove the destroyed will because unable to prove the entire contents thereof (*In re* Hedgepeth, 150 N. C. 245, 63 S. E. 1025), surely she is entitled to recover of the defendants for the wrong they have done her by the conspiracy and destruction of the will, and the measure of her damages will be the legacy of which she has been deprived. It may be very difficult for her to prove her allegations by legal evidence and satisfactory to a jury, but with that we have nothing to do. The only question presented to us is the ruling of the court below that the complaint does not state a cause of action, and in this we think the court below was mistaken.

As the action is not to set up the will, nor against the estate, but against the defendants individually for their tort, the action could be brought in the county where the plaintiff resides.

Reversed.

RATCLIFFE *v.* EVANS

In the Court of Appeal, May 26, 1892.

Reported in [1892] 2 *Queen's Bench*, 524.

Motion to enter judgment for the defendant, or for a new trial, by way of appeal from the judgment entered by Mr. Commissioner Bompas, Q. C., in an action tried with a jury at the Chester Summer Assizes, 1891.

The statement of claim in the action alleged that the plaintiff had for many years carried on the business, at Hawarden in the county of Flint, of an engineer and boiler-maker under the name of "Ratcliffe & Sons," having become entitled to the good-will of the business upon the death of his father, who, with others, had formerly carried on the business as "Ratcliffe & Sons;" that the defendant was the registered proprietor, publisher, and printer of a weekly newspaper called the "County Herald," circulated in Flintshire and some of the adjoining counties, and that the plaintiff had suffered damage by the defendant falsely and maliciously publishing and printing of the plaintiff in relation to his business, in the "County Herald," certain words set forth which imported that the plaintiff had ceased to carry on his business of engineer and boiler-maker, and that the firm of Ratcliffe & Sons did not then exist.

At the trial the learned commissioner allowed the statement of claim to be amended by adding that "by reason of the premises the plaintiff was injured in his credit and reputation, and in his said business of an engineer and boiler-maker, and he thereby lost profits which he otherwise would have made in his said business." The plaintiff proved the publication of the statements complained of, and that they were untrue. He also proved a general loss of business since the publication; but he gave no specific evidence of the loss of any particular customers or orders by reason of such publication. In answer to questions left to them by the commissioner, the jury found that the words did not reflect upon the plaintiff's character, and were not libellous; that the statement that the firm of Ratcliffe & Sons was extinct was not published *bona fide;* and that the plaintiff's business suffered injury to the extent of £120 from the publication of that statement. The commissioner, upon those findings, gave judgment for the plaintiff, for £120, with costs. The defendant appealed.[1]

The following judgment of the court (LORD ESHER, M. R., BOWEN, and FRY, L. JJ.), was read by

BOWEN, L. J. This was a case in which an action for a false and malicious publication about the trade and manufactures of the plaintiff was tried at the Chester assizes, with the result of a verdict for the plaintiff for £120. Judgment having been entered for the plaintiff for that sum and costs, the defendant appealed to this court for a new trial, or to enter a verdict for the defendant, on the ground, amongst others, that no special damage, such as was necessary to support the action, was proved at the trial. The injurious statement complained of was a publication in the "County Herald," a Welsh newspaper. It was treated in the pleadings as a defamatory statement or libel; but this suggestion was negatived, and the verdict of the jury proceeded upon the view that the writing was a false statement purposely made about the manufactures of the plaintiff, which was intended to, and did in fact, cause him damage. The only proof at the trial of such damage consisted, however, of evidence of general loss of business without specific proof of the loss of any particular customers or orders, and the question we have to determine is, whether in such an action such general evidence of damage was admissible and sufficient. That an action will lie for written or oral falsehoods, not actionable *per se* nor even defamatory, where they are maliciously published, where they are calculated in the ordinary course of things to produce, and where they do produce, actual damage, is established law. Such an action is not one of libel or of slander, but an action on the case for damage wilfully and intentionally done without just occasion or excuse, analogous to an action for slander of title. To support it actual damage must be shown, for it is an action which only lies in respect of such damage as has actually occurred. It was contended before us that in such an action it is not enough to allege and prove general loss of business arising from the publication, since such general loss is general and not special damage, and special damage, as often has been said, is the gist of such an action on the case. Lest we should be led astray in such a matter by mere words, it is desirable to recollect that the term "special damage," which is found for centuries in the books, is not always used with reference to similar subject-matter, nor in the same context. At times (both in the law of tort and of contract) it is employed to denote that damage arising out of the special circumstances of the case which, if properly pleaded, may be superadded to the general damage which the law implies in every breach of contract and every infringement of an absolute right: see Ashby *v.* White, 2 Ld. Raym. 938; 1 Sm. L. C. 9th ed. p. 268, *per* Holt, C. J. In all such cases the law presumes that *some* damage will flow in the ordinary course of things from the mere invasion of the plaintiff's rights, and calls it general damage. Special damage in such a context means the particular damage (beyond the general damage), which results from the particular circum-

[1] The arguments of counsel are omitted.

stances of the case, and of the plaintiff's claim to be compensated, for which he ought to give warning in his pleadings in order that there may be no surprise at the trial. But where no actual and positive right (apart from the damage done) has been disturbed, it is the damage done that is the wrong; and the expression "special damage," when used of this damage, denotes the actual and temporal loss which has, in fact, occurred. Such damage is called variously in old authorities, "express loss," "particular damage:" Cane *v.* Golding, Sty. 169; "damage in fact," "special or particular cause of loss:" Law *v.* Harwood, Cro. Car. 140; Tasburgh *v.* Day, Cro. Jac. 484.

The term "special damage" has also been used in actions on the case brought for a public nuisance, such as the obstruction of a river or a highway, to denote that actual and particular loss which the plaintiff must allege and prove that he has sustained beyond what is sustained by the general public, if his action is to be supported, such particular loss being, as is obvious, the cause of action: see Iveson *v.* Moore, 1 Ld. Raym. 486; Rose *v.* Groves, 5 M. & G. 613. In this judgment we shall endeavor to avoid a term which, intelligible enough in particular contexts, tends, when successively employed in more than one context and with regard to different subject-matter, to encourage confusion in thought. The question to be decided does not depend on words, but is one of substance. In an action like the present, brought for a malicious falsehood intentionally published in a newspaper about the plaintiff's business — a falsehood which is not actionable as a personal libel and which is not defamatory in itself — is evidence to show that a general loss of business has been the direct and natural result admissible in evidence, and, if uncontradicted, sufficient to maintain the action? In the case of a personal libel, such general loss of custom may unquestionably be alleged and proved. Every libel is of itself a wrong in regard of which the law, as we have seen, implies general damage. By the very fact that he has committed such a wrong, the defendant is prepared for the proof that some general damage may have been done. As is said by Gould, J., in Iveson *v.* Moore, 1 Ld. Raym. 486, in actions against a wrong-doer a more general mode of declaring is allowed. If, indeed, over and above this general damage, further particular damage is under the circumstances to be relied on by the plaintiff, such particular damage must of course be alleged and shown. But a loss of general custom, flowing directly and in the ordinary course of things from a libel, may be alleged and proved generally. "It is not special damage" — says Pollock, C. B., in Harrison *v.* Pearce, 32 L. T. (O. S.) 298, — "it is general damage resulting from the kind of injury the plaintiff has sustained." So in Bluck *v.* Lovering, 1 Times L. R. 497, under a general allegation of loss of credit in business, general evidence was received of a decline of business presumably due to the publication of the libel, while loss of particular customers, not having been pleaded, was held rightly to have been rejected at the trial: see also Ingram *v.* Lawson, 6 Bing. N. C. 212. Akin to, though distinguishable in a respect which will be mentioned from, actions of libel are those actions which are brought for oral slander, where such slander consists of words actionable in themselves and the mere use of which constitutes the infringement of the plaintiff's right. The very speaking of such words, apart from all damage, constitutes a wrong and gives rise to a cause of action. The law in such a case, as in the case of libel, presumes, and in theory allows, proof of general damage. But slander, even if actionable in itself, is regarded as differing from libel in a point which renders proof of general damage in slander cases difficult to be made good. A person who publishes defamatory matter on paper or in print puts in circulation that which is more permanent and more easily transmissible than oral slander. Verbal defamatory statements may, indeed, be intended to be repeated, or may be uttered under such circumstances that their repetition follows in the ordinary course of things from their original utterance. Except in such cases, the law does not allow the plaintiff to recover damages which flow, not from the original slander, but from its unauthorized repetition: Ward *v.* Weeks, 7 Bing. 211; Holwood *v.* Hopkins, Cro. Eliz. 787; Dixon *v.* Smith, 5 H. & N. 450. General loss of custom cannot properly be proved in respect of a slander of this kind when it has been uttered under such circumstances that its repetition does not flow directly and naturally from the circumstances under which the slander itself was uttered. The doctrine that in slanders actionable *per se* general damage may be alleged and proved with generality must be taken, therefore, with the qualification that the words complained of must have been spoken under circumstances which might in the ordinary course of things have directly produced the general damage that has in fact occurred. Evans *v.* Harries, 1 H. & N. 251, was a slander uttered in such a manner. It consisted of words reflecting on an innkeeper in the conduct of his business spoken openly in the presence of divers persons, guests and customers of the inn — a floating and transitory class. The court held that general evidence of the decline of business was rightly receivable. "How," asked Martin, B., "is a public-house keeper, whose only customers are persons passing by, to show a damage resulting from the slander, unless he is allowed to give general evidence of a loss of custom?" Macloughlin *v.* Welsh, 10 Ir. L. Rep. 19, was an instance of excommunication in open church. General proof was held to be rightly admitted that the plaintiff was shunned and his mill abandoned, though no loss of particular customers was shown. Here the very nature of the slander rendered it necessary that such general proof should be allowed. The defamatory words were spoken openly and publicly, and were intended to have the exact effect which was produced. Unless such general evidence was admissible, the injury done could not be proved at all. If, in addition to this general loss, the loss of particular customers was to be relied on, such particular losses would, in accordance with the ordinary rules of pleading, have been required to be mentioned in the statement of claim: see Ashley *v.* Harrison, 1 Esp. 50. From libels and slanders actionable *per se*, we pass to the case of slanders not actionable *per se*, where actual damage done is the very gist of the action. Many old authorities may be cited for the proposition that in such a case the actual loss must be proved specially and with certainty: Law *v.* Harwood, Cro. Car. 140. Many such instances are collected in the judgments in Iveson *v.* Moore, 1 Ld. Raym. 486, where, although there was a difference as to whether the general rule had been fulfilled in that particular kind of action on the case, no doubt was thrown on the principle itself. As was there said — in that language of old pleaders which has seen its day, but which connoted more accuracy of legal thought than is produced by modern statements of claim — "damages in the '*per quod*,' where the '*per quod*' is the gist of the action, should be shown certainly and specially." But such a doctrine as this was always subject to the qualification of good sense and of justice. Cases may here, as before, occur where a general loss of custom is the natural and direct result of the slander, and where it is not possible to specify particular instances of the loss. Hartley *v.* Herring, 8 T. R. 130, is probably a case of the kind, although it does not appear from the report under what circumstances, or in the presence of whom, the slanderous words were uttered. But if the words are uttered to an individual, and repetition is not intended except to a limited extent, general loss of custom cannot be ordinarily a direct and natural result of the limited slander: Dixon *v.* Smith, 5 H. & N. 450; Hopwood *v.* Thorn, 19 L. J. (C. P.) 95. The broad doctrine is stated in Buller's Nisi Prius, p. 7, that where words are not actionable, and the special damage is the gist of the action, saying generally that several persons left the plaintiff's house is not laying the special damage. Slanders of title, written or oral, and actions such as the present, brought for damage done by falsehoods, written or oral, about a man's goods or business, are similar in many respects to the last-mentioned class of slanders not actionable in themselves. Damage is the gist of both actions alike, and it makes no difference in this respect whether the falsehood is oral or in writing: Malachy *v.* Soper. The necessity of alleging and proving actual temporal loss with certainty and precision in all cases of the sort has been insisted upon for centuries: Lowe *v.* Harewood, W. Jones, 196; Cane *v.* Golding, Sty. 176; Tasburgh *v.* Day, Cro. Jac. 484; Evans *v.* Harlow, 5 Q. B. 624. But it is an ancient and established rule of pleading that the question of generality of pleading must depend on the general subject-matter: Janson *v.* Stuart, 1 T. R. 754; Lord Arlington *v.* Merricke, 2 Saund. 412, n. 4; Grey *v.* Friar, 15 Q. B. 907; see Co. Litt. 303 d; Westwood *v.* Cowne, 1 Stark. 172; Iveson *v.* Moore, 1 Ld. Raym. 486. In all actions accordingly on the case where the damage actually done is the gist of the action, the character of the acts themselves which produce the damage, and the circumstances under which these acts are done, must regulate the degree of certainty and particularity with which the damage done ought to be stated and proved. As much certainty and particularity must be insisted on, both in pleading and proof of damage, as is reasonable, having regard to the circumstances and to the nature of the acts themselves by which the damage is done. To insist upon less would be to relax old and intelligible principles. To insist upon more would be the vainest pedantry. The rule to be laid down with regard to malicious falsehoods affecting property or trade is only an instance of the doctrines of good sense applicable to all that branch of actions on the case to which the class under discussion belongs. The nature and circumstances of the publication of the falsehood may accordingly require the admission of evidence of general loss of business as the natural and direct result produced, and perhaps intended to be produced. An instructive illustration, and one by which the present appeal is really covered, is furnished by the case of Hargrave *v.* Le Breton, 4 Burr. 2422, decided a century and a half ago. It was an example of slander of title at an auction. The allegation in the declaration was that divers persons who would have purchased at the auction left the place; but no particular persons were named. The objection that they were not specially mentioned was, as the report tells us, " easily " answered. The answer given was that in the nature of the transaction it was impossible to specify names; that the injury complained of was in effect that the bidding at the auction had been prevented and stopped, and that everybody had gone away. It had, therefore, become impossible to tell with certainty who would have been bidders or purchasers if the auction had not been rendered abortive. This case shows, what sound judgment itself dictates, that in an action for falsehood producing damage to a man's trade, which in its very nature is intended or reasonably likely to produce, and which in the ordinary course of things does produce, a general loss of business, as distinct from the loss of this or that known customer, evidence of such general decline of business is admissible. In Hargrave *v.* Le Breton it was a falsehood openly promulgated at an auction. In the case before us to-day, it is a falsehood openly disseminated through the press — probably read, and possibly acted on, by persons of whom the plaintiff never heard. To refuse with reference to such a subject-matter to admit such general evidence would be to misunderstand and warp the meaning of old expressions; to depart from, and not to follow, old rules; and, in addition to all this, would involve an absolute denial of justice and of redress for the very mischief which was intended to be committed. It may be added that, so far as the decision in Riding *v.* Smith can be justified, it must be justified on the ground that the court (rightly or wrongly) believed the circumstances under which the falsehood was uttered to have brought it within the scope of a similar principle. In our opinion, therefore, there has been no misdirection and no improper admission of evidence, and this appeal should be dismissed with costs. *Appeal dismissed.*[1]

DUDLEY *v.* BRIGGS

SUPREME JUDICIAL COURT, MASSACHUSETTS, MAY 8, 1886.

Reported in 141 *Massachusetts Reports*, 582.

TORT. Writ dated Sept. 18, 1885. The declaration was as follows:

"And the plaintiff says that he is, and has been for many years, a compiler and publisher of directories of cities, towns, and counties in this Commonwealth and elsewhere; that by care, attention, skill, and faithfulness, and after great labor and expense, he had acquired a large number of subscribers among business men and other people, throughout the cities and towns of Bristol County, and elsewhere in this Commonwealth, for 'The Bristol County Directory,' which the plaintiff has compiled and published biennially for many years, and until the acts and doings of the defendant hereinafter complained of; that, at great labor and expense, he had acquired a large and valuable list of advertisers in his said directory, from whom, as well as from the said subscribers to said directory, he obtained a large income, and would have continued to do so, but for the acts and doings of the defendant hereinafter alleged and set forth.

[1] See American Ins. Co. *v.* France, 111 Ill. App. 382; Davis *v.* New England Pub. Co., 203 Mass. 470; Haney Mfg. Co. *v.* Perkins, 78 Mich. 1; Benton *v.* Pratt, 2 Wend. 385.

"[If, from the nature of the case, the amount of damage caused to a plaintiff by the tort of a defendant cannot be estimated with certainty, shall the defendant therefore be exonerated from liability?] Certainty, it is true, would thus be attained, but it would be the certainty of injustice." Christiancy, J., in Allison *v.* Chandler, 11 Michigan, 542, 555. See also pp. 553–556.

"And the plaintiff says that, according to his usual and ordinary custom in the compilation and publication of the said 'The Bristol County Directory,' he would have compiled and published the same in this year, A. D. 1885, and he made his preparations therefor, but he says that the defendant and his canvassers, and other servants and agents, in order to injure the plaintiff, and to deprive him of the opportunity of compiling and publishing said directory for said year of 1885, and thereafterwards, and receiving the gains and profits therefrom, and to secure the same to the defendant, together with all the gains and profits arising therefrom, and otherwise to injure the plaintiff and get gain, profit, and advantage to the defendant, knowingly and wilfully, falsely and fraudulently, pretended and represented to many persons, and particularly to the plaintiff's patrons, the advertisers in said directory and the subscribers thereto throughout said Bristol County, that the plaintiff had gone out of the business of compiling and publishing said directory, that the plaintiff had sold out said business to the defendant, that the said canvassers and the defendant's other servants and agents were compiling the materials for the plaintiff's directory, the same as formerly, and other false and fraudulent representations then and there made, of which the plaintiff is not yet fully informed, and thereby deceitfully and wrongfully induced the plaintiff's said patrons, advertisers, and subscribers, in and throughout said Bristol County, to give to the defendant their advertisements and subscriptions, and to pay him instead of the plaintiff therefor.

"Whereas, in truth and in fact, the said representations were wholly false and untrue; the plaintiff had neither gone out of the business of compiling and publishing the said directory, as he had done for years before, nor had he sold out to the defendant, nor had he any intention of doing so; nor were the defendant and his canvassers, and other agents and servants, compiling the said directory the same as formerly or for the plaintiff; all of which the defendant, as well as his said canvassers and other servants and agents, well knew. And the defendant did knowingly, wrongfully, injuriously, and deceitfully compile and publish the said 'The Bristol County Directory,' for the year A. D. 1885, and vend and sell the same to the plaintiff's patrons, advertisers, subscribers, and other persons, as aforesaid. And the plaintiff says that thereby he has been prevented from compiling, publishing, and selling his said directory this year, A. D. 1885, as he has always done heretofore; that he has lost the great gains and profits which he would otherwise have made and received from the sale thereof, and from advertisers in and subscribers to said directory, and has been put to great loss and expense in preparing for said compilation and publication, till he learned of the defendant's said act and doings, and thereby he will be hereafter prevented from compiling and publishing said directory except at an increased expense and with diminished profits."

The defendant demurred to the declaration, on the ground that it did not set forth a legal cause of action.

The Superior Court sustained the demurrer; and ordered judgment for the defendant. The plaintiff appealed to this court.

FIELD, J. The plaintiff in his declaration does not allege that, by the acts of the defendant, he has been deprived of the benefit of any contract he had made, or of any property in existence and in his possession, or that the defendant published his directory for 1885 as a directory prepared and published by the plaintiff; and does not bring his case within such decisions as Lumley *v.* Gye, Marsh *v.* Billings, 7 Cush. 322; Thomson *v.* Winchester, 19 Pick. 214; Blofeld *v.* Payne, 4 B. & A. 410; Morison *v.* Salmon, 2 M. & G. 385; and Sykes *v.* Sykes, 3 B. & C. 541.

He does not allege that he had any copyright in the previous publications which the publication of the defendant infringed; and the courts of the Commonwealth have no jurisdiction over infringements of copyright. If each publication of a directory by the plaintiff every two years was a separate publication, then the plaintiff's declaration amounts to this, — that he intended to publish a directory for 1885, whereby he expected to make profits, but, by reason of the acts of the defendant, he abandoned such an intention, and lost the profits he otherwise would have made. But an intention in the mind of the plaintiff to compile and publish a directory is not property, and the abandonment of such an intention is not a loss of property. Bradley *v.* Fuller, 118 Mass. 239.

An attempt has been made to bring this case within what is called slander of goods, manufactured and sold by another. See Western Counties Manure Co. *v.* Lawes Chemical Manure Co., L. R. 9 Ex. 218. This implies that the plaintiff was engaged in the business of making and selling directories, and that the defendant made statements disparaging the plaintiff's business. We think that the declaration does not show that the business of the plaintiff, in publishing a new directory every two years, was a continuous business. The directory to be published in 1885 was to be a new compilation and publication. From the nature of the book, perhaps this could not well be otherwise. New subscribers and new advertisements were to be obtained. We have been shown no case where it has been held that a false statement that the plaintiff had gone out of business, or sold out his business to the defendant, was an actionable slander of a person in his trade; but upon this we express no opinion. It may be said that such statements tend to injure a man in his business, because they tend to prevent customers from resorting to him for trade, and to injure the value of the good-will of his business. However this may be, the difficulty is in attaching good-will as a valuable thing to the publication every two years of a new directory. Such a directory could be published by anybody. It is perhaps a question of degree whether the publication by the plaintiff had been so frequent and regular that there can be said to be a good-will that would be protected in law. There is no allegation of any continuing contract, express or implied, of subscribing for, or advertising in, the directories, as a publication periodically issued; there is no allegation of any place of business to which customers resorted to purchase directories. Until the plaintiff had entered upon the compilation of the directory for 1885, we do not think that there was any business of publishing a directory for 1885 carried on by the plaintiff, or anything that, for example, could have been sold as a going concern by an assignee in insolvency, if the plaintiff had become an insolvent debtor. The cases upon liability for wrongful interference with the business of another are largely collected in Walker *v.* Cronin; but in that case there was an actual business, with the carrying on of which the defendant wrongfully interfered. The declaration in this case, indeed, alleges that the plaintiff made his preparations for compiling and publishing a directory for 1885, but it does not allege what those preparations were, or that they were anything valuable. The averment that he " has been put to great loss and expense in preparing for said compilation and publication," near the end of the declaration, appears to be a part of the damages.

The plaintiff cites Swan *v.* Tappan, 5 Cush. 104, but there the declaration was held insufficient, because there was no allegation of special damage. The declaration in the present case cannot well be distinguished in this respect from the declaration in Swan *v.* Tappan, but we do not deem it necessary to reconsider the decision in that case on this point. There, the plaintiff was actually engaged in selling his book, which had already been printed and put upon the market, and the action was the ordinary action for the malicious disparagement of the goods of another, manufactured and kept for sale.

The plaintiff relies upon Benton *v.* Pratt, 2 Wend. 385, which perhaps may be considered as an extreme case. See Randall *v.* Hazelton, 12 All. 412. In Benton *v.* Pratt, Seagraves and Wilson, at Allentown, had orally agreed to purchase of the plaintiff two hundred hogs, at the market price, if delivered within three or four weeks, and they had not been previously supplied; and, " about the time for the delivery," the plaintiff was proceeding with his drove of hogs to Allentown for the purpose of delivering to them two hundred hogs. The defendant, by his falsehood and deceit, intentionally prevented the performance of this contract, by persuading Seagraves and Wilson that the plaintiff was not intending to drive his hogs to Allentown, whereby they were induced to buy the hogs of the defendant, instead of buying the hogs of the plaintiff, as they otherwise would have done. The court say, that it was " not material whether the contract of the plaintiff with Seagraves and Wilson was binding upon them or not; " but the agreement, if there was an agreement, although not in writing, was an actual offer by Seagraves and Wilson, not revoked, and which they would have performed, and the plaintiff was in the actual possession of the property which Seagraves and Wilson had offered to buy, and was actually proceeding to deliver this property to them, in accordance with their offer.

The fatal objection to the present case is, that it is entirely problematical whether the plaintiff would actually have published a directory if the defendant had not made the fraudulent misrepresentations alleged. The plaintiff abandoned his intention to compile and publish a directory in consequence of the defendant's acts; but this, upon the principles stated in Bradley *v.* Fuller, 118 Mass. 239, and the cases therein cited, is not sufficient to support an action.

Judgment affirmed.

GARRET *v.* TAYLOR

IN THE KING'S BENCH, EASTER TERM, 1620.

Reported in Croke, James, 567.

ACTION on the case. Whereas he was a Freemason, and used to sell stones, and to make stone buildings, and was possessed of a lease for divers years to come of a stone-pit in Hedington, in the county of Oxford, and digged divers stones there, as well to sell as to build withal; that the defendant, to discredit and to deprive him of the commodity of the said mine, imposed so many and so great threats upon his workmen, and all comers disturbed, threatening to mayhem and vex them with suits if they bought any stones; whereupon they all desisted from buying, and the others from working, &c.

After judgment by *nihil dicit* for the plaintiff, and damages found by inquisition to fifteen pounds, it was moved in arrest of judgment, that this action lay not; for nothing is alleged but only words, and no act nor insult: and causeless suits on fear are no cause of action.

Sed non allocatur: for the threatening to mayhem, and suits, whereby they durst not work or buy, is a great damage to the plaintiff, and his losing the benefit of his quarries a good cause of action: and although it be not shown how he was possessed for years, by what title, &c., yet that being but a conveyance to this action, was held to be well enough. And adjudged for the plaintiff.[1]

[1] Standard Oil Co. *v.* Doyle, 118 Ky. 662; Dickson *v.* Dickson, 33 La. Ann. 1261 *Accord.*

Threats of vexatious suits against customers: Emack *v.* Kane, 34 Fed. 46; Lewin *v.* Welsbach Light Co., 81 Fed. 904; Farquhar Co. *v.* National Harrow Co., 99 Fed. 160; Adriance *v.* National Harrow Co., 121 Fed. 827, 98 Fed. 118; Dittgen *v.* Racine Paper Goods Co., 164 Fed. 85; Electric Renovator Co. *v.* Vacuum Cleaner Co., 189 Fed. 754; Atlas Underwear Co. *v.* Cooper Underwear Co., 210 Fed. 347; Shoemaker *v.* South Bend Spark Arrester Co., 135 Ind. 471; Pratt Food Co. *v.* Bird, 148 Mich. 631.

TARLETON *v.* M'GAWLEY

AT NISI PRIUS, CORAM LORD KENYON, C. J., DECEMBER 21, 1804.

Reported in Peake, 205.

THIS was a special action on the case. The declaration stated that the plaintiffs had sent a vessel called the "Bannister," with a crew on board, under the command of one Thomas Smith, and loaded with goods proper for trading with the natives, to a part of the coast of Africa called Cameroon, to trade with the natives there. That while the last-mentioned ship was lying off Cameroon, a canoe with some natives on board came to the same for the purpose of establishing a trade, and went back to the shore, of which defendant had notice. And that he well knowing the premises, but *contriving and maliciously intending to hinder and deter the natives from trading* with the said Thomas Smith, for the benefit of the plaintiffs, with force and arms, fired from a certain ship called the "Othello," of which he was master and commander, a certain cannon loaded with gunpowder and shot, at the said canoe, and killed one of the natives on board the same. *Whereby the natives of the said coast were deterred and hindered from trading with the said T. Smith for the benefit, &c., and plaintiffs lost their trade.*

LORD KENYON. This action is brought by the plaintiffs to recover a satisfaction for a civil injury which they have sustained. The injury complained of is, that by the improper conduct of the defendant the natives were prevented from trading with the plaintiffs. The whole of the case is stated on the record, and if the parties desire it, the opinion of the court may hereafter be taken whether it will support an action. I am of opinion it will. Had this been an accidental thing, no action could have been maintained; but it is proved that the defendant had expressed an intention not to permit any to trade, until a debt due from the natives to himself was satisfied. If there was any court in that country to which he could have applied for justice he might have done so, but he had no right to take the law into his own hands.[1]

HART *v.* ALDRIDGE

IN THE KING'S BENCH, MAY 3, 1774.

Reported in Cowper, 54.

THIS came before the court on a case reserved upon the following question: Whether under the circumstances of this case the plaintiff was entitled to recover? It was an action of trespass on the case for enticing away several of the plaintiff's servants, who used to work for

[1] St. Johnsbury Co. *v.* Hunt, 55 Vt. 570 (arrest of plaintiff's engineer on a malicious and baseless charge, whereby the running of plaintiff's train was delayed) *Accord.*

him in the capacity of journeymen shoemakers. The jury found that Martin and Clayton were employed as journeymen shoemakers by the plaintiff, but for no determinate time, but only by the piece, and had, at the time of the trespass laid, each of them a pair of shoes unfinished; that the defendant persuaded them to enter into his service, and to leave these shoes unfinished, which they accordingly did.

Mr. Darwell, for the plaintiff, stated it to be a question of common law, and that the only point for the opinion of the court was, "whether a journeyman was such a servant as the law takes notice of?" In support of which proposition he insisted that a journeyman is as much a servant as any other person who works for hire or wages; that neither in reason nor at common law is there any distinction between a servant in one capacity or another, and that the injury of seduction is in all cases the same, though the recompense in damages may be different. He pressed the argument *ab inconvenienti*, stating that it would be of great detriment to the town, where the whole trade was in a great measure carried on by this sort of servant. That the verdict had found the defendant to be apprised of the retainer of the servants, it being in proof that he had desired them to leave their work then in hand unfinished.

Mr. Willes, contra. The single question is, whether the enticing away a journeyman shoemaker, who is hired to make a single pair of shoes, is such an injury to his master as that an action will lie for it. Now the jury have found that there was no hiring for any determinate time, but only by the piece: if so, they could not be the plaintiff's servants; for the term "journeyman" does not import that they belong to any particular master.

LORD MANSFIELD interrupted him. The question is, whether saying that such a one is a man's journeyman, is as much as to say that he is such a man's servant; that is, whether the jury, by finding him to be the plaintiff's journeyman, do not *ex vi termini* find him to be his servant. A journeyman is a servant by the day; and it makes no difference whether the work is done by the day or by the piece. He was certainly retained to finish the work he had undertaken, and the defendant knowingly enticed him to leave it unfinished.

What is the gist of the action? That the defendant has enticed a man away who stood in the relation of servant to the plaintiff, and by whom he was to be benefited. I think the point turns upon the jury finding that the persons enticed away were employed by the plaintiff as his journeymen. It might perhaps have been different if the men had taken work for everybody, and after the plaintiff had employed them the defendant had applied to them, and they had given the preference to him in point of time. For if a man lived in his own house and took in work for different people, it would be a strong ground to say that he was not the journeyman of any particular master; but the gist of the present action is that they were attached to this particular master.

ASTON, J. It is clear that a master may maintain an action against any one for taking and enticing away his servant, upon the ground of the interest which he has in his service and labor.[1] And even supposing, as my lord has stated, that the servant did live in his own house, if he were employed to finish a certain number of shoes for a particular person by a fixed time, and a third person enticed him away, I think an action would lie. If not, it might be of very bad consequence in trade. He is a servant *quoad hoc*, and though the seducer and enticer is much the worse, yet the law inflicts a penalty upon workmen leaving their work undone.

Mr. Justice WILLES and Mr. Justice ASHHURST concurred.

Per Curiam. Let the *postea* be delivered to the plaintiff.[2]

EAGER *v.* GRIMWOOD

IN THE EXCHEQUER, JUNE 1, 1847.

Reported in 1 *Exchequer Reports,* 61.

TRESPASS for assaulting and debauching the daughter and servant of the plaintiff, whereby she then became pregnant, &c., and the plaintiff lost and was deprived of her services. Plea: Not guilty.

At the trial before Pollock, C. B., at the London sittings after last Michaelmas term, the following facts appeared: The connection between the defendant and the plaintiff's daughter took place for the

[1] Gunter *v.* Astor, 4 Moore, 12; Hartley *v.* Cummings, 5 C. B. 247; Jones *v.* Blocker, 43 Ga. 331; Wharton *v.* Jossey, 46 Ga. 578; Lee *v.* West, 47 Ga. 311 (*semble*); Smith *v.* Goodman, 75 Ga. 198; Bundy *v.* Dodson, 28 Ind. 295; Jones *v.* Tevis, 4 Litt. 25; Tyson *v.* Ewing, 3 J. J. Marsh, 185; Carew *v.* Rutherford, 106 Mass. 1; Bixby *v.* Dunlap, 56 N. H. 456; Stille *v.* Jenkins, 3 Green, (N. J.) 302; Scidmore *v.* Smith, 13 John. 322; Covert *v.* Gray, 34 How. Pr. 450; Johnston Co. *v.* Meinhardt, 9 Abb. N. C. 393; Stout *v.* Woody, 63 N. C. 37; Haskins *v.* Royster, 70 N. C. 601; Robinson *v.* Culp, 3 Brev. 302; Daniel *v.* Swearengen, 6 S. C. 297; Fowler *v.* Stonum, 6 Tex. 60; Thacker Co. *v.* Burke, 59 W. Va. 253; Cowper *v.* Macfarlane, 6 Sess. Cas., 4th Series, 683 *Accord.*

See, also, Martinez *v.* Gerber, 3 M. & G. 88.

An action will lie against one who induces a servant to violate his duty not to communicate the trade secrets of his employer. Jones *v.* Westervelt, 7 Cow. 445; Kerr *v.* Roxburgh, 3 Murr. (Scotland) 126; Roxburgh *v.* McArthur, 3 Sess. Cas., 2d Series, 556.

[2] In Blake *v.* Lanyon, 6 T. R. 221, a journeyman, while his work was unfinished, left plaintiff and hired with defendant, who then did not know the facts. Defendant was held liable for retaining the journeyman after notice. Fawcet *v.* Beavres, 2 Lev. 63; Pilkington *v.* Scott, 15 M. & W. 657; Kennedy *v.* McArthur, 5 Ala. 151; Dacy *v.* Gay, 16 Ga. 203; Everett *v.* Sherfey, 1 Ia. 356; Stowe *v.* Heywood, 7 All. 118; Sargent *v.* Mathewson, 38 N. H. 54; Dickson *v.* Taylor, 1 Murr. (Scotland) 141 *Accord.* Adams *v.* Bafeald, 1 Leon. 240; Caldwell *v.* O'Neal, 117 Ga. 775 (if contract is oral only) *Contra.*

It was said also that there was no liability for the hiring of plaintiff's journeyman without notice of the facts. Eades *v.* Vandeput, 5 East, 39 n. (*a*); Sherwood *v.* Hall, 3 Sumn. 127; Ferguson *v.* Tucker, 2 Har. & G. 182; Butterfield *v.* Ashley, 6 Cush. 249; Sargent *v.* Mathewson, 38 N. H. 54; Clark *v.* Clark, 63 N. J. Law, 1; Stuart *v.* Simpson, 1 Wend. 376; Caughey *v.* Smith, 47 N. Y. 244; Bell *v.* Lakin, 1 McMull. 364; Conant *v.* Raymond, 2 Aik. 243 *Accord.*

first time two days after Christmas day, 1844. In June, 1845, the plaintiff's daughter gave birth to a child, which, according to the evidence of a surgeon, was a full-grown child. It also appeared that the plaintiff had been put to some expense in consequence of his daughter's illness. The learned Chief Baron left it to the jury to say whether or no the defendant was the father of the child; and he told them that if they believed he was not the father of the child, they should find a verdict for him. The jury having found for the defendant,

Prentice obtained a rule *nisi* for a new trial, on the ground of misdirection, against which

Humfrey showed cause.

Prentice, in support of the rule.[1]

POLLOCK, C. B. The case of Grinnell *v.* Wells, 7 Man. & G. 1033, is precisely in point. That case decided that an action for seduction cannot be maintained without proof of loss of service. Tindal, C. J., in delivering the judgment of the court, says: "The foundation of the action by a father to recover damages against the wrong-doer, for the seduction of his daughter, has been uniformly placed from the earliest time hitherto, not upon the seduction itself, which is the wrongful act of the defendant, but upon the loss of service of the daughter, in which service he is supposed to have a legal right or interest." The rule must be absolute to enter a nonsuit, unless the plaintiff will consent to a *stet processus*.

ALDERSON, B., ROLFE, B., and PLATT B., concurred.

Rule accordingly.[2]

[1] The arguments of counsel are omitted.

[2] "The rule which governs the numerous cases upon this subject is, that where the proximate effect of the criminal connection is an incapacity to labor, by reason of which the master loses the services of his servant, such loss of service is deemed to be the immediate effect of the connection, and entitles the master to his action. The same principle which gives a master an action where the connection causes pregnancy or sexual disease applies to all cases where the proximate consequence of the criminal act is a loss of health resulting in a loss of service. There may be cases in which the seduction, without producing pregnancy or sexual disease, causes bodily injury, impairing the health of the servant, and resulting in a loss of services to her master. So the criminal connection may be accomplished under such circumstances, as, for instance, of violence or fraud, that its proximate effect is mental distress or disease, impairing her health and destroying her capacity to labor. In either of these cases the master may maintain an action, because the loss of services is immediately caused by the connection, as much as in cases of pregnancy or sexual disease. Vanhorn *v.* Freeman, 1 Halst. 322. But if the loss of health is caused by mental suffering, which is not the consequence of the seduction, but is produced by subsequent intervening causes, such as abandonment by the seducer, shame resulting from exposure, or other similar causes, the loss of services is too remote a consequence of the criminal act, and the action cannot be maintained. Boyle *v.* Brandon, 13 M. & W. 738; Knight *v.* Wilcox, 14 N. Y. 413.

"In the case at bar, as the ruling appears to have been general that the action could not be maintained unless pregnancy or sexual disease was proved, we think a new trial should be granted." Morton, J., in Abrahams *v.* Kidney, 104 Mass. 222. See to the same effect Blagge *v.* Ilsley, 127 Mass. 191; Clark *v.* Clark, 63 N. J. Law, 1; White *v.* Nellis, 31 N. Y. 405; Ingerson *v.* Miller, 47 Barb. 47.

EVANS *v.* WALTON

IN THE COMMON PLEAS, JUNE 11, 1867.

Reported in Law Reports, 2 *Common Pleas*, 615.

THE first count of the declaration stated that Louisa Evans was and still is the servant of the plaintiff in his business of a publican and victualler; and that the defendant, well knowing the same, wrongfully enticed and procured the said Louisa Evans unlawfully and without the consent and against the will of the plaintiff, her said master, to depart from the service of the plaintiff; whereby the plaintiff had lost the service of the said Louisa Evans in his said business.

Pleas: Not guilty; and that Louisa Evans was not the servant of the plaintiff, as alleged. Issue thereon.

The cause was tried before Pigott, B., at the last Spring Assizes at Oxford. The plaintiff was a licensed victualler in Birmingham, and was assisted in his business by his daughter Louisa, a girl about nineteen years of age, who served in the bar and kept the accounts. On the 10th of November, 1866, the daughter, with her mother's permission, which was procured by means of a fabricated letter purporting to be an invitation to her to spend a few days with a friend at Manchester, left the plaintiff's house and went to a lodging-house in the neighborhood of Birmingham, where she cohabited with the defendant, at whose dictation the above-mentioned letter had been written. On the 19th of November the daughter returned home, and resumed her duties for a short time, but ultimately left her home again, and on the 9th of February was again found cohabiting with the defendant at the same lodging-house.

On the part of the defendant it was submitted that, in order to sustain the action, in the absence of an allegation that the defendant had debauched the plaintiff's daughter, it was necessary to show a binding contract of service.

The learned Baron, after consulting Blackburn, J., intimated an opinion that the action would lie upon the declaration as framed; but he reserved to the defendant leave to move to enter a nonsuit if the court should be of opinion that in point of law the action was not maintainable, — the court to have power to draw any inferences of fact, and to amend the declaration if necessary, according to the facts proved.

The case was then left to the jury, who returned a verdict for the plaintiff, damages, £50.

Huddleston, Q. C., in Easter term, obtained a rule *nisi*.

Powell, Q. C., and *J. O. Griffits* (June 11) showed cause, submitting that the action would lie upon the declaration as it stood.

The court called on

H. James and *Jelf*, in support of the rule. There are two kinds of action for loss of service, viz., an action for the seduction and consequent loss of service of a daughter, and an action for enticing away a servant. In order to sustain the first, it is not enough that there has been criminal intercourse, but it must be shown that that intercourse has resulted in pregnancy or other illness so as to cause a disability in the daughter to perform her accustomed duties: Eager *v.* Grimwood; Boyle *v.* Brandon, 13 M. & W. 738; but an actual contract of service need not be proved. It is not suggested that there is any such cause of action here. In Sedgwick on Damages (2d ed.), page 543, it is said that " although the defendant be guilty of the seduction, but the jury are of opinion that the child is not his, the plaintiff cannot recover. In other words, without some damage to the plaintiff or master occasioned by the illness of the female, and resulting from the illicit intercourse, the plaintiff is without relief." And for this Eager *v.* Grimwood is cited.

[BOVILL, C. J. Eager *v.* Grimwood is cited in Smith's Leading Cases (6th ed.), vol. i. p. 260, with evident disapprobation.]

No precedent is to be found without the allegation *per quod servitium amisit.* The action for seduction is an anomalous one.

[WILLES, J. Upon the first point, I think we are bound by the case of Eager *v.* Grimwood. The question is, whether the action may not be maintained for enticing the girl away from her father's service.]

To sustain an action for enticing away a servant, it is necessary to show a valid and binding contract of service, which has been broken through the procurement of the defendant. Actual service is not enough. Here, there was no contract, express or implied, for the breach of which the father could have sued his daughter. All that the defendant can be charged with having done is, inciting the daughter to do that which in the exercise of her own free will she had an undoubted right to do. If an action would lie for this, it would equally lie for inducing a daughter to quit her father's house for the purpose of marrying her.[1] See Fitz. N. B. 90 H. In Cox *v.* Muncey, 6 C. B. N. S. 375, it was held by this court that no action will lie for enticing away an apprentice, unless there be a valid contract of apprenticeship; and the like was held as to a servant by the Court of Queen's Bench in Sykes *v.* Dixon, 9 Ad. & E. 693; 1 P. & D. 463.

[BOVILL, C. J. At the end of Lord Denman's judgment, in Sykes *v.* Dixon, there is a remark which seems to be adverse to your view. " Then," says his Lordship, " it was argued, on the authority of Keane *v.* Boycott, 2 H. Bl. 511, that the objection " (that is, to the validity of the contract) " was not one which a third person could take: and that might be so in a case where the servant was *de facto* continuing in the service; but not here, where he had quitted his

[1] The father can maintain no action in such a case: Goodwin *v.* Thompson, 2 Greene, 329; Jones *v.* Tevis, 4 Litt. 25; Hervey *v.* Moseley, 7 Gray, 479; Beard *v.* Holland, 59 Miss. 161, 164; Wilkinson *v.* Dellinger, 126 N. C. 462. Unless the daughter was induced to marry the defendant by the latter's fraud. Hills *v.* Hobert, 2 Root, 48; Goodwin *v.* Thompson, *supra.*

master, and taken his chance in hiring himself to the defendant." Here the daughter was *de facto* continuing in the service of her father when the defendant seduced her therefrom.]

All the authorities were referred to in Lumley *v.* Gye, and amongst them Blake *v.* Lanyon; but in none of them was the action held to lie in the absence of a binding contract of service.[1]

BOVILL, C. J. The rule in this case was granted principally on the contention of the defendant's counsel that, in order to sustain the action, it was necessary to show that there was a binding contract of service between the father and the daughter. And for this proposition various text-books were referred to, and several cases cited, amongst which was that of Sykes *v.* Dixon, 9 Ad. & E. 693; 1 P. & D. 463. But, when that case is looked at, I find no such principle involved in the decision. Indeed, in each of the cases, from the form of the declaration, it became necessary to prove some contract for service beyond that which the law would imply from the relation of the parties. No authority is to be found where it has been held that in an action for enticing away the plaintiff's daughter a binding contract of service must be alleged and proved. But there are abundant authorities to show the contrary. It is said that the case of seduction is anomalous in this respect. There is, however, no foundation for that assertion. In the case of an action for the seduction of a daughter, no proof of service is necessary beyond the services implied from the daughter's living in her father's house as a member of his family. So, in the case of an action for assaulting the plaintiff's infant son or daughter, no evidence of service is necessary beyond that which the law will imply as between parent and child. In Barber *v.* Dennis, 6 Mod. 69; 1 Salk. 68, the widow of a waterman, who, as was said, by the usage of Waterman's Hall, may take an apprentice, had her apprentice taken from her and put on board a Queen's ship, where he earned two tickets, which came to the defendant's hands, and for which the mistress brought trover. It was agreed that the action would well lie if the apprentice were a legal apprentice, for his possession would be that of his master, and whatever he earns shall go to his master; but it was objected that the company of watermen is a voluntary society, and that being free of it does not make a man free of London, so that the custom of London for persons under one and twenty to bind themselves apprentices does not extend to watermen; which was agreed by all. Then it was said that the supposed apprentice here was no legal apprentice, if the indentures be not enrolled pursuant to the 5 Eliz. c. 4, and, if he were not a legal apprentice, the plaintiff had no title. But Holt, C. J., said he would understand him an apprentice or servant *de facto*, and that would suffice against them, being wrong-doers. Again, in Fitz. N. B. 91 G. it is laid down that,

[1] A part of the argument and the concurring opinion of Montague Smith, J., with which Keating, J., agreed, are omitted.

"if a man ought to have toll in a fair, &c., and his servants are disturbed in gathering the same, he shall have trespass for assault of his servants, and for the loss of their service," &c. To this is appended a note by Lord Hale: "Trespass for beating his servants, *per quod servitium amisit*, lies, although he was not retained, but served only at will. 11 Hen. IV. fol. 2, *per* Hull, accordant. And so if A. retains B. to be his servant, who departs into another county and serves C., A., before any request or seizure, cannot beat B.; and, if he does, C. shall have trespass against him (21 Hen. VI. fol. 9), and recover damages, having regard to the loss of service (22 Ass. 76): and the retainer is traversable. 11 Hen. VI. fol. 30." These authorities, and the principle upon which the action for assaulting a servant is founded, would seem to show that an actual binding contract is not necessary. There is no allegation in this declaration of a hiring for any definite time. All that is alleged is, that the girl was the daughter and servant of the plaintiff. It cannot be doubted that the jury would infer from the facts that the relation of master and servant did exist, without any evidence of a contract for a definite time; and, if we are to draw inferences from the facts, I should come to the same conclusion. Then, was that relation put an end to? The service, no doubt, was one which would be determinable at the will of either party, as is said by Bramwell, B., in Thompson *v.* Ross, 5 H. & N. 16. That this kind of service is sufficient, I should gather from the language used by this court in Hartley *v.* Cummings, 5 C. B. 247, and particularly from the judgment of Maule, J. That was an action for seducing workmen from the service of the plaintiff, a glass and alkali manufacturer, and harboring them after notice. It appeared that one Pike was in the service of the plaintiff, and the defendant induced him to leave. In giving judgment, Maule, J., says: "The objection urged on the part of the defendant is, that the agreement entered into by Pike with the plaintiff was one that gave the latter no right to compel Pike to serve him, inasmuch as it was void either for want of mutuality or because it was a contract to an unreasonable extent operating in restraint of trade. On the other side, it was insisted, upon the authority of Keane *v.* Boycott, 2 H. Bl. 511, that it is quite immaterial, for the purpose of this action, whether the agreement was void or not; for that it is not competent to the defendants, who are wrong-doers, to take advantage of its invalidity. In answer to this, the case of Sykes *v.* Dixon, 9 Ad. & E. 693; 1 P. & D. 463, was cited on the part of the defendants, where it is said to have been decided by the Court of Queen's Bench that such an objection may be set up by a third person not a party to the agreement. It is unnecessary to say whether that case may not be distinguished from the present, — there being no subsisting service that was interrupted by the act of the defendant, — because I am of opinion that in this case there was a contract between Hartley and Pike, which was perfectly valid, notwithstanding the objections that have been urged." Whether or not there was a subsisting service seems to be the test. I think the jury properly assumed that there was a subsisting service here. It is said that the girl's services were not lost to the plaintiff by reason of the defendant's having enticed her away; for that, inasmuch as she afterwards returned to her father's house, the relation of master and servant was not put an end to by any act of the defendant's. I think however, there was a sufficient interruption of the service to entitle the plaintiff to maintain the action, and that the rule to enter a nonsuit should be discharged.

WILLES, J. I am of the same opinion. I cannot look at it as an anomaly to hold that the daughter was the servant of her father at the time the defendant by his enticement induced her to forbear from rendering to her father the services which were due to him from her. There is a series of cases in the books, of which that in the Year-Book of 11 Hen. IV, fol. 2, is probably the first, to show that this action is maintainable. This case was followed by a very remarkable one of M. 22 Hen. VI, fol. 30, in which that doctrine is fully recognized, and where service at will and service upon a retainer are put upon the same footing with regard to any complaint of being wrongfully deprived of their fruits, and it is pointed out that the writ at common law ran, "*quare un tiel servientem meum in servitio meo existentem cepit et abduxit,*" without alleging any contract or retainer. That runs so completely with the earlier case, and also with the doctrine of Lord Denman in Sykes v. Dixon, 9 Ad. & E. 693, 699; 1 P. & D. 463, and of Maule, J., in Hartley v. Cummings, 5 C. B. 247, and also with the observations of Bramwell, B., in Thompson v. Ross, that I feel no difficulty in holding that, upon authority, as well as in good sense, the father of a family, in respect of such service as his daughter renders him from her sense of duty and filial gratitude, stands in the same position as an ordinary master. If she is in his service, whether *de son bon gre* or *sur retainer*, he is equally entitled to her services, and to maintain an action against one who entices her away. Assuming that the service was at the will of both parties, like a tenancy at will, the relation must be put an end to in some way before the rights of the master under it can be lost. As a question of fact, was the daughter in the service of her father at the time the cause of action arose? Was the relation of master and servant put an end to by her quitting her father's house by means of the false pretence to which the defendant induced her to resort? There was no proof that she quitted without any intention to return to her home. What pretence, then, was there for assuming that the service at will was put an end to? To use the language of Newton, J., in the case of 22 Hen. VI, fol. 30, it is no more than if a servant should absent herself for the purpose of going to church on the Sabbath day. Then, was the defendant guilty of any wrong in keeping her away from the plaintiff's service? I apprehend that, where the relation of master and servant exists, any fraud whereby the servant is induced to absent herself affords a ground of action. Somewhat the same sort of question arose in Winsmore *v.* Greenbank, where, in an action on the case for inducing the plaintiff's wife to continue absent, it was held to be sufficient to state that "the defendant unlawfully and unjustly persuaded, procured, and enticed the wife to continue absent, &c., by means of which persuasion, &c., she did continue absent, &c., whereby the plaintiff lost the comfort and society of his wife," &c., without setting forth the means used by the defendant, or alleging that any adultery had been committed. There is really no difficulty when once the relation of master and servant at the time of the acts complained of is established. It was said that, inasmuch as none of the usual consequences, such as sickness or the birth of a child, resulted from the defendant's acts, no action is maintainable for the mere improper intercourse. Be it so, as there is an authority in favor of that position; but that only removes the charge of debauching the plaintiff's daughter out of the way. It does seem to me to be an extraordinary thing, and to reduce the argument to an absurdity, to say that the plaintiff would have had a sufficient cause of action against the defendant if the daughter had proved with child by him, and had gone back to her father's house and been confined there, and that the fact of the father having through his fraud been deprived of his daughter's services during the nine days' concubinage affords no ground of action. The conclusion I arrive at is, that it was a question for the jury whether at the time the daughter left her father's house there was an existing service *de facto*, and whether by the defendant's means and procurement that service was denied to the plaintiff. If both those questions were found against the defendant, the plaintiff was clearly entitled to the verdict. I think there was abundant evidence to support the finding, and that the rule must be discharged. *Rule discharged.*[1]

[1] Whether it is an excess of fair competition to induce a servant at will to leave the plaintiff, and enter the service of the defendant, cannot be said to be definitely settled. In Salter *v.* Howard, 43 Ga. 601, the plaintiff prevailed; but in Campbell *v.* Cooper, 34 N. H. 49, the defendant was successful. The other cases commonly cited for the plaintiff are distinguishable. In Sykes *v.* Dixon, 9 A. & E. 693, and Peters *v.* Lord, 18 Conn. 337, the servant had left the plaintiff of his own head before entering the service of the defendant. In Keane *v.* Boycott, 2 H. Bl. 512, the defendant, a recruiting officer, officiously induced the servant to leave the plaintiff, in order to enlist as a soldier. In Speight *v.* Oliviera, 2 Stark. 493; Morgan *v.* Molony, 7 Ir. L. R. N. S. 101, 240; Ball *v.* Bruce, 21 Ill. 161; and Noice *v.* Brown, 39 N. J. Law, 569, as in the principal case, the enticement was for an immoral purpose. In Cox *v.* Muncey, 6 C. B. N. S. 375, a father induced an apprentice at will to leave the master, but the motive of the father does not appear.

"[Keane *v.* Boycott, 2 H. Bl. 512] seems contrary to the general principle and is certainly opposed to the decision of the Court of Appeals in DeFrancesco *v.* Barnum, 45 Ch. D. 430. The defendant there had enticed away an apprentice of the plaintiff. But the indenture contained unreasonable stipulations, and it was held that it might be avoided by the apprentice, and that it was not unlawful for the defendant to persuade the apprentice to do that which was lawful. It is different, however, if malice, force or fraud be used to take or decoy the servant away. In that case the master has a right of action, even though the servant be under no

LUMLEY v. GYE

IN THE QUEEN'S BENCH, TRINITY TERM, 1853.

Reported in 2 Ellis & Blackburn, 216.

CROMPTON, J.[1] The declaration in this case consisted of three counts. The two first stated a contract between the plaintiff, the proprietor of the Queen's Theatre, and Miss Wagner, for the performance by her for a period of three months at the plaintiff's theatre; and it then stated that the defendant, knowing the premises and with a malicious intention, whilst the agreement was in full force, and before the expiration of the period for which Miss Wagner was engaged, wrongfully and maliciously enticed and procured Miss Wagner to refuse to sing or perform at the theatre, and to depart from and abandon her contract with the plaintiff and all service thereunder, whereby Miss Wagner wrongfully, during the full period of the engagement, refused and made default in performing at the theatre; and special damage arising from the breach of Miss Wagner's engagement was then stated. The third count stated that Miss Wagner had been hired and engaged by the plaintiff, then being the owner of her Majesty's Theatre, to perform at the said theatre for a certain specified period as the dramatic artiste of the plaintiff for reward to her in that behalf, and had become and was such dramatic artiste for the plaintiff at his said theatre for profit to the plaintiff in that behalf; and that the defendant, well knowing the premises and with a malicious intention, whilst Miss Wagner was such artiste of the plaintiff, wrongfully and maliciously enticed and procured her, so being such artiste of the plaintiff, to depart from and out of the said employment of the plaintiff, whereby she wrongfully departed from and out of the said service and employment of the plaintiff, and remained and continued absent from such service and employment until the expiration of her said hiring and engagement to the plaintiff by effluxion of time; and special damage arising from the breach of Miss Wagner's engagement was then stated. To this declaration the defendant demurred; and the question for our decision is, Whether all or any of the counts are good in substance ?

The effect of the two first counts is, that a person, under a binding contract to perform at a theatre, is induced by the malicious act of the defendant to refuse to perform and entirely to abandon her contract; whereby damage arises to the plaintiff, the proprietor of the

binding obligation. Per *Willes*, J., Evans *v.* Walton, L. R. 2 Com. Pl., pp. 621–622." Clerk and Lindsell, Torts, 5 ed. 227.

To induce a servant who is under contract with the plaintiff to leave the latter at the expiration of the term of service, and to enter the defendant's service, is no more than lawful competition. Nichol *v.* Martyn, 2 Esp. 732; Boston Manufactory *v.* Binney, 4 Pick. 425.

[1] The statement of the case and the arguments of counsel are omitted.

theatre. The third count differs, in stating expressly that the performer had agreed to perform as the dramatic artiste of the plaintiff, and *had become and was* the dramatic artiste of the plaintiff for reward to her; and that the defendant maliciously procured her to depart out of the employment of the plaintiff as such dramatic artiste; whereby she did depart out of the employment and service of the plaintiff; whereby damage was suffered by the plaintiff. It was said, in support of the demurrer, that it did not appear in the declaration that the relation of master and servant ever subsisted between the plaintiff and Miss Wagner; that Miss Wagner was not averred, especially in the two first counts, to have entered upon the service of the plaintiff; and that the engagement of a theatrical performer, even if the performer has entered upon the duties, is not of such a nature as to make the performer a servant, within the rule of law which gives an action to the master for the wrongful enticing away of his servant. And it was laid down broadly, as a general proposition of law, that no action will lie for procuring a person to break a contract, although such procuring is with a malicious intention and causes great and immediate injury. And the law as to enticing servants was said to be contrary to the general rule and principle of law, and to be anomalous, and probably to have had its origin from the state of society when serfdom existed, and to be founded upon, or upon the equity of, the Statute of Laborers. It was said that it would be dangerous to hold that an action was maintainable for persuading a third party to break a contract, unless some boundary or limits could be pointed out; and that the remedy for enticing away servants was confined to cases where the relation of master and servant, in a strict sense, subsisted between the parties; and that, in all other cases of contract, the only remedy was against the party breaking the contract.

Whatever may have been the origin or foundation of the law as to enticing of servants, and whether it be, as contended by the plaintiff, an instance and branch of a wider rule, or whether it be, as contended by the defendant, an anomaly and an exception from the general rule of law on such subjects, it must now be considered clear law that a person who wrongfully and maliciously, or, which is the same thing, with notice, interrupts the relation subsisting between master and servant by procuring the servant to depart from the master's service, or by harboring and keeping him as servant after he has quitted it and during the time stipulated for as the period of service, whereby the master is injured, commits a wrongful act for which he is responsible at law. I think that the rule applies wherever the wrongful interruption operates to prevent the service during the time for which the parties have contracted that the service shall continue; and I think that the relation of master and servant subsists, sufficiently for the purpose of such action, during the time for which there is in existence a binding contract of hiring and service between the parties; and I think that it is a fanciful and technical and unjust distinction to say that the not having actually entered into the service, or that the service not actually continuing, can make any difference. The wrong and injury are surely the same, whether the wrong-doer entices away the gardener, who has hired himself for a year, the night before he is to go to his work, or after he has planted the first cabbage on the first morning of his service; and I should be sorry to support a distinction so unjust, and so repugnant to common sense, unless bound to do so by some rule or authority of law plainly showing that such distinction exists. . . .[1]

The objection as to the actual employment not having commenced would not apply in the present case to the third count, which states that Miss Wagner had become the artiste of the plaintiff, and that the defendant had induced her to depart from the employment. But it was further said that the engagement, employment or service, in the present case, was not of such a nature as to constitute the relation of master and servant, so as to warrant the application of the usual rule of law giving a remedy in case of enticing away servants. The nature of the injury and of the damage being the same, and the supposed right of action being in strict analogy to the ordinary case of master and servant, I see no reason for confining the case to services or engagements under contracts for services of any particular description; and I think that the remedy, in the absence of any legal reason to the contrary, may well apply to all cases where there is an unlawful and malicious enticing away of any person employed to give his personal labor or service for a given time under the direction of a master or employer who is injured by the wrongful act; more especially when the party is bound to give such personal services exclusively to the master or employer; though I by no means say that the service need be exclusive. . . .[2]

In deciding this case on the narrower ground, I wish by no means to be considered as deciding that the larger ground taken by Mr. *Cowling* is not tenable, or as saying that in no case except that of master and servant is an action maintainable for *maliciously* inducing another to break a contract to the injury of the person with whom such contract has been made. It does not appear to me to be a sound answer, to say that the act in such cases is the act of the party who breaks the contract; for that reason would apply in the acknowledged case of master and servant. Nor is it an answer, to say that there is a remedy against the contractor, and that the party relies on the contract; for, besides that reason also applying to the case of master and servant, the action on the contract and the action against the malicious wrong-doer may be for a different matter; and the damages occasioned by such malicious injury might be calculated on a very different principle from

[1] The learned judge here discussed and approved of Blake *v.* Lanyon, 6 T. R. 221.

[2] The rest of the opinion on this point is omitted.

the amount of the debt which might be the only sum recoverable on the contract. Suppose a trader, *with a malicious intent to ruin a rival trader*, goes to a banker or other party who owes money to his rival, and begs him not to pay the money which he owes him, and by that means ruins or greatly prejudices the party: I am by no means prepared to say that an action could not be maintained, and that damages, beyond the amount of the debt if the injury were great, or much less than such amount if the injury were less serious, might not be recovered. Where two or more parties were concerned in inflicting such injury, an indictment, or a writ of conspiracy at common law, might perhaps have been maintainable; and, where a writ of conspiracy would lie for an injury inflicted by two, an action on the case in the nature of conspiracy will generally lie; and in such action on the case the plaintiff is entitled to recover against one defendant without proof of any conspiracy, the malicious injury and not the conspiracy being the gist of the action.[1] In this class of cases it must be assumed that it is the malicious act of the defendant, and that malicious act only, which causes the servant or contractor not to perform the work or contract which he would otherwise have done. The servant or contractor may be utterly unable to pay anything like the amount of the damage sustained entirely from the wrongful act of the defendant; and it would seem unjust, and contrary to the general principles of law, if such wrong-doer were not responsible for the damage caused by his wrongful and malicious act. Several of the cases cited by Mr. *Cowling* on this part of the case seem well worthy of attention.

Without however deciding any such more general question, I think that we are justified in applying the principle of the action for enticing away servants to a case where the defendant *maliciously procures* a party, who is under a valid contract to give her exclusive personal services to the plaintiff for a specified period, to refuse to give such services *during the period for which she had so contracted*, whereby the plaintiff was injured.

I think, therefore, that our judgment should be for the plaintiff.

ERLE, J. The question raised upon this demurrer is, Whether an action will lie by the proprietor of a theatre against a person who maliciously procures an entire abandonment of a contract to perform exclusively at that theatre for a certain time; whereby damage was sustained? And it seems to me that it will. The authorities are numerous and uniform, that an action will lie by a master against a person who procures that a servant should unlawfully leave his service. The principle involved in these cases comprises the present; for there, the right of action in the master arises from the wrongful act of the defendant in procuring that the person hired should break his contract, by putting an end to the relation of employer and employed;

[1] See note (4) to Skinner *v.* Gunton, 1 Wms. Saund. 230. — Reporter's note.

and the present case is the same. If it is objected that this class of actions for procuring a breach of contract of hiring rests upon no principle, and ought not to be extended beyond the cases heretofore decided, and that, as those have related to contracts respecting trade, manufactures, or household service, and not to performance at a theatre, therefore they are no authority for an action in respect of a contract for such performance; the answer appears to me to be, that the class of cases referred to rests upon the principle that the procurement of the violation of the right is a cause of action, and that, when this principle is applied to a violation of a right arising upon a contract of hiring, the nature of the service contracted for is immaterial. It is clear that the procurement of the violation of a right is a cause of action in all instances where the violation is an actionable wrong, as in violations of a right to property, whether real or personal, or to personal security; he who procures the wrong is a joint wrong-doer, and may be sued, either alone or jointly with the agent, in the appropriate action for the wrong complained of. Where a right to the performance of a contract has been violated by a breach thereof, the remedy is upon the contract against the contracting party; and, if he is made to indemnify for such breach, no further recourse is allowed; and, as in case of the procurement of a breach of contract the action is for a wrong and cannot be joined with the action on the contract, and as the act itself is not likely to be of frequent occurrence nor easy of proof, therefore the actions for this wrong, in respect of other contracts than those of hiring, are not numerous; but still they seem to me sufficient to show that the principle has been recognized. In Winsmore *v.* Greenbank it was decided that the procuring of a breach of the contract of a wife is a cause of action. The only distinction in principle between this case and other cases of contracts is, that the wife is not liable to be sued; but the judgment rests on no such grounds; the procuring a violation of the plaintiff's right under the marriage contract is held to be an actionable wrong. In Green *v.* Button, 2 C. M. & R. 707, it was decided that the procuring a breach of a contract of sale of goods by a false claim of lien is an actionable wrong. Sheperd *v.* Wakeman, 1 Sid. 79, is to the same effect, where the defendant procured a breach of a contract of marriage by asserting that the woman was already married. In Ashley *v.* Harrison, 1 Peake's N. P. C. 194; s. c. 1 Esp. N. P. C. 48, and in Taylor *v.* Neri, 1 Esp. N. P. C. 386, it was properly decided that the action did not lie, because the battery, in the first case, and the libel, in the second case, upon the contracting parties were not shown to be with intent to cause those persons to break their contracts, and so the defendants by their wrongful acts did not procure the breaches of contract which were complained of. If they had so acted for the purpose of procuring those breaches, it seems to me they would have been liable to the plaintiffs. To these decisions, founded on the principle now relied upon, the cases for procuring breaches of contracts of hiring should be added; at least Lord Mansfield's judgment in Bird *v.* Randall, 3 Burr. 1345, is to that effect. This principle is supported by good reason. He who maliciously procures a damage to another by violation of his right ought to be made to indemnify; and that, whether he procures an actionable wrong or a breach of contract. He who procures the non-delivery of goods according to contract may inflict an injury, the same as he who procures the abstraction of goods after delivery; and both ought on the same ground to be made responsible. The remedy on the contract may be inadequate, as where the measure of damages is restricted; or in the case of non-payment of a debt where the damage may be bankruptcy to the creditor who is disappointed, but the measure of damages against the debtor is interest only; or, in the case of the non-delivery of the goods, the disappointment may lead to a heavy forfeiture under a contract to complete a work within a time, but the measure of damages against the vendor of the goods for non-delivery may be only the difference between the contract price and the market value of the goods in question at the time of the breach. In such cases, he who procures the damage maliciously might justly be made responsible beyond the liability of the contractor.

With respect to the objection that the contracting party had not begun the performance of the contract, I do not think it a tenable ground of defence. The procurement of the breach of the contract may be equally injurious, whether the service has begun or not, and in my judgment ought to be equally actionable, as the relation of employer and employed is constituted by the contract alone, and no act of service is necessary thereto.

The result is that there ought to be, in my opinion, judgment for the plaintiff.

[The concurring opinion of WIGHTMAN, J., is omitted.]

COLERIDGE, J. It may simplify what I have to say, if I first state what are the conclusions which I seek to establish. They are these: that in respect of breach of contract the general rule of our law is to confine its remedies by action to the contracting parties, and to damages directly and proximately consequential on the act of him who is sued;[1] that, as between master and servant, there is an admitted exception; that this exception dates from the Statute of Laborers, 23 Edw. III., and both on principle and according to authority is limited by it. If I am right in these positions, the conclusion will be for the defendant, because enough appears on this record to show, as to the first, that he, and, as to the second, that Johanna Wagner, is not within the limits so drawn.

[1] Only the opinion of Coleridge, J., on this point is given. It is now generally admitted that this learned judge, although wrong on this point, was right in maintaining that the actress was not a servant.

First, then, that the remedy for breach of contract is by the general rule of our law confined to the contracting parties. I need not argue that, if there be any remedy by action against a stranger, it must be by action on the case. Now, to found this, there must be both injury in the strict sense of the word (that is a wrong done), and loss resulting from that injury: the injury or wrong done must be the act of the defendant; and the loss must be a direct and natural, not a remote and indirect consequence of the defendant's act. Unless there be a loss thus directly and proximately connected with the act, the mere intention, or even the endeavor, to produce it will not found the action. The existence of the intention, that is the malice, will in some cases be an essential ingredient in order to constitute the wrongfulness or injurious nature of the act; but it will neither supply the want of the act itself, or its hurtful consequences: however complete the *injuria*, and whether with malice or without, if the act be after all *sine damno*, no action on the case will lie. The distinction between civil and criminal proceedings in this respect is clear and material; and a recollection of the different objects of the two will dispose of any argument founded merely on the allegation of malice in this declaration, if I shall be found right in thinking that the defendant's act has not been the direct or proximate cause of the damage which the plaintiff alleges he has sustained. If a contract has been made between A. and B. that the latter should go supercargo for the former on a voyage to China, and C., however maliciously, persuades B. to break his contract, but in vain, no one, I suppose, would contend that any action would lie against C. On the other hand, suppose a contract of the same kind made between the same parties to go to Sierra Leone, and C. urgently and *bona fide* advises B. to abandon his contract, which on consideration B. does, whereby loss results to A.; I think no one will be found bold enough to maintain that an action would lie against C. In the first case no loss has resulted; the malice has been ineffectual; in the second, though a loss has resulted from the act, that act was not C.'s, but entirely and exclusively B.'s own. If so, let malice be added, and let C. have persuaded, not *bona fide* but *mala fide* and maliciously, still, all other circumstances remaining the same, the same reason applies; for it is *malitia sine damno*, if the hurtful act is entirely and exclusively B.'s, which last circumstance cannot be affected by the presence or absence of malice in C. Thus far I do not apprehend much difference of opinion: there would be such a manifest absurdity in attempting to trace up the act of a free agent breaking a contract to all the advisers who may have influenced his mind, more or less honestly, more or less powerfully, and to make them responsible civilly for the consequences of what after all is his own act, and for the whole of the hurtful consequences of which the law makes him directly and fully responsible, that I believe it will never be contended for seriously. This was the principle on which Lord Kenyon proceeded in Ashley *v.* Harrison, 1 Peake's N. P. C. 194; s. c. 1 Esp. N. P. C. 48. There the defendant libelled Madame Mara; the plaintiff alleged that, in consequence, she, from apprehension of being hissed and ill-treated, forbore to sing for him, though engaged, whereby he lost great profits. Lord Kenyon nonsuited the plaintiff: he thought the defendant's act too remote from the damage assigned. But it will be said that this declaration charges more than is stated in the case last supposed, because it alleges, not merely a persuasion or enticement, but a procuring. In Winsmore *v.* Greenbank the same word was used in the first count of the declaration, which alone is material to the present case; and the Chief Justice, who relied on it, and distinguished it from enticing, defined it to mean "persuading with effect;" and he held that the husband might sue a stranger for persuading with effect his wife to do a wrongful act directly hurtful to himself. Although I should hesitate to be bound by every word of the judgment, yet I am not called on to question this definition or the decision of the case. Persuading with effect, or effectually or successfully persuading, may no doubt sometimes be actionable — as in trespass — even where it is used towards a free agent; the maxims, *qui facit per alium facit per se*, and *respondeat superior*, are unquestionable; but, where they apply, the wrongful act done is properly charged to be the act of him who has procured it to be done. He is sued as a principal trespasser, and the damage, if proved, flows directly and immediately from his act, though it was the hand of another, and he a free agent, that was employed. But, when you apply the term of effectual persuasion to the breach of a contract, it has obviously a different meaning; the persuader has not broken and could not break the contract, for he had never entered into any; he cannot be sued upon the contract; and yet it is the breach of the contract only that is the cause of damage: Neither can it be said that in breaking the contract the contractor is the agent of him who procures him to do so; it is still his own act; he is principal in so doing, and is the only principal. This answer may seem technical; but it really goes to the root of the matter. It shows that the procurer has not done the hurtful act; what he has done is too remote from the damage to make him answerable for it. The case itself of Winsmore *v.* Greenbank seems to me to have little or no bearing on the present: a wife is not, as regards her husband, a free agent or separate person; if to be considered so for the present purpose, she is rather in the character of a servant, with this important peculiarity, that, if she be induced to withdraw from his society and cohabit with another or do him any wrong, no action is maintainable by him against her. In the case of criminal conversation, trespass lies against the adulterer as for an assault on her, however she may in fact have been a willing party to all that the defendant had done. No doubt, therefore, effectual persuasion to the wife to withdraw and conceal herself from her husband is in the eye of the law an actual withdrawing and concealing her; and so, in other counts of the declaration, was it charged in this very case of Winsmore *v.* Greenbank. A case explainable and explained on the same principle is that of ravishment of ward. The writ for this lay against one who procured a man's ward to depart from him; and, where this was urged in a case hereafter to be cited (Mich. 11 H. 4, fol. 23 A. pl. 46, 2 E. & B. 255), Judge Hankford [1] gives the answer: the reason is, he says, because the ward is a chattel, and vests in him who has the right. None of this reasoning applies to the case of a breach of contract; if it does, I should be glad to know how any treatise on the law of contract could be complete without a chapter on this head, or how it happens that we have no decisions upon it. Certainly no subject could well be more fruitful or important; important contracts are more commonly broken with than without persuaders or procurers, and these often responsible persons when the principals may not be so. I am aware that with respect to an action on the case the argument *primæ impressionis* is sometimes of no weight. If the circumstances under which the action would be brought have not before arisen, or are of rare occurrence, it will be of none, or only of inconsiderable weight; but, if the circumstances have been common, if there has been frequently occasion for the action, I apprehend it *is* important to find that the action has yet never been tried. Now we find a plentiful supply both of text and decision in the case of seduction of servants; and what inference does this lead to, contrasted with the silence of the books and the absence of decisions on the case of breach of ordinary contracts? Let this too be considered: that, if by the common law it was actionable effectually to persuade another to break his contract to the damage of the contractor, it would seem on principle to be equally so to uphold him, after the breach, in continuing it. Now upon this the two conflicting cases of Adams *v.* Bafeald, 1 Leon. 240, and Blake *v.* Lanyon, 6 T. R. 221, are worth considering. In the first, two judges against one decided that an action does not lie for retaining the servant of another, unless the defendant has first procured the servant to leave his master; in the second, this was overruled; and, although it was taken as a fact that the defendant had hired the servant in ignorance and, as soon as he knew that he had left his former master with work unfinished, requested him to return, which we must understand to have been a real, earnest request, and only continued him after his refusal, which we must take to have been his independent refusal, it was held that the action lay; and this reason is given: "The very act of giving him employment is affording him the means of keeping out of his former service." Would the judges who laid this down have held it actionable to give a stray servant food or clothing or lodging out of charity? Yet these would have been equally

[1] William Hankford, Justice of the Common Pleas in 1398, afterwards, in 1414 (1 H. 5), Chief Justice of England. — Reporter's note.

means of keeping him out of his former service. The true ground on which this action was maintainable, if at all, was the Statute of Laborers, to which no reference was made. But I mention this case now as showing how far courts of justice may be led if they allow themselves, in the pursuit of perfectly complete remedies for all wrongful acts, to transgress the bounds which our law, in a wise consciousness as I conceive of its limited powers, has imposed on itself, of redressing only the proximate and direct consequences of wrongful acts. To draw a line between advice, persuasion, enticement and procurement is practically impossible in a court of justice; who shall say how much of a free agent's resolution flows from the interference of other minds, or the independent resolution of his own ? This is a matter for the casuist rather than the jurist; still less is it for the juryman. Again, why draw the line between bad and good faith ? If advice given *mala fide*, and loss sustained, entitle me to damages, why, though the advice be given honestly, but under wrong information, with a loss sustained, am I not entitled to them ? According to all legal analogies the *bona fides* of him who, by a conscious wilful act, directly injures me will not relieve him from the obligation to compensate me in damages for my loss. Again, where several persons happen to persuade to the same effect, and in the result the party persuaded acts upon the advice, how is it to be determined against whom the action may be brought, whether they are to be sued jointly or severally, in what proportions damages are to be recovered ? Again, if, instead of limiting our recourse to the agent, actual or constructive, we will go back to the person who immediately persuades or procures him one step, why are we stop there ? The first mover, and the malicious mover too, may be removed several steps backward from the party actually induced to break the contract; why are we not to trace him out ? Morally he may be the most guilty. I adopt the arguments of Lord Abinger and my brother Alderson in the case of Winterbottom *v.* Wright, 10 M. & W. 109; if we go the first step, we can show no good reason for not going fifty. And, again, I ask how is it that, if the law really be as the plaintiff contends, we have no discussions upon such questions as these in our books, no decisions in our reports ? Surely such cases would not have been of rare occurrence; they are not of slight importance, and could hardly have been decided without reference to the Courts in Banc. Not one was cited in the argument bearing closely enough upon this point to warrant me in any further detailed examination of them. I conclude therefore what occurs to me on the first proposition on which the plaintiff's case rests.

Judgment for plaintiff.[1]

[1] Cattle *v.* Stockton Co., L. R. 10 Q. B. 453, 458 (*semble*); Angle *v.* Chicago R. Co., 151 U. S. 1; Bitterman *v.* Louisville R. Co., 207 U. S. 205, 222–23; Dr. Miles Medical Co. *v.* Park & Sons Co., 220 U. S. 373, 394 (*semble*); Heaton Co. *v.* Dick, 55 Fed. 23, 52 Fed. 667; Heath *v.* American Book Co., 97 Fed. 533; Tubular Co. *v.* Exeter Co., 159 Fed. 824; Motley *v.* Detroit Co., 161 Fed. 389; Chipley *v.* At-

BOWEN *v.* HALL

IN THE COURT OF APPEAL, FEBRUARY 5, 1881.

Reported in 6 *Queen's Bench Division,* 333.

BRETT, L. J.[1] The Lord Chancellor agrees with me in the judgment I am about to read, and it is to be taken therefore as the judgment of the Lord Chancellor as well as of myself.

In this case, we were of opinion at the hearing, that the contract was one for personal service, though not one which established strictly for all purposes the relation of master and servant between the plaintiff and Pearson. We were of opinion that there was evidence to justify a finding that Pearson had been induced by the defendants to break his contract of service, that he had broken it, and had thereby, in fact, caused some injury to the plaintiff. We were of opinion that the act of the defendants was done with knowledge of the contract between the plaintiff and Pearson, was done in order to obtain an advantage for one of the defendants at the expense of the plaintiff, was done from a wrong motive, and would therefore justify a finding that it was done in that sense maliciously. There remained nevertheless the question, whether there was any evidence to be left to the

kinson, 23 Fla. 206; Doremus *v.* Hennessy, 176 Ill. 608; Heywood *v.* Tillson, 75 Me. 225, 236 (*semble*); Knickerbocker Ice Co. *v.* Gardiner Dairy Co., 107 Md. 556; Walker *v.* Cronin, 107 Mass. 555; Beekman *v.* Marsters, 195 Mass. 205; Joyce *v.* Great Northern R. Co., 100 Minn. 225; Mealey *v.* Bemidji Lumber Co., 118 Minn. 427; Lally *v.* Cantwell, 30 Mo. App. 524; Van Horn *v.* Van Horn, 52 N. J. Law, 284; Haskins *v.* Royster, 70 N. C. 601; Jones *v.* Stanly, 76 N. C. 355; Flaccus *v.* Smith, 199 Pa. St. 128; Delz *v.* Winfree, 80 Tex. 400, 405; Raymond *v.* Yarrington, 96 Tex. 443; Brown Co. *v.* Indiana Stove Works, 96 Tex. 453; Duffies *v.* Duffies, 76 Wis. 374, 377 (*semble*); Martens *v.* Reilly, 109 Wis. 464; Hewitt *v.* Ontario Co., 44 Up. Can. Q. B. 287 *Accord.*

Boyson *v.* Thorn, 98 Cal. 578; Barron *v.* Collins, 49 Ga. 580 (*semble*); Chambers *v.* Baldwin, 91 Ky. 121; Bourlier *v.* Macauley, 91 Ky. 135; Kline *v.* Eubanks, 109 La. 241 (*semble*); Ashley *v.* Dixon, 48 N. Y. 430; De Jong *v.* Behrman, 148 App. Div. 37; Laskey Feature Play Co. *v.* Fox, 93 Misc. 364; Swain *v.* Johnson, 151 N. C. 93; Sleeper *v.* Baker, 22 N. D. 386 *Contra.*

It was decided before the case of Lumley *v.* Gye that an action for slander of title was maintainable where the only special damage laid was the breach by a third person of his contract with the plaintiff. Green *v.* Button, 2 C. M. & R. 707. But see, *contra*, Kendall *v.* Stone, 5 N. Y. 14; Brentman *v.* Note, 3 N. Y. Sup. 420 (N. Y. City Court).

So an action would doubtless lie for defamatory words, not actionable *per se*, which induced a third person to break his contract to marry the plaintiff. But compare Davis *v.* Condit, 124 Minn. 365 (seduction of plaintiff's fiancée).

As to justification, see Leonard *v.* Whetstone, 34 Ind. App. 383.

On the general subject, see also Sweeney *v.* Smith, 167 Fed. 385; Mahoney *v.* Roberts, 86 Ark. 130; Citizens' Light, &c. Co. *v.* Montgomery Light, &c. Co., 171 Fed. 553, 560, 561; McGurk *v.* Cronenwett, 199 Mass. 457; Globe Ins. Co. *v.* Fireman's Ins. Co., 97 Miss. 148; Biggers *v.* Matthews, 147 N. C. 299; Thacker Coal Co. *v.* Burke, 59 W. Va. 253; Huffcutt, Interference with Contracts and Business in New York, 18 Harvard Law Rev. 423.

[1] The statement of facts and the dissenting opinion of Lord Coleridge, C. J., are omitted.

jury against the defendants Hall and Fletcher, it being objected that Pearson was not a servant of the plaintiff. The case was accurately within the authority of the case of Lumley *v.* Gye. If that case was rightly decided, the objection in this case failed. The only question then which we took time to consider was whether the decision of the majority of the judges in that case should be supported in a Court of Error. That case was so elaborately discussed by the learned judges who took part in it, that little more can be said about it, than whether, after careful consideration, one agrees rather with the judgments of the majority, or with the most careful, learned, and able judgment of Mr. Justice Coleridge. The decision of the majority will be seen, on a careful consideration of their judgments, to have been founded upon two chains of reasoning. First, that wherever a man does an act which in law and in fact is a wrongful act, and such an act as may, as a natural and probable consequence of it, produce injury to another, and which in the particular case does produce such an injury, an action on the case will lie. This is the proposition to be deduced from the case of Ashby *v.* White, 1 Sm. L. C. (8th ed.), p. 264. If these conditions are satisfied, the action does not the less lie because the natural and probable consequence of the act complained of is an act done by a third person: or because such act so done by the third person is a breach of duty or contract by him or an act illegal on his part, or an act otherwise imposing an actionable liability on him. It has been said that the law implies that the act of the third party, being one which he has free will and power to do or not to do, is his own wilful act, and therefore is not the natural or probable result of the defendants' act. In many cases that may be so, but if the law is so to imply in every case, it will be an implication contrary to manifest truth and fact. It has been said that if the act of the third person is a breach of duty or contract by him, or is an act which it is illegal for him to do, the law will not recognize that it is a natural or probable consequence of the defendant's act. Again, if that were so held in all cases, the law would in some refuse to recognize what is manifestly true in fact. If the judgment of Lord Ellenborough in Vicars *v.* Wilcocks, 8 East, 1, requires this doctrine for its support, it is in our opinion wrong.

We are of opinion that the propositions deduced above from Ashby *v.* White, 1 Sm. L. C. (8th ed.), p. 264, are correct. If they be applied to such a case as Lumley *v.* Gye, the question is whether all the conditions are by such a case fulfilled. The first is that the act of the defendants which is complained of must be an act wrongful in law and in fact. Merely to persuade a person to break his contract, may not be wrongful in law or fact as in the second case put by Coleridge, J., *supra*. But if the persuasion be used for the indirect purpose of injuring the plaintiff, or of benefiting the defendant at the expense of the plaintiff, it is a malicious act which is in law and in fact a wrong act, and therefore a wrongful act, and therefore an actionable act if injury ensues from it. We think that it cannot be doubted that a malicious act, such as is above described, is a wrongful act in law and in fact. The act complained of in such a case as Lumley *v.* Gye, and which is complained of in the present case, is therefore, because malicious, wrongful. That act is a persuasion by the defendant of a third person to break a contract existing between such third person and the plaintiff. It cannot be maintained that it is not a natural and probable consequence of that act of persuasion that the third person will break his contract. It is not only the natural and probable consequence, but by the terms of the proposition which involves the success of the persuasion, it is the actual consequence. Unless there be some technical doctrine to oblige one to say so, it seems impossible to say correctly, in point of fact, that the breach of contract is too remote a consequence of the act of the defendants. The technical objections alluded to above have been suggested as the consequences of the judgment in Vicars *v.* Wilcocks, 8 East, 1. But that judgment when so used or relied on seems to us to be disapproved in the opinions given in the House of Lords in Lynch *v.* Knight, 9 H. L. C. 577, and seems to us when so used to be unreasonable. In the case of Lumley *v.* Gye, and in the present case, the third condition is fulfilled, namely, that the act of the defendant caused an injury to the plaintiff, unless again it can be said correctly that the injury is too remote from the cause. But that raises again the same question as has been just dismissed. It is not too remote if the injury is the natural and probable consequence of the alleged cause. That is stated in all the opinions in Lynch *v.* Knight, 9 H. L. C. 577. The injury is in such a case in law as well as in fact a natural and probable consequence of the cause, because it is in fact the consequence of the cause, and there is no technical rule against the truth being recognized. It follows that in Lumley *v.* Gye, and in the present case, all the conditions necessary to maintain an action on the case are fulfilled.

Another chain of reasoning was relied on by the majority in Lumley *v.* Gye, and powerfully combated by Coleridge, J. It was said that the contract in question was within the principle of the Statute of Laborers, that is to say, that the same evil was produced by the same means, and that as the statute made such means when employed in the case of master and servant, strictly so called, wrongful, the common law ought to treat similar means employed with regard to parties standing in a similar relation as also wrongful. If, in order to support Lumley *v.* Gye, it had been necessary to adopt this proposition we should have much doubted, to say the least. The reasoning of Coleridge, J., upon the second head of his judgment seems to us to be as nearly as possible, if not quite, conclusive. But we think it is not necessary to base the support of the case upon this latter proposition.

We think the case is better supported upon the first and larger doctrine. And we are therefore of opinion that the judgment of the Queen's Bench Division was correct, and that the principal appeal must be dismissed. *Appeal dismissed.*[1]

GLAMORGAN COAL CO., LIMITED *v.* SOUTH WALES MINERS' FEDERATION

IN THE COURT OF APPEAL, AUGUST 11, 1903.

Reported in [1903] 2 *King's Bench*, 545.

SOUTH WALES MINERS' FEDERATION *v.* GLAMORGAN COAL CO., LIMITED

IN THE HOUSE OF LORDS, APRIL 14, 1905.

Reported in [1905] *Appeal Cases*, 239.

APPEAL by the plaintiffs from the decision of BIGHAM, J., [1903] 1 K. B. 118.[2]

The action was brought by the Glamorgan Coal Company, Limited, and seventy-three other plaintiffs, owners of collieries in South Wales, against the South Wales Miners' Federation, its trustees, its officers, and a number of members of its executive council, claiming damages for wrongfully and maliciously procuring and inducing workmen employed in the plaintiffs' collieries to break their contracts of service with the plaintiffs. In the alternative the plaintiffs sued the defendants for wrongfully, unlawfully, and maliciously conspiring together to do the acts complained of. The plaintiffs claimed both damages and an injunction.

The defence consisted of denials of the material allegations in the statement of claim, and of a plea that the acts complained of were done, if at all, with reasonable justification and excuse. The trial

[1] "That this was a wrongful interference on the part of the Omaha Company, and that it resulted directly in loss to the contractor and to the Portage Company, is apparent. It is not an answer to say that there was no certainty that the contractor would have completed his contract, and so earned these lands for the Portage Company. If such a defence were tolerated, it would always be an answer in case of any wrongful interference with the performance of a contract, for there is always that lack of certainty. It is enough that there should be, as there was here, a reasonable assurance, considering all the surroundings, that the contract would be performed in the manner and within the time stipulated, and so performed as to secure the land to the company.

"It certainly does not lie in the mouth of a wrongdoer, in the face of such probabilities as attend this case, to say that perhaps the contract would not have been completed even if no interference had been had, and that, therefore, there being no certainty of the loss, there is no liability." Brewer, J., in Angle *v.* Chicago R. Co., 151 U. S. 1, 12.

[2] Statement abridged. Arguments omitted; also part of opinions.

of the action was commenced with a special jury; but ultimately the jury was discharged, and all questions of law and fact, as well as the ascertainment of damages, if any, were by consent left to the determination of the learned judge.

The following facts (*inter alia*) were stated, in substance, by BIGHAM, J., in his written opinion: —

The plaintiffs are seventy-four limited liability companies associated together for the protection of their own interests under the style of the Monmouthshire and South Wales Coal Owners' Association. They work upwards of 200 collieries in the South Wales district, and in these collieries they employ about 100,000 men.

For the last twenty or twenty-five years the masters and the men in the South Wales colliery district have worked together under an agreement, called the sliding scale agreement, by which the rate of wages paid to the men is made to depend on the price for the time being of a certain agreed class of coal — that is to say, as the price of that coal rises or falls so the rate of wages moves up or down. Clause 23 of the sliding scale agreement is as follows: "It is hereby agreed that all notices to terminate contracts on the part of the employers as well as employed, shall be given only on the first day of any calendar month, and to terminate on the last day of the same month."

The defendant federation was formed in 1898, and in 1899 was registered under the Friendly Societies Act. Practically all the miners in the South Wales district became members of it. There are about 128,000 members; including all, or very nearly all, the men who work for the plaintiffs. In 1900 the federation was in the possession of funds amounting to 100,000*l*. By its rules its objects are declared to be to provide funds to carry on the business of the federation; taking into consideration the question of trade and wages; to protect workmen generally, and regulate the relations between them and employers; and to call conferences to deal with questions affecting the workmen of a trade, wage, and legislative character.

In November, 1900, the executive council of the federation requested the workmen to hold meetings for the purpose of electing delegates to attend a conference on November 12. Delegates were accordingly elected, and at the conference a resolution was passed authorizing the council of the federation to declare a general holiday at any time they might think it necessary for the protection of wages and of the industry generally.

On October 23, 1901, a "manifesto" to the workmen was published, stating that it had been resolved that the workmen shall observe as general holidays Friday and Saturday next. Subsequently two other stop-days were ordered, viz.: for October 31 and November 6. (The reasons for issuing the manifesto are stated in the opinion of STIRLING, L. J., *post.*) The result was that the men stayed away from work on the four days, and so broke their contracts with the masters.

The manifesto purported to be issued by the sliding scale committee, and was signed by the members of that committee, who were also members of the executive council of the federation. But in fact the issuing of the manifesto was caused by the executive council of the federation. In truth it was the federation who were acting; the name of the sliding scale committee being used as a blind, with the purpose of securing the funds of the federation from possible liability under the decision in the Taff Vale Case, [1901] App. Cas. 426.

BIGHAM, J., concluded his findings of fact with the following statement: —

"The evidence satisfies me that the action of the federation, and of the other defendants in 1901, was dictated by an honest desire to forward the interest of the workmen, and was not, in any sense, prompted by a wish to injure the masters. Neither the federation nor the other defendants had any prospect of personal gain from the operation of the stop-days. Having been requested by the men by the resolution of November 12, 1900, to advise and direct them as to when to stop work, the federation and the other defendants, who were its officers, in my opinion, did to the best of their ability advise and direct the men. Whether they advised them wisely I cannot say, though I am inclined to think not. But I am satisfied that they advised them honestly, and without malice of any kind against the plaintiffs.

"I have to decide, in these circumstances, whether an action in tort will lie against the defendants. The advice and guidance of the defendants was solicited and given. If followed, it involved, as the defendants knew, the breaking of the subsisting contracts. It was followed, as the defendants wished it should be, and damage resulted to the masters; but there was no malicious intention to cause injury, no profit was gained for themselves by the defendants, and their sole object was to benefit the men whom they were advising and directing."

The learned judge gave judgment for the defendants on both branches of the plaintiffs' claim. His opinion is reported in [1903] 1 K. B. 118.

Plaintiffs appealed.

[The opinion of VAUGHAN WILLIAMS, L. J., in favor of affirmance, is omitted.]

ROMER, L. J. The law applicable to this case is, I think, well settled. I need only refer to two passages in which that law is shortly and comprehensively stated. In Quinn *v.* Leathem [1901], A. C. 495, at p. 510, Lord Macnaghten said: "A violation of legal right committed knowingly is a cause of action, and it is a violation of legal right to interfere with contractual relations recognized by law if there be no sufficient justification for the interference." And in Mogul Steamship Co. *v.* McGregor, Gow & Co., 23 Q. B. D. 598, at p. 614, Bowen, L. J., included in what is forbidden "the intentional procurement of a violation of individual rights, contractual or other, assuming always that there is no just cause for it." But although, in my judgment, there is no doubt as to the law, yet I fully recognize that considerable difficulties may arise in applying it to the circumstances of any particular case. When a person has knowingly procured another to break his contract, it may be difficult under the circumstances to say whether or not there was "sufficient justification or just cause" for his act. I think it would be extremely difficult, even if it were possible, to give a complete and satisfactory definition of what is "sufficient justification," and most attempts to do so would probably be mischievous. I certainly shall not make the attempt. In particular I do not think it necessary or useful to discuss the point as to how far the question of justification can be assimilated to the question of malice in cases of libel and slander. As Collins, M. R., said in Read *v.* Friendly Society of Operative Stonemasons, [1902] 2 K. B. 732, at p. 739: "It is not at all necessary in this case to embark upon the question whether 'without just cause' is a complete equivalent for what was meant in the common law by 'malice.' I am inclined to think that, though in many cases adequate as a description, it is not co-extensive with it, nor do I think that in civil actions any more than in criminal it will be possible to eliminate motives from the discussion." I respectfully agree with what Bowen, L. J., said in the Mogul Case, when considering the difficulty that might arise whether there was sufficient justification or not: "The good sense of the tribunal which had to decide would have to analyze the circumstances and to discover on which side of the line each case fell." I will only add that, in analyzing or considering the circumstances, I think that regard might be had to the nature of the contract broken; the position of the parties to the contract; the grounds for the breach; the means employed to procure the breach; the relation of the person procuring the breach to the person who breaks the contract; and I think also to the object of the person in procuring the breach. But, though I deprecate the attempt to define justification, I think it right to express my opinion on certain points in connection with breaches of contract procured where the contract is one of master and servant. In my opinion, a defendant sued for knowingly procuring such a breach is not justified of necessity merely by his showing that he had no personal animus against the employer, or that it was to the advantage or interest of both the defendant and the workman that the contract should be broken. I take the following simple case to illustrate my view. If A. wants to get a specially good workman, who is under contract with B., as A. knows, and A. gets the workman to break his contract to B.'s injury by giving him higher wages, it would not, in my opinion, afford A. a defence to an action against him by B. that he could establish he had no personal animus against B., and that it was both to the interest of himself and of the workman that the contract with B. should be broken. I think that the principle involved in this simple case, taken by me by way of illustration, really governs the present case. For it is to be remembered that what A. has to justify is his action, not as between him and the workman, but as regards the employer B. And, if I proceed to apply the law I have stated to the circumstances of the present case, what do I find? On the findings of fact it is to my mind clear that the defendants, the federation, procured the men to break their contracts with the plaintiffs — so that I need not consider how the question would have stood if what the federation had done had been merely to advise the men, or if the men, after taking advice, had arranged between themselves to break their contracts, and the federation had merely notified the men's intentions to the plaintiffs. The federation did more than advise. They acted, and by their agents actually procured the men to leave their work and break their contracts. In short, it was the federation who caused the injury to the plaintiffs. This was practically admitted before us by the counsel for the federation, and, indeed, such an admission could not, in my opinion, be avoided, having regard to the facts stated by the learned judge in his judgment. And it is not disputed that the federation acted as they did knowingly. So that the only question which remains is one of justification. Now the justification urged is that it was thought, and I will assume for this purpose rightly thought, to be in the interest of the men that they should leave their work in order to keep up the price of coal, on which the amount of wages of the men depended. As to this, I can only say that to my mind the ground alleged affords no justification for the conduct of the federation towards the employers; for, as I have already pointed out, the absence on the part of the federation of any malicious intention to injure the employers in itself affords no sufficient justification. But it was said that the federation had a duty towards the men which justified them in doing what they did. For myself I cannot see that they had any duty which in any way compelled them to act, or justified them in acting, as they did towards the plaintiffs. And the fact that the men and the federation, as being interested in or acting for the benefit of the men, were both interested in keeping up prices, and so in breaking the contracts, affords in itself no sufficient justification for the action of the federation as against the plaintiffs, as I have already pointed out. I think, therefore, that the appeal must succeed.

STIRLING, L. J.

. . . .

That interference with contractual relations known to the law may in some cases be justified is not, in my opinion, open to doubt. For example, I think that a father who discovered that a child of his had entered into an engagement to marry a person of immoral character would not only be justified in interfering to prevent that contract from being carried into effect, but would greatly fail in his duty to his child if he did not. This duty is recognized by the courts; for the Court of Chancery and the Chancery Division of the High Court of Justice have continually so interfered on behalf of wards of Court, sometimes with a heavy hand; and the principle on which the judges of those courts have acted is simply that of doing on behalf of the ward that which a right-minded father would do in the true interest of his child. I conceive that circumstances might occur which would give rise to the same duty in the case of a contract of service. I need not say that the present is a very different case from that which I have just put. It would no doubt be desirable if a general rule could be formulated which would determine in what cases such a justification exists; but no such rule has been laid down, and I doubt whether this can be done; so far as I can see it must be left (in the language of Lord Bowen) to the tribunal to analyze the circumstances of each particular case and discover whether a justification exists or not.

In the present case the learned judge finds that the federation and the other defendants "had lawful justification or excuse for what they did in this, that having been solicited by the men to advise and guide them on the question of stop-days, it was their duty and right to give them advice, and to do what might be necessary to secure that the advice should be followed;" and the existence of this duty has been strongly pressed upon us in argument by the learned counsel for the several defendants. It will be observed that the learned judge expressly finds that the defendants were not merely advisers, but also agents "to do what might be necessary to secure that the advice should be followed." In the view which I take of the facts the defendants not only gave advice, but acted, and their action took the form of interfering with the contractual relations between the masters and the men. If in so doing they committed a tort, it would be no answer to say that they acted upon the advice of a third person, as, for example, their own solicitor; and it is difficult to see how they can be in a better position simply because the advice on which they acted emanated from themselves.

In my judgment the liability of the defendants must turn on the answer to be given to the question whether the circumstances of the case were in fact such as to justify the defendants, or any of them, in acting as they did.

The circumstances were these: Middlemen at Cardiff were attempting to reduce the price of coal, and it was feared that some employers might yield to the pressure of competition and enter into agreements for the sale of coal at prices lower than those existing at the time, with the result that the wages of the miners, which were regulated by a sliding scale, would be reduced.

To counteract this it was considered desirable by the men's advisers that prices should be sustained by diminishing the output of coal, and that this should be effected by the men taking the holidays complained of. It was not contended or suggested that a limitation of the output of coal was an illegitimate object or aim on the part of the men, or that, if it could have been attained without the breach of contracts (as, for example, by the service of proper notices putting an end to those contracts), the men would not have been within their legal rights. The difficulty which presented itself was this,—that one of the terms of the arrangement under which the sliding scale of wages existed was that notices of the determination of contracts of employment should only be given on the first day of a calendar month to terminate on the last day, and this prevented notices of determination being effective at the desired moment. The critical period was known to occur in October or November. The men persuaded themselves that it was the masters' interest as well as their own that they should have power to take holidays at this period; but this was a point on which the masters were entitled to have their own opinion; and from what occurred in November, 1900, it was known to the men that the masters' view did not agree with that of the men. If the men had faith in the soundness of their opinion, their course was to negotiate through the defendants for a modification of the sliding scale arrangement; what they actually thought fit to do was that while insisting on the benefit of the sliding scale they treated themselves as emancipated from the observance of one of the terms on which that scale had been agreed to, although the masters objected, and although the course taken by the men might result in serious damages to the masters, or some of them. This is, I think, a difficult position to maintain. The justification set up seems to me to amount to no more than this — that the course which they took, although it might be to the detriment of the masters, was for the pecuniary interest of the men; and I think it wholly insufficient. The defendants took active steps to carry this policy into effect, and, as I have said, interfered to bring about the violation of legal rights. In my judgment they fail to justify those acts, and the appeal ought to be allowed.

THE COURT declined to grant an immediate injunction, but reserved liberty to the plaintiffs to apply for an injunction in case it should be necessary to do so. *Appeal allowed.*

The defendants appealed to the House of Lords.

The EARL OF HALSBURY, L. C., gave an opinion in favor of dismissing the appeal.

LORD MACNAGHTEN.

. . . .

But what is the alleged justification in the present case? It was said that the council — the executive of the federation — had a duty cast upon them to protect the interests of the members of the union, and that they could not be made legally responsible for the consequences of their action if they acted honestly in good faith and without any sinister or indirect motive. The case was argued with equal candor and ability. But it seems to me that the argument may be disposed of by two simple questions. How was the duty created? What in fact was the alleged duty? The alleged duty was created by the members of the union themselves, who elected or appointed the officials of the union to guide and direct their action; and then it was contended that the body to whom the members of the union have thus committed their individual freedom of action are not responsible for what they do if they act according to their honest judgment in furtherance of what they consider to be the interest of their constituents. It seems to me that if that plea were admitted there would be an end of all responsibility. It would be idle to sue the workmen, the individual wrong-doers, even if it were practicable to do so. Their counsellors and protectors, the real authors of the mischief, would be safe from legal proceedings. The only other question is, What is the alleged duty set up by the federation? I do not think it can be better described than it was by Mr. Lush. It comes to this — it is the duty on all proper occasions, of which the federation or their officials are to be the sole judges, to counsel and procure a breach of duty.

I agree with Romer and Stirling, L.JJ., and I think the appeal must be dismissed.

LORD JAMES.

. . . .

In order, therefore, to establish the existence of good cause and excuse, all the defendants can say is, "We, the federation, had the duty cast upon us to advise the workmen. We did advise them to commit an unlawful act, but in giving that advice we honestly believed that they would be in a better financial position than if they acted lawfully and fulfilled their contracts." Even if it be assumed that such allegations are correct in fact, I think that no justification in law is established by them. The intention of the defendants was directly to procure the breach of contracts. The fact that their motives were good in the interests of those they moved to action does not form any answer to those who have suffered from the unlawful act. During the arguments that have been addressed to your Lordships I do not think quite sufficient distinction was drawn between the intention and the motives of the defendants. Their intention clearly was that the workmen should break their contracts. The defendants' motives, no doubt, were that by so doing wages should be raised. But if in carrying out the intention the defendants purposely procured an unlawful act to be committed, the wrong that is thereby inflicted cannot be obliterated by the existence of a motive to secure a money benefit to the wrong-doers.

For these reasons I think the judgment of the Court of Appeal should be affirmed.[1]

[1] As to the distinction between intent and motive, see Smith, Crucial Issues in Labor Litigation, 20 Harvard Law Rev. 253, 256–259.

Lord Lindley. My Lords, I agree so entirely with the judgments of Romer and Stirling, L.JJ., that I should say no more were it not for the great importance of some of the arguments addressed to your Lordships on this appeal and which deserve notice.

It is useless to try and conceal the fact that an organized body of men working together can produce results very different from those which can be produced by an individual without assistance. Moreover, laws adapted to individuals not acting in concert with others require modification and extension if they are to be applied with effect to large bodies of persons acting in concert. The English law of conspiracy is based upon and is justified by this undeniable truth.

But the possession of great power, whether by one person or by many, is quite as consistent with its lawful as with its unlawful employment; and there is no legal presumption that it will be or has been unlawfully exercised in any particular case. Some illegal act must be proved to be threatened and intended, or to have been committed, before any court of justice in the United Kingdom can properly make such conduct the basis of any decision.

These remarks are as applicable to trade unions as to other less powerful organizations. Their power to intimidate and coerce is undoubted; its exercise is comparatively easy and probable; but it would be wrong on this account to treat their conduct as illegal in any particular case without proof of further facts which make it so. It is not incumbent on a trade union to rebut any presumption of illegality based only on their power to do wrong. Freedom necessarily involves such a power; but the mere fact of its existence does not justify any legal presumption that it will be abused.

In the case before your Lordships there is proof that the members of the mining federation combined to break and did break their contracts with their employers by stopping work without proper notice and without proper leave. There is also proof that the officials of the federation assisted the men to do this by ordering them to stop work on particular days named by the officials. To break a contract is an unlawful act, or, in the language of Lord Watson in Allen *v.* Flood, [1898] A. C. at p. 96, "a breach of contract is in itself a legal wrong." The form of action for such a wrong is quite immaterial in considering the general question of the legality or illegality of a breach of contract. Any party to a contract can break it if he chooses; but in point of law he is not entitled to break it even on offering to pay damages. If he wants to entitle himself to do that he must stipulate for an option to that effect. Non-lawyers are apt to think that everything is lawful which is not criminally punishable; but this is an entire misconception. A breach of contract would not be actionable if nothing legally wrong was involved in the breach.

The federation by its officials are clearly proved in this case to have been engaged in intentionally assisting in the concerted breach of a number of contracts entered into by workmen belonging to the federation. This is clearly unlawful, according to Lumley *v.* Gye, 2 E. & B. 216, and Quinn *v.* Leathem, [1901] A. C. 495, and the more recent case of Read *v.* Friendly Society of Stonemasons, [1902] 2 K. B. 732. Nor is this conclusion opposed to Allen *v.* Flood, [1898] A. C. 1, or the Mogul Steamship Company's Case, [1892] A. C. 25, where there was no unlawful act committed.

The appellants' counsel did not deny that, in his view of the case, the defendants' conduct required justification, and it was contended (1) that all which the officials did was to advise the men, and (2) that the officials owed a duty to the men to advise and assist them as they did.

As regards advice, it is not necessary to consider when, if ever, mere advice to do an unlawful act is actionable when the advice is not libellous or slanderous. Nor is it necessary to consider those cases in which a person, whose rights will be violated if a contract is performed, is justified in endeavoring to procure a breach of such contract. Nor is it necessary to consider what a parent or guardian may do to protect his child or ward. That there are cases in which it is not actionable to exhort a person to break a contract may be admitted; and it is very difficult to draw a sharp line separating all such cases from all others. But the so-called advice here was much more than counsel; it was accompanied by orders to stop, which could not be disobeyed with impunity. A refusal to stop work as ordered would have been regarded as disloyal to the federation. This is plain from the speeches given in evidence on the trial; and in my opinion it is a very important element in the case which cannot be ignored.

As regards duty the question immediately arises — duty to do what ? The defendants have to justify a particular line of conduct, which was wrongful, i. e., aiding and abetting the men in doing what both the men and the officials knew was legally wrong. The constitution of the union may have rendered it the duty of the officials to advise the men what could be legally done to protect their own interests; but a legal duty to do what is illegal and known so to be is a contradiction in terms. A similar argument was urged without success in the case of the Friendly Society of Stonemasons, [1902] 2 K. B. 732, already referred to.

Then your Lordships were invited to say that there was a moral or social duty on the part of the officials to do what they did, and that, as they acted *bona fide* in the interest of the men and without any ill-will to the employers, their conduct was justifiable; and your Lordships were asked to treat this case as if it were like a case of libel or slander on a privileged occasion. My Lords, this contention was not based on authority, and its only merits are its novelty and ingenuity. The analogy is, in my opinion, misleading, and to give effect to this contention would be to legislate and introduce an entirely new law, and not to expound the law as it is at present. It would be to render many acts lawful which, as the law stands, are clearly unlawful.

My Lords, I have purposely abstained from using the word "malice." Bearing in mind that malice may or may not be used to denote ill-will, and that in legal language presumptive or implied malice is distinguishable from express malice, it conduces to clearness in discussing such cases as these to drop the word "malice" altogether, and to substitute for it the meaning which is really intended to be conveyed by it. Its use may be necessary in drawing indictments; but when all that is meant by malice is an intention to commit an unlawful act without reference to spite or ill-feeling, it is better to drop the word malice and so avoid all misunderstanding.

The appeal ought to be dismissed with costs.

Order of the Court of Appeal affirmed and appeal dismissed with costs.[1]

JERSEY CITY PRINTING CO. *v.* CASSIDY

COURT OF CHANCERY, NEW JERSEY, DECEMBER 11, 1906.

Reported in 63 *New Jersey Equity Reports,* 759.

ON motion, on order to show cause, for an injunction to restrain defendants, former employes of the complainant, and now on strike, from unlawful interference with the complainant's business, the employment of workmen, &c. Heard on bill, answer and affidavits.

Upon filing the bill an order was made restraining the defendants "from in any manner knowingly and intentionally causing or attempting to cause by threats, offers of money, payment of money, offering to pay or the payment of transportation expenses, inducements or persuasions to any employe of the complainant under contract to render service to it to break such contract by quitting such service; from any and all personal molestation of persons willing to be employed by complainant with intent to coerce such persons to refrain from entering such employment; from addressing persons willing to be employed by complainant against their will and thereby causing them personal annoyance with a view to persuade them to refrain from such employment; from loitering or picketing in the streets near the premises of

[1] Compare Tunstall *v.* Sterns Coal Co., (C. C. A.) 192 Fed. 808. Section 3 of the Trade Disputes Act, 6 Edward 7, Chap. 47, enacted Dec. 21, 1906, is as follows: —

"Sect. 3. An act done by a person in contemplation or furtherance of a trade dispute shall not be actionable on the ground only that it induces some other person to break a contract of employment or that it is an interference with the trade, business, or employment of some other person, or with the right of some other person to dispose of his capital or his labor as he wills."

See Smith, Crucial Issues in Labor Litigation, 20 Harvard Law Rev. 253, 345, 429.

complainant, Nos. 68 and 70 York street, and No. 37 Montgomery street, Jersey City, with intent to procure the personal molestation and annoyance of persons employed or willing to be employed by complainant and with a view to cause persons so employed to quit their employment, or persons willing to be employed by complainant to refrain from such employment; from entering the premises of complainant, Nos. 68 and 70 York street, Jersey City, against its will with intent to interfere with its business; from violence, threats of violence, insults, indecent talk, abusive epithets practiced upon any persons without their consent with intent to coerce them to refrain from entering the employment of complainant, or to leave its employment."

STEVENSON, V. C. (orally). The bill is filed to restrain a body of workmen, who are on a strike, and other persons associated with them, from doing certain things which are alleged to be injurious to the complainant, their former employer. The things that they are restrained from doing are specified in the restraining order. That order was not made hastily. It was formulated with care on the part of the court, and I do not understand that counsel for the defendant criticises its terms on the ground that they are too broad. The defence is that the persons who are enjoined have not been doing, and are not threatening now to do, any of those things that are interdicted. That is the sum and substance of the defence, which has been presented by a great many affidavits and with very great force.

The order does not interfere with the right of the workman to cease his employment for any reasons that he deems sufficient. It does not undertake to say that workmen may not refuse to be employed if certain other classes of workmen are retained in employment. It leaves the workman absolutely free to abstain from work — for good reasons, for bad reasons, for no reasons. His absolute freedom to work, or not to work, is not in any way impaired. The restraining order is based upon the theory that the right of the workman to cease his employment, to refuse to be employed, and to do that in conjunction with his fellow-workmen, is just as absolute as is the right of the employer to refuse further to employ one man, or ten men, or twenty men who have theretofore been in his employment. From an examination of the cases and a very careful consideration of the subject I am unable to discover any right in the courts, as the law now stands, to interfere with this absolute freedom on the part of the employer to employ whom he will, and to cease to employ whom he will; and the corresponding freedom on the part of the workman, for any reason or no reason, to say that he will no longer be employed; and the further right of the workmen, of their own free will, to combine and meet as one party, as a unit, the employer who, on the other side of the transaction, appears as a unit before them. Any discussion of the motives, purposes or intentions of the employer in exercising his absolute right to employ or not to employ as he sees fit, or of the free combination of employes in exercising the corresponding absolute right to be employed or not as they see fit, seems to me to be in the air.

Thus, there is a wide field in which employes may combine and exercise the arbitrary right of " dictating " to their common employer " how he shall conduct his business." The exact correlative of this right of the employe exists, in an equal degree, in the employer. He may arbitrarily " dictate " to five thousand men in his employ in regard to matters in respect of which their conduct ought, according to correct social and ethical principles, to be left entirely free. But if the " dictation " is backed up solely by the announcement that, if it is not submitted to, the dictating party will refrain from employing, or refrain from being employed, as the case may be, no legal or equitable right belonging to the party dictated to, which I am able to discern, is thereby invaded.

Some of the expressions which I have used, and which are commonly used, in relation to this subject seem to me to be misleading. Union workmen who inform their employer that they will strike if he refuses to discharge all non-union workmen in his employ are acting within their absolute right, and, in fact, are merely dictating the terms upon which they will be employed. All such terms necessarily relate both to " how the employer shall conduct his business " and how the employes shall conduct their business.

The doctrine of the old cases, of which we have in New Jersey an interesting example in State *v.* Donaldson, 3 Vr. 151, which placed the employe, when acting in combination with his fellow-workmen, at a tremendous disadvantage as compared with his employer, I think may be regarded as entirely exploded. The authority of the deliverances of the supreme court in State *v.* Donaldson was largely, if not entirely, abolished by statute in 1883.

The principles which I have endeavored to state are all recognized in the restraining order in this case, and are so plainly recognized that the intelligent and industrious counsel for the defendants is unable to point out any respect wherein the terms of the order should be modified. The things which the restraining order interdicts are things which, for the purposes of this argument, it is practically conceded the defendants have no right to do.

In this situation of the case it would seem to be unnecessary to further consider the legal propriety of the restraining order, much less to take it up clause by clause. I have, however, pointed out what conduct on the part of the defendants is excluded from the operation of this order, and I think that it is fair to all the parties to this suit who are concerned in the maintenance of the restraining order to explain, at least in a general way, what conduct is included within its prohibition. This can be most conveniently done by making plain the most important principles embodied in the order — principles which practically have been developed by the courts of this country and England during the last five or ten years.

The injunction in strike and boycott cases is of very recent use. Already a wide difference of opinion has been developed among judges in regard to the liability of a combination of workmen to actions at law for damages and suits in equity for an injunction.

It is only very recently, I think, that one of the most important rights which now are vindicated by the injunction in a strike case has been differentiated; in many cases it has been apparently half recognized or indirectly enforced.

That the interest of an employer or an employe in a contract for services is property is conceded. Where defendants, in combination or individually, undertake to interfere with and disrupt existing contract relations between the employer and the employe, it is plain that a property right is directly invaded. The effect is the same whether the means employed to cause the workman to break his contract, and thus injure the employer, are violence or threats of violence against the employe or mere molestation, annoyance, or persuasions. In all these cases, whatever the means may be, they constitute the cause of the breaking of a contract, and consequently they constitute the natural and proximate cause of damage. The intentional doing of anything by a third party which is the natural and proximate cause of the disruption of a contract relation, to the injury of one of the contracting parties, is now very generally recognized as actionable, in the absence of a sufficient justification, and the question, in every case, seems to turn upon justification alone.

Where the tangible property of an employer is seized or directly injured by violence, with intent to interfere with the carrying on of his business, the case, also is free from embarrassment.

In the case of Frank *v.* Herold, 18 Dick. Ch. Rep. 443, Vice-Chancellor Pitney amply discussed the whole subject of the unlawfulness of molestation and annoyance of employes, with intent and with the effect to induce them to abandon their employment, to the injury of their employer's business.

But the difficult case presents itself when the workmen in combination undertake to interfere with the freedom of action on the part of other workmen who naturally would seek employment where they (the workmen in combination) desire and intend that no man shall be employed excepting upon their terms.

The difficulty is in perceiving how molestation and annoyance, not of the employes of a complainant, but of persons who are merely looking for work and may become employes of the complainant, can be erected into a legal or equitable grievance on the part of the complainant. But the difficulty is still further increased where the possible employes make no complaint to any court for protection, and the conduct of the molesting party does not afford a basis which the ancient common law recognized as sufficient to support an action of tort on their behalf, such as for an assault and battery or a slander. Abusive language is not necessarily actionable at the common law. If to call a man a "scab" in the street or to follow him back and forth from his home to his place of employment was formerly not actionable on behalf of the victim of this petty annoyance, the problem is to understand how one who is merely the victim's possible employer can complain, either at law or in equity, there being no actual contract for service, but only a potential one, interfered with.

It is easier, I think, to obtain a correct idea of the legal and equitable right which underlies many of the injunctions which have been granted in these strike cases restraining combinations of workmen from interfering with the natural supply of labor to an employer, by means of molestation and personal annoyance, if we exclude from consideration the conduct of the defendants as a cause of action on behalf of the immediate victims of their molestation — *i. e.*, of the workman or workmen whom the combination are seeking to deter from entering into the employment which is offered to them, and which they, if let alone, would wish to accept. I say this, although I firmly believe that the molested workman, seeking employment and unreasonably interfered with in this effort by a combination, has an action for damages at common law, and, where the molestation is repeated and persistent, has the same right to an injunction, in equity, which, under the same circumstances, is accorded to his contemplated employer.

The underlying right in this particular case under consideration, which seems to be coming into general recognition as the subject of protection by courts of equity, through the instrumentality of an injunction, appears to be the right to enjoy a certain free and natural condition of the labor market, which, in a recent case in the House of Lords, was referred to, in the language of Lord Ellenborough, as a "probable expectancy." This underlying right has otherwise been broadly defined or described as the right which every man has to earn his living, or to pursue his trade or business, without undue interference, and might otherwise be described as the right which every man has, whether employer or employe, of absolute freedom to employ or to be employed. The peculiar element of this perhaps newly-recognized right is that it is an interest which one man has in the freedom of another. In the case before this court the Jersey City Printing Company claims the right, not only to be free in employing labor, but also the right that labor shall be free to be employed by it, the Jersey City Printing Company.

A large part of what is most valuable in modern life seems to depend more or less directly upon "probable expectancies." When they fail, civilization, as at present organized, may go down. As social and industrial life develops and grows more complex these "probable expectancies" are bound to increase. It would seem to be inevitable that courts of law, as our system of jurisprudence is evolved to meet the growing wants of an increasingly complex social order, will discover, define and protect from undue interference more of these "probable expectancies."

In undertaking to ascertain and define the rights and remedies of employers and employes, in respect of their "probable expectancies" in relation to the labor market, it is well not to lose sight altogether of any other analogous rights and remedies which are based upon similar "probable expectancies." It will probably be found in the end, I think, that the natural expectancy of employers in relation to the labor market and the natural expectancy of merchants in respect to the merchandise market must be recognized to the same extent by courts of law and courts of equity and protected by substantially the same rules.

It is freedom in the market, freedom in the purchase and sale of all things, including both goods and labor, that our modern law is endeavoring to insure to every dealer on either side of the market. The valuable thing to merchant and to customer, to employer and to employe, manifestly is freedom on both sides of the market. The merchant, with his fortune invested in goods and with perfect freedom to sell, might be ruined if his customers were deprived of their freedom to buy; the purchaser, a householder, seeking supplies for his family, with money in his pocket and free to buy, might find his liberty of no value and might suffer from lack of food and clothing if the shopmen who deal in these articles were so terrorized by a powerful combination as to be coerced into refusing to sell either food or clothing to him.

It is, however, the right of the employer and employe to a free labor market that is the particular thing under consideration in this case.

A man establishes a large factory where working people reside, taking the risk of his being able to conduct his industry and offer these working people employment which they will be willing to accept. He takes the risk of destructive competition and a large number of other risks, out of which, at any time, may come his financial ruin and the suspension of his manufacturing works. But our law, in its recent development, undertakes to insure to him, not only that he may employ whom he pleases, but that all who wish to be employed by him may enter into and remain in such employment freely, without threats of harm, without unreasonable molestation and annoyance from the words, actions or other conduct of any other persons *acting in combination.* What is the measure or test by which the conduct of a combination of persons must be judged in order to determine whether or not it is an unlawful interference with freedom of employment in the labor market, and as such injurious to an employer of labor in respect of his "probable expectancies," has not as yet been clearly defined. Perhaps no better definition could be suggested than that which may be framed by conveniently using that important legal fictitious person who has taken such a large part in the development of our law during the last fifty years — the reasonably prudent, reasonably courageous and not unreasonably sensitive man. Precisely this same standard is employed throughout the law of nuisance in determining what degree of annoyance on the part of one's neighbor one must submit to, and what degree of such annoyance is excessive and the subject of an action for damages or a suit for an injunction.

A man may not be liable to an action for slander for calling a workman a "scab" in the street, but if a hundred men combine to have this workman denounced as a "scab" in the street, or followed in the streets to and from his home, so as to attract public attention to him and place him in an annoyingly conspicuous position, such conduct, the result of such combination, is held to be an invasion of the "probable expectancy" of his employer or contemplated employer, an invasion of this employer's *right to have labor flow freely to him.* Without any regard to the rights and remedies which the molested workman may have, the injunction goes at the suit of the employer to protect his "probable expectancy" — to secure freedom in the labor market to employ and to be employed, upon which the continuance of his entire industry may depend.

I think it is safe to say that all through this development of strike law, during the last decade, no principle becomes established which does not operate equally upon both employer and employe. The rights of both classes are absolutely equal in respect of all these "probable expectancies." An operator upon printing machines has the right to offer his labor freely to any of the printing shops in Jersey City. These shops may all combine to refuse to employ him on account of his race, or membership in a labor union, or for any other reason, or for no reason, precisely as twenty employes in one printing shop may combine and arbitrarily refuse to be further employed unless the business is conducted in accordance with their views. But in the case of the operative seeking employment, he has a right to have the action of the masters of the printing shops, in reference to employing him, left absolutely free. If, after obtaining, or seeking to obtain, employment in a shop, the master of that shop should be subjected to annoyances and molestation, instigated by the proprietors of other printing shops, who combine to compel by such molestation and annoyance, this one master printer, against his will and wish, to exclude the operative from employment, this operative, in my judgment, would have a right to an action at law for damages, and would have a right to an injunction if his case presented the other ordinary conditions upon which injunctions issue. But the common law courts have not had time to speak distinctly on this subject as yet, and it is necessary to be cautious in dealing with a subject in which both courts of law and courts of equity as yet are feeling their way.

I think that the leading principle enforced in the restraining order in this case is not inconsistent with any authorities which control this court. This principle is that a combination of employers, or a combination of employes, the object of which is to interfere with the freedom of the employer to employ, or of the employe to be employed (in either of which cases there is an interference with the enjoyment of a "probable expectancy," which the law recognizes as something in the nature of property), by means of such molestation or personal annoyance as would be liable to coerce the person upon whom it was inflicted, assuming that he is reasonably courageous and not unreasonably sensitive, to refrain from employing or being employed, is illegal and founds an action for damages on the part of any person knowingly injured in respect of his "probable expectancy" by such interference, and also, when the other necessary conditions exist, affords the basis of an injunction from a court of equity.

The doctrine which supports that portion of the restraining order in this case which undertakes to interdict the defendants from molesting applicants for employment as an invasion of a right of the complainant, is applicable to a situation presenting either an employer or an employe as complainant, and containing the following elements:

First. Some person or persons desiring to exercise the right of employing labor, or the right of being employed to labor.

Second. A combination of persons to interfere with that right, by molestation or annoyance, of the employers who would employ, or of the employes who would be employed, in the absence of such molestation.

How far the element of combination of a number of persons will finally be found necessary, in order to make out the invasion of a legal or equitable right in this class of cases, need not be discussed. We are dealing with cases where powerful combinations of large numbers, in fact, exist.

Third. Such a degree of molestation as might constrain a person having reasonable fortitude, and not being unreasonably sensitive, to abandon his intention to employ or to be employed, in order to escape such molestation.

Fourth. As the result of the foregoing conditions, an actual pecuniary loss to the complaining party, by the interference with his enjoyment of his "probable expectancies" in respect of the labor market.

I do not think that the constraining force brought to bear upon the employer or employe which the law can interdict can ever include the power of public opinion or even of class opinion. Every man, whether an employer or an employe, constitutes a part of a great industrial system, and his conduct is open to the criticism of the members of his own class. While, therefore, a combination of union men have no right to cry "scab" in the streets to non-union employes, or follow them in the street in a body to and from their homes, or do many other things *in combination*, which, if done once by a single individual, would not found an action of tort, such combinations, I think, have left a fairly wide field of effort towards the creation and application of public opinion as a constraining force upon conduct of any kind which they wish to discourage.

I have endeavored to explain, in a general way, my own view of the most important and least understood principle embodied in the restraining order in this case, in order that the defendants, and, in fact, all parties interested, may have all possible light in construing and applying the exact terms of the order. What I have said may be found to be subject to modifications, without subjecting the terms of the order to any change. All generalizations on such a subject — such a novel subject as the one under consideration — are dangerous. There may be conduct on the part of a combination of employers, or of employes, which would seem to come within the general definition or description of illegal and prohibited conduct, which I have attempted to frame, but which conduct, nevertheless, might be justified, and hence could not be adjudged illegal. Molestation and personal annoyance, however, the terms which I have employed, do not seem to be inclusive of any justifiable conduct, especially if no one is allowed to complain that he is molested or annoyed by being subjected peaceably to the judgment and criticism of public opinion.

The vice-chancellor then discussed at length the effect of the answer of the defendants and the affidavits annexed thereto, which denied all the charges of interference with existing labor contracts or molestation practiced to prevent new workmen from being employed. The conclusion was that, notwithstanding such denials, even when sustained by the greater weight of evidence, the restraining order should be held in force as to those defendants who stood fairly charged, under oath, with the interdicted misconduct, and should be vacated as to any other defendants not so charged; that the sole issue appeared to be one of fact, viz., whether the defendants had done, and were threatening to do, the acts complained of or not, and that such an issue could not properly be tried on *ex parte* affidavits, but should be reserved for the final hearing; that in a case like this, where the defendants were the only persons in sight apparently interested in having the unlawful conduct complained of continued, and were therefore subjected to a temptation to cause such conduct to be continued, an injunction which merely prevented them from doing acts which they disclaimed any right to do, and denied that they had done or threatened to do, should be retained until the final hearing.

THE MOGUL STEAMSHIP COMPANY LIMITED v. McGREGOR & COMPANY

In the Court of Appeal, July 13, 1889.

Reported in Law Reports, 23 Queen's Bench Division, 598.

Bowen, L. J.[1] We are presented in this case with an apparent conflict or antinomy between two rights that are equally regarded by the law — the right of the plaintiffs to be protected in the legitimate exercise of their trade, and the right of the defendants to carry on their business as seems best to them, provided they commit no wrong to others. The plaintiffs complain that the defendants have crossed the line which the common law permits; and inasmuch as, for the purposes of the present case, we are to assume some possible damage to the plaintiffs, the real question to be decided is whether, on such an assumption, the defendants in the conduct of their commercial affairs have done anything that is unjustifiable in law. The defendants are a number of ship-owners who formed themselves into a league or conference for the purpose of ultimately keeping in their own hands the control of the tea carriage from certain Chinese ports, and for the purpose of driving the plaintiffs and other competitors from the field. In order to succeed in this object, and to discourage the plaintiffs' vessels from resorting to those ports, the defendants during the "tea harvest" of 1885 combined to offer to the local shippers very low freights, with a view of generally reducing or "smashing" rates, and thus rendering it unprofitable for the plaintiffs to send their ships thither. They offered, moreover, a rebate of five per cent to all local shippers and agents who would deal exclusively with vessels belonging to the Conference, and any agent who broke the condition was to forfeit the entire rebate on all shipments made on behalf of any and every one of his principals during the whole year — a forfeiture of rebate or allowance which was denominated as "penal" by the plaintiffs' counsel. It must, however, be taken as established that the rebate was one which the defendants need never have allowed at all to their customers. It must also be taken that the defendants had no personal ill-will to the plaintiffs, nor any desire to harm them except such as is involved in the wish and intention to discourage by such measures the plaintiffs from sending rival vessels to such ports. The acts of which the plaintiffs particularly complained were as follows: — First, a circular of May 10, 1885, by which the defendants offered to the local shippers and their agents a benefit by way of rebate if they would not deal with the plaintiffs, which was to be lost if this condition was not fulfilled. Secondly, the sending of special ships to Hankow in order by competition to deprive the plaintiffs' vessels of profitable freight.

[1] Only the opinion of Bowen, L. J., is given. Fry, L. J., concurred, but Lord Esher, M. R., dissented. The decision was afterwards affirmed in the House of Lords, [1892] A. C. 25.

Thirdly, the offer at Hankow of freights at a level which would not repay a shipowner for his adventure, in order to " smash " freights and frighten the plaintiffs from the field. Fourthly, pressure put on the defendants' own agents to induce them to ship only by the defendants' vessels, and not by those of the plaintiffs. It is to be observed with regard to all these acts of which complaint is made that they were acts that in themselves could not be said to be illegal unless made so by the object with which, or the combination in the course of which, they were done; and that in reality what is complained of is the pursuing of trade competition to a length which the plaintiffs consider oppressive and prejudicial to themselves. We were invited by the plaintiffs' counsel to accept the position from which their argument started — that an action will lie if a man maliciously and wrongfully conducts himself so as to injure another in that other's trade. Obscurity resides in the language used to state this proposition. The terms " maliciously," " wrongfully," and " injure " are words all of which have accurate meanings, well known to the law, but which also have a popular and less precise signification, into which it is necessary to see that the argument does not imperceptibly slide. An intent to " injure " in strictness means more than an intent to harm. It connotes an intent to do wrongful harm. " Maliciously," in like manner, means and implies an intention to do an act which is wrongful, to the detriment of another. The term " wrongful " imports in its turn the infringement of some right. The ambiguous proposition to which we were invited by the plaintiffs' counsel still, therefore, leaves unsolved the question of what, as between the plaintiffs and defendants, are the rights of trade. For the purpose of clearness, I desire, as far as possible, to avoid terms in their popular use so slippery, and to translate them into less fallacious language wherever possible.

The English law, which in its earlier stages began with but an imperfect line of demarcation between torts and breaches of contract, presents us with no scientific analysis of the degree to which the intent to harm, or, in the language of the civil law, the *animus vicino nocendi*, may enter into or affect the conception of a personal wrong; see Chasemore *v.* Richards, 7 H. L. C. 349, at p. 388. All personal wrong means the infringement of some personal right. " It is essential to an action in tort," say the Privy Council in Rogers *v.* Rajendro Dutt, 13 Moore, P. C. 209, " that the act complained of should under the circumstances be legally wrongful as regards the party complaining; that is, it must prejudicially affect him in some legal right; merely that it will, however directly, do a man harm in his interests, is not enough." What, then, were the rights of the plaintiffs as traders as against the defendants ? The plaintiffs had a right to be protected against certain kind of conduct; and we have to consider what conduct would pass this legal line or boundary. Now, intentionally to do that which is calculated in the ordinary course of events to damage, and which does, in fact, damage another in that other person's property or trade, is actionable if done without just cause or excuse. Such intentional action when done without just cause or excuse is what the law calls a malicious wrong (see Bromage *v.* Prosser; Capital and Counties Bank *v.* Henty, *per* Lord Blackburn, 7 App. Cas. 741, at p. 772). The acts of the defendants which are complained of here were intentional, and were also calculated, no doubt, to do the plaintiffs damage in their trade. But in order to see whether they were wrongful we have still to discuss the question whether they were done without any just cause or excuse. Such just cause or excuse the defendants on their side assert to be found in their own positive right (subject to certain limitations) to carry on their own trade freely in the mode and manner that best suits them, and which they think best calculated to secure their own advantage.

What, then, are the limitations which the law imposes on a trader in the conduct of his business as between himself and other traders? There seem to be no burdens or restrictions in law upon a trader which arise merely from the fact that he is a trader, and which are not equally laid on all other subjects of the Crown. His right to trade freely is a right which the law recognizes and encourages, but it is one which places him at no special disadvantage as compared with others. No man, whether trader or not, can, however, justify damaging another in his commercial business by fraud or misrepresentation. Intimidation, obstruction, and molestation are forbidden; so is the intentional procurement of a violation of individual rights, contractual or other, assuming always that there is no just cause for it. The intentional driving away of customers by show of violence, Tarleton *v.* M'Gawley, Peake, 205; the obstruction of actors on the stage by preconcerted hissing, Clifford *v.* Brandon, 2 Camp. 358, Gregory *v.* Brunswick, 13 L. J. C. P. 34; the disturbance of wild fowl in decoys by the firing of guns, Carrington *v.* Taylor, 11 East, 571, and Keeble *v.* Hickeringill, 11 East, 574 note; the impeding or threatening servants or workmen, Garret *v.* Taylor, Cro. Jac. 567; the inducing persons under personal contracts to break their contracts, Bowen *v.* Hall, Lumley *v.* Gye, — all are instances of such forbidden acts. But the defendants have been guilty of none of these acts. They have done nothing more against the plaintiffs than pursue to the bitter end a war of competition waged in the interest of their own trade. To the argument that a competition so pursued ceases to have a just cause or excuse when there is ill-will or a personal intention to harm, it is sufficient to reply (as I have already pointed out) that there was here no personal intention to do any other or greater harm to the plaintiffs than such as was necessarily involved in the desire to attract to the defendants' ships the entire tea freights of the ports, a portion of which would otherwise have fallen to the plaintiffs' share. I can find no authority for the doctrine that such a commercial motive deprives of "just cause or excuse " acts done in the course of trade which would but for such a motive be justifiable. So to hold would be to convert into an illegal motive the instinct of self-advancement and self-protection, which is the very incentive to all trade. To say that a man is to trade freely, but that he is to stop short at any act which is calculated to harm other tradesmen, and which is designed to attract business to his own shop, would be a strange and impossible counsel of perfection. But we were told that competition ceases to be the lawful exercise of trade, and so to be a lawful excuse for what will harm another, if carried to a length which is not fair or reasonable. The offering of reduced rates by the defendants in the present case is said to have been " unfair." This seems to assume that, apart from fraud, intimidation, molestation, or obstruction, of some other personal right *in rem* or *in personam*, there is some natural standard of " fairness " or " reasonableness " (to be determined by the internal consciousness of judges and juries) beyond which competition ought not in law to go. There seems to be no authority, and I think, with submission, that there is no sufficient reason, for such a proposition. It would impose a novel fetter upon trade. The defendants, we are told by the plaintiffs' counsel, might lawfully lower rates provided they did not lower them beyond a " fair freight," whatever that may mean. But where is it established that there is any such restriction upon commerce ? And what is to be the definition of a " fair freight ? " It is said that it ought to be a normal rate of freight, such as is reasonably remunerative to the shipowner. But over what period of time is the average of this reasonable remunerativeness to be calculated ? All commercial men with capital are acquainted with the ordinary expedient of sowing one year a crop of apparently unfruitful prices, in order by driving competition away to reap a fuller harvest of profit in the future; and until the present argument at the bar it may be doubted whether shipowners or merchants were ever deemed to be bound by law to conform to some imaginary " normal " standard of freights or prices, or that law courts had a right to say to them in respect of their competitive tariffs, " Thus far shalt thou go, and no further." To attempt to limit English competition in this way would probably be as hopeless an endeavor as the experiment of King Canute. But on ordinary principles of law no such fetter on freedom of trade can in my opinion be warranted. A man is bound not to use his property so as to infringe upon another's right. *Sic utere tuo ut alienum non lædas.* If engaged in actions which may involve danger to others, he ought, speaking generally, to take reasonable care to avoid endangering them. But there is surely no doctrine of law which compels him to use his property in a way that judges and juries may consider reasonable: see Chasemore *v.* Richards, 7 H. L. C. 349. If there is no such fetter upon the use of property known to the English law, why should there be any such a fetter upon trade ?

It is urged, however, on the part of the plaintiffs, that even if the acts complained of would not be wrongful had they been committed by a single individual, they become actionable when they are the result of concerted action among several. In other words, the plaintiffs, it is contended, have been injured by an illegal conspiracy. Of the general proposition, that certain kinds of conduct not criminal in any one individual may become criminal if done by combination among several, there can be no doubt. The distinction is based on sound reason, for a combination may make oppressive or dangerous that which if it proceeded only from a single person would be otherwise, and the very fact of the combination may show that the object is simply to do harm, and not to exercise one's own just rights. In the application of this undoubted principle it is necessary to be very careful not to press the doctrine of illegal conspiracy beyond that which is necessary for the protection of individuals or of the public; and it may be observed in passing that as a rule it is the damage wrongfully done, and not the conspiracy, that is the gist of actions on the case for conspiracy: see Skinner *v.* Gunton, 1 Wms. Saund. 229; Hutchins *v.* Hutchins, 7 Hill, 104. But what is the definition of an illegal combination? It is an agreement by one or more to do an unlawful act, or to do a lawful act by unlawful means: O'Connell *v.* The Queen, 11 Cl. & F. 155; Reg. *v.* Parnell, 14 Cox, Criminal Cases, 508; and the question to be solved is whether there has been any such agreement here. Have the defendants combined to do an unlawful act? Have they combined to do a lawful act by unlawful means? A moment's consideration will be sufficient to show that this new inquiry only drives us back to the circle of definitions and legal propositions which I have already traversed in the previous part of this judgment. The unlawful act agreed to, if any, between the defendants must have been the intentional doing of some act to the detriment of the plaintiffs' business without just cause or excuse. Whether there was any such justification or excuse for the defendants, is the old question over again, which, so far as regards an individual trader, has been already solved. The only differentia that can exist must arise, if at all, out of the fact that the acts done are the joint acts of several capitalists, and not of one capitalist only. The next point is whether the means adopted were unlawful. The means adopted were competition carried to a bitter end. Whether such means were unlawful is in like manner nothing but the old discussion which I have gone through, and which is now revived under a second head of inquiry, except so far as a combination of capitalists differentiates the case of acts jointly done by them from similar acts done by a single man of capital. But I find it impossible myself to acquiesce in the view that the English law places any such restriction on the combination of capital as would be involved in the recognition of such a distinction. If so, one rich capitalist may innocently carry competition to a length which would become unlawful in the case of a syndicate with a joint capital no larger than his own, and one individual merchant may lawfully do that which a firm or a parnership may not. What limits, on such a theory, would be imposed by law on the competitive action of a joint-stock company limited, is a problem which might well puzzle a casuist. The truth is, that the combination of capital for purposes of trade and competition is a very different thing from such a combination of several persons against one, with a view to harm him, as falls under the head of an indictable conspiracy. There is no just cause or excuse in the latter class of cases. There is such a just cause or excuse in the former. There are cases in which the very fact of a combination is evidence of a design to do that which is hurtful without just cause — is evidence — to use a technical expression — of malice. But it is perfectly legitimate, as it seems to me, to combine capital for all the mere purposes of trade for which capital may, apart from combination, be legitimately used in trade. To limit combinations of capital, when used for purposes of competition, in the manner proposed by the argument of the plaintiffs, would, in the present day, be impossible — would be only another method of attempting to set boundaries to the tides. Legal puzzles which might well distract a theorist may easily be conceived of imaginary conflicts between the selfishness of a group of individuals and the obvious well-being of other members of the community. Would it be an indictable conspiracy to agree to drink up all the water from a common spring in a time of drought; to buy up by preconcerted action all the provisions in a market or district in times of scarcity: see Rex *v.* Waddington, 1 East, 143; to combine to purchase all the shares of a company against a coming settling-day; or to agree to give away articles of trade gratis in order to withdraw custom from a trader? May two itinerant match-vendors combine to sell matches below their value in order by competition to drive a third match-vendor from the street? In cases like these, where the elements of intimidation, molestation, or the other kinds of illegality to which I have alluded are not present, the question must be decided by the application of the test I have indicated. Assume that what is done is intentional, and that it is calculated to do harm to others. Then comes the question, Was it done with or without "just cause or excuse?" If it was *bona fide* done in the use of a man's own property, in the exercise of a man's own trade, such legal justification would, I think, exist not the less because what was done might seem to others to be selfish or unreasonable: see the summing-up of Erle, J., and the judgment of the Queen's Bench in Reg. *v.* Rowlands, 17 Q. B. 671. But such legal justification would not exist when the act was merely done with the intention of causing temporal harm, without reference to one's own lawful gain, or the lawful enjoyment of one's own rights. The good sense of the tribunal which had to decide would have to analyze the circumstances and to discover on which side of the line each case fell. But if the real object were to enjoy what was one's own, or to acquire for one's self some advantage in one's property or trade, and what was done was done honestly, peaceably, and without any of the illegal acts above referred to, it could not, in my opinion, properly be said that it was done without just cause or excuse. One may with advantage borrow for the benefit of traders what was said by Erle, J., in Reg. *v.* Rowlands, 17 Q. B. 671, at p. 687, n., of workmen and of masters: "The intention of the law is at present to allow either of them to follow the dictates of their own will, with respect to their own actions, and their own property; and either, I believe, has a right to study to promote his own advantage, or to combine with others to promote their mutual advantage."

Lastly, we are asked to hold the defendants' Conference or association illegal, as being in restraint of trade. The term "illegal" here is a misleading one. Contracts, as they are called, in restraint of trade, are not, in my opinion, illegal in any sense, except that the law will not enforce them. It does not prohibit the making of such contracts; it merely declines, after they have been made, to recognize their validity. The law considers the disadvantage so imposed upon the contract a sufficient shelter to the public. The language of Crompton, J., in Hilton *v.* Eckersley, 6 E. & B. 47, is, I think, not to be supported. No action at common law will lie or ever has lain against any individual or individuals for entering into a contract merely because it is in restraint of trade. Lord Eldon's equity decision in Cousins *v.* Smith, 13 Ves. 542, is not very intelligible, even if it be not open to the somewhat personal criticism passed on it by Lord Campbell in his "Lives of the Chancellors." If indeed it could be plainly proved that the mere formation of "conferences," "trusts," or "associations" such as these were always necessarily injurious to the public—a view which involves, perhaps, the disputable assumption that, in a country of free trade, and one which is not under the iron *régime* of statutory monopolies, such confederations can ever be really successful — and if the evil of them were not sufficiently dealt with by the common law rule, which held such agreements to be void as distinct from holding them to be criminal, there might be some reason for thinking that the common law ought to discover within its arsenal of sound commonsense principles some further remedy commensurate with the mischief. Neither of these assumptions are, to my mind, at all evident, nor is it the province of judges to mould and stretch the law of conspiracy in order to keep pace with the calculations of political economy. If peaceable and honest combinations of capital for purposes of trade competition are to be struck at, it must, I think, be by legislation, for I do not see that they are under the ban of the common law.

In the result, I agree with Lord Coleridge, C. J., and differ, with regret, from the Master of the Rolls. The substance of my view is this, that competition, however severe and egotistical, if unattended by circumstances of dishonesty, intimidation, molestation, or such illegalities as I have above referred to, gives rise to no cause of action at common law. I myself should deem it to be a misfortune if we were to attempt to prescribe to the business world how honest and peaceable trade was to be carried on in a case where no such illegal elements as I have mentioned exist, or were to adopt some standard of judicial "reasonableness," or of "normal" prices, or "fair freights," to which commercial adventurers, otherwise innocent, were bound to conform.

In my opinion, accordingly, this appeal ought to be dismissed with costs. *Appeal dismissed.*[1]

PASSAIC PRINT WORKS *v.* ELY & WALKER DRY GOODS COMPANY

United States Circuit Court of Appeals, Eighth Circuit, November 14, 1900.

Reported in 44 *U. S. Circuit Court of Appeals Reports*, 426, s. c. 105 *Federal Reporter*, 163.

In U. S. Circuit Court of Appeals, Eighth Circuit. Before Caldwell, Sanborn, and Thayer, Circuit Judges.[2]

In error to U. S. Circuit Court for Eastern District of Missouri.

This case was determined below on a demurrer to the plaintiff's petition, which was sustained; and a final judgment was entered against the Passaic Print Works, the plaintiff below, it having declined to plead further.

The plaintiff's petition contained, in substance, the following allegations (*inter alia*): —

Plaintiff is a corporation engaged in the manufacture of prints or calicoes which it sells to jobbers or wholesale dealers in St. Louis and elsewhere, who in turn sell the same to the retail trade. In 1899 it had fixed on certain prices for certain specified brands of calicoes; and it had, prior to Feb. 25, 1899, received from several wholesale dealers in St. Louis orders for large amounts of said brands at the prices specified. On February 25, 1899, the defendant company, combining and conspiring among themselves and with others to the plaintiff unknown, and maliciously intending to injure the business of the said plaintiff, and to cause it great loss in money, and to break up and ruin the plaintiff's trade among the jobbers in St. Louis, maliciously caused a circular, in the name of the said defendant corporation, to be issued and sent out to the retail trade tributary to St. Louis. In the circular defendant company offered for sale several brands of calicoes

[1] Payne *v.* Railroad Co., 13 Lea, 507 (Freeman and Turney, JJ., dissenting); South Royalton Bank *v.* Suffolk Bank, 27 Vt. 505; Delz *v.* Winfree, 80 Tex. 400, 405 (*semble*) *Accord.* See Lough *v.* Outerbridge, 143 N. Y. 271.

[2] Statement rewritten.

manufactured by plaintiff at prices lower than those fixed by plaintiff. The brands were offered "as long as they last" at these reduced prices: "Prices for all items subject to change without notice, and orders accepted only for stock on hand." Plaintiff further alleged that it was informed and believed that defendant had but a small quantity of such goods to sell, and for that reason qualified its offer as above stated.

The petition further averred, that the effect of issuing this circular was to compel jobbers to whom plaintiff had already sold either to cancel their orders or to compel plaintiff to make a rebate on price, and to thereby break up the trade of plaintiff in St. Louis and the adjacent country, and to make the other jobbers in St. Louis afraid to deal in said brands except at greatly reduced prices and then in comparatively small quantities; and upon information and belief the plaintiff alleged "that the quotations of this plaintiff's said goods in the said circular were made by the said defendants with the end and object in this paragraph stated, and not for any legitimate trade purpose."

THAYER, Circuit Judge, [after stating the case] delivered the opinion of the court.

The complaint filed in the lower court, the substance of which has been stated, shows by necessary intendment that when the circular of the defendant company was issued it had in stock a limited quantity of the four brands of calico of the plaintiff's manufacture which are therein described. The circular stated, in substance, that the defendant had such calicoes in stock, and the complaint did not deny that fact, but admitted it by averring that "the defendant corporation had but a small quantity of such goods to sell, and for that reason qualified its offer to sell by inserting in the circular after the name of the goods the words 'as long as they last.'" Moreover, the owner of property, real or personal, has an undoubted right to sell it and to offer it for sale at whatever price he deems proper, although the effect of such offer may be to depreciate the market value of the commodity which he thus offers, and incidentally to occasion loss to third parties who have the same kind or species of property for sale. The right to offer property for sale, and to fix the price at which it may be bought, is incident to the ownership of property, and the loss which a third party sustains in consequence of the exercise of that right is *damnum absque injuria.* We are thus confronted with the inquiry whether the motive which influenced the defendant company to offer for sale such calicoes of the plaintiff's manufacture as they had in stock at the price named in its circular, conceding such motive to have been as alleged in the complaint, changed the complexion of the act, and rendered the same unlawful, when, but for the motive of the actor, it would have been clearly lawful. It is common learning that a bad motive — such as an intent to hinder, delay, and defraud creditors, by virtue of St. 13 Eliz. c. 5, and possibly by the rules of the common law — will render a conveyance or transfer of property void which, but for the bad motive, would have been valid. So, also, one who sets the machinery of the law in motion without probable cause, and for the sole purpose of injuring the reputation of another, or subjecting him to loss and expense, is guilty of an unlawful act which would have been lawful but for the improper motive. And one who, by virtue of his situation, has a qualified privilege to make defamatory statements concerning another, may be deprived of the benefit of that privilege by proof that it was not exercised in good faith, but in pursuance of a malicious intent to injure the person concerning whom the defamatory statement or statements were made. Poll. Torts (Webb's Ed.) pp. 331–335, and cases there cited. There is also some authority for saying that one who maliciously (that is, with intent to obtain some personal benefit at another's loss or expense) induces another to break his contract with a third party thereby commits an actionable wrong if special damage is disclosed, although the act done would have been lawful if the wrongful motive had been absent. Lumley *v.* Gye, 2 El. & Bl. 216; Bowen *v.* Hall, 6 Q. B. Div. 333; Walker *v.* Cronin, 107 Mass. 555. And see Poll. Torts (Webb's Ed.) pp. 668–673. Aside from cases of the latter kind, it is a general rule that the bad motive which inspires an act will not change its complexion, and render it unlawful, if otherwise the act was done in the exercise of an undoubted right. Or, as has sometimes been said, " when an act done is, apart from the feelings which prompted it, legal, the civil law ought to take no cognizance of its motive." The question as to how far and under what circumstances a bad purpose will render an act actionable which, considered by itself, and without reference to the purpose which prompted it, is lawful, has been so much discussed since the decision in Allen *v.* Flood, [1898] 1 App. Cas. 1, that it would be profitless to indulge in further comment. It has been well observed that it would be dangerous to the peace of society to admit the doctrine that any lawful act can be transformed *prima facie* into an actionable wrong by a simple allegation that the act was inspired by malice or ill will, or by an improper motive. It is wiser, therefore, to exclude any inquiry into the motives of men when their actions are lawful, except in those cases where it is well established that malice is an essential ingredient of the cause of action, or in those cases where, the act done being wrongful, proof of a bad motive will serve to exaggerate the damages.

The case at bar falls within neither of the exceptions to the general rule above stated, — that, if an act is done in the exercise of an undoubted right, and is lawful, the motive of the actor is immaterial. No one can dispute the right of the defendant company to offer for sale goods that it owned and were in its possession, whether the quantity was great or small, for such a price as it deemed proper. This was the outward visible act of which complaint is made, and, being lawful, the law will not hold it to be otherwise because of a secret purpose entertained by the defendant company to inflict loss on the plaintiff by compelling it to reduce the cost of a certain kind of its prints or calicoes.

Nor is the complaint aided in any respect by reference to the law of conspiracy, since the only object that the defendants had in view which the law will consider was the disposition or sale of certain goods which the defendant corporation had the right to sell; and the means employed to accomplish that end, namely, placing them on the market at a reduced cost, were also lawful.

In the brief filed in behalf of the plaintiff in error it is suggested finally that the complaint may be sustained on the ground that it states a good cause of action for maliciously causing certain persons to break or cancel their contracts with the plaintiff, but we think it quite obvious that the complaint was not framed with a view of stating a cause of action of that nature, and that it is insufficient for that purpose. It does not give the name of any person or corporation with whom the plaintiff had a contract for the sale of its prints which was subsequently broken in consequence of the wrongful acts of the defendant. Neither does it show that it had accepted any orders for goods which the jobber was not privileged to cancel at his pleasure. Nor does it allege any special damage incident to the breach of any particular contract. In view of all the allegations which the complaint contains it is manifest, we think, that it was framed with a view of recovering on the broad ground that the issuance of the circular was unlawful and actionable, provided the motive of the defendant company in issuing it was to occasion loss or inconvenience to the plaintiff.

We are of opinion that the complaint did not state a cause of action, as the trial court held, and the judgment below is therefore affirmed.

SANBORN, Circuit Judge (dissenting). I cannot concur in the opinion of the majority in this case because the petition alleges that the defendants by their advertisement of the goods manufactured by plaintiff, without any legitimate trade purpose, prevented jobbers from purchasing goods of the plaintiff, and caused those who had agreed to purchase from it to cancel their orders unless the plaintiff would make them a rebate, so that the plaintiff sustained damage in the sum of $19,000. In my opinion, the gravamen of this cause of action is not the malicious intent or purpose of the defendants, but it is their wrongful act of interfering with the plaintiff's business, of preventing sales that it would have made, and of causing the cancellation of orders to, or contracts of purchase from, the plaintiff already made. This act, without any allegation or averment of intent or purpose, was itself wrongful, unless it was done for a justifiable purpose. The act of interfering with and injuring the trade or business of the plaintiff without justifiable cause entitled the plaintiff to damages. It is conceded that, if the defendants had advertised these prints for any legitimate trade purpose, for the purpose of selling them for gain for themselves, for the purpose of converting them into money because they preferred their advertised price to the goods, or for the purpose of competing in trade with the plaintiff, they would have had a justifiable cause for inflicting upon it the damages of which it complains, and these damages would then have been *damnum absque injuria*. But, if they had advertised them for any of these purposes, this case would have constituted an exception to the general rule of law. The general rule is that whenever one injures a man's business, profession, or occupation he is liable for the damages he inflicts. The exception is that, where the injury is caused by competition in trade or the lawful exercise of a right which the inflictor has, then the injury is justifiable, and no damages can be recovered. But, where such an injury is inflicted, the presumption always is that the rule, and not the exception, applies, and, if the inflictor would justify, he must show that he falls within the exception. The question in this case, therefore, is not whether or not the motive or intent of the defendants will make acts unlawful which were otherwise lawful, but whether or not the intent and purpose of the defendants will justify an otherwise unlawful act, and excuse them from the payment of damages for which, under the general rule of law, they are liable to the plaintiff. It is whether or not the petition shows that they advertised the goods for legitimate trade purposes, so that their acts fell within the exception, which justifies the infliction of damages, and not under the general rule, which requires them to compensate the plaintiff for the injury they have caused. The opinion of the majority assumes that the defendants advertised the prints for a legitimate trade purpose, so that their acts fell within the exception to the general rule. It overlooks the legal presumption that injury to one's business entitles him to compensatory damages, and the plain averment of the petition that the acts of the defendants were not done for any justifiable cause, but were committed for the sole purpose of inflicting upon the plaintiff the injury they caused.

[After quoting from the averments in the petition.]

Now, no one will dispute the rules of law that the plaintiff in this action had the right to conduct its business of manufacturing and selling prints without the injurious interference of strangers, and that the defendants were subject to the universal rule that they must so use their own property and rights as to inflict no unnecessary injury upon their neighbors. The averments of this petition are that they were not using any of their property or exercising any of their rights for any legitimate trade purpose, but that they were using them for the express purpose of inflicting injury upon the plaintiff, and that they succeeded in imposing the infliction. These allegations seem to me to bring this case under the general rule of law, and to clearly negative the claim that it falls within the exception. They seem to state a good cause of action.

[The learned Judge here cited, and quoted from, various authorities.]

The proposition is sustained by respectable authority; it is just, and I believe it is sound, — that an action will lie for depriving a man of custom (that is, of possible contracts), when the result is effected by persuasion as well as when it is accomplished by fraud or force, if the harm is inflicted without justifiable cause, such as competition in trade. Walker *v.* Cronin, 107 Mass. 555, 565; Morasse *v.* Brochu, 151 Mass. 567, 25 N. E. 74, 8 L. R. A. 524; Hartnett *v.* Association, 169 Mass. 229, 235, 47 N. E. 1002, 38 L. R. A. 194; Delz *v.* Winfree, 80 Tex. 400, 405, 16 S. W. 111; Doremus *v.* Hennessy, 62 Ill. App. 391, 403; Van Horn *v.* Van Horn, 52 N. J. Law, 284, 20 Atl. 485; Temperton *v.* Russell, 62 Law J. (Q. B. Div. 1893) 412, 419.

Under the legal principles to which reference has been made, and under the authorities which have been cited, the petition in this case states a good cause of action for interference with and injury to the business of the plaintiff by preventing it from obtaining custom it would otherwise have obtained, without any justifiable cause or excuse, and for this reason the demurrer should have been overruled, and the case sent to trial.

There is another reason why the judgment below should be reversed. It is that the petition sufficiently states a cause of action for maliciously interfering with contracts between jobbers in St. Louis and the plaintiff, and inducing the former to break their contracts to the injury of the latter.

. . . .

For the reasons which have now been briefly stated, the judgment below should, in my opinion, be reversed, and the defendants should be required to answer the petition.[1]

TUTTLE *v.* BUCK

SUPREME COURT, MINNESOTA, FEBRUARY 19, 1909.

Reported in 107 *Minnesota Reports*, 145.

ACTION in the District Court for Wright County to recover $10,000 damages. Defendant demurred to the complaint on the ground it did not state a cause of action. From an order, Buckham, J., overruling the demurrer, defendant appealed. Affirmed.

This appeal was from an order overruling a general demurrer to a complaint in which the plaintiff alleged: —

[1] See Boggs *v.* Duncan Furniture Co., 163 Ia. 106; Rogers, Predatory Price Cutting as Unfair Trade, 27 Harvard Law Rev. 139.

That for more than ten years last past he has been and still is a barber by trade, and engaged in business as such in the village of Howard Lake, Minnesota, where he resides, owning and operating a shop for the purpose of his said trade. That until the injury hereinafter complained of his said business was prosperous, and plaintiff was enabled thereby to comfortably maintain himself and family out of the income and profits thereof, and also to save a considerable sum per annum, to wit, about $800. That the defendant, during the period of about twelve months last past, has wrongfully, unlawfully, and maliciously endeavored to destroy plaintiff's said business, and compel plaintiff to abandon the same. That to that end he has persistently and systematically sought, by false and malicious reports and accusations of and concerning the plaintiff, by personally soliciting and urging plaintiff's patrons no longer to employ plaintiff, by threats of his personal displeasure, and by various other unlawful means and devices, to induce, and has thereby induced, many of said patrons to withhold from plaintiff the employment by them formerly given. That defendant is possessed of large means, and is engaged in the business of a banker in said village of Howard Lake, at Dassel, Minnesota, and at divers other places, and is nowise interested in the occupation of a barber; yet in the pursuance of the wicked, malicious, and unlawful purpose aforesaid, and for the sole and only purpose of injuring the trade of the plaintiff, and of accomplishing his purpose and threats of ruining the plaintiff's said business and driving him out of said village, the defendant fitted up and furnished a barber shop in said village for conducting the trade of barbering. That failing to induce any barber to occupy said shop on his own account, though offered at nominal rental, said defendant, with the wrongful and malicious purpose aforesaid, and not otherwise, has during the time herein stated hired two barbers in succession for a stated salary, paid by him, to occupy said shop, and to serve so many of plaintiff's patrons as said defendant has been or may be able by the means aforesaid to direct from plaintiff's shop. That at the present time a barber so employed and paid by the defendant is occupying and nominally conducting the shop thus fitted and furnished by the defendant, without paying any rent therefor, and under an agreement with defendant whereby the income of said shop is required to be paid to defendant, and is so paid in partial return for his wages. That all of said things were and are done by defendant with the sole design of injuring the plaintiff, and of destroying his said business, and not for the purpose of serving any legitimate interest of his own. That by reason of the great wealth and prominence of the defendant, and the personal and financial influence consequent thereon, he has by the means aforesaid, and through other unlawful means and devices by him employed, materially injured the business of the plaintiff, has largely reduced the income and profits thereof, and intends and threatens to destroy the same altogether, to plaintiff's damage in the sum of $10,000.[1]

ELLIOTT, J. (after stating the facts as above).

In has been said that the law deals only with externals, and that a lawful act cannot be made the foundation of an action because it was done with an evil motive. In Allen *v.* Flood, [1898] A. C. 1, 151, Lord Watson said that, except with regard to crimes, the law does not take into account motives as constituting an element of civil wrong. In Mayor *v.* Pickles, [1895] A. C. 587, Lord Halsbury stated that if the act was lawful, " however ill the motive might be, he had a right to do it." In Raycroft *v.* Tayntor, 68 Vt. 219, 35 Atl. 53, 33 L. R. A. 225, 54 Am. St. 882, the court said that, " when one exercises a legal right only, the motive which actuates him is immaterial." In Jenkins *v.* Fowler, 24 Pa. St. 308, Mr. Justice Black said that " malicious motives make a bad act worse, but they cannot make that wrong which, in its own essence, is lawful." This language was quoted in Bohn Mnfg. Co. *v.* Hollis, 54 Minn. 223, 233, 55 N. W. 1119, 21 L. R. A. 337, 40 Am. St. 319, and in substance in Ertz *v.* Produce Exchange, 79 Minn. 140, 143, 81 N. W. 737, 48 L. R. A. 90, 79 Am. St. 433. See also 2 Cooley, Torts (3d Ed.) 1505; Auburn *v.* Douglass, 9 N. Y. 444.

Such generalizations are of little value in determining concrete cases. They may state the truth, but not the whole truth. Each word and phrase used therein may require definition and limitation. Thus, before we can apply Judge Black's language to a particular case, we must determine what act is " in its own essence lawful." What did Lord Halsbury mean by the words " lawful act " ? What is meant by " exercising a legal right " ? It is not at all correct to say that the motive with which an act is done is always immaterial, providing the act itself is not unlawful. Numerous illustrations of the contrary will be found in the civil as well as the criminal law.

We do not intend to enter upon an elaborate discussion of the subject, or become entangled in the subtleties connected with the words " malice " and " malicious." We are not able to accept without limitations the doctrine above referred to, but at this time content ourselves with a brief reference to some general principles.

It must be remembered that the common law is the result of growth, and that its development has been determined by the social needs of the community which it governs. It is the resultant of conflicting social forces, and those forces which are for the time dominant leave their impress upon the law. It is of judicial origin, and seeks to establish doctrines and rules for the determination, protection, and enforcement of legal rights. Manifestly it must change as society changes and new rights are recognized. To be an efficient instrument, and not a mere abstraction, it must gradually adapt itself to changed

[1] The arguments are omitted.

conditions. Necessarily its form and substance have been greatly affected by prevalent economic theories.

For generations there has been a practical agreement upon the proposition that competition in trade and business is desirable, and this idea has found expression in the decisions of the courts as well as in statutes. But it has led to grievous and manifold wrongs to individuals, and many courts have manifested an earnest desire to protect the individual from the evils which result from unrestrained business competition. The problem has been to so adjust matters as to preserve the principle of competition and yet guard against its abuse to the unnecessary injury to the individual. So the principle that a man may use his own property according to his own needs and desires, while true in the abstract, is subject to many limitations in the concrete. Men cannot always, in civilized society, be allowed to use their own property as their interests or desires may dictate without reference to the fact that they have neighbors whose rights are as sacred as their own. The existence and well-being of society require that each and every person shall conduct himself consistently with the fact that he is a social and reasonable person. The purpose for which a man is using his own property may thus sometimes determine his rights, and applications of this idea are found in Stillwater Water Co. *v.* Farmer, 89 Minn. 58, 93 N. W. 907, 60 L. R. A. 875, 99 Am. St. 541, Id., 92 Minn. 230, 99 N. W. 882, and Barclay *v.* Abraham, 121 Iowa, 619, 96 N. W. 1080, 64 L. R. A. 255, 100 Am. St. 365.

Many of the restrictions which should be recognized and enforced result from a tacit recognition of principles which are not often stated in the decisions in express terms. Sir Frederick Pollock notes that not many years ago it was difficult to find any definite authority for stating as a general proposition of English law that it is wrong to do a wilful wrong to one's neighbor without lawful justification or excuse. But neither is there any express authority for the general proposition that men must perform their contracts. Both principles, in this generality of form and conception, are modern, and there was a time when neither was true. After developing the idea that law begins, not with authentic general principles, but with the enumeration of particular remedies, the learned writer continues: "If there exists, then, a positive duty to avoid harm, much more must there exist the negative duty of not doing wilful harm, subject, as all general duties must be subject, to the necessary exceptions. The three main heads of duty with which the law of torts is concerned, namely, to abstain from wilful injury, to respect the property of others, and to use due diligence to avoid causing harm to others, are all alike of a comprehensive nature." Pollock, Torts (8th Ed.), p. 21. He then quotes with approval the statement of Lord Bowen that "at common law there was a cause of action whenever one person did damage to another, wilfully and intentionally, without just cause or excuse."

In Plant *v.* Woods, 176 Mass. 492, 57 N. E. 1011, 51 L. R. A. 339, 79 Am. St. 330, Mr. Justice Hammond said: "It is said also that, where one has the lawful right to do a thing, the motive by which he is actuated is immaterial. One form of this statement appears in the first headnote in Allen *v.* Flood, as reported in [1898] A. C. 1, as follows: 'An act lawful in itself is not converted by a malicious or bad motive into an unlawful act so as to make the doer of the act liable to a civil action.' If the meaning of this and similar expressions is that where a person has the lawful right to do a thing irrespective of his motive, his motive is immaterial, the proposition is a mere truism. If, however, the meaning is that where a person, if actuated by one kind of a motive, has a lawful right to do a thing, the act is lawful when done under any conceivable motive, or that an act lawful under one set of circumstances is therefore lawful under every conceivable set of circumstances, the proposition does not commend itself to us as either logically or legally accurate."

Similar language was used by Mr. Justice Wells in Walker *v.* Cronin, 107 Mass. 555; by Lord Coleridge in Mogul Steamship Co. *v.* McGregor, 21 Q. B. Div. 544–553; by Lord Justice Bowen in the same case, 23 Q. B. Div. 593; by Mr. Justice Holmes in Aikens *v.* Wisconsin, 195 U. S. 194, 204, 25 Sup. Ct. 3, 49 L. Ed. 154; by Chief Justice McSherry, in Klingel *v.* Sharp, 104 Md. 233, 64 Atl. 1029, 7 L. R. A. (N. S.) 976, 118 Am. St. 399; and by Judge Sanborn in his dissenting opinion in Passaic Print Works *v.* Ely & Walker Dry Goods Co., 105 Fed. 163, 44 C. C. A. 426, 62 L. R. A. 673. Numerous cases will be found referred to in the note to this case in 62 L. R. A. 673, and in an article in 18 Harvard Law Rev. 411.

It is freely conceded that there are many decisions contrary to this view; but, when carried to the extent contended for by the appellant, we think they are unsafe, unsound, and illy adapted to modern conditions. To divert to one's self the customers of a business rival by the offer of goods at lower prices is in general a legitimate mode of serving one's own interest, and justifiable as fair competition. But when a man starts an opposition place of business, not for the sake of profit to himself, but regardless of loss to himself, and for the sole purpose of driving his competitor out of business, and with the intention of himself retiring upon the accomplishment of his malevolent purpose, he is guilty of a wanton wrong and an actionable tort. In such a case he would not be exercising his legal right, or doing an act which can be judged separately from the motive which actuated him. To call such conduct competition is a perversion of terms. It is simply the application of force without legal justification, which in its moral quality may be no better than highway robbery.

Nevertheless, in the opinion of the writer this complaint is insufficient. It is not claimed that it states a cause of action for slander. No question of conspiracy or combination is involved. Stripped of the adjectives and the statement that what was done was for the sole purpose of injuring the plaintiff, and not for the purpose of serving a legitimate purpose of the defendant, the complaint states facts which in themselves amount only to an ordinary every day business transaction. There is no allegation that the defendant was intentionally running the business at a financial loss to himself, or that after driving the plaintiff out of business the defendant closed up or intended to close up his shop. From all that appears from the complaint he may have opened the barber shop, energetically sought business from his acquaintances and the customers of the plaintiff, and as a result of his enterprise and command of capital obtained it, with the result that the plaintiff, from want of capital, acquaintance, or enterprise, was unable to stand the competition and was thus driven out of business. The facts thus alleged do not, in my opinion, in themselves, without reference to the way in which they are characterized by the pleader, tend to show a malicious and wanton wrong to the plaintiff.

A majority of the justices, however, are of the opinion that, on the principle declared in the foregoing opinion, the complaint states a cause of action, and the order is therefore affirmed.

Affirmed.

JAGGARD, J., dissents.[1]

WEAVER, J., IN DUNSHEE *v.* STANDARD OIL COMPANY

(1911) 152 *Iowa Reports*, 618.

As we understand appellants' contention, it is that their conduct did not transgress the bounds of legitimate competition, and that so long as they kept within this limitation the question of the alleged malice or motive inspiring their acts is wholly immaterial. Cases involving the question thus suggested have frequently arisen, both in this country and in England, and there is much in harmony in the expressions of judicial opinion thereon. Many authorities may be found holding without apparent qualification or exception, that the law takes no account whatever of motives as constituting an element of civil wrong. In other words, if a man do a thing which is otherwise lawful, the fact that he does it maliciously and for the express purpose of injuring his neighbor affords the latter no remedy at law. Such is the net effect of Raycroft *v.* Tayntor, 68 Vt. 219, 35 Atl. 53, 33 L. R. A. 225, 54 Am. St. Rep. 882; Jenkins *v.* Fowler, 24 Pa. 308, and others of that class. If this be the correct view of the law, a man may excavate the earth near the boundary of his own land for the mere purpose of seeing the foundation of the house of his neighbor slide into the pit thus prepared for it; he may dig through his

[1] In Holbrook *v.* Morrison, 214 Mass. 209, a land owner put a sign on her land reading, " For Sale. Best Offer From Colored Family." Defendant wished to sell but was also moved by ill will toward plaintiffs, whose real estate business was seriously interfered with by the threatened sale. See Ames, How Far an Act May Be a Tort Because of the Wrongful Motive of the Actor, 18 Harvard Law Rev. 411, 420; Smith, Crucial Issues in Labor Litigation, 20 Harvard Law Rev. 429, 453, 455.

own soil to the subterranean sources of his neighbor's spring or well and divert the water into a ditch, where it will serve no purpose of use or profit to himself or any one else; if a banker or merchant, he may punish the blacksmith who refuses to patronize him by temporarily establishing a shop on the next lot and hiring men to shoe horses without money and without price, until he has driven the offending smith to come to his terms or to go out of business; and if a farmer, dependent upon a subterranean supply of water for the irrigation of his soil or watering of his live stock, he may contrive to ruin his competing neighbor by wasting the surplus not reasonably required for his own use. The laws of competition in business are harsh enough at best; but if the rule here suggested were to be carried to its logical and seemingly unavoidable extreme there is no practical limit to the wrongs which may be justified upon the theory that "it is business." Fortunately, we think, there has for many years been a distinct and growing tendency of the courts to look beneath the letter of the law and give some effect to its beneficent spirit, thereby preventing the perversion of the rules intended for the protection of human rights into engines of oppression and wrong. It is doubtless true that under many circumstances an act is legally right and defensible without regard to the motive which induces or characterizes it; but there is abundance of authority for saying that this is by no means the universal rule, and that an act which is legally right when done without malice may become legally wrong when done maliciously, wantonly, or without reasonable cause. In Panton *v.* Holland, 17 Johns. (N. Y.) 92, 8 Am. Dec. 369, it is stated as a general rule that, "In the exercise of a lawful right, a party may become liable to an action where it appears that the act was done maliciously." See also, Greenleaf *v.* Francis, 18 Pick. (Mass.) 117; Chesley *v.* King, 74 Me. 164, 43 Am. Rep. 569; Flaherty *v.* Moran, 81 Mich. 52, 45 N. W. 381, 8 L. R. A. 183, 21 Am. St. Rep. 510; Sankey *v.* St. Marys, 8 Mont. 265, 21 Pac. 23; Harbison *v.* White, 46 Conn. 106; Stillwater *v.* Farmer, 89 Minn. 58, 93 N. W. 907, 60 L. R. A. 875, 99 Am. St. Rep. 541; Ohio Oil Company *v.* Indiana, 150 Ind. 698, 50 N. E. 1124; Barclay *v.* Abraham, 121 Iowa, 619, 96 N. W. 1080, 64 L. R. A. 255, 100 Am. St. Rep. 365. The same principle has been frequently applied in the decision of trade and labor controversies, though not without other instances in which it has been repudiated. See People *v.* Petheram, 64 Mich. 252, 31 N. W. 188; Walker *v.* Cronin, 107 Mass. 555; Van Horn *v.* Van Horn, 52 N. J. Law, 284, 20 Atl. 485, 10 L. R. A. 184; Hawarden *v.* Coal Co., 111 Wis. 545, 87 N. W. 472, 55 L. R. A. 828; Graham *v.* Railroad Co., 47 La. Ann. 214, 16 South. 806, 27 L. R. A. 416, 49 Am. St. Rep. 366; Tuttle *v.* Buck, 107 Minn. 145, 119 N. W. 946, 22 L. R. A. (N. S.) 599, 131 Am. St. Rep. 446; Plant *v.* Woods, 176 Mass. 492, 57 N. E. 1011, 51 L. R. A. 339, 79 Am. St. Rep. 330; Barr *v.* Council, 53 N. J. Eq. 101, 30 Atl. 881; Toledo, &c. Ry. Co. *v.* Penn. Co., (C. C.) 54 Fed. 730, 19 L. R. A. 387; Stevens *v.* Kelly, 78 Me. 445, 6 Atl. 868, 57 Am. Rep. 813; Purington *v.* Hinchcliffe, 219 Ill. 159, 76 N. E. 47, 2 L. R. A. (N. S.) 824, 109 Am. St. Rep. 322. In the Van Horn Case, *supra*, the court says: "While a trader may engage in the sharpest competition with those in like business by holding out extraordinary inducements, . . . yet, when he oversteps that line and commits an act with the malicious intent of inflicting injury upon his rival's business, his conduct is illegal, and if damage results from it the injured party is entitled to redress. Nor does it matter whether the wrongdoer effects his object by persuasion or by false representation. The court looks through the instrumentality or means used to the wrong perpetrated with the malicious intent and bases the right of action on that." Quoting this language in Barr *v.* Council, *supra*, the same court adds: "The right of action depends, then, not so much upon the nature of the act, as upon the intent with which it is done, always assuming that injury has attended the doing of it." In Parkinson *v.* Council, 154 Cal. 581, 98 Pac. 1027, 21 L. R. A. (N. S.) 550, the court, while reaching the opposite conclusion generally, concedes it to be the law that: "Any injury to a lawful business, whether the result of conspiracy or not, is *prima facie* actionable, but may be defended on the ground that it was merely a lawful effort of the defendants to promote their own welfare. To defeat this plea of justification, the plaintiff may offer evidence that the acts of the defendants were inspired by express malice, and were done for the purpose of injuring the plaintiff, and not to benefit themselves."

Dealing with the perplexities arising in the effort to sustain, on the one hand, the widest practicable liberty of men to engage in any and every line of business, and, on the other, to protect the business of each from wrongful encroachment or interference by others, the New Hampshire court after reference to many of the decided cases, has lately said: "The more recent authorities reason that, as the right to deal or not to deal with others is inherent in the idea of Anglo-Saxon liberty, *prima facie* a man may demand an open market, and, since this is so, one who interferes with this open market must justify his acts, or respond in damages. Thus far these authorities are uniform, but when they proceed to the determination of what amounts to a justification they differ widely. The cause is not far to seek. The rule they apply is that of reasonable conduct; yet they decide each case as though it involved only a question of law. In reality, the issue is largely one of fact, and the result is what would be expected. Judges are men, and their decisions upon complex facts must vary as those of juries might on the same facts. Calling one determination an opinion and the other a verdict does not alter human nature, nor make that uniform and certain which from its nature must remain variable and uncertain. While these cases go too far in what they decide as questions of law, yet the test they constantly declare they are applying is the true one. The standard is reasonable conduct under all the circumstances of the case." Huskie *v.* Griffin, 75 N. H. 345, 74 Atl. 595, 27 L. R. A. (N. S.) 966. See, also, Doremus *v.* Hennesy, 176 Ill. 608, 52 N. E. 924, 54 N. E. 524, 43 L. R. A. 797, 802, 68 Am. St. Rep. 203; Horan *v.* Burns, 72 N. H. 93, 54 Atl. 945, 62 L. R. A. 602, 101 Am. St. Rep. 670; Ertz *v.* Produce Exchange, 79 Minn. 140, 81 N. W. 737, 48 L. R. A. 90, 79 Am. St. Rep. 433. As suggested in the foregoing quotation, no definition or standard of reasonable cause can be stated which will insure absolute uniformity or even consistency in the decision of such cases, because the issue presented is in its essence one of fact, and the same facts and circumstances will not always appeal with like effect to the minds of all jurors or of all judges. It is for this reason that, save in those exceptional cases where the case of the plaintiff or the defendant is so clear and undisputable that all fair-minded persons are forced to the same conclusion, controversies of this nature, in a trial at law, are for the jury, and not for the court.

Coming to the case in hand, we may concede to the appellants the undoubted right to establish a retail oil business in Des Moines, to employ agents and drivers, and send them out over the same routes and make sales to the same people with whom the Crystal Oil Company was dealing; but in so doing it was bound to conduct such business with reasonable regard and consideration for the equal right of the Crystal Company to continue supplying oil to such of its customers as desired to remain with it. If, however, there was no real purpose or desire to establish a competing business, but, under the guise or pretence of competition, to accomplish a malicious purpose to ruin the Crystal Company or drive it out of business, intending themselves to retire therefrom when their end had been secured, then they can claim no immunity under the rules of law which recognize and protect competition between dealers in the same line of business seeking in good faith the patronage of the same people. And if, under such pretence of competition, defendants maliciously interfered with the business of the Crystal Oil Company, in the manner charged, and injury to the latter was thereby inflicted, a right of action exists for the recovery of damages. It may be conceded that authorities are not wanting to sustain the position that, even though the Standard Oil Company had no intention of becoming a retail dealer in oil in Des Moines, but entered the business of selling oil in this manner temporarily, for the sole purpose of driving the Crystal Company out, it is a matter into which the courts will not inquire; but we think such precedents are out of harmony with fundamental principles of justice, which, as we have said, underlie the law, as well as out of harmony with the later and better-considered cases. True the Standard Company, as a wholesale dealer, would violate no law in offering its product for sale at retail at half price in the territory supplied by the Crystal Company, but such fact, if proven, would have a distinct bearing upon the reasonableness of its methods employed in diverting trade from said company, as well as upon the charge that in interfering between the Crystal Company and its customers the Standard Company was actuated by malice or spirit of wanton assault upon the business of another, who had given it offence.[1]

KUZNIAK v. KOZMINSKI

Supreme Court, Michigan, December 17, 1895.

Reported in 107 *Michigan Reports*, 444.

Bill by John Kuzniak against Jacob Kozminski and Frances Kozminski to abate an alleged nuisance. From a decree for complainant, defendants appeal. Reversed.

Long, J. The parties to this cause own adjoining lots in the city of Grand Rapids. Defendants' lot is on the southeasterly corner of Eleventh and Muskegon streets, and upon which is a large tenement house facing both streets. The complainant owns the lot immediately south and adjoining the defendants', and upon which he has a dwelling house facing Muskegon street, and also a tenement house about 60 feet back from Muskegon street, and within 22 inches of the north line, being the line of defendants' lot. At the time this tenement house was erected, defendants had upon their lot what was called a "chicken shed"; and, after complainant's tenement house was

[1] In this case, however, the means used by defendant involved trespasses and fraud. See American Waltham Watch Co. v. United States Watch Co., 173 Mass. 85.

erected, defendants moved this chicken shed upon a part of their lot directly opposite complainant's tenement house, and within 24 inches of the lot line, and converted it into a coal and wood house for the use of their tenants, who occupied the dwelling on said lot. This bill was filed by complainant for the purpose of having this coal and wood house of defendants declared a nuisance, and to compel them to remove the same. The claim made by the bill is that the defendants removed the building to that place through spite and from a malicious motive, and not because it was needed for any useful purpose. Defendants answered the bill, denying that they were actuated by malice in putting the building there, and averred that it was so placed for the use of their tenants for wood and coal. The testimony was taken in open court, and the court found that the building was a nuisance, and a decree was entered directing the defendants to remove the building within 60 days from the date of the decree, and that, in default of such removal, the sheriff of the county remove the same, at the cost and expense of defendants. The complainant was awarded the costs of the suit. Defendants appeal.

It was held in Flaherty *v.* Moran, 81 Mich. 52, that a fence erected maliciously, and with no other purpose than to shut out the light and air from a neighbor's window, was a nuisance, and the decree of the court below ordering its removal was affirmed; but that decision was placed on the ground that the fence served no useful purpose, and was erected solely from a malicious motive. In the present case the building erected by the defendants was for a useful purpose; and, while there may have been some malice displayed in putting it so near the complainant's house as to shut off some of the light, that would not be a sufficient reason upon which to found a right in complainant to have the building removed. Defendants had a right to erect a building upon their own premises, and the decisions have been quite uniform to the effect that the motives of a party in doing a legal act cannot form the basis upon which to found a remedy. In Allen *v.* Kinyon, 41 Mich. 282, it was held that the motive is of no consequence when the party does not violate the rights of another. In Hawkins *v.* Sanders, 45 Mich. 491, it was held that there was no right of prospect which would prevent the erection of an awning on a neighboring lot. The case does not fall within the rule of Flaherty *v.* Moran, *supra*, and the court below was in error in directing the removal of the building. That decree must be reversed, and a decree entered here dismissing complainant's bill, with costs of both courts to the defendants.

The other Justices concurred.[1]

[1] See Faloon *v.* Schilling, 29 Kan. 292.

"*Spite fence.*" Malicious use of property to the injury of a neighbor was held not actionable in Capital Bank *v.* Henty, 7 A. C. 741, 766 (*semble*); Giller *v.* West, 162 Ind. 17; Brostrom *v.* Lauppe, 179 Mass. 315; Bordeaux *v.* Greene, 22 Mont. 254; Mahan *v.* Brown, 13 Wend. 261; Auburn Co. *v.* Douglass, 9 N. Y. 444 (*semble*); Pickard *v.* Collins, 23 Barb. 444; Levy *v.* Brothers, 4 Misc. 48; Letts *v.*

HORAN *v.* BYRNES

SUPREME COURT, NEW HAMPSHIRE, APRIL 7, 1903.

Reported in 72 *New Hampshire Reports*, 93.

CASE, under sections 28 and 29, chapter 143, Public Statutes, for maintaining a structure in the nature of a fence, in violation of the statute.

Upon the trial, defendant moved for a nonsuit, on the ground that the statute is unconstitutional. The motion was denied, and defendant excepted.

Kessler, 54 Ohio St. 73; Koblegard *v.* Hale, 60 W. Va. 37; Metzger *v.* Hochrein, 107 Wis. 267.

Contra Norton *v.* Randolph, 176 Ala. 381; Burke *v.* Smith, 69 Mich. 380; Flaherty *v.* Moran, 81 Mich. 52; Kirkwood *v.* Finegan, 95 Mich. 543; Peek *v.* Roe, 110 Mich. 52; Barger *v.* Barringer, 151 N. C. 433. See Wilson *v.* Irwin, 144 Ky. 311; Metz *v.* Tierney, 13 N. M. 363; Smith *v.* Speed, 11 Okl. 95; Haverstick *v.* Sipe, 33 Pa. St. 368; Shell *v.* Kemmerer, 13 Phila. 502; McCorkle *v.* Driskell, (Tenn.) 60 S. W. 172.

Malicious diversion of percolating water was held to give no right of action in Corporation of Bradford *v.* Pickles, [1895] A. C. 587; Meeker *v.* East Orange, 76 N. J. Law, 435; Phelps *v.* Nowlen, 72 N. Y. 39; Chatfield *v.* Wilson, 28 Vt. 49; Huber *v.* Merkel, 117 Wis. 355.

Contra Chasemore *v.* Richards, 7 H. L. Cas. 349, 388 (*semble*); Roath *v.* Driscoll, 20 Conn. 533, 540–44 (*semble*); Chesley *v.* King, 74 Me. 164 (*semble*); Stevens *v.* Kelley, 78 Me. 445, 452; Greenleaf *v.* Francis, 18 Pick. 119 (*semble*); Swett *v.* Cutts, 50 N. H. 439, 447 (*semble*); Wyandot Club Co. *v.* Sells, 3 Ohio N. P. 210; Wheatley *v.* Baugh, 25 Pa. St. 528, 533 (*semble*); Haldeman *v.* Bruckhart, 45 Pa. St. 514 (*semble*); Lybe's Appeal, 106 Pa. St. 626 (*semble*); Williams *v.* Laden, 161 Pa. St. 283 (*semble*); Miller *v.* Black Rock Co., 99 Va. 747 (*semble*).

But cases of this type are now coming to be treated on a different principle of waste or unreasonable use of water underlying neighboring tracts. Gagnon *v.* French Lick Hotel Co., 163 Ind. 687; Barclay *v.* Abraham, 121 Ia. 619; Stillwater Water Co. *v.* Farmer, 89 Minn. 58; Springfield Waterworks Co. *v.* Jenkins, 62 Mo. App. 74.

(1) Has the owner of land the same ownership and control of percolating water (water passing, or filtering, through the ground beneath the surface of the earth, without flowing in definite channels), that he has of the soil, *e.g.*, the sand and the rocks ?

Or (2) has he only a limited and qualified right in the percolating water; a right of reasonable user limited by the correlative rights of his neighbors ?

On those questions there is, in recent cases, a conflict of authority. For illustrative cases endorsing the first theory, see Acton *v.* Blundell, 12 M. & W. 324; Mayor of Bradford *v.* Pickles, [1895] A. C. 587; Meeker *v.* East Orange, 76 N. J. Law, 435. For illustrative cases favoring the second theory, see Bassett *v.* Salisbury Mfg. Co., 43 N. H. 569 (where the question related to the right of the defendant to prevent water percolating under the surface of plaintiff's land from passing off through defendant's land); Katz *v.* Walkinshaw, 141 Cal. 116, 140, 141.

We are concerned here only to point out how the adoption of one or the other of the above conflicting views may affect the materiality of the landowner's motive in the use of percolating water.

If the first theory is adopted, then, in some jurisdictions, the landowner would not be held liable, even though actuated by bad motive (Mayor of Bradford *v.* Pickles, [1895] A. C. 587); and, in all other jurisdictions, he would be liable only when, and because, he was actuated by bad motive.

But if the second theory is adopted, the landowner might frequently be held liable, irrespective of motive. On the second theory percolating water might be regarded as, in a certain sense, the common property of the adjoining owners (bear-

Verdict for the plaintiff.[1]

PARSONS, C. J. "Any fence or other structure in the nature of a fence, unnecessarily exceeding five feet in height, erected or maintained for the purpose of annoying the owners or occupants of adjoining property, shall be deemed a private nuisance.

"Any owner or occupant, injured either in his comfort or the enjoyment of his estate by such nuisance, may have an action of tort for the damage sustained thereby.

"If the plaintiff recovers judgment in the action, the defendant shall cause the removal of the nuisance within thirty days from the date of the judgment, and for each day he shall permit the nuisance to remain after the expiration of said thirty days he shall incur a penalty of ten dollars for the use of the party injured." P. S. c. 143, ss. 28, 29, 30.

The act forbids the use by one landowner of his land for the unnecessary erection of a fence exceeding five feet in height, when the purpose of such unnecessary height is the annoyance of the adjoining owner or occupant, if such unnecessary height injures the adjoining owner in his comfort or the enjoyment of his estate. The claim of the defendant in support of his motion for a nonsuit, that the statute is unconstitutional, raises the question whether the statutory prohibition is an interference with the defendant's "natural, essential, and inherent" right of "acquiring, possessing, and protecting property," or deprives him of that protection in its enjoyment, which is the right of "every member of the community." Bill of Rights, arts. 2, 12.

. . . .

The constitutional objection made to the present statute raises the question, if it appears that the statute is an interference with the defendant's property right, whether the interference is or not one which the legislature might properly make as a regulation of the use of property. The constitutionality of similar statutes has been upheld upon the latter ground, as being merely a small limitation of existing rights incident to property, which under the police power may be im-

ing some analogy to an underground lake); and it would be held that each owner is entitled to only a reasonable share, and is entitled to use that share only for certain purposes. See 3 Farnham, Waters, § 935. Upon this view an owner who uses more than his share, or who uses it for purposes outside those legally allowable, would be liable entirely irrespective of motive. "Later American cases," says Professor Huffcut, "transfer the emphasis from the showing of 'malice' to a showing of 'unreasonable user,' which may or may not be accompanied by malice." 13 Yale Law Journal, 222.

We may add that if bad motive should not be held, in itself, a substantive ground of liability, yet the existence of bad motive might be a piece of evidence bearing upon the question of reasonable user. User for the sole purpose of gratifying ill will might not be deemed reasonable.

On the general question of liability for malevolent acts in reference to percolating water, see, Ames, How Far an Act May Be a Tort Because of the Wrongful Motive of the Actor, 18 Harvard Law Rev. 411, 414–415; Huffcut, Percolating Waters: the Rule of Reasonable User, 13 Yale Law Journ. 222.

[1] Statements abridged. Portions of opinion omitted.

posed for the sake of preventing a manifest evil. "It is hard," it has been said, "to imagine a more insignificant curtailment of the rights of property." Rideout *v.* Knox, 148 Mass. 368, 372, 373; Karasek *v.* Peier, 22 Wash. 419; Western &c. Co. *v.* Knickerbocker, 103 Cal. 111. Similar statutes in Maine, Vermont, and Connecticut have been before the courts, but it has not been suggested that the power of the legislature to adopt them has been attacked in those states. Lord *v.* Langdon, 91 Me. 221; Harbison *v.* White, 46 Conn. 106; Gallagher *v.* Dodge, 48 Conn. 387, 40 L. R. A. 181–183, note.

The present statute was passed in 1887. Laws 1887, c. 91. In Hunt *v.* Coggin, 66 N. H. 140, the verdict was for the defendant; and in Horan *v.* Byrnes, 70 N. H. 531, the defendant waived any objection to the statute upon this ground. In Lovell *v.* Noyes, 69 N. H. 263, the question was whether a building was within the terms of the statute. The constitutional question is now presented for the first time.

It is objected in answer to the argument that statutes like the present are within the constitutional exercise of the police power, involving for the general good some slight limitation of existing property rights, that if one incident of the property right in real estate is the right to use it maliciously for the sole purpose of injuring another, it is as much an invasion of the right to take it from a small portion as from the whole of one's property; and that the matter in question concerns private individuals and not the public in general, and hence does not come within the police power. State *v.* White, 64 N. H. 48, 50. It may be thought these objections are successfully answered in the cases cited, or that, if not there answered, a satisfactory answer can be found. But a discussion of these objections does not reach the fundamental question in the case.

"The statute was designed to prevent an act the sole effect of which would be to annoy or injure another." Lovell *v.* Noyes, 69 N. H. 263. The primary question, therefore, is whether one's right to use property solely to injure another is a part of his property right in real estate, which is so protected by the constitution that the prohibition of such use is not within the general power of legislation "for the benefit and welfare of this state and for the governing and ordering thereof." Const. art. 5. Upon the question whether a fence on or near the division line between adjoining landowners, maliciously built to an unreasonable height for the sole purpose of annoying and injuring the adjoining owner or occupant, is a nuisance which can in the absence of statutory authority be abated by an injunction, the courts are in conflict. Letts *v.* Kessler, 54 Ohio St. 73, answers the question in the negative, while an opposite conclusion is reached in Michigan. Burke *v.* Smith, 69 Mich. 380; Flaherty *v.* Moran, 81 Mich. 52; Kirkwood *v.* Finegan, 95 Mich. 543. In Rideout *v.* Knox, 148 Mass. 368, and Karasek *v.* Peier, 22 Wash. 419, cases in which the power of the legislature to enact a statute similar to that under consideration is attacked and upheld, it is conceded "that to a large extent the power to use one's property malevolently, in any way which would be lawful for other ends, is an incident of property which cannot be taken away even by legislation." Rideout *v.* Knox, *supra*, 372.

The conclusion that a landowner's property right in real estate includes the right to use it solely for the injury and annoyance of his neighbor, without intending to subserve any useful purpose of his own, is "based upon a narrow view of the effect of the land titles," and is reached "by the strict enforcement of a technical rule of ownership briefly expressed in an ancient maxim," *cujus est solum, ejus est usque ad coelum.* The courts of this state have had in some respects, at least, a different understanding of the elements of land-ownership. As to the use of land in the control of surface water, the enjoyment of water percolating beneath the surface, and the use generally that may be rightfully made of real estate by the owner or occupant, the test has been considered to be not merely whether the act was an exercise of dominion on the land regardless of the injury to other land, but the reasonableness of the use under all the circumstances, including the necessity and advantage to one and the unavoidable injury to the other. Franklin *v.* Durgee, 71 N. H. 186; Ladd *v.* Brick Co., 68 N. H. 185; Swett *v.* Cutts, 50 N. H. 439; Bassett *v.* Company, 43 N. H. 569, 577. It has been said that the rule of absolute dominion is easier of application. Chase *v.* Silverstone, 62 Me. 175, 183. This view, however, does not seem to be upheld by the difficulties met in its application in reference to surface waters. See Franklin *v.* Durgee, 71 N. H. 186, 189. But however that may be, difficulty in administration is not a sufficient reason for the denial of justice. Cases like Chatfield *v.* Wilson, 28 Vt. 49, and Phelps *v.* Nowlen, 72 N. Y. 39, in which the principle of the maxim relied upon is applied to waters in the soil, are not authority here, where a contrary view is entertained. Franklin *v.* Durgee and Bassett *v.* Company, *supra.*

Aside from the authorities in cases in which the control of waters was in question, the leading case appears to be Mahan *v.* Brown, 13 Wend. 261. Here, although the plaintiff alleged that the fence complained of was erected solely to injure her, the decision is upon the ground that by the erection of the fence the plaintiff is deprived of no right, but is merely prevented from acquiring a right. If by enjoyment of light and air across his neighbor's land for the prescriptive period a landowner could acquire a right to such enjoyment, the building of a fence as an assertion of a contrary right and to prevent the acquiring of such easement would be a building for a necessary and useful purpose, and not for the sole purpose of annoying another. The case standing upon a view of the effect of non-user of a right to build, now generally abandoned in this country (Wash. Ease. 490,

497, 498), is not of value in the present discussion. The argument generally is, that the motive with which one does an act otherwise lawful is immaterial; and hence, as it must be conceded that a landowner has the right to build on his land as he conceives may best subserve his interests, the act lawful for a useful purpose is not made unlawful and a nuisance merely by the intent accompanying it.

Whether the first proposition is entirely true may perhaps be doubted. Cases cited to support the proposition (Walker *v.* Cronin, 107 Mass. 555; Phelps *v.* Nowlen, 72 N. Y. 39) do not support it in its entirety. See Chesley *v.* King, 74 Me. 164. In Houston *v.* Laffee, 46 N. H. 505, which was trespass for cutting an aqueduct pipe maintained by the plaintiff upon the defendant's land by a parol license, it was held that if the cutting of the pipe was done simply for the purpose of putting an end to the license, and without any malice or intentional wrong, the defendant would not be liable; but if the pipe was cut "wantonly, unnecessarily, maliciously, and with a view . . . to injure the plaintiff," the defendant would be liable. It is true that an act which one has the right to do under all circumstances, like the bringing of a suit upon a valid claim (Friel *v.* Plumer, 69 N. H. 498), cannot be made actionable by the motive which accompanies it. But as applied to the use of real estate the argument begs the question which is whether the enjoyment of real estate includes the right to use it solely to injure another. Because when employed for a useful purpose such use may rightfully injure another, it does not follow that the same use for a wrongful purpose may also rightfully injure another, except upon the theory of absolute dominion, for the character of the use is an element of the right.

"As a general proposition, it is safe to say that the owner of land has a right to make a reasonable use of his property; and that right extends as well to an unlimited distance above the earth's surface as to an unlimited distance below. He may not only dig for a foundation and a cellar as deep as he pleases, but he may erect his building as high as he pleases into the air, subject all the time, of course, to a proper application of the doctrine contained in the maxim, *sic utere tuo ut alienum non lædas.* The erection and maintenance of buildings for habitation or business is a customary and reasonable use of land. Of course the landowner, in making such erections, must be held to the exercise of all due care against infringing the legal rights of others, to be determined by the nature of the rights and interests to be affected, and all the circumstances of each particular case." Ladd, J., in Garland *v.* Towne, 55 N. H. 55, 58.

"Property in land must be considered, for many purposes, not as an absolute, unrestricted dominion, but as an aggregation of qualified privileges, the limits of which are prescribed by the equality of rights and the correlation of rights and obligations necessary for the highest enjoyment of land by the entire community of proprietors. . . . The soil is often called property, and this use of language is sufficiently accurate for some purposes. But the proposition that the soil is property conveys a very imperfect idea of the numerous and variously limited rights comprised in landed estate; and it is sometimes necessary to remember that the name of property belongs to some of the essential proprietary rights vested in the person called the owner of the soil. . . . So these proprietary rights, which are the only valuable ingredients of a landowner's property, may be taken from him, without an asportation or adverse personal occupation of that portion of the earth which is his in the limited sense of being the subject of certain legally recognized proprietary rights which he may exercise for a short time. . . . One of Eaton's proprietary rights was the correlative of R.'s duty of abstaining from such a use of air and water, and from such an interference with their quality and circulation, as would be unreasonable and injurious to the enjoyment of Eaton's farm." Thompson *v.* Androscoggin Co., 54 N. H. 545, 551, 552, 554. "Excavations maliciously made in one's own land, with a view to destroy a spring or well in his neighbor's land, could not be regarded as reasonable." Swett *v.* Cutts, 50 N. H. 439, 447.

"If a man has no right to dig a hole upon his premises, not for any benefit to himself or his premises, but for the express purpose of destroying his neighbor's spring, why can he be permitted to shut out light and air from his neighbor's windows maliciously, and without profit or benefit to himself ? By analogy, it seems to me that the same principle applies in both cases, and that the law will interpose and prevent the wanton injury in both cases. . . . It must be remembered that no man has a legal right to make a malicious use of his property . . . for the avowed purpose of damaging his neighbor. To hold otherwise would make the law a convenient engine in cases like the present to injure and destroy the peace and comfort, and to damage the property, of one's neighbor, for no other than a wicked purpose, which in itself is or ought to be unlawful. The right to do this cannot, in an enlightened country, exist either in the use of property or in any way or manner. . . . The right to breathe the air, and to enjoy the sunshine, is a natural one; and no man can pollute the atmosphere, or shut out the light of heaven, for no better reason than that the situation of his property is such that he is given the opportunity of so doing, and wishes to gratify his spite and malice towards his neighbor." Morse, J., in Burke *v.* Smith, 69 Mich. 380, approved and unanimously adopted in Flaherty *v.* Moran, 81 Mich. 52, above cited.

"While one may in general put his property to any use he pleases not in itself unlawful, his neighbor has the same right to the undisturbed enjoyment of his adjoining property. . . . What standard does the law provide ? . . . Whatever may be the law in other jurisdictions, it must be regarded as settled in this state that the test is the reasonableness or unreasonableness of the business in question under all the circumstances." Ladd *v.* Brick Co., 68 N. H. 185, 186. "The common-law right of the ownership of land, in its relationship to the control of surface water, as understood by the courts of this state for many years, does not sanction or authorize practical injustice to one landowner by the arbitrary and unreasonable exercise of the right of dominion by another" (Franklin *v.* Durgee, *supra*), but makes the test of the right the reasonableness of the use under all the circumstances. In such case the purpose of the use, whether understood by the landowner to be necessary or useful to himself, or merely intended to harm another, may be decisive upon the question of right. It cannot be justly contended that a purely malicious use is a reasonable use. The question of reasonableness depends upon all the circumstances — the advantage and profit to one of the use attacked, and the unavoidable injury to the other. Where the only advantage to one is the pleasure of injuring another, there remains no foundation upon which it can be determined that the disturbance of the other in the lawful enjoyment of his estate is reasonable or necessary. There is no sound ground upon which a distinction can be made against the plaintiff's right to use his land for the enjoyment of the air and light which naturally come upon it, in favor of his right to use it to enjoy the waters which naturally flow upon or under it, except the fact that the use of land for buildings necessarily cuts off air and light from the adjoining estate. The fact that the improvement of real estate in this way for a useful purpose, universally conceded to be reasonable, may affect the adjoining owner's enjoyment of his estate to the same extent as a like act done solely to injure the other, is not a sufficient reason for distinguishing the right to build upon the surface from the right to dig below it or to control the surface itself. Jurisdictions which reject the doctrine of reasonable necessity, reasonable care, and reasonable use, which "prevail in this state in a liberal form, on a broad basis of general principle" (Haley *v.* Colcord, 59 N. H. 7), as applied to the ownership of real estate, in favor of the principle of absolute dominion, may properly consider a malicious motive immaterial upon the rightfulness of a particular use; but in this state, to do so would be to reject the principle announced in Bassett *v.* Company, 43 N. H. 569, and repeatedly reaffirmed during the last forty years.

It is to be conceded that the maxim *sic utere tuo ut alienum non lædas* is to be applied as forbidding injury, not merely to the property, but to the right of another. Ladd *v.* Brick Co., 68 N. H. 185; Pittsburg, &c. R'y *v.* Bingham, 29 Ohio St. 364; Letts *v.* Kessler, 54 Ohio St. 73; Bonomi *v.* Backhouse, E. B. & E. 622, 643; Jeffries *v.* Williams, 5 Exch. 792. But the landowner's right in the enjoyment of his estate being that of reasonable use merely, there attaches at once to each the correlative right not to be disturbed by the malicious, and hence unreasonable, use made by another. To hold that a right is infringed because, by the noxious use made by another, the air coming upon a landowner's premises is made more or less injurious, and to deny the invasion of a right by an unreasonable use which shuts off air and light entirely, is an attempt to bound a right inherent and essential to the common enjoyment of property by the limitations of an ancient form of action. An unreasonable use of one estate may constitute a nuisance by its diminution of the right of enjoyment of another, without furnishing all the elements necessary to maintain an action *quare clausum fregit;* though in particular cases it may be said that no right is invaded unless something comes from the one lot to the other. Lane *v.* Concord, 70 N. H. 485, 488, 489; Thompson *v.* Androscoggin Co., 54 N. H. 545, 552; Wood, Nuis., s. 611. As, therefore, the statute does not deprive the plaintiff of any right to reasonable use, it does not deprive him of any property right. Hence it is not necessary to inquire whether, as an invasion of property rights, the limitation of the statute is one which might properly be made for the general good.

. . . .

The objection based upon the unconstitutionality of the statute is not sustained, and the exception to the denial of the motions for a nonsuit and to direct a verdict upon that ground is overruled.

[The verdict was set aside on account of an erroneous ruling as to the admission of evidence.] [1]

KEEBLE *v.* HICKERINGILL

IN THE QUEEN'S BENCH, TRINITY TERM, 1706.

Reported in 11 *East,* 574, *note.*

ACTION upon the case. Plaintiff declares that he was, 8th November in the second year of the Queen, lawfully possessed of a close of land called Minott's Meadow, *et de quodam vivario, vocato* a decoy pond, to which divers wild fowl used to resort and come; and the plaintiff had at his own costs and charges prepared and procured divers decoy ducks, nets, machines, and other engines for the decoying and taking of the wild fowl, and enjoyed the benefit in taking them: the defendant knowing which, and intending to damnify the plaintiff in his vivary, and to fright and drive away the wild fowl used to resort thither, and deprive him of his profit, did, on the 8th of November, resort to the head of the said pond and vivary, and did discharge six

[1] In Rideout *v.* Knox, 148 Mass. 368, where a similar statute was held constitutional, it was held error to charge that defendant could not justify building the fence unless his sole motive was a legitimate use; malice must be the dominant motive. See also Ingwerson *v.* Barry, 118 Cal. 342; Gallagher *v.* Dodge, 48 Conn. 387; Holmes *v.* Fuller, 68 Vt. 207; Karasek *v.* Peier, 22 Wash. 419; Jones *v.* Williams, 56 Wash. 588; Ames, How Far an Act May Be a Tort Because of the Wrongful Motive of the Actor, 18 Harvard Law Rev. 411, 414–415.

guns laden with gunpowder, and with the noise and stink of the gunpowder did drive away the wild fowl then being in the pond: and on the 11th and 12th days of November the defendant, with design to damnify the plaintiff, and fright away the wild fowl, did place himself with a gun near the vivary, and there did discharge the said gun several times that was then charged with the gunpowder against the said decoy pond, whereby the wild fowl were frighted away, and did forsake the said pond. Upon not guilty pleaded, a verdict was found for the plaintiff and £20 damages.

Holt, C. J. I am of opinion that this action doth lie. It seems to be new in its instance, but is not new in the reason or principle of it. For, first, this using or making a decoy is lawful. Secondly, this employment of his ground to that use is profitable to the plaintiff, as is the skill and management of that employment. As to the first, every man that hath a property may employ it for his pleasure and profit, as for alluring and procuring decoy ducks to come to his pond. To learn the trade of seducing other ducks to come there in order to be taken is not prohibited either by the law of the land or the moral law; but it is as lawful to use art to seduce them, to catch them, and destroy them for the use of mankind, as to kill and destroy wild fowl or tame cattle. Then when a man useth his art or his skill to take them, to sell and dispose of for his profit; this is his trade; and he that hinders another in his trade or livelihood is liable to an action for so hindering him. Why otherwise are scandalous words spoken of a man in his profession actionable, when without his profession they are not so ? Though they do not affect any damage, yet are they mischievous in themselves; and therefore in their own nature productive of damage; and therefore an action lies against him. Such are all words that are spoken of a man to disparage him in his trade, that may bring damage to him; though they do not charge him with any crime that may make him obnoxious to punishment; as to say a merchant is broken, or that he is failing, or is not able to pay his debts, 1 Roll. 60, 1; all the cases there put. How much more, when the defendant doth an actual and real damage to another when he is in the very act of receiving profit by his employment. Now there are two sorts of acts for doing damage to a man's employment, for which an action lies; the one is in respect of a man's privilege; the other is in respect of his property. In that of a man's franchise or privilege whereby he hath a fair, market, or ferry, if another shall use the like liberty, though out of his limits, he shall be liable to an action; though by grant from the King. But therein is the difference to be taken between a liberty in which the public hath a benefit, and that wherein the public is not concerned. 22 H. 6, 14, 15. The other is where a violent or malicious act is done to a man's occupation, profession, or way of getting a livelihood; there an action lies in all cases. But if a man doth him damage by using the same employment; as if Mr. Hickeringill had set up another decoy on his own ground near the plaintiff's, and that had spoiled the custom of the plaintiff, no action would lie, because he had as much liberty to make and use a decoy as the plaintiff. This is like the case of 11 H. 4, 47. One schoolmaster sets up a new school to the damage of an ancient school, and thereby the scholars are allured from the old school to come to his new. (The action there was held not to lie.) But suppose Mr. Hickeringill should lie in the way with his guns, and fright the boys from going to school, and their parents would not let them go thither; sure that schoolmaster might have an action for the loss of his scholars. 29 E. 3, 18. A man hath a market, to which he hath toll for horses sold: a man is bringing his horse to market to sell: a stranger hinders and obstructs him from going thither to the market: an action lies, because it imports damage. Action upon the case lies against one that shall by threats fright away his tenants at will. 9 H. 7, 8; 21 H. 6, 31; 9 H. 7, 7; 14 Ed. 4, 7; Vide Rastal. 662; 2 Cro. 423. Trespass was brought for beating his servant, whereby he was hindered from taking his toll; the obstruction is a damage, though not the loss of his service.[1]

IBOTTSON *v.* PEAT

In the Exchequer, May 1, 1865.

Reported in 3 *Hurlstone & Coltman*, 644.

Bramwell, B.[2] I am also of opinion that the plaintiff is entitled to judgment. The declaration states that the plaintiff being possessed of certain land, the defendant unlawfully and with intent to drive and frighten away game then being on the land of the plaintiff, and to prevent him from shooting them, fired rockets and combustibles close to and over the land of the plaintiff, so as to be a nuisance to him. The defendant by his plea admits that the matter alleged is true, but sets up a right to do what is complained of for the purpose attributed to the defendant in the declaration, viz., to prevent him from shooting the game. Then what is the reason given? It is this: — "The game which I frightened was game which you enticed away from the Duke of Rutland's land, by placing corn and other food for them on your land; and therefore I, as the servant of the Duke, in order to prevent you from shooting the game, and from continuing to entice them, did the acts complained of." In my opinion that is a bad plea. There is nothing in point of law to prevent the plaintiff from doing that which the plea alleges he has done. I say "in point of law," because it can-

[1] The rest of the opinion is omitted. This case was followed in Carrington *v.* Taylor, 11 East, 571. See Lamprey *v.* Danz, 86 Minn. 317; Whittaker *v.* Stangvick, 100 Minn. 386; Meredith *v.* Triple Island Gun Club, 113 Va. 80.

[2] Only the opinion of Bramwell, B., is given. Pollock, C. B., Martin and Pigott, BB., concurred.

not be contended for a moment that any action would lie against the plaintiff. As to the propriety of such conduct between gentlemen and neighbors I say nothing. Where a person's game is attracted from his land, he ought to offer them stronger inducements to return to it. It is like the case I referred to in the course of the argument, Chasemore *v.* Richards, 2 H. & N. 168, 7 H. L. 349, which shows that if a man has the misfortune to lose his spring by his neighbor digging a well, he must dig his own well deeper.

Judgment for the plaintiff.

FISHER *v.* FEIGE

SUPREME COURT, CALIFORNIA, JULY 14, 1902.

Reported in 137 *California Reports,* 39.

APPEAL by defendants from a judgment in favor of plaintiff.

Plaintiff is a lower riparian proprietor on a certain watercourse, and defendants are upper riparian proprietors thereon. The action was brought to recover damages in the sum of five thousand dollars for certain alleged interferences by defendants with the flow of the water in the stream, and for a perpetual injunction restraining defendants from their repetition of the alleged wrongs.[1]

It is averred that along and adjacent to the stream as it flows through defendants' land there is a heavy growth of timber, which, before the alleged wrongful acts of defendants, protected the waters of the stream from evaporation by drying winds and the rays of the sun, and that the defendants have cut and felled a large number of trees, and thus let in the sun and the wind and caused the waters to be diminished by evaporation, so that not as much flowed down on to plaintiff's land as formerly; and that they threatened to fell more of said trees in the future.

It is also averred, and found by the court, that said acts were done by defendants "solely for the purpose of injuring the plaintiff and damaging his said property, and out of spite and ill-will towards the plaintiff."

The court found that plaintiff was damaged in the sum of one cent by the alleged wrongs, for which amount judgment was rendered. By the judgment the defendants were also "perpetually enjoined" . . . "from cutting or felling the timbers and trees growing in the channel and upon the immediate banks of said stream at any point above the said lands of the plaintiff, whereby the said stream will be exposed to the rays of the sun and the waters thereof lost or materially diminished by evaporation."

[1] Statement rewritten. Only so much of the case is given as relates to a single point.

Defendants appealed from the judgment.

McFarland, J. [After discussing the question of motive.]

. . . Under the facts found we cannot see how the lawfulness of the acts enjoined can depend upon the motives by which they were done, or may be done in the future.

It is found that the defendants did fell trees on their lands, and threatened to fell more, the effect of which was, and would be, to let in the sun and winds, and thus increase evaporation.

. . . .

It is quite apparent that cutting trees upon one's own land is a lawful act, which cannot be restrained because it "lets in the sun" and causes more evaporation; any incidental damage which might come to a lower riparian owner from such lawful act would clearly be *damnum absque injuria.*

. . . .

Judgment reversed.

Temple, J., and Henshaw, J., concurred.

ALLEN *v.* FLOOD

In the House of Lords, December 14, 1897.

Reported in [1898] *Appeal Cases,* 1.

The plaintiffs (now the respondents), Flood and Taylor, are members of the Shipwrights' Provident Union.[1] The defendant (now the appellant), Allen, is a member and the London delegate of the Independent Society of Boilermakers and Iron and Steel Shipbuilders. The latter society restricts the labor of its members to ironwork. The society of shipwrights permits its members to work either in wood or iron. The members of the boilermakers' society are accustomed to claim that the proper business of shipwrights is to work in wood only, and that shipwrights who work in iron are trespassing on the trade of the boilermakers' union.[2]

In April, 1894, about forty men of the boilermakers' society were engaged at the Regent Dock, Millwall, in repairing an iron ship, on the employment of the Glengall Iron Company. Flood and Taylor were at the same time employed by the Glengall Company to execute repairs upon the woodwork of the vessel. By the terms of their employment they were entitled to leave at the close of any day; and the Glengall Company might, at the close of any day cease to employ them further. The ironworkers were employed on similar terms.[3]

[1] Statement rewritten. Arguments omitted. Some of the opinions are entirely omitted, and none are given in full.

[2] . . . "The litigants are members of two rival associations of workingmen, registered under the Trade Unions Act of 1871." . . . Lord Watson, [1898] A. C., p. 90. "It is not a dispute between employers and employed, — between capital and labor, — but rather one between the members of one trade union and of another trade union." . . . Lord Ashbourne, *ibid.* p. 109. "Each party had the financial support of their union." Lord Macnaghten, p. 147.

[3] As to the terms of the ironworkers' employment, see Lord Watson, pp. 90, 99, and Lord Herschell, p. 130.

The boilermakers, on discovering that Flood and Taylor had shortly before been employed by another firm (Mills & Knight) on the Thames in doing ironwork on a ship, became much excited, and began to talk of leaving their employment. One of them telegraphed for Allen, their London delegate. Allen came, dissuaded them from leaving work at dinner-time, and told them that they must wait and see how things were settled. Allen then had an interview with Halkett, the Glengall Company's manager. As to what took place at this interview, the testimony at the subsequent trial was conflicting. The version most favorable to the plaintiffs was substantially as follows: —

Allen told Halkett that he (Allen) had been sent for because Flood and Taylor were known to have done ironwork in Mills & Knight's yard, and that unless Flood and Taylor were discharged all the members of the boilermakers' society would be "called out" or "knock off" work that day; that Halkett had no option; that there was no ill-feeling towards the Glengall Company or towards Flood and Taylor personally,[1] but that the iron-men were doing their best to put an end to the practice of shipwrights doing ironwork, and that wherever these men were employed, or other shipwrights who had done ironwork, the boilermakers would cease work, — in every yard on the Thames.

If the boilermakers had been called out, it would have stopped the Glengall Company's business. For fear that the threat would be carried out, Halkett discharged Flood and Taylor at the close of the day.

An action was then brought by Flood and Taylor against three persons, viz., Allen, the London delegate; Jackson, the chairman; and Knight, the general secretary of the Boilermakers' Society.[2] The plaintiffs' allegations were: that the defendants, maliciously and wrongfully and with intent to injure the plaintiffs, procured and induced the Glengall Company to break their contract with the plaintiffs and not to enter into new contracts with them; and also, maliciously, etc., intimidated and coerced the Glengall Company to break their contract with plaintiffs and not to enter into new contracts, and also unlawfully and maliciously conspired with others to do the above acts.

The case was tried by jury before KENNEDY, J.

The learned judge ruled that there was not "a shred of evidence of any conspiracy at all;" that there was "no evidence of anything amounting to intimidation or coercion in any legal sense of the term;"[3] and that there was no breach of contract.

The following questions, among others, were put to the jury: —

1. Did the defendant Allen maliciously induce the Glengall Iron Company to discharge the plaintiffs or either of them from their employment?

2. Did the defendant Allen maliciously induce the Glengall Iron Company not to engage the plaintiffs or either of them?

In putting these questions to the jury, KENNEDY, J., gave some explanations, portions of which are, in substance, as follows:[4] "The word 'malice' is a word of art in law, and it does not mean in this case a personal dislike, a personal feeling of resentment against the two plaintiffs. It is clear from the

[1] See Lord Macnaghten, p. 146.

[2] It was *held*, both by Kennedy, J., and by the Court of Appeal, that Jackson and Knight were not liable. Upon this branch of the case there was no appeal to the House of Lords.

[3] See Lord Macnaghten, p. 148.

[4] The statement here given is compiled from extracts recited in the opinions of Lord Shand, p. 162, Lord Halsbury, p. 82, and Lord Macnaghten, p. 149.

evidence of the men and of their employers that there was no such personal feeling in this case. The question that I want you to answer is, that, if you find he induced the Glengall Iron Company, by the threat which is suggested by the plaintiffs of calling out all the men on strike, did he do that with the malicious intention which I have endeavored to explain, that is, merely, not for the purpose of forwarding that which he believed to be his interest as a delegate of his union in the fair consideration of that interest but for the purpose of injuring these plaintiffs, and preventing them doing that which they were each of them entitled to do. 'Maliciously' means, connected with the word 'induce,' this, — that it was not for the mere purpose of forwarding fairly Allen's own interests, but from the indirect motive of doing a mischief to the plaintiffs in their lawful business."

The jury answered both questions in the affirmative; and also found that each plaintiff had suffered 20*l.* damages.

After consideration, KENNEDY, J., entered judgment for the plaintiffs against Allen for 40*l.* This decision was affirmed by the Court of Appeal (LORD ESHER, M. R., LOPES and RIGBY, L. JJ.); L. R. (1895) 2 Q. B. 21.

Against these decisions, Allen brought the present appeal to the House of Lords. The appeal was first argued in December, 1895. Their Lordships having required further argument, the appeal was reargued in March and April, 1897. The following Judges were summoned to attend [1] at the second argument: HAWKINS, MATHEW, CAVE, NORTH, WILLS, GRANTHAM, LAWRENCE, and WRIGHT, JJ.

At the close of the arguments, the following question was propounded to the Judges: Assuming the evidence given by the plaintiffs' witnesses to be correct, was there any evidence of a cause of action fit to be left to the jury?

MATHEW, J., and WRIGHT, J., answered the question in the negative; and the other six Judges in the affirmative.

After the delivery of the opinions of the Judges, the House took time for consideration.

Dec. 14, 1897. LORD HALSBURY, L. C. . . . The first objection made to the plaintiff's right to recover for the loss which they thus undoubtedly suffered is that no right of the plaintiffs was infringed, and that the right contended for on their behalf is not a right recognized by law, or, at all events, only such a right as every one else is entitled to deprive them of if they stop short of physical violence or obstruction. I think the right to employ their labor as they will is a right both recognized by the law and sufficiently guarded by its provisions to make any undue interference with that right an actionable wrong.

Very early authorities in the law have recognized the right; and, in my view, no authority can be found which questions or qualifies it. The schoolmaster who complained that his scholars were being assaulted and brought an action, the quarry owner who complained that his servants were being menaced and molested, were both held to have a right of action. And it appears to me that the importance of those cases, and the principle established by them, have not been sufficiently considered. It is said that threats of violence or actual violence were unlawful means: the lawfulness of the means I will discuss hereafter. But the point on which these cases are important is the

[1] See Veeder, Advisory Opinions of the Judges in England, 13 Harv. Law Rev. 358.

existence of the right. It was not the schoolmaster who was assaulted; it was not the quarry owner who was assaulted or threatened; but, nevertheless, the schoolmaster was held entitled to bring an action in respect of the loss of scholars attending his school, and the quarry owner in respect of the loss of workmen to his quarry. They were third persons; no violence or threats were applied to them, and the cause of action, which they had a right to insist on, was the indirect effect upon themselves of violence and threats applied to others.

My Lords, in my view these are binding authorities to show that the preliminary question, namely, whether there was any right of the plaintiffs to pursue their calling unmolested, must be answered in the affirmative. The question of what is the right invaded would seem to be reasonably answered, and the universality of the right to all Her Majesty's subjects seems to me to be no argument against its existence. It is, indeed, part of that freedom from restraint, that liberty of action, which, in my view, may be found running through the principles of our law.

. . . .

First it is said that the company were acting within their legal rights in discharging the plaintiffs. So they were; but does that affect the question of the responsibility of the person who caused them so to act by the means he used? The scholars who went away from the school were entitled to do so. The miners were entitled to cease working at the quarry. The natives were entitled to avoid running the risk of being shot; but the question is, What was the cause of their thus exercising their legal right?

The question must be whether what was done in fact, and what did in fact procure the dismissal of the plaintiff, was an actionable wrong or not. I have never heard that a man who was dismissed from his service by reason of some slander could not maintain an action against the slanderer because the master had a legal right to discharge him.

. . . .

It will be observed that Kennedy, J., draws a distinction between the conduct which he assumes to be lawful on Allen's part to do what he did do if it were merely for the purpose of forwarding that which he believed to be his interest as a delegate of his union in fair consideration of that interest on the one hand, and on the other hand his conduct if what he did was done for the purpose of injuring these plaintiffs.

My Lords, it appears to me that that is a direction of which the defendants cannot complain, since it puts what is to my mind an alternative more favorable to them. In my view, his belief that what he was doing was for his interest as a delegate of his union would not justify the doing of what he did do. It is alleged, and to my mind and to the mind of the jury proved, that the employers were compelled under pressure of the threats that he used to discharge the plaintiffs.

. . . .

But the objection made by the defendants appears to be that the word "malicious" adds nothing; that if the thing was lawful it was lawful absolutely; if it was not lawful it was unlawful, — the addition of the word "malicious" can make no difference. The fallacy appears to me to reside in the assumption that everything must be absolutely lawful or absolutely unlawful. There are many things which may become lawful or unlawful according to circumstances.

In a decision of this House it has undoubtedly been held that whatever a man's motives may be, he may dig into his own land and divert subterranean water which but for his so treating his own land might have reached his neighbor's land. But that is because the neighbor had no right to the flow of the subterranean water in that direction, and he had an absolute right to do what he would with his own property. But what analogy has such a case with the intentional inflicting of injury upon another person's property, reputation, or lawful occupation ? To dig into one's own land under the circumstances stated requires no cause or excuse. He may act from mere caprice, but his right on his own land is absolute, so long as he does not interfere with the rights of others.

But, referring to Bowen, L. J.'s observation, which to my mind is exactly accurate, " in order to justify the intentional doing of that which is calculated in the ordinary course of events to damage, and which does, in fact, damage another in that other person's property or trade," you must have some just cause or excuse.

Now, the word " malicious " appears to me to negative just cause or excuse; and without attempting an exhaustive exposition of the word itself, it appears to me that, if I apply the language of Bowen, L. J., it is enough to show that this was within the meaning of the law " malicious."

It appears to me that no better illustration can be given of the distinction on which I am insisting between an act which can be legally done and an act which cannot be so done because tainted with malice, than such a colloquy between the representative of the master and the representative of the men as might have been held on the occasion which has given rise to this action. If the representative of the men had in good faith and without indirect motive pointed out the inconvenience that might result from having two sets of men working together on the same ship, whose views upon the particular question were so diverse that it would be inexpedient to bring them together, no one could have complained; but if his object was to punish the men belonging to another union because on some former occasion they had worked on an iron ship, it seems to me that the difference of motive may make the whole difference between the lawfulness or unlawfulness of what he did.

I see it is suggested by one of your Lordships that the action for malicious prosecution is supposed to be an exception. I am not quite certain that I understand what is the proposition to which it is an exception. If it means that there is no other form of procedure known to the law wherein malice may make the distinction between a lawful and an unlawful act, I am unable to agree. Maliciously procuring a person to be made a bankrupt, maliciously and without reasonable or probable cause presenting a petition to wind up a company, or maliciously procuring an arrest, are equally cases wherein the state of mind of the person procuring the arrest may affect the question of the lawfulness or unlawfulness of the act done.

Again, in slander or libel the right to preserve one's character or business from attack appears to me quite as vague and general a right as it is suggested is the right to pursue one's occupation unmolested; and it cannot be denied that in both these cases the lawfulness or unlawfulness of what is said or written may depend upon the absence or presence of malice.

Doubtless there are cases in which the mere presence of malice in an act done will not necessarily give a right of action, since no damage may result; and in this case, however malicious Allen's intervention may have been, if the employers had defied Allen's threats instead of yielding to them, the plaintiffs could not have succeeded in an action, because they would not have been injured: see Quartz Hill Co. *v.* Eyre, 11 Q. B. D. 674; Gibbs *v.* Pike, 9 M. & W. 351; Jenings *v.* Florence, (1857) 2 C. B. (N. S.) 467.

. . . .

LORD WATSON. . . . There is no expression in the verdict which can be held, either directly or by implication, to impeach the legality of the company's conduct in discharging the respondents. The mere fact of an employer discharging or refusing to engage a workman does not imply or even suggest the absence of his legal right to do either as he may choose. It is true that the company is not a party to this suit; but it is also obvious that the character of the act induced, whether legal or illegal, may have a bearing upon the liability in law of the person who procured it. The whole pith of the verdict, in so far as it directly concerns the appellant, is contained in the word "maliciously," — a word which is susceptible of many different meanings. The expression "maliciously induce," as it occurs upon the face of the verdict, is ambiguous: it is capable of signifying that the appellant knowingly induced an act which of itself constituted a civil wrong, or it may simply mean that the appellant procured, with intent to injure the respondents, an act which, apart from motive, would not have amounted to a civil wrong; and it is, in my opinion, material to ascertain in which of these senses it was used by the jury.

Although the rule may be otherwise with regard to crimes, the law of England does not, according to my apprehension, take into account motive as constituting an element of civil wrong. Any invasion of the civil rights of another person is in itself a legal wrong, carrying with it liability to repair its necessary or natural consequences, in so far as these are injurious to the person whose right is infringed, whether the motive which prompted it be good, bad, or indifferent. But the existence of a bad motive, in the case of an act which is not in itself illegal, will not convert that act into a civil wrong for which reparation is due. A wrongful act, done knowingly and with a view to its injurious consequences, may, in the sense of law, be malicious; but such malice derives its essential character from the circumstance that the act done constitutes a violation of the law. There is a class of cases which have sometimes been referred to as evidencing that a bad motive may be an element in the composition of civil wrong; but in these cases the wrong must have its root in an act which the law generally regards as illegal, but excuses its perpetration in certain exceptional circumstances from considerations of public policy. These are well known as cases of privilege, in which the protection which the law gives to an individual who is within the scope of these considerations consists in this, — that he may with immunity commit an act which is a legal wrong and but for his privilege would afford a good cause of action against him, all that is required in order to raise the privilege and entitle him to protection being that he shall act honestly in the discharge of some duty which the law recognizes, and shall not be prompted by a desire to injure the person who is affected by his act. Accordingly, in a suit brought by that person, it is usual for him to allege and necessary for him to prove an intent to injure in order to destroy the privilege of the defendant. But none of these cases tend to establish that an act which does not amount to a legal wrong, and therefore needs no protection, can have privilege attached to it; and still less that an act in itself lawful is converted into a legal wrong if it was done from a bad motive.

[After quoting from BOWEN, L. J., in Mogul Steamship Co. *v.* McGregor, and BAYLEY, J., in Bromage *v.* Prosser.]

The root of the principle is that, in any legal question, malice depends, not upon evil motive which influenced the mind of the actor, but upon the illegal character of the act which he contemplated and committed. In my opinion it is alike consistent with reason and common sense that when the act done is, apart from the feelings which prompted it, legal, the civil law ought to take no cognizance of its motive.

It does not appear to me to admit of doubt that the jury, in finding the action of the company to have been maliciously induced by the appellant, simply meant to affirm that the appellant was influenced by a bad motive, namely, an intention to injure the respondents in their trade or calling of shipwrights.

. . . .

There are, in my opinion, two grounds only upon which a person who procures the act of another can be made legally responsible for its consequences. In the first place, he will incur liability if he knowingly and for his own ends induces that other person to commit an actionable wrong. In the second place, when the act induced is within the right of the immediate actor, and is therefore not wrongful in so far as he is concerned, it may yet be to the detriment of a third party; and in that case, according to the law laid down by the majority in Lumley *v.* Gye, 2 E. & B. 216, the inducer may be held liable if he can be shown to have procured his object by the use of illegal means directed against that third party.

. . . .

Asssuming that the Glengall Iron Company, in dispensing with the further services of the respondents, were guilty of no wrong, I am willing to take it that any person who procured their act might incur responsibility to those who were injuriously affected by it, if he employed unlawful means of inducement directed against them. According to the decision of the majority in Lumley *v.* Gye, 2 E. & B. 216, already referred to, a person who by illegal means, that is, means which in themselves are in the nature of civil wrongs, procures the lawful act of another, which act is calculated to injure, and does injure, a third party, commits a wrong for which he may be made answerable. So long as the word " means " is understood in its natural and proper sense, that rule appears to me to be intelligible; but I am altogether unable to appreciate the loose logic which confounds internal feeling with outward acts, and treats the motive of the actor as one of the means employed by him.

It has been maintained, and some of the learned judges who lent their assistance to the House have favored the argument, that the appellant used coercion as a means of compelling the Glengall Iron Company to terminate their connection with the respondents; but that conclusion does not appear to me to be the fair result of the evidence. If coercion, in the only legal sense of the term, was employed, it was a wrong done as much to the Glengall Iron Company, who are the parties said to have been coerced, as to the respondents. Its result might be prejudicial to the respondents, but its efficacy wholly depended upon its being directed against and operating upon the company. It must be kept in view that the question of what amounts to wrongful coercion in a legal sense involves the same considerations which I have discussed in relation to the elements of a civil wrong as committed by the immediate actor. According to my opinion, coercion, whatever be its nature, must, in order to infer the legal liability of the person who employs it, be intrinsically and irrespectively of its motive a wrongful act. According to the doctrine ventilated in Temperton *v.* Russell, [1893] 1 Q. B. 715, and the present case it need not amount to a wrong, but will become wrongful if it was prompted by a bad motive.

. . . .

I have already indicated that, in my opinion, no light is thrown upon the decision of the present question by Pitt *v.* Donovan, 1 M. & S. 639, and other cases of that class. The defendant had in that case represented, contrary to the fact, that the plaintiff was insane at the time when he executed a particular deed. The communication was made to a person to whom the defendant was under a legal duty to make the disclosure if it had been true; and the defendant was in law absolved from the ordinary consequences of his having circulated a libel which was false and injurious, if he honestly believed it to be true. The law applicable in cases of that description is, I apprehend, beyond all doubt; but the rule by which the law in certain exceptional cases excuses the perpetration of a wrong, by reason of the absence of evil motive, is insufficient to establish or to support the converse and very different proposition, that the presence of an evil motive will convert a legal act into a legal wrong.

. . . .

[The opinions of LORD ASHBOURNE, and LORD MORRIS, concurring with LORD HALSBURY, are omitted.]

LORD HERSCHELL.

. . . .

Great stress was laid at the bar on the circumstance that in an action for maliciously and without reasonable and probable cause putting in motion legal process an evil motive is an essential ingredient. I have always understood and I think that has been the general understanding, that this was an exceptional case. The person against whom proceedings have been initiated without reasonable and probable cause is *prima facie* wronged. It might well have been held that an action always lay for thus putting the law in motion. But I apprehend that the person taking proceedings was saved from liability if he acted in good faith because it was thought that men might otherwise be too much deterred from enforcing the law, and that this would be disadvantageous to the public. Some of the learned judges cite actions of libel and slander as instances in which the legal liability depends on the presence or absence of malice. I think this is a mistake. The man who defames another by false allegations is liable to an action, however good his motive, and however honestly he believed in the statement he made. It is true that in a limited class of cases the law, under certain circumstances, regards the occasion as privileged, and exonerates the person who has made false defamatory statements from liability if he has made them in good faith. But if there be not that duty or interest which in law creates the privilege, then, though the person making the statements may have acted from the best of motives, and felt it his duty to make them, he is none the less liable. The gist of the action is that the statement was false and defamatory. Because in a strictly limited class of cases the law allows the defence that the statements were made in good faith, it seems to me, with all deference, illogical to affirm that malice constitutes one of the elements of the torts known to the law as libel and slander. But even if it could be established that in cases falling within certain well-defined categories, it is settled law that an evil motive renders actionable acts otherwise innocent, that is surely far from showing that such a motive always makes actionable acts prejudicial to another which are otherwise lawful, or that it does so in cases like the present utterly dissimilar from those within the categories referred to.

. . . .

If the fact be that malice is the gist of the action for inducing or procuring an act to be done to the prejudice of another, and not that the act induced or procured is an unlawful one as being a breach of contract or otherwise, I can see no possible ground for confining the action to cases in which the thing induced is the not entering into a contract. It seems to me that it must equally lie in the case of every lawful act which one man induces another to do where his purpose is to injure his neighbor or to benefit himself at his expense. I cannot hold that such a proposition is tenable in principle, and no authority is to be found for it. I should be the last to suggest that the fact that there was no precedent was in all cases conclusive against the right to maintain an action. It is the function of the Courts to apply established legal principles to the changing circumstances and conditions of human life. But the motive of injuring one's neighbor or of benefiting one's self at his expense is as old as human nature. It must for centuries have moved men in countless instances to persuade others to do or to refrain from doing particular acts. The fact that under such circumstances no authority for an action founded on these elements has been discovered does go far to show that such an action cannot be maintained.

. . . .

I now proceed to consider on principle the proposition advanced by the respondents, the alleged authorities for which I have been discussing. I do not doubt that every one has a right to pursue his trade or employment without "molestation" or "obstruction," if those terms are used to imply some act in itself wrongful. This is only a branch of a much wider proposition, namely, that every one has a right to do any lawful act he pleases without molestation or obstruction. If it be intended to assert that an act not otherwise wrongful always becomes so if it interferes with another's trade or employment, and needs to be excused or justified, I say that such a proposition in my opinion has no solid foundation in reason to rest upon. A man's right not to work or not to pursue a particular trade or calling, or to determine when or where or with whom he will work, is in law a right of precisely the same nature, and entitled to just the same protection as a man's right to trade or work. They are but examples of that wider right of which I have already spoken. That wider right embraces also the right of free speech. A man has a right to say what he pleases, to induce, to advise, to exhort, to command, provided he does not slander or deceive or commit any other of the wrongs known to the law of which speech may be the medium. Unless he is thus shown to have abused his right, why is he to be called upon to excuse or justify himself because his words may interfere with some one else in his calling?

. . . .

[After stating the case of Mogul Steamship Co. *v.* McGregor.]

It was said that this was held lawful because the law sanctions acts which are done in furtherance of trade competition. I do not think the decision rests on so narrow a basis, but rather on this, that the acts by which the competition was pursued were all lawful acts, that they were acts not in themselves wrongful, but a mere exercise of the right to contract with whom, and when, and under what circumstances and upon what conditions they pleased. I am aware of no ground for saying that competition is regarded with special favor by the law; at all events, I see no reason why it should be so regarded. It may often press as hardly on individuals as the defendant's acts are alleged to have done in the present case. But if the alleged exception could be established, why is not the present case within it ? What was the object of the defendant, and the workmen he represented, but to assist themselves in their competition with the shipwrights ? A man is entitled to take steps to compete to the best advantage in the employment of his labor, and to shut out, if he can, what he regards as unfair competition, just as much as if he was carrying on the business of a shipowner. The inducement the appellant used to further his end was the prospect that the members of his union would not work in company with what they deemed unfair rivals in their calling. What is the difference between this case and that of a union of shipowners who induce merchants not to enter into contracts with the plaintiffs, by the prospect that if at any time they employ the plaintiffs' ships they will suffer the penalty of being made to pay higher charges than their neighbors at the time when the defendants' ships alone visit the ports? In my opinion there is no difference in principle between the two cases.

. . . .

LORD MACNAGHTEN. My Lords, I am sorry to say that I must begin by recapitulating the facts of the case. For the findings of the jury, taken by themselves, do not convey to my mind any definite meaning. The jury have found that the appellant Allen " maliciously induced " the Glengall Iron Company to discharge the respondents from their service, and they have awarded damages in consequence. I do not know what the jury meant by the word " induced; " I am not sure that I know what they meant by the word " maliciously." Sometimes, indeed, I rather doubt whether I quite understand that unhappy expression myself. I am therefore compelled to turn for help to the evidence at the trial, accepting, as I suppose the jury must have accepted, the account given by the respondents in preference to that offered by the appellant wherever there may be any shadow of difference between them.

[After a full statement of the evidence.]

Now before I proceed to consider the legal grounds on which Kennedy, J., and the Court of Appeal decided the case against Allen, I should like to ask what there was wrong in Allen's conduct. He had nothing to do with the origin of the ill-feeling against Flood and Taylor. He did nothing to increase it. He went to the dock simply because he was sent for by one of the men of his union. It seems to be considered the duty of a district delegate to listen to the grievances of the members of his union within his district, and to settle the difficulty if possible. The jury found that the settlement of this dispute was a matter within Allen's discretion. The only way in which he could settle it was by going and seeing the manager. There was surely nothing wrong in that. There was nothing wrong in his telling the manager that the iron-men would leave their work unless the two shipwrights against whom they had a grudge were dismissed, if he really believed that that was what his men intended to do. As far as their employers were concerned, the iron-men were perfectly free to leave their work for any reason, or for no reason, or even for a bad reason; any one of them might have gone singly to the manager, or they might have gone to him all together (if they went quietly and peaceably), and told him that they would not stay any longer with Flood and Taylor at work among them.

If so, it is difficult to see why fault should be found with Allen for going in their place and on their behalf and saying what they would have said themselves.

. . . .

As regards the meaning of the word "induce," I do not think the jury got much assistance. I rather gather from the summing-up that the jury were given to understand that if they thought that Allen merely represented the state of things as it was — and the feeling of the iron-men at the Regent's Dock — they would be at liberty to answer the questions put to them about Allen in the negative. But the answer must be the other way if they thought that Allen went further, and assumed to represent the union, and to speak as if he had the power of the union at his back; that would be a threat and would amount to "inducing." Now, I must say that I do not think it can be said that Allen did "induce" the company to discharge the plaintiffs. Certainly it cannot be truly said that he procured them to be discharged. It was not his act that prevented the company from continuing to employ them. If the whole story had been a fiction and an invention on his part I could have understood the finding of the jury. But I do not think there was any misrepresentation on Allen's part. I do not think there was any exaggeration. Nor, indeed, was any such point made at the trial.

. . . .

So we see now, I think, what the findings of the jury come to, if they are to be treated as being in accordance with the evidence. They must mean that Allen induced the company to discharge the plaintiffs, by representing to the manager, not otherwise than in accordance with the truth, the state of feeling in the yard, and the intentions of the workmen, and that he did so "maliciously," because he must have known what the issue of his communication to the manager would be, and naturally perhaps he was not sorry to see an example made of persons obnoxious to his union. But is his conduct actionable? It would be very singular if it were. No action would lie against the company for discharging the two shipwrights. No action would lie against the iron-men for striking against them. No action would lie against the officers of the union for sanctioning such a strike. But if the respondents are right the person to answer in damages is the man who happened to be the medium of communication between the iron-men and the company, — the most innocent of the three parties concerned, for he neither set the "agitation" on foot, nor did he do anything to increase it, nor was his the order that put an end to the connection between employer and employed. It seems to me that the result would have been just the same if Edmonds had told Mr. Halkett what was going on in the yard, or if Mr. Halkett had learned it from Flood and Taylor themselves.

Even if I am wrong in my view of the evidence and the verdict, if the verdict amounts to a finding that Allen's conduct was malicious in every sense of the word, and that he procured the dismissal of Flood and Taylor, that is, that it was his act and conduct alone which caused their dismissal, and if such a verdict were warranted by the evidence, I should still be of opinion that judgment was wrongly entered for the respondents. I do not think that there is any foundation in good sense or in authority for the proposition that a person who suffers loss by reason of another doing or not doing some act which that other is entitled to do or to abstain from doing at his own will and pleasure, whatever his real motive may be, has a remedy against a third person who, by persuasion or some other means not in itself unlawful, has brought about the act or omission from which the loss comes, even though it could be proved that such person was actuated by malice towards the plaintiff, and that his conduct, if it could be inquired into, was without justification or excuse.

The case may be different where the act itself to which the loss is traceable involves some breach of contract or some breach of duty, and amounts to an interference with legal rights. There the immediate agent is liable, and it may well be that the person in the background who pulls the strings is liable too, though it is not necessary in the present case to express any opinion on that point.

But if the immediate agent cannot be made liable, though he knows what he is about, and what the consequences of his action will be, it is difficult to see on what principle a person less directly connected with the affair can be made responsible unless malice has the effect of converting an act not in itself illegal or improper into an actionable wrong. But if that is the effect of malice, why is the immediate agent to escape? Above all, why is he to escape when there is no one else to blame and no one else answerable? And yet many cases may be put of harm done out of malice without any remedy being available at law. Suppose a man takes a transfer of a debt with which he has no concern for the purpose of ruining the debtor, and then makes him bankrupt out of spite, and so intentionally causes him to lose some benefit under a will or settlement, — suppose a man declines to give a servant a character because he is offended with the servant for leaving, — suppose a person of position takes away his custom from a country tradesman in a small village merely to injure him on account of some fancied grievance not connected with their dealings in the way of buying and selling, — no one, I think, would suggest that there could be any remedy at law in any of those cases. But suppose a customer, not content with taking away his own custom, says something not slanderous or otherwise actionable or even improper in itself to induce a friend of his not to employ the tradesman any more. Neither the one nor the other is liable for taking away his own custom. Is it possible that the one can be made liable for inducing the other not to employ the person against whom he has a grudge? If so, a fashionable dressmaker might now and then, I fancy, be plaintiff in a very interesting suit. The truth is, that questions of this sort belong to the province of morals rather than to the province of law. Against spite and malice the best safeguards are to be found in self-interest and public opinion. Much more harm than good would be done by encouraging or permitting inquiries into motives when the immediate act alleged to have caused the loss for which redress is sought is in itself innocent or neutral in character, and one which anybody may do or leave undone without fear of legal consequences. Such an inquisition would, I think, be intolerable, to say nothing of the probability of injustice being done by juries in a class of cases in which there would be ample room for speculation and wide scope for prejudice.

In order to prevent any possible misconstruction of the language I have used, I should like to add that in my opinion the decision of this case can have no bearing on any case which involves the element of oppressive combination. The vice of that form of terrorism commonly known by the name of "boycotting," and other forms of oppressive combination, seems to me to depend on considerations which are, I think, in the present case, conspicuously absent.

. . . .

LORD SHAND. . . . The case was one of competition in labor, which, in my opinion, is in all essentials analogous to competition in trade, and to which the same principles must apply; and I ask myself what would be the thought of the application of the word " malicious " to the conduct of a tradesman who induces the customer of another tradesman to cease making purchases from one with whom he had long dealt, and instead to deal with him, a rival in trade. The case before the jury was, in my view, in no way different, except that in the one case there was competition in labor, — in the other there would be competition in trade.

Some of the learned consulted judges speak of Allen's conduct as having been caused by a desire to inflict " punishment " on the shipwrights for past acts, and indicate that, if the shipwrights had been actually working at iron-work on the vessel at the time, the case would have been different.[1]

I cannot agree in any such view. " Punishment " in a wide and popular sense may possibly be used, though incorrectly, to describe the boilermakers' action; but it is quite clear that what they were resolved to do, and really did, was, while marking their sense of the injury which they thought (rightly or wrongly is not the question) the shipwrights were doing to them in trenching on their proper lines of business, to take a practical measure in their own defence. Their object was to benefit themselves in their own business as working boilermakers, and to prevent a recurrence in the future of what they considered an improper invasion on their special department of work. How this could possibly be regarded as " malicious," even in any secondary sense that can reasonably be attributed to that term, I cannot see.

. . . .

Coming now directly to the merits of the question in controversy in the case, the argument of the plaintiffs and the reasons for the opinions of the majority of the consulted judges seem to me to fail, because, although it is no doubt true that the plaintiffs were entitled to pursue their trade as workmen " without hindrance," their right to do so was qualified by an equal right, and indeed the same right, on the part of other workmen. The hindrance must not be of an unlawful character. It must not be by unlawful action. Amongst the rights of all workmen is the right of competition. In the like manner and to the same extent as a workman has a right to pursue his work or labor without hindrance, a trader has a right to trade without hindrance. That right is

[1] . . . " There is no ground for even a suggestion that the defendant's acts were due to competition in trade or employment. There could be no competition between the two sets of men in the circumstances under which they were then working, the one at wood, the other at iron only; and even if they were competing, the plaintiffs were working well within their right." Hawkins, J., p. 23. " Now, although according to the principles of the Mogul Case the action of Allen might have been justified on the principles of trade competition, if it had been confined to the time when the respondents were doing ironwork, and were therefore acting in competition with the boilermakers, it appears to me that as soon as he overstepped those limits, and induced their employers to dismiss them by way of punishment, his action was without just cause or excuse, and, consequently, malicious within the legal meaning of that word." Cave, J., p. 37. "This action was not an effort, by competition, to enable the boilermakers to get the work instead, but to punish the plaintiffs by causing the employment of other shipwrights in their room." Lord Ashbourne, p. 111.

subject to the right of others to trade also, and to subject him to competition, — competition which is in itself lawful, and which cannot be complained of where no unlawful means (in the sense I have already explained) have been employed. The matter has been settled in so far as competition in trade is concerned by the judgment of this House in the Mogul Steamship Co. Case, [1892] A. C. 25. I can see no reason for saying that a different principle should apply to competition in labor. In the course of such competition, and with a view to secure an advantage to himself, I can find no reason for saying that a workman is not within his legal rights in resolving that he will decline to work in the same employment with certain other persons, and in intimating that resolution to his employers.

. . . .

[The opinions of LORD DAVEY and LORD JAMES OF HEREFORD, in favor of reversing the order of the Court of Appeal are omitted.]

Order of the Court of Appeal reversed and judgment entered for the appellant with costs here and below including the costs of the trial; cause remitted to the Queen's Bench Division.[1]

LEATHEM *v.* CRAIG

QUEEN'S BENCH DIVISION, IRELAND, NOVEMBER 22, 1898.
COURT OF APPEAL, IRELAND, MAY 2, 1899.

Reported in [1899] 2 *Irish Reports*, 667, 744.

QUINN *v.* LEATHEM

IN THE HOUSE OF LORDS, AUGUST 5, 1901.

Reported in [1901] *Appeal Cases*, 495.[2]

THIS was an action tried before FitzGibbon, L. J., at the Belfast Summer Assizes, 1896, brought against the defendants for damages for maliciously and wrongfully procuring certain persons to break contracts into which they had entered with the plaintiff, and not to enter into other contracts with the plaintiff; and for maliciously and wrongfully enticing and procuring certain workmen in the employment of such persons to leave the service of their employers and to break their contracts of service, with intent to injure the plaintiff,

[1] GERMAN CIVIL CODE, §§ 226, 826.

226. The exercise of a right is not permitted, when its sole object is to injure another.

826. Whoever intentionally inflicts damage upon another in a morally reprehensible manner is bound to compensate the other for the damage.

See also Digest, xxxix, 3, 1, § 12, xxxix, 3, 2, § 9; L. 17, 55; Domat, Civil Law (Cushing's ed.) § 158; Erskine, Institutes of the Law of Scotland, Bk. II, tit. 1, § 2; Bell, Principles of the Law of Scotland, § 966; Planiol, Traité Elémentaire de droit civil, (4 ed.), II, §§ 870–72; Windscheid, Lehrbuch des Pandektenrechts, I, § 121; Ames, How Far an Act May Be a Tort Because of the Wrongful Motive of the Actor, 18 Harvard Law Rev. 411; Walton, Motive as an Element in Torts in the Common and in the Civil Law, 22 Harvard Law Rev. 349.

[2] Some opinions are omitted. None are given in full. Arguments omitted.

and to prevent such persons from carrying out their contracts with the plaintiff, and from entering into other contracts with the plaintiff; and for maliciously and wrongfully intimidating such persons, and coercing them to break their contracts with the plaintiff; and intimidating such servants in their employ, and coercing them to leave the service of their employers, to the injury of the plaintiff; and for unlawfully conspiring, together with other persons, to do the acts aforesaid, with intent to injure the plaintiff.

There was also a paragraph in the statement of claim, claiming damages for the publication of the plaintiff's name in a " black list," issued by the defendants, and a prayer for an injunction to prevent the continuance and repetition of the acts complained of.

The following facts were proved. The plaintiff was a butcher at Lisburn, in the county of Antrim, about eight miles from Belfast, where he had carried on business for a number of years. He had in his employment one Robert Dickie, his foreman, who had been with him for ten years. The plaintiff had been in the habit of sending large quantities of meat to Andrew Munce, a butcher in Belfast, and had been doing so for some twenty years. There was no contract in writing between them; but, whatever amount the plaintiff sent, Munce took and paid for — the amount being, on an average, of the value of £30 a week.

The defendants John Craig, John Davey, and Joseph Quinn were butchers' assistants in Belfast; and the defendants, Henry Dornan and Robert Shaw, butchers' assistants in Lisburn. In the spring of 1895 these defendants and several others in the same occupation formed themselves into an association, which was duly registered under the Trade Union Acts, 1871 and 1876, under the title of " The Belfast Journeymen Butchers' Assistants' Association," of which the defendant Davey became the Secretary. The plaintiff's men were not members of the association. At the commencement of July, 1895, the defendants' association required the plaintiff to dismiss Robert Dickie from his employment, which he refused to do. Upon that the defendants' society threatened to withdraw the plaintiff's men from his service. A deputation was sent down to meet the plaintiff at Lisburn, and a meeting was held in Magill's public-house, Lisburn, on the 9th July, at which the defendants Craig, Quinn, Dornan, and Shaw were present — Craig being in the chair. The plaintiff stated that he had come on behalf of his men, and was ready to pay all fines and demands against them, and asked to have them admitted into the society. The defendant Shaw objected, and said that the plaintiff's men should be punished, and should be put out to walk the streets for twelve months. The plaintiff objected to this, as Dickie was a married man with a family. Shaw moved, and Morgan seconded a resolution that the plaintiff's assistants should be called out, and it was carried. The defendants stated that they could pick out plenty of men to work for the plaintiff from their list; the plaintiff replied that they were not suitable for his business, and refused to put his own men out. Craig then said that the plaintiff's meat would be stopped at Munce's, if the plaintiff would not comply with their wishes. The plaintiff still refused. The defendants then called out some of the plaintiff's employees. Edward Dickie, a servant of the plaintiff, was brought to a meeting of the defendants' society, held over Dornan's shop in Lisburn, and was ordered to leave the plaintiff, the society undertaking to pay him the same wages as he had been receiving from the plaintiff. Dickie, yielding to this order, left the plaintiff without notice. "Black lists" were issued by the society upon which the names of persons were posted who had offended against the society's rules. Leathem's name was posted, and also the name of John M'Bride, a flesher in Lisburn, who was dealing with the plaintiff. Subsequently, however, Dornan and others of the defendants came to M'Bride; and on his undertaking not to deal any more with Leathem, his name was struck out.

On the 6th September, 1895, the defendant Davey wrote to the plaintiff the following letter: —

"I have been instructed to write you if you would be kind enough to reply on or before Tuesday, 10th, whether you have made up your mind to continue to employ non-union labour. If you continue as at present, our society will be obliged to adopt extreme measures in your case. Trusting that you will see the wisdom of acceding to our views at once, I remain," &c.

On the 13th September, Davey wrote to Munce: —

"A deputation has been appointed to wait on you, or your responsible representative, on Monday evening, the 16th inst., at 6.30 p. m., to come to a decision in regard to this case of Leathem & Sons, as we are anxious to have a settlement at once."

To this Munce replied: —

"In reply to your letter *re* Leathem & Sons, I cannot see my way to attend any deputation of the sort, as it is quite out of my province to interfere with the liberty of any man. But why refer to me in this matter? I do not think it fair for you to come at me in the matter, seeing it appears to be the Messrs. Leathem that you wish to interfere with."

On the 16th September a deputation of the defendants' society went to Munce's establishment, and had an interview with W. F. Munce, the son of Andrew Munce, and asked him to put pressure on his father to stop dealing with the plaintiff. W. F. Munce replied by letter on the 17th September: —

"A deputation of the Journeymen Butchers' Association waited at Corn Market yesterday evening, with reference to the case of the purchase of meat from Henry Leathem, Lisburn. In accordance with promise, I placed the views of the deputation before Mr. Munce, and in reply he wishes to state he could not interfere to bring pressure to bear on Mr. Leathem to employ none but society men, by refusing to purchase meat from him, as that would be outside his province, and would be interfering with the liberty of another man; but at the same time he will strongly recommend Mr. Leathem to adopt the views of the Journeymen Butchers' Association, and employ men belonging to the society."

On the 18th September Davey wrote to Andrew Munce: —

" Have submitted your letter to committee. They are of opinion that in the main it is unsatisfactory, but thanking you kindly for your recommendation to Mr. Leathem, with whom we have endeavoured to make a satisfactory arrangement, but have failed; so therefore have no other alternative but to instruct your employees to cease work immediately Leathem's beef arrives."

On the 19th September Munce telegraphed to Leathem: —

" Unless you arrange with society you need not send any beef this week, as men are ordered to quit work."

Munce ceased to deal with the plaintiff, and the plaintiff was obliged to sell off the meat he had on hand at a heavy loss at any price he could get. In consequence of these transactions the plaintiff's business was ruined.

The case was tried before FitzGibbon, L. J., at the Summer Assizes of 1896, at Belfast. The defendants did not offer any evidence, their counsel asking for a direction on the grounds: 1, that to sustain the action a contract made with Leathem must be proved to have been made and broken through the acts of the defendants, and that there was no evidence of such contract or breach; 2, that there was no evidence of pecuniary damage to the plaintiff through the acts of the defendants; 3, that the ends of the defendants and the means taken by them to promote those ends as appearing in evidence were legitimate, and there was no evidence of actual damage to the plaintiff.

The learned Lord Justice declined to withdraw the case from the jury, and left to them the following questions: —

1. Did the defendants, or any of them, wrongfully and maliciously induce the customers or servants of the plaintiff named in the evidence to refuse to deal with the plaintiff? *Answer:* Yes.

2. Did the defendants, or any two or more of them maliciously conspire to induce the plaintiff's customers or servants named in the evidence, or any of them, not to deal with the plaintiff or not to continue in his employment; and were such persons so induced not so to do? *Answer:* Yes.

3. Did the defendants Davey, Dornan, and Shaw, or any of them, publish the " black lists " with intent to injure the plaintiff in his business; and, if so, did the publication so injure him? *Answer*. Yes.

FitzGibbon, L. J., in summing up, told the jury that pecuniary loss, directly caused by the conduct of the defendants, must be proved in order to establish a cause of action; and he advised them to require to be satisfied that such loss to a substantial amount had been proved by the plaintiff. He declined to tell them that, if actual and substantial pecuniary loss was proved to have been directly caused to the plaintiff by the wrongful acts of the defendants, they were bound to limit the amount of damages to the precise sum so proved. He told them that, if the plaintiff gave the proof of actual and substantial loss necessary to maintain the action, they were at liberty in assessing damages to take all the circumstances of the case, including the conduct of the defendants, reasonably into account. The Lord Justice did not tell the jury that the liability of the defendants depended on any question of law. He told them that the questions left to them were questions of fact to be determined on the evidence; but that they included questions as to the intent of the defendants, and, in particular, their intent to injure the plaintiff in his trade as distinguished from the intent of legitimately advancing their own interests. The Lord Justice did not tell the jury that the defendants could be directly asked what their own intention was, but he did tell them that their intention was to be inferred from their acts and conduct as proved, and that, in acting upon the evidence given by the plaintiff, they were at liberty to have regard to the fact that the defendants, who might have given the best evidence on the subject, had not been produced to explain, qualify, or contradict any of the evidence given for the plaintiff as to their own acts. Upon the meaning of the words "wrongfully and maliciously" in the questions, the Lord Justice told the jury that they had to consider whether the intent and actions of the defendants went beyond the limits which would not be actionable, namely, securing or advancing their own interests, or those of their trade, by reasonable means, including lawful combination, or whether their acts, as proved, were intended and calculated to injure the plaintiff in his trade, through a combination and with a common purpose, to prevent the free action of his customers and servants in dealing with him, with the effect of actually injuring him, as distinguished from acts legitimately done to secure or advance their own interests. Finally, he told the jury that acts done with the object of increasing the profits or raising the wages of any combination of persons such as the society to which the defendants belonged, whether employers or employed, by reasonable and legitimate means, were perfectly lawful and were not actionable so long as no wrongful act was maliciously — that is intentionally — done to injure a third party. To constitute such a wrongful act for the purposes of this case, the Lord Justice told the jury that they must be satisfied that there had been a conspiracy, a common intention, and a combination, on the part of the defendants to injure the plaintiff in his business; and that acts must be proved to have been done by the defendants in furtherance of that intention which had inflicted actual money loss upon the plaintiff in his trade; and that whether the acts of the defendants were or were not in that sense actionable, was the question which the jury had to try upon the evidence.

The jury found for the plaintiff with £250 damages, of which £50 was separately assessed for damages on the cause of action relating to the " black list," and £200 for damages on the other causes of action and judgment was thereupon entered for the plaintiff for £250 damages and costs.

The defendants now moved to set aside the verdict and judgment so had, and that judgment should be entered for them on the ground of misdirection; or for a new trial, on the ground that the damages were excessive, and that the jury were allowed to take the " black lists " into account.

WILLIAM O'BRIEN, J. . . .

The right infringed is the right to live by labor.

. . . .

Physical hindrances, or prevention of labor by physical means, it was conceded, would be the invasion of a right, and that would certainly be the case whether the restraint was applied to the employer or to the workman.

. . . .

If temporal loss were not coercion, it could be used to the degree of a person being starved. The proposition on which the judgment of the majority (in Allen *v.* Flood) was founded in this respect is opposed to the whole analogy of the law that makes duress of property, or menace of temporal loss, as effectual as physical violence to avoid all kinds of acts.

. . . .

In The Mogul Steamship Company *v.* M'Gregor, [1892] A. C. 25, the trade of the defendants was the primary object, and the injury to the plaintiffs was the result of the means taken to advance that object. There, as in Allen *v.* Flood, [1898] A. C. 1, the injury to others was the thing intended, as the means of carrying out another object.

. . . .

There is an observation which appears to me to gather up several of the fallacies which are scattered through the arguments in the judgments of the majority in Allen *v.* Flood, [1898] A. C. 1. The case is put by Lord Watson as if it were a question whether a person could be made liable for doing, from a malicious motive, what, without such motive he could do lawfully. In fact there are cases in law in which the malice makes the distinction of what is lawful or unlawful, as in malicious prosecution, or takes away the right that otherwise exists, as in the instance of privileged communication. But that is not the present case at all, as it was not that of Allen *v.* Flood, [1898] A. C. 1. The defendant, who maliciously instigated the thing, is not the person who possessed the power of dismissal. Therefore the supposed constitutional objection, that the law could not enter into a man's mind, has no place. The same point meets the case of the butler and the cook that was put in the argument. The butler tells his master he will leave unless the cook is dismissed. Lord Herschell snatched at the admission of counsel, that the cook could bring an action, as being the logical conclusion from his argument. With great respect, it is neither logical nor the law. The servant is the master of his own actions. He can choose his own company, though even for that object he cannot use threats. But in this case it was another person that assumed to choose his company for him. Allen was not a boiler-maker, as Craig was not a butcher, who wished to leave. Each was a member of a trade organization, and had no duty or interest of his own to interfere. What relation could such a position assume but that of intimidation?

. . . .

. . . a confusion of relations, in applying the proposition that a person cannot be made liable for maliciously exercising a right which he possesses. The action here is for maliciously causing another person to exercise a right which that other person possessed. In one case, the right may be said to absorb the malice, though there are exceptions to the rule in the common law. But how can it absorb another man's malice?

. . . .

What wrong can be conceived more cruel and grievous than wilfully depriving men of their employment? There must be a right, correlative to the wrong. What right can be more sacred than the right to live by a man's labor? But then, it is said, the wrong and the right are subject to the legal power of another person. That is the case in many instances, in which the law nevertheless gives a remedy for wrong that requires the exercise of another person's will. That is the case of a person who is defamed; the damage comes from those who hear. That is the case of malicious prosecution; the agency is that of the law. The servant who is enticed away from his master, leaves of his own will. The woman who left her husband, in Winsmore *v.* Greenbank, Willes, 577, did so with her own consent; the actress who broke her engagement, in Lumley *v.* Gye, 2 E. & B. 216, could have performed, if she liked. That is the case of tenants leaving their holdings on account of threats, which is put in 1 Rolle's Abridgment, 108; Action sur Case, (N.) pl. 21.

Many other examples could be given where the law allows a remedy, though the wrongful act requires the concurrence of another person's will. The rule is the same as to crimes. The law does not excuse instigation to crime because the other person need not commit the crime, or for the reason that it is impossible to separate the effect of the instigation and natural pravity of will, which was the ground erroneously assigned by Coleridge, J., for his opinion in Lumley *v.* Gye, 2 E. & B. 216. In fact the law makes no distinction between moral and physical agency, or the degrees of the influence, when the cause is attached to the consequence by the verdict of the jury.

. . . .

The law of conspiracy, which is traced down, in Comyn's Digest, and after him in the notes to Saunders' Reports, and in several English judgments as well as in the judgment in Kearney *v.* Lloyd, 26 L. R. Ir. 268, from the obsolete writ of conspiracy, through the action on the case in the nature of conspiracy, with their several distinctions, and which was originally confined to false accusations of crime, has widened out by the expansion of social conditions and the increase of wickedness, until it embraces in its modern extent every kind of wrong committed by several against another, and has been applied in a multitude of instances where the law gives no remedy against an individual, which was the utmost that was determined by Allen *v.* Flood, [1898] A. C. 1.

. . . .

. . . a malicious design to deprive a person of his livelihood, the malice being compounded both of the object, and the want of any just motive of personal right. For no one contended at any time that the object of drawing all persons into the pen of a trade union, was a ground of privilege like that which excused the act in The Mogul Steamship Co. *v.* M'Gregor, [1892] A. C. 25, where the defendants merely waged a war of rivalry in their trade. However, if " civil wrong " be understood in the sense of actionable wrong, the rule, so confined, is contrary to a multitude of cases, in which the action was adopted, and in which nevertheless it is most certain there was no legal remedy against a single defendant, even before the decision of Allen *v.* Flood, [1898] A. C. 1. Indeed, that is the express and special use of the action of conspiracy, without which it would find no real place in practice, though it is not impossible such an action could be maintained for what is actionable also in the case of an individual.

. . . .

There was in this case a direct design to injure the plaintiff. That was malice alone. The act was not done in exercise of any right the defendants possessed. It was done through the agency of another person by improperly influencing his will; and that will was moved solely by their act, and would not otherwise have been exercised. It was done by numbers, to which the law attaches a new and altered quality of more formidable wrong — the foundation of conspiracy — which is a difference in things themselves that can never be taken out of the law, civil or criminal, whilst there is a difference between a man and an army. Lastly, there was the damage which was so unjust as itself to make the act malicious.

. . . .

For the case put, of a person maliciously digging on his own land, and draining the well of his neighbor, is no exception, and demonstrates the weakness of the argument which is founded on it. In that case the act could not be prohibited without interfering with the inherent right of property; and the right of the neighbor was subject to the right of the contiguous owner. The two rights were equal. The right absorbed the malice, and could not otherwise co-exist with it. Here the defendants possessed no right which they could not otherwise exercise; and the right of the plaintiff to carry on his trade was not subject to any right in them. No right of interference with others, which the law could recognize, could attach to the aggressions of a trade union — to their plans for the revision of the relations between employers and employed — to proceedings conducting, by inevitable sequence, to what was lately expressed, with no less energy than the weight attaching to the author, as " the destructive demands of a class upon the fundamental laws on which civil order rests."

SIR P. O'BRIEN, L. C. J., and ANDREWS, J., delivered opinions in favor of denying defendants' motion.

PALLES, C. B., dissented, because he felt himself " coerced by the judgment of the House of Lords in Allen *v.* Flood. . . ."

The defendants' motion was refused with costs.

The case was then carried to the Irish Court of Appeal. In accordance with the opinions there delivered by LORD ASHBOURNE, CHANCELLOR, PORTER, M. R., WALKER, L. J., and HOLMES, L. J., the decision below, as to the verdict and judgment for £200, was affirmed with costs; the judgment for the plaintiff being amended by omitting the part as to the recovery of £50 damages which was separately assessed on account of the " black list."

HOLMES, L. J., said: " The ' black list ' was only an overt act of the conspiracy, and the sum awarded for it is included in the £200."

One of the defendants, Quinn, appealed to the House of Lords.

LORD CHANCELLOR HALSBURY, LORDS MACNAGHTEN, SHAND, BRAMPTON, ROBERTSON, and LINDLEY delivered opinions in favor of dismissing the appeal.

EARL OF HALSBURY, L. C.

. . . .

[As to the effect of the decision in Allen *v.* Flood.]

Now the hypothesis of fact upon which Allen *v.* Flood was decided by a majority in this House was that the defendant there neither uttered nor carried into effect any threat at all: he simply warned the plaintiff's employers of what the men themselves, without his persuasion or influence, had determined to do, and it was certainly proved that no resolution of the trade union had been arrived at at all, and that the trade union official had no authority himself to call out the men, which in that case was argued to be the threat which coerced the employers to discharge the plaintiff. It was further an element in the decision that there was no case of conspiracy or even combination.

What was alleged to be done was only the independent and single action of the defendant, actuated in what he did by the desire to express his own views in favor of his fellow-members. It is true that I personally did not believe that was the true view of the facts, but, as I have said, we must look at the hypothesis of fact upon which the case was decided by the majority of those who took part in the decision.

. . . .

LORD MACNAGHTEN.

. . . .

I do not think that the acts done by the defendants were done "in contemplation or furtherance of a trade dispute between employers and workmen." So far as I can see, there was no trade dispute at all. Leathem had no difference with his men. They had no quarrel with him. For his part he was quite willing that all his men should join the union. He offered to pay their fines and entrance moneys. What he objected to was a cruel punishment proposed to be inflicted on some of his men for not having joined the union sooner. There was certainly no trade dispute in the case of Munce. But the defendants conspired to do harm to Munce in order to compel him to do harm to Leathem, and so enable them to wreak their vengeance on Leathem's servants who were not members of the union.

. . . .

LORD LINDLEY.[1] My Lords, the case of Allen *v.* Flood, [1898] A. C. 1, has so important a bearing on the present appeal that it is necessary to ascertain exactly what this House really decided in that celebrated case. It was an action by two workmen of an iron company against three members of a trade union, namely, Allen and two others, for maliciously, wrongfully, and with intent to injure the plaintiffs, procuring and inducing the iron company to discharge the plaintiffs.[2] The action was tried before Kennedy, J., who ruled that there was no evidence to go to the jury of conspiracy, intimidation, coercion, or breach of contract. The result of the trial was that the plaintiffs obtained a verdict and judgment against Allen alone. He appealed, and the only question which this House had to determine was whether what he had done entitled the plaintiffs to maintain their action against him. What the jury found that he had done was, that he had maliciously induced the employers of the plaintiffs to discharge them, whereby the plaintiffs suffered damage. Different views were taken by the noble Lords who heard the appeal as to Allen's authority to call out the members of the union, and also as to the means used by Allen to induce the employers of the plaintiffs to discharge them; but, in the opinion of the noble Lords who formed the majority of

[1] Read by Lord Davey in Lord Lindley's absence.
[2] [1895] 2 Q. B. 22, 23; [1898] A. C. 3.

Your Lordships' House, all that Allen did was to inform the employers of the plaintiffs that most of their workmen would leave them if they did not discharge the plaintiffs.[1] There being no question of conspiracy, intimidation, coercion, or breach of contract, for consideration by the House, and the majority of their Lordships having come to the conclusion that Allen had done no more than I have stated, the majority of the noble Lords held that the action against Allen would not lie; that he had infringed no right of the plaintiffs; that he had done nothing which he had no legal right to do, and that the fact that he had acted maliciously and with intent to injure the plaintiffs did not, without more, entitle the plaintiffs to maintain the action.

My Lords, this decision, as I understand it, establishes two propositions: one a far-reaching and extremely important proposition of law, and the other a comparatively unimportant proposition of mixed law and fact, useful as a guide, but of a very different character from the first.

The first and important proposition is that an act otherwise lawful, although harmful, does not become actionable by being done maliciously in the sense of proceeding from a bad motive, and with intent to annoy or harm another. This is a legal doctrine not new or laid down for the first time in Allen *v.* Flood, [1898] A. C. 1; it had been gaining ground for some time, but it was never before so fully and authoritatively expounded as in that case. In applying this proposition care, however, must be taken to bear in mind, first, that in Allen *v.* Flood, [1898] A. C. 1, criminal responsibility had not to be considered. It would revolutionize criminal law to say that the criminal responsibility for conduct never depends on intention. Secondly, it must be borne in mind that even in considering a person's liability to civil proceedings the proposition in question only applies to "acts otherwise lawful," i. e., to acts involving no breach of duty, or, in other words, no wrong to any one. I shall refer to this matter later on.

The second proposition is that what Allen did infringed no right of the plaintiffs, even although he acted maliciously and with a view to injure them. I have already stated what he did, and all that he did, in the opinion of the majority of the noble Lords. If their view of the facts was correct, their conclusion that Allen infringed no right of the plaintiffs is perfectly intelligible, and indeed unavoidable. Truly, to inform a person that others will annoy or injure him unless he acts in a particular way cannot of itself be actionable, whatever the motive or intention of the informant may have been.

My Lords, the questions whether Allen had more power over the men than some of their Lordships thought, and whether Allen did more than they thought, are mere questions of fact. Neither of these questions is a question of law, and no court or jury, is bound as a

[1] [1898] A. C. p. 19, Lord Watson; p. 115, Lord Herschell; pp. 147–150, Lord Macnaghten; pp. 161, 165, Lord Shand; p. 175, Lord Davey; p. 178, Lord James.

matter of law to draw from the facts before it inferences of fact similar to those drawn by noble Lords from the evidence relating to Allen in the case before them.

I will pass now to the facts of this case, and consider (1) what the plaintiff's rights were; (2) what the defendants' conduct was; (3), whether that conduct infringed the plaintiff's rights. For the sake of clearness it will be convenient to consider these questions in the first place apart from the statute which legalizes strikes, and in the next place with reference to that statute.

1. As to the plaintiff's rights. He had the ordinary rights of a British subject. He was at liberty to earn his own living in his own way, provided he did not violate some special law prohibiting him from so doing, and provided he did not infringe the rights of other people. This liberty involved liberty to deal with other persons who were willing to deal with him. This liberty is a right recognized by law; its correlative is the general duty of every one not to prevent the free exercise of this liberty, except so far as his own liberty of action may justify him in so doing. But a person's liberty or right to deal with others is nugatory, unless they are at liberty to deal with him if they choose to do so. Any interference with their liberty to deal with him affects him. If such interference is justifiable in point of law, he has no redress. Again, if such interference is wrongful, the only person who can sue in respect of it is, as a rule, the person immediately affected by it; another who suffers by it has usually no redress; the damage to him is too remote, and it would be obviously practically impossible and highly inconvenient to give legal redress to all who suffered from such wrongs. But if the interference is wrongful and is intended to damage a third person, and he is damaged in fact — in other words, if he is wrongfully and intentionally struck at through others, and is thereby damnified — the whole aspect of the case is changed: the wrong done to others reaches him, his rights are infringed although indirectly, and damage to him is not remote or unforeseen, but is the direct consequence of what has been done. Our law, as I understand it, is not so defective as to refuse him a remedy by an action under such circumstances. The cases collected in the old books on actions on the case, and the illustrations given by the late Bowen, L. J., in his admirable judgment in the Mogul Steamship Company's Case, 23 Q. B. D. 613, 614, may be referred to in support of the foregoing conclusion, and I do not understand the decision in Allen *v.* Flood, [1898] A. C. 1, to be opposed to it.

If the above reasoning is correct, Lumley *v.* Gye, 2 E. & B. 216, was rightly decided, as I am of opinion it clearly was. Further, the principle involved in it cannot be confined to inducements to break contracts of service, nor indeed to inducements to break any contracts. The principle which underlies the decision reaches all wrongful acts done intentionally to damage a particular individual and actually damaging him. Temperton *v.* Russell, [1893] 1 Q. B. 715, ought to have been decided and may be upheld on this principle. That case was much criticised in Allen *v.* Flood, [1898] A. C. 1, and not without reason; for, according to the judgment of Lord Esher, the defendants' liability depended on motive or intention alone, whether anything wrong was done or not. This went too far, as was pointed out in Allen *v.* Flood, [1898] A. C. 1. But in Temperton *v.* Russell, [1893] 1 Q. B. 715, there was a wrongful act, namely, conspiracy and unjustifiable interference with Brentano, who dealt with the plaintiff. This wrongful act warranted the decision, which I think was right.

2. I pass on to consider what the defendants did. The appellant and two of the other defendants were the officers of a trade union, and the jury have found that the defendants wrongfully and maliciously induced the customers of the plaintiff to refuse to deal with him, and maliciously conspired to induce them not to deal with him. There were similar findings as to inducing servants of the plaintiff to leave him. What the defendants did was to threaten to call out the union workmen of the plaintiff and of his customers if he would not discharge some non-union men in his employ. In other words, in order to compel the plaintiff to discharge some of his men, the defendants threatened to put the plaintiff and his customers, and persons lawfully working for them, to all the inconvenience they could without using violence. The defendants' conduct was the more reprehensible because the plaintiff offered to pay the fees necessary to enable his non-union men to become members of the defendants' union; but this would not satisfy the defendants. The facts of this case are entirely different from those which this House had to consider in Allen *v.* Flood, [1898] A. C. 1. In the present case there was no dispute between the plaintiff and his men. None of them wanted to leave his employ. Nor was there any dispute between the plaintiff's customers and their own men, nor between the plaintiff and his customers, nor between the men they respectively employed. The defendants called no witnesses, and there was no evidence to justify or excuse the conduct of the defendants. That they acted as they did in furtherance of what they considered the interests of union men may probably be fairly assumed in their favor, although they did not come forward and say so themselves; but that is all that can be said for them. No one can, I think, say that the verdict was not amply warranted by the evidence. I have purposely said nothing about the black list, as the learned judge who tried the case considered that the evidence did not connect the appellant with that list. But the black list was, in my opinion, a very important feature in the case.

3. The remaining question is whether such conduct infringed the plaintiff's rights so as to give him a cause of action. In my opinion, it plainly did. The defendants were doing a great deal more than exercising their own rights: they were dictating to the plaintiff and his customers and servants what they were to do. The defendants were

violating their duty to the plaintiff and his customers and servants, which was to leave them in the undisturbed enjoyment of their liberty of action as already explained. What is the legal justification or excuse for such conduct? None is alleged and none can be found. This violation of duty by the defendants resulted in damage to the plaintiff — not remote, but immediate and intended. The intention to injure the plaintiff negatives all excuses and disposes of any question of remoteness of damage. Your lordships have to deal with a case, not of *damnum absque injuria*, but of *damnum cum injuria*.

Every element necessary to give a cause of action on ordinary principles of law is present in this case. As regards authorities, they were all exhaustively examined in the Mogul Steamship Co. *v.* MacGregor, [1892] A. C. 25, and Allen *v.* Flood, [1898] A. C. 1, and it is unnecessary to dwell upon them again. I have examined all those which are important, and I venture to say that there is not a single decision anterior to Allen *v.* Flood, [1898] A. C. 1, in favor of the appellant. His sheet anchor is Allen *v.* Flood, [1898] A. C. 1, which is far from covering this case, and which can only be made to cover it by greatly extending its operation.

It was contended at the bar that if what was done in this case had been done by one person only, his conduct would not have been actionable, and that the fact that what was done was affected by many acting in concert makes no difference. My Lords, one man without others behind him who would obey his orders could not have done what these defendants did. One man exercising the same control over others as these defendants had could have acted as they did, and, if he had done so, I conceive that he would have committed a wrong towards the plaintiff for which the plaintiff could have maintained an action. I am aware that in Allen *v.* Flood, [1898] A. C. 1, Lord Herschell, [1898] A. C. at pp. 128, 138, expressed his opinion to be that it was immaterial whether Allen said he would call the men out or not. This may have been so in that particular case, as there was evidence that Allen had no power to call out the men, and the men had determined to strike before Allen had anything to do with the matter. But if Lord Herschell meant to say that as a matter of law there is no difference between giving information that men will strike, and making them strike, or threatening to make them strike, by calling them out when they do not want to strike, I am unable to concur with him. It is all very well to talk about peaceable persuasion. It may be that in Allen *v.* Flood, [1898] A. C. 1, there was nothing more; but here there was very much more. What may begin as peaceable persuasion may easily become, and in trades union disputes generally does become, peremptory ordering, with threats open or covert of very unpleasant consequences to those who are not persuaded. Calling workmen out involves very serious consequences to such of them as do not obey. Black lists are real instruments of coercion, as every man whose name is on one soon discovers to his cost. A combination not to work is one thing, and is lawful. A combination to prevent others from working by annoying them if they do is a very different thing, and is *prima facie* unlawful. Again, not to work oneself is lawful so long as one keeps off the poor-rates, but to order men not to work when they are willing to work is another thing. A threat to call men out given by a trade union official to an employer of men belonging to the union and willing to work with him is a form of coercion, intimidation, molestation, or annoyance to them and to him very difficult to resist, and, to say the least, requiring justification. None was offered in this case.

My Lords, it is said that conduct which is not actionable on the part of one person cannot be actionable if it is that of several acting in concert. This may be so where many do no more than one is supposed to do. But numbers may annoy and coerce where one may not. Annoyance and coercion by many may be so intolerable as to become actionable, and produce a result which one alone could not produce. I am aware of the difficulties which surround the law of conspiracy both in its criminal and civil aspects; and older views have been greatly and, if I may say so, most beneficially modified by the discussions and decisions in America and this country. Amongst the American cases, I would refer especially to Vegelahn *v.* Guntner, 167 Mass. 92, where coercion by other means than violence, or threats of it, was held unlawful. In this country it is now settled by the decision of this House in the case of the Mogul Steamship Co., [1892] A. C. 25; 23 Q. B. D. 598, that no action for a conspiracy lies against persons who act in concert to damage another and do damage him, but who at the same time merely exercise their own rights and who infringe no rights of other people. Allen *v.* Flood, [1898] A. C. 1, emphasizes the same doctrine. The principle was strikingly illustrated in the Scottish Coöperative Society *v.* Glasgow Fleshers' Association, 35 Sc. L. R. 645, which was referred to in the course of the argument. In this case some butchers induced some salesmen not to sell meat to the plaintiffs. The means employed were to threaten the salesmen that if they continued to sell meat to the plaintiffs, they, the butchers, would not buy from the salesmen. There was nothing unlawful in this, and the learned judge held that the plaintiffs showed no cause of action, although the butchers' object was to prevent the plaintiffs from buying for coöperative societies in competition with themselves, and the defendants were acting in concert.

The cardinal point of distinction between such cases and the present is that in them, although damage was intentionally inflicted on the plaintiffs, no one's right was infringed — no wrongful act was committed; whilst in the present case the coercion of the plaintiff's customers and servants, and of the plaintiff through them, was an infringement of their liberty as well as his, and was wrongful both to them and also to him, as I have already endeavored to show.

Intentional damage which arises from the mere exercise of the rights of many is not, I apprehend, actionable by our law as now settled. To hold the contrary would be unduly to restrict the liberty of one set of persons in order to uphold the liberty of another set. According to our law, competition, with all its drawbacks, not only between individuals, but between associations, and between them and individuals, is permissible, provided nobody's rights are infringed. The law is the same for all persons, whatever their callings: it applies to masters as well as to men; the proviso, however, is all-important, and it also applies to both, and limits the rights of those who combine to lock-out as well as the rights of those who strike. But coercion by threats, open or disguised, not only of bodily harm but of serious annoyance and damage, is *prima facie*, at all events, a wrong inflicted on the persons coerced; and in considering whether coercion has been applied or not, numbers cannot be disregarded.

. . . .

I conclude this part of the case by saying that, in my opinion, the direction given to the jury by the learned judge who tried the case was correct, so far as the liability of the defendants turns on principles of common law, and that the objection taken to it by the counsel for the appellant is untenable. I mean the objection that the learned judge did not distinguish between coercion to break contracts of service, and coercion to break contracts of other kinds, and coercion not to enter into contracts.

I pass now to consider the effect of the statute 38 & 39 Vict. c. 86. [The opinion on this point is omitted.]

My Lords, I will detain your Lordships no longer. Allen *v.* Flood, [1898] A. C. 1, is in many respects a very valuable decision, but it may be easily misunderstood and carried too far.

Your Lordships are asked to extend it and to destroy that individual liberty which our laws so anxiously guard. The appellant seeks by means of Allen *v.* Flood, [1898] A. C. 1, and by logical reasoning based upon some passages in the judgments given by the noble Lords who decided it, to drive your Lordships to hold that boycotting by trades unions in one of its most objectionable forms is lawful, and gives no cause of action to its victims although they may be pecuniarily ruined thereby.

My Lords, so to hold would, in my opinion, be contrary to well-settled principles of English law, and would be to do what is not yet authorized by any statute or legal decision.

In my opinion this appeal ought to be dismissed with costs.

Order appealed from affirmed, and appeal dismissed with costs.[1]

[1] ENGLAND, TRADE DISPUTES ACT, 1906, 6 Ed. 7, c. 47.

1. — The following paragraph shall be added as a new paragraph after the first paragraph of section three of the Conspiracy and Protection of Property Act, 1875: —

"An act done in pursuance of an agreement or combination by two or more

VEGELAHN *v.* GUNTNER

SUPREME JUDICIAL COURT, MASSACHUSETTS, OCTOBER 26, 1896.

Reported in 167 *Massachusetts Reports*, 92.

BILL IN EQUITY against fourteen individual defendants and two trades unions.[1]

. . . .

The following decree was entered at a preliminary hearing upon the bill: "This cause came on to be heard upon the plaintiff's motion for a temporary injunction; and after due hearing, at which the several defendants, were represented by counsel, it is ordered, adjudged, and decreed that an injunction issue *pendente lite*, to remain in force until the further order of this court, or of some justice thereof, restraining the respondents and each and every of them, their agents

persons shall, if done in contemplation or furtherance of a trade dispute, not be actionable unless the act, if done without any such agreement or combination, would be actionable."

2. — (1) It shall be lawful for one or more persons, acting on their own behalf or on behalf of a trade union or of an individual employer or firm in contemplation or furtherance of a trade dispute, to attend at or near a house or place where a person resides or works or carries on business or happens to be, if they so attend merely for the purpose of peacefully obtaining or communicating information, or of peacefully persuading any person to work or abstain from working.

(2) Section seven of the Conspiracy and Protection of Property Act, 1875, is hereby repealed from "attending at or near" to the end of the section.

3. — An act done by a person in contemplation or furtherance of a trade dispute shall not be actionable on the ground only that it induces some other person to break a contract of employment or that it is an interference with the trade, business, or employment of some other person, or with the right of some other person to dispose of his capital or his labor as he wills.

4. — (1) An action against a trade union, whether of workmen or masters, or against any members or officials thereof on behalf of themselves and all other members of the trade union in respect of any tortious act alleged to have been committed by or on behalf of the trade union, shall not be entertained by any court.

(2) Nothing in this section shall affect the liability of the trustees of a trade union to be sued in the events provided for by the Trades Union Act, 1871, section nine, except in respect of any tortious act committed by or on behalf of the union in contemplation or in furtherance of a trade dispute.

5. — (1) This Act may be cited as the Trade Disputes Act, 1906, and the Trade Union Acts, 1871 and 1876, and this Act may be cited together as the Trade Union Acts, 1871 to 1906.

(2) In this Act the expression "trade union" has the same meaning as in the Trade Union Acts, 1871 and 1876, and shall include any combination as therein defined, notwithstanding that such combination may be the branch of a trade union.

(3) In this Act and in the Conspiracy and Protection of Property Act, 1875, the expression "trade dispute" means any dispute between employers and workmen, or between workmen and workmen, which is connected with the employment or non-employment, or the terms of the employment, or with the conditions of labor, of any person, and the expression "workmen" means all persons employed in trade or industry, whether or not in the employment of the employer with whom a trade dispute arises; and, in section three of the last-mentioned Act, the words "between employers and workmen" shall be repealed.

See Smith, Crucial Issues in Labor Litigation, 20 Harvard Law Rev. 345, 351, note 3.

[1] The statement has been abridged.

and servants, from interfering with the plaintiff's business by patrolling the sidewalk or street in front or in the vicinity of the premises occupied by him, for the purpose of preventing any person or persons who now are or may hereafter be in his employment, or desirous of entering the same, from entering it, or continuing in it; or by obstructing or interfering with such persons, or any others, in entering or leaving the plaintiff's said premises; or by intimidating, by threats or otherwise, any person or persons who now are or may hereafter be in the employment of the plaintiff, or desirous of entering the same, from entering it, or continuing in it; or by any scheme or conspiracy among themselves or with others, organized for the purpose of annoying, hindering, interfering with, or preventing any person or persons who now are or may hereafter be in the employment of the plaintiff, or desirous of entering the same, from entering it, or from continuing therein."

Hearing upon the bill and answers before Holmes, J., who reported the case for the consideration of the full court, as follows: —

"The facts admitted or proved are that, following upon a strike of the plaintiff's workmen, the defendants have conspired to prevent the plaintiff from getting workmen, and thereby to prevent him from carrying on his business unless and until he will adopt a schedule of prices which has been exhibited to him, and for the purpose of compelling him to accede to that schedule, but for no other purpose. If he adopts that schedule he will not be interfered with further. The means adopted for preventing the plaintiff from getting workmen are, (1) in the first place, persuasion and social pressure. And these means are sufficient to affect the plaintiff disadvantageously, although it does not appear, if that be material, that they are sufficient to crush him. I ruled that the employment of these means for the said purpose was lawful, and for that reason refused an injunction against the employment of them. If the ruling was wrong, I find that an injunction ought to be granted.

"(2) I find also, that, as a further means for accomplishing the desired end, threats of personal injury or unlawful harm were conveyed to persons seeking employment or employed, although no actual violence was used beyond a technical battery, and although the threats were a good deal disguised, and express words were avoided. It appeared to me that there was danger of similar acts in the future. I ruled that conduct of this kind should be enjoined.

"The defendants established a patrol of two men in front of the plaintiff's factory, as one of the instrumentalities of their plan. The patrol was changed every hour, and continued from half-past six in the morning until half-past five in the afternoon, on one of the busy streets of Boston. The number of men was greater at times, and at times showed some little inclination to stop the plaintiff's door, which was not serious, but seemed to me proper to be enjoined. The patrol proper at times went further than simple advice, not obtruded beyond the point where the other person was willing to listen, and conduct of that sort is covered by (2) above, but its main purpose was in aid of the plan held lawful in (1) above. I was satisfied that there was probability of the patrol being continued if not enjoined. I ruled that the patrol, so far as it confined itself to persuasion and giving notice of the strike, was not unlawful, and limited the injunction accordingly.

"There was some evidence of persuasion to break existing contracts. I ruled that this was unlawful, and should be enjoined.

"I made the final decree appended hereto. If, on the foregoing facts, it ought to be reversed or modified, such decree is to be entered as the full court may think proper; otherwise, the decree is to stand."

The final decree was as follows: "This cause came on to be heard, and was argued by counsel; and thereupon, on consideration thereof, it is ordered, adjudged, and decreed that the defendants, and each and every of them, their agents and servants, be restrained and enjoined from interfering with the plaintiff's business by obstructing or physically interfering with any persons in entering or leaving the plaintiff's premises numbered 141, 143, 145, 147 North Street in said Boston, or by intimidating, by threats, express or implied, of violence or physical harm to body or property, any person or persons who now are or hereafter may be in the employment of the plaintiff, or desirous of entering the same, from entering or continuing in it, or by in any way hindering, interfering with, or preventing any person or persons who now are in the employment of the plaintiff from continuing therein, so long as they may be bound so to do by lawful contract."

ALLEN, J. The principal question in this case is whether the defendants should be enjoined against maintaining the patrol. The report shows that, following upon a strike of the plaintiff's workmen, the defendants conspired to prevent him from getting workmen, and thereby to prevent him from carrying on his business, unless and until he should adopt a certain schedule of prices. The means adopted were persuasion and social pressure, threats of personal injury or unlawful harm conveyed to persons employed or seeking employment, and a patrol of two men in front of the plaintiff's factory, maintained from half-past six in the morning till half-past five in the afternoon, on one of the busiest streets of Boston. The number of men was greater at times, and at times showed some little disposition to stop the plaintiff's door. The patrol proper at times went further than simple advice, not obtruded beyond the point where the other person was willing to listen; and it was found that the patrol would probably be continued, if not enjoined. There was also some evidence of persuasion to break existing contracts.

The patrol was maintained as one of the means of carrying out the defendants' plan, and it was used in combination with social pressure, threats of personal injury or unlawful harm, and persuasion to break existing contracts. It was thus one means of intimidation indirectly to the plaintiff, and directly to persons actually employed, or seeking to be employed, by the plaintiff, and of rendering such employment unpleasant or intolerable to such persons. Such an act is an unlawful interference with the rights both of employer and of employed. An employer has a right to engage all persons who are willing to work for him, at such prices as may be mutually agreed upon; and persons employed or seeking employment have a corresponding right to enter into or remain in the employment of any person or corporation willing to employ them. These rights are secured by the Constitution itself. Commonwealth *v.* Perry, 155 Mass. 117; People *v.* Gillson, 109 N. Y. 389; Braceville Coal Co. *v.* People, 147 Ill. 66, 71; Ritchie *v.* People, 155 Ill. 98; Low *v.* Rees Printing Co., 41 Neb. 127. No one can lawfully interfere by force or intimidation to prevent employers or persons employed or wishing to be employed from the exercise of these rights. In Massachusetts, as in some other States, it is even made a criminal offence for one by intimidation or force to prevent or seek to prevent a person from entering into or continuing in the employment of a person or corporation. Pub. Sts. c. 74, § 2. Intimidation is not limited to threats of violence or of physical injury to person or property. It has a broader signification, and there also may be a moral intimidation which is illegal. Patrolling or picketing, under the circumstances stated in the report, has elements of intimidation like those which were found to exist in Sherry *v.* Perkins, 147 Mass. 212. It was declared to be unlawful in Regina *v.* Druitt, 10 Cox C. C. 592; Regina *v.* Hibbert, 13 Cox C. C. 82; and Regina *v.* Bauld, 13 Cox C. C. 282. It was assumed to be unlawful in Trollope *v.* London Building Trades Federation, 11 T. L. R. 228, though in that case the pickets were withdrawn before the bringing of the bill. The patrol was an unlawful interference both with the plaintiff and with the workmen, within the principle of many cases, and, when instituted for the purpose of interfering with his business, it became a private nuisance. See Carew *v.* Rutherford, 106 Mass. 1; Walker *v.* Cronin, 107 Mass. 555; Barr *v.* Essex Trades Council, 8 Dick. 101; Murdock *v.* Walker, 152 Penn. St. 595; Wick China Co. *v.* Brown, 164 Penn. St. 449; Cœur d'Alene Consolidated & Mining Co. *v.* Miners' Union, 51 Fed. Rep. 260; Temperton *v.* Russell, [1893] 1 Q. B. 715; Flood *v.* Jackson, 11 T. L. R. 276; Wright *v.* Hennessey, a case before Baron Pollock, 52 Alb. L. J. 104; Judge *v.* Bennett, 36 W. R. 103; Lyons *v.* Wilkins, [1896] 1 Ch. 811.

The defendants contend that these acts were justifiable, because they were only seeking to secure better wages for themselves by compelling the plaintiff to accept their schedule of wages. This motive or purpose does not justify maintaining a patrol in front of the plaintiff's premises, as a means of carrying out their conspiracy. A combination among persons merely to regulate their own conduct is within allowable competition, and is lawful, although others may be indirectly affected thereby. But a combination to do injurious acts expressly directed to another, by way of intimidation or constraint either of himself or of persons employed or seeking to be employed by him, is outside of allowable competition, and is unlawful. Various decided cases fall within the former class, for example: Worthington *v.* Waring, 157 Mass. 421; Snow *v.* Wheeler, 113 Mass. 179; Bowen *v.* Matheson, 14 Allen, 499; Commonwealth *v.* Hunt, 4 Met. 111; Heywood *v.* Tillson, 75 Maine, 225; Cote *v.* Murphy, 159 Penn. St. 420; Bohn Manuf. Co. *v.* Hollis, 54 Minn. 223; Mogul Steamship Co. *v.* McGregor, [1892] A. C. 25; Curran *v.* Treleaven, [1891] 2 Q. B. 545, 561. The present case falls within the latter class.

Nor does the fact that the defendants' acts might subject them to an indictment prevent a court of equity from issuing an injunction. It is true that ordinarily a court of equity will decline to issue an injunction to restrain the commission of a crime; but a continuing injury to property or business may be enjoined, although it may also be punishable as a nuisance or other crime. Sherry *v.* Perkins, 147 Mass. 212; *In re* Debs, 158 U. S. 564, 593, 599; Baltimore & Potomac Railroad *v.* Fifth Baptist Church, 108 U. S. 317, 329; Cranford *v.* Tyrell, 128 N. Y. 341, 344; Gilbert *v.* Mickle, 4 Sandf. Ch. 357; Mobile *v.* Louisville & Nashville Railroad, 84 Ala. 115, 126; Arthur *v.* Oakes, 63 Fed. Rep. 310; Toledo, Ann Arbor, & North Michigan Railway *v.* Pennsylvania Co., 54 Fed. Rep. 730, 744; Emperor of Austria *v.* Day, 3 DeG., F. & J. 217, 239, 240, 253; Hermann Loog *v.* Bean, 26 Ch. D. 306, 314, 316, 317; Monson *v.* Tussaud, [1894] 1 Q. B. 671, 689, 690, 698.

A question is also presented whether the court should enjoin such interference with persons in the employment of the plaintiff who are not bound by contract to remain with him, or with persons who are not under any existing contract, but who are seeking or intending to enter into his employment. A conspiracy to interfere with the plaintiff's business by means of threats and intimidation, and by maintaining a patrol in front of his premises in order to prevent persons from entering his employment, or in order to prevent persons who are in his employment from continuing therein, is unlawful, even though such persons are not bound by contract to enter into or to continue in his employment; and the injunction should not be so limited as to relate only to persons who are bound by existing contracts. Walker *v.* Cronin, 107 Mass. 555, 565; Carew *v.* Rutherford, 106 Mass. 1; Sherry *v.* Perkins, 147 Mass. 212; Temperton *v.* Russell, [1893] 1 Q. B. 715, 728, 731; Flood *v.* Jackson, 11 L. T. R. 276.

In the opinion of a majority of the court the injunction should be in the form originally issued. *So ordered.*

[The opinion of FIELD, C. J., is omitted. His conclusion was, "that the decree entered by Mr. Justice Holmes should be affirmed without modification."]

HOLMES, J. In a case like the present, it seems to me that, whatever the true result may be, it will be of advantage to sound thinking to have the less popular view of the law stated, and therefore, although when I have been unable to bring my brethren to share my convictions my almost invariable practice is to defer to them in silence, I depart from that practice in this case, notwithstanding my unwillingness to do so in support of an already rendered judgment of my own.

In the first place, a word or two should be said as to the meaning of the report. I assume that my brethren construe it as I meant it to be construed, and that, if they were not prepared to do so, they would give an opportunity to the defendants to have it amended in accordance with what I state my meaning to be. There was no proof of any threat or danger of a patrol exceeding two men, and as of course an injunction is not granted except with reference to what there is reason to expect in its absence, the question on that point is whether a patrol of two men should be enjoined. Again, the defendants are enjoined by the final decree from intimidating by threats, express or implied, of physical harm to body or property, any person who may be desirous of entering into the employment of the plaintiff so far as to prevent him from entering the same. In order to test the correctness of the refusal to go further, it must be assumed that the defendants obey the express prohibition of the decree. If they do not, they fall within the injunction as it now stands, and are liable to summary punishment. The important difference between the preliminary and the final injunction is that the former goes further, and forbids the defendants to interfere with the plaintiff's business "by any scheme . . . organized for the purpose of . . . preventing any person or persons who now are or may hereafter be . . . desirous of entering the [plaintiff's employment] from entering it." I quote only a part, and the part which seems to me most objectionable. This includes refusal of social intercourse, and even organized persuasion or argument, although free from any threat of violence, either express or implied. And this is with reference to persons who have a legal right to contract or not to contract with the plaintiff, as they may see fit. Interference with existing contracts is forbidden by the final decree. I wish to insist a little that the only point of difference which involves a difference of principle between the final decree and the preliminary injunction which it is proposed to restore, is what I have mentioned, in order that it may be seen exactly what we are to discuss. It appears to me that the judgment of the majority turns in part on the assumption that the patrol necessarily carries with it a threat of bodily harm. That assumption I think unwarranted, for the reasons which I have given. Furthermore, it cannot be said, I think, that two men walking together up and down a sidewalk and speaking to those who enter a certain shop do necessarily and always thereby convey a threat of force. I do not think it possible to discriminate and to say that two workmen, or even two representatives of an organization of workmen, do, — especially when they are, and are known to be, under the injunction of this court not to do so. See Stimson, Handbook to Labor Law, § 60, esp. pp. 290, 298, 299, 300; Regina *v.* Shepherd, 11 Cox C. C. 325. I may add, that I think the more intelligent workingmen believe as fully as I do that they no more can be permitted to usurp the State's prerogative of force than can their opponents in their controversies. But if I am wrong, then the decree as it stands reaches the patrol, since it applies to all threats of force. With this I pass to the real difference between the interlocutory and the final decree.

I agree, whatever may be the law in the case of a single defendant, Rice *v.* Albee, 164 Mass. 88, that when a plaintiff proves that several persons have combined and conspired to injure his business, and have done acts producing that effect, he shows temporal damage and a cause of action, unless the facts disclose, or the defendants prove, some ground of excuse or justification. And I take it to be settled, and rightly settled, that doing that damage by combined persuasion is actionable, as well as doing it by falsehood or by force. Walker *v.* Cronin, 107 Mass. 555; Morasse *v.* Brochu, 151 Mass. 567; Tasker *v.* Stanley, 153 Mass. 148.

Nevertheless, in numberless instances the law warrants the intentional infliction of temporal damage because it regards it as justified. It is on the question of what shall amount to a justification, and more especially on the nature of the considerations which really determine or ought to determine the answer to that question, that judicial reasoning seems to me often to be inadequate. The true grounds of decision are considerations of policy and of social advantage, and it is vain to suppose that solutions can be attained merely by logic and the general propositions of law which nobody disputes. Propositions as to public policy rarely are unanimously accepted, and still more rarely, if ever, are capable of unanswerable proof. They require a special training to enable any one even to form an intelligent opinion about them. In the early stages of law, at least, they generally are acted on rather as inarticulate instincts than as definite ideas for which a rational defence is ready.

To illustrate what I have said in the last paragraph, it has been the law for centuries that a man may set up a business in a country town too small to support more than one, although he expects and intends thereby to ruin some one already there, and succeeds in his intent. In such a case he is not held to act "unlawfully and without justifiable cause," as was alleged in Walker *v.* Cronin and Rice *v.*

Albee. The reason, of course, is that the doctrine generally has been accepted that free competition is worth more to society than it costs, and that on this ground the infliction of the damage is privileged. Commonwealth *v.* Hunt, 4 Met. 111, 134. Yet even this proposition nowadays is disputed by a considerable body of persons, including many whose intelligence is not to be denied, little as we may agree with them.

I have chosen this illustration partly with reference to what I have to say next. It shows without the need of further authority that the policy of allowing free competition justifies the intentional inflicting of temporal damage, including the damage of interference with a man's business, by some means, when the damage is done not for its own sake, but as an instrumentality in reaching the end of victory in the battle of trade. In such a case it cannot matter whether the plaintiff is the only rival of the defendant, and so is aimed at specifically, or is one of a class all of whom are hit. The only debatable ground is the nature of the means by which such damage may be inflicted. We all agree that it cannot be done by force or threats of force. We all agree, I presume, that it may be done by persuasion to leave a rival's shop and come to the defendant's. It may be done by the refusal or withdrawal of various pecuniary advantages which, apart from this consequence, are within the defendant's lawful control. It may be done by the withdrawal, or threat to withdraw, such advantages from third persons who have a right to deal or not to deal with the plaintiff, as a means of inducing them not to deal with him either as customers or servants. Commonwealth *v.* Hunt, 4 Met. 111, 132, 133; Bowen *v.* Matheson, 14 Allen, 499; Heywood *v.* Tillson, 75 Maine, 225; Mogul Steamship Co. *v.* McGregor, [1892] A. C. 25.

I pause here to remark that the word "threats" often is used as if when it appeared that threats had been made, it appeared that unlawful conduct had begun. But it depends on what you threaten. As a general rule, even if subject to some exceptions, what you may do in a certain event you may threaten to do,[1] that is, give warning of your

[1] "The defendant associations had the absolute right to threaten to do that which they had the right to do." Parker, C. J., in National Protective Association *v.* Cumming, 170 New York, 315, p. 329.

"It will be said that a man has the absolute right to threaten to do that which he has a right to do. Granted that what you may absolutely do you may absolutely threaten to do (give unqualified notice of your intention to do). But it does not follow that you may conditionally threaten to do it. The right to absolutely refuse to work and the right to conditionally refuse do not, as against third persons, *i. e.*, persons other than the employer, stand to each other in the relation of the greater to the less. The former does not necessarily include the latter. They are distinct from each other; and the latter may sometimes be the more important and the more dangerous right of the two." 20 Harvard Law Rev., p. 273.

"The right to quit an employment which is terminable at will may include a right to give absolute and unqualified notice of intention to leave."

"It may also include, *as against an employer*, a right to annex any possible condition to an offer to work or to a threat to refrain from working. By 'right as against an employer' we mean that an employer could not maintain an action intention to do in that event, and thus allow the other person the chance of avoiding the consequences. So as to "compulsion," it depends on how you "compel." Commonwealth *v.* Hunt, 4 Met. 111, 133. So as to "annoyance" or "intimidation." Connor *v.* Kent, Curran *v.* Treleaven, 17 Cox C. C. 354, 367, 368, 370. In Sherry *v.* Perkins, 147 Mass. 212, it was found as a fact that the display of banners which was enjoined was part of a scheme to prevent workmen from entering or remaining in the plaintiff's employment, "by threats and intimidation." The context showed that the words as there used meant threats of personal violence, and intimidation by causing fear of it.

I have seen the suggestion made that the conflict between employers and employed is not competition. But I venture to assume that none of my brethren would rely on that suggestion. If the policy on which our law is founded is too narrowly expressed in the term free competition, we may substitute free struggle for life. Certainly the policy is not limited to struggles between persons of the same class competing for the same end. It applies to all conflicts of temporal interests.

So far, I suppose, we are agreed. But there is a notion which latterly has been insisted on a good deal, that a combination of persons to do what any one of them lawfully might do by himself will make the otherwise lawful conduct unlawful. It would be rash to say that some as yet unformulated truth may not be hidden under this proposition. But in the general form in which it has been presented and accepted by many courts, I think it plainly untrue, both on authority

against a laborer for annexing such conditions. The employer is not legally damaged by such an offer. He is not bound to accept it. As between B and C, the person with whom B is directly dealing, it may be true that 'the right to refuse to deal involves the right to name any terms which one pleases, and to refuse to deal except on these terms.' C cannot maintain an action against B for insisting on unreasonable terms. But the terms or conditions annexed to an offer may relate to the offeree's relations to a third person, and [if the offeree accepts and performs the conditions] that may raise a question whether such third person has any ground of complaint."

"We think that the right to work or not to work does not include, *as against third persons*, the right to annex any possible condition to an offer to work or to a notice of intention to refrain from work. Suppose that B offers to work for C on condition that C commits a battery on A. Could B effectively deny that he instigated the commission of the battery? Could B escape liability to A on the ground that he was merely stating to C the conditions on which he was willing to exercise his right to labor or not to labor?" 20 Harvard Law Rev. 270–271.

The contrary view is open to several objections: —

"1. It assumes that, if certain conduct of B does not violate any legal right of C, it cannot infringe a legal right of A.

"2. It overlooks the distinction between unconditionally exercising a right, and offering to exercise it (or to refrain from exercising it) on condition that the offeree shall take action which is intended to produce (and does produce) damage to a third person.

"3. It assumes that one who intentionally instigates a second person to inflict damage on a third person can escape responsibility by putting the instigation in the form of a conditional offer to exercise, or to refrain from exercising, a right which he had against the second person." 20 Harvard Law Rev. 269.

and on principle.[1] Commonwealth *v.* Hunt, 4 Met. 111; Randall *v.* Hazelton, 12 Allen, 412, 414. There was combination of the most flagrant and dominant kind in Bowen *v.* Matheson and in the Mogul Steamship Company's case, and combination was essential to the success achieved. But it is not necessary to cite cases; it is plain from the slightest consideration of practical affairs, or the most superficial reading of industrial history, that free competition means combination, and that the organization of the world, now going on so fast, means an ever increasing might and scope of combination. It seems to me futile to set our faces against this tendency. Whether beneficial on the whole, as I think it, or detrimental, it is inevitable, unless the fundamental axioms of society, and even the fundamental conditions of life, are to be changed.

One of the eternal conflicts out of which life is made up is that between the effort of every man to get the most he can for his services, and that of society, disguised under the name of capital, to get his services for the least possible return. Combination on the one side is patent and powerful. Combination on the other is the necessary and desirable counterpart, if the battle is to be carried on in a fair and equal way. I am unable to reconcile Temperton *v.* Russell, [1893] 1 Q. B. 715, and the cases which follow it, with the Mogul Steamship Company case. But Temperton *v.* Russell is not a binding authority here, and therefore I do not think it necessary to discuss it.

If it be true that workingmen may combine with a view, among other things, to getting as much as they can for their labor, just as capital may combine with a view to getting the greatest possible return, it must be true that when combined they have the same liberty that combined capital has to support their interests by argument, persuasion, and the bestowal or refusal of those advantages which they otherwise lawfully control. I can remember when many people thought that, apart from violence or breach of contract, strikes were wicked, as organized refusals to work. I suppose that intelligent economists and legislators have given up that notion to-day. I feel pretty confident that they equally will abandon the idea that an organized refusal by workmen of social intercourse with a man who shall

[1] "In many of the cases the element of combination or conspiracy is found. If the act be lawful, the combination or conspiracy to commit it does not make the act unlawful; if it be unlawful, the combination to commit it may render its commission easier and may aggravate the injury; but it does not change the character of the act. The fact of combination is treated by the courts as of great evidentiary value in deciding the question of coercion or duress." Burke, J., in Sumwalt Ice Co. *v.* Knickerbocker Ice Co., 114 Md. 403, 414.

"The gist of a civil action of this sort is not the conspiracy but the deceit or fraud causing damage to the plaintiff, the combination being charged merely for the purpose of fixing joint liability on the defendants." Rugg, J., in New England Foundation Co. *v.* Reed, 209 Mass. 556.

See also Romer, L. J., in Giblan *v.* National Amalgamated Union, [1903] 2 K. B. 600, 619–620. But compare Henshaw, J., in Vallejo Ferry Co. *v.* Solano Club, 165 Cal. 255.

enter their antagonist's employ is wrong, if it is dissociated from any threat of violence, and is made for the sole object of prevailing if possible in a contest with their employer about the rate of wages. The fact, that the immediate object of the act by which the benefit to themselves is to be gained is to injure their antagonist, does not necessarily make it unlawful, any more than when a great house lowers the price of certain goods for the purpose, and with the effect, of driving a smaller antagonist from the business. Indeed, the question seems to me to have been decided as long ago as 1842 by the good sense of Chief Justice Shaw, in Commonwealth *v.* Hunt, 4 Met. 111. I repeat at the end, as I said at the beginning, that this is the point of difference in principle, and the only one, between the interlocutory and the final decree. See Regina *v.* Shepherd, 11 Cox C. C. 325; Connor *v.* Kent, Gibson *v.* Lawson, Curran *v.* Treleaven, 17 Cox C. C. 354.

The general question of the propriety of dealing with this kind of case by injunction I say nothing about, because I understand that the defendants have no objection to the final decree if it goes no further, and that both parties wish a decision upon the matters which I have discussed.[1]

PLANT *v.* WOODS

SUPREME JUDICIAL COURT, MASSACHUSETTS, SEPTEMBER 5, 1900.

Reported in 176 *Massachusetts Reports*, 492.

BILL IN EQUITY filed in the Superior Court, by the officers and members " of the voluntary association known as Union 257, Painters and Decorators of America of Springfield, Massachusetts, which Union is affiliated with a national organization of the same name, with headquarters at Lafayette in the State of Indiana," against the officers and members " of the voluntary association known as Union 257, Painters and Decorators of America, which Union is affiliated with a national organization of the same name, with headquarters at Baltimore in the State of Maryland," to restrain the defendants from any acts or the use of any methods tending to prevent the members of the plaintiff

[1] *Intimidation.* See Springhead Co. *v.* Riley, 6 Eq. 551 (intimidating placards); Southern R. Co. *v.* Machinists Union, 111 Fed. 49; Knudsen *v.* Benn, 123 Fed. 636; Atchison R. Co. *v.* Gee, 139 Fed. 582; Pope Motor Co. *v.* Keegan, 150 Fed. 148 (collection of large crowd); Allis Chalmers Co. *v.* Iron Molders' Union, 150 Fed. 155 (crowds); Goldfield Consolidated Mines Co. *v.* Goldfield Miners' Union, 159 Fed. 500; Kolley *v.* Robinson, (C. C. A.) 187 Fed. 415; Fortney *v.* Carter, (C. C. A.) 203 Fed. 454; Bittner *v.* West Virginia Coal Co., (C. C. A.) 214 Fed. 716; Goldberg *v.* Stablemen's Union, 149 Cal. 429; Underhill *v.* Murphy, 117 Ky. 640; Sherry *v.* Perkins, 147 Mass. 212 (intimidating banner); Ideal Mfg. Co. *v.* Ludwig, 149 Mich. 133 (crowd); Baltic Mining Co. *v.* Judge, 177 Mich. 632; Minnesota Stove Co. *v.* Cavanaugh, 131 Minn. 458; Jones *v.* Maher, 62 Misc. 388; O'Neil *v.* Behanna, 182 Pa. St. 236; Jensen *v.* Cooks' Union, 39 Wash. 531; Commercial Printing Co. *v.* Tacoma Typographical Union, 85 Wash. 234.

Picketing, see American Steel Co. *v.* Wire Drawers' Union, 90 Fed. 608; Iron Molders' Union *v.* Allis Chalmers Co., (C. C. A.) 166 Fed. 45; Sona *v.* Aluminum association from securing employment or continuing in their employment. Hearing before Dewey, J., who entered the following decree:

"The cause came on to be heard, and was argued by counsel; and thereupon, on consideration thereof, it is ordered adjudged and decreed that the defendant association, the defendants, and each and every of them, their committees, agents, and servants, be restrained and strictly enjoined from interfering and from combining, conspiring, or attempting to interfere, with the employment of members of the plaintiffs' said association, by representing or causing to be represented in express or implied terms to any employer of said members of plaintiffs' association, or to any person or persons or corporation who might become employers of any of the plaintiffs, that such employers will suffer or are likely to suffer some loss or trouble in their business for employing or continuing to employ said members of plaintiffs' said association; or by representing, directly or indirectly, for the purpose of interfering with the employment of members of the plaintiffs' said association, to any who have contracts or may have contracts for services to be performed by employers of members of plaintiffs' said association that such persons will or are likely to suffer some loss or trouble in their business for allowing such employers of members of plaintiffs' said association (and because they are such employers) to obtain or perform such contracts; or by intimidating or attempting to intimidate, by threats, direct or indirect, express or implied, of loss or trouble in business, or otherwise, any person or persons or corporation who now are employing or may hereafter employ or desire to employ any of the members of the plaintiffs' said association; or by attempting by any scheme or conspiracy, among themselves or with others, to annoy, hinder, or interfere with, or prevent any person or persons or corporation from employing or continuing to employ a member or members of plaintiffs' said association; or by causing, or attempting to cause, any person to discriminate against any employer of members of plaintiffs' said association (because he is such employer) in giving or allowing the performance of contracts to or by such employer; and from any and all acts, or the use of any methods, which by putting or attempting to put any person or persons or corporation in fear of loss or trouble, will tend to hinder, impede, or obstruct members, or any member, of the plaintiffs' said association

Castings Co., (C. C. A.) 214 Fed. 936; Karges Furniture Co. *v.* Woodworkers' Union, 165 Ind. 421; Beck *v.* Teamsters' Union, 118 Mich. 497.

Annoyance of workers resorting to plaintiff. Union P. R. Co. *v.* Ruef, 120 Fed. 102; Frank *v.* Herold, 63 N. J. Eq. 443; Jonas Glass Co. *v.* Glass Blowers' Ass'n, 77 N. J. Eq. 219.

Inducing employer to break contracts. Read *v.* Friendly Society, [1902] 2 K. B. 732; Jonas *v.* Glass Blowers' Ass'n, 77 N. J. Eq. 219; Flaccus *v.* Smith, 199 Pa. St. 128.

Inducing employees to break contract. Hardie Tynes Mfg. Co. *v.* Cruse, 189 Ala. 66; Folsom *v.* Lewis, 208 Mass. 336; Jonas Glass Co. *v.* Glass Blowers' Ass'n, 77 N. J. Eq. 219; Grassi Contracting Co. *v.* Bennett, 160 N. Y. Suppl. 279.

from securing employment or continuing in employment. And that the plaintiffs recover their costs, taxed as in an action of law."

The case was reported, at the request of both parties, for the determination of this court. The facts appear in the opinion.

HAMMOND, J. This case arises out of a contest for supremacy between two labor unions of the same craft, having substantially the same constitution and by-laws. The chief difference between them is that the plaintiff union is affiliated with a national organization having its headquarters in Lafayette in the State of Indiana, while the defendant union is affiliated with a similar organization having its headquarters in Baltimore in the State of Maryland. The plaintiff union was composed of workmen who in 1897 withdrew from the defendant union.

There does not appear to be anything illegal in the object of either union as expressed in its constitution and by-laws. The defendant union is also represented by delegates in the Central Labor Union, which is an organization composed of five delegates from each trade union in the city of Springfield, and had in its constitution a provision for levying a boycott upon a complaint made by any union.

The case is before us upon a report after a final decree in favor of the plaintiffs, based upon the findings stated in the report of the master.

The contest became active early in the fall of 1898. In September of that year, the members of the defendant union declared "all painters not affiliated with the Baltimore headquarters to be non-union men," and voted to "notify the bosses" of that declaration. The manifest object of the defendants was to have all the members of the craft subjected to the rules and discipline of their particular union, in order that they might have better control over the whole business, and to that end they combined and conspired to get the plaintiffs and each of them to join the defendant association, peaceably if possible but by threat and intimidation if necessary. Accordingly, on October 7, they voted that "if our demands are not complied with, all men working in shops where Lafayette people are employed refuse to go to work." The plaintiffs resisting whatever persuasive measures, if any, were used by the defendants, the latter proceeded to carry out their plan in the manner fully set forth in the master's report. Without rehearsing the circumstances in detail it is sufficient to say here that the general method of operations was substantially as follows: —

A duly authorized agent of the defendants would visit a shop where one or more of the plaintiffs were at work and inform the employer of the action of the defendant union with reference to the plaintiffs, and ask him to induce such of the plaintiffs as were in his employ to sign application for reinstatement in the defendant union. As to the general nature of these interviews the master finds that the defendants have been courteous in manner, have made no threats of personal violence, have referred to the plaintiffs as non-union men, but have not otherwise represented them as men lacking good standing in their craft; that they have not asked that the Lafayette men be discharged, and in some cases have expressly stated that they did not wish to have them discharged, but only that they sign the blanks for reinstatement in the defendant union. The master, however, further finds, from all the circumstances under which those requests were made, that the defendants intended that employers of Lafayette men should fear trouble in their business if they continued to employ such men, and that employers to whom these requests were made were justified in believing that a failure on the part of their employees who were Lafayette men to sign such reinstatement blanks, and a failure on the part of the employers to discharge them for not doing so, would lead to trouble in the business of the employers in the nature of strikes or a boycott, and the employers to whom these requests were made did believe that such results would follow, and did suggest their belief to the defendants, and the defendants did not deny that such results might occur; that the strikes which did occur appear to have been steps taken by the defendants to obtain the discharge of such employees as were Lafayette men who declined to sign application blanks for reinstatement; that these defendants did not in all cases threaten a boycott of the employers' business, but did threaten that the place of business of at least one such employer would be left off from a so-called "fair list" to be published by the Baltimore Union. The master also found that, from all the evidence presented, the object which the Baltimore men and the defendant association sought to accomplish in all the acts which were testified to was to compel the members of the Lafayette Union to join the Baltimore Union, and as a means to this end they caused strikes to be instituted in the shops where strikes would seriously interfere with the business of the shops, and in all other shops they made such representations as would lead the proprietors thereof to expect trouble in their business.

We have, therefore, a case where the defendants have conspired to compel the members of the plaintiff union to join the defendant union, and to carry out their purpose have resolved upon such coercion and intimidation as naturally may be caused by threats of loss of property by strikes and boycotts, to induce the employers either to get the plaintiffs to ask for reinstatement in the defendant union, or, that failing, then to discharge them. It matters not that this request to discharge has not been expressly made. There can be no doubt, upon the findings of the master and the facts stated in his report, that the compulsory discharge of the plaintiffs in case of non-compliance with the demands of the defendant union is one of the prominent features of the plan agreed upon.

It is well to see what is the meaning of this threat to strike, when taken in connection with the intimation that the employer may "expect trouble in his business." It means more than that the strikers will cease to work. That is only the preliminary skirmish. It means that those who have ceased to work will, by strong, persistent, and organized persuasion and social pressure of every description, do all they can to prevent the employer from procuring workmen to take their places. It means much more. It means that, if these peaceful measures fail, the employer may reasonably expect that unlawful physical injury may be done to his property; that attempts in all the ways practised by organized labor will be made to injure him in his business, even to his ruin, if possible; and that, by the use of vile and opprobrious epithets and other annoying conduct, and actual and threatened personal violence, attempts will be made to intimidate those who enter or desire to enter his employ; and that whether or not all this be done by the strikers or only by their sympathizers, or with the open sanction and approval of the former, he will have no help from them in his efforts to protect himself.

However mild the language or suave the manner in which the threat to strike is made under such circumstances as are disclosed in this case, the employer knows that he is in danger of passing through such an ordeal as that above described, and those who make the threat know that as well as he does. Even if the intent of the strikers, so far as respects their own conduct and influence, be to discountenance all actual or threatened injury to person or property or business, except that which is the direct necessary result of the interruption of the work, and even if their connection with the injurious and violent conduct of the turbulent among them or of their sympathizers be not such as to make them liable criminally or even answerable civilly in damages to those who suffer, still with full knowledge of what is to be expected they give the signal, and in so doing must be held to avail themselves of the degree of fear and dread which the knowledge of such consequences will cause in the mind of those — whether their employer or fellow workmen — against whom the strike is directed; and the measure of coercion and intimidation imposed upon those against whom the strike is threatened or directed is not fully realized until all those probable consequences are considered.

Such is the nature of the threat, and such the degree of coercion and intimidation involved in it.

If the defendants can lawfully perform the acts complained of in the city of Springfield, they can pursue the plaintiffs all over the State in the same manner, and compel them to abandon their trade or bow to the behests of their pursuers.

It is to be observed that this is not a case between the employer and employed, or, to use a hackneyed expression, between capital and labor, but between laborers all of the same craft, and each having the same right as any one of the others to pursue his calling. In this, as in every other case of equal rights, the right of each individual is to be exercised with due regard to the similar right of all others, and the right of one be said to end where that of another begins.

The right involved is the right to dispose of one's labor with full freedom. This is a legal right, and it is entitled to legal protection. Sir William Erle in his book on Trade Unions, page 12, has stated this in the following language, which has been several times quoted with approval by judges in England: " Every person has a right under the law, as between him and his fellow subjects, to full freedom in disposing of his own labor or his own capital according to his own will. It follows that every other person is subject to the correlative duty arising therefrom, and is prohibited from any obstruction to the fullest exercise of this right which can be made compatible with the exercise of similar rights by others. Every act causing an obstruction to another in the exercise of the right comprised within this description — done, not in the exercise of the actor's own right, but for the purpose of obstruction — would if damage should be caused thereby to the party obstructed, be a violation of this prohibition."

The same rule is stated with care and discrimination by Wells, J., in Walker *v.* Cronin, 107 Mass. 555, 564: " Every one has a right to enjoy the fruits and advantages of his own enterprise, industry, skill, and credit. He has no right to be protected against competition; but he has a right to be free from malicious and wanton interference, disturbance, or annoyance. If disturbance or loss come as a result of competition, or the exercise of like rights by others, it is *damnum absque injuria*, unless some superior right by contract or otherwise is interfered with. But if it come from the merely wanton or malicious acts of others, without the justification of competition or the service of any interest or lawful purpose, it then stands upon a different footing."

In this case the acts complained of were calculated to cause damage to the plaintiffs, and did actually cause such damage; and they were intentionally done for that purpose. Unless, therefore, there was justifiable cause, the acts were malicious and unlawful. Walker *v.* Cronin, *ubi supra*, Carew *v.* Rutherford, 106 Mass. 1, and cases cited therein.

The defendants contend that they have done nothing unlawful, and, in support of that contention, they say that a person may work for whom he pleases; and, in the absence of any contract to the contrary, may cease to work when he pleases, and for any reason whatever, whether the same be good or bad; that he may give notice of his intention in advance, with or without stating the reason; that what one man may do several men acting in concert may do, and may agree beforehand that they will do, and may give notice of the agreement; and that all this may be lawfully done notwithstanding such concerted action may, by reason of the consequent interruption of the work, result in great loss to the employer and his other employees, and that such a result was intended. In a general sense, and without reference to exceptions arising out of conflicting public and private interests, all this may be true.

It is said also that, where one has the lawful right to do a thing, the motive by which he is actuated is immaterial. One form of this statement appears in the first head-note in Allen *v.* Flood, as reported in [1898] A. C. 1, as follows: "An act lawful in itself is not converted by a malicious or bad motive into an unlawful act so as to make the doer of the act liable to a civil action." If the meaning of this and similar expressions is that where a person has the lawful right to do a thing irrespective of his motive, his motive is immaterial the proposition is a mere truism. If, however, the meaning is that where a person, if actuated by one kind of a motive, has a lawful right to do a thing, the act is lawful when done under any conceivable motive; or that an act lawful under one set of circumstances is therefore lawful under every conceivable set of circumstances, the proposition does not commend itself to us as either logically or legally accurate.

In so far as a right is lawful, it is lawful, and in many cases the right is so far absolute as to be lawful whatever may be the motive of the actor, as where one digs upon his own land for water (Greenleaf *v.* Francis, 18 Pick. 117), or makes a written lease of his land for the purpose of terminating a tenancy at will (Groustra *v.* Bourges, 141 Mass. 7), but in many cases the lawfulness of an act which causes damage to another may depend upon whether the act is for justifiable cause; and this justification may be found sometimes in the circumstances under which it is done irrespective of motive, sometimes in the motive alone, and sometimes in the circumstances and motive combined.

This principle is of very general application in criminal law, and also is illustrated in many branches of the civil law, as in cases of libel and of procuring a wife to leave her husband. Tasker *v.* Stanley, 153 Mass. 148, and cases therein cited. Indeed the principle is a prominent feature underlying the whole doctrine of privilege, malice, and intent. See on this an instructive article in 8 Harvard Law Review, 1, where the subject is considered at some length.

It is manifest that not much progress is made by such general statements as those quoted above from Allen *v.* Flood, whatever may be their meaning.

Still standing for solution is the question, Under what circumstances, including the motive of the actor, is the act complained of lawful, and to what extent?

In cases somewhat akin to the one at bar this court has had occasion to consider the question how far acts, manifestly coercive and intimidating in their nature, which cause damage and injury to the business or property of another, and are done with intent to cause such injury and partly in reliance upon such coercion, are justifiable.

In Bowen *v.* Matheson, 14 Allen, 499, it was held to be lawful for persons engaged in the business of shipping seamen to combine together into a society for the purpose of competing with other persons engaged in the same business, and it was held lawful for them, in pursuance of that purpose, to take men out of a ship, if men shipped by a non-member were in that ship; to refuse to furnish seamen through a non-member; to notify the public that they had combined against non-members, and had " laid the plaintiff on the shelf "; to notify the plaintiff's customers and friends that the plaintiff could not ship seamen for them; and to interfere in all these ways with the business of the plaintiff as a shipping agent, and compel him to abandon the same. The justification for these acts, so injurious to the business of the plaintiff and so intimidating in their nature, is to be found in the law of competition. No legal right of the plaintiff was infringed upon, and, as stated by Chapman, J., in giving the opinion of the court (p. 503), " if their effect is to destroy the business of shipping-masters who are not members of the association, it is such a result as in the competition of business often follows from a course of proceeding that the law permits." The primary object of the defendants was to build up their own business, and this they might lawfully do to the extent disclosed in that case, even to the injury of their rivals.

Similar decisions have been made in other courts where acts somewhat coercive in their nature and effect have been held justifiable under the law of competition. Mogul Steamship Co. *v.* McGregor, [1892] A. C. 25; Bohn Manuf. Co. *v.* Hollis, 54 Minn. 223; Macauley *v.* Tierney, 19 R. I. 255.

On the other hand, it was held in Carew *v.* Rutherford, 106 Mass. 1, that a conspiracy against a mechanic, — who is under the necessity of employing workmen in order to carry on his business, — to obtain a sum of money from him which he is under no legal obligation to pay, by inducing his workmen to leave him or by deterring others from entering into his employ, or by threatening to do this so that he is induced to pay the money demanded, under a reasonable apprehension that he cannot carry on his business without yielding to the demands, is an illegal, if not a criminal conspiracy; that the acts done under it are illegal, and that the money thus obtained may be recovered back. Chapman, C. J., speaking for the court, says that there is no doubt that, if the parties under such circumstances succeed in injuring the business of the mechanic, they are liable to pay all the damages done to him.

That case bears a close analogy to the one at bar. The acts there threatened were like those in this case, and the purpose was, in substance, to force the plaintiff to give his work to the defendants, and to extort from him a fine because he had given some of his work to other persons.

Without now indicating to what extent workmen may combine and in pursuance of an agreement may act by means of strikes and boycotts to get the hours of labor reduced or their wages increased, or to procure from their employers any other concession directly and immediately affecting their own interests, or to help themselves in competition with their fellow-workmen, we think this case must be governed by the principles laid down in Carew *v.* Rutherford, *ubi supra.* The purpose of these defendants was to force the plaintiffs to join the defendant association, and to that end they injured the plaintiffs in their business, and molested and disturbed them in their efforts to work at their trade. It is true they committed no acts of personal violence, or of physical injury to property, although they threatened to do something which might reasonably be expected to lead to such results. In their threat, however, there was plainly that which was coercive in its effect upon the will. It is not necessary that the liberty of the body should be restrained. Restraint of the mind, provided it would be such as would be likely to force a man against his will to grant the thing demanded, and actually has that effect, is sufficient in cases like this. As stated by Lord Bramwell in Regina *v.* Druitt, 10 Cox C. C. 592, 600, "No right of property, or capital, . . . was so sacred, or so carefully guarded by the law of this land, as that of personal liberty. . . . That liberty was not liberty of the body only. It was also a liberty of the mind and will; and the liberty of a man's mind and will, to say how he should bestow himself and his means, his talents, and his industry, was as much a subject of the law's protection as was that of his body."

It was not the intention of the defendants to give fairly to the employer the option to employ them or the plaintiffs, but to compel the latter against their will to join the association, and to that end to molest and interfere with them in their efforts to procure work by acts and threats well calculated by their coercive and intimidating nature to overcome the will.

The defendants might make such lawful rules as they please for the regulation of their own conduct, but they had no right to force other persons to join them.

The necessity that the plaintiffs should join this association is not so great, nor is its relation to the rights of the defendants, as compared with the right of the plaintiffs to be free from molestation, such as to bring the acts of the defendants under the shelter of the principles of trade competition. Such acts are without justification, and therefore are malicious and unlawful, and the conspiracy thus to force the plaintiffs was unlawful. Such conduct is intolerable, and inconsistent with the spirit of our laws.

The language used by this court in Carew *v.* Rutherford, 106 Mass. 1, 15, may be repeated here with emphasis, as applicable to this case: "The acts alleged and proved in this case are peculiarly offensive to the free principles which prevail in this country; and if such practices could enjoy impunity, they would tend to establish a tyranny of irresponsible persons over labor and mechanical business which would be extremely injurious to both." See, in addition to the authorities above cited, Commonwealth *v.* Hunt, 4 Met. 111; Sherry *v.* Perkins, 147 Mass. 212, 214; Vegelahn *v.* Guntner, 167 Mass. 92, 97; St. 1894, c. 508, § 2;[1] State *v.* Donaldson, 3 Vroom, 151; State *v.* Stewart, 59 Vt. 273; State *v.* Glidden, 55 Conn. 46; State *v.* Dyer, 67 Vt. 690; Lucke *v.* Clothing Cutters & Trimmers' Assembly, 77 Md. 396.

As the plaintiffs have been injured by these acts, and there is reason to believe that the defendants contemplate further proceedings of the same kind which will be likely still more to injure the plaintiffs, a bill in equity lies to enjoin the defendants. Vegelahn *v.* Guntner, *ubi supra.*

Some phases of the labor question have recently been discussed in the very elaborately considered case of Allen *v.* Flood, *ubi supra.* Whether or not the decision made therein is inconsistent with the propositions upon which we base our decision in this case, we are not disposed, in view of the circumstances under which that decision was made, to follow it. We prefer the view expressed by the dissenting judges, which view, it may be remarked, was entertained not only by three of the nine lords who sat in the case, but also by the great majority of the common law judges who had occasion officially to express an opinion.

There must be, therefore, a decree for the plaintiffs. We think, however, that the clause, " or by causing or attempting to cause, any person to discriminate against any employer of members of plaintiffs' said association (because he is such employer) in giving or allowing the performance of contracts to or by such employer," is too broad and indefinite, inasmuch as it might seem to include mere lawful persuasion and other similar and peaceful acts; and for that reason, and also because so far as respects unlawful acts it seems to cover only such acts as are prohibited by other parts of the decree, we think it should be omitted.

Inasmuch as the association of the defendants is not a corporation, an injunction cannot be issued against it as such, but only against its members, their agents and servants.

As thus modified, in the opinion of the majority of the court, the decree should stand. *Decree accordingly.*

HOLMES, C. J. When a question has been decided by the court, I think it proper, as a general rule, that a dissenting judge, however strong his convictions may be, should thereafter accept the law from

[1] This section is as follows: " No person shall, by intimidation or force, prevent or seek to prevent a person from entering into or continuing in the employment of any person or corporation."

the majority and leave the remedy to the Législature, if that body sees fit to interfere. If the decision in the present case simply had relied upon Vegelahn *v.* Guntner, 167 Mass. 92, I should have hesitated to say anything, although I might have stated that my personal opinion had not been weakened by the substantial agreement with my views to be found in the judgments of the majority of the House of Lords in Allen *v.* Flood, [1898] A. C. 1. But much to my satisfaction, if I may say so, the court has seen fit to adopt the mode of approaching the question which I believe to be the correct one, and to open an issue which otherwise I might have thought closed. The difference between my brethren and me now seems to be a difference of degree, and the line of reasoning followed makes it proper for me to explain where the difference lies.

I agree that the conduct of the defendants is actionable unless justified. May *v.* Wood, 172 Mass. 11, 14, and cases cited. I agree that the presence or absence of justification may depend upon the object of their conduct, that is, upon the motive with which they acted. Vegelahn *v.* Guntner, 167 Mass. 92, 105, 106. I agree, for instance, that if a boycott or a strike is intended to override the jurisdiction of the courts by the action of a private association, it may be illegal. Weston *v.* Barnicoat, 175 Mass. 454. On the other hand, I infer that a majority of my brethren would admit that a boycott or strike intended to raise wages directly might be lawful, if it did not embrace in its scheme or intent violence, breach of contract, or other conduct unlawful on grounds independent of the mere fact that the action of the defendants was combined. A sensible workingman would not contend that the courts should sanction a combination for the purpose of inflicting or threatening violence or the infraction of admitted rights. To come directly to the point, the issue is narrowed to the question whether, assuming that some purposes would be a justification, the purpose in this case of the threatened boycotts and strikes was such as to justify the threats. That purpose was not directly concerned with wages. It was one degree more remote. The immediate object and motive was to strengthen the defendants' society as a preliminary and means to enable it to make a better fight on questions of wages or other matters of clashing interests. I differ from my brethren in thinking that the threats were as lawful for this preliminary purpose as for the final one to which strengthening the union was a means. I think that unity of organization is necessary to make the contest of labor effectual, and that societies of laborers lawfully may employ in their preparation the means which they might use in the final contest.

Although this is not the place for extended economic discussion, and although the law may not always reach ultimate economic conceptions, I think it well to add that I cherish no illusions as to the meaning and effect of strikes. While I think the strike a lawful instrument in the universal struggle of life, I think it pure phantasy to suppose that there is a body of capital of which labor as a whole secures a larger share by that means. The annual product, subject to an infinitesimal deduction for the luxuries of the few, is directed to consumption by the multitude, and is consumed by the multitude always. Organization and strikes may get a larger share for the members of an organization, but, if they do, they get it at the expense of the less organized and less powerful portion of the laboring mass. They do not create something out of nothing. It is only by divesting our minds of questions of ownership and other machinery of distribution, and by looking solely at the question of consumption, — asking ourselves what is the annual product, who consumes it, and what changes would or could we make, — that we can keep in the world of realities. But, subject to the qualifications which I have expressed, I think it lawful for a body of workmen to try by combination to get more than they now are getting, although they do it at the expense of their fellows, and to that end to strengthen their union by the boycott and the strike.[1]

MARTELL v. WHITE

SUPREME JUDICIAL COURT, MASSACHUSETTS, MARCH 1, 1904.

Reported in 185 *Massachusetts Reports*, 255.

TORT for alleged conspiracy to injure plaintiff's business. In the Superior Court, Bishop, J., ordered a verdict for defendants, and plaintiff excepted.

HAMMOND, J. The evidence warranted the finding of the following facts, many of which were not in dispute. The plaintiff was engaged in a profitable business in quarrying granite and selling the same to granite workers in Quincy and vicinity. About January, 1899, his customers left him, and his business was ruined through the action of the defendants and their associates.

The defendants were all members of a voluntary association known as the Granite Manufacturers' Association of Quincy, Mass., and some

[1] In accord with the prevailing opinion, see Tunstall v. Stearns Coal Co., 192 Fed. 808; Folsom v. Lewis, 208 Mass. 336; Burnham v. Dowd, 217 Mass. 351; Fairbanks v. McDonald, 219 Mass. 291; Cornellier v. Haverhill Mfr's Assn, 221 Mass. 554; Blanchard v. Newark District Council, 77 N. J. Law, 389; Ruddy v. United Journeyman Plumbers, 79 N. J. Law, 467, 81 N. J. Law, 574. Compare Giblan v. National Amalgamated Union, [1903] 2 K. B. 600; National Fire Proofing Co. v. Mason Builders' Ass'n, 169 Fed. 259; Gill Engraving Co. v. Doerr, 214 Fed. 111.

Contra, Kemp v. Division No. 241, 255 Ill. 213.

Purpose of gaining control of the labor market. New England Cement Co. v. McGivern, 218 Mass. 198; Jacobs v. Cohen, 183 N. Y. 207; McCord v. Thompson Starrett Co., 129 App. Div. 130; Schwarcz v. International Union, 68 Misc. 528; Newton v. Erickson, 70 Misc. 291.

Compare Reynolds v. Davis, 198 Mass. 294.

of them were on the executive committee. The association was composed of " such individuals, firms, or corporations as are, or are about to become manufacturers, quarriers, or polishers of granite." There was no constitution, and, while there were by-laws, still, except as hereinafter stated, there was in them no statement of the objects for which the association was formed. The by-laws provided among other things for the admission, suspension and expulsion of members, the election of officers, including an executive committee, and defined the respective powers and duties of the officers. One of the by-laws read as follows: " For the purpose of defraying in part the expense of the maintenance of this organization, any member thereof having business transactions with any party or concern in Quincy or its vicinity, not members hereof, and in any way relating to the cutting, quarrying, polishing, buying or selling of granite (hand polishers excepted), shall for each of said transactions contribute at least $1 and not more than $500. The amount to be fixed by the association upon its determining the amount and nature of said transaction."

Acting under the by-laws, the association investigated charges which were made against several of its members that they had purchased granite from a party " not a member " of the association. The charges were proved, and under the section above quoted it was voted that the offending parties " should respectively contribute to the funds of the association " the sums named in the votes. These sums ranged from $10 to $100. Only the contribution of $100 has been paid, but it is a fair inference that the proceedings to collect the others have been delayed only by reason of this suit. The party " not a member " was the present plaintiff, and the members of the association knew it. Most of the customers of the plaintiff were members of the association, and after these proceedings they declined to deal with him. This action on their part was due to the course of the association in compelling them to contribute as above stated, and to their fear that a similar vote for contribution would be passed should they continue to trade with the plaintiff.

The jury might properly have found also that the euphemistic expression " shall contribute to the funds of the association " contained an idea which could be more tersely and accurately expressed by the phrase " shall pay a fine," or, in other words, that the plain intent of the section was to provide for the imposition upon those who came within its provisions of a penalty in the nature of a substantial fine. The bill of exceptions recites that "there was no evidence of threats or intimidation practiced upon the plaintiff himself, and the acts complained of were confined to the action of the society upon its own members." We understand this statement to mean simply that the acts of the association concerned only such of the plaintiff's customers as were members, and that no pressure was brought to bear upon the plaintiff except such as fairly resulted from action upon his customers. While it is true that the by-law was not directed expressly against the plaintiff by name, still he belonged to the class whose business it was intended to affect, and the proceedings actually taken were based upon transactions with him alone, and in that way were directed against his business alone. It was the intention of the defendants to withdraw his customers from him, if possible, by the imposition of fines upon them, with the knowledge that the result would be a great loss to the plaintiff. The defendants must be presumed to have intended the natural result of their acts.

Here, then, is a clear and deliberate interference with the business of a person with the intention of causing damage to him and ending in that result. The defendants combined and conspired together to ruin the plaintiff in his business, and they accomplished their purpose. In all this have they kept within lawful bounds ? It is elemental that the unlawfulness of a conspiracy may be found either in the end sought or the means to be used. If either is unlawful within the meaning of the term as applied to the subject, then the conspiracy is unlawful. It becomes necessary, therefore, to examine into the nature of the conspiracy in this case, both as to the object sought and the means used.

The case presents one phase of a general subject which gravely concerns the interests of the business world and indeed those of all organized society, and which in recent years has demanded and received great consideration in the courts and elsewhere. Much remains to be done to clear the atmosphere, but some things at least appear to have been settled, and certainly at this stage of the judicial inquiry it cannot be necessary to enter upon a course of reasoning or to cite authorities in support of the proposition that while a person must submit to competition he has the right to be protected from malicious interference with his business. The rule is well stated in Walker *v.* Cronin, 107 Mass. 555, 564, in the following language: " Every one has a right to enjoy the fruits and advantages of his own enterprise, industry, skill and credit. He has no right to be protected against competition; but he has a right to be free from malicious and wanton interference, disturbance or annoyance. If disturbance or loss come as a result of competition, or the exercise of like rights by others, it is *damnum absque injuria*, unless some superior right by contract or otherwise is interfered with. But if it come from the merely wanton or malicious acts of others, without the justification of competition or the service of any interest or lawful purpose, it then stands upon a different footing."

In a case like this, where the injury is intentionally inflicted, the crucial question is whether there is justifiable cause for the act. If the injury be inflicted without just cause or excuse, then it is actionable. Bowen, L. J., in Mogul Steamship Co. *v.* McGregor, 23 Q. B. D. 598, 613; Plant *v.* Woods, 176 Mass. 492. The justification must be as broad as the act and must cover not only the motive and the purpose, or in other words the object sought, but also the means used.

The defendants contend that both as to object and means they are justified by the law applicable to business competition. In considering this defence it is to be remembered, as was said by Bowen, L. J., in Mogul Steamship Co. *v.* McGregor, L. R. 23 Q. B. D. 598, 611, that there is presented " an apparent conflict or antimony between two rights that are equally regarded by the law — the right of the plaintiff to be protected in the legitimate exercise of his trade and the right of the defendants to carry on their business as seems best to them, provided they commit no wrong to others." Here, as in most cases where there is a conflict between two important principles, either of which is sound and to be sustained within proper bounds, but each of which must finally yield to some extent to the other, it frequently is not possible by a general formula to mark out the dividing line with reference to every conceivable case, and it is not wise to attempt it. The best and only practicable course is to consider the cases as they arise, and, bearing in mind the grounds upon which the soundness of each principle is supposed to rest, by a process of elimination and comparison to establish points through which at least the line must run and beyond which the party charged with trespass shall not be allowed to go.

While the purpose to injure the plaintiff appears clearly enough, the object or motive is left somewhat obscure upon the evidence. The association had no written constitution, and the by-laws do not expressly set forth its objects. It is true that from the by-laws it appears that none but persons engaged in the granite business can be members, and that a member transacting any business of this kind with a person not a member is liable to a fine; from which it may be inferred that it is the idea of the members that for the protection of their business it would be well to confine it to transactions among themselves, and that one at least of the objects of the association is to advance the interests of the members in that way. The oral testimony tends to show that one object of the association is to see that agreements made between its members and their employees and between this association and similar associations in the same line of business be kept and " lived up to." Whether this failure to set out fully in writing the objects is due to any reluctance to have them clearly appear or to some other cause, is of course not material to this case. The result, however, is that its objects do not so clearly appear as might be desired; but in view of the conclusion to which we have come as to the means used, it is not necessary to inquire more closely as to the objects. It may be assumed that one of the objects was to enable the members to compete more successfully with others in the same business, and that the acts of which the plaintiff complains were done for the ultimate protection and advancement of their own business interests, with no intention or desire to injure the plaintiff except so far as such injury was the necessary result of measures taken for their own interests. If that was true, then so far as respects the end sought the conspiracy does not seem to have been illegal.

The next question is whether there is anything unlawful or wrongful in the means used as applied to the acts in question. Nothing need be said in support of the general right to compete. To what extent combination may be allowed in competition is a matter about which there is as yet much conflict, but it is possible that in a more advanced stage of the discussion the day may come when it will be more clearly seen and will more distinctly appear in the adjudication of the courts than as yet has been the case; that the proposition that what one man lawfully can do any number of men acting together by combined agreement lawfully may do, is to be received with newly disclosed qualifications arising out of the changed conditions of civilized life and of the increased facility and power of organized combination, and that the difference between the power of individuals acting each according to his own preference and that of an organized and extensive combination may be so great in its effect upon public and private interests as to cease to be simply one of degree and to reach the dignity of a difference in kind. Indeed, in the language of Bowen, L. J., in the Mogul Steamship case, *ubi supra*, page 616: "Of the general proposition that certain kinds of conduct not criminal in one individual may become criminal if done by combination among several, there can be no doubt. The distinction is based on sound reason, for a combination may make oppressive or dangerous that which if it proceeded only from a single person would be otherwise, and the very fact of the combination may show that the object is simply to do harm, and not to exercise one's own just rights." See also opinion of Stirling, L. J., in Giblan *v.* National Amalgamated Laborers' Union, [1903] 2 K. B. 600, 621. Speaking generally, however, competition in business is permitted, although frequently disastrous to those engaged in it. It is always selfish, often sharp, and sometimes deadly. Conspicuous illustrations of the destructive extent to which it may be carried are to be found in the Mogul Steamship case above cited, and in Bowen *v.* Matheson, 14 Allen, 499. The fact therefore that the plaintiff was vanquished is not enough, provided that the contest was carried on within the rules allowable in such warfare.

It is a right, however, which is to be exercised with reference to the existence of a similar right on the part of others. The trader has not a free lance. He may fight, but as a soldier, not as a guerilla. The right of competition rests upon the doctrine that the interests of the great public are best subserved by permitting the general and natural laws of business to have their full and free operation, and that this end is best attained when the trader is allowed in his business to make free use of these laws. He may praise his wares, may offer more advantageous terms than his rival, may sell at less than cost, or, in the words of Bowen, L. J., in the Mogul Steamship case, *ubi supra*, may adopt " the expedient of sowing one year a crop of apparently unfruitful prices in order by driving competition away to realize a fuller harvest of profit in the future." In these and many other obvious ways he may secure the customers of his rival, and build up his own business to the destruction of that of others, and so long as he keeps within the operation of the laws of trade his justification is complete.

But from the very nature of the case it is manifest that the right of competition furnishes no justification for an act done by the use of means which in their nature are in violation of the principle upon which it rests. The weapons used by the trader who relies upon this right for justification must be those furnished by the laws of trade, or at least must not be inconsistent with their free operation. No man can justify an interference with another man's business through fraud or misrepresentation, nor by intimidation, obstruction or molestation. In the case before us the members of the association were to be held to the policy of refusing to trade with the plaintiff by the imposition of heavy fines, or in other words they were coerced by actual or threatened injury to their property. It is true that one may leave the association if he desires, but if he stays in it he is subjected to the coercive effect of a fine to be determined and enforced by the majority. This method of procedure is arbitrary and artificial, and is based in no respect upon the grounds upon which competition in business is permitted, but on the contrary it creates a motive for business action inconsistent with that freedom of choice out of which springs the benefit of competition to the public, and has no natural or logical relation to the grounds upon which the right to compete is based. Such a method of influencing a person may be coercive and illegal. Carew *v.* Rutherford, 106 Mass. 1.

Nor is the nature of the coercion changed by the fact that the persons fined were members of the association. The words of Munson, J., in Boutwell *v.* Marr, 71 Vt. 1, 9, are applicable here: " The law cannot be compelled by any initial agreement of an associate member to treat him as one having no choice but that of the majority, nor as a willing participant in whatever action may be taken. The voluntary acceptance of by-laws providing for the imposition of coercive fines does not make them legal and collectible, and the standing threat of their imposition may properly be classed with the ordinary threats of suits upon groundless claims. The fact that the relations and processes deemed essential to a recovery are brought within the membership and proceedings of an organized body cannot change the result. The law sees in the membership of an association of this character both the authors of its coercive system and the victim of its unlawful pressure. If this were not so, men could deprive their fellows of established rights, and evade the duty of compensation, simply by working through an association."

In view of the considerations upon which the right of competition is based, we are of opinion that as against the plaintiff the defendants have failed to show that the coercion or intimidation of the plaintiff's customers by means of a fine is justified by the law of competition. The ground of the justification is not broad enough to cover the acts of interference in their entirety, and the interference being injurious and unjustifiable is unlawful.

We do not mean to be understood as saying that a fine is of itself necessarily or even generally an illegal implement. In many cases it is so slight as not to be coercive in its nature; in many it serves a useful purpose to call the attention of a member of an organization to the fact of the infraction of some innocent regulation; and in many it serves as an extra incentive to the performance of some absolute duty or the assertion of some absolute right. But where, as in the case before us, the fine is so large as to amount to moral intimidation or coercion, and is used as a means to enforce a right not absolute in its nature but conditional, and is inconsistent with those conditions upon which the right rests, then the coercion becomes unjustifiable and taints with illegality the act.

The defendants strongly rely upon Bowen *v.* Matheson, 14 Allen, 499; Mogul Steamship Co. *v.* McGregor, [1892] A. C. 25; Bohn Mfg. Co. *v.* Hollis, 54 Minn. 223; Macauley Bros. *v.* Tierney, 19 R. I. 255, and Cote *v.* Murphy, 159 Penn. St. 420. In none of these cases was there any coercion by means of fines upon those who traded with the plaintiff. Inducements were held out, but they were such as are naturally incident to competition, for instance, more advantageous terms in the way of discounts, increased trade, and otherwise. In the Minnesota case there was among the rules of the association a clause requiring the plaintiff to pay 10 per cent, but the propriety or the legality of that provision was not involved. In Bowen *v.* Matheson, it is true that the by-laws provided for a fine, but the declaration did not charge that any coercion by means of a fine had been used. A demurrer to the declaration was sustained upon the ground that there was no sufficient allegation of an illegal act. The only allegation which need be noticed here was that the defendants "did prevent men from shipping with" the plaintiff, and as to this the court said: "This might be done in many ways which are legal and proper, and as no illegal methods are stated the allegation is bad." This comes far short of sustaining the defendants in their course of coercion by means of fines. As to the other cases cited by the defendant it may be said that, while bearing upon the general subject of which the present case presents one phase, they are not inconsistent with the conclusion to which we have come. Among the authorities bearing upon the general subject and having some relation to the questions involved in this case, see, in addition to those hereinbefore cited, Slaughter-House Cases, 16 Wall. 116; United States *v.* Addystone, 175 U. S. 211; Doremus *v.* Hennessy, 176 Ill. 608; Inter-Ocean Pub. Co. *v.* Associated Press, 184 Ill. 438; State *v.* Stewart, 59 Vt. 273; Olive *v.* Van Patten, 7 Tex. Civ. App. 630; Barr *v.* Essex Trades Council, 53 N. J. Eq. 101; Jackson *v.* Stanfield, 137 Ind. 592; Bailey *v.* Master Plumbers, 103 Tenn. 99; Brown *v.* Jacobs Pharmacy Co., 115 Ga. 429; Mogul Steamship Co. *v.* McGregor, 15 Q. B. D. 476; s. c. 21 Q. B. D. 544; s. c. 23 Q. B. D. 598; s. c. [1892] A. C. 25.

For the reasons above stated a majority of the court are of opinion that the case should have been submitted to the jury.

Exceptions sustained.[1]

PICKETT *v.* WALSH

SUPREME JUDICIAL COURT, MASSACHUSETTS, OCTOBER 16, 1906.

Reported in 192 *Massachusetts Reports*, 572

THE plaintiffs were brick and stone "pointers." The defendants were officers and members of bricklayers' unions and stonemasons' unions.[2]

One ground of complaint was that the defendants prevented the employment of the plaintiffs as "pointers" by notifying contractors that they would not lay the bricks or do the mason work on any building unless they were also employed to do the pointing of the brick and stone masonry. "The defendants in effect say we want the work of pointing the brick and stone laid by us, and you must give us all or none of the work."[3] The court held that this conduct, although disastrous to the plaintiffs and damaging to the building contractors, was justifiable. ". . . it was within the rights of these unions to compete for the work of doing the pointing, and, in the exercise of their right of competition, to refuse to lay bricks and set stone unless they were given the work of pointing them when laid."[4]

The other ground of action in Pickett *v.* Walsh was quite distinct from the foregoing. The firm of L. P. Soule & Son Company were the general contractors for the erection of the Ford building; but they had nothing to do with the employment of "pointers." The pointing of that building was being done under a contract between the owners of the building and Pickett, a pointer who was one of the plaintiffs. Other buildings were being erected for other owners, on which the Soule Company were the general contractors, and as to which no complaint existed in reference to the pointing. The bricklaying and masonry on these other buildings were being done by members of the defendants' union. The defendant officials induced all the bricklayers and masons to quit working for the Soule Company on these other buildings, because that company "was doing work on another building [the Ford building] in which

[1] See majority and minority opinions in the later case of Willcut & Sons Co. *v.* Driscoll, 200 Mass. 110, also Booth *v.* Burgess, 72 N. J. Eq. 181. Compare Rhodes *v.* Musicians' Union, 37 R. I. 281.

[2] The following condensed statement is taken from 20 Harvard Law Review, 445–447.

[3] Loring, J., p. 583. [4] Ibid.

work was being done by pointers, employed not by the L. P. Soule & Son Company but [by] the owners of the building." The evident purpose was to thus induce the Soule Company to exert pressure on the owners of the Ford building to discontinue the employment of the pointers (Pickett *et als.*). The court held that this conduct was not justifiable. The decision is not based on the ground that the defendants were intentionally inducing, or attempting to induce, a breach of contract; but on the broad ground that the forcing a neutral third person to exert a pressure on the plaintiff's employer was not a lawful means of competition.

LORING, J.[1]

That strike has an element in it like that in a sympathetic strike, in a boycott, and in a blacklisting, namely: It is a refusal to work for A, with whom the strikers have no dispute, for the purpose of forcing A to force B to yield to the strikers' demands. In the case at bar the strike on the L. P. Soule & Son Company was a strike on that contractor to force it to force the owner of the Ford building to give the work of pointing to the defendant unions. That passes beyond a case of competition where the owner of the Ford building is left to choose between the two competitors. Such a strike is in effect compelling the L. P. Soule & Son Company to join in a boycott on the owner of the Ford building. It is a combination by the union to obtain a decision in their favor by forcing third persons who have no interest in the dispute to force the employer to decide the dispute in their (the defendant union's) favor. Such a strike is not a justifiable interference with the right of the plaintiffs to pursue their calling as they think best. In our opinion organized labor's right of coercion and compulsion is limited to strikes on persons with whom the organization has a trade dispute; or to put it in another way, we are of the opinion that a strike on A, with whom the striker has no trade dispute, to compel A to force B to yield to the strikers' demands, is an unjustifiable interference with the right of A to pursue his calling as he thinks best.[2]

[1] Only a part of the opinion is given (pp. 587–88).

[2] Bossert *v.* Dhuy, 166 App. Div. 261, 221 N. Y. 342 *Accord.* But see Grassi Contracting Co. *v.* Bennett, 160 N. Y. Suppl. 279.

In Bohn Mfg. Co. *v.* Hollis, 54 Minn. 223, "a large number of retail lumber dealers formed a voluntary association, by which they mutually agreed that they would not deal with any manufacturer or wholesale dealer who should sell lumber directly to consumers not dealers, at any point where a member of the association was carrying on a retail yard; and they provided in their by-laws that, whenever any wholesale dealer or manufacturer made any such sale, the secretary should notify all the members of the fact. The plaintiff, a wholesaler, having made such a sale directly to a consumer, the secretary threatened to send notice of the fact, as provided in the by-laws, to all the members of the association." (This statement is copied from 17 Green Bag, 218. See also statement by Professor Lewis, 44 Am. L. Reg. N. S. 469.) The court refused to grant an injunction against sending out the notice. Here the retail dealers did not threaten to cease dealing with any one except their competitors, *i. e.*, wholesale dealers who should attempt to sell directly to consumers. They used no lever but their own conduct. They did not threaten to induce outsiders to refrain from working for, or selling goods to, the wholesalers. And even as to their own conduct, they did not threaten to abstain from dealings with wholesalers in all matters, but only in the purchase of lumber. Much less did they threaten to abstain from dealing with persons who dealt with the wholesalers. In a subsequent case the same court said: "It is to be noted that the defendants in the Bohn case had similar legitimate interests to protect which were menaced by the practice of wholesale dealers in selling lumber to contractors and consumers; and that the defendants' efforts to induce parties

BARR v. THE ESSEX TRADES COUNCIL

COURT OF CHANCERY, NEW JERSEY, OCTOBER TERM, 1894.

Reported in 53 New Jersey Equity Reports, 101.

ON order to show cause why injunction should not issue.[1]

The original complainant was the sole proprietor and publisher of a daily morning newspaper called the "Newark Times."

The defendants are eighteen bodies known as "labor unions," embracing many trades in the city of Newark, affiliated in a society or representative body known as "Essex Trades Council."

The Essex Trades Council is a voluntary association, composed of delegates chosen thereto by each of the eighteen defendant unions. Meetings are held weekly. Every organization represented in the council is required to make a monthly report of union purchases, and failing to do so for two consecutive months, its products are not to be considered as "fair."

A circular, issued by the Council in 1893, addressed to the public, states: —

"The Essex Trades Council has for some time past been concentrating the trade of its members and those whom these could influence, upon the goods made and recommended by organized fair labor, and the stores and places where these goods are sold. The regular system of purchase reports from individual consumers, transmitted through their organization, places the council in a position to announce that it is already turning thousands of dollars of trade every week away from those indifferent to the welfare of the worker, and into the pockets of labor's proven friends. That these friends may receive greater support by being made more readily known to organized working men and their many sympathizers among lovers of justice, together forming the great bulk of the consuming public, the Essex Trades Council will shortly issue a series of cards for free display in all business establishments especially deserving the patronage of organized fair consumers, their families, associates and friends."

The plan of operation, as developed by the papers and exhibits filed in the cause, is that each individual member of the different unions is

not to deal with offending wholesale dealers were limited to the members of the association having similar interests to conserve, and that there was no agreement or combination or attempt to induce other persons not members of the association to withhold their patronage from such wholesale dealers." Ertz v. Produce Exchange Co., 79 Minn. 140, 144. See also Jackson v. Stanfield, 137 Ind. 592; Brown v. Jacobs Pharmacy Co., 115 Ga. 429; and other cases collected by Professor Wyman, 17 Green Bag, 210, 222.

Strike unless plaintiff is discharged, as a means toward better conditions in the shop, see Minasian v. Osborne, 210 Mass. 250.

Strike to get rid of personally objectionable foreman. De Minico v. Craig, 207 Mass. 593.

[1] Statement abridged. Portions of opinion omitted.

required at stated periods to fill out a blank slip furnished for that purpose, stating the amount expended by him in purchase, the character of the articles bought, and the names of the tradesmen with whom he has dealt. These cards, when filled in, are returned by the members to their own union, and by the union reported to the council. A failure by a union to so report for two consecutive months, places its products under the ban of organized labor as represented in the council. These reports place the trades council in possession of data as to the amount of purchases by the members of the unions, and the tradesmen with whom their dealing is carried on, from which its officers are enabled to estimate, with some degree of accuracy, the volume of purchases by the members of the several organizations within a stated period of time.

The next step is an agreement in writing purporting to be made between the Essex Trades Council and a tradesman, by which the latter, " in return for the patronage of united fair consumers," promises and agrees to buy as consumer, engage as employer, keep as dealer, as exclusively as he can, such labor and goods as may be announced as fair by a particular union and endorsed by the council of consumers of the Essex Trades Council.

Cards are then issued to the tradesmen, under the seal of the trades council, addressed " to all fair consumers," each certifying that the person to whom it is issued " is a fair consuming dealer," and is entitled to their fraternal support until a specified date. Coupons are annexed for certification by particular industries. These cards are of such size, color and appearance that, if publicly displayed in stores or places of business, they will attract attention.

There was issued, under date of March 31, 1894, " by the Essex Trades Council and auxiliary circle bodies," a small pamphlet of convenient size to be carried in the pocket, which is entitled " The Fair List of Newark, N. J.," and to be " for the information of people who buy service or product and who have enterprise enough to seek to place their money where it will do them most good." It contains names and addresses of tradesmen and persons in business, including lawyers, interspersed with items of information and advice.

. . . .

The plaintiff Barr determined to employ " plate matter " in making up part of his daily paper. (This consists of reading matter edited, set up and stereotyped in New York.) All plaintiff's employees were members of the local typographical union. This union had declared against the use of plate matter in the city of Newark, which fact was known to Mr. Barr. Through his foreman, he sought to have this resolution of the union relaxed in favor of his paper, but on its refusal so to do adhered to his determination, and, by letter dated March 13, 1894, informed his foreman that he would use plate matter on and after March 17th, saying further, that, not desiring to lose any of the men in his department, the union scale of wages would be maintained, and that he would gladly retain the services of such as might be willing to stay. Some of the employees determined to remain, others, however, left in consequence of his disregard of the union's determination, and the union withdrew its endorsement of the newspaper. The union thereupon, through its delegates, informed the Essex Trades Council of this fact and requested its assistance. In response, the council appointed a committee in reference to the controversy, and, on March 30, 1894, issued a circular addressed to the public, which, after giving its version of the dispute, concludes with this appeal: —

"Friends, one and all, leave this council-boycotting 'Newark Times' alone. Cease buying it! Cease handling it! Cease advertisin it! Keep the money of fair men moving only among fair men. Boycott the boycotter of organized fair labor."

This circular was distributed in the city of Newark.

In April, 1894, the trades council issued a small four-page sheet entitled "The Union Buyer. Official bulletin of united fair custom of Newark and vicinity. Issued by the Essex Trades Council." It is impressed at the heading with the union label. It purports to be volume I, number 1, issued at Newark, N. J., April, 1894. Its first announcement is as follows: —

"Our mission — To support the supporters and boycott the boycotters of organized fair labor. To promote the public welfare by the diffusion of common cents, urging all to carry these in trade only to those who will return them to the people in the shape of living wages."

The whole paper is devoted to the controversy between the unions and the "Newark Times," no other object being considered. It refers throughout to that paper either by reversing the letters of the name "Times" as "Semit," or by turning the type bottom side up. The first article after the declaration of its mission is a statement from Typographical Union No. 103, under the heading of "'The Times' Trouble." The only grievance stated against the "Times" grows out of the use of plate matter, and ends with "workingmen and advertisers, remember that plate matter means forty-five cents a day, and understand why the 'Newark Times' is an unfair office." Then follow five columns of "Notes and Comments." These are all directed to the controversy, and are in vigorous and denunciatory language, and conclude as follows: —

"In conclusion, the council desires to state that the issue between it and the 'Semit' is now wide open. It is a fight between the 'Semit' and its supporters and the council and its supporters. We give the great public absolute freedom in the choice of its side, but not a single cent of our money will be knowingly let pass to any one who buys the 'Semit,' keeps the 'Semit,' advertises in the 'Semit,' or in any other way leads us to believe that a portion of our honestly-earned money may find its way into the pockets to furnish support to the unfair management of the 'Semit' or any of those who have so foully betrayed the cause of organized fair labor."

At the foot of this document is placed, in large type, the request, "When through reading, please pass to your neighbor."

This paper was circulated in Newark. There were other publications, but the defendants deny any responsibility for them, and there is no evidence to connect them with their issue or circulation.

Various labor unions represented in the trades council then passed a prepared set of resolutions, which were printed and distributed in Newark. One of these requested all enterprising business houses to abstain from advertising in the "Times" until the trouble had been adjusted, stating that hundreds of their friends had refused to buy and read the "Times," and that its circulation had become considerably reduced because of its alleged unfair stand. Another asked such advertisers as had made contracts with the "Times" for definite periods, to consider whether it would not be far more advantageous for them in the end to take out their advertisements, leave their space entirely blank and pay the few cents their contracts called for, than to jeopardize thousands of dollars of trade that fair labor would be "compelled to withhold so long as such advertisements appeared, and for an indefinite period thereafter," adding that "those who now continue to advertise in the 'Times' merely succeed in making themselves conspicuous as persons to carefully and studiously keep away from."

These resolutions found their way into the hands of the advertisers in the "Times."

The various trades unions, affiliated in the council, represent, as is claimed by them, a purchasing power amounting to over $400,000 in each and every week. Owing to the issue and distribution of the aforesaid circular and resolutions, the individual members of the union, and their friends and sympathizers, withheld their patronage from the "Newark Times." The circulation of the paper was thereby considerably reduced.

The issue and distribution of said circular and resolutions caused certain persons, who had theretofore advertised in the "Times," to cease advertising in that paper.

GREEN, V. C.

. . . .

[After stating the testimony of Mr. Beckmeyer, secretary of the Essex Trades Council, as to the signification of the word "boycott," as used in the circular and publications.]

From which it is to be gathered that the use of the word "boycott" in the publications, as applied to the "Times," would be regarded by the members of the various unions to mean only that they should refrain from trading or dealing with the complainant, and with those who oppose the organizations in their actions and doings with reference to the complainant.

I do not see that this changes the character of the injury, but even if it does, so far as the members of the organizations are concerned, the difficulty is that these communications were addressed to the public and indiscriminately circulated. They were not intended only for members of the order by whom a technical signification would be given to the word "boycott," but to the general public who would read them and give the word its accepted meaning.

[After quoting various definitions of "boycott"] Mr. Justice Taft, in Toledo Co. *v.* Penn. Co., 54 Fed. Rep. 746, says: "As usually understood a boycott is a combination of many to cause a loss to one person by coercing others against their will, to withdraw from him their beneficial business intercourse, through threats that, unless those others do so, the many will cause similar loss to them."

But the defendants insist, and counsel vigorously urge, that this particular boycott is not open to such adverse criticism, because "there was no violence, intimidation, coercion or threats used, and that everything was done in a peaceful and orderly manner." How far is this claim borne out by the facts? It is true, there was no public disturbance, no physical injury, no direct threats of personal violence or of actual attack on or destruction of tangible property as a means of intimidation or coercion. Force and violence, however, while they may enter largely into the question in a criminal prosecution, are not necessary factors in the right to a civil remedy. But even in criminal law, I do not understand that intimidation, even when a statutory ingredient of crime, necessarily presupposes personal injury or the fear thereof. The clear weight of authority undoubtedly is that a man may be intimidated into doing, or refraining from doing, by fear of loss of business, property or reputation, as well as by dread of loss of life, or injury to health or limb; and the extent of this fear need not be abject, but only such as to overcome his judgment, or induce him not to do, or to do, that which otherwise he would have done or have left undone.

There can be no reasonable dispute that the whole proceeding or boycott in this controversy is to force Mr. Barr, by fear of loss of business, to conduct that business, not according to his own judgment, but in accordance with the determination of the typographical union, and, so far as he is concerned, it is an attempt to intimidate and coerce.

Next as to the members of the various labor unions. According to Mr. Beckmeyer, all the organizations represented in the trades council and the individual members thereof, in strict conformity with the purpose and object for which the said council was organized, withheld their patronage from the said newspaper on the mere announcement by the typographical union to the trades council that that union had withdrawn its endorsement from the "Times." Why? It is said that it was only the exercise by each person of his right to spend his money as his own will dictated. The fallacy of this is apparent. It loses sight of the combination, the whole strength of which lies in the fact that each individual has surrendered his own discretion and will to the direction of the accredited representative of all the organizations. He no longer uses his own judgment, but, by entering into the combination, agrees to be bound by its decree. As is said in Templeton *v.* Russell, *supra*, " those men had bound themselves to obey, and they knew they had done so, and that if they did not obey they would be fined, or expelled from the union to which they belonged." It is common knowledge, if indeed it does not amply so appear by the papers in this case, that a member of a labor organization who does not submit to the edict of his union asserts his independence of judgment and action at the risk, if not the absolute sacrifice, of all association with his fellow-members. They will not eat, drink, live or work in his company. Branded by the peculiarly offensive epithets adopted, he must exist ostracized, socially and industrially, so far as his former associates are concerned. Freedom of will under such circumstances cannot be expected.

Next as to the advertising public. Tradesmen advertise in newspapers for the sole purpose of drawing customers to their stores. An authoritative announcement, not from one, but from many sources, that the body of organized labor in the city or county representing a purchasing power of $400,000 a week would cease to deal with those whose advertisements appeared in the newspaper, would have a much more deterrent effect than any threat of violence. To say that this is only advice, or an intimation, to the advertiser for his guidance if he sees fit to accept it, is trifling with the language. Advice, behind which lurks the threat of the withdrawal of such a volume of business, could have no other effect than to intimidate and coerce, as it did in fact make several change their judgment, which had previously led them to advertise in the paper. The claim that this boycott was attempted to be enforced without intimidation or coercion will not bear the light of examination.

A legal excuse for the action of the defendants is next sought in the claim that the Essex Trades Council is a business institution, and that what it has done has been in prosecution of such business, seeking, I suppose, to bring the case within the rule of Mogul Steamship Co. *v.* McGregor, 15 Q. B. Div. 476; 23 Q. B. Div. 598. That case proceeded on the doctrine of a lawful competition in business, both parties being engaged in carrying on the same character of business, and the acts complained of having been adopted for the advancement of the defendant's own trade, viz., carrying goods on a steamship line, although thereby damage to the other party necessarily ensued.

I see no similarity in the business of these parties. That of the complainant is the publisher of a newspaper. Members of the typographical union, and stereotypers' and pressmen's union, are skilled workmen, whose services might be employed in such business, but they are not carrying on any enterprise in competition with that of the complainant. So far as the other unions are concerned, the most, if not all of them, have no connection with such trade.

Neither does the claim of the Essex Trades Council, that it is a business institution, stand on any firmer ground. The only element of business which it is engaged in would appear from the facts to be the furnishing to tradesmen of printed cards, certifying that they are proper persons for the members of trades unions to deal with, suitable to be displayed in conspicuous places in such tradesmen's places of business. This was supplemented by the issue, under date of March 31, 1894, of the small pocket pamphlet entitled "The Fair List of Newark, N. J.," containing the names and addresses of tradesmen and persons in business in Newark, with items of information and advice. Why this is called a business does not appear. It is not stated that any compensation is either required or received by the trades council from the tradespeople for granting or continuing those endorsements, but whether this is so or not, it is in no sense a competing business with the publication of a daily newspaper, and therefore does not come within the principle of the case referred to.

The order to show cause, as far as relates to [eight specified organizations], they having all disclaimed any participation in the acts complained of, must be discharged, with costs. The said order to show cause, so far as relates to the other defendants, must be made absolute, with costs, and an injunction may issue against them, restraining them from distributing or circulating any circulars, printed resolutions, bulletins, or other publications containing appeals or threats against the "Newark Times," or the complainants, its publishers, with the design and tending to interfere with their business in publishing said paper, and from making any threats or using any intimidation to the dealers or advertisers in such newspaper tending to cause them to withdraw their business from such newspaper.[1]

PIERCE v. THE STABLEMEN'S UNION LOCAL NO. 8760

SUPREME COURT, CALIFORNIA, JULY 6, 1909.

Reported in 156 *California Reports*, 70.

HENSHAW, J. The plaintiff went into equity seeking an injunction to restrain the defendants from illegal interference with its business. Plaintiff conducted a livery, board and feed stable in the city and county of San Francisco. The officers and representatives of defend-

[1] Gompers *v.* Bucks Stove & Range Co., 221 U. S. 418; Baldwin *v.* Escanaba Dealers' Ass'n, 165 Mich. 98; Fink *v.* Butchers' Union, 84 N. J. Eq. 638; McCormick *v.* Local Unions, 32 Ohio Cir. Ct. R. 165 *Accord.*
Compare *Ex parte* Heffron, 179 Mo. App. 639.

ant made request of him to " unionize " his stable by discharging his non-union employees and employing union men in their places. Upon his refusal, a strike of the union men was declared. Following the strike, a boycott was decreed. A patrol about plaintiff's place of business was established, and, under the findings, these representatives of the defendants, the pickets, " called forth in loud, threatening, and menacing tones to the patrons and customers of plantiffs not to patronize plaintiffs in their said business; defendant, the Stablemen's Union, through its agents and representatives, has stated to and threatened patrons and customers and other persons dealing with plaintiffs that if said patrons and customers and other persons continued to patronize and do business with plaintiffs, said Stablemen's Union would cause them respectively to be boycotted in their business." Menacing terms and threatening language were made use of by the agents, representatives, and pickets of the union toward the employees of the plaintiff, such as: " Unfair stable; union men locked out and non-union men put in; look at this stable, the only unfair stable on Market Street; the stable that always was and always will be unfair. This is a scab stable. When we catch you outside, we will finish you. We will get you yet. It is a scab stable, full of scabs. We will fix you yet. It is a matter of time when we will get you all right. You will never get out of the stable alive. We will break you in half. We will beat you to death. When we catch you outside, we will finish you." A judgment for an injunction followed upon these findings, and that judgment by its terms commanded the defendant, its agents and employees, to desist and refrain " from in any wise interfering with, or harassing, or annoying, or obstructing plaintiff in the conduct of the business of their stable, known as the Nevada Stables and situated at number 1350 Market Street, in the city and county of San Francisco; or from in any wise molesting, interfering with, threatening, intimidating, or harassing any employee or employees of plaintiffs; or from intimidating, harassing, or interfering with any customer or customers, patron or patrons of plaintiffs in connection with the business of plaintiffs, either by boycott or by threats of boycott, or by any other threats; or by any kind of force, violence, or intimidation, or by other unlawful means, seeking to induce any employee or employees of plaintiffs to withdraw from the service of plaintiffs; or by any kind of violence, threats, or intimidation inducing, or seeking to induce, any customer or customers, patron or patrons, of plaintiffs to withdraw their patronage or business from them, or from stationing or placing in front of said plaintiffs' place of business any picket, or pickets, for the purpose of injuring, obstructing, or in any wise interfering with, the business of plaintiffs, or for the purpose of preventing any customer or customers, patron or patrons, of plaintiffs from doing business with them; or from in any other way molesting, intimidating, or coercing, or attempt to molest or intimidate or coerce any customer, patron, or employee of plaintiffs now or hereafter dealing with, or any employee now or hereafter employed by, or working for plaintiffs in their said business."

This appeal is from the judgment. The findings are not attacked. Certain objections to the complaint are presented upon demurrer, and these may be briefly disposed of. The complaint is sufficient to invoke the interposition of a court of equity. It is in this respect similar to the complaint considered in Goldberg-Bowen Co. *v.* Stablemen's Union, 149 Cal. 429. The complaint alleges specific acts calling for preventive relief, and is not confined to mere generalities, as was the case in Davitt *v.* American Bakers' Union, 124 Cal. 99. The fact that certain of the acts charged amount to crimes or threatened crimes, does not offer reason why equity will refuse to restrain them. While equity will not attempt to restrain the commission of a crime as such, the fact that an act threatening irreparable injury to property rights, is of itself criminal, does not deprive a court of equity of its right and power to enjoin its commission. (*In re* Debs, 158 U. S. 564; Sherry *v.* Perkins, 144 Mass. 212; Vegelahn *v.* Guntner, 167 Mass. 92.) In like manner, while equity will not enjoin against a trespass as such, yet when the acts committed and threatened are in the nature of a continuing trespass, working irreparable injury, they will be enjoined. (Boston R. R. *v.* Sullivan, 177 Mass. 230; Lembeck *v.* Nye, 47 Ohio, 336.)

Appellants' principal contentions upon the appeal, however, are the following: First, that, as the controversy between these parties arises from and over a trade dispute, the court is powerless to grant any injunction under the language of "An act to limit the meaning of the word 'conspiracy' and also the use of restraining orders and injunctions as applied to disputes between employers and employees in the State of California, approved March 20, 1903" (Pen. Code, page 581); second, that the boycott is a legal weapon in a trade dispute and, therefore, an injunction should not issue to restrain its use or threatened use; third, that "picketing" as an adjunct to the boycott is itself legal and may not be forbidden.

1. As to the first of these contentions, this court had occasion in Goldberg, etc., Co. *v.* Stablemen's Union, 149 Cal. 429, to consider the statute above referred to and relied upon by appellants, and declared that if the construction there contended for (and here contended for) was the proper construction, this provision of the court was void. Not only would it be void as violative of one's constitutional right to acquire, possess, enjoy, and protect property, but as well would it be obnoxious to the constitution in creating arbitrarily and without reason a class above and beyond the law which is applicable to all other individuals and classes. It would legalize a combination in restraint of trade or commerce, entered into by a trades union, which would be illegal if entered into by any other persons or associations. It would

exempt trades unions from the operation of the general laws of the land, under circumstances where the same laws would operate against all other individuals, combinations, or associations. It is thus not only special legislation, obnoxious to the constitution (Art. IV, sec. 25, subds. 3 and 33), but it still further violates the constitution in attempting to grant privileges and immunities to certain citizens or classes of citizens which, upon the same terms, have not been granted to all citizens (Art. I, sec. 21).

2. In considering the second proposition, whether or not a court of equity may enjoin a boycott, the meaning of the word is of primary importance. It is defined in 4 Am. & Eng. Enc. of Law, 2d ed., page 85, as follows: " The boycott is a conspiracy, the direct object of which is to occasion loss to the party or parties against whom the conspiracy is directed, and the means commonly used is the inducing of others to withdraw from such party or parties their patronage and business intercourse by threats that, unless they so withdraw, the members of the combinaton will cause, directly or indirectly, loss of a similar character to them." Appellants announce their willingness to accept this definition, substituting the word " confederacy " or " combination " for " conspiracy." But the definition, even as so amended, it will be noted is not complete. The " means commonly used " are specified, but other means may be and frequently are employed. A boycott may adopt illegal means and thus become a " conspiracy," a word which imports illegality; or a boycott may employ legal means and methods, and thus be merely a legitimate combination by a number of men to accomplish, within the law, a legal result. The crux of the question and the strain in every case turns, then, upon the means employed. We think that to-day no court would question the right of an organized union of employes, by concerted action, to cease their employment (no contractual obligation standing in the way), and this action constitutes a " strike." We think, moreover, that no court questions the right of those same men to cease dealing by concerted action, either socially or by way of business, with their former employer, and this latter act, in its essence, constitutes the " primary boycott." But what acts organized labor may do, and what means it may adopt to accomplish its end, without violation of the law, have presented questions of much nicety, over which the courts have stood, and still stand, widely divided. It would not be profitable to discuss and analyze these widely divergent cases. It is sufficient to formulate briefly the principles adopted in this state, many of which have recently found elaborate expression in the case of Parkinson *v.* Building & Trades Council of Santa Clara, 36 Cal. Dec. 445. The right of united labor to strike, in furtherance of their trade interests (no contractual obligation standing in the way) is fully recognized. The reason for the strike may be based upon the refusal to comply with the employees' demand for the betterment of wages, conditions,

hours of labor, the discharge of one employee, the engagement of another — any one of the multifarious ends which in good faith may be believed to tend toward the advancement of the employees. After striking, the employees may engage in a boycott, as that word is here employed. As here employed it means not only the concerted right to the withdrawal of social and business intercourse, but the right by all legitimate means of fair publication, and fair oral or written persuasion, to induce others interested in or sympathetic with their cause, to withdraw their social intercourse and business patronage from the employer. They may go even further than this, and request of another that he withdraw his patronage from the employer, and may use the moral intimidation and coercion of threatening a like boycott against him if he refuse so to do. This last proposition necessarily involves the bringing into a labor dispute between A and B, C who has no difference with either. It contemplates that C, upon the demand of B, and under the moral intimidation lest B boycott him, may thus be constrained to withdraw his patronage from A, with whom he has no controversy. This is the "secondary boycott," the legality of which is vigorously denied by the English courts, the federal courts, and by the courts of many of the states of this nation. Without presenting the authorities, which are multitudinous, suffice it to state the other view in language of the President of the United States but recently uttered: "A body of workmen are dissatisfied with the terms of their employment. They seek to compel their employer to come to their terms by striking. They may legally do so. The loss and inconvenience he suffers he cannot complain of. But when they seek to compel third persons, who have no quarrel with their employer, to withdraw from all association with him by threats that, unless such third persons do so, the workmen will inflict similar injury on such third persons, the combination is oppressive, involves duress, and if injury results, it is actionable." (President Taft, McClure's Magazine, June, 1909, page 204.) Notwithstanding the great dignity which attaches to an utterance such as this, which, as has been said, is but the expression of numerous courts upon the subject-matter, this court, after great deliberation, took what it believed to be the truer and more advanced ground above indicated and fully set forth in Parkinson *v.* Building & Trades Council, etc., *supra.* In this respect this court recognizes no substantial distinction between the so-called primary and secondary boycott. Each rests upon the right of the union to withdraw its patronage from its employer and to induce by fair means any and all other persons to do the same, and in the exercise of those means, as the unions would have the unquestioned right to withhold their patronage from a third person who continued to deal with their employer, so they have the unquestioned right to notify such third person that they will withdraw their patronage if he continues so to deal. However opposed to the weight of federal authority the views of this court are, that they are not unique may be noted by reading National Protective Association *v.* Cumming, 170 N. Y. 315; Lindsay *v.* Montana Federation of Labor, (Mont.) 18 L. R. A. (N. S.) 707, where the highest courts of those states formulate and adopt like principles.

It has been said that it is important to any correct understanding of or adjudication upon such questions that a definition of the word "boycott" should be first stated. Thus, to say that a boycott is a "conspiracy" immediately implies illegality, and puts the conduct of the boycotters under the ban of the law. So also does the definition which describes boycotting as "illegal coercion" designed to accomplish a certain end. As we have undertaken to define boycott, it is an organized effort to persuade or coerce, which may be legal or illegal, according to the means employed. In other jurisdictions where a definition is given to a boycott which imports illegality the injunction will of course lie against boycotting as such. In this state the injunction will issue, depending upon the circumstances whether the means employed, or threatened to be employed, are legal or illegal.

3. We are thus brought to consider the method of "picketing," the use of which appellants contend is a legal weapon in their hands. So far in this discussion we have dealt exclusively with the respective rights of the employer and of the employee. There are other parties, however, whose rights are entitled to equal consideration, and whose rights always become involved and imperilled when picketing is adopted as a coercive measure in aid of a boycott.

If the strikers have the right, as above indicated, to withdraw patronage themselves and by fair publication, written and oral persuasion to induce others to join in their cause, and finally by threat of like boycott to coerce others into so doing, their rights go no further than this. It is the equal right of the employer to insist before the law that his business shall be subject at the hands of the strikers to no other detriment than that which follows as a consequence of the legal acts of the strikers so above set forth. It is not to be forgotten that when the employees have struck, they occupy no contractual relationship whatsoever to their former employer, and have no right to coerce him or attempt to coerce him by the employment of any other means than those which are equally open to any other individual or association of individuals. No sanctity attaches to a trades union which puts it above the law, or which confers upon it rights not enjoyed by any other individual or association. The two classes of persons to whom we have adverted and whose rights necessarily become involved where a picket or patrol is established, are, first, the rights of those employed or seeking employment in the place of the striking laborers, and, second, the rights of the general public. It is the absolute, unqualified right of every employee, as well as of every other person, to go about his legal business unmolested and unobstructed and free from intimidation, force, or duress. The right of a labor association to strike is no higher than the right of a non-union workman to take employment in place of the strikers. Under the assurance and shield of the Constitution and of the laws, the non-union laborer may go to and from his labor and remain at his place of labor in absolute security from unlawful molestations, and wherever the laws fail to accord such protection, in so far is their execution to be blamed. In this country a man's constitutional liberty means far more than his mere personal freedom. It means that, among other rights, his is the right freely to labor and to own the fruits of his toil. (*Ex parte* Jentzsch, 112 Cal. 468.) Any act of boycotting, therefore, which tends to impair this constitutional right freely to labor, by means passing beyond moral suasion, and playing by intimidation upon the physical fears, is unlawful.

The inconvenience which the public may suffer by reason of a boycott lawfully conducted is in no sense a legal injury. But the public's rights are invaded the moment the means employed are such as are calculated to and naturally do incite to crowds, riots, and disturbances of the peace.

A picket, in its very nature, tends to accomplish, and is designed to accomplish, these very things. It tends to and is designed, by physical intimidation, to deter other men from seeking employment in the places vacated by the strikers. It tends, and is designed, to drive business away from the boycotted place, not by the legitimate methods of persuasion, but by the illegitimate means of physical intimidation and fear. Crowds naturally collect; disturbances of the peace are always imminent and of frequent occurrence. Many peaceful citizens, men and women, are always deterred by physical trepidation from entering places of business so under a boycott patrol. It is idle to split hairs upon so plain a proposition, and to say that the picket may consist of nothing more than a single individual peacefully endeavoring by persuasion to prevent customers from entering the boycotted place. The plain facts are always at variance with such refinements of reason. Says Chief Justice Shaw in Commonwealth *v.* Hunt, 4 Met. 111: "The law is not to be hoodwinked by colorable pretences; it looks at truth and reality through whatever disguise it may assume." If it be said that neither threats nor intimidations are used, no man can fail to see that there may be threats, and there may be intimidations, and there may be molesting, and there may be obstructing, without there being any express words used by which a man should show violent threats toward another, or any express intimidation. We think it plain that the very end to be attained by picketing, however artful may be the means to accomplish that end, is the injury of the boycotted business through physical molestation and physical fear caused to the employer, to those whom he may have employed or who may seek employment from him, and to the general public.

The boycott, having employed these means for this unquestioned purpose, is illegal, and a court will not seek by over-niceties and refinements to legalize the use of this unquestionably illegal instrument. (Vegelahn *v.* Guntner, *supra,* Crump *v.* Commonwealth, 84 Va. 927; Union Pacific *v.* Ruef, 120 Fed. Rep. 124; 18 Ency. of Law, 2d ed., page 85.)

In conclusion, then, and applying these principles to the injunction here under consideration, it appears that, while the injunction was properly granted, it was broader in its terms than the law warrants. It was, for example, too broad in restraining defendants from " in any wise interfering with " plaintiff's business, since the interference which we have discussed, of publication, reasonable persuasion, and threat to withdraw patronage, is legal and such as defendants could employ. So, also, was the injunction too broad in restraining defendants from " intimidating any customer by boycott or threat of boycott," since, as has been said, the secondary boycott is likewise a legal weapon. In all other respects, however, the injunction was proper.

The trial court is directed to modify its injunction in the particulars here specified, and in all other respects the judgment will stand affirmed.

We concur: LORIGAN, J.; BEATTY, C. J.; MELVIN, J.

SHAW, J. I agree with all that is said by Justice Henshaw in his opinion, except the part relating to the so-called " secondary boycott " and the attempt to draw a distinction between the compulsion of third persons caused by picketing, and the compulsion of third persons produced by a boycott. My views concerning the " secondary boycott " are expressed in my dissenting opinion in Parkinson *v.* Building Trades Council, (Cal.) 98 Pac. 1040. The means employed for the coercion or intimidation of a third person in a " secondary boycott " are unlawful whenever they are such as are calculated to, and actually do, destroy his free will and cause him to act contrary to his own volition in his own business, to the detriment of the person toward whom the main boycott or strike is directed; in other words, whenever the means used constitute duress, menace, or undue influence. Whether this coercion or compulsion comes from fear of physical violence, as in the case of picketing, or from fear of financial loss, as in the secondary boycott, or from fear of any other infliction, is, in my opinion, immaterial, so long as the fear is sufficiently potent to control the action of those upon whom it is cast. I can see no logical or just reason for the distinction thus sought to be made. There is no such distinction in cases where contracts or wills are declared void, because procured by duress, menace, or undue influence. There should be none where actual injury is produced or threatened through such means acting upon third persons. Nor do I believe any well-considered case authorizes any such distinction. The opinions in the case of National Protective Association *v.* Cummings, 170 N. Y. 315, are devoted to a discussion of the right to strike and the limitations of that right and not to a discussion of the "secondary boycott." A close analysis of the cases on the subject will, as I believe, show that this court stands alone on this point.

For these reasons I do not agree to that part of the judgment directing a modification of the injunction. I believe that it should stand in the form as given by the court below.

ANGELLOTTI, J., and SLOSS, J.

We concur in the judgment. The modification of the judgment is in line with the views announced in the Parkinson case. So far as "picketing" is concerned, while we are not prepared to hold that there may not be acts coming within that term as it is accepted and understood in labor disputes, that are entirely lawful and should not be enjoined, we believe that as to such "picketing" as is described in both findings and judgment in this case, the views expressed in the opinion of the court are correct.[1]

[1] Bossert *v.* Dhuy, 221 N. Y. 342; Cohn & Roth Electric Co. *v.* Bricklayers' Union, 92 Conn. 161 *Accord.* See Iron Molders' Union *v.* Allis Chalmers Co., (C. C. A.) 166 Fed. 45. Also Wigmore, The Boycott as Ground for Damages, 21 American Law Rev. 509, and Interference with Social Relations, 21 American Law Rev. 764.

INDEX

Bei Fragen zur Produktsicherheit wenden Sie sich bitte an:
If you have any questions regarding product safety,
please contact:

Walter de Gruyter GmbH
Genthiner Straße 13
10785 Berlin
productsafety@degruyterbrill.com